THE 

Crossword Puzzle Dictionary

THE 

Crossword Puzzle Dictionary

Charles Preston
Crossword Puzzle Editor of USA TODAY, and
Barbara Ann Kipfer
with Paul Magoulas, Assistant Editor

A Stonesong Press Book

HYPERION

NEW YORK

A Stonesong Press Book

 For information address: Hyperion, 114 Fifth Avenue, New York, New York 10011.

Library of Congress Cataloging-in-Publication Data

Preston, Charles, 1921–
The USA today crossword puzzle dictionary / Charles Preston and Barbara Ann Kipfer.—1st ed.
p. cm.
"A Stonesong Press book."
ISBN 0-7868-8060-0 (pbk.)
1. Crossword puzzles—Glossaries, vocabularies, etc. I. Kipfer, Barbara Ann. II. USA today (Arlington, Va.) III. Title.
GV1507.C7P72 1995
793.73'2'03—dc20 95-21583
CIP

FIRST EDITION

10 9

A

AAL: **8** morindin, mulberry

AARDVARK: **3** pig **6** farrow **7** ant bear **8** anteater, earth pig, edentate

AARDWOLF: **5** hyena

AARON:
brother: **5** Moses
burial place: **3** Hor **8** Mount Hor
father: **5** Amram
made: **10** golden calf
mother: **8** Jochebed
sister: **6** Miriam
son: **5** Abihu, Nadab **7** Eleazar, Ithamar
wife: **8** Elisheba

AARON'S ROD: **4** wand **7** molding, mullein

ABACA: **4** hemp **5** fiber, lupis **6** linaga

ABACK: **5** short **6** behind, sudden **7** unaware **8** suddenly, unawares **12** unexpectedly

ABACUS: **4** slab **7** swanpan **8** cupboard **10** calculator

ABADDON: **3** pit **4** hell **5** hades, Sheol **8** Apollyon

ABAFT: **3** aft **4** back **5** after, arear **6** astern, behind **8** rearward

ABALONE: **5** awabi, ormer, shell, uhllo **6** sea ear **7** mollusk **8** ear shell

ABANDON: **4** drop, elan, flee, junk, quit, stop **5** chuck, ditch, leave, remit, scrap, waive, yield **6** abjure, depart, desert, disuse, give up, maroon, reject, resign, vacate **7** discard, forsake, freedom, liberty, license, neglect **8** abdicate, forswear, rashness, renounce **9** repudiate, surrender, turpitude **10** enthusiasm, exuberance, relinquish, wantonness **11** spontaneity

ABANDONED: **3** bad **4** left, lewd, lost **6** sinful, wanton **7** corrupt, forlorn, immoral, put down **8** derelict, deserted, flagrant, forsaken, stranded **9** destitute, dissolute, humiliate, shameless **10** degenerate, dissipated **12** incorrigible

ABASE: **4** mock, sink **5** cower, lower **6** humble, malign **9** downgrade

ABASH: **4** faze **5** shame, upset **6** dismay, humble, put out **7** chagrin, confuse, mortify **8** bewilder, confound **9** discomfit, embarrass **10** disconcert, discourage

ABATE: **3** ebb, end **4** ease, fall, lull, omit, slow, void, wane **5** allay, annul, let up, lower, quash, relax, remit, slake, taper **6** deduct, lessen, recede, reduce, weaken **7** assuage, die down, nullify, slacken, subside, vitiate **8** decrease, diminish, mitigate, moderate **9** alleviate, eradicate **10** invalidate

ABATEMENT: **5** letup **6** myosis, rebate **8** decrease **9** allowance, deduction, lessening, reduction **10** diminution, relaxation, subsidence

ABBA: **5** abbot **6** father

ABBEY: **6** chapel, church, friary, priory **7** convent, nunnery **8** cloister, seminary **9** hermitage, monastery, sanctuary
concerning: **8** abbatial
assistant: **5** prior **8** prioress
head: **5** abbot **6** abbess

ABBREVIATE: **3** cut **4** clip **5** prune **6** digest **7** abridge, curtail, cut back, shorten **8** compress, condense, contract, simplify, truncate **9** epitomize

ABDICATE: **4** cede, quit **5** demit, leave, forgo **6** resign, retire, vacate **7** abandon **8** disclaim, renounce, withdraw **9** surrender **10** relinquish

ABDOMEN: **3** gut, pot **5** belly **6** middle, paunch, venter **7** midriff, stomach **8** pot belly **9** bay window
concerning: **6** pelvic, ventri, ventro **7** gastric, ventral **8** visceral

ABDUCT: **5** seize, steal **6** kidnap, snatch

ABECEDARIAN: **4** tyro **6** novice **7** amateur, dabbler, learner **8** beginner, neophyte **9** fledgling **10** tenderfoot **12** alphabetical

ABEL:
brother: **4** Cain, Seth
father: **4** Adam
mother: **3** Eve
slayer: **4** Cain

ABELARD:
wife: **7** Heloise

ABERRANT: **3** odd **7** deviant, devious, strange, unusual **8** abnormal, atypical, peculiar **9** anomalous, different, disparate

ABERRATION: **4** slip **5** error, fault, lapse, mania, quirk **6** lunacy, oddity **7** madness **8** delusion, insanity **9** deviation **11** psychopathy **12** eccentricity **13** hallucination

ABET: **3** aid, egg **4** back, goad, help **5** egg on **6** assist, foment, incite, second, uphold **7** endorse, espouse, further, support, sustain **8** advocate **9** encourage, instigate **11** countenance

ABETTOR: **6** patron **8** promoter **9** accessory, auxiliary, supporter **10** accomplice **11** confederate, conspirator **13** coconspirator

ABEYANCE: **4** stay **5** break, letup, pause **7** latency, respite **10** suspension **12** intermission

ABHOR: **4** hate, shun **6** detest, eschew, loathe **7** despise, disdain, dislike **8** execrate **9** abominate

ABHORRENCE: **4** hate **5** odium **7** disgust **8** aversion **9** antipathy, repulsion, revulsion **10** repugnance

ABI:
father: **9** Zechariah
husband: **4** Ahaz
mother: **8** Hezekiah

ABIDE: **4** bear, last, live, stay **5** await, delay, dwell, exist, pause, stand, tarry, visit **7** stomach

ABIES: **4** firs **5** pines, trees **8** conifers **10** evergreens

ABIGAIL:
brother: **5** David
husband: **5** David, Nabal

role: **4** maid **7** servant
son: **5** Amasa

ABILITY: **4** bent, gift **5** force, knack, power, skill **6** energy, talent **7** caliber, faculty, know-how, prowess **8** aptitude, capacity, strength **9** dexterity, expertise, ingenuity, potential **10** capability, competence, efficiency **11** proficiency

ABJECT: **3** low **4** base, mean, poor **6** humble, paltry **7** servile, slavish **8** beggarly, contrite, cringing, degraded, wretched **9** ignorable, miserable **10** submissive

ABJURE: **4** deny **5** avoid, spurn **6** desert, eschew, give up, recall, recant, reject, resign, revoke **7** abandon, disavow, retract **8** disclaim, forswear, renounce, withdraw **9** repudiate

ABLAZE: **5** afire, fiery **6** aflame, ardent **7** blazing, burning, glowing, ignited, radiant **8** inflamed

ABLE: **3** apt, fit **4** good **5** adept, smart **6** au fait, clever, strong, suited **7** capable, learned **8** dextrous, skillful, suitable, talented, vigorous **9** competent, dexterous, effective, efficient, masterful, qualified, versatile **10** proficient

ABLUTION: **4** bath, wash **12** purification

ABNEGATE: **4** deny **5** forgo, waive **6** abjure, eschew, forego, refuse, reject **7** disavow **8** disclaim, forswear, renounce **10** relinquish

ABNER:
cousin: **4** Saul
father: **3** Ner
killer: **4** Joab

ABNORMAL: **3** odd **4** rare **5** queer, weird **7** deviant, erratic, offbeat, unusual **8** aberrant, uncommon **9** anomalous, eccentric, irregular, unnatural **11** exceptional **13** extraordinary

ABOARD: **4** onto **6** across, on deck **7** astride, athwart, present **9** alongside

ABODE: **3** pad **4** flat, home **5** house, manor **6** estate **7** address, cottage, habitat, mansion **8** domicile, dwelling **9** apartment, residence
of Dead: **3** Dar **4** Aalu, Aaru, Hell **5** Aralu, Hades, Orcus, Sheol **6** Heaven **7** Abaddon **8** Valhalla **9** perdition, Purgatory

ABOLISH: **3** end **4** kill **5** abate, annul, erase, quash **6** cancel, repeal, revoke, vacate **7** destroy, nullify, rescind, wipe out **8** abrogate **9** eradicate **10** annihilate, do away with, invalidate **11** discontinue, exterminate

ABOMINABLE: **4** evil, vile **6** horrid, odious **8** damnable **9** atrocious, execrable, loathsome, revolting **12** disagreeable

ABOMINABLE SNOWMAN: **4** yeti **7** monster

ABOMINATE: **4** hate **5** abhor, scorn **6** detest, loathe **7** despise **8** execrate

ABOMINATION: **4** evil **5** crime **6** horror, infamy, plague **7** disgust, outrage **8** anathema, atrocity, disgrace **9** antipathy, bete noire **10** odiousness, repugnance

ABORIGINAL: **5** first **7** endemic **8** primeval **9** primitive **10** indigenous, primordial

ABORIGINE: **3** abo **6** native, savage **10** autochthon

ABORTION: **7** failure **8** misbirth **11** miscarriage, termination

ABORTIVE: **4** idle, vain **6** futile **7** useless **9** fruitless **11** ineffective **12** unproductive

ABOUND: **4** gush, teem **5** crawl, swarm **8** flourish, overflow

ABOUNDING: **4** full, rich, rife **5** alive, flush **6** jammed, packed **7** replete **8** abundant **9** plentiful

ABOUT: **4** in re, near, some **5** anent, astir, circa **6** active, almost, around **7** apropos, close to **9** as regards **10** concerning, respecting, throughout **11** surrounding **13** approximately

ABOUT-FACE: **5** shift **6** switch **8** flip-flop, reversal **9** turnabout, volte-face

ABOVE: **4** atop, over, past, upon **5** aloft, north **6** beyond, higher **8** overhead, superior **9** exceeding **12** transcendent

ABOVE ALL: **4** most **6** indeed, mostly **7** chiefly **9** primarily **10** especially

ABOVEBOARD: **4** open **5** blunt, frank, overt **6** candid, honest **7** ethical **8** bona fide, truthful

ABRACADABRA: **5** charm, magic, spell **6** jargon **7** sorcery **10** hocus-pocus, mumbo jumbo **11** incantation

ABRADE: **3** irk, rub **4** file, fray, fret, gall, rasp **5** annoy, chafe, erode, grate, grind **6** ruffle, scrape **7** corrode **8** irritate **9** excoriate

ABRAHAM: **9** patriarch
brother: **5** Haran, Nahor
father: **5** Terah
grandfather: **5** Nahor
grandson: **4** Esau **5** Jacob
nephew: **3** Lot
shrine: **5** Caaba, Kaaba
son: **5** Isaac, Medan, Shuah **6** Midian, Zimran **7** Ishmael
wife: **4** Sara **5** Hagar, Sarah **7** Keturah

ABRASIVE: **4** sand **5** emery, harsh **6** coarse, quartz **8** annoying **9** provoking, sandpaper **10** irritating

ABREAST: **4** even **5** abeam **6** au fait, beside, modern **7** aligned, popular **8** informed, parallel **9** alongside, au courant **10** side by side **12** contemporary

ABRI: **4** shed **6** cavity, dugout **7** shelter

ABRIDGE: **3** cut **4** trim **5** limit **6** lessen, reduce, shrink **7** capsule, curtail, shorten **8** condense, diminish, minimize, retrench **10** abbreviate

ABRIDGMENT: **5** brief **6** digest, precis, sketch **7** epitome, outline, summary **8** decrease, synopsis **9** lessening, reduction **10** compendium

ABROAD: **3** off, out **4** asea, away **5** astir, forth **6** astray **7** distant **8** overseas

ABROGATE: **4** undo, void **5** annul, quash, remit **6** cancel, negate, repeal, revoke **7** abolish, nullify, rescind **8** dissolve, overrule **9** repudiate

ABRUPT: **4** curt, fast, rude **5** blunt, brief, brisk, gruff, hasty, quick, sharp, short, steep, swift, terse **6** snippy, sudden **7** brusque **8** headlong, impolite **9** impetuous **10** unexpected **11** precipitous **13** unceremonious

ABSALOM:
brother: **7** Solomon **8** Adonijah
captain: **5** Amasa
father: **5** David
killer: **4** Joab
mother: **6** Maacah
sister: **5** Tamar

ABSCESS: **4** boil, sore **5** botch, ulcer **6** lesion

ABSCOND: **3** fly, run **4** bolt, flee, skip **5** elope, scram, split **6** decamp, escape, vanish **12** absquatulate

ABSENCE: **3** cut **4** AWOL, lack, void, want **5** leave **6** vacuum **7** truancy **8** omission **10** deficiency, withdrawal

ABSENT: **3** off **4** away, gone **5** empty **6** truant **7** lacking, missing

ABSENTMINDED: **4** lost **5** blank **6** dreamy **7** bemused, far away **8** distrait, dreaming, unseeing **9** oblivious **10** abstracted **11** inattentive

ABSENT WITHOUT LEAVE: **4** AWOL

ABSOLUTE: **4** pure, real, sure, true **5** sheer, stark, total, utter, whole **6** actual, entire, simple **7** perfect **8** complete, definite, despotic, explicit, implicit, outright, positive **9** arbitrary, downright, imperious, undoubted **10** autocratic **11** categorical **13** unconditional

ABSOLUTELY: **3** yea, yes **4** amen **5** quite, truly **6** indeed, really, wholly **9** certainly, perfectly **10** definitely, positively, thoroughly **13** unequivocally

ABSOLUTION: **5** mercy **6** pardon **7** amnesty, release **9** cleansing, remission **11** condonation, exculpation, forgiveness

ABSOLVE: **4** free **5** clear, remit **6** acquit, excuse, exempt, pardon **7** forgive, release **8** dispense, liberate, overlook **9** discharge, exculpate, exonerate, vindicate **10** disculpate

ABSORB: **5** merge, unite **6** engage, enwrap, imbibe, soak up **7** combine, consume, engross, immerse, occlude **8** permeate **10** assimilate **11** incorporate

ABSORBED: **4** deep, rapt **6** intent **7** riveted **8** immersed, involved **9** engrossed **11** preoccupied

ABSTAIN: **4** curb, deny, fast **5** avoid, cease, forgo, spurn, waive **6** desist, eschew, pass up, refuse, reject **7** forbear, refrain **8** teetotal

ABSTEMIOUS: **3** dry **5** sober **7** ascetic, austere, sparing **8** moderate **9** abstinent, temperate **11** straitlaced

ABSTINENCE: **8** sobriety **9** restraint **10** abstention, self-denial **12** renunciation

ABSTRACT: **4** cull, deed, pure **5** brief, ideal **6** deduct, divert, remove, unreal **7** abridge, excerpt, obscure, purloin, summary **8** abstruse, detached, esoteric, separate, synopsis, withdraw **9** epitomize, imaginary, recondite, summarize **10** compendium **11** theoretical **12** non-objective **13** expressionism

ABSTRACTED: **4** lost **7** bemused, pensive **8** absorbed **9** engrossed, oblivious **11** preoccupied **12** absentminded

ABSTRUSE: **4** deep **5** ideal **6** remote, subtle **7** complex, obscure **8** abstract, esoteric, profound **9** recondite **10** mysterious, perplexing

ABSURD: **4** wild **5** crazy, inane, kooky, loony, silly, wacky **6** stupid **7** asinine, foolish, idiotic **9** ludicrous, senseless **10** irrational, ridiculous **11** meaningless, nonsensical **12** preposterous

ABUNDANCE: **4** glut, mass **5** store **6** oodles, plenty, riches, wealth **7** surplus **8** fullness, opulence **9** affluence, amplitude, plenitude, profusion **10** prosperity

ABUNDANT: **4** lush, rich, rife **5** ample **6** galore, lavish **7** copious, fertile, profuse, replete, teeming **8** brimming, fruitful, generous, numerous, prolific **9** abounding, bountiful, plenteous, plentiful **11** overflowing

ABUSE: **3** mar, tax **4** flay, harm, hurt, maul **5** curse, fault, scold, wrong **6** berate, defame, defile, injure, insult, misuse, punish **7** affront, bedevil, calumny, cruelty, exploit, obloquy, pervert, slander, violate **8** belittle, derogate, maltreat, misapply, mistreat **9** blaspheme, castigate, desecrate, disparage, invective, objurgate **10** manipulate, opprobrium, scurrility **12** vituperation

ABUSIVE: **4** foul, vile **5** harsh, rough **6** savage **7** corrupt, profane **8** insolent, libelous, scornful **9** insulting, offensive **10** calumnious, scurrilous **11** blasphemous

ABUT: **4** join **5** flank, touch **6** adjoin, border **8** adjacent

ABYSMAL: **4** deep **6** dreary **7** endless **8** infinite, profound, unending **9** boundless **10** bottomless

ABYSS: **3** pit **4** deep, gulf, hell, void **5** chasm, Hades **6** bottom, cavity, depths, vorago **7** inferno **8** crevasse, deepness

ACACIA: **4** tree **5** babul, boree, cooba, myall, thorn **6** legume, locust, mimosa, wattle **7** catechu **9** boobyalla, gum arabic

ACADEMIC: **5** rigid **6** formal, unreal **7** bookish, classic, erudite, learned **8** educated, pedantic **9** professor, scholarly **10** collegiate **11** quodlibetic, theoretical

year division: **4** term **7** quarter **8** semester **9** trimester

ACADEMY: **6** lyceum, manege, school **7** college, society **8** academie, seminary **9** institute **10** university **11** institution

ACAUDAL: **7** anurous **8** tailless

ACCEDE: **3** let **5** admit, agree, allow, enter, grant, yield **6** assent, attain, comply, concur, permit **7** approve, consent **9** acquiesce **11** acknowledge

ACCELERATE: **3** gun, rev **4** race, rush **5** hurry **6** hasten **7** advance, forward, further, quicken, speed up **8** dispatch, expedite, increase **9** stimulate **11** precipitate

ACCELERATOR: **5** pedal **8** gas pedal, throttle **9** activator, cyclotron

ACCENT: **4** beat, mark, tone **5** drawl, ictus, pitch, pulse, sound, throb, twang **6** brogue, rhythm, stress **7** cadence, dialect **8** emphasis, tonality **9** emphasize **10** inflection, intonation

mark: **5** acute, grave **10** circumflex

syllable: **5** arsis

ACCENTUATE: **6** set off, stress **7** feature, sharpen **8** bring out **9** emphasize, intensify

ACCEPT: **3** buy **4** bear, take **5** admit, adopt, agree, allow, brant, honor **6** assent, endure, ratify, submit, suffer **7** approve, believe, embrace, espouse, receive, sustain **8** tolerate **9** acquiesce, undertake, withstand **10** understand **11** acknowledge

ACCEPTABLE: **4** fair **6** decent, viable **7** average **8** adequate, all right, pleasant, suitable **9** palatable, tolerable **10** sufficient **12** satisfactory

ACCEPTED: **5** valid **6** chosen, normal, proper **7** correct, popular, routine **8** approved, credited, standard **9** canonical, customary, prevalent **10** sanctioned **12** conventional

ACCESS: **3** way **4** adit, door, gate, path, road **5** entry, onset, route, spell **6** attack, avenue, entree, portal, street, tunnel **7** passage **8** approach, entrance, eruption, increase, paroxysm **10** admittance, right of way

ACCESSIBLE: **4** near, open **5** handy **6** nearby, patent, public **8** pervious **9** available, reachable **10** attainable, convenient, obtainable, procurable **12** approachable, unrestricted

ACCESSION: **5** enter **7** arrival **8** addition, approach **9** agreement, inaugural, increment, induction **10** usurpation **11** acquisition **12** installation

ACCESSORY: **4** aide, ally, plus, tool **5** extra **6** helper **7** abettor, adjunct **8** additive **9** appendage, assistant, auxiliary, component, secondary **10** accomplice, additional, attachment, incidental, subsidiary, supplement **11** concomitant, contingency, contributor, subordinate, subservient **12** appurtenance, contributory **13** accompaniment

ACCIDENT: **3** hap **4** case, fate, luck **5** event, fluke, wreck **6** chance, hazard, mishap **7** smashup **8** calamity, disaster, incident **9** collision **10** misfortune **11** catastrophe, contingency, contretemps **12** misadventure

ACCIDENTAL: **3** odd **6** casual, chance, random **9** extrinsic, haphazard, secondary, unplanned **10** coincident, extraneous, fortuitous, incidental, unexpected, unintended **11** conditional, inadvertent, subordinate **12** adventitious **13** serendipitous, unintentional

ACCLAIM: **4** clap, fame, hail, laud **5** cheer, extol, honor, kudos **6** bravos, homage, praise, repute, salute **7** applaud, approve, commend, glorify, ovation **8** plaudits **10** compliment **11** approbation

ACCLIMATE: **5** adapt, inure **6** harden, season **7** toughen **8** accustom **9** climatize, condition, habituate **11** accommodate

ACCLIVITY: **4** bank, hill, rise **7** incline, upgrade **9** elevation

ACCOLADE: **5** award, honor, medal **6** eulogy, praise, salute **7** laurels, tribute **8** ceremony, citation, encomium **9** laudation **10** compliment, decoration, salutation **11** recognition

ACCOMMODATE: **3** fit **4** give, help, hold, lend, suit **5** adapt, board, defer, house, lodge, serve, yield **6** adjust, change, comply, modify, oblige, settle, tailor **7** conform, contain **9** reconcile

ACCOMPANY: **4** join, lead **5** usher **6** assist, attend, convey, convoy, escort, follow, squire **7** conduct **8** chaperon **9** associate **10** supplement

ACCOMPLICE: **4** aide **5** crony **6** cohort, flunky, helper **7** abettor, partner **8** henchman **9** accessory, assistant, associate, colleague **11** confederate

ACCOMPLISH: **3** end, win **4** gain **5** reach **6** attain, effect, finish, manage **7** achieve, execute, fulfill, furnish, perform, produce, realize, succeed **8** complete, dispatch, engineer **10** consummate

ACCOMPLISHED: **3** apt **4** able, done **5** adept, ended **6** expert, gifted, proven **7** skilled **8** finished, polished, talented **9** brilliant **10** proficient

ACCOMPLISHMENT: **3** art **4** deed, feat **5** craft, skill **7** success, triumph **8** learning **11** culmination, performance, realization

ACCORD: **4** deal, give **5** agree, allot, award, grant, merge, tally **6** accede, adjust, bestow, concur, treaty, unison **7** concede, concert, consent, rapport **8** affinity, volition **9** harmonize, reconcile **10** compliance, conformity, correspond

ACCORDANT: **4** like **7** attuned **8** coherent, parallel, suitable **9** assenting, congruous, consonant **10** compatible, consistent, harmonious **13** corresponding

ACCORDINGLY: **4** ergo, then, thus **5** hence **6** whence **9** therefore, thereupon, wherefore **12** consequently

ACCOST: **4** dare, hail, meet **5** greet, hound, speak **6** bother, salute, waylay **7** address, solicit **8** approach, confront **9** encounter

ACCOUNT: **3** tab, use **4** bill, item, rank, rate, tale, view **5** basis, count, score, story, value, worth **6** assess, client, detail, esteem, ledger, profit, reason, record, report, repute **7** believe, history, invoice, recital **8** business, customer, estimate **9** advantage, chronicle, discourse, inventory, narrative, statement **10** commentary, importance, recitation **11** bookkeeping, description, explanation

ACCOUNTABLE: **6** liable **8** amenable, culpable **10** answerable, explicable **11** responsible

ACCOUNTANT: **3** CPA **5** clerk **7** actuary, auditor **8** reckoner **10** bookkeeper, controller

ACCOUTRE: **3** arm, rig **4** gear **5** array, dress, equip **6** attire, clothe, outfit **7** costume, furnish **8** decorate **9** embellish

ACCREDIT: **4** okay **6** assign, charge, empower, ratify **7** approve, certify, confirm, endorse, license **8** deputize, notarize, sanction, validate **9** attribute, authorize **10** commission

ACCRETION: **4** gain, rise **6** growth **8** addition, increase **9** coherence, expansion, increment **11** enlargement **12** accumulation

ACCRUE: **3** add **4** earn, gain, grow **5** amass, swell **7** acquire, collect, redound **8** increase, multiply, snowball

ACCUMULATE: **4** bank, fund, heap, mass, pile **5** stack, stock, store **7** backlog **8** dividend, interest, treasure **9** inventory **11** aggregation

ACCUMULATION: **7** accrual, buildup **9** gathering **10** collecting

ACCURATE: **4** true **5** exact, right **7** certain, correct, precise **8** reliable **9** authentic, errorless **10** dependable, meticulous

ACCURSED: **4** vile **6** damned, doomed, odious **7** hellish **8** infamous **9** abhorrent, loathsome, repugnant, revolting **10** abominable, detestable

ACCUSE: **4** cite **5** blame **6** allege, attack, charge, defame, finger, indict **7** arraign, impeach **8** denounce, reproach **9** inculpate **10** calumniate **11** incriminate, recriminate

ACCUSER: **8** libelant **9** plaintiff **10** prosecutor **11** complainant **12** incriminator

ACCUSTOM: **3** use **4** want **5** adapt, drill, inure **6** harden, orient **7** toughen **9** acclimate, condition, habituate **11** familiarize

ACE: **3** jot, one, pip **4** hero, star, tops **5** adept, flyer, point **6** expert, tiptop **7** aviator **8** topnotch **9** hole-in-one **11** crackerjack

ACERBATE: **3** vex **7** envenom **8** embitter, irritate **9** infuriate **10** exasperate

ACERBIC: **3** dry **4** acid, sour, tart **5** acrid, harsh, sharp **6** bitter **9** corrosive, sarcastic **10** astringent

ACETIC ACID: **7** acetate, vinegar **8** vesicant **9** corrosive

ACHE: **4** hurt, long, pain, pang **5** mourn, smart, throb **6** desire, grieve, hunger, suffer, twinge **7** agonize, anguish **8** soreness

ACHIEVE: **3** get **4** earn, gain **5** reach **6** attain, effect, obtain **7** fulfill, produce, realize, succeed, triumph **8** complete **9** actualize **10** accomplish

ACHIEVEMENT: **3** act **4** coup, deed, feat **7** mastery **10** attainment **11** realization, tour de force **14** accomplishment

ACHILLES:
advisor: **6** Nestor
father: **6** Peleus **7** Phoenix
fought: **9** Trojan War
friend: **9** Patroclus
grandfather: **6** Aeacus
hero in: **5** Iliad
horse: **7** Xanthus
killed: **6** Hector
killer: **5** Paris
lover: **7** Briseis
mother: **6** Thetis
teacher: **6** Chiron **7** Centaur
vulnerable part: **4** heel

ACHROMATIC: **4** gray **7** neutral **8** diatonic **9** achromous, colorless

ACID: **3** LSD **4** acyl, base, sour, tart **5** acerb, acrid, amino, boric, harsh, iodic, malic, oleic, sharp **6** acetic, acetyl, alkali, biting, bitter, citric, cyanic, formic, lactic **7** acetose, acetous, benzoic, malonyl, pungent, stearic **8** benzolyl, carbolic, tartaric **9** corrosive

ACIS:
father: **6** Faunus
killer: **10** Polyphemus
lover: **7** Galatea

ACKNOWLEDGE: **3** nod **4** tell **5** admit, allow, thank **6** accept, affirm, answer, assent, avouch, reveal **7** concede, confess, declare, divulge, profess **8** disclose, proclaim **9** recognize

ACME: **3** top **4** apex, peak **5** crest, crown **6** apogee, climax, height, heyday, summit, zenith **7** maximum **8** pinnacle **11** culmination

ACOLYTE: **3** fan **6** helper, novice **7** devotee **8** altar boy, follower **9** assistant, attendant

ACONITE: **8** cammarum **9** monkshood, wolfsbane

ACORN: **3** nut, oak **4** mast **6** camata **7** ballote, bellote **8** balanoid, camatina

ACQUAINT: **4** meet, tell **5** teach **6** advise, inform, notify **7** apprise, present **8** disclose **9** enlighten, introduce **11** familiarize

ACQUAINTANCE: **4** kith, mate **6** friend **7** comrade **9** associate, companion **10** friendship **11** familiarity

ACQUAINTED: **6** au fait, versed **8** familiar, informed **10** conversant

ACQUIESCE: **3** bow **5** abide, agree, allow, grant, yield **6** accede, accept, comply, concur, submit **7** concede, conform, succumb

ACQUIRE: **3** add, get **4** earn, gain, grab, make, reap **5** amass, learn, reach **6** attain, garner, gather, obtain, secure **7** collect, procure **8** contract

ACQUISITIVE: **4** avid **6** greedy **7** selfish **8** covetous **10** prehensile

ACQUIT: **3** act **4** free **5** clear **6** excuse, pardon, parole **7** absolve, amnesty, conduct, release **8** liberate, reprieve **9** discharge, exonerate, vindicate

ACRID: **4** sour **5** harsh, sharp **6** biting, bitter **7** pungent, reeking **8** stinging, virulent **9** acidulous, corrosive **10** astringent, irritating

ACRIMONIOUS: **3** mad **5** angry, cross, harsh, irate, nasty, sharp, surly, testy **6** bitter, cranky **7** caustic **8** spiteful, stinging **9** rancorous, resentful **11** belligerent, contentious, quarrelsome

ACROSS: **4** over **5** total **6** beyond, wholly **7** athwart **8** opposite, sweeping **10** altogether, transverse

ACROSTIC: **4** game **6** cipher, phrase, puzzle **7** acronym **8** wordplay **11** composition

ACT: **3** gig, law **4** bill, deed, fake, feat, move, play, skit, turn, work **5** doing, edict, feign, serve, stunt **6** behave, bestir, decide, decree **7** comport, exploit, perform, portray, pretend, statute **8** function, simulate **9** alternate, ordinance, represent **10** observance, theatrical **11** impersonate, performance

ACTION: **3** fun **4** bowl, case, deed, fray, step, suit, work **5** arena, cause, fight, force, means, stage **6** affair, battle, motion, trover, unused **7** conduct, dormant, process, stadium **8** behavior, conflict, disabled, fighting, function, maneuver, movement, replevin **9** adventure, animation, sidelined **10** deportment, enterprise, excitement, litigation, proceeding **11** inoperative, transaction

ACTIVATE: **4** stir **5** impel, rouse, start **6** arouse, charge, prompt **8** energize, vitalize

ACTIVE: **4** busy, spry **5** agile, alert, brisk, peppy, quick, zippy **6** hearty, lively, moving, nimble **7** dynamic, kinetic, working **8** animated, athletic, spirited, vigorous **9** assiduous, energetic, sprightly, vivacious **11** industrious

ACTIVITY: **3** ado **4** life, stir, work **6** bustle, flurry, tumult **7** pursuit **8** business, exercise, function, movement **10** occupation **11** undertaking

ACTOR: **3** bit, ham **4** cast, diva, doer, hero, hint, lead, mime, role, side, star, word **5** extra, heavy, mimic, super **6** emoter, mummer, player, prompt, troupe **7** artiste, company, heroine, histrio, ingenue, stand-in, starlet, trouper, villain **8** comedian, juvenile, thespian **9** performer, portrayer, soubrette, tragedian **10** understudy **11** barnstormer, entertainer

ACTUAL: **4** real, true **6** extant **7** certain, factual, genuine **8** bona fide, concrete, existing, material, positive, tangible **9** authentic, veritable **10** prevailing **11** substantial **12** indisputable

ACTUALITY: **4** fact **5** being, truth **6** verity **7** reality **9** existence

ACTUATE: **4** move, stir **5** cause, drive, enact, impel, spark, start **6** arouse, incite, prompt, propel **7** agitate, animate, enliven, inspire, provoke, trigger **8** motivate **9** instigate, stimulate

ACUMEN: **3** wit **6** wisdom **7** insight **8** keenness, sagacity **9** acuteness **10** astuteness, perception, shrewdness **11** discernment, percipience **12** perspicacity

ACUTE: **4** dire, keen **5** canny, piked, quick, sharp, smart **6** astute, clever, severe, shrewd, subtle, urgent **7** crucial, extreme, intense, pointed **8** critical, incisive, piercing **9** ingenious, intuitive, knifelike, sensitive **10** discerning, perceptive **11** intelligent, penetrating

ADAGE: **3** saw **4** quip **5** axiom, motto **6** cliche, dictum, homily, saying, truism **7** bromide, precept, proverb **8** aphorism, apothegm

ADAH:
husband: **4** Esau **6** Lamech
son: **5** Jabal, Jubal **7** Eliphaz **9** Bashemath

ADAM:
grandson: **4** Enos **5** Enoch
son: **4** Abel, Cain, Seth
wife: **3** Eve **6** Lilith

ADAMANT: **3** set **4** firm, hard **5** rigid, stony **8** stubborn **9** immovable **10** inflexible, relentless, unbendable, unyielding

ADAM BEDE: **11** George Eliot

ADAPT: **3** fit **4** suit **5** alter, inure, shape **6** adjust, change, modify, tailor, temper **7** arrange, conform, convert, qualify, reshape **9** acclimate, harmonize, reconcile **10** assimilate **11** accommodate

ADAPTABLE: **6** mobile, pliant, supple **8** amenable, flexible **9** alterable, malleable, resilient, tractable, versatile **10** adjustable, changeable **11** conformable **12** reconcilable

ADD: **3** sum **4** fuse, join, plus **5** affix, annex, recap, tally, total, unite **6** append, attach, expand, figure, reckon **7** amplify, augment, combine, compile, compute, connect, subjoin **8** compound, increase **9** calculate, summarize **10** strengthen, supplement

ADDICT: **3** fan **4** buff, head, user **5** fiend, hound, slave **6** junkie **7** druggie, fanatic, habitue, hophead, pothead **8** acidhead **9** mainliner **10** aficionado, enthusiast

ADDICTION: **5** habit **6** fetish **8** fixation **9** obsession, surrender **10** compulsion **11** enslavement

ADDITION: **4** plus, wing **5** annex, extra, rider **6** prefix, suburb, suffix **7** adjunct, codicil, joining **8** addendum, increase, totaling **9** accession, accretion, amendment, appendage, expansion, extension, summation **11** calculation

ADDITIONAL: **3** new **4** more **5** extra **7** another **9** auxiliary **12** supplemental

ADDLED: **5** dizzy, giddy, silly **7** foolish, muddled **8** confused **9** befuddled, flustered **10** bewildered

ADDRESS: **3** aim, sue, wit, woo **4** call, hail, home, send, talk **5** abode, greet, orate, poise, skill, speak **6** adjust, aplomb, appeal, direct, eulogy, manner, salute **7** lecture, oration **8** approach, converse, dispatch, harangue, location, petition, presence **9** dexterity, discourse, residence, statement **10** allocution, peroration

ADDUCE: **4** cite, name **5** offer, quote **6** allege, submit, tender **7** advance, mention, present, produce, propose, suggest **8** document

ADEPT: **3** ace, apt **5** handy, sharp **6** adroit, artist, expert, master **7** capable, skilled **8** skillful **9** dexterous, masterful, tolerable **10** acceptable, consummate, proficient **12** professional

ADEQUATE: **4** fair, okay **5** ample **6** decent, plenty **8** possible, suitable **9** competent, effective, tolerable **10** acceptable, answerable, sufficient **12** commensurate, satisfactory

ADHERE: **3** fix **4** glue **5** cling, stick **6** cleave, cohere, fasten

ADHERENCE: **4** bond **7** loyalty **8** cohesion, devotion, fidelity **9** constancy, obedience **10** attachment **12** faithfulness

ADHERENT: **3** fan **4** ally **5** pupil **6** votary **7** acolyte **8** believer, disciple, follower, partisan, upholder **9** supporter

ADHESIVE: **3** gum **4** bond, glue, tape **5** epoxy, gooey, paste **6** cement, mastic, sticky **7** stickum **8** birdlime, clinging, mucilage **9** tenacious

ADIEU: **3** bye **4** ta-ta **5** adios, aloha **6** so long **7** cheerio, good-bye **8** au revoir, farewell, godspeed **11** leave-taking, valediction

ADIT: **3** way **5** entry, stulm **6** access, tunnel **7** channel, opening **8** approach, entrance **9** admission **10** passageway

ADJACENT: **4** next **5** close **6** beside, nearby **7** against, meeting **8** abutting, touching **9** adjoining, bordering **10** juxtaposed **11** coterminous, neighboring

ADJECTIVE: **8** modifier **9** dependent, gerundive, qualifier

ADJOIN: **3** add **4** meet **5** touch, unite, verge **6** append, attach, border **7** connect, contact **8** neighbor **9** juxtapose

ADJOURN: **3** end **5** close, defer, delay **6** recess, shelve **7** disband, dismiss **8** dissolve, postpone, prorogue **9** terminate **11** discontinue

ADJUDGE: **4** deem, rule **5** award **6** decide, decree, settle **7** referee **8** consider **9** arbitrate, determine **10** adjudicate

ADJUNCT: **4** aide **5** affix, annex **7** quality **8** addition, appendix **9** accessory, appendage, associate, auxiliary, colleague **10** complement, supplement **11** subordinate **12** appurtenance

ADJURE: **3** ask, beg **5** plead **6** appeal, charge, exhort **7** beseech, entreat, implore **8** petition

ADJUST: **3** fix, rig, set **4** bend, move, suit, trim, true, tune **5** adapt, align, amend **6** attune, change, tailor, temper **7** address, arrange, balance, conform, correct, justify, rectify **8** accustom, modulate, regulate **9** harmonize **10** coordinate, straighten **11** accommodate

ADJUTANT: **4** aide **5** stork **6** helper **7** hurglia, officer **9** assistant, auxiliary

ADMETUS:
father: **6** Pheres
ruled: **8** Thessaly
wife: **8** Alcestis

ADMINISTER: **3** run **4** boss, dose, rule **5** apply, issue, treat **6** direct, govern, manage **7** conduct, control, execute, furnish, oversee **8** dispense **9** supervise **10** distribute **11** superintend

ADMINISTRATOR: **7** manager, officer, provost, trustee **8** director, executor, official **9** executrix

ADMIRABLE: **5** great **6** worthy **8** laudable, splendid **9** deserving, excellent, venerable **12** praiseworthy

ADMIRE: **4** like **5** adore, prize, value **6** esteem, praise, regard, revere **7** approve, cherish, idolize, respect **8** treasure, venerate

ADMIRER: **3** fan **4** buff **5** lover **6** backer, votary **7** booster, devotee, fancier **8** follower

ADMISSION: **3** fee **4** gate **5** entry **6** access, charge, entree, ticket **8** entrance **9** testimony **10** admittance, concession, confession, disclosure

ADMIT: **3** let, own **4** avow **5** agree, allow, enter, grant **6** accept, avouch, enroll, induct, permit **7** adhibit, concede, confess, declare, include, profess, receive, welcome **9** recognize **11** acknowledge

ADMONISH: **4** warn **5** alert, chide, scold **6** advise, enjoin, exhort, rebuke, remind **7** caution, counsel, lecture, reprove, upbraid **8** reproach **9** criticize, reprehend, reprimand

ADO: **4** fuss, stir **5** tizzy **6** bother, bustle, flurry, hassle, hubbub, racket, ruckus, uproar **7** turmoil **9** commotion, confusion **10** excitement, hullabaloo

ADOBE: **3** mud **4** clay, tile **5** brick, house **6** mudcap

ADOLESCENCE: **5** teens, youth **6** nonage **7** puberty **12** youthfulness

ADOLESCENT: **3** boy, lad **4** girl, lass **5** green, minor **6** callow **8** immature, juvenile, teenager, youthful **9** pubescent

ADONIS:
father: **7** Cinyras
killed by: **4** boar
loved: **5** Venus **9** Aphrodite
mother: **5** Myrrh **6** Smyrna

ADOPT: **3** use **4** pass, take **5** enact **6** accept, assume, borrow, choose, employ, select **7** approve, embrace, espouse, receive, support **8** advocate, practice **10** naturalize **11** appropriate

ADORABLE: **4** cute **5** sweet **6** divine, lovely **7** lovable, winsome **8** charming, precious **10** cuddlesome, delightful **12** irresistible

ADORATION: **6** homage **7** worship **8** devotion, idolatry **10** veneration

ADORE: **4** love **5** exalt, honor **6** admire, esteem, praise, revere **7** cherish, glorify, idolize, respect, worship **8** enshrine, venerate

ADORN: **4** deck, trim **5** array, begem, grace, primp, prink **6** bedeck, emboss, enrich **7** bedizen, bejewel, dignify, enhance, furbish, garnish **8** beautify, decorate, ornament **9** caparison, embellish, glamorize

AD REM: **8** relevant **9** pertinent **10** applicable **15** straightforward

ADRIFT: **4** lost **5** loose **6** afloat, astray, aweigh **7** aimless **8** derelict, insecure, straying **9** wandering

ADROIT: **3** apt **4** deft **5** adept, canny, handy, quick, sharp, slick **6** artful, astute, brainy, clever, facile **7** cunning **8** dextrous, skillful **9** dexterous, ingenious, masterful **10** proficient **11** intelligent, resourceful

ADULT: **4** aged, ripe **5** elder, grown **6** mature, nubile **8** seasoned, tempered **9** developed

ADULTERATE: **3** cut, mix **4** thin **5** alter, spike, taint, water **6** debase, dilute, doctor, impure, weaken **7** falsify **8** denature, spurious **11** counterfeit

ADUMBRATE: **3** fog **4** bode, mist **5** augur, cloud **6** darken, sketch **7** obscure, outline, portend, presage, suggest **8** foretell, indicate, intimate **9** obfuscate **10** foreshadow

ADVANCE: **3** aid **4** cite, gain, help, inch, lend, loan **5** boost, creep, raise, serve **6** adduce, allege, assign, better, hasten, prepay, uplift **7** elevate, forward, further, improve, proceed, promote, propose, upgrade **8** increase, overture, progress **9** encourage, evolution **10** accelerate, aggrandize **11** improvement

ADVANCED: **4** aged **5** ahead **7** elderly, liberal **8** farthest, foremost, precious, tolerant **9** premature **11** enlightened, progressive

ADVANTAGE: **3** aid, use **4** boot, edge, gain, odds **5** favor, start, stead **6** behalf, profit **7** account, benefit **8** handicap, interest, leverage **11** opportunity, superiority

ADVANTAGEOUS: **6** useful **7** gainful **8** valuable **9** conducive, expedient, favorable **10** auspicious, beneficial, commodious, profitable **11** encouraging

ADVENT: **5** onset **6** coming **7** arrival **8** approach **9** beginning **11** incarnation **12** commencement

ADVENTITIOUS: **5** alien **6** casual **7** foreign **9** extrinsic **10** accidental, fortuitous **12** nonessential

ADVENTURE: **4** dare, feat, risk **5** event, quest, stunt **6** chance, danger, hazard **7** exploit **8** escapade **10** enterprise, experience **11** undertaking

ADVENTURER: **4** hero **7** gambler **9** daredevil, mercenary, sportsman **12** swashbuckler

ADVENTUROUS: **4** bold, rash **5** brash, brave **6** daring, errant **8** perilous, reckless **9** audacious, foolhardy, hazardous **10** courageous

ADVERSARY: **3** foe **4** anti **5** enemy, rival **8** opponent **9** assailant **10** antagonist, competitor

ADVERSE: **3** con **7** against, counter, harmful, opposed **8** contrary, critical, inimical, negative, opposing, opposite **9** difficult **11** conflicting, detrimental, disinclined **12** inauspicious

ADVERSITY: **3** woe **5** trial **6** misery, sorrow **7** setback, tragedy, trouble **8** calamity, hardship **9** suffering **10** affliction, misfortune **11** catastrophe

ADVERT: **4** note **5** refer **6** attend, notice **7** observe **8** consider

ADVERTISE: **4** plug, push, show **5** boast **6** blazon, inform, notify, report **7** declare, display, exploit, promote, publish **8** announce, ballyhoo, proclaim **9** broadcast, publicize

ADVERTISEMENT: **4** bill, sign, spot **5** blurb, flyer, promo **6** banner, dodger, insert, notice, poster, teaser **7** handout, leaflet, placard, release, stuffer **8** circular, handbill **9** billboard, broadside **10** commercial, skywriting

ADVICE: **3** tip **4** news, rede, word **6** notice **7** caution, consult, counsel, opinion, pointer, warning **8** guidance **9** direction **10** admonition, suggestion **11** information, instruction **12** intelligence

ADVISABLE: **4** wise **5** sound **6** proper **7** fitting, politic, prudent **8** sensible **9** desirable, expedient

ADVISE: **4** clue, post, tell, urge, warn **5** guide **6** inform, notify **7** apprise, caution, counsel, suggest **8** acquaint, admonish, advocate **9** encourage, recommend

ADVISER, ADVISOR: **4** aide, tout **5** coach **6** mentor, nestor **7** tipster **9** confidant, counselor **10** consultant, instructor

ADVISORY: **5** board, panel **6** notice, report **7** cabinet, council, warning **8** ministry **9** committee **11** instructive

ADVOCATE: **3** pro **4** back, urge **5** favor, plead **6** advise, backer, defend, lawyer, uphold **7** endorse, espouse, promote **8** champion, defender, partisan **9** barrister, counselor, neonomian, paraclete, proponent, recommend, supporter **11** intercessor

ADZ, ADZE: **3** axe **6** pickax **7** hatchet

AEACUS:
father: **4** Zeus
lived: **5** Hades
mother: **6** Aegina
son: **6** Peleus, Phocus **7** Telamon
wife: **6** Endeis

AEETES:
daughter: **5** Medea **9** Chalciope
father: **6** Helios
kept: **12** Golden Fleece
kingdom: **7** Colchis
mother: **5** Perse
son: **8** Absyrtus, Apsyrtus
wife: **5** Idyia **9** Asterodea

AEGEAN SEA: **5** Crete, Psara, Psyra, Saros **6** Greece, Rhodes,

Samian, Turkey **7** Argolis, Corinth, Leleges, Samiote, Saronic

AEGIS: **4** Zeus **5** armor **6** Athena, shield **7** backing, control, defense **8** auspices, guidance **9** safeguard **10** protection **11** sponsorship

AEGISTHUS:
daughter: **7** Erigone
father: **8** Thyestes
killer: **7** Orestes
lover: **12** Clytemnestra
mother: **7** Pelopia
victim: **6** Atreus **9** Agamemnon

AEGYPTUS:
brother: **6** Danaus
father: **5** Belus
kingdom: **5** Egypt
mother: **8** Anchinoe

AELLO: **5** Harpy **7** Harpies, monster

AENEAS:
hero: **4** Troy
antagonist: **6** Turnus
father: **8** Anchises
friend: **7** Achates
loved: **4** Dido
mother: **5** Venus **9** Aphrodite
son: **5** Iulus **7** Silvius **8** Ascanius
wife: **6** Creusa **7** Lavinia

AENEID:
author: **6** Vergil, Virgil
first word: **4** arma
protagonist: **6** Aeneas
second word: **8** virumque
third word: **4** cano

AEON: **3** age **8** eternity

AERATE: **3** air **6** aerify, charge **7** freshen, inflate **9** oxygenate, ventilate

AERIAL: **3** air **4** airy **5** lofty **6** dreamy, unreal **7** antenna, soaring **8** ethereal **9** imaginary **11** atmospheric **13** unsubstantial

AERIE, EYRIE: **4** nest **5** brood **9** penthouse

AERONAUT: **4** Fogg **5** pilot **7** aviator **10** balloonist

AESCULAPIUS:
daughter: **6** Hygeia **7** Panacea
father: **6** Apollo
god of: **7** healing **8** medicine
killer: **4** Zeus **7** Jupiter
mother: **7** Coronis
son: **7** Machaon **9** Podalirus
teacher: **6** Chiron
wife: **6** Epione

AESTHETE: **8** virtuoso **10** dilettante **11** connoisseur

AESTHETIC: **8** artistic, esthetic, pleasing, tasteful **9** beautiful

AETHER:
father: **6** Erebus
personifies: **3** air, sky

AFFABLE: **4** warm **5** civil **6** benign, genial, polite, social **7** amiable, cordial, likable **8** charming, friendly, gracious, pleasant **9** agreeable, courteous, easygoing **10** accessible **11** complaisant

AFFAIR: **4** ball, gala, love **5** amour, event, issue, party, tryst **6** action **7** blowout, concern, liaison, romance, shindig **8** activity, business, endeavor, interest, occasion **9** gathering **10** engagement, proceeding **11** celebration, transaction **12** relationship

AFFECT: **3** act, hit **4** move, stir, sway **5** alter, bluff, fancy, feign, touch **6** assume, change, regard, strike **7** actuate, concern, embrace, operate, pretend, profess **8** frequent, interest, simulate **9** cultivate, influence **11** counterfeit

AFFECTATION: **4** airs, pose, sham **6** facade, fakery **8** artifice, pretense **9** hypocrisy, mannerism **10** pretension

AFFECTED: **4** vain **5** moved, upset **7** changed, mincing, stilted, touched **8** impaired, involved, mannered, precious **9** afflicted, unnatural **10** artificial, influenced **11** pretentious

AFFECTION: **4** love **5** fancy **6** esteem, liking, malady, regard, virtue, warmth **7** ailment, emotion, feeling, passion **8** devotion, fondness, sickness, weakness **10** friendship, propensity, tenderness

AFFECTIONATE: **4** dear, fond, warm **6** ardent, caring, loving, tender **7** adoring, amorous, devoted **8** attached, romantic **11** sentimental

AFFIANCED: **7** pledged **8** intended, plighted, promised **9** betrothed **10** engagement

AFFIDAVIT: **4** oath **5** jurat **8** document **9** statement **10** deposition **11** attestation

AFFILIATE: **3** arm **4** ally, join **5** group, merge, unite **6** attach, branch, relate **7** chapter, consort **9** associate, colleague **10** fraternize, subsidiary

AFFINITY: **3** kin **4** bias **5** fancy **6** accord, liking **7** analogy, rapport **8** fondness, relation, sympathy **10** attraction, connection, fellowship, preference, propensity, similarity **11** inclination, resemblance

AFFIRM: **3** say **4** aver, avow **5** claim, state, swear **6** allege, assert, attest, avouch, depose, ratify, uphold **7** contend, declare, profess, testify **8** maintain, validate **9** predicate **10** asseverate

AFFIRMATIVE: **3** aye, nod, yes **4** amen, yeah **7** hopeful **8** dogmatic, emphatic, positive **9** approving, assertive **10** conclusive **11** categorical, predicative

AFFIX: **3** add **4** glue, join, nail, seal **5** annex, paste, rivet, unite **6** anchor, append, attach, fasten, staple **7** connect, subjoin

AFFLICT: **3** try **4** hurt, pain **5** annoy, beset, gripe, smite, wound **6** bother, burden, harass, pester, plague **7** oppress, torment, trouble **8** distress

AFFLICTED: **3** sad **5** ailed **6** cursed, dolent **7** doleful, grieved **8** impaired, stricken **9** depressed, suffering **10** distressed

AFFLICTION: **3** rue **4** evil, pain **5** cross, grief, trial **6** misery, mishap, ordeal, sorrow **7** anguish, disease, illness, scourge **8** calamity, distress, hardship, sickness **9** adversity, heartache, martyrdom **10** misfortune **11** tribulation

AFFLUENCE: **4** flow **5** money **6** riches, wealth **7** fortune **8** opulence **9** abundance, plenitude **10** prosperity

AFFLUENT: **3** fat **4** rich **5** flush, river **6** loaded, stream **7** copious **9** pecunious, tributary

AFFORD: **4** bear, give, risk **5** grant, incur, spare, yield **6** invest, manage, supply **7** furnish, provide, sustain

AFFRAY: **4** feud, riot **5** brawl, clash, fight, melee **6** attack, battle, fracas, ruckus, tumult **7** assault, quarrel, scuffle **8** skirmish **9** encounter **10** donnybrook **11** altercation, disturbance

AFFRIGHT: **3** awe **5** alarm, daunt, panic, scare, spook **6** fright **7** startle, terrify **10** intimidate

AFFRONT: **3** cut **4** defy, meet, slap, snub **5** abuse, anger **6** injury, insult, nettle, offend, slight **7** outrage, provoke **8** disgrace, dishonor, irritate **9** humiliate, indignity **10** defamation

AFGHAN: **5** shawl, throw **7** blanket, crochet **8** covering, coverlet

AFGHANISTAN:
capital: **5** Kabul
cities: **5** Herat **8** Kandahar **12** Hazar-i-Sharif
continent: **4** Asia
ethnic groups: **5** Tajik, Uzbek **6** Hazara, Pathan **7** Pashtun, Sistani **8** Pashtoon
features: **4** Oxus **5** Kabul, Kunar **6** Khyber, Peiwar, Saberi, Salang **7** Helmand, Sikaram **8** Amu Darya **9** Hindu Kush **10** Shah Fuladi
languages: **4** Dari **6** Pashto, Pashtu, Pushtu, Turkic **7** Persian
monetary unit: **7** afghani

AFICIONADO: **3** fan **4** buff **5** hound, pupil **7** admirer, devotee, student **8** follower **10** enthusiast

AFIELD: **4** away **5** amiss **6** astray, beyond

AFIRE: **5** aglow **6** ablaze, aflame, ardent **7** burning, flaming, flaring, ignited

AFLOAT: **5** awash **6** adrift, buoyed, natant **7** rumored, sailing **9** operating **11** circulating

AFOOT: **5** about, astir **6** abroad **7** brewing, walking **9** happening

AFRAID: **4** wary **5** loath, sorry, timid **6** aghast, craven, scared **7** alarmed, chicken, fearful **8** cowardly, hesitant **9** concerned, petrified, reluctant, terrified **10** frightened **12** apprehensive, fainthearted

AFRESH: **4** anew, over **5** again, newly **6** encore, de novo, lately **8** repeated

AFRICA:
cities: **5** Cairo, Lagos, Tunis **7** Abidjan, Algiers, Nairobi **8** Cape Town, Kinshasa **10** Alexandria, Casablanca **12** Johannesburg
countries: **4** Chad, Mali, Togo **5** Benin, Congo, Egypt, Gabon, Ghana, Kenya, Libya, Niger, Sudan, Zaire **6** Angola, Gambia, Guinea, Malawi, Rwanda, Uganda, Zambia **7** Algeria, Burundi, Comoros, Lesotho, Liberia, Morocco, Nigeria, Senegal, Somalia, Tunisia **8** Botswana, Cameroon, Djibouti, Ethiopia, Tanzania, Zimbabwe **9** Cape Verde, Mauritius, Swaziland **10** Ivory Coast, Madagascar, Mauritania, Mozambique, Seychelles **11** Sierra Leone, South Africa **12** Guinea-Bissau,
ethnic groups: **3** Dru, Edo, Ewe, Fbo, Fon, Ijo, Vai, Vei, Yao **4** Agau, Agni, Akim, Akka, Akra, Alur, Arab, Asha, Bari, Beja, Boer, Boni, Copt, Efik, Egba, Ekoi, Fula, Hutu, Igbo, Kafa, Lozi, Luri, Madi, Moor, Nama, Nuba, Nupe, Qung, Riff, Saho, Sara, Yaka, Zulu **5** Bantu, Bassa, Batwa, Dinka, Fanti, Felup, Galla, Grebo, Gurma, Hausa, Inkra, Kafir, Mande, Masai, Mossi, Pygmy, Rundi, Shluh, Temne, Tutsi **6** Bariba, Basuto, Berber, Damara, Dorobo, Dyerma, Fulani, Hamite, Harari, Herero, Kabyle, Kikuyu, Nilote, Senufo, Somali, Tuareg, Ubangi, Watusi, Yoruba, Zenaga **7** Akwapim, Ashango, Ashanti, Bedouin, Malinke, Sandawe, Songhai, Swahili **8** Mandingo **9** Hottentot
features: **6** Nubian, Sahara **8** Kalahari **11** Kilimanjaro **15** Great Rift Valley
water: **3** Omo **4** Aden, Chad, Nile, Tana **5** Abaya, Congo, Gabes, Kyoga, Mweru, Ngami, Niger, Nyasa, Sidra, Tumba, Volta, Zaire **6** Albert, Chilwa, Dilolo, Guinea, Kariba, Moeris, Orange, Rudolf, Ruvuma, Shirwa, Ubangi **7** Leopold, Lualaba, Senegal, Tur-

kana, Zambezi **8** Banweulu, Victoria **10** Tanganyika

AFT: **4** back, past, rear **6** astern, behind **9** posterior

AFTER: **3** for **4** anon, back, next, past, soon **5** later, since **6** behind, beyond, hinder **8** rearward **9** following **10** concerning, subsequent

AFTERMATH: **5** issue **6** impact, payoff, result, sequel, upshot **7** outcome **8** offshoot **9** remainder **11** consequence

AFTERTHOUGHT: **6** review, sequel **10** postscript **15** reconsideration

AFTERWARDS: **4** next, then **5** later **9** following, thereupon **10** eventually **12** subsequently

AGA, AGHA: **4** lord **5** chief **6** leader **7** officer **8** official **9** authority, commander

AGAG:
killer: **6** Samuel
kingdom: **10** Amalekites

AGAIN: **4** also, more, over **5** recur **6** afresh, de novo, encore **7** besides, further **8** moreover **12** additionally

AGAINST: **3** con **4** anti, from, near, upon **6** beside, facing, versus **7** opposed **8** opposite, touching **10** concerning, respecting

AGAMEMNON:
antagonist: **9** Aegisthus
brother: **8** Menelaus
daughter: **7** Electra **9** Iphigenia **12** Chrysothemis
father: **6** Atreus
killer: **12** Clytemnestra
kingdom: **7** Mycenae
son: **7** Orestes
wife: **12** Clytemnestra

AGAPE: **4** agog, ajar, open **6** amazed **7** shocked, yawning **9** awestruck **10** astonished, bewildered, confounded **11** overwhelmed

AGATE: **3** eye, mib **4** Ider, ruby **6** achate, Brazil, marble, quartz **9** landscape **10** chalcedony

AGE: **3** eon, era **4** date, grow, span, time, wane **5** cycle, epoch, ripen, years **6** mature, mellow, period, wither **7** century, develop, interim **8** duration, eternity, lifetime, majority **10** generation, millennium
same: **6** coeval

AGED: **3** old **4** ripe, shot **5** anile, dated, hoary, passe **6** feeble, infirm, senile **7** ancient, antique, elderly **8** seasoned, timeworn **9** venerable **10** antiquated

AGELESS: **7** classic, eternal **8** dateless, enduring, timeless

AGENCY: **4** firm, news **5** cause, means **6** bureau, charge, medium, office **7** channel, company, vehicle **9** influence, operation

AGENDA: **4** card, list, plan **5** slate **6** docket, lineup **7** program **8** calendar, schedule **9** timetable

AGENOR:
brother: **5** Belus
daughter: **6** Europa
father: **7** Antenor **8** Poseidon
kingdom: **9** Phoenicia
mother: **5** Libya **6** Theano
son: **5** Cilix **6** Cadmus **7** Phoenix

AGENT: **3** fed, spy **4** doer, nark **5** cause, envoy, force, means, organ, proxy **6** broker, dealer, deputy, medium, seller **7** bailiff, channel, facient, steward **8** advocate, assignee, emissary, executor, operator **9** surrogate **10** commissary, instrument **11** facilitator, underwriter **12** intermediary, middleperson

AGGLOMERATE: **4** clot, lump, mass, pile **5** bunch **7** cluster **8** mobilize **9** aggregate **10** collection

AGGRANDIZE: **4** lift **5** boost, widen **6** dilate, extend, parlay **7** augment, broaden, dignify, elevate, enlarge, glorify, magnify, promote **8** increase, multiply

AGGRAVATE: **3** irk, nag **4** gall, rile **5** anger, annoy, peeve, rouse, upset **6** nettle, pester **7** enlarge, incense, inflame, magnify **8** aggrieve, heighten, increase, irritate **9** intensify **10** exacerbate, exasperate

AGGREGATE: **3** all, sum **4** bulk, mass **5** blend, bunch, gross, total, unite, whole **6** amount **8** compound **9** composite, summation **10** accumulate

AGGREGATION: **4** army, gang, herd **5** crowd, flock, group **7** cluster, company **8** assembly, quantity **9** congeries, gathering **10** cumulation **11** association, combination

AGGRESSION: **3** war **4** push, raid **5** fight **6** attack, injury **7** assault, offense **8** forceful, invasion **9** hostility, intrusion **10** antagonism **11** provocation

AGGRESSIVE: **4** bold, flip **7** intense, scrappy, zealous **8** barbaric, militant **9** ambitious, bellicose **10** pugnacious **12** enterprising

AGGRESSOR: **7** invader **8** attacker **9** assailant **10** antagonist

AGGRIEVE: **3** sad, try **4** hurt, pain **5** annoy, wrong **6** injure, woeful **7** afflict, oppress, trouble, unhappy **8** distress, mournful **9** aggravate, persecute **10** maltreated

AGHAST: **4** awed **6** afraid **7** anxious, shocked, stunned **8** appalled, startled **9** astounded, horrified, stupefied, terrified

AGILE: **4** deft, fast, keen, spry **5** brisk, fleet, light, lithe, quick, zippy **6** active, limber, nimble, supple **7** springy **8** athletic, dextrous **9** dexterous

AGITATE: **3** bug, irk **4** goad, move, rile, rock, seek **5** alarm, churn, drive, harry, rouse, shake, upset **6** bother, debate, excite, harass, rattle, ruffle **7** discuss, disturb, fluster, inflame, perturb, provoke, trouble **8** activate, convulse, disquiet, distress, irritate **10** discompose

AGITATION: **4** flap, fury **5** storm **6** bustle, flurry, tumult, unrest **7** ferment, flutter, rampage, tempest, turmoil **8** upheaval, violence **9** commotion, confusion, emotional **10** turbulence, uneasiness **11** trepidation

AGLAIA:
daughter: **7** Idomene
father: **7** Jupiter
husband: **4** Abas
mother: **8** Eurynome
son: **7** Proteus **8** Acrisius

AGNATE: **4** akin, like **6** allied **7** connate, kindred, related **10** affiliated

AGNOMEN: **4** name **5** alias **7** epithet, surname **8** nickname

AGNOSTIC: **5** pagan **7** doubter, heathen, infidel, skeptic **10** empiricist, unbeliever **11** freethinker

AGO: **4** back, erst, gone, past **5** since **6** before

AGOG: **4** avid, keen **5** eager **6** lively **7** excited **8** bursting, thrilled **9** awestruck, expectant, impatient **10** breathless

AGONIZE: **3** try **4** fret, rack **5** labor **6** lament, strain **7** crucify **8** struggle **10** excruciate

AGONY: **3** woe **4** pain **5** grief, pangs, trial **6** misery, sorrow **7** anguish, despair, torment, torture **8** distress **9** heartache, suffering **11** tribulation

AGRARIAN: **5** rural **7** natural **8** pastoral **10** campestral **12** agricultural

AGREE: **3** fit, yes **4** jibe, suit **5** admit, allow, equal, grant, match, yield **6** accede, accord, attune, comply, concur, square, submit, unison **7** arrange, concede, conform, consent **8** coincide **9** acquiesce, congruous, cooperate, harmonize, reconcile **10** correspond, homologate

AGREEABLE: **4** nice, fair **7** amiable, dulcify, willing **8** amenable, charming, pleasant, pleasing **9** appealing, compliant, congenial, consonant **10** acceptable, compatible, consenting, satisfying **11** consentient

AGREEMENT: **3** nod **4** deal, pact, writ **5** lease **6** accord, avowal, cartel, treaty **7** bargain, charter, consent, entente, harmony, promise, rapport **8** alliance, contract, covenant **9** consensus, indenture **10** accordance, conspiracy **11** arrangement **13** understanding

AGRICULTURE: **4** Dago, farm **5** Dagan, flora, grove, Picus, ranch **6** Grigit, Saturn, Vacuna **7** farming, orchard, tillage **8** agrology, agronomy, vineyard **9** gardening **11** arviculture, cultivation **12** horticulture
concerning: **7** georgic **8** geoponic
deity: **3** Ops **4** Nabu, Nebo, Thor **5** Ceres **6** Faunus, Tammuz **7** Demeter **8** Amaethon
device: **4** disk, plow **5** baler, drill, mower **6** binder, harrow, header, reaper, seeder, tedder **7** combine, tractor **8** thrasher, thresher **9** separator **10** cultivator **11** Caterpillar

AGROUND: **6** ashore, reefed **7** beached **8** stranded **11** shipwrecked

AGUE: **5** chill, fever **7** malaria **9** shivering

AHAB:
antagonist: **6** Elijah
daughter: **8** Athaliah
father: **4** Omri
killer: **4** Aram
kingdom: **6** Israel
son: **7** Ahaziah
wife: **7** Jezebel

AHASUERUS:
alias: **6** Xerxes **8** Cyaxares
kingdom: **6** Persia
son: **6** Darius
wife: **6** Esther, Vashti

AHAZ:
father: **6** Jotham
kingdom: **5** Judah
son: **8** Hezekiah
wife: **3** Abi

AHAZIAH:
father: **4** Ahab
killer: **4** Jehu
mother: **7** Jezebel
sister: **9** Jehosheba **11** Jehosobeath

AHEAD: **4** ante, fore **5** early **6** before, onward **7** forward, leading **8** advanced, foremost, previous **9** preceding **10** beforehand

AHINOAM:
father: **7** Ahimaaz
husband: **4** Saul **5** David
son: **5** Ammon

AID: **4** abet, alms, care, help **5** allay, coach, favor, grant, serve **6** assist, backup, relief, remedy, rescue, succor, uphold **7** advance, charity, forward, subsidy, support **8** befriend, benefact **9** alleviate **10** facilitate **11** collaborate

AIDA:
antagonist: **7** Amneris
composer: **5** Verdi

father: **8** Amonasro
lover: **7** Radames

AIDE: **5** gofer **6** deputy, helper, second **7** orderly **8** sidekick **9** assistant **10** apprentice, coadjutant **11** subordinate

AIL: **3** ill **4** ache, pain **5** awful, upset **6** affect, bother, falter **7** afflict, decline

AILMENT: **3** bug **6** malady **7** disease, ferment, illness **8** disorder, sickness, syndrome, weakness **9** complaint, condition, infirmity **10** affliction, disability

AIM: **3** try **4** bent, goal, plan, want **5** covet, essay, level, point, sight **6** aspire, course, design, direct, intend, strive, target **7** address, attempt, purpose **8** ambition **9** intention, objective **11** destination

AIMLESS: **4** idle **5** blind, stray **6** chance, random **7** erratic **8** careless, drifting, goalless **9** frivolous, haphazard, senseless **10** undirected

AINE: **5** elder **6** eldest, senior

AIR: **3** fan, sky **4** aria, aura, haze, neon, smog, tell, tune, vent, wind **5** aloft, angry, blast, draft, ether, ozone, speak, voice, xenon **6** aerate, allure, breeze, broach, cachet, expose, helium, manner, melody, oxygen, regard, vanity, welkin, zephyr **7** display, divulge, draught, exhibit, krypton, publish **8** agitated, behavior, demeanor, nitrogen, proclaim **9** broadcast, katabatic, semblance, unsettled **10** appearance, atmosphere, cloudiness, deportment **11** affectation, haughtiness

AIRCRAFT: **3** jet **5** blimp, drone, plane **6** copter, glider **7** balloon, chopper **8** aerostat, airplane, zeppelin **9** dirigible **10** helicopter, whirlybird

AIRPLANE: **3** jet, MIG, SST **4** gyro, zero **5** liner **6** bomber, glider **7** clipper, fighter **8** Enola Gay **9** transport **12** Memphis Belle
battle: **8** dogfight
flier: **5** flyer, pilot **7** aviator **8** aeronaut, Concorde
inventor: **6** Wright
trick: **3** dip **4** buzz, dive, loop, roll **8** hedgehop, nosedive, sideslip, tailspin **10** barrel roll

AIRPORT: **5** drome **8** airdrome, airfield **9** aerodrome
area: **5** apron, tower **6** runway **7** taxiway

AIRS: **4** show **5** front **6** vanity **7** hauteur **8** pretense **9** arrogance, pomposity **10** uppishness

AIRTIGHT: **4** shut **6** closed, sealed **8** hermetic **12** impenetrable

AIRY: **3** gay **4** cool, rare, thin **5** empty, fresh, happy, light, merry **6** breezy, jaunty, jocund, lively **7** haughty, tenuous **8** animated, cheerful, debonair, delicate, ethereal, graceful **9** sprightly, visionary, vivacious

AISLE: **3** way **4** lane, path, walk **5** alley **6** avenue **7** passage, walkway **8** clearing, corridor **10** passageway

AJAR: **4** open **6** unshut **9** unlatched

AJAX:
alias: **4** Aias
father: **6** Oileus **7** Telamon
kingdom: **7** Locrius
mother: **8** Periboea
saved: **8** Achilles

AKIN: **4** like **5** alike, close **6** agnate, allied **7** connate, kindred, related, similar **9** analogous, connected **10** affiliated, comparable, correlated

ALABAMA:
bird: **12** yellowhammer
capital: **10** Montgomery
cities: **6** Mobile **10** Birmingham, Huntsville, Tuscaloosa

explorer: **6** De Soto
features: **12** Appalachians
flower: **8** camellia
native: **9** Alabamian
nickname: **11** Cotton State **12** Heart of Dixie **17** Yellowhammer State
tree: **12** southern pine
water: **3** Pea **6** Mobile **7** Alabama **9** Tennessee

ALACRITY: **4** zest **5** speed **6** fervor, gaiety **7** avidity **8** celerity, dispatch, rapidity **9** briskness, eagerness, readiness **10** enthusiasm, nimbleness **11** willingness

A LA MODE: **4** chic **6** trendy **7** stylish, voguish **11** fashionable

ALARM: **3** SOS **4** bell, fear, yell **5** alert, clock, panic, scare, siren, upset **6** buzzer, dismay, excite, outcry, signal, stress **7** disturb, startle, unnerve, warning **8** frighten, surprise **11** disturbance, trepidation

ALAS: **3** ach, woe **4** pity **8** welladay **9** alackaday **12** interjection

ALASKA:
bird: **15** yellow ptarmigan
capital: **6** Juneau
cities: **4** Nome **6** Seward **9** Anchorage, Fairbanks, Fort Yukon, Holy Cross, Ketchikan
explorer: **6** Bering
features: **11** Mount Katmai **13** Mount McKinley
flower: **11** forget-me-not
islands: **3** Fox, Rat **4** Adak, Atka, Attu, Near **5** Kiska, Umnak **6** Agattu, Kodiak, Shuyak **7** Afognak, Baronof, Diomede, Fur Seal, Nunivak **8** Aleutian, Andreaof, Pribilof **9** Alexander
native: **3** Auk **4** Dene, Tene **5** Aleut, Inuit **6** Ahtena, Eskimo, Indian **7** Alaskan, Ingalik, Khotana, Koyukon, Tlingit
nickname: **12** Last Frontier
tree: **11** Sitka spruce
water: **5** Yukon **6** Copper **7** Chukchi, Susitna **9** Matanuska, Porcupine

ALBANIA:
capital: **6** Tirane
cities: **5** Vlore **6** Durres **7** Elbasan, Shkoder
continent: **6** Europe
features: **11** Dinaric Alps
languages: **4** Tosk **5** Greek **8** Albanian
monetary unit: **3** lek **6** qintar
native: **8** Albanian

ALBATROSS: **4** bird **5** nelly **6** gooney **7** pelican **8** handicap, seabirds **9** hindrance, mallemuck

ALBEIT: **3** but **5** altho, while **6** though **7** whereas **8** although

ALBERTA:
bird: **9** horned owl
capital: **8** Edmonton
cities: **7** Calgary, Red Deer **10** Lethbridge **11** Medicine Hat
country: **6** Canada
features: **5** Banff **6** Jasper **9** Elk Island **10** Drumheller **11** Wood Buffalo **12** Waterton Lake
flower: **8** wild rose
water: **4** Cold, Milk **5** Peace, Slave, Smoky **6** Battle, Legend, Louise, Oldman, Pigeon, Wapiti **7** Red Deer, Wabasca **8** Peerless **9** Athabasca

ALBION: **7** Britain, England **9** Britannia **12** Great Britain

ALBUM: **4** book **5** index **6** record **7** memento **8** register **9** anthology, portfolio, scrapbook **10** collection

ALCAZAR: **6** palace **8** fortress

ALCESTIS:
father: **6** Pelias
husband: **7** Admetus
mother: **8** Anaxibia **10** Phylomache
protagonist: **8** Hercules
son: **7** Eumelus **8** Hippasus

ALCHEMY: **5** magic **6** change **7** sorcery **8** wizardry **10** witchcraft **13** transmutation

ALCINOUS:
brother: **8** Rhexenor
daughter: **8** Nausicaa
father: **10** Nausithous
kingdom: **10** Phaeacians
mother: **8** Periboea
son: **8** Laodamas
wife: **5** Arete

ALCMAEON:
brother: **11** Amphilochus
daughter: **10** Trisiphone
father: **10** Amphiaraus
mother: **8** Eriphyle
son: **7** Acarnan **10** Amphoterus
wife: **10** Callirrhoe

ALCMENE:
father: **9** Electryon
husband: **10** Amphitryon
mother: **5** Anaxo
son: **8** Heracles, Hercules

ALCOHOL: **4** beer, wine **5** allyl, booze, butyl, ethyl, proof, vinyl **6** liquor, methyl, pentyl **7** butanol, ethanol, spirits, whiskey **8** cocktail, glycerol, methanol **9** moonshine

ALCOHOLIC: **5** drunk **6** addict, barfly, brewed **9** inebriant, spiritous **11** dipsomaniac **12** intoxicating

ALCOVE: **3** bay **4** nook **5** arbor, niche, study **6** corner, cranny, recess **7** cubicle, dinette **11** compartment

ALDER: **4** tree **5** alnus, shrub

ALE: **3** nog **4** beer, brew, malt, suds **5** lager, stout **6** porter, stingo **8** beverage

ALEA: **6** Athena **9** sanctuary

ALEHOUSE: **3** bar, pub **4** cafe **6** bistro, saloon, tavern **7** cabaret, taproom **9** nightclub

ALERT: **4** flag, keen, warn, wary **5** alarm, awake, eager, ready, sharp, siren **6** active, bright, inform, lively, nimble, signal **7** heedful, wakeful **8** spirited, vigilant, watchful **9** observant

ALEUTIAN ISLANDS: **3** Fox, Rat **4** Adak, Atka, Attu, Near **5** Amlia, Kiska, Umnak **6** Akutan, Amukta, Kodiak, Seguam **7** Kagamil **8** Amchitka, Unalaska **9** Andreanof

ALEXANDER THE GREAT:
birthplace: **5** Pella
father: **6** Philip
horse: **10** Bucephalus
kingdom: **9** Macedonia
mother: **8** Olympias
teacher: **9** Aristotle
warred with: **4** Gaza **5** Egypt, Issus **6** Persia **7** Babylon
wife: **6** Roxana

ALFALFA: **3** hay **6** fodder **7** lucerne

ALGA, ALGAE: **4** scum, kelp **5** dulse **6** desmid, diatom, lichen **7** seaweed **8** algology, plankton, rockweed **9** stonewort

ALGERIA:
capital: **7** Algiers **8** al-Jazair
cities: **4** Bone, Oran **5** Medea **6** Annaba **7** Quahran **9** Qacentina **11** Constantine
continent: **6** Africa
ethnic groups: **4** Arab **6** Berber, Kabyle
features: **6** Sahara **7** Melrhir **12** Barbary Coast **14** Atlas Mountains **15** Hoggar Mountains
languages: **6** Arabic
monetary unit: **5** dinar
native: **8** Algerian
water: **7** Cheliff, Sheliff

ALI BABA: **6** sesame **8** Morgiana **10** woodcutter **13** Arabian Nights

ALIAS: **3** AKA **6** anonym, handle **7** epithet, pen name **9** pseudonym

ALIBI: **4** plea **5** proof **6** excuse **7** pretext **9** statement **11** explanation

ALIEN: **6** exotic, remote **7** foreign, hostile, invader, opposed, refugee, strange, unusual **8** outsider, stranger **9** different, foreigner, immigrant, outlander

ALIENATE: **4** part, wean **6** detach, devest, remise **8** disunite, estrange, separate, transfer **9** disaffect, hostility

ALIGHT: **3** sit **4** land, rest **5** aglow, perch, roost **6** arrive, bright, settle **7** blazing, deplane, lighted, radiant **8** dismount **9** disembark

ALIGN: **3** fix **4** join, true **5** agree, level **6** adjust **7** marshal **8** regulate **9** affiliate **10** straighten

ALIKE: **4** akin, same **5** ditto, equal **7** similar, uniform **8** parallel **9** congruent, duplicate, identical **10** comparable **11** homogeneous

ALIMENT: **3** pap **4** food **7** pabulum **9** nutriment **10** digestible, sustenance **11** nourishment

ALIMONY: **4** keep **6** upkeep **9** allowance, provision **10** settlement **11** maintenance

ALIVE: **4** keen, spry **5** alert, awake, aware, brisk, eager, vivid **6** active, extant, lively **7** dynamic, vibrant, zestful **8** animated, existent, vigorous **9** abounding, breathing, sprightly, unexpired

ALKALINE: **4** lime **5** borax, salty **6** alkali **7** antacid **12** neutralizing

ALKALOID: **4** base **5** ergot **6** eserin, heroin **7** caffein, cocaine, codeine, harmine, sinapin **8** atropine, caffeine, morphine **9** quinidine **10** strychnine

ALL: **3** any, sum **4** full **5** alone, gross, group, quite, total, whole **6** entire, solely, wholly **8** complete, entirely, everyone, totality **9** aggregate, everybody **10** altogether, completely, everything, thoroughly **11** exclusively

ALL IN: **4** beat **5** spent, tired, weary **6** bleary, bushed, pooped **7** drained **8** fatigued **9** exhausted

ALL OUT: **5** broad **7** maximum **8** thorough **9** extensive **10** unreserved

ALL OVER: **4** done **5** ended **8** finished **9** concluded, universal **10** everywhere, throughout

ALL RIGHT: **3** yes **4** good, okay **5** swell **6** agreed **7** average **8** adequate

ALLAY: **4** calm, ease, lull **5** abate, quiet, still **6** pacify, reduce, settle, soften, soothe **7** appease, comfort, compose, relieve **8** diminish, mitigate **9** alleviate

ALLEGE: **3** lay, say **4** aver, avow **5** claim, offer, plead, state **6** affirm, assert, charge, impute **7** advance, declare, present, profess, testify **8** maintain **9** attribute **10** asseverate

ALLEGIANCE: **3** tie **4** duty **5** ardor, honor **6** fealty, homage **7** loyalty, tribute **8** devotion, fidelity **9** obedience **10** obligation **12** faithfulness

ALLEGORY: **4** myth, tale **5** fable, moral, story **6** symbol **7** parable **8** apologue

ALLEVIATE: **4** dull, ease, help **5** abate, blunt, slake **6** lessen, soften, subdue **7** assuage, lighten, relieve **8** diminish, mitigate, palliate

ALLEY: **3** way **4** lane, path, slum, walk **5** byway **7** passage **10** passageway

ALLIANCE: **3** tie **4** bond, pact **5** union **6** accord, fusion, league, treaty **7** compact, society **8** affinity, covenant, marriage **9** agreement, coalition **10** federation **11** affiliation, association, partnership

ALLIED: **3** wed **4** akin **5** alike, bound **6** agnate, joined, linked, united **7** cognate, connate, kindred, related, similar, unified **9** connected

ALLOCATE: **4** deal, give **5** allot, allow, divvy, share, slice **6** assign **7** earmark **9** apportion **10** distribute

ALLOT: **4** dole, give **5** award, grant, share **6** accord, assign, design, ordain, ration **7** appoint, present, provide, reserve, specify **8** allocate, dispense **9** apportion, prescribe **10** distribute

ALLOW: **3** let **4** bear, pass **5** admit, defer, grant, stand **6** accept, endure, oblige, permit, suffer **7** approve, concede, confess, suppose **8** consider, tolerate **9** authorize **11** acknowledge

ALLOWANCE: **3** aid, cut, fee **4** edge, gift, odds, part **5** leave, quota, share **6** bounty, margin, ration, rebate, salary **7** alimony, annuity, pension, portion, stipend **8** discount, handicap, sanction **9** deduction, reduction, tolerance **10** concession, permission

ALLOY: **3** mix **4** fuse **5** blend **6** debase, impair, reduce **7** mixture **8** compound **9** composite **10** adulterate, amalgamate

carbon and iron: **5** steel

copper and aluminum: **9** duralumin

copper and tin: **6** bronze, oreide, ormolu, oroide, pewter

copper and zinc: **5** brass **6** tombac **8** arsedine

copper, iron and zinc: **4** aich **7** rheotan

costume jewelry: **4** aich **6** oreide, ormolu, oroide, tombac **8** arsedine

fusible: **6** solder

gold and silver: **4** asem **8** electrum

lead and tin: **5** calin, terne **6** pewter

nickel and iron: **7** elinvar

nickel and silver: **8** alfenide

sulfuric: **6** niello

ALLUDE: **4** hint **5** imply, infer, point **6** advert, relate **7** connote, mention, suggest, touch on **8** indicate, intimate **9** insinuate

ALLURE: **3** win, woo **4** bait, coax, draw, lead, lure, sway **5** angle, charm, court, snare, tempt **6** cajole, entice, induce, seduce **7** attract, beguile **8** blandish, intrigue, persuade **9** captivate, influence, magnetize

ALLUSION: **4** hint **6** remark **7** mention **8** innuendo, instance **9** reference **10** denotation, intimation **11** insinuation

ALLY: **3** pal **4** join **5** unite **6** backer, friend, helper **7** comrade, connect, partner **8** adherent, relative **9** affiliate, assistant, associate, colleague, supporter **10** accomplice **11** confederate

ALMIGHTY: **3** God **5** great **6** mighty **7** Creator, eternal, extreme, supreme **8** absolute, powerful, puissant **10** omnipotent

ALMOST: **4** nigh **5** about, close **6** around, nearly **7** roughly **9** virtually **11** practically **13** approximately

ALMS: **3** aid **4** dole, gift **6** relief **7** charity, handout **8** donation, offering, pittance **11** benefaction **12** contribution

ALMSMAN: **5** tramp **6** beggar, pauper **10** panhandler

ALOFT: **4** high **5** above **7** skyward **8** airborne, overhead

ALOHA: **4** hail, love **5** hello **7** goodbye **8** farewell, greeting **9** affection **10** salutation

ALONE: **4** only, solo **5** aloof, apart **6** hermit, single, unique **7** forlorn, removed, widowed **8** desolate, detached, isolated, lonesome, separate, solitary **9** unrivaled **10** unescorted **11** exclusively **12** incomparable, unparalleled

ALONG: **3** too **4** also, near, with **5** ahead **6** beside, onward **7** forward **8** adjacent, advanced, likewise, together **10** lengthwise **11** approaching

ALONGSIDE: **4** near **6** beside **7** abreast, against **8** parallel

ALOOF: **3** shy **4** cold, cool **5** alone, apart **6** chilly, frosty, remote, uppity **7** distant, removed **8** arrogant, detached, reserved **9** withdrawn **11** indifferent

ALOUD: **4** oral **5** vocal **7** audible, clearly, lustily, noisily

ALP: **4** peak, pike **5** mount **6** summit **8** mountain

ALPHA: **4** dawn **5** first, start **9** beginning **11** Greek letter

ALPHABET: **4** ABCs **5** order, signs **6** basics, primer **7** letters, symbols **8** elements **9** ideograph, rudiments

ALPINE:
climber: **10** alpestrian
dance: **5** gavot
dress: **6** dirndl
herdsman: **4** senn
pass: **3** col **7** Brenner, Simplon, Splugen **9** Semmering **10** St. Gotthard **14** Great St. Bernard **15** Little St. Bernard
plant: **9** edelweiss
wind: **4** bise, bora **5** foehn

ALPS: **4** Rosa **5** Eiger **7** Bernina **8** Jungfrau **10** Matterhorn **13** mountain range
countries of: **5** Italy **6** Bosnia, France **7** Austria, Croatia, Germany **11** Switzerland **13** Liechtenstein
peak: **9** Mont Blanc
river source: **5** Rhine, Rhone

ALREADY: **3** now **4** once **5** early **6** before **7** earlier **8** formerly **10** beforehand, previously

ALSO: **3** and, too, yet **4** more, plus **5** again, ditto **7** besides, further **8** likewise, moreover **9** including, similarly

ALTAR: **4** font **5** table **6** shrine **7** chantry **9** sanctuary **10** tabernacle

ALTER: **4** spay, turn, vary **5** adapt, amend, reset **6** adjust, change, doctor, modify, neuter, revamp, revise **7** convert **8** castrate **9** transform

ALTER EGO: **4** mate, twin **5** agent **6** double, friend **9** confidant **10** complement

ALTERCATION: **3** row **4** beef, feud, spat, tiff **5** brawl, fight, melee, scrap, words **6** fracas, strife **7** dispute, quarrel, wrangle **8** argument, squabble **9** bickering **11** controversy

ALTERNATE: **3** sub **4** else, vary **5** other, proxy, shift, waver **6** backup, change, double, rotate, seesaw **7** standby **8** intermit **9** fluctuate, surrogate **10** substitute

ALTERNATIVE: **4** pick **6** choice, either, option **8** druthers, elective, loophole **9** selection **10** preference

ALTHAEA:
brother: **9** Plexippus
daughter: **8** Deianira
father: **8** Thestius
husband: **6** Oeneus
son: **6** Tydeus **8** Meleager

ALTHOUGH: **3** but **5** still, while **6** albeit **7** despite, however, whereas **8** granting

ALTITUDE: **4** apex, peak **6** height, zenith **7** ceiling **9** elevation, loftiness

ALTOGETHER: **4** fully **5** quite **6** wholly **7** totally, utterly **8** entirely **10** completely, thoroughly **12** collectively

ALTRUISM: **7** charity **8** kindness **10** generosity **11** benevolence **12** philanthropy

ALUMINUM: **4** alum **7** alumina, epidote

ALUMNUS: **4** grad **5** pupil **8** graduate **12** postgraduate

ALWAYS: **4** ever **7** forever **8** evermore **9** eternally, regularly, uniformly **10** constantly, habitually, invariably **11** continually, everlasting, perpetually **13** everlastingly

AMALGAMATE: **3** mix **4** fuse, join, meld, pool **5** alloy, blend, merge, unite **6** mingle **7** combine **8** coalesce, compound **10** synthesize **11** consolidate

AMALTHEA:
form: **4** goat **5** nymph
horn: **10** cornucopia
raised: **4** Zeus

AMASA:
father: **6** Jether
killer: **2** Joab
mother: **7** Abigail

AMASS: **4** hive, pile, save **5** hoard, stack, store **6** corral, gather **7** acquire, collect, compile **8** assemble **9** stockpile **10** accumulate

AMATEUR: **3** ham **4** tyro **6** novice, votary **7** admirer, dabbler, learner **8** beginner, neophyte, tinkerer **9** greenhorn **10** apprentice, dilettante

AMAZE: **3** awe **4** stun **5** alarm, shock **6** wonder **7** astound, impress, stagger, stupefy **8** astonish, confound, surprise **9** dumbfound, overwhelm **11** flabbergast

AMAZEMENT: **8** unbelief **9** marveling **12** astonishment

AMAZON: **5** harpy, river, vixen **6** female **9** mythology **12** woman warrior
headstreams: **7** Maranon, Ucayali
inhabited: **7** Scythia
location: **12** South America
warrior: **5** queen **9** Hippolyta **11** Penthesilea

AMBASSADOR: **5** agent, envoy **6** consul, deputy **7** attache **8** diplomat, emissary **9** messenger **12** intermediary

AMBER: **3** tan **5** brown, resin **6** golden, yellow

AMBIENCE: **3** air **4** mood **6** flavor, milieu **7** setting **10** atmosphere **11** environment

AMBIGUITY: **5** doubt **6** enigma **7** duality, dubiety, evasion **9** duplicity, obscurity **12** doubtfulness

AMBIGUOUS: **4** dark **5** muddy, vague **6** unsure **7** cryptic, dubious, unclear **8** doubtful, puzzling **9** equivocal, uncertain, unsettled **10** indefinite

AMBIT: **5** limit, range, scope, space **6** bounds, extent, sphere **7** compass **8** boundary **9** extension

AMBITION: **3** aim **4** goal, hope, mark, plan **5** dream, drive **6** desire, target **7** purpose **9** intention **10** aspiration

AMBITIOUS: **4** avid, bold, keen **5** eager **6** ardent **8** aspiring **9** demanding, energetic **12** enterprising

AMBLE: **4** mope, pace **5** mosey **6** dawdle, loiter, ramble, stroll **7** meander, saunter

AMBROSIA: **5** honey **6** nectar **7** dessert, perfume **8** delicacy

AMBROSIAL: **4** lush **5** sweet, tasty **6** aromal, divine **8** fragrant, heavenly, luscious **9** delicious **10** delightful

AMBULATORY: **6** mobile **7** nomadic, walking

AMBUSH: **3** mug **4** trap **5** await, snare, trick **6** attack, waylay **7** assault, lurking **8** surprise **10** camouflage

AMELIORATE: **4** ease, help **6** better, reform, uplift **7** advance, improve, promote **8** progress **10** recuperate

AMEN: **3** yes **5** truly **6** assent, verily **7** exactly **8** approval, response **9** certainly

AMENABLE: **4** open **6** docile, liable, pliant **7** subdued, subject, willing **8** yielding **9** receptive, tractable **10** responsive **11** accountable, complaisant, cooperative

AMEND: **3** fix **4** edit, lift **5** alter, right **6** better, change, polish, reform, repair, revise **7** correct, improve, rectify

AMENDS: **7** apology, payment **8** requital **9** atonement, expiation, indemnity **10** recompense, reparation **11** restitution **12** compensation

AMENITIES: **7** manners **8** comforts, luxuries, mildness, niceties **9** etiquette, geniality **10** courtesies, refinement **11** formalities **12** conveniences, pleasantries

AMENT: **4** fool **5** idiot, moron **6** catkin **7** cattail **8** imbecile **9** simpleton

AMERCE: **4** fine **6** punish **8** penalize

AMERICAN: **4** Yank **6** gringo, native, Yankee

AMETHYST: **3** gem **6** purple, quartz **7** onegite

AMFORTAS:
father: **7** Titurel
quest: **9** holy grail
led: **7** knights

AMIABLE: **4** cozy, easy, kind, warm **6** genial, polite **7** affable, cordial, winsome **8** charming, engaging, friendly, gracious, pleasing, sociable **9** agreeable, courteous

AMICABLE: **5** civil **8** empathic, friendly **9** brotherly, peaceable **10** benevolent, harmonious

AMID: **3** mid **4** over **5** among, midst **6** during **7** between **10** surrounded, throughout **11** encompassed

AMISS: **3** bad, ill **4** awry, foul **5** askew, false, wrong **6** astray, unfair **7** haywire, wrongly **8** improper, mistaken **9** defective, erroneous, incorrect **10** inaccurate

AMITY: **5** peace **6** accord **7** harmony **8** goodwill, sympathy **9** simpatico **10** friendship **11** brotherhood

AMMUNITION: **4** ammo, arms, fuse, shot **5** bombs, round **6** charge, powder, shells **7** bullets, rockets **8** grenades, material, missiles, shrapnel **9** artillery, cartridge **10** cannonball

AMNESIA: **4** daze **5** fugue **6** stupor **8** blackout

AMNESTY: **6** pardon **8** immunity **10** absolution **11** condonation, forgiveness

AMOEBA, AMEBA: **4** cell, germ **5** virus **7** proteus **8** bacteria, organism

AMONG: **3** mid **4** amid, with **5** midst **7** between

AMOROUS: **4** fond, sexy **6** ardent, erotic, loving, tender **7** lustful **8** attached, lovesick **10** passionate **11** aphrodisiac **12** affectionate

AMORPHOUS: **5** baggy, vague **8** formless, inchoate **9** irregular, shapeless, undefined **11** nondescript

AMOUNT: 3 all, lot, sum, tab 4 bulk, cost, mass, unit 5 chunk, price, store, tally, total, whole 6 dosage, extent, number, volume 7 measure, portion 8 comprise, quantity 9 aggregate

AMOUR PROPRE: 5 pride 6 egoism, vanity 10 narcissism

AMPERE UNIT: 4 volt, watt

AMPHETAMINE: 5 benny, speed, upper

AMPHIBIAN: 4 frog, hyla, newt, rana, toad 7 caudate, proteus 8 seaplane 9 caecilian 10 salamander
family: 7 Hylidae, Pipidae, Ranidae 9 Bufonidae, Proteidae, Sirenidae
young: 6 larvae 7 tadpole 8 polliwog

AMPHION:
brother: 6 Zethus
father: 4 Zeus
mother: 7 Antiope
wife: 5 Niobe

AMPHITHEATER: 4 bowl, oval 5 arena, cavea 7 stadium 8 coliseum 10 auditorium

AMPHITRITE:
father: 6 Nereus
goddess: 3 sea
husband: 7 Neptune 8 Poseidon
mother: 5 Doris
son: 6 Triton

AMPHITRYON:
daughter: 8 Perimede
father: 7 Alcaeus
son: 8 Iphicles
wife: 7 Alcmene

AMPHORA: 3 jar, jug, urn 4 vase 8 ornament

AMPLE: 3 big 4 full, good, much, rich, vast 5 broad, great, large, roomy 6 enough, galore, lavish, plenty 7 copious, liberal, opulent 8 abundant, generous, handsome, spacious 9 bountiful, extensive, plentiful 10 sufficient

AMPLIFY: 3 add 5 boost, raise, swell, widen 6 dilate, expand, extend 7 augment, enlarge, inflate 8 increase, lengthen 9 intensify

AMPUTATE: 3 cut, lop 5 sever 6 excise, remove 7 curtail 8 truncate 9 eliminate

AMULET: 3 gem 4 luck, mojo 5 charm, token 6 fetish 8 ornament, talisman 10 protection

AMUSE: 3 wow 4 kill 5 cheer 6 divert, engage, please, tickle 7 beguile, delight, enliven, gratify 8 distract, interest 9 entertain, fascinate 10 exhilarate

AMUSEMENT: 3 fun 4 game, jest, lark, play 5 hobby, sport 7 pastime 8 pleasure 9 diversion, merriment 10 recreation, relaxation

AMUSING: 4 riot 5 boffo, droll, funny, merry 7 comical 8 humorous, pleasant 9 absorbing, laughable, ludicrous, priceless 10 delightful, ridiculous

AMYCUS:
antagonist: 5 Lycus 8 Dascylus
father: 7 Neptune 8 Poseidon
friend: 8 Hercules
mother: 5 Melia

ANA: 5 books 6 events 7 sayings 9 anecdotes 10 collection 11 memorabilia

ANABASIS: 5 march 7 advance, headway 8 progress 10 expedition

ANADEM: 5 crown 6 diadem, wreath 7 chaplet

ANAGOGIC: 6 mystic, occult 8 mystical 10 symbolical

ANAGRAM: 4 code, game 6 cipher, puzzle

ANALGESIC: 4 drug 5 opium 7 anodyne, aspirin, codeine, soother 8 sedative 10 anesthetic

ANALOGOUS: **4** akin, like **5** alike **6** allied **7** kindred, related, similar **8** agreeing, parallel **10** comparable, equivalent, resembling **11** correlative

ANALOGY: **6** simile **8** metaphor, parallel **10** comparison, congruence **11** resemblance

ANALYSIS: **4** scan, test **5** audit, brief, study **6** review **7** finding, inquiry **9** breakdown, criticism, diagnosis, reasoning, reduction **10** dissection **11** examination

ANALYZE: **4** sift **5** assay, study, weigh **6** search **7** dissect, examine, inspect **8** diagnose, evaluate **9** determine, subdivide **10** scrutinize

ANANIAS: **4** liar **6** fibber **8** perjurer **11** storyteller **12** prevaricator
deceived: **5** Peter
father: **9** Nedebaeus
wife: **8** Sapphira

ANARCHIST: **5** rebel **7** radical **8** agitator, mutineer, nihilist, revolter **9** insurgent, terrorist **10** malcontent **13** revolutionary

ANARCHY: **4** riot **5** chaos **6** revolt **7** turmoil **8** disorder, nihilism **9** confusion, rebellion **11** lawlessness **13** nongovernment

ANATHEMA: **3** ban **4** bane, hate, oath **5** curse, taboo **6** pariah, phobia **7** censure, outcast **10** abhorrence **11** imprecation, malediction **12** condemnation

ANATOMY: **4** body, form **7** biology, zoology **8** analysis, cytology, etiology, skeleton **9** diagnosis, framework, histology, structure **10** dissection, physiology

ANCESTOR: **8** forebear **9** ascendant, patriarch, precursor, prototype **10** antecessor, forefather, foremother, forerunner, progenitor **11** predecessor

ANCESTRY: **4** line, race **5** blood, stock **6** family, origin **7** descent, lineage **8** breeding, heredity, heritage, pedigree **9** genealogy, parentage **10** extraction **11** antecedents

ANCHISES:
father: **5** Capys
kingdom: **4** Troy
mother: **8** Themiste
son: **5** Lyrus **6** Aeneas

ANCHOR: **3** fix, tie **4** bind, dock, hook, moor **5** berth, plant, rivet **6** attach, fasten **7** ballast, connect, grapnel, killick, support **9** safeguard

ANCHORAGE: **3** key **4** dock, port, slip **5** haven, wharf **6** harbor, refuge **7** mooring **9** roadstead

ANCIENT: **3** old **4** aged **5** passe, relic **6** bygone, senior **7** antique, archaic, classic, elderly **8** historic, primeval, timeworn **9** classical, primitive **10** antiquated **11** patriarchal

ANCILLARY: **5** minor **9** attendant, auxiliary, satellite, secondary **10** subsidiary **11** subordinate

AND: **3** too **4** also, plus **7** besides, further **8** moreover **9** including **10** connective **11** furthermore

ANDORRA:
capital: **14** Andorra la Vella
continent: **6** Europe
features: **8** Pyrenees
languages: **7** Catalan
monetary unit: **5** franc **6** peseta **7** centime, centimo
water: **6** Valira

ANDROID: **5** robot **9** automaton

ANDROMACHE:
antagonist: **8** Hermione
father: **6** Eetion
husband: **6** Hector
son: **8** Molossus, Pergamus

ANDROMEDA:
daughter: **10** Gorgophone
father: **7** Cepheus
husband: **7** Perseus
mother: **10** Cassiopeia
protagonist: **7** Perseus
son: **6** Mestor **7** Heleius

ANECDOTE: **3** gag **4** tale, yarn **5** story **6** sketch **7** episode **8** chestnut **9** narrative **12** reminiscence

ANEMIC: **3** wan **4** pale, weak **5** frail **6** feeble, watery **8** lifeless **9** bloodless

ANEMONE: **4** lily **6** flower **9** buttercup **10** windflower

ANENT: **4** with **5** about **7** apropos **8** touching **9** regarding **10** concerning

ANESTHETIC: **3** gas **4** dope, drug, dull **5** ether, local **6** obtuse, opiate, spinal **7** anodyne, general **8** morphine, narcotic, sedative **9** analgesic, novocaine **10** chloroform, palliative **12** unperceptive

ANEW: **4** over **5** again, fresh **6** afresh, de novo, lately **8** recently

ANGEL: **3** gem **4** dear, lamb **5** saint **6** backer, cherub, seraph, spirit **7** darling, sponsor **8** guardian **9** messenger

ANGELIC: **4** good, holy, pure **5** sweet **6** divine **7** saintly **8** cherubic, heavenly, innocent **9** beautiful, celestial

ANGER: **3** irk, mad, vex **4** fury, gall, goad, rage, rile **5** annoy, cross, wrath **6** choler, dander, enrage, offend, rancor, ruffle, temper **7** burning, incense, inflame, outrage, provoke, tantrum **8** acrimony, irritate **9** aggravate, animosity, infuriate **10** antagonize, exasperate **11** displeasure

ANGLE: **3** aim, bow **4** bend, cast, fish, hook, plan, turn **5** bevel, facet, phase, point, slant, twist **6** aspect, dogleg, jockey, zigzag **7** gimmick **8** intrigue, position **9** viewpoint **10** standpoint
math: **5** acute, right **6** obtuse **8** straight
measure: **7** degrees

ANGLO-SAXON:
group: **4** fyrd, moot **5** gemot **6** gemote **9** heptarchy
kingdom: **4** Kent **5** Essex **6** Mercia, Sussex, Wessex **10** East Anglia **11** Northumbria
kings: **3** Ine **4** Edwy **5** Edred **6** Alfred, Egbert, Harold **8** Ethelred
people: **4** Jute **5** Angle, Saxon
person: **4** earl, esne **5** thane, thegn **8** atheling

ANGOLA:
capital: **6** Luanda
cities: **6** Huambo, Lobito **7** Lubango **8** Benguela
continent: **6** Africa
features: **4** Moco **7** Cabinda
languages: **5** Bantu **10** Portuguese
monetary unit: **6** kwanza
native: **5** Bantu, Kongo **7** Angolan
water: **5** Cuito, Kasai **6** Cuanza, Cunene **7** Cubango

ANGRY: **3** hot, mad **4** grim, sore **5** cross, huffy, irate, livid, upset, vexed **6** ireful, raging **7** annoyed, furious **8** incensed, inflamed, outraged, storming **9** indignant, irascible, perturbed, resentful **11** exasperated

ANGUISH: **3** rue, woe **4** ache, dole, pain, pang **5** agony, grief **6** misery, sorrow **7** despair, torment **8** distress **10** heartbreak

ANGULAR: **4** bent, bony, lean, thin **5** gaunt, lanky, rough, sharp **6** abrupt, skewed, skinny **7** awkward, crooked, pointed, scraggy, scrawny **8** rawboned

ANIMA: **4** life, soul **6** psyche, spirit

ANIMADVERSION: **3** rap **4** flak, slur **5** blame, knock **7** censure **8** judgment **9** aspersion, criticism **10** accusation, perception **11** observation **12** faultfinding

ANIMAL:
class: **5** genus **6** genera
coat: **3** fur **4** fell, hair, hide, pelt, skin, wool
collection: **3** zoo **9** menagerie
day-active: **7** diurnal
doctor: **3** vet **12** veterinarian
home: **3** pen, sty **4** barn, cage, coop, fold, yard **5** stall **6** corral **7** paddock, pasture
invertebrate: **6** insect **7** mollusk **10** crustacean
land-living: **11** terrestrial
life: **4** bios **5** fauna
meat-eating: **9** carnivore
mythical: **4** faun, yeti **5** hydra, snark **6** dragon, sphinx **7** centaur, griffin, mermaid, phoenix, unicorn **8** Loch Ness, Minotaur
night-active: **9** nocturnal
one-celled: **5** ameba, monad **6** amoeba **9** protozoan
plant-eating: **9** herbivore
science: **7** zoology **8** ethology
tree-living: **8** arboreal
vertebrate: **4** bird, fish **6** mammal **7** reptile **9** amphibian, marsupial
water-living: **6** marine **7** aquatic

ANIMATE: **4** move, perk, spur, stir **5** alive, rouse **6** ensoul, excite, kindle, living, prompt, vivify **7** actuate, enliven, inspire, quicken **8** activate, energize, vitalize **9** enhearten, stimulate **10** exhilarate, invigorate

ANIMATED: **3** gay **4** keen **5** brisk, happy, peppy, vivid, zippy **6** active, blithe, lively, snappy **7** dynamic, glowing, zestful **8** spirited, vigorous **9** sprightly, vivacious **12** enthusiastic

ANIMATION: **3** vim, zap **4** glow, life, zing **5** vigor **6** action **7** sparkle

ANIMOSITY: **4** hate **5** anger **6** animus, malice, rancor **7** dislike **9** hostility **10** antagonism, resentment

ANIUS:
daughter: **4** Oeno **5** Elais
father: **6** Apollo
mother: **5** Rhoeo

ANKLE: **4** bone **5** talus **6** tarsus **10** astragalus

ANNALS: **7** account, history, journal, records **8** archives **10** chronicles **11** publication

ANNEAL: **4** bake, fuse, heat **6** harden, temper **7** toughen **10** strengthen

ANNEX: **3** add, tag, win **4** hook, join, wing **5** affix, seize, unite **6** append, attach, fasten, secure **7** acquire, connect, procure **8** addition, arrogate **9** extension **11** appropriate

ANNIE OAKLEY: **4** pass **7** freebie

ANNIHILATE: **3** end **4** kill, rout, slay **5** crush, erase **6** devour, murder, negate, squash **7** abolish, destroy, nullify **8** decimate, demolish, massacre **9** eradicate, slaughter **10** extinguish, obliterate **11** exterminate

ANNIVERSARY: **8** ceremony, festival **10** recurrence **11** celebration **13** commemoration
tenth: **9** decennial
twentieth: **12** vigentennial
hundredth: **9** centenary **10** centennial
one hundred fiftieth: **16** sesquicentennial
thousandth: **10** millennial **11** millenniary

ANNOTATE: **4** note **5** gloss **6** define, remark **7** comment, explain, expound **8** footnote **9** interpret **10** illustrate

ANNOUNCE: **3** bid **4** drum, tell **5** blast, sound, state **6** assert, blazon, herald, inform, report **7** declare, divulge, present, publish, signify, trumpet **8** foretell, proclaim **9** advertise, broadcast, introduce **10** promulgate

ANNOUNCEMENT: **4** news **5** blurb **6** decree, notice **7** message **8** briefing, bulletin **9** manifesto, statement **10** communique **11** declaration **12** notification, proclamation

ANNOUNCER: **5** emcee **10** newscaster **11** broadcaster **12** anchorperson

ANNOY: **3** bug, get, ire, irk, nag, vex **4** bait, fret, gall, ride, rile **5** chafe, harry, peeve, tease, upset **6** badger, harass, heckle, needle, offend, pester **7** agitate, disturb, provoke, trouble **8** distress, irritate **9** aggravate, displease **10** exasperate

ANNOYANCE: **4** pain, pest **5** thorn, worry **6** bother **8** headache, irritant, nuisance **11** disturbance **13** inconvenience

ANNUAL: **4** book, weed **5** plant **6** flower, yearly **7** journal **8** periodic, yearlong **11** anniversary

ANNUL: **3** nix **4** undo, void **5** blank, erase **6** cancel, negate, recall, repeal **7** abolish, nullify, rescind **8** abrogate, dissolve **9** disaffirm **10** annihilate, extinguish, invalidate **11** countermand

ANODYNE: **4** balm **7** comfort, soother **8** narcotic, sedative **10** anesthetic, painkiller **12** tranquilizer

ANOINT: **3** oil, rub **5** anele, bless, crown **6** grease **8** sanctify **10** consecrate

ANOMALOUS: **3** odd **4** rare **7** bizarre, deviant, strange, unusual **8** aberrant, abnormal, atypical, peculiar **9** eccentric **11** incongruous

ANON: **4** soon, then **5** again, later **7** shortly **8** directly, tomorrow **9** afterward, presently **11** immediately

ANONYMOUS: **6** pseudo, secret **7** unknown, unnamed **8** nameless, unsigned **9** incognito **12** unidentified

ANOTHER: **3** new **4** more **5** added, extra, fresh **6** second **7** further **9** different **10** additional

ANSWER: **3** lip, say **4** meet, plea, suit **5** argue, react, reply, serve, write **6** refute, retort, return **7** defense, fulfill, respond, satisfy **8** rebuttal, response, solution **9** wisecrack **11** acknowledge

ANSWERABLE: **6** liable **7** obliged, subject **8** amenable **10** chargeable **11** accountable

ANT: **4** army, atta **5** emmet **6** amazon, driver **7** pismire, soldier, termite **9** carpenter
male: **8** micraner **9** ergataner
nest: **4** hill **5** drone, mound **6** colony **9** formicary
queen: **4** gyne
worker: **6** ergate

ANTAEUS:
appears as: **5** giant
father: **7** Neptune **8** Poseidon
killer: **8** Hercules
mother: **4** Gaea

ANTAGONISM: **5** spite **6** animus, hatred, rancor **7** dislike, rivalry **8** conflict, friction **9** animosity, antipathy, hostility **10** contention, opposition **11** competition

ANTAGONIST: **3** foe **5** enemy, match, rival **7** battler **8** attacker, opponent **9** adversary **10** competitor

ANTAGONISTIC: **4** anti **6** bitter **7** counter, hostile, opposed **8** clashing, contrary, inimical **9** dissonant **10** unfriendly

ANTARCTICA:
explorers: **4** Byrd, Cook, Ross **5** Fuchs, Scott **6** Mawson **7** Weddell, Wilkins **8** Amundsen **9** Ellsworth
features: **5** Siple **9** Admiralty **11** Mount Erebus **12** Vinson Massif **18** Ellsworth Mountains
water: **4** Ross **7** Weddell **8** Amundsen

ANTE: **3** bet, pay **5** price, stake, wager

ANTECEDENT: **4** fore, line, past **5** blood, cause, prior **6** former, reason **7** earlier, premise **8** ancestor, previous **9** foregoing, precursor **10** forerunner **11** predecessor

ANTEDATE: **4** pace **7** precede **8** antecede, backdate **10** anticipate

ANTEDILUVIAN: **3** old **7** ancient, archaic **8** obsolete, timeworn **10** antiquated

ANTELOPE: **3** gnu **4** koba, oryx, puku, tora **5** bongo, eland, nagor, takin, yakin **6** grimme, impala **7** blesbok, chamois, defassa, gazelle, grysbok **8** agacella, bushbuck, reedbuck **9** springbok, waterbuck **10** hartebeest
female: **3** doe
four-horned: **6** chouka **7** chikara **10** chousingha
male: **4** buck
young: **3** kid

ANTENNA: **4** ears, palp, wire **6** aerial, feeler **8** receiver

ANTERIOR: **4** past **5** front, prior **6** before, former **7** earlier, forward **8** atlantal, previous **9** foregoing, preceding **10** antecedent

ANTHEM: **4** hymn, song **5** chant, music, psalm **6** choral, melody **9** antiphony **10** responsory

ANTHOLOGY: **3** ana **4** book **5** album **6** choice **7** analect, garland **8** excerpts, treasury **9** potpourri, selection **10** collection, miscellany **11** compilation

ANTHROPOID: **3** ape **6** gibbon, monkey **7** gorilla, primate **8** humanoid **9** orangutan **10** chimpanzee

ANTI: **3** con, foe **7** against, opposed **9** adversary **10** antagonist

ANTIC: **4** dido, joke, lark, romp **5** comic, droll, prank, stunt **7** playful **9** escapades, ludicrous **10** shenanigan

ANTICIPATE: **3** see **4** balk, hope **5** augur, await **6** assume, expect, figure, thwart **7** counter, foresee, obviate, predict, prepare **8** forecast, outguess **9** apprehend, forestall, foretaste **11** precipitate

ANTICIPATION: **4** hope **6** augury **7** inkling **9** foresight, intuition, readiness **11** expectation **12** presentiment

ANTIDOTE: **4** cure **6** remedy **7** negator **9** antitoxin, antivenin **10** corrective, preventive **11** neutralizer

ANTIGONE:
brother: **8** Eteocles **9** Polynices
father: **7** Oedipus
mother: **7** Jocasta
sister: **6** Ismene

ANTIGUA AND BARBUDA:
capital: **7** St. John's
cities: **10** Codrington
features: **7** Redonda
monetary unit: **6** dollar
water: **9** Caribbean

ANTIPATHY: **6** enmity, hatred, rancor **7** allergy, disgust, dislike **8** aversion, distaste, loathing **9** animosity, hostility **10** abhorrence, antagonism

ANTIPODAL: **5** polar **7** counter, opposed **8** contrary, opposite **9** diametric

ANTIQUATED: **3** old **4** aged **5** dated, hoary, passe **7** ancient, archaic, elderly, outworn **8** obsolete, outdated, outmoded **9** primitive **12** antediluvian

ANTIQUE: **3** old **5** relic, virtu **7** classic, vestige, vintage **8** artifact, heirloom **9** venerable

ANTISEPTIC: **4** dull, pure **6** iodine, phenol **7** alcohol, sterile **8** hygienic, peroxide, sanitary **9** germicide, purifying **12** disinfectant

ANTISOCIAL: **4** cold **7** hostile **8** solitary **9** alienated, reclusive **10** rebellious **11** anarchistic, belligerent, introverted **12** misanthropic

ANTITHESIS: **7** reverse **8** antipode, contrast, opposite, reversal

ANTITOXIN: **5** serum **7** vaccine **8** antidote **10** antibiotic

ANTLER: **4** horn, knob, rack **5** point, spike **8** deerhorn
section: **3** bay **4** brow, snag **5** crown, royal **8** trestine

ANTONY AND CLEOPATRA:
author: **11** Shakespeare
characters: **4** Eros **5** Menas, Philo **6** Caesar, Taurus **7** Agrippa, Octavia

ANVIL: **5** block, forge **6** smithy, stithy **7** bickern **8** includes **9** converter

ANXIETY: **4** care, fear, fuss **5** anger, doubt, dread, panic, worry **7** anguish, caution, chagrin, concern, jitters **8** suspense **9** misgiving **10** foreboding, uneasiness **11** butterflies **12** apprehension

ANXIOUS: **4** agog, keen **5** antsy, eager, hyper **6** ardent, uneasy **7** fearful, unquiet, uptight **8** restless, watchful, yearning **9** disturbed, expectant, impatient

ANY: **3** all **4** each, much, part, some **5** every **6** either **8** quantity, whatever

ANYBODY: **3** one **6** masses **7** someone **8** everyone

ANYWAY: **5** about **6** anyhow, random **10** regardless **12** nevertheless

A-ONE, A1: **3** ace **4** tops **5** great, prime **6** superb **8** superior **9** excellent **10** tremendous

APACE: **4** fast **7** quickly, rapidly, swiftly **8** speedily **9** posthaste

APACHE: **4** Yuma **6** Indian **14** Native American
chief: **7** Cochise **8** Geronimo

APART: **4** away **5** alone, aside, riven, split **6** freely **7** asunder, enisled, removed **8** detached, distinct, divorced, isolated, reserved, secluded, separate **9** divergent **10** separately **11** dissociated **12** individually

APARTMENT: **3** den, pad **4** coop, digs, flat **5** abode, rooms, suite **6** rental **7** chamber **8** building, dwelling, tenement **9** penthouse

APATHETIC: **3** dry **4** blah, cold, dull, flat, limp **5** inert, stoic **7** callous, passive, unmoved **8** listless, sluggish **9** impassive, unfeeling **10** insensible **11** indifferent, unemotional **12** uninterested

APATHY: **6** acedia, phlegm, torpor **7** languor **8** coolness, doldrums, lethargy, uncaring **9** disregard, lassitude, unconcern **10** detachment **11** impassivity **12** heedlessness

APE: **4** copy, mime **5** ditto, mimic **6** baboon, gelada, gibbon, mirror, monkey, parrot, simian **7** emulate, gorilla, imitate, portray, primate **8** pongidae **9** orangutan **10** chimpanzee **11** impersonate

APERCU: **6** digest, glance, sketch **7** insight, outline **8** syllabus **10** conspectus

APERITIF: **4** whet **5** drink **8** cocktail **9** antipasto, appetizer

APERTURE: **3** eye, gap **4** hole, leak, slit, slot, vent **5** chasm, cleft, crack, space **6** outlet, window **7** fissure, opening, orifice **8** puncture **11** perforation

APEX: **3** cap, max, tip **4** acme, cusp, peak, tops **5** crest, crown, point **6** apogee, climax, summit, vertex, zenith **8** meridian, pinnacle **11** culmination **12** quintessence

APHAREUS:
brother: **7** Lynceus
kingdom: **8** Messenia
son: **4** Idas **7** Lynceus
wife: **5** Arene

APHORISM: **3** saw **5** adage, axiom, maxim, moral, motto **6** dictum, saying, slogan, truism **7** precept, proverb **8** apothegm

APHRODITE:
daughter: **8** Harmonia
father: **4** Zeus
goddess: **4** love
mother: **5** Dione
son: **4** Eros **5** Cupid, Eneas **6** Aeneas

APIARY: **4** hive **7** beehive **8** beehouse

APIECE: **3** all, per **4** each **6** singly **9** severally **12** individually, respectively

APISH: **5** silly **7** slavish **8** affected **9** emulative

APLOMB: **4** ease, tact **5** nerve, poise **6** surety **7** balance **8** coolness **9** assurance, stability **10** confidence, equanimity **11** nonchalance

APOCALYPTIC: **4** dire **7** fateful, ominous **8** oracular **9** prophetic, revealing **10** predictive

APOCRYPHAL: **4** fake, sham **5** false **6** unreal, untrue **7** dubious **8** disputed, doubtful **9** ungenuine **10** fabricated, fictitious **11** counterfeit, unauthentic

APOGEE: **3** top **4** acme, apex, peak **5** crest **6** climax, summit, zenith **8** pinnacle

APOLLO: **6** Delius **7** Phoebus, Pythius **9** Musagetes
birthplace: **5** Delos
father: **4** Zeus **7** Jupiter
god: **5** light, music **6** beauty **8** prophecy
instrument: **4** lute, lyre
loved: **6** Cyrene, Daphne **8** Calliope
mother: **4** Leto **6** Latona
sister: **5** Diana **7** Artemis
son: **3** Ion **7** Orpheus

APOLLYON: **5** devil, Satan **6** diablo **7** Abaddon, Lucifer **9** Beelzebub

APOLOGETIC: **5** sorry **7** atoning **8** contrite, penitent **9** regretful **10** remorseful **11** vindicatory **12** supplicating

APOLOGUE: **4** myth **5** fable, story **6** legend **7** parable **8** allegory

APOLOGY: **4** plea **6** amends, excuse, regret **7** remorse **9** atonement, penitence **11** explanation, vindication

APOSTATE: **3** rat **7** heretic, traitor **8** deserter, disloyal, renegade, turncoat **9** dissident, faithless

APOSTLE: **4** John, Jude, Paul **5** James, Judas, Peter, Silas, Simon **6** Andrew, Philip, Thomas **7** Matthew, pioneer, teacher, witness **8** Barnabas, disciple, follower, Matthias, preacher **9** companion, messenger **10** evangelist, missionary **11** Bartholomew

APOTHECARY: **7** chemist **8** druggist, gallipot **9** dispenser **10** pharmacist

APOTHEGM: **3** saw **5** adage, axiom, maxim, moral **6** dictum, saying, truism **7** proverb **8** aphorism

APPALL, APPAL: **3** awe **4** faze, stun **5** daunt, repel, shock **6** dismay, insult, revolt **7** astound, disgust, horrify, terrify **8** frighten

APPALLING: **3** bad **4** dire **5** awful, gross **7** fearful **8** alarming, dreadful, outraged, shocking, terrible **9** frightful

APPANAGE: **5** grant, right **7** adjunct **9** endowment, privilege **10** perquisite **11** prerogative

APPARATUS: **3** rig **4** gear, tool **5** gizmo, setup **6** device, gadget, outfit, system **7** network, utensil **8** material **9** appliance, doohickey, equipment, machinery, trappings **11** contraption

APPAREL: **4** clad, duds, garb, robe, suit, togs, wear **5** adorn, dress **6** attire, outfit **7** clothes, costume, garment, vesture **8** clothing, wardrobe **9** embellish **11** furnishings

APPARENT: **4** open **5** clear, overt, plain **6** likely, patent **7** blatant, evident, glaring, obvious, seeming **8** distinct, manifest, probable, supposed **10** noticeable, ostensible **11** discernible, unconcealed, unequivocal

APPARITION: **5** ghost, haunt, spook **6** shadow, spirit, wraith **7** eidolon, fantasy, phantom, specter **8** bogeyman, delusion, illusion, revenant **9** hobgoblin **10** appearance, phenomenon

APPEAL: **3** ask, beg, bid **4** call, plea, seek **5** plead **6** allure, beauty, entice, prayer, summon **7** address, beseech, implore, propose, request, solicit **8** approach, petition **10** attraction, supplicate

APPEALING: **4** cute **7** lovable **8** alluring, engaging, pleading, pleasing, tempting **9** agreeable, imploring **10** attractive, entrancing

APPEAR: **4** look, loom, seem **5** arise, enter, issue, occur **6** arrive, emerge **7** emanate, present, surface **11** materialize

APPEARANCE: **3** air **4** look, show, view **5** debut, front, shape, sight **6** advent, aspect, facade, manner **7** arrival, display **8** attitude, demeanor, illusion, presence **9** semblance **10** disclosure **11** countenance

APPEASE: **4** calm, ease **5** allay, quell, quiet, slake **6** pacify, please, soften, solace, soothe, subdue **7** assuage, gratify, mollify, placate, satisfy **8** diminish, mitigate **10** conciliate, propitiate **11** tranquilize

APPELLATION: **3** tag **4** name **5** label, title **6** handle **7** epithet, moniker **8** cognomen, nickname **11** designation

APPEND: **3** add, fix **4** clip, hang, join **6** attach, fasten

APPENDAGE: **3** arm, ear, leg, tab, tag **4** limb, tail, wing **5** extra, rider **6** branch, member, suffix **7** adjunct, antenna **8** addition, offshoot, parasite, tentacle **9** accessory, extension, extremity **10** supplement

APPENDIX: **5** index, organ, rider, table **8** addendum, addition, epilogue **10** postscript, supplement

APPERTAIN: **4** bear, vest **5** apply, refer **6** belong, relate **7** concern, pertain

APPETITE: **3** yen **4** lust, urge, zest **5** gusto, taste **6** desire, hunger, liking, relish **7** craving, longing, passion, wanting **8** gluttony, penchant, tendency, weakness **9** hankering **10** propensity

APPETIZER: **3** dip **5** snack **6** canape, sample, savory, tidbit **8** cocktail, delicacy, munchies **9** antipasto **11** hors d'oeuvre

APPLAUD: **4** clap, hail, kudo, plug, root **5** boost, cheer, extol **6** praise **7** acclaim, approve, commend, endorse **9** encourage **10** compliment

APPLAUSE: **4** hand **5** kudos **6** bravos, cheers, praise **7** hurrahs, ovation **8** clapping **9** accolades

APPLE: **4** crab, pome **6** Esopus, pippin, russet **7** Baldwin, costard, Duchess, Fameuse, Stayman, Wealthy, Winesap **8** Cortland, Greening, Jonathan, McIntosh, pearmain **9** Delicious, Oldenberg **11** Gravenstein, Spitzenburg
beverage: **5** cider, juice **8** Calvados **9** Applejack
dessert: **3** pie **5** crisp **7** strudel
genus: **5** malus

APPLE OF ONE'S EYE: **3** pet **5** pupil **7** darling **8** favorite

APPLESAUCE: **3** rot **4** bunk, pulp **5** fudge, hokum, hooey **7** baloney, hogwash, rubbish **8** malarkey, nonsense **9** poppycock

APPLIANCE: **4** gear, tool **6** device, gadget **7** fixture, utensil **9** apparatus **10** instrument

APPLICABLE: **3** apt, fit **4** meet **6** kosher, proper, useful **7** fitting, germane **8** apposite, relative, relevant, suitable **9** befitting, pertinent

APPLICANT: **6** seeker, suitor **8** aspirant, prospect **9** appellant, candidate

APPLICATION: **3** use **4** form, play **5** blank, claim, study **6** appeal, debate, effort **7** request **8** dressing, industry, ointment, petition **9** diligence, operation, relevance **10** employment

APPLY: **3** ask, fit, rub, use **4** bend, suit **5** cover **6** allude, appeal, bestow, commit, devote, direct, employ, impose, relate **7** address, conform, overlay, pertain, request, solicit, utilize **8** exercise, petition **9** persevere **10** administer **11** superimpose

APPOINT: **3** fix, set, tap **4** name **5** allot, elect, equip **6** assign, choose, decree, detail, direct, ordain, outfit, select **7** arrange, confirm, furnish **8** delegate, nominate **9** authorize, designate **10** commission

APPOINTMENT: **3** gig, job **4** date, post **5** berth **6** office **7** meeting, nominee, station **8** position **9** selection **10** assignment, engagement, rendezvous

APPORTION: **3** cut, lot **5** allot, award, quota, share, split **6** assess, assign, divide, ration **7** consign, prorate **8** allocate **10** distribute

APPORTIONMENT: **4** deal, part **5** share **7** measure **8** dividend, division **9** allotment, allowance

APPOSITE: **3** apt **6** timely **7** fitting, germane **8** relevant, suitable **9** pertinent **10** applicable

APPRAISE: **4** deem, rate **5** check, gauge, judge, value **6** assess, survey **7** analyze, examine, inspect **8** estimate, evaluate **10** adjudicate

APPRECIABLE: **5** clear, large **7** evident, obvious **8** apparent, definite, tangible **10** noticeable **11** discernible

APPRECIATE: **4** feel, gain, like, love **5** adore, enjoy, judge, prize, value **6** admire, esteem **7** cherish, realize, respect, welcome **8** increase, treasure **9** recognize **10** understand

APPRECIATION: **5** grasp **6** growth, thanks **7** tribute **9** enjoyment, gratitude **10** admiration **11** recognition, testimonial

APPREHEND: **3** bag, get, nab, see **4** bust, know, nail, take, view **5** catch, seize **6** arrest, collar, detain, fathom **7** capture, foresee **8** perceive **9** recognize **10** anticipate, comprehend

APPREHENSION: **4** fear, idea **5** alarm, doubt, dread, worry **6** arrest, dismay, taking **7** anxiety, capture, concern **8** distrust, mistrust **9** misgiving, suspicion **10** uneasiness **11** premonition, trepidation **12** anticipation, intellection

APPREHENSIVE: **5** aware, jumpy, stiff **6** afraid, morbid **7** anxious, fearful, nervous **9** cognizant, conscious, misgiving **10** suspicious

APPRENTICE: **4** tyro **5** pupil **6** novice, rookie **7** amateur, learner, student, trainee **8** beginner, neophyte **9** novitiate **10** tenderfoot

APPRISE: **4** clue, tell, warn **5** value **6** advise, inform, notify **8** acquaint, disclose **9** enlighten

APPROACH: **3** try, way **4** come, feel, gate, loom, near **5** reach, start **6** access, advent, avenue, impend **7** address, advance, landing, passage, solicit **8** overture **9** procedure **11** approximate

APPROBATION: **4** okay **5** favor **6** esteem, praise, regard **7** respect, support **8** applause, approval, blessing **10** admiration, compliment

APPROPRIATE: **3** apt, due, fit, use **4** grab, meet, take **5** annex, claim, right, usurp **6** borrow, pilfer, pirate, pocket, proper, timely, worthy **7** convert, earmark, fitting, germane, preempt, purloin, related, reserve **8** becoming, deserved, embezzle, relevant, suitable **9** pertinent **10** applicable, confiscate, convenient

APPROPRIATION: **5** grant **7** seizure, stipend, subsidy **8** takeover **9** allotment, allowance, budgeting

APPROVAL: **4** amen, okay **5** favor **6** assent, liking **7** consent, support **8** blessing, sanction **10** permission **11** approbation

APPROVE: **3** buy **4** back, like, okay, pass, sign **5** adopt, agree, allow, clear, favor **6** accept, admire, handle, ratify, uphold **7** applaud, confirm, consent, endorse, initial **8** accredit, sanction, validate **9** authorize **10** compliment

APPROXIMATE: **4** like, near **5** about, close, guess, reach **6** almost **7** similar **8** approach, estimate, resemble, surmised

APPROXIMATELY: **5** about **6** almost, around, nearly **7** roughly **9** bordering, generally, virtually **10** relatively **11** practically

APPURTENANCE: **4** gear **5** annex **8** addition, appendix **9** accessory, apparatus, appendage, component **10** attachment

A PRIORI: **6** theory **9** deductive **11** inferential, presumptive **12** hypothetical

APRON: **3** bib **4** tier **5** cover, smock **6** shield **8** airstrip, pinafore **10** protection, stagefront

APROPOS: **3** apt, fit **4** meet **5** about **6** proper, seemly, timely **7** correct, fitting, germane **8** relevant, suitable **10** concerning **11** appropriate

APT: **3** fit, pat **4** able, keen **5** adept, alert, prone, quick, ready, savvy **6** astute, clever, gifted, likely **7** apropos, capable, fitting **8** disposed, inclined, skillful, suitable, talented, tendency **9** competent, pertinent **10** proficient **11** appropriate

APTITUDE: **4** bent, gift **5** flair, knack **6** genius, talent **7** ability, leaning **8** capacity, instinct **10**

propensity **11** disposition, inclination

AQUARIUM: 4 bowl, pool, tank **8** fishbowl

AQUEDUCT: 4 race **5** canal **7** channel, conduit, passage **8** pipeline **9** conductor **10** waterworks **11** watercourse

ARABIA: 11 Saudi Arabia
countries of: **4** Oman **5** Qatar, Yemen **6** Kuwait **11** Saudi Arabia **18** United Arab Emirates

ARABLE: 7 fertile **8** farmable, plowable, tillable **10** cultivable

ARACHNID: 4 crab, mite, tick **6** spider **8** scorpion **9** tarantula **10** harvestman

ARAM: 5 Syria

ARBITER: 5 fixer, judge, maven **6** umpire **7** referee **9** moderator **12** middleperson

ARBITRARY: 4 rash **5** bossy **6** chance, random **7** erratic, offhand, willful **8** absolute **9** imperious, whimsical **10** autocratic, capricious, highhanded, irrational, tyrannical **12** unreasonable

ARBITRATE: 5 judge **6** decide, settle, smooth **7** mediate **9** determine, intercede, negotiate

ARBITRATOR: 5 judge **6** umpire **8** mediator **9** moderator **11** conciliator

ARBOR: 3 bar **4** axle, beam **5** bower **6** gazebo **7** pergola, retreat, spindle **9** pavillion **11** summerhouse

ARC: 3 bow **4** arch, bend, halo **5** curve, orbit **7** azimuth, rainbow **8** halfmoon

ARCADE: 4 hall **6** loggia **7** gallery, skywalk **9** colonnade **10** passageway

ARCADIA: 4 Eden, Zion **6** utopia **8** paradise

ARCANE: 6 hidden, mystic, occult, secret **8** esoteric **9** enigmatic **10** cabalistic

ARCAS:
father: **4** Zeus
mother: **8** Callisto
son: **4** Azan **6** Elatus **8** Apheidas
wife: **5** Erato

ARCH: 3 arc, bow, sly **4** bend, hump, main, span **5** chief, curve, great, prime, vault **6** bridge, clever, extend **7** cunning, eminent, roguish **8** foremost **9** principal

ARCHAIC: 3 old **5** dated, passe **7** ancient, antique **8** historic, obsolete, outmoded **9** venerable **10** antiquated

ARCHANGEL: 5 Satan, Uriel **7** Gabriel, Michael, Raphael

ARCHER: 5 Cupid **6** bowman **9** Robin Hood **11** Sagittarius

ARCHETYPE: 4 form, idea **5** ideal, model **7** example, pattern **8** exemplar, original, paradigm **9** prototype

ARCHITECT: 5 maker **6** artist, author **7** builder, creator, founder, planner **8** designer, engineer **9** innovator **12** draftsperson

ARCHITECTURE: 5 style **6** design **8** building, planning **9** framework **12** constitution

ARCHIVE: 5 annal **6** museum, papers, record **7** library, scrolls **8** document, registry, writings **9** chronicle

ARCTIC: 3 icy **4** cold, cool **5** gelid, nippy, polar **6** bitter, boreal, chilly, frigid, frosty **7** glacial **8** freezing
explorers: **3** Nay, Rae **4** Byrd, Eric, Kane, Ross **5** David, Peary **6** Baffin, Bering, Button, Greely, Henson, Hudson, Nansen, Nobile **7** Bennett, McClure, Wilkins, Wrangel **8** Amundsen, Ericsson,

Franklin **9** Frobisher, Rasmussen **10** Stefansson, Willoughby **11** Nordenskold
features: **16** Northwest Passage
islands: **5** Banks, Devon **6** Baffin **7** Wrangel **8** Bathurst
natives: **5** Aleut, Inuit **6** Eskimo, Indian **7** Alaskan, Chukchi, Samoyed **9** Laplander
water: **4** Kara **6** Laptev **7** Barents, Chukchi, Lincoln **8** Beaufort

ARDENT: **3** hot **4** avid, fond, keen, warm **5** eager, fiery **6** ablaze, fervid, torrid **7** burning, devoted, earnest, feeling, fervent, flaming, intense, shining, zealous **8** desirous, spirited, vehement **9** impetuous, steadfast **10** passionate **12** enthusiastic

ARDOR: **4** dash, fire, glow, heat, love, zest **5** gusto, oomph, verve **6** desire, fervor, spirit **7** feeling, passion **8** devotion, keenness, vivacity **9** animation, intensity **10** enthusiasm

ARDUOUS: **4** hard **5** lofty, steep, tight, tough **6** murder, tiring, trying, uphill **8** exacting, grueling **9** difficult, laborious, strenuous **10** exhausting **12** backbreaking

AREA: **4** belt, city, size, turf, zone **5** block, field, range, realm, scene, scope, space, state, tract **6** county, extent, locale, parcel, region, sector, sphere **7** expanse, section **8** district, province, township, vicinity **9** bailiwick, territory **12** neighborhood

ARENA: **3** pit **4** bowl, oval, ring, rink **5** court, field, stage **6** sphere, square **7** stadium, theater **8** coliseum, gridiron, province **10** hippodrome **11** battlefield **12** amphitheater

ARES: **4** Mars
daughter: **8** Harmonia **9** Melanippe
father: **4** Zeus **7** Jupiter
god: **3** War
mother: **4** Enyo, Hero
son: **6** Cycnus, Phobos **8** Diomedes, Thestius

ARGENT: **5** money, white **6** silver **7** shining, silvery

ARGENTINA:
capital: **6** Viedma **11** Buenos Aires
cities: **7** Cordoba, La Plata, Mendoza, Rosario, Santa Fe, Tucuman **11** Bahia Blanca
continent: **12** South America
explorers: **5** Cabot **7** De Solis
features: **4** Mayo **5** Andes, Cachi, Laudo **6** Bonete, Pissis **9** Aconcagua, Patagonia
languages: **6** French, German **7** English, Italian, Spanish
monetary unit: **4** peso
water: **4** Coig **5** Atuel, Chico, Dulce, Limay **6** Quinto **7** La Plata **8** Colorado, Gallegos **9** Rio Grande **11** Iguacu Falls, Iguaza Falls

ARGONAUT: **8** wanderer **10** adventurer
leader: **5** Jason
quest: **12** Golden Fleece
ship: **4** Argo

ARGOT: **4** cant **5** lingo, slang **6** jargon, patois **7** dialect **10** vernacular

ARGUE: **4** feud, moot, spar **5** claim, clash, cross, plead **6** battle, bicker, debate, defend, hassle, induce, reason **7** contend, contest, discuss, dispute, quarrel, quibble, wrangle **8** conflict, disagree, maintain, persuade **11** expostulate, remonstrate

ARGUMENT: **3** row **4** beef, case, fuss, plea, plot, stew, tiff **5** brawl, fight, proof, scene **6** combat, debate, hassle, reason **7** defense, quarrel, rhubarb, summary **8** abstract, squabble **9** discourse, statement **10** difference **11** altercation, controversy

ARGUMENTATIVE: **5** salty **6** shrill, touchy **7** eristic, scrappy **8**

contrary **10** indicative, rhetorical **11** belligerent, contentious **12** disputatious

ARGUTE: **4** high **5** acute, savvy, sharp **6** shrewd

ARIA: **4** hymn, solo, song, tune **6** melody **7** excerpt

ARID: **3** dry **4** bald, bare, dull, flat, lean **5** dusty **6** barren, boring, jejune, meager **7** parched, sterile **8** lifeless, withered **9** waterless **10** desiccated, spiritless **12** moistureless

ARIES: **3** ram **4** Mars **5** April, March

ARISE: **4** dawn, lift, soar **5** awake, begin, mount, raise, stand, surge **6** accrue, amount, appear, ascend, derive, emerge, happen, spring **7** develop, emanate, proceed **9** originate

ARISTOCRACY: **5** elite **6** gentry **8** nobility **9** oligarchy

ARISTOCRAT: **4** lady, peer **5** noble, ritzy **8** nobleman **9** blue-blood, patrician **12** gentleperson

ARISTOTLE: **5** Greek **11** philosopher
taught: **6** ethics **7** physics, poetics **8** politics, rhetoric

ARIZONA:
bird: **10** cactus wren
capital: **7** Phoenix
cities: **4** Mesa **5** Tempe **6** Tucson **7** Nogales **8** Glendale, Prescott **9** Flagstaff **10** Scottsdale
explorer: **6** De Niza **8** Coronado
features: **9** Hoover Dam **10** Boulder Dam **11** Grand Canyon **12** London Bridge, Roosevelt Dam **13** Painted Desert **15** Colorado Plateau
flower: **13** Saguaro cactus
native: **4** Hopi, Pima, Yuma **6** Apache, Navaho, Navajo, Papago
nickname: **16** Grand Canyon State
tree: **9** paloverde
water: **8** Lake Mead **13** Colorado River

ARK: **3** box **4** boat, ship **5** barge, chest, hutch **6** basket, coffer, refuge, vessel **7** retreat, shelter **9** Noah's boat
resting place: **6** Ararat

ARKANSAS:
bird: **11** mockingbird
capital: **10** Little Rock
cities: **9** Fort Smith, Pine Bluff **12** Fayetteville
explorer: **6** De Soto, Joliet **7** La Salle **9** Marquette
features: **6** Ozarks **10** Hot Springs
flower: **12** apple blossom
nickname: **17** Land of Opportunity
tree: **13** shortleaf pine
water: **13** Quachita River **16** Mississippi River

ARM: **3** bay **4** hook, limb, pack, spur, wing **5** bough, equip, force, inlet, might, power, sound **6** branch, weapon **7** fortify, furnish, prepare, protect, support **9** appendage, extension **10** instrument, projection, strengthen
bone: **4** ulna **6** radius **7** humerus
joint: **4** ares **5** elbow, wrist
muscle: **6** biceps **7** triceps

ARMADA: **4** navy **5** fleet, force **8** flotilla, squadron, warships

ARMADILLO: **4** peba, tatu **5** poyou, tatou **6** mulita, peludo **7** tatouay **8** pangolin **10** pichiciago **11** quirquincho
family: **11** Dasypodidae

ARMAMENT: **4** arms, heat **6** shield **7** defense, weapons **8** ordnance, security **9** munitions, safeguard

ARMAMENTARIUM: **4** data, fund **5** stock, store **6** armory, supply **7** arsenal **9** apparatus, equipment, inventory **10** collection

ARMENIA:
also called: **5** Minni **8** Anatolia
capital: **7** Yerevan

cities: **7** Kumayri **9** Kirovakan, Leninakan
features: **7** Aragats **11** Mount Ararat
republic of: **6** Russia
water: **5** Araks, Sevan, Zanga **6** Razdan

ARMISTICE: **5** peace, truce **9** cessation

ARMOIRE: **8** cupboard, wardrobe **10** repository **12** clothespress

ARMOR: **4** mail **5** guard, plate **6** sheath, shield **7** bulwark, defense **8** covering **10** protection
arm: **6** couter **8** vambrace **9** rerebrace
chest: **7** cuirass **11** breastplate
foot: **7** sabaton **8** poulaine
hand: **8** gauntlet
helmet: **4** comb, nose **5** armet, crest, skull, visor **6** beaver, gorget **7** ventail
leg: **6** cuisse, greave, poleyn
shoulder: **8** pauldron
waist: **5** skirt, tunic **6** tasset

ARMORY: **4** dump **5** depot, plant, range **6** center **7** arsenal, factory **8** magazine **9** warehouse

ARMPIT: **5** oxter **6** axilla **8** underarm

ARMY: **3** mob **4** band, gang, pack **5** array, crowd, force, horde **6** legion, troops **7** cavalry, militia **8** soldiers, warriors **9** battalion
chaplain: **5** padre
commission: **6** brevet
enlisted man: **3** Joe, NCO **7** private **8** doughboy
mascot: **4** mule
meal: **4** chow, mess
officer: **5** major **7** captain, colonel, general **8** sergeant **10** lieutenant
post: **4** base, camp, fort
school: **3** OCS, OTS **7** academy **9** West Point
unit: **5** corps, squad, troop **6** detail, outfit **7** brigade, company, platoon **8** division, regiment **10** detachment
vehicle: **4** jeep, tank **9** half-track

AROMA: **4** balm, odor **5** savor, scent, smell, spice **6** flavor **7** bouquet, perfume **9** fragrance, redolence

AROMATIC: **5** balmy, spicy, sweet **6** fruity, savory **7** odorous, pungent, scented **8** fragrant, redolent **9** ambrosial

AROUND: **4** near **5** about, circa **6** nearby **7** through **10** encircling, enveloping, everywhere **11** neighboring, surrounding **12** encompassing

AROUSE: **3** fan **4** call, fire, stir, whet **5** alarm, alert, awake, pique, raise, rally, spark **6** excite, foment, incite, kindle, summon, thrill **7** actuate, agitate, animate, enliven, inflame, provoke **9** challenge, stimulate

ARPEGGIO: **5** chord, scale **7** roulade **8** division, flourish

ARRAIGN: **3** try **4** cite **5** blame **6** accuse, charge, indict **7** impeach **9** challenge **11** incriminate

ARRANGE: **3** fix, set **4** edit, file, plan, rank, sort, tidy **5** adapt, align, array, group, order, score **6** adjust, codify, design, devise, scheme, settle **7** catalog, compose, prepare, seriate **8** classify, conclude, organize, position, tabulate **9** collocate **10** categorize, instrument **11** alphabetize, orchestrate

ARRANGEMENT: **4** deal **5** chart, index, order, terms **6** design, format, layout, scheme, treaty **7** pattern **8** contract, grouping **10** allocation **11** composition, disposition **12** distribution

ARRANT: **3** bad **5** gross, utter **6** brazen, wicked **7** blatant, vagrant **8** flagrant, rascally **9** confirmed, downright, notorious, shameless **11** unmitigated

ARRAY: **3** lot, set **4** clad, deck, garb, host, robe, show **5** adorn, drape, dress, habit, order **6** attire, clothe, outfit, parade, series **7** apparel, arrange, display, furnish, marshal **8** grouping **10** assemblage

ARREARS: **3** IOU **4** debt **5** claim **9** liability **10** obligation **12** indebtedness

ARREST: **3** bag, can, nab, net **4** bust, grab, halt, jail, nail, stay, stop **5** catch, pinch, seize **6** collar, detain, hinder, secure **7** capture, custody, suspend **8** imprison, obstruct, restrain **9** apprehend, intercept **11** incarcerate

ARRIVE: **4** come, land, show **5** occur, reach, visit **6** appear, attain **7** prosper, succeed **8** approach, dismount, flourish

ARROGANCE: **4** gall **5** nerve, pride **6** hubris, vanity **7** bluster, conceit, egotism, hauteur **9** assurance, insolence, pomposity **11** affectation

ARROGANT: **4** vain **5** bossy, cocky, lofty, proud **6** lordly, snooty, uppity **7** haughty, pompous **8** insolent, superior **9** conceited, egotistic, insulting, presuming **10** disdainful **11** domineering, highfalutin, overbearing **12** contemptuous, presumptuous

ARROGATE: **4** grab, take **5** claim, seize, usurp **6** assume, demand **7** preempt **9** sequester **10** commandeer, confiscate

ARROW: **3** bow, pin, rod **4** bolt, dart, reed **6** sprite, weapon **7** missile, pointer **9** direction, indicator
section: **4** butt, head **5** shaft **7** feather

ARROYO: **3** gap **5** brook, creek, gorge, gully **6** ravine, stream **7** channel **11** watercourse

ARSENAL: **4** dump **5** depot, stock **6** armory, supply **7** weapons **8** dockyard, magazine **9** stockpile **10** storehouse

ARSENIC: **6** poison **8** chemical

ARSONIST: **7** firebug **10** pyromaniac

ART: **3** pop **4** wile **5** craft, genre, knack, magic, skill, trade **6** cubism **7** baroque, calling, cunning, faculty, fauvism, finesse, methods, realism, science, surreal **8** abstract, business, learning, vocation **9** classical, expertise, ingenuity **10** humanities, profession, surrealism **11** contrivance, cultivation, objectivism, primitivism, Renaissance, romanticism **13** impressionism

ARTEMIS: **5** Diana **7** Cynthia **9** Astrateia
brother: **6** Apollo
father: **4** Zeus
mother: **4** Leto

ARTERY: **3** way **4** path, road, tube, vein **5** aorta, canal, route **6** course, street, vessel **7** carotid, conduit, highway, passage **8** coronary **9** maxillary

ARTFUL: **3** apt, sly **4** deft, foxy, wily **5** slick, smart, suave **6** clever, crafty, gifted, smooth, tricky **7** crooked, cunning, vulpine **8** slippery, stealthy, talented **9** deceitful, deceptive, dexterous, underhand **10** contriving **11** imaginative

ARTICLE: **3** one, the **4** beat, item, term **5** essay, paper, piece, point, story, theme, thing **6** column, matter, object, report **7** feature **8** doctrine **9** condition, statement **10** particular **11** composition, stipulation

ARTICULATE: **3** say **4** link **5** clear, speak, state, utter, vocal **6** convey, fluent, spoken, verbal **7** express **8** distinct, eloquent **9** enunciate, pronounce **10** formulated, meaningful **12** intelligible

ARTIFICE: **3** con **4** hoax, ploy, ruse **5** trick **6** deceit, tactic **7** cunning, gimmick **8** foxiness, intrigue, wiliness **9** cageyness, chicanery, deception

ARTIFICIAL: **4** fake, mock, sham **5** bogus, false, phony **6** ersatz, hollow, pseudo, unreal **7** assumed, feigned **8** spurious **9** imitation, insincere, pretended, simulated, synthetic, unnatural **10** factitious, fictitious **11** counterfeit

ARTILLERY: **4** arms, guns **5** force **6** cannon **7** battery, bazooka, rockets **8** missiles, ordnance, weaponry

ARTISAN: **6** expert, master **7** builder, plumber **9** carpenter **12** craftsperson, professional

ARTIST: **3** ace **4** star **5** actor **6** dancer, expert, master, singer **7** painter **8** composer, musician, sculptor, virtuoso **9** performer **12** professional

ARTLESS: **4** free, open, pure **5** frank, naive, plain **6** candid, direct, humble, simple **7** natural **8** innocent, trusting **9** childlike, guileless, ingenuous **10** unaffected, unschooled

ARTY: **5** showy **6** dainty **7** popular **8** highbrow, imposing **9** imitative, overblown, tasteless **11** pretentious, superficial

ASA: **6** healer **9** physician
father: **4** Abia **6** Abijam **7** Elkanah

AS A RULE: **7** usually **8** commonly **9** generally **10** frequently, ordinarily

AS GOOD AS: **5** about **6** almost, nearly **9** nearabout **11** essentially

AS LONG AS: **3** for **5** since **7** because, whereas **11** considering

ASCEND: **4** lift, rise, soar **5** climb, mount, scale, tower **6** aspire, sprout **8** escalate, progress

ASCENDANCY: **4** rule, sway **5** power **7** control, mastery, success **8** dominion, prestige **9** authority, influence, supremacy **10** domination **11** superiority

ASCENT: **4** hill, ramp, rise **5** grade, slope **6** spring, stairs **7** incline, upgrade **8** progress **9** acclivity, elevation, uplifting **11** advancement

ASCERTAIN: **3** get **5** learn **6** verify **7** unearth **8** discover, identify **9** determine **11** doublecheck

ASCETIC: **3** nun **4** monk, yogi **5** fakir, stark, stoic **6** hermit, severe, strict **7** austere, eremite, recluse, stylite **8** celibate **9** abstinent, anchorite **11** disciplined

ASCRIBE: **3** lay **4** cite **5** blame, infer, refer **6** accuse, allege, attach, charge, impute **9** attribute, reference

ASEA: **4** lost **6** addled, adrift **7** puzzled, sailing **8** confused **9** befuddled, uncertain **10** bewildered

ASEPTIC: **4** cold **5** clean **6** barren **7** sterile **8** lifeless **9** purifying, shrinking **10** restrained

ASH: **4** dust, soot, tree **5** ember **6** cinder **7** clinker, residue

ASHAMED: **5** sorry **7** abashed, humbled **8** contrite **9** flustered, mortified **10** humiliated, remorseful **11** embarrassed

ASHEN: **3** wan **4** gray, pale **5** faded, pasty, waxen **6** pallid **7** ghastly **8** blanched

ASHER:
brother: **3** Dan **5** Judah **8** Benjamin
daughter: **5** Serah **6** Beriah

father: **5** Jacob
mother: **6** Zilpah
son: **4** Isui, Usui **6** Jimnah

ASIA:
cities: **5** Osaka, Seoul, Tokyo **6** Bombay, Tehran **7** Bangkok, Beijing, Jakarta **8** Calcutta, Hong Kong, Shanghai
countries: **4** Iran, Iraq, Laos, Oman **5** Burma, China, Egypt, India, Japan, Nepal, Qatar, Syria, Tibet, Yemen **6** Bhutan, Brunei, Cyprus, Israel, Jordan, Kuwait, Russia, Taiwan, Turkey **7** Bahrain, Lebanon, Vietnam **8** Cambodia, Malaysia, Maldives, Mongolia, Pakistan, Sri Lanka, Thailand **9** Indonesia, Singapore **10** Bangladesh, North Korea, South Korea **11** Afghanistan, Philippines, Saudi Arabia **12** Arab Emirates
dynasties: **5** Gupta, Indus, Mogul, Sumer **9** Babylonia, Tamerlane **10** Kublai Khan **11** Mesopotamia
ethnic groups: **3** Han, Lao, Mon, Tai **4** Arab, Kurd, Shan, Thai, Turk **5** Khmer, Malay, Tajik, Tamil, Uzbek **6** Indian, Lepcha, Manchu, Mongol, Sindhi **7** Baluchi, Bengali, Persian, Punjabi, Tibetan **8** Armenian, Kanarese **9** Chungchia, Dravidian, Indo-Aryan, Sinhalese
features: **5** Altai **6** Pamirs **7** Khingan **8** Tien Shan **9** Annapurna, Himalayas, Hindu Kush **10** Gobi Desert, Takla Makan **12** Mount Everest **13** Arabian Desert
languages: **4** Urdu **5** Hindi **6** Arabic **7** Chinese **8** Japanese **11** Indo-Iranian
water: **4** Amur, Lena **6** Baikal **7** Aral Sea, Huang He, Yenisei **8** Balkhash, Hsi River, Ili River, Ob-Irtysh **9** Ural River **10** Caspian Sea, Chang Jiang, Indus River **11** Ganges River, Mekong River, Tigris River, Yellow River **12** Yangtze River **14** Euphrates River, Irrawaddy River

ASIA MINOR: **7** Phrygia, Pisidia **8** Anatolia, Bithynia, Pergamum
cities: **4** Myra, Myus, Teos, Troy **5** Issus, Perga **6** Mylasa, Patara, Priene, Sardis, Tarsus **7** Ephesus, Miletus **8** Colophon
features: **3** Ida **6** Sultan, Taurus
kingdoms: **5** Caria, Ionia, Lydia, Mysia, Troad, Troas **6** Pontus **7** Cilicia
now called: **6** Turkey
water: **5** Halys **7** Marmara **8** Black Sea, Bosporus, Monderez **9** Aegean Sea **11** Dardanelles **13** Mediterranean

ASIDE: **3** off **4** afar, away, gone **5** aloof, apart **6** beside **7** private, tangent, whisper **8** reserved, secretly, separate **9** alongside, obliquely

ASIDE FROM: **4** save **6** except **7** barring, besides **9** excluding

ASININE: **4** dull **5** dense, inept, silly **6** absurd, simple, stupid **7** doltish, foolish, idiotic **8** mindless **9** imbecilic, senseless **11** lamebrained **12** simpleminded

ASK: **3** bid **4** call, pray, quiz, seek **5** claim, crave, exact, grill, order, press, utter **6** adjure, demand, expect, summon **7** beseech, consult, entreat, implore, inquire, request, solicit **8** petition, question **11** interrogate

ASKANCE: **4** awry **5** askew **7** crooked **8** sideways **9** cynically **10** critically, doubtfully **11** skeptically

ASKEW: **4** alop, awry, bent **5** amiss **6** aslant, zigzag **7** asquint, crooked, knotted **8** cockeyed, lopsided **9** distorted

ASLEEP: **3** out **4** dead, idle **6** dozing, latent, numbed **7** napping, resting, unaware **8** dreaming, inactive **9** unfeeling **10** motionless, slumbering **11** hibernating, unconscious

ASPECT: **3** air **4** face, form, look, side, view **5** angle, phase, point **6** manner **7** bearing, feature, outlook **8** carriage, prospect **9** semblance, situation **10** appearance **11** countenance

ASPEN: **4** tree, wood **6** poplar **7** quaking **9** quivering, trembling

ASPERITY: **8** acerbity, acrimony, hardness, sourness, tartness **9** briskness, harshness, hostility, roughness **10** bitterness, crabbiness, difficulty, unevenness

ASPERSION: **4** muck, slur **5** abuse **6** insult **7** baptism, calumny, slander **8** innuendo, reproach **9** invective **10** backbiting

ASPHALT: **4** pave **7** bitumen **8** blacktop, uintaite

ASPHYXIATE: **5** choke, drown **7** smother **8** strangle **9** suffocate

ASPIRANT: **6** seeker **7** hopeful **9** applicant, candidate **10** competitor

ASPIRATION: **3** aim **4** goal, hope, wish **5** dream, ideal **6** desire **7** craving, pursuit **8** ambition, yearning

ASPIRE: **3** try **4** long, rise, seek, soar, want **5** mount, tower **6** ascend, desire, hanker, thirst

ASS: **4** dolt, duff, fool **5** burro, chump, dunce, idiot, jenny, moron **6** donkey, nitwit **7** jackass **8** imbecile, numskull **9** blockhead, simpleton **10** nincompoop

ASSAIL: **4** bash, beat, pelt **5** abuse, beset, pound, stone, storm, whack **6** accuse, attack, invade, malign, scathe, strike **7** assault, bombard **8** lambaste **9** encounter

ASSAILANT: **5** enemy **6** mugger **8** attacker **9** aggressor, assaulter **10** antagonist

ASSAM:
capital: **6** Dispur
cities: **4** Ledo **7** Gauhati, Nowgong **8** Shillong
country: **5** India
language: **8** Assamese
natives: **6** Nepali **7** Bengali **8** Assamese

ASSASSIN: **3** gun **6** gunman, hit man, killer, slayer **8** gunwoman, hitwoman, murderer **9** cutthroat **10** hatchet man, triggerman **11** executioner **12** triggerwoman

ASSASSINATION: **8** Huey Long **9** commandos **10** John Lennon **11** John Kennedy, Mark Chapman **12** Anwar El-Sadat, Indira Gandhi, James Earl Ray, Leon Czolgosz, Sirhan Sirhan **13** James Garfield, Robert Kennedy **14** Abraham Lincoln, Charles Guiteau, Gavrilo Princip, Mohandas Gandhi **15** Carl Austin Weiss, John Wilkes Booth, Lee Harvey Oswald, William McKinley **16** Martin Luther King **20** Nathuram Vinayak Godse **24** Archduke Francis Ferdinand

ASSAULT: **3** mug **4** beat, jump, push, raid, slug **5** beset, fight, onset, pound, siege, smite, storm **6** assail, attack, breach, charge, invade, strike **7** advance, violate **9** bushwhack, incursion, onslaught **10** aggression **11** bombardment

ASSAY: **3** try **4** test **5** check, offer, prove **6** survey **7** analyze, examine, eyeball **8** analysis, appraise, estimate, evaluate **9** determine, undertake **10** experiment

ASSEMBLAGE: **4** army, crew, herd, mass, pack **5** batch, bunch, crowd, flock, stock, swarm **6** convoy, throng **7** cluster, collage, turnout **8** assembly **9** community, gathering **11** aggregation **12** congregation

ASSEMBLE: **3** fit **4** call, join, make, mass, meet **5** build, flock, piece, rally, unite **6** couple, gather, huddle, muster, summon **7** collect, convene, recruit **8** congress **9** construct

ASSEMBLY: **4** band, body, hall **5** forum, group, junta, party, rally, troop **7** company, council, meeting, session, society **8** audience, conclave, congress, tribunal **10** auditorium, collection, convention, parliament **11** convocation, legislature

ASSENT: **3** bow, nod, yes **4** amen **5** admit, agree, grant, yield **6** accede, accept, chorus, comply, concur **7** consent **8** adhesion, sanction **9** acquiesce, admission, subscribe **10** compliance, condescend, permission **11** acknowledge, endorsement

ASSERT: **3** say **4** aver, cite **5** argue, claim, plead, state, utter, vaunt, voice **6** affirm, assure, avouch, defend, depose, stress, submit, uphold **7** advance, contend, declare, protest, support **8** advocate, champion, maintain **9** emphasize, predicate, vindicate

ASSERTIVE: **4** firm, sure **5** pushy **8** absolute, dogmatic, forceful, positive **9** confident, defensive, pragmatic **10** aggressive **11** affirmative

ASSESS: **3** tax **4** levy, rate, toll **5** price, value, weigh **6** charge, impose **7** account, measure **8** appraise, estimate, evaluate

ASSESSMENT: **3** fee, tax **4** dues, duty, fine **6** impost, surtax, tariff **9** reckoning, valuation

ASSET: **3** aid **4** help **6** credit **7** benefit **8** treasure **9** advantage **11** distinction

ASSETS: **4** cash **5** goods, money, worth **6** credit, equity, riches, wealth **7** capital **8** accounts, property **9** resources, valuables **10** belongings

ASSIDUOUS: **4** busy **6** active, steady **7** devoted, earnest **8** diligent, plugging **9** laborious, tenacious, unwearied **10** determined, persistent **11** hardworking, industrious, painstaking, persevering

ASSIGN: **3** fix, set, tag **4** deed, give, rate, seal, sign **5** allot, allow, award, grant, order **6** affect, charge, choice, convey, depute, detail, invest, select **7** adjudge, advance, appoint, ascribe, consign, dispose, specify, tribute **8** allocate, delegate, transfer **9** apportion, attribute, designate **10** distribute **11** appropriate

ASSIGNATION: **4** date **6** affair **7** meeting **10** engagement, rendezvous **11** appointment

ASSIGNMENT: **3** job **4** beat, duty, task **5** chore, stint **6** lesson **7** mission **8** homework **9** selection **11** appointment **13** authorization

ASSIMILATE: **4** fuse **5** adopt, alter, blend, grasp, learn, merge **6** absorb, digest **8** resemble **9** integrate, transform **10** comprehend, metabolize, understand **11** acclimatize, appropriate

ASSIST: **3** aid **4** back, help, plug **5** avail, boost **6** uphold **7** benefit, comfort, relieve, support, sustain **8** abetment, befriend **9** reinforce **10** facilitate **11** collaborate

ASSISTANT: **4** aide, ally, hand **6** deputy, helper, lackey, second **7** abettor, orderly, partner **8** adjutant, henchman **9** associate, colleague, secretary **10** accomplice, apprentice **11** confederate, subordinate

ASSIZE: **3** law **4** rule **5** court, trial **6** decree **7** hearing, inquest, measure, session, statute **8** assembly, tribunal **9** enactment, ordinance **10** regulation

ASSOCIATE: **3** pal **4** aide, ally, chum, join, link, peer **5** buddy, crony **6** cohort, fellow, friend, helper, hobnob, mingle, relate **7** adjunct, bracket, comrade, connect, consort, partner **8** federate, identify, intimate, sidekick **9** affiliate, assistant, colleague, companion, confidant, socialize **10** fraternize **11** counterpart

ASSOCIATION: **4** body, bond, clan, club, coop, gang, pool, ring **5** cabal, guild, lodge, order, tribe, union **6** cartel, league, lyceum, pledge **7** company, council, society **8** alliance, converse, intimacy, sorority **9** coalition, syndicate **10** assemblage, connection, fellowship, fraternity **11** affiliation, combination, confederacy, conjunction, partnership

ASSORT: **4** file, rank, suit, type **5** class, group **8** classify **10** categorize

ASSORTED: **5** mixed **6** hybrid, motley, varied **9** different

ASSORTMENT: **3** lot, set **4** kind **5** array, batch, combo, group **6** medley **7** melange, mixture, variety **8** mishmash **9** diversity, potpourri **10** collection, miscellany

ASSUAGE: **4** calm, ease, fill, lull **5** abate, quiet **6** lessen, modify, pacify, reduce, soften, solace, soothe **7** appease, comfort, mollify, relieve, satisfy, sweeten **8** diminish, mitigate **9** alleviate **11** tranquilize

ASSUME: **3** don **4** deem, mask, take **5** adopt, cloak, guess, infer, raise, seize, think, usurp **6** accept, affect, deduce, expect **7** acquire, believe, pretend, suppose, surmise **8** arrogate, simulate **9** speculate, undertake **11** appropriate, counterfeit

ASSUMED: **5** alias, bogus, false, tacit **8** affected, expected, supposed **9** fictional **10** artificial, fictitious, understood **12** hypothetical

ASSUMING: **4** bold, rude **5** lofty **6** brazen **8** arrogant, superior **9** egotistic **11** overbearing, pretentious **12** presumptuous

ASSURANCE: **3** vow **4** oath, word **5** brass, faith, nerve, trust **6** belief, credit, pledge, surety **7** promise **8** audacity, boldness, coolness **9** certainty, cockiness, guarantee, impudence, insurance **10** confidence, effrontery **11** affirmation

ASSURE: **3** bag **4** lock **6** assert, attest, avouch, clinch, secure **7** confirm, declare **8** convince **9** encourage **10** strengthen, underwrite

ASSYRIA:
also called: **5** Ashur, Assur **6** Asshur
capital: **12** Calah Nineveh
cities: **4** Hara, Opis **5** Al sur **6** Arbela, Asshur, Kalakh **9** Dur Sargon
gods/goddesses: **3** Ira, Sin **4** Adad, Anet, Nana, Nebo, Nine **5** Ashur, Hadad, Istar, Ninip **6** Allatu, Asshur, Ishtar, Nergal, Shamas **9** Sarpanitu
kings/queens: **3** Pul **5** Belus **6** Sargon **9** Semiramis **10** Adadnirari **11** Sennacherib, Shalmaneser **12** Ashur-uballit **13** Tukulti-enurta **14** Nebuchadnezzar, Tiglathpileser
water: **6** Tigris

ASTERIUS: **8** argonaut
alias: **8** Asterion
daughter: **5** Crete
father: **4** Anax **10** Hyperasius
kingdom: **5** Crete
mother: **8** Pasiphae
son: **5** Minos **8** Sarpedon
wife: **6** Europa

ASTERN: **3** aft **4** back, rear **6** behind

ASTEROID: **6** debris **9** meteorite

ASTIR: **5** about, alert, awake **6** active, moving, roused

ASTONISH: **3** awe **4** daze **5** amaze, floor **6** boggle, dazzle **7** impress, perplex, startle **8** confound, surprise **11** flabbergast

ASTONISHING: **7** amazing **8** fabulous, shocking, wondrous **9** confusing, wonderful **10** incredible, miraculous, stupendous **11** spectacular **12** breathtaking

ASTOUND: **4** stun **5** amaze, shock **6** appall **7** stagger, terrify **8** astonish, confound **9** dumbfound, electrify

ASTRAL: **6** dreamy, remote **7** stellar **8** starlike **9** celestial, stellular, visionary

ASTRAY: **3** off **4** awry, lost **5** amiss, aside, wrong **6** abroad, adrift, afield, errant, faulty **8** mistaken **9** wandering

ASTRINGENT: **4** acid, sour, tart **5** brisk, harsh, stern **6** biting, severe, tannin **7** binding, styptic **8** piercing **10** antiseptic **11** compressive, contracting **12** constrictive, invigorating

ASTROLOGER: **6** Merlin **9** stargazer **10** star reader **11** Nostradamus

ASTRONAUT: **9** cosmonaut
Apollo 1 fire: **11** Edward White **12** Roger Chaffee **13** Virgil Grissom
Challenger explosion: **12** Michael Smith, Ronald McNair **13** Francis Scobee, Gregory Jarvis, Judith Resnick **14** Ellison Onizuka **16** Christa McAuliffe
first American in space: **11** Alan Shepard
first American space walk: **11** Edward White
first American woman in space: **9** Sally Ride
first on moon: **13** Neil Armstrong
first orbital flight: **11** Yuri Gagarin
first space shuttle: **9** John Young **13** Robert Crippen
first woman in space: **19** Valentina Tereshkova
U.S.-U.S.S.R. rendezvous: **10** Vance Brand **12** Alexei Leonov **13** Valeri Kubasov, Donald Slayton **14** Thomas Stafford

ASTRONOMER: **5** Adams **6** Halley, Hubble, Newton **7** Galileo **8** Einstein **10** Copernicus, Hipparchus

ASTUTE: **3** sly **4** able, foxy, keen, wily **5** acute, cagey, canny, quick, sharp, smart **6** bright, clever, crafty **7** cunning, skilled **9** sagacious **10** discerning, perceptive **11** intelligent

ASUNDER: **4** torn **5** apart, loose, split **7** divided **9** separated **12** disconnected

ASYLUM: **3** den **4** home **5** cover, haven **6** bedlam, harbor, refuge, safety **7** retreat, shelter **8** madhouse **9** sanctuary **10** sanatorium **11** institution

ASYMMETRIC: **4** skew **6** uneven, warped **8** lopsided **9** distorted

AT ALL: **3** any **4** ever **6** anyway **7** anytime

ATHAMAS:
daughter: **5** Helle
father: **6** Aeolus

kingdom: **6** Thebes
son: **5** Ptous **7** Phrixos, Phrixus **8** Learchus
wife: **3** Ino **7** Nephele

AT HAND: **4** here, near **5** close, ready **7** present **10** accessible

ATHEIST: **5** pagan **7** doubter, infidel **8** agnostic **11** non-believer

ATHENA, ATHENE: **4** Alea, Nike **5** Areia, Xenia **6** Ergane, Hippia, Hygeia, Pallas, Polias **7** Agoraea, Minerva **8** Apaturia, Athenaia, Zosteria **9** Oxyderces, Parthenos, Poliuchos **10** Axiopoenus, Chalinitis

ATHENS:
ancient capital: **6** Attica
famous people: **4** Zeus **5** Plato, Solon **7** Cecrops, Hadrian, Phidias **8** Pericles, Socrates **9** Aristides, Aristotle
features: **4** Nike **5** Agora, Odeum **6** Lyceum, Parnes **9** Acropolis, Parthenon
native: **5** Metic **8** Athenian
place: **6** Greece

ATHLETE: **3** pro **4** jock, star **8** champion **12** professional, sportsperson

ATHLETIC: **3** fit **4** team **5** agile, burly, husky, vital **6** active, brawny, robust, strong **8** muscular, powerful, vigorous **9** acrobatic, energetic

ATHLETICS: **5** games, sport **6** events **7** contest, workout **8** exercise **10** recreation

ATHWART: **4** over **6** across **7** against **8** sideways, traverse **9** crosswise **10** crisscross

ATLAS:
daughter: **4** Maia **6** Merope **7** Alcyone, Calypso, Electra **8** Asterope, Pleiades **10** Hesperides
father: **7** Iapetus
kingdom: **10** Mauretania
mother: **7** Clymeme
wife: **7** Pleione

ATMOSPHERE: **3** air, sky **4** aura, mood, tone **5** scene, sense **6** spirit **7** climate, feeling **8** ambiance, envelope **10** background **11** environment

ATOLL: **4** belt, reef **6** island

ATOM: **3** bit, dot, jot **4** iota, mite, mote, whit **5** crumb, shade, speck, tinge, trace **6** little **8** fragment **9** molecular **13** infinitesimal
parts: **6** proton **7** neutron **8** electron

ATOMIC: **4** bomb, tiny **6** energy, fusion, minute **7** fission, nuclear **8** granular **9** molecular, submarine

ATOMIZE: **4** ruin **5** grate, smash, spray **6** reduce **7** destroy **8** vaporize **9** pulverize

ATONE: **3** pay **6** answer, repent, square **7** correct, expiate **10** compensate

ATONEMENT: **6** amends **7** apology, penance **10** recompense, reparation **11** restitution **12** satisfaction

ATREUS:
brother: **8** Thyestes
daughter: **8** Anaxibia
father: **6** Pelops
killed: **6** Aglaus
killer: **9** Aegisthus
kingdom: **7** Mycenae
mother: **10** Hippodamia
son: **8** Menelaus **9** Agamemnon **11** Pleisthenes
wife: **6** Aerope

ATRIUM: **4** hall, room **5** court **6** cavity **7** chamber, passage **8** entrance

ATROCIOUS: **3** bad **4** dark, evil, foul, rank, vile **5** awful, cruel, gross **6** brutal, rotten, savage, wicked **7** heinous, inhuman, ungodly, violent **8** fiendish, grievous, horrible, ruthless, terrible **9** frightful, loathsome **10** abominable, diabolical

ATROPHY: **6** shrink, wither **7** decline **8** decaying, downfall **10** diminution, emaciation **13** deterioration

ATTACH: **3** add, fix, put **4** bind, glue, join, link, weld **5** affix, hitch, paste, seize **6** addict, adhere, append, arrest, cement, fasten, indict **7** ascribe, connect **8** allocate, appoint **9** affiliate, associate, attribute

ATTACHMENT: **3** tie **4** love **5** amore, clamp **6** liking **7** fixture, loyalty **8** affinity, devotion, fondness **9** accessory, affection, extension **10** allegiance, engagement **11** inclination

ATTACK: **3** fit **4** bash, bout, fray, raid, rush **5** assay, begin, blame, blitz, drive, fight, onset, storm **6** accuse, action, affray, assail, battle, charge, invade, sortie, strike, stroke, thrust **7** ailment, assault, besiege, bombard, offense, seizure, slander **8** denounce, paroxysm, skirmish **9** criticize, incursion, onslaught **10** aggression

ATTAIN: **3** get, hit, win **4** earn, gain, rise, snag **5** reach, touch **6** accede, arrive, aspire, obtain, secure, strike **7** achieve, acquire, fulfill, procure, succeed **8** overtake **10** accomplish

ATTAINMENT: **4** feat **5** skill **6** finish, talent, wisdom **7** mastery, reaping

ATTEMPT: **3** aim, try **4** shot, stab, wage **5** assay, begin, start **6** effort, pursue, strive **7** venture **8** endeavor **9** undertake **10** experiment

ATTEND: **3** aid, see **4** heed, mind, tend **5** await, guard, serve, treat, usher, watch **6** appear, assist, convoy, follow, harken, listen, shadow **7** consort, oversee **8** chaperon, minister **9** accompany

ATTENDANCE: **4** draw, gate **5** crowd **6** number, regard **7** company, turnout **8** presence **9** attention **11** application

ATTENDANT: **4** aide, maid, page **5** guide, usher, valet **6** escort, helper, porter, squire **7** courier, orderly, related, servant **8** follower **9** assistant, associate, companion **10** consequent, subsequent, waitperson **11** chamberlain

ATTENTION: **4** care, heed, note **5** study **6** notice, regard **7** respect, thought **8** courtesy **9** diligence, obedience, vigilance **11** mindfulness, observation **13** concentration, consideration

ATTENTIVE: **4** kind, wary **5** alert, awake, glued **6** intent, polite **7** careful, gallant **8** diligent, studious, watchful **9** assiduous, courteous, listening **10** interested, respectful **11** circumspect

ATTENUATE: **3** sap **4** thin **5** water **6** dilute, lessen, reduce, shrink, weaken **7** deflate, slender **8** decrease, diminish, tapering **9** constrict, undermine

ATTEST: **4** seal, show **5** prove, swear, vouch **6** affirm, invoke, verify **7** confirm, support, testify, witness **8** indicate **9** subscribe **11** corroborate **12** authenticate

ATTIC: **3** top **4** loft **6** garret **7** mansard **8** cockloft

ATTIRE: **3** don **4** clad, garb, robe **5** dress **6** clothe, outfit **7** apparel, clothes, threads **8** wardrobe

ATTITUDE: **3** air, set **4** mood, pose, view **5** angle, slant, stand **6** action, aspect, manner **7** feeling, mindset, posture **8** approach, behavior, position **11** disposition, perspective

ATTORNEY: **5** agent, proxy **6** chaser, factor, lawyer **8** advocate **9** barrister, counselor, solicitor

ATTRACT: **3** wow **4** bait, draw, pull **5** catch, charm, tempt **6** allure, beckon, engage, entice, seduce **7** enchant **8** enthrall, interest **9** captivate, fascinate, influence

ATTRACTION: **4** card, lure **6** appeal, magnet **7** glamour **8** affinity, charisma **9** chemistry

ATTRACTIVE: **4** chic, cute, sexy **5** bonny **6** lovely, pretty **7** elegant, winsome **8** alluring, charming, graceful, handsome, pleasant **9** appealing, beautiful **11** captivating

ATTRIBUTE: **3** fix **4** mark, sign **5** badge, blame, grace, place, point, quirk, refer **6** allege, aspect, assert, assign, bestow, charge, symbol, talent, virtue **7** ascribe, feature, quality **8** property **10** reputation **11** peculiarity **12** idiosyncrasy

ATTRITION: **4** loss, wear **5** grief **6** regret, sorrow **7** penance, remorse, rubbing **8** friction, thinning **9** weakening **10** repentance

ATTUNE: **3** key **4** tune **5** adapt, agree **6** accord, adjust, tailor **7** balance **9** harmonize **10** compensate

AUCTION: **3** bid **4** sale, sell **5** block, trade **6** barter **7** bidding **8** offering

AUDACIOUS: **4** bold, rude, wild **5** brash, gutsy, hardy, risky **6** brazen, daring **7** defiant, forward **8** arrogant, fearless, impudent, insolent, reckless, spirited, uncurbed **9** daredevil, foolhardy, imprudent, shameless **10** courageous **11** adventurous, venturesome **12** presumptuous

AUDACITY: **4** gall, grit, guts **5** brass, moxie, nerve, spunk **6** spirit **7** courage **8** backbone, boldness **9** assurance, cockiness, insolence, sauciness **10** effrontery, imprudence **12** fearlessness

AUDIBLE: **4** loud **5** aural, clear, heard, plain **10** resounding **11** discernible

AUDIENCE: **4** fans **5** crowd, house **6** market, public **7** gallery, patrons **8** assembly, audition, tribunal **9** clientele, following, interview, listeners **10** spectators

AUDIT: **4** scan **5** check, probe **6** reckon, report, review, survey **7** balance, examine, inspect **8** analysis, estimate **10** accounting, scrutinize **11** investigate

AUDITION: **4** demo, test **5** trial **6** tryout **7** hearing, reading

AUDITOR: **3** CPA **6** hearer **7** actuary **8** listener **10** accountant, bookkeeper

AUDITORIUM: **4** hall, room **5** arena **7** theater **8** coliseum **12** amphitheater

AUGER: **3** bit **4** bore, tool **5** drill, grill **6** gimlet

AUGHT: **3** zip **4** nada, zero **5** zilch **6** cipher **7** nothing **8** anything

AUGMENT: **3** add **4** grow, rise **5** build, exalt, swell **6** deepen, dilate, expand, extend **7** amplify, develop, enhance, enlarge, improve, inflate **8** heighten, increase, multiply

AUGUR: **4** bode, omen, seer **6** divine, herald **7** betoken, foresee, predict, presage, promise, prophet, signify **8** forebode, foreshow, foretell, forewarn, indicate, intimate, prophesy **9** harbinger, predictor **10** anticipate, conjecture

AUGURY: **4** rite, sign **5** token **6** ritual **7** portent, warning **8** ceremony, forecast **9** sortilege **10** divination, forerunner, prognostic

AUGUST: **5** awful, grand, noble, regal **6** solemn **7** eminent, exalted, stately **8** baronial, imposing, majestic, splendid **9** brilliant, dignified, venerable **10** monumental

AU NATUREL: **3** raw **4** nude **5** naked **9** undressed

AURA: **3** air **4** glow, halo, mood, tone **5** aroma, scent **6** aspect, nimbus **7** essence, feeling, quality **8** ambience, mystique **9** emanation **10** atmosphere

AUREATE: **6** gilded, golden, ornate, yellow **7** flowery **8** splendid **9** brilliant, overblown

AURICULAR: **4** otic **6** phonic **7** audible, hearsay

AUSPICES: **3** aid **4** care **5** aegis **7** backing, support **8** advocacy, guidance **9** influence, patronage **10** protection **11** sponsorship

AUSPICIOUS: **4** fair, good **5** happy **6** golden **7** hopeful **9** favorable, fortunate **10** propitious, prosperous, successful **11** encouraging **12** advantageous

AUSTERE: **4** cold, hard **5** bleak, grave, harsh, rigid, rough, sharp, stiff **6** barren, bitter, formal, severe, strict **7** ascetic, earnest, serious **8** rigorous **9** abstinent, unadorned **10** astringent, forbidding, relentless

AUSTRALIA:

animal: **4** joey, laap, lerp, mako, tait **5** galah, goana, koala, panda, tungo **6** bunyip, cuscus, elapid, wombat, yabbie **7** beetong, brumbee, dasqure, dasyure, wallaby **8** duckbill, kangaroo, platypus **9** bandicoot, phalanger

bird: **3** emu **4** emeu, lary, lory **5** arara, crake, grebe, stint **6** budgie, gannet, leipoa **7** bittern, boobook, bustard, corella, figbird, lorilet **8** berigora, dabchick, dotterel, lorikeet, lyrebird **9** cockateel, cockatiel **10** budgerigar

capital: **8** Canberra

cities: **5** Perth **6** Darwin, Hobart, Sydney **7** Geelong **8** Adelaide, Brisbane **9** Melbourne, Newcastle **10** Townsville, Wollongong **12** Alice Springs

explorers: **4** Cook

features: **9** Ayers Rock **10** Arnhem Land **13** Simpson Desert **14** Australian Alps **16** Great Barrier Reef, Great Sandy Desert **19** Great Victoria Desert **20** Great Australian Bight

food: **3** roa **4** java **5** nonda **8** piripiri

islands: **5** Cocos, Heard **7** Ashmore, Cartier, Keeling, Norfolk **8** Coral Sea, McDonald **9** Christmas

monetary unit: **4** cent **6** dollar

native: **6** Binghi **9** aborigine

products: **6** colane **9** boomerang

state: **8** Tasmania, Victoria **10** Queensland **13** New South Wales

tree: **4** toon **5** belar, boree, penda **6** marara **7** alipata **8** beefwood, curajong, flindosa, ironbark **9** koorajong

water: **4** Eyre **5** Carey, Coral, Cowan, Frome, Timor **6** Austin, Barlee, Mackay, Tasman **7** Amadeus, Arafura, Eyerard, Torrens **8** Carnegie **9** Billabong **12** Darling River

AUSTRIA:

capital: **6** Vienna

cities: **4** Graz, Linz **8** Salzburg **9** Innsbruck

continent: **6** Europe

ethnic groups: **5** Croat **7** Slovene

famous people: **5** Freud, Haydn **6** Mahler, Mozart **7** Strauss **8** Bruckner, Schubert

features: **4** Alps **6** Carnic **7** Brenner **8** Aligauer **9** Lechtaler, Semmering **13** Grossglockner

languages: **6** German

monetary unit: **9** schilling

native: **8** Austrian

nobility: **6** Ritter **8** Habsburg, Hapsburg **9** Esterhazy
water: **3** Inn, Mur **4** Enns, Lech, Murz, Raba **5** Atter, Traun **6** Danube **9** Constance

AUTHENTIC: **4** pure, real, sure, true **5** valid **6** actual, proper **7** certain, correct, genuine **8** bonafide, credible, original, reliable **10** authorized, legitimate **11** trustworthy

AUTHENTICATE: **4** seal **5** prove, vouch **6** attest, verify **7** confirm, endorse, justify **8** document, validate **9** guarantee

AUTHOR: **4** doer, poet **5** maker **6** scribe, source, writer **7** creator, founder **8** compiler, composer, inventor, novelist, producer **9** architect, wordsmith **10** journalist, originator, playwright **11** ghostwriter

AUTHORITATIVE: **5** sound **6** proven, ruling **7** factual, learned **8** dogmatic, imposing, official, positive **9** authentic, effectual, imperious, scholarly **10** commanding, conclusive, convincing, legitimate **11** dictatorial, magisterial

AUTHORITY: **4** boss, rule, sway **5** force, might, power, right **6** expert, source, weight **7** command, control, kingpin, scepter **8** dominion, strength **9** influence **10** competence, government, importance **12** jurisdiction

AUTHORIZE: **3** let **4** okay, vest **5** allow **6** permit, ratify **7** approve, endorse, justify, license, warrant **8** accredit, delegate, legalize **10** commission, legitimize **11** rubberstamp

AUTOBIOGRAPHY: **3** bio **4** life, vita **5** diary **6** memoir **7** journal, letters

AUTOCHTHONOUS: **5** first **6** native **7** endemic **8** earliest **10** aboriginal

AUTOCRAT: **4** czar **5** mogul, ruler **6** despot **7** monarch **8** dictator **9** sovereign

AUTOCRATIC: **5** bossy **8** absolute, arrogant, despotic **9** arbitrary, tyrannous **10** oppressive

AUTOGRAPH: **3** ink, pen **4** name, sign **9** signature **11** endorsement, John Hancock

AUTOMATIC: **7** assured, natural, robotic, routine **8** habitual **9** intuitive **10** mechanical **11** instinctive, involuntary, unconscious

AUTOMATION: **4** tool **5** robot **7** android, machine **15** computerization

AUTOMOBILE: **3** car **4** auto, heap, jeep **5** coupe, lemon, racer, sedan **6** hot rod, jalopy, wheels **7** clunker, hardtop, machine, vehicle **8** motorcar, roadster **11** convertible
inventor: **4** Ford, Otto **6** Cugnot, Lenoir **7** Daimler, Panhard **8** Levassor **10** Trevithick

AUTONOMOUS: **4** free **8** separate **9** sovereign **11** independent **12** self-governed, uncontrolled

AUTUMN: **4** fall **6** season **11** harvest-time **12** Indian summer

AUXILIARY: **3** sub **4** aide, ally **5** spare **6** backup, branch, helper **7** partner, reserve **8** adjutant **9** accessory, ancillary, assistant, emergency, secondary **10** additional, supporting **11** subordinate, subservient

AVAIL: **3** aid, use **4** help, meet, work **5** serve, value **6** profit **7** account, benefit, service, suffice, utilize **9** advantage **10** assistance

AVAILABLE: **3** fit **4** free, open **5** handy, ready **6** usable **7** present **8** feasible, possible **9** effectual **10** accessible, attainable, convenient, obtainable, procurable **11** efficacious

AVALANCHE: **4** pile **5** flood, slide **6** deluge **7** torrent **8** mudslide **9** cataclysm, landslide, snowslide **10** inundation

AVANT-GARDE: **3** hip, new, van **7** leaders, offbeat **8** original, pioneers, vanguard **10** innovative **11** forerunners, progressive **12** trailblazing, trendsetting

AVARICE: **4** lust **5** greed **7** avidity **8** cupidity, rapacity **9** frugality **10** stinginess

AVE MARIA: **4** song **6** prayer **8** Hail Mary **10** rosary bead

AVENGE: **5** repay **6** injure, punish **7** chasten, redress, revenge **9** retaliate, vindicate

AVENUE: **3** ave, way **4** gate, mall, road **5** drive, entry, means **6** access, artery, course, outlet, street **7** opening **8** approach **10** passageway

AVER: **3** say **5** claim, prove, state, swear **6** affirm, assert, avouch, insist, verify **7** certify, contend, declare, justify **8** maintain, proclaim **9** emphasize, predicate

AVERAGE: **3** par **4** fair, mean, norm, rule **5** usual **6** common, median, medium, middle, normal **7** balance, humdrum, typical **8** mediocre, ordinary, standard **10** proportion

AVERSE: **5** balky, loath **6** afraid **7** against, opposed **8** contrary, hesitant **9** reluctant, unwilling **11** disinclined, unfavorable **12** antagonistic

AVERSION: **4** hate **5** dread **6** enmity, hatred **7** disdain, disgust, dislike **8** distaste **9** animosity, antipathy, hostility **10** repugnance **11** abomination

AVERT: **4** bend, foil, halt, turn, veer **5** avoid, deter, dodge, evade, shunt **6** thwart **7** deflect, prevent **8** preclude **9** forestall, frustrate

AVIARY: **4** cage **6** volary **8** ornithon **9** birdhouse, columbary, dovehouse

AVIATION: **6** flight **8** piloting **10** navigation **11** aeronautics

AVIATOR: **3** ace **5** flier, pilot **6** airman, fly-boy, Wright **7** birdman, Earhart, hotshot **8** airwoman, Red Baron **9** Lindbergh **10** Richthofen **11** barnstormer **12** Rickenbacker

AVID: **4** agog, keen, warm **5** eager **6** ardent, greedy, hungry **7** anxious, craving, devoted **8** covetous, grasping, ravenous **9** impatient, voracious **10** insatiable

AVIDITY: **4** zeal **6** fervor **7** avarice, longing **8** cupidity **10** enthusiasm, greediness

AVOCATION: **4** kick **5** hobby, thing **7** pastime **8** sideline **9** amusement, diversion **10** occupation, recreation

AVOID: **4** duck, shun **5** avert, ditch, dodge, elude, evade, shirk, skirt **6** bypass, escape **7** abstain, boycott, forsake, refrain **8** preclude, sidestep, withdraw

AVOIDANCE: **5** delay **6** flight **7** eluding, evasion **9** annulment, runaround **10** preventing, withdrawal

AVOW: **3** own **5** grant, state, swear **6** affirm, assert, avouch **7** concede, confess, declare, profess **8** announce, maintain, proclaim **11** acknowledge

AWAIT: **4** hope, pend, stay **5** abide, sweat **6** attend, expect, impend **10** anticipate

AWAKE: **5** alert, alive, rouse **6** active, arouse, excite **7** careful, heedful, mindful **9** attentive, conscious

AWAKENING: **7** arising, rebirth, revival **9** eye-opener **10** enlivening

AWARD: **4** give **5** grant, honor, kudos, medal, prize **6** accord, assign, bestow, degree **7** appoint, diploma, laurels, present, tribute **8** accolade, citation, judgment **9** apportion, sheepskin **10** decoration **11** scholarship
Academy Award: **5** Oscar
broadcasting: **7** Peabody
children's literature: **12** Newbery Medal
commercials: **4** Clio
journalism, letters, music: **8** Pulitzer
mystery story: **5** Edgar
off-Broadway: **4** Obie
performing arts: **13** Kennedy Center
recording: **6** Grammy
science fiction: **4** Hugo
television: **4** Emmy
theatre: **4** Tony

AWARE: **3** hip **4** wise **5** alert, alive **6** groovy **7** knowing, mindful **8** apprised, informed, sensible, vigilant, watchful **9** cognizant, conscious **11** intelligent

AWAY: **3** far, off, out **4** gone **5** along, apart, aside **6** abroad, absent, begone, onward **7** distant, missing **8** directly **9** elsewhere, endlessly **10** tirelessly

AWE: **3** cow **4** fear **5** alarm, amaze, panic, scare **6** fright, regard **7** respect **8** astonish, bewilder, overcome, showboat **9** fascinate, overpower, quivering, terrorize, trembling **10** intimidate

AWESOME: **5** awful, grand, hairy **6** solemn **7** amazing, dreaded, ghostly, uncanny **8** imposing, majestic, terrible **9** appalling **12** breathtaking

AWFUL: **3** bad **4** dire, ugly **5** gross, lousy, nasty **6** horrid **7** awesome, fearful **8** dreadful, shocking, terrible **9** appalling, frightful, revolting **10** horrendous, impressive, tremendous

AWFULLY: **4** very **5** badly, quite **6** poorly **7** greatly **9** extremely **10** dreadfully

AWKWARD: **5** bulky, gawky, inept **6** clumsy, klutzy, rustic, uneasy, wooden **7** boorish, stilted, uncouth **8** bumbling, bungling, lubberly, unwieldy **9** difficult, graceless, lumbering, ponderous **10** backhanded, blundering, cumbersome, ungraceful, unskillful **11** heavyhanded **12** embarrassing, inconvenient **13** butterfingers

AWNING: **4** hood, tent **5** shade **6** canopy, screen **7** marquee, shelter **8** covering, velarium **10** protection

AWRY: **4** bent **5** amiss, askew, wrong **6** faulty, uneven **7** crooked, haywire, oblique, twisted **8** cockeyed, slanting **9** distorted

AX, AXE: **4** chop, fell, fire, sack **5** split **6** handle, piolet **7** cleaver, dismiss, hatchet **8** tomahawk **9** discharge

AXIOM: **3** law **4** rule **5** adage, maxim, motto, truth **6** dictum, saying, truism **7** precept, proverb **8** aphorism, sentence **9** principle **11** proposition

AXIS: **3** hub **4** axle, deer, pole, stem **5** hinge, pivot **7** fulcrum, spindle, support **8** alliance **9** coalition

AXLE: **3** cod, pin, rod **4** axis **5** arbor, shaft, wheel **7** gudgeon, mandrel, spindle

AYAH: **4** maid **5** nurse **9** governess, nursemaid **11** chambermaid

AYE: **3** yea, yes **4** okay, vote **6** always **11** affirmative, continually

AZERBAIJAN:
capital: **4** Baku
cities: **7** Gyanzha, Sumgait **9** Kirovabad
features: **17** Caucasus Mountains
languages: **6** Turkic
republic of: **6** Russia
water: **10** Caspian Sea

AZORES:
capital: **12** Ponta Delgada
cities: **5** Horta
islands: **4** Pico **5** Corvo, Faial **6** Flores **9** San Miguel
territory of: **8** Portugal
water: **8** Atlantic

AZTEC:
capital: **12** Tenochtitlan
conquerors: **9** Spaniards
famous: **7** temples **8** calendar **11** agriculture
god: **4** Xipe **6** Tlaloc **8** Tonatiuh
language: **7** Nahuatl
location: **13** central Mexico
ruler: **8** Itzcoatl **9** Montezuma

AZURE: **4** blue **6** cobalt **7** celeste **8** cerulean **9** cloudless

B

BAAL: **3** god **4** idol **5** deity **7** Baalath

BABBITT: **4** boob **5** alloy, metal **9** bourgeois **10** conformist, philistine **11** materialist
author: **13** Sinclair Lewis

BABBLE: **3** coo, gab, yak **4** blab, chat, prat, rant, talk **6** drivel, gibber, gossip, mutter, rattle **7** blabber, blather, chatter, prattle, twaddle **8** nonsense **9** gibberish, murmuring

BABEL: **3** din **5** clang, tower **6** bedlam, hubbub, jargon, racket, tumult **7** discord, turmoil **9** confusion **10** hullabaloo **11** pandemonium

BABOON: **3** ape **6** chacma, monkey **7** babuina **8** mandrill

BABUSHKA: **4** veil **5** scarf **8** kerchief

BABY: **3** kid, tot, wee **4** babe, doll **5** child, humor, nurse, small, spoil **6** coddle, fondle, infant, little, nipper, pamper **7** bambino, newborn, papoose **8** youthful

BABY BED: **4** crib **6** cradle **8** bassinet

BABY CARRIAGE: **4** pram **5** buggy **8** stroller **12** perambulator

BABYISH: **5** silly **6** simple **7** puerile **8** childish, immature **9** infantile

BABYLONIA:
also called: **5** Aralu
capital: **7** Babylon (now Baghdad)
cities: **5** Erech, Larsa **6** Calneh, Cunaxa, Cuthah, Lagash, Nippur, Sippar
empire: **11** Mesopotamia
features: **7** zikurat **8** ziggurat **11** Mount Ararat **12** Tower of Babel **14** Hanging Gardens
gods/goddesses: **3** Anu, Aya, Bel, Hea, Hes, Ira, Ler, Sin, Utu **4** Adad, Anat, Apsu, Baal, Erua, Gula, Irra, Nana, Nebo, Nina, Utug **5** Alala, Alalu, Belit, Dagan, Enlil, Etana, Istar, Ninib, Nusku, Siris, Urash **6** Belili, Beltis, Ishtar, Nergal, Oannes, Tammuz **7** Mylitta, Ninurta, Shamash **8** Merodach **10** Adramelech
heroes: **5** Adapa, Etana **9** Gilgamesh
kingdoms: **5** Akkad, Sumer
kings/queens: **5** Gudea **6** Sargon **8** Naram-Sin **9** Hammurabi **14** Nebuchadnezzar
languages: **8** Akkadian, Sumerian
water: **4** Apsu **6** Tigris **9** Euphrates

BACCALAUREATE: **6** degree, sermon **7** address **8** bachelor

BACCHANAL: **4** orgy **5** feast, party **6** frolic **7** debauch, reveler **8** carnival **11** merrymaking

BACHELOR: **6** single **8** celibate, eligible **9** unmarried **10** unattached

BACILLUS: **3** bug **4** germ **5** virus **7** microbe **9** bacterium

BACK: **3** aft, aid **4** abet, fund, help, hind, rear, tail **5** abaft, arear, favor, final, rural, stern **6** assist, astern, dorsum, lumbar, return, second, uphold, verify **7** bolster, delayed, endorse, finance, postern, rebound, sponsor, support, sustain, warrant **8** advocate, bankroll **9** encourage, extremity, posterior, reinforce **10** strengthen, underwrite

BACKBITE: **3** lie **5** abuse, spite **6** defame, gossip, vilify **7** abusive, hurtful, slander **8** backstab, badmouth **9** denigrate, malicious

BACKBONE: **4** grit, guts, will **5** heart, nerve, spine, spunk **6** spirit **7** courage, stamina, support **8** mainstay, tenacity **9** character, vertebrae **10** foundation

BACKCOUNTRY: **4** bush, farm **5** rural **6** sticks **7** boonies **9** boondocks

BACK DOWN: **3** ebb **4** balk **5** admit, welsh **6** recant, renege **7** back off, retract, retreat **8** move away, withdraw **9** surrender

BACKER: **4** ally **5** angel **6** patron **7** sponsor **8** advocate, investor, promoter **9** supporter **11** protagonist

BACKFIRE: **4** fail, flop **5** crash **6** fizzle **8** miscarry **9** boomerang

BACKGROUND: **4** past, rear **5** deeds **7** culture, history, scenery, setting **8** distance, training **9** education, landscape **10** experience, upbringing **11** credentials

BACKING: **3** aid **4** help **5** grant **6** lining **7** support **8** abetment, auspices **9** financing **10** assistance **11** endorsement

BACKLASH: **4** snag **6** fizzle, recoil, tangle **8** reaction **11** retaliation

BACKLOG: **5** store **6** assets, excess **7** reserve, surplus **9** inventory, stockpile **12** accumulation

BACKPACK: **4** hike, pack **5** pouch **8** knapsack **9** haversack

BACKSIDE: **3** can **4** buns, butt, rear, seat, tush **5** fanny, heiny **6** behind, bottom, heinie **7** keister **8** buttocks, derriere

BACKSLIDE: **4** fall **5** lapse **6** desert, return **7** regress, relapse **11** deteriorate

BACK TALK: **3** lip **4** sass **5** cheek, mouth

BACKUP: **4** help **5** spare **6** second **7** standby **9** alternate **10** substitute, supporting, understudy

BACKWARD: **3** shy **4** dull, slow **5** arear, dense, loath **6** astern, behind, stupid **7** bashful, laggard, reverse **8** hesitant, sluggish **9** dimwitted, recessive, reluctant, unwilling, withdrawn **10** behindhand **11** undeveloped **13** retrospective

BACKWATER: **3** ebb **5** bayou, slack **7** retract, retreat **8** holdback

BACKWOODSMAN: **4** hick **5** yokel **7** bumpkin **9** hillbilly

BACON: **3** pig **4** loin, pork **5** prize **6** flitch, gammon, rasher **8** porkslab **11** porkbellies

BACTERIA, BACTERIUM: **3** bug **4** germ **5** cocci, virus **6** aerobe **7** bacilli, microbe **8** organism, spirilla

BAD: **3** big, ill **4** dire, evil, foul, lewd, poor, sick, vile **5** awful, grave, gross, lousy, nasty, sorry **6** arrant, cruddy, faulty, rotten, severe, sinful, unruly, wicked **7** baleful, baneful, corrupt, harmful, hurtful, immoral, naughty, spoiled, tainted, unlucky, vicious **8** annoying, contrite, criminal, depraved, dreadful, flagrant, inferior **9** abandoned, atrocious, blemished, dangerous, defective, hazardous, offensive, perverted, repulsive, worthless **10** aggravated, deplorable, distressed, inadequate, melancholy, unpleasant **11** displeasing, ineffective, misbehaving, troublesome, unfavorable **12** contaminated, disagreeable, inauspicious

BAD BLOOD: **4** feud, hate **5** anger **6** enmity, rancor **10** bitterness, resentment

BADGE: **3** pin **4** mark, sign **5** brand, kudos, motto, token **6** emblem, ensign, symbol **7** laurels, scepter **8** insignia **9** medallion

BADGER: **3** nag **4** bait, ride **5** annoy, brock, bully, chivy, hound, tease, worry **6** bother, harass, heckle, needle, pester, wombat **7** torment **8** huckster, irritate **9** bandicoot
group: **4** cete

BADGER STATE: **9** Wisconsin

BADINAGE: **4** fool **6** banter, joking **7** joshing, kidding, ribbing, teasing **8** raillery, repartee

BADLY: **4** awry, illy **6** feebly, poorly, unwell **7** crudely, harshly, ineptly **8** faultily, severely, shoddily **9** corruptly, seriously **10** carelessly, dreadfully, shamefully **11** defectively, imperfectly, unfavorably **12** inadequately, unskillfully

BADMOUTH: **4** barb, slur **6** insult **9** criticize, disparage

BAFFLE: **4** balk, daze, faze, foil **5** amaze, elude, evade, stump **6** defeat, outwit, puzzle, rattle, thwart **7** astound, confuse, deceive, mystify, perplex **8** astonish, bewilder, confound, dumfound **9** confusion, discomfit, dumbfound, frustrate **10** circumvent, disconcert

BAG: **3** get, kit, net, pot, sac **4** gain, kill, land, poke, sack, trap **5** catch, pouch, purse, seize, snare, steal **6** entrap, obtain, pocket, wallet **7** capture, collect, reticle, satchel **8** reticule **9** apprehend, cartridge, container, gladstone, haversack, specialty **10** pocketbook, speciality

BAGATELLE: **3** toy **4** game **6** trifle **7** trinket **10** knickknack

BAGGAGE: **4** arms, gear, tote **5** huzzy, nasty, tents, trash **6** harlot, refuse, trunks **7** effects, luggage, rubbish **8** carriage, packages, utensils **9** munitions, suitcases **10** belongings, prostitute **11** impedimenta

BAGGY: **4** limp **5** loose, roomy **6** droopy, flabby, puffed **7** bloated, sagging **9** unpressed

BAGHDAD:
capital of: **4** Iraq
formerly: **7** Babylon
water: **6** Tigris

BAGNIO: **4** bath **6** prison **7** brothel **8** bordello, cathouse, hothouse **10** whorehouse

BAGPIPE: **5** drone **7** musette **8** zampogna **10** doodlesack, instrument

BAHAMAS:
capital: **6** Nassau
cities: **8** Freeport, Hope Town, Moss Town **9** Alice Town **10** Andros Town, George Town **12** Spanish Wells
islands: **3** Cat **4** Long **6** Rum Cay **7** Acklins, Crooked **9** Eleuthera, Mayaguana **11** Grand Bahama,

Great Inagua, San Salvador **12** Berry Islands **13** New Providence
monetary unit: **14** Bahamian dollar

BAHRAIN:
capital: **6** Manama
cities: **7** Isa Town **8** Jidd Hafs, Muharraq **10** Mina Sulman
continent: **4** Asia
features: **11** Sitra Island
islands: **6** Sitra **7** Bahrain **8** Umm Na'san **10** Al-Muharraq
languages: **4** Urdu **5** Farsi **6** Arabic
monetary unit: **5** dinar
native: **8** Bahraini
water: **11** Persian Gulf

BAIL: **3** dip **4** bond, hoop, pawn, ring **5** ladle, scoop, throw **6** bucket, pledge, secure, surety **7** custody, deliver, release **8** bailsman, bulwarks, security **9** guarantee **10** collateral

BAILIFF: **5** agent, bobby **6** deputy **7** sheriff, steward **8** marshall, overseer **9** constable **10** magistrate

BAILIWICK: **4** area, beat **5** realm **6** domain **7** diocese **8** district, province **9** territory **12** jurisdiction, neighborhood

BAIT: **3** irk **4** bite, chum, draw, feed, halt, lure, trap, worm **5** bribe, decoy, tempt **6** allure, attack, badger, entice, harass **7** fulcrum, provoke, torment **10** allurement, enticement, exasperate, inducement, temptation

BAKE: **3** dry, fry **4** boil, cook, fire, heat, stew **5** broil, grill, parch, roast, toast **6** harden, simmer

BAKER: **4** chef, cook, oven **7** furnace, roaster, utensil

BAKER'S DOZEN: **8** thirteen

BALAAM:
beast: **3** ass **6** donkey
father: **4** Beor
killer: **6** Israel

BALANCE: **3** due, pay **4** even, hang, rest **5** level, poise, scale, total, weigh **6** adjust, equate, excess, offset, parity, square **7** residue **8** equality, equalize, leftover **9** composure, remainder, stability **10** antithesis, neutralize, steadiness **11** equilibrium

BALCONY: **4** deck **5** foyer, porch, stoop **6** piazza **7** catwalk, gallery, mirador, pergola, terrace, veranda **8** brattice, platform **9** mezzanine

BALD: **4** bare **5** crude, naked, plain, stark **6** barren, callow, shaven, simple, smooth **7** exposed, literal, sheared **8** hairless **9** unadorned, uncovered **11** undisguised

BALDER:
alias: **5** Baldr **6** Baldur
brother: **5** Hoder, Hodur
father: **4** Odin
killer: **4** Hoth, Loke **5** Hoder, Hodur
mother: **5** Frigg
murder weapon: **9** mistletoe
son: **7** Forsete
wife: **5** Nanna

BALDERDASH: **3** rot **4** bull, bunk **5** crock, trash **6** drivel, jargon **8** claptrap, malarkey, nonsense **9** poppycock, rigmarole

BALDNESS: **8** alopecia **11** phalacrosis **12** hairlessness

BALE: **3** woe **4** case, evil, harm, pack **5** bunch, crate, death **6** bundle, parcel, sorrow **7** package **8** compress, disaster **9** influence

BALEARIC ISLANDS:
capital: **15** Palma de Mallorca
islands: **5** Ibiza **7** Cabrera, Majorca, Minorca **8** Mallorca **10** Formentera
language: **7** Catalan

BALEFUL: **3** bad **4** cold, evil **6** deadly, malign **7** harmful, ruinous **8** sinister, wretched **9** malicious **10**

calamitous, vindictive **11** apocalyptic, coldhearted, destructive

BALK: **3** bar, shy **4** beam, bilk, foil, loft **5** block, check, cramp, demur, hunch, stall, waver **6** baffle, defeat, falter, hinder, impede, outwit, recoil, refuse, thwart **7** inhibit, quibble, stumble **9** discomfit, frustrate

BALKAN MOUNTAINS:
ethnic groups: **4** Serb, Slav **5** Croat **8** Albanian, Romanian
features: **5** Botev
states: **6** Greece, Turkey (European) **7** Albania, Romania **8** Bulgaria **10** Yugoslavia

BALKY: **5** loath **6** mulish, ornery **7** wayward **8** contrary, negative, stubborn **9** obstinate **10** rebellious

BALL: **3** fly, fun, orb, toy **4** bead, game, prom, snow **5** dance, globe, round **6** bullet, muddle, pellet, pompon, sphere **7** confuse, hoedown, mandrel, shindig **8** spheroid **9** promenade

BALL OF FIRE: **4** whiz **6** dynamo, genius

BALLAD: **3** lay **4** lied, poem, song **5** ditty **6** sonnet **7** canzone **8** serenade

BALLAST: **4** load, trim **5** brace, poise, stone **6** steady, weight **7** balance, sandbag, support **10** stabilizer

BALLERINA: **6** dancer **8** coryphee, danseuse **9** figurante

BALLET: **5** dance, drama **9** pantomime **12** choreography
clothing: **4** tutu **6** tights **7** costume **8** leotards, toe shoes
famous: **6** Apollo **7** Giselle **8** Swan Lake **9** Monotones **12** Rite of Spring **13** The Nutcracker **14** Sleeping Beauty
knee bend: **4** plie
leap: **4** jete **5** saute **9** entrechat
position: **6** pointe **7** fouette **8** batterie **9** arabesque
turns: **5** tours **6** double, single, triple **9** pirouette
types: **6** modern **7** Russian **8** Romantic **12** neoclassical

BALLOON: **3** bag **5** blimp, swell **6** billow, expand, gasbag **7** airship, distend, inflate **8** zeppelin

BALLOT: **4** poll, vote **5** elect, tally, voice **6** choice, lineup, ticket

BALLYHOO: **4** hype, plug, tout **6** hoopla **7** buildup, promote, trumpet **9** advertise, publicity **10** propaganda

BALM: **3** oil **4** cure, lull **5** cream, spice **6** lotion, potion, relief, solace **7** comfort, perfume, soother, unction **8** medicine, ointment **9** fragrance

BALMY: **3** odd **4** calm, daft, mild, soft **5** bland, daffy, moist, silly, spicy, sunny, sweet, weird **6** gentle **7** healing **8** aromatic, fragrant, pleasant, soothing, tropical **9** eccentric **10** refreshing

BALONEY: **4** bull, bunk **5** hooey **6** humbug **7** hogwash **8** nonsense, sandwich

BALSAM: **3** fir **4** tree **5** cream, resin **6** storay **7** copaiba **8** ointment

BALTIC SEA:
cities on: **3** Abo **4** Kiel, Riga **6** Gdansk, Gdynia **7** Tallinn **8** Klaipeda **9** Stockholm
gulf: **4** Riga **7** Bothnia, Finland
islands: **4** Dago **5** Faron, Oland, Visby **6** Karlso, Sarema **7** Gotland **8** Bornholm
rivers: **4** Neva, Oder, Odra **5** Dvina, Narva **6** Hieman **7** Vistula

BALTIC STATES: **6** Latvia **7** Estonia **9** Lithuania

BALUSTRADE: **4** post **8** handrail

BAMBOOZLE: 3 con 4 dupe, fool, hoax, rook 5 cheat, grill 6 cajole, humbug, puzzle 7 buffalo, deceive, defraud, swindle 8 flimflam

BAN: 3 bar 4 halt, veto 5 block, taboo 6 enjoin, forbid, invoke, outlaw 7 boycott, condemn, exclude, prevent 8 denounce, execrate, prohibit, suppress 9 exclusion 11 malediction 12 denunciation

BANAL: 4 blah, dull, flat 5 corny, inane, silly, stale, trite 6 watery 7 cliched, humdrum, insipid, mundane, trivial 8 ordinary 9 hackneyed 10 pedestrian 11 commonplace

BANANA: 4 musa, saba 5 bunch 6 ensete 8 plantain

BAND: 3 set, tie 4 belt, bevy, cord, crew, gang, hoop, pack, ring 5 bunch, combo, group, label, merge, posse, strap, strip, unite 6 bundle, collar, collet, fillet, outfit, string, stripe 7 binding, company, garland, orphrey 8 bracelet, cincture, ligament, symphony 9 aggregate, orchestra 10 collection

BANDAGE: 4 bind, cast, tape 5 blind, clout, dress, gauze, truss 6 fillet, ligate, swathe 7 plaster, swaddle 8 cincture, compress 9 blindfold

BANDANNA: 4 silk 5 scarf 8 kerchief 12 handkerchief

BANDEAU: 3 bra 5 strip 6 fillet 9 brassiere

BANDIT: 4 caco 5 bravo, crook, thief 6 banish, outlaw, pirate, robber 7 bandido 8 gangster, marauder 9 cutthroat, desperado 10 highwayman

BANDLEADER: 5 Sousa 6 master 7 maestro 8 choragus, director 9 conductor

BANDY: 4 cart, swap, toss 5 trade 6 banter, barter 7 discuss 8 carriage, exchange

BANE: 3 woe 4 evil, harm, pest, ruin 5 curse, death 6 blight, injury, murder, poison 7 nemesis, torment, undoing 8 downfall, mischief, nuisance

BANEFUL: 3 bad, ill 4 dire, evil, vile 5 fatal 6 deadly 7 harmful, hurtful, noxious, ruinous 8 venomous 9 pestilent, poisonous 10 malevolent

BANG: 3 hit, rap, wow 4 beat, blow, clap, dock, drub, echo, kick, slam 5 clash, crash, drive, excel, force, pound, sound, thump, whack 6 bounce, energy, strike, thrash, thwack 7 collide, surpass 9 explosion 10 detonation

BANGLADESH:
capital: 5 Dhaka (Dacca)
cities: 6 Khulna 10 Chittagong
continent: 4 Asia
ethnic groups: 6 Bihari 7 Bengali
features: 6 Sylhet 10 Chittagong, Mymensingh
languages: 4 Magh 6 Bangla, Chakma 7 Bengali
monetary unit: 4 taka
water: 5 Padma 6 Jamuna 11 Brahmaputra, Ganges River

BANGLE: 4 roam 5 charm, droop, waste 6 tinsel 7 fritter, trinket 8 bracelet, ornament 10 knickknack

BANISH: 3 ban, bar 4 oust 5 eject, exile, expel 6 deport, dispel 7 abandon, condemn, dismiss, exclude 8 displace, relegate 9 ostracize, proscribe 10 expatriate

BANISTER: 7 railing, support 8 handrail 10 balustrade

BANK: 3 bay, cop, row 4 bink, brew, dike, dune, edge, hill, mass, pile, ramp, rive, sand, tier 5 banco, bench, brink, coast, fence, funds, levee, money, mound, ridge, river, share, shelf, shore, slope, stack, stage, trust, vault **6** degree, depend, invest, margin, reckon, strand, teller, thrift **7** anthill, deposit, pottery, savings, shallow **8** deposits, platform **9** acclivity, elevation **10** depository, embankment, repository

BANKROLL: **3** wad **4** back **5** funds, stake **7** finance **8** currency **9** grubstake, subsidize **10** capitalize

BANKRUPT: **3** sap **5** broke, drain, strip **6** busted, devour, ruined **7** default, failure **8** depleted **9** destitute, insolvent, penniless **11** liquidation **12** impoverished

BANNER: **4** flag, jack **6** colors, ensign **7** leading, pennant, salient **8** foremost, gonfalon, headline, standard **9** banderole, exemplary **10** profitable, surpassing

BANQUET: **4** dine, meal **5** feast, treat **6** dinner, junket, regale **8** carousal, festival, jamboree **9** reception

BANTAM: **3** hen **4** cock, tiny **5** dwarf, saucy, small, teeny **6** little, petite **7** chicken **9** combative **10** diminutive

BANTER: **3** kid, rag, rib **4** fool, jest, jive, joke, ride **5** chaff, jolly, tease **7** mockery **8** badinage, chitchat, satirize **10** persiflage, pleasantry **11** playfulness

BANTU:
ethnic groups: **4** Baya, Bihe, Bule, Fang, Gogo, Gola, Guha, Hehe, Jaga, Luba, Maka, Nama, Vira, Yaka, Zulu **5** Duala, Kafir **6** Banyai, Damara, Kaffir, Waguha, Yakala **7** Swahili, Wachaga **8** Bechuana
languages: **3** Ila **4** Suto, Zulu **5** Ronga, Xhosa **6** Chwana, Thonga **7** Nyanaja, Swahili **8** Nyamwezi, Sechuana **10** Wanymawezi

BANZAI: **3** cry **5** hello **6** attack, charge

BAPTISM: **6** ritual **7** dunking **9** beginning, cleansing, immersion, sacrament **10** initiation **11** christening **12** purification

BAPTIZE: **3** dip, dub **4** full, name, term **5** admit **6** purify **7** cleanse **8** christen, sprinkle

BAR: **3** ban, dam, inn, law, pub, rod **4** axle, band, bank, bolt, cake, deny, gate, joke, lock, oust, pole, rail, sand, save, shut, stop **5** arbor, bench, block, brake, close, court, deter, fence, hedge, juice, lever, shade, shaft, stake, strap, strip **6** billet, except, fasten, grille, hinder, lounge, saloon, stripe **7** barrage, barrier, cabaret, confine, exclude, prevent, taproom **8** conclude, handicap, obstruct, preclude, prohibit, restrain, restrict, surround **9** barricade, blackball, fastening, gatehouse, hindrance, nightclub, ostracize, speakeasy **10** barristers, crosspiece, difficulty, impediment, portcullis **11** obstruction **13** establishment

BARB: **3** awn, bur, cut, jag **4** burr, clip, dart, file, hook, jagg, snag **5** beard, horse, point, ridge, scoff, shaft, spike, thorn **6** insult **7** bristle, kingish, sarcasm **10** projection

BARBADOS:
capital: **10** Bridgetown
ethnic groups: **7** African
features: **12** Mount Hillaby
languages: **7** English
monetary unit: **6** dollar
place: **10** West Indies
water: **9** Caribbean

BARBARIAN: **3** Hun **4** boor, clod, Goth, punk, rude, wild **5** alien, brute, bully **6** savage, vandal **7** hoodlum, vicious **8** hooligan **9** untutored **10** philistine **11** uncivilized

BARBARISM: **4** cant **6** misuse **7** cruelty **8** atrocity, solecism **9** brutality **10** corruption, savageness **11** catachresis

BARBARITY: **7** cruelty **8** atrocity, ferocity, rudeness, savagery **9** brutality **10** inhumanity **11** boorishness **12** ruthlessness

BARBAROUS: **4** fell, mean, rude, wild **5** cruel, rough **6** brutal, unholy **7** Hunnish, slavish, uncivil **8** ignorant, impolite, inhumane, ruthless **9** ferocious, heartless, primitive, truculent **10** outlandish, unpolished **11** uncivilized **12** uncultivated

BARBECUE: **4** bake, spit **5** broil, grill, party **6** picnic **7** cookout **9** fireplace **10** rotisserie

BARBER: **3** cut **4** trim **5** shave **6** poller, tonsor **7** scraper, stylist, tonsure **8** coiffeur **10** beautician, haircutter **11** chirotonsor, hairdresser **13** cosmetologist

BARBER'S ITCH: **8** ringworm

BARD: **4** poet **5** druid, scald **6** singer, writer **8** minstrel, musician **10** troubadour

BARE: **3** all **4** bald, cold, nude, worn **5** alone, clear, empty, naked, plain, stark, strip **6** barren, callow, divert, divest, expose, meager, paltry, reveal, scanty, simple, unclad **7** austere, divulge, exposed, unarmed, uncover, undress **8** desolate, disclose, stripped **9** unadorned, uncovered, worthless **10** threadbare **11** bareskinned, defenseless, unfurnished

BAREFACED: **4** bold, open **5** blunt, brash, frank, sassy **6** brazen, candid **7** blatant, glaring **8** flagrant, impudent **9** audacious, shameless **11** undisguised

BAREFOOTED: **6** unshod **8** shoeless **9** discalced

BARELY: **4** just, only **5** faint **6** almost, hardly, poorly **8** narrowly, scantily, scarcely, slightly

BARFLY: **4** lush **5** drunk, stiff **8** carouser **9** alcoholic

BARGAIN: **4** deal, pact, sale **5** cheap, steal, trade **6** barter, dicker, haggle **7** contend, contest **8** closeout, contract, covenant, discount, giveaway, struggle **9** agreement, negotiate, stipulate **11** transaction

BARGAIN FOR: **6** expect **7** imagine **10** anticipate **11** contemplate

BARGE: **3** ark, tow **4** boat, dory, raft, scow, ship **5** ferry, lunge, lurch **6** lumber, thrust, vessel **7** lighter **8** flagship, flatboat

BARK: **3** arf, bag, bay, cry, rub, yap **4** case, coat, howl, peel, pelt, rind, roar, skin, snap, woof, yell **5** cough, shell, shout **6** abrade, cortex, holler **7** solicit **8** covering

BARLEY: **4** food, malt, seed **5** grain

BARMY: **5** foamy, silly **6** frothy, screwy **7** flighty, foolish

BARN: **3** bay **4** loft, shed **5** stall **6** corral, stable **7** hayloft **10** storehouse **11** outbuilding

BARNACLE: **5** leech **8** hanger-on, parasite **9** appendage **10** crustacean, freeloader **11** bloodsucker

BARNSTORM: **4** tour **5** actor, pilot **6** troupe **8** campaign

BARON: **4** king, peer **5** mogul, noble **6** tycoon **7** magnate **10** capitalist

BAROQUE: **4** gilt **6** ornate, rococo **7** bizarre **9** elaborate, grotesque, irregular **10** flamboyant **11** extravagant

BARRACK: **3** hut **4** base, camp **8** garrison, quarters **9** dormitory

BARRACUDA: **4** fish, spet **5** barry, pelon **6** becuna, picuda, sennet **10** guaguanche

BARRAGE: **4** fire, hail **5** burst, salvo **6** attack, deluge, shower, volley **7** barrier, torrent **9** broadside, cannonade, onslaught **10** outpouring **11** bombardment

BARREL: **3** fat, keg, tub, tun, vat **4** butt, cask, drum, hoop **5** hurry **6** vessel **7** cistern, rundlet **8** cylinder, hogshead **9** container **10** receptacle

BARREN: **3** dry **4** arid, bare, dull, vain **5** empty, stark, stern, vapid, waste **6** desert, fallow, jejune, meager **7** badland, sterile, useless **8** depleted, desolate, impotent, treeless **9** childless, exhausted, fruitless, infertile **10** unfruitful **12** unproductive

BARRICADE: **3** bar **4** stop, wall **5** block, fence **6** defend **7** barrier, bulwark, fortify **8** blockade, stockade **11** obstruction

BARRIER: **3** bar, dam **4** door, gate, line, moat, wall **5** bound, chain, fence, limit **6** hurdle, screen, trench **7** defense, parapet, railing **8** boundary, confines, drawback, fortress, handicap, stockade **9** barricade, palisades, restraint, roadblock **11** obstruction

BARRING: **3** but **6** saving **7** besides **9** excepting, excluding

BARRISTER: **6** lawyer **7** counsel **8** advocate, attorney **9** counselor, solicitor

BARROOM: **3** pub **4** cafe **6** lounge, saloon, tavern **7** taproom **8** dramshop

BARROW: **3** hog **4** bank, dune, hill, mote, pile **5** grave, gurry, mound **7** trolley, tumulus **8** mountain, pushcart

BARTER: **4** chop, hawk, sell, swap, vend **5** trade, truck **6** dicker, haggle **7** bargain, permute, traffic **8** commerce, exchange **11** reciprocate

BASAL: **4** easy **5** basic **6** lowest **7** initial **9** beginning, necessary **10** elementary **11** fundamental

BASE: **3** bed, low **4** camp, clam, foot, foul, home, lewd, mean, root, site, stem, step, vile **5** basis, cheap, dirty, gross, muddy, snide, stand, strip **6** abject, bottom, common, ground, hangar, locate, menial, podium, shabby, sordid, vulgar, wicked **7** bedrock, corrupt, housing, install, lowdown, servile, slavish, support **8** backbone, degraded, garrison, infamous, inferior, pedestal, shameful, stepping, unworthy, wretched **9** absorbent, degrading, essential, establish, predicate, principle **10** despicable, foundation, villainous **11** disgraceful, ignominious **12** contemptible, dishonorable, headquarters

BASEBALL:

equipment: **3** bat **4** ball, mitt

inventor: **9** Doubleday

officials: **3** ump **6** umpire

place: **7** diamond

positions: **7** catcher, pitcher **9** firstbase, left-field, shortstop, thirdbase **10** right-field, second-base **11** center-field, pinch-hitter

terms: **3** bag, bat, fan, hit, lob, out, peg, RBI, run **4** bean, bunt, foul, high, home, pole, save, walk, wild **5** bench, count, curve, drive, error, field, force, homer, mound, pitch, plate, popup, score, slide, swing **6** assist, batter, bottom, double, dugout, inside, popout, putout, single, sinker, stance, strike, triple, windup **7** battery, blooper, bullpen, circuit, cleanup, diamond, infield, outside, sidearm, squeeze, stretch **8** delivery, grounder, knuckler, outfield, pinchhit, spitball **9** full count, sacrifice, strikeout

BASELESS: **4** idle **5** false **9** pointless, unfounded, untenable **10** gratuitous, groundless, reasonless **11** unwarranted

BASH: **3** bat **4** beat, blow, dent, mash, swat, whop **5** blast, party, smash **6** strike, wallop **7** blowout, clobber **8** wingding

BASHEMATH:
father: **7** Ishmael
husband: **4** Esau

BASHFUL: **3** coy, shy **5** timid **6** demure, humble, modest **7** daunted **8** blushing, dismayed, reserved, retiring, sheepish **9** diffident, shrinking **11** embarrassed, unassertive

BASIC: **3** key **4** main **5** chief, vital **7** central, primary **8** inherent **9** elemental, essential **10** underlying **11** fundamental, rudimentary

BASICALLY: **6** mostly **7** firstly **9** primarily, radically **11** essentially **13** fundamentally

BASIL: **4** herb **5** plant, royal **6** Ocimum, tulasi

BASILICA: **5** title **6** church, shrine, temple

BASIN: **3** bay, pan, tub **4** bowl, dish, dock, font, sink, tank **5** stoup **6** crater, lagoon, marina, valley, vessel **8** lavatory, receptor, washbowl **9** reservoir, watershed **10** depression

BASIS: **3** bed **4** root **5** axiom, cause, heart, proof **6** bottom, ground, motive, reason **7** essence, footing, premise **9** principle **10** antecedent, foundation, groundwork

BASK: **3** sun **4** laze, warm **5** bathe, enjoy, relax, revel **6** lounge, relish, wallow **7** delight, indulge, rejoice

BASKET: **3** ark, bin **5** cesta, chest, crate, scull **6** barrel, cradle, dosser, hamper **7** canasta, pannier, scuttle **8** bassinet **9** container **10** receptacle

BASKETBALL:
inventor: **8** Naismith
nicknames: **5** cager **8** hoopster
officials: **3** ref **6** umpire **7** referee
place: **5** court
positions: **5** guard **6** center **7** forward
terms: **3** key, tap **4** cage, dunk, pass **5** layup, stuff, tipin **7** dribble, rebound, timeout **8** jump ball **9** backboard, backcourt, field goal, free throw **10** front court

BASQUE:
cities: **4** Irun **5** Eibar **6** Bermeo, Bilbao, Sestao, Tolosa **7** Vitoria
language: **7** Euskara
place: **5** Spain **6** France **8** Pyrenees **11** Atlantiques

BASS: **3** low **4** alto, deep, fish **5** black, voice **6** singer **7** jewfish

BASSINET: **4** crib, pram **6** cradle **12** perambulator

BASTARD: **4** fake **5** false **6** galley, hybrid, impure **7** lowbred, mongrel **8** bantling, baseborn, spurious **9** scoundrel **10** artificial, fatherless **11** adulterated **12** illegitimate

BASTE: **3** sew **4** beat, cane, cook, lard, pelt, tack **5** roast **6** batter, punish, season, stitch, thrash **8** lambaste

BASTION: **4** fort, rock **6** pillar **7** citadel **8** mainstay **10** stronghold

BAT: **3** bop, fox, hit, wad **4** beat, blow, club, gait, sock, swat, wink **5** billy, binge, brick, speed, spree, stick **6** beetle, cudgel, racket, strike, stroke, wander **7** clobber, flutter, vampire **8** bludgeon **10** battledore, packsaddle **11** rattlemouse

BATCH: **3** lot **4** mass, sort **5** array, bunch, group **6** bundle, parcel, volume **7** mixture **8** quantity **10** assemblage, collection

BATH: **3** dip, spa, tub **4** wash **6** plunge, shower, sponge, toilet **7** Turkish **9** cleansing

BATHE: **3** tub, wet **4** bask, lave, soak, wash **5** douse, rinse **6** shower **7** immerse, pervade, suffuse **8** irrigate, permeate, submerge

BATHING SUIT: **5** thong, **6** bikini, trunks **7** maillot **8** swimsuit

BATHROOM: **3** can, lav **4** head, john **6** toilet **7** commode, latrine **8** restroom, sudatory

BATHSHEBA:
father: **5** Eliam
husband: **5** David, Uriah
son: **7** Solomon

BATON: **3** rod **4** bend, wand **5** billy, staff, stick **6** cudgel **7** bourdon, scepter **9** truncheon **10** nightstick

BATRACHIAN: **4** frog, toad **9** amphibian

BATTEN: **3** fix, tie **4** down **5** gloat **6** enrich, thrive **7** prosper

BATTER: **3** ram **4** beat, dent, maim **5** crush, paste, pound **6** bruise, hammer, hitter, pummel **7** assault, bombard, clobber, cripple, destroy, shatter **8** demolish **10** concoction

BATTERY: **4** army, cell, grid, ring **5** group **6** series **7** assault, brigade **8** division, violence **9** artillery **11** bombardment

BATTLE: **3** cry, war **4** duel, fray, meet **5** brush, clash, fight, joust, onset, press **6** affray, combat, sortie **7** bombard, carnage, contend, contest, crusade, warfare **8** campaign, conflict, skirmish, struggle **9** encounter **10** blitzkrieg, engagement **11** competition, hostilities

BATTY: **4** nuts **5** crazy, silly, wacky **6** insane **7** foolish **8** deranged

BAUBLE: **3** toy **4** bead **6** doodad, gewgaw, trifle **7** novelty, trinket **8** gimcrack **9** plaything **10** knickknack

BAVARIA:
capital: **6** Munich
cities: **5** Furth **8** Augsburg, Wurzburg **9** Nuremberg **10** Regensburg
country: **7** Germany
feature: **6** Lunder **8** Bayreuth **10** Allgau Alps **11** Wetterstein **12** Oberammergau **14** Bohemian Forest
water: **3** Alz, Ilz, Inn, Nab **4** Eger, Isar, Lech, Main **5** Ammer, Amper, Chiem, Iller, Regen, Saale **6** Danube **7** Altmuhl, Regnitz **9** Starnberg

BAWDY: **4** foul, lewd, rude **5** dirty **6** coarse, erotic, risque, vulgar **7** lustful, obscene **8** indecent

BAWL: **3** cry **4** bark, howl, wail, weep, yell **5** shout **6** bellow, boohoo, scream **7** blubber

BAWL OUT: **5** scold **6** berate **7** upbraid **9** castigate, reprimand

BAY: **3** arm, cry **4** bank, bark, cove, gulf, hole, howl, nook, tree, wail, wing, yawp **5** award, bight, creek, fiord, fleet, haven, horse, niche, oriel, sinus **6** alcove, laurel, recess, strait, window **7** enclose **11** compartment, indentation

BAY OF BISCAY:
cities: **7** Hendaye **8** Biarritz
islands: **3** Yeu **5** Belle, Groix **6** Oleron
rivers: **5** Adour, Loire **7** Garonne

BAYONET: **4** stab **5** knife, lance, spear **6** pierce, weapon

BAYOU: **4** cove **5** brook, creek, marsh, river **6** harbor, outlet, slough, stream **7** channel **9** backwater

BAYOU STATE: **9** Louisiana **11** Mississippi

BAY STATE: **13** Massachusetts

BAZAAR: **4** fair, fete **6** market **7** canteen **8** emporium, exchange **10** exposition **11** marketplace

BAZOO: **3** boo **4** hiss, razz, talk **5** kazoo, mouth, raspberry

BEACH: **4** bank, moor, ripa, sand **5** coast, shore **6** ground, strand **7** seaside, shingle **8** lakeside **9** shipwreck **10** oceanfront, waterfront

BEACHED: **7** aground **8** deserted, grounded, marooned

BEACON: **4** flag, mark, sign **5** alarm, flare, guide, light **6** pharos, signal **7** cresset, lantern, seamark, warning **8** landmark, signpost **10** lighthouse, watchtower

BEAD: **3** dab, dot **4** drop, foam **5** sight **6** bauble, bubble, prayer, rosary **7** chaplet, droplet, sparkle, trinket **8** necklace, particle

BEAK: **3** neb, nib **4** bill, nose, peak, prow **5** snout, spout **7** rostrum **8** mandible **9** proboscis, schnozzle **10** magistrate, projection

BEAKER: **3** cup **5** glass **6** bareca, vessel

BE-ALL AND END-ALL: **3** sum **4** acme, root **5** total, whole **7** essence **8** entirety, ultimate **9** aggregate **10** everything

BEAM: **3** bar, ray **4** balk, emit, glow, grin, stud **5** brace, caber, flash, gleam, joist, light, plank, shine, smile, smirk **6** binder, column, girder, rafter, walker **7** chevron, radiate, support, trimmer **8** emission, transmit

BEAMING: **3** gay **4** rosy **5** sunny **6** joyous, lucent **7** radiant, shining **8** animated, cheerful **9** beautiful, brilliant

BEAN: **3** dry, urd, wax **4** chap, head, lima, navy **5** baked, black, brain, cacao, jelly, pinto, skull **6** caster, coffee, collar, fellow, kidney, lentil, noggin, strike, string, thrash, trifle **7** calabar, jumping

BEANTOWN: **6** Boston

BEAR: **3** cat, cub, lug **4** buck, bush, down, haul, have, tote **5** abide, allow, brave, breed, bring, brown, bruin, carry, drive, koala, polar, press, stand, yield **6** afford, behave, endure, render, suffer, thrust **7** cherish, condone, conduct, grizzly, produce, stomach, support, sustain **8** forbear, shoulder, tolerate **9** propagate, reproduce, transport **13** constellation

BEAR DOWN: **4** push **5** exert **6** defeat, stress **9** overpower

BEARD: **4** barb, defy, face, fuzz **5** brave, decoy **6** goatee **7** stubble, Vandyke **8** confront, whiskers **9** challenge

BEARDED: **5** hairy **6** barbed, shaggy **7** barbate, hirsute **8** unshaven **9** whiskered

BEARING: **3** aim, air, way **4** look, mien, port **5** birth, front, habit, poise, track, trend **6** allure, aspect, course, manner, orient, thrust, weight **7** address, conduct, meaning, posture, purport, support **8** attitude, behavior, carriage, demeanor, pressure, relation **9** direction, influence, producing **10** deportment, importance **11** countenance **12** significance

BEAST: **3** cad, hun, pig **4** lion **5** brute, demon, fiend, tiger **6** animal, savage **7** monster, varmint **8** gargoyle **9** barbarian

BEASTLY: **3** bad **4** foul **5** awful, feral, gross, nasty **6** animal, brutal, vulgar **7** boorish, inhuman, obscene, swinish **8** dreadful, sadistic **9** loathsome, offensive **10** abominable, disgusting

BEAT: **3** bat, cob, fan, hit, tap, top, win **4** area, baff, bang, bash, belt, best, blow, bolt, bray, cane, club, ding, drub, dump, flap, flax, flog, haze, lash, lump, maul, pant, pelt, rout, scat, slam, tack, wave, whip, whop **5** baste, churn, clink, crush, douse, excel, fight, filch, kaput, knock, meter, pound, pulse, repel, round, scoop, throb, thump, trump, worst **6** accent, batter, beetle, better, buffet, cotton, cudgel, defeat, hammer, hamper, outrun, patrol, pummel, quiver, raddle, rhythm, ripple, squash, strike, stroke, switch, thrash, thresh **7** assault, beatnik, blister, cadence, canvass, clobber, conquer, exhaust, fatigue, pulsate, repulse, shellac, surpass, trounce **8** fatigued, lambaste, malleate, overcome, shellack, suppress, vanquish **9** exhausted, fluctuate, throbbing **10** assignment

BEAT IT: **4** scat, shoo **5** leave, scram **6** begone **7** vamoose

BEATITUDE: **3** joy **5** bliss **7** ecstasy **8** euphoria **9** happiness **10** exaltation **11** blessedness

BEATNIK: **4** beat **6** hippie **7** dropout **8** Bohemian, maverick, peacenik

BEAU: **3** guy **4** buck, dude **5** beaux, blade, dandy, flame, honey, lover, spark **6** escort, fellow, steady, suitor **7** admirer, bravery, coxcomb, cupidon **8** truelove **9** boyfriend, caballero, gentleman **10** sweetheart

BEAU IDEAL: **5** model **7** example **8** standard

BEAU MONDE: **5** elite **7** fashion, society **11** aristocracy

BEAUTIFUL: **4** cute, fair, fine **5** belle, bonny, elite **6** blithe, choice, decore, freely, lovely, poetic, pretty **7** angelic, elegant, radiant **8** charming, delicate, gorgeous, graceful, handsome, splendid, stunning **9** exquisite **10** attractive

BEAUTIFY: **4** deck, gild **5** adorn, grace, prune **6** bedeck **7** adonize, enhance, garnish **8** decorate **9** embellish, glamorize

BEAUTY: **4** doll **5** belle, charm, grace, merit, style, Venus **6** Apollo, eyeful, looker, polish **7** goddess **8** knockout **9** Aphrodite, dreamboat **10** goodliness, loveliness **11** pulchritude

BEAVER: **3** hat, kit **4** coin, plew, skin **6** rodent

BEAVER STATE: **6** Oregon

BECAUSE: **3** for **4** that, thus **5** being, since **8** inasmuch **9** therefore

BECKON: **3** ask, bid, bow, nod **4** call, coax, wave **5** tempt **6** curtsy, entice, motion, summon **7** bidding, command, curtsey, gesture **10** salutation

BECLOUD: **3** fog **4** hide **5** muddy **6** darken, puzzle **7** conceal, confuse, mystify, obscure, perplex **8** confound, overcast **10** camouflage

BECOME: **3** get, wax **4** grow, pass, rise, suit **5** adorn, befit, grace, shift **6** accord, befall, betide, change, evolve **7** augment, behoove, enhance, flatter **8** heighten

BECOMING: 3 fit **4** good **5** right **6** gainly, worthy **7** decorum **8** handsome, suitable, tasteful **9** befitting **10** attractive, convenient, flattering **11** appropriate

BED: 3 cot, hay, pad, row **4** base, bunk, crib, plot, sack, twin **5** basis, berth, couch, layer **6** bottom, cradle, double, flower, litter, matrix, pallet, retire **7** channel, feather, lodging, stratum **8** bassinet, mattress, rollaway **9** davenport, stretcher **10** foundation

BEDAZZLE: 4 daze, stun **5** blind **7** astound, enchant, stagger **8** bewilder **9** captivate, overwhelm

BEDDING: 5 cover, linen, quilt **6** afghan, pillow, sheets **7** blanket **9** bedspread, comforter **10** bedclothes

BEDECK: 3 gem **4** trim **5** adorn, array, grace **8** decorate, ornament **9** embellish

BEDEVIL: 3 hex **5** abuse, annoy, tease, worry **6** harass, muddle, pester **7** bewitch, torment

BEDIM: 3 fog **4** blur, fade, mist **5** cloud, gloom **6** darken **7** becloud, obscure

BEDLAM: 3 din **4** riot **5** chaos, furor, noise **6** asylum, racket, tumult, uproar **7** lunatic, madness, turmoil **8** madhouse **9** confusion

BEDRIDDEN: 3 ill **6** ailing, feeble **8** confined, disabled **13** incapacitated

BEDROCK: 4 base **5** basis **6** bottom, ground **10** substratum

BEDROOM: 4 flat **5** berth **7** boudoir, chamber, cubicle **11** compartment

BEE:
food: **7** flowers
group: **5** swarm **6** colony
live: **4** hive, skep **6** apiary
produces: **5** honey
type: **6** cuckoo, worker **8** honeybee **9** bumblebee, carpenter
young: **5** grubs

BEEF: 3 arm **4** meat **5** brawl, gripe, vigor **6** cattle **7** dispute, quarrel, rhubarb **8** complain **9** objection
cuts: **4** loin, rump, side **5** chuck, flank, roast, round, shank, steak **6** cutlet **7** brisket, quarter, sirloin **8** short rib, shoulder **10** tenderloin **11** porterhouse

BEEFY: 5 bulky, hefty, husky **6** brawny, robust, stolid

BEEHIVE STATE: 4 Utah

BEEKEEPER: 8 apiarist **12** apiculturist

BEER: 3 ale, keg, mug, mum **4** bock, brew, case, dark, grog, hops, malt, near, suds, yard **5** glass, kvass, lager, stein, stout, wheat, yeast **6** barley, brewer, liquor, porter, swanky **7** bottled, brewski, pitcher **8** beverage

BEET: 4 beta **5** chard, sugar **6** mangel **7** borscht, mangold **8** beetrave **9** vegetable

BEETHOVEN, LUDWIG VAN:
birthplace: **4** Bonn **7** Germany
opera: **7** Fidelio
sonata: **5** Laube **6** Spring **9** Moonlight
symphony: **5** fifth, first, sixth, third **6** Choral, Eroica, fourth, second **7** seventh **8** Pastoral

BEETLE: 3 bat, bug, jut **4** beat, hang, June, maul, stag **5** bulge, drive, meloe **6** chafer, golach, jutout, mallet, pestle, scarab, weevil **7** firefly, goldbug, ladybug, prinoid, project **8** Japanese, lowering, overhang, protrude, skipjack **9** tumblebug **10** battledore

BEFALL: 3 gel, hap **4** come **5** occur **6** become, betide, happen **7** develop, pertain **8** bechance **9** transpire

BEFITTING: **3** apt **4** just **5** right **6** kosher, seemly **7** correct **8** becoming, suitable **10** conforming **11** appropriate

BEFOG: **3** dim **5** cloud **6** puzzle **7** conceal, confuse, mystify, obscure **8** confound

BEFORE: **3** ere **4** back, past, till **5** afore, ahead, avant, first, front, prior **6** facing, former, rather, sooner **7** already, earlier, forward, vanward **8** anterior, hitherto **9** preceding **10** heretofore, previously

BEFOUL: **4** soil **5** dirty, stain **6** defile, malign **7** corrupt, pollute, slander **11** contaminate

BEFRIEND: **3** aid **4** abet, back, help **5** favor **6** advise, assist, defend **7** benefit, embrace, protect, support, sustain

BEFUDDLE: **4** daze **5** addle **6** baffle, muddle **7** confuse, fluster, mystify, stupefy **8** distract, unsettle **9** inebriate **10** intoxicate

BEG: **3** ask, bid, bum, nag **4** coax, pray, urge **5** crave, mooch, plead **6** adjure, hustle **7** beseech, entreat, request, solicit **8** petition **9** panhandle **10** supplicate

BEGET: **4** bear, sire **5** breed, bring, spawn, yield **6** afford, create, father **7** produce **8** engender, generate **9** germinate, procreate

BEGGAR: **3** bum **4** hobo, ruin **5** asker, rogue **6** bidder, canter, pauper, wretch **7** almsman, moocher, vagrant **8** deadbeat, indigent, palliard, vagabond **9** almswoman, mendicant, schnorrer, scrounger, suppliant **10** freeloader, impoverish, panhandler, supplicant

BEGGARLY: **3** low **4** mean, poor **5** cheap, petty, sorry **6** cheesy, paltry, vulgar **8** bankrupt, indigent, infamous, wretched **10** despicable

BEGIN: **3** bud, set **4** dawn, lead, open, rise **5** arise, enter, start **6** attack, create, spring **7** emanate, trigger **8** commence, initiate **9** germinate, institute, introduce, originate **10** inaugurate

BEGINNER: **4** tyro **6** novice, rookie **7** amateur, entrant, founder, recruit, student, trainee **8** freshman **9** candidate, debutante, greenhorn, postulate **10** apprentice

BEGINNING: **3** day, egg, new **4** dawn, germ, rise, root, seed **5** alpha, birth, cause, debut, heart, start **6** origin, outset, spring **7** genesis, initial, kickoff **8** entrance **9** embryonic, inception **10** conception, elementary, foundation, initiation **12** commencement

BEGONE: **3** off, out **4** away, scat, shoo **5** leave, scoot, scram **6** depart **7** skiddoo, vamoose **8** hightail

BEGRUDGE: **4** envy **5** covet, pinch **6** loathe, resent **7** grumble

BEGUILE: **3** con, fox, gyp **4** burn, coax, foil, fool, lure **5** amuse, bluff, charm, cheat, elude, evade, trick **6** delude, divert, entrap, seduce **7** deceive, flatter, mislead **8** maneuver **9** entertain **10** manipulate

BEHALF: **3** aid **4** part, sake, side **6** matter, profit **7** account, benefit, defense, support **8** interest **9** advantage **10** assistance

BEHAVE: **3** act **4** bear, work **5** carry, react, treat **6** demean, deport, direct, handle, manage **7** conduct, gesture, manager **8** function, regulate, restrain

BEHAVIOR: **3** air **4** code, deed, port, tact **5** guise **6** action, manner, morals **7** bearing, comport, conduct, decorum, routine **8** attitude, demeanor **9** etiquette **10** deportment

BEHEAD: **4** kill **7** execute **9** decollate **10** decapitate, guillotine

BEHEMOTH: **3** big **4** huge **5** beast, giant **7** mammoth, monster

BEHEST: **3** bid **4** rule, wish **5** edict, order **6** decree, demand, desire **7** command, mandate **9** direction, prompting **10** injunction **12** solicitation

BEHIND: **3** aft **4** past, rear, rump, seat, tush, ward **5** abaft, after, arear, fanny, tardy **6** arrear, astern **7** backing, laggard **8** backward, buttocks, derriere, trailing **9** posterior **10** afterwards **11** instigating

BEHOLD: **3** eye, see **4** gaze, hold, look, scan, view, wait **5** catch, sight, watch **6** notice, regard, retain **7** discern, earmark, observe, witness **8** consider, maintain, perceive

BEHOLDEN: **5** bound, owing **7** obliged **8** grateful, indebted **11** accountable

BEHOOVE: **3** fit **4** need, suit **5** befit, ought **6** proper **7** benefit, require **8** suitable

BEIGE: **3** tan **4** ecru **5** camel, color, cream, khaki **8** brownish

BEING: **3** one **4** life, self, soul **5** angel, human, thing **6** animal, entity, living, matter, mortal, nature, person, spirit **7** because, essence, present, reality, supreme **8** creature, ontology, organism, standing **9** actuality, existence **11** subsistence

BELABOR: **3** ply **4** beat, drub, lash, work **5** pound **6** assail, buffet, cudgel, hammer, thrash **9** reiterate

BELARUS:
capital: **5** Minsk
cities: **5** Gomen, Homel **7** Mahilou, Mogilev

BELATED: **4** late **5** tardy **6** remiss **7** delayed, overdue **8** deferred

BELCH: **4** burp, rasp, spew, vent **5** expel, vomit **6** hiccup, repeat **10** eructation

BELEAGUER: **3** nag **5** annoy, beset **6** bother, harass, invest, plague **7** assault, besiege **8** blockade, surround **9** persecute

BELFRY: **4** dome **5** tower **6** turret **7** clocher **8** carillon **9** campanile

BELGIUM:
capital: **8** Brussels
cities: **4** Mons **5** Ghent, Liege, Namur **6** Bruges, Leuven, Ostend **7** Antwerp **9** Charleroi, Zeebrugge
continent: **6** Europe
ethnic groups: **7** Flemish, Walloon
features: **14** Ardennes Forest
kings: **6** Albert **7** Leopold **8** Baudouin
languages: **5** Dutch **6** French, German **7** Flemish, Italian
monetary unit: **5** franc
native: **7** Belgian
provinces: **5** Liege, Namur **7** Antwerp, Brabant, Hainaut, Limburg **9** Luxemburg **10** Luxembourg **12** East Flanders, West Flanders
water: **5** Meuse **7** Scheldt

BELIE: **4** deny, hide **5** color **6** belong, betray, defame **7** besiege, deceive, distort, falsify, pertain, slander **8** disguise, disprove, negative, surround **10** camouflage, contradict, contravene **11** counterfeit

BELIEF: **4** hope, idea, mind, sect, view **5** axiom, credo, creed, dogma, faith, trust **6** gospel, theory **7** feeling, opinion **8** credence, doctrine, position, reliance, religion **9** admission, assurance, certainty **10** confidence, conviction, persuasion

BELIEVABLE: **6** likely **8** credible, possible, straight **9** authentic, plausible **10** acceptable **11** conceivable, trustworthy

BELIEVE: **3** buy **4** deem, hold **5** judge, think, trust **6** accept, affirm, assume, credit **7** imagine, suppose, swallow **8** accredit, consider, theorize

BELIEVER: **6** zealot **7** admirer, apostle, devotee **8** adherent, disciple **9** supporter

BELITTLE: **3** pan **5** decry, knock, sneer **6** slight, squash **7** detract, disdain **8** diminish, minimize **9** criticize, denigrate, discredit, disparage, downgrade **10** depreciate

BELIZE:
capital: **8** Belmopan
cities: **7** Corozal **8** Dangriga **10** Belize City, Orange Walk, Punta Gorda
continent: **14** Central America
ethnic groups: **4** Maya **6** Creole **7** Mestizo
features: **8** Victoria
languages: **6** Creole **7** English, Spanish
monetary unit: **6** dollar

BELL: **3** cow **4** call, door, gong, ring, roar, toll **5** chime, cloak, flare, swell, tower **6** bellow, church, curfew, dinner, school, tocsin, tongue **7** blossom, clapper, corolla **9** beautiful

BELLEROPHON:
brother: **7** Deliade
father: **8** Poseidon
home: **7** Corinth
horse: **7** Pegasus
killed: **7** Chimera
son: **11** Hippolochus

BELLES LETTRES: **8** classics **10** literature

BELLICOSE: **3** mad **7** hostile, scrappy, warlike **8** militant **9** combative **10** pugnacious, rebellious **11** belligerent

BELLIGERENT: **3** hot **4** mean **5** nasty **6** fierce, ornery **7** hostile, warlike, warring **8** fighting **9** adversary, bellicose, combative, litigious, wrangling **10** aggressive, pugnacious **11** contentious, quarrelsome **12** antagonistic

BELLOW: **3** cry, yap **4** bark, bawl, bell, call, roar, rout, yawp, yell **5** blare, shout **6** clamor, holler, scream, shriek **7** bluster **10** vociferate

BELLWETHER: **4** lead **5** doyen, guide, sheep **6** leader **10** forerunner

BELLY: **3** bag, gut, pot **4** beer **5** bingy, bulge, tummy **6** hunger, paunch **7** abdomen, stomach **8** appetite **11** breadbasket

BELONG: **3** fit, set **4** bear, vest **5** apply, match **6** accord, relate **7** concern, pertain **9** appertain, correlate, harmonize **10** affiliated

BELONGINGS: **4** gear **5** goods **6** assets, estate, family, things **7** effects **8** property **9** household **10** appendages **11** possessions

BELOVED: **3** pet **4** dear, idol, love **5** flame **6** adored, spouse, steady **7** admired, darling, revered **8** precious **9** boy friend, cherished, inamorata, valentine **10** girl friend, sweetheart

BELOW: **4** down, less **5** lower, under **7** beneath **8** downward, inferior **10** downstairs, underneath **11** subordinate

BELT: **4** area, band, bash, beat, blow, mark, ring, sash, zone **5** girth, strap, strip, tract, whack **6** circle, girdle, invest, region, strait, stripe **7** circuit, clobber, highway, passage **8** cincture, conveyor, encircle, surround **9** bandoleer, encompass, waistband **10** cummerbund

BEMOAN: **3** rue **4** pity, wail **5** mourn **6** grieve, lament, regret, sorrow **7** deplore

BEMUSE: **4** stun **5** addle **7** confuse, fluster **8** distract **9** overwhelm

BENCH: **3** bar, pew **4** seat, work **5** board, court, ledge, stool **6** settee **7** discard **8** sideline, tribunal

BENCHMARK: **5** gauge, model **7** example **8** standard **9** yardstick **10** touchstone

BEND: **3** bow, ply, sag **4** arch, flex, kink, loop, tilt, turn, wind **5** angle, crimp, curve, stoop, twist **6** buckle, compel, crouch, direct, divert, fasten, submit, zigzag **7** incline, refract **8** persuade **9** curvature

BENEATH: **5** below, lower, under **6** lesser **8** inferior **11** subordinate, underground

BENEDICTION: **4** amen **5** grace **6** praise, prayer, thanks **8** approval, blessing **9** gratitude **10** invocation **12** thanksgiving

BENEFACTION: **4** alms, gift **5** grant **7** charity, present **8** donation, gratuity, kindness **9** endowment **11** approbation, benevolence **12** philanthropy

BENEFACTOR: **3** aid **5** angel, donor **6** friend, helper, patron, savior **7** sponsor **8** promoter **10** grubstaker **12** humanitarian

BENEFICIAL: **4** good **6** useful **7** gainful, helpful **8** valuable **9** desirable, enjoyable, favorable, healthful, lucrative **10** profitable **11** serviceable **12** advantageous, remunerative

BENEFICIARY: **4** heir, user **5** donee **7** heiress, legatee **9** recipient, successor

BENEFIT: **3** aid, use **4** boot, gain, gift, help, perk, sake **5** avail, boost **6** assist, behalf, better, profit, raffle **7** advance, concert, deserve, enhance, improve, relieve, service, utility, welfare **8** befriend, blessing, interest **9** advantage, emolument **10** exhibition **11** performance

BENEVOLENT: **4** good, kind **6** benign, caring, humane, loving **7** liberal **8** generous **9** unselfish **10** altruistic, charitable, chivalrous **11** considerate **13** philanthropic

BENIGN: **4** good, kind, mild **5** bland **6** genial, gentle, slight, tender **7** affable, amiable **8** benedict, gracious, harmless, salutary **9** favorable, healthful, wholesome **10** benevolent, charitable

BENIN:
capital: **7** Cotonou **9** Porto Novo
cities: **6** Abomey **7** Parakou **10** Natitingou
continent: **6** Africa
ethnic groups: **3** Fon **4** Adja **6** Bariba, Yoruba
features: **7** Atakora
languages: **3** Fon **5** Somba **6** French, Yoruba
monetary unit: **5** franc
water: **9** Mono River **10** Niger River

BENJAMIN:
father: **5** Jacob
mother: **6** Rachel
progeny: **3** Ehi **4** Aher, Gera, Rosh

BENT: **3** aim, bow, set **4** bias, gift, nose, turn **5** bound, crank, flair, knack, prone, taste, trend **6** angled, braced, course, curved, energy, genius, hooked, swayed, talent **7** crooked, decided, hunched, impetus, leaning, leveled, pronate, purpose, settled, stooped **8** aptitude, declined, penchant, tendency **9** contorted, curvature, direction, insistent, prejudice **10** determined, proclivity, propensity **11** disposition, inclination

BENUMB: **4** daze, numb, stun **5** blunt, chill **6** cumber, deaden **7** stupefy **11** desensitize

BEQUEATH: **4** give, will **5** endow, grant, leave, offer **6** bestow, commit, demise, legate **7** bequest, commend **8** transmit **9** testament

BEQUEST: **4** gift, will **5** dower **6** estate, legacy **8** bequeath, heritage **9** endowment **11** inheritance

BERATE: **3** jaw, nag **4** lash, rail **5** abuse, chide, scold, score **6** revile, scorch **7** blister, censure, upbraid **8** chastise **9** castigate

BEREAVE: **3** rob **4** oust **5** leave, strip **6** divest, sadden **7** deprive **10** dispossess

BEREAVEMENT: **5** death **6** sorrow **8** distress **10** affliction

BEREFT: **4** lorn, lost, poor **6** devoid, robbed **7** fleeced, forlorn, lacking, missing **9** destitute

BERMUDA:
capital: **8** Hamilton
language: **7** English
monetary unit: **6** dollar

BERRY: **3** bay, dew, mul **4** bean, beat, blue, cran, rasp, seed **5** black, fruit, goose, grain, mound, straw **6** boysen, huckle, kernel

BERSERK: **3** mad **4** wild **5** crazy **7** enraged, violent **8** demented, frenzied, maniacal **10** distraught

BERTH: **3** bed, job **4** bunk, dock, slip **5** niche, place, wharf **6** billet, harbor, office **7** mooring **8** position **9** situation **10** profession **11** appointment

BERYL: **3** gem **5** green, jewel **6** yellow **7** emerald

BESEECH: **3** ask, beg **4** pray **5** plead **6** adjure, appeal, invoke **7** entreat, implore, solicit **8** petition **9** obsecrate **10** supplicate

BESET: **3** bug, ply **4** sail **5** allot, harry, hound, siege, spend, storm **6** assail, attack, circle, harass, infest, pester, plague **7** arrange, besiege **8** blockade, obstruct, surround **9** beleaguer

BESIDE: **4** near **5** along, aside **6** except **7** abreast **8** adjacent, opposite **9** excluding

BESIDES: **3** and, but, too **4** also, else, plus, then **5** added, extra **6** beyond, except **8** moreover **9** otherwise **10** additional **11** furthermore

BESIEGE: **3** nag **4** girt, trap **5** annoy, belay, beset, siege, storm **6** attack, pester, plague **7** assault, confine, solicit **8** blockade, surround **9** beleaguer

BESMIRCH: **4** blot, soil **5** smear, taint **6** defile, smudge **7** blacken, slander **8** discolor, dishonor

BESOTTED: **5** drunk **6** buzzed, cooked, wasted, zonked **7** sloshed, smashed **10** inebriated, infatuated **11** intoxicated

BESPANGLE: **3** dot **4** star, stud, trim **5** adorn, light **7** garnish **8** decorate, sprinkle **9** embellish

BESPATTER: **4** blot, dash, slur, soil, spot **5** dirty, muddy, stain **6** malign, sparge **7** condemn, scatter **8** reproach, sprinkle **10** stigmatize

BESPEAK: **3** ask **4** cite, hint, show **5** argue, imply, speak **6** accost, attest, engage **7** address, arrange, discuss, exclaim, request, reserve **8** announce, foretell, indicate **9** stipulate

BEST: **3** ace, bad, pip, top **4** boss, most, pick **5** cream, elite, excel, primo **6** choice, defeat, exceed, finest, flower, utmost **7** conquer, largest, optimum, surpass **8** champion, greatest, outmatch, outstrip, topnotch, vanquish **9** excellent, paramount

BESTIAL: 3 low **4** vile, wild **5** cruel **6** brutal, filthy **7** brutish **8** barbaric, depraved, ruthless

BESTOW: 3 add, put, use **4** deal, gift, give **5** allot, allow, apply, award, beset, grant **6** accord, confer, devote, divide, donate, entail, extend, harbor, render **7** deliver, dispose, entrust, present, quarter, tribute **8** bequeath, dispense

BET: 3 lay, pot **4** ante, odds, play, risk, wage **5** stake, wager **6** chance, gamble, pledge, raffle **7** lottery **9** speculate

BETE NOIRE: 4 hate, ogre **5** dread **6** plague, terror **7** bugaboo, outcast **8** bogeyman **11** abomination

BETHINK: 4 mind **6** devise, recall **7** reflect **8** consider, remember **9** recollect, reminisce **10** deliberate

BETHUEL:
father: **5** Nahor
mother: **6** Milcah
son: **5** Laban

BETIDE: 4 fall **5** befit, occur **6** become, befall, chance, happen **7** develop, presage **9** transpire

BETIMES: 4 soon **5** early **7** shortly **8** speedily **9** sometimes **10** seasonably **11** prematurely **12** occasionally

BETOKEN: 4 note, omen, show **6** assert, betide, denote, import **7** bespeak, express, presage, signify, witness **8** forebode, indicate **9** symbolize **10** foreshadow

BETRAY: 3 rat **4** blab, blow, fink, sell, sile, sing, tell, undo **5** cross, peach, snare, spill **6** accuse, delude, expose, finger, reveal, seduce, snitch, squeal, tattle **7** abandon, beguile, deceive, divulge, falsify, mislead **8** disclose, discover

BETRAYAL: 7 sellout, treason **9** chicanery, deception **10** dishonesty, disloyalty

BETRAYER: 4 nark **5** Judas, skunk **7** stoolie, traitor **8** informer, turncoat

BETROTH: 3 vow **4** bind **6** assure, engage, pledge **7** espouse, promise **8** affiance, contract

BETTER: 3 aid, top, win **4** good, half, more, well **5** amend, excel, outdo, safer, wiser **6** bigger, choice, exceed **7** advance, correct, elevate, greater, improve, promote, rectify, support, surpass **8** increase, superior, worthier **9** desirable, excelling, healthier **10** ameliorate, preferable

BETTERMENT: 6 reform **7** mastery **8** revision **10** correction **11** improvement

BETWEEN: 4 amid **5** among **6** amidst, within **7** average, betwixt, halfway **12** intermediate

BEVEL: 4 blow, cant, edge, ream **5** angle, bezel, miter, mitre, slope **7** chamfer, incline, oblique, slanted **8** diagonal

BEVERAGE: 3 ade, ale, nog, pop, tea **4** beer, grog, milk, soda, wine **5** cider, cocoa, draft, drink, juice, lager, leban, negus, punch, tonic, treat, water **6** coffee, cooler, eggnog, liquid, liquor, malted, nectar, potion **7** cordial, potable, seltzer **8** cocktail, lemonade

BEVY: 4 band, crew, herd, pack **5** covey, crowd, flock, group, party, swarm **6** flight, school, troupe **7** company **8** assembly **9** gathering **10** collection

BEWAIL: 3 cry, rue **4** moan, sigh, weep **5** mourn **6** bemoan, grieve, lament, repent, sorrow **7** deplore

BEWARE: 4 cave, heed, mind, shun **5** avoid, spend **6** eschew, notice **7** warning

BEWILDER: **3** fog **4** daze, foil, stun **5** abash, addle, amaze, amuse, floor, upset **6** baffle, bother, dazzle, muddle, puzzle, rattle **7** buffalo, confuse, fluster, mystify, perplex, stupefy **8** astonish, confound, distract, surprise **9** embarrass, obfuscate

BEWITCH: **3** hex **4** hook, jinx, wile **5** charm, spook, trick **6** allure, dazzle, entice, thrill, voodoo **7** attract, bedevil, control, delight, enchant **9** captivate, fascinate, hypnotize, spellbind

BEYOND: **4** free, hope, over, past **5** above, after, aside, ultra **6** across, remote, yonder **7** besides, further, outside **8** moreover, question, superior **9** hereafter, otherwise

BHUTAN:
capital: **6** Thimbu **7** Thimphu **9** Paro Dzong
cities: **4** Paro **6** Mongar **7** Punakha
continent: **4** Asia
ethnic groups: **5** Bhote **8** Napalese
features: **4** Duar **9** Himalayas **13** Gangkar Punsum
languages: **6** Gurung, Nepali **7** Bumthap **8** Assamese, Dzongkha, Sharchop
monetary unit: **8** ngultrum
water: **11** Brahmaputra

BIAS: **4** awry, bent, skew, sway **5** color, slant, slope **7** bigotry, incline, leaning, oblique **8** diagonal, tendency **9** influence, prejudice, procedure **10** favoritism, partiality, prepossess, propensity, standpoint **11** declination, disposition, intolerance **12** predetermine

BIBLE:
animal: **4** reem **5** daman **6** hydrax **8** behemoth
apocrypha: **5** Tobit **6** Baruch, Esdras, Jeremy, Judith, Syriac, Wisdom **7** Vulgate **8** Manasses **9** Maccabees **10** Septuagint **14** Ecclesiasticus
books: **3** Job **4** Acts, Amos, Ezra, Joel, John, Jude, Luke, Mark, Ruth **5** Hosea, James, Jonah, Kings, Micah, Peter, Titus **6** Daniel, Esther, Exodus, Haggai, Isaiah, Joshua, Psalms, Romans, Samuel **7** Ezekiel, Genesis, Hebrews, Matthew, Numbers, Obadiah, Timothy **8** Habakkuk, Jeremiah, Nehemiah, Philemon, Proverbs **9** Apocrypha, Ephesians, Galatians, Leviticus, Zechariah **10** Chronicles, Colossians, Revelation **11** Corinthians, Deuteronomy, Philippians **12** Ecclesiastes, Lamentations **13** Song of Solomon, Thessalonians
characters: **3** Eli, Eve, Hor, Koa, Reu **4** Abel, Adam, Aher, Anam, Cain, Edes, Enos, Esau, Iram, Mary, Noah, Oreb, Paul, Sara, Seth **5** Aaron, Caleb, Elias, Ephai, Esrom, Hadad, Isaac, Jacob, Nahum, Rahad **6** Elijah, Lamech, Levite, Pilate **7** Abigail, Antioch, Ezekial, Sidrach, Tabitha
kingdoms: **4** Elam, Moab **5** Judah, Judea **6** Israel **8** Chaldeae
kings/queens: **4** Saul **5** David, Herod, Hiram, Tidal **7** Solomon
versions: **4** Geez **5** Douay **7** Vulgate **9** Apocrypha, King James **10** New English **15** Revised Standard
water: **4** Nile **6** Jordan, Red Sea **7** Dead Sea, Galilee **8** Tiberias **10** Gennesaret

BICKER: **3** war **4** spar, tiff **5** argue, brawl, fight, scrap **6** assail, attack, battle, haggle, rattle **7** dispute, quarrel, wrangle **8** skirmish, squabble **9** altercate **10** contention

BICYCLE: **4** bike **5** cycle, wheel **6** racing, tandem **8** mountain, ten-speed **10** two-wheeler

BID: **3** ask, beg **4** call, pray, warn, wish **5** offer, order, price **6** adjure, beckon, charge, direct, invite, reveal, summon **7** command, declare, request **8** announce, proclaim, proposal

BIDE: **4** face, stay, wait **5** await, dwell, tarry **6** endure, linger, remain, reside, suffer **8** continue, tolerate **9** withstand

BIER: **4** pyre **5** grave **6** coffin, hearse **7** support **10** catafalque

BIG: **3** fat **4** bold, huge, tall, vast **5** adult, bulky, chief, grand, great, gross, hefty, jumbo, large, major, roomy **6** mature, mighty **7** eminent, leading, massive, pompous **8** boastful, enormous, generous, gigantic, imposing, pregnant **9** important **10** altruistic, tremendous **11** heavyweight, magnanimous, outstanding, pretentious

BIG APPLE: **11** New York City

BIG BEND STATE: **9** Tennessee

BIG DIPPER: **9** Ursa Major

BIGFOOT: **4** Omah, Yeti **9** Sasquatch

BIGHEARTED: **7** liberal **8** generous **9** unselfish **10** benevolent, charitable, openhanded

BIGHT: **3** bay **4** bend, gulf, loop, road **5** angle, bayou, curve, inlet, noose **6** corner

BIGOT: **6** racist, zealot **7** fanatic **9** hypocrite **10** intolerant

BIGOTRY: **4** bias **6** racism, sexism **9** ignorance, prejudice

BIG SHOT: **3** VIP **5** mogul **6** bigwig, tycoon **7** magnate **8** somebody **9** celebrity

BILGE: **3** rot **4** bull, scum **5** bulge, trash **7** malarky, rubbish **8** nonsense **10** balderdash

BILK: **3** con, gyp **4** balk, dupe, hoax **5** cheat, dodge, shake, trick **6** escape, fleece **7** deceive, defraud, swindle **8** flimflam **9** bamboozle, frustrate

BILL: **3** act, fee, fin, law, neb, nib, tab **4** beak, buck, card, debt, note, post **5** check, flyer, libel, score **6** charge, dollar, indict, poster, strike **7** invoice, lampoon, mattock, placard, program, sawbuck, statute **8** document, headland, petition **9** greenback, reckoning, statement

BILLET: **3** bar, job, log **4** camp, loop, note, pass, post, slab **5** berth, house, lodge, order, strip **6** ballot, canton, enroll, harbor, letter, notice, office, ticket **7** bearing, pollack, quarter **8** document, dwelling, firewood, position, quarters **9** residence **11** appointment, requisition

BILLIARDS: **4** game, pool

term: **3** cue, run **4** miss, rack **5** break, carom, chalk, masse **6** bridge, cannon, miscue, pocket, string **7** cue ball, cushion, English, scratch **8** rotation **9** eight ball

BILLOW: **3** sea **4** roll, toss, wave **5** crest, float, surge, swell **6** bounce, ripple **7** breaker

BILLY CLUB: **3** bat **5** baton, stick **8** bludgeon **10** nightstick

BIN: **3** box **4** bing, cart, crib **5** crate, frame, hutch, stall, store **6** basket, bunker, hamper, trough, within **9** container **10** receptacle

BINARY: **4** dual **6** double, number **7** twofold

BIND: **3** jam, tie **4** gird, hold, join, tape **5** stick **6** cement, fasten, fetter, hogtie, secure **7** confine, dilemma **8** obligate **9** constrict **10** difficulty **11** predicament

BINDER: **4** band, bond **5** cover, frame, lever **6** folder, girder **8** notebook **9** guarantee

BINDING: **4** belt, cord, rope, tape **5** valid **6** edging, ribbon **8** fastener, limiting **9** mandatory, necessary, stringent **10** astringent, obligatory **11** restraining, restrictive

BINGE: **3** bat, bow, hit **4** blow, bust, soak **5** fling, party, spree **6** affair, bender, cringe **7** blowout, indulge, splurge **8** carousal **9** obeisance **10** indulgence

BIOGRAPHY: **3** bio **4** life, saga **5** diary **6** memoir **7** account, history, journal, recount

BIRD: **3** ani, daw, nun, pie, tit **4** avis, crow, kite, lark, ruff, tern, wren **5** brant, egret, finch, hobby, pewee, raven, robin, snipe, terek, vireo **6** bulbul, falcon, hoopoe, linnet, marten, mocker, oriole, phoebe, plover, shrike, thrush **7** bluejay, bustard, buzzard, catbird, flicker, halcyon, jackdaw, kinglet, peacock, redwing, skylark, sparrow, swallow, tanager, warbler, waxwing **8** airplane, bluebird, boatbill, bobolink, bobwhite, grosbeak, kingbird, pheasant, redstart, starling, thrasher **9** blackbird, bullfinch, chickadee, goldfinch, partridge, sandpiper **10** woodpecker **11** hummingbird

African: **4** coly, fink, taha, tock **6** quelea **7** marabou, touraco **8** unbrette **10** hammerhead

Antarctic: **4** skua **7** penguin

aquatic: **3** auk, cob, ern, mew **4** duck, gull, loon, swan, tern **5** goose, grebe, small, terne **6** petrel **7** penguin **8** dabchick, flamingo **9** cormorant

Arctic: **3** auk **4** skua **6** fulmar **7** dovekey **9** guillemot

Asian: **4** mine, myna **5** pitta **7** courser, lapwing **8** dotterel, parakeet **9** brambling, feng-huang, fenghwang

Australian: **3** emu, roa **4** lory **5** arara, pitta **6** leipoa **7** boobook, bustard, waybung **8** bellbird, bushlark, lorikeet, lyrebird, manucode **9** cassowary, coachwhip, friarbird, frogmouth, pardalote

black: **3** ani, daw, pie **4** crow, rook **5** merle, ouzel, raven **6** magpie, oriole **7** grackle, jackdaw **8** starling

Central American: **3** daw **4** crow, guan, ibis, rave, rook **5** booby, macaw, raven **6** magpie **7** corvine, jacamar **8** curassow, puffbird

combining form: **3** avi **4** orni

concerning: **5** avian, avine **8** ornithic **9** volucrine

crow family: **3** daw, jay, kae, pie **4** craw, rook **5** raven **6** corbie, magpie **7** jackdaw

diving: **3** auk **5** grebe **6** dipper, petrel **9** merganser

European: **3** ani, daw, emu, mag, mew, nun, qua **4** darr, emeu, gled, kite, mall, rook, stag, yite **5** amsel, glede, mavis, merle, ouzel, serin, tarin, terek, terin, whaup **6** avocet, godwit, linnet, loriot, marten, merlin, missel, redcap, whewer, windle, winnel **7** bittern, bustard, haybird, kestrel, martlet, ortolan, sakeret, starnel, witwall **8** bargoose, chepster, dotterel, garganey, nuthatch, redstart, wheybird, whimbrel **9** brambling, gallinule, goldfinch, goosander, peregrine **10** chiffchaff, turtledove, whitterick **11** lammergeier, lammergeyer

extinct: **3** moa **4** dodo, mamo **5** didus **7** offbird **9** solitaire

flightless: **3** emu, moa **4** dodo, kiwi, rhea **6** kakapo, ratite **7** apteryx, ostrich, penguin **9** cassowary

game: **4** duck **5** goose, quail **6** grouse, turkey **8** pheasant, wildfowl, woodcock **9** merganser, partridge

genus: **4** alca, crax, otis **7** certhia **9** apatornis

Hawaiian: **3** ava, iwa **4** iiwi, koae, mamo, moho, omao

Indian: **4** baya **6** bulbul, luggar **7** peacock **8** adjutant

large: **3** emu, moa **4** guan, rhea **5** eagle **6** curlew, willet **7** bustard, ostrich, pelican **8** curassow, shoebill

male: **3** cob, tom **4** cock **5** drake **6** gander **7** peacock, rooster
marsh: **4** coot, rail, sora **5** crane, snipe, stilt
Mexican: **6** jacana, towhee **7** jacamar
mythical: **3** roc **5** hansa **6** simurg **7** phoenix, simurgh **9** feng-huang
New Zealand: **3** ihi, kea, moa, poe, tui **4** kaka, kiwi, kulu, ruru, titi, weka **6** kakapo **7** apteryx **8** morepork, notornis
North American: **4** coot, wren **5** crane, egret, junco, robin, stork, swift **7** bittern **8** flamingo
of paradise: **8** manucode
of peace: **4** dove
of prey: **3** owl **4** hawk, kite **5** eagle, elant, harpy, owlet **6** eaglet, elanet, falcon, osprey, raptor **7** goshawk, vulture **9** accipiter
parts: **3** neb, nib **4** bill, knee, lora, mala **5** lores **6** pecten, pileum, pinion, rostra, syrinx
poultry: **3** hen **4** duck **5** goose **6** pigeon, turkey **7** chicken, rooster **8** pheasant
rare: **8** rara avis
sea: **3** auk, ern, ree **4** erne, gony, gull, rail, ruff, sora, tern **5** eider, snipe, solan, stilt, wader **6** avocet, curlew, gannet, petrel, plover, puffin **7** pelican **9** albatross, sandpiper **10** shearwater
small: **3** tit **4** tody, wren **5** finch, pipit, vireo **6** canary **7** creeper, humming, sparrow **8** starling, titmouse **9** chickadee
songbird: **3** jay, tit **4** crow, lark, wren **5** finch, mavis, robin, shama, vireo **6** canary, linnet, oriole, oscine, shrike, thrush **7** mocking, restart, sparrow **8** bobolink, cardinal, starling **11** nightingale **12** whippoorwill
South American: **3** ara, hia **4** anna, guan, mina, myna, toco **5** chaja, mynah **6** toucan **7** cariama **8** boatbill, caracara, guacharo, hoactzin **9** trumpeter
talking: **4** crow, myna **5** mynah **6** parrot
tropical: **3** ani **4** tody **6** barbet, motmot, quezal, toucan, trogon **7** cacique, manakin, quetzal, waxbill
unfledged: **3** gor **4** eyas **6** gorlin **8** nestling
wading: **4** ibis, rail **5** crane, egret, heron, snipe, stilt, stork **6** avocet, jacana **7** bittern **8** flamingo **9** sandpiper
webbed-foot: **3** auk **4** duck, loon, swan **5** drake, goose, murre **6** avocet, avoset, gander, puffin **9** albatross, razorbill
West Indian: **3** ani **4** tody
young: **4** eyas, gull **5** chick, piper, poult, squab **7** flapper, nestler **8** birdikin, nestling **9** fledgling

BIRTH: **4** bear, stem **5** source, start **6** burden, origin, spring **7** genesis, lineage **8** breeding, dawning, delivery, nascency, nativity, prenatal **9** beginning, naissance, parentage, postnatal **10** extraction **11** renaissance

BIRTH CONTROL: **3** IUD **4** foam, pill **6** condom, sponge **9** diaphragm, vasectomy **10** abstinence **13** contraception

BIRTH FLOWER:
April: **5** daisy
August: **9** gladiolus
December: **10** poinsettia
February: **8** primrose
January: **9** carnation
July: **8** sweet pea
June: **4** rose
March: **6** violet
May: **15** lily of the valley
November: **13** chrysanthemum
October: **6** dahlia
September: **5** aster

BIRTHMARK: **4** mole **5** naeve, nevus **7** blemish, feature, spiloma **10** hemangioma, strawberry

BIRTHRIGHT: **6** legacy **9** privilege **11** inheritance

BIRTHSTONE:
April: **7** diamond **8** sapphire
August: **7** peridot **8** sardonyx **9** carnelian
December: **4** ruby **6** zircon **9** turquoise
February: **8** amethyst
January: **6** garnet
July: **4** onyx, ruby
June: **5** pearl **7** emerald **9** moonstone **11** alexandrite
March: **6** jasper **10** aquamarine, bloodstone
May: **5** agate **7** emerald
November: **5** topaz
October: **4** opal **5** beryl **10** aquamarine, tournaline
September: **8** sapphire **10** chrysolite

BISCUIT: **3** bun, dog **4** bake, cake, roll, snap **5** scone, wafer **6** cookie, muffin **7** cracker, pentile, pretzel **8** hardtack, zwieback

BISECT: **4** fork **5** cross, halve, split **6** divide **7** furcate **8** separate **9** intersect

BISHOP: **4** abba, pope **5** angel **6** archer, cleric, priest **7** pontiff, prelate, primate **8** director, overseer **9** clergyman, patriarch **13** administrator
cap: **5** miter, mitre **7** biretta
district: **7** diocese
robe: **6** chimar **7** chimere
throne: **8** cathedra

BISON: **4** urus **6** wisent **7** aurochs, buffalo

BISTRO: **3** bar **4** cafe **6** tavern **7** barroom, cabaret **9** nightclub **10** restaurant **11** discotheque

BIT: **3** ace, jot, wee **4** atom, bite, chip, curb, iota, item, mite, part, snap, time, tool **5** blade, check, crumb, drill, jiffy, scrap, shred, speck, spell, while **6** bridle, morsel, smidge, splice, tittle, trifle **7** portion, scatche, smidgen **8** fraction, fragment, molecule, particle, quantity **9** restraint

BITE: **3** cut, eat, nip **4** bait, chew, food, gash, gnaw, hold, meal, rust, snap **5** cheat, chomp, decay, pinch, seize, smart, snack, sting, taste, trick, wound **6** crunch, nibble, pierce **7** corrode, impress **8** lacerate, mouthful, puncture **9** allotment

BITING: **3** raw **4** cold **5** sharp **6** bitter, severe **7** caustic, cutting, mordant, nipping, pungent **8** incisive, scathing, stinging **9** corrosive, sarcastic, trenchant **11** penetrating

BITTER: **3** bad **4** acid, keen, sore, sour, tart **5** acrid, bleak, cruel, harsh, irate, nasty, sharp **6** crabby, severe **7** austere, caustic, hostile, painful **8** grievous, piercing, poignant, sardonic, stinging, virulent **9** malicious, offensive, resentful **10** afflictive, unpleasant **11** acrimonious, distasteful

BITTERNESS: **3** rue **5** agony, scorn **6** enmity, malice, rancor **7** anguish **8** acerbity, acrimony, severity **9** animosity, hostility, poignancy, virulence **10** antagonism **11** malevolence

BIVALVE: **4** clam, spat **6** cockle, mussel, oyster **7** mollusk, scallop **10** brachiopod

BIZARRE: **3** odd **4** wild **5** antic, kinky, queer, weird **6** absurd **7** curious, offbeat, strange **8** fanciful, peculiar **9** eccentric, fantastic, grotesque **10** outlandish, ridiculous **11** extravagant

BLAB: **3** gab, rat **4** chat, tell **6** babble, betray, gossip, jabber, reveal, snitch, squeal, tattle **7** blabber, chatter

BLABBERMOUTH: **6** magpie **7** windbag **8** bigmouth, busybody **10** chatterbox, tattletale

BLACK: **3** jet **4** dark, grim, inky, onyx **5** color, dirty, dusky, ebony, murky, negro, pitch, raven, sable, slate, sooty **6** dismal, gloomy, sullen **7** spotted, swarthy, unclean **8** charcoal, mournful, sinister **9** atrocious **10** forbidding, oppressive **12** Afro-American

BLACKBALL: **3** ban, bar **4** shun, snub **5** expel **6** banish **7** boycott, exclude **9** blacklist, ostracize

BLACKEN: **3** tar **4** soot **5** cloud, smear, stain, sully **6** darken, defame, defile, malign **7** slander **8** disgrace **10** stigmatize

BLACKGUARD: **3** cad **4** shag **5** louse **6** rascal **7** lowlife, vagrant, villain **8** vagabond **9** scoundrel

BLACKLIST: **3** ban, bar **4** shun, snub **5** expel **6** banish **7** boycott, exclude **9** blackball, ostracize

BLACK MAGIC: **6** voodoo **7** sorcery **8** wizardry **10** witchcraft

BLACKMAIL: **5** bleed, bribe **6** coerce, extort, payoff, ransom **7** squeeze **8** threaten **9** shakedown

BLACK OUT: **5** erase, faint, shade **6** darken **7** conceal, eclipse **10** censorship

BLACK SEA:
also called: **6** Pontus
cities: **5** Varna **6** Batumi, Burgas, Odessa **8** Istanbul **10** Sevastopol
land: **6** Crimea
linked to: **4** Azov **7** Marmara **8** Bosporus **11** Dardanelles
rivers: **3** Don **5** Kuban **6** Danube **7** Dnieper, Sakarya **8** Dniester

BLACK SHEEP: **7** deviate **9** reprobate

BLACKSMITH: **5** anvil, shoer **6** plover, smithy **10** horseshoer

BLACKWATER STATE: **8** Nebraska

BLADDER: **3** bag, sac **5** pouch **6** pocket **7** blister, inflate, vesicle

BLADE: **3** bit, oar **4** blow, bone, edge, leaf **5** grain, knife, razor, spear, spire, sword **6** cutter, scythe, sickle **7** cutlass, gallant, scapula **9** propeller

BLAH: **4** bunk, dull, flat, yawn **5** bland **6** boring **7** humdrum, tedious **8** lifeless, nonsense **10** monotonous **11** uninspiring

BLAME: **4** call, hurt, onus **5** chide, fault, guilt **6** accuse, charge, impute, rebuke, revile **7** ascribe, censure, condemn, reprove **8** admonish, reproach **9** castigate, challenge, criticize, inculpate, liability **10** accusation **11** culpability, reprobation **12** reprehension

BLAMELESS: **4** good, pure **5** clear **7** perfect, upright **8** innocent, spotless **9** faultless, righteous, unstained **10** immaculate

BLANCH: **4** fade, pale **5** chalk, wince **6** argent, bleach, recoil, whiten **7** lighten **9** whitewash

BLAND: **4** blah, dull, flat, kind, mild, oily, soft **5** suave **6** benign, gentle, smooth, urbane **7** affable, amiable, insipid, lenient **8** gracious, tranquil **9** courteous, tasteless **10** unexciting **12** ingratiating

BLANDISH: **4** coax, urge **5** charm **6** allure, cajole, entice **7** beguile, flatter, wheedle

BLANK: **4** bare, form, idle, shot, skip, void **5** abyss, annul, blind, break, clean, clear, empty, space **6** hollow, vacant **7** muddled **8** omission, unfilled **9** colorless, fruitless, frustrate, scoreless **10** expression

BLANKET: **4** coat, film, mask, wrap **5** cover, layer, quilt, sheet, throw

6 afghan, poncho, serape, stroud 8 coverlet, sweeping 9 comforter

BLARE: 4 boom, peal, roar, toot 5 blast, blaze, noise, shout 6 scream 7 fanfare, trumpet

BLARNEY: 4 coax, line 6 butter, cajole 7 flatter, wheedle 8 flattery 12 exaggeration

BLASÉ: 5 bored, sated, weary 6 casual 7 mundane 8 mondaine, satiated 9 apathetic, unexcited 10 nonchalant 11 indifferent

BLASPHEMY: 7 calumny, cursing, impiety, shaming 8 anathema, scoffing, swearing 9 profanity, sacrilege, violation 10 execration 11 irreverence, malediction 12 vituperation

BLAST: 3 pop 4 bang, blow, bomb, gale, gust, ruin, wind 5 party, shell, stunt 6 attack, blight 7 blowout, bluster, explode, shatter, shindig, trumpet 8 dynamite, lambaste, outburst, proclaim 9 criticize, discharge, explosion 10 detonation

BLATANT: 4 loud 5 gaudy, gross, noisy, overt, vocal 6 brazen, coarse, vulgar 7 obvious 8 brawling, flagrant 9 clamorous, deafening, obtrusive, shameless 10 vociferous 11 conspicuous

BLATHER: 4 stir 6 babble 7 blither, chatter, prattle 8 nonsense

BLAZE: 4 burn, fire, glow, rush, shot 5 flame, flare, flash, glare, gleam, glory, shine, torch 7 bonfire, declare, pioneer, sparkle 9 coruscate, firebrand, holocaust 10 brilliance, effulgence, illuminate

BLAZER: 4 coat 6 jacket

BLAZON: 4 deck, show 5 adorn, blare, boast 6 depict, shield 7 declare, display, exhibit, publish 8 announce, inscribe, proclaim 9 broadcast, embellish 11 description

BLEACH: 3 sun 4 fade 6 blanch, purify, whiten 7 decolor, lighten 8 etiolate

BLEACHERS: 5 boxes, seats, stand 7 benches 8 scaffold 10 grandstand

BLEAK: 3 dim, raw 4 blay, cold, dour, gray, grim, pale 6 barren, bitter, dismal, dreary, gloomy, pallid 7 austere, cutting, joyless 8 blighted, desolate 10 depressing, melancholy

BLEAR: 3 dim, fog 4 blur, dull 5 faint 6 darken 7 deceive, mislead, obscure 8 protrude

BLEAT: 3 baa, cry 4 blat, fuss 5 gripe, whine 7 blather, bluster

BLEED: 3 run 4 flow, gush, leak, pity 5 drain, exude 6 extort, fleece 7 agonize, exhaust, extract, overtax 9 blackmail 10 hemorrhage

BLEMISH: 3 mar, zit 4 blot, blur, dent, flaw, hurt, mark, mole, scar, slur, spot, vice, want, wart 5 blame, crack, fault, speck, stain, sully, taint 6 blotch, breach, defame, defect, impair, injure, pimple, smirch, stigma 7 blister, default, failing, freckle 8 pockmark 9 birthmark, blackhead, deformity, discredit, disfigure 10 defacement, deficiency 12 imperfection

BLEND: 3 fit, mix 4 blot, brew, fuse, join, meld 5 blind, cream, merge, shade, spoil, stain, unite 6 dazzle, fusion, mingle 7 combine, mixture, pollute 8 compound 9 associate, commingle, harmonize, integrate 10 amalgamate, concoction, synthesize 11 incorporate

BLESS: 4 give 5 adore, cross, extol, favor, grace, grant, guard, thank

6 anoint, hallow, praise 7 absolve, approve, baptize, confirm, glorify, protect 8 dedicate, eulogize, preserve, sanctify 9 celebrate 10 consecrate, felicitate

BLESSED: 4 holy 5 happy 6 divine, joyful, sacred 7 endowed, exalted, revered 8 benedict, blissful, hallowed 9 venerated 10 sanctified 11 consecrated

BLESSING: 4 boon, gift, okay 5 grace 6 bounty, praise, thanks 7 benison, consent, godsend, worship 8 approval, felicity, windfall 10 benedicite 11 benediction

BLIGHT: 3 mar, nip 4 bane, kill, ruin, rust, smut 5 blast, frost, spoil 6 plague, wither 7 cripple, destroy, disease, eyesore 9 frustrate 10 affliction

BLIMP: 5 fatso 7 airship, balloon 8 zeppelin

BLIND: 4 dark, daze, dull, hood, snow 5 blank, blend, cloak, color, decoy, front, shade 6 ambush, bisson, dazzle, hidden, myopic, screen, secret 7 aimless, bandage, benight, eclipse, eyeless, obscure, shutter, unaware 8 hoodwink, ignorant, involved, outshine, unseeing 9 concealed, deceitful, defective, insensate, senseless, sightless 10 camouflage, incomplete, inebriated, misleading 11 intoxicated, nearsighted 12 shortsighted

BLIND ALLEY: 7 dead end, impasse 8 blockade, cul-de-sac 10 standstill

BLINDER: 4 flab, hood 5 bluff, shade 9 blindfold 11 obstruction

BLINDFOLD: 4 dark 5 blink 6 darken 7 bandage, blinder, obscure 8 heedless, reckless 9 concealed

BLINK: 3 bat 4 omit, peek, shun, wink 5 blush, flash, gleam, shine, trick 6 bypass, falter, glance, ignore, squint 7 condone, flicker, glimmer, neglect, nictate, sparkle, twinkle 8 overlook 9 blindfold

BLINTZ: 5 crepe 7 pancake

BLIP: 3 tap 4 echo, spot 6 censor, glitch

BLISS: 3 joy 4 Eden 5 glory 6 heaven, utopia 7 delight, ecstasy, gladden, rapture 8 euphoria, gladness, paradise, pleasure 9 happiness 10 jubilation 11 contentment

BLISSFUL: 4 holy 5 happy 6 blithe, divine, dreamy, elated 7 blessed 8 ecstatic, euphoric 9 enchanted, glorified

BLISTER: 3 sac 4 beat, blob, boil, cyst, lash 5 blain 6 bubble, canker, scorch 7 abscess, vesicle 8 lambaste, vesicate 9 castigate

BLITHE: 3 gay 4 glad 5 bonny, happy, jolly, merry 6 jovial, joyous, lively 7 gleeful, jocular, radiant, winsome 8 carefree, cheerful 9 vivacious

BLITZ: 4 raid 6 attack, red dog, strike 8 football 9 offensive 10 blitzkrieg 11 bombardment

BLIZZARD: 4 blow, gale, wind 6 squall 8 snowfall, whiteout 9 snowstorm

BLOAT: 5 puffy, swell 6 expand 7 balloon, inflate

BLOATED: 6 stuffy, turgid 7 pompous, swollen 8 arrogant

BLOB: 3 wen 4 blot, boil, daub, drop, lump, mark, mass 6 pimple, splash 7 blemish, blister, globule, pustule, splotch

BLOC: 4 ring 5 cabal, group, party, union 6 clique 7 faction 8 alliance 9 coalition 11 combination

BLOCK: **3** bar, cob, dam, row **4** cake, clog, cube, fill, foil, head, plug, road, stop **5** annex, check, deter, nudge, spike, stump **6** hamper, hinder, impede, oblong, oppose, square, street, stymie, thwart **7** buckler, inhibit, outline, prevent **8** blockade, obstacle, obstruct **9** barricade, frustrate, hindrance, intercept, stonewall **11** obstruction

BLOCKADE: **3** bar, dam **4** snag, wall **5** beset, block, fence, siege **7** barrier, closure, embargo **8** obstruct **9** barricade, beleaguer, roadblock **10** checkpoint **11** obstruction, restriction

BLOCKHEAD: **3** ass, oaf **4** bust, dolt, fool, putz **5** chump, dummy, dunce, idiot, moron, ninny **6** noodle **7** halfwit, tomfool **8** beefhead, bonehead, hardhead, numskull **9** harebrain, screwball **10** nincompoop **11** knucklehead

BLOND, BLONDE: **4** fair, gold **5** color, light, sandy, straw **6** flaxen, golden, yellow **8** bleached **9** towheaded

BLOOD: **3** kin, red, sap **4** blue, cell, clot, gore, life, race, type **5** fluid, serum, stock, white **6** family, friend **7** brother, kinship, kinsman, lineage **8** pedigree, pressure, relation, vitality **9** lifeblood, poisoning **10** hemoglobin

BLOODBATH: **3** war **5** purge **7** carnage **8** massacre **9** slaughter

BLOODLESS: **4** cold, pale **6** anemic, pallid, torpid **8** lifeless **9** unfeeling **11** passionless

BLOODSHED: **4** gore **5** death **6** murder **7** killing **8** violence

BLOODSUCKER: **4** tick **5** leech **6** sponge **7** vampire **8** parasite **10** freeloader

BLOODTHIRSTY: **5** cruel **6** carnal, savage **7** vicious **8** barbaric, ruthless, sanguine **9** murderous

BLOODY: **4** gory **6** damned **7** crimson, wounded **8** bleeding **9** cutthroat, ferocious, murderous

BLOOM: **3** bud **4** blow, grow **5** blush, flare, flush **6** floret, flower, luster, sprout, thrive **7** blossom, develop **8** flourish

BLOOPER: **4** goof **5** boner, error **6** bungle **7** blunder, mistake

BLOSSOM: **3** bud **4** blob, grow, open **5** bloom, spike **6** flower, mature **7** burgeon, develop, prosper **8** flourish **10** effloresce

BLOT: **3** dry, mar **4** blob, blue, daub, flaw, onus, soil, spot **5** blend, smear, speck, stain, sully **6** absorb, blotch, defect, efface, impair, smudge, smutch **7** blemish, eclipse, obscure, tarnish **8** discolor, disgrace, reproach **10** obliterate, stigmatize

BLOTCH: **3** dab **4** acne, blot, mark, spot **5** patch, smear, stain **6** smirch, smudge, stigma **7** blemish, splotch **8** eruption

BLOUSE: **5** middy, shirt, smock, tunic **7** casaque

BLOW: **3** dub, fan, hit, jab, pop, rap, wap **4** baff, bang, bash, beat, belt, brag, buff, bump, chap, conk, cuff, daud, drub, gale, gasp, goof, huff, jolt, lash, pant, plug, puff, scud, slam, slap, slug, sock, toot, wind **5** blast, bloom, boast, botch, break, burst, clink, clout, clump, draft, flack, flick, impel, knock, punch, shock, slipe, sound, spend, split, storm, swipe, thump, treat, whack **6** betray, bounce, buffet, depart, exhale, expand, flower, frolic, stream, wallop **7** assault, attaint, bluster, boaster, breathe, destroy, inflate, publish, setback, shatter, trumpet **8** boasting, calamity, confound, disaster, disclose, squander **10** concussion, misfortune

BLOWHARD: **6** gascon **7** boaster, windbag **8** braggart

BLOWOUT: **4** bash, leak, meal **5** feast, party, spree **6** valley **7** rupture, shindig

BLOW UP: **4** bomb, rage, rave **7** balloon, explode, inflate **8** dynamite, outburst **10** exaggerate

BLUBBER: **3** cry, fat **4** blub, flab, wail, weep **5** swell, thick, whale, whine **6** flitch, nettle, seethe **7** swollen, whimper

BLUDGEON: **3** bat, hit **4** club **5** stick **6** coerce, cudgel **7** clobber **9** truncheon

BLUE: **3** low, sad, sky **4** aqua, bice, glum, lewd, navy, teal **5** azure, color, ocean, royal **6** cobalt, gloomy, indigo **7** celeste, gentian **8** cerulean, dejected, downcast **9** turquoise **10** despondent, melancholy

BLUE BLOOD: **5** elite, noble **9** socialite **10** aristocrat

BLUEBONNET: **3** cap **4** Scot **8** Scotsman **10** cornflower

BLUEGRASS STATE: **8** Kentucky

BLUE HEN STATE: **8** Delaware

BLUE LAW STATE: **11** Connecticut

BLUE-PENCIL: **3** cut **4** edit **6** delete, revise **7** abridge **8** condense

BLUEPRINT: **3** map **4** plan **5** chart, draft **6** sketch **7** diagram **8** strategy **9** schematic

BLUES: **5** dumps, music **10** depression, melancholy

BLUFF: **4** bank, brag, fool, hill, hoax, rude, sham **5** blunt, boast, burly, cliff, fraud, front, gruff, trick **6** abrupt, assume, candid, facade **7** deceive, pretend **8** impolite **9** bamboozle, outspoken

BLUNDER: **3** err **4** balk, bull, flub, goof, mess, slip, stir **5** boner, botch, break, error, fault **6** blotch, boggle, bumble, bungle, muddle, wallow **7** blooper, confuse, failure, mistake, stumble **8** flounder **9** mismanage, oversight **11** disturbance

BLUNT: **4** bald, curt, dull, flat, numb **5** bluff, frank, plain **6** dampen, deaden, obtuse, stupid, weaken **7** rounded **8** explicit, hebetate **9** depressed, downright, pointless **10** point-blank **11** insensitive

BLUR: **3** dim, fog **4** blob, blot, mask, soil, spot **5** blear, cloud, smear, stain, sully, taint **6** smudge **7** blemish, confuse **9** disfigure **10** stigmatize

BLURB: **4** plug, puff, spot **5** brief **12** announcement, commendation **13** advertisement

BLUSH: **4** glow, pink, rose **5** color, gleam, rouge, tinge **6** glance, redden **7** crimson **10** appearance

BLUSHING: **3** coy, red **4** rosy **6** modest **7** bashful **8** flushing **9** rosaceous **11** embarrassed

BLUSTER: **4** blow, brag, huff, rage, rant, rave, roar **5** blast, boast, bully, gloat, noise, storm **6** babble, bellow, tumult **7** blubber, swagger **8** threaten **9** confusion **10** intimidate, turbulence

BOAR: **3** hog, sus **4** gore, wild **5** swine **6** barrow, hogget **8** sanglier **9** hoggaster

BOARD: **3** bed **4** eats, food, keep, slat **5** brass, enter, house, lodge, meals, mount, panel, plank, table **6** embark, shield **7** cabinet, council **8** approach, tribunal **9** authority **10** commission, management, provisions **11** accommodate

BOAST: **3** gab, own **4** blow, brag, crow, rave **5** exult, glory, strut, vaunt **6** bounce, clamor, flaunt, shovel **7** bluster, clamour, display, glorify **8** flourish **9** gasconade

BOASTER: **5** skite **6** crower, gascon **7** bouncer, cracker, egotist, ruffler **8** blowhard, braggart, rodomont

BOASTFUL: **3** big **5** cocky **7** pompous **8** arrogant, bragging **9** conceited, gasconade, loudmouth **11** pretentious, rodomontade, swellheaded

BOAT: **3** ark, cat, row, tub, tug **4** bark, brig, dory, junk, life, raft, sail, scow, ship, skag, tack, trow **5** barge, bully, canoe, coble, craft, ferry, kayak, ketch, liner, motor, river, scull, shell, skiff, sloop, steam, yacht **6** cruise, cutter, dinghy, garvey, vessel **7** gondola, inboard, lighter, scooter, steamer **8** outboard, schooner **9** catamaran, submarine, transport **10** Hovercraft, watercraft

BOATMAN: **4** mate **5** poler **6** barger **7** hobbler, huffler, oarsman, paddler **8** deckhand **9** gondolier, yachtsman

BOAZ:
father: **6** Salmon
son: **4** Obed
wife: **4** Ruth

BOB: **3** bow, cut, hop, tap **4** ball, buff, clip, duck, jeer, jest, leap, mock, sled, worm **5** bunch, dance, float, shake, trick **6** bounce, buffet, curtsy, hairdo, seesaw, weight, wobble **7** haircut, pendant, refrain **8** shilling

BOBBIE, BOBBY: **3** cop **4** bull **6** copper, peeler **7** officer **8** flatfoot **9** policeman

BOBBIN: **3** pin **4** coil, cord, reel **5** braid, quill, spool **7** ratchet, spindle **8** cylinder

BODE: **4** omen, stop **5** augur, offer **6** herald **7** message, predict, signify **8** forecast, foreshow, foretell, indicate

BODILY: **5** solid **6** actual, carnal **7** fleshly, sensual, somatic, totally **8** corporal, entirely, physical, tangible **10** completely **11** substantial

BODY: **4** bulk, core, form, hull, mass, nave, stem **5** being, flesh, frame, group, stiff, torso, trunk **6** corpse, extent, object, person **7** anatomy, cadaver, carcass, company, remains **8** argument, beefcake, fuselage, heavenly, majority **9** substance **10** assemblage, foundation **11** association, corporation

BODY OF WATER: **3** bay, sea **4** gulf, lake, pond **5** ocean, river **6** lagoon **7** channel **9** reservoir

BOG: **3** bug, fen, gog **4** bold, cess, mire, moor, ooze, sink, sump **5** marsh, swamp **6** morass, slough **8** quagmire, wetlands **9** everglade

BOG DOWN: **4** halt, mire **5** delay, stall **6** impede

BOGGLE: **3** jib, shy **4** balk, foil, muff **5** alarm, botch, scare **6** baffle, bungle, falter **7** blunder, perplex, stagger **8** frighten, hesitate **9** dissemble, dumbfound, embarrass, overwhelm

BOGUS: **4** fake, sham **5** false, phony **6** forged, pseudo **8** spurious **9** imitation **10** artificial, fictitious **11** counterfeit

BOHEMIAN: **4** arty **6** hippie **7** beatnik **8** maverick **9** eccentric **10** dilettante **13** nonconformist

BOIL: **4** blob, burn, cook, rage, sore, stew **5** anger, botch, poach, steam **6** bubble, burble, fester, pimple, seethe, simmer **7** abscess, inflame **10** effervesce

BOILER: **16** copper, geyser, kettle, retort **7** furnace **8** cauldron

BOISTEROUS: **4** loud, rude **5** burly, noisy, rough, rowdy **6** coarse, stormy, strong, unruly **7** furious, massive, roaring, violent **8** vehement **9** clamorous, excessive, excitable, turbulent **10** blustering, disorderly, unyielding, vociferous **11** loudmouthed, mischievous

BOLD: **3** big **4** rude, wise **5** bardy, brash, brave, fresh, hardy, large, manly, steep, stout **6** abrupt, brassy, brazen, bright, daring, fierce, heroic, spunky, strong **7** assured, dashing, defiant, forward, haughty, massive, valiant **8** arrogant, colorful, fearless, immodest, impudent, insolent, intrepid, powerful, resolute, striking, unafraid **9** audacious, bodacious, confident, dauntless, imprudent, undaunted **10** courageous **11** adventurous **12** presumptuous

BOLDNESS: **4** grit **5** nerve, valor, vigor **6** daring **7** bravery, courage **8** audacity **9** assurance, hardihood, hardiness **10** brazenness, confidence **11** intrepidity, presumption

BOLIVIA:

capital: **5** La Paz, Sucre
cities: **5** Oruro **6** Potosi **9** Santa Cruz **10** Cochabamba
continent: **12** South America
ethnic groups: **6** Aymara **7** Quechua
features: **5** Andes, Cuzco **9** Altiplano
languages: **6** Aymara **7** Quechua, Spanish
monetary unit: **9** boliviano
native: **8** Bolivian
water: **5** Poopo **8** Titicaca

BOLSTER: **3** aid, pad **4** help, prop **5** boost **6** assist, pillow, uphold **7** cushion, support **8** maintain **9** reinforce **10** strengthen

BOLT: **3** bar, nut, pin, rod, run **4** beat, dart, flee, lock, rush **5** close, flash, gorge, latch, rivet, shaft **6** decamp, desert, devour, fasten, flight, refine, secure, sprint, strong, toggle **7** consume, missile, shackle, thunder **8** fastener, separate, stampede **9** lightning

BOMB: **3** dud, egg **4** atom, bust, flop, pass **5** blare, shell **6** device, fiasco **7** bombard, destroy, failure, grenade, nuclear **8** hydrogen **10** projectile

BOMBARD: **4** bomb, pelt **5** beset, blitz, pound, shell **6** attack, batter, strike **7** assault, besiege **10** blitzkrieg

BOMBAST: **3** pad **4** rage, rant, rave **5** stuff **6** cotton, padded **7** bluster, stuffed **8** boasting, rhapsody, rhetoric **9** turgidity **12** exaggeration

BOMBASTIC: **5** tumid, vocal, wordy **6** fluent, heroic, turgid **7** flowery, pompous, ranting **8** inflated **9** flatulent, grandiose, overblown **10** balderdash, rhetorical **11** highfalutin

BONA FIDE: **4** real **5** legal **7** genuine **9** authentic **10** legitimate

BONANZA: **4** mine, mint **6** eureka **7** jackpot **8** eldorado, windfall

BONANZA STATE: **7** Montana

BONBON: **5** candy, cream, sweet **6** dainty **7** caramel **8** confetti

BOND: **3** tie, vow **4** bail, blue, duty, knot, link **5** bound, chain, irons, union **6** binder, cement, engage, fasten, surety **7** network, shackle **8** adhesive, contract, covenant, ligament, marriage, security **9** agreement, composure, guarantee **10** allegiance, constraint, friendship, obligation **11** association, certificate

BONDAGE: **4** yoke **6** chains, thrall **7** helotry, serfdom, slavery **9** captivity, restraint, servitude **11** enslavement

BONE: **3** rib **4** coxa, ulna **5** dorsa, femur, ilium, jugal, malar, nasal, pubis, skull, talus, tibia **6** carpal, cervix, chorax, coccyx, fibula, lumbar, pelvis, radius, sacrum, tarsal **7** cranium, frontal, humerus, ischium, maxilla, patella, scapula, sternum **8** clavicle, mandible, parietal, phalange, sphenoid, temporal **9** calcaneus, occipital, vertebrae, zygomatic **10** acetabulum, astragalus, metacarpal, metatarsal

BONEHEAD: **4** clod, fool **5** dunce, idiot, moron **6** nitwit **8** imbecile **9** blockhead **10** nincompoop

BONER: **4** goof **5** error **6** bungle **7** blooper, blunder, faux pas, mistake

BONEYARD: **4** dump **5** grave, stock, store **8** cemetery

BONNET: **3** cap, hat **4** blue, hood **5** cover, decoy **6** capote, string **7** chapeau, coronet **8** headgear **9** headdress

BONNY: **3** gay **4** fair, fine **5** merry, plump **6** pretty, strong **7** healthy **8** handsome **9** beautiful, ravishing **11** goodlooking

BONUS: **3** tip **4** gift, perk **5** award, bribe, gravy, prize **6** reward **7** benefit, premium, signing, subsidy **8** dividend, gratuity **9** allowance **12** compensation

BON VIVANT: **5** sport **7** epicure, gourmet **8** hedonist, sybarite

BONY: **4** hard, lank, lean, thin **5** lanky, stiff, tough **6** skinny **7** angular, scrawny

BOO: **4** hiss, hoot, jeer **5** decry **6** heckle, holler **7** catcall **9** raspberry

BOOB: **3** ass **4** fool, goof, goon, jerk **5** dunce, idiot **6** nitwit **7** fathead **8** imbecile

BOOBY HATCH: **3** can **4** jail **6** asylum, cooler **8** hoosegow, madhouse

BOODLE: **4** bilk, loot, swag **5** cheat, crowd, graft **6** chisel **7** plunder **8** flimflam

BOOHOO: **3** coo, cry, sob **4** fret, hoot, weep **6** snivel

BOOK: **3** log **4** bill, hire, note, opus, text **5** album, atlas, bible, diary, folio, novel, story **6** arrest, charge, indict, manual, primer, record, tablet, volume **7** catalog, fiction, reserve, writing **8** brochure, document, register, schedule **9** hardcover, paperback **10** dictionary, nonfiction

BOOKISH: **7** learned **8** academic, educated, highbrow, pedantic **9** scholarly

BOOKKEEPER: **3** CPA **5** clerk **7** auditor **10** accountant

BOOM: **3** jib **4** bang, clap, grow, pole, roar **5** blast, crash **6** thrive, upturn **7** explode, resound, support, thunder **8** flourish **9** expansion **10** prosperity

BOOMERANG: **5** kalie, kiley, wango **6** recoil **7** rebound, reverse **8** backfire, backlash, ricochet **10** projectile

BOOMER STATE: **8** Oklahoma

BOON: **3** fun, gay **4** gift, good, kind **5** favor, grant, merry **6** benign, bounty, jovial, prayer **7** benefit, festive, godsend, present **8** blessing, donation, intimate, offering, windfall **9** advantage, congenial, favorable **10** prosperous

BOONDOCKS: **4** bush **6** sticks **7** boonies, country **9** backwoods **10** hinterland **11** wildnerness

BOOR: **3** cad, oaf **4** clod, dork, goon, hick, lout **5** churl, clown, slave, yokel **6** lummox, rustic **7** buffoon, peasant, villein **9** barbarian, roughneck **10** clodhopper, countryman

BOORISH: **4** rude **5** crude, gawky, rough **6** clumsy, coarse, vulgar **7** awkward, uncivil, uncouth **8** churlish, cloddish, clownish, inurbane **9** bourgeois **10** uncultured, uneducated, ungracious, unpolished

BOOST: **3** aid **4** abet, back, help, laud, lift, plug, push, rise **5** exalt, hoist, raise **6** assist, foster, praise **7** advance, amplify, commend, elevate, endorse, further, improve, promote, upgrade **8** increase **9** encourage, promotion

BOOT: **3** cut **4** camp, fire, help, kick, oust, punt, shoe, sock **5** avail, eject, evict, spoil **6** bootie, buskin, casing, cowboy, fumble, novice, thrill, waders **7** benefit, dismiss **8** beginner, covering, footwear, galoshes **9** advantage, discharge, dismissal

BOOTH: **3** box **4** nook, shed, shop **5** cabin, crame, house, stall, stand, table **9** cubbyhole

BOOTLEG: **5** booze, hooch **6** liquor **7** alcohol, illegal, illicit, smuggle **9** moonshine **11** clandestine

BOOTLESS: **4** vain **6** futile **7** useless **9** fruitless, worthless **10** unavailing

BOOTLICK: **4** fawn **5** toady **6** grovel **7** flatter **9** brownnose

BOOTY: **4** gain, loot, swag **5** graft, prize **6** spoils **7** pillage, plunder **8** pickings

BOOZE: **4** bout, grog **5** drink, hooch, spree **6** liquor **7** alcohol **8** cocktail

BOOZER: **4** lush, wino **5** drunk, toper **6** sponge **8** drunkard **9** alcoholic

BORDER: **3** end, hem, lip, rim **4** curb, dado, edge, line, side, trim **5** bound, braid, brink, coast, costa, flank, frame, plait, skirt, strip **6** edging, fringe, impale, margin **7** outline **8** boundary, frontier, neighbor, outskirt, sideline, surround **9** extremity, periphery, threshold

BORDERLINE: **5** vague, verge **7** inexact, unclear **8** marginal **9** ambiguous, undecided **10** ambivalent

BORE: **3** bit, irk, tap **4** cloy, drag, hole, poke, size, tide, tire, tool, wimp **5** annoy, drill, gauge, prick, punch **6** bummer, pierce, thrust, tunnel **7** caliber, fatigue **8** nuisance **9** penetrate, perforate

BOREAS: **4** wind **7** norther
daughter: **9** Cleopatra
father: **8** Astraeus
mother: **3** Eos
son: **5** Zetes **6** Calais

BOREDOM: **6** apathy, tedium **7** fatigue **8** dullness, lethargy **9** weariness **11** disinterest

BORING: **3** dry **4** drag, flat **6** tiring **7** humdrum, irksome, mundane, tedious **8** piercing, tiresome **9** colorless, wearisome **11** displeasing

BORN: **6** inbred, innate **7** hatched, nascent, natural **8** inherent **9** delivered **10** congenital

BORNE: **4** rode **6** braved, narrow **7** carried, endured **8** produced **9** tolerated

BOROUGH: **4** burg, town **6** castle, county, parish **7** citadel, village **8**

district, fortress, precinct, township

BORROW: **3** tap, use **4** copy, loan, pawn, take **5** adopt, mooch, steal **6** pirate, pledge, surety **7** hostage **10** plagiarize, substitute

BOSOM: **4** bust, dear **5** chest, close, heart **6** breast, circle, desire **7** beloved, embrace **8** emotions, intimate **9** cherished **11** inclination

BOSS: **3** bur, pad **4** head **5** bully, chief, order, owner **6** direct, groovy, leader, manage, master, shield **7** awesome, cushion, foreman, headman, kingpin, manager **8** director, employer, overseer, superior **9** excellent, supervise **10** politician, supervisor

BOSSY: **3** cow **10** tyrannical **11** dictatorial, domineering

BOTANY: **7** ecology **8** cytology, genetics **12** horticulture

BOTCH: **3** err, mar, mux **4** blow, fail, goof, mend, mess, sore **5** spoil **6** boggle, bumble, bungle, fiasco, fumble, jumble **7** blunder

BOTH: **3** two **4** pair **5** alike **6** couple **7** equally

BOTHER: **3** ado, ail, bug, nag, try, vex **4** fret, fuss, goad **5** annoy, taunt, tease, upset, worry **6** badger, harass, pester, puzzle, tamper **7** confuse, disturb, perplex, provoke, trouble **8** bewilder, headache, irritate, nuisance **9** aggravate

BOTSWANA:
capital: **8** Gaborone
cities: **6** Serowe, Tutume **8** Mahalpye **11** Francistown
continent: **6** Africa
ethnic groups: **6** Tswana **7** Kalanga
features: **5** Orapa **7** Jwaneng **12** Makgadikgadi **13** Okavango Swamp **14** Kalahari Desert
languages: **7** English **8** Setswana
monetary unit: **4** pula
water: **5** Ngami **8** Okavango

BOTTLE: **3** jug **4** ewer, vial **5** ampul, cruet, flask, glass, phial **6** carafe, carboy, flagon, magnum, vessel **7** canteen **8** decanter, preserve, restrain **9** container

BOTTLENECK: **3** jam **4** clog **7** barrier, impasse **8** gridlock **10** congestion

BOTTOM: **3** bed, can **4** base, butt, foot, root, rump, seat **5** abyss, basal, basis, dregs, fanny, floor **6** ground **7** bedrock, essence, lowland, surface **8** buttocks, derriere, sediment **9** underside **10** foundation, groundwork, underneath

BOUGH: **3** arm, leg **4** limb, twig **5** sprig **6** branch **8** offshoot

BOULEVARD: **3** way **4** drag, road **6** avenue, street **7** highway **9** concourse

BOUNCE: **3** bob, hop **4** fire, jump, leap, sack **5** boast, bound, eject, evict, knock, scold, thump, vault **6** spirit, spring, strike **7** rebound **8** vitality **9** discharge, expulsion, terminate **10** elasticity, resilience

BOUND: **3** end **4** area, bind, bond, dart, edge, jump, leap, ramp, skip, stem **5** going, limit, sting, tiled, vault, verge **6** border, bounce, define, domain, finite, fringe, hurdle, liable, prance, spring **7** barrier, certain, closure, confine, dressed, rebound, secured **8** boundary, confined, destined, enclosed, frontier, prepared, restrict, shackled **9** committed, compelled, inhibited, obligated **10** indentured **11** apprenticed, constrained, termination **12** circumscribe

BOUNDARY: **3** end, rim **4** dole, edge, line, term, wall **5** ambit, fence, hedge, limit, march, verge **6** border, define, extent, margin **7**

barrier, horizon **8** confines, environs, frontier, precinct **9** perimeter **11** termination

BOUNDLESS: **4** vast **5** great **6** untold **7** endless, eternal **8** infinite, unending **9** limitless, unlimited **10** unconfined, unmeasured **11** everlasting, measureless **12** immeasurable

BOUNTIFUL: **4** free, good, lush, rich **5** ample **6** galore, lavish, plenty **7** aplenty, fertile, liberal **8** abundant, generous **9** plentiful

BOUNTY: **3** fee, pay **4** boon, gift **5** award, bonus, grant **6** reward, virtue **7** charity, largess, premium, present, subsidy **8** donation, goodness, gratuity, kindness **9** allowance **10** generosity **11** munificence

BOUQUET: **4** aura, balm, odor, posy **5** aroma, spray **7** corsage, essence, nosegay, perfume **9** fragrance **10** compliment **11** arrangement, boutonniere

BOURGEOIS: **6** common **7** boorish **8** mediocre, ordinary **11** commonplace, middle-class **12** capitalistic

BOUT: **3** job **4** fray, term, turn **5** binge, booze, clash, essay, fight, match, round, siege, spell, spree, trial **6** attack, period **7** attempt, carouse, circuit, contest **8** conflict

BOW: **3** arc, dip, nod, tie **4** arch, bend, bent, cave, duck, fold, knot, stem, turn **5** cross, crush, curve, defer, stoop, yield **6** archer, buckle, curtsy, fiddle, ribbon, salaam, submit, weapon **7** concede, inflict, rainbow, succumb **8** crescent, greeting

BOWED: **4** bent **6** arched, curved **7** bulging, hunched, rounded

BOWELS: **4** guts **5** belly, colon **6** depths **7** innards, stomach **8** entrails **10** intestines

BOWER: **4** jack, nook **5** abode, arbor, joker, knave **6** alcove, anchor **7** chamber, cottage, pergola, retreat, shelter **8** dwelling

BOWL: **3** cup, pan, urn **5** arena, basin **6** beaker, crater, saucer, tureen, vessel **7** helping, stadium **9** container **12** amphitheater

BOWLING:
place: **5** alley
terms: **5** frame, spare, split **6** strike **7** ninepin, skittle, tenpins

BOX: **3** bin, hit, lug **4** cage, case, crib, cuff, cyst, duke, pack, seat, slap, slug, spar, till, tray, wrap **5** barge, boist, caddy, chest, clout, crate, fight, punch, stall, trunk **6** buffet, bunker, carton, casket, coffin, square, strike **7** confine, enclose, package **9** container, fisticuff **10** receptacle

BOXING:
official: **7** referee
terms: **3** jab, pug, TKO **4** blow, bout **5** feint, glove, match, punch **6** bantam **7** fighter, sparrer **8** knockout, pugilism, pugilist **10** fisticuffs **11** heavyweight, lightweight **12** middleweight **13** prizefighting

BOY: **3** bat, lad, son **4** buck, chap, page **5** buddy, child, knave, valet, water, youth **6** junior, nipper, rascal, urchin **7** servant **9** youngster

BOYCOTT: **4** shun **5** avoid **6** reject **7** embargo, exclude, protest **9** blackball, blacklist **10** ostracized

BOYFRIEND: **4** beau, date **5** flame, lover **6** fellow, fiance, steady **9** inamorato

BRACE: **3** arm, leg, tie **4** bind, case, gird, mark, pair, prop, stay **5** nerve, steel **6** clench, couple, crutch, fasten, rafter, splint, steady **7** fortify, stiffen, support **8** buttress **9** reinforce, suspender **10** strengthen

BRACELET: **4** band, ring **5** chain, charm **6** armlet, bangle **7** trinket **8** handcuff

BRACING: **5** brisk, crisp, tonic **8** arousing **10** quickening, refreshing **11** stimulating **12** exhilarating, invigorating

BRACKET: **4** join, prop **5** class, group, level, shelf **6** couple, sconce **7** compare, fixture **8** category, classify

BRAG: **4** blow, crow, defy, huff **5** boast, exult, strut, vaunt **6** bounce, hotdog **7** display, swagger **8** braggart, flourish, pretense, threaten **9** gasconade **10** exaggerate

BRAGGART: **4** brag **5** boast **6** crower, gasbag, gascon **7** boaster, cracker, egotist, windbag **8** bigmouth, blowhard, rodomont **9** loudmouth **11** braggadocio

BRAID: **3** cue **4** band, knit, lace, mesh, trim **5** fancy, pleat, start, tress, trick, twine, twist, weave **6** border, moment, plight, ribbon, snatch, string **7** entwine, pigtail **8** ornament, reproach, soutache, trimming **9** deceitful, interlace **10** interweave

BRAIN: **4** bean, mind, wits **5** skull **6** psyche **7** cranium **8** cerebrum **9** intellect

parts: **3** pia **4** alba, aula, dura, iter, lura **6** cortex **8** cerebrum, meninges **10** encephalon, gray matter **11** pericranium

related: **8** cerebral **10** cerebellar, encephalic

BRAINLESS: **4** dumb **5** silly **6** stupid **7** asinine, foolish, witless **8** mindless **9** senseless **11** thoughtless

BRAINWASH: **5** alter **7** control, convert **8** convince, persuade **9** influence

BRAKE: **4** curb, drag, rein, skid, slow, stop **5** block, check, delay **6** anchor, bridle, hinder, impede, retard **10** decelerate

BRAMBLE: **4** burr, bush, sage **5** brier, rough, shrub, thorn **6** nettle **8** prickers

BRANCH: **3** arm, bow, leg, out **4** bush, fork, limb, part, snag, spur, stem, twig **5** annex, bough, creek, sprig **6** bureau, divide, member, outlet, stream **7** diverge, section **8** district, offshoot **10** department

BRAND: **4** blot, burn, flaw, kind, make, mark, name, sear, sign, sort **5** label, stain, stamp, sword, taint, torch **6** emblem **7** species **8** hallmark **9** character, trademark **10** stigmatize

BRANDISH: **4** show, wave **5** flash, shake, swing, wield **6** flaunt **7** display, flutter, glitter, swagger **8** flourish **9** irradiate

BRANDY: **4** marc **6** cognac, grappa **7** sidecar, stinger **9** alexander, applejack

BRANNIGAN: **5** brawl, fight, spree **6** bender, ruckus **7** quarrel **11** altercation

BRASH: **4** bold, rash **5** cocky, sassy, storm **6** attack, brazen, uppity **7** forward **8** cocksure, tactless **9** impetuous, impulsive, irascible **10** indiscreet **11** thoughtless **12** presumptuous

BRASS: **3** top **4** cash, gall **5** alloy, money, nerve **6** brazen **7** officer **8** audacity **9** impudence **10** confidence, effrontery

BRASS TACKS: **4** meat **5** facts **7** details **10** essentials

BRASSY: **4** bold **5** showy **6** arrant, brazen **7** blatant **8** arrogant, impudent **9** outspoken

BRAT: **3** imp **5** apron, child, cloak **6** infant, rascal, urchin **7** garment, spoiled **8** clothing

BRAVADO: **4** pomp **5** pride, storm **6** daring **7** bluster, bravery, swagger **8** boasting **9** gasconade **11** braggadocio

BRAVE: **4** bold, dare, defy, face, game, good **5** adorn, boast, gutsy, hardy, manly, stout **6** breast, daring, endure, heroic **7** dashing, gallant, soldier, stomach, swagger, valiant, warrior **8** cavalier, defiance, fearless, intrepid, stalwart, superior, unafraid, virtuous **9** challenge, confident, dauntless, excellent, undaunted, withstand **10** courageous **11** venturesome **12** stouthearted

BRAVERY: **4** grit, guts **5** spunk, valor **6** spirit, valour **7** bravado, courage, heroism **8** boldness **9** fortitude, gallantry

BRAWL: **4** fray, riot, spat, tiff **5** broil, fight, melee **6** affray, bicker, fracas, revile, ruckus, rumble, shindy, strife, tumult, uproar **7** dispute, quarrel, scuffle, wrangle **8** argument, complain, dogfight, squabble, upheaval **10** donnybrook, fisticuffs **11** altercation, disturbance

BRAWN: **5** clout, flesh, might, moxie **6** muscle **7** breadth **8** strength **10** ruggedness

BRAWNY: **5** beefy, bulky, husky, tough **6** robust, strong, sturdy **8** muscular, powerful, stalwart

BRAZEN: **4** bold, loud **5** brass, cocky, sassy **6** brassy, flashy **7** callous, chintzy, forward **8** arrogant, immodest, impudent, metallic **9** shameless, unashamed

BRAZIL:
capital: **8** Brasilia
cities: **5** Belem **6** Manaus, Recife **8** Curitiba, Salvador, Sao Paulo **9** Fortaleza **11** Porto Alegre **12** Rio de Janeiro **13** Belo Horizonte
continent: **12** South America
ethnic groups: **7** African **10** Portuguese
explorer: **6** Cabral
features: **5** Xingu **12** Mount Roraima
islands: **6** Maraca, Marajo **7** Caviana, Mexiana
languages: **6** German **7** English, Italian **10** Portuguese
monetary unit: **8** cruzeiro
native: **9** Brazilian
water: **6** Amazon

BREACH: **3** gap **4** chip, flaw, hole, rift **5** chasm, cleft, crack, pause, split, wound **6** harbor, hiatus, inroad, offend **7** assault, blemish, dispute, opening, parting, quarrel, rupture, violate **8** breaking, fracture, interval, trespass **9** violation **10** disruption, dissension, infraction, transgress **12** infringement, interruption

BREAD: **3** bun, rye **4** diet, fare, food, loaf, pita, roll **5** dough, money, toast, wheat, white **6** basket, French, staple **7** crouton, Italian **8** zwieback **9** greenback, sourdough **10** livelihood, sustenance

BREAD AND BUTTER: **3** job **4** keep, work **5** basic **6** career, living **10** profession

BREADTH: **4** span **5** gamut, range, scope, width **6** extent, spread **7** stretch **8** diameter, latitude **9** amplitude, broadness, dimension

BREAK: **3** cut, gap, off, out **4** boon, bust, chip, dash, down, flee, fold, lull, pick, plow, rent, rift, ruin, shot, slip, snap, stop, tame, tear **5** alter, blank, burst, cleft, crack, lapse, pause, pluck, point, sever, smash, wound **6** bruise, cleave, cutoff, defeat, escape, hiatus, impair, pierce **7** blunder, crackle, crevice, cripple, crumble, destroy, disable, disrupt, exhaust, fissure, opening, respite, rupture, shatter **8** announce, breather, division, fraction, fracture, interval, separate **9** advantage, eradicate, interrupt, penetrate **10** alienation, invalidate, separation, transgress **11** opportunity **12** intermission, interruption

BREAKABLE: **4** weak **5** frail **6** flimsy **7** brittle, fragile **8** delicate

BREAKDOWN: **5** crash **6** mishap **7** failure, nervous, smashup **8** analysis, collapse **9** diagnosis **11** itemization

BREAKER: **4** surf, wave **6** billow, roller **9** destroyer

BREAK IN: **5** train **6** invade **7** intrude **8** trespass **9** condition, interject, interrupt **10** burglarize

BREAKNECK: **4** fast **5** quick, risky **6** speedy **8** reckless **9** daredevil

BREAK OF DAY: **4** dawn **5** sunup **7** morning, sunrise **8** daybreak

BREAK OUT: **4** bolt, flee **5** arise, start **6** escape, flight **7** getaway

BREAKTHROUGH: **4** find, leap **5** boost **7** advance **8** progress **9** discovery **11** development, improvement

BREAKUP: **4** part **5** split **7** disband, divorce **8** separate **10** separation

BREAST: **4** bust **5** bosom, brave, chest, heart, udder **8** emotions, mammilla **9** encounter

BREATH: **4** blow, gasp, huff, pant, puff, sigh, wind **5** aroma, pause, smell, vapor, whiff **6** breeze, second, wheeze **7** respite **9** lifeblood **10** exhalation

BREATHE: **3** fan **4** live, pant, puff, sigh **5** exist, speak, utter **6** aspire, exhale, inhale, murmur **7** emanate, instill, respire, whisper **10** articulate

BREATHER: **4** lull, rest **5** break, pause **6** recess **7** respite

BREATHLESS: **4** dead, keen **5** eager, spent, stale, tense **7** airless, excited **9** astounded, exhausted

BREATHTAKING: **7** amazing, awesome **8** stunning **9** thrilling **10** impressive **11** astonishing, hairraising

BREED: **3** ilk, lot **4** bear, kind, race, rear, sire, type **5** beget, class, hatch, raise, spawn, stock, train **6** create, family, strain **7** lineage, nourish, nurture, produce, species, variety **8** engender, instruct, multiply **9** cultivate, offspring, originate, procreate

BREEDING: **4** line **6** mating, origin **7** conduct, culture, descent, manners, rearing **8** behavior, civility, training **9** education, genealogy, schooling **10** extraction, upbringing **11** development, instruction

BREEZE: **3** air, zip **4** aura, blow, gale, gust, sail, stir, wind **5** blast, draft, glide, waltz **6** breath, cruise, report **7** current, freshen, whisper **8** pushover

BREEZY: **4** airy **5** brisk, fresh, sunny, windy **6** lively **7** relaxed **8** carefree, debonair **9** easygoing, vivacious

BREVITY: **8** laconism **9** briefness, crispness, shortness, terseness **11** conciseness, pointedness **12** succinctness

BREW: **3** ale, mix **4** beer, boil, grog, loom, make, plot, pour **5** blend, hatch **6** devise, gather, liquor, seethe **7** concoct, distill, ferment, prepare **8** beverage, contrive **10** miscellany

BRIBE: **3** buy, fee, fix, oil **4** bait, gift, hire, meed **5** bonus, graft, offer, steal, tempt **6** entice, extort, grease, payola **7** corrupt **8** kickback **9** blackmail **10** allurement

BRIC-A-BRAC: 8 trinkets **9** artifacts, ornaments **11** knickknacks

BRICK: 4 oven, tile **5** adobe, block, house, layer, stone

BRIDAL: 4 song **6** shower **7** nuptial, wedding **8** espousal, hymeneal, marriage **9** connubial

BRIDE: 3 tie **4** loop, rein, wife **6** bridle **8** newlywed

BRIDEGROOM: 7 husband **8** newlywed

BRIDESMAID: 9 attendant

BRIDGE: 3 tie, way **4** band, game, link, span **5** cross, union **7** auction, bascule, catwalk, connect, pontoon, trestle, viaduct **8** contract, overpass, traverse **10** suspension

BRIDLE: 3 bit **4** curb, rein, rule **5** brake, bride, check, guard, guide, leash **6** direct, govern, halter, muzzle, subdue **7** blinder, control, harness, repress, swagger **8** restrain, suppress **9** restraint

BRIEF: 3 few **4** case, curt, list, writ **5** blurb, charm, crisp, quick, short **6** abrupt, advise, common, letter, update **7** abridge, compact, compose, concise, invoice, limited, mandate, outline, passing, summary **8** argument, condense, fleeting, succinct, syllabus **9** condensed, momentary, temporary **10** abridgment, compendium, memorandum, transitory **12** condensation

BRIG: 4 boat, jail, ship **6** prison, vessel **7** slammer **8** stockade **10** guardhouse

BRIGADE: 4 army, crew, unit **5** corps, posse, squad **6** outfit **7** company **8** regiment **10** detachment

BRIGAND: 5 thief **6** bandit, outlaw, pirate, robber **7** hoodlum, soldier **8** marauder, pillager **9** desperado **10** highwayman

BRIGHT: 3 apt, gay **4** glad, rosy, wise **5** acute, aglow, alert, beamy, clear, fresh, light, lucid, quick, sharp, smart, sunny, vivid, witty **6** ablaze, cheery, clever, lively, lucent **7** blazing, forward, radiant, ringing, shining **8** animated, cheerful, colorful, flashing, gleaming, luminous, splendid **9** brilliant, cloudless, promising, sparkling, twinkling **10** glistening, glittering, optimistic, precocious **11** illustrious, intelligent, psychedelic, transparent

BRIGHTEN: 4 gild, lift **5** cheer, clear, light, liven, shine **6** polish **7** animate, enliven, lighten **9** intensify, irradiate **10** illuminate

BRIGHTNESS: 5 eclat, flame, gleam, gloss, sheen, shine **6** luster **7** clarity, sparkle **8** radiance, splendor **9** clearness **10** brilliance

BRILLIANT: 3 gay **4** good, keen, wise **5** smart **6** bright, clever, genius, gifted, glossy, lucent, signal **7** eminent, learned, radiant, shining **8** dazzling, glorious, luminous **9** sparkling **10** celebrated, glittering **12** incandescent **13** distinguished

BRIM: 3 hem, lip, rim, sea **4** edge **5** bluff, brink, ocean, verge, water **6** border, margin **8** overflow

BRIMMING: 4 full **5** flush **6** jammed **7** crowded, flooded **8** swelling

BRINE: 3 sea **4** blue, main, salt **5** ocean **6** alkali, saline **8** marinade

BRING: 3 lug **4** bear, lead, take **5** carry, fetch **6** convey, escort, summon **7** deliver, procure, produce **9** accompany, institute, transport

BRING ABOUT: **4** make **5** cause, start **6** attain, create, effect **7** achieve, realize **8** organize **9** establish **10** accomplish

BRING AROUND: **3** get **4** cure **6** induce, revive **7** convert **8** convince

BRING BACK: **6** effect, recall, return, revive **7** restore **8** remember, retrieve, transact **9** recollect, surrender

BRING DOWN: **4** drop **5** level **6** humble **9** overthrow

BRING IN: **3** get **4** earn **5** gross, usher, yield **6** import, report **7** acquire, realize

BRING OFF: **7** achieve, execute, perform, succeed **8** complete **10** accomplish

BRING OUT: **4** tell **5** state **7** declare, display, publish

BRING TOGETHER: **4** join **5** amass, blend, unite **7** combine, compile **9** harmonize **10** accumulate **11** consolidate

BRING UP: **4** rear **5** nurse, offer, raise, train, vomit **6** foster **7** discuss, educate, nurture **11** regurgitate

BRINK: **3** end, eve, lip, rim, sea **4** bank, brim, edge **5** limit, point, shore, verge **6** border, margin **8** boundary

BRINY: **3** sea **5** ocean, salty **6** saline

BRISEIS:
husband: **5** Mynes
lover: **8** Achilles

BRISK: **3** gay **4** busy, fast, keen, spry, walk, yern **5** agile, alert, alive, crisp, fresh, nippy, perky, quick, sharp, smart **6** active, breezy, lively, nimble, snappy **7** chipper **8** animated, spirited **9** energetic, vivacious **10** refreshing **11** stimulating

BRISTLE: **4** barb, fume, hair **5** anger, brush, fiber, strut, toast **6** feeler, ruffle **7** stubble, whisker

BRITISH COLUMBIA:
capital: **8** Victoria
cities: **6** Duncan **7** Kelowna **8** Kamloops **9** Vancouver **12** Prince George
country: **6** Canada
explorers: **4** Cook **5** Drake
features: **14** Rocky Mountains **15** Vancouver Island
water: **6** Fraser **8** Columbia

BRITOMARTIS: **7** Artemis **8** Dictynna
father: **4** Zeus
mother: **5** Carme

BRITTLE: **4** prim, weak **5** brash, candy, crisp, eager, frail, short **6** crispy, feeble, fickle, slight **7** crunchy, fragile, nervous **8** delicate **9** breakable, crumbling, irritable **10** perishable

BROACH: **3** cut, pin, tap **4** moot, open, ouch, spur, stab, veer **5** begin, dress, drift, prick, spool, voice **6** pierce, submit **7** mention, publish, spindle, suggest, violate **8** approach, incision **9** interject, introduce

BROAD: **4** deep, full, vast, wide **5** ample, large, plain, roomy, thick, woman **6** coarse **7** evident, general, liberal, obvious **8** spacious, sweeping, tolerant **9** expansive, extensive, universal **11** nonspecific

BROADCAST: **4** send, show **5** radio **6** report **7** declare, program, publish **8** announce, newscast, televise **10** television **11** communicate

BROAD-MINDED: **4** open **7** lenient, liberal **8** flexible, tolerant **9** receptive **11** progressive

BROBDINGNAGIAN: **3** big **4** huge **5** giant **7** mammoth **8** colossal, gigantic **10** tremendous

BROCHURE: **4** book **5** flyer **8** circular, pamphlet

BROIL: **4** bake, burn, char, fray, heat, sear **5** brawl, fight, grill, melee, roast, scrap **6** affray **7** contest, discord, dispute, quarrel **8** conflict **10** contention, dissension **11** altercation, disturbance

BROKE: **4** flat, poor **6** busted **8** bankrupt, strapped **9** destitute, insolvent, penniless

BROKEN: **3** arm, leg **4** down, rent, torn, weak **5** burst, kaput, rough, tamed **6** busted, ruined, shaken **7** cracked, crushed, damaged, erratic, injured, subdued **8** ruptured **9** defective, dispersed, fractured, shattered **10** incomplete **11** discouraged **12** disconnected

BROKER: **5** agent, stock **6** dealer, factor, jobber **7** realtor, scalper **8** broacher, marriage, merchant **10** negotiator **12** intermediary, middleperson

BROMIDE: **5** trite **6** cliche **8** banality, compound, sedative **9** platitude **10** stereotype **11** commonplace

BRONX CHEER: **3** boo **4** hiss **9** raspberry

BRONZE: **3** tan **4** bust **5** alloy, metal **6** copper, statue **8** brownish

BROOCH: **3** bar, pin **4** clip **5** cameo, clasp **6** shield **7** jewelry **8** ornament

BROOD: **3** fry **4** fret, mope, nest, race, sulk, weep **5** breed, dwell, flock, group, hatch, issue, worry, young **6** clutch, family, litter, ponder **7** agonize, progeny **8** children, daydream, incubate, languish, meditate **9** multitude, offspring **11** contemplate

BROOK: **3** run **4** bear, beck, burn, rill, rush, take **5** abide, creek, river, stand **6** accept, endure, gutter, stream, suffer **7** stomach **8** tolerate **11** watercourse

BROOM: **3** mop **4** swab **5** besom, brush, sweep, whisk **8** splinter

BROTH: **4** bree, soup **5** stock, water **8** bouillon, consomme

BROTHEL: **4** crib, stew **6** bordel **8** bordello, cathouse **10** whorehouse

BROTHER: **3** bro, bub, kin, pal **4** mate, monk, peer, twin **5** billy, blood, buddy, cadet, friar **6** fellow **7** comrade, sibling **8** relative

BROTHERHOOD: **4** clan, club, gang **5** guild, lodge, order, union **7** society **10** fellowship, fraternity **11** association

BROTHERLY: **4** kind, love **6** tender **8** amicable, friendly **9** fraternal **10** neighborly **12** affectionate

BROW: **3** eye, rim, top **4** brim, edge **5** bound, brink, front, ridge, slope **6** temple **8** forehead

BROWBEAT: **3** nag **5** bully **6** coerce, harass **7** depress, henpeck **8** frighten **10** disconcert, intimidate

BROWN: **3** tan **4** coin, cook, dark, puce, sear **5** amber, beige, color, dusky, hazel, khaki, light, penny, sugar, toast **6** auburn, bronze, coffee, gloomy, tanned **7** swarthy **8** brunette, chestnut, mahogany **9** chocolate

BROWNIE: **3** elk **4** cake **5** cooky, fairy, pixie **6** goblin **9** Girl Scout, sandpiper

BROWSE: **4** brut, crop, feed, flip, scan, shop, skim **5** graze, thumb **6** forage, glance, nibble **7** pasture

BRUISE: **3** mar **4** bash, dent, hurt, maim, maul **5** abuse, black, break, crush, pound **6** batter, breach, injury, mangle, shiner **7** disable **9** contusion, pulverize

BRUNEI:
also called: **16** Brunei Darussalam
capital: **17** Bandar Seri Gegawan
cities: **5** Seria **6** Tutong **11** Kuala Belait
continent: **4** Asia
ethnic groups: **5** Malay **7** Chinese
features: **10** Mount Pagon
languages: **5** Malay **7** Chinese, English
monetary unit: **6** dollar
water: **6** Belait, Tutong **9** Temburong

BRUNETTE, BRUNET: **4** dark **5** brown **6** tanned **7** swarthy **11** brown-haired

BRUNT: **3** jar **4** blow, crux, jolt **5** clash, force, shock **6** attack, burden, impact, stress **7** assault, tension

BRUSH: **3** rub **4** comb, fray, hair, skim **5** broom, clash, clean, fight, graze, groom, paint, sweep, tooth, touch, whisk **6** stroke **7** scuffle **8** conflict, skirmish **9** encounter, sideswipe **11** undergrowth

BRUSH ASIDE: **4** snub **5** spurn **6** reject, slight **7** neglect **9** disregard

BRUSH OFF: **3** cut **4** deny **6** reject **9** dismissal

BRUSH UP: **4** cram **5** study **6** polish, reread, review **7** refresh

BRUSQUE: **4** curt, rude **5** bluff, blunt, frank, gruff, rough, short, surly, terse **6** abrupt, snippy **7** violent **8** cavalier, impolite **12** discourteous

BRUTAL: **5** cruel, gross **6** bloody, carnal, coarse, savage, severe **7** beastly, caddish, callous, inhuman, uncivil **8** ruthless **9** atrocious, barbarous, ferocious, unfeeling

BRUTE: **4** ogre **5** beast, demon, feral, fiend, force **6** animal, savage **7** ruffian **8** physical **9** scoundrel

BUBBLE: **3** air, sac **4** bead, blob, boil, fizz, foam, seed, suds **5** empty, froth, slosh **6** seethe, trifle **7** blister, blubber, deceive, globule **8** delusive **9** percolate **10** effervesce **11** speculation

BUCCANEER: **5** rover **6** pirate, rifler, robber, viking **7** corsair, spoiler **10** freebooter

BUCK: **3** ram **4** boil, butt, deer, dude, male, rear, soak, stag, wash **5** blade, carry, knife, naked, repel, steep **6** basket, dollar, oppose, resist **7** private, unhorse **8** antelope, prickett, sawhorse **9** pulverize

BUCKET: **3** can, tub **4** bail, cage, pail **5** cheat, hurry, scoop, skeel **6** barrel, drench, kettle, vessel **7** swindle **9** container

BUCKEYE STATE: **4** Ohio

BUCKLE: **3** bow **4** belt, bend, curl, down, kink, warp **5** clasp, twist, under, yield **6** fasten **7** contend, grapple, harness **8** fastener, struggle **10** distortion

BUCOLIC: **4** hick, idyl **5** local, rural **6** farmer, native, poetic, rustic, simple **7** bumpkin **8** herdsman, pastoral

BUD: **3** eye, gem, pip **4** bulb, germ, grow, knop, seed **5** child, shoot, youth **6** button, flower, sprout **7** blossom, brother, burgeon, develop **8** bourgeon **9** debutante, germinate, incipient

BUDDHISM:
Buddha: **7** Gautama **10** Shakyamuni, Siddhartha
disciple: **6** Ananda
evil spirit: **4** Mara
language: **4** Pali

monk: **4** lama **5** arhat, yahan **7** mahatma, poongee **8** talapoin **9** dalai lama
schools: **3** Zen **8** Hinayana, Mahayana **9** Theravada, Vipassana **11** Jodo-shinshu
terms: **4** mani, raga, tope **5** bodhi, karma, stupa, sutra **6** bhikku, bo tree, dharma, mantra, tantra **7** bhikshu, krikaya, nirvana **11** bodhissatva, prayer wheel

BUDDY: **3** pal **4** chum, mate **5** crony **6** friend **7** brother, comrade **8** sidekick **9** companion

BUDDY-BUDDY: **4** cozy **5** close **6** chummy **8** friendly, intimate

BUDGE: **3** fur **4** move, push, stir **6** propel **8** convince, movement, persuade

BUDGET: **4** pack, plan **5** funds, stock, store **6** amount, ration, wallet **7** program **8** allocate, estimate, finances **9** allowance, resources

BUFF: **3** fan, nut, rub **4** bare, nude **5** naked, shine **6** expert, polish, smooth **7** devotee, leather **10** enthusiast

BUFFALO: **4** anoa, meat, stag **5** bison, stump **6** hamper, puzzle **7** caribao, gazelle **8** bewilder **9** bamboozle, frustrate

BUFFER: **3** pad **4** zone **6** bumper, fender, screen **7** cushion **8** backstop **9** safeguard

BUFFET: **3** bar, box **4** beat, blow, cuff, jolt, meal, slap, toss **5** lunch, smite, spank, stool **6** batter, brunch, dinner, strike, strive, supper, thrash **7** counter **8** cupboard, lambaste **9** sideboard **11** smorgasbord

BUFFOON: **3** wag **4** bozo, fool, jerk, mime **5** antic, buffo, clown, comic, droll, idiot **6** jester, mummer, stooge **7** playboy **8** humorist, ridicule **9** harlequin, prankster

BUG: **3** ant, fad, fly, nag, off **4** flaw, flea, germ, gnat, idea, June, mite, rage, wire **5** annoy, roach, virus **6** beetle, bother, insect, needle, pester, scheme, spider **7** forward, pompous, wiretap **8** hemipter, hobbyist, mosquito **9** conceited, eavesdrop, infection, lightning **10** enthusiast

BUGABOO: **4** fear, ogre **5** alarm, bogey, scare **6** goblin **7** bugbear, specter **8** bogeyman **9** hobgoblin, scarecrow

BUGGY: **4** cart, shay **5** nutty, wagon **7** caboose, foolish, vehicle **8** carriage, demented, infested

BUGLE: **4** bead, call, horn **6** cornet **7** clarion, trumpet **10** instrument

BUILD: **4** body, form, make, rear **5** erect, found, frame, raise, shape **6** create, expand **7** develop, fashion **8** assemble, engineer, increase, physique **9** construct, establish, fabricate, undertake **11** manufacture

BUILDER: **5** maker, mason **7** artisan, erector **9** architect, carpenter **10** contractor

BUILDING: **3** hut **4** barn, casa, pile **5** hotel, house **6** casino, castle, church, fabric, museum, palace, temple **7** edifice, factory, library, theater **8** dwelling, tenement **9** apartment, structure **10** storehouse **12** architecture, construction

BULB: **3** bud, nub **4** corm, knob, lamp, root, seed **5** globe, onion, plant, swell, tuber, tulip **6** garlic **9** expansion

BULGARIA:
capital: **5** Sofia
cities: **4** Ruse **5** Varna **6** Burgas **7** Plovdiv
continent: **6** Europe
ethnic groups: **4** Turk **9** Bulgarian

features: **7** Balkans **16** Rhodope Mountains
languages: **7** Turkish **9** Bulgarian
monetary unit: **4** leva
native: **9** Bulgarian
water: **6** Danube, Struma **7** Maritsa **8** Black Sea

BULGE: **3** bag, bug **4** bump, cask, hump, knob, lump **5** belly, bilge, bloat, flask, pouch, swell **6** billow, dilate, expand, extend, growth, wallet **7** blister **8** protrude, swelling **9** appendage **10** projection **12** protuberance

BULK: **3** sum **4** body, heap, hulk, lump, mass, pile, size **5** cargo, might, power, swell **6** amount, expand, extent, figure, volume **8** majority, quantity **9** aggregate, dimension, largeness, magnitude, substance **11** massiveness

BULKY: **3** big **4** huge **5** beefy, burly, gross, heavy, hefty, large, stodgy, stout **6** clumsy **7** awkward, massive, weighty **8** enormous **9** corpulent **10** cumbersome **11** substantial

BULL: **3** cop **4** bunk, jest, male, seal, slip, toro **5** error, whale **6** humbug **7** baloney **8** nonsense **9** detective, policeman

BULLDOZE: **3** cow, dig, ram **4** push **5** bully, drive, force, grade, level, scoop **6** thrust **7** flatten **8** browbeat, threaten **10** intimidate

BULLET: **3** zip **4** ball, fast, lead, shot, slug **5** hurry **6** pellet, sinker, tracer **7** missile **9** cartridge **10** ammunition

BULLETIN: **4** memo **5** flash, scoop **6** notice, poster, report **7** message, program, release **9** statement **10** communique **12** announcement

BULLFIGHTER: **6** torero **7** matador, picador **8** toreador **12** banderillero

BULLHEADED: **8** stubborn **9** obstinate, pigheaded **10** headstrong

BULL'S-EYE: **6** center, pulley, target, window **9** precisely

BULLY: **4** boss, good, huff, punk, ride **5** annoy, bravo, great, meany, tease **6** bounce, harass, menace, tyrant **7** bluster, bullock, dashing, ruffian **8** browbeat, domineer, frighten **9** excellent, terrorize **10** antagonize, intimidate

BULWARK: **4** fort, wall **5** fence, guard **6** buffer, defend, secure, shield **7** citadel, defense, parapet, protect, support **8** fortress **10** breakwater, stronghold

BUM: **4** hobo, idle **5** drone, idler, mooch, tramp **6** frolic, loafer, lounge, sponge **8** vagabond **10** panhandler

BUMBLE: **3** bee **4** veil **5** botch **6** bobble, bungle, jumble, muffle **7** blunder, bramble, stumble

BUMMER: **4** flop **6** beggar **7** moocher, washout

BUMP: **3** hit, jar **4** bang, blow, jolt, lump, oust, thud **5** clash, knock, smash, thump **6** bounce, demote, impact, nodule, strike **7** collide, pothole, replace **8** dislodge, swelling **9** downgrade **10** concussion **12** protuberance

BUMP INTO: **3** hit **4** luck, meet **7** collide, stumble **9** encounter

BUMPKIN: **3** oaf **4** hick **5** yokel **6** lummox **7** country **10** clodhopper

BUMP OFF: **4** kill **6** finish, murder **9** liquidate **11** assassinate

BUMPTIOUS: **4** bold **5** cocky **6** brazen **8** arrogant, insolent **9** conceited, obtrusive **10** aggressive

BUMPY: **5** rocky, rough **6** bouncy, uneven **7** jolting

BUN: **4** hair, knot, roll **5** bread **7** biscuit

BUNCH: **3** lot, set **4** body, crew, herd, mass, pack **5** batch, clump, crowd, flock, group, swarm **6** bundle **7** bouquet, cluster **8** assemble, quantity **9** aggregate **10** assortment, collection

BUNDLE: **3** bag, lot, tie, wad **4** bale, band, bind, pack, pile, roll **5** bunch, group **6** packet, parcel **7** fortune, package **10** collection

BUNGLE: **3** err **4** flub, goof, muff, slip **5** botch, spoil **6** boggle, bumble, fumble **7** blunder, butcher, mistake **9** mismanage

BUNK: **3** bed, cot, hay **4** bull **5** berth, hooey, lodge, sleep **6** billet, trough **7** baloney, hogwash, malarky, twaddle **8** nonsense **10** balderdash **11** foolishness

BUNKER: **4** army, hold **6** dugout **7** shelter **8** sandtrap

BUNT: **3** bat, tap **4** butt, meet, push **5** shove **6** strike **9** spearhead

BUOY: **3** dan **4** bell **5** elate, float, raise **6** marker, signal, uplift **7** elevate, support, sustain

BUOYANT: **3** gay **4** airy **5** happy, light **6** joyous, lively **7** elastic, hopeful, lilting, springy **8** animated, cheerful, floating, spirited, volatile **9** resilient, vivacious **10** unsinkable **12** lighthearted

BURBLE: **3** yak **4** boil, gush **6** babble, bubble, jabber **7** chatter, confuse

BURDEN: **3** tax, try, vex **4** care, clog, duty, load, pile **5** cargo, worry **6** bother, charge, hamper, impede, saddle, strain, stress, weight **7** afflict, oppress, trouble **8** capacity, encumber, handicap, overhead **9** aggravate, grievance **10** imposition

BURDENSOME: **5** heavy **6** tiring **7** arduous, onerous, weighty **8** grievous, grinding, wearying **9** demanding, difficult, laborious **10** exhausting, oppressive **11** troublesome

BUREAU: **4** desk **5** chest **6** agency, branch, office **7** dresser **8** division **10** chiffonier, department

BUREAUCRAT: **8** official, stickler **10** politician **12** civil servant

BURGEON: **3** bud **4** grow **5** bloom **6** expand, flower, sprout, thrive **7** blossom, prosper **8** increase, mushroom, snowball

BURGLAR: **4** yegg **5** crook, thief **6** robber **7** prowler **11** safecracker

BURGLARY: **5** caper, crime, heist, theft **6** felony **7** break-in, larceny, robbery

BURIAL: **5** rites **7** funeral **9** interment, sepulture **10** deposition, entombment

BURIAL GROUND: **4** tomb **5** grave **7** pyramid **8** boneyard, catacomb, cemetery **9** graveyard **10** necropolis

BURKINA FASO:
capital: **11** Ouagadougou
cities: **9** Koudougou **13** Bobo-Dioulasso
continent: **6** Africa
ethnic groups: **4** Bobo **5** Mande, Mossi **7** Voltaic
languages: **6** French **7** Sudanic
monetary unit: **5** franc
water: **5** Volta

BURLAP: **3** bag **5** cloth, gunny **6** fabric **7** sacking **8** wrapping

BURLESQUE: **4** mime, mock **5** farce, mimic, revue, spoof, strip **6** comedy, parody, satire **7** lampoon, overact, takeoff **8** comedian, ridicule, travesty **9** slapstick **10** caricature, exaggerate, vaudeville

BURLY: **3** big **5** beefy, bulky, heavy, hefty, husky, stout **6** brawny, hearty, portly, stocky, sturdy **8** imposing, muscular

BURMA: **7** Myanmar

BURN: **3** sun, tan **4** bake, beat, brew, char, fire, raze, sear, skin **5** anger, blaze, broil, brown, cheat, flame, parch, scald, singe, sting, waste, water **6** chisel, desire, kindle, scorch, tingle **7** combust, consume, cremate, flicker, oxidize, smolder, swindle **8** squander **9** cauterize **10** incinerate

BURNING: **3** hot **4** fire **5** angry, blaze, eager, fiery, flame **6** ablaze, ardent, desire, fervid, torrid, urgent **7** arduous, boiling, fervent, flaming, glaring, glowing, intense, shining **8** exciting, feverish, sizzling, stinging **9** consuming, inflaming **10** combustion, irritating

BURNISH: **3** rub, wax **4** buff **5** glaze, gloss, shine **6** luster, polish **7** furbish **8** brighten

BURR: **3** cut, nut, pad, rib **4** buzz, halo, knob, ring **5** briar, notch **6** circle, tunnel, washer **7** sticker **9** whetstone

BURRO: **3** ass **4** mule **6** donkey **7** jackass

BURROW: **3** den, dig **4** cave, hole, mine, mole, root, tube **5** couch, delve **6** tunnel **7** passage, shelter **8** excavate

BURSAR: **6** purser **7** cashier **9** paymaster, treasurer **10** cashkeeper, controller

BURST: **3** fit, out, pop **4** blow, bust, gush, rush, scat **5** blast, break, erupt, flash **6** broken, damage, injury **7** explode, rupture, shatter **8** outbreak, puncture **9** explosion, interrupt

BURUNDI:
capital: **9** Bujumbura
cities: **5** Ngozi **6** Bururi, Gitega **7** Muyinga
continent: **6** Africa
ethnic groups: **3** Twa **4** Hutu **5** pygmy, Tutsi
features: **15** Great Rift Valley
languages: **5** Rundi **6** French
native: **9** Burundian
water: **10** Tanganyika

BURY: **4** hide, sink **5** cover, embed, plant, rivet, stash **6** entomb, inhume, shroud **7** conceal, engross, immerse, repress **8** inundate, submerge **9** overwhelm

BUSH: **5** bosch, clump, grove, plant, shrub **6** branch, forest, league **7** cluster, outback, thicket **9** backwoods **11** backcountry

BUSHED: **4** beat, worn **5** spent, tired **6** pooped **8** fatigued **9** exhausted

BUSHWA: **4** bull, bunk **5** hooey, trash **7** baloney, hogwash, rubbish **8** nonsense **9** poppycock

BUSHWHACKER: **6** bandit, outlaw, scythe, sniper **7** pioneer **9** guerrilla

BUSHY: **5** furry, hairy **6** shaggy, woolly **7** bushman

BUSINESS: **3** art, bag, job **4** care, duty, firm, game, task, work **5** cause, field, trade **6** affair, career, custom, office, outfit, racket **7** beeswax, calling, capital, concern, trading, traffic, venture **8** activity, commerce, industry, vocation **9** patronage, situation, syndicate **10** employment, enterprise, occupation, profession **11** disturbance, partnership, transaction **13** establishment

BUSINESSLIKE: **6** intent **7** careful, earnest, routine, serious **8** diligent **9** efficient, organized **10** purposeful **12** professional

BUSINESSMAN/WOMAN: **4** suit **5** baron **6** dealer, tycoon **8** merchant **9** executive **10** capitalist **12** entrepreneur **14** businessperson

BUST: **3** nab **4** fail, flop, raid, ruin, tame **5** bosom, break, burst, chest, flunk, lemon, loser, pinch **6** arrest, breast, bronze, reduce, statue **7** capture, failure **8** bankrupt **9** sculpture

BUSTLE: **3** ado **4** dash, fuss, stir, todo **5** frisk, furor, haste **6** clamor, flurry, hubbub, hustle, racket, rumpus, scurry, tumult, unrest, uproar **7** clatter, scamper, turmoil **8** activity **9** agitation, commotion, whirlwind

BUSY: **4** nosy **5** brisk **6** active, intent, lively **7** engaged, hopping, humming, swamped, working **8** absorbed, diligent, employed, occupied, sedulous, tireless, untiring **9** assiduous, attentive, energetic, laborious **11** distracting, industrious, unavailable

BUSYBODY: **3** pry **5** snoop **6** gossip **7** meddler, snooper **9** buttinsky **10** fussbudget, pragmatist, rubberneck **12** blabbermouth

BUT: **3** yet **4** just, mere, only, save **5** still **6** except, unless **7** besides, however **9** otherwise **11** nonetheless **12** nevertheless

BUTCHER: **4** kill, ruin, slay **5** botch **6** bungle, killer, murder **8** merchant, murderer, mutilate **9** slaughter **11** executioner

BUTT: **3** end, pit, ram **4** buck, cart, cask, goat, head, horn, jolt, push, rump, stub, tush **5** cigar, fanny, hinge, joint, patsy, shaft, stump **6** adjoin, behind, bottom, sucker, target, thrust, victim **7** project **8** buttocks, derriere, flounder **9** cigarette

BUTTER: **3** fat, ghi, oil **4** food, ghee, oleo **6** spread **7** flatter **9** margarine

BUTTERFINGERED: **6** clumsy **7** awkward **8** bungling, careless

BUTTERFLY: **4** kiho **5** giant, satyr, tiger, zebra **6** apollo, morpho, ursula **7** admiral, alfalfa, buckeye, monarch, skipper, viceroy **8** arthemis, grayling **9** aphrodite, underwing **10** swim stroke **12** lepidopteran

BUTTOCKS: **4** buns, butt, rear, seat **5** fanny **6** behind, bottom, heinie **7** keister **8** derriere

BUTTON: **3** bud **4** chin, hook, knob, stud **5** badge, pearl **6** bauble, buckle, emblem, fasten **8** fastener

BUTTONHOLE: **4** loop, slip, stop **6** accost, detain, eyelet **8** approach

BUTTRESS: **4** pier, pile, prop, stay **5** boost, brace, strut **6** uphold **7** bolster, support **8** abutment **9** reinforce

BUXOM: **5** built, busty, hefty, plump **6** bosomy, robust **7** shapely, stacked **8** bouncing **10** curvaceous, voluptuous **11** full-figured

BUY: **3** get **4** chap, coup, gain, shop **5** bribe, score, trade **6** market, ransom, redeem, secure **7** acquire, bargain **8** purchase

BUYER: **5** agent, fence **6** client, patron, sucker, vendee **7** shopper **8** consumer, customer, prospect **9** purchaser

BUZZ: **3** hum, saw **4** call, hiss, ring, whir **5** phone, rumor **6** gossip, notion **7** hearsay, scandal, whisper **9** telephone

BYGONE: **3** old **4** past **5** olden **6** former **7** ancient, archaic **8** backward, departed, obsolete **9** forgotten **10** oldfangled

BYPASS: **4** miss, omit, shun **5** avoid, dodge **6** detour, ignore **8** sidestep

BYPATH: **3** way **4** lane **5** byway, trail **7** pathway **8** shortcut

BY-PRODUCT: **7** spin-off **8** offshoot **9** aftermath

BYSTANDER: **7** witness **8** observer, onlooker, passerby **9** spectator **10** eyewitness

BYWORD: **3** saw **4** rule **5** adage, axiom, motto **6** byname, dictum, phrase, saying, slogan **7** epithet, proverb **8** nickname **9** catchword

BYZANTINE: **6** church, tricky **7** complex **8** involved **9** intricate **12** architecture

C

CAB: **4** hack, taxi **6** hansom **8** carriage **10** locomotive

CABAL: **4** camp, clan, plot, ring **5** junta, party **6** circle, clique, scheme **7** coterie, council, faction **8** intrigue **9** collusion **10** conspiracy

CABALISTIC: **6** mystic, occult **7** strange **8** esoteric **10** mysterious **12** supernatural

CABALLERO: **5** lover **6** escort, knight **8** cavalier, horseman **9** gentleman

CABARET: **4** cafe, club **6** tavern **9** nightclub, speakeasy **10** restaurant **11** discotheque

CABBAGE: **3** nab **4** crib, hook, kale **5** filch, money, steal **6** pilfer **7** purloin **8** coleslaw, colewort **10** sauerkraut

CABIN: **3** boy, den, hut, log **4** camp, shed **5** booth, coach, lodge, shack **6** shanty **7** caboose, cottage **9** stateroom

CABINET: **3** box **4** case, file **5** board, chest **6** bureau, closet, vanity **7** armoire, commode, console, council, dresser, kitchen **8** cupboard, ministry **9** committee **11** chiffonnier

CABLE: **4** boom, cord, link, rope, wire **5** chain, wires **6** stitch **7** coaxial **8** telegram **10** television

CACHE: **4** bury, hide **5** cover, kitty, store **7** conceal, reserve, secrete **8** treasure **9** stockpile **10** storehouse

CACHET: **4** seal **5** stamp **6** design, status **7** capsule, stature **8** prestige **11** distinction

CACKLE: **3** gab, jaw **4** blab, chat, crow **5** cluck, laugh **6** babble, giggle, gossip, titter **7** chackle, chatter, snicker, twaddle **8** laughter

CACOPHONOUS: **4** sour **5** harsh, noisy **6** offkey **7** raucous **8** strident **9** dissonant **10** discordant

CACTUS: **3** sun **4** bleo, moon, toad **5** nopal, plant, snake **6** cereus, chaute, chende, cholla, cochal, Easter, mescal, peyote, spider **7** airampo, rainbow, saguaro **8** chichipe, snowdrop **9** Christmas, porcupine

CAD: **3** cur **4** boor, heel, lout, worm **5** creep, louse **6** rascal **7** bounder, dastard, villain **9** scoundrel

CADAVER: **4** body **5** stiff **6** corpse **7** carcass, remains

CADAVEROUS: **4** pale **5** gaunt **6** wasted **7** deathly, ghastly, haggard, shadowy **9** emaciated **10** corpselike

CADENCE: **4** beat, pace, tone **5** count, meter, pulse, sound, swing, tempo **6** rhythm **7** measure **10** inflection, modulation

CADET: **5** plebe, youth **6** junior **7** recruit, student **10** midshipman

CADGE: **3** beg, bum **4** hawk **5** mooch **6** peddle, sponge **8** huckster, scrounge **9** panhandle

CADMUS:
daughter: **3** Ino **5** Agave **6** Semele **7** Autonoe
father: **6** Agenor
killed: **6** dragon
kingdom: **9** Phoenicia
mother: **10** Telephassa
sister: **6** Europa
son: **8** Illyrius **9** Polydorus
wife: **8** Harmonia

CADRE: **4** core, unit **5** force, frame, group, panel, staff **7** nucleus **9** framework **14** infrastructure

CADUCITY: **3** age **5** lapse **8** senility **10** feebleness, perishable, transitory

CAESAR, JULIUS: **6** tyrant **7** emperor
killer: **6** Brutus **7** Cassius
kingdom: **4** Rome
lover: **9** Cleopatra
murdered on: **11** Ides of March
son: **8** Augustus, Octavian
wife: **7** Pompeia **8** Cornelia **9** Calpurnia

CAESURA: **4** rest, stop **5** break, pause **8** interval **12** interruption

CAFE: **3** bar **5** diner **6** saloon, tavern **7** cabaret **8** teahouse **9** cafeteria, nightclub **10** restaurant **11** coffeehouse

CAGE: **3** box, mew, pen **4** coop, jail **5** brake, pound **6** basket, bucket, prison **7** chantry, confine **8** imprison **9** enclosure **11** incarcerate

CAGEY: **3** sly **4** foxy, wary, wily **5** canny, sharp **6** astute, crafty, shrewd **7** cunning **8** discreet

CAIN:
brother: **4** Abel, Seth
father: **4** Adam
home: **4** Eden
killed: **4** Abel
land: **3** Nod
mother: **3** Eve
son: **5** Enoch

CAISSON: **3** box **4** case **5** chest, float, wagon **7** chamber

CAITIFF: **3** rat **4** base, mean, vile **5** louse **6** wicked **7** dastard **8** cowardly **9** scoundrel **10** despicable

CAJOLE: **3** con **4** coax, lure **5** jolly, tease **6** entice **7** beguile, flatter **8** blandish, persuade **9** brownnose, sweettalk

CAKE: **3** bar, bun, cup, set **4** bake, food, lump, mass, slab **5** block, crust, patty, wedge **6** coffee, cookie, eclair, harden, pastry **7** thicken **8** compress, solidify **9** coagulate

CAKEWALK: **4** rout **5** cinch, dance, march, strut **6** prance

CALABOOSE: **3** jug, pen **4** brig, jail **5** clink **6** cooler, lockup, prison **7** slammer **8** hoosegow

CALAMITOUS: **3** sad **4** dire, evil **5** fatal **6** bitter, deadly, dismal, tragic, woeful **7** adverse, direful, ruinous, unlucky **8** wretched **9** miserable **10** afflictive, deplorable, disastrous **11** cataclysmic, distressful, unfortunate **12** catastrophic

CALAMITY: **3** ill **4** blow, ruin **5** storm, wreck **6** misery, mishap, sorrow **7** scourge, tragedy **8** accident, disaster, hardship **9** adversity **10** affliction, misfortune **11** catastrophe **12** misadventure

CALCIUM: **7** element **8** compound

CALCULATE: **3** add, aim **4** plan, rate **5** count, tally, think **6** assess, devise, divide, expect, figure, number **7** average, compute, project **8** consider, estimate, evaluate, forecast, multiply, subtract **9** determine, enumerate **10** anticipate

CALCULATED: **4** risk **7** planned, studied **8** measured **10** deliberate **12** premeditated

CALCULATING: **3** sly **4** safe, wily **6** artful, crafty **7** careful, cunning **8** cautious, scheming **9** computing **10** contriving

CALCULATION: **6** answer, result **8** forecast, prudence, totaling **9** ciphering, deduction, logistics, reckoning **10** adjustment, estimation, precaution, prediction **11** computation

CALCULATOR: **5** table **6** abacus **8** computer

CALDRON, CAULDRON: **3** pot, vat **6** boiler, kettle

CALEB:
daughter: **6** Achash
father: **8** Jepunneh
son: **3** Hur, Iru

CALEDONIA: **8** Scotland

CALENDAR: **3** log **4** ordo **5** annal, diary, slate **6** agenda, docket, Julian **7** almanac, journal, program **8** menology, schedule **9** Gregorian, timetable **10** chronology

CALF: **4** dolt, veal **5** dogie, youth **6** muscle **7** fatling, foreleg **8** maverick, yearling

CALIBER: **4** bore, rank **5** class, gauge, grade, merit, scope, skill, value, worth **6** degree, talent, weight **7** ability, dignity, quality, stature **8** capacity, diameter, prestige **9** character **10** prominence

CALIFORNIA:
bird: **11** valley quail
capital: **10** Sacramento
cities: **6** Carmel, Fresno, Malibu **7** Oakland, San Jose **8** San Diego **10** Los Angeles **12** San Francisco
explorer: **5** Drake **8** Cabrillo
features: **6** Sonora **8** Alcatraz, Monterey, Yosemite **10** Napa Valley **12** Mojave Desert **14** Colorado Desert **15** San Andreas Fault
flower: **11** golden poppy
native: **11** Californian
nickname: **11** Golden State
tree: **7** redwood
water: **3** Eel, Pit **5** Kings **6** Salmon **7** Feather **9** Lake Tahoe **10** Sacramento, San Jacinto, Stanislaus

CALINKY STATE: **13** South Carolina

CALL: **3** bid, cry, dub **4** buzz, dial, hail, name, page, plea, ring, stop, yell **5** alarm, claim, elect, order, phone, rouse, shout, utter, visit, waken, yodel, yodle **6** accuse, appeal, arouse, decree, demand, invite, invoke, muster, reason, summon **7** address, appoint, baptize, collect, command, convene, entitle, grounds, impeach, request, solicit **8** announce, assemble, identify, nominate, proclaim, subpoena, vocation **9** challenge, telephone

CALL FOR: **4** need, want **5** crave **6** demand, entail **7** request, require, suggest

CALL FORTH: **5** evoke **6** awaken, elicit, summon **7** command

CALLING: **3** art, job **4** rank, work **5** craft, trade **6** career, metier, naming **7** mission, pursuit, station, summons **8** business, devotion, function, lifework, position, shouting, vocation **9** condition, utterance **10** employment, occupation, profession **11** appellation, convocation, undertaking

CALLIOPE:
father: **4** Zeus
mother: **9** Mnemosyne
son: **7** Orpheus

CALLISTO:
killer: **7** Artemis
lover: **4** Zeus
son: **5** Arcas

CALL OFF: **3** end **4** halt **5** scrub **6** cancel

CALLOUS: **4** cold, hard **5** cruel, horny, tough **6** brawny, obtuse, torpid **8** stubborn **9** apathetic, unfeeling **11** hardhearted, indifferent, insensitive

CALL OUT: **3** cry **4** yell **5** shout **6** holler, muster

CALLOW: **3** raw **4** bald, bare **5** crude, green, naive **6** marshy **7** shallow **8** immature, juvenile, youthful **9** infantile, unfledged **10** tenderfoot

CALL TO: **4** hail **5** greet **7** address

CALL TO ORDER: **4** open **5** begin **7** convene

CALL UPON: **3** ask **4** urge **5** visit **6** invite **7** request

CALM: **4** cool, easy, fair, hush, lull, mild, rest **5** abate, allay, charm, peace, quell, quiet, sober, still, stoic **6** defuse, docile, gentle, lowkey, pacify, placid, sedate, serene, smooth, soothe, steady **7** appease, assuage, collect, halcyon, patient, placate, restful, silence, unmoved **8** composed, pastoral, peaceful, restrain, tranquil **9** collected, easygoing, impassive, temperate, unexcited, unruffled **10** harmonious, nonchalant, unconfused **11** complacence, levelheaded, tranquilize, undisturbed

CALMNESS: **5** poise **6** repose **8** ataraxia, coolness, serenity **9** composure, placidity, quietness, sangfroid, stillness **10** equanimity **11** tranquility **12** peacefulness

CALUMNIATE: **4** slur **5** libel, smear **6** accuse, defame, malign, revile, vilify **7** asperse, blacken, slander **9** blaspheme **10** scandalize

CALYX: **4** husk, leaf **5** petal, sepal

CAM: **3** cog **4** awry, disk **5** askew, shaft **6** tappet **7** crooked, trippet **8** cylinder

CAMARADERIE: **5** cheer **7** jollity **10** fellowship, sisterhood **11** brotherhood, sociability **12** friendliness

CAMBODIA:
also called: **9** Kampuchea **13** Khmer Republic
capital: **9** Phnom Penh
cities: **10** Battambang, Kompong Som
continent: **4** Asia
ethnic groups: **5** Ehmer **7** Chinese **9** Cambodian **10** Vietnamese
features: **9** Angkor Wat
languages: **5** Khmer **6** French
leaders: **6** Lon Nol, Pol Pot **8** Sihanouk
monetary unit: **4** riel
native: **9** Cambodian
water: **8** Tonle Sap **10** Gulf of Siam **11** Mekong River

CAMEL:
driver: **6** sarwan **8** cameleer
one-humped: **9** dromedary
two-humped: **8** Bactrian

CAMELOT:
king: **6** Arthur
knights: **8** Lancelot, Percival
magician: **6** Merlin
queen: **9** Guinevere
quest: **9** Holy Grail
sword: **9** Excalibur

CAMEROON:
capital: **6** Younde
cities: **6** Douala, Garova **8** Victoria **10** Nkongsamba
continent: **6** Africa
ethnic groups: **5** Bantu **6** Fulani **7** Hamitic **8** Bamileke
features: **13** Mount Cameroon **16** Adamawa Mountains
languages: **6** French **7** English
monetary unit: **5** franc
water: **5** Nyong **6** Guinea, Sanaga

CAMOUFLAGE: **4** fake, hide **5** cloak, cover **6** screen **7** conceal **8** disguise **9** deceptive **10** masquerade **11** smokescreen

CAMP: **3** mod, pop **4** fire, tent, wild **5** siege **6** ground **7** barrack, bivouac, lodging, shelter **8** quarters **10** settlement

CAMPAIGN: **3** run **5** drive, fight **7** canvass, crusade, solicit, warfare **8** muckrake, politick **9** barnstorm, offensive, operation

CAMPANILE: **5** tower **6** belfry **7** steeple

CAMPUS: **4** quad **5** field **7** college, grounds

CAN: **3** cup, jug, may, tin **4** able, boot, butt, fire, jail, john, keep, rump, tush **5** could, fanny **6** bottom, toilet, vessel **7** ability, capable, dismiss **8** aluminum, buttocks, preserve, restroom **9** competent, container, discharge, terminate **10** receptacle

CANADA:
capital: **6** Ottawa
cities: **6** Quebec **7** Calgary, Halifax, Toronto **8** Edmonton, Hamilton, Montreal, Winnipeg **9** Saskatoon, Vancouver
continent: **12** North America
ethnic groups: **6** French **7** British **8** European
explorers: **5** Cabot **7** Cartier
features: **11** Great Plains (Prairies) **14** Canadian Shield, Rocky Mountains **17** Arctic Archipelago
languages: **6** French **7** English
monetary unit: **4** cent **6** dollar
native: **5** Inuit, Metis **6** Canuck, Eskimo, Indian **8** Canadian, Canadien
provinces: **6** Quebec **7** Alberta, Ontario **8** Manitoba **10** Nova Scotia **12** New Brunswick, Newfoundland, Saskatchewan **15** British Columbia **18** Prince Edward Island
symbol: **9** maple leaf
territories: **5** Yukon **20** Northwest Territories
water: **3** Red **5** Yukon **6** Nelson, Ottawa **8** Columbia **10** Great Lakes **12** Niagara Falls **14** Mackenzie River **16** St. Lawrence Seaway

CANAILLE: **3** mob **6** masses, rabble **8** riffraff, unwashed **9** commoners

CANAL: **3** cut **4** duct, Suez, tube **5** ditch, drain **6** Panama, strait, trench **7** channel, conduit, towpath **8** aqueduct **10** bottleneck **11** watercourse

CANARD: **3** fib **4** hoax **5** rumor, spoof **7** swindle **11** fabrication **12** exaggeration

CANARY: **4** bird, fink, wine **5** dance **6** singer, yellow **7** stoolie **8** informer, songbird, squealer

CANARY ISLANDS:
cities: **6** Laguna **9** Santa Cruz
islands: **4** Roca **5** Clara, Ferro, Lobos, Palma **6** Gomera, Hierro **7** Inferno **8** Graciosa, Tenerife **9** Lanzarote **10** Allegranza **11** Gran Canaria **13** Fuerteventura
Spanish provinces: **9** Las Palmas **19** Santa Cruz de Tenerife

CANCEL: **3** end **4** drop, omit, void **5** abort, annul, erase, quash, remit, trash **6** delete, efface, negate, recall, remove, revoke **7** abolish, destroy, expunge, nullify, rescind, retract, scratch **8** abrogate **10** neutralize, obliterate

CANCER: **5** tumor **7** disease, sarcoma **8** sickness **9** carcinoma, radiation **10** corruption, malignancy **12** chemotherapy

CANDESCENT: **3** hot **5** shine, white **7** glowing **8** dazzling **11** luminescent

CANDID: **4** fair, just, open, pure **5** blunt, clear, frank **6** direct, honest **7** genuine, sincere **8** splendid, truthful **9** honorable, impartial, outspoken **10** aboveboard, immaculate **11** unconcealed

CANDIDATE: **6** bidder **7** nominee **8** aspirant, prospect **9** applicant, contender, postulant **10** campaigner

CANDLE: **3** dip, wax **5** light, Roman, stick, taper **6** bougie, tallow **8** bayberry **9** chandelle

CANDLEHOLDER: **6** lampad, sconce **7** menorah, pricket **9** girandole **10** candelabra, chandelier **11** candlestick

CANDOR: **6** purity **7** honesty **8** fairness, kindness, openness, veracity **9** frankness, innocence, integrity, sincerity **10** brightness, brilliance, kindliness **12** impartiality

CANDY: **3** bar **4** kiss, mint, rock **5** fudge, sweet, taffy **6** bonbon, comfit, nougat, toffee **7** brittle, caramel, congeal, flatter, fondate, gumdrop, sweeten **8** licorice, lollipop, sourball **9** chocolate, granulate, jelly bean, sweetmeat **10** confection, jawbreaker **11** crystallize, sugarcoated

CANE: **3** hit, rod **4** beat, flog, pipe, pole, stem, whip **5** birch, lance, staff, stick, sugar **6** bamboo, punish, strike **7** hickory, scourge **9** pikestaff

CANINE: **3** cur, dog, fox, pup **4** lobo, mutt, wolf **5** dingo, hound, hyena, pooch **6** coyote **7** doglike

CANKER: **4** boil, sore **5** decay, stain, ulcer **6** cancer, infect, lesion **7** consume, corrode, corrupt, pollute, tarnish

CANNABIS: **3** pot, tea **4** hemp **5** bhang, grass **6** reefer **7** hashish **9** marijuana

CANNIBAL: **5** brute **6** savage **8** man-eater **9** primitive **10** headhunter **15** anthropophagite

CANNON: **3** bit, gun **4** ball **5** crack, thief **6** mortar **7** bastard, firearm, robinet **8** howitzer, ordnance **9** artillery **10** pickpocket

CANNONADE: **4** bomb **5** blitz, burst, salvo **6** shower, volley **7** barrage, battery **11** bombardment

CANNY: **3** sly **4** able, cozy, wary, wily, wise **5** cagey, lucky **6** astute, clever, frugal, gentle, shrewd **7** careful, cunning, knowing, prudent, thrifty **8** skillful, watchful **9** carefully, dexterous, fortunate, ingenious, sagacious **11** sharpwitted

CANOE: **4** boat, proa, waka **5** birch, bungo, kayak, skiff **6** ballam, dugout, pitpan **7** almadia, coracle, currane, pirogue

CANON: **3** law **4** code, list, rule **5** axiom, dogma, edict, maxim, model, tenet **6** decree **7** command, precept, statute **8** decision, doctrine, standard **9** catalogue, criterion, principle **10** regulation **12** constitution

CANONICAL: **5** legal **6** proper **8** accepted, orthodox **9** customary **10** authorized, sanctioned

CANOPY: **3** sky **4** hood **5** cover, shade **6** awning, tester **7** marquee, shelter **8** covering, umbrella **9** baldachin, pavillion

CANT: **3** tip **4** coax, heel, lean, rise, tilt, turn **5** argot, bevel, grade, idiom, lingo, lusty, merry, niche, pitch, plead, share, slang, slant, slope, whine **6** corner, herald, jargon, patter, snivel **7** dialect, incline **8** cheerful, language, pretense, vigorous **9** hypocrisy, pomposity, vulgarism **10** dishonesty, vernacular, vocabulary

CANTALOUPE: **5** fruit, melon **9** muskmelon

CANTANKEROUS: **4** mean, sour **5** surly **6** cranky, ornery **7** fretful **8** choleric **9** irritable, malicious **11** contentious

CANTEEN: **3** bar, jug **5** flask **6** bottle **7** cantina, thermos **10** commissary

CANTER: **3** bum, jog, run **4** pace, rack, trot **6** beggar, gallop, whiner **7** drifter **8** vagabond

CANTON: **4** part **6** billet, corner, county **7** quarter, section **8** district, division **11** subdivision

CANTOR: **5** hazan **6** leader, singer **7** chanter, soloist **8** vocalist **9** precentor

CANUCK: **8** Canadian **14** French Canadian

CANVAS: **3** oil **4** duck, sail, tarp, tent **6** burlap **7** artwork, picture **8** painting **9** tarpaulin

CANVASS: **4** case, hawk, poll, seek, sift **5** check, study **6** debate, peddle, search, survey **7** agitate, analyze, discuss, examine, solicit **8** campaign **10** scrutinize **11** electioneer, investigate

CANYON: **4** glen **5** gorge, Grand, gulch, gully **6** arroyo, divide, ravine, valley

CAP: **3** fez, hat, lid, taj, tip, top **4** best, coif, cork, dome, hood, pass, seal **5** beret, cover, crest, crown, excel, outdo, seize, topee, trump **6** arrest, beanie, better, bonnet, climax, cornet, helmet, summit, turban **7** montero, surpass **8** headgear, outshine, yarmulke **9** detonator, headpiece **11** mortarboard

CAPABILITY: **3** art **5** craft, knack, means, skill **7** ability **8** aptitude, capacity, efficacy **9** potential **10** competence

CAPABLE: **3** apt, can **4** able **5** adept **6** expert, fitted, suited **7** skilled **8** masterly **9** competent, effective, qualified **10** proficient **11** experienced **12** accomplished

CAPACIOUS: **4** full, vast, wide **5** ample, broad, large, roomy **7** massive **8** abundant, generous, spacious **9** extensive, plentiful **10** commodious, expandable **12** considerable **13** comprehensive

CAPACITY: **4** bulk, full, gift, room, size **5** knack, limit, power, skill, space **6** burden, extent, spread, talent, volume **7** ability, caliber, content, faculty **8** aptitude, strength **9** intellect, potential **10** capability, competence

CAPANEUS:
father: **9** Hipponous
killer: **4** Zeus
mother: **8** Astynome
son: **9** Sthenelus
wife: **6** Evadne

CAPARISON: **4** deck **5** adorn **7** harness **8** clothing, covering **9** trappings **10** decoration

CAPE: **4** head, neck **5** cloak, point, shawl, stole, talma **6** bertha, chapel, mantle, poncho, sontag, tabard, tippet **8** headland, lambskin, mantilla, pelerine **9** peninsula, sheepskin **10** projection, promontory

CAPER: **3** gag, hop **4** dido, jump, lark, leap, romp, skit **5** antic, dance, fling, frisk, prank, stunt **6** cavort, frisco, frolic, gambol, prance, spring **8** escapade, mischief **9** adventure, devilment **11** monkeyshine, shenanigans

CAPE VERDE:
capital: **5** Praia
cities: **6** Sal-Rei **7** Mindelo **9** Porto Novo
continent: **6** Africa
ethnic groups: **6** Creole **7** African
features: **3** Sal **4** Fogo, Maio **5** Grava **8** Boa Vista, Sao Tiago **10** Santa Luzia, Santo Antao, Sao Nicolau, Sao Vicente
languages: **7** Crioulo **10** Portuguese
monetary unit: **6** escudo
water: **13** Atlantic Ocean

CAPILLARY: **4** tube **6** minute **7** slender, tension **8** hairlike **11** blood vessel

CAPITAL: **3** cap, top **4** cash, city, good, main **5** basic, chief, funds, great, major, money, stake, stock, vital **6** letter, wealth **7** central, leading, serious, supreme, weighty **8** dominant, foremost **9** excellent, paramount, principal, prominent, resources **11** scrumptious **12** headquarters

CAPITALISM: **9** democracy, economics **10** free market, government **11** competition **14** free enterprise

CAPITALIST: **6** tycoon **8** investor **9** financier, plutocrat **12** entrepreneur **14** businessperson

CAPITALIZE: **4** back, fund, gain **5** stake **6** profit **7** exploit, finance, sponsor **8** bankroll **9** subsidize

CAPITAL PUNISHMENT: **3** gas **6** murder **7** hanging **10** guillotine **12** death penalty **13** electrocution **15** lethal injection

CAPITOL: **4** dome **6** center **10** statehouse **11** legislature

CAPITOL HILL: **5** House **6** Senate

CAPITULATE: **3** bow **4** cave, fall, fold **5** agree, yield **6** submit **7** concede, succumb **8** headline **9** enumerate, surrender

CAPRICE: **3** fad **4** kink, mood, whim **5** antic, craze, fancy, humor, quirk, trait **6** notion, sudden, temper, vagary, whimsy **7** impulse, whimsey **9** capriccio, crotchets **11** willfulness **12** inconsistent

CAPRICIOUS: **4** iffy **5** dizzy, doddy, fluky, moody **6** fickle, quirky **7** erratic, flighty, wayward **8** fanciful, unstable, unsteady, volatile, wavering **9** arbitrary, crotchety, fantastic, impulsive, whimsical **10** changeable **12** inconsistent

CAPSIZE: **4** coup, keel, roll **5** upset **6** invert **8** overturn **9** overthrow

CAPSULE: **3** pod **4** case, dose, pill, time **5** shell **6** ampule, sheath **7** cockpit, outline, tabloid **8** abridged, membrane **9** cartridge, condensed

CAPTAIN: **3** boh **4** boss, head **5** chief, guide, pilot **6** leader, master **7** foreman, headman, manager, officer, skipper **8** governor **9** centurion, commander, principal **10** headwaiter

CAPTION: **5** title **6** legend **7** cutline, heading **8** headline, subtitle **9** underline **11** explanation

CAPTIOUS: **4** mean **5** cross, testy **6** crabby, crafty, ornery, severe **7** cynical, fretful, peevish **8** contrary, critical, perverse, petulant **9** demanding, insidious, irascible, sarcastic **10** capricious, nit-picking **12** fault-finding

CAPTIVATE: **3** win **4** draw, hook, lure, take **5** catch, charm **6** allure, dazzle, please, seduce, subdue **7** attract, bewitch, capture, enamour, enchant **8** enthrall, overtake **9** entertain, fascinate, hypnotize, infatuate, mesmerize, spellbind

CAPTIVE: **5** slave **7** hostage **8** enslaved, prisoner **9** oppressed **10** imprisoned **12** incarcerated

CAPTIVITY: **6** duress **7** bondage, custody, serfdom, slavery **9** servitude **11** confinement **12** imprisonment

CAPTURE: **3** bag, cop, get, nab, net, win **4** grab, hook, land, nail, snag, take, trap **5** catch, prize, seize, snare **6** arrest, collar, obtain **9** apprehend, captivate

CAR: **4** auto, heap, jeep, race **5** buggy, cable, coach, coupe, motor, sedan, train **6** basket, hotrod, jalopy, wheels **7** armored, chariot, hardtop, midsize, trailer, trolley, vehicle **8** dragster, fullsize, railroad, roadster **9** hatchback, limousine **10** automobile, subcompact **11** convertible **12** station wagon

CARAVAN: **4** band, line, trek, trip **5** fleet **6** convoy, parade, safari, travel **7** journey **9** motorcade **10** procession

CARAVANSARY: **3** inn **4** khan **5** hotel, lodge, serai **6** hostel **8** hostelry **9** resthouse

CARBOHYDRATE: **5** sugar **6** simple, starch **7** complex, glucose, maltose **8** compound, dextrose, glycogen **9** cellulose

CARBON: **4** coal, coke, copy, lead, soot **7** element, replica **8** charcoal, graphite

CARBONATE: **4** burn, char, sear **6** aerate, scorch

CARBUNCLE: **4** boil, sore **6** pimple, stones **7** abscess

CARCASS: **4** body **5** stiff **6** corpse **7** cadaver, carrion

CARCINOMA: **5** tumor **6** cancer **10** malignancy

CARD: **3** map **4** menu, plan, post, wild **5** chart, joker, tally, trump **6** ticket **7** program **8** birthday, business, comedian, schedule **9** character **10** attraction

CARD GAME: **3** pan, pig, war **4** faro, fish, frog, skat, trio, tunk **5** chile, cinch, ombre, pedro, pitch, poker, rummy, samba, stops, whist **6** boodle, bridge, clubby, eights, euchre, fan tan, hearts, hombre, kaluki, memory, piquet, pounce, red dog, sevens, slough, smudge, spider **7** auction, authors, belotte, bezique, Bolivia, canasta, cassino, Chicago, garbage, kalougi, low ball, old maid, pool nap, seven-up, shotgun, Uruguay, wipe-off **8** all fours, baccarat, big forty, canfield, chouette, conquian, crapette, cribbage, gin rummy, kaloochi, Klondike, Michigan, Napoleon, Oklahoma, pinochle, Saratoga, sixty-six, slapjack **9** accordion, argington, black jack, forty-five, kalabrias, monte bank, Newmarket, old sledge, play or pay, shasta sam, sir garnet, solitaire, spoil five, stud poker, twenty-one, vingt-et-un, zioncheck **10** blind tiger, crazy jacks, deuces wild, five finger, five or nine, klaberjass, parliament, panguingue, put and take, schafskopf, sheepshead, tournament **11** calculation, crazy eights, five hundred, red and black, Russian bank **12** forty thieves **13** concentration, dealer's choice, Michigan rummy **14** Earl of Coventry, spite and malice

terms: **3** ace, bid, bue, cat, cut, pic, ten **4** book, deal, draw, hand, jack, king, pair, pass, skat, slam, suit, wild **5** check, deuce, flush, joker, knave, queen, raise, royal, trump, widow **6** tenace **7** auction, holding **8** straight **9** duplicate **11** progressive **13** international

CARDIGAN: **6** fabric, jacket **7** sweater

CARDINAL: **3** key, red **4** bird, head, main **5** basic, chief, cloak, vital **6** cleric, number, ruling **7** central, highest **9** essential, important, principal, uppermost **10** preeminent, underlying **11** fundamental

CARE: **4** cure, dole, duty, heed, like, mind, reck, tend, wish **5** alarm, grief, guard, nurse, pains, trust, worry **6** burden, desire, dismay, effort, foster, lament, regard, sorrow **7** anxiety, auspice, caution, chagrin, cherish, concern, keeping, nurture, sadness, tension, thought **8** business, distress, minister, tutelage **9** attention, diligence, direction, heartache, oversight **10** enthusiasm, management, solicitude **11** safekeeping, tribulation **12** guardianship, watchfulness

CAREEN: **3** tip **4** bend, cant, keel, lean, list, sway, tilt, veer **5** lurch, pitch, slant, slope, swing, weave **7** incline, stagger

CAREER: **3** bag, job, run **4** path, road, work **5** field, trade **6** course, gallop, racket **7** calling, pursuit **8** business, vocation **10** livelihood, occupation, profession

CARE FOR: **4** like, love, mind, tend **5** fancy, guard, nurse **6** foster, relish **7** nurture

CAREFREE: **3** gay **4** easy, wild **5** happy **6** breezy **7** relaxed **8** careless, reckless **9** easygoing **10** untroubled **12** lighthearted

CAREFUL: **4** safe, wary **5** alert, canny, exact, leery **6** frugal, intent **7** anxious, guarded, heedful, mindful, prudent, thrifty **8** accurate, cautious, diligent, discreet, gingerly, thorough, vigilant, watchful **9** advertent, attentive, exquisite, observant, provident **10** economical, meticulous, particular, respective, scrupulous, thoughtful **11** considerate, painstaking **12** conservative

CARELESS: **3** lax **4** cool, easy **5** hasty, messy, slack, unfit **6** casual, remiss, supine, untidy, unwary **7** languid **8** heedless, listless, reckless, slipshod, wasteful **9** forgetful, haphazard, negligent, unheeding, unmindful **10** disorderly, neglectful, nonchalant, regardless **11** inadvertent, inattentive, indifferent, spontaneous, thoughtless, unconcerned **12** absentminded **13** irresponsible

CARESS: **3** coy, hug, pet, toy **4** feel, kiss, neck **5** flirt, touch **6** coddle, cosset, fondle, pamper, stroke **7** embrace, massage

CARETAKER: **5** super **6** keeper **7** curator, janitor **8** watchman **9**

concierge, custodian **11** housekeeper

CAREWORN: **5** jaded **7** haggard **8** fatigued, troubled, tuckered **9** exhausted **10** distressed

CARGO: **4** bulk, haul, load **5** goods **6** burden, lading **7** freight, payload **8** contents, shipment **9** truckload

CARIBBEAN:
gulfs: **6** Darien
island groups: **7** Leeward **8** Antilles, Windward
islands: **4** Cuba **5** Aruba, Haiti **6** Belize, Guyana, Nassau, Tobago **7** Antigua, Curacao, Grenada, Jamaica, St. Lucia **8** Anguilla, Barbados, Dominica, Trinidad **9** Monserrat, St. Vincent **10** Hispaniola, Puerto Rico **12** Santo Domingo **18** St. Christopher-Nevis

CARICATURE: **3** art **4** copy, mock, skit **5** farce, mimic **6** overdo, parody, satire **7** cartoon, lampoon, takeoff **8** travesty **9** burlesque **12** exaggeration

CARILLON: **4** peal **5** bells **6** belfry, chimes **7** angelus **9** bell tower **12** glockenspiel

CARK: **3** ail, vex **4** fret, heed, load, stew **5** annoy, pains, worry **6** burden, charge, harass **7** anxiety, trouble **8** distress

CARMEN:
author: **14** Prosper Merimee
composer: **5** Bizet

CARMINE: **3** red **5** color **6** cherry **7** crimson, scarlet

CARNAGE: **5** blitz, havoc **6** murder **8** butchery, massacre **9** bloodshed, holocaust, slaughter **12** annihilation

CARNAL: **4** lewd **6** animal, bodily, erotic, sexual, wanton **7** earthly, fleshly, immoral, lustful, obscene, sensual, worldly **8** material, sensuous, temporal **9** corporeal

CARNIVAL: **4** fair, fete, show **5** carny **6** circus **7** revelry **8** festival, sideshow **9** Mardi Gras **11** merrymaking

CARNIVORE: **3** cat, dog, fox **4** bear, coon, lion, lynx, mink, puma, seal, wolf **5** civit, dingo, easel, hyena, otter, panda, sable, skunk, tiger **6** cougar, coyote, ermine, feline, ferret, jackal, jaguar, marten, ocelot, possum, weasel **7** leopard, opossum, raccoon, tigress **8** mongoose

CARNIVOROUS: **9** predatory, rapacious **11** flesh-eating

CAROL: **4** hymn, noel, sing, song **5** dance, ditty **6** ballad, chorus, warble

CAROM: **4** bump, skim **5** graze **6** bounce, glance, strike **7** rebound **8** ricochet

CAROUSAL: **4** orgy, romp **5** binge, drunk, feast, revel, spree **6** bender, frolic, shindy **7** banquet, carouse **8** festival, jamboree **10** debauchery

CAROUSE: **4** hell, riot **5** drink, party, quaff, revel, spree **7** wassail

CAROUSEL: **4** ride **8** conveyor **10** tournament **12** merry-go-round

CARP: **3** nag **4** fish, fuss, talk **5** cavil, knock, scold, speak **6** bother, censor, nibble **7** censure, chatter, condemn, henpeck, nitpick, quibble **8** complain **9** criticize

CARPE DIEM: **11** seize the day

CARPENTER: **3** ant, bee **5** mason **6** framer, joiner **7** artisan, builder **10** woodworker **12** cabinetmaker

CARPET: **3** rug **4** shag **5** magic, tapis **6** fabric, flying, indoor **7** matting, outdoor, Persian **8** covering, tapestry **9** broadloom

CARRIAGE: **3** air, rig **4** hack, load, look, pace **5** buggy, coach, front, poise, wagon **6** aspect, burden, manner **7** baggage, bearing, chariot, conduct, gesture, posture, vehicle **8** attitude, behavior, carrying, demeanor, stroller **9** behaviour, execution, transport **10** conveyance, deportment

CARRIED: **5** borne, toted **6** carted, lugged, wafted **8** drifting **11** transported

CARRIER: **3** bus, car **4** mail, rack, ship **5** barge, plane, train, truck **6** bearer, pigeon, porter **7** airline, courier, flattop, mailman, postman **8** aircraft, emissary, railroad, teamster **9** mailwoman, messenger, postwoman

CARRION: **4** vile **5** bones **6** corpse, rotten **7** cadaver, carcass, corrupt, remains **9** loathsome

CARROLL, LEWIS:
character: **5** Alice **11** White Rabbit **12** Humpty Dumpty **22** Charles Lutwidge Dodgson

CARROT: **3** top **4** root **5** plant **6** reward **10** enticement

CARRY: **3** lug, win **4** bear, cart, haul, have, hold, lead, move, send, take, tote **5** bring, guide, poise, stock **6** behave, convey, convoy, derive, extend, supply **7** bolster, conduct, contain, prevail, produce, schlepp, support, sustain, undergo **8** continue, shoulder, transfer, transmit **9** transport

CARRY AWAY: **5** steal **6** abduct, kidnap, remove **9** transport

CARRY OFF: **5** seize **6** finish **7** destroy, succeed

CARRY ON: **4** rant, rave **6** endure, engage **7** perform, persist, proceed **8** continue **9** horseplay

CARRY OUT: **6** effect **7** execute, fulfill **8** complete, transact **9** implement **10** accomplish

CART: **3** lug **4** dray, haul, tote **5** bring, carry, sulky, truck, wagon **6** convey **7** chariot, trolley, trundle, tumbler, vehicle **11** wheelbarrow

CARTE BLANCHE: **5** power **7** freedom, license **9** authority **10** permission

CARTE DU JOUR: **4** menu

CARTEL: **3** mob **4** bloc, defy, pact, pool, ring, ship **5** group, paper, trust **6** letter **8** contract, monopoly **9** challenge, syndicate **10** federation

CARTHAGE:
continent: **6** Africa
gods/goddesses: **5** Tanit **6** Moloch, Tanith **10** Baal-Hammon **14** Tyrian Meklarth
kings/queens: **4** Dido **8** Hannibal
place: **7** Tunisia
related: **5** Punic **12** Carthaginian
water: **13** Mediterranean

CARTILAGE: **6** tissue **7** gristle

CARTON: **3** bin, box **4** case **5** crate **6** packet **9** container **10** receptacle

CARTOON: **6** sketch **7** drawing **9** animation **10** caricature, comic strip

CARTOONIST: **6** Al Capp **7** B. Kliban **8** Bil Keane **9** Bud Fisher, Chic Young, Tom Wilson **10** Gary Larson, Johnny Hart, Mort Walker, Walt Disney **12** Bill Waterson, Garry Trudeau, Rube Goldberg **13** Charles Addams, Charles Schulz

CARTRIDGE: **4** case, tube **5** blank, shell **7** capsule **8** cassette, cylinder

CARTWHEEL: **4** coin **6** tumble **10** handspring, somersault

CARVE: **3** cut, saw **4** chip, etch, mold **5** sever, shape, slice, split **6** chisel, sculpt **7** dissect, engrave, whittle **9** sculpture

CASA: **5** house **8** dwelling

CASANOVA: **3** cad **4** roue, wolf **5** lover, Romeo **7** admirer, Don Juan **8** lothario, lover boy, paramour **9** ladies' man, womanizer

CASCADE: **4** gush **5** falls, spout **6** rapids, tumble **8** cataract **9** waterfall

CASE: **3** box, pod **4** deed, file, pack, pair, suit **5** brace, brief, cause, claim, cover, crate, event, folio, state, study, trial **6** action, affair, binder, carton, coffin, quiver, sheath, survey **7** capsule, compact, enclose, episode, example, holster, humidor, inclose, lawsuit, satchel **8** argument, envelope, instance **9** cartridge, condition, container **10** conditions, occurrence, proceeding, receptacle **11** contingency

CASH: **4** coin, draw **5** brass, bread, clink, dough, funds, money **6** change, dinero **7** capital, coinage **8** banknote, currency **9** principal

CASHIER: **3** can **4** boot, cast, fire **5** clerk, expel **6** bursar, purser, reject, teller **7** discard **9** treasurer

CASING: **4** boot, skin, tire **5** frame **6** coffin, lining, sheath **8** covering

CASK: **3** keg, tub, tun, vat **4** butt, pipe **5** bulge **6** barrel, casket, casque, firkin **8** hogshead, puncheon

CASKET: **3** box **4** case, cask, pall, tomb **5** chest **6** coffer, coffin

CASPIAN SEA:
also called: **5** Tates
place: **4** Iran **6** Russia
ports: **4** Baku **9** Astrakhan
rivers: **4** Kura, Ural **5** Volga

CASSANDRA:
father: **5** Priam
husband: **9** Agamemnon
killer: **12** Clytemnestra
mother: **6** Hecuba
son: **6** Pelops **9** Teledamus

CASSEROLE: **4** dish, food, hash **6** tureen **7** goulash, potluck

CASSIOPEIA:
daughter: **9** Andromeda
husband: **7** Cepheus
kingdom: **8** Ethiopia

CAST: **3** lob **4** emit, fire, form, hurl, look, mold, name, shed, spew, tint, toss **5** chart, eject, fling, found, heave, pitch, shade, shape, sling, throw **6** actors, launch, spread, visage **7** cashier, company, compute, deposit, discard, plaster, players, project **8** jettison **10** characters, expression, impression

CAST ABOUT: **4** hunt, seek **6** search **8** contrive

CASTAWAY: **4** waif **5** leper **6** maroon, outlaw **7** outcast **8** derelict, renegade **9** shipwreck

CAST AWAY: **4** jilt, shed **5** scrap **6** reject, strand **7** abandon, discard

CAST DOWN: **4** sink **5** abase, lower **6** droopy, sadden **7** humbled **8** dejected, dispirit **9** depressed, disgraced **10** humiliated

CAST OFF: **4** free, shed **5** untie **7** discard **8** unfasten **9** repudiate

CAST OUT: **4** oust **5** eject, exile, expel **6** banish **9** ostracize

CAST UP: **3** add **4** spew **5** total, vomit **7** measure **8** disgorge

CASTE: **4** race, rank **5** breed, class, grade **6** degree, status **8** position, standing

CASTIGATE: **4** flog, lash, ream **5** chide, scare **6** berate, pummel, punish, revise, scathe, subdue, thrash **7** censure, chasten **8** admonish, chastise, lambaste **9** criticize, reprimand

CASTLE: **4** fort, rook **5** manor, villa **6** palace **7** chateau, citadel, mansion **8** bastille, fortress **10** stronghold

CASTOR:
father: **4** Zeus
horse: **8** Cyllaros
killer: **4** Idas
mother: **4** Leda
sister: **5** Helen
twin brother: **6** Pollux

CASTRATE: **3** fix **4** geld, spay **5** alter **6** change, neuter **8** caponize, mutilate **9** sterilize

CASUAL: **5** aloof, blase, homey, loose, stray **6** chance, random **7** natural, offhand, relaxed **8** informal **9** easygoing, impromptu, uncertain **10** accidental, contingent, fortuitous, incidental, nonchalant, occasional **11** indifferent

CASUALTY: **4** blow, loss **5** death **6** chance, hazard, injury, mishap, victim **7** wounded **8** accident, disaster, fatality **10** misfortune

CASUISTRY: **6** deceit **7** evasion, fallacy **8** delusion **9** chicanery, sophistry

CAT: **4** lion, lynx, puma, puss **5** kitty, pussy, tiger **6** cougar, feline, jaguar, kitten **7** cheetah, leopard, panther, tigress **11** caterpillar
breed: **4** Manx **5** alley, civet, tabby **6** Angora, calico **7** Maltese, Persian, Siamese **8** Cheshire, longhair **9** Himalayan, shorthair
extinct: **12** saber-toothed
female: **5** queen **7** lioness, tigress **9** grimalkin
genus: **5** felis
male: **3** gib **6** tomcat
tailless: **4** Manx

CATACLYSM: **4** ruin **6** deluge, tragic **7** debacle **8** calamity, collapse, upheaval **10** disastrous **11** catastrophe

CATACOMB: **4** tomb **5** crypt, vault **7** chamber **8** cemetery **10** passageway

CATAFALQUE: **3** box **4** bier **6** casket, coffin

CATALOG, CATALOGUE: **4** book, file, list, roll **5** brief, flyer, index, tally **6** record, roster **7** arrange, itemize **8** classify, register, schedule **9** directory, enumerate, inventory **10** prospectus

CATALYST: **4** goad, spur **5** spark **8** stimulus **9** activator, incentive, synergist **10** motivation

CATAMARAN: **4** raft **5** float **6** vessel **8** sailboat

CATAPULT: **4** hurl **5** fling, heave, throw **6** launch, propel **8** ballista **9** slingshot

CATARACT: **5** falls, flood **6** deluge, rapids **7** cascade **8** downpour **9** waterfall **10** eye disease

CATASTROPHE: **4** blow, doom **6** fiasco, mishap **7** tragedy **8** accident, calamity, disaster, fatality **9** cataclysm, emergency **10** misfortune

CATCALL: **3** boo **4** hiss, hoot, razz **6** heckle **9** raspberry **10** Bronx cheer

CATCH: **3** bag, get, nab, net, wed **4** bait, bust, clip, draw, haul, hoax, hold, hook, land, nail, pass, snap, stop, trap **5** clamp, grasp, hitch, ketch, knack, lasso, marry, seize, snare, trick **6** arrest, clutch, corner, detect, entrap, snatch **7** attract, capture, develop, receive **8** drawback, entangle, overtake, surprise **9** apprehend, intercept **10** comprehend

CATCHER IN THE RYE:
author: **10** J.D. Salinger

CATCHING: **6** taking **8** epidemic **10** contagious, infectious **11** captivating

CATCH ON: **3** get, see **5** grasp, learn **6** fathom **8** discover **10** assimilate

CATCH-22: **7** paradox
author: **12** Joseph Heller

CATCHWORD: **3** cue **5** maxim, motto **6** byword, cliche, phrase, slogan

CATCHY: **6** fitful, tricky **7** popular **9** appealing **11** captivating

CATEGORICAL: **4** sure **7** certain **8** absolute, emphatic, explicit, specific **11** unequivocal, unmitigated, unqualified

CATEGORY: **4** rank, type **5** class, genus, order **6** family **7** heading, species **8** division, grouping **14** classification

CATER: **4** feed, help **5** humor, serve, spoil **6** pamper, purvey, supply **7** indulge, provide

CATERPILLAR: **4** moth, worm **5** larva **6** canker **7** tractor **9** butterfly

CATERWAUL: **3** cry **4** bawl, wail, yell **5** whine **6** scream

CATFISH: **3** mud **4** cusk, pout, shal **5** bagre, banjo **6** sucker **8** flathead

CATHARSIS: **7** release **9** cleansing, purgation **10** abreaction

CATHARTIC: **8** laxative **9** cleansing, purgative, purifying

CATHEDRAL: **5** duomo **6** church, temple **8** basilica **9** sanctuary

CATHOLIC: **5** broad, papal, whole **6** global **7** general, liberal **8** tolerant **9** inclusive, universal **10** charitable, ecumenical **11** unsectarian

CATLIKE: **5** quiet **6** feline, silent **8** stealthy

CATNAP: **4** doze **5** sleep **6** siesta, snooze **10** forty winks

CATNIP: **3** nep **6** catnep **7** cataria, catwort

CATREUS:
daughter: **6** Aerope **7** Clymene **9** Apemosyne
father: **5** Minos
kingdom: **5** Crete
mother: **8** Pasiphae
son: **11** Althaemenes

CAT'S-CRADLE: **4** game **7** ribwort

CAT'S-PAW: **4** dupe, gull, pawn, rush, tool **5** cloud, patsy **6** breeze, stooge **7** bulrush, matreed

CATTAIL: **4** rush **5** cloud, plant **7** bulrush, matreed **8** reed mace

CATTLE: **4** cows, herd, kine, neat, oxen **5** beefs, bovid, bulls, stock **6** beasts, calves, steers **8** longhorn **9** livestock
brand: **4** duff **5** buist
breed: **4** Zebu **5** Angus, Devon, Dutch **6** Belted, Durham, Jersey, Sussex **7** Brahman, Brangus **8** Ayrshire, Bradford, Charbray, Guernsey, Hereford, Longhorn **9** Red Polled, Shorthorn **10** Beefmaster, Brown Swiss **11** Charollaise, Dutch Belted **12** water buffalo
female: **3** cow
genus: **3** Bos
goddess: **6** Bubona
group: **4** herd **5** drove
male: **4** bull
steal: **6** rustle
young: **4** calf **6** heifer **8** yearling

CATTLEMAN: **6** cowboy, drover, gaucho **8** wrangler **10** cowpuncher

CATTY: **4** evil, mean **5** nasty **6** bitchy **7** hateful **8** spiteful, venomous **9** malicious **10** backbiting

CATWALK: **6** bridge **7** footway, walkway

CAUCUS: **6** powwow **7** council, meeting, primary, session **8** assembly, election **9** gathering

CAUDAL: **4** back, rear **9** posterior

CAUSE: **3** aim, key, let **4** call, case, goal, move, root, spur, suit **5** agent, basis, ideal **6** agency, belief, create, effect, induce, malady, motive, object, origin, reason, source **7** concern, disease, lawsuit, produce, provoke, purpose **8** business, engender, movement, occasion **9** originate, principle **10** conviction, mainspring

CAUSTIC: **4** tart **5** acrid, crisp, rough, sharp **6** biting, bitter, ironic, severe **7** burning, cutting, gnawing, pungent **8** abrasive, alkaline, scathing, stinging **9** corrosive, sarcastic, satirical **10** astringent, malevolent **11** acrimonious

CAUTERIZE: **4** burn, char, sear **5** brand, singe

CAUTION: **4** care, flag, heed, hint, warn **6** advice, caveat, exhort, notify **7** anxiety, counsel, warning **8** admonish, forecast, prudence, wariness **9** attention, diligence, vigilance **10** admonition, discretion, providence **11** calculation, reservation **12** watchfulness

CAUTIOUS: **4** safe, wary **5** alert, canny, leery **7** careful, guarded, mindful, prudent **8** discreet, vigilant **10** scrupulous **11** circumspect

CAVALCADE: **5** drill, march **6** column, parade, safari **7** caravan, journey **8** sequence **9** spectacle **10** procession

CAVALIER: **3** gay **4** curt, fine **5** brave, cocky, frank, lofty, proud, rider **6** escort, knight **7** gallant, haughty, offhand, soldier **8** arrogant, horseman **9** caballero, chevalier **10** disdainful, nonchalant **12** supercilious

CAVALRY: **4** army **6** horses, troops **7** lancers, rangers **8** horsemen, soldiers **10** knighthood

CAVE: **3** den **4** cove, give, hole, lair, rear, toss **5** crypt, upset **6** cavern, cavity, cellar, grotto, hollow, luster, plunge **7** crumple **8** collapse, overturn
dweller: **3** bat **4** bear, lion **6** hermit **10** troglodyte
explorer: **9** spelunker
researcher: **12** speleologist

CAVEAT: **4** flag, sign **5** alarm **6** beware, notice **7** caution, warning **10** admonition

CAVE IN: **5** yield **6** buckle, submit **7** crumple, implode, succumb **8** collapse

CAVERN: **3** den **4** cave, hole **5** croft **6** cavity, grotto, hollow **10** subterrane

CAVERNOUS: **4** deep, huge, vast, wide **5** broad **6** gaping, hollow **7** immense, yawning

CAVIAR: **3** roe **4** eggs **6** relish **8** delicacy

CAVIL: **6** bicker, haggle **7** nitpick, quibble **8** belittle **9** criticize, exception, objection

CAVITY: **3** bag, pit, sac **4** cave, dent, hole, mine, sink, vein, void **5** bursa, decay, mouth, sinus **6** antrum, atrium, cavern, crater, grotto, hollow, pocket, vacuum **7** chamber, orifice, vesicle **10** depression, excavation

CAVORT: **4** play, romp **5** caper, revel **6** frolic, gambol, prance **9** horseplay

CEASE: **3** end **4** halt, quit, rest, stop **5** abate, pause, peter **6** desist, finish **7** abstain, refrain, suspend **9** cessation, culminate, terminate **11** discontinue

CEASE-FIRE: 5 truce **9** armistice

CEASELESS: 7 endless, nonstop **8** enduring, unending, untiring **9** continual, incessant, perpetual **11** everlasting, unremitting

CECROPS:
daughter: **5** Herse **8** Aglaurus **9** Pandrasos
father: **14** King Erechtheus
kingdom: **6** Attica
son: **11** Erysichthon
wife: **8** Aglaurus

CEDAR: 4 tree, wood **5** savin **6** deodar, sabine **9** evergreen
genus: **5** Thuja **6** Cedrus **9** Juniperus

CEDE: 4 fold, give **5** award, grant, leave, waive, yield **6** assign, resign, submit **7** abandon **8** renounce, transfer **9** surrender **10** relinquish

CEILING: 4 acme, dome, roof **5** limit **6** lining **7** maximum, plafond, plaster **8** covering

CELEBRATE: 4 keep, laud **5** bless, cheer, extol, feast, honor, revel **6** praise **7** applaud, glorify, observe, rejoice **8** eulogize, proclaim **9** ritualize **11** commemorate

CELEBRATED: 4 kept **5** famed, noted **6** famous **7** eminent, popular **8** glorious, observed, renowned **9** important, prominent, venerable **11** illustrious **13** distinguished

CELEBRATION: 4 fete, gala, rite **5** party **7** jubilee, triumph **8** birthday, ceremony, festival, jamboree **11** anniversary

CELEBRITY: 3 VIP **4** fame, hero, name, star **6** renown, repute **7** hotshot, notable **8** prestige, somebody **9** dignitary, superstar **11** heavyweight

CELERITY: 5 haste, hurry, speed **6** hustle **8** legerity, rapidity, velocity **9** quickness, swiftness

CELESTIAL: 3 sky **4** holy **6** divine, uranic **7** angelic **8** beatific, blissful, empyrean, ethereal, heavenly, Olympian **9** planetary, spiritual **12** astronomical, supernatural

CELESTIAL BEING: 3 god **5** angel **6** cherub, seraph **7** goddess

CELESTIAL BODY: 3 sun **4** moon, star **5** comet **6** nebula, planet

CELIBACY: 5 unwed **6** purity **8** chastity **9** virginity **10** abstinence

CELIBATE: 4 pure **6** chaste **8** virginal, virtuous **9** continent, unmarried

CELL: 3 egg **4** cage, germ, hold, jail **5** group, vault **6** embryo, lockup, prison **7** cellule, chamber, cubicle, dungeon **9** bacterium **11** compartment
blood: **3** red **5** white **8** hemocyte
part: **7** nucleus, vacuole **8** lysosome, membrane **9** centriole, cytoplasm **10** chromosome **11** chloroplast
study: **8** cytology

CELLAR: 4 cave **5** vault **8** basement **9** storeroom **10** downstairs, subterrane

CELLOPHANE: 7 wrapper **9** packaging **11** transparent

CELLULOID: 4 film **6** plastic

CELSIUS: 10 centigrade **11** thermometer

CELT: 4 Gael, Gaul, Manx, Scot **5** Irish, Welsh **6** Breton, Briton **7** Cornish **10** Highlander

CEMENT: 4 bind, glue, join, lime, lute **5** epoxy, imbed, paste, putty, stick, unify, unite **6** cohere, fasten, mastic, mortar, solder **8** adhesive, concrete, solidify

CEMETERY: **6** litten **7** charnel **8** boneyard, catacomb, Golgotha, mortuary **9** graveyard **10** churchyard, necropolis **11** polyandrium **12** potter's field

CENOBITE: **3** nun **4** monk **8** celibate, monastic **9** religious

CENSOR: **4** blip, edit **5** bleep, purge **6** critic, delete, forbid **7** control **8** restrict, suppress, withhold **10** blue-pencil

CENSORIOUS: **6** severe **7** abusive, carping **8** blameful, critical **10** denouncing **11** disparaging, reproachful **12** faultfinding

CENSURE: **4** carp **5** blame, chide, judge, scold **6** accuse, attack, berate, charge, rebuff, rebuke, tirade **7** chasten, condemn, impeach, reprove **8** admonish, disallow, reproach **9** castigate, challenge, criticize, reprimand **11** disapproval **12** reprehension

CENSUS: **4** list, poll **5** count, tally **6** number **11** enumeration

CENTAUR: **6** Chiron, Nessus **8** man-horse

CENTENNIAL STATE: **8** Colorado

CENTER: **3** hub, mid **4** axis, core, mean, nave **5** focus, heart, midst, pivot, point **6** hotbed, middle **7** capital, halfway, nucleus **8** focalize, midpoint **12** headquarters

CENTIGRADE: **5** scale **6** degree **7** Celsius **11** thermometer

CENTIPEDE: **4** boat **6** insect **9** arthropod, chilopoda

CENTRAL: **3** key, mid **4** main **5** basic, chief, focal, prime **6** median, middle **7** capital, leading, pivotal, primary **8** dominant, foremost, interior **9** essential **11** fundamental, significant

CENTRAL AMERICA:
countries: **6** Belize, Panama **8** Honduras, Salvador **9** Costa Rica, Guatemala, Nicaragua **10** El Salvador
explorers: **8** Columbus
features: **4** Maya **11** Cordilleras
water: **11** Panama Canal

CENTRALIZE: **5** focus **6** gather **8** assemble, condense **10** accumulate, streamline **11** concentrate

CENTRIFUGAL: **6** spiral **8** efferent **9** divergent, radiating, spreading

CENTURY: **3** age **10** one hundred

CEPHALOPOD: **5** squid **7** inkfish, mollusk, octopus **10** cuttlefish

CEPHEUS: **13** constellation
daughter: **9** Andromeda
kingdom: **8** Ethiopia
wife: **10** Cassiopeia

CERAMIC: **4** clay **5** brick, tiles **7** pottery **9** porcelain, stoneware **11** earthenware
oven: **4** kiln

CERATE: **3** wax **4** balm, lard **5** cream **8** ointment

CERBERUS:
father: **6** Typhon
form: **14** three-headed dog
guarded: **5** Hades
mother: **7** Echidna

CEREAL: **3** rye **4** bran, corn, food, mush, oats, rice **5** grain, wheat **6** barley, farina **7** oatmeal, soybean **8** porridge **9** buckwheat

CEREBRAL: **5** brain **7** psychic **8** highbrow **12** intellectual

CEREMONIAL: **5** lofty **6** formal, ritual **7** stately **8** mannered **12** conventional

CEREMONIOUS: **5** civil, exact, grand, lofty, stiff **6** proper, solemn **7** precise, studied **9** dignified, grandiose **10** respectful **11** punctilious

CEREMONY: **4** rite, show, sign **5** state **6** custom, parade, ritual **7** display, liturgy, pageant, prodigy **8** accolade, function, marriage, occasion, protocol **9** etiquette, formality, solemnity **10** observance **11** celebration

CERTAIN: **4** firm, real, sure, true **5** bound, clear, exact, fixed **6** actual, secure, stated **7** assured, precise, settled **8** absolute, apparent, constant, definite, positive, reliable **9** confident, convinced, satisfied, steadfast **10** dependable, inevitable, infallible, undeniable **11** determinate, indubitable, trustworthy, unequivocal **12** indisputable

CERTAINLY: **3** yes **5** truly **6** indeed, really, surely, verily **7** hardily **10** absolutely

CERTAINTY: **5** faith **8** credence, firmness, foregone, sureness **9** actuality, assurance, dogmatism **10** confidence, conviction

CERTIFICATE: **4** bond, deed **5** check **6** permit, ticket, verify **7** diploma, license, voucher **8** document **9** statement, testimony **10** credential **11** declaration

CERTIFY: **4** avow **5** swear **6** affirm, assure, attest, depose, verify **7** confirm, endorse, license, testify, witness **8** notarize **9** determine, guarantee **12** authenticate

CESSATION: **4** halt, lull, rest, stop **5** letup, pause, truce **6** ending, recess **7** ceasing, respite **8** interval, stoppage **9** armistice, remission **10** conclusion, suspension **11** termination **12** intermission, interruption

CETACEAN: **4** cete, orca **5** whale **6** beluga, mammal **7** dolphin, grampus **8** porpoise

CEYLON: **8** Sri Lanka

CHAD:
capital: **8** N'djamena (Fort Lamy)
cities: **4** Sarh **6** Abeche **7** Moundou
continent: **6** Africa
features: **12** Sahara Desert
languages: **6** Arabic, French
monetary unit: **5** franc
water: **5** Chari **6** Logone **8** Lake Chad

CHAFE: **3** irk, rub, vex **4** fret, fume, gall, rage, wear **5** anger, annoy, grind, scold **6** abrade, banter, bother, excite, harass, injury, nettle **7** incense, inflame, scratch **8** friction, irritate

CHAFF: **3** kid, rag **4** jest, joke, josh, ride **5** taunt, tease, trash, waste **6** banter, debris, refuse **7** rubbish **8** ridicule

CHAGRIN: **5** shame **6** dismay **7** mortify **8** irritate **11** displeasure, humiliation **15** dissatisfaction

CHAIN: **3** saw, set, tie **4** bind, bond, file, gang, iron, join, link, mail, moor **5** cable, leash, train **6** collar, fasten, letter, secure, series, string, tether **7** connect, embrace, enslave, manacle, network, shackle **8** bracelet, handcuff, restrain, sequence **9** constrain **10** chatelaine

CHAIR: **4** seat **5** bench, sedan, stool **6** office, rocker, throne **7** preside **8** recliner

CHAIRPERSON: **4** head **5** emcee **7** monitor, speaker **8** director **9** executive, moderator **10** supervisor **11** toastmaster

CHALCEDONY: **3** gem **4** onyx, opal, sard **5** agate, stone **6** jasper, quartz **7** mineral, opaline **8** hematite **9** carnelian **10** bloodstone

CHALDEA:
features: **6** Tigris **9** Euphrates
part of: **9** Babylonia

CHALET: **3** hut **5** cabin, house **7** cottage

CHALICE: **3** ama, cup **5** calix, grail **6** goblet

CHALK: **4** draw, talc, tick **5** point, score **6** blanch, bleach, crayon, credit, record, sketch, whiten **9** limestone

CHALK UP: **3** win **4** earn **5** score **6** obtain **7** achieve, acquire

CHALLENGE: **4** call, dare, defy, test **5** brave, claim, query, stump **6** accuse, appeal, charge, demand, forbid, invite **7** arraign, censure, protest, provoke, reclaim, summons **8** confront, question, reproach **9** exception, objection **10** controvert

CHAMBER: **4** cave, cell, flat, hall, room **5** bower, solar **6** alcove, atrium, camera, hollow, parlor **7** bedroom, caisson, cubicle **8** assembly **9** apartment, camarilla, vestibule **11** compartment, legislature

CHAMBERLAIN: **4** lord **7** officer, servant, steward **9** attendant, treasurer **10** camerlengo

CHAMOIS: **4** skin **5** cloth **6** chammy, fabric, shammy **7** leather **8** antelope

CHAMPAGNE: **4** wine **5** color **6** bubbly

with orange juice: **6** Mimosa

CHAMPION: **3** ace **4** hero **6** assert, backer, defend, squire, victor, winner **7** fighter, heroine, protect **8** advocate, defender, greatest, medalist, unbeaten **9** challenge, combatant, firstrate **10** undefeated **11** outstanding, titleholder

CHAMPIONSHIP: **3** cup **5** crown, title **7** defense, pennant **8** advocacy, World Cup **9** Super Bowl, supremacy **10** Stanley Cup **11** World Series

CHANCE: **3** hap, lot **4** case, fate, luck, odds, risk **5** fluke, stake **6** gamble, happen, hazard, mishap, raffle, random **7** fortune, lottery, outcome, outlook, stumble, venture **8** accident, casualty, fortuity **9** adventure, happening, unplanned **10** contingent **11** opportunity, possibility, probability

CHANCY: **4** iffy **5** hairy, risky, rocky **6** touchy, tricky **7** dubious, erratic **8** perilous **9** dangerous **10** auspicious, precarious

CHANDELIER: **5** light **6** luster **7** fixture **11** candelabrum **12** candleholder

CHANGE: **4** move, swap, turn, vary, veer **5** adapt, alter, amend, break, shift **6** evolve, modify, mutate, remove, revamp, revise, switch **7** commute, convert, deviate, replace **8** castrate, reversal, revision, transfer **9** deviation, diversity, rearrange, transform, transpose, variation **10** alteration, conversion, correction, difference, innovation, substitute, transition **13** metamorphosis

CHANGEABLE: **5** giddy **6** fickle, fitful, mobile **7** erratic, mutable, variant **8** amenable, unstable, unsteady, volatile **9** alterable, impulsive, irregular, uncertain, unsettled **10** capricious, irresolute **11** convertible

CHANGELESS: **4** same **5** fixed **6** stable, steady **7** regular **8** constant, enduring **9** steadfast **10** invariable

CHANGE OF HEART: **8** reversal **10** conversion

CHANGEOVER: **5** shift **6** switch **10** alteration, conversion, transition

CHANNEL: **4** duct, main, pipe, send, tube, vein **5** canal, chase, ditch, drain, drill, flume, flute, river, route, sinus, steer **6** arroyo, artery, canyon, furrow, groove, gutter, medium, strait, stream, trough **7** conduct, conduit, passage, tideway **8** aqueduct, guideway, transmit **10** instrument **11** watercourse

CHANNEL ISLANDS: **4** Herm **5** Lihou **6** Jersey, Jethou **7** Brechou **8** Alderney, Guernsey **9** Great Sark **10** Little Sark
place: **14** English Channel

CHANT: **4** cant, hymn, sing, song, tune **5** carol, croon, psalm, trill **6** anthem, chorus, Hallel, warble **7** worship **8** canticle, vocalize **9** plainsong **10** cantillate, intonation

CHAOS: **4** mess, void **5** babel, chasm **6** bedlam, jumble, uproar **7** anarchy, entropy, turmoil **8** disorder, shambles **9** confusion **10** unruliness **11** lawlessness, pandemonium

CHAOTIC: **7** muddled, riotous **8** confused **9** turbulent **10** disordered **13** helter-skelter

CHAP: **3** boy, dry, jaw, lad, man **4** baby, band, chip, chop, gent, mash **5** buyer, child, chink, cleft, crack, knock, lover, split, trade, youth **6** barter, fellow, redden, strike, stroke **7** fissure, roughen **8** customer **9** gentleman

CHAPEL: **6** bethel, church, shrine, vestry **7** chantry, oratory **9** sanctuary **10** tabernacle

CHAPERON: **4** hood **5** guard, guide **6** attend, escort, matron **7** oversee **8** guardian **9** companion, governess, protector, safeguard

CHAPLAIN: **5** padre, rabbi **6** pastor, priest **8** minister, preacher, reverend **9** clergyman **11** clergywoman

CHAPLET: **4** band, bead **5** crown **6** circle, fillet, rosary, wreath **7** coronet, garland **8** necklace, ornament

CHAPMAN: **5** buyer **6** dealer, trader **7** peddler **8** merchant

CHAPTER: **3** era **4** body **5** lodge, phase, topic **6** branch, member, period **7** episode, meeting, section **8** assembly **9** affiliate

CHAR: **4** burn, sear **5** broil, singe, trout **6** scorch **7** blacken **9** carbonize

CHARACTER: **4** bent, card, fame, kind, lead, logo, mold, part, role, sign, sort, soul, star, tone, type **5** brand, ethos, fiber, stamp, style, trait **6** aspect, figure, letter, nature, repute, spirit, symbol, weirdo **7** courage, engrave, essence, impress, oddball, quality **8** identity, original **9** attribute, eccentric **10** appearance, reputation **11** personality, temperament **12** constitution, intelligence

CHARACTERISTIC: **4** cast, mark **5** trait **6** inborn, nature, unique **7** feature, quality, special, typical **8** inherent, property, symbolic, tendency **9** attribute, mannerism, trademark **11** distinctive, inclination, peculiarity **13** individuality

CHARACTERIZE: **4** mark **6** define, depict, typify **7** imprint, outline, portray **8** describe, indicate, typecast **9** delineate, designate, represent, symbolize **10** pigeonhole **11** distinguish

CHARADE: **4** fake, game **5** trick **6** enigma, puzzle, riddle **7** picture **8** disguise, pretense

CHARGE: **3** bid, fee **4** bill, cost, dues, duty, fill, levy, load, rate, rush, toll **5** debit, gripe, onset, order, price, storm, weigh **6** accuse, aerate, allege, attack, burden, credit, damage, demand, finger, impute, indict, invade, saddle, sortie, tariff **7** arraign, command, custody, expense, impeach, mandate **8** chastise, overload **9** challenge, onslaught, penetrate **10** commission, injunction, management **11** arraignment, incriminate, instruction

CHARGEABLE: **6** liable **10** answerable, burdensome **11** responsible, troublesome

CHARGED: **4** live **5** tense **6** filled, loaded **7** excited **9** emotional **10** purposeful

CHARGER: **4** dish **5** horse, mount, steed **7** accuser, platter **10** instrument

CHARIOT: **3** car **4** biga, cart, char **5** buggy, wagon **6** charet, essede **7** vehicle **8** carriage, quadriga

CHARISMA: **4** gift **5** charm, power **6** allure, appeal, dazzle **7** glamour, pizzazz **9** magnetism **11** fascination

CHARITABLE: **4** kind **6** benign, giving, humane **7** lenient, liberal **8** generous **9** forgiving **10** altruistic, benevolent, thoughtful **11** considerate, sympathetic **12** eleemosynary **13** philanthropic

CHARITY: **4** alms, gift, love, pity **5** mercy **6** relief **7** handout **8** donation, goodwill, kindness **10** almsgiving, assistance, compassion, generosity **11** fundraising **12** philanthropy

CHARLATAN: **4** sham **5** cheat, faker, fraud, phony, quack **8** impostor **9** pretender **10** medicaster, mountebank

CHARM: **4** calm, draw, song **5** allay, freet, freit, grace, lucky, magic, spell **6** allure, amulet, beauty, caract, entice, fetish, melody, please, saphie, seduce, soothe, subdue, summon **7** attract, beguile, bewitch, conjure, control, delight, enamour, enchant, enthral, flatter, glamour, sorcery **8** charisma, enthrall, entrance, talisman **9** agreeable, captivate, fascinate, magnetism, seduction **10** attraction

CHARMING: **4** cute **6** lovely **7** winning, winsome **8** adorable, delicate, enticing, inviting **9** agreeable, beautiful, glamorous, ravishing, seductive **10** attractive, enchanting **11** captivating, titillating **12** electrifying

CHARON:
father: **6** Erebus
job: **7** boatman **8** ferryman
mother: **3** Nox
river: **4** Styx

CHART: **3** map **4** plan, plot **5** draft, graph, table **6** design, devise, record, scheme **7** diagram, explore, outline, project **8** document, platform **9** blueprint

CHARTER: **4** deed, hire, pact, rent **5** grant, lease **6** member, permit **7** license **8** sanction **9** agreement, privilege **10** commission **12** constitution

CHARY: **3** shy **4** dear, safe, wary **5** leery, scant **6** frugal **7** careful, guarded, prudent, sparing **8** cautious, discreet, hesitant, reserved, vigilant **9** reluctant, treasured **10** economical, scrupulous, suspicious

CHARYBDIS:
associated with: **6** Scylla **9** whirlpool
father: **8** Poseidon
form: **7** monster
mother: **4** Gaea

CHASE: **4** hunt, shag, shoo, sick **5** catch, harry, hound, track **6** follow, gallop, harass, pursue, quarry, shadow **7** pursuit

CHASM: **3** gap, pit **4** gulf, rift, void **5** abyss, blank, cleft, gorge **6** arroyo, canyon, cavity, crater, hiatus **7** fissure **8** aperture, crevasse **9** oversight

CHASTE: **4** pure **5** clean, moral **6** decent, honest, proper, vestal **7** refined **8** celibate, innocent, spotless, virginal, virtuous **9** continent, incorrupt, undefiled, wholesome **10** immaculate

CHASTEN: **4** rate **5** abase, scold, smite **6** humble, punish, refine, subdue **7** censure, correct, upbraid **8** chastise **9** castigate, humiliate, reprimand **10** discipline

CHASTISE: **4** beat, flog, lash, ream, whip **5** blame, scold, spank, strap, taunt **6** accuse, berate, pummel, punish, rebuke, thrash **7** chasten, correct, reprove, scourge **8** admonish **9** castigate **10** discipline

CHASTITY: **5** honor **6** purity, virtue **7** modesty **8** celibacy, devotion, goodness, morality **9** innocence, integrity, virginity **10** abstinence

CHAT: **3** gab, rap **4** coze, gist, talk **5** dally, point, prate, speak **6** babble, cackle, gabble, gibber, gossip, jabber **7** chatter, palaver, prattle **8** converse, dialogue **11** confabulate **12** conversation

CHATEAU: **5** house, manor, villa **6** castle, estate **7** mansion

CHATEAUBRIAND: **4** beef **5** steak **10** tenderloin

CHATTEL: **4** gear **5** goods, slave, wares **7** capital, effects **8** property **10** belongings

CHATTER: **3** gab, yap **4** blab, chat, talk **5** clack, prate, shake **6** babble, cackle, gabble, gibber, gossip, jabber, palter, rattle, tattle **7** blabber, brabble, chipper, prabble, prattle, twaddle **8** chitchat, schmooze, verbiage **11** goosecackle

CHATTERBOX: **5** clack **6** gossip, magpie **7** windbag **8** busybody **9** talkative **12** blabbermouth

CHATTY: **5** gabby, windy, wordy **7** gossipy, verbose **8** friendly **9** garrulous, talkative **10** loquacious

CHAUVINISM: **8** jingoism **9** fanatical, prejudice **10** partiality, patriotism **11** nationalism

CHEAP: **4** poor, vile **5** gaudy, petty, price, tacky, tight **6** abject, cheesy, common, shoddy, stingy, trashy **7** bargain, chintzy **8** inferior, purchase **9** worthless **10** economical **11** depreciated, inexpensive

CHEAPEN: **6** reduce **7** corrupt **8** belittle, diminish **9** denigrate, devaluate, downgrade

CHEAT: **3** con, gyp **4** bilk, dupe, fake, flam, fool, hoax, jilt, liar, rook, sham, take **5** crook, dodge, fling, fraud, gouge, rogue, scamp, screw, shark, short, spoil, trick, welsh **6** baffle, chisel, deride, doodle, fiddle, fleece, humbug, renege, shaver **7** beguile, deceive, defraud, finesse, gudgeon, mislead, plunder, quibble, scammer, shyster, swindle **8** artifice, delusion, flimflam, hoodwink, impostor **9** bamboozle, chicanery, scoundrel, victimize **10** mountebank

CHECK: **3** tab **4** balk, curb, hold, mark, rein, stem, stop, stub, test **5** allay, audit, block, brake, daunt, delay, deter, frisk, limit, plaid, probe, quell, quilt, repel, stall, still, study, tally, taunt **6** arrest, bridle, defeat, detain, hinder, impede, oppose, quench, rebate, review, stifle, survey, verify **7** confirm, control, examine, inhibit, inquiry, inspect, monitor, repress, reprove, setback **8** research, scrutiny, withhold **9** constrain, hindrance, restraint, supervise **10**

neutralize **11** certificate, examination

CHECKERED: **4** pied **5** plaid **6** motley, varied **7** quilted **9** patchwork **10** variegated **11** diversified

CHECKMATE: **4** gain, stop, undo **6** corner, defeat, outwit, thwart **7** triumph **9** frustrate **11** countermove

CHEEK: **4** gall, jowl **5** nerve **8** audacity, boldness, temerity **9** brashness, impudence, sauciness **10** effrontery

CHEEP: **3** pip, yap **4** peep **5** chirp, tweet **6** shrill, squeak, tattle **7** chipper, chirrup, twitter

CHEER: **3** ole, rah **4** clap, food, hope, root, yell **5** bravo, drink, elate, feast, heart, shout **6** gaiety, hurrah, solace, uplift **7** acclaim, animate, applaud, cherish, comfort, console, hearten, inspire, ovation, refresh, rejoice, support **8** brighten, inspirit **9** encourage, happiness, merriment **10** exhilarate, invigorate **11** hospitality

CHEERFUL: **3** gay **4** airy, glad, rosy **5** cadgy, happy, jolly, merry, sunny **6** blithe, bouncy, bright, cheery, chirpy, genial, hearty, lively **7** chipper **8** pleasant **9** contented, sprightly **10** enlivening **11** comfortable **12** lighthearted

CHEERLESS: **3** sad **4** cold, glum, gray **5** bleak **6** dismal, dreary, gloomy, solemn, sullen **7** austere, forlorn **8** dejected **10** depressing, dispirited, melancholy **11** comfortless

CHEESE: **3** pot **4** blue, Brie, Edam, feta, Goya, hand, Jack **5** brick, churn, cream, Dutch, Gouda, Swiss **6** Cantal, Dunlop, farmer, Leyden, Mysost, Romano, Saanen, Sbrinz, Spalen, Tilsit **7** cheddar, cottage, gervais, Gruyere, Munster, Primost, ricotta, Sapsago, Stilton **8** American, Bel Paese, Cheshire, Parmesan, pimiento, Sorrento, St. Paulin, Trappist, Vacherin **9** Camembert, gammelost, Limburger, provolone, reblochon, Roquefort **10** Gorgonzola, Lancashire, mozzarella, Neufchatel **11** Emmenthaler, Liederkranz, Pont l'Eveque, Port du Salut, schmierkase, Wensleydale **13** Cucciocavallo

concerning: **6** caseic **7** caseous

dishes: **4** cake **6** fondue, omelet **7** rarebit, souffle

types: **4** hard, soft **8** semihard, very hard **9** processed

CHEESY: **4** poor **5** cheap **6** caseic, shabby, sleazy, trashy **7** caseous **8** inferior **9** worthless

CHEMICAL: **3** sal **4** acid, base, salt **5** amide, azine, ester, imine, purin **6** alkali, boride **7** element, metamer **8** catalyst, compound

measure: **4** dram, gram **5** liter, titer

CHEMISE: **5** dress, shirt, smock **8** camisole, lingerie **12** undergarment

CHERISH: **3** hug, pet **4** like, love, save **5** adore, cling, guard, honor, nurse, prize, value **6** admire, caress, coddle, esteem, fondle, foster, harbor, nestle, pamper, revere **7** comfort, embrace, indulge, nourish, nurture, protect, support, sustain **8** inspirit, preserve, treasure **9** cultivate **10** appreciate

CHERRY:

genus: **6** prunus

types: **4** bing, duke, gean **5** morel **7** capulin, lambert, marasca, mazzard, morello, oxheart **8** amarelle, Napoleon **9** bigarreau **10** maraschino

CHERUB: **5** angel, saint **6** seraph, spirit

CHESS:
pieces: **3** man **4** king, pawn, rook **5** horse, queen **6** bishop, castle, knight
terms: **4** draw, mate, move **5** debut **6** castle, fidate, gambit, gardez **7** en prise, endgame, j'adoube, opening, zugwang **8** scacchic **9** checkmate, stalemate **10** fianchetto

CHEST: **3** ark, box **4** bust, fund, safe **5** bosom, front, hutch, trunk **6** basket, breast, bureau, casket, coffer, coffin, hamper, locker, shrine, thorax **7** cabinet, commode, dresser **8** cupboard, treasury **9** container, strongbox **10** chiffonier, receptacle

CHESTERFIELD: **4** coat, sofa **5** couch, divan **7** topcoat **8** overcoat **9** cigarette, davenport

CHESTNUT: **3** bay **4** joke, tree **5** brown, color, horse **6** cliche, sorrel
genus: **8** Castanea

CHEVALIER: **4** lord **5** cadet, noble **6** knight **7** gallant **8** cavalier, horseman **9** gentleman

CHEVRON: **4** beam, mark **5** badge, glove **6** stripe, zigzag **7** molding **8** insignia

CHEW: **3** cud, eat **4** bite, gnaw, mull **5** champ, chomp, crush, grind, munch **6** ponder **8** ruminate **9** manducate, masticate **10** deliberate

CHEW OUT: **5** scold **6** berate **7** upbraid **9** castigate, criticize

CHIC: **4** posh, trim **5** nifty, smart, swank, vogue **6** classy, dapper, modish, trendy **7** elegant, faddish, stylish **11** fashionable

CHICAGO:
features: **5** O'Hare **9** Gold Coast **10** Sears Tower **12** Fort Dearborn
native: **9** Chicagoan
nickname: **9** Windy City
place: **8** Illinois
water: **12** Lake Michigan

CHICANERY: **4** ploy, ruse, wile **5** fraud, trick **6** deceit **7** cunning **8** artifice, cheating, trickery **9** deception **10** dishonesty

CHICHI: **4** arty **5** showy, swank **6** frilly **7** pompous, splashy **9** grandiose **10** flamboyant **11** pretentious

CHICK: **4** girl **5** child, woman **6** moppet, sprout **7** chicken **9** youngster

CHICKEN: **3** hen **4** cock, fowl **5** biddy, capon, chick, fryer, sissy, timid **6** afraid, chicky, coward, pullet, yellow **7** broiler, gutless, poultry, rooster **8** cockerel

CHICKENHEARTED: **5** sissy, timid **6** afraid, yellow **7** fearful, gutless **8** cowardly

CHICORY: **4** bunk, herb, root **5** plant **6** endive **7** witloof **9** radicchio

CHIDE: **4** rail **5** blame, scold **6** berate, rebuke **7** censure, lecture, reprove, upbraid, wrangle **8** admonish, reproach **9** castigate, criticize, reprehend, reprimand

CHIEF: **3** big, key **4** arch, boss, duce, duke, head, high, king, lord, main **5** elder, first, great, major, prime, ruler, vital **6** bigwig, leader, master, rector, sachem **7** capital, captain, central, crucial, eminent, foreman, kingpin, premier, supreme **8** dominant, foremost **9** commander, paramount, president, principal, prominent **10** ringleader

CHIFFONIER: **5** chest **6** bureau **7** cabinet, commode, dresser **8** cupboard

CHIGNON: **3** bun **4** knot **5** twist **6** hairdo

CHILD: **3** ben, boy, bud, cub, imp, kid, lad, son, tad, tot **4** babe, baby, brat, girl, lass, page, tyke, waif **5** chick, minor, youth **6** cherub, infant, moppet, orphan, squirt, urchin **7** bambino, progeny, tadpole, toddler **8** bantling, daughter **9** offspring, youngster **10** adolescent, descendant

CHILDBIRTH: **5** labor **7** lying-in, travail **8** delivery, nativity **9** producing **11** confinement, parturition

CHILDISH: **5** naive, petty, silly, young **6** puling, senile, simple **7** asinine, babyish, foolish, kiddish, puerile **8** immature, juvenile **9** childlike, credulous, frivolous, infantile

CHILE:
capital: **8** Santiago
cities: **5** Arica **6** Temuco **7** Iquique **10** Concepcion, Valparaiso, Vina del Mar **11** Antofagasta, Punta Arenas
conqueror: **8** Valdivia
continent: **12** South America
ethnic groups: **6** Indian **7** mestizo, Spanish
features: **4** Maco, Toro **5** Andes, Maipu, Pular, Torre, Yogan **6** Llaima **13** Atacama Desert
languages: **7** Spanish
monetary unit: **4** peso
native: **7** Chilean
territories: **10** Antarctica (part) **12** Easter Island **14** Tierra del Fuego **20** Juan Fernandez Islands
water: **3** Loa **5** Itata, Maipu, Maule **6** Chuapa **8** Valdivia

CHILL: **3** icy, raw **4** cold, cool **5** fever, rigor, shake **6** arctic, dampen, freeze, frigid, frosty, shiver **7** depress, distant, glacial, hostile **8** coldness, dispirit, gelidity **11** refrigerate

CHILLER: **5** eerie **7** shocker **8** thriller **11** frightening

CHILL OUT: **5** relax

CHILLY: **3** raw **4** cold, cool **5** bleak, crisp, nippy **6** arctic, biting, drafty, frigid, frosty **8** freezing **10** unfriendly

CHIME: **4** bell, edge, gong, ring, ting, toll **5** knell, sound **6** accord, cymbal, jingle, melody **7** concord, harmony **9** agreement

CHIME IN: **4** tell **5** offer, state **6** remark **7** declare **9** interrupt

CHIMERA: **5** dream **6** mirage **7** fantasy, monster **8** delusion, illusion **11** fabrication

CHIMERICAL: **4** wild **6** absurd, unreal **7** utopian **8** delusive, fabulous, fanciful, mythical **9** fantastic, fictional, imaginary, unfounded, visionary

CHIMNEY: **3** lum **4** flue, pipe, tube, vent **5** gully, stack **6** funnel, hearth **7** furnace **9** fireplace **10** smokestack

CHIMPANZEE: **3** ape **5** chimp **6** animal, bonobo, monkey **7** primate **10** anthropoid, troglodyte

CHIN: **3** jaw, rap **4** chat, talk **6** button, mentum **8** chitchat, mandible

CHINA: **4** ware **6** dishes **7** ceramic, pottery, service **8** crockery **9** porcelain, tableware **11** earthenware
also called: **4** Tsao **5** Seres **6** Cathay
autonomous regions: **6** Xizang (Tibet) **9** Nei Mongol **10** Ningxia Hui **13** Guangxi Zhuang, Xinjiang Uygur
boat: **4** bark, junk **6** sampan
capital: **7** Beijing (Peking)
cities: **4** Luda (Lu-ta) **5** Wuhan **6** Harbin **7** Nanjing (Nanking), Qingdao (Tsingtao), Tianjin (Tientsin) **8** Shanghai, Shenyang

(Mukden) **9** Chongqing (Chungking), Guangzhou (Canton)
continent: **4** Asia
cooking: **5** Hunan **6** Fukien, Peking **8** Szechuan **9** Cantonese
dynasties: **3** Han, Qin, Sui, Wei, Yin **4** Chin, Chou, Hsia, Ming, Song, Tang, Tsin, Yuan **5** Shang, Wu Tai **6** Manchu, San Kuo
ethnic groups: **6** Korean, Manchu, Mongol **10** Han Chinese
features: **9** Great Wall, Ming Tombs **10** Gobi Desert **11** Gezhouba Dam **18** Terra-Cotta Warriors
islands: **4** Amoy **5** Macao **6** Hainan, Taiwan **7** Formosa
languages: **3** Gan, Hui, Min, Yue **5** Hakka, Xiang **6** Zhuang **8** Mandarin **9** Cantonese
leaders: **3** Mao **9** Mao Zedong, Sun Yat-sen, Zhou Enlai (Chou Enlai) **10** Hua Guofeng **11** Den Xiaoping **13** Chiang Kai-shek
monetary unit: **4** yuan
municipalities: **7** Beijing, Tianjin **8** Shanghai
native: **7** Chinese
provinces: **5** Anhui (Anhwei), Gansu (Kansu), Hebei (Hopei), Henan (Honan), Hubei (Hupei), Hunan, Jilin (Kirin) **6** Hainan, Yunnan, Fujian (Fukien), Shanxi (Shansi) **7** Guizhou (Kweichow), Jiangsu (Kiangsu), Jiangxi (Kiangsi), Qinghai (Tsinghai), Shaanxi (Shensi), Sichuan (Szechwan) **8** Liaoning, Shandong (Shantung) **9** Guangdong (Kwantung), Zheijiang (Chekiang) **12** Heilongjiang

CHINE: **4** back, meat **5** spine **6** cleave **8** backbone

CHINK: **3** gap **4** bore, cash, coin, gash, rent, rift, rime, slit **5** cleft, crack, money **6** cranny, jingle **7** chinkle, crevice, fissure **8** aperture

CHINOOK STATE: **10** Washington

CHINTZY: **4** mean **5** cheap, gaudy, petty, tight **6** sleazy, stingy

CHIP: **3** bit, cut, hew **4** clip, coin, flaw, nick, pare **5** chaff, chunk, crack, flake, money, piece, scrap, shard, token **6** chisel, damage, marker **7** shaving, whittle **8** fragment, splinter

CHIPS: **4** coin **5** money, token **7** markers

CHIP IN: **3** pay **9** interpose, subscribe **10** contribute

CHIPMUNK: **6** chippy, gopher, rodent **8** squirrel

CHIPPER: **3** gay **4** spry **5** alert, alive, chirp, cocky, happy, perky **6** frisky, lively **7** chatter, twitter **8** cheerful **9** energetic, sprightly

CHIROGRAPHY: **7** writing **10** penmanship **11** calligraphy, handwriting

CHIRP: **4** call, peep, pipe, sing **5** cheep, chirt, sound, tweet **7** chipper, chirrup, chitter, twitter

CHIRRUP: **4** call, peep, pipe, sing **5** cheep, chirt, sound, tweet **7** chipper, chitter, twitter

CHISEL: **3** cut, gyp **4** bilk, chip, form, rook, tool **5** carve, cheat, gouge, knife, shape **7** bargain, defraud, engrave, intrude **9** sculpture

CHISELER: **4** fake **5** cheat, crook **8** swindler

CHIT: **3** IOU, kid, tab **4** bill, memo, note **5** check, child, draft **6** infant, moppet, sprout **7** voucher **9** offspring **10** memorandum

CHITCHAT: **4** talk **6** babble, banter, drivel, gossip **7** chatter, prattle **12** conversation

CHIVALROUS: **5** brave, noble **6** gentle, heroic, polite **7** gallant, valiant **8** generous, knightly **9** courteous, honorable **10** courageous **11** considerate

CHIVALRY: **5** valor **7** courage **8** fairness **10** knighthood

CHIVY, CHIVVY: **4** bait, hunt, race **5** annoy, chase, hound, tease **6** badger, bother, harass, pursue **7** pursuit, scamper, torment **9** confusion

CHLORIDE: **4** salt **5** ester **7** muriate **8** chemical, compound

CHLORINE: **6** bleach **7** element, halogen **12** disinfectant

CHLOROFORM: **4** kill **5** toxic **6** poison **7** solvent **10** anesthetic

CHOCOLATE: **3** bar **4** food **5** candy, cocoa, color, drink **8** beverage **10** confection

CHOICE: **4** best, fine, pick, rare **5** cream, elite, prime, stock, voice **6** better, flower, option, picked, select, winner **7** popular, variety, verdict **8** deciding, decision, delicate, druthers, election, judgment, uncommon, volition **9** excellent, exquisite, selection **10** assortment, preferable, preference, substitute **11** alternative

CHOIR: **4** band **5** quire **6** chorus **7** singers
leader: **6** cantor **9** precentor

CHOKE: **3** gag **4** clog, fail, fill, lose, plug **5** block, close, crack, wring **6** hinder, impede, stifle **7** congest, silence, smother **8** obstruct, stoppage, strangle, suppress **9** constrict, neckcloth, suffocate **10** asphyxiate

CHOLERIC: **3** mad **5** angry, cross, huffy, irate, testy **6** cranky, grumpy, touchy **7** enraged, grouchy, peevish **8** wrathful **9** impatient, irascible **11** belligerent, quarrelsome

CHOMP: **4** bite, chew **6** crunch **9** masticate

CHOOSE: **3** opt **4** cull, pick, take, vote **5** adopt, elect, fancy **6** decide, prefer, select **7** embrace **9** determine

CHOOSY: **5** fussy, picky **7** finicky **9** selective **10** fastidious, particular

CHOP: **3** cut, hew, lop **4** chip, dice, gash, hack, meat, slit **5** carve, cleft, crack, grade, knock, mince, sever, slash, split **6** barter, change, cleave **7** quality **8** exchange

CHOP-CHOP: **4** fast **7** quickly, rapidly **8** promptly **12** lickety-split

CHOPIN, FREDERIC FRANCOIS:
birthplace: **6** Poland
lover: **10** George Sand
occupation: **7** pianist, teacher **8** composer

CHOPPY: **4** wavy **5** jerky, rough **6** ripply **7** chapped, violent

CHORD: **4** cord, note, rope, tone **5** major, minor, music, nerve, triad **6** accord, string, tendon **9** harmonize

CHORE: **3** job **4** duty, task, work **5** stint **6** effort, errand **8** scutwork **9** housework **10** assignment

CHOREOGRAPHY: **7** dancing **11** composition

CHOROGRAPHY: **5** chart **7** diagram, mapping **9** mapmaking

CHORTLE: **5** laugh, snort **6** cackle, giggle **7** chuckle, snicker

CHORUS: **4** echo, song **5** choir **6** accord, melody, unison **7** concert, harmony, refrain, singers **8** carolers, ensemble, response **9** agreement, consensus

CHOSEN: **5** elite, named **6** called, picked, tabbed **7** elected **8** selected **9** preferred

CHOW: **3** bye, dog **4** eats, food, grub, meal **8** victuals

CHRIST: **3** God, Son **4** Lord **5** Jesus **7** Messiah, Saviour

CHRISTEN: **4** name **5** bless **7** baptize, immerse

CHRISTIAN: **5** pious **7** devoted **8** disciple, faithful **9** religious **10** charitable

CHRISTIANIA:
former capital of: **6** Norway
new name: **4** Oslo

CHRISTMAS: **4** Noel, Xmas, yule **7** holiday **8** festival, Nativity, yuletide

CHRISTMAS CAROL, A:
author: **14** Charles Dickens
characters: **7** Tiny Tim **10** Bob Crachit **13** Christmas Past **15** Christmas Future, Ebenezer Scrooge **16** Christmas Present

CHROMIUM: **7** element, mineral

CHRONIC: **5** fixed, usual **6** inbred, severe **7** intense, lasting, routine **8** constant, habitual, stubborn **9** confirmed, continual, incessant, incurable, lingering, prolonged, recurring **10** continuous

CHRONICLE: **4** epic, tell **5** diary, story **6** annals, record **7** account, history, journal **8** archives, describe, register **9** narrative

CHRONOLOGICAL: **5** dated **7** ordered **9** tabulated **10** classified, sequential, successive **11** consecutive

CHRONOMETER: **5** clock, timer, watch **9** hourglass, metronome, timepiece

CHUBBY: **5** plump, pudgy, round, tubby **6** chunky, flabby, rotund **8** heavyset, rolypoly **10** overweight

CHUCK: **3** pat **4** beef, cast, food, hurl, jerk, junk, oust, shed, toss **5** cluck, ditch, fling, pitch, scrap, throw **7** discard **9** dismissal

CHUCKLE: **5** exult, laugh **6** cackle, giggle, teehee, titter **7** chortle, snicker

CHUM: **3** pal **4** mate **5** buddy, crony **6** friend **7** comrade **8** sidekick **9** associate, companion, confidant

CHUMP: **3** oaf, sap **4** boob, dolt, fool, goof **6** sucker **8** lunkhead **9** blockhead

CHUNK: **3** gob, wad **4** mass, slab, slug **5** piece, whang **7** portion

CHUNKY: **5** beefy, dumpy, husky, lumpy, plump, squat, stout **6** chubby, stocky, stubby

CHURCH: **4** sect **5** creed, faith **6** temple **7** edifice, synaxis **8** basilica **9** sanctuary **10** house of god **12** congregation
concerning: **9** ecclesial **14** ecclesiastical
division: **3** see **5** synod **6** parish **7** diocese, prelacy **10** episcopacy, episcopate, sacerdotum
parts: **3** pew **4** apse, bema, font, nave **5** aisle, altar, bench, solea **6** belfry, chapel, pulpit, vestry **7** balcony, chancel, galilee, narthex, oratory, reredos, steeple **8** cantoria, sacristy, transept **9** bell tower **10** clerestory
service: **4** mass, rite **5** matin **7** baptism, nocturn, vespers **8** evensong **9** communion
workers: **4** dean, pope **5** abbot, elder, vicar **6** beadle, bishop, curate, deacon, lector, priest, reader, sexton, warden **7** ostiary, prelate, primate, sacrist **8** altarboy, minis-

ter, reverend **9** clergyman, presbyter

CHURCHYARD: **8** cemetery **9** graveyard

CHURL: **3** cad **4** boor, lout, serf **5** carle, ceorl, chuff, knave, miser, yokel **6** rustic **7** haskard, husband, niggard, peasant, skimper, villain **8** tightwad **10** countryman

CHURLISH: **4** mean **5** blunt, crude, gruff, rough, surly **6** crabby, crusty, ornery, rustic, sullen, vulgar **7** boorish, crabbed, grouchy, lowbred, uncivil, violent **10** ungracious

CHURN: **4** beat, foam, stir, whip **5** shake, swirl **6** vessel **7** agitate, ferment

CHUTE: **4** ramp, rush, tube **5** flume, rapid, slide, slope **6** trough **7** cascade, channel **9** parachute, waterfall **11** watercourse

CICERONE: **5** guide, pilot **6** mentor **9** conductor

CIDER: **5** apple **7** alcohol **8** beverage

CIGAR: **4** toby, weed **5** claro, smoke, stogy **6** boquet, Corona, Havana, stogie **7** bouquet, cheroot, tobacco **8** panatela, perfecto **9** Belvedere
storage: **7** humidor

CIGARETTE: **3** fag **4** biri, butt, puff **5** cubeb, smoke **6** gasper, reefer

CILIUM: **4** hair **7** eyelash

CINCH: **4** grip, sash, snap **5** girth **6** assure, breeze, fasten **8** pushover **9** certainty

CINCTURE: **4** band, belt **5** girth **6** collar, girdle **8** encircle **9** enclosure **11** surrounding

CINDER: **4** coal, gray, slag, soot **5** ashes, dross **6** embers, scoria **7** clinker

CINEMA: **4** film, show **5** bijou, flick, movie **6** screen **7** picture, theater **13** motion picture

CINNAMON: **4** bark, tree **5** brown, spice **6** cassia

CIPHER: **3** nil **4** code, nada, null, zero **5** aught, blank, zilch, zippo **6** decode, figure, letter, naught, number, symbol **7** nothing, unravel **9** nonentity **10** cryptogram

CIRCA: **4** near **5** about **6** around **7** roughly **13** approximation

CIRCE:
brother: **6** Aeetes
father: **3** Sol **6** Helios
form: **9** sorceress
island: **5** Aeaea
lover: **7** Ulysses **8** Odysseus
mother: **5** Perse
son: **5** Comus **6** Agrius **9** Telegonus

CIRCLE: **3** lap, orb, set **4** bowl, disc, disk, gyre, halo, hoop, loop, ring, rink, turn **5** crowd, cycle, globe, group, orbit, pivot, realm, round, swirl, twirl, wheel **6** clique, collet, cordon, corona, girdle, radius, rotary, rotate, sphere, spiral, system **7** circlet, circuit, company, compass, coronet, coterie, enclose, equator, friends, revolve, ringlet **8** encircle, insiders, sorority, surround **9** circulate, encompass **10** associates, companions, fraternity, revolution **13** circumference

CIRCLET: **4** band, hoop, ring **6** bangle, wreath **8** bracelet, headband

CIRCUIT: **3** lap **4** area, beat, loop, tour, zone **5** ambit, cycle, jaunt, orbit, round, route, track, whirl **6** course, hookup **7** compass **8** boundary, district **9** excursion **10** revolution **13** circumference

CIRCUITOUS: **4** mazy **6** curved **7** crooked, devious, turning, twisted, winding **8** circular, indirect, rambling **9** ambiguous, deceitful, underhand, wandering **10** meandering, roundabout, serpentine **11** complicated **12** labyrinthine

CIRCULAR: **4** bill **5** flier, flyer, round **6** curved, insert, ringed **7** annular, leaflet, perfect, rounded **8** brochure, complete, handbill, pamphlet, spheroid, spinning **10** roundabout **11** publication

CIRCULATE: **3** air, mix **4** move, turn **6** report, rotate, spread **7** publish, radiate **8** disperse **9** broadcast, propagate **10** distribute, promulgate

CIRCUMFERENCE: **3** arc, rim **4** edge **5** ambit, girth, verge **6** border, bounds, limits **7** circuit, outline **8** boundary, surround **9** perimeter, periphery

CIRCUMLOCUTION: **7** winding **8** rambling, verbiage **9** euphemism, verbality, wordiness **10** periphrase, redundancy, roundabout

CIRCUMSCRIBE: **4** curb **5** bound, fence, limit **6** define, impede **7** confine, enclose, trammel **8** encircle, restrain, restrict, surround **9** delineate, encompass

CIRCUMSPECT: **4** safe, wary, wise **5** alert, cagey, canny, chary **7** careful, guarded **8** cautious, discreet, watchful **9** attentive, observant **10** deliberate, discerning

CIRCUMSTANCE: **4** fact, fate, item **5** event, point, state **6** affair, detail, factor **7** destiny, element **8** incident, position **9** condition, happening, situation **10** occurrence, particular **11** coincidence, environment, opportunity

CIRCUMSTANTIAL: **5** exact **6** minute **7** deduced, precise **8** accurate, detailed, presumed **10** ceremonial, contingent, incidental, particular **11** inferential **12** nonessential

CIRCUMVENT: **4** balk, dupe, foil, fool **5** avoid, cheat, check, evade, trick **6** baffle, bypass, detour, entrap, outwit, stymie, thwart **7** deceive, defraud, mislead, prevent **8** surround **9** encompass, frustrate, overreach

CIRCUS: **4** ring, show **5** arena **6** bazaar, big top, cirque **8** carnival **9** spectacle **10** hippodrome **12** amphitheater

CIRQUE: **5** basin **6** circle, circus **7** circlet

CISTERN: **3** sac, tub, vat **4** tank, well **5** chest **6** cavity, vessel **9** reservoir

CITADEL: **4** fort **5** manor, tower **6** castle **7** bastion **8** fastness, fortress **10** stronghold **13** fortification

CITATION: **4** writ **5** award, honor **6** notice **7** excerpt, mention, summons **8** encomium **9** quotation, reference **10** allegation

CITE: **4** call, note, tell **5** quote, refer **6** adduce, allege, arouse, notify, praise, repeat, summon **7** arraign, excerpt, extract, mention, specify **8** document, indicate, subpoena

CITIZEN: **5** voter **6** native **7** burgess, burgher, denizen, settler, subject **8** civilian, commoner, national, occupant, resident, taxpayer, villager **10** inhabitant

CITRON: **4** lime, rind, tree **5** fruit, lemon **6** cedrat, yellow **10** watermelon

CITRUS FRUIT: **4** lime **5** lemon **6** orange **7** kumquat **8** mandarin **9** tangerine **10** grapefruit

CITY: **10** metropolis **11** megalopolis **12** municipality
Bells: **10** Strasbourg

Brotherly Love: **12** Philadelphia
city-state: **5** polis
concerning: **5** civic, urban **9** municipal
David: **9** Jerusalem
Seven Hills: **4** Rome

CIVIC: **5** civil, local, urban **6** public, urbane **7** borough **8** national **9** community

CIVIL: **5** civic, suave **6** formal, polite, urbane **7** affable, cordial, courtly, politic, refined **8** discreet, gracious, mannerly, obliging, polished **9** civilized, courteous **10** cultivated, diplomatic, respectful **11** complaisant

CIVILIAN: **7** citizen, subject **8** commoner, pacifist **11** nonmilitant **12** noncombatant, practitioner

CIVILITY: **4** tact **7** amenity, decorum, respect **8** courtesy **9** propriety **10** affability, compliance, politeness

CIVILIZATION: **5** mores **6** people **7** culture, society **8** progress **9** education **10** refinement **11** cultivation, development

CIVILIZE: **4** tame **5** teach, train **6** polish, refine, uplift **7** develop, educate, improve **8** acquaint, humanize, idealize **9** cultivate, enlighten

CLACK: **3** jaw, yak **4** blab **5** cluck, prate **6** babble, cackle, gossip, rattle **7** chatter, clatter, prattle **10** chatterbox

CLAD: **4** face **5** robed **6** garbed **7** adorned, arrayed, attired, clothed, covered, dressed **8** sheathed

CLAIM: **3** ask **4** call, case, dibs, lien, mine, name, take **5** exact, right, title **6** allege, assert, charge, demand, elicit **7** acclaim, declare, pretend, profess **8** maintain, pretence, pretense, proclaim, property **9** challenge, ownership, postulate, privilege, vindicate **10** birthright

CLAIMANT: **9** plaintiff, pretender **10** petitioner

CLAIRVOYANCE: **3** ESP **7** feeling, insight **9** telepathy **11** discernment, premonition

CLAIRVOYANT: **4** seer **6** medium **7** prophet, psychic **9** intuitive, visionary **10** perceptive, telepathic

CLAM: **4** base, hush **5** clamp, clasp, crash, grasp **6** dollar, mussel **7** bivalve, mollusk **9** shellfish
type: **4** hard, soft **5** giant, razor, round **6** quahog **7** geoduck, steamer, stuffed **10** little neck **11** cherrystone

CLAMANT: **4** dire **6** urgent **7** blatant **8** pressing **9** clamorous **10** imperative

CLAMMY: **4** cool, damp, dank **5** moist, slimy **6** sticky

CLAMOR: **3** cry **4** bunk, roar, wail, yell **5** blare, boast, noise, shout **6** bellow, hubbub, outcry, racket, ruckus, tumult, uproar **7** discord **8** brouhaha **9** commotion **10** hullabaloo

CLAMP: **3** pin **4** bolt, grip, hold, lock, nail, snap, vise **5** block, brace, clasp **6** clench, fasten, secure **7** grapple **8** fastener, holdfast

CLAN: **4** band, cult, gang, race, ring, sect, unit **5** class, group, horde, house, party, stock, tribe **6** circle, clique, family **7** coterie, society **8** kinfolks **10** fraternity **11** brotherhood

CLANDESTINE: **3** sly **4** foxy **6** artful, covert, hidden, secret, sneaky **7** cloaked, furtive, illicit **8** stealthy **9** concealed **10** fraudulent, undercover **11** underground **13** surreptitious

CLANG: **4** call, ding, peal, ring **5** clank, noise, sound **6** jangle **10** resounding

CLANK: **4** bang, ring **5** clang, clink, sound **7** clatter

CLANNISH: **4** akin **5** close **6** narrow, secret, select, united **9** exclusive, sectarian

CLAP: **4** bang, boom, flap, peal, roar, slap **5** cheer, clack, clink, crack, smack **6** praise, strike, stroke **7** applaud, chatter, thunder **9** explosion

CLAPTRAP: **4** bull, bunk **5** hokum, hooey, trash **6** drivel, humbug **7** baloney, fustian, hogwash **8** malarkey, nonsense **9** poppycock **10** pretension **11** insincerity

CLARIFY: **5** clean, clear **6** purify, rarefy, refine, settle **7** analyze, cleanse, explain **8** simplify **9** delineate, elucidate, interpret **10** illuminate

CLARINET: **4** wind **8** woodwind **10** instrument

CLARION: **5** acute, clear, sharp **7** ringing **8** definite **9** inspiring

CLARITY: **8** accuracy, literacy, openness, radiance **9** clearness, precision **10** brightness, brilliance **12** explicitness

CLASH: **4** bang, dolt, feud, slam **5** argue, brawl, crash, fight, melee **6** affray, battle, differ, impact, strife, strike **7** collide, discord, dispute, scandal **8** conflict, contrast, disagree, showdown, struggle **9** collision, interfere

CLASP: **3** hug, pin **4** clip, fold, grab, grip, hold, hook, hoop, lock **5** clamp, cling, grasp **6** brooch, buckle, clench, clutch, fasten, infold, secure **7** embrace, entwine **8** fastener, surround **9** constrain

CLASS: **4** clan, form, kind, race, rank, sect, sort, type **5** breed, caste, gauge, genre, genus, grade, group, index, order, style **6** circle, family, gender, rating, status **7** bracket, species, subject, variety **8** category, division, position, standing **9** hierarchy **11** description, fashionable **12** denomination

CLASSIC: **3** top **5** ideal, model, prime **7** ancient, perfect, vintage **8** flawless, standard **11** composition, masterpiece

CLASSICAL: **4** pure **5** Greek, Latin, Roman **6** chaste, simple **7** elegant **8** academic, masterly, standard **10** scholastic **11** traditional

CLASSIFICATION: **4** file, rank, rate, sort **5** genre, genus, grade, group, order **6** family, rating, system **7** species **8** analysis, category, division, taxonomy **11** arrangement **12** confidential

CLASSIFY: **4** list, rank, size, sort, type **5** grade, group, label, range **6** assort, codify, divide, number **7** arrange, catalog **8** register **9** segregate **10** categorize, distribute, pigeonhole **11** alphabetize

CLASSY: **4** chic, posh, tony **5** slick, smart **7** elegant, stylish **11** fashionable

CLATTER: **4** bang, roar **5** clack, noise **6** babble, gabble, gossip, rattle **7** blatter, chatter, clutter, prattle, turmoil **9** commotion **11** disturbance

CLAUDIUS:
killer: **6** Hamlet
nephew: **6** Hamlet
successor: **4** Nero

CLAUSE: **4** part, term **5** point, rider **6** phrase **7** article, heading, passage, proviso **8** sentence **9** condition, dependent, provision, ultimatum **10** conclusion **11** independent, stipulation

CLAUSTROPHOBIA: **4** fear **12** closed spaces

CLAVICLE: **10** collarbone

CLAW: **3** dig, paw **4** foot, hand, hook, maul, nail, sere, tear **5** grasp, griff, grope, seize, slash, talon **6** clutch, nipper, scrape, ungula **7** scratch **8** lacerate

CLAY: **3** cob, mud **4** bole, galt, loam, marl **5** adobe, argil, brick, earth, gault, loess, ochre, paste, rabat, tasco, tiles **6** clunch, kaolin **7** pottery

CLEAN: **3** mop **4** dust, pure, smug, swab, tidy, trim, wash, wipe **5** bathe, clear, empty, scour, scrub, smart **6** chaste, kosher, purify, spruce, vacuum **7** cleanse, clearly, perfect, squeaky, sterile **8** brightly, entirely, innocent, renovate, sanitary, spotless, unsoiled **9** dexterous, guiltless, laundered, speckless, undefiled, wholesome **10** immaculate **11** butterworth, disinfected, untarnished **13** unadulterated

CLEAN-CUT: **7** defined **8** chiseled, explicit, outlined **9** wholesome

CLEANER, CLEANSER: **4** soap **5** borax, purer **6** bleach, polish **7** ammonia, janitor **8** abrasive **9** detergent **10** antiseptic

CLEANSE: **4** free, heal, soap, wash **5** brush, erase, purge, rinse, scour, scrub **6** purify, refine **7** absolve, baptize, clarify, sweeten **9** disinfect, expurgate, sterilize

CLEAR: **3** net, rid **4** earn, free, gain, open, over, void **5** alert, clean, erase, lucid, plain, sharp, sunny, vivid **6** acquit, bright, candid, exempt, lucent, profit, purify, settle, smooth, vacate **7** absolve, clarify, clarion, crystal, evident, glaring, legible, lighten, obvious, release, unblock **8** apparent, brighten, definite, distinct, explicit, innocent, pellucid, positive, relevant **9** cloudless, convinced, discharge, disengage, elucidate, exonerate, extricate, vindicate **10** articulate, unconfused, unhampered, unobscured **11** disentangle, translucent, transparent **12** intelligible, unmistakable

CLEARANCE: **4** sale **7** consent **8** approval, headroom **10** permission **13** authorization

CLEAR-CUT: **4** open **5** exact, lucid, sharp **7** concise, evident, obvious **8** chiseled, definite, distinct, explicit **10** unconfused **11** categorical **12** unquestioned

CLEARHEADED: **5** alert, awake **6** astute **8** sensible **10** perceptive

CLEARING: **5** glade, tract **6** assart **7** opening

CLEARLY: **6** surely **7** plainly **9** evidently, obviously, seemingly **10** apparently, noticeably **12** unmistakably

CLEAR OUT: **4** sort **5** scram **6** decamp, remove **7** vamoose **8** hightail **9** eliminate, skedaddle

CLEAR UP: **5** solve **6** settle **7** explain, improve, resolve **8** brighten, decipher, untangle

CLEAT: **4** bitt, wood **5** block, chock, metal, wedge **6** batten **7** bollard, support **8** spurlike

CLEAVAGE: **3** gap **4** slit **5** break, cleft, split **6** schism **7** crevice **8** division **10** separation

CLEAVE: **3** cut, rip **4** chop, hack, join, link, part, rend, rift, slit, tear **5** break, carve, cleft, cling, clove, sever, shear, slice, split, whack **6** adhere, bisect, divide, pierce, remain, sunder **8** separate

CLEAVER: **3** axe **5** knife **7** hatchet

CLEFT: **3** gap **4** flow, reft, rift, rive, torn **5** break, chasm, chink, clove, crack, gorge, split **6** breach, cleave, cranny, crotch, divide, ravine, recess, trough **7** crevice, divided, fissure, opening **8** aperture, division, fracture **11** indentation

CLEMENCY: **5** mercy **8** fairness, humanity, kindness, leniency, mildness **10** compassion, indulgence **11** forgiveness

CLEMENT: **4** calm, easy, kind, mild, warm **6** benign, gentle **7** lenient **8** merciful, peaceful **9** forgiving, indulgent **10** benevolent

CLENCH: **4** grip, grit, hold **5** clamp, clasp, clint, close, grasp **6** clinch, clutch **7** grapple, tighten

CLEOPATRA:
husband: **7** Ptolemy
killed by: **7** suicide
killer: **3** asp
kingdom: **5** Egypt
lover: **10** Mark Antony **12** Julius Caesar
river: **4** Nile

CLERGY: **5** cloth **7** canonry, clerics **8** deaconry, ministry **9** rabbinate **10** priesthood **11** cardinalate

CLERGYMAN/WOMAN: **3** nun **4** dean, monk **5** canon, clerk, padre, rabbi, vicar **6** bishop, cleric, deacon, father, parson, pastor, priest, rector **7** cassock, pontiff **8** cardinal, chaplain, minister, preacher, reverend **9** blackcoat, dignitary, monsignor, presbyter **10** evangelist, missionary **12** ecclesiastic

CLERK: **5** agent, steno **6** cleric, layman, teller, typist **7** auditor, cashier, scholar **8** employee, recorder, salesman **9** assistant, registrar, secretary **10** accountant, bookkeeper, saleswoman **11** salesperson **12** receptionist, stenographer

CLEVER: **3** apt, sly **4** able, cute, deft, keen **5** agile, alert, clean, clear, funny, handy, quick, slick, smart, witty **6** active, artful, astute, bright, gifted, nimble, pretty, shrewd **7** cunning **8** creative, dextrous, handsome, obliging, skillful, talented **9** dexterous, ingenious **11** imaginative, intelligent

CLICHÉ: **5** adage, motto, trite **6** slogan, truism **7** bromide **8** banality, buzzword, timeworn **9** hackneyed **11** stereotyped

CLICK: **4** bang, beat, tick **5** agree, clack, match **7** succeed

CLIENT: **5** buyer **6** patron **7** patient, shopper **8** consumer, customer **9** dependent

CLIENTELE: **6** public **7** cortege **8** regulars **9** following, patronage

CLIFF: **4** crag, face, hill, rock, scar, wall **5** bluff, cleve, ledge, scarp, slope **8** hillside, palisade **9** precipice

CLIMATE: **4** mood, tone **6** temper **7** feeling, weather **8** ambience, attitude **9** condition **11** environment

CLIMAX: **3** cap, top **4** acme, apex, peak **6** apogee, ascend, crisis, finish, summit, zenith **7** maximum **8** conclude, pinnacle **9** gradation, highlight **11** culmination

CLIMB: **4** rise, shin, soar **5** crawl, creep, mount, scale **6** ascend, ascent **7** clamber **8** escalate, struggle

CLIMBING PLANT: **3** ivy **4** vine **6** bryony **7** creeper

CLINCH: **3** hug, win **4** bind, grip, nail, seal **5** clamp, cling, grasp, rivet, seize **6** clench, clutch, decide, fasten, secure **7** confirm, embrace, grapple, scuffle **8** complete, conclude **9** culminate, establish

CLING: **3** hug **4** bond, hang, hold, last **5** clasp, stick, trust **6** adhere, clinch, cohere, depend, fasten, linger **7** cherish, embrace **8** cohesion, maintain **9** persevere

CLINIC: **8** hospital **9** infirmary **10** dispensary

CLINK: **3** can **4** bang, beat, brig, clap, jail, ring **5** latch, noise, pokey, sound **6** cooler, jingle, lockup, prison, tinkle **8** hoosegow **9** calaboose **10** guardhouse

CLINQUANT: **4** gold **5** showy **6** tinsel **10** glittering

CLIP: **3** bob, cut, hit, mow, nip **4** barb, crop, hold, hook, pace, rate, snip, sock, time, trim **5** block, clasp, prune, punch, shave, shear **6** clutch, excise, fasten, hinder, reduce **7** curtail, embrace, scissor, shorten, swindle **8** decrease, diminish, truncate **9** encompass **10** abbreviate, overcharge

CLIPPER: **4** boat, ship **6** vessel **7** shearer **8** sailboat

CLIQUE: **3** mob, set **4** bloc, clan, club, crew, gang, ring **5** cabal, crowd, group **6** circle **7** coterie, faction **8** conclave, insiders **9** camarilla

CLOAK: **3** aba **4** cape, coat, hide, mant, mask, robe, veil, wrap **5** blind, capot, cover, guise, manta, shawl **6** capote, dolman, mantle, poncho, screen, shield, shroud, tabard **7** conceal, garment, manteau, obscure, pretext, shelter **8** burnoose, disguise, mantilla, palliate **9** dissemble **10** camouflage **11** portmanteau

CLOBBER: **4** beat, belt, lick, rout, slug, whip **5** pound, smash **6** defeat, strike, wallop **7** shellac, trounce

CLOCK: **3** hit **4** time **5** alarm, meter, punch, watch **6** attain, Big Ben, cuckoo, wallop **7** digital, realize, sundial **8** odometer, ornament, recorder **9** hourglass, indicator, stopwatch, timepiece **11** chronometer, grandfather, speedometer
maker: **9** horologer **10** horologist

CLOCKWORK: **9** precision **10** regularity **11** consistency

CLOD: **3** oaf **4** dolt, dull, fool, lout, lump, soil **5** clown, divot, dummy, earth, moron, yokel **6** dimwit, stupid **7** bumpkin **8** numskull **9** blockhead

CLODHOPPER: **4** boor, boot, hick, shoe **6** lummox, rustic **7** bumpkin, plowman, redneck

CLOG: **3** jam **4** curb, halt, load, lump, plug, shoe, snag, stop **5** block, check, choke, close, dance **6** fetter, hamper, impede, sandal, weight **7** barrier, shackle, trammel **8** blockage, obstruct, overload, overshoe, restrain **9** hindrance, restraint **10** difficulty **11** encumbrance

CLOISTER: **4** hall, stoa **5** abbey, aisle, order **6** arcade, friary **7** convent, nunnery, retreat, seclude, shelter **8** lamasery, monastic **9** enclosure, hermitage, monastery, sanctuary, sequester **10** passageway

CLOISTERED: **5** alone **7** recluse **8** confined, hermitic, isolated, secluded, shielded, solitary **9** withdrawn **11** sequestered

CLONE: **4** copy **6** double **7** android, replica **9** duplicate

CLOSE: **3** cap, end **4** firm, hard, link, near, quit, seal, shut, slam, snug, stop **5** block, cease, cheap, dense, muggy, musty, stale, thick, tight **6** allied, button, chummy, clause, clench, finale, finish, loving, narrow, nearby, packed, period, secure, stingy, windup **7** adjourn, airless, compact, connect, context, cramped, extreme, precise, similar **8** accurate, adjacent, complete, conclude, familiar, friendly, imminent, intimate, stagnant **9** barricade, congested, extremity, proximate, secretive **10** avaricious, completion, conclusion, convenient **11** approaching, culmination, discontinue, termination **12** parsimonious

CLOSED: **6** folded, locked **7** private, settled **8** bankrupt, resolved **9** exclusive

CLOSED-MINDED: **5** rigid **8** stubborn **9** obstinate, pigheaded **10** inflexible

CLOSEFISTED: **5** cheap, tight **6** stingy **8** clinging **9** tenacious

CLOSELY: **6** almost, barely, nearly **7** exactly, sharply **9** carefully, heedfully, similarly

CLOSEMOUTHED: **5** quiet **6** sedate, silent **7** bashful **8** reserved **9** secretive, withdrawn

CLOSENESS: **7** secrecy **8** intimacy, nearness **9** proximity **10** stinginess, strictness

CLOSET: **4** room, safe **5** ambry, cuddy **6** armary, hidden, locker, pantry, recess, secret **7** cabinet, chamber, conceal, private **8** coatroom, cupboard, wardrobe **9** storeroom **11** theoretical **12** confidential

CLOSURE: **3** end **4** plug **5** bound, cover, limit **6** finish **7** sealing **9** agreement, cessation, enclosure **10** conclusion **11** confinement, containment

CLOT: **3** gel **4** clod, curd, gout, jell, lump, mass **5** array, clump, group, grume **7** agulate, clodder, cluster, congeal, embolus, thicken **8** blockage, coagulum, concrete, solidify, thrombus **9** blockhead, coagulate

CLOTH: **4** bolt **6** fabric, shroud, swatch **7** bunting, drapery, remnant, textile **8** material **10** upholstery

CLOTHE: **3** don, rig **4** clad, deck, garb, gown, robe, vest **5** adorn, array, couch, cover, dress, endow, guise, habit **6** attire, outfit, swathe **7** apparel, bedrape, vesture **8** accouter **10** habilitate

CLOTHES: **4** duds, garb, gear, rags, suit, wear, work **5** dress **6** attire, casual, formal **7** apparel, baggage, civvies, costume, raiment, regalia, threads, vesture **8** clothing, garments, wardrobe **9** vestments **10** bedclothes, sportswear **11** habiliments

CLOUD: **3** fog **4** blur, dust, film, haze, hide, mist, smog, veil **5** befog, cover, gloom, shade, sully, swarm, taint, vapor **6** billow, cirrus, darken, nebula, nimbus, screen, shadow, stigma **7** blacken, blemish, confuse, cumulus, distort, obscure, ominous, perplex, stratus, tarnish **8** befuddle, overcast **9** obfuscate **11** thunderhead

CLOUDBURST: **5** storm **6** deluge **7** torrent **8** downpour **9** rainstorm

CLOUDLESS: **4** fair **5** clear, sunny **6** bright

CLOUDY: **4** dark, dull, gray, hazy **5** filmy, murky, shady, vague **6** dimmed, dismal, dreary, gloomy, opaque **7** obscure **8** overcast **10** indistinct

CLOUT: **3** bat, hit **4** bash, beat, blow, clod, club, nail, pull, slap, slug, sock, swat **5** power, punch, smite, whack **6** strike, target, thrash **7** bandage **9** influence

CLOVERLEAF: **7** freeway **11** interchange

CLOWN: **4** boor, card, fool, hick, joke, lout, mime, zany **5** comic **6** jester, rustic, stooge **7** buffoon, bumpkin **8** comedian, ignorant **9** harlequin **11** Emmett Kelly, merry-andrew, punchinello, wisecracker

CLOY: **4** glut, nail, pall, sate **5** gorge **6** overdo **7** satiate, satisfy, surfeit **8** overfill, saturate

CLUB: **3** bat, hit **4** beat, cane, gang, maul, team **5** baton, billy, bunch, clout, lodge, order, staff, stick, union, unite **6** circle, clique, cudgel, mallet, weapon **7** hangout **8** bludgeon, sorority **9** blackjack, truncheon **10** fraternity, nightstick, sisterhood **11** association, brotherhood

CLUCK: **3** hen **4** call, dumb **5** clack, click, naive, sound **6** nitwit, stupid

CLUE: **3** key, tip **4** hint, idea, lead, sign, warn **5** guide, trace **6** notify **7** inkling **8** evidence, indicate, innuendo, telltale **10** intimation, suggestion **11** fingerprint

CLUMP: **4** blob, bush, heap, lump, mass, thud **5** array, bunch, group, scuff, stomp, thump **6** clunch, lumber **7** cluster, galumph **10** hodgepodge

CLUMSY: **5** blunt, bulky, gawky, hulky, inept, stiff **6** gauche, klutzy **7** awkward, unhandy **8** bumbling, bungling, inexpert, tactless, ungainly, unwieldy **9** lumbering, maladroit, stumbling **10** blundering, cumbersome

CLUSTER: **4** band, heap, knot, lump **5** bunch, clump, flock, group, swarm **6** gather **7** cluther, package **8** converge **10** accumulate, collection

CLUTCH: **3** nab **4** clam, claw, grab, grip, hold **5** catch, clasp, grasp, gripe, seize, talon **6** clench, clinch, retain, snatch **7** control, embrace, grapple **8** coupling

CLUTTER: **4** mess **5** dirty, strew **6** bustle, litter **7** rummage **8** disarray, disorder **9** confusion **10** hodgepodge

CLYMENE:
daughter: **8** Alcimede
father: **6** Mimyas **7** Oceanus
form: **5** nymph
husband: **7** Iapetus **8** Cephalus
inhabited: **5** ocean
mother: **6** Tethys
son: **5** Atlas **9** Palamedes **10** Prometheus

CLYTEMNESTRA:
brother: **6** Castor, Pollux
daughter: **7** Electra **9** Iphigenia
father: **9** Tyndareus
husband: **9** Agamemnon
killed: **9** Agamemnon
killer: **7** Orestes
lover: **9** Aegisthus
mother: **4** Leda
sister: **5** Helen
son: **7** Orestes

COACH: **3** bus **4** help **5** cabin, drill, guide, prime, ready, stage, teach, train, tutor **6** advise, direct, mentor **7** adviser, prepare, tallyho **8** carriage, instruct **10** instructor

COAGULATE: **3** gel, set **4** clod, clot, curd, jell **6** cotter, curdle, harden **7** clabber, congeal, thicken **8** concrete, solidify

COAL: **3** ash **4** bass, char, fuel, smut **5** ember, spark, stoke **6** carbon, cinder **8** charcoal
color: **5** black, brown
distillate: **3** tar
grade: **3** egg, nut, pea **4** duff, lump **5** chunk, stove **6** broken **9** briquette

lump: **3** cob
mine: **5** drift, seams, shaft, strip
miner: **7** collier
smokeless fuel: **4** coke
types: **3** pit **4** hard, peat, soft **6** cannel **7** lignite **10** anthracite, bituminous

COALESCE: **3** mix **4** fuse, join **5** blend, merge, unite **7** combine **9** associate, integrate **10** amalgamate, fraternize **11** incorporate

COALITION: **4** bloc **5** trust, union **6** fusion, league, merger **7** faction **8** alliance **9** syndicate **10** federation **11** association, combination, conjunction

COARSE: **3** low, raw **4** foul, hard, lewd, loud, mean, rank, rude, vile **5** bawdy, crass, crude, dirty, gross, gruff, harsh, loose, thick **6** brutal, callow, common, filthy, impure, ribald, vulgar **7** blatant, obscene, raucous, raunchy, uncouth **8** homespun, immodest, indecent, inferior, unchaste **9** inelegant, offensive, repulsive, unrefined **10** disgusting, indelicate, unpolished **12** scatological

COAST: **4** bank, land, sail **5** beach, glide, shore, skirt, slide **6** border, cruise, strand **7** seaside **8** littoral, seaboard, seashore **9** freewheel
feature: **4** cave, dune **5** cliff, marsh, stack **6** bleach, lagoon **8** headland

COASTER: **3** mat **4** sled, tray **5** plate, wagon **9** container

COAT: **3** car, pea **4** cape, robe, toga **5** cloak, parka, tails, tunic **6** duster, jacket, reefer **7** cutaway, garment, vesture **8** overcoat **12** chesterfield
living: **3** fur **4** bark, hair, hide, husk, pelt, rind, wool **5** bloom, shell **6** mantle, pelage **8** membrane, pellicle, tegument **10** integument
non-living: **4** daub **5** crust, glaze, layer, plate **6** enamel, veneer **7** overlay, plaster **8** laminate
parts: **4** cuff **5** lapel **6** collar, pocket, sleeve

COATING: **4** film, skin **5** crust, glaze, layer **6** patina, veneer **7** blanket **8** covering

COAT OF ARMS: **5** crest **6** ensign, shield **7** pennant **8** insignia

COAX: **3** beg, con **4** dupe, hook, lure, urge **5** press, tease, tempt **6** cajole, entice, induce, soothe **7** beguile, flatter, implore, wheedle **8** blandish, inveigle, persuade **9** influence **10** manipulate

COB: **4** coin, heap, lump, mass, swan **5** horse

COBALT: **4** blue **5** azure **7** element

COBBLER: **3** pie **5** drink, soler **6** mender **7** botcher, dessert, saddler **8** chuckler **9** bootmaker, shoemaker **10** cordwainer

COBRA: **3** asp, Naq **4** naja **5** snake **6** uraeus
enemy: **8** mongoose **14** Rikki-Tikki-Tavi

COBWEB: **3** net **4** mesh, trap **5** fiber **7** network **8** gossamer **9** labyrinth, spiderweb

COCCYX: **8** tailbone

COCK: **3** tap **4** fowl, heap, pile, tilt **5** capon, fight, slant, stack, strut, valve **6** faucet, leader **7** chicken, rooster, swagger **11** chanticleer

COCKADE STATE: **8** Maryland

COCK-AND-BULL STORY: **3** fib, lie **4** yarn **6** canard **7** untruth, whopper **9** falsehood **11** fabrication

COCKEYED: **4** awry **5** askew, drunk, goofy, weird **6** absurd, tilted **7** crooked **8** lopsided **9** ludicrous **10** inebriated, topsy-turvy **11** intoxicated

COCKLE: **5** shell **6** pucker, ripple **7** bivalve, mollusk, wrinkle

COCKPIT: **3** pit **5** cabin **8** quarters **11** compartment

COCKSURE: **4** sure, vain **5** brash, cocky **7** certain **8** arrogant, positive **9** conceited, confident

COCKTAIL: **4** wine **5** drink, horse **6** gimlet **7** martini, Molotov, sidecar, stinger **8** daiquiri, highball **9** appetizer, Manhattan, Margarita **10** Bloody Mary, pina colada **11** boilermaker

COCKY: **4** pert **5** brash **6** crouse, jaunty **8** arrogant, cocksure **9** conceited **10** hotdogging **11** egotistical **12** presumptuous

COCOA: **3** hot **4** bean **5** brown **8** beverage **9** chocolate

COCONUT:
drink: **4** milk
family: **6** Palmae **9** Arecaceae
fiber: **4** coir
meat: **5** copra

COCOON: **3** pod **4** wrap **6** encase **7** envelop, swaddle **8** covering

CODDLE: **3** pet **4** baby, brew, cook **5** humor, nurse, poach, spoil **6** caress, cuddle, fondle, pamper, simmer **7** indulge **11** mollycoddle

CODE: **3** law **5** canon, codex **6** cipher, custom, ethics, secret, signal **7** precept **9** standards **10** regulation **12** instructions
inventor: **11** Samuel Morse
types: **3** red, zip **4** area, blue, book, name **5** penal

CODGER: **5** crank, miser **6** fellow **7** elderly **9** eccentric

CODICIL: **5** rider **6** sequel **8** addition, appendix, modifier **9** postcript **10** supplement

CODIFY: **4** rank **5** index, order **6** digest **7** arrange **8** classify, condense **9** summarize **10** categorize **11** systematize

COERCE: **3** cow **4** make, push, urge **5** bully, drive, force **6** compel, menace **7** enforce, repress **8** bulldoze, dominate, pressure, restrain, restrict, suppress, threaten **9** blackmail, constrain, terrorize **10** intimidate

COERCION: **5** force **6** duress **8** violence **10** compulsion, persuasion **12** intimidation

COEXISTENCE: **5** order, peace **7** harmony **11** conjunction

COFFEE: **4** cafe, drip, java **5** mocha **7** chicory, instant **8** espresso **9** demitasse **10** cappuccino **13** decaffeinated

COFFER: **3** box **4** case **5** chest, hutch, trunk **6** casket **7** caisson **8** treasury **9** strongbox **10** depository

COFFIN: **3** box, urn **4** pall **6** casing, casket **7** pine box **11** sarcophagus

COG: **3** cam, lie **4** fang, gear **5** cheat, prong, tenon, tooth, wedge, wheel **6** cajole **7** connect, deceive, wheedle **11** subordinate

COGENT: **5** solid, valid **6** potent, strong **8** forcible, powerful **9** effective, justified, momentous, trenchant **10** convincing, legitimate, persuasive **11** influential

COGITATE: **4** mull, plan **5** study, think **6** ponder, reason **7** imagine, reflect **8** consider, meditate, ruminate **9** speculate **10** brainstorm, deliberate **11** contemplate

COGNATE: **4** akin **5** alike, close **6** allied, common **7** kindred, related, similar **9** affiliate, universal

COGNIZANCE: **4** heed, mark **5** grasp **6** notice, regard **7** bearing, insight **9** attention, awareness, cognition, knowledge **10** perception **11** observation, recognition **12** jurisdiction

COGNIZANT: **5** alive, awake, aware **6** versed **7** knowing **8** informed, sensible **9** conscious **11** enlightened, intelligent **12** apprehensive

COGNOMEN: **4** name **5** title **6** handle **7** epithet, moniker, surname **8** nickname

COGNOSCENTE: **5** judge **6** critic, expert **7** insider **9** authority **10** specialist **11** connoisseur

COHERE: **3** fit **4** bind, glue, join, suit **5** agree, blend, cling, stick, unite **6** cement, cleave, concur, relate **7** combine, conform, connect **8** dovetail, solidify

COHERENT: **5** clear, lucid, sound **7** logical, orderly **8** rational **14** understandable

COHORT: **4** ally, chum, mate **5** buddy **6** fellow, friend **7** comrade, partner **8** sidekick **9** associate **10** accomplice

COIF: **3** cap **4** hood **5** cover **6** hairdo **7** arrange **8** skullcap **9** headdress

COIFFURE: **4** Afro, buzz, perm, shag, trim **6** braids, dreads, hairdo **7** beehive, flattop, haircut **8** pigtails, ponytail **9** hairstyle **10** dreadlocks

COIL: **4** curl, fuss, loop, roll, wind **5** tense, twine, twist **6** rotate, scroll, spiral, tumult, windup **7** entwine, ringlet, wreathe **8** encircle **9** confusion, corkscrew **10** difficulty, intertwine **11** convolution

COIN: **3** bob, die, lap, ora, ori, rap, sou **4** cash, dime, doit, mint, mite, obol, pina, real, rial, rosa, tara **5** bezzo, chink, cuyne, daric, disme, ducat, eagle, groat, metal, noble, quoin, taler, token **6** besant, bezant, change, florin, nickel, sequin, specie, stater, tanner, thaler, tickey **7** carolus, moidore, quarter, solidus, striver **8** currency, denarius, doubloon, groschen, louis d'or, napoleon, sesterce, zecchino **9** dandiprat, sovereign **10** castellano, krugerrand

collecting: **11** numismatics

concerning: **10** numismatic

fake: **9** brummagem **11** counterfeit

parts: **4** head, tail **5** verso **7** obverse

COINAGE: **6** coined **7** mintage **9** invention, neologism

COINCIDE: **4** jibe, sync **5** agree, tally **6** accord, concur **7** coexist **9** harmonize **10** correspond **11** synchronize

COINCIDENCE: **4** fate **5** fluke **6** chance **8** accident **9** concourse **11** concurrence, parallelism

COINCIDENT: **9** ancillary, attending, consonant **10** concurring, coordinate **11** concomitant **12** contemporary, simultaneous

COINCIDENTAL: **6** casual, chance **9** unplanned **10** accidental **13** unintentional **14** circumstantial

COLANDER: **5** sieve **6** sifter **7** utensil **8** strainer **10** bowl-shaped

COLD: **3** flu, raw **4** cool, dead **5** algid, bleak, brisk, crisp, frore, gelid, nippy, virus **6** arctic, chilly, frigid, frosty, frozen, wintry **7** chilled, distant, glacial, shivers **8** freezing, reserved, unheated **9** apathetic, cheerless, unfeeling **10** insensible, spiritless, unfriendly **11** hyperborean, indifferent, penetrating, unemotional **13** refrigeration

COLD-BLOODED: **4** evil **5** cruel **6** brutal, savage **7** callous, satanic **8** ruthless **9** heartless, unfeeling **10** diabolical **11** insensitive

COLD FEET: **4** fear **5** alarm, doubt, panic **6** fright **9** cowardice, nerveless

COLD SHOULDER: **4** shun **6** ignore, slight

COLD SWEAT: **4** fear **5** panic, shock, worry **7** anxiety, jitters **11** nervousness, trepidation

COLD TURKEY: **4** quit, stop **10** withdrawal

COLIC: **4** pain **5** gripe **9** bellyache **11** stomachache

COLISEUM: **4** bowl **5** arena **7** stadium, theater **10** hippodrome **12** amphitheater

COLLABORATE: **3** aid **4** join **6** assist **8** conspire **9** cooperate, interface

COLLAPSE: **4** cave, fall, fold, wilt **5** crash, wreck **6** buckle, topple **7** crumple, debacle, deflate, failure **8** downfall **9** breakdown, ruination **11** prostration **12** disintegrate

COLLAR: **3** nab **4** band, Eton, gill, grab, nail, ruff, sort, tree **5** catch, chain, fichu, jabot, match, order, seize **6** bertha, tackle, torque **7** capture, shackle, Vandyke **8** assemble, neckband, necklace **9** apprehend, neckpiece **10** turtleneck

COLLARBONE: **8** clavicle

COLLATE: **4** sort **5** match, order **6** bestow, verify **7** arrange, bracket, compare **8** assemble **9** integrate

COLLATERAL: **4** bond **5** added **6** pledge **8** indirect, security **9** ancillary, guarantee, secondary **10** subsidiary **11** concomitant, subordinate

COLLEAGUE: **4** aide, ally **5** buddy, crony **6** cohort **7** consort, partner **8** teammate **9** assistant, associate **10** compatriot

COLLECT: **3** get, tax **4** call, levy, pile, pool, save **5** amass, flock, group, hoard, raise **6** accrue, garner, gather, muster, obtain, sheave **7** acquire, compile, impound **8** assemble, contract **9** aggregate, stockpile **10** accumulate, congregate

COLLECTED: **4** calm, cool **5** quiet, sober **6** poised, serene **8** composed, peaceful **9** aggregate, clustered, confident **11** levelheaded, unflappable

COLLECTION: **3** ana **4** bevy, clan, mass, olio, pile **5** batch, crowd, group, store, suite **6** bundle, conger, medley, sorite **7** cluster, omnibus **8** assembly, caboodle **9** aggregate, anthology, collation, gathering, repertory **10** assemblage, assortment, cancionero **11** acquisition

COLLECTIVE: **5** group, joint **6** mutual, shared **8** multiple **9** aggregate, composite **10** cumulative **12** consolidated

COLLEGE: **5** lycee **6** school **7** academy **10** university **11** institution
graduate: **6** alumna, doctor, master **7** alumnae, alumnus **8** bachelor
oldest: **7** Harvard **9** Mt. Holyoke
parts: **4** dorm, quad **6** campus **9** dormitory **10** quadrangle
terms: **4** term **5** class, major, minor **7** lecture, seminar **8** academic, semester, sorority, tutorial **9** alma mater **10** collegiate, fraternity
workers: **3** don **4** dean, prof **6** bursar, docent, doctor, regent **7** proc-

tor **9** president, professor, registrar

COLLIDE: **3** hit **4** bang, bump, jolt, meet **5** carom, clash, crash **6** strike **7** impinge **8** conflict, disagree

COLLISION: **4** blow, butt **5** clash, crash, shock **6** impact, pileup **7** contact, crackup, smashup **8** accident **9** encounter, insurance **10** percussion

COLLOCATE: **5** place **6** gather **7** arrange, collect, compile **8** parallel, position

COLLOQUIAL: **5** plain **6** casual, common **8** familiar, informal, ordinary **10** particular, vernacular **14** conversational

COLLOQUY: **4** chat, talk **6** debate, parley **8** converse, dialogue **10** conference, discussion **12** conversation

COLLUDE: **4** plot **6** devise, scheme **7** connive **8** conspire **11** collaborate

COLLUSION: **5** fraud, graft **6** scheme **7** cahoots **9** agreement **10** complicity, connivance, conspiracy

COLOMBIA:
capital: **6** Bogota
cities: **4** Cali **8** Medellin **9** Cartagena **11** Bucaramanga **12** Barranquilla, Buenaventura
continent: **12** South America
ethnic groups: **7** mestizo
features: **5** Andes **9** Zipaquira
islands: **6** Mapelo **9** San Andres **11** Providencia
languages: **7** Spanish
monetary unit: **4** peso
native: **9** Colombian
water: **9** Caribbean, Magdalena **13** Lake Guatavita

COLON: **4** line **6** farmer **8** colonist **9** intestine **11** punctuation

COLONIAL: **7** pilgrim **9** immigrant **10** pioneering

COLONIZE: **5** found **6** gather, settle **7** migrate **8** populate **9** establish **10** transplant

COLONY: **4** band **5** group, swarm **7** outpost **8** dominion, province **9** community, satellite **10** settlement

COLOPHON: **6** device **11** inscription

COLOR: **3** dye, hue **4** cast, flag, tint, tone **5** paint, shade, stain, tinge **7** pigment **8** tincture **10** complexion
achromatic: **4** gray **5** beige, black, white **7** neutral
changing: **10** iridescent, opalescent
concerning: **9** chromatic
primary: **3** red **4** blue **6** yellow
secondary: **5** green **6** orange, purple

COLORADO:
bird: **11** lark bunting
capital: **6** Denver
cities: **4** Vail **5** Aspen **6** Aurora, Pueblo **7** Greeley **8** Lakewood **11** Fort Collins **15** Colorado Springs
explorer: **4** Pike
features: **9** Mesa Verde, Pikes Peak **14** Rocky Mountains **15** Garden of the Gods
flower: **9** columbine
nickname: **15** Centennial State
tree: **10** blue spruce
water: **13** Colorado River

COLORANT: **3** dye **7** pigment

COLOR BLINDNESS: **9** oblivious **11** achromatism, insensitive **12** dichromatism **14** monochromatism

COLORED: **4** dyed **6** biased, tinted **7** bigoted, painted, stained **9** distorted, prismatic **10** prejudiced **14** misrepresented

COLORFUL: **3** gay **4** loud **5** jazzy, vivid **6** bright, flashy **7** dynamic **8** animated **9** brilliant, glamorous **11** psychedelic

COLORING: **5** guise **7** quality **9** influence **10** coloration, complexion

COLORLESS: **3** wan **4** drab, dull, pale **5** ashen, blank, faded, plain, white **6** albino, anemic, pallid **7** neutral, prosaic **8** blanched, bleached, lifeless **10** achromatic **11** transparent

COLOSSAL: **3** big **4** huge, vast **5** grand, great **7** immense, mammoth **8** enormous, gigantic **9** humongous, monstrous **10** behemothic, monumental

COLT: **3** gun **4** foal **5** horse **6** pistol **7** sapling **8** beginner, yearling **9** fledgling, youngster

COLUMBINE: **5** plant **6** flower **9** buttercup **11** red-flowered **12** blue-flowered

COLUMBUS:
birthplace: **5** Genoa
burial site: **7** Seville
discovered: **7** America **9** Caribbean
family: **5** Diego
friend: **5** Ojeda
patrons: **8** Isabella **9** Ferdinand
ships: **4** Nina **5** Pinta **10** Santa Maria
visited: **4** Cuba **7** Bahamas, Jamaica **8** Trinidad **9** Caribbean, Venezuela **10** Hispaniola: **11** San Salvador **13** Canary Islands

COLUMN: **3** row **4** file, line, post **5** brace, stack, totem **6** parade, pillar **7** article, support **8** monolith, pilaster **9** formation **10** procession
parts: **4** base **5** shaft **7** capital
types: **5** Doric, Ionic, Roman, round **6** fluted, Gothic, square **8** Egyptian **10** Corinthian

COLUMNIST: **10** journalist **11** commentator **12** newspaperman **13** correspondent **14** newspaperwoman **15** newspaperperson

COMA: **5** sleep **6** stupor, torpor, trance **7** slumber **8** blackout, lethargy **10** somnolence **13** insensibility **15** unconsciousness

COMATOSE: **4** lazy **6** drowsy, torpid **7** drugged **8** listless **9** catatonic, lethargic, soporific **10** insensible **11** unconscious

COMB: **4** card, rake **5** brush, clean, curry, groom, probe, sweep, tease **6** search, smooth **7** ransack **11** investigate

COMBAT: **3** war **4** bout, cope, duel, fray **5** brush, clash, fight, joust, repel **6** action, battle, oppose, resist, strife **7** contend, contest, scuffle **8** argument, conflict, struggle **9** encounter, withstand **11** controversy

COMBATANT: **6** dueler **7** battler, fighter, soldier **8** champion **10** serviceman **12** servicewoman **13** serviceperson

COMBATIVE: **7** hawkish, scrappy **8** militant **9** agonistic, bellicose **10** pugnacious **11** belligerent **12** antagonistic

COMBINATION: **3** key, mix **4** bloc, brew, gang, lock, pact, pool, ring **5** blend, combo, party, union **6** cartel, merger **7** amalgam, combine, consort, faction **8** alliance, compound, ensemble **9** aggregate, coalition, composite, composure, synthesis **10** concoction **11** affiliation, association, coalescence, composition, confederacy, conjunction, unification

COMBINE: **3** add, dub, mix **4** bind, fuse, join, pool **5** blend, group, marry, merge, unite **6** couple, merger, mingle, splice **7** conjoin, conjure **8** coalesce, compound, condense, intermix **9** construct, cooperate **10** amalgamate **11** combination, consolidate

COMBUSTIBLE: **4** fuel **5** fiery **8** burnable, volatile **9** excitable, explosive, flammable **11** inflammable

COMBUSTION: **4** fire, heat **6** tumult **7** burning **8** ignition, volatile **9** agitation, consuming, cremation, oxidation **11** candescence **12** incineration

COME: **4** grow, loom **5** arise, enter, occur, reach **6** accrue, amount, appear, arrive, befall, emerge, extend, happen, mature, spring **7** advance, develop, emanate, proceed **8** approach **9** transpire

COME ABOUT: **5** occur **6** happen, result

COME ACROSS: **4** find **6** notice **7** uncover **8** discover

COME AFTER: **5** ensue **6** follow **7** succeed

COME ALONG: **4** mend **6** attend **7** improve, recover **8** progress **9** accompany

COME APART: **6** detach **8** separate **12** disintegrate

COME AT: **4** rush **5** grasp, reach **6** attack, charge **7** achieve

COMEBACK: **4** quip **5** rally, reply **6** answer, return **7** rebound, revival, triumph **8** recovery, repartee **10** resurgence

COME BEFORE: **6** sooner **7** precede **8** antecede

COME BETWEEN: **4** part **6** divide, meddle **8** alienate, separate

COME BY: **3** see **5** visit **6** attain, obtain **7** inherit

COME CLEAN: **5** admit **6** reveal **7** confess **11** acknowledge

COMEDIAN: **3** wag, wit **4** card, fool **5** actor, clown, comic, joker **6** jester **8** humorist **9** prankster **11** entertainer, wisecracker

COMEDOWN: **4** dive, fall, land **5** crash **6** reduce, worsen **7** descend, letdown, setback **8** collapse **10** anticlimax

COMEDY: **5** farce, humor, revue **6** satire, sitcom **8** travesty **9** burlesque, slapstick

COME FORWARD: **6** appear, emerge **9** volunteer

COME FROM: **4** stem **5** arise **6** derive, result **7** emanate

COME IN: **5** enter **6** arrive, finish **7** intrude

COMELY: **4** fair **5** bonny **6** decent, lovely, pretty, proper **8** becoming, charming, gorgeous, graceful, handsome, pleasing, stunning, suitable **9** agreeable, beautiful **10** attractive, gratifying, personable **11** good-looking

COME OFF: **5** break, click **7** develop, severed, succeed **9** transpire

COME ON: **4** bait, gain **5** decoy **9** seduction **10** inducement, temptation **11** flimflammer

COME OUT: **4** leak **6** appear **8** conclude, protrude, revealed **9** disclosed

COMESTIBLE: **4** food **6** edible **7** eatable, victual **8** esculent **10** provisions

COME THROUGH: **6** endure **7** achieve, persist, prevail, succeed, survive **10** accomplish

COME TO: **5** total **6** awaken **7** recover **10** recuperate

COME TOGETHER: **4** join, meet **6** gather **7** collide **8** assemble

COME UPON: **4** find **6** locate **8** discover, identify

COMFORT: **3** aid **4** ease, help **5** cheer **6** assist, endure, relief, solace, soothe, succor **7** console, enliven, gladden, refresh, relieve, support **8** pleasure, reassure, serenity **9** alleviate, encourage **10** strengthen, sympathize

COMFORTABLE: **4** cozy, easy, rich, snug **5** ample, comfy **6** well-off **7** relaxed, wealthy, well-to-do **8** adequate, cheerful, pleasant, suitable **9** contented, satisfied **10** acceptable, complacent, gratifying

COMFORTER: **4** puff **5** cover, quilt, scarf **6** afghan **7** blanket **8** pacifier **11** sympathizer

COMIC: **3** wag, wit **4** card **5** droll, funny, joker **6** ironic **8** comedian, humorist **9** laughable, ludicrous

COMICAL: **4** zany **5** crazy, droll, funny, goofy, silly, witty **7** amusing, jocular **8** farcical, humorous, ticklish **9** laughable, ludicrous, whimsical **10** capricious, ridiculous **12** entertaining

COMING: **4** next **6** advent, future, likely **7** arrival, certain **8** deserved, imminent **9** impending, promising **11** approaching, progressing

COMMA: **4** mark **5** pause **8** interval **11** punctuation

COMMAND: **3** bid **4** beck, call, duty, rule, sway, tell **5** beken, edict, exact, force, might, order, power **6** adjure, charge, compel, demand, direct, enjoin, govern, impose, manage, master, ordain **7** appoint, bidding, conquer, control, dictate, mandate, officer, request **8** domineer, regulate, restrain **9** authority, direction, expertise, influence, knowledge, ordinance, prescribe, supremacy **10** commission **11** instruction **12** proclamation

COMMANDEER: **4** take **5** seize, usurp **6** hijack, snatch **8** arrogate **10** confiscate **11** appropriate

COMMANDER: **4** boss, czar, guru, head **5** chief, ruler **6** leader, master **7** captain, emperor, general, kingpin, officer **10** commandant

COMMANDMENT: **3** law **4** rule **5** edict, order **7** mitzvah, precept **8** mandates **9** commanded

COMMEMORATE: **4** hail, keep **5** honor **6** salute **7** observe **8** remember **9** celebrate, solemnize **11** immortalize, memorialize

COMMENCE: **4** open **5** arise, begin, found, start **6** incept, launch, spring **8** initiate **9** originate **10** inaugurate

COMMENCEMENT: **4** dawn **5** alpha, onset, start **7** genesis, kick-off, opening **9** admission, beginning **10** graduation **11** celebration

COMMEND: **4** give, laud **5** adorn, boost, extol, yield **6** bestow, commit, praise **7** acclaim, applaud, approve, entrust, support **8** bequeath, eulogize, relegate **9** recommend **10** compliment, ingratiate

COMMENDABLE: **6** worthy **7** notable **8** laudable **9** deserving, excellent, exemplary, honorable **12** praiseworthy

COMMENDATION: **5** award, honor **7** tribute **11** acclamation

COMMENSURATE: **4** even **5** equal **6** square **8** adequate, balanced, parallel **10** equivalent **11** appropriate **12** proportional **13** corresponding

COMMENT: **4** note, talk, word **6** notate, remark **7** discuss, explain, expound, observe, opinion **9** criticize, discourse, editorial, interject, statement, wisecrack **10** animadvert, annotation, commentary, illustrate, reflection

COMMENTARY: **5** gloss **6** review **7** account **8** analysis, critique, treatise **9** criticism **11** explanation

COMMENTATOR: **6** critic, writer **7** analyst **8** observer, reporter **9** annotator, announcer, columnist, expositor **13** correspondent

COMMERCE: **5** trade **6** barter **7** traffic **8** business, exchange, industry **9** marketing, retailing

COMMERCIAL: **7** popular **9** exploited **10** mercantile **13** advertisement

COMMINGLE: **3** mix **4** fuse, join **5** blend, merge, unite **7** combine **9** integrate **10** amalgamate

COMMISERATE: **4** pity **7** console, empathy **10** sympathize **13** compassionate

COMMISSION: **3** fee **4** duty, hire, task, work **5** board, order, trust **6** agency, charge, demand, office, ordain, permit **7** appoint, charter, command, consign, license, mandate, mission, payment, royalty, stipend, warrant **8** delegate, deputize **9** allowance, authorize, brokerage, establish **10** assignment, constitute, obligation **11** instruction **12** compensation, dispensation

COMMIT: **4** bind, give **5** allot, place, refer **6** assign, invest, pursue **7** command, confide, consign, entrust **8** bequeath, delegate, practice, relegate **10** perpetrate

COMMITMENT: **4** bond, duty **6** pledge **7** promise **8** warranty **9** guarantee **10** obligation

COMMITTEE: **4** body, jury **5** board, group, junta, panel **6** bureau **7** council **8** trustees **9** gathering

COMMODE: **3** cap **6** toilet **7** dresser **8** bathroom, cupboard **9** washstand **10** chiffonier

COMMODIOUS: **3** big, fit **4** wide **5** ample, handy, roomy **8** spacious, suitable **9** capacious **10** convenient **11** comfortable, serviceable

COMMODITY: **3** lot **4** ware **5** asset, goods, stock **6** staple **7** article, chattel, product **8** quantity **10** possession

COMMON: **4** base, mean, poor **5** banal, cheap, daily, joint, plain, stale, trite, usual **6** coarse, mutual, normal, ornery, shared, vulgar **7** average, current, general, generic, popular, regular, trivial, typical **8** everyday, familiar, frequent, habitual, informal, mediocre, ordinary, plebeian, trifling **9** bourgeois, customary, hackneyed, prevalent, universal, unrefined **10** collective, monotonous, prevailing, widespread **11** traditional **12** conventional

COMMONER: **5** plebe **7** citizen, peasant, student **8** civilian

COMMON LAW: **6** custom, system **9** precedent, tradition

COMMONLY: **5** often **6** widely **7** popular, usually **9** generally, regularly, routinely **10** frequently

COMMONPLACE: **4** dull, worn **5** banal, daily, plain, stale, trite, usual **6** truism **7** cliched, humdrum, obvious, prosaic, trivial **8** everyday, ordinary **9** hackneyed **10** mainstream, uneventful **11** stereotyped, unimportant

COMMON SENSE: **6** wisdom **8** judgment, prudence, sensible **9** realistic, soundness

COMMONWEALTH: **5** state **6** nation, people, public **7** society **8** republic **9** community **10** res publica

COMMOTION: **3** ado **4** flap, fray, fuss, heat, riot, stir **5** alarm, flare, hurry, storm **6** bustle, flurry, fracas, mutiny, racket, revolt, tumult, unrest, uproar **7** clatter, tempest, turmoil **8** brouhaha, disorder, upheaval, uprising **9** agitation, confusion **10** excitement, turbulence **11** disturbance, pandemonium

COMMUNE: **4** area, chat, talk **5** share **6** advise, confer, debate, parley, reveal **7** consult, discuss, divulge, kibbutz **8** converse **10** collective **11** communicate, cooperative, participate **12** conversation

COMMUNICABLE: **8** catching, pandemic, sociable **9** expansive, talkative **10** contagious, infectious **12** transferable **13** transmittable

COMMUNICATE: **4** talk, tell **5** reach, write **6** answer, bestow, convey, inform, reveal, signal **7** dictate, divulge, network **8** converse **9** broadcast, interface **10** correspond

COMMUNICATION: **3** ESP **4** link, news, note **5** ideas **6** letter, report **7** contact, message **8** bulletin, exchange, language, telegram **9** directive **10** communique, connection **12** conversation, intelligence

COMMUNION: **4** mass, sect, talk **5** creed, faith, share, union, unity **6** church **7** concord, harmony **8** affinity, converse, religion **9** agreement, Eucharist, sacrament **10** confession, fellowship **12** conversation, denomination **13** communication

COMMUNIQUE: **4** note, wire **5** cable **6** letter, report **7** message **8** bulletin, dispatch **12** announcement **13** communication

COMMUNISM: **7** Marxism **8** Leninism **10** Bolshevism **12** collectivism

COMMUNIST: **3** Red **5** pinko **6** commie, Maoist **7** comrade, Marxist **8** Leninist

COMMUNITY: **4** body, city, town **5** state **6** colony, hamlet, nation, people, polity, public **7** enclave, society, village **8** district, identity, likeness, province, township **10** population **11** association **12** commonwealth, neighborhood

COMMUTE: **3** fly **4** ride **5** alter, drive, trade **6** change, travel **7** convert, shorten **8** decrease, exchange **9** transform **10** substitute **11** interchange **12** metamorphose

COMOROS:
capital: **6** Moroni
cities: **6** Domoni **7** Fomboni **9** Mutsamudu
continent: **6** Africa
ethnic groups: **6** Arabic **7** African **10** East Indian
features: **9** Njazidiji
islands: **5** Mwali **6** Nzwani **8** Njazidja
languages: **5** Makua **6** Arabic, French **8** Comorian
monetary unit: **5** franc
water: **17** Mozambique Channel

COMPACT: **4** bond, case, cram, firm, hard, pact, snug, trim **5** brief, close, dense, pithy, short, small, solid, terse, thick, tight **6** packed **7** bargain, concise, concord, stuffed **8** alliance, condense, contract, covenant, solidify, succinct **9** agreement **10** compressed, conspiracy, federation **11** concentrate, consolidate **13** understanding

COMPANION: **3** pal **4** chum, mate, peer, wife **5** amigo, buddy, crony, matey **6** cohort, comate, escort, fellow, friend, spouse **7** comrade, husband, partner **8** chaperon, compadre, playmate, sidekick **9** associate, attendant **10** accomplice

COMPANY: **3** mob **4** band, body, core, crew, firm, gang, host, team

5 crowd, flock, group, guest, horde, party, squad, troop 6 actors, circle, clique, outfit, throng, troupe 7 concern, consort, society, visitor 8 assembly, business 9 concourse, gathering 10 enterprise, fellowship 11 association, corporation, partnership 13 companionship

COMPARABLE: 4 like 5 close 7 similar 8 parallel 9 analogous 10 equivalent, tantamount 13 corresponding

COMPARATIVE: 4 near, than 5 equal, rival 8 relative 9 qualified 11 approaching, approximate

COMPARE: 5 liken, match, scale, weigh 6 confer, equate, ponder, relate 7 analyze, collate, examine, inspect 8 contrast, estimate 9 correlate 10 assimilate

COMPARISON: 6 simile 7 analogy, parable 8 allegory, likeness, metaphor 9 collation 10 connection, similarity 11 contrasting, examination 14 distinguishing

COMPARTMENT: 3 bay, bin 4 cell, hold, nook 5 berth, stall 6 alcove, bunker, locker 7 chamber, cubicle, section 8 division 10 pigeonhole

COMPASS: 4 area, gain, land 5 annex, field, range, reach, scope 6 arrive, attain, bounds, circle, curved, degree, device, obtain, radius, sphere 7 achieve, circuit, confine, divider, enclose, environ, fulfill, horizon 8 boundary, surround 10 accomplish, comprehend, instrument 13 circumference

COMPASSION: 4 pity 5 heart, mercy, sorry 6 lenity 7 empathy, remorse 8 clemency, humanity, sympathy 10 condolence, tenderness 11 benevolence 13 consideration

COMPATIBLE: 7 fitting, harmony 8 suitable, together 9 agreeable, congenial, congruous 10 consistent 12 reconcilable

COMPEL: 4 bind, make, move, tell, urge 5 cause, drive, exact, force, press 6 coerce, enjoin, extort, impose, oblige 7 command, dragoon, enforce, require, squeeze 8 persuade 9 constrain, influence, overpower 11 necessitate

COMPENDIUM: 4 list 5 brief 6 apercu, digest, sketch 7 outline, summary 8 abstract, handbook, syllabus, synopsis 10 abridgment 11 compilation 12 abbreviation

COMPENSATE: 3 pay 5 agree, repay, tally 6 recoup, redeem, refund, reward, square 7 balance, correct, restore, satisfy 9 indemnify, reimburse 10 neutralize, recompense, remunerate

COMPENSATION: 3 fee, pay 5 bonus, wages 6 amends, income, offset, salary 7 damages, payment, redress 8 stipened 9 allowance, indemnity 10 settlement 11 restitution 12 counterpoise, remuneration, satisfaction

COMPETE: 3 pit, vie 4 face 5 clash, fight, match, rival 6 battle, oppose, strive 7 contend, contest 9 challenge, encounter

COMPETENT: 3 apt, fit 4 able, good, meet, sane 5 adept, smart 6 expert, worthy 7 capable, skilled, trained 8 complete, suitable 9 effective, qualified 10 proficient, sufficient

COMPETITION: 4 game 5 match, sport 6 debate 7 contest, rivalry 8 conflict, struggle 9 emulation 10

contention, opposition, tournament

COMPETITOR: **3** foe **5** enemy, rival **6** player **8** emulator, opponent **9** adversary, combatant **10** antagonist, challenger, contestant, opposition

COMPILE: **3** add **4** cull, edit **5** amass **6** gather **7** abridge, arrange, collect, compose **8** assemble **10** accumulate **11** anthologize, consolidate

COMPLACENT: **4** calm, smug **6** serene **9** confident, contented, egotistic, satisfied **11** comfortable, self-assured

COMPLAIN: **4** beef, fret, fuss, kick, moan, yelp **5** brawl, gripe, grunt, whine **6** grouch, lament, object, squawk, yammer **7** deplore, grumble, protest **9** bellyache, criticize

COMPLAINT: **6** malady **7** ailment, disease, illness, protest **8** disorder **9** criticism, exception, grievance, infirmity, objection **10** accusation

COMPLEMENT: **4** crew, gang **5** whole **7** balance **8** addition **10** completion, enrichment, supplement **11** counterpart

COMPLETE: **3** all, end **4** done, fill, full **5** close, every, ripen, total, uncut, utter, whole **6** effect, entire, finish, mature, settle **7** achieve, execute, fulfill, perfect, realize **8** absolute, circular, conclude, flawless, implicit, thorough **9** implement, terminate **10** accomplish, consummate **12** wholehearted

COMPLEX: **4** fear, hard **5** mixed **6** knotty, phobia **7** anxiety, cryptic, network, tangled **8** compound, involved, manifold, puzzling, syndrome **9** composite, difficult, entangled, intricate, perplexed **10** convoluted **11** complicated **12** labyrinthine **13** sophisticated

COMPLEXION: **3** hue **4** glow, look, tint, tone **5** color, state, tinge **6** aspect, makeup, temper **7** texture **10** appearance

COMPLIANCE: **7** consent, harmony **8** civility, docility **9** agreement, obedience, passivity **10** concession, conformity, submission **12** acquiescence

COMPLIANT: **4** easy **7** willing **8** flexible, yielding **10** manageable

COMPLICATE: **5** ravel **6** jumble, puzzle, tangle **7** confuse, involve, perplex **8** bewilder, confound **9** intricate

COMPLICATED: **4** hard **6** knotty **7** arduous, complex, snarled **9** difficult, elaborate, embroiled **10** disordered **11** troublesome

COMPLICATION: **5** hitch, snarl **7** dilemma, illness, problem **8** drawback, obstacle **9** confusion, intricacy **10** difficulty **11** development

COMPLIMENT: **4** laud **5** extol, kudos **6** eulogy, notice, praise, salute **7** applaud, commend, tribute **8** flattery, gratuity, respects **9** adulation, sentiment **12** commendation, congratulate

COMPLY: **4** bend, fold, mind, obey **5** abide, agree, apply, yield **6** accede, accord, follow, submit **7** conform, observe **8** obedient **9** acquiesce, courteous **11** accommodate

COMPONENT: **4** item, part, unit **5** basic, piece **6** factor, member, vector **7** element **8** inherent **9** substance **10** ingredient **11** constituent, fundamental

COMPOSE: **3** pen **4** calm, form, make **5** brief, build, quiet, relax, write **6** accord, adjust, author, create, design, pacify, settle, soothe **7** arrange, concoct, conform, control, dispose, fashion, produce **8** compound, comprise, restrain **9** alleviate, construct, formulate, originate **10** constitute **11** orchestrate

COMPOSED: **4** calm, cool **5** quiet, staid **6** demure, placid, poised, sedate, serene **8** compound, together, tranquil **9** collected, composite, unruffled **10** controlled **11** unflappable

COMPOSER: **4** bard, poet **5** odist **6** author, writer **7** elegist **8** lyricist, monodist, musician **9** wordsmith **10** compositor

COMPOSITE: **5** combo **6** hybrid, medley, mosaic **7** mixture **8** compound **11** synthesized

COMPOSITION: **4** opus, play, work **5** ditty, drama, essay, paper, piece, score, style, theme **6** accord, design, lesson, make-up, melody, thesis **7** article, mixture, writing **8** compound, concerto, creation, fantasia, symphony **9** aggregate, congruity, formation, invention, structure, synthesis **10** concoction, manuscript **11** arrangement, combination, conjunction **12** architecture, constitution, construction

COMPOST: **4** pile, soil **5** blend, mulch **6** manure **7** mixture **8** compound **10** fertilizer **11** composition

COMPOSURE: **5** quiet **6** repose **7** balance, control, posture **8** calmness, coolness, serenity **9** sangfroid, stability **10** equanimity **11** tranquility **13** collectedness

COMPOUND: **4** join, link, meld **5** alloy, blend, unite **6** fusion, jumble, settle, worsen **7** amalgam, augment, combine, complex, compose, compost, compute, goulash **8** acerbate, increase **9** aggregate, composite, enclosure, residence, substance **10** amalgamate, commixture, concoction, confection, constitute, synthesize

COMPREHEND: **3** get, see **4** know, read **5** click, grasp, savvy, sense **6** absorb, attain, digest, embody, fathom **7** contain, discern, embrace, imagine, involve, realize **8** comprise, conceive, conclude, perceive **9** apprehend **10** appreciate, assimilate, understand

COMPREHENSIBLE: **5** clear, lucid **8** coherent **10** understood **11** conceivable, unambiguous **12** intelligible

COMPREHENSIVE: **4** full, wide **5** broad, grand, large **7** blanket, concise, copious **8** complete, thorough, umbrella **9** expansive, extensive, inclusive **11** compendious **12** encyclopedic

COMPRESS: **4** bale, bind, cram, firm **5** cramp, crowd, crush, press, stuff **6** shrink **7** abridge, bandage, compact, curtail, deflate, embrace, flatten, squeeze **8** astringe, condense, contract **9** constrain, dehydrate, epitomize, summarize **10** abbreviate **11** consolidate

COMPRISE: **4** form, hold **5** cover, imply **6** embody **7** compose, contain, embrace, enclose, include, involve **10** comprehend, constitute

COMPROMISE: **4** deal, risk **5** truce **6** hazard, settle **7** sellout **8** compound, endanger **9** agreement, negotiate **10** concession

COMPTROLLER: **7** auditor **9** treasurer **10** accountant, controller

COMPULSION: **4** need, urge **5** drive, force **6** duress **7** impulse **8** coercion **9** addiction, compelled, necessity, obsession **10** constraint, obligation

COMPULSORY: **7** binding **8** coercive, required **9** mandatory **10** obligatory

COMPUNCTION: **4** pity **5** qualm **6** regret, sorrow **7** anxiety, concern, remorse **8** sympathy **9** misgiving, penitence **10** conscience, contrition, repentance

COMPUTE: **3** add, sum **5** count, tally **6** figure, number, reckon **8** estimate **9** calculate, enumerate

COMPUTER: **5** brain, gauge, total **6** cipher **7** machine **9** ascertain **10** calculator
inventor: **6** Turing **7** Babbage **9** Hollerith
primitive: **6** abacus
terms: **4** code, data **5** debug, input **6** access, analog, memory, output **7** digital, program **8** hardware, software **10** compatible, programmer, simulation **11** silicon chip

COMRADE: **3** pal **4** ally, chum, mate, peer **5** buddy, crony **6** fellow, friend **7** brother, partner **8** sidekick **9** associate, companion, confidant

CON: **3** gyp, rap **4** anti, bilk, dupe, fool, know, rook, scam **5** bluff, cheat, guide, learn, steer, study, trick **6** direct, master, peruse, regard, versus **7** against, convict, deceive, examine, mislead, opposed, swindle **9** bamboozle

CONCATENATION: **4** link **5** chain, nexus, union **6** series **8** coupling, sequence **10** connection **11** integration

CONCAVE: **6** arched, cupped, dished, hollow, sunken **7** bowlike, scooped **9** depressed

CONCEAL: **4** bury, hide, mask, stow, veil **5** cache, cloak, couch, cover, stash **6** closet, harbor, screen, shroud **7** secrete **8** disguise, ensconce, withhold **9** dissemble **10** camouflage

CONCEALED: **5** blind, privy **6** covert, hidden, latent, occult, perdue, unseen **8** abstruse **9** blindfold, incognito, recondite **11** clandestine

CONCEDE: **3** own **4** quit **5** admit, agree, allow, grant, waive, yield **6** accord, resign **7** confess **9** recognize, surrender, vouchsafe **10** relinquish **11** acknowledge

CONCEIT: **5** pride **6** vanity **7** egotism **8** snobbery **9** arrogance, pomposity **10** self-esteem

CONCEITED: **3** ham **4** smug, vain **5** cocky, proud **6** snooty **7** pompous **8** arrogant, bragging, snobbish **9** loudmouth, whimsical **11** egotistical, opinionated **12** narcissistic

CONCEIVE: **4** form, make, plan **5** begin, dream, frame, start, think **6** create, design, devise, ponder **7** develop, imagine, realize, suppose, suspect **8** comprise, contrive, envisage, envision **9** apprehend, formulate, visualize **10** comprehend, understand

CONCENTRATE: **4** mass, pile **5** focus, unify **6** attend, center, fixate, gather **7** compact, essence, examine, thicken **8** assemble, condense, meditate **9** intensify **10** accumulate, centralize, scrutinize **11** consolidate **12** conglomerate

CONCENTRATED: **4** deep, real **5** whole **6** potent, robust **7** intense, reduced **8** straight **9** condensed, undiluted

CONCENTRATION: **5** array, study **7** extract **8** fixation, focusing **9** diligence **10** absorption **11** application, convergence

CONCEPT: **4** idea **5** image, slant **6** notion, theory **7** opinion, thought **10** brainchild, conviction

CONCEPTION: **4** idea, plan **5** image, start **6** belief, design, origin **7** genesis, purpose **8** notation **9** beginning, inception, invention **10** impression **12** apprehension, impregnation **13** comprehension, fertilization

CONCERN: **4** bear, care, firm **5** cause, touch, worry **6** affair, affect, behold, bother, burden, charge, matter, regard, unease **7** anxiety, company, disturb, involve, pertain, trouble **8** business, distress, interest **9** implicate, misgiving **10** solicitude **11** corporation **12** apprehension **13** consideration, establishment

CONCERNED: **6** active **7** anxious, fearful, worried **8** affected, involved **10** distressed

CONCERT: **3** gig **4** plan, show, tune **5** union, unite **6** accord, chorus **7** concord, harmony, recital **9** agreement, cooperate **11** performance **13** collaboration, entertainment
hall: **5** odeum **7** theater **9** music hall **10** auditorium

CONCERTED: **5** joint **6** mutual **8** combined **11** prearranged

CONCESSION: **4** boon **5** favor, grant, lease **6** assent, gambit, permit **7** buyback **8** giveback, rollback, yielding **9** admission, allowance, privilege **10** compromise **12** acquiescence **13** condescension

CONCIERGE: **6** porter **7** doorman, janitor **9** attendant

CONCILIATORY: **4** calm **6** gentle, giving, irenic, placid **7** lenient **9** appeasing, forgiving, placating **10** mollifying, reassuring

CONCISE: **4** curt **5** brief, crisp, pithy, short, terse **7** compact, laconic, pointed, precise, summary **8** abridged, succinct **9** condensed **10** compedious **11** abbreviated **12** epigrammatic **13** comprehensive

CONCLAVE: **6** huddle, parley **7** meeting, session **8** assembly **13** secret meeting

CONCLUDE: **3** end **4** rule, stop **5** cease, close, infer, judge, limit **6** clinch, decide, deduce, figure, finish, gather, reason, settle **7** achieve, arrange, confine, resolve, suppose **8** complete **9** determine, speculate, terminate **11** discontinue

CONCLUSION: **3** end **6** finale, finish, period, result **7** finding, opinion, outcome **8** decision, epilogue, judgment **9** diagnosis, inference, summation **10** completion, settlement **11** culmination, probability, termination

CONCLUSIVE: **4** last **5** final **6** cogent **7** certain, obvious, telling **8** absolute, decisive, definite, ultimate **9** revealing **10** compelling, convincing, definitive **11** irrefutable

CONCOCT: **4** brew, cook, plan, plot, vamp **5** frame, hatch **6** create, devise, invent, scheme **7** compose, perfect, prepare **8** compound, intrigue **9** fabricate, formulate, originate

CONCOMITANT: **6** fellow **7** consort **9** accessory, associate, attendant, belonging, companion, conjoined, connected, satellite **10** coincident, concurrent **11** synchronous, synergistic **12** accompanying, contributing

CONCORD: **4** pact **5** agree, amity, peace, unity **6** accord, treaty, unison **7** concert, consent, harmony, oneness, rapport **8** covenant, protocol **9** agreement, communion, consensus **10** consonance, friendship **11** cooperation

CONCOURSE: **4** path **5** crowd, foyer **6** throng **7** company, linkage, merging **8** junction **9** gathering **10** assemblage, concursion, confluence, passageway **11** conjunction

CONCRETE: **4** firm, real **5** solid, unite **6** actual, cement, harden **7** combine, congeal, factual, precise **8** coalesce, compound, material, solidify, tangible **10** particular
made of: **4** sand **5** water **6** cement, gravel **9** aggregate

CONCUR: **4** band, jibe, join, meet **5** agree, chime, unite **6** accord **7** approve, combine, consent **8** coincide **9** acquiesce, cooperate **11** collaborate

CONCURRENT: **6** allied, coeval, mutual, united **8** parallel **10** associated, coexistent, coincident, compatible, consistent **11** concomitant, synchronous **12** simultaneous

CONCUSSION: **4** blow, bump, jolt **5** clash, crash **6** impact, injury, trauma **8** pounding **9** collision

CONDEMN: **4** damn, doom **5** blame, decry, judge, knock **6** banish, detest, punish **7** adjudge, censure, convict **8** belittle, denounce, reproach, sentence **9** castigate, criticize **10** disapprove

CONDEMNATION: **4** doom **6** rebuke **7** blaming, censure **8** judgment **11** reprobation **12** denunciation

CONDENSATION: **5** brief **7** summary **8** rainfall, synopsis **9** reduction **10** abridgment **11** precipitate

CONDENSE: **3** cut **4** chop, trim **5** unite **6** digest, harden, lessen, reduce, shrink **7** abridge, compact, shorten, thicken **8** compress, contract, diminish **9** capsulize, constrict, epitomize **10** abbreviate **11** concentrate, consolidate

CONDESCEND: **5** deign, stoop **6** oblige, submit, unbend **7** concede **9** patronize, vouchsafe

CONDESCENDING: **6** snobby **8** arrogant, superior **9** egotistic **12** supercilious

CONDIMENT: **3** soy **4** herb, salt **5** sauce, spice **6** catsup, pepper, relish **7** ketchup, mustard **9** seasoning

CONDITION: **4** case, mode, must, rank, rote, rule **5** adapt, angle, cause, shape, state, terms **6** action, aspect, estate, fettle, malady, plight, repair, status **7** article, premise, station **8** occasion, position, sickness **9** agreement, exception, necessity, provision, requisite, situation **10** limitation **11** predicament, requirement, stipulation **13** circumstances

CONDITIONAL: **4** iffy **9** dependent, qualified, tentative **10** contingent, fortuitous, incidental

CONDOLENCE: **4** pity, ruth **6** solace **7** comfort **8** sympathy **10** compassion **13** commiseration

CONDONE: **5** remit **6** excuse, forget, ignore, pardon **7** absolve, forgive **8** overlook, tolerate

CONDUCIVE: **6** useful **7** helpful **9** accessory, favorable **10** beneficial **12** contributory

CONDUCT: **4** bear, deed, lead, mien, move, plan, rule, send, wage **5** carry, guide, pilot, steer, usher **6** action, attend, behave, charge, convey, convoy, direct, escort, funnel, govern, manage **7** bearing, channel, comport, conduit, control, execute, operate, oversee, regimen **8** attitude, behavior, carriage, demeanor, guidance, regulate, strategy, transact **9** accompany, supervise **10** administer, deportment, government, proceeding **11** comportment, superintend

CONDUCTOR: **5** guard, guide **6** convoy, copper, escort, leader **7** cathode, maestro **8** aqueduct, cicerone, director, material, motorman **9** collector **10** bandleader, impresario, propagator **11** transmitter

CONDUIT: **4** duct, main, pipe, tube, wire **5** cable, canal, drain, gully, sewer **6** trough **7** channel, conduct, passage **8** aqueduct **11** watercourse

CONE: **5** solid, spire **6** bobbin, conoid, funnel, object **7** fissure, pyramid **8** strobile **9** container

CONFECTION: **5** candy, icing, jelly, sweet **6** bonbon, dainty **7** caramel, mixture, praline, sherbet **8** compound, delicacy, preserve, sherbert **9** marmalade, sweetmeat **11** preparation

CONFEDERACY:
capital: **8** Richmond
leaders: **3** Lee **4** Hill, Hood **5** Bragg, Davis, Price **6** Morgan **7** Jackson, Pickett **8** Stephens **10** Beauregard, Longstreet
states: **5** Texas **7** Alabama, Florida, Georgia **8** Arkansas, Virginia **9** Louisiana, Tennessee **11** Mississippi **13** North Carolina, South Carolina

CONFEDERATE: **3** pal, reb **4** ally **5** rebel, unite **6** cohort **7** abettor, comrade, conjure, leagued, partner **8** conspire **9** accessory, assistant, associate, auxiliary, colleague **10** accomplice, syndicated **12** collaborator

CONFER: **4** give, meet, talk **5** award, endow, grant, speak, treat **6** advise, bestow, donate, invest, parley, powwow **7** commune, compare, consult, discuss, present, provide **8** comprise, converge **10** brainstorm, contribute, deliberate

CONFERENCE: **4** talk **5** forum **6** huddle, league, parley **7** council, meeting, palaver, seminar **8** colloquy, congress **9** collation, comparing, interview, symposium **10** convention, discussion **11** association **12** consultation, conversation, organization

CONFESS: **4** aver, avow, sing **5** admit, grant **6** attest, recant, reveal, shrive, unload **7** concede, confide, declare, divulge **8** disclose **11** acknowledge

CONFESSION: **5** creed **6** avowal, shrive **9** admission, assertion, communion, statement **10** disclosure, profession, revelation

CONFIDANT: **5** amigo, crony **6** friend **7** adviser **8** intimate

CONFIDE: **4** tell **5** admit, trust **6** commit **7** believe, confess, entrust **8** intimate, relegate

CONFIDENCE: **4** guts, hope **5** faith, heart, nerve, poise, spunk, trust **6** aplomb, belief, credit, morale, secret, spirit **7** courage **8** backbone, boldness, credence, personal, reliance, sureness **9** assurance, hardihood **10** conviction, effrontery

CONFIDENT: **4** bold, smug, sure **5** brash, cocky, hardy **6** secure **7** assured, certain, hopeful, reliant **8** cocksure, constant, fearless, intrepid, sanguine, trustful **9** undaunted **10** courageous, determined **11** trustworthy **12** presumptuous

CONFIDENTIAL: **5** privy **6** covert, hushed, secret **7** private **8** esoteric, intimate **10** classified **11** trustworthy

CONFIGURATION: **4** form **5** shape **6** design, figure **7** contour, gestalt, outline, pattern **9** apparatus **11** arrangement

CONFINE: **3** dam, pen, tie **4** bind, cage, coop, hold, jail, keep, lock, seal **5** bound, cramp, limit, scope, stint **6** border, corral, detain, ground, hurdle, immure, intern, tether **7** enclose, impound, repress, shorten **8** boundary, imprison, regulate, restrain **9** constrain, restraint **11** incarcerate, restriction **12** circumscribe

CONFINED: **3** ill **4** pent, sick **7** limited **8** hampered **9** bedridden **10** indisposed

CONFINEMENT: **4** curb **7** custody, lying-in **9** captivity, detention, isolation, restraint **10** childbirth, constraint, immuration, internment, limitation **11** parturition **12** accouchement, imprisonment

CONFINES: **5** range **6** bounds, limits, region **8** boundary, environs **10** dimensions

CONFIRM: **4** firm, okay, seal **5** bless, prove, vouch **6** affirm, assure, attest, clinch, ratify, settle, uphold, verify **7** approve, certify, endorse, fortify, sustain **8** sanction, validate **9** approbate, establish, reinforce **10** strengthen **11** corroborate, countersign **12** authenticate, substantiate

CONFISCATE: **4** take **5** seize, usurp **7** impound, preempt **8** arrogate **9** sequester **10** commandeer **11** appropriate

CONFLAGRATION: **3** war **4** fire **5** blaze **7** burning, inferno **8** conflict, wildfire **9** holocaust

CONFLICT: **3** war **4** bout, duel, fray, rift **5** brush, clash, fight, melee **6** action, battle, combat, mutiny, oppose, strife **7** contend, contest, discord, dispute, faction, scuffle, warfare **8** argument, contrast, disagree, friction, struggle, tug-of-war **9** animosity, collision, encounter, hostility, rebellion **10** antagonism, difference, dissension **11** competition, controversy

CONFLICTING: **7** adverse, warring **8** clashing, contrary, opposing **12** incompatible, inconsistent **13** contradictory

CONFLUENCE: **5** crowd, union **7** conflux, flowing, meeting **8** junction **9** concourse, gathering **10** assembling **11** conjunction

CONFORM: **3** fit **4** obey, suit **5** adapt, agree, apply, yield **6** adjust, assent, comply, follow, settle, submit, tailor **7** compose **9** acquiesce, harmonize **10** correspond **11** accommodate

CONFORMABLE: **5** alike **8** amenable, matching, obedient, suitable **9** agreeable **10** submissive

CONFORMATION: **5** shape **6** figure **7** harmony, outline **9** structure **10** adaptation **13** configuration

CONFORMITY: **6** accord **7** decorum, harmony **8** affinity, docility, likeness **9** agreement, congruity, obedience **10** compliance, similarity, submission **11** consistency, resemblance, willingness **12** acquiescence

CONFOUND: **4** faze **5** amaze, spoil, waste **6** baffle, dismay, muddle, puzzle, rattle, refute **7** astound, confuse, consume, destroy, mystify, perplex, stupefy **8** astonish, bewilder, surprise **9** dumbfound, embarrass, frustrate **10** disconcert **11** flabbergast

CONFRONT: **4** dare, defy, face, meet **5** brave, repel **6** oppose, resist **8** threaten **9** challenge, encounter

CONFRONTATION: **5** clash **6** battle **7** contest, dispute **8** conflict, showdown

CONFUSE: **4** daze, maze **5** amaze, befog, blend, cloud, muddy, snarl, stump, upset **6** baffle, bemuse, fuddle, jumble, muddle, puzzle, rattle **7** blunder, disrupt, fluster, mislead, mystify, nonplus, perplex, stupefy, unhinge **8** befuddle, bewilder, confound, distract **9** dumbfound, misinform, obfuscate **10** complicate, disarrange, discompose, disconcert

CONFUSED: **4** lost **5** foggy, muddy, vague **6** misled **7** chaotic, obscure, unglued **8** mistaken **10** bewildered, tumultuous **12** disorganized **13** helter-skelter

CONFUSION: **4** fuss, mess, muck, riot **5** chaos, deray, havoc, mixup, snafu, snarl **6** babble, bedlam, hubbub, huddle, jumble, muddle, pother, rumpus, tumult, uproar **7** anarchy, blunder, bluster, chagrin, clutter, farrage, flutter, turmoil **8** disarray, disorder, shambles **9** agitation, commotion **10** hullabaloo **11** disturbance, pandemonium, trepidation **12** perturbation, razzle-dazzle

CONFUTE: **4** deny **5** rebut **6** expose, negate, refute **7** counter, silence **8** confound, disprove, overcome **9** overwhelm **10** contradict, invalidate

CONGEAL: **3** gel, set **4** cake, jell **6** curdle, freeze, harden **7** stiffen, thicken **8** concrete, condense, solidify **9** coagulate **10** gelatinize **11** refrigerate

CONGENIAL: **4** good, like **6** social **7** affable, cordial, kindred **8** friendly, pleasant **9** agreeable **10** compatible, delightful **11** sympathetic

CONGENITAL: **6** inborn, inbred, innate **7** connate **8** inherent **9** intrinsic **10** hereditary

CONGESTED: **6** packed **7** blocked, clogged, crowded, plugged **10** gridlocked

CONGESTION: **3** jam **5** snarl **8** crowding, stoppage **9** gathering **10** bottleneck **12** overcrowding

CONGLOMERATE: **4** heap, mass, pile **5** group, stack, trust **6** cartel, melded, varied **7** combine **8** assemble, assorted **9** clustered, composite **10** assemblage **11** agglomerate **12** accumulation

CONGO:
capital: **11** Brazzaville
cities: **5** N'Kayi **7** Loubomo **11** Pointe-Noire
continent: **6** Africa
ethnic groups: **6** Bateke **7** Bakongo
languages: **4** Teke **5** Kongo **6** French
monetary unit: **5** franc
water: **4** Uele **6** Ubangi **10** Zaire (Congo) River

CONGRATULATE: **4** laud **5** toast **6** praise, salute **10** compliment, felicitate

CONGREGATE: **4** mass, meet, teem **5** flock, swarm **6** gather, muster **7** collect, convene **8** assemble, converge **10** rendezvous

CONGREGATION: **4** body, mass **5** flock, group, laity, swarm **6** church, parish **7** meeting **8** assembly, audience, brethren **9** following, gathering **10** collection **11** churchgoers **12** parishioners

CONGRESS: **4** diet **5** synod **6** caucus, league **7** council, meeting **8** assembly, conclave **10** convention, fellowship, parliament, sisterhood **11** brotherhood, convocation, legislature
divisions: **5** House **6** Senate

member: **7** senator **14** representative (House)
place: **15** Capitol Building

CONGRUITY: **6** accord **7** concord **8** symmetry **9** agreement, coherence **10** compatible, conformity, consonance, harmonious **11** consistency

CONJECTURE: **4** deem, idea, plot, view **5** fancy, guess, think **6** belief, theory **7** imagine, opinion, presume, surmise, suspect **8** conceive, judgment **9** inference, speculate, suspicion **10** assumption, conclusion, estimation **11** hypothesize, speculation, supposition

CONJUGAL: **6** bridal, wedded **7** marital, married, nuptial, spousal **8** hymeneal **9** connubial **11** matrimonial

CONJUNCTION: **2** if, or, so **3** and, but, for, nor, yet **4** than, that, till, when **5** after, since, where, while **6** either **7** because **8** although

CONJURE: **4** pray **5** charm, crave, raise **6** adjure, appeal, invoke, summon, voodoo **7** combine, command, imagine, implore **8** conspire, contrive, exorcise **9** importune **10** supplicate

CONJUROR: **4** mage, sear **5** witch **6** shaman, wizard **7** juggler, warlock **8** magician, sorcerer **9** enchanter

CONK: **3** die, hit **4** fail, swat **5** faint, knock, stall **6** fungus **7** decease **9** hairstyle **10** straighten

CONNECT: **3** tie, wed **4** ally, bind, join, link **5** chain, marry, merge, unite **6** attach, bridge, cohere, couple, fasten, relate **7** combine, network, rapport **9** affiliate, associate, correlate, interface, interlock

CONNECTICUT:
bird: **5** robin
capital: **8** Hartford
cities: **7** Danbury, Milford **8** New Haven, Stamford **9** Greenwich, Waterbury **10** Bridgeport
explorer: **5** Block
features: **4** Yale **13** Mystic Seaport
flower: **14** mountain laurel
nickname: **11** Nutmeg State **17** Constitution State
tree: **8** white oak
water: **15** Housatonic River, Long Island Sound **16** Connecticut River

CONNECTION: **4** bond, link, seam **5** nexus, union **6** family, hookup **7** contact, kinship **8** affinity, alliance, coupling, junction, relative **9** coherence, relevance **10** attachment, continuity **11** affiliation, association, conjunction **12** intermediary, relationship

CONNIVE: **4** plan, plot, wink **5** blink **6** foment, incite, scheme **7** collude, finagle **8** conspire, intrigue **9** machinate

CONNOISSEUR: **4** buff **5** judge, maven **6** critic, expert **7** epicure, gourmet **9** authority, collector **10** specialist

CONNOTATION: **4** hint **6** intent, spirit **7** essence, meaning **8** coloring, overtone **10** suggestion **11** implication

CONNOTE: **5** imply, spell **7** signify **8** indicate **9** insinuate

CONNUBIAL: **6** bridal, wedded **7** marital, married, nuptial, spousal **8** conjugal, hymeneal **11** matrimonial

CONQUER: **4** beat, best, down, lick, rout, tame, whip **5** cream, crush, daunt **6** defeat, humble, master, occupy, subdue, victor **7** achieve, acquire, clobber, prevail, succeed, triumph **8** overcome, surmount, vanquish **9** checkmate, overpower, overthrow, subjugate

CONQUEROR: **4** hero **6** master, victor, winner **8** champion **10** subjugator **12** conquistador

CONQUEST: **4** rout **5** catch, score **6** defeat **7** mastery, victory **8** invasion **11** enchantment

CONSANGUINITY: **5** blood **7** kinship, lineage **8** affinity **10** sisterhood **11** affiliation, brotherhood **12** relationship

CONSCIENCE: **5** heart, qualm, sense **6** morals, psyche, virtue **7** thought **8** scruples **10** principles **11** compunction

CONSCIENTIOUS: **4** fair, just **5** exact, pious **6** honest **7** careful, dutiful, upright **8** diligent, faithful, punctual, reliable **10** meticulous, scrupulous **11** painstaking

CONSCIOUS: **4** felt, keen **5** alert, alive, awake, aware **7** feeling, knowing **8** sensible **9** attentive, cognizant **10** deliberate, perceptive **11** intentional

CONSCIOUSNESS: **4** mind **7** concern **9** awareness, knowledge **11** realization

CONSECRATE: **3** vow **4** seal **5** bless, deify, exalt, honor **6** anoint, devote, hallow, ordain **7** glorify **8** dedicate, sanctify, venerate

CONSECUTIVE: **5** after **6** serial **7** ensuing **8** unbroken **9** following **10** continuous, succeeding **11** progressive

CONSENSUS: **5** unity **6** accord **7** harmony **9** unanimity

CONSENT: **5** agree, allow, yield **6** accede, accord, assent, comply, permit, submit **7** approve, concede **8** blessing **9** allowance **10** permission **12** acquiescence **13** authorization

CONSEQUENCE: **3** end **4** rank **5** event, fruit, issue, worth **6** cachet, effect, moment, result, sequel, weight **7** account, concern, fallout, outcome, payback, stature **8** prestige **9** aftermath **10** importance, prominence **11** aftereffect, consecution **12** repercussion **13** consideration

CONSEQUENT: **5** sound **7** ensuing **8** indirect, rational **9** following, resultant

CONSEQUENTIAL: **3** big **7** crucial, pompous **8** eventful **9** important **10** meaningful **11** substantial

CONSEQUENTLY: **4** then, thus **5** later **9** therefore, thereupon, wherefore **11** accordingly

CONSERVATION: **4** care **6** saving **7** storage **8** managing **9** husbandry **10** cherishing, protection **12** preservation

CONSERVATIVE: **4** safe **6** square, stable **7** diehard, guarded **8** cautious, moderate, old liner **9** bourgeois, right-wing **11** reactionary, right-winger, traditional

CONSERVATORY: **6** school **7** academy, nursery **10** glasshouse, greenhouse

CONSERVE: **4** save **5** guard, hoard, skimp **6** scrimp **7** husband, protect, sustain **8** maintain, preserve, squirrel **9** safeguard

CONSIDER: **4** deem, heed, mull, muse, note **5** judge, study, think, weigh **6** debate, expend, impute, ponder, reason, reckon, review **7** analyze, believe, consult, examine, inspect, reflect **8** cogitate, estimate, meditate **9** entertain, speculate **10** adjudicate, deliberate **11** contemplate

CONSIDERABLE: **5** ample, large, major, super **7** notable, several **8**

abundant **9** bountiful, capacious, important **10** noteworthy, remarkable **11** significant, substantial

CONSIDERATE: **4** kind, mild **6** gentle, polite **7** careful, heedful, mindful, prudent, tactful **8** generous **9** attentive, concerned, observant **10** benevolent, respectful, thoughtful **11** sympathetic

CONSIDERATION: **4** perk **5** cause, mercy, point **6** aspect, motive, notice, reason, regard, review, reward **7** concern, respect, thought **8** scrutiny **9** attention, incentive **10** advisement, commission, importance, recompense

CONSIGN: **4** give, mail, send, ship **5** allot, remit, shift, yield **6** assign, commit, devote **7** address, confide, deliver, deposit, entrust, forward **8** delegate, relegate, transfer **9** authorize, recommend **10** commission

CONSIST: **3** lie **4** hold **5** abide, exist, stand **6** inhere, reside **7** contain, include **8** comprise, dovetail **9** harmonize

CONSISTENCY: **4** body **5** union, unity **7** concord, density, harmony **8** firmness, symmetry **9** adherence, coherence, congruity, stability, viscosity **10** consonance, regularity, uniformity **11** composition

CONSISTENT: **4** even, firm, same **6** steady **7** logical, regular, uniform **8** constant, expected, suitable **9** congruous, consonant, unfailing, unvarying **10** changeless, dependable, harmonious, persistent

CONSOLATION: **5** cheer **6** relief, solace **7** comfort **8** sympathy **10** compassion

CONSOLE: **4** calm, lift **5** allay, cheer, table **6** solace, soothe **7** cabinet, comfort, relieve, support **9** alleviate, encourage **11** tranquilize

CONSOLIDATE: **4** fuse, join, pool **5** blend, merge, unify, unite **6** harden **7** combine, compact, fortify **8** coalesce, compress, condense, solidify **9** reinforce **10** amalgamate, centralize, strengthen **11** concentrate

CONSONANCE: **5** chime, unity **6** accord, chorus **7** concord, harmony **9** agreement

CONSONANT: **5** alike **6** letter, sonant **7** phoneme, similar, unified **8** parallel, resonant, suitable **9** agreeable, congruous **10** coincident, compatible, consistent, harmonious

sound: **5** click, glide, nasal, trill **6** apical, dental, voiced **7** frontal, glottal, palatal, spirant **9** retroflex, voiceless

CONSORT: **4** aide, join, mate, play, wife **5** agree, group, tally, unite **6** accord, escort, mingle, spouse **7** concert, conform, husband, partner **8** assembly, sidekick **9** accompany, associate, colleague, companion, harmonize **10** correspond, fraternize **11** association, conjunction

CONSPICUOUS: **4** loud **5** clear, plain **6** famous, flashy, marked, patent, signal **7** blatant, eminent, evident, notable, obvious, pointed, salient, visible **8** apparent, flagrant, manifest, striking **9** important, notorious, prominent **10** celebrated, noticeable **11** discernible, distinctive, outstanding **13** distinguished

CONSPIRACY: **4** coup, plan, plot **5** cabal, covin **6** scheme **7** treason **8** intrigue **9** agreement, collusion **10** connivance **11** confederacy, machination

CONSPIRE: **4** join, plot **5** agree **6** concur, devise, league, scheme **7** collude, complot, conjure, connive, consort **8** contrive **9** cooperate **11** confederate

CONSTANCY: **5** ardor **6** fealty **7** honesty, loyalty **8** devotion, fidelity, tenacity **9** adherence, eagerness, fixedness, fortitude, integrity, stability **10** allegiance, attachment **11** earnestness **12** faithfulness

CONSTANT: **4** even, firm, true **5** fixed, loyal, solid **6** stable, steady **7** certain, chronic, durable, endless, eternal, forever, lasting, nonstop, regular, staunch, uniform **8** enduring, faithful, habitual, stalwart **9** confident, continual, incessant, permanent, perpetual, steadfast, sustained, unvarying **10** continuous, dependable, invariable, persistent, relentless, unwavering **11** everlasting

CONSTELLATION: **4** star **6** dipper **7** cluster, pattern **8** asterism, northern, southern **13** configuration
archer: **11** Sagittarius
bull: **6** Taurus
champion: **7** Perseus
charioteer: **6** Auriga
crab: **6** Cancer
dragon: **5** Draco
eagle: **6** Aquila
fish: **6** Pisces
flying horse: **7** Pegasus
goat: **11** Capricornus
great bear: **9** Ursa Major
herdsman: **6** Bootes
hunter: **5** Orion
lady in chains: **9** Andromeda
lady in chair: **10** Cassiopeia
lion: **3** Leo
little bear: **9** Ursa Minor
ram: **5** Aries
scales: **5** Libra
scorpion: **8** Scorpius
southern cross: **4** Crux
swan: **6** Cygnus
twins: **6** Gemini
virgin: **5** Virgo
water bearer: **8** Aquarius
whale: **5** Cetus

CONSTERNATION: **4** fear **5** alarm, dread, panic, shock **6** dismay, fright, horror, terror, wonder **7** anxiety **8** distress **9** amazement, confusion **11** distraction, trepidation

CONSTITUENT: **4** item, part, unit **5** piece, voter **6** factor, member **7** citizen, element, portion **8** division, integral **9** component **10** ingredient

CONSTITUTE: **3** fix, set **4** form, make **5** draft, enact, found, shape **6** create, embody, ordain **7** appoint, compose, develop **8** compound, comprise **9** authorize, determine, establish, legislate **10** commission

CONSTITUTION: **3** law **4** code **5** being, build, state **6** custom, health, nature, temper **7** charter, essence, stamina **8** physique, vitality **9** character, enactment, structure **11** composition **12** organization **13** establishment

CONSTITUTIONAL: **4** walk **6** inborn, innate, lawful, stroll **7** natural, organic **8** inherent **9** essential, intrinsic **10** congenital

CONSTITUTION STATE: **11** Connecticut

CONSTRAIN: **4** curb, deny, fain, urge **5** check, clasp, deter, force, impel, limit, press **6** coerce, compel, oblige, ravish, secure, squash, stifle, subdue **7** confine, deprive, enforce, inhibit, oppress, repress, violate **8** compress, distress, restrain, restrict **9** constrict

CONSTRAINT: **4** bond **5** force **6** duress **7** driving, modesty, reserve, shyness **8** coercion, distress, pressure, timidity **9** captivity, necessity, restraint **10** compulsion, obligation **11** confinement, suppression

CONSTRICT: **4** bind, curb, grip **5** choke, cramp, limit, tense **6** hamper, shrink **7** confine, inhibit, squeeze, tighten **8** astringe, compress, contract, restrict, strangle **9** constrain **10** constipate, constringe

CONSTRUCT: **4** form, make, rear **5** build, erect, frame **6** create, devise **7** arrange, combine, compose, fashion **8** assemble, engineer, envision **9** fabricate, originate

CONSTRUCTION: **4** cast, mold **6** design, makeup **7** contour, version **8** building, creation, roadwork **9** framework, inference, structure **11** development **12** architecture **14** prefabrication

CONSTRUCTIVE: **7** helpful **9** effective, practical **10** beneficial

CONSTRUE: **5** infer, parse **6** deduce, render **7** analyze, explain, expound, resolve **8** decipher **9** interpret, translate **10** comprehend

CONSUL: **5** envoy **8** delegate, emissary, minister, official **10** magistrate **14** representative

CONSULT: **3** ask **5** refer **6** advise, confer, devise, huddle **7** counsel, discuss, meeting **8** consider, decision **9** determine, negotiate **10** brainstorm, deliberate

CONSUME: **3** eat, use **4** down, gulp **5** crush, drink, scarf, spend, waste **6** absorb, devour, engage, expend, hoover, inhale, perish, ravage **7** deplete, destroy, dwindle, engross, exhaust, swallow, utilize **8** squander **9** dissipate **10** annihilate, monopolize

CONSUMER: **4** user **5** buyer **6** client **7** shopper **8** customer **9** purchaser

CONSUMMATE: **4** ripe **5** crown, ideal **6** effect, finish **7** achieve, fulfill, perfect, perform **8** absolute, complete, conclude **9** culminate, exquisite **10** accomplish, undisputed

CONSUMPTION: **3** use **5** decay, waste **6** eating **8** drinking **9** depletion, devouring **11** destruction, expenditure **12** tuberculosis

CONTACT: **4** abut, join, meet **5** reach, touch, union **6** impact, relate **7** meeting, network, rapport **8** approach, junction, touching **9** collision **10** connection, contiguity **11** contingency **12** acquaintance **13** communication

CONTAGION: **3** pox **5** taint, virus **6** miasma, poison **7** disease, illness **8** epidemic **9** infection **10** corruption, pestilence **13** contamination

CONTAGIOUS: **8** catching **9** epizootic, spreading **10** infectious **12** communicable **13** transmittable

CONTAIN: **4** have, hold, keep, stop **5** bound, check, house **6** embody, retain, stifle **7** control, embrace, enclose, harness, include, subsume **8** comprise, restrain **10** comprehend **11** accommodate

CONTAINER: **3** bag, bin, box, can, cup, jug, keg, pod, pot, tub, urn, vat **4** cage, case, cask, crib, drum, pail, sack, silo, tank, vase, vial **5** crate, flask, pouch **6** barrel, basket, bottle, bucket, carafe, carton, casket, hamper, holder, magnum, shaker **7** canteen, capsule, inkwell **8** canister, decanter **10** receptacle

CONTAMINATE: **4** foul, soil **5** spoil, stain, sully, taint **6** befoul, blight, debase, defile, infect, poison **7** corrupt, debauch, deprave, pollute, tarnish, vitiate **9** desecrate **10** adulterate

CONTEMPLATE: **4** muse, plan, view **5** probe, study, think, weigh **6** ponder, regard, survey **7** examine, inspect, propose, reflect **8** consider, meditate, ruminate **9** speculate **10** deliberate, scrutinize

CONTEMPLATION: **5** study **6** gazing, musing, prayer **7** purpose, thought **8** scanning **9** awareness, intention **10** meditation **11** observation, speculation **12** deliberation **13** consideration

CONTEMPORARY: **4** peer **5** equal **6** coeval, modern, recent **7** abreast, current, voguish **10** coexistent, newfangled, synchronal

CONTEMPT: **5** scorn, shame, sneer, spite **6** hatred, slight, stigma **7** disdain, mockery **8** aversion, disgrace, loathing **10** disrespect **11** indignation

CONTEMPTIBLE: **3** low, sad **4** base, evil, mean, vile **5** cheap, crass, petty, sorry **6** abject, scummy, scurvy, shabby, sordid **7** hateful, pitiful **8** beggarly, infamous, sneaking, wretched **9** revolting, worthless **10** despicable, disgusting **12** dishonorable

CONTEMPTUOUS: **7** haughty **8** arrogant, cavalier, derisive, insolent, sardonic, scornful **9** insulting **10** disdainful **12** supercilious **13** condescending

CONTEND: **3** tug, vie **4** avow, cope, face, wage **5** argue, brawl, claim, cross, fight **6** assert, battle, buffet, bustle, combat, debate, oppose, reason **7** bargain, compete, contest, dispute, quarrel **8** conflict, maintain, skirmish, squabble, struggle **9** encounter, vindicate

CONTENT: **4** calm, cozy, ease, gist, load, smug, text **5** happy, peace **6** amount, please, volume **7** appease, essence, gratify, meaning, satiate, satisfy, willing **8** capacity **9** satisfied

CONTENTION: **3** war **4** beef, feud, flak, riot, tiff **5** fight, scrap **6** combat, debate, ground, rumpus, strife **7** contest, discord, dispute, opinion, rivalry, wrangle **8** argument, conflict, friction, squabble, struggle **9** rebellion **10** difference, dissension **11** altercation, competition, controversy, explanation **12** disagreement

CONTENTIOUS: **7** hostile **8** militant, perverse **9** bellicose, wrangling **10** pugnacious **11** belligerent, quarrelsome **12** cantankerous

CONTENTMENT: **4** ease **5** bliss **7** comfort **8** gladness, pleasure **9** happiness **11** complacency **12** satisfaction

CONTEST: **4** bout, duel, feud, fray, game, meet, pitt, race, spar, tiff **5** clash, fight, match, trial **6** action, affray, battle, combat, debate, defend, oppose, resist, strife, strive **7** compete, contend, dispute, protest, rivalry, warfare **8** argument, conflict, question, skirmish, struggle **9** challenge, encounter **10** tournament **11** altercation, competition

CONTESTANT: **5** rival **6** player **7** entrant, warrior **8** finalist, prospect **9** adversary, candidate, combatant, contender, defendant **10** challenger, competitor **11** participant

CONTEXT: **7** climate, meaning **9** framework, situation, substance **10** background, vocabulary

CONTIGUOUS: **5** close **6** nearby **7** besides, meeting **8** abutting, adjacent, touching **9** bordering **11** neighboring

CONTINENT: **4** mass, pure **6** chaste **8** celibate, mainland **9** abstinent, temperate **10** restrained **11** restrictive

CONTINENTS: **4** Asia **6** Africa, Europe **7** Oceania **9** Australia **10** Antarctica **12** North America, South America

CONTINGENCY: **4** odds **5** event **6** chance **8** accident, fortuity, incident, juncture, prospect **9** emergency **10** crossroads, likelihood **11** possibility, predicament, uncertainty

CONTINGENT: **4** body **6** casual, chance, likely **8** possible **9** dependent, empirical **10** accidental, delegation, detachment, fortuitous **11** conditional, provisional **13** unanticipated, unpredictable

CONTINUAL: **7** endless, eternal, lasting **8** constant, enduring, unbroken, unwaning **9** ceaseless, connected, incessant, perennial, permanent, perpetual, recurrent, unceasing **10** continuous **11** everlasting, unremitting

CONTINUANCE: **4** stay, term **6** extent, sequel **8** duration, postpone **9** endurance, extension, longevity, procedure **10** continuity **11** adjournment **12** perseverance

CONTINUE: **4** last, live, stay **5** abide, carry, exist, renew **6** endure, extend, pursue, remain, resume **7** connect, outlast, persist, proceed, prolong, survive, sustain **8** maintain **9** persevere **11** reestablish

CONTINUITY: **5** chain **6** script **7** linking, stamina **8** cohesion **9** endurance **10** connection, succession **11** progression

CONTORT: **4** bend, coil, knot, turn, warp **5** curve, gnarl, twist, wrest **6** deform, writhe **7** distort **9** convolute, disfigure

CONTOUR: **4** form, line **5** curve, graph, shape **6** figure **7** outline, profile **9** lineament, structure **10** silhouette **14** characteristic

CONTRABAND: **5** cause **6** banned, piracy **7** acquire, bootleg, deflate, develop, illegal, illicit **8** smuggled, unlawful **9** moonshine **10** prohibited

CONTRACT: **3** get **4** bond, deal, pact **5** catch, cause, lease, limit, proof **6** engage, lessen, narrow, pledge, reduce, shrink, treaty **7** abridge, acquire, compact, curtail, deflate, develop, promise, shorten, shrivel, wrinkle **8** condense, covenant, restrict **9** agreement, constrict, handshake **10** abbreviate, constringe, convention, obligation, settlement **11** arrangement, concentrate, stipulation

CONTRACTION: **5** cramp, spasm **6** twitch **7** elision, tensing **8** decrease, omission **9** reduction, shrinkage **10** abridgment, convulsion, shortening, tightening **11** confinement **12** abbreviation

CONTRADICT: **4** deny **5** belie, rebut **6** differ, impugn, negate, oppose, refute **7** counter, dispute **8** disclaim, disprove **9** repudiate **10** controvert

CONTRADICTION: **6** denial **7** paradox **8** antilogy, conflict **10** gainsaying **11** discrepancy **12** disagreement **13** contravention

CONTRADICTORY: **5** polar **7** against, reverse **8** contrary, opposite **9** diametric **10** antipodean **12** antagonistic, incompatible, inconsistent

CONTRAPTION: **4** tool **5** thing **6** device, gadget **7** machine **9** apparatus **10** instrument **11** contrivance

CONTRARY: **5** balky, polar **6** averse, ornery **7** adverse, counter, hostile, opposed, reverse, wayward **8** converse, opposite, perverse, stubborn **9** antipodal, unpopular **10** discordant, discrepant, rebellious, refractory **11** conflicting, paradoxical, unfavorable **12** antagonistic, disagreeable **13** insubordinate

CONTRAST: **6** differ **7** deviate **8** mismatch, opposite, separate **9** diversity **10** antithesis, comparison, difference, divergence **13** dissimilarity

CONTRAVENE: **4** defy **5** spurn **6** breach, hinder, offend, oppose, thwart **7** gainsay, violate **8** infringe, overstep, trespass **9** disregard, repudiate **10** contradict, transgress

CONTRIBUTE: **3** aid **4** give, help, tend **5** cause, endow **6** assist, bestow, donate, factor, submit, supply, tender **7** augment, furnish, further, provide **9** subscribe, subsidize **10** strengthen

CONTRIBUTION: **4** alms, gift **5** grant, share **7** article, charity, handout, payment, present, writing **8** donation, offering **10** supplement **11** benefaction

CONTRITE: **5** sorry **6** humble, rueful **8** penitent **9** regretful, repentant, sorrowful **10** apologetic, remorseful **12** compunctious

CONTRIVANCE: **4** gear, plan, tool **5** gizmo, shift **6** design, device, doodad, gadget, scheme, widget **7** machine, project **8** artifice, creation **9** apparatus, appliance, doohickey, invention **10** instrument **11** contraption

CONTRIVE: **4** brew, fake, make, plan, plot **5** fudge **6** design, devise, invent, manage, scheme, wangle **7** achieve, agitate, concoct, connive, consult, contend, fashion, finagle, project **8** conspire, engineer, intrigue, maneuver **9** construct, fabricate, machinate **10** accomplish, manipulate

CONTROL: **4** curb, hold, rein, rule, sway **5** check, clout, grasp, guide, juice, leash, power, steer **6** bridle, direct, govern, handle, manage, subdue **7** command, conduct, contain, mastery, preside **8** dominate, dominion, monopoly, overlook, regulate, restrain **9** influence, ordinance, supervise **10** discipline, domination, manipulate, regulation **11** predominate **12** jurisdiction

CONTROVERSIAL: **7** eristic, suspect **8** arguable **9** contended, debatable, polemical **12** disputatious, questionable

CONTROVERSY: **3** row **4** beef, flak, spat, tiff **6** debate, strife **7** dispute, quarrel, wrangle **8** argument **10** contention, difference, discussion **11** altercation **12** disagreement

CONTROVERT: **4** deny, moot **5** argue, rebut **6** debate, oppose, refute **7** contest, counter, dispute, gainsay **8** question **9** challenge **10** contradict

CONTUMACIOUS: **6** unruly **7** haughty, riotous **8** insolent, mutinous, stubborn **9** alienated, insurgent, obstinate, seditious **10** headstrong, rebellious, refractory **11** disobedient **12** unmanageable **13** insubordinate

CONTUMELY: **5** abuse, scorn **6** remark **7** disdain **8** contempt, reproach, rudeness **9** arrogance, insolence, insulting **11** humiliation

CONTUSION: **4** bump **5** knock, mouse **6** bruise, injury

CONUNDRUM: **6** enigma, puzzle, riddle **7** mystery, paradox **8** question

CONVALESCE: **4** mend **6** revive **7** improve, recover, restore **10** recuperate, rejuvenate

CONVENE: **3** sit **4** call, meet, open **5** rally, unite **6** gather, muster, summon **7** convoke **8** assemble **10** congregate

CONVENIENCE: **4** ease **6** luxury **7** amenity, benefit, comfort, leisure, service **9** appliance, enjoyment **10** preference, usefulness **12** availability

CONVENIENT: **5** handy, ready **6** nearby, proper, useful **7** helpful **8** suitable **9** adaptable, agreeable, available, favorable **10** accessible, beneficial **11** appropriate

CONVENT: **4** easy **5** abbey **6** priory **7** nunnery, retreat **8** cloister **9** community, monastery, sanctuary

CONVENTION: **4** rule **5** usage **6** caucus, custom, treaty **7** meeting, members, precept **8** assembly, congress, contract, practice, protocol **9** agreement, delegates, etiquette, gathering, tradition **10** conference **11** convocation

CONVENTIONAL: **5** trite, usual **6** common, decent, formal, normal, proper **7** correct, regular, routine, typical **8** accepted, everyday, orthodox, standard **9** customary, developed **10** ceremonial **11** contractual, established, traditional

CONVERGE: **4** join, meet **5** focus, merge, rally **6** concur, gather **8** assemble **11** concentrate

CONVERSANT: **3** hip **5** adept, awake, aware **6** au fait, expert, versed **7** abreast, skilled **8** familiar, informed **9** cognizant, practiced **10** acquainted, proficient **11** experienced

CONVERSATION: **4** chat, talk **6** gossip, parley **7** palaver **8** chitchat, colloquy, dialogue, exchange, repartee, shoptalk **9** discourse **10** conference, discussion **11** association, interchange **13** communication

CONVERSE: **4** chat, chin, talk **5** speak **6** confer, parley **7** commune, consort, convert, obverse, palaver, reverse **8** antipode, colloquy, dialogue, exchange, opposite **10** antithesis **11** association

CONVERSION: **4** flux **6** change, switch **8** mutation **10** adaptation, alteration **13** metamorphosis

CONVERT: **4** sway, turn **5** adapt, alter, amend, renew **6** change, modify, novice, reform, revise **7** restore, reverse **8** converse, disciple, follower, neophyte, persuade **9** acetalize, brainwash, transform, translate, transpose **11** proselytize

CONVEX: **4** bent **5** bowed **6** arched, curved, raised **7** bulging, gibbous, rounded **9** outcurved **11** protuberant

CONVEY: **4** bear, cart, give, lead, mean, move, send, tell, tote, will **5** bring, carry, grant, guide, steal **6** assign, convoy, devise, impart, import, relate, remove, reveal **7** conduct, deliver, dispose, project, support **8** alienate, bequeath, transfer, transmit **9** transport **11** communicate

CONVEYANCE: **3** bus, car **4** auto, cart, deed, sled **5** grant, train, truck, wagon **7** charter, conduct, trailer, transit, trolley, vehicle **8** airplane, carriage, carrying, railroad, transfer **9** transport **10** automobile

CONVICT: **3** con **4** find **5** felon, lifer, prove **6** attain, inmate **7** adjudge, attaint, captive, condemn, culprit

8 criminal, jailbird, prisoner, sentence **10** malefactor

CONVICTION: **4** mind, view **5** creed, dogma, faith, tenet **6** belief, fervor **7** opinion **8** position, sentence **9** certainty, principle, sentiment **10** confidence

CONVINCE: **4** sell, sway **5** prove **6** assure, change **7** satisfy **8** persuade

CONVINCING: **5** sound, valid **6** cogent **7** evident, telling **8** powerful **9** authentic, plausible **10** believable, conclusive, persuasive

CONVIVIAL: **3** gay **5** jolly, merry **6** festal, genial, jovial, joyous, lively **7** festive, jocular **8** cheerful, friendly **9** hilarious, vivacious **12** entertaining

CONVOCATION: **5** synod **6** caucus **7** calling, council, meeting **8** assembly, congress **9** concourse, gathering **10** convention

CONVOKE: **4** call, cite, meet **6** gather, muster, summon **7** convene, request **8** assemble

CONVOLUTE: **4** coil, loop, wind **5** cloud, twist **6** spiral, tangle **7** contort, snaking **9** intricate

CONVOY: **4** lead **5** carry, guard, guide, pilot, usher **6** attend, convey, escort, manage **9** accompany, formation, safeguard **10** protection

CONVULSION: **3** fit **5** furor, spasm, throe **6** attack, tumult, uproar **7** seizure, shaking **8** epilepsy, laughter, paroxysm **9** commotion, tottering **11** contraction, disturbance

COO: **4** woot **5** sound, utter **6** murmur

COOK: **3** fix, fry **4** bake, boil, chef, heat, make, sear, stew **5** baker, baste, broil, curry, grill, poach, roast, saute, steam **6** braise, happen, simmer **7** concoct, develop, parboil, prepare, process, servant **8** barbecue, contrive **9** microwave

COOKIE: **4** cake, Oreo **5** sugar, wafer **7** biscuit, brownie **8** macaroon **9** Toll House **10** confection, gingersnap

COOKING: **7** cuisine **8** magirics **10** cordon bleu, gastronomy **13** haute cuisine

terms: **3** fry **4** bake, bard **5** broil, brule, chine, devil, farci, garni, puree, saute **6** au bleu, blanch, coddle, dredge, flambe **7** al dente, bouchee, bouquet, parboil **8** bouillon, culinary, marinade, marinate **9** medallion **10** jardiniere

tools: **3** pan, pot, wok **5** range, stove **6** galley, trivet, tureen **7** broiler, griddle, kitchen, ramekin, roaster, skillet, spatula, steamer, terrine **8** colander **9** casserole **9** Dutch oven **10** rotisserie

COOK UP: **4** brew, plot **6** devise, invent, scheme **8** contrive **9** formulate

COOL: **3** air, fan, ice **4** calm, cold, keen **5** algid, chill, dandy, gelid, nippy, poise **6** chilly, frigid, placid, sedate, serene **7** assured, relaxed, unmoved **8** composed, moderate **9** apathetic, collected, confident, excellent, temperate, unexcited, unruffled **10** deliberate, nonchalant, unfriendly, unsociable **11** indifferent, refrigerate, sensational, unconcerned, unemotional, unflappable **12** unresponsive

COOLER: **4** icer, jail **5** drink **6** icebox, lockup, prison **9** container **11** refrigerant **12** refrigerator

COOLNESS: **4** cold **5** nerve **6** aplomb **8** calmness, serenity **9** assurance, composure **12** indifference

COOP: **3** pen **4** cage, jail, yard **5** cramp **6** corral, prison **7** confine **9** enclosure **11** cooperative

COOPERATE: **4** band, join, tend **5** agree, unite **6** assist, concur **7** combine, conduce **8** coadjute **10** contribute **11** collaborate, participate

COOPERATION: **5** union **7** concert, synergy **8** teamwork **11** partnership **12** partisanship

COORDINATE: **4** mesh, tune **5** adapt, alike, equal **6** adjust **7** arrange **8** organize **9** correlate, harmonize, integrate, reconcile **10** equivalent **11** synchronize

COP: **3** bag, nab, rob, top **4** bank, grab, lift, pile, trap **5** bobby, catch, crest, filch, snare, steal, stock, swipe **6** peeler, strike **7** capture, officer **8** purchase **9** patrolman, policeman **11** patrolwoman, policewoman

COPE: **4** deal, face **5** cloak, cover, dress, equal, match, notch, vault **6** canopy, chapel, endure, handle, manage, strive **7** contend, survive, weather **8** complete, confront, struggle **9** encounter

COPIOUS: **4** full, lush, rich **5** ample, wordy **6** galore, lavish, plenty **7** flowing, profuse, replete **8** abundant, affluent, generous, numerous **9** bountiful, exuberant, plenteous, plentiful **11** overflowing

COPPER: **3** cop **4** bull, cent **5** bobby, metal, penny **6** peeler **7** element **8** farthing **9** butterfly, policeman **11** policewoman

COPPICE: **4** bosk, wood **5** copse, firth, grove **6** forest, growth, regrow **7** thicket **8** woodland **9** underwood

COPULATE: **4** join, mate **5** breed, unite **7** cohabit **9** fornicate

COPY: **3** ape **4** echo, edit, mime **5** cheat, clone, ditto, image, mimic, phony, Xerox **6** carbon, effigy, follow, mirror, parrot **7** emulate, forgery, imitate, redraft, replica, reprint, takeoff, tracing **8** likeness, simulate **9** duplicate, facsimile, imitation, personify, reproduce **10** mimeograph, plagiarize, transcribe, transcript **11** counterfeit **12** reproduction

COQUET, COQUETTE: **3** coy, toy **4** fool, vamp **5** dally, flirt **6** trifle, wanton **9** philander

CORAL: **3** red **4** pink **5** horny, polyp **8** skeleton, zoophyte **9** limestone, madrepore

CORD: **4** band, bind, bond, line, rope, wire, wood, yarn **5** cable, fiber, nerve, twine **6** fabric, sennet, spinal, string, tendon, thread **7** measure

CORDIAL: **4** real, warm **5** drink, vital **6** genial, hearty, polite **7** amiable, liqueur, sincere, zealous **8** friendly, gracious, sociable, vigorous **9** agreeable, courteous **10** hospitable

liqueur: **4** ouzo **6** Kahlua **7** Sambuca **8** amaretto, anisette **9** Cointreau, Triple Sec **10** chartreuse **11** Benedictine **12** Grand Marnier

CORDIALITY: **5** ardor **6** regard, warmth **7** amenity **8** sympathy **9** geniality **10** heartiness **11** sociability **12** friendliness, pleasantness

CORDON: **4** cord, tree **5** group, guard, shrub **6** ribbon **12** stringcourse

CORE: **3** cob, hub, nub **4** base, gist, guts, meat, pith, root **5** focus, heart **6** center, kernel, middle, nodule, staple **7** essence, nucleus **9** substance

CORK: **3** oak **4** plug, seal, stop **5** close, float, shive, spike **6** bobber

7 phellem, stopper, stopple **8** suppress

CORKER: **4** lulu, whiz **5** dandy **9** excellent, humdinger **10** remarkable **11** crackerjack

CORKSCREW: **4** coil, wind **5** twist **6** spiral **7** entwine

CORMORANT: **4** bird **6** greedy **8** gourmand, ravenous **9** rapacious **10** gluttonous

CORN: **3** cob, ear, zea **4** samp **5** grain, maize, mealy **6** kernel, nubbin
product: **4** meal, pone **5** bread, grist **6** hominy **8** tortilla

CORNCRACKER STATE: **8** Kentucky

CORNER: **3** box, nab **4** bend, edge, fool, nook, spot, trap, tree, veer **5** angle, catch, elbow, niche, trick, trust **6** bottle, collar, cranny, recess **7** dilemma, retreat **8** junction, monopoly

CORNERSTONE: **4** base **5** basis, quoin **7** marking, support **10** foundation

CORNET: **4** horn **7** trumpet **9** headdress **10** instrument

CORNHUSKER STATE: **8** Nebraska

CORNICE: **4** band, drip, eave **5** crown, frame **6** geison **7** furnish, molding

CORNUCOPIA: **4** horn **8** ornament **9** abundance **10** receptacle

CORNY: **5** banal, dated, stale, trite **6** square, stupid **7** cliched **11** sentimental

COROLLARY: **6** effect, result **7** analogy, theorem **9** deduction, inference **10** conclusion, consequent **11** proposition

CORONA: **4** halo, ring **5** cigar, crown, light **6** circle, rosary, wreath **7** aureole

CORONATION: **8** ceremony, crowning **9** accession **12** inauguration

CORONER: **7** officer **8** examiner

CORONET: **4** band **5** crown, tiara **6** anadem, circle, diadem, wreath **7** chaplet **8** headband **9** headdress

CORPORAL: **4** rank **6** bodily **8** physical, tangible **9** corporeal **10** anatomical

CORPORATION: **4** firm **5** trust **7** company **8** business **9** syndicate **10** enterprise **11** association, combination

CORPOREAL: **4** real **6** actual, bodily, carnal **7** somatic **8** corporal, material, physical, tangible **11** substantial

CORPS: **4** band, unit **5** squad, troop **6** outfit **7** brigade, company **8** division

CORPSE: **4** body **5** stiff **7** cadaver, carcass, remains

CORPULENT: **3** fat **5** blimp, bulky, heavy, husky, large, obese, plump, stout, tubby **6** chubby, fleshy, portly, rotund **7** weighty **10** overweight

CORPUS: **4** body, bulk, mass **5** whole **7** capital **8** writings **9** principal **11** compilation

CORPUSCLE: **4** cell

CORRAL: **3** pen **4** coop **5** fence **7** confine, round up **8** stockade, surround **9** enclosure

CORRECT: **3** fit, fix **4** edit, nice, okay, true **5** amend, check, exact, right **6** adjust, better, change, inform, proper, punish, reform, remedy, repair, revamp, revise **7**

improve, perfect, precise, rectify, redress, reprove, upgrade **8** accurate, chastise, regulate, truthful **9** castigate, faultless **10** acceptable, counteract, neutralize, scrupulous **11** comme il faut, punctilious **12** conventional

CORRECTION: **10** adjustment, alteration, discipline, punishment **12** modification

CORRELATE: **5** match **6** equate **7** compare **8** parallel **9** associate **10** coordinate

CORRELATION: **8** analogue **11** equivalence **12** relationship **13** correspondent

CORRESPOND: **3** fit **4** jibe, suit **5** agree, equal, match, reply, tally, write **6** accord, answer, square **7** conform, respond **8** coincide, parallel, resemble **9** harmonize **10** complement **11** communicate

CORRESPONDENCE: **4** mail **7** analogy, letters **8** messages **9** agreement, bulletins, coherence, congruity **10** similarity

CORRESPONDENT: **5** match **6** pen pal, writer **8** reporter, suitable **10** equivalent, freelancer, journalist **11** conformable, contributor, correlation

CORRIDOR: **4** hall, path **5** aisle, foyer **7** couloir, gallery, hallway **10** passageway

CORROBORATE: **4** back **5** prove **6** verify **7** confirm, support, sustain **8** validate **9** establish **10** strengthen **12** authenticate, substantiate

CORRODE: **4** bite, gnaw, rust **5** decay, erode, scour, waste **6** canker **7** consume, corrupt, destroy, eat away, oxidize **8** wear away **11** deteriorate

CORROSIVE: **6** biting **7** acerbic, caustic, erosive, mordant **8** abrasive, venomous **9** sarcastic **11** destructive

CORRUGATED: **6** folded, ridged **7** creased, grooved **8** crinkled, crumpled

CORRUPT: **3** bad, low, mar, rot **4** evil, vile **5** bribe, spoil, stain, taint, venal **6** debase, impure, poison, ravish, rotten **7** abusive, corrode, crooked, debauch, defiled, degrade, deprave, immoral, pervert, pollute, violate, vitiate **9** dishonest, falsified, unethical **10** adulterate, demoralize, flagitious, fraudulent, profligate **11** contaminate, underhanded

CORRUPTION: **4** vice **5** fraud, graft **6** payola **7** jobbery **8** fiddling **9** turpitude **10** debauchery **11** impropriety

CORSAIR: **6** pirate, robber **8** marauder, picaroon **9** buccaneer **10** freebooter

CORSET: **4** belt **5** laced **6** bodice, girdle **7** control, support **8** restrict **12** undergarment

CORSICA:
capital: **7** Ajaccio
cities: **5** Calvi, Corte **6** Bastia
place: **6** France

CORTEGE: **4** line **5** train **7** caravan, retinue **10** procession

CORTEX: **4** bark, rind **5** layer **8** peridium

CORUSCATE: **4** beam **5** blaze, flash, gleam **7** glisten, glitter, radiate, sparkle

COSA NOSTRA: **3** mob **5** Mafia **9** syndicate

COSMETIC: **5** blush, cream, henna, liner, rouge **6** makeup, powder **7** mascara **8** beautify, lipgloss, lipstick **9** eye shadow **10** decorative, nail polish **11** restorative, superficial

COSMIC: **4** huge, vast **6** global **7** immense **8** catholic, infinite **9** limitless, planetary, universal **12** cosmopolitan

COSMONAUT: **9** astronaut

COSMOPOLITAN: **6** cosmic, global, urbane **7** worldly **8** cultured **9** universal **10** ecumenical **13** sophisticated

COSMOS: **5** earth, globe, order, realm, stars, world **6** flower, galaxy, nature, scheme **7** harmony **8** creation, universe **9** structure

COSSET: **3** pet **4** lamb, love **5** spoil **6** caress, cuddle, fondle, pamper

COST: **3** fee **4** harm, loss, pain, toll **5** price, value **6** charge, damage **7** expense, penalty **8** estimate **9** sacrifice, suffering **11** expenditure

COSTA RICA:
capital: **7** San Jose
cities: **5** Limon **10** Puntarenas
continent: **14** Central America
ethnic groups: **7** mestizo, Spanish
features: **11** Poas volcano
languages: **7** Spanish
monetary unit: **7** colones
native: **10** Costa Rican

COSTLY: **4** dear, high, rich **5** steep **6** lavish **7** opulent, ruinous **8** damaging, gorgeous, precious, splendid, valuable **9** expensive, priceless, sumptuous **10** disastrous, exorbitant **11** extravagant

COSTUME: **4** garb, robe, suit **5** dress, getup, guise **6** attire, outfit **7** apparel, clothes, uniform **8** clothing, disguise, ensemble

COT: **3** bed, hut **4** bunk **5** berth, cabin, couch, house, stall **6** sheath **7** cottage, shelter **8** bedstead, covering, dwelling **9** stretcher

COTERIE: **4** club, gang, ring **5** junto **6** circle, clique **7** society

COTTAGE: **3** hut **5** cabin, house, lodge, shack **6** chalet, shanty **7** shelter **8** bungalow, dwelling **10** guesthouse

COTTON:
fabric: **4** duck, leno, pima **5** denim, terry **6** calico, canvas, chintz, muslin **7** etamine, nankeen, percale
gin inventor: **7** Whitney
plant: **4** boll **5** bolly

COTTON STATE: **7** Alabama

COTTONTAIL: **4** hare **6** rabbit

COUCH: **3** bed, cot, lie **4** hide, lurk, sofa, word **5** divan, floor, frame, grain, lodge, paint, slink, sneak, squat, stoop, utter **6** daybed, lounge, pallet **7** conceal, express, ottoman, recline, varnish **9** davenport **12** chesterfield

COUGAR: **3** cat **4** puma **7** panther **9** catamount **12** mountain lion

COUGH: **4** ahem, bark, cold, hack **5** whoop **6** tussis **9** pertussis

COUGH UP: **4** ante **7** confess, deliver **8** disclose **10** relinquish

COUNCIL: **4** body **5** board, divan, junta, panel, synod **6** senate **7** cabinet, meeting **8** assembly, conclave, congress, ministry **9** committee **10** conference, consistory, discussion, federation **11** convocation **12** deliberation

COUNSEL: **4** rule, urge, warn **5** steer **6** advice, advise, confer, exhort, lawyer **7** caution, suggest **8** admonish, advocate, attorney, guidance **9** barrister, counselor, prescribe, recommend **10** counsellor **11** instruction **12** consultation, deliberation

COUNSELOR, COUNSELLOR: **6** lawyer, mentor **7** adviser, advisor, counsel, teacher **8** attorney **9** barrister **10** instructor, supervisor

COUNT: **3** add, sum **4** bank, cast, deem, foot, name, poll, rate, rely, tell, tote **5** await, judge, score, tally, total **6** census, depend, esteem, expect, figure, impute, matter, number, reckon, result **7** compute, include, outcome, signify **8** numerate **9** calculate, enumerate

COUNTENANCE: **3** aid **4** back, face, help, mien, okay, show **5** favor, front **6** accept, aspect, uphold, visage **7** approve, bearing, conduct, endorse, feature, support **8** advocate, befriend, calmness, sanction **9** composure, encourage, semblance **11** physiognomy

COUNTER: **5** asset, match, stand, table, token **6** marker, offset, oppose **7** adverse, against, contend, current, nullify, respond, reverse **8** contrary, opposite **9** antipodal, retaliate **10** contradict

COUNTERACT: **4** foil **5** annul, check **6** cancel, hinder, negate, oppose, resist, thwart **7** balance, correct **8** antidote, negative, overcome **9** frustrate **10** neutralize

COUNTERBALANCE: **5** check **6** offset **7** correct, rectify **8** equalize **10** compensate

COUNTERFEIT: **4** coin, copy, fake, mock, sham **5** bogus, dummy, false, fraud, fudge, phony **6** affect, assume, forged, pseudo **7** falsify, feigned, forgery, imitate, pretend **8** simulate, spurious **9** brummagem, deception, disguised **10** artificial, fictitious, fraudulent **11** impersonate **12** reproduction

COUNTERMAND: **4** stop, void **5** annul **6** cancel, recall, repeal, revoke **7** rescind, reverse **8** abrogate, override **9** frustrate

COUNTERPART: **4** copy, like, mate, twin **5** equal, match **6** carbon, double **8** parallel **9** correlate, duplicate **10** complement, equivalent

COUNTERPOISE: **6** offset **7** balance, ballast **8** equalize **9** stabilize **10** compensate, counteract **11** equilibrium **13** counterweight

COUNTERSIGN: **4** mark, seal, sign **7** certify, confirm, endorse **8** password **9** authorize, signature, watchword **11** corroborate

COUNTLESS: **6** untold **7** umpteen **8** infinite **9** limitless **10** numberless **11** innumerable **12** incalculable

COUNTRY: **4** bush, farm, home, land **5** realm, rural, state **6** nation, people, region, sticks **7** outland **8** citizens, district, homeland, pastoral **9** backwoods, boondocks, territory **10** fatherland, motherland **12** commonwealth

COUNTY: **4** seat **5** shire **6** canton, parish **7** borough **8** district, division **11** subdivision

COUP: **4** feat, plan, plot **6** attack, strike, stroke **7** mastery **8** overturn, takeover **9** overthrow, stratagem **10** revolution **11** achievement

COUP DE GRACE: **7** quietus **8** clincher, knockout **9** deathblow **11** mercy stroke

COUP D'ETAT: **6** mutiny, revolt **9** overthrow, stratagem **10** revolution

COUPLE: **3** duo, tie, two **4** bond, dyad, join, link, mate, pair, team, twin, yoke **5** brace, hitch, marry, unite **6** fasten **7** bracket, combine, connect, harness, twosome **8** assemble, copulate

COUPLER: **4** link, ring **6** device **7** drawbar, shackle **8** fastener

COUPLET: **4** pair, poem, unit **5** verse **7** distich

COUPON: **4** form, slip, stub **5** stamp, token **7** voucher **11** certificate **13** advertisement

COURAGE: **4** elan, grit, guts, soul **5** heart, nerve, spine, spunk, valor **6** daring, mettle **7** bravery, heroism, prowess **8** audacity, backbone, boldness, firmness, gameness, tenacity **9** braveness, fortitude, gallantry, hardihood **10** resolution **12** fearlessness

COURAGEOUS: **4** bold, game **5** brave, hardy **6** daring, heroic **7** gallant, spartan, valiant **8** fearless, intrepid, unafraid, valorous **9** daredevil, undaunted, venturous **11** adventurous, lionhearted **12** stouthearted

COURIER: **3** spy **4** post **5** envoy, gofer, guide, scout **6** runner **7** carrier, mailman, postman **9** attendant, mailwoman, messenger, postwoman

COURSE: **3** lap, run, way **4** flow, game, heat, line, path, plan, race, rink, road **5** class, cycle, drift, orbit, route, track, trail **6** artery, career, design, gallop, manner, method, policy, scheme, series, stream, street, system **7** beeline, circuit, conduct, highway, passage, pathway, routine, running, subject **8** movement, progress, sequence, tendency **9** direction, itinerary, procedure **10** curriculum, proceeding

COURT:
cases: **4** moot, suit **5** cause, trial **6** action, docket **7** celebre, hearing, sitting **10** litigation **11** arraignment
officials: **4** jury **5** crier, judge **7** bailiff, pleader **8** advocate, marshall **9** defendant, plaintiff **12** amicus curiae
terms: **3** sue **4** bond, oyez, ward, writ **5** brief **6** decree, recess, remand **7** finding, perjury, session, summons, testify, verdict **8** citation, forensic, in camera, judgment, mandamus, recourse, subpoena **9** committal, embracery, interdict, testimony **10** cognizance, injunction **12** cross-examine, recognizance
types: **5** forum **7** circuit **8** kangaroo, tribunal **9** appellate, judiciary **10** judicature **11** star chamber

COURTEOUS: **4** fair, kind **5** civil, suave **6** gentle, polite, urbane **7** cordial, gallant, genteel, refined **8** debonair, gracious, mannerly, polished **9** attentive **10** respectful, thoughtful **11** complaisant, considerate

COURTIER: **4** beau **5** wooer **7** courter **9** attendant, flatterer

COURTLY: **4** prim **5** civil, lofty, suave **6** polite **7** elegant, refined, stately **8** cultured, debonair, decorous, gracious, polished **9** dignified **10** flattering **12** aristocratic

COURTSHIP: **4** suit **6** dating **7** pursuit, romance

COURTYARD: **4** area, quad **5** patio, space **9** curtilage, enclosure **10** quadrangle

COUSIN: **3** coz, kin **7** kinsman **8** nobleman, relative **9** kinswoman **11** counterpart

COUTURIER: **8** designer **10** couturiere, dressmaker, seamstress

COVE: **3** bay **4** cave, gulf, hole, nook, pass **5** basin, bight, creek, inlet, sound **6** cavern, harbor, lagoon, recess, valley **7** molding, retreat

COVENANT: **4** bind, bond, deal, oath, pact **5** agree **6** accord, engage, pledge, treaty **7** bargain, compact, promise **8** contract, document **9** agreement, concordat, condition, testament **10** commitment, convention **11** stipulation

COVER: **3** cap, lid **4** coat, hide, mask, pave, roof, span, veil, wrap **5** cloak, drape, hatch, shade, track **6** clothe, defend, detail, screen, shield **7** blanket, conceal, eclipse, obscure, overlay, protect, shelter **8** disguise **9** sanctuary **10** camouflage

COVERAGE: **5** scope **6** report **8** analysis, observed **9** inclusion, indemnity, insurance **11** description **12** broadcasting

COVERING: **3** rug, wig **4** bark, boot, case, hood, hull, husk, pall, tarp, tile **5** apron, armor, crust, quilt, shell, testa **6** awning, bonnet, canopy, helmet, jacket, screen, sheath, shroud, toupee **7** capsule, ceiling **8** clothing, coverlet, umbrella **10** integument **11** explanatory, smokescreen

COVERLET: **5** quilt, throw **6** afghan, spread **7** blanket **9** comforter

COVERT: **5** privy **6** asylum, harbor, hidden, latent, masked, refuge, secret **7** covered, defense, feather, guarded, private, thicket **9** concealed, disguised, incognito, insidious, sheltered **10** underbrush, undercover **11** camouflaged, clandestine, underhanded **12** confidential

COVET: **4** ache, envy, lust, want, wish **5** crave, yearn **6** aspire, desire, hanker, thirst

COVETOUS: **4** avid, keen **5** eager, itchy **6** greedy, stingy **7** envious, jealous, selfish **8** desirous, grasping, ravenous **9** mercenary **10** avaricious, gluttonous **11** acquisitive

COVEY: **4** bevy **5** brood, bunch, flock, group **6** family **7** company

COW:
female: **5** milch **6** farrow **8** springer
group: **4** herd, kine **6** cattle
habitat: **3** pen **4** barn, byre **6** corral **7** pasture, vaccary
young: **4** calf **5** stirk **6** heifer **4** beef **6** bovine **8** ruminant **9** quadruped

COWARD: **4** wimp **5** sissy **7** caitiff, chicken, gutless, quitter **9** jellyfish **10** scaredy-cat **11** yellowbelly

COWARDLY: **3** shy **5** timid **6** afraid, craven, yellow **7** fearful, nervous **9** dastardly **10** frightened **11** lily-livered **12** fainthearted **13** pusillanimous

COWBOY, COWGIRL: **5** rider, roper, waddy **6** driver, gaucho, herder, huasos **7** charros, cowpoke, llanero, puncher, vaquero **8** buckaroo, guardian, herdsman, stockman, wrangler **9** cattleman **10** cowpuncher, herdswoman, stockwoman **11** cattlewoman **12** broncobuster, frontiersman **14** frontierswoman
dress: **3** hat **5** boots, chaps, spurs **7** bandana **9** long johns
equipment: **4** rope, whip **5** quirt **6** lariat, pistol, saddle, six gun **7** gun belt, holster, shotgun **10** boleadoras **13** branding irons

COWER: **4** fawn, hide **5** quail, stoop, toady, wince **6** cringe, crouch, grovel, recoil, shrink **7** tremble

COWL: **3** cap **4** hood, monk, robe **5** cloak **6** bonnet **7** capuche

COXCOMB: **3** cap, fob **4** buck, dude, fool **5** dandy, hinge **8** popinjay

COY: **3** shy **4** arch **5** quiet, still, timid **6** allure, demure, modest **7** bashful, distant, evasive **8** reserved, skittish **9** diffident, kittenish **10** coquettish, hesitating **11** unassertive

COYOTE STATE: **11** South Dakota

COZEN: **3** con, gyp **4** bilk, dupe **5** cheat, fraud, trick **6** chisel **7** beguile, deceive, defraud, swindle **8** flimflam, hoodwink **9** bamboozle

COZY: **4** easy, safe, snug, soft, warm **5** cushy, homey **6** secure, toasty **8** covering, familiar, friendly, intimate, relaxing **9** contented **10** buddy-buddy, palsy-walsy **11** comfortable

CRAB: **6** hermit, robber, spider **7** decapod, fiddler **8** arachnid **9** arthropod, horseshoe **10** crustacean **11** soft-shelled
division: **9** brachyura
parts: **5** chela **6** nipper

CRABBY: **4** dour, glum **5** cross, huffy, surly, testy **6** bitter, cranky, sullen **7** cynical, grouchy **9** difficult, irritable

CRACK: **3** gag, gap, pop, try **4** bang, blow, chip, chop, clap, cuff, fail, flaw, jest, joke, leak, quip, rend, rift, snap, stab **5** break, check, chine, clack, cleft, craze, elite, noise, solve, split **6** chance, cleave, cranny, damage, insult, remark, thwack, wallop **7** blemish, crevice, fissure, instant, succumb **8** division, fracture **9** explosion **10** proficient

CRACKED: **3** mad **4** nuts **5** break, crazy **6** insane **7** bonkers **8** collapse, deranged **10** unbalanced

CRACKER: **4** poor **5** baked, wafer **7** biscuit, pretzel, redneck, saltine

CRACKERJACK: **3** ace **4** fine **5** adept, nifty, super **6** expert **7** skilled **8** splendid **9** excellent

CRACKER STATE: **7** Georgia

CRACKLE: **4** snap **5** break, noise, sound **7** brustle, crinkle, sparkle **9** crepitate

CRACKPOT: **3** nut **4** kook **5** flake, wacko **6** insane, maniac **7** lunatic, oddball **9** eccentric, screwball

CRACKUP: **5** amuse, smash, wreck **6** pileup **8** collapse **9** breakdown

CRADLE: **3** bed, cot, hug **4** crib, lull, tend **6** cuddle, nestle, origin **7** infancy, nourish, nursery, nurture **8** bassinet **10** wellspring

CRAFT: **3** art, job **4** boat, ruse, ship **5** fraud, skill, trade **6** deceit, talent, vessel **7** ability, cunning **8** airplane, aptitude, artifice, foxiness, vocation, wiliness **9** dexterity, expertise **10** employment, occupation, profession

CRAFTSPERSON: **5** smith **6** artist, master, worker, writer **7** artisan **8** mechanic **9** carpenter **10** specialist

CRAFTY: **3** sly **4** arch, foxy, wily **5** acute, adept, cagey, canny, slick **6** adroit, astute, clever, shrewd, smooth, subtle, tricky **7** cunning, vulpine **8** scheming **9** deceitful, designing, ingenious **10** fraudulent **11** calculating

CRAGGY: **5** harsh, rocky, rough, steep **6** rugged **7** unlevel

CRAM: **3** jam **4** fill, glut, load, pack **5** crowd, crush, drive, force, gorge, grind, learn, press, study, stuff **6** review **7** overeat, squeeze **8** compress, overfill

CRAMP: **3** bar **4** ache, iron, kink, pain **5** crick, crowd, frame, limit, spasm **6** hamper, hinder, impede, stymie **7** confine, prevent **8** compress, restrain, restrict **9** constrict, interfere, stiffness **10** constraint **11** contraction

CRANE: **4** bird **5** davit, heron, raise, wader **6** device **7** derrick, machine, stretch **8** hesitate

CRANIUM: **4** head **5** skull **8** brainpan **9** braincase

CRANK: **4** bend, crab, kook, turn, wind **5** brace, start, winch **6** grouch, handle **7** bracket, fanatic **8** crackpot, sourpuss, unstable **9** eccentric **10** vigorously

CRANKY: **4** ugly **5** cross, testy **6** crabby, ornery, touchy **7** grouchy **9** crotchety, difficult, irascible, irritable **12** cantankerous, disagreeable

CRANNY: **4** hole, nook **5** cleft, crack, niche **6** corner **7** byplace, crevice, fissure, opening

CRASH: **3** ram **4** bang, bust, fall **5** blast, crack, crush, noise, shock, sleep, smash, sound, wreck **6** crunch, fabric, pileup, topple **7** collide, failure, lodging, shatter, shelter, smashup **8** accident, collapse **9** collision **10** depression

CRASS: **3** raw **4** rude **5** crude, gross, rough **6** coarse, stupid, vulgar **7** uncouth **9** unrefined **10** unpolished **11** insensitive

CRATE: **3** box, car **4** case **5** chest **6** basket, carton, cradle, jalopy, pallet **7** package, vehicle **8** aircraft, airplane **9** container **10** receptacle

CRATER: **3** pit **4** bowl, hole **5** abyss **6** cavity, hollow **7** caldera, opening **10** depression

CRAVAT: **3** tie **4** band **5** ascot, scarf **7** necktie, overlay **11** neckerchief

CRAVE: **3** ask, beg **4** ache, long, lust, need, pray, want **5** covet, dream, fancy, yearn **6** desire, hanker, hunger, thirst **7** beseech, implore, request, require, solicit **10** supplicate

CRAVEN: **4** weak, wimp **5** timid **6** afraid, scared, yellow **7** chicken, dastard, gutless **8** cowardly, defeated, overcome, poltroon, recreant **12** fainthearted

CRAWL: **3** lag, pen **4** drag, fawn, inch, poke, slow, swim, teem **5** creep **6** cringe, grovel, writhe **7** slither **8** lollygag

CRAYON: **3** wax **5** chalk, color **6** pastel, pencil, sketch **7** drawing **8** charcoal

CRAZE: **3** fad **4** chic, kick, loco, mode, rage, wild **5** break, furor, mania, style, trend, vogue **6** frenzy, madden **7** derange, fashion, novelty, passion **8** bewilder **9** unbalance **11** infatuation

CRAZY: **3** mad **4** gaga, nuts **5** batty, daffy, flaky, goofy, inane, loony, silly, wacky, weird **6** absurd, cuckoo, insane, looney, maniac, psycho **7** bananas, bizarre, bonkers, cracked, erratic, foolish, lunatic, strange, touched **8** crackpot, demented **9** fanatical, senseless **10** unbalanced **11** harebrained **12** preposterous

CREAK: **4** rasp **5** croak, grate, grind, groan, noise, sound **6** squeak **7** screech **8** complain

CREAM: **3** top **4** beat, best, pick, whip **5** elite, froth **6** choice, defeat, lotion **7** trounce **8** cosmetic, emulsion, ointment **11** moisturizer

CREAMY: **4** lush, rich **5** foamy, thick **6** fluffy, smooth

CREASE: **4** bend, fold, line, ruck, seam, tuck **5** crimp, pleat **6** furrow, groove, ruffle **7** crumple, wrinkle

CREATE: **4** form, make, mold, plan **5** beget, build, cause, found, shape, start **6** design, invent **7** compose, concoct, fashion, imagine **8** conceive, generate **9** establish, originate, procreate

CREATION: **4** opus, work **5** world **6** cosmos, nature **7** genesis **8** universe **9** formation, macrocosm **10** brainchild, production **11** achievement, masterpiece

CREATIVE: **6** clever, gifted **8** artistic, inspired, original **9** inventive **10** innovative, productive **11** imaginative

CREATOR: **5** maker **6** author, father **7** founder **8** designer, inventor **9** architect **10** mastermind, originator

CREATURE: **3** man **4** ogre, tool **5** alien, beast, being, giant, gnome, human, thing, troll **6** animal, mammal, person **7** gremlin, mermaid, monster, varmint **10** individual

CREDENCE: **5** faith, shelf, table, trust **6** belief, credit **8** reliance **9** certainty **10** acceptance, confidence **15** trustworthiness

CREDENTIALS: **4** card, deed **5** proof **6** papers, permit **7** license, voucher **9** documents, reference **11** certificate

CREDIBLE: **5** valid **6** likely **7** seeming **8** probable, reliable, straight **9** authentic, plausible **10** aboveboard, believable **11** trustworthy **12** satisfactory

CREDIT: **4** deem, loan **5** asset, faith, glory, honor, kudos, merit, trust **6** assign, belief, charge, esteem, points, thanks, weight **7** ascribe, believe **8** credence **9** attention, attribute **10** estimation **11** distinction, recognition

CREDITABLE: **6** worthy **8** suitable **9** deserving, reputable **12** praiseworthy

CREDO: **4** code **5** creed **6** belief **10** philosophy

CREDULOUS: **5** naive **6** unwary **8** gullible, trusting **9** accepting **12** unsuspecting

CREED: **4** cult **5** canon, credo, dogma, faith, tenet **6** belief **8** doctrine, ideology **10** confession, principles

CREEK: **3** bay, rio **4** burn, cove, race, rill **5** bayou, brook, crick, inlet **6** arroyo, rindle, spring, stream **7** channel, estuary, rivulet **11** watercourse

CREEP: **4** inch, lurk **5** crawl, prowl, skulk, slink, snake, sneak, steal **6** grovel, tiptoe, writhe **7** gumshoe, slither **9** pussyfoot

CREEPY: **5** eerie, nasty, scary **6** spooky **7** macabre, ominous **8** ghoulish, sinister **10** disgusting

CREMATE: **4** burn, char **6** scorch **10** incinerate

CREOLE STATE: **9** Louisiana

CREPE: **4** band **5** crape, paper **6** fabric **7** pancake **8** crinkled, wrinkled

CRESCENT: **4** arch, horn, lune, moon **5** curve, lunar **6** convex **7** concave **8** meniscus **10** increasing, semicircle

CREST: **3** tip, top **4** acme, apex, arms, comb, edge, noon, peak, seal, tuft **5** crown, plume, ridge **6** apogee, climax, emblem, height, helmet, summit, symbol **7** bearing **8** insignia, pinnacle, whitecap **11** culmination

CRESTFALLEN: **3** low, sad **4** blue, down **8** dejected, downcast **9** depressed **10** dispirited **11** downhearted **12** disappointed

CRETE:
also called: **6** Candia
capital: **8** Iraklion
cities: **6** Aghios, Khania (Canea) **8** Nikolaos **9** Rethymnon
continent: **6** Europe
famous people: **5** Minos **7** Ariadne **8** Dictynna, minotaur **9** Idomeneus **11** Britomartis
features: **5** Minoa **7** Knossos
languages: **6** Cretan, Minoan

place: **6** Greece
water: **13** Mediterranean

CRETIN: **4** fool **5** idiot, moron **8** deformed, imbecile

CREVASSE: **4** rift **5** abyss, chasm, crack, gully, split **6** breach **7** fissure

CREVICE: **4** leak, nook, rent, seam, slit **5** break, chink, cleft, crack **6** cranny **7** fissure, opening **8** cleavage, crevasse, division **10** interstice

CREW: **3** mob **4** band, gang, herd, team **5** covey, crowd, group, hands, horde, party, posse, squad, troop **6** rowers, rowing, throng **7** company, members, retinue, sailors, workers **8** mariners **10** assemblage, complement

CRIB: **3** bed, box, cot, hut **4** bunk, pony, rack, room **5** cheat, crate, frame, stall, steal, theft **6** basket, manger, pilfer **7** cottage **8** building **10** plagiarism, plagiarize, storehouse

CRICK: **4** ache, kink **5** cramp, spasm **6** twinge

CRICKET:
officials: **6** umpire
positions: **5** cover, gully, mid on **6** bowler, long on, mid off **7** batsman, captain, fielder, fine leg, leg slip, long leg, long off **8** short leg, silly mid, third man **9** first slip, mid wicket, square leg **10** cover point, extra cover, second slip, silly mid on **12** wicket keeper
terms: **3** bat, bye, off, ons, rot, run **4** bowl, over **5** bails, pitch, smick **6** attack, crease, yorker **7** strumps

CRIME: **3** act, sin **4** evil, tort, vice **5** abuse, arson, caper, wrong **6** breach, felony, murder **7** misdeed, offense, scandal **8** atrocity, iniquity **9** violation **10** corruption, illegality **11** abomination, misdemeanor **13** transgression

CRIMEA:
also called: **4** Krym **7** Taurida
capital: **10** Simferopol
cities: **5** Kerch, Yalta **9** Balaklava **10** Sevastopol
country: **6** Russia
water: **4** Alma, Azof, Azov

CRIMINAL: **3** con **4** hood, thug **5** crook, felon **6** guilty, inmate, outlaw **7** convict, corrupt, culprit, hoodlum, illegal, lawless, mobster **8** culpable, fugitive, gangster, jailbird, repeater **9** desperado, wrongdoer **10** delinquent, deplorable, malefactor **13** reprehensible

CRIMP: **4** bend, curl, fold, friz, mold, snag, wave **5** cramp, frizz, pinch, plait, pleat **6** crease, hamper, ruffle, thwart **7** crinkle, wrinkle **8** obstacle **9** corrugate

CRIMSON: **3** dye, red **4** rose **5** blush, color, rouge **6** bloody, maroon, redden

CRINGE: **4** bend **5** cower, crawl, dodge, quail, sneak, stoop, toady, wince **6** crouch, flinch, grovel, quiver, recoil, shrink **7** crinkle, tremble, truckle **8** bootlick

CRINKLE: **4** bend, coil, curl, fold, kink, seam, turn **5** crimp, ridge, twist **6** crease, pucker, ripple, rumple, rustle **7** crackle, wrinkle

CRIPPLE: **3** mar **4** harm, hurt, lame, maim **6** impair, injure, weaken **7** crumpet, disable **8** enfeeble, handicap, mutilate, paralyze, sideline **9** dismember **10** debilitate, immobilize **12** incapacitate

CRISIS: **4** crux, pass **5** panic, peril, pinch, trial **6** climax, trauma **7** dilemma, impasse, trouble **8** juncture **9** emergency **10** crossroads **11** catastrophe, predicament

CRISP: **4** cold, firm **5** brisk, clear, fresh, nippy, plump, sharp, short, terse **6** biting, chilly, lively, spruce **7** bracing, brittle, concise, cutting, friable **8** clearcut, incisive **9** crackling **10** refreshing **12** invigorating

CRISSCROSS: **4** awry **8** confused, traverse **9** intersect **11** conflicting

CRITERION: **4** norm, rule, test **5** canon, gauge, proof, scale **7** example, measure **8** standard **9** benchmark, precedent, yardstick **10** touchstone

CRITIC: **5** judge **6** carper, censor, expert **7** analyst **8** reviewer **9** authority, detractor, evaluator, muckraker, nitpicker **10** antagonist, mudslinger **11** commentator, connoisseur, faultfinder

CRITICAL: **4** dire **5** acute, exact, fussy **6** urgent **7** carping, crucial, cynical, finicky, pivotal, serious **8** captious, decisive, exacting, pressing **9** dangerous, sarcastic, strategic **10** precarious **11** significant

CRITICISM: **5** blame, knock **6** review **7** comment **8** critique, judgment **9** objection **10** assessment, evaluation **13** animadversion

CRITICIZE: **4** bash, carp, slam, slur **5** blame, blast, cavil, judge, knock, roast **6** assess, rebuke, review, scathe **7** censure, comment, examine **8** badmouth, reproach **9** castigate, disparage, interpret

CROAK: **3** caw, die **4** gasp, kill, moan **5** grunt, noise, quark, sound **6** grouch, hoarse, mutter **7** grumble **8** complain

CROATIA:
capital: **6** Zagreb
cities: **5** Agram, Rieka **6** Osijek
continent: **6** Europe
ethnic groups: **7** Serbian **8** Croatian
features: **10** Julian Alps **11** Styrian Alps
languages: **8** Croatian
native: **8** Croatian
place: **10** Yugoslavia
water: **11** Adriatic Sea

CROCK: **3** pot **4** bull, soil, soot **6** smudge, vessel **8** nonsense, potsherd **9** container **11** earthenware

CROCODILE: **5** gator **6** cayman, gavial, mugger **7** reptile **9** alligator

CRONE: **4** ugly **5** woman

CRONY: **3** pal **4** ally, chum **5** buddy **6** cohort, friend **7** partner **8** sidekick **9** associate, companion, confidant **10** accomplice

CROOK: **4** bend, hook, thug, turn **5** cheat, curve, snake, thief **6** outlaw, robber **7** burglar, meander, shyster **8** criminal, swindler

CROOKED: **4** agee, awry, bent **5** askew, false, lying, shady, snide **6** angled, crafty, curved, errant, shifty, skewed, tricky, zigzag **7** corrupt, devious, knavish, turning, twisted, winding **8** tortuous, unlawful **9** dishonest, distorted, irregular, unethical **10** fraudulent, misleading **11** underhanded **12** dishonorable, unscrupulous

CROON: **3** hum **4** lull, roar, sing, wail **6** bellow, murmur

CROP: **3** cut, lop, mow, top **4** clip, reap, trim, whip **5** fruit, grain, prune, shear, yield **6** gather **7** curtail, haircut, harvest, produce **8** truncate **9** vegetable

CROSS: **3** mad, mix **4** crux, ford, lace, sign, span **5** angry, blend, testy, trial **6** betray, bisect, bridge, burden, crabby, cranky, delete, divide, emblem, grumpy, hinder, hybrid, sullen, symbol, thwart, touchy **7** annoyed, fretful **8** crucifix, navigate, petulant, snappish, traverse **9** crotchety, frustrate, half-breed, intersect, irritable **10**

affliction, interbreed, transverse **11** combination **12** disagreeable

CROSS-EXAMINE: **4** pump **5** grill **7** debrief **8** question **11** interrogate

CROSS-EYE: **7** walleye **9** esotropia **10** strabismus

CROSSING: **4** loop, pass **7** passage **8** junction, opposing, traverse **12** intersection

CROSS OUT: **5** erase **6** cancel, delete **9** eliminate

CROSSROADS: **4** pass **6** crisis **12** intersection, turning point

CROSS SECTION: **4** part **8** side view **14** representation

CROSSWISE: **6** across, aslant **7** athwart **8** diagonal, longways, sideways **10** vertically **13** perpendicular

CROTCHET: **4** whim **5** fancy, quirk, trait **6** notion, vagary **11** peculiarity **12** eccentricity

CROTCHETY: **5** cross, surly **6** cranky, ornery **7** grouchy **9** difficult, irritable, obstinate **12** cantankerous

CROUCH: **3** dip **4** bend, duck **5** cower, squat, stoop **6** grovel

CROW: **3** caw, cry, jay **4** bird, brag, rook **5** boast, exult, gloat, raven, sound, strut **6** cackle, magpie, squawk **7** corvine, grapnel, jackdaw, swagger **8** jubilate **9** blackbird

CROWBAR: **3** pry **5** jimmy, lever **6** chisel, remove **7** extract

CROWD: **3** jam, mob, set **4** cram, gang, herd, host, pack, push **5** bunch, cramp, crush, drove, flock, group, horde, party, posse, press, shove, swarm, three **6** circle, clique, deluge, huddle, legion, scores, stream, throng **7** cluster, company, sellout, squeeze **9** gathering, multitude **10** assemblage

CROWDED: **3** SRO **4** full **5** close, dense, thick, tight **6** filled, loaded **7** compact, stuffed, teeming **8** swarming **9** congested, jampacked **11** overflowing

CROWN: **3** cap, tip, top **4** apex, best, coin, king, peak, roof **5** adorn, crest, exalt, knock, queen, tiara, tooth **6** circle, climax, diadem, invest, laurel, reward, summit, trophy, wreath, zenith **7** chaplet, coronet, dignify, garland, install **8** enthrone, pinnacle, surmount **9** headdress, sovereign

CRUCIAL: **4** dire **5** acute, final, grave, vital **6** severe, trying, urgent **7** pivotal, serious, telling **8** critical, decisive **9** climactic, difficult, essential, important, necessary

CRUCIBLE: **4** dish, test **5** trial **6** ordeal, vessel **7** furnace **10** affliction

CRUCIFY: **4** hang, kill **5** smite **6** martyr **7** execute, lampoon, torment, torture **8** browbeat, ridicule **9** persecute

CRUDE: **3** raw **4** foul, lewd, rude **5** cheap, crass, dirty, gross, harsh, rough **6** callow, coarse, savage, vulgar **7** obscene, raunchy, uncouth **8** ignorant, impolite **9** primitive, unrefined **10** incomplete, unpolished **11** undeveloped

CRUEL: **4** evil, hard, mean **5** harsh **6** bloody, brutal, fierce, savage, unjust, unkind **7** brutish, callous, inhuman, vicious **8** barbaric, depraved, fiendish, inhumane, pitiless, ruthless, sadistic, vengeful **9** atrocious, ferocious, heartless, merciless, unfeeling **10** diabolical **11** hardhearted

CRUISE: **4** boat, sail, scud, ship, trip **5** coast, glide, jaunt **6** voyage, wander **9** gallivant

CRUMB: **3** bit **4** drop **5** break, piece, scrap, shred, speck **6** little, morsel **7** remnant, smidgen **8** fragment, particle **9** loathsome

CRUMBLE: **3** rot **5** break, crush, decay, spoil **6** molder, perish, powder, tumble **8** collapse, splinter **9** decompose, pulverize **12** disintegrate

CRUMBLY: **4** worn **5** frail **7** brittle, fragile, friable

CRUMPLE: **4** cave, fold, ruck **5** break, crush **6** crease, rumple **7** crinkle, crunkle, shrivel, wrinkle **8** collapse **9** corrugate

CRUNCH: **4** bite, chew, crux, gnaw **5** chomp, crush, gnash, grind, munch, press, tread **6** crisis **7** scrunch **8** ruminate **9** masticate **13** confrontation

CRUSADE: **3** war **4** push **5** cause, jihad, march, rally **8** campaign, movement

CRUSADER: **6** knight **7** pilgrim, Templar **8** champion, reformer

CRUSH: **4** cram, dump, hurt, mash, mill, pulp **5** break, crash, crowd, drove, force, grind, press, quell, smash, tread **6** crunch, defeat, reduce, squash, subdue, thwack **7** conquer, crumble, destroy, oppress, passion, repress, squelch, trample **8** compress, demolish, suppress **9** granulate, overpower, overwhelm, pulverize **10** annihilate, obliterate **11** infatuation

CRUST: **4** film, hull, rind, scab **5** layer, shell **6** caking, harden **7** coating

CRUSTACEAN: **4** crab **5** louse, prawn **6** shrimp **7** lobster, pillbug, squilla **8** barnacle **9** water flea
part: **4** claw **5** alima, chela, exite **6** endite, feeler, pincer, podite **7** antenna, pleopod **8** nauplius, podomere

CRUSTY: **4** curt, dour, hard **5** blunt, brief, crisp, gruff, harsh, stern, surly, testy **6** abrupt, crabby, morose **7** crabbed, peevish **8** choleric, snappish **9** irascible, irritable

CRUX: **3** nub **4** core, gist, meat **5** basis, cross, point **6** crunch, kernel, matter, moment **7** essence, problem **8** puzzling **10** difficulty

CRY: **3** boo, caw, coo, sob **4** bark, bawl, call, fret, hawk, hoot, howl, hype, keen, meow, moan, ouch, puff, rage, wail, weep, yell, yelp **5** blame, groan, plead, rumor, shout, sound, tears, utter, vogue, whine **6** bellow, boohoo, cackle, clamor, demand, hurrah, lament, scream, shriek, snivel, squall, squeal, yammer **7** blubber, exclaim, protest, screech, whimper **8** complain, proclaim **9** advertise, broadcast **11** acclamation, lamentation

CRYING: **4** dire **6** action, urgent **7** burning, heinous **8** pressing **9** annoyance, attention, desperate, insistent **10** imperative **12** astonishment

CRYPT: **3** pit **4** cave, cell, tomb **5** grave, vault **6** cavern, cavity, grotto, recess **7** chamber **8** catacomb **9** sepulcher

CRYPTIC: **4** dark **5** murky, vague **6** hidden, occult, secret **7** obscure **8** esoteric, mystical **9** ambiguous, enigmatic **10** apocryphal, camouflage, mysterious

CRYPTOGRAM: **4** code **6** cipher, figure **7** writing **14** representation

CRYSTAL: **3** ice **4** hard **5** clear, glass, lucid **6** limpid, quartz **7** diamond, mineral **8** pellucid **9** unblurred **10** oscillator **11** crystalline, transparent

CRYSTALLIZE: **4** coat, form, jell **5** candy, sugar **8** solidify **9** granulate

CUB: **3** fox, pup **4** bear, lion, wolf **5** moose, scout, shark, tiger, whelp **6** novice **7** giraffe **8** reporter **9** youngster

CUBA:
capital: **6** Havana
cities: **8** Camaguey **10** Guantanamo **14** Santiago de Cuba
ethnic groups: **7** Spanish **8** Africans
explorer: **8** Columbus
features: **11** Isle of Youth **22** Sierra Maestra Mountains
languages: **7** Spanish
monetary unit: **4** peso
native: **5** Cuban
water: **8** Atlantic **9** Bay of Pigs, Caribbean

CUBBYHOLE: **4** nook **5** niche **6** cranny **7** cubicle **8** category

CUBE: **3** die **4** dice **5** block **7** cubicle **9** tenderize **10** hexahedron

CUBICLE: **7** bedroom, chamber **11** compartment

CUCKOO: **4** bird, fool, nuts **5** batty, clock, crazy, daffy, silly, wacky **6** insane **9** screwball

CUD: **4** chew, food, quid **5** bolus

CUDDLE: **3** hug, pet **4** kiss, love **5** touch **6** caress, fondle, nestle, nuzzle **7** embrace, snuggle

CUDGEL: **3** bat **4** beat, cane, club **5** baton, drive, staff, stick **6** weapon **8** bludgeon **9** bastinado, blackjack, truncheon **10** nightstick, shillelagh

CUE: **3** nod, rod, tip **4** clue, hint, prod, sign, wink **5** queue **6** notion, prompt, signal **7** gesture, warning **8** reminder **9** catchword **10** intimation, suggestion

CUFF: **3** box, hit **4** band, belt, blow, slam, slap, slug, swat **5** clout, smack, smite, spank **6** buffet, pummel, strike, wallop **7** clobber, scuffle **8** handcuff

CUISINE: **4** fare, food, menu **7** cookery

CUL-DE-SAC: **4** tube **6** cavity, pocket **7** deadend, impasse

CULL: **3** opt **4** pick, sift, sort **5** elect, glean **6** choose, gather, prefer, reject, remove, select **7** collect, extract **8** separate

CULMINATE: **3** end **6** climax, finish, result **8** conclude

CULMINATION: **4** acme, apex, noon, peak **5** crown **6** apogee, finale, summit, zenith **7** maximum **8** pinnacle **10** completion **11** ne plus ultra **12** consummation

CULPABLE: **6** guilty **8** blamable, criminal **10** answerable, censurable **11** blameworthy, responsible

CULPRIT: **7** convict, villain **8** criminal, offender **9** miscreant **10** delinquent, malefactor **12** transgressor

CULT: **4** clan, sect **5** creed, faith **6** church, clique, ritual, school **7** faction, faddish, worship **8** religion **9** followers, obsessive

CULTIVATE: **3** hoe, sow **4** farm, grow, plow, rear, tend, till, work **5** labor, nurse, plant, raise, study **6** foster **7** acquire, bolster, cherish, develop, educate, improve, nourish, prepare **8** civilize **9** encourage

CULTIVATION: **6** polish **7** culture, manners, nurture, tillage **8** advocacy, agrology **9** gentility, husbandry **10** refinement **11** advancement, agriculture **12** horticulture

CULTURE: **3** art **5** mores, music **6** polish **7** farming, society **8** agronomy, breeding, folklore, learning **9** education, knowledge

10 lifestyles, literature, refinement 11 savoir faire 12 civilization

CULTURED: 7 elegant, genteel 8 educated, literate, polished 11 enlightened 13 sophisticated

CULVERT: 5 drain, sewer 6 gutter 7 channel, conduit

CUMBERSOME: 5 bulky, heavy 6 clumsy 7 awkward, massive, weighty 8 cumbrous 9 ponderous 10 burdensome

CUMULATIVE: 7 amassed 8 accruing 10 augmenting, collective, increasing 11 multiplying

CUNNING: 3 sly 4 foxy, keen, wary, wily 5 guile, savvy, sharp, slick, smart 6 adroit, artful, astute, clever, crafty, deceit, pretty, shifty, shrewd, smooth, subtle 7 devious 8 dextrous, skillful, slippery 9 chicanery, deceptive, designing, ingenious, insidious 11 imaginative 13 Machiavellian

CUP:
concerning: 9 oalicular
parts: 3 ear, lug, mug, tig, tyg 4 shot, zarf 5 calix, glass, grail, jorum, stein, stoup 6 beaker, goblet, noggin, vessel 7 chalice, stirrup, tankard 8 cannikin, pannikin 9 demitasse, Holy Grail, kantharos, porringer

CUPBOARD: 5 ambry, cuddy 6 buffet, bureau, closet, locker, pantry 7 armoire, cabinet, dresser 9 sideboard 10 chiffonier

CUPID:
lover: 6 Psyche
mother: 5 Venus
symbolizes: 3 Dan 4 Amor, Eros, love 6 cherub 7 Amorino

CUPIDITY: 4 lust 5 greed 6 desire 7 avarice, craving, passion 8 rapacity, yearning 12 covetousness

CUR: 3 bum, cad, dog 4 mutt, toad 6 canine, coward, rotten 7 mongrel, stinker, villain 9 scoundrel, yellow dog

CURATE: 4 abbe 6 cleric, pastor, priest 7 dominie 8 minister 9 assistant, clergyman

CURATIVE: 6 curing 7 healing 8 remedial, salutary 9 healthful, medicinal 10 beneficial 11 restorative, therapeutic 12 invigorating

CURATOR: 6 keeper 7 manager 8 director, guardian, overseer 9 caretaker, custodian

CURB: 4 edge, rein, tame 5 brake, brink, check, curve, limit 6 arrest, border, bridle, hamper, hinder, thwart 7 abstain, barrier, control, inhibit, repress, shackle 8 moderate, restrain, restrict, suppress, withhold 9 constrain

CURDLE: 4 clot, curd, sour, turn 5 quail, quarl, spoil 6 change 7 clabber, congeal, ferment, thicken 8 condense 9 coagulate

CURE: 3 age, dry 4 care, heal, help, kick, mend, salt, save 5 agent, smoke 6 kipper, physic, remedy, season 7 recover, rectify, restore, therapy 8 antidote, corrects, preserve, solution 9 treatment

CURE-ALL: 4 balm 6 elixir, remedy 7 panacea 8 medicine 10 catholicon

CURFEW: 4 bell, time 6 signal 10 regulation 11 restriction

CURIO: 5 relic 6 bauble 7 antique, bibelot, trinket 8 keepsake, souvenir 9 bric-a-brac, curiosity 10 knick-knack 11 collectible

CURIOSITY: 5 curio 6 marvel, wonder 7 concern 8 interest, meddling, nosiness, snooping 9 objet d'art

CURIOUS: 3 odd 4 nosy, rare 5 eager, novel, queer, weird 6 exotic, prying, snoopy, unique **7** peeping, strange, unusual **8** peculiar, singular **9** intrusive, wondering **10** unorthodox **11** inquisitive

CURL: 4 bend, coil, kink, lock, loop, roll, wave, wind **5** crisp, frizz, swirl, twist **6** ripple, spiral, writhe **7** crimple, meander, ringlet **9** corkscrew **11** convolution

CURRENCY: 4 cash, coin **5** bills, bread, dough, money **6** dinero, moolah **7** cabbage **10** greenbacks, prevalence **11** circulation

CURRENT: 3 now, run **4** flow, flux, gust, rife, rush, tide **5** draft, drift, rapid, trend, usual **6** common, course, living, modern, motion, moving, recent, stream, trendy **7** counter, general, instant, ongoing, popular, present, running, topical, torrent **8** accepted, tendency **9** customary, prevalent **10** prevailing **11** electricity **12** contemporary

CURRY: 4 comb **5** clean, favor, groom, sauce **6** powder, relish **7** prepare **9** condiment, seasoning

CURSE: 4 bane, cuss, damn, jinx, oath **5** spell, swear **6** burden, plague, voodoo, whammy **7** condemn, malison **8** anathema **9** blasphemy, expletive, obscenity, profanity, swearword **10** affliction, execration **11** malediction

CURSED: 4 vile **6** damned **7** doggone, hateful **8** blighted, infamous **9** execrable, loathsome **10** confounded, foredoomed **13** blankety-blank

CURSORY: 4 fast **5** brief, hasty, quick, rapid, scant, short **6** sloppy, speedy **7** hurried, passing, shallow, sketchy **8** careless, rambling **9** depthless, desultory, haphazard **11** superficial

CURT: 4 rude, tart **5** bluff, blunt, brief, gruff, pithy, short, terse **6** abrupt, snappy, snippy **7** concise, summary **8** succinct **9** condensed

CURTAIL: 3 cut, lop **4** chop, clip, crop, dock, halt, stop **5** slash **6** lessen, reduce **7** abridge, shorten **8** decrease, diminish, downsize, restrict, retrench **10** abbreviate

CURTAIN: 4 boom, mask, veil, wall **5** blind, drape, shade **6** purdah, screen, shroud **7** barrier, conceal, shutter **8** backdrop **10** decoration

CURTAINS: 3 end **4** ruin **5** death **7** drapery

CURTSY, CURTSEY: 3 bob, bow, dip **7** bending, gesture **9** obeisance

CURVACEOUS: 5 buxom, curvy **7** endowed, shapely, stacked **9** well-built **10** attractive, voluptuous

CURVATURE: 3 arc **4** arch, bend **5** curve, ratio **10** deflection

CURVE: 3 arc, bow **4** arch, bend, curb, curl, hook, turn, veer **5** bight, crook, crump, sweep, swirl, twist **6** spiral, swerve **7** circuit, concave, contour, deviate, ellipse, hairpin **8** parabola **9** curvature

CURVED: 4 bent **5** round, snaky **6** humped, looped, turned **7** arcuate, arrondi, crooked **8** aquiline, arciform **9** declinate **10** elliptical

CUSHION: 3 mat, pad **4** seat **5** quiet, squab **6** buffer, insole, pillow, soften **7** bolster, hassock, protect **8** insulate, mitigate **9** upholster

CUSP: 3 end, tip **4** apex, flap, fold, horn, peak **5** angle, point, tooth **6** corner

CUSTODIAN: 5 guard **6** keeper, warden **7** cleaner, curator, janitor, steward **8** cerberus, guardian **9** attendant, caretaker, protector

CUSTODY: 4 care **5** trust, watch **6** arrest, charge **7** control, keeping

10 protection **11** confinement, safekeeping, supervision

CUSTOM: **3** law, use, way **4** duty, form, mode, more, rite, rule, toll, wont **5** habit, style, usage **6** groove, method, ritual, system **7** costume, fashion, routine **8** business, practice **9** formality **10** consuetude, convention, observance, tailor-made

CUSTOMARY: **5** usual **6** common, normal **7** general, popular, regular **8** accepted, familiar, habitual, orthodox, standard **10** accustomed, understood **11** established, traditional **12** conventional

CUSTOMER: **5** buyer **6** client, patron **7** regular, shopper **8** consumer, prospect **9** clientele, purchaser

CUSTOMS: **3** tax **4** duty, levy, rate, toll **5** mores **6** tariff **10** inspection

CUT: **3** mow, nip, saw **4** bite, chip, chop, clip, dice, dock, fell, form, gash, hack, mode, nick, part, raze, slit, snip, snub, tear, trim, type **5** carve, knife, lance, mince, piece, prune, sever, share, shear, slash, slice, split **6** bisect, chisel, cleave, delete, dilute, divide, excise, ignore, incise, insult, lessen, reduce, slight **7** affront, curtail, opening, section, segment, shorten, whittle **8** condense, incision, kickback, lacerate, lowering, retrench **9** allotment

CUT-AND-DRIED: **5** trite **7** routine, settled **8** ordinary **9** cut-and-dry

CUTAWAY: **4** coat, dive **5** model **7** diagram

CUTBACK: **4** clip, trim **5** lower, prune **7** curtail, shorten **8** decrease, reversal **9** economize, reduction

CUT DOWN: **4** clip, kill **5** clear, level, limit **6** reduce **8** diminish **9** slaughter

CUTE: **3** coy **5** sharp **6** clever, dainty, pretty, shrewd **7** cunning **8** adorable, precious **9** beautiful **10** attractive

CUT IN: **7** connect, include, intrude **9** interrupt, intervene

CUTLASS: **5** sword **6** machee, weapon

CUT OFF: **4** clip, halt, trim **5** block **6** detach **7** deprive, isolate, prevent **8** amputate, insulate **9** sequester **10** disinherit **11** discontinue **12** interception

CUT OUT: **3** fit **4** exit, suit **5** scram **6** escape, excise, remove **7** deprive **8** supplant **9** eliminate

CUT SHORT: **3** end **4** clip, dock **5** abort, shear **7** curtail **9** terminate **10** abbreviate

CUTTER: **4** boat, sled **5** sloop **6** editor, sleigh, slicer, tailor, vessel **7** clipper

CUTTHROAT: **5** cruel **7** hoodlum, ruffian **8** murderer, ruthless **10** relentless

CUTTING: **3** raw **4** curt **5** crisp, nasty, sharp **6** biting, bitter, severe **7** editing, hateful, pointed **8** chilling, incisive, piercing, sardonic **9** malicious, sarcastic **11** penetrating

CUTTING EDGE: **5** blade **7** element, quality **9** forefront **13** state-of-the-art

CUT UP: **4** chop, joke **5** carve, clown, knock, split **6** divide **7** crucify **8** ridicule **9** criticize, horseplay, misbehave

CYCLE: **3** age, eon, era **4** aeon, bike, ring, time **5** chain, orbit, phase, round, wheel **6** circle, course, period, series **7** bicycle, circuit, vehicle **8** sequence **10** revolution

CYCLONE: **4** gale, gust, wind **5** blast, storm **7** tornado, twister, typhoon, weather **9** whirlwind, windstorm

CYCLOPS: **5** giant **6** Titans **8** Cyclopes
feature: **6** one eye
forged: **12** thunderbolts
inhabited: **6** Sicily

CYLINDER: **4** drum, pipe, roll, tube **6** barrel, bobbin, piston, platen, roller

CYLINDRICAL: **5** round **6** terete **7** tubular **8** circular **11** coordinates

CYNIC: **6** mocker **7** doubter, skeptic **9** pessimist **10** misogamist, unbeliever **11** misanthrope

CYNICAL: **3** wry **6** ironic **8** doubtful, sardonic, scornful, snarling **9** sarcastic **10** suspicious

CYPRUS:
capital: **7** Nicosia
cities: **6** Paphos **7** Kyrenia, Larnaca, Morphou **8** Limassol **9** Famagusta
continent: **4** Asia **6** Europe
ethnic groups: **4** Turk **5** Greek **8** Armenian, Maronite
features: **12** Mount Olympus
languages: **5** Greek **7** English, Turkish
monetary unit: **5** pound
native: **7** Cypriot
water: **13** Mediterranean

CYST: **3** bag, sac, wen **4** cist, sore **5** pouch, spore **7** blister, vesicle

CZAR: **4** king **5** baron, ruler **6** tycoon **7** emperor, monarch **8** autocrat

CZECHOSLOVAKIA:
also called: **7** Bohemia, Moravia
capital: **6** Prague
cities: **4** Brno **7** Ostrava **10** Bratislava
continent: **6** Europe
ethnic groups: **5** Czech **6** Slovak
water: **4** Labe (Elbe) **6** Danube, Morava, Vltava (Moldau)

D

DAB: **3** hit, pat **4** daub, drop, lump, peck, spot, swab, wipe **5** smear **6** blotch **7** portion, smidgen **8** flatfish, flounder

DABBLE: **4** idle **5** dally **6** fiddle, meddle, putter, splash, tinker, trifle **7** moisten, spatter **8** sprinkle

DABBLER: **6** novice **7** amateur **8** beginner **10** dilettante

DACTYLOGRAM: **11** fingerprint

DAD: **3** pop **5** pappy, poppy **6** father, old man

DAEDAL: **4** fine **6** varied **7** complex **8** artistic, involved, skillful **9** ingenious, intricate

DAFT: **3** mad **4** loco, wild **5** crazy, daffy, fried, giddy, nutty, silly **6** absurd, cuckoo, insane, stupid **7** cracked, foolish, idiotic, unsound **8** demented, imbecile **10** frolicsome

DAGGER: **4** dirk, snee **5** blade, knife **6** anlace, bodkin, weapon **8** stiletto **10** misericord

DAILY: **7** diurnal, journal, routine **8** periodic **9** circadian, newspaper, quotidian, regularly

DAINTY: **4** airy, cute, nice, rare, trim **5** frail **6** choice, pretty, select **7** elegant, finicky, fragile **8** delicacy, delicate, graceful **9** beautiful, exquisite **10** attractive, fastidious **11** persnickety

DAIRY: **4** farm **8** creamery
products: **4** milk **5** cream **6** butter, cheese, yogurt

DAIS: **4** seat **5** bench, stage, table **6** podium **7** terrace **8** platform

DALE: **4** dell, dene, glen, vale **5** spout **6** dingle, ravine, trough, valley

DALLY: **3** toy **4** chat, drag, fool, idle, play, romp **5** delay, flirt, sport **6** dabble, dawdle, frivol, frolic, linger, loiter, trifle **8** lollygag

DAM: **3** bar **4** clog, dike, plug, slow, stem, stop, weir **5** block, check, choke, levee **6** hinder, impede **7** barrier, repress **8** blockade, obstacle, obstruct, restrain **9** barricade

DAMAGE: **3** mar **4** bill, cost, harm, hurt, loss, maim, ruin **5** award, cloud, spoil, wound **6** charge, defile, impair, injury, scathe, weaken **7** blemish, corrupt, expense, pollute, scratch, tarnish **8** accident, sabotage **9** indemnity, undermine, vandalism **10** reparation **11** deleterious, destruction

DAME: **4** lady, miss **5** title, woman **6** female, matron

DAMN: **4** cuss, darn, doom **5** curse **6** attack, punish **7** condemn **8** denounce, penalize, sentence **9** castigate

DAMNABLE: **6** blamed, odious, wicked **7** hateful **8** culpable **9** atrocious, execrable **10** detestable

DAMNED: **6** cursed, doomed, fallen **7** doggone, dratted **8** accursed, infamous **9** loathsome, revolting

DAMP: **3** fog, wet **4** dank, dewy, mist **5** humid, moist, muggy, musty, rainy, soggy **6** clammy, hinder, soaked **7** drizzly **8** drenched, moisture **9** saturated

DAMPEN: **4** dull **5** cloud, spray **6** deaden, muffle **7** depress, moisten **8** dispirit **10** discourage

DAMSEL: **4** girl, lass, miss **5** woman **6** female, maiden **8** princess **10** demoiselle

DANCE: **3** hop, jig **4** ball, hoof, prom, shag **5** stomp **7** hoedown **9** cotillion
arrangement: **12** choreography
ballroom: **5** mambo, polka, rumba, samba, tango **6** chacha, shimmy **7** beguine, carioca, foxtrot, lancers **8** merengue **9** quickstep
Brazil: **5** samba **6** maxixe **9** bossa nova
Cuba: **8** habanera
folk: **3** jig **4** hula, reel **5** belly, fling, sword **6** morris, square **7** hoedown **8** hornpipe **11** streathspey
footwear: **4** taps **5** pumps **8** slippers, toeshoes
France: **5** galop **9** Farandole, tambourin
historical: **5** volta **6** minuet, pavane **7** bourree, gavotte **8** chaconne, courante, galliard, rigadoon **9** allemande, cotillion, ecossaise, passepied, quadrille, sarabande **10** Charleston, turkey trot **11** passacaglia, schottische
Hungary: **7** Czardas
India: **6** nautch
Israel: **4** hora
Italy: **8** courante **9** rigoletto **10** saltarello, tarantella
Latin America: **5** conga, limbo, mambo, rumba, samba, tango **6** chacha, maxixe **7** carioca, criolla
modern: **3** bop **4** gogo **5** break, salsa, twist **6** boogie, hustle **7** shuffle **9** jitterbug, rock n roll **12** mashed potato
performance: **3** tap **6** ballet
Peru: **5** cueca
Poland: **7** mazurka **9** polonaise
Spain: **6** bolero **8** cachucha, fandango, flamenco **9** malaguena, zapateado **10** seguidilla
waltz: **7** mazurka, twostep

DANDELION: **4** weed **5** color, plant **6** yellow

DANDER: **5** anger, scurf **6** temper **7** provoke

DANDLE: **4** love, rock **6** caress, cuddle, nuzzle, pamper

DANDRUFF: **4** snow **5** scurf **6** flakes, furfur **9** seborrhea

DANDY: **3** fop **4** beau, buck, dude, fine, yawl **5** grand, great, nifty, swell **6** peachy, superb **7** capital, coxcomb **8** popinjay, sailboat, splendid, terrific **9** excellent, exquisite, humdinger **11** crackerjack

DANGER: **4** fear, risk **5** peril **6** crisis, hazard, threat **7** pitfall **8** jeopardy **9** adventure, emergency **11** uncertainty

DANGEROUS: **5** hairy, nasty **6** chancy, deadly, touchy, unsafe **7** parlous, unsound **8** insecure, perilous **9** hazardous **10** precarious **11** speculative, treacherous

DANGLE: **4** hang, loll, lure **5** droop, hover, swing, tempt **6** entice **7** suspend

DANK: **3** wet **4** cold, damp **5** humid, moist, soggy **6** chilly, clammy **8** dripping

DANUBE:
place: **6** Europe
ports: **3** Ulm **4** Linz, Ruse **6** Braila, Galati, Vienna **8** Belgrade, Budapest **10** Bratislava
rivers: **4** Main **5** Rhine

DAP: **3** bob, dip **4** fish, skip **6** bounce **7** rebound

DAPPER: **4** chic, neat, prim, trim **5** natty, sharp, swank **6** classy, spiffy, spruce **7** dashing, stylish

DAPPLED: **6** dotted **7** flecked, mottled, piebald, spotted **8** freckled, speckled **10** variegated **12** multicolored

DARE: **4** defy, face, goad, risk **5** brave **7** attempt, venture **8** confront **9** challenge, disregard, speculate, undertake

DAREDEVIL: **4** bold **6** daring **8** reckless, stuntman **10** stuntwoman **11** adventurous **12** swashbuckler

DARING: **4** bold, rash **5** brave, cocky, gutsy, nerve **6** heroic **7** dashing, valiant **8** devilish, fearless, intrepid **9** audacious, daredevil, dauntless **10** courageous **11** adventurous, venturesome **12** death-defying

DARK: **3** dim, sad, wan **4** evil, grim **5** black, blind, brown, dingy, dusky, faint, murky, shady, unlit, vague **6** brunet, cloudy, dismal, dreary, gloomy, hidden, morbid, occult, opaque, sombre, wicked **7** corrupt, obscure, ominous, stygian, sunless, swarthy **8** abstruse, hopeless, ignorant, infamous, overcast, sinister **9** ambiguous, secretive, uncertain **10** forbidding, mysterious, mystifying **12** caliginosity

DARKEN: **4** dull, tint **5** bedim, cloud, gloom, shade, umber **6** deepen, shadow **7** benight, blacken, eclipse, obscure, tarnish **8** overcast **9** obfuscate **10** overshadow

DARKNESS: **4** dusk, murk **5** night **6** shadow **7** privacy, secrecy **8** twilight **9** blackness, isolation **10** wickedness **11** concealment, unawareness

DARLING: **3** pet **4** cute, dear, love **5** honey, sugar, sweet **6** dreary **7** beloved, dearest, sweetie **8** adorable, favorite, precious, truelove **10** attractive, honeybunch, sweetheart

DARN: **4** damn, mend **5** patch, weave **6** cussed, repair, stitch **9** downright

DART: **4** bolt, dash, flit, leap, race **5** bound, fling, hurry, scoot, speed **6** hasten, launch, propel, scurry, spring, sprint **7** missile, stinger **8** movement **9** flechette

D'ARTAGNAN:
author: 14 Alexandre Dumas
companion: **5** Athos **6** Aramis **7** Porthos
group: **18** The Three Musketeers

DARWIN:
birthplace: **7** England
field: **9** evolution **15** Origin of Species **16** natural selection

DASH: **3** run, vim, zip **4** bang, bolt, dart, ding, drop, elan, hurl, race, ruin, rush, slam **5** abash, break, crash, flair, fling, grain, hurry, knock, lunge, oomph, smack, smash, speed, spice, style, swash, throw, trace **6** baffle, energy, hurtle, little, pizazz, spirit, splash, sprint, stroke, thrust **7** collide, depress, panache, scamper, shatter, smidgen, spatter, splotch **8** confound, splinter, sprinkle, strength **9** animation, frustrate, overthrow **10** discourage

DASHING: **3** gay **4** bold, chic **5** showy **6** dapper, daring, jaunty **7** gallant, stylish **8** debonair, fearless, spirited **9** vivacious **10** courageous, flamboyant **11** fashionable

DASTARD: **3** cad **4** wimp **5** sneak **6** coward, craven **7** chicken **8** poltroon, recreant

DASTARDLY: **4** base, foul, mean, vile **6** rotten, yellow **8** cowardly **9** malicious **10** despicable

DATA: **4** info **5** facts, input, scoop **6** charts, values **7** figures **8** material **10** statistics **11** information **12** compilations

DATE: **3** age, day, era, woo **4** time, year **5** court, epoch, fruit, lover **6** escort, moment, steady **7** century **8** duration **9** chronicle, companion, originate **10** engagement, rendezvous **11** anniversary, appointment

DATED: **4** aged **5** faded, passe **6** demode **7** archaic **8** obsolete, outmoded **10** antiquated **12** old-fashioned

DAUB: **3** dab **4** blot, blur, coat, soil **5** apply, cover, fleck, paint, smear, sully **6** grease, smudge **7** besmear, plaster, splotch **8** splatter

DAUGHTER: **4** girl **5** child **6** female **9** offspring **10** descendant

DAUNT: **3** awe, cow **4** faze, foil, stun, tame **5** alarm, break, bully, check, deter **6** dismay, subdue **7** conquer, control, depress, horrify, stupefy, terrify **8** dispirit, frighten **10** disconcert, discourage, dishearten, intimidate

DAUNTLESS: **4** bold **5** brave **6** daring **7** aweless, valiant **8** fearless, intrepid, unafraid **10** courageous **11** lionhearted **12** stouthearted

DAVENPORT: **3** bed **4** desk, sofa **5** couch **11** convertible **12** chesterfield

DAVID:
king of: **6** Israel
knew: **4** Saul **5** Asaph, Ittai, Jesus, Nabal, Uriah **6** Hushai, Nathan **7** Goliath, Shavsha **11** Athithophel
relatives: **5** Jesse, Tamar **6** Michal **7** Abigail, Absalom, Solomon **9** Bathsheba

DAWDLE: **4** idle, loaf, poke **5** dally, delay, mosey **6** diddle, linger, loiter, lounge, putter **8** lollygag **9** vacillate **10** dilly-dally **13** lackadaisical, procrastinate

DAWN: **4** morn, rise **5** birth, occur, start, sunup **6** aurora, emerge, unfold **7** genesis, morning, sunrise **8** daybreak **9** beginning **10** understand

DAY: **3** age, era **4** date, time **5** cycle, epoch **6** period **8** lifetime, sunlight **10** generation

DAYBREAK: **4** dawn, morn **5** sunup **6** aurora **7** morning, sunrise

DAYDREAM: **4** muse, wish **6** vision **7** imagine, reverie **8** envision **9** fantasize

DAZE: **3** fog **4** numb, stun **5** dizzy, shock **6** bemuse, benumb, muddle, puzzle, stupor, trance **7** confuse, stupefy **8** befuddle, bewilder **9** disorient, dumbfound, overwhelm

DAZED: **5** dopey, woozy **6** addled, groggy, punchy **7** dazzled **8** confused

DAZZLE: **4** blur **5** amaze, blind, shine **6** excite **7** eclipse, impress **8** bewilder, outshine **9** electrify

DAZZLING: **5** vivid **6** bright **7** fulgent, glaring, glowing, radiant **8** gorgeous **9** brilliant, sparkling **10** foudroyant **12** breathtaking

DEACON: **5** elder, vicar **6** cleric **9** layperson

DEAD: **4** beat, cold, dull, flat, gone, lost, numb **5** bleak, inert, quiet, slain, spent, stiff, utter **6** asleep, barren, buried, doomed, fallen, lapsed **7** defunct, drained, exactly, expired, extinct, useless **8** absolute, complete, deceased, departed, inactive, lifeless, obsolete, perished **9** bloodless, exhausted, inanimate **10** breathless, discharged, lackluster, motionless, spiritless, unexciting **11** indifferent, inoperative **12** extinguished, unproductive

DEADBEAT: **3** bum **4** lazy **6** loafer **7** sponger, vagrant **10** freeloader

DEADEN: **4** dope, dull, kill, numb, stun **5** blunt, quiet **6** benumb, freeze, lessen, muffle, obtund, retard, soothe, weaken **7** petrify, repress, stupefy **8** diminish, paralyze **11** anesthetize, desensitize **12** incapacitate

DEAD END: **4** stop **5** rowdy, tough **7** impasse **8** cul-de-sac

DEADLOCK: **4** draw **7** dilemma, impasse **8** gridlock **9** stalemate **10** standstill **11** predicament

DEADLY: **4** dire **5** awful, fatal, toxic **6** lethal, mortal **7** extreme, ghostly, harmful, ruinous, tedious, violent **8** ruthless, terrible, venomous, virulent **9** dangerous, pestilent, poisonous **10** implacable, pernicious **11** destructive **12** carcinogenic

DEADPAN: **5** blank **6** vacant **9** impassive **11** unemotional **14** expressionless

DEAL: **4** dole, hand, pact, part, sale, swap **5** allot, board, plank, share, trade, treat, wield **6** barter, behave, bestow, divide, handle, manage **7** bargain, control, deliver, portion, wrestle **8** dispense, separate **9** agreement, apportion, negotiate, treatment **10** administer, compromise, distribute **11** arrangement, transaction

DEALER: **5** agent **6** broker, jobber, seller, trader, vendor **8** merchant, operator, retailer **9** middleman, tradesman **10** negotiator, trafficker **11** businessman, distributor, middlewoman, tradeswoman **12** middleperson, tradesperson **13** businesswoman **14** businessperson

DEALINGS: **6** doings **7** affairs, matters, traffic **8** business, commerce **9** relations **11** proceedings

DEAN: **5** doyen **6** senior **9** authority, dignitary, principal **10** headmaster

DEAR: **3** pet **4** fond, high, love, near **5** angel, honey, loved **6** costly, prized, scarce, worthy **7** beloved, darling, lovable, special **8** esteemed, precious, treasure, valuable **9** cherished, expensive, heartfelt, important **10** honeybunch, sweetheart **12** affectionate

DEARLY: **6** deeply **8** heartily **9** earnestly **10** profoundly, yearningly **14** affectionately

DEARTH: **4** lack, need, want **6** famine **7** paucity, poverty **8** scarcity, shortage, sparsity **10** deficiency, scantiness **13** insufficiency

DEATH: **3** end **4** bane, doom, exit, loss **5** decay, sleep **6** demise, murder **7** decease, passage **8** biolysis, curtains, fatality **9** departure **10** euthanasia, expiration, extinction, grim reaper

DEATH-DEFYING: **4** bold, rash **5** risky **6** daring **9** audacious, daredevil

DEATHLESS: **7** eternal, undying **8** immortal **11** everlasting

DEATHLY: **4** grim **5** fatal **6** grisly, lethal, mortal **7** ghastly, macabre **8** gruesome, terrible **9** appalling, extremely **10** cadaverous

DEBACLE: **4** rout **5** crash, flood, havoc, wreck **6** defeat, fiasco **7** failure, washout **8** collapse, disaster, downfall **9** breakdown, cataclysm **11** catastrophe

DEBAR: **4** deny **6** forbid, hinder, refuse, reject **7** deprive, exclude, prevent, suspend **8** preclude, prohibit **9** blackball

DEBASE: **4** sink **5** lower, shame, spoil, stoop **6** defile, demean, humble, impair, reduce, revile, vilify **7** cheapen, corrupt, debauch, degrade, deprave, pervert, pollute, vitiate **8** disgrace, dishonor **9** humiliate **10** adulterate, degenerate **11** contaminate, deteriorate

DEBATABLE: **4** moot **6** unsure **7** dubious **8** arguable **9** uncertain **10** disputable **12** questionable **13** controversial

DEBATE: **4** moot **5** argue, fight, rebut **6** oppose, ponder, reason **7** canvass, contend, contest, discuss, dispute, examine, quarrel, wrangle **8** argument, consider, question **10** deliberate **11** controversy

DEBAUCH: **4** lure, orgy, warp **5** abuse, revel, spree, taint **6** debase, defile, seduce **7** corrupt, deprave, mislead, pollute, violate, vitiate **9** bacchanal **10** demoralize **11** contaminate

DEBAUCHED: **4** lewd **6** wanton, wicked **9** abandoned, lecherous **10** profligate

DEBAUCHERY: **6** excess **10** indulgence **11** dissipation

DEBILITATED: **5** frail **6** feeble, infirm, sapped **8** decrepit, weakened **9** enervated, enfeebled **13** incapacitated

DEBILITY: **7** disease, fatigue, languor, malaise **8** weakness **9** infirmity **10** affliction, feebleness, sickliness

DEBIT: **4** debt **6** charge **8** drawback **9** detriment, liability **10** obligation

DEBONAIR: **5** suave **6** dapper, jaunty, smooth, urbane **7** affable, dashing, elegant **8** charming, gracious

DEBOUCHE: **4** exit **5** issue **6** emerge, outlet **7** opening **9** discharge

DEBRIS: **4** junk **5** trash, waste **6** litter, pieces, refuse, rubble **7** garbage, remains, rubbish **8** wreckage

DEBT: **3** sin **4** bill, note, owed **5** debit, wrong **7** arrears, baggage, deficit, offense **9** liability **10** commitment, obligation

DEBUNK: **4** mock, sham **5** strip **6** expose, unmask **7** lampoon **8** disprove, ridicule

DEBUT: **6** opener **7** opening **8** entrance, premiere **9** beginning, launching **12** introduction, presentation

DECADENCE: **5** decay **7** decline **8** downfall **10** corruption, perversion, regression **13** deterioration

DECADENT: **6** effete, sinful, wanton, wicked **7** immoral **8** depraved **10** degenerate **13** self-indulgent

DECAMP: **4** bolt, flee, move **5** leave, scoot **6** depart, desert, escape **7** vamoose **8** evacuate, hightail **9** skedaddle

DECANTER: **6** bottle, carafe, flagon, vessel

DECAPITATE: **4** kill **6** behead **7** execute **10** guillotine

DECAY: **3** rot **4** fade, fail, mold, ruin, rust, sour **5** death, spoil, waste **6** caries, mildew, molder, wither **7** atrophy, corrode, crumble, decline, dwindle, putrefy **8** collapse, decrease **9** decadence, decompose **11** destruction, deteriorate **12** dilapidation, disintegrate

DECEASED: **4** dead, gone **7** defunct, expired **8** departed, finished **9** succumbed

DECEIT: **4** hoax **5** fraud **7** swindle **8** flimflam, trickery **9** chicanery, deception **10** dishonesty, entrapping, misleading

DECEITFUL: **4** foxy **5** false, lying, slick **6** crafty, shifty, sneaky **7** cunning **9** dishonest, insidious, insincere **10** fallacious, fraudulent, mendacious **11** underhanded

DECEIVE: **3** con, gyp, lie **4** bilk, dupe, fool, gull, hoax, jilt, scam **5** bluff, catch, cheat, cozen, trick **6** baffle, betray, delude, humbug **7** beguile, buffalo, defraud, mislead, swindle **8** flimflam, hoodwink **9** bamboozle, victimize **11** double-cross **12** misrepresent

DECELERATE: **4** slow **5** brake **8** slow down

DECENCY: **6** virtue **7** decorum **8** civility, courtesy **9** etiquette, propriety

DECENT: **4** fair, good, kind, pure **5** clean, moral **6** chaste, common, honest, modest, proper **7** average, correct, ethical, fitting **8** adequate, suitable **9** competent **10** acceptable, conforming, sufficient, thoughtful **11** appropriate, respectable

DECEPTION: **4** jive, ruse, scam, sham, wile **5** cheat, covin, craft, fraud, guile, magic, sting, trick **6** deceit, humbug, hustle, mirage **7** cunning, fallacy, sleight, slyness, sophism **8** artifice, illusion, intrigue, subtlety, trickery **9** chicanery, collusion, duplicity, falsehood, hypocrisy, imposture, treachery **10** artfulness, camouflage, dishonesty, misleading **11** contrivance, counterfeit

DECEPTIVE: **5** false, phony, slick, snide **6** crafty **7** cunning **8** illusory **9** dishonest **10** fallacious, misleading

DECIDE: **4** rule **5** judge **6** choose, select **7** resolve **8** conclude **9** determine, establish

DECIDED: **4** firm, sure **5** fixed **6** formed, intent **7** certain **8** absolute, decisive, definite, emphatic, positive **11** prearranged, unequivocal

DECIMATE: **4** kill **5** wreck **6** reduce **7** destroy **8** demolish, massacre **9** slaughter **10** annihilate

DECIPHER: **4** read **5** break, solve **6** decode, deduce, reveal **7** analyze, decrypt, explain, unravel **9** interpret, translate **10** understand

DECISION: **6** choice, crisis, decree, result, ruling **7** finding, opinion, verdict **8** judgment, sentence, volition **9** agreement, precedent, selection **10** conclusion, resolution **12** adjudication, perseverance **13** determination

DECISIVE: **4** firm **5** final **6** intent **7** crucial **8** absolute, critical, resolute **10** conclusive, definitive **12** unmistakable

DECK: **4** drop, fall, trim **5** adorn, array, cover, dress, equip, floor **6** blazon, clothe, outfit **7** apparel, festoon, present **8** beautify, decorate, platform **9** embellish **11** pack of cards

DECLAIM: **4** rant, rave **5** orate, speak **6** attach, recite **7** inveigh, lecture **8** denounce, harangue, perorate, proclaim **11** pontificate

DECLARATION: **4** oath, word **5** edict, pitch **6** charge, oracle **8** document **9** admission, affidavit, assertion, statement, ultimatum **10** allegation, deposition, disclosure **11** affirmation **12** announcement, proclamation

DECLARE: **3** bid **4** aver, avow, show, tell, vent **5** admit, state, voice **6** affirm, allege, assert, assure, avouch, herald, indict, notify, relate, reveal **7** certify, confess, confirm, divulge, express, profess, signify, testify **8** advocate, announce, describe, indicate, maintain, manifest, proclaim **9** advertise, broadcast, pronounce **10** annunciate, asseverate, promulgate **11** acknowledge

DECLINE: **3** dip, ebb, sag **4** drop, fade, fail, fall, sink, slip, wane **5** chute, decay, droop, lower, slant, slide, slope, slump, stoop **6** lessen, refuse, reject, shrink, weaken **7** abstain, cheapen, descend, descent, dwindle, failure, forbear **8** decrease, diminish, languish, withdraw **9** decadence, declivity, downslide, recession, repudiate **10** depression **13** deterioration

DECLIVITY: **4** drop, fall **5** cliff, slope **6** plunge **7** decline, descent **8** gradient **9** downgrade **10** descending

DECOMPOSE: **3** rot **5** decay, spoil **6** fester, molder **7** putrefy **8** dissolve, separate **12** disintegrate

DECOR: **6** colors **7** scenery, setting **9** adornment **10** background **11** furnishings

DECORATE: **4** cite, deck, trim **5** adorn, color, dress, paint **6** emboss, parget **7** enhance, festoon, furbish, garnish **8** beautify, ornament **9** embellish

DECORATION: **4** lace **5** award, frill, medal **6** lights, plaque, ribbon, tinsel **7** garnish, laurels, spangle, trinket **8** accolade, citation, ornament, trimming **9** furniture, paintings

DECOROUS: **4** calm, good, nice, prim **5** moral, quiet, sober, staid **6** decent, demure, modest, polite, proper, seemly, steady **7** fitting, orderly, regular, settled **8** composed, mannerly, suitable **9** befitting, dignified, unruffled **10** respectful **11** appropriate

DECORUM: **4** tact **7** decency **8** civility, protocol **9** etiquette, formality, gentility, propriety

DECOY: **4** bait, fake, lure, trap **5** drill, plant, tempt **6** allure, entice, entrap, seduce **7** mislead **8** inveigle **10** camouflage

DECREASE: **4** curb, drop, fall, loss, sink, wane **5** abate, taper, waste **6** lessen, reduce, shrink **7** curtail, cutback, decline, dwindle, slacken, subside **8** diminish, discount, subtract **9** devaluate

DECREE: **3** act, law **4** rule **5** canon, edict, order, tenet, ukase **6** dictum, impose, indict, ordain **7** adjudge, appoint, command, mandate, require, statute **8** decision, judgment, sentence **9** authorize, determine, directive, enactment, ordinance **10** adjudicate, regulation **12** announcement, proclamation

DECREPIT: **4** lame, weak, worn **5** frail **6** creaky, feeble, flimsy, shabby **7** failing, fragile, rickety, rundown, unsound **8** battered **9** bedridden **11** dilapidated

DECRY: **4** slur **5** blame, lower **6** lessen **7** asperse, censure, condemn, degrade **8** belittle, derogate, diminish **9** criticize, deprecate, discredit, disparage **10** depreciate, disapprove, undervalue

DEDICATE: **6** anoint, assign, devote, direct, donate, hallow, pledge **7** present **8** inscribe, sanctify **10** consecrate

DEDUCE: **4** draw **5** infer, trace **6** derive, evolve, gather, reason **7** analyze, extract, presume, surmise **8** conclude **10** comprehend

DEDUCT: **4** dock, take **5** abate **6** reduce, remove **8** abstract, discount, subtract, withdraw

DEDUCTION: **6** rebate **8** markdown, write-off **9** exemption, inference **10** conclusion **11** calculation **13** understanding

DEED: **3** act **4** case, fact, feat **5** proof, quest, title **6** action, convey, escrow, remise **7** charter, crusade, exploit **8** contract, document, transfer **9** adventure **11** achievement, certificate, performance

DEEM: **3** say **4** feel, hold, hope, tell, view **5** allow, judge, sense, think **6** esteem, expect, reckon, regard **7** account, believe, suppose, surmise **8** consider, judgment, proclaim

DEEP: **3** low, sea, sly **4** dark **5** abyss, below, grave, heavy, ocean, vivid **6** intent **7** abysmal, complex, cunning, focused, intense, serious **8** absorbed, abstruse, complete, involved, profound, thorough **9** entangled, insidious **10** bottomless **11** penetrating **13** philosophical

DEEPEN: **6** expand **7** broaden, enhance, thicken **9** intensify **10** strengthen

DEEP-SEATED: **6** inbred, innate, rooted **7** lasting **8** inherent **9** ingrained **10** congenital, entrenched

DEER: **6** cervid, mammal **7** cervine **8** ruminant

African: **5** Okapi

Asian: **4** maha, napu, sika **6** chitra, hangul, sambar **10** chevrotain

Eurasian: **3** red, roe **6** fallow **7** caribou **8** reindeer

family: **8** cervidae

female: **3** doe **4** hind

male: **4** buck, hart, spay, stag **7** roebuck

meat: **5** jerky **7** charqui, venison

North American: **3** elk **4** mule **5** moose **7** caribou **8** reindeer **11** white-tailed

South American: **4** pudu **6** guemal, vanada **7** brocket

track: **4** slot

young: **3** kid **4** fawn, spay **7** pricket, spitter

DEFACE: **3** mar **4** mark, ruin, scar **5** spoil **6** damage, deform, impair, injure **7** blemish, distort, tarnish **8** mutilate **9** disfigure, vandalize

DE FACTO: **4** real **5** truly **6** actual **8** existing, tangible

DEFAMATION: **4** slur **5** libel **7** calumny, slander **10** derogatory **12** backstabbing

DEFAME: **4** foul **5** libel, smear **6** damage, injure, malign, vilify **7** asperse, blemish, degrade, scandal, slander, traduce **8** besmirch, disgrace, dishonor **9** denigrate **10** calumniate, stigmatize

DEFAULT: **4** fail, omit, skip, want **5** shirk, welsh **6** slight **7** blemish, failure, forfeit, mistake **8** omission **10** negligence, nonpayment **11** delinquency, dereliction **12** imperfection

DEFEAT: **4** beat, best, foil, lick, loss, rout, ruin, undo **5** break, check, crush, floor, quell **6** baffle, master, thwack **7** conquer, deprive, destroy, outplay, prevail, reverse, setback, shellac, triumph, trounce **8** decimate, overcome, vanquish **9** frustrate, overpower, overthrow, overwhelm, subjugate **10** defeasance, disappoint

DEFECT: **4** flaw, vice, want **5** break, error, fault **6** blotch, damage, desert, glitch, injury, reject **7** abandon, blemish, forsake **8** drawback, renounce **9** birthmark, deformity **10** deficiency **11** shortcoming **12** imperfection

DEFEND: **4** back, save, wear **5** guard, hedge, repel, watch **6** assert, screen, secure, shield, uphold **7** contest, justify, protect, shelter, support **8** advocate, champion, conserve, maintain, preserve **9** exculpate, safeguard, vindicate **11** rationalize

DEFENDANT: **7** accused, defense **8** litigant, offender **9** appellant

DEFENDER: **6** patron **7** sponsor **8** advocate, champion, guardian, upholder **9** protector

DEFENSE: **4** fort, plea, wall **5** aegis, alibi, armor, fence, guard **6** answer, covert, excuse **7** bulwark, shelter **8** armament, boundary, security **9** barricade, safeguard **10** protection **11** explanation **13** justification

DEFENSELESS: **4** bare **5** naked **7** exposed, unarmed **8** helpless **9** powerless **10** vulnerable **11** unprotected

DEFER: **4** stay, wait **5** adapt, delay, stall, table, yield **6** shelve, submit **7** suspend **8** postpone, prorogue, protract **10** capitulate **13** procrastinate

DEFERENCE: **5** honor **6** homage, regard **7** respect **9** attention, obedience, obeisance **10** submission, veneration

DEFERMENT: **4** stay **5** delay, pause **9** extension **10** suspension

DEFIANCE: **6** revolt **8** audacity, boldness, contempt **9** disregard, hostility, insolence, rebellion **10** insurgency **12** disobedience

DEFICIENCY: **4** flaw, lack, want **5** minus **6** dearth, defect, glitch **7** frailty **8** scarcity, shortage, weakness **10** inadequacy **11** shortcoming **12** imperfection **13** insufficiency

DEFICIT: **7** arrears, default **8** shortage **9** shortfall **10** impairment, inadequacy **12** disadvantage

DEFILE: **4** soil **5** abuse, dirty, gorge, smear, taint **6** debase, ravish **7** corrupt, degrade, deprave, pollute, tarnish, violate **8** discolor, disgrace, dishonor, maculate **9** desecrate **10** adulterate **11** contaminate

DEFINE: **3** fix, set **4** term **5** bound, label, limit, state **6** assign, decide, detail **7** clarify, explain, expound, outline, specify **8** construe, describe **9** determine, interpret, prescribe **10** illustrate **11** distinguish **12** characterize

DEFINITE: **4** sure **5** clear, exact, fixed, sharp **7** certain, limited, precise, settled **8** distinct, explicit, positive **10** conclusive **11** categorical, determinate, unequivocal **12** unmistakable

DEFINITION: **7** clarity **11** description, explanation, terminology, translation **14** interpretation

DEFINITIVE: **5** final **8** absolute, complete, decisive, explicit, specific **10** conclusive

DEFLATE: **6** humble, lessen, reduce **8** diminish, puncture **9** devaluate, humiliate

DEFLECT: **4** bend, veer **5** avert **6** bounce, detour, divert, swerve **7** deviate, refract **8** ricochet

DEFORM: **3** mar **4** flaw, maim **6** deface, impair, mangle **7** contort, distort **8** misshape **9** disfigure **10** disarrange

DEFRAUD: **3** con, gyp, rob **4** bilk, rook **5** cheat, trick **6** fleece **7** deceive, swindle **8** embezzle **9** bamboozle, victimize

DEFT: **4** able, neat **5** agile, fleet, handy, quick **6** adroit, clever, expert, nimble **8** dextrous, skillful **9** dexterous **10** proficient

DEFUNCT: **4** dead **5** kaput **7** extinct **8** deceased, finished, inactive, lifeless **11** inoperative

DEFY: **4** dare, face **5** beard, brave, flout, front, scorn **6** ignore, oppose, resist **9** challenge, frustrate

DÉGAGÉ: **4** easy, free **6** casual **7** relaxed **8** detached, informal **10** uninvolved

DEGENERATE: **3** rot **4** sink **5** decay **6** debase, effete, worsen **7** corrupt, immoral, regress, vitiate **8** decadent, depraved **9** perverted **11** deteriorate

DEGRADATION: **7** descent **8** demotion, disgrace, ignominy **9** depravity **12** degeneration

DEGRADE: **4** bust **5** abase, lower, shame **6** debase, demean, depose, humble, lessen, reduce, vilify **7** cheapen, corrupt, decline **8** belittle, diminish, dishonor **9** discredit, disparage, humiliate **10** depreciate **11** deteriorate

DEGREE: **4** rank, rate, rung, step, term, tier, unit **5** class, grade, honor, level, notch, order, phase, pitch, point, ratio, scale, stage, title **6** extent **7** caliber, measure **8** interval, quantity, relation, standing **9** gradation **10** attainment **11** temperature **14** classification
achievement: **8** cum laude **13** magna cum laude, summa cum laude

DEHYDRATE: **3** dry **5** drain, parch **8** preserve **9** anhydrous, desiccate, evaporate

DEIFY: **5** adore, exalt **6** revere **7** elevate, glorify, idolize, worship **8** venerate **11** immortalize

DEIGN: **5** stoop **9** patronize, vouchsafe **10** condescend

DEITY: **3** god **4** idol **7** creator, demigod, goddess, godhead **8** Almighty, divinity, immortal **9** celestial **11** demigoddess **12** supreme being

DEJA VU: **8** illusion **11** familiarity

DEJECTED: **3** low, sad **4** blue, down, glum **6** dismal, gloomy, somber **7** humbled, hurting, unhappy **8** dampened, wretched **9** cheerless, depressed, sorrowful, woebegone **10** despondent, melancholy, spiritless **11** crestfallen, discouraged, downhearted **12** disconsolate, disheartened

DELAWARE:
bird: **7** blue hen
capital: **5** Dover
cities: **6** Newark **10** Wilmington
explorer: **4** Penn
features: **13** Rehoboth Beach
flower: **12** peach blossom
nickname: **10** First State **12** Diamond State

tree: **5** holly
water: **8** Delaware, Rehoboth **9** Broadkill **13** Atlantic Ocean

DELAY: **4** drag, slow, stay, stop, wait **5** block, check, dally, defer, deter, stall, table, tarry **6** arrest, dawdle, detain, hinder, impede, logjam, loiter, retard, shelve, temper, weaken **7** inhibit, prevent, prolong **8** demurral, hesitate, obstruct, postpone, reprieve, stoppage **9** deferment, detention, lingering **10** dillydally, filibuster, moratorium, suspension **12** interruption **13** procrastinate

DELECTABLE: **5** tasty **6** divine, savory **8** heavenly, pleasing **9** delicious, enjoyable, exquisite, palatable **10** appetizing, delightful, satisfying **11** pleasurable, scrumptious

DELEGATE: **4** name, send **5** agent, proxy **6** assign, commit, deputy **7** appoint, consign, empower, entrust **8** emissary, relegate, transfer **9** authorize, designate

DELEGATION: **7** mission **9** committee **10** commission, contingent, nomination **11** appointment

DELETE: **4** edit, omit **5** annul, bleep, erase, purge **6** cancel, remove **7** expunge **9** eliminate **10** obliterate

DELETERIOUS: **7** harmful, hurtful, ruining **8** damaging, ruinous **9** injurious **10** pernicious **11** destructive, detrimental, prejudicial

DELIBERATE: **4** cool, slow **5** meant, study, think, weigh **6** advise, confer, debate, ponder **7** consult, examine, planned, reflect **8** consider, designed, measured, meditate **9** determine, leisurely, voluntary **10** calculated, meticulous, purposeful **11** intentional **12** premeditated

DELIBERATION: **4** care **7** counsel **9** attention **10** discussion

DELICACY: **4** tact **5** goody, taste **6** caviar, luxury, nicety **7** delight, finesse, frailty **8** elegance, pleasure **9** exactness, precision, propriety **10** daintiness, refinement **11** savoir faire, slenderness

DELICATE: **4** airy, fine, lacy, nice, soft, weak **5** faint, light, silky **6** choice, dainty, petite, sickly, slight, tender, touchy **7** elegant, fragile, refined, tenuous **8** cautious, charming, critical, ethereal, graceful, luscious, pleasant, volatile **9** beautiful, exquisite, sensitive **10** delightful, diplomatic, precarious **11** considerate, persnickety, susceptible

DELICIOUS: **5** yummy **6** divine, savory **8** enticing, heavenly, luscious, tasteful, tempting **9** ambrosial, exquisite, nectarous, toothsome **10** appetizing, delectable, delightful **11** scrumptious

DELIGHT: **3** joy, wow **4** glee **5** amuse, bliss, charm, feast, mirth, revel **6** please, regale, relish, thrill **7** ecstasy, enchant, gladden, gratify, rapture, rejoice, satisfy **8** gladness, pleasure, savoring **9** enjoyment, enrapture, entertain, fascinate, happiness

DELIGHTFUL: **4** nice **6** dreamy, lovely **8** adorable, alluring, delicate, engaging, pleasant **9** delicious, ravishing **10** delectable, enchanting, refreshing

DELILAH:
betrayed: **6** Samson
cut Samson's: **4** hair
lover: **6** Samson

DELINEATE: **3** map **4** draw **5** chart, draft, trace **6** depict, design, sketch, survey **7** outline, picture, portray **8** describe **9** represent

DELINQUENCY: **7** default, failure, misdeed, neglect, offense **9** violation **10** misconduct, wrongdoing **11** dereliction, misbehavior, misdemeanor

DELINQUENT: **3** lax **4** late, punk **5** tardy **6** behind, remiss **7** culprit, hoodlum, overdue **8** criminal **9** negligent **13** irresponsible

DELIRIOUS: **3** mad **4** wild **6** crazed, insane, raving **7** excited, frantic, lunatic **8** demented, deranged, ecstatic, frenzied, thrilled **9** unsettled **10** hysterical, irrational **11** lightheaded **12** unreasonable

DELIRIUM: **5** fever, furor, mania **10** aberration, enthusiasm **13** hallucination

DELIRIUM TREMENS: **6** shakes **7** horrors **9** trembling **10** withdrawal

DELIVER: **4** cart, deal, free, give, save, send, tell **5** bring, carry, pitch, serve, speak, throw, voice **6** broach, convey, redeem, render, rescue, resign, supply **7** inflict, present, release **8** announce, dispatch, liberate, transfer, transmit **9** pronounce, surrender, transport **10** distribute, emancipate

DELIVERY: **4** drop **5** birth, labor **6** rescue **7** address, diction **8** emphasis, shipment **9** elocution, salvation **11** parturition **12** accouchement

DELL: **4** dale, glen, vale **5** glade **6** dingle, valley

DELUDE: **4** bilk, dupe, fool **5** cheat, cozen, trick **7** beguile, deceive, mislead **8** hoodwink

DELUGE: **4** soak **5** drown, flood, swamp **6** engulf **7** niagara, torrent **8** downpour, inundate, overflow, overload, submerge **9** cataclysm, overpower, overwhelm

DELUSION: **5** dream, ghost, trick **6** mirage, vision **7** fallacy, fantasy, figment, phantom **8** illusion **9** deception **10** aberration, apparition **13** hallucination, misconception

DELUSIVE: **5** false **6** unreal **8** fanciful, illusory, quixotic **9** deceptive, imaginary **10** misleading

DELUXE: **4** posh **5** grand, plush, ritzy **6** choice **7** elegant, opulent **8** palatial, superior **9** exclusive, luxurious, sumptuous

DELVE: **3** dig **4** mine, seek **5** probe **6** search **7** examine, explore, inquire **8** research **11** investigate

DEMAGOGUE: **6** leader **7** fanatic, hothead, inciter, radical **8** agitator, fomenter **10** instigator **12** rabble-rouser, troublemaker

DEMAND: **4** call, need, plea, urge **5** claim, crave, exact, force, order **6** charge, coerce, compel, expect, insist, summon **7** command, implore, inquire, mandate, request, require **8** question **9** challenge **11** requisition

DEMARCATE: **5** bound, limit, split **6** define, detach, divide **7** delimit **8** separate **11** distinguish

DEMEAN: **5** abase, lower **6** debase, humble **7** degrade **8** belittle **9** disparage, humiliate

DEMEANOR: **4** mien **5** poise **6** manner **7** bearing, conduct **8** attitude, behavior, carriage **9** treatment **10** appearance, deportment **11** comportment, countenance, disposition

DEMIGOD, DEMIGODDESS: **4** hero **5** deity **7** godling, heroine

DEMISE: **4** fall, ruin **5** death, dying **6** expire **7** decease **8** collapse **11** termination

DEMOBILIZE: **7** disband **8** disperse **9** discharge **12** demilitarize

DEMOCRACY: **7** freedom **8** equality **12** commonwealth

DEMOCRATIC: **7** popular **10** autonomous, self-ruling **11** egalitarian

DEMOLISH: **4** raze, ruin **5** crush, level, total, waste, wreck **7** consume, destroy **8** bulldoze, decimate **9** devastate, pulverize **10** obliterate

DEMON: **3** hag, imp **4** evil, ogre **5** devil, fiend, genie, Satan, witch **6** goblin **7** incubus, vampire, villain, warlock **8** diligent, skillful, succubus

DEMONIC, DEMONIAC: **6** wicked **7** satanic **8** devilish, fiendish **9** possessed **10** diabolical, serpentine

DEMONSTRATE: **4** show **5** prove, rally **6** flaunt, parade, picket, strike **7** display, exhibit, explain, protest **8** validate **10** illustrate

DEMONSTRATIVE: **4** open **5** frank **8** definite, effusive, outgoing **9** emotional, expansive **10** conclusive, expressive **12** affectionate, unrestrained

DEMORALIZE: **5** daunt, upset **6** dampen, deject, weaken **7** corrupt, deprave, depress, pervert, unnerve, vitiate **8** dispirit **9** undermine **10** discourage, dishearten

DEMOTE: **4** bump, bust **5** bench, break **6** reduce **7** degrade, dismiss **9** downgrade

DEMUR: **5** delay, doubt, pause **6** linger, object, oppose, resist **7** protest, scruple **8** disagree, hesitate, question **9** challenge, vacillate

DEMURE: **3** coy, shy **4** prim **5** staid, timid **6** modest **7** bashful, earnest **8** affected, composed, decorous, reserved **11** unassertive

DEN: **4** cave, hole, lair, nest, room **5** cabin, couch, haunt, study **6** burrow, cavern, grotto, hollow **7** library, retreat, shelter **8** dwelling, hideaway, playroom, workroom

DENIAL: **7** refusal **8** rebuttal **9** rejection **10** abstinence, retraction **11** repudiation **13** contradiction

DENIGRATE: **5** libel, smear **6** defame, malign **7** degrade, disdain, slander **8** belittle, ridicule **9** disparage **10** stigmatize

DENIZEN: **6** native **7** citizen, dweller **8** occupant, resident **10** inhabitant

DENMARK:
capital: **10** Copenhagen
cities: **6** Aarhus, Odense, Silund **7** Aalborg, Esbjerg **8** Elsinore
continent: **6** Europe
ethnic groups: **12** Scandinavian
features: **6** Amager **8** Bornholm, Legoland **9** Sjaelland **13** Tivoli Gardens **14** Kronborg Castle
islands: **3** Als, Fyn **4** Aero **5** Samso **7** Falster, Lolland **8** Bornholm **9** Langeland
languages: **6** Danish
monetary unit: **5** krone
territories: **9** Greenland **13** Faeroe Islands
water: **8** North Sea **9** Baltic Sea

DENOMINATION: **4** cult, kind, name, sect, size **5** class, creed, faith, title, value **6** church **8** category, religion **10** persuasion **11** appellation **14** classification

DENOTATION: **4** sign **6** symbol **7** meaning **10** signifying **11** description, explanation

DENOTE: **4** mark, mean, name, show **5** imply **6** intend, signal **7** betoken, connote, express **8** indicate **9** designate, insinuate, represent **10** denominate

DENOUNCE: **5** blame, decry, knock **6** accuse, attack **7** arraign, condemn, upbraid **8** announce **9** criticize, fulminate **10** denunciate, stigmatize

DE NOVO: **4** anew **5** again, newly **6** afresh **9** beginning

DENSE: **4** firm, slow **5** close, foggy, heavy, solid, thick **6** obtuse, opaque, simple, stupid **7** compact, crowded **8** ignorant **11** substantial, thickheaded **12** impenetrable

DENSITY: **4** bulk, mass **6** weight **10** complexity **11** consistency

DENT: **4** chip, dint, nick **5** dinge, gouge, notch, tooth **6** dimple, hallow, indent **7** blemish, depress, headway **8** progress **10** depression, impression

DENUDE: **4** bare **5** erode, strip **6** divest, expose **8** unclothe **9** dismantle

DENUNCIATION: **7** censure **8** denounce **9** criticism, invective, reprimand **10** accusation **11** castigation **12** condemnation

DENY: **4** veto **6** abjure, disown, forbid, impugn, negate, recant, refuse, refute, reject, renege **7** decline, deprive, disavow, dispute, forsake, gainsay **8** disagree, disclaim, negative, renounce, restrain, traverse, withhold **9** disaffirm **10** contradict, contravene

DEPART: **3** die **4** exit, pass, vary, veer **5** leave, split, stray **6** bygone, decamp, divide, expire, perish, recede, retire, secede, sunder, vacate **7** abandon, abscond, deviate, digress, forsake, retreat, succumb, vamoose **8** farewell, separate, withdraw **9** disappear

DEPARTMENT: **4** part, unit, word **5** niche, realm **6** agency, branch, bureau, domain, office **7** section **8** division, province **9** specialty **10** assignment, commission

DEPARTURE: **4** exit **5** death, going, shift, twist **6** change, egress, exodus **7** goodbye **8** farewell **9** deviation **10** aberration, divergence, evacuation **11** abandonment

DEPEND: **4** bank, hang, lean, rely, rest **5** count, hinge, trust **7** confide **10** contingent **11** conditioned

DEPENDABLE: **4** sure **5** loyal, solid, tried **6** secure, stable, steady **8** constant, faithful, reliable **9** steadfast **11** responsible, trustworthy

DEPENDENCY: **4** need **6** colony **8** reliance **9** addiction

DEPENDENT: **4** ward **5** child **6** minion, vassal **7** subject **8** clinging, helpless, relative **9** secondary **10** contingent, sequacious **11** conditional, provisional, subordinate, susceptible

DEPICT: **4** draw, limn **5** draft, image, paint **6** detail, sketch **7** express, picture, portray **8** describe **9** delineate, represent **10** illustrate **12** characterize

DEPLETE: **5** bleed, drain, empty, waste **6** reduce **7** consume, exhaust **8** bankrupt, diminish, enervate, squander **10** impoverish

DEPLORABLE: **6** tragic, woeful **8** dreadful, grievous, terrible, wretched **9** sickening **10** calamitous **11** distressing, intolerable, unfortunate **13** reprehensible

DEPLORE: **4** hate, moan, wail **5** abhor, mourn **6** bemoan, bewail, grieve, lament, regret **7** condemn **10** disapprove

DEPLOY: **6** unfold **7** arrange, display **8** position **12** redistribute

DEPORT: **5** exile, expel **6** banish, behave **7** bearing, dismiss **8** displace **9** extradite, transport

DEPORTMENT: **3** air **4** mien **6** action, manner **7** address, bearing, conduct, posture **8** behavior, carriage, demeanor, presence **10** appearance

DEPOSE: 4 aver, oust **6** assert, bounce, divest, remove, unseat **7** degrade, dismiss, impeach, subvert, testify **8** dethrone

DEPOSIT: 4 bank, dump, fund, hock, pawn, silt **5** place, stash, store **6** pledge, settle **7** consign, entrust, payment **8** retainer, security, sediment, squirrel **12** accumulation

DEPOSITION: 6 burial **7** opinion, removal **8** evidence, sediment **9** affidavit, overthrow, statement, testimony **10** allegation **11** declaration

DEPOSITORY: 4 bank, safe, tomb **5** cache, vault **6** locker **7** trustee **8** archives **9** strongbox **10** repository

DEPOT: 4 base, yard **5** annex **6** armory **7** arsenal, station **8** junction, magazine, terminal, terminus **9** warehouse **10** storehouse

DEPRAVED: 4 base, evil, lewd, vile **6** rotten, wicked **7** bestial, corrupt, immoral, vicious **8** vitiated **9** abandoned, debauched, perverted **10** degenerate **11** demoralized **12** incorrigible

DEPRECATE: 7 deplore **8** belittle, derogate **9** denigrate, downgrade, underrate **10** depreciate, disapprove

DEPRECIATE: 5 abase, decry, smear **6** lessen, reduce, shrink **7** cheapen, degrade, depress, devalue **8** belittle, derogate, diminish, ridicule **9** deprecate, disparage, downgrade **10** undervalue

DEPREDATION: 4 raid **5** crime, theft **6** rapine, ravage **7** looting, pillage, plunder **8** stealing **9** marauding **11** devastation

DEPRESS: 4 dash, dent, fall, sink **5** abase, crush, droop, lower, slump **6** dampen, deject, dismay, indent, lessen, sadden, weaken **7** cheapen, degrade, trouble **8** diminish, dispirit, enfeeble **10** depreciate, discourage, dishearten

DEPRESSED: 3 low, sad **4** blue, down, glum **6** bummed, gloomy, hollow, somber **7** unhappy **8** dejected, downcast **9** destitute **10** despondent, melancholy, spiritless **11** downhearted

DEPRESSING: 5 bleak **6** dismal, dreary **7** joyless **9** upsetting **11** distressing, melancholic

DEPRESSION: 3 dip, pit **4** fall, hole **5** basin, blahs, dumps, slump **6** cavity, crater, dimple, dismay, gulley, pocket, ravine, valley **7** blowout, despair **8** doldrums, downturn **9** dejection, recession **10** impression **11** despondency **12** hopelessness

DEPRIVATION: 4 loss, need, want **6** denial **7** poverty **8** hardship **9** privation **11** destitution, withholding

DEPRIVE: 3 rob **4** deny, dock **5** stiff, strip **6** divest, remove **7** bereave **9** dismantle **10** disinherit, dispossess

DEPTH: 5 abyss, pitch, sense **6** bottom, wisdom **7** insight, measure **8** deepness, strength **9** intensity **11** penetration, perspective **12** abstruseness, profoundness

DEPUTATION: 9 committee **10** delegation

DEPUTY: 4 aide **5** agent, envoy, proxy **6** second **7** bailiff **8** delegate, minister **9** appointee, assistant, surrogate **10** substitute

DERANGED: 3 mad **4** loco, nuts **5** crazy **6** insane **7** berserk **8** demented **9** delirious, disturbed **10** irrational, unbalanced

DERBY: **3** hat **4** race, town **7** contest

DERELICT: **3** bum **4** hobo, wino **5** dingy, seedy, tramp **6** remiss, shabby **7** drifter, outcast, uncouth, vagrant **8** careless, castaway, deserted, forsaken, vagabond **9** abandoned, negligent **10** delinquent **11** dilapidated

DERIDE: **4** gibe, hoot, jeer, mock, razz, twit **5** chaff, fleer, rally, scoff, scorn, taunt **6** insult **8** ridicule

DE RIGUEUR: **5** right **6** proper **7** correct, fitting **8** becoming, required **10** obligatory **11** fashionable

DERISION: **5** scorn **6** insult **7** disdain, mockery **8** contempt, ridicule **10** disrespect

DERIVATION: **4** root **6** origin, source **8** ancestry **9** etymology, genealogy **10** beginnings, wellspring

DERIVATIVE: **6** copied **7** adapted, evolved, fluxion **8** borrowed, offshoot **9** outgrowth, secondary **10** unoriginal

DERIVE: **4** draw, stem **5** glean, infer, reach, trace **6** arrive, deduce, evolve, gather, obtain **7** acquire, extract, receive **8** conclude **9** determine, originate

DERNIER CRI: **3** fad **4** chic, mode, rage **5** craze, style, vogue **8** last word **9** latest cry **11** latest thing

DEROGATORY: **5** snide **7** detract **8** damaging, decrying, diminish **9** degrading, malicious, offensive **10** belittling, defamatory **11** disparaging **12** unflattering

DERRICK: **3** rig **4** lift **5** crane, hoist **7** machine

DERRING-DO: **5** nerve **6** daring **7** courage **8** audacity, reckless

DESCANT: **4** sing **6** melody, remark **7** comment **9** criticism, discourse **11** observation **12** counterpoint

DESCEND: **4** dive, drop, fall, sink **5** lower, slope, stoop **6** derive **7** decline, incline **9** originate, penetrate

DESCENDANT: **4** heir, seed **5** brood, child, scion **7** progeny **8** children, offshoot **9** genealogy, offspring

DESCENT: **4** drop, fall, raid **5** chute, issue, slope, stock **6** origin **7** advance, assault, decline, lineage **8** ancestry, breeding, downfall, invasion, lowering, pedigree **9** declivity, genealogy, onslaught **10** extraction, generation **11** degradation, inclination

DESCRIBE: **4** tell **5** state **6** define, depict, detail, recite, relate, report **7** explain, express, narrate, picture, portray, recount **8** construe, rehearse **9** designate, discourse, interpret, represent **10** illustrate **12** characterize

DESCRIPTION: **3** ilk **4** kind, sort, type **5** brief, class, order **6** nature **7** account, recital, variety **8** category, vignette **9** chronicle **10** definition

DESCRY: **3** see **4** note, spot **5** sight **6** behold, detect, reveal **7** discern, observe **8** disclose, discover, perceive **9** determine

DESECRATE: **5** abuse **6** defile, ravage **7** pollute, profane, violate **8** dishonor **9** blaspheme

DESERT: **4** arid, bolt, flee, sand **5** leave, split, waste **6** barren, decamp, defect, renege, reward **7** abandon, abscond, badland, forsake, merited **8** deserved, renounce **9** wasteland **10** punishment, relinquish, wilderness

DESERTED: **4** AWOL, bare **6** lonely, vacant **7** forlorn **8** forsaken, marooned **9** abandoned, neglected **11** uninhabited

DESERTER: **3** rat **6** bolter, truant **7** runaway, traitor **8** apostate, betrayer, defector, fugitive, renegade, turncoat

DESERVE: **4** earn, rate **5** merit **7** procure, warrant

DESERVING: **6** worthy **7** fitting **9** admirable

DESICCATE: **3** dry **4** sear **5** parch **6** wither **7** deplete, shrivel **9** dehydrate, evaporate **10** devitalize

DESIGN: **3** end, map **4** draw, goal, idea, plan, plot **5** chart, decor, draft, model, motif, shape **6** create, device, intend, intent, invent, layout, motive, object, sketch, tailor **7** arrange, diagram, fashion, outline, pattern, project, propose, purpose **8** conceive, contrive, scenario, strategy **9** blueprint, delineate, intention **11** contemplate, perspective **12** architecture

DESIGNATE: **3** dub, set **4** call, mark, mean, name, show **5** elect, label, style, title **6** assign, choose, denote, intend, select, settle **7** appoint, entitle, specify **8** allocate, identify, indicate **9** authorize **10** commission, denominate **12** characterize

DESIGNATION: **5** label, title **7** moniker **9** selection **10** indication, nomination **11** appellation, appointment

DESIGNING: **5** sharp **6** artful, astute, crafty **7** cunning, devious **8** planning, scheming **9** conniving **10** foreseeing

DESIRABLE: **6** suited **7** welcome **8** alluring, eligible, pleasing **9** advisable, agreeable, seductive **10** attractive, beneficial, gratifying, worthwhile **12** advantageous

DESIRE: **4** care, hope, itch, lust, need, urge, want, will, wish **5** ardor, covet, crave, fancy, mania **6** aspire, hunger, prefer, thirst **7** craving, fantasy, longing, passion, request **8** appetite, cupidity, petition, yearning **9** appetency, hankering **10** preference **11** inclination

DESIROUS: **4** avid **5** eager **6** ardent, greedy **7** envious, hopeful, wishful **8** aspiring **9** ambitious **10** solicitous **11** acquisitive

DESIST: **4** halt, quit, stop **5** cease, pause, yield **7** abandon, abstain, forbear, suspend **11** discontinue

DESK: **4** ambo **5** booth, table **6** carrel, pulpit **7** counter, lectern, tambour **8** vargueno **9** davenport, furniture, secretary **10** escritoire

DESOLATE: **4** bare, ruin **5** alone, bleak, empty, gaunt **6** barren, devoid, dismal, dreary, gloomy, lonely, ravage, unused **7** destroy, forlorn, plunder **8** deprived, deserted, forsaken, lifeless, solitary **9** abandoned, depressed, destitute, woebegone **10** depopulate, melancholy, unoccupied **11** uninhabited **12** disconsolate

DESPAIR: **4** pain **5** gloom **6** burden **9** surrender **10** depression, melancholy **11** desperation, despondency **12** hopelessness **14** discouragement

DESPERADO: **4** thug **6** bandit, outlaw **7** hoodlum, ruffian **8** gangster **10** lawbreaker

DESPERATE: **4** dire, rash, vain **6** futile, urgent **7** drastic, extreme, frantic **8** critical, headlong, hopeless, reckless **9** audacious, dangerous **10** despairing, despondent, outrageous **11** precipitate

DESPERATION: **6** frenzy **7** anguish, concern, despair **12** hopelessness

DESPICABLE: **3** low **4** base, mean, vile **5** cheap, slimy **6** abject, scurvy, shabby, sordid **7** caitiff, hateful, pitiful **8** unworthy, wretched **9** loathsome, miserable **10** detestable **12** contemptible

DESPISE: **4** hate, shun **5** abhor, scorn, scout, spurn **6** detest, loathe, slight **7** contemn, disdain **8** misprize **9** abominate, disregard, repudiate

DESPITE: **4** hate, hurt, snub **6** grudge, injury, insult, malice, slight **8** although, contempt **9** insolence **10** regardless

DESPOIL: **3** rob **4** loot, raid, ruin, sack **5** rifle, strip **6** divest, ravage, ravish, remove **7** deprive, destroy, pillage, plunder **8** disarray **9** depredate, vandalize

DESPONDENCY: **5** gloom **6** misery **7** despair, sadness **10** depression, melancholy **11** desperation **12** hopelessness

DESPONDENT: **3** sad **4** blue, down **6** bummed **7** doleful, forlorn **8** dejected, hopeless **9** depressed, woebegone **10** dispirited **11** discouraged **12** disconsolate

DESPOT: **4** czar **5** ruler **6** tyrant **7** monarch **8** autocrat, dictator, monocrat **9** oppressor

DESPOTIC: **8** absolute, dominant **9** arbitrary **10** oppressive, tyrannical **13** authoritarian

DESSERT: **3** pie **4** cake, tart **5** fruit, pasty, sweet **6** cookie, eclair, mousse **7** pudding, sherbet, strudel **8** ice cream **10** cheesecake **11** final course

DESTINATION: **3** aim, end **4** fate, goal **6** target **7** purpose **8** terminal **9** objective

DESTINE: **6** decree, direct, intend, ordain **7** certain, purpose **9** preordain **12** predetermine

DESTINY: **4** doom, fate **5** karma **6** design, kismet **7** fortune **11** expectation **13** inevitability

DESTITUTE: **4** poor **5** broke, empty, needy **6** bereft, devoid, wasted **7** lacking, wanting **8** bankrupt, defeated, deprived, desolate, forsaken, indigent **9** abandoned, defaulted, exhausted, insolvent, penniless **10** devastated **12** impoverished

DESTROY: **3** end **4** blow, kill, nuke, raze, ruin, rush, slay, undo **5** break, erase, erode, level, quell, smash, smite, spoil, waste, wreck **6** blight, damage, deface, defeat, famish, finish, ravage **7** abolish, consume, expunge, overrun **8** decimate, demolish, desolate, dissolve, dynamite, mutilate, overturn, sabotage, vaporize **9** depredate, devastate, dismantle, eradicate, extirpate, liquidate **10** annihilate, extinguish **11** exterminate

DESTROYER: **6** vandal, vessel **7** warship **8** saboteur **9** terrorist **10** iconoclast

DESTRUCTION: **4** bane, doom, ruin **5** decay, havoc, waste **7** carnage **8** downfall, genocide, massacre, shambles, wreckage **9** holocaust **10** demolition, extinction, subversion **11** devastation

DESTRUCTIVE: **5** fatal **6** deadly, lethal **7** baleful, harmful, hurtful, noxious, ruinous, vicious **8** damaging, wasteful **9** discredit, poisonous, truculent **10** pernicious, shattering **11** cataclysmic, deleterious, detrimental, internecine

DESUETUDE: **6** disuse **10** inactivity

DESULTORY: **6** casual, chance, random, roving **7** aimless, erratic **8** rambling, sporadic, unsteady, wavering **9** irregular, unsettled **10** incidental, inconstant **11** haphazardly **12** disconnected

DETACH: **5** sever **6** sunder **7** disjoin, divorce, isolate, unhitch **8** dismount, disunite, separate, unfasten **9** disengage **10** disconnect **12** disassociate

DETACHED: **4** free **5** alone, aloof, apart **6** remote **7** distant, neutral, removed **8** unbiased **9** impartial, withdrawn **10** uninvolved **11** emancipated, unconcerned, unconnected **13** disinterested, dispassionate

DETACHMENT: **4** unit **6** detail, patrol **8** coolness, division **10** separation **11** disinterest **12** indifference

DETAIL: **4** fact, item, unit **5** point, squad **6** aspect, assign, relate **7** account, appoint, article, element, feature, itemize, minutia, narrate, specify **8** rehearse **9** elaborate **10** detachment **11** stipulation

DETAILED: **4** full **6** minute **7** precise **8** accurate, itemized, thorough **10** meticulous, particular **13** comprehensive **14** circumstantial

DETAIN: **4** hold, keep, mire, stop **5** check, delay **6** arrest, hinder, impede, retard **7** confine, inhibit **8** imprison, restrain

DETECT: **3** see **4** espy, find, spot **5** catch **6** descry, expose, notice, reveal, unmask **7** discern, uncover **8** discover, identify **9** ascertain

DETECTIVE: **3** tec **4** bull, dick **6** shamus, sleuth, tracer **7** gumshoe, scenter, spotter **8** flatfoot, operator **12** investigator

famous: **8** Sam Spade, The Saint **9** James Bond, Nero Wolfe, Pinkerton **10** Martin Kane, Miss Marple, Nick Carter, Perry Mason, Peter Salem, Philo Vance **11** Charlie Chan, Ellery Queen, Green Hornet, Nick Charles **12** Simon Templar **13** Hercule Poirot, Michael Shayne, Philip Marlowe **14** Sherlock Holmes

story writer: **8** Rex Stout **10** Ian Fleming **11** Ellery Queen **14** Agatha Christie **15** Dashiell Hammett, Raymond Chandler **16** Arthur Conan Doyle **18** Erle Stanley Gardner

DETENTE: **5** pause **6** policy **8** easement **9** passivity **10** precaution

DETENTION: **5** delay **7** custody **9** hindrance, restraint **10** detainment, quarantine **11** confinement **12** imprisonment **13** incarceration

DETER: **4** stop **5** avert, block, check, delay, spoil **6** dampen, debase, divert, weaken **7** decline **8** frighten, obstruct, prohibit **10** degenerate

DETERIORATE: **4** wane **6** worsen **7** corrode, crumble, regress **9** decompose

DETERMINATION: **4** grit, will **5** heart, spunk **7** resolve, verdict **8** decision, judgment, tenacity **9** fortitude **10** conclusion, conviction, settlement **11** persistence

DETERMINE: **3** end, fix **5** award **6** assess, assign, choose, decide, decree, define, settle **7** analyze, appoint, arrange, control, dictate, resolve **8** conclude, discover, regulate **9** arbitrate, ascertain, calculate, establish **10** adjudicate, deliberate, predestine

DETERMINED: **3** set **4** bent, firm **6** driven, intent, mulish **7** decided, serious, settled **8** decisive, foregone, resolute, stubborn **9** obstinate, pigheaded, tenacious **10** persistent, unyielding

DETERRENT: 4 curb **5** block **6** hurdle **8** obstacle **9** hindrance, restraint **10** impediment

DETEST: 4 damn, hate **5** abhor, curse **6** loathe, reject **7** despise, dislike **8** execrate **9** abominate

DETESTABLE: 4 foul, vile **5** lousy **6** horrid, odious **7** heinous **8** shocking **9** loathsome, obnoxious, repulsive, revolting **10** despicable, disgusting

DETHRONE: 4 oust **6** depose, remove **7** uncrown **8** displace

DETONATE: 4 bang, fire **5** blast **6** ignite **7** explode **9** discharge

DETOUR: 5 avoid, skirt **6** branch, bypass, divert **9** deviation **10** circumvent

DETRACT: 5 decry **6** divert, lessen, vilify **7** cheapen **8** belittle, derogate, diminish, minimize **9** disparage, underrate **10** depreciate

DETRACTION: 5 libel **6** damage **7** calumny, slander **8** innuendo, ridicule **10** backbiting **11** traducement

DETRIMENT: 4 cost, harm, hurt, loss **6** damage, injury **8** drawback **9** liability **10** disability, impairment, impediment **12** disadvantage

DETRIMENTAL: 4 evil **7** adverse, baleful **8** damaging, negative **10** pernicious **11** deleterious, destructive

DETRITUS: 4 tuff **5** waste **6** debris, matter **7** garbage, rubbish **9** fragments

DE TROP: 6 excess **7** surplus **11** superfluous

DEVALUE: 5 lower **6** debase, defile **7** cheapen, degrade **8** decrease **10** depreciate

DEVASTATE: 4 ruin, stun **5** wreck **6** ravage **7** destroy, pillage, plunder **8** demolish, desolate **9** desecrate, overwhelm

DEVASTATION: 5 havoc **9** confusion **11** destruction

DEVELOP: 4 form, grow **5** occur, ripen **6** evolve, expand, flower, happen, mature, refine, reveal, unfold, unfurl **7** advance, augment, broaden, educate, expound, prosper, uncover, untwist **8** disclose, discover, flourish, generate, manifest **9** elaborate, transpire **10** strengthen **11** materialize

DEVELOPMENT: 5 phase **6** growth **8** incident, increase, progress **9** dwellings, evolution, expansion, formation, situation **11** elaboration

DEVIANT: 7 wayward **8** abnormal, atypical **9** different, irregular

DEVIATE: 4 vary, veer **5** drift, lapse, sheer, stray **6** change, depart, detour, swerve, wander **7** deflect, digress, diverge, meander **9** sidetrack

DEVIATION: 7 anomaly **9** departure **10** aberration, deflection **11** abnormality

DEVICE: 4 plan, tool **5** angle, means, meter, motto, shift **6** design, emblem, figure, gadget, scheme, symbol **7** gimmick, machine, pattern, project, vehicle **8** artifice, fastener, insignia, maneuver **9** accessory, apparatus, appliance, doohickey, equipment, expedient, invention, mechanism, technique **10** concoction, instrument **11** contraption, contrivance, thingamajig

DEVIL: **3** imp **4** haze **5** annoy, demon, error, fiend, knave, ruler, Satan, tease **6** Azazel, Diablo, pester, rascal, wicked **7** Amaimon, dickens, Lucifer, Old Nick, torment, villain **8** Apollyon, Mephisto **9** adversary, Archfiend, Beelzebub, scoundrel

DEVILISH: **4** evil **6** wicked **7** demonic, extreme, hellish, satanic **8** demoniac, fiendish **9** atrocious, excessive, malicious, nefarious **10** diabolical, unhallowed **11** mischievous

DEVIL-MAY-CARE: **4** bold, rash **5** risky **6** jovial, rakish **8** heedless

DEVIOUS: **3** sly **4** foxy, wily **6** crafty, errant, shifty, sneaky, tricky **7** crooked, cunning, winding **8** indirect, rambling, tortuous **9** deceitful, dishonest, underhand **10** fraudulent, misleading, roundabout

DEVISE: **4** form, plan, plot, will **5** chart, forge, frame **6** convey, create, design, invent, scheme **7** appoint, arrange, concoct, consult, imagine, prepare, suppose **8** bequeath, conspire, contrive **9** construct, fabricate, formulate

DEVITALIZE: **6** deaden, weaken **7** destroy **8** diminish

DEVOID: **5** empty **6** barren, bereft, needed, vacant **7** lacking, wanting, without **9** destitute

DEVOTE: **3** vow **4** ally, give **5** apply **6** attach, bestow, commit, depute, direct, pledge, resign **7** address, destine, entrust **8** dedicate, venerate **10** consecrate **11** appropriate

DEVOTED: **4** true **5** loyal, pious **6** ardent, devout **7** adoring, arduous, dutiful, earnest, zealous **8** attached, constant, faithful **9** assiduous, dedicated, religious **10** unwavering **12** affectionate, wholehearted

DEVOTEE: **3** fan **4** buff **6** votary, zealot **7** admirer, amateur, booster, fanatic, groupie **8** advocate, believer, disciple, follower **9** supporter **10** aficionado, enthusiast

DEVOTION: **4** love **5** piety **6** fealty, prayer **7** loyalty, passion **8** fidelity, sanctity **9** adherence, adoration, reverence **10** allegiance, commitment, dedication **12** faithfulness

DEVOUR: **3** eat **5** stuff, waste **6** engulf, gobble, guzzle, ravage, relish **7** consume, swallow **10** annihilate

DEVOUT: **4** holy, warm **5** pious **6** ardent, hearty, solemn **7** cordial, devoted, earnest, serious, sincere **8** faithful, reverent **9** heartfelt, religious, righteous, spiritual **10** venerating

DEW: **3** wet **4** pure **5** fresh, tears, water **8** moisture, renewing **12** condensation

DEXTERITY: **3** art **4** tact **5** craft, knack, skill, touch **7** ability, agility, cunning, finesse **8** aptitude, deftness, facility **9** adeptness, expertise, quickness, readiness **10** adroitness, cleverness, nimbleness **11** proficiency

DEXTEROUS: **4** deft **5** handy **6** active, nimble, smooth

DHARMA: **3** law **7** conduct **8** Buddhism, Hinduism **9** principle, teachings **10** obligation **13** enlightenment

DIABLERIE: **7** devilry, sorcery **8** devilish, deviltry, satanism **10** black magic, witchcraft

DIABOLICAL: **4** evil, vile **5** cruet **6** wicked **7** heinous, hellish, satanic, vicious **8** demoniac, devilish, fiendish, infernal **10** serpentine

DIACRITICAL: **7** marking **14** discriminating, distinguishing

DIADEM: **4** halo **5** crown, tiara **6** anadem, fillet **7** coronet, dignity **8** headband

DIAGNOSIS: **7** opinion **8** analysis **10** conclusion **11** examination **14** identification

DIAGONAL: **4** bias **6** angled **7** beveled, slanted **11** transversal

DIAGRAM: **3** map **4** plan **5** chart, graph **6** design, layout **7** drawing, outline **9** blueprint **11** description **12** illustration

DIALECT: **4** cant **5** argot, idiom, lingo, slang **6** accent, jargon, patois, speech **8** language **10** vernacular

DIALOGUE: **4** chat, talk **6** parley, script, speech **7** passage **10** discussion **11** composition **12** conversation

DIAMETER: **5** width **7** breadth, caliber **9** thickness

DIAMETRICAL: **5** polar **7** counter, opposed **8** contrary **11** conflicting, contrasting

DIAMOND: **3** gem, ice **4** rock **5** jager, jewel **7** lozenge, rhombus **8** corundum, gemstone **9** brilliant, solitaire
fake: **6** zircon **9** schlenter **10** rhinestone
good: **7** paragon
industrial: **4** bort **5** balas, bortz **9** carbonado **12** black diamond
weight: **5** carat

DIAMOND STATE: **8** Delaware

DIAPHANOUS: **4** airy, fine **5** clear, gauzy, lucid, sheer, vague **6** flimsy **8** delicate, gossamer **11** transparent **13** insubstantial

DIARY: **3** log **6** record **7** journal, minutes **8** register **9** chronicle

DIATRIBE: **5** abuse **6** screed, tirade **8** harangue **9** criticism, invective **11** castigation **12** denunciation

DICEY: **4** iffy **5** risky **6** chancy, tricky **9** dangerous, uncertain

DICKER: **4** deal, swap **5** trade **6** barter, haggle **7** bargain, chaffer, quibble **8** exchange **9** negotiate

DICTATE: **3** say **4** rule, tell **5** order, utter **6** decree, impose, ordain, record **7** command, compose, control, mandate, require **9** prescribe **11** communicate

DICTATOR: **4** czar, duce **6** despot, fuhrer, tyrant **7** fascist **8** autocrat **12** totalitarian **13** authoritarian

DICTATORIAL: **5** bossy **6** lordly **7** pompous **8** absolute, arrogant, despotic, dogmatic, positive **9** arbitrary, imperious, masterful **10** oppressive, tyrannical **11** doctrinaire, domineering, magisterial, overbearing **13** authoritative

DICTION: **5** style **7** fluency, oratory, wording **8** language, phrasing, rhetoric, verbiage **10** intonation, vocabulary **11** enunciation, phraseology **12** articulation

DICTIONARY: **5** words **7** lexicon **8** glossary, wordbook **9** reference **10** vocabulary **11** onomasticon
compiler: **13** lexicographer

DICTUM: **5** adage, axiom, edict, moral, motto **6** decree, saying, truism **7** proverb **8** apothegm **9** statement **11** declaration **13** pronouncement

DIDACTIC: **7** preachy **8** academic, pedantic, sermonic, tutorial **9** homiletic **10** moralistic **11** educational, instructive

DIDDLE: **3** gyp **5** cheat **6** dawdle, jiggle, loiter **7** swindle **9** worthless

DIE: **3** ebb **4** long, mold, stop, wane **5** abate, cease, croak, yearn **6** demise, depart, expire, finish, perish, vanish, wither **7** decease, dwindle, succumb **8** languish **10** degenerate

DIE-HARD: **4** Tory **8** hardnose, mossback, standpat, stubborn **9** obstinate, pigheaded, resisting **10** inflexible **11** reactionary **12** conservative **14** uncompromising

DIET: **4** fare, fast, food **5** drink **6** reduce, viands **7** regimen **8** assembly **10** convention, provisions, starvation **11** legislature, nourishment

DIFFER: **4** vary **5** clash **6** debate, oppose **7** contend, discord, dissent **8** conflict, distinct **10** dissimilar

DIFFERENCE: **6** hassle **7** discord, dispute, quarrel **8** argument, conflict, squabble **9** disparity, variation **10** alteration, dissension, divergence, unlikeness **11** controversy, discrepancy, distinction **12** disagreement **13** heterogeneity

DIFFERENT: **5** novel, other **6** divers, sundry, unique, unlike **7** diverse, offbeat, several, strange, unalike, unusual, variant, various **8** assorted, atypical, contrary, distinct, peculiar, separate **9** divergent, unrelated **10** dissimilar **12** incomparable

DIFFERENTIATE: **5** alter **6** change, modify **8** contrast, separate **10** comprehend **11** distinguish **12** discriminate

DIFFICULT: **4** hard **5** fussy, hairy, rough, tough **6** cranky, knotty, trying, uphill **7** arduous, complex, labored, painful **8** involved, puzzling, stubborn **9** demanding, intricate, laborious **11** complicated, troublesome

DIFFICULTY: **3** ado, fix, jam **4** mess, snag **5** fight, nodus, pinch, rigor **6** hassle, pickle, scrape **7** barrier, dilemma, dispute, paradox, pitfall, problem, quarrel, setback, trouble **8** hardship, obstacle, quagmire, struggle **9** hindrance **10** impediment **11** aggravation, controversy, frustration, obstruction, vicissitude **12** complication

DIFFIDENCE: **4** fear **5** doubt **7** modesty, reserve, shyness **8** humility, meekness **9** timidness **10** hesitation, insecurity **11** bashfulness **12** apprehension

DIFFUSE: **4** full **5** wordy **6** divide, extend, prolix, soften, spread, strewn **7** copious, scatter, verbose **8** disperse, expanded, rambling, waffling **9** dissipate, expatiate, irradiate, propagate **10** circulated, palaverous, widespread **11** disseminate

DIG: **3** get, hoe, jab **4** gibe, hole, like, mine, poke, prod, quip, root, till **5** crack, delve, enjoy, grasp, nudge, probe, spade, taunt **6** burrow, exhume, groove, insult, plunge, quarry, shovel, thrust, tunnel **7** explore, unearth **8** bulldoze, discover, excavate, prospect **9** extricate **10** understand **11** investigate

DIGEST: **4** code **5** grasp **6** absorb, codify, endure, ponder, precis **7** abridge, analyze, epitome, pandect, stomach, summary **8** condense, dissolve, organize, synopsis, tolerate **10** assimilate, comprehend

DIGIT: **3** toe **4** unit **5** thumb **6** figure, finger, number, pinkie, symbol **7** numeral **9** extremity

DIGNIFIED: **4** prim **5** grant, lofty, noble, staid **6** august **7** courtly, exalted, stately, upright **8** majestic **9** honorable, respected

DIGNIFY: **5** adorn, honor, raise **7** elevate, ennoble, glorify, promote **11** distinguish

DIGNITARY: **3** VIP **6** leader **7** notable **8** eminence, luminary, official

DIGNITY: **4** rank **5** grace, honor, poise, pride, worth **6** virtue **7** decorum, majesty, stature **8** elegance, prestige, standing **9** character, etiquette, nobleness **10** excellence

DIGRESS: **4** roam, veer **5** drift, shift, stray **6** swerve, wander **7** deviate, diverge, meander

DIGRESSION: **6** detour **7** episode **9** excursion **10** deflection

DIKE: **4** bank, dyke **5** ditch, levee **7** barrier, channel **8** causeway **10** embankment **11** watercourse

DILAPIDATED: **5** dingy **6** shabby **7** damaged, run-down **8** battered, decrepit **9** neglected **10** ramshackle, threadbare

DILATE: **5** swell, widen **6** expand, extend **7** amplify, augment, broaden, enlarge, expound, inflate, prolong, stretch **8** lengthen, protract **9** expatiate

DILATORY: **4** lazy, slow **5** slack, tardy **6** remiss **7** laggard **8** delaying, inactive, sluggish **9** leisurely, unhurried **15** procrastinating

DILEMMA: **3** fix **4** bind, mess, mire, spot **6** crisis, pickle **7** problem **8** quandary **11** predicament **12** complication **13** Hobson's choice

DILETTANTE: **6** rookie **7** admirer, amateur, dabbler, dabster, trifler **11** connoisseur, superficial

DILIGENCE: **4** heed, zeal **5** vigor **6** effort **8** industry **9** assiduity, attention, intensity **10** dedication **11** application, earnestness **12** perseverance

DILIGENT: **4** busy **5** eager **6** active **7** careful, heedful, operose **8** sedulous, studious, thorough **9** assiduous, steadfast **10** persistent, unflagging **11** hardworking, industrious, painstaking

DILLY: **3** pip **4** lulu **5** beaut, dandy, peach **6** doozer **9** humdinger **12** lollapalooza

DILLYDALLY: **3** lag **4** idle, loaf **5** delay, stall **6** dawdle, linger, loiter **9** vacillate

DILUTE: **3** cut **4** thin **5** alter, water **6** lessen, reduce, weaken **8** diminish **9** attenuate **10** adulterate

DIM: **4** blur, dull, fade, hazy, mist, pale, soft **5** bleak, dense, dusky, faint, foggy, vague **6** cloudy, darken, dreary, gloomy, obtuse, somber **7** blurred, darkish, eclipse, obscure, shadowy, subdued, tarnish, unclear **8** negative, overcast **9** obfuscate **10** depressing, lackluster, mysterious **11** unfavorable **12** disapproving

DIMENSION: **4** bulk, size **5** range, scope **6** aspect, extent, height, volume **7** element, measure, quality **8** capacity **9** magnitude, thickness **10** importance, proportion

DIMENSIONS: **4** mass, time **6** length

DIMINISH: **3** ebb **4** ease, fade, sink, wane **5** abate, lower, peter, taper **6** dilute, lessen, narrow, recede, reduce, wither **7** abridge, cheapen, curtail, deplete, detract, dwindle, subside **8** condense, decrease, derogate, minimize, moderate, retrench, subtract **9** alleviate, extenuate

DIMINUTION: **5** decay **7** decline **8** decrease **9** abatement, lessening **11** curtailment

DIMINUTIVE: **4** tiny **5** dwarf, small, teeny **6** bantam, little, petite, slight **9** miniature, minuscule, pintsized **11** lilliputian

DIM-WITTED: **4** dull, dumb, slow **6** stupid **7** idiotic **12** feebleminded

DIN: **4** loud, riot **5** noise, sound **6** babble, clamor, hubbub, racket, rattle, steven, tumult, uproar **7** clangor, clatter, instill, turmoil **9** commotion, confusion **10** hullabaloo **11** pandemonium

DINE: **3** eat, sup **5** feast, lunch **6** dinner **7** consume, partake **9** breakfast

DINER: **4** cafe **5** guest **6** eatery, patron **7** canteen **8** train car **10** restaurant **11** greasy spoon **12** luncheonette

DING: **4** beat, dash, dent, nick, ring **5** clang, drive, knock, pound, thump **6** stroke, thrust

DINGHY: **4** boat **5** skiff **7** rowboat **8** life raft, lifeboat

DINGY: **4** dark, drab **5** dirty, dusty, grimy, seedy, smoky, tacky **6** dreary, gloomy, shabby, soiled **7** squalid **10** discolored **11** dilapidated

DINKY: **4** cute, poor, tiny **5** minor, small **6** petite, shabby **9** miniature **13** insignificant

DINNER: **4** food, meal **5** feast **6** entree, supper **7** banquet, potluck
course: **4** soup **5** salad **6** entree **7** dessert **8** main dish **9** appetizer, vegetable **11** hors d'oeuvre

DINT: **4** dent, nick, will **5** drive, force, power **6** effort, energy **8** strength **10** impression **11** indentation

DIOCESE: **3** see **7** prelacy **8** benefice, district **9** bishopric **10** episcopate **12** jurisdiction

DIP: **3** sag **4** bail, drop, duck, dunk, fade, lade, sink, soak, swim, veer **5** delve, douse, droop, ladle, lower, sauce, slope, souse **6** browse, candle, dabble, plunge **7** decline, descend, immerse, moisten **8** decrease, downturn, submerge **10** depression

DIPLOMA: **5** award, honor **6** degree **7** charter **8** document **9** sheepskin **11** certificate

DIPLOMACY: **4** tact **5** poise, skill **8** delicacy **9** dexterity **10** artfulness, graciosity **11** savoir-faire **13** statesmanship

DIPLOMAT: **5** agent, envoy **6** consul, nuncio **7** attache **8** mediator, minister **10** ambassador **14** representative

DIPSOMANIA: **7** craving **10** alcoholism

DIRE: **4** grim **5** awful **6** dismal, tragic, urgent, woeful **7** crucial, doleful, drastic, fearful, ominous **8** critical, dreadful, horrible, terrible **9** desperate **10** calamitous **11** apocalyptic, devastating

DIRECT: **3** aim **4** bend, even, head, helm, lead, rein, sway, turn **5** apply, blank, blunt, clear, coach, focus, frank, guide, order, point, refer, steer, train, utter **6** advise, candid, ensign, govern, honest, lineal, manage, prompt **7** address, appoint, beeline, command, conduct, control, nonstop, oversee, preside **8** dedicate, instruct, marshall, regulate, straight **9** immediate **10** administer, point-blank **11** compendious, superintend, superscribe

DIRECTION: **3** way **4** bent, care, east, path, plan, road, rule, west **5** label, north, route, south, trend **6** course **7** bearing, command, control, mandate, outlook **8** guidance, tendency **10** leadership, management, regulation, trajectory **11** inclination, information, instruction

DIRECTIVE: **4** memo **5** edict, order, ukase **6** decree, ruling **8** bulletin **10** injunction **11** instruction **13** communication

DIRECTLY: **3** now **4** soon **7** exactly, quickly, shortly, totally **8** candidly, promptly, straight **9** instantly, literally, presently **11** immediately

DIRECTOR: **4** boss, head **5** chief, coach **6** leader **7** manager, prefect **8** chairman, governor **9** commander, conductor **10** chairwoman, supervisor **11** chairperson **13** administrator

DIRECTORY: **4** list, ordo **5** atlas, guide, index **6** lineup, roster **7** almanac **8** register **11** yellow pages **13** telephone book

DIRGE: **4** hymn, keen, poem, song **5** chant, elegy **6** lament **7** requiem **8** threnody

DIRT: **3** mud **4** clay, dust, muck, sand, scum, smut, soil, soot **5** dregs, earth, filth, grime, rumor, trash **6** gossip, gravel, ground, refuse **7** scandal **9** excrement, obscenity **10** corruption

DIRTY: **3** low **4** base, foul, vile **5** dingy, foggy, grimy, messy, muddy, nasty, stain **6** bemire, defile, filthy, greasy, grubby, impure, risque, sloppy, smutty, soiled, sordid, stormy, vulgar **7** begrime, clouded, corrupt, illicit, obscene, raunchy, squalid, sullied, tarnish, unclean **8** polluted **9** dishonest **10** despicable, unsanitary **11** distasteful

DISABILITY: **6** defect, malady **8** drawback, handicap **10** affliction, deficiency, impediment, incapacity **12** disadvantage

DISABLE: **4** lame, maim **5** wreck **6** damage, disarm, hinder, hogtie, weaken **7** cripple **9** hamstring, undermine **10** immobilize **12** incapacitate

DISABUSE: **4** free **6** debunk, expose **7** correct, rectify **8** liberate **9** enlighten **10** disenchant **11** disillusion

DISADVANTAGE: **4** hurt, loss **6** damage **7** penalty **8** drawback, handicap, hardship, obstacle, weakness **9** detriment, prejudice **10** difficulty **11** deprivation

DISADVANTAGED: **8** deprived **12** impoverished **15** underprivileged

DISADVANTAGEOUS: **5** wrong **7** harmful, hurtful **9** slighting **11** deleterious, detrimental, prejudicial, unfavorable

DISAFFECTED: **8** disloyal, mutinous, recreant **9** alienated, estranged, faithless, resentful, withdrawn **10** perfidious, rebellious **11** treacherous

DISAFFIRM: **4** deny **5** annul **6** negate **7** gainsay, reverse **8** disclaim, renounce **9** repudiate **10** contradict

DISAGREE: **4** vary **5** argue, clash **6** differ, oppose **7** contend, counter, dispute, quarrel, wrangle **8** conflict

DISAGREEABLE: **4** sour, vile **5** awful, cross, harsh, nasty **7** grouchy, hateful, peevish **8** annoying, petulant, unsavory **9** difficult, irritable, offensive, repugnant **10** unpleasant **11** displeasing, distasteful **12** cantankerous

DISAGREEMENT: **4** rift, spat **5** clash, fight **6** debate, strife **7** discord, dispute **8** argument, conflict, squabble, variance **9** bickering, diversity **10** contention, difference, difficulty, disharmony, dissension **11** controversy, discrepancy, displeasure

DISALLOW: **3** nix **4** deny, veto **6** censor, forbid, refuse, reject **7** censure, exclude **8** prohibit **9** repudiate

DISAPPEAR: **4** fade, flee **5** cease, leave **6** depart, vanish **7** vamoose **8** diminish, dissolve, evanesce, withdraw **9** evaporate

DISAPPOINT: **4** dash, fail, fall **6** baffle, bungle, defeat, dismay, sadden, thwart **9** frustrate **10** disenchant, dishearten, dissatisfy

DISAPPOINTMENT: **6** defeat, fiasco, regret **7** failure, letdown, setback, washout **8** delusion, obstacle **10** anticlimax **11** displeasure

DISAPPROVAL: **4** hiss **5** blame **7** boycott, catcall, censure, dissent, grumble **9** criticism, disliking, rejection

DISAPPROVE: **4** veto **6** reject **7** condemn, protest **8** denounce, disallow **9** deprecate **11** expostulate

DISARM: **5** charm **6** allure, defuse, subdue **7** cripple, disable **8** convince **9** fascinate, influence **10** demobilize, immobilize **12** demilitarize, incapacitate

DISARRANGE: **4** muss **5** upset **6** jumble, ruffle **7** confuse, disturb **8** dishevel, scramble, unsettle **9** dislocate **10** disconcert **11** disorganize

DISARRAY: **4** mess **5** chaos **6** muddle **7** anarchy, turmoil **8** disorder **9** confusion **11** pandemonium

DISASSEMBLE: **7** disband, scatter **8** separate **9** dismantle

DISASSOCIATE: **4** part **7** divorce **8** separate, uncouple **10** disconnect **12** disaffiliate

DISASTER: **4** bale, blow, ruin **6** blight, fiasco, mishap **7** debacle, tragedy **8** accident, calamity, casualty, fatality **9** adversity, cataclysm, holocaust **10** misfortune **11** catastrophe **12** misadventure

DISASTROUS: **4** dire **7** hapless, harmful, ruinous **8** terrible **10** horrendous **11** devastating, unfortunate

DISAVOW: **4** deny **6** abjure, negate, recant, refuse, reject **7** gainsay, retract **8** disclaim, forswear, renounce **9** repudiate **10** contradict

DISBAND: **4** part **7** dismiss, scatter **8** disperse, dissolve, separate **9** dissipate **11** disassemble **12** disintegrate

DISBELIEVE: **5** doubt **6** reject **7** suspect **8** distrust, mistrust, question **9** skeptical

DISBELIEVER: **5** cynic **7** atheist, doubter, infidel, skeptic **8** agnostic **9** dissident

DISBURSE: **5** divvy, spend **6** defray, divide, expend, outlay **8** allocate, dispense **10** distribute

DISCARD: **4** dump, jilt, junk, oust, shed, toss **5** chuck, ditch, fling, scrap, shuck **6** divest, reject, remove, unload **7** abandon, cashier, divorce **8** jettison **9** eliminate, repudiate

DISCERN: **3** see **4** espy **6** behold, descry, detect **7** foresee, observe, uncover **8** discover, perceive **9** ascertain **10** anticipate, understand **11** distinguish

DISCERNIBLE: **7** evident, obvious, visible **8** apparent, distinct, tangible **10** noticeable **11** perceptible **14** comprehensible

DISCERNING: **4** wise **5** acute **6** astute, clever **9** sagacious, sensitive **10** insightful **11** clairvoyant **14** discriminating

DISCHARGE: **3** can **4** boot, dump, emit, fire, free, ooze, oust, pour, sack, void **5** blast, eject, expel, exude, quash, shoot **6** bounce, defray, exempt, launch, pardon, unload **7** absolve, cashier, dismiss, execute, release, relieve, seepage **8** detonate, disgorge, dispense, displace, emptying, evacuate, supplant **9** acquittal, execution, exonerate, explosion, liquidate, terminate **10** liberation **11** performance

DISCIPLE: **3** ite **5** chela **7** apostle, epigone, scholar, student **8** adherent, believer, follower, imitator
of Jesus: **4** John, Jude, Mark, Paul **5** James, Judas, Peter, Simon **6** Andrew, Philip, Thomas **7** Matthew **8** Barnabas, Matthias **11** Bartholomew

DISCIPLINARIAN: **4** czar **6** tyrant **8** enforcer, martinet **10** taskmaster **13** authoritarian

DISCIPLINARY: **7** ordered **8** punitive **9** punishing **10** corrective

DISCIPLINE: **4** area, flog, whip **5** drill, teach, train **6** punish, school **7** chasten, control, correct **8** chastise, instruct, penalize, regiment, restrain, training **9** education, obedience, specialty, willpower **10** strictness **11** self-control

DISCLAIM: **4** deny **6** abjure, disown, negate, recant **7** disavow, gainsay, retract **8** abnegate, renounce **9** repudiate **10** contradict

DISCLOSE: **4** bare, leak, open, tell **5** admit, spill, utter **6** betray, expose, impart, reveal, squeal, unveil **7** confess, display, divulge, exhibit, publish, uncover **8** discover, indicate **11** acknowledge

DISCLOSURE: **6** expose **7** arrival **9** admission **10** revelation **11** declaration **13** enlightenment

DISCOLOR: **4** blot, fade, spot **5** smear, stain, sully **6** bleach, defile, streak **7** tarnish **8** besmirch

DISCOMFIT: **5** annoy, upset **6** baffle, bother, defeat, outwit, rattle, thwart **7** confuse, disturb, fluster **8** confound **9** embarrass, frustrate, humiliate **10** disconcert

DISCOMFORT: **4** ache, pain **5** agony **6** dismay **7** disturb, malaise, trouble **8** distress, soreness **9** annoyance, embarrass **10** irritation, uneasiness **11** displeasure

DISCOMMODE: **5** upset **6** bother, burden **7** fluster, trouble **13** inconvenience

DISCOMPOSE: **5** upset **6** pester, rattle, ruffle **7** agitate, confuse, disturb, fluster, perturb, provoke, unhinge **8** disarray, disorder, displace, disquiet, unsettle **10** disarrange, disconcert **11** disorganize

DISCONCERT: **4** faze **5** abash **6** baffle, rattle, ruffle **7** confuse, disturb, nonplus, perplex, perturb **8** bewilder, confound, unsettle **9** discomfit, embarrass, frustrate, unbalance **10** disarrange, discompose

DISCONNECT: **4** undo **5** sever **6** detach, sunder, unplug **8** separate, uncouple **9** disengage, interrupt

DISCONNECTED: **5** loose **6** broken **7** muddled, removed **8** rambling **9** illogical **10** abstracted, disjointed, incoherent, irrational

DISCONSOLATE: **3** sad **4** blue, down **6** dreary, gloomy, somber **7** forlorn, unhappy **8** dejected, hopeless **9** cheerless, depressed, miserable, woebegone **10** despairing, dispirited, melancholy **11** pessimistic

DISCONTENTED: **5** bored **7** unhappy **8** restless **9** miserable **10** displeased, malcontent **12** dissatisfied

DISCONTINUE: **3** end **4** drop, halt, quit, stop **5** break, cease, pause, scrub **6** desist **7** abandon, suspend **9** interrupt, terminate

DISCORD: **5** clash, noise **6** differ, enmity, static, strife **8** conflict, friction, variance **9** animosity, cacophony, hostility **10** antagonism, contention, difference, disharmony, dissension **12** disagreement

DISCORDANT: **5** harsh **6** hoarse **7** jarring **8** contrary, jangling **9** dissonant, untenable **10** discrepant **11** conflicting, incongruous, quarrelsome **12** incompatible, inconsistent, inharmonious **13** heterogeneous

DISCOUNT: **6** forget, ignore, lessen, rebate **7** dismiss **8** decrease, minimize, rollback, subtract **9** allowance, deduction, disregard, exemption, reduction **12** depreciation

DISCOURAGE: **5** daunt, deter **6** dampen, deject, hinder **7** depress, inhibit **8** dispirit, dissuade, frighten, restrain **10** demoralize, dishearten, intimidate

DISCOURSE: **4** chat, talk, tell **5** orate, paper, speak **6** eulogy, homily, parley, preach, sermon, thesis **7** address, comment, descant, discuss, dissert, expound, lecture, oration, prelect **8** argument, colloquy, converse, dialogue, rhetoric, treatise **9** expatiate, monologue, narration, soliloquy **10** discussion **11** description **12** conversation, dissertation

DISCOURTEOUS: **4** rude **5** crude **7** ill-bred, uncivil, uncouth **8** impolite **9** inaffable **10** ungracious, unmannerly **11** ill-mannered **13** disrespectful

DISCOVER: **3** see, spy **4** espy, find, spot **5** learn **6** define, descry, detect, expose, locate, reveal, unmask **7** confess, discern, divulge, explore, observe, pioneer, realize, uncover, unearth **8** disclose, identify, perceive **9** ascertain, determine, recognize

DISCOVERY: **6** espial, method, strike **8** analysis, sighting, treasure **9** diagnosis, invention **10** revelation **11** origination **12** breakthrough

DISCREDIT: **5** blame, decry, doubt, shame, smear, taint **6** damage, defame, expose **7** asperse, blemish, impeach, slander, suspect **8** belittle, disgrace, dishonor, distrust, ignominy, question **9** disparage **10** disbelieve

DISCREET: **5** civil **6** modest, polite **7** careful, guarded, politic, prudent **8** cautious, reserved, sensible **9** judicious **10** controlled, reasonable **11** circumspect

DISCREPANCY: **3** gap **5** error **8** conflict **9** disparity **10** difference **12** disagreement **13** inconsistency

DISCRETE: **7** diverse, various **8** detached, distinct, separate **10** individual

DISCRETION: **4** tact **5** sense **6** choice, wisdom **7** caution, privacy, secrecy **8** judgment, maturity, prudence **9** diplomacy, restraint

DISCRIMINATE: **4** hate **5** favor **7** discern **8** contrast, perceive, separate **9** demarcate, segregate, victimize **11** distinguish **13** differentiate

DISCRIMINATING: **6** astute, shrewd **7** bigoted, careful, choosey, finicky **8** critical **9** selective **10** analytical, perceptive, prejudiced **11** distinctive

DISCRIMINATION: **4** bias, heed **6** acumen, hatred **8** inequity, keenness, sagacity **9** injustice **10** partiality **14** understandment

DISCURSIVE: **6** roving **7** verbose **8** rambling **10** digressive, meandering

DISCUSS: **3** air **5** argue **6** confer, debate, parley **7** agitate, consult, contend, dispute, examine, explain, expound **8** consider, talk over **9** discourse, elaborate

DISCUSSION: **3** rap **4** talk **6** huddle, parley, powwow **7** canvass, meeting **8** argument, colloquy, dialogue **9** symposium **10** conference, exposition **12** conversation, deliberation **13** confabulation

DISDAIN: **4** hate **5** abhor, flout, scorn **6** detest, loathe, slight **7** contemn, despise **8** contempt, derision, ridicule **9** arrogance **11** haughtiness **12** indifference

DISEASE: **5** virus **6** malady **7** ailment, illness **8** debility, epidemic, pandemic, sickness **9** complaint, infirmity

animal: **3** rot **4** gout **5** cleft **6** canker, surrah **7** anthrax, fistula **8** hysteria

bone: **8** bursitis **9** scoliosis, synovitis

circulation: **5** edema **6** anemia, angina, dropsy **7** toxemia **8** aneurism, leukemia **9** phlebitis **10** hemophilia

digestive: **7** colitis **9** cirrhosis, hepatitis

finding: **9** diagnosis, prognosis

nervous: **8** dementia, dyslexia **9** catalepsy, catatonia **10** Alzheimer's, meningitis

plant: **3** pox, rot **4** bunt, cork, rust, smut **5** ergot, speck **6** blight, canker, mildew **7** blister

respiratory: **4** mono **8** pleurisy **12** tuberculosis

skin: **4** acne, rash **5** hives, lupus **6** eczema, herpes, thrush **7** scabies **8** impetigo, ringworm **9** psoriasis, seborrhea

viral: **4** AIDS **7** anthrax, rubella, rubeola, tetanus **9** gonorrhea **10** diphtheria

DISEMBARK: **4** land **6** arrive **7** deplane **8** dismount

DISENCHANTED: **5** blase **7** knowing, mundane, unhappy **10** undeceived **11** enlightened, worldly-wise **12** disappointed **13** disillusioned

DISENCUMBER: **3** rid **6** unload **7** lighten, relieve **8** unburden **9** alleviate, disengage

DISENGAGE: **4** free, undo, wean **5** clear, sever **6** detach, loosen **7** release **8** liberate, unfasten, withdraw **9** extricate **11** disencumber

DISENTANGLE: **4** comb, free **5** loose, solve, untie **6** evolve, sunder **7** unravel, untwist **8** separate **9** extricate **10** disconnect

DISFAVOR: **5** odium **7** dislike **8** aversion, disgrace **9** disesteem, repulsion **11** disapproval, displeasure

DISFIGURE: **3** mar **4** maim, mark, scar **6** deface, defile, deform, injure **7** blemish, distort **8** mutilate

DISGRACE: **4** blot, mock, slur, spot **5** abase, odium, shame, stain **6** debase, infamy **7** degrade, obloquy, scandal, slander **8** contempt, disfavor, dishonor, ignominy, reproach **9** desecrate, discredit, disrepute, embarrass, humiliate **10** stigmatize **11** humiliation

DISGRACEFUL: **4** base **5** shady **6** shoddy **8** shameful, unworthy **9** appalling **10** unbecoming

DISGRUNTLED: **4** sore **6** grumpy **7** peevish, unhappy **9** irritated **10** malcontent **12** dissatisfied

DISGUISE: **4** hide, mask, veil **5** alter, belie, cloak, cover **6** facade, veneer **7** charade, conceal, falsify, obscure, pretend **8** artifice, pretense **9** dissemble, incognito, whitewash **10** camouflage, masquerade **11** dissimulate

DISGUST: **5** repel, shock **6** appall, offend, revolt, sicken **7** dislike, outrage, surfeit **8** aversion, distaste, loathing, nauseate **9** antipathy, repulsion **10** abhorrence, repugnance **11** abomination

DISGUSTING: **4** foul, vile **5** awful, gross, nasty, yucky **6** creepy **7** beastly, hateful, hideous, obscene **8** shocking **9** offensive

DISH: **3** cup **4** bowl, food, girl, tray **5** basin, china, plate, serve, woman **6** course, entree, looker, recipe, saucer, tureen **7** ceramic, charger, helping, platter **8** dispense, favorite **9** casserole, container

DISHABILLE: **7** undress **8** careless, disarray, disorder

DISHARMONY: **5** chaos, clash **7** discord **8** conflict, disarray, friction **10** dissension

DISHEARTEN: **5** crush, daunt, deter **6** dampen, deject, humble, sadden **7** depress **8** dispirit **10** demoralize, discourage

DISHEVELED: **5** messy, ratty **6** frowsy, sloppy, untidy **7** ruffled, tousled, unkempt **8** slovenly, straggly, uncombed, wrinkled **10** disorderly **11** disarranged

DISHONEST: **5** false, lying **6** shifty **7** corrupt, crooked, devious, knavish **8** cheating **9** deceitful, deceptive **10** fraudulent, misleading, untruthful **11** underhanded **12** unscrupulous **13** untrustworthy

DISHONESTY: **5** fraud **7** cunning **8** stealing **9** chicanery, improbity, mendacity

DISHONOR: **5** shame, stain **6** defame, defile, infamy **7** blemish, debauch, degrade, obloquy, tarnish **8** disgrace, ignominy **9** discredit, disrepute, humiliate **10** opprobrium

DISHONORABLE: **4** base, foul **5** shady **7** corrupt, ignoble **8** cowardly, shameful **9** unethical **10** despicable **12** contemptible, unprincipled **13** reprehensible

DISILLUSIONED: **7** wakened **9** shattered **11** enlightened **12** disappointed, disenchanted

DISINCLINATION: **6** hatred **7** dislike **8** aversion **9** antipathy **10** reluctance, resistance **11** disinterest **13** unwillingness

DISINCLINED: **5** loath **7** balking, bashful, uneager **9** reluctant, unwilling **10** indisposed, protesting

DISINFECT: **6** purify **7** cleanse **8** fumigate, sanitize **9** sterilize

DISINHERIT: **6** cut off, disown **7** deprive, exclude **12** disaffiliate

DISINTEGRATE: **4** melt **5** decay, erode **7** crumble, shatter **8** dissolve, splinter **9** decompose, pulverize **11** fragmentize

DISINTER: **3** dig **5** delve **6** exhume, expose **7** uncover, unearth **8** disclose

DISINTERESTED: **4** fair **7** neutral, passive **8** detached, unbiased **9** apathetic, impartial **10** uninvolved **11** indifferent, nonpartisan **12** uninfluenced

DISJOINTED: **5** apart, loose **7** chaotic, muddled, tangled **8** confused, unhinged **10** dislocated, disordered, incoherent, unattached **11** unorganized **12** disconnected

DISK, DISC: **4** dial, puck **5** CD-ROM, paten, plate, sabot, wheel **6** circle, harrow, record, washer **8** diskette **9** faceplate, medallion
types: **4** hard **5** brake **6** floppy **7** compact, optical **8** magnetic

DISLIKE: **4** hate **6** detest, loathe, resent **7** despise **8** aversion, distaste **9** animosity, antipathy, disrelish, prejudice **10** antagonism **12** disaffection

DISLOCATE: **4** move **5** upset **6** uproot **7** disrupt **8** disjoint, displace, separate, transfer

DISLODGE: **4** oust **5** expel **6** remove **7** disturb **9** extricate

DISLOYAL: **5** false **6** untrue **8** recreant **9** faithless, undutiful **10** subversive, traitorous, unfaithful **11** treacherous, treasonable

DISLOYALTY: **6** mutiny **7** perfidy, treason **8** apostasy, betrayal **9** rebellion **10** infidelity **12** insurrection

DISMAL: **3** sad **4** blue, dark, dire, dull, glum, gray, grim **5** black, bleak **6** cloudy, dreary, gloomy, somber **7** doleful, ghastly, joyless, ominous, unhappy **8** funereal, hopeless, lonesome **9** cheerless, sorrowful **10** calamitous, depressing, melancholy **13** disheartening

DISMANTLE: **4** raze, undo **5** annul, level, strip **6** denude, divest **7** deprive, destroy, rescind **8** dismount **11** disassemble

DISMAY: **4** fear **5** alarm, daunt, dread, panic, shake, upset **6** appall, fright, rattle, subdue, terror **7** anxiety, deprive, horrify, terrify, unhinge **8** affright, confound **10** disappoint, discomfort, discourage **11** disillusion, trepidation **12** apprehension **13** consternation **14** disenchantment

DISMEMBER: **4** maim **5** sever **6** mangle, sunder **7** dissect **8** amputate, disjoint, mutilate

DISMISS: **3** can **4** boot, drop, fire, free, oust, sack **5** clear, eject, expel **6** banish, dispel, reject, remove **7** cashier, disband, discard **8** delegate **9** discharge, terminate

DISMISSAL: **5** conge **6** layoff, waiver **7** release **9** discharge, disregard, expulsion **11** adjournment, deportation

DISMOUNT: **6** alight **7** deplane, descend, unhorse **9** dismantle

DISNEY:
characters: **4** Huey **5** Dewey, Dumbo, Goofy, Louie, Pluto **10** Donald Duck **11** Mickey Mouse, Minnie Mouse
entertainment: **10** Disneyland, Euro Disney **11** Disney World
films: **5** Bambi **7** Aladdin **8** Fantasia, Lion King **9** Pinocchio, Snow White **10** Pocahontas **11** Mary Poppins **13** Little Mermaid **15** Steamboat Willie

DISOBEDIENT: **6** unruly **7** defiant, naughty, wayward, willful **8** mutinous **9** insurgent **10** disorderly, rebellious, refractory **11** mischievous **12** noncompliant **13** insubordinate, undisciplined

DISOBEY: **6** ignore, resist **9** disregard, misbehave

DISORDER: **4** fuss, mess, riot **5** chaos **6** fracas, jumble, malady, mayhem, mucker, muddle, ruffle, tousle, tumult **7** ailment, anarchy, clutter, confuse, disease, disturb, illness, trouble **8** disarray, dishevel, shambles, sickness, syndrome **9** commotion, complaint, confusion **10** affliction, disarrange, disconcert, misconduct **11** disorganize

DISORDERLY: **5** rowdy **6** unruly, untidy **7** unkempt **8** unlawful **9** unsettled **11** disobedient **12** hugger-mugger, ungovernable, unmanageable **14** uncontrollable

DISORGANIZED: **5** upset **7** chaotic, muddled **8** confused **9** haphazard **10** disorderly, fragmental **12** unmethodical **13** helter-skelter

DISORIENTED: **4** lost **8** confused, unstable **10** unbalanced

DISOWN: **4** deny **5** expel **6** reject **7** abandon, disavow, forsake **8** abdicate, renounce **9** repudiate **10** disinherit

DISPARAGE: **4** slur **5** abuse, decry **6** demean, slight **7** degrade, disdain **8** belittle, derogate, dishonor, minimize, ridicule **9** criticize, discredit, underrate **10** demoralize

DISPARITY: **3** gap **8** contrast **9** imbalance **10** difference, inequality, unevenness **11** discrepancy **13** dissimilarity

DISPASSIONATE: **4** calm, cool, fair, just **6** serene **7** unmoved **8** composed, moderate, unbiased **9** collected, impartial, unexcited, unfeeling, unruffled **10** unimpaired **11** levelheaded, unemotional, unflappable **12** unprejudiced

DISPATCH: **4** free, kill, note, post, send **5** flash, haste, hurry, speed, story **6** devour, finish, hasten, murder, report **7** consume, deliver, dispose, message **8** bulletin, celerity, expedite, transmit **9** eliminate, quickness, swiftness **10** accelerate, communique, promptness **11** assassinate, instruction **13** communication

DISPEL: **5** allay, eject, expel **6** banish **7** dismiss, scatter **8** disperse **9** dissipate, drive away

DISPENSABLE: **5** minor **7** trivial **8** needless **10** disposable, expendable **11** superfluous, unessential

DISPENSATION: **6** decree, relief, scheme, system **9** allotment, exemption **10** management, permission **11** arrangement **12** distribution

DISPENSE: **4** deal **5** spare **6** assign, direct, divide, excuse, exempt, manage **7** absolve, arrange, dole out, measure, prepare, provide, release **9** exonerate **10** administer, distribute, manipulate

DISPENSE WITH: **4** dump, omit **5** scrap **6** shelve **7** abandon, discard **9** eliminate **10** relinquish

DISPERSE: **5** strew **6** dispel, spread, vanish **7** diffuse, disband, scatter **8** separate **9** circulate, disappear, dissipate **10** distribute **11** disseminate

DISPIRITED: **3** low, sad **4** blue, down, flat **6** bummed **7** forlorn **8** dejected, downcast **9** cheerless, depressed, woebegone **10** melancholy **11** crestfallen, demoralized **12** disheartened

DISPLACE: **4** move **5** evict, exile, shift, usurp **6** banish, depose, remove, uproot **8** dislodge, supplant, unsettle **9** discharge, dislocate, supersede

DISPLAY: **4** pomp, show **5** boast, model, sight, sport, stage **6** blazon, expose, extend, flaunt, parade, reveal, sample, unfold, unveil **7** example, exhibit, pageant, promote, uncover **8** ceremony, disclose, discover, emblazon, flourish, indicate, manifest, splendor **9** advertise, spectacle **10** exhibition **11** affectation, demonstrate

DISPLEASE: **4** miff **5** anger, annoy, pique **6** bother, offend **7** disturb, provoke **8** irritate **9** aggravate **10** dissatisfy, exasperate

DISPLEASURE: **5** anger, wrath **6** sorrow **7** disgust, dislike, offense, umbrage **8** aversion, distaste, vexation **10** discomfort, discontent, resentment **11** disapproval, indignation, unhappiness

DISPORT: **4** play **6** frolic **9** amusement, entertain, merriment **10** recreation

DISPOSAL: **5** power **7** command, dumping **8** jettison, riddance **9** authority, clearance **10** conclusion, discarding, settlement **11** arrangement

DISPOSE: **4** bend, give **5** array, order, place **6** adjust, bestow, settle **7** abandon, arrange, incline, prepare **8** dispatch, organize, regulate **9** determine **10** distribute **11** systematize

DISPOSITION: **4** bent, bias, mood **5** heart, humor **6** makeup, nature, temper **7** concept **8** aptitude, attitude, tendency **9** affection, character, direction **10** adjustment, management, proclivity, propensity **11** arrangement, inclination, personality, temperament **12** constitution, idiosyncrasy, organization

DISPROPORTION: **8** mismatch **9** disparity, imbalance **10** difference, inadequacy, inequality

DISPROPORTIONATE: **6** uneven **7** unequal **9** excessive, irregular **10** asymmetric, unbalanced, unrelative

DISPROVE: **5** belie, rebut **6** negate, refute, weaken **7** confute **8** puncture **9** discredit **10** controvert, invalidate

DISPUTABLE: **4** moot **6** unsure **7** dubious **8** arguable, doubtful, fallible **9** debatable, uncertain **12** questionable

DISPUTATION: **6** debate **7** mooting, polemic **8** argument **10** discussion, dissension **11** controversy

DISPUTE: **4** deny, feud, fuss, moot **5** argue, brawl, doubt **6** bicker, debate, differ, haggle, oppose, resist **7** contend, contest, discuss, faction, gainsay, quarrel, wrangle **8** argument, question, squabble **9** challenge, encounter **10** contravene **11** altercation, controversy **12** disagreement

DISQUALIFICATION: **10** disability **11** elimination **13** ineligibility

DISQUALIFY: **5** debar **6** outlaw **7** exclude, suspend **8** prohibit **10** invalidate **12** incapacitate

DISQUIET: **4** fear, fret, pain **5** worry **6** excite, unrest **7** anxiety, disturb, fluster, trouble, turmoil **8** distress **10** discompose, discontent, uneasiness **12** restlessness

DISREGARD: **4** omit, skip **5** waive **6** forget, ignore, slight **7** disobey, neglect **8** defiance, discount, overlook **9** lassitude, oversight **11** inattention **12** indifference

DISREPUTABLE: **4** base **5** lowly, seamy, seedy, shady **8** shameful, unsavory **9** notorious **11** disgraceful **12** contemptible, dishonorable

DISRESPECT: **8** boldness, contempt, dishonor, rudeness **10** incivility **11** discourtesy

DISRESPECTFUL: **4** rude **7** uncivil **8** impolite, impudent **9** insulting **10** ungracious **11** impertinent

DISROBE: **4** shed **5** strip **6** denude, divest, remove **7** undress

DISRUPT: **5** break, upset **7** disturb **8** disorder, unsettle **9** interrupt **11** disorganize

DISSATISFACTION: **7** dislike **8** distaste **9** annoyance **10** discontent **11** displeasure, frustration, unhappiness

DISSATISFIED: **5** irked **11** disgruntled, unfulfilled **12** malcontented

DISSECT: **5** carve, probe, study **6** sunder **7** analyze, examine **8** separate **9** anatomize **11** dichotomize, investigate

DISSEMBLE: **4** hide, mask, veil **5** cloak, cover, feign **6** screen **7** conceal, pretend **8** disguise, simulate **10** camouflage **11** counterfeit

DISSEMINATE: **3** sow **6** blazon, spread **7** diffuse, scatter **8** disperse, transmit **9** broadcast, circulate, propagate, publicize **10** distribute, promulgate

DISSENSION: **6** static, strife **7** discord **8** conflict, friction **10** contention, disharmony **12** disagreement

DISSENT: **4** buck, vary **6** differ, divide, oppose **7** protest **9** exception, objection **10** dissidence **12** disagreement **13** nonconformity

DISSENTER: **5** rebel **7** heretic, sectary **8** mutineer, recusant **9** dissident, protester **10** schismatic **13** nonconformist

DISSERTATION: **5** essay, tract **6** debate, thesis **7** lecture **8** critique, treatise **9** discourse, monograph **10** discussion, exposition

DISSERVICE: **4** harm **5** wrong **6** damage, injury **7** outrage **9** injustice **10** unkindness

DISSIDENT: **5** rebel **7** heretic, sectary **8** agitator **9** dissenter, fractious **10** schismatic **11** disagreeing **13** nonconformist

DISSIMILAR: **6** unique, unlike **7** diverse **8** contrary, distinct **9** different **13** heterogeneous

DISSIMULATE: **4** hide **5** cloak, feign **7** conceal, pretend **8** disguise **9** dissemble **10** camouflage

DISSIPATE: **5** spend, waste **6** dispel, expend, misuse **7** consume, deplete, diffuse, fritter, scatter **8** disperse, dissolve, squander **9** disappear, evaporate **11** overindulge

DISSIPATION: **9** amusement, diversion **10** debauchery, wantonness **12** intemperance **13** entertainment

DISSOCIATE: **5** sever **8** alienate, distance, estrange, separate **10** disconnect

DISSOLUTE: **3** lax **4** wild **5** loose, slack **6** rakish, wanton **7** corrupt, immoral, lustful **9** abandoned, debauched **10** profligate **12** unprincipled, unrestrained

DISSOLUTION: **3** end **4** ruin **5** death, decay **6** demise **7** breakup, decease, divorce, rupture **8** division **9** annulment, dismissal **10** extinction, separation **11** termination **12** liquefaction **14** disintegration

DISSOLVE: **4** fade, fuse, melt, thaw, undo, void **5** annul **6** relent, vanish **7** adjourn, destroy, disband, divorce, dwindle, liquefy **8** evanesce, separate **9** decompose, disappear, dissipate **10** invalidate **11** discontinue **12** disintegrate

DISSONANCE: **5** noise **6** strife **7** discord, jarring **8** conflict **10** difference **12** disagreement

DISSONANT: **5** harsh **7** grating, raucous **8** jangling, strident **9** irregular **10** discordant **11** cacophonous, incongruous, unmelodious **12** inconsistent, inharmonious

DISSUADE: **4** stop **5** deter **6** divert, thwart **7** caution, prevent **8** restrain **10** discourage, disincline

DISTANCE: **4** span **5** depth, range, space **6** degree, extent, length, outrun, period, radius **7** farness, horizon, mileage, yardage **8** coldness, interval, latitude, outstrip **9** aloofness, longitude **10** difference, dissociate, remoteness **12** disagreement

DISTANT: **3** far **4** afar, away, cold **5** aloof **6** remote **7** faraway, removed **8** isolated, reserved **9** separated, withdrawn **10** unfriendly, unsociable

DISTASTE: **4** hate **6** offend **7** disgust, dislike **8** aversion, loathing **9** displease, disrelish, hostility **10** abhorrence, opprobrium, repugnance

DISTASTEFUL: **4** flat **6** bitter **7** hateful **8** unsavory **9** offensive, repulsive **10** detestable, nauseating, unpleasant **11** undesirable, unpalatable **12** disagreeable **13** objectionable

DISTEMPER: **5** paint **6** malady **7** ailment, disease, illness **8** disorder **9** infection, testiness **10** affliction **11** disturbance

DISTEND: **5** bloat, bulge, swell, widen **6** dilate, expand, spread **7** augment, balloon, enlarge, inflate, stretch **8** elongate, increase

DISTILL: **4** drop **5** exude **6** purify **7** extract, ferment, trickle **8** condense, separate

DISTINCT: **5** clear, plain, vivid **6** unique **7** diverse, obvious, special, unusual **8** apparent, discrete, explicit, separate **9** different **10** dissimilar, individual, particular **11** categorical, distinguish **12** recognizable, unmistakable

DISTINCTION: **4** mark, rank **5** glory, honor, merit **6** renown **7** feature, laurels **8** eminence **9** greatness **10** excellence, prominence, reputation, separation **12** significance

DISTINCTIVE: **6** unique **7** typical **8** original, peculiar, uncommon **11** outstanding **14** characteristic, discriminating

DISTINGUÉ: **7** refined **8** cultured, polished **10** cultivated **13** distinguished

DISTINGUISH: **4** note **5** exalt **6** admire, define, praise **7** discern **8** classify, distinct, identify, perceive, separate **9** ascertain, designate, punctuate **12** characterize **13** differentiate

DISTINGUISHED: **5** grand **6** famous, marked **7** eminent, notable, shining, special, stately **8** distinct, imposing, renowned **9** acclaimed, brilliant, dignified, distingue, prominent **10** celebrated **11** illustrious

DISTORT: **4** bend, warp **5** alter, belie, twist **6** deform, doctor, garble, mangle **7** deceive, falsify **8** misstate **9** disfigure **12** misrepresent

DISTORTED: **4** awry **5** askew **7** colored, crooked, gnarled **8** cockeyed **9** perverted **10** anamorphic

DISTRACT: **5** addle, amuse, stall, upset **6** divert, harass, puzzle **7** agitate, confuse, disturb, fluster, perplex, unnerve **8** bewilder, confound **9** entertain

DISTRACTION: **9** commotion, diversion **10** aberration **11** disturbance **12** interruption **13** preoccupation

DISTRAUGHT: **5** upset **6** crazed **7** frantic, unglued, worried **8** deranged, frenzied, troubled **9** flustered **10** distressed, hysterical

DISTRESS: **4** hurt, need, pain **5** anger, annoy, dolor, grief, upset, worry **6** danger, grieve, harass, misery, sorrow, suffer **7** afflict, agonize, anguish, anxiety, perplex, torment, torture, trouble **8** calamity **9** adversity, constrain, necessity **10** affliction, constraint, discomfort, distraught, heartbreak **11** tribulation

signal: **3** SOS **4** flag **5** alarm, siren **6** flares, mayday **9** broadcast

DISTRESSING: **3** sad **6** woeful **7** fearful, nagging, painful **8** dreadful **10** deplorable **11** frightening, regrettable, troublesome

DISTRIBUTE: **4** deal, dole, sort **5** allot, group, issue, share **6** assign, divide, donate, parcel, ration, spread, supply **7** arrange, deliver, dispose **8** allocate, classify, dispense, disperse, separate **9** apportion, circulate **10** administer **11** disseminate

DISTRIBUTOR: **3** cap **6** dealer, jobber, seller **8** merchant **9** publisher **10** wholesaler **14** businessperson

DISTRICT: **4** area, turf, ward, zone **5** tract **6** canton, parish, region, sector **7** diocese, quarter **8** locality, precinct, province, vicinity **9** community, territory **12** neighborhood

DISTRUST: **4** fear **5** doubt, qualm **7** suspect **8** question **9** suspicion **10** skepticism

DISTRUSTFUL: **5** leery **7** cynical, dubious **10** suspicious **12** disbelieving

DISTURB: **5** alarm, annoy, upset **6** arouse, bother, harass, ruffle, tamper **7** agitate, disrupt, intrude, perturb, trouble, unnerve **8** distract, distress, unsettle **9** discomfit, interfere, interrupt **10** disarrange, discompose, disconcert

DISTURBANCE: **4** riot **5** brawl, quake, storm **6** affray, fracas, hubbub, rumpus, tumult, uproar **7** cyclone, ferment, tornado, turmoil **8** disorder, eruption, violence **9** commotion, confusion, hurricane **10** excitement **11** derangement, distraction, trepidation **12** insurrection, interruption, perturbation

DISUNITE: **4** part **5** sever **6** detach, divide, sunder **7** disband, disjoin, divorce **8** alienate, dissolve, estrange, separate **9** disengage **10** disconnect, dissociate

DITCH: **4** dike, junk, moat, skip **5** canal, chuck, gully, scrap **6** gutter, reject, trench, trough **7** abandon, channel, discard, forsake, foxhole **8** jettison **10** excavation

DITHER: **4** flap **5** panic, shake, tizzy, waver **6** babble, shiver **7** fluster, tremble, whiffle **8** hesitate **9** agitation, confusion, vacillate **10** irresolute

DITHYRAMBIC: **4** wild **8** elevated, euphoric **10** boisterous **12** unrestrained

DITTO: **4** copy, same **5** alike **6** repeat **9** agreement, duplicate

DITTY: **4** poem, song **6** ballad, melody

DIURNAL: **5** daily, diary **7** daytime, journal **9** ephemeral

DIVAGATE: **5** drift, stray **6** ramble, wander **7** deviate, digress

DIVAN: **4** book, seat, sofa **5** couch **6** lounge **7** chamber **8** tribunal **9** davenport **11** coffeehouse

DIVE: **4** dump, fall, jump, leap, swan **5** lunge, swoop **6** gainer, plunge, spring **7** descent, hangout, plummet **8** submerge, tailspin **9** belly flop, jackknife **10** cannonball

DIVERGE: **4** veer **5** split **6** branch, differ, divide, oppose, spread, swerve **7** deflect, deviate, digress **8** contrast, disagree

DIVERGENT: **7** unequal, variant **8** aberrant, atypical, separate **9** different **11** conflicting

DIVERSE: **6** motley, sundry, varied **7** several **8** assorted, distinct, opposite, separate **9** different **13** heterogeneous

DIVERSIFY: **4** vary **6** change, expand, rotate **7** variate

DIVERSION: **4** game, play **5** hobby, sport **6** detour, levity **7** pastime **8** sideshow **9** amusement, departure, merriment **10** deflection, digression, recreation, relaxation **11** distraction **13** entertainment

DIVERSITY: **6** change **7** variety **10** assortment, difference **11** variegation **12** multiformity

DIVERT: **4** veer **5** amuse, avoid, relax, stall **6** swerve **7** beguile, deflect **8** distract, redirect **9** entertain

DIVEST: **4** bare, free **5** bleed, spoil, strip **6** denude, unload **7** deprive, despoil, dispose, disrobe, uncover **8** dethrone, unclothe **9** dismantle **10** dispossess

DIVIDE: **4** deal, fork, part **5** carve, cleft, divvy, halve, ridge, sever, share, slice, split **6** bisect, branch, cleave, differ, parcel, sunder **7** dissent, diverge, fissure, isolate, quarter, section, segment, trisect **8** alienate, allocate, classify, disunite, fraction, graduate, separate **9** apportion, intersect, partition **10** categorize, distribute **11** dichotomize

DIVIDED: **4** reft **5** apart **7** partite **8** branched, detached, disunity, prorated **10** incomplete, unattached

DIVIDEND: **5** bonus, share **6** carrot, profit, return, reward **7** earning

DIVINATION: **4** omen **5** guess **6** augury **7** insight **8** forecast, prophecy **9** intuition, prognosis **10** prediction **11** premonition **12** clairvoyance **14** fortune-telling
on a crystal ball: **7** scrying
on consulting ghosts: **9** sciomancy
on drawing lots: **9** sortilege
on dreams: **11** oneiromancy
on fire: **9** pyromancy
on numbers: **10** numerology
on tarot cards: **10** cartomancy
on the palm: **9** palmistry **10** chiromancy
on the planets: **9** horoscope
on the stars: **9** astrology

DIVINE: **4** holy **5** guess, pious **6** priest, sacred **7** angelic, blessed, discern, foresee, godlike, perfect, portend, predict **8** forebode, foreknow, foretell, heavenly, immortal, minister, mystical, perceive **9** celestial, religious, spiritual, wonderful **10** anticipate, conjecture, delightful, superhuman, theologian, understand **11** magnificent **12** supernatural **13** prognosticate

DIVINE COMEDY:
author: **14** Dante Alighieri

DIVINITY: **3** god **5** deity **7** demigod, goddess, godhead **8** religion, sanctity, theology

DIVISION: **4** dole, part, rift, unit **5** group, realm, share, split **6** border, branch, breach, schism, sector **7** discord, fission, section **8** category, cleavage, district **9** allotment, partition, reduction, territory **10** department, disharmony, separation **11** bifurcation, compartment

DIVORCE: **5** annul, sever, split **6** sunder **7** nullify **8** dissolve, disunion, disunite, separate **10** separation

DIVULGE: **4** bare, blab, show, tell **5** spill, voice **6** expose, gossip, impart, reveal, squeal, tattle **7** confess, confide, publish, uncover **8** disclose, proclaim **9** broadcast

DIZZY: **5** crazy, giddy, haste, rapid, silly, tipsy **6** groggy, wobbly **7** flighty, foolish, reeling **8** confused, swimming, unsteady **10** bewildered **11** harebrained, lightheaded, vertiginous **14** scatterbrained

DJIBOUTI:
capital: **8** Djibouti
cities: **5** Obock **6** Dikhil **8** Tadjoura
continent: **6** Africa
ethnic groups: **4** Afar **6** Somali
languages: **4** Afar **6** Arabic, French, Somali
monetary unit: **5** franc
water: **8** Aden Gulf, Lac Assal

DNA: **4** acid, gene **7** nucleic **11** double helix **20** deoxyribonucleic acid

DO AWAY WITH: **4** drop, kill **5** erase **6** banish, cancel, murder, revoke **7** abolish, discard **8** dissolve **9** eliminate, liquidate **10** annihilate **11** discontinue, exterminate

DOCENT: **5** guide **7** teacher **8** lecturer **10** instructor

DOCILE: **4** calm, meek, mild, tame **6** gentle **7** willing **8** obedient, resigned **9** agreeable, compliant, tractable **10** manageable, submissive

DOCK: **4** clip, moor, pier, quay, slip **5** basin, berth, wharf **6** anchor, couple, marina **7** landing, shorten **8** platform, withhold

DOCKET: **4** card, list **5** label, slate, tally **6** agenda, roster **7** program **8** calendar, schedule **9** timetable

DOCTOR: **3** PhD **4** mend **5** medic, quack, treat **6** change, dilute, expert, healer, medico, repair **7** falsify, rebuild, scholar, surgeon **8** sawbones **9** clinician, internist, physician, professor, scientist **10** administer, adulterate
anesthesia: **16** anesthesiologist
back: **12** chiropractor
blood: **12** hematologist
bones: **11** orthopedist
cancer: **10** oncologist
childbirth: **12** obstetrician
children's: **12** pediatrician
digestive system: **12** gastrologist
disease: **11** pathologist
ears: **9** otologist
ears, nose, throat: **16** otolaryngologist
eyes: **11** optometrist **15** ophthalmologist
family doctor: **19** general practitioner
feet: **10** podiatrist
female reproduction: **12** gynecologist
glands: **15** endocrinologist
heart: **12** cardiologist
kidneys: **12** nephrologist
mental health: **12** psychiatrist
skin: **13** dermatologist
specialized training: **8** resident
teeth: **7** dentist **12** orthodontist
throat: **13** laryngologist
urinary tract: **9** urologist
x-ray: **11** radiologist

DOCTRINE: **4** rule **5** canon, credo, creed, dogma, maxim, tenet **6** belief, gospel, ritual, theory **7** article, concept, precept **8** attitude, teaching **9** principle, statement **10** discipline, philosophy **11** fundamental

DOCUMENT: **4** bill, book, deed, writ **5** lease, paper **6** record, report, verify **7** certify, confirm, diploma, license, voucher **8** contract, covenant, evidence, mortgage, passport, validate **9** indenture, testimony **10** manuscript **12** substantiate

DODDERING: **3** old **4** aged, weak **5** shaky **6** feeble, infirm, senile **8** decrepit **9** trembling

DODECANESE ISLANDS: **3** Kos **4** Syme **5** Leros, Telos **6** Kassos, Khalke, Lipsos, Rhodes **7** Nisyros **8** Kalymnos **9** Karpathos
where: **6** Aegean, Greece

DODGE: **4** duck **5** avoid, cheat, ditch, elude, evade, shift, shirk, skirt, trick **6** escape, swerve **7** deceive **8** artifice, sidestep **9** pussyfoot **10** equivocate **11** prevaricate

DODGER: **6** shifty **7** haggler **8** circular, handbill **9** dishonest, trickster

DOE: **4** deer, fawn **6** female

DOER: **5** actor **6** dynamo, worker **7** hustler **8** activist, go-getter **9** performer

DOFF: **3** tip **4** shed **5** strip **6** remove **7** discard, disrobe, undress

DOG: **3** cur, pug, pup **4** mutt, Spot **5** hound, pooch, puppy, rover **6** canine **7** mongrel

breeds: **4** dane **5** boxer, corgi, dingo, husky **6** afghan, basset, beagle, borzoi, collie, heeler, kelpie, poodle, saluki, setter **7** bulldog, mastiff, pointer, spaniel **8** Airedale, doberman, elkhound, keeshond, Labrador, malamute, pinscher, sheepdog, shepherd **9** chihuahua, dachshund, pekingese, retriever, wolfhound **10** bloodhound, Pomeranian **13** cocker spaniel

famous: **4** Toto **5** Benji **6** Feller, Lassie **9** Beethoven, Old Yeller, Rin-Tin-Tin

kinds: **3** toy **4** herd, work **5** hound **7** mongrel, terrier **8** sporting

DOGGED: **7** adamant, staunch **8** stubborn **9** insistent, obstinate, steadfast, tenacious **10** determined, persistent, unshakable, unyielding **11** persevering

DOGGONE: **4** damn, darn **6** shucks **7** blasted **10** confounded

DOGMA: **4** rule **5** canon, credo, creed, tenet **6** belief, gospel **8** doctrine **9** principle, statement, teachings **10** philosophy

DOGMATIC: **6** biased **8** arrogant, despotic **9** arbitrary, doctrinal, fanatical **10** intolerant, pontifical, prejudiced **11** dictatorial, opinionated **12** totalitarian **13** authoritative

DO IN: **4** kill, ruin, tire **6** finish, murder **7** destroy, exhaust **8** bankrupt **9** eliminate, liquidate

DOLDRUMS: **5** blues, dumps, ennui, slump **6** apathy, tedium **7** boredom **9** lassitude **10** depression, melancholy, stagnation **12** listlessness

DOLE: **4** alms, give **5** allot, grief, share **6** relief, sorrow **7** charity, handout, welfare **8** dispense, donation **10** distribute

DOLEFUL: **3** sad **4** dour, down **5** bleak **6** dismal, dreary, gloomy **7** forlorn, unhappy **8** downcast, mournful **9** depressed, plaintive, sorrowful, woebegone **10** lugubrious, melancholy

DOLL: **3** toy **4** baby **5** woman **6** figure, moppet, puppet **7** darling **8** figurine, mistress **9** mannequin **10** sweetheart

DOLLAR: **3** one **4** bean, buck **5** money **8** currency, simoleon **9** greenback

DOLLOP: **3** bit **4** blob, dash, lump **6** splash **7** modicum

DOLLY: **3** car **4** cart, tool **5** truck **10** locomotive **14** mobile platform

DOLOR: **5** grief **6** misery, sorrow **7** anguish, sadness **8** distress **9** suffering **10** heartbreak

DOLOROUS: **6** dismal, woeful **7** doleful, painful **8** grievous, mournful **10** lamentable, melancholy

DOLT: **3** ass, oaf **4** clod, dork, fool, goof **5** chump, dummy, idiot, moron **7** dullard, jughead **8** bonehead, imbecile, lunkhead, meathead, numskull **9** blockhead, ignoramus, simpleton **11** chowderhead

DOMAIN: **4** area, land, turf **5** field, realm **6** empire, estate, sphere **7** kingdom **8** dominion, property, province **9** authority, bailiwick, territory **12** jurisdiction

DOME: **3** cap **4** roof **5** vault **6** bubble, cupola, mosque **7** ceiling

DOMESTIC: **4** maid **6** common, native **7** servant **8** homebred, homemade, tranquil **9** household **10** homeworker **13** chamberperson

DOMESTICATE: **4** tame **5** adapt, break, teach, train **6** master, subdue **9** habituate **10** housebreak, naturalize

DOMICILE: **3** pad **4** home **5** abode, house **6** castle, palace **8** dwelling **9** residence **10** habitation

DOMINANCE: **4** edge, rule **5** power **9** advantage, supremacy **10** ascendancy **11** superiority

DOMINANT: **5** bossy, chief **6** master **7** central, primary, regnant **8** despotic, foremost **9** ascendant, paramount, prevalent, principal **10** commanding, preeminent, prevailing **11** controlling, outweighing **12** preponderant **13** authoritative

DOMINATE: **4** rule **5** reign **6** direct, govern, manage **7** control, dictate **8** domineer **10** monopolize, overshadow

DOMINATION: **4** sway **5** might, power **7** command, mastery, tyranny **9** influence **10** prepotency, repression, subjection **11** sovereignty

DOMINEER: **4** boss, rule **5** bully **7** command, control, henpeck, oppress **8** bulldoze, dominate **9** tyrannize **10** intimidate

DOMINEERING: **6** lordly **8** arrogant, despotic, imperial, insolent **9** egotistic, imperious, masterful **10** autocratic, tyrannical **11** dictatorial, overbearing

DOMINICA:
capital: **6** Roseau
cities: **7** Marigot **10** Portsmouth
continent: **9** Caribbean **12** South America
ethnic groups: **5** Carib **7** African, mulatto
languages: **6** creole, French **7** English
monetary unit: **6** dollar
water: **9** Caribbean **11** Boiling Lake

DOMINICAN REPUBLIC:
capital: **12** Santo Domingo
continent: **14** Central America
features: **10** Cordillera, Pico Duarte
languages: **7** Spanish
monetary unit: **4** peso
water: **9** Caribbean

DOMINION: **4** land, rule, sway, turf **5** field, realm, right **6** domain, empire, sphere **7** command, control, kingdom **9** authority, bailiwick, ownership, privilege, supremacy, territory **10** ascendancy **11** sovereignty **12** jurisdiction

DOMINO: **4** game, mask **7** costume

DON: **4** wear **5** dress, put on, title, tutor **6** assume, clothe, take on **9** gentleman, professor **10** instructor

DONATE: **4** dole, give **5** award, grant **6** bestow, supply **7** present, provide **8** bequeath **10** contribute

DONATION: **4** alms, gift **6** relief **7** bequest, charity **8** offering **9** endowment **10** assistance **11** benefaction **12** contribution

DONE: **5** ready, spent **6** cooked, doomed **7** settled, through **8** depleted, finished, prepared, rendered **9** completed, concluded, exhausted **12** accomplished

DONE FOR: **4** dead, sunk **5** ended, goner, kaput **6** beaten, licked, ruined **7** wrecked **8** defeated

DONE IN: **4** beat **5** spent, tired **6** pooped **7** drained **8** frazzled, murdered **9** exhausted

DON JUAN: **5** lover, Romeo **6** suitor **8** Casanova **9** libertine, womanizer **10** profligate

DONKEY: **3** ass **4** fool, moke, mule **5** burro, jenny **7** jackass **8** imbecile, numskull

DONOR: **5** giver **6** backer, patron **7** donator **10** benefactor **11** contributor **12** humanitarian **14** philanthropist

DON QUIXOTE:
author: **17** Miguel de Cervantes
characters: **10** Pedro Perez **11** Sancho Panza **17** Dulcinea del Toboso
horse: **9** Rosinante

DOODLE: **4** dolt, draw **6** fiddle, putter, tinker **7** trifler **8** scribble

DOOHICKEY: **5** gizmo, thing **6** doodad, gadget, widget **7** trinket **11** thingamajig

DOOM: **4** damn, fate, ruin **5** curse, death **6** kismet **7** condemn, destine, destiny, fortune, statute, tragedy **8** calamity, decision, disaster, judgment, sentence **9** ordinance **10** predestine **11** destruction

DOOMED: **3** fey **5** fatal **7** forlorn **8** hopeless **9** abandoned

DOOR: **4** exit, gate **5** entry **6** egress, portal **7** barrier, opening, passage **8** entrance, hatchway **11** opportunity

DOPE: **4** drug, fool, news **5** dummy, dunce, facts, idiot, opium, scoop **6** heroin, opiate, uppers **7** cocaine, details, downers, lowdown **8** narcotic **9** marijuana, stimulant, substance **11** anesthetize

DOPEY: **4** dumb **5** dazed, silly **6** stupid, torpid **7** asinine, doltish, foolish **8** comatose, sluggish **9** lethargic

DOPPELGANGER: **5** ghost **6** double, spirit **10** apparition

DORMANT: **4** idle **5** quiet **6** asleep, latent, torpid **7** passive, resting **8** inactive, sleeping **9** quiescent, suspended, unaroused **10** motionless **11** hibernating

DORSUM: **4** back **9** posterior

DOSE: **4** dram, part, pill **5** slice **6** amount, potion, remedy **7** capsule, draught, measure **8** quantity, spoonful **12** prescription

DOT: **4** iota, mark, mote, spot **5** dowry, point, speck **6** period, pimple **7** freckle, speckle **8** particle, sprinkle

DOTAGE: **6** old age **8** senility **10** feebleness **11** decrepitude, elderliness

DOTE ON: **5** adore, fancy, spoil **6** admire, lavish, pamper, revere **7** idolize, indulge, worship **8** treasure

DOTING: **4** dear, fond **6** loving, struck **7** devoted, fatuous, serving **12** affectionate

DOTTY: **5** crazy, wacky **6** absurd, insane **8** enamored **9** eccentric **10** ridiculous, unbalanced **12** feebleminded

DOUBLE: **4** bend, copy, dual, fold, twin **5** clone, duple, twice **6** binary, binate, duplex, paired, second, wraith **7** enlarge, twofold **8** geminate, increase **9** duplicate **10** reciprocal, understudy **11** counterpart **12** doppelganger, impersonator

DOUBLE-CROSS: **5** cheat, trick **6** betray **7** deceive, defraud, mislead, swindle

DOUBLE-DEALING: **6** deceit, sneaky **7** devious **8** betrayal, disloyal, trickery **9** chicanery, dishonest, duplicity, treachery **12** hypocritical

DOUBLE ENTENDRE: **3** pun **8** innuendo **9** ambiguity **12** equivocation

DOUBLE-TALK: **4** bull, bunk, jazz **5** hokum **6** drivel **7** baloney, twaddle **8** nonsense **9** gibberish, rigmarole **10** balderdash **11** doublespeak

DOUBT: **4** fear **5** demur, qualm, waver **7** suspect **8** distrust, mistrust, question, unlikely **9** discredit, misgiving, skeptical, suspicion **10** difficulty, disbelieve, hesitation, indecision **11** uncertainty **12** apprehension

DOUBTER: **5** cynic **7** skeptic **8** agnostic **10** headshaker, unbeliever

DOUBTFUL: **4** hazy, iffy **5** shaky, vague **6** unsure **7** dubious, fearful, unclear **9** ambiguous, equivocal, uncertain, undecided **10** hesitating, improbable, irresolute, suspicious **11** distrustful, unconvinced **12** apprehensive, questionable, undetermined

DOUCEUR: **3** tip **4** gift **5** bonus, bribe **7** present **8** gratuity

DOUGH: **4** cash **5** bread, money **6** batter **7** cabbage

DOUGHNUT: **6** Danish, dunker, pastry, sinker **7** cruller

DOUGHTY: **4** bold **5** brave **6** heroic **7** awesome, valiant **8** fearless, intrepid **10** courageous **12** stouthearted

DOUR: **4** glum, grim, sour **5** bleak, stern **6** dismal, gloomy, morose, severe, sullen **9** cheerless, obstinate **10** forbidding, inflexible, unyielding

DOUSE: **4** doff, duck, dunk, soak **5** rinse, slosh **6** deluge, drench, plunge, splash **7** immerse, smother **8** downpour, saturate **10** extinguish

DOVETAIL: **4** jibe, join, mesh **5** agree, tally, tenon **7** combine, connect **9** harmonize, interlock **10** correspond

DOWAGER: **5** widow **6** matron **9** matriarch **12** elderly woman

DOWDY: **4** drab **5** dated, dingy, tacky **6** frumpy, homely, shabby, untidy **7** unkempt **8** slovenly **9** unstylish **10** antiquated, slatternly

DOWN: **4** blue, fell, fuzz, hill **5** below, drink, floor, level **6** defeat **7** destroy, plumage, unhappy **8** dejected, suppress **9** depressed, overthrow **10** dispirited, underneath **11** crestfallen

DOWN-AND-OUT: **5** broke, needy **6** beaten **7** outcast **9** destitute, penniless, prostrate **13** incapacitated

DOWNBEAT: **4** grim **5** bleak **8** inactive, negative, stagnant **9** cheerless **11** pessimistic

DOWNCAST: **3** low, sad **4** blue **5** moody **6** gloomy, morose **7** forlorn, unhappy **8** dejected **9** depressed, woebegone **10** chapfallen, dispirited, melancholy **11** discouraged **12** disheartened

DOWNER: **6** bummer **8** sedative **10** depressant **11** barbiturate, predicament

DOWNFALL: **4** drop, ruin **5** abyss, storm **6** deluge, shower, topple **7** atrophy, decline, descent, undoing **8** collapse, disgrace **10** cloudburst **11** destruction **12** degeneration **14** disintegration

DOWNGRADE: **4** bump, drop, hill **5** lower, pitch, slope **6** debase, demote, lessen, reduce **7** declass, decline, descent, devalue **8** belittle, decrease **9** denigrate **10** depreciate

DOWNHEARTED: **3** sad **4** blue **7** unhappy **8** dejected **9** depressed, woebegone **11** discouraged

DOWNLOAD: **4** move **6** unload **8** transfer

DOWNPOUR: **4** rain **5** flood **6** deluge, shower **7** monsoon **10** cloudburst

DOWNRIGHT: **4** open, pure, sure **5** blunt, frank, plain, stark **6** candid, direct, honest **7** utterly **8** absolute, complete, entirely, positive **10** aboveboard, absolutely, forthright, thoroughly **11** categorical, undisguised, unequivocal, unmitigated

DOWNSTAIRS: **5** below **6** cellar **8** basement

DOWN-TO-EARTH: **4** easy, nice **5** plain **6** casual, simple **8** sensible **9** practical, realistic **10** reasonable

DOWNTREND: **3** dip, sag **4** drop, fall, slip **5** slide, slump **6** plunge **7** decline, setback **8** downturn **9** downslide

DOWNY: **4** soft **5** light, nappy, quiet, silky **6** fluffy, placid **7** plumate **8** feathery, soothing

DOZE: **3** nap **5** sleep **6** catnap, drowse, siesta, snooze **7** slumber

DRAB: **4** dull, flat **5** bleak, dingy, faded, mousy, whore **6** boring, dismal, dreary **8** lifeless, slattern **9** cheerless, colorless **10** lackluster, monotonous, prostitute, uninspired **11** commonplace

DRACONIAN: **5** harsh **6** severe, strict

DRAFT: **4** gust, pick, plan, swig, toot, wind **5** drink, swill **6** breeze, design, devise, drench, induct, redact, sketch **7** compose, diagram, draught, drawing, lottery, outline, pattern, prepare, project, version **8** beverage **9** formulate, selection **12** registration

DRAG: **3** lug, tow, tug **4** bore, draw, haul, pull, road, yank **5** brake, crawl, delay **6** anchor, bother, bummer, burden, dredge, linger, loiter, search, street **7** schlepp **8** drawback, nuisance, tiresome **9** tediously **10** inhalation

DRAGON: **4** Puff **5** hydra **6** wyvern **7** monster **8** basilisk, quaviver, tarragon
slayer: **6** Cadmus, Sigurd **7** Beowulf, Perseus

DRAGOON: **6** coerce **7** soldier, trooper **8** pressure **9** persecute, subjugate **10** cavalryman, intimidate

DRAIN: **3** dry, sap **4** fade, leak, pipe, pour, pump, seep, sink, tire, tube **5** bleed, canal, empty, sewer, spout **6** burden, guzzle, outlet, siphon, trench, weaken **7** channel, deplete, dwindle, exhaust **8** aspirate, bankrupt **9** discharge **11** watercourse

DRAINED: **4** beat **5** spent, weary **6** bushed, devoid, pooped, used up **7** worn out **8** depleted

DRAM: **3** nip, sip **4** drop, mite, slug, swig **5** draft, drink **6** weight **7** measure, smidgen, snifter **8** quantity

DRAMA: **4** play, show **5** movie, opera **6** acting, climax **7** program, tension, theater, tragedy **8** conflict **10** excitement **11** composition

DRAMATIC: **5** stagy, vivid **6** moving, scenic **8** powerful, striking, thespian **9** emotional, thrilling **10** histrionic, theatrical **11** suspenseful **12** breathtaking

DRAMATIST: **6** author, writer **10** dramaturge, playwright

DRAPE: **3** don **4** deck, hang **5** adorn, cloak, cover, dress **6** clothe, dangle, enwrap, shroud, sprawl, swathe **7** curtain, suspend

DRASTIC: **4** dire, rash **5** harsh **6** severe **7** extreme, radical **9** dangerous, desperate

DRAW: **3** lug, tie, tow, tug **4** drag, earn, gain, haul, hook, lead, lure, pull **5** catch, charm, color, paint, trace, train **6** allure, deduce, depict, derive, design, entice, extend, induce, inhale, select, sketch **7** attract, compose, express, extract, portray **8** deadlock, standoff **9** allowance, captivate, delineate, influence, stalemate **10** attraction

DRAWBACK: **4** flaw **5** fault **6** refund **8** handicap, obstacle **9** detriment, hindrance **10** impediment **11** shortcoming **12** disadvantage

DRAW BACK: **6** flinch, recede, recoil **7** retreat, sheathe

DRAWERS: **5** pants **6** shorts **7** panties **8** bloomers **9** underwear **10** underpants

DRAWING: **3** art **4** plan **5** draft **6** doodle, sketch **7** cartoon, hauling, lottery, picture, pulling **8** graphics, magnetic **9** depiction **10** attracting, storyboard **11** captivating, delineation **12** illustration

DRAWING POWER: **4** lure, pull **6** appeal **9** magnetism **11** fascination

DRAWING ROOM: **5** salon **6** parlor **9** stateroom **13** reception room

DRAWL: **5** utter **6** accent, intone **8** lengthen, Southern

DRAWN: **3** wan **4** worn **5** tense, tired **6** sapped **7** haggard **8** fatigued, stressed

DRAW OFF: **4** pump **5** drain **6** siphon

DRAW ON: **5** cause **6** employ, prompt **8** approach, convince

DRAW OUT: **4** drag **5** educe **6** extend **7** attract, extract, stretch **8** lengthen, protract

DRAW UP: **4** halt **5** draft, write **7** compose, diagram, prepare **9** formulate

DRAY: **4** cart **5** wagon **7** vehicle

DREAD: **4** fear **5** alarm, panic **6** cringe, fright, horror, terror **7** anguish, anxiety, shudder **11** trepidation **12** apprehension

DREADFUL: **4** dire, grim **5** awful **6** grisly, tragic **7** ghastly, hideous **8** horrible, shocking, terrible **9** appalling, frightful, revolting **10** abominable, formidable, unpleasant **11** distasteful

DREADNOUGHT: **7** gunboat, warship **10** battleship

DREAM: **4** goal, hope, wish **5** fancy, ideal, image **6** desire, trance, vision **7** chimera, fantasy, reverie, surreal **8** illusion **9** nightmare **10** apparition, aspiration **11** expectation **13** hallucination

DREAMER: **7** fantast **8** idealist **9** visionary **10** ideologist **11** romanticist

DREAM UP: **6** create, invent **7** imagine **8** conceive

DREAMY: **4** airy, hazy, soft **5** great, ideal, super, vague **6** divine, serene, unreal **7** pensive, utopian **8** ethereal, romantic, soothing **9** beautiful, fantastic, marvelous **10** delightful **11** imaginative

DREARY: **3** sad **4** blah, damp, dull, glum **5** bleak **6** boring, dismal, gloomy, lonely, somber **7** doleful, forlorn **9** cheerless, sorrowful **10** depressing, melancholy, monotonous, oppressive **11** distressful

DREDGE: **3** dig, net **4** coat, drag, fish, sift **5** scoop **6** deepen **8** excavate

DREGS: **4** lees, scum **5** dross, slags, trash **6** rabble, refuse **7** deposit, grounds, residue **8** riffraff, sediment, settling

DRENCH: **3** wet **4** dose, dunk, hose, soak **5** douse, draft, drown, flood, souse, steep **6** deluge **7** immerse **8**

inundate, permeate, saturate, submerge, waterlog

DRESS: **3** don, tog **4** garb, gear, gown, robe **5** adorn, frock, getup, preen, primp, toile, train **6** attire, clothe, invest, outfit **7** apparel, clothes, garment, toggery **8** clothing, ornament, vestment **9** vestiture **10** habiliment **12** accouterment
law: **4** robe
religious: **4** robe **5** cloth

DRESS DOWN: **4** lash **5** scold **6** berate **7** upbraid **9** castigate, reprimand **10** tongue-lash

DRESSER: **5** chest **6** bureau **7** cabinet, commode **8** cupboard **10** chiffonier **14** chest of drawers

DRESSING: **5** gauze, sauce **7** bandage **8** stuffing **10** fertilizer

DRESSMAKER: **5** sewer **6** tailor **7** modiste **9** couturier **10** couturiere, seamstress

DRESS UP: **5** adorn, primp **6** clothe **7** enhance **9** embellish

DRESSY: **4** chic **5** fancy, showy, smart **6** classy, formal **7** elegant, stylish **11** fashionable

DRIBBLE: **4** drop, move **5** drool **6** bounce, slaver **7** fritter, slobber, trickle

DRIBLET: **3** bit **4** drip, tear **8** pittance

DRIFT: **4** dune, flow, tide, waft **5** amble, coast, float, flock, mosey, tenor, trend **6** course, design, linger, ramble, scheme, tunnel, wander **7** cluster, impulse, meander, meaning, purport **8** tendency **9** deviation, intention **12** accumulation

DRIFTER: **3** bum **4** hobo **5** tramp **6** roamer **7** vagrant **8** vagabond, wanderer

DRILL: **3** bit, hit **4** bore, tool **5** auger, borer, punch, teach, train, tutor **6** pierce, stoper **7** channel, workout **8** exercise, instruct, practice, puncture, rehearse **9** maneuvers, perforate **10** repetition

DRINK: **3** lap, sip, tea **4** brew, grog, gulp, shot, swig, tiff **5** booze, draft, punch, quaff, slurp, toast **6** absorb, chaser, coffee, guzzle, liquid, liquor, potion, salute **7** alcohol, carouse, consume, draught, potable, swallow **8** beverage, cocktail, highball, libation

DRINKER: **4** lush, wino **5** drunk, toper **6** bibber, boozer, sponge **7** imbiber, quaffer, tosspot **8** drunkard **9** alcoholic

DRIP: **4** bore, drop, jerk, leak, seep **5** exude, klutz **7** dribble, trickle

DRIVE: **3** run **4** bang, butt, goad, herd, move, push, ride, roll, spin, spur, urge **5** force, hurry, impel, pound, press, shove, stamp, surge, vigor **6** attack, compel, hammer, outing, plunge, propel, thrust **7** commute, impulse, operate, suggest **8** campaign, momentum **9** chauffeur, constrain, excursion, steamroll **10** initiative

DRIVE AWAY: **4** shoo **5** chase, deter, exile, repel **8** alienate

DRIVEL: **4** bunk, mush **6** babble, slaver **7** prating, rubbish, slobber, twaddle **8** nonsense **9** gibberish

DRIVER: **6** cabbie, cowboy, hackie, hammer, jockey, mallet **7** autoist **8** coachman, engineer, golf club, motorist, operator **9** chauffeur, propeller **10** charioteer

DRIZZLE: **4** mist, rain **5** spray **6** shower **8** sprinkle

DROLL: **3** odd **4** zany **5** comic, funny, queer **6** absurd **7** amusing, buffoon, comical, jocular, offbeat, strange **8** farcical, humorous **9** eccentric, laughable, ludicrous, whimsical **10** ridiculous

DRONE: **3** bee, bum **4** buzz, drum, slug **5** idler, leech, sound **6** bumble, lubber **7** bagpipe, humming, shirker, speaker **8** loiterer, parasite

DROOL: **4** gush **5** froth **6** desire, drivel, slaver **7** dribble, slobber **8** salivate

DROOP: **3** sag **4** bend, drop, fade, hang, sink, wilt **5** lower, slump, stoop **6** dangle, slouch, wither **7** decline **8** diminish, languish

DROP: **4** bead, blob, dash, down, drip, dump, fall, omit, plop, sack, shed, sink, stop **5** abyss, droop, knock, lower, slope, slump **6** fumble, plunge, unload **7** abandon, certain, descent, dismiss, dribble, forsake, globule, incline, plummet, release **8** collapse, decrease **9** terminate **10** relinquish **11** discontinue

DROP IN: **4** call **5** visit **6** arrive, stop by **8** come over, surprise

DROPLET: **4** bead, tear **7** globule

DROPOFF: **3** nod, sag **4** doze, slip **5** slide **6** snooze, unload **7** decline, deliver, dwindle, slacken

DROP OUT: **4** quit **5** leave **6** resign **8** withdraw

DROSS: **4** lees, scum **5** dregs, trash, waste **6** refuse, scoria, sinter **7** cinders, remains **8** impurity, sediment **9** recrement, worthless **11** commonplace

DROUGHT: **4** lack **6** dearth, thirst **7** aridity, dryness **8** scarcity, shortage

DROVE: **3** mob **4** herd **5** crowd, flock, horde, press, swarm **6** chisel **9** following **10** assemblage, collection

DROVER: **6** cowboy **7** cowpoke **8** shepherd

DROWN: **4** soak **5** flood, swamp **6** deluge, drench, muffle **7** immerse **8** inundate, submerge **9** overwhelm, suffocate

DROWSY: **4** dull, lazy **5** tired **6** sleepy, supine **7** lulling **8** comatose, indolent, listless, oscitant, sluggish **9** lethargic, somnolent, soporific

DRUB: **4** beat, drum, flay, flog, lick, whip **5** pound, stamp, throb **6** berate, defeat, pummel, thrash **7** belabor, instill, shellac **8** lambaste

DRUDGE: **4** grub, hack, moil, peon, plod **5** grind, labor, scrub, slave **6** menial, slavey, toiler **9** workhorse

DRUDGERY: **4** toil, work **5** chore, grind, labor **8** struggle **10** tedious job

DRUG: **3** LSD **4** acid, dope, numb, pill **5** crack, opium, upper **6** downer, heroin, opiate, peyote, poison **7** cocaine, generic, hashish, stupefy **8** medicine, narcotic, relaxant, sedative **9** analgesic, marijuana **10** medication **11** amphetamine, anesthetize, barbiturate, desensitize **12** hallucinogen, prescription **14** pharmaceutical

DRUGGED: **4** high **6** loaded, stoned, wasted, zonked **7** freaked **8** turned on **9** spaced out

DRUM: **3** keg, tap **4** beat, cask **5** bongo, drone, strum, tabor, throb **6** barrel, gather, tom-tom **7** capstan, pulsate, tambour, thunder, timbrel **8** cylinder **9** reiterate **10** instrument, tambourine

DRUNKARD: **3** sot **4** lush, soak, wino **5** souse, stiff, toper **6** barfly, bibber, boozer, sponge **7** drinker, tippler, tosspot **9** alcoholic, inebriate **11** dipsomaniac

DRUNKEN: **4** gone **5** tight, tipsy **6** buzzed, loaded, tanked, wasted **7** pickled, sloshed, totaled **8** groggied **9** plastered **10** inebriated **11** intoxicated

DRY: **4** arid, bare, dull, sere, wipe **5** baked, drain, droll, dusty, empty, towel, vapid, wizen **6** barren, biting, boring, harden **7** cynical, parched, sapless, thirsty **8** depleted, rainless, withered **9** dehydrate, desiccate, drinkless, fruitless, sarcastic, shriveled, waterless **10** dehumidify, evaporated, monotonous, siccaneous, teetotaler **11** xerothermic **12** moistureless, unproductive **13** uninteresting

DRY GOODS: **5** cloth **7** fabrics **8** clothing, textiles **9** soft goods

DRY RUN: **4** test **5** trial **8** maneuver **9** rehearsal

DRY UP: **4** sear **6** welter, wither **7** shrivel **9** dehydrate, desiccate, evaporate

DUAL: **4** twin **6** binary, double, duplex, paired **7** coupled, twofold **10** reciprocal

DUB: **4** call, copy, flub, muff, name, poke **5** botch, fluff, label **6** bestow, boggle, duffer, knight, thrust **7** baptize, bungler, entitle **8** nickname, rerecord **9** designate

DUBIOUS: **4** iffy **5** fishy, shady, shaky, vague **6** chancy, unsure **7** unclear **8** doubtful **9** ambiguous, equivocal, skeptical, uncertain, undecided **10** disputable, indecisive, suspicious **12** questionable, undetermined

DUCK: **4** teal **5** drake, eider, scaup **6** canard, peking, wigeon **7** dabbler, gadwall, mallard, pintail **8** duckling, mandarin, shelduck, shoveler **9** blackjack, merganser
group: **3** tea **4** sord **5** brood, skein
movement: **3** bob, bow **4** dive **5** avoid, dodge, evade, shirk **6** plunge **8** sidestep

DUCT: **3** vas **4** pipe, tube **5** canal, chute **6** outlet **7** channel, conduit, passage

DUCTILE: **4** soft **6** docile, pliant, supple **7** plastic, pliable **8** flexible, moldable, yielding **9** adaptable, compliant, malleable, tractable **10** manageable, responsive

DUD: **4** bomb, bust, drag, flop **5** lemon, loser **6** bummer, turkey **7** debacle, washout

DUDE: **3** fop **4** buck, chap **5** dandy, swell **6** fellow **7** coxcomb, hotshot **8** popinjay **12** clotheshorse **12** Beau Brummell

DUDGEON: **4** fury, huff, rage **5** anger, wrath **6** malice **7** umbrage **10** bitterness, irritation, resentment

DUDS: **4** garb, gear, togs **6** attire **7** apparel **8** clothing **10** belongings

DUE: **4** debt, owed **5** merit **6** earned, mature, proper, rights, unpaid **7** deserts, fitting, payable, revenge **8** adequate, becoming, deserved, directly, rightful, suitable **9** justified, scheduled **11** appropriate, collectible **12** attributable, compensation

DUEL: **4** spar **5** fence, fight, joust **6** combat, oppose **7** contest, dispute **8** conflict **10** engagement **15** affaire d'honneur

DUES: **3** fee, tax **4** ante, debt, duty, toll **7** payment **10** assessment, collection, initiation **12** contribution

DUET: **3** duo **4** pair **11** piece for two

DUFF: **4** coal **5** slack **7** pudding **8** buttocks

DUFFER: **3** dub **4** dope **5** dunce **7** peddler, useless **9** worthless **10** dullwitted **11** incompetent

DUGOUT: **4** boat, cave **5** canoe **6** cellar, hollow **7** foxhole, pirogue, shelter

DULCET: **4** soft **5** sweet **7** musical, tuneful **8** charming, pleasing, sonorous, soothing **9** agreeable, melodious **10** harmonious

DULL: **3** dim, dry **4** blah, down, drab, dumb, flat, gray, numb, slow, tame **5** banal, blind, blunt, dense, dingy, foggy, heavy, inert, murky, muted, prosy, stale, trite **6** boring, cloudy, common, deaden, dismal, dreary, drowsy, gloomy, miffle, obtuse, simple, square, stolid, stuffy, stupid, torpid, weaken **7** humdrum, insipid, prosaic, routine, shallow, tedious, vacuous **8** inactive, lifeless, listless, monotone, overcast, sluggish, stagnant, tiresome **9** apathetic, brainless, colorless, depressed, inanimate, lethargic, pointless **10** dispirited, insensible, lackluster, monotonous, pedestrian, uneventful, unexciting, uninspired **11** desensitize, insensitive, thickheaded **13** unimaginative

DULLARD: **4** boor, clod, dolt, fool **5** dummy, dunce, idiot, moron **6** dimwit, nitwit **8** dumbbell **9** simpleton

DULLNESS: **6** apathy, tedium, torpor **8** evenness, lethargy, monotony **9** bluntness, lassitude **13** insensibility

DULY: **6** justly **7** rightly **8** mannerly, properly, suitable **10** punctually **11** accordingly, befittingly **13** appropriately

DUMB: **3** mum **4** dull, mute **5** dense **6** silent, stupid **7** asinine, foolish, idiotic, moronic **8** ignorant, taciturn **9** senseless, voiceless **10** speechless **12** inarticulate **13** unintelligent, unintentional

DUMBBELL: **4** boob, dolt, dope, fool **5** clown, idiot, moron **6** nitwit **7** dullard **8** lunkhead **9** blockhead, ignoramus

DUMBFOUND: **4** daze, stun **5** amaze **6** boggle **7** confuse, perplex, stagger, startle **8** astonish, bewilder, surprise **9** overwhelm **11** flabbergast

DUMBFOUNDED: **5** agape **6** aghast **7** puzzled, shocked **8** overcome **9** astounded **10** speechless

DUMMY: **4** copy, doll, dolt, fake, fool **5** dunce, front, idiot, klutz **6** dimwit, effigy, puppet, stooge **9** ignoramus, imitation, mannequin, simpleton **10** substitute

DUMP: **4** beat, cast, drop, hole, junk **5** chuck, ditch, empty, hovel, scrap **6** pigsty, reject, unload **7** deposit, discard, eyesore **8** junkyard, transfer

DUMPY: **5** ninny, pudgy, short, squat, stout **6** stocky, stubby **9** shapeless **12** disreputable

DUNCE: **3** oaf **4** boob, dolt, dope, fool, goof, goon **5** chump, dummy, idiot **7** buffoon, jackass, jughead **8** bonehead, dumbbell, lunkhead, numskull **9** blockhead, ignoramus **10** dunderhead, hammerhead, nincompoop

DUNE: **4** bank, hill **5** ridge **8** sandbank

DUNGEON: **4** cell, jail **5** vault **6** donjon, prison **7** chamber **8** stockade **9** oubliette

DUNK: **3** dip **4** duck, slam, soak **5** douse, souse **6** drench **7** baptize, immerse **8** saturate, submerge

DUO: **4** duet, dyad, pair **5** combo **6** couple **7** twosome

DUPE: **3** con **4** bilk, fool, gull, hoax **5** cheat, chump, patsy, shaft, trick

6 baffle, betray, delude, pigeon, sucker, victim 7 deceive, mislead, swindle 8 flimflam, hoodwink, pushover 9 bamboozle

DUPLE: 3 two 4 dual 6 binary, double

DUPLICATE: 4 copy, echo, mate 5 alike, clone, ditto, spare 6 carbon, double, mirror, repeat 7 imitate, replica 8 parallel 9 facsimile, identical, photocopy, reproduce 10 transcript 11 counterpart

DUPLICITY: 5 fraud, guile 6 deceit 7 cunning, duality, perfidy, twofold 9 chicanery, deception, treachery 10 dishonesty 13 double-dealing

DURABILITY: 4 grit 7 stamina 9 constancy, endurance, fortitude 11 reliability

DURABLE: 5 hardy, tough 6 stable, staple, strong, sturdy 7 lasting 8 constant, enduring 9 permanent 10 dependable

DURATION: 3 run 4 span, term, time 6 length, period 7 stretch 8 lifetime 9 endurance, longevity 11 continuance, persistence

DURESS: 5 force 6 threat 8 coercion, pressure 9 captivity, detention 10 compulsion, constraint 11 confinement 12 stranglehold

DURING: 4 amid, when 5 midst, while 9 meanwhile 10 throughout

DUSK: 5 gloom 6 darken, sunset 7 evening, sundown 8 darkness, gloaming, twilight 9 nightfall

DUSKY: 3 dim 4 dark 5 bleak, murky, shady, tawny 6 cloudy, gloomy 7 obscure, shadowy, swarthy 8 blackish, overcast

DUST: 4 coat, dirt, film, sift, soot 5 ashes, clean, cover, earth, flour, strew 6 pollen, powder 7 eburine, remains, turmoil 8 sprinkle 9 agitation, commotion, confusion, particles

DUSTY: 3 dim, dry 4 arid 5 stale 6 chalky 7 unswept 8 timeworn

DUTIFUL: 5 loyal 6 devout, docile 8 faithful, obedient, reverent, trustful 9 complaint, compliant 10 obligatory, respectful 13 conscientious

DUTY: 3 job, tax 4 levy, onus, role, task, toll 5 chore, shift, stint 6 burden, charge, devoir, excise, office, pledge, tariff 7 calling, customs, mission, purpose, respect, service, station 8 function 9 objective 10 allegiance, assignment, obligation 11 undertaking 14 responsibility

DWARF: 3 elf 4 runt, tiny 5 gnome, pygmy, small, stunt, troll 6 bantam, goblin, midget, peanut, peewee 8 belittle, diminish, minimize, Tom Thumb 9 miniature, tower over 10 homunculus, leprechaun, overshadow 11 lilliputian

in Snow White: 3 Doc 5 Dopey, Happy 6 Grumpy, Sleepy, Sneezy 7 Bashful

DWELL: 4 harp, live, stay 5 abide, brood, delay, tarry 6 linger, occupy, remain, reside 7 inhabit 9 expatiate

DWELLING: 3 hut, pad 4 casa, flat, home, nest, tent 5 abode, cabin, condo, haunt, house, hovel, igloo, manor, tepee, villa 6 castle, chalet, duplex, palace, shanty 7 chateau, cottage, mansion, trailer 8 building, bungalow, domicile, tenement 9 apartment, residence 10 habitation

DWINDLE: 3 ebb 4 fade, wane 5 abate, waste 6 lessen, shrink 7 decline, shorten 8 decrease, diminish

DYE: 4 tint 5 color, imbue, shade, stain, tinge 6 litmus, ruddle, tracer 7 pigment 8 colorant, tincture

black: **9** lampblack, nigrosine
blue-violet: **4** anil, woad **6** indigo **7** cyanine **11** ultramarine
brown: **5** umber **6** bister, sienna
green: **5** sumac **8** viridian **10** terre-verte
red: **5** henna **6** kermes, madder, orcein **8** brazilin, cinnabar
white: **8** titanium
yellow-orange: **6** flavin, fustic **7** annatto, saffron

DYED-IN-THE-WOOL: **5** sworn **7** devoted **9** ingrained **13** thoroughgoing

DYING: **6** doomed **7** ceasing **8** expiring, moribund **9** dwindling, perishing

DYNAMIC: **5** vital **6** active **7** driving, intense, kinetic **8** forceful, vigorous **9** energetic **10** compelling **11** charismatic, influential, progressive

DYNAMITE: **3** TNT **5** blast **6** superb **7** destroy, shatter **8** demolish, exciting **9** explosive, wonderful **15** trinitrotoluene
inventor: **11** Alfred Nobel

DYNAMO: **4** doer **5** mover **7** hustler **8** go-getter **9** generator

DYNASTY: **4** rule **5** realm, reign **6** empire, regime **7** control **8** dominion **9** dominance, supremacy
British: **7** Windsor
Chinese: **4** Chou, Ming, Tang
Egyptian: **6** Hyksos
English: **4** York **5** Tudor **9** Lancaster
French: **6** Valois
German: **12** Hohenstaufen
Hellenic: **8** Seleucid
Italian: **5** Savoy
North African: **8** Fatimids
Portuguese: **4** Aviz
Russian: **7** Romanov
Turkish: **7** Ottoman

DYSPEPTIC: **4** mean **6** crabby, ornery **7** grouchy **9** irritable

DYSPHORIA: **7** anxiety **10** depression, melancholy **12** restlessness

E

EACH: **3** per **5** every **6** apiece **8** everyone, separate, specific **12** individually

EAGER: **4** agog, avid, keen **5** antsy, itchy, ready, sharp **6** ardent, intent **7** anxious, athirst, excited, fervent, intense, willing, zealous **8** desirous, restless, spirited, vigorous, yearning **9** impatient, impetuous **10** expectancy **11** hardworking **12** enthusiastic

EAGERNESS: **4** elan, zeal **5** ardor, gusto **6** fervor, hunger **7** avidity, urgency **8** alacrity, fervency **9** readiness **10** enthusiasm, impatience

EAGLE: **3** ern **4** crow, erne, gier, hawk **6** aquila, falcon, raptor **8** bateleur, pygargus
nest: **5** aerie, eyrie

EAR: **3** neb **4** drum, lobe **5** auris, pinna **6** concha, stapes **7** auricle, cochlea, stirrup **8** tympanum
doctor: **9** otologist
vegetable: **3** cob **5** caper, risom, spica, spici, spike **6** mealie, nubbin, rizzom

EARACHE: **7** otalgia

EARL: **4** lord, peer **7** British **8** nobleman
wife: **8** countess

EARLIER: **6** before, sooner **7** already **8** formerly, previous **9** preceding **10** beforehand

EARLY: **4** soon **5** first, prior **6** primal, timely **7** ancient, betimes, initial, nascent **8** advanced, immature, untimely **9** matutinal, premature, primitive **11** immediately **12** unexpectedly

EARMARK: **3** tag **4** band **5** label, stamp, trait **6** aspect **7** feature, quality **9** attribute, signature **11** distinction **14** identification

EARN: **3** get, net, win **4** gain, make, reap **5** clear, gross, merit **6** attain, obtain, profit **7** achieve, acquire, collect, deserve, procure, realize

EARNEST: **5** grave, sober, staid, token **6** ardent, honest, intent, sedate, solemn **7** devoted, serious, sincere, zealous **8** diligent, resolute **9** heartfelt **10** determined, meaningful **11** industrious **12** affectionate, wholehearted

EARNINGS: **3** pay **4** gate **5** wages **6** income, salary **7** profits **8** proceeds **9** dividends

EARSPLITTING: **4** loud **6** shrill **7** blaring **8** piercing **9** deafening

EARTH: **4** clay, dirt, land, loam, soil, turf, vale **5** globe, layer, loess, terra **6** ground, planet **7** topsoil **8** alluvium, telluric **10** terra firma **11** terrestrial
satellite: **4** moon
study: **7** geodesy, geology **9** geography

EARTHENWARE: **5** china, delft **7** biscuit, faience, pottery **8** ceramics, crockery, majolica **9** porcelain, stoneware

EARTHLY: **5** human **6** bodily, global, mortal **7** mundane, secular, worldly **8** material, physical, possible, telluric, temporal **10** imaginable **11** conceivable, terrestrial

EARTHQUAKE: **5** seism, shock **6** tremor **8** movement, trembler, upheaval **10** aftershock
center: **9** epicenter
detecting instrument: **11** seismograph
measuring device: **12** Richter scale
science: **10** seismology

EARTHWORK: **7** bulwark **10** embankment, excavation **13** fortification

EARTHY: **5** crude, gross **6** coarse, folksy, hearty, simple, vulgar **7** natural, obscene, worldly **8** indecent **9** practical, realistic, unrefined **11** terrestrial, uninhibited

EASE: **4** calm, inch, rest, snap **5** allay, guide, knack, quiet, relax **6** breeze, loosen, pacify, reduce, relief, smooth, soften, soothe **7** appease, comfort, content, faculty, freedom, leisure, liberty, lighten, relieve **8** diminish, facility, maneuver, mitigate, moderate, relieved, security, simplify, unburden **9** affluence, alleviate, composure, enjoyment, expertise, readiness **10** relaxation **11** comfortable, contentment, naturalness, tranquility **12** satisfaction

EASILY: **6** coolly, freely, simply **7** handily, readily **8** smoothly **9** certainly, decidedly **10** undeniably **11** indubitably **12** effortlessly

EAST: **4** Asia **6** Levant, Orient **7** sunrise

EASY: **4** calm, cozy, glib, mild, snap **5** basic, cinch, cushy, light **6** facile, gentle, secure, simple, smooth **7** amiable, lenient, natural, obvious, relaxed **8** carefree, careless, familiar, friendly, moderate, painless, tolerant, tranquil, unforced **9** compliant, tractable, unhurried **10** effortless, manageable **11** comfortable, complaisant, susceptible, unconcerned

EASYGOING: **4** calm **6** casual, placid **7** patient, relaxed **8** carefree, careless, composed, flexible **9** collected, unhurried **10** nonchalant, unaffected **12** happy-go-lucky

EAT: **4** bite, chow, dine, feed, fret, gnaw, rust **5** erode, feast, graze, lunch, munch, snack, taste **6** absorb, devour, dinner, forage, gobble, ingest, nibble, ravage, supper **7** banquet, consume, corrode, destroy, swallow **9** breakfast **10** gormandize

EATABLE: **6** edible, savory **8** esculent, tasteful **9** delicious, palatable, succulent **10** appetizing, comestible

EATING DISORDER: **7** bulimia **15** anorexia nervosa

EATING PLACE: **3** inn **4** cafe **5** diner, hotel **6** tavern **7** automat, beanery, drive-in, tea-room **8** mess hall, pizzeria **9** cafeteria, chophouse, lunchroom **10** restaurant **12** delicatessen, luncheonette

EAVESDROP: **3** bug, spy, tap **5** snoop **6** listen **7** wiretap **8** overhear

EBB: **4** sink, tide, wane **5** abate **6** recede, reflux, retire **7** decline, retreat, subside **8** decrease, diminish, languish, withdraw **10** diminution, regression

EBONY: **3** jet **4** inky, wood **5** black, raven

EBULLIENCE: **6** gaiety **7** elation, ferment, zestful **8** vitality **9** animation **10** enthusiasm, excitement, exuberance **12** exhilaration

EBULLIENT: **6** bouncy, joyous, lively **7** gushing **8** agitated, bubbling, ecstatic **11** overflowing **12** effervescent, high-spirited

ECCENTRIC: **3** odd **5** flaky, kooky, queer, weird **7** bizarre, erratic, offbeat, strange, unusual **8** abnormal, peculiar, singular **9** anomalous, character, irregular, quizzical, whimsical **10** capricious **13** nonconformist **14** unconventional

ECCENTRICITY: **5** quirk **6** oddity **9** deviation **10** aberration, hereticism **12** idiosyncrasy

ECCLESIASTIC: **4** abbe **5** abbot **6** cleric, divine, parson, pastor, priest **8** chaplain, minister, preacher, reverend **9** religious

ECDYSIAST: **8** stripper **11** stripteaser

ECHELON: **4** rank, tier **5** class, level **8** position **9** formation, hierarchy

ECHO: **4** ring **5** mimic **6** mirror, parrot, repeat, second **7** imitate, resound, revoice **8** response **9** duplicate, imitation, reiterate **11** impersonate, reverberate

ECLECTIC: **5** broad, mixed **6** choosy, varied **7** diverse, jumbled, mingled **8** assorted, combined **9** selective, universal **13** comprehensive, heterogeneous

ECLIPSE: **4** blot, hide, mask, veil **5** cloud, cover, outdo, shade, sully **6** darken, dazzle, exceed **7** conceal, obscure **9** transcend **10** extinguish, overshadow **11** obscuration

ECLOGUE: **4** idyl, poem **5** idyll **8** dialogue, pastoral

ECOLOGY: **7** science **9** bionomics

ECONOMIC: **8** material **9** efficient, financial **10** commercial, productive, profitable

ECONOMICAL: **5** chary, sound, tight **6** frugal, meager, modest **7** careful, prudent, sparing, thrifty **9** penurious, practical, provident **11** inexpensive

ECONOMICS: **4** bond, fund, loan **5** stock **6** credit, equity, system **7** futures **8** interest, treasury **9** arbitrage, deflation, inflation, plutonomy, portfolio, recession **10** management, securities **14** macroeconomics

ECONOMIZE: **3** eke **4** save **5** pinch, skimp **6** manage, scrape, scrimp **7** husband, squeeze **8** conserve, entrench

ECONOMY: **4** plan **6** saving, thrift **8** prudence **9** austerity, frugality **10** discretion

ECSTASY: **3** joy **5** bliss **6** heaven **7** delight, elation, rapture **8** euphoria, paradise, pleasure **9** happiness, transport **10** exaltation

ECSTATIC: **5** happy **6** dreamy **7** excited **9** delirious, enchanted, entranced, rhapsodic **10** enraptured

ECUADOR:
capital: **5** Quito
cities: **6** Cuenca, Tulcan **7** Salinas **9** Guayaquil

conqueror: **7** Pizarro
continent: **12** South America
ethnic groups: **6** Indian **7** African, mestizo, Spanish
features: **5** Andes **8** Antisana, Cotopaxi, Illiniza **14** Cordillera Real **16** Galapagos Islands, Mount Chimborazzo
languages: **7** Spanish **8** Jivaroan, Quechuan
monetary unit: **5** sucre
water: **6** Amazon, Guayas, Zamora

ECUMENICAL: **6** global **7** general, liberal **8** unifying **9** inclusive, planetary, universal, worldwide **12** cosmopolitan

ECZEMA: **4** rash **6** tetter **10** dermatitis **12** inflammation

EDDY: **4** turn **5** shift, swirl **6** gyrate, vortex **7** counter, current, reverse **9** maelstrom, whirlpool **14** countercurrent

EDEN: **5** bliss **6** garden, heaven, utopia **8** paradise **9** innocence
home of: **3** Eve **4** Adam

EDENTATE: **5** sloth **8** aardvark, anteater **9** armadillo, toothless

EDGE: **3** hem, rim **4** bank, brim, inch, line, side, trim, whet **5** bevel, blade, brink, crest, grind, ledge, sidle, verge **6** adjoin, border, flange, fringe, margin **7** keeness, molding, outline, selvage, sharpen, valance **8** boundary **9** advantage, perimeter, periphery, sharpness, threshold

EDGY: **5** tense **6** touchy, uneasy **7** anxious, jittery, nervous, uptight **8** restless **9** excitable, impatient, irritable

EDIBLE: **4** food **7** eatable **8** esculent **10** comestible, digestible

EDICT: **3** ban, law **4** bull, fiat, writ **5** order, ukase **6** decree, dictum, notice, ruling **7** command, mandate, program, statute **9** directive, enactment, ordinance **10** regulation **12** announcement, proclamation

EDIFICATION: **8** teaching **9** direction, education, knowledge **11** improvement **12** illumination **13** enlightenment

EDIFICE: **8** building, monument **9** cathedral, structure **10** skyscraper

EDIFY: **5** teach **6** inform, uplift **7** educate, elevate, improve **8** instruct **9** enlighten **10** illuminate

EDIT: **5** adapt, check, emend **6** censor, delete, modify, review, revise, reword, rework **7** compile, correct, prepare, publish, rewrite **8** copyread **9** proofread **10** bluepencil

EDITION: **4** copy, kind **5** issue **6** number, volume **7** version **8** printing **9** broadcast **10** impression

EDITOR: **6** writer **7** reviser **8** redactor **10** journalist

EDUCATE: **4** rear **5** coach, edify, teach, train **6** foster, inform, school **7** develop, explain **8** civilize, instruct **9** cultivate, enlighten **10** discipline **12** indoctrinate

EDUCATED: **4** bred **6** taught **7** learned **8** enriched, literate, nurtured **9** broadened **11** experienced **13** knowledgeable

EDUCATION: **5** study **8** breeding, learning, pedagogy, training, tutelage **9** erudition, schooling **10** background, discipline **14** apprenticeship
method: **8** Socratic **9** heuristic **10** Montessori

EDUCE: **5** evoke, wrest **6** arrive, deduce, derive, elicit, evolve **7** extract, procure **8** conclude

EERIE, EERY: **5** scary, weird **6** creepy, gloomy, spooky **7** bizarre, ghostly, macabre, ominous, strange, uncanny **8** eldritch **9** unearthly **10** mysterious **11** frightening **12** supernatural

EFFACE: **4** raze **5** erase **6** cancel, delete, remove **7** destroy, expunge **9** eliminate, eradicate **10** indistinct, obliterate

EFFECT: **4** make, mark **5** avail, cause, enact **6** impact, import, intent, invoke, result, sequel, upshot **7** achieve, acquire, conduce, emotion, execute, fulfill, operate, outcome, perform, produce, purport, realize, redound **8** complete, generate, initiate **9** advantage, influence **10** accomplish, expression, hypothesis, impression, phenomenon **11** consequence

EFFECTIVE: **4** able **5** valid **6** active, actual, causal, direct, moving, potent **7** capable, telling **8** adequate, forceful, powerful, striking, vigorous **9** competent, effectual, efficient, operative **10** persuasive, productive **11** efficacious, influential

EFFECTS: **5** goods **6** assets, things **8** chattels, movables, property **10** belongings **11** commodities, possessions

EFFECTUAL: **5** valid **6** potent, useful **7** capable **8** adequate **9** efficient, effective **10** fulfilling, functional **11** efficacious, influential, practicable **13** authoritative

EFFEMINATE: **4** soft, weak **5** sissy, timid **6** gentle, prissy **7** epicene, unmanly, womanly **8** feminine, womanish **9** sissified

EFFERVESCENT: **4** airy **5** fizzy, happy **6** breezy, bubbly, frothy, lively **7** buoyant, foaming, zestful **8** animated, bouncing, mirthful, spirited, volatile **9** ebullient, exuberant, vivacious **10** carbonated **12** enthusiastic

EFFETE: **5** spent **6** barren **7** drained, sterile **8** consumed, decadent **9** exhausted, infertile **10** unfruitful **12** unproductive

EFFICACIOUS: **5** valid **6** active, potent, useful **7** capable **8** forcible, powerful, vigorous, virtuous **9** effective, effectual, efficient, prevalent

EFFICIENT: **4** able **5** adept **6** expert **7** capable **8** economic, skillful **9** competent, effective, effectual, organized **10** productive **12** businesslike

EFFIGY: **5** dummy, image, model **6** figure **8** likeness **14** representation

EFFLORESCENCE: **4** rash **7** redness **8** anthesis, blooming **9** flowering, sprouting, unfolding **10** developing

EFFLUVIUM: **4** aura, odor **5** fumes, scent, smell, vapor, waste **7** exhaust **9** byproduct **10** exhalation

EFFLUX: **7** outflow **9** discharge, effluence, emanation

EFFORT: **3** try **4** push, task, toil, work **5** chore, drive, force, labor, pains, power, sweat, trial **6** battle, energy, strain, stress **7** arduous, attempt, trouble **8** endeavor, exercise, exertion, struggle **11** achievement, application, undertaking

EFFORTLESS: **4** easy, snap **6** facile, fluent, simple, smooth **7** flowing **8** graceful, painless

EFFRONTERY: **4** gall **5** brass, cheek, nerve **8** audacity, boldness, temerity **9** arrogance, brashness, hardihood, insolence, sassiness **10** brazenness **11** presumption

EFFULGENCE: **5** blaze **6** dazzle, luster **8** radiance, splendor **10** brightness, brilliance

EFFULGENT: **6** bright **7** beaming, glowing, radiant **8** luminous **11** resplendent

EFFUSIVE: **5** gushy **7** profuse **8** bubbling **9** ebullient, emotional, exuberant, talkative **10** expressive **11** overflowing **12** unrestrained **13** demonstrative

EFT: **4** newt **10** salamander

EGG: **4** food, goad, ovum, prod, seed, spur, urge **5** ovule, spawn **6** embryo, fellow, incite, person **9** encourage, instigate

parts: **4** yolk **5** shell **6** embryo **7** albumen, chalaza **8** air space, membrane, vitellus

EGGHEAD: **5** brain **8** highbrow **12** intellectual

EGG-SHAPED: **4** oval **5** ovoid **6** oblong **7** oviform, rounded **10** elliptical

EGO: **4** self **6** psyche **7** conceit **11** personality **10** self-esteem **13** individuality

EGOCENTRIC: **7** pompous **11** egotistical **12** megalomaniac, narcissistic **13** self-absorbed, self-centered

EGOTISM: **6** vanity **7** conceit **8** self-love **9** arrogance **10** narcissism **11** self-worship **12** boastfulness

EGOTISTIC: **4** vain **5** cocky **7** haughty, stuck-up **8** boastful, superior **9** conceited **11** opinionated, pretentious **12** self-admiring, self-centered, vainglorious

EGREGIOUS: **5** gross **7** blatant, extreme, heinous **8** flagrant, infamous, shocking **9** notorious, offensive **10** deplorable, outrageous **12** preposterous

EGRESS: **4** exit, vent **6** escape, outlet **7** doorway, passage **9** departure, emergence

EGYPT:

animals: **4** adda, apis, haje, ibis, lynx **5** bubal, genet, hyena, skink **6** jackal, jerboa, saluki, scarab, sicsac **7** gazelle **8** cerastes **9** ichneumon

boats: **5** baris **7** felucca **8** dahabeah

capital: **5** Cairo

cities: **4** Gaza, Giza, Qena, Said, Suez **5** Aswan, Asyut, Benha, Luxor, Tanta **6** Faiyum **7** Mansura, Memphis **10** Alexandria

cosmetic: **4** kohl

cotton: **4** pima

cross: **4** ankh

dancers: **4** alme **7** ghawazi **8** ghawazee

deserts: **6** Libyan **7** Arabian, Western

drinks: **4** bosa, boza **5** bozah **6** zythum

dynasty: **5** Saite **7** Ayyubid, Fatimid **8** Mameluke **9** Ptolemaic

ethnic groups: **4** Arab, Copt **5** Nilot **6** Nubian **7** Bedouin

Giza pyramids: **6** Cheops, Khafre **7** Menkure

goddesses: **3** Mut, Nut **4** Anta, Apet, Bast, Isis, Maat, Sati **5** Athor, Pakht **6** Sekhet **8** Nekhebet

gods: **3** Bes, Geb, Min, Set, Shu **4** Amen, Ptah, Seth **5** Ammon, Horus, Thoth **6** Amen-Ra, Anubis **7** Serapis

gulfs: **4** Suez **5** Aqaba

islands: **4** Roda **6** Philae **7** Shadwan

kings: **3** Tut **4** Fuad, Mena **5** Menes **6** Ramses **7** Ptolemy, Rameses **9** Amenhotep **11** Tutankhamen

lakes: **4** Edku **5** Qarun **6** Bitter, Nasser **7** Manzala **8** Burullus **11** Birket Qarun

languages: **6** Arabic, French **7** English

leaders: **5** Jawar, Pasha, Sadat **6** Fa-

rouk, Ismail, Nasser, Tawfig **7** Saladin
monarch: **7** pharaoh
monetary unit: **5** pound **7** piaster
months: **4** Apap, Tybi **5** Payni, Thoth **6** Choiak, Hathor, Mechir, Mesore, Paophi **7** Pachons **9** Phamenoth, Pharmuthi
monument: **7** obelisk
mountains: **5** Sinai, Uekia **6** Gharib, Nugrus
oasis: **4** Siwa **6** Dakhla, Kharga **7** Farafra **8** Bahariya
paper: **6** papyri **7** papyrus
peninsula: **5** Sinai **6** Pharos
plants: **3** kat **5** anise, calla, cumin, lotus **6** cummin, lentil
queens: **9** Cleopatra, Nefertiti, Nofretete **10** Hatshepsut, Hetepheres
rivers: **4** Bahr, Nile, Qena **7** Rosetta **8** Damietta
ruins: **5** Miroe, Tanis **6** Abydos, Karnak, Sphinx, Thebes **7** Memphis **8** Berenice **13** Valley of Kings, Valley of Tombs
seasons: **4** Ahet, Pert **5** Shemu
stone: **7** Rosetta
symbol: **3** uta **4** ankh, aten **5** lotus **6** scarab
temple: **4** Idfu **5** Edoon, Luxor, Thoth **6** Abydos, Karnak, Osiris **7** Dendera
tomb: **7** mastaba, pyramid
waterway: **9** Suez Canal
weights: **3** ket, oka **4** heml **5** artal, artel, deben, kerat **7** drachma, quintal
wind: **7** chamsin, khamsin, sirocco **8** skamseen

EIGHT-SIDED: **7** octagon **9** octagonal **10** octahedral, octahedron

EIGHTY-SIX (86): **5** eject **6** refuse **7** discard **8** throw out

EJACULATE: **4** call, howl, yell **5** eject, utter **7** exclaim **9** discharge

EJACULATION: **5** shout **6** bellow **9** utterance **11** exclamation

EJECT: **4** boot, cast, emit, jilt, oust, shun, spew, void **5** erupt, evict, expel, spurt, vomit **6** banish, bounce, disbar, remove **7** dismiss, exclude, extrude **8** disgorge **9** discharge, eighty-six, ejaculate, ostracize **10** dispossess

EKE: **4** also, fill **7** augment, husband, magnify, stretch **8** increase, lengthen **9** economize **10** supplement

ELABORATE: **5** fancy, plush **6** expand, flashy, ornate **7** clarify, comment, develop, elegant, enhance, explain **8** detailed, involved **9** embellish, intricate **11** complicated, painstaking

ELAN: **4** dash, zeal, zest **5** ardor, flair, gusto, style, verve, vigor **6** spirit **7** panache **9** eagerness **10** enthusiasm, liveliness

ELAPSE: **4** go by, pass, slip **5** glide **6** expire **9** transpire

ELASTIC: **6** bouncy, limber, pliant **7** buoyant, springy **8** flexible, stretchy, tolerant **9** expansive, resilient **10** rebounding

ELATE: **4** buoy, lift **5** cheer, exalt, raise **6** excite, please **7** delight, elevate, gladden, inflate, inspire **8** heighten **10** exhilarate

ELATED: **5** happy, proud **6** jovial, joyful **7** aroused, jocular **8** animated, ecstatic, jubilant, spirited **9** overjoyed

ELBOW: **4** bend, push **5** angle, joint, nudge, shove **6** jostle

ELBOWROOM: **4** room **5** range, space, sweep **6** leeway

ELDER: **4** head, tree **5** shrub **6** senior **7** oldster, veteran **8** ancestor, superior **9** matriarch, patriarch, presbyter **10** forefather

ELDERLY: **3** old **4** aged, gray **5** hoary **7** ancient **9** venerable **13** superannuated

ELECT: **4** call, name, pick, vote **6** assume, choose, decide, prefer, select **7** embrace **8** nominate **9** designate, determine, legislate

ELECTION: **6** choice, voting **7** primary **9** balloting **10** referendum **11** alternative

ELECTIVE: **8** optional **9** electoral, voluntary **11** constituent **13** discretionary

ELECTRIC: **6** static **8** magnetic
current: **6** direct **11** alternating
device: **3** arc **4** coil, core, fuse, plug **5** anode, diode, meter, motor **6** dynamo, switch **7** ammeter, battery, booster, cathode, circuit **8** resistor, rheostat **9** amplifier, capacitor, condenser, conductor, electrode, generator, rectifier, voltmeter **10** alternator **11** transformer **12** galvanometer **13** semiconductor **14** superconductor
unit: **3** amp **4** volt, watt **5** farad, henry **6** ampere **7** coulomb, siemens

ELECTRIFY: **4** jolt, stun **5** amaze **6** charge, dazzle, excite, thrill **7** amplify, astound, startle **8** astonish, energize **9** galvanize, stimulate

ELECTRON: **4** atom **17** subatomic particle

ELEEMOSYNARY: **10** benevolent, charitable, gratuitous **13** philanthropic

ELEGANCE: **5** class, grace, style, taste **6** beauty, luxury, polish **7** dignity **8** courtesy, grandeur, splendor, urbanity **10** concinnity, refinement **11** cultivation **12** gracefulness

ELEGANT: **4** chic, fine, posh **5** grand, swank **6** dainty, dapper, lavish, urbane **7** courtly, genteel, refined, stately, stylish **8** debonair, delicate, graceful, handsome, lapidary, majestic, polished, tasteful **9** beautiful, exquisite **10** attractive, cultivated **11** fashionable

ELEGY: **4** poem, song **5** dirge **6** lament, monody **7** requiem **8** threnody

ELEMENT: **3** air **4** fire, line **5** basic, earth, group, metal, plane, point, water **6** aspect, detail, domain, factor, matter, member **7** feature, quality **8** material, particle **9** component, essential, principle **10** ingredient **11** constituent, environment, fundamental
Periodic Table: **3** tin (Sn) **4** gold (Au), iron (Fe), lead (Pb), neon (Ne), zinc (Zn) **5** argon (Ar), boron (B), radon (Rn), xenon (Xe) **6** barium (Ba), carbon (C), cerium (Ce), cesium (cs), cobalt (Co), copper (Cu), curium (Cm), erbium (Er), helium (He), indium (In), iodine (I), nickel (Ni), osmium (Os), oxygen (O), radium (Ra), silver (Ag), sodium (Na), sulfur (S) **7** arsenic (As), bismuth (Bi), bromine (Br), cadmium (Cd), calcium (Ca), fermium (Fm), gallium (Ga), hafnium (Hf), holmium (Ho), iridium (Ir), krypton (Kr), lithium (Li), mercury (Hg), niobium (Nb), rhenium (Re), rhodium (Rh), silicon (Si), terbium (Tb), thorium (Th), thulium (Tm), uranium (U), yttrium (Y) **8** actinium (Ac), aluminum (Al), americum (Am), antimony (Sb), astatine (At), berylium (Be), chlorine (Cl), chromium (Cr), europium (Eu), fluorine (F), francium (Fr), hydrogen (H), lutecium (Lu), nitrogen (N), nobelium (No), platinum (Pt), polonium (Po), rubidium (Rb), samarium (Sm), scandium (Sc), selenium (Se), tantalum (Ta), thallium (Tl), tita-

nium (Ti), tungsten (W), vanadium (V) **9** berkelium (Bk), beryllium (Be), germanium (Ge), lanthanum (La), magnesium (Mg), manganese (Mn), neodymium (Nd), neptunium (Np), palladium (Pd), plutonium (Pu), potassium (K), ruthenium (Ru), strontium (Sr), tellurium (Te), ytterbium (Yb), zirconium (Zr) **10** dysprosium (Dy), gadolinium (Gd), lawrencium (Lr), molybdenum (Mo), phosphorus (P), promethium (Pm), technetium (Tc) **11** californium (Cf), einsteinium (Es), mendelevium (Md) **12** praseodymium (Pr), protactinium (Pa)

ELEMENTARY: **4** easy **5** basal, basic, crude, plain **6** simple **7** initial, primary **8** original **9** elemental, essential, primitive **10** rudimental, underlying **11** fundamental, preliminary

ELEPHANT: **4** boar **6** tusker **7** mammoth **8** mastodon **9** pachyderm
female: **3** cow
keeper: **6** mahout
male: **4** bull
young: **4** calf

ELEPHANTINE: **4** huge **6** clumsy, strong **7** immense, mammoth **8** colossal, enormous, gigantic, ungainly

ELEVATE: **4** lift, rise **5** boost, elate, erect, exalt, hoist, honor, raise **6** uphold, uplift **7** advance, dignify, enhance, glorify, improve, promote **8** heighten, idyllize **10** exhilarate

ELEVATED: **4** high, tall **5** great, lofty, noble, steep **6** aerial, elated, formal, raised **7** eminent, ethical **8** majestic, towering **9** dignified, prominent, righteous

ELEVATION: **3** top **4** hill, rise **5** ridge **6** ascent, height **8** altitude, eminence, mountain, platform **9** acclivity, promotion, sublimity **10** exaltation, prominence **11** advancement

ELEVATOR: **4** cage, lift, silo **5** hoist **10** dumbwaiter

ELF: **3** fay, hob, imp **4** pixy, puck **5** dwarf, fairy, gnome, nisse, pixie **6** goblin, kobold, sprite **7** brownie **10** leprechaun

ELFIN: **4** tiny **5** small **9** fairylike, sprightly **11** mischievous

ELICIT: **4** draw **5** educe, evoke, exact, wrest, wring **6** deduce, derive, entice, extort, induce **7** extract **8** bring out, discover

ELIDE: **4** omit, skip, slur **5** annul, erase **6** delete, ignore **7** abridge, curtail, nullify **9** eliminate **10** abbreviate

ELIGIBLE: **4** meet **6** fitted, worthy **8** entitled, suitable **9** available, competent, desirable, qualified **10** acceptable

ELIMINATE: **4** drop, omit, oust, sift **5** erase, expel, purge **6** banish, cancel, delete, except, ignore, remove **7** abolish, destroy, exclude, excrete, expunge **9** eradicate, liquidate **10** annihilate, disqualify

ELITE: **3** top **4** best **5** cream **6** choice, flower, gentry, select **7** quality, royalty, society, wealthy **9** blue blood, topflight **10** upper class, upper crust **11** aristocracy

ELIXIR: **5** tonic **6** potion, remedy **7** arcanum, cure-all, nostrum, panacea **8** medicine, solution **9** principle

ELK: **4** deer **5** moose **6** wapiti

ELLIPTICAL: **4** oval **5** ovate, ovoid **6** oblong **7** concise **8** abridged **9** egg-shaped

ELOCUTION: **6** speech **7** oratory **8** rhetoric **9** eloquence **10** expression **12** articulation

ELONGATE: **6** extend **7** prolong, stretch **8** lengthen, protract

ELOPE: **4** flee **6** run off **7** abscond, run away **10** go secretly

ELOQUENCE: **6** fervor **7** fluency, oratory **8** rhetoric **9** discourse, elocution **10** expression **12** articulation

ELOQUENT: **5** lofty, vivid **6** ardent, facund, fervid, moving, poetic **7** voluble **8** forceful **10** expressive, passionate, persuasive **11** impassioned

EL SALVADOR:
capital: **11** San Salvador
cities: **8** Santa Ana **9** San Miguel
continent: **14** Central America
ethnic groups: **6** Indian **7** Mestizo
features: **5** Mayan
languages: **7** Spanish
monetary unit: **5** colon
water: **7** Pacific

ELSE: **4** also, more **5** extra, other **7** besides, instead **9** different, otherwise **10** additional

ELSEWHERE: **4** away, gone **7** outside **8** formerly

ELUCIDATE: **5** clear **6** detail **7** clarify, explain, expound **8** describe **9** enlighten, interpret **10** illustrate

ELUDE: **4** duck, flee, foil, hide, slip **5** avoid, ditch, dodge, evade **6** baffle, escape, outwit **8** sidestep **9** frustrate

ELUSIVE: **4** eely, foxy, wily **5** cagey **6** subtle, tricky **7** cunning, evasive **8** fleeting, slippery **10** lubricious, mysterious

EMACIATED: **4** lean, thin **5** gaunt **6** sickly, skinny, wasted **7** scrawny, wizened **8** anorexic, famished, starving, underfed

EMANATE: **4** flow, stem **5** arise, issue **6** effuse, emerge, spring **7** proceed, radiate **8** initiate **9** discharge, originate

EMANCIPATE: **4** free **5** loose **7** manumit, release, unchain **8** liberate, unfetter **11** enfranchise, untrammeled

EMASCULATE: **3** fix **4** geld **5** alter **6** soften, weaken **8** castrate **10** devitalize

EMBALM: **4** wrap **6** freeze **7** perfume **8** preserve **11** immortalize

EMBANKMENT: **4** dike, fill, quay, wall **5** levee, mound **7** ravelin **9** banquette

EMBARGO: **3** ban **5** edict, order **7** barrier **8** blockade, blockage, stoppage **11** prohibition, restriction

EMBARK: **5** begin, board, enter, start **6** depart, engage, enlist, invest, launch **8** commence

EMBARRASS: **4** faze, stun **5** abash, annoy, shame, tease, upset **6** demean, rattle **7** chagrin, confuse, flummox, fluster, mortify, nonplus **8** bewilder, confound **9** discomfit, dumbfound **10** disconcert **11** contretemps

EMBARRASSMENT: **5** shame **6** unease **7** mistake, scandal **8** distress **9** confusion **10** discomfort, perplexity **11** awkwardness, humiliation **12** bewilderment, discomposure **13** mortification

EMBASSY: **5** envoy **7** mission **8** diplomat **9** consulate **10** ambassador, delegation

EMBATTLED: **5** beset **8** fighting, prepared **9** embroiled, fortified **10** crenelated

EMBEDDED: **5** fixed **6** nested **7** planted **8** enclosed, inserted **9** ingrained, installed **10** deep-seated, entrenched

EMBELLISH: **4** deck, gild, grim **5** adorn, color, dress, grace **6** bedeck, blazon, emboss, enrich, polish **7** apparel, enhance, garnish, magnify **8** beautify, brighten, decorate, ornament **9** elaborate, embroider **10** exaggerate

EMBER: **3** ash **4** coal, slag **5** brand **6** cinder

EMBEZZLE: **4** bilk **5** forge, steal **6** misuse, thieve **7** defraud, purloin, swindle **8** peculate **9** defalcate **14** misappropriate

EMBITTER: **4** sour **5** anger, upset **7** envenom **8** acerbate **9** acidulate, aggravate **10** exacerbate

EMBLEM: **4** arms, flag, logo, mace, sign **5** badge, crest, cross, image, motto, token **6** banner, colors, device, figure, symbol **7** scepter **8** allegory, colophon, insignia, monogram **9** trademark

EMBODIMENT: **6** avatar **7** epitome, example **9** inclusion **11** incarnation, integration, realization **13** manifestation **14** representation **15** personification

EMBODY: **4** fuse **5** blend, merge **6** absorb, mirror, typify **7** contain, embrace, include **8** coalesce, organize **9** actualize, incarnate, represent, symbolize **10** assimilate **11** incorporate, materialize

EMBOLDEN: **4** abet, spur **5** liven **6** excite **7** bolster, hearten, inspire, support **8** motivate **9** encourage, stimulate

EMBOSOM: **7** embrace, enclose **8** envelope, surround

EMBOSS: **5** adorn, carve, chase **7** engrave **8** decorate, ornament **9** embellish

EMBRACE: **3** hug **4** clip, fold, love **5** adopt, clasp, cling, grasp, reach **6** accept, caress, clinch, clutch, cradle, cuddle, embody, enfold, huddle **7** cherish, enclose, espouse, include, snuggle, squeeze, support, welcome **8** comprise, encircle **9** encompass **10** comprehend **11** incorporate

EMBROIDER: **3** sew **4** lace **5** adorn **6** overdo, stitch **8** beautify, decorate, ornament **9** dramatize, elaborate, embellish **10** exaggerate **11** romanticize

EMBROIDERY: **4** lace, purl **7** orphrey, tambour **8** applique, couching, smocking, tapestry **10** needlework **11** needlepoint

EMBROIL: **4** mire **6** muddle, tangle **7** confuse, involve **8** entangle **9** implicate **10** complicate

EMBROILMENT: **4** fray, spat, tiff **5** brawl, clash, fight **7** dispute, quarrel **8** argument, conflict, squabble **11** altercation

EMBRYO: **3** egg **4** germ, seed **5** fetus, ovule **8** organism

EMEND: **4** edit **6** better, redact, reform, revise **7** correct, improve, rectify

EMERALD: **5** beryl, color, green **8** gemstone

EMERGE: **4** dawn, loom, rise, show **5** arise, issue, surge **6** appear, arrive, evolve **7** develop, emanate, surface **11** materialize

EMERGENCY: **3** fix **5** pinch **6** crisis, crunch **7** squeeze, urgency **8** accident, exigency, juncture **10** flashpoint

EMERGENT: **6** rising, urgent **9** resulting

EMIGRANT: **5** alien **6** emigre **7** pilgrim, pioneer, refugee, settler **8** colonist **9** foreigner, immigrant

EMINENCE: **4** hill, note, rank, rise **5** bluff, honor, knoll **6** height, renown, summit **8** standing **9** elevation, greatness, loftiness **10** projection, prominence, promontory **11** distinction

EMINENT: **4** high **5** great, lofty, noble, noted **6** famous **7** exalted **8** dominant, glorious, imposing, renowned, towering **9** acclaimed, important, paramount, prominent **10** celebrated, formidable, noteworthy **11** illustrious, outstanding, prestigious **13** distinguished

EMIR: **5** ruler, title **6** leader, prince **8** governor **9** chieftain

EMISSARY: **5** agent, envoy **6** consul, deputy, legate **8** delegate **9** messenger **10** ambassador **12** intermediary **14** representative

EMISSION: **5** fumes **8** ejection, emitting, issuance **9** discharge, radiation

EMIT: **4** beam, cast, give, glow, pour, reek, send, vent **5** eject, expel, exude, issue, utter, voice **6** exhale, expire **7** emanate, express, radiate, release **8** transmit **9** discharge **10** disembogue

EMOLLIENT: **4** balm **5** salve **6** lotion **8** ointment, soothing **9** softening **10** mollifying

EMOLUMENT: **3** fee **4** wage **6** income, profit, salary **7** payment, stipend **8** earnings **10** recompense **12** compensation

EMOTION: **3** joy **4** fear, hate, love, pity **5** agony, anger, grief, pride, shame **6** relief, sorrow, warmth **7** anxiety, concern, despair, ecstasy, empathy, feeling, passion, remorse, sadness **8** jealousy, surprise **9** affection, agitation, happiness, sensation **10** melancholy **11** despondency, mental state **12** satisfaction

EMOTIONAL: **5** mushy, upset **6** moving, trauma **7** nervous **8** arousing, effusion, neurosis, stirring, touching **9** sensitive **10** distraught, hysterical, vulnerable **11** sentimental **12** heartwarming

EMOTIONLESS: **4** cold **5** staid **6** stolid **7** deadpan, distant, unmoved **8** reserved **9** apathetic, heartless, impassive, unfeeling **10** impersonal **11** indifferent

EMPATHY: **4** pity, ruth **7** insight, rapport **8** sympathy **10** compassion **11** sensitivity **13** understanding

EMPEROR: **4** czar, king **5** ruler **6** Caesar, kaiser, sultan **7** monarch **8** autocrat, dictator, imperial **9** sovereign

EMPHASIS: **5** focus **6** accent, stress, weight **8** strength **9** attention **10** importance, prominence

EMPHASIZE: **6** hammer **7** amplify, feature, impress **8** pinpoint **9** highlight, italicize, punctuate, reiterate, underline **10** accentuate, underscore

EMPHATIC: **6** marked **7** certain, decided, earnest **8** absolute, decisive, definite, distinct, explicit, forceful, positive, stressed **9** insistent **11** categorical, unequivocal

EMPIRE: **4** rule **5** realm, reign **6** domain **7** control, dynasty, kingdom **8** dominion **9** territory **10** federation **11** sovereignty

EMPIRE STATE: **7** New York

EMPIRICAL: **7** factual **8** provable **9** practical **10** verifiable **12** experimental, hypothetical **13** observational

EMPLOY: **3** use **4** hire **5** apply **6** bestow, engage, occupy, retain, supply **7** involve, operate, procure, service, utilize **8** exercise **10** manipulate

EMPLOYEE: **4** hand, help **6** worker **7** laborer **8** factotum **9** assistant, jobholder **10** apprentice

EMPLOYER: **4** boss, firm **5** owner **7** company, manager **8** business **11** corporation **12** entrepreneur, organization

EMPLOYMENT: **3** job, use **4** line, task, work **5** craft, trade, usage **7** calling **8** adoption, business, vocation **9** operation **10** occupation, profession **11** utilization

EMPORIUM: **4** mart, shop **5** store **6** bazaar, market **8** boutique, galleria **11** marketplace

EMPOWER: **5** allow, grant **6** enable, invest **7** entitle, license **8** delegate, deputize **9** authorize **10** commission

EMPRESS: **5** queen, ruler **7** czarina **8** maharani

EMPTINESS: **4** void **6** hunger, vacuum **7** vacancy **8** bareness **9** blankness, inanition **10** hollowness

EMPTY: **4** bare, dump, idle, pour, void **5** blank, clear, drain, expel **6** barren, devoid, unload, vacate **7** deplete, exhaust, release, vacuous **8** deserted, evacuate, starving **9** discharge, fruitless **10** unoccupied **11** meaningless

EMPTY-HEADED: **5** dizzy, silly, vapid **6** simple, stupid **7** fatuous, flighty **8** ignorant **9** brainless **14** featherbrained, scatterbrained

EMPYREAN: **3** sky **5** ether **6** cosmos **8** heavenly, paradise **9** celestial, firmament

EMULATE: **4** copy **5** equal, excel, rival **6** follow, strive **7** compete, contend, imitate

ENABLE: **5** allow, ready **6** permit **7** empower, entitle, prepare **8** activate **9** authorize **10** capacitate

ENACT: **4** pass **6** decree, effect, ratify **7** appoint, approve, execute, perform **8** proclaim **9** establish, legislate, personate, represent **10** constitute

ENACTMENT: **3** law **5** edict **6** decree **7** statute **9** ordinance, portrayal **10** regulation **14** representation

ENAMEL: **5** glaze, gloss, japan, paint **6** finish **7** coating, lacquer **9** cloisonne

ENAMORED: **6** loving **7** charmed, smitten **9** attracted, enchanted, entranced **10** captivated, enthralled, fascinated, infatuated

ENCAMP: **4** tent **6** billet, settle **7** bivouac, quarter

ENCEINTE: **7** gestate **8** pregnant **9** expecting **13** fortification

ENCHANT: **5** charm **6** allure, enamor **7** attract, bewitch, delight **8** enthrall **9** captivate, fascinate, hypnotize, mesmerize, spellbind

ENCHANTING: **7** winsome **8** charming **9** glamorous, ravishing, seductive, wonderful **10** delightful, intriguing

ENCIRCLE: **4** band, belt, loop, ring **5** fence, orbit **6** engird **7** contain, embrace, enclose, environ, wreathe **8** cincture, surround **9** encompass **12** circumscribe

ENCLOSE: **3** box, hem, pen **4** cage, coop, pale, wall **5** bound, fence, hedge, house **6** circle, corral, encase, enwrap, insert **7** contain, embosom, embrace, envelop, harness **8** blockade, comprise, conclude, encircle, imprison, surround **9** encompass **12** circumscribe

ENCLOSURE: **4** bawn, cell, cote, fold, trap, weir, yard, zone **5** court, crawl, fence, pound, stall

6 aviary, corral, garden, kennel, prison, runway **7** barrier, paddock **8** cincture, cloister, stockade **9** cofferdam, courtyard **10** quadrangle

ENCOMIUM: **6** eulogy, praise **7** tribute **8** accolade **9** laudation, panegyric **10** compliment, salutation **12** commendation

ENCOMPASS: **4** belt, clip, ring, span **5** beset **6** circle, embody, engird **7** achieve, contain, embrace, enclose, envelop, environ, include, involve **8** comprise, encircle, surround **9** circulate **10** circumvent, constitute **11** incorporate **12** circumscribe

ENCORE: **5** again **6** cheers, recall, repeat, return **10** repetition **12** reappearance

ENCOUNTER: **4** bout, espy, face, meet **5** brush, close, fight **6** action, affray, assail, attack, battle, combat, detect, oppose, suffer **7** address, affront, contest, dispute, undergo **8** conflict, confront, skirmish, struggle **9** collision **10** engagement, rendezvous

ENCOURAGE: **4** abet, back, help, push, spur **5** boost, cheer, rally **6** advise, assure, exhort, foster, incite, induce, uphold **7** advance, animate, applaud, bolster, comfort, confirm, console, forward, further, hearten, inspire, nurture, promote, restore, support, sustain **8** embolden, energize, inspirit, reassure **9** instigate, stimulate **10** strengthen

ENCOURAGEMENT: **4** hope, lift, push **5** faith **6** praise, relief **8** approval **9** incentive, patronage **10** confidence, motivation **11** reassurance

ENCROACH: **5** seize, usurp **6** invade, meddle **7** impinge, intrude **8** infringe, overstep, trespass **10** motivation

ENCUMBER: **3** tax **4** clog, load **5** beset **6** bother, burden, hamper, hinder, impede, saddle **7** oppress **8** entangle, handicap, obstruct, overload **9** embarrass **10** overburden

ENCYCLOPEDIC: **5** broad **7** general **8** complete, thorough **9** extensive, scholarly, universal **10** exhaustive **13** comprehensive

END: **3** aim, tip **4** butt, edge, goal, rump, stop, tail **5** cease, close, death, limit, omega, point, quash, scrap, sever **6** define, design, expire, finale, finish, period, result, upshot, windup **7** abolish, achieve, closure, extreme, lineman, outcome, purpose, remnant **8** boundary, complete, conclude, dissolve, finality, position, terminal **9** cessation, determine, extremity, intention, objective, remainder, terminate **10** completion, conclusion, expiration, extinction **11** achievement, culmination, destruction, discontinue **14** accomplishment

of the world: **8** doomsday **10** Armageddon **11** apocalyptic, eschatology

ENDANGER: **4** risk **6** chance, expose, hazard **7** imperil **8** threaten **10** compromise, jeopardize

ENDEARING: **5** sweet **7** lovable **8** charming, engaging **12** affectionate

ENDEAVOR: **3** aim, job **4** seek, work **5** exert, fling, labor, study **6** affair, effort, strife, strive **7** attempt, pursuit, venture **8** business, exertion, struggle, vocation **10** enterprise **11** undertaking

ENDED: **4** done, over **7** destroy, through **8** finished **9** completed

ENDLESS: **6** untold **7** eternal, forever **8** enduring, immortal, infinite **9** boundless, continual, perpetual, unceasing, unlimited **10** continuous, indefinite **11** everlasting, measureless **12** interminable **13** uninterrupted

ENDORSE: **4** back, okay, sign **5** bless, vouch **6** attest, pledge, second **7** approve, certify, support **8** advocate, notarize, validate **9** authorize, guarantee, recommend **11** countersign

ENDORSEMENT: **4** fiat **5** rider **7** backing **8** sanction **9** amendment, signature **10** acceptance **11** approbation **12** ratification

ENDOW: **4** fund, will **5** award, endue, equip, grant, leave **6** bestow, enrich, invest, supply **7** finance, furnish, provide, support **8** bequeath **10** contribute

ENDOWMENT: **4** gift **5** dower, dowry, trust **6** talent **7** ability, chantry, quality **8** aptitude, donation **10** foundation **11** inheritance

ENDURANCE: **5** pluck **7** stamina **8** capacity, patience, strength, tenacity, vitality **9** fortitude, hardihood, longevity, suffering, tolerance **10** durability **11** continuance, lastingness, persistence **12** perseverance

ENDURE: **4** bear, bide, last, live **5** abide, allow, brave, stand **6** remain, suffer **7** outlast, persist, prevail, stomach, survive, sustain, toughen, undergo, weather **8** continue, tolerate **9** withstand **10** strengthen

ENDURING: **5** sound **6** biding, sturdy **7** durable, eternal, lasting, staunch **8** stubborn **9** perennial, permanent, steadfast **10** continuing

ENEMY: **3** foe **5** rival **7** nemesis, opponent **9** adversary, combatant, detractor **10** antagonist

ENERGETIC: **4** fast, spry **5** brisk, peppy **6** active, hearty, lively, robust **7** charged, dynamic **8** forcible, tireless, vigorous **9** strenuous, vivacious **11** hardworking, industrious **12** enterprising, enthusiastic

ENERGIZE: **4** fuel **5** prime **7** animate **8** activate, vitalize **9** electrify, stimulate **10** invigorate

ENERGY: **3** pep, zip **4** bang, fuel, heat, zest **5** drive, force, juice, might, numen, power, solar, steam, vigor **6** atomic, effort, spirit **7** current, stamina, voltage **8** activity, friction, strength, vitality **9** fortitude **10** geothermal **11** electricity

ENERVATE: **3** sap **4** tire **5** drain **6** weaken **7** deplete, exhaust, fatigue **8** enfeeble **10** debilitate, devitalize

ENFANT TERRIBLE: **4** brat **5** scamp **6** rascal **7** hellion **12** trouble-maker **13** embarrassment

ENFEEBLE: **5** drain **6** impair, soften, weaken **7** cripple, deplete, disable, exhaust **8** enervate **9** attenuate **10** debilitate **12** incapacitate

ENFOLD: **3** hug **4** wrap **5** cover, drape **6** clutch, cuddle, encase, enwrap, swathe **7** embrace, enclose, envelop **8** encircle, surround

ENFORCE: **5** exact **6** coerce, compel, demand, impose, invoke, stress **7** execute, require, support **9** implement, prosecute **10** administer

ENFRANCHISE: **4** free **7** deliver, manumit **8** liberate **10** emancipate

ENGAGE: **4** book, hire, join, lock, mesh **5** agree, enter **6** absorb, arrest, battle, embark, employ, fasten, occupy, pledge, secure **7** betroth, conduce, engross, involve, promise, reserve **8** affiance, contract, entangle, interest, persuade **9** fascinate, interlock, undertake **11** participate

ENGAGEMENT: **3** gig, job, vow **4** date **5** fight, stint, tryst **6** affair, battle **7** booking, contest, meeting **8** skirmish **9** betrothal, encounter **10** commitment, employment, rendezvous **11** appointment, assignation, involvement

ENGAGING: **5** sweet **7** likable **8** charming, pleasant **10** attractive **11** captivating, fascinating, interesting

ENGENDER: **5** beget, breed, cause **6** create, excite, incite **7** develop, produce **8** generate **9** cultivate, originate, procreate, propagate

ENGINE: **3** ion, jet, ram **4** beam **5** motor, steam **6** bypass, diesel, donkey, plasma, radial, ramjet, wankel **7** booster, Lenoir's, turbine, vernier **8** gasoline, internal, Newcomen, outboard, thruster, turbojet **9** induction, sustainer, turboprop **10** combustion, locomotive **11** retrorocket, synchronous **13** fuel injection

ENGINEER: **4** plan **5** pilot **6** driver, manage **7** arrange, builder, operate, planner **8** contrive, designer, inventor, maneuver **9** conductor, construct, negotiate **10** manipulate **11** constructor, motorperson

ENGLAND:
air force: **3** RAF
also called: **6** Albion **7** Britain **9** Britannia **12** Great Britain **13** United Kingdom
artists: **4** Opie **6** Romney, Turner **7** Hogarth, Millais, Poynter **8** Reynolds **9** Constable **12** Gainsborough
bed: **4** doss
capital: **6** London
channels: **6** Solent **7** Bristol, English **8** Spithead
china: **5** Spode **8** Wedgwood
cities: **4** Bath, Hull, York **5** Dover, Leeds **6** Exeter, Oldham, Oxford **7** Bristol, Chelsea, Croydon, Ipswich, Preston, Reading **8** Brighton, Coventry **9** Greenwich, Liverpool, Newcastle, Sheffield **10** Birmingham, Manchester
conservative: **4** Tory
continent: **6** Europe
counties: **4** Avon, Kent **5** Devon, Essex, Salop **6** Dorset, Durham, Surrey, Sussex **7** Cambria, Norfolk, Suffolk **8** Cheshire, Cornwall, Hereford, Somerset **9** Cleveland, Hampshire, Wiltshire, Worcester, Yorkshire **10** Derbyshire, East Sussex, Humberside, Lancashire, West Sussex **11** Oxfordshire, Tyne and Wear **12** Bedfordshire, Lincolnshire, Warwickshire, West Midlands **13** Hertfordshire, Staffordshire
explorers: **4** Cook, Ross **5** Cabot, Drake, Scott **6** Hudson
features: **6** Big Ben **10** Stonehenge **12** Hadrian's Wall **14** Madame Tussauds **16** Piccadilly Circus
forests: **5** Arden **6** Exmoor **8** Dartmoor, Sherwood
invaders: **4** Dane **5** Norse, Roman, Saxon **6** Norman
islands: **3** Man **4** Holy **5** Farne, Lundy, Wight **6** Coquet, Mersea, Scilly, Thanet, Tresco, Walney **7** Bardsey, Channel, Hayling, Ireland, Sheppey **8** Anglesea, Foulness, Grasmere, Holyhead
kings: **3** Hal **4** Bran, Brut, Cnut, Cole, John, Lear **5** Brunt, Henry, James, Sweyn **6** Alfred, Arthur, Canute, Edmund, Edward, Eg-

bert, George, Harold **7** Charles, Richard, Stephen, William
lakes: **8** Coniston **9** Ullswater **10** Windermere
languages: **7** English
monetary unit: **5** pound
mountains: **5** Black **7** Scafell, Snowdon **8** Cambrian, Cumbrian **9** Cotswolds, Cross Fell
nobility titles: **4** dame, duke, earl, king, lady, lord, peer **5** baron, noble, queen **6** knight, prince **7** baronet, duchess, marquis **8** baroness, countess, marquess, princess, viscount **11** marchioness, viscountess
people: **4** Celt, Jute, Pict **5** Angle, Saxon **6** Briton, Norman, Viking **8** Norseman
pertaining to: **6** Briton **7** British, English **8** Anglican **10** Anglophile, Anglo-Saxon
pirates: **4** Kidd **5** Drake **6** Morgan **7** Hawkins
political parties: **4** Tory, Whig **7** Liberal **8** Laborite **9** Labourite **12** Conservative
queens: **4** Anne, Bess, Jane, Mary **8** Victoria **9** Catherine, Elizabeth, Guinevere
rivers: **3** Cam, Dee, Don, Esk, Exe, Lea, Ure, Wye **4** Aire, Avon, Eden, Foss, Hull, Lune, Nene, Ouse, Tyne **5** Stour, Trent, Tweed **6** Humber, Kennet, Mersey, Severn, Thames **7** Derwent, Welland **9** Yorkshire
royal houses: **4** York **5** Tudor **6** Stuart **7** Hanover, Windsor **9** Lancaster **11** Plantagenet
schools: **4** Eton **5** Leeds, Rugby **6** Exeter, London, Oxford **9** Cambridge
soldier: **5** tommy **7** redcoat **8** fusilier
statesmen: **4** Eden, Grey, Lamb, Peel, Pitt **5** Heath **6** Attlee, Wilson **7** Asquith, Baldwin, Canning, Spencer, Walpole **8** Disraeli, Stanhope, Thatcher **9** Cavendish, Churchill, Gladstone, Grenville, MacDonald, Macmillan **10** Wellington **11** Chamberlain, Lloyd George
water: **4** Aire, Avon, Hull, Tyne **5** Trent **6** Mersey, Severn, Thames **8** Atlantic **14** English Channel
writers: **4** Bede, Hume, Shaw **5** Auden, Bacon, Byron, Defoe, Eliot, Hardy, Joyce, Keats, Swift, Waugh, Wilde, Woolf **6** Austen, Bronte, Bunyan, Conrad, Dryden, Huxley, Milton **7** Boswell, Chaucer, Dickens, Johnson, Kipling, Marlowe, Shelley **8** Browning, Fielding, Tennyson **9** Coleridge **10** Wordsworth **11** Shakespeare

ENGRAVE: **3** cut **4** etch, mark **5** carve, chase, print, stamp **6** chisel **7** impress, imprint, stipple **8** inscribe, ornament **9** sculpture

ENGRAVING: **5** cameo **7** enchase, glyptic **8** drypoint, intaglio **9** cerograph, mezzotint, xylograph **11** hyalography, stylography

ENGROSS: **4** grip, hold **6** absorb, engage, occupy **7** consume, immerse **8** enthrall, submerge **9** captivate, fascinate, preoccupy **10** monopolize

ENGULF: **4** bury **5** drown, flood, swamp **6** deluge **7** consume, swallow **8** inundate, overflow, submerge **9** overwhelm

ENHANCE: **4** lift **5** raise **6** deepen **7** amplify, augment, elevate, enlarge, improve, magnify, sharpen **8** beautify, heighten, increase **9** embellish, intensify **10** exaggerate

ENIGMA: **4** crux **6** riddle, secret **7** mystery, problem **8** puzzling **9** conundrum **12** inexplicable

ENIGMATIC: **7** cryptic, elusive, obscure **8** baffling, mystical **9** ambiguous, equivocal, recondite **10** perplexing **12** inexplicable

ENJOIN: **3** ban, bid **4** deny **5** order **6** decree, direct, forbid, impose, outlaw **7** command **8** admonish, prohibit, restrict

ENJOY: **3** own **4** have, like **5** fancy, savor **6** relish **7** benefit, command, possess **10** appreciate **11** pleasurable

ENJOYMENT: **3** fun **4** zest **5** gusto **6** liking, relish **7** delight **8** felicity, pleasure **9** amusement, happiness, merriment **10** possession, recreation **11** delectation **12** satisfaction **13** entertainment

ENLARGE: **3** add **4** grow, ream **5** boost, swell, widen **6** dilate, expand, extend, fatten, spread **7** amplify, augment, broaden, develop, enhance, greaten, inflate, magnify, stretch **8** increase, lengthen, multiply **9** elaborate, expatiate, intumesce **10** aggrandize, exaggerate

ENLARGEMENT: **6** growth **8** addition **9** accretion, expansion, extension **10** elongation **13** magnification

ENLIGHTEN: **5** edify, guide, teach **6** advise, inform, preach, uplift **7** apprise, educate **8** disclose, instruct **10** illuminate

ENLIGHTENMENT: **5** bodhi, truth **6** wisdom **7** insight, nirvana **9** awareness, knowledge **13** understanding

ENLIST: **4** hire, join **5** draft, enter, serve **6** employ, engage, enroll, induct, secure **7** recruit **8** register **9** volunteer

ENLIVEN: **4** warm **5** cheer, renew, rouse, spice **6** excite, revive **7** animate, inspire, refresh **8** brighten, vitalize **9** stimulate **10** exhilarate, invigorate, rejuvenate

EN MASSE: **7** jointly **8** as a group, ensemble, in a group, together **11** all together

ENMESH: **4** trap **5** catch, snare **7** involve, trammel **8** entangle **9** implicate

ENMITY: **5** spite **6** animus, hatred, malice, rancor **7** dislike **8** acrimony, aversion, loathing **9** animosity, antipathy, hostility **10** antagonism, bitterness, resentment **11** malevolence

ENNUI: **5** blues **6** apathy, tedium **7** boredom, fatigue, languor **8** doldrums **9** lassitude, weariness **10** melancholy **12** listlessness **15** dissatisfaction

ENORMITY: **8** evilness **9** depravity, immensity **10** wickedness **11** abomination, heinousness, massiveness, monstrosity **12** horribleness

ENORMOUS: **4** huge, vast **5** great, large **7** immense, mammoth, massive, titanic **8** abnormal, behemoth, colossal, gigantic **9** excessive, herculean, monstrous **10** gargantuan, stupendous, tremendous **11** elephantine

ENOUGH: **4** very **5** ample, fully, quite **6** fairly, plenty **8** adequate, passably, suitable **9** tolerably **10** acceptable, sufficient **12** satisfactory

ENRAGE: **5** anger, annoy **6** incite, madden, needle **7** incense, inflame, provoke **9** infuriate **10** exasperate

ENRAPTURE: **5** charm **6** allure, please, ravish, thrill **7** bewitch, delight, enchant **8** enthrall, entrance **9** captivate, fascinate, spellbind, transport

ENRICH: **5** adorn **6** fatten **7** augment, enhance, improve, upgrade **8** decorate, ornament **9** embellish, fertilize **10** ameliorate, supplement

ENROLL: **4** join, list **5** enter **6** accept, enlist, induct, record **7** engross, recruit **8** inscribe, register **9** subscribe **11** matriculate

EN ROUTE: **5** bound **6** midway **8** on the way **9** on the road, traveling

ENSCONCE: **4** hide **5** cover, embed, stash **6** nestle, settle, shield **7** conceal **9** establish

ENSEMBLE: **4** band, suit **5** getup, group **6** outfit, troupe **7** company, costume **9** aggregate, gathering **10** altogether, collection

ENSHRINE: **7** cherish, idolize **8** sanctify **10** consecrate

ENSIGN: **4** flag, rank, sign **5** title **6** banner, symbol **7** officer, pennant **8** gonfalon, insignia, standard **9** oriflamme

ENSILED: **5** alone, apart **8** isolated, solitary **9** separated **10** segregated

ENSLAVE: **5** chain **7** capture, oppress, shackle **8** imprison, suppress **9** subjugate

ENSLAVEMENT: **7** bondage, serfdom, slavery **9** servitude, thralldom

ENSNARE: **4** hook, mesh, snag, trap **5** catch, snarl **6** enmesh, entrap **7** capture, springe **8** entangle

ENSUE: **4** flow, stem **6** appear, follow, result **7** emanate, proceed

ENSUING: **4** next **5** after, later **9** resultant **10** subsequent, succeeding

ENSURE: **5** guard **6** assure, clinch, secure **7** certify, protect **9** guarantee, safeguard

ENTAIL: **5** cause, evoke **6** bestow, demand, impose **7** involve, require **9** encompass **11** necessitate

ENTANGLE: **4** knot, mesh, mire, trap **5** catch, ravel, snare, snarl, twist **6** enmesh, entrap, impede, muddle, puzzle **7** confuse, embroil, ensnarl, entwine, involve, perplex **8** bewilder **9** embarrass, implicate **10** complicate, intertwine

ENTANGLEMENT: **3** web **4** knot, maze **6** affair, jumble **7** liaison, problem **8** intrigue, obstacle **10** difficulty

ENTENTE: **6** accord, treaty **7** harmony **8** alliance **9** agreement, coalition

ENTER: **4** come, join, list, post **5** admit, begin **6** appear, arrive, engage, enlist, enroll, insert, invade, irrupt, pierce, record, submit **7** intrude **8** initiate, inscribe, register, trespass **9** introduce, penetrate **10** infiltrate

ENTERPRISE: **4** firm, push, zeal **5** cause, drive, vigor **6** action, effort, spirit **7** attempt, company, courage, project, pursuit, venture **8** boldness, business, campaign, endeavor **9** adventure, operation **10** initiative **11** undertaking

ENTERPRISING: **4** bold, busy **5** alert **6** active, daring **7** driving **8** aspiring **9** ambitious, energetic **10** aggressive, courageous **11** hardworking, industrious **12** enthusiastic

ENTERTAIN: **4** dine, host **5** amuse, treat **6** divert, harbor, occupy, ponder, regale **7** beguile, comfort, receive **8** consider **9** stimulate **11** contemplate

ENTERTAINER: **4** geek, host, mime **5** actor, emcee **6** artist, dancer, player, singer **7** actress, hostess, juggler, trouper **8** comedian, magician, minstrel, musician **9** performer **10** comedienne, troubadour **13** contortionist, ventriloquist

ENTERTAINMENT: **4** fair, gala, play, show **5** cheer, feast, hobby, opera, party, revue, sport, treat **7** banquet, concert, pastime **8** function, pleasure **9** amusement, diversion, enjoyment, festivity, merriment, reception **10** recreation **11** celebration, performance **12** extravaganza

ENTHRALL: **4** hold, hook **5** charm **6** absorb, thrill **7** enchant, enslave **8** intrigue **9** captivate, enrapture, fascinate, mesmerize, spellbind, subjugate

ENTHUSIASM: **4** elan, fire, love, zeal, zest **5** ardor, mania, verve **6** energy, fervor, kindle, spirit **7** passion **8** devotion, vivacity **9** eagerness, intensity **10** excitement, exuberance, fanaticism

ENTHUSIAST: **3** fan, nut **4** buff **5** lover **6** maniac, rooter **7** admirer, devotee, fanatic **8** follower, optimist **9** supporter **10** aficionado

ENTHUSIASTIC: **4** avid, keen **5** eager, rabid **6** ardent, gung ho **8** obsessed **9** ebullient, emotional, rhapsodic **10** interested **12** wholehearted

ENTICE: **4** bait, coax, lure, wile **5** charm, tempt **6** allure, cajole, incite, induce, invite, seduce **7** attract, solicit, wheedle **8** inveigle, persuade **9** fascinate

ENTIRE: **3** all **4** full **5** every, gross, sound, total, uncut, whole **6** choate, intact **7** perfect, plenary **8** absolute, complete, integral, thorough, unbroken, unmarred **9** undivided **10** unimpaired **12** undiminished

ENTIRELY: **4** only **5** alone, quite **6** solely **7** utterly **10** altogether, reservedly **11** exclusively, undividedly

ENTITLE: **3** dub **4** call, name, term **5** allow, label **6** enable, permit **7** appoint, empower, qualify **8** nominate **9** authorize, designate

ENTITY: **4** body, unit **5** being **6** matter **7** essence **8** material, presence **9** existence, structure, substance **10** individual

ENTOMB: **4** bury **5** cover, inter, inurn **6** inhume **7** confine **9** sepulture

ENTOURAGE: **5** staff, train **6** escort **7** retinue **8** groupies **9** following, retainers **10** associates, attendants, companions, procession

ENTRANCE: **4** adit, door, gate, hall **5** charm, debut, foyer, lobby, mouth **6** access, portal, ravish **7** delight, doorway, gateway, hallway, ingress, opening **8** approach **9** admission, beginning, captivate, enrapture, fascinate, hypnotize, induction, mesmerize, threshold, vestibule **10** admittance, appearance **12** introduction

ENTRANT: **6** player **9** candidate **10** competitor, contestant **11** participant

ENTRAP: **4** bait, hook, lure, nail **5** catch, decoy, snare, tempt **6** allure, ambush **7** beguile, capture **8** entangle, inveigle

ENTREAT: **3** ask, beg **4** coax, pray, seek **5** crave, plead **6** adjure, appeal, exhort, invoke **7** beseech, conjure, implore, request, solicit **8** persuade, petition **9** importune **10** supplicate

ENTREE: **4** dish **5** entry **6** access **8** entrance **9** admission, induction **10** admittance, main course

ENTRENCH: **3** fix **5** embed **6** anchor, invade **7** fortify, implant, ingrain, protect **8** infringe, trespass **9** establish

ENTREPRENEUR: **7** manager **8** employer, operator **9** executive, organizer **11** enterpriser **14** businessperson

ENTRUST: **4** give **6** assign, commit, depend, permit **7** commend, confide, consign, deposit **8** delegate, encharge **9** authorize

ENTRY: **4** adit, door, item, memo, note **5** foyer, lobby **6** access, entree, record **7** account, ingress, opening, passage **8** entrance, register **9** candidate, vestibule **10** adjustment, contestant, passageway **11** participant

ENTWINE: **4** coil, lace, wind **5** braid, twist, weave **6** spiral **8** encircle **9** interlace **10** interweave

ENUMERATE: **4** list, tell **5** count, tally, total **6** detail, figure, number, recite, reckon **7** catalog, compute, itemize, recount **8** estimate **9** calculate

ENUNCIATE: **5** speak, state, voice **6** intone **7** declare, express **8** announce, proclaim, vocalize **9** pronounce **10** articulate

ENVELOP: **4** cage, hide, mask, veil **5** cloak, cover **6** cocoon, encase, enfold, engulf, enwrap, sheath, shroud, swathe **7** blanket, conceal, enclose, environ, swaddle **8** surround **9** encompass

ENVELOPE: **5** pouch, shell **6** jacket, pocket **7** wrapper **8** covering

ENVIOUS: **5** green **6** greedy **7** jealous **8** covetous, spiteful **9** resentful **10** begrudging

ENVIRON: **5** fence, limit **7** enclose, envelop **8** encircle, surround **9** encompass **12** circumscribe

ENVIRONMENT: **6** medium, milieu **7** climate, element, setting, terrain **8** ambience **10** atmosphere, background, conditions **12** neighborhood, surroundings

ENVIRONS: **4** turf **7** suburbs **8** district, precinct, vicinity **9** outskirts, territory

ENVISAGE: **5** image **6** regard **7** picture **8** confront, consider **9** visualize

ENVISION: **5** dream **7** foresee, imagine, picture, predict **8** conceive **13** conceptualize

ENVOY: **5** agent **6** consul, deputy, legate **7** attache, courier **8** diplomat, emissary, minister **9** messenger **10** ambassador **14** representative

ENVY: **5** covet **8** begrudge, jealousy **10** discontent, resentment

ENZYME: **6** lipase, olease, pepsin **7** adenase, amylase, diatase, protein **8** catalyst, protease, racemase

EON, AEON: **3** age, era **4** time **8** eternity

EPHEMERAL: **5** brief, short, vague **7** passing **8** fleeting **9** momentary, temporary, transient **10** evanescent, transitory, unenduring

EPIC: **4** epos, poem, saga, tale **5** grand, great, noble **6** heroic **8** imposing, majestic **9** legendary, narrative **11** composition

EPICURE: **7** glutton, gourmet **8** gourmand, hedonist, sybarite **10** gastronome, voluptuary **11** connoisseur

EPIDEMIC: **4** rash **6** plague **8** catching, outbreak **10** contagious, infectious, pestilence, widespread **12** communicable

EPIDERMIS: **4** skin **5** layer

EPIGRAM: **4** poem **5** adage **6** saying **9** statement, witticism

EPIGRAMMATIC: **5** pithy, terse, witty **7** concise

EPILOGUE: **6** ending **8** appendix, postlude **9** afterword, summation **10** conclusion

EPISODE: **5** event, scene, story **7** passage **8** incident **9** adventure **10** experience, occurrence

EPISTLE: **4** note **6** letter **7** message **11** composition **13** communication

EPITAPH: **6** eulogy **8** memoriam **11** inscription, remembrance

EPITHET: **4** name, term **5** title **6** insult, phrase **8** nickname **9** expletive, sobriquet **11** appellation, description

EPITOME: **5** brief, model **6** digest, resume **7** summary **8** abstract, exemplar, synopsis **10** abridgment **12** abbreviation, condensation, illustration

EPOCH: **3** age, era **4** time **5** event **6** period **8** interval

EQUABLE: **4** calm, even **6** placid, serene, smooth, stable, steady **7** regular **8** constant, tranquil **9** easygoing, unruffled **10** consistent, methodical, unchanging **11** unflappable

EQUAL: **4** even, fair, like, mate, meet, peer, same **5** alike, level, match, rival **7** abreast, compeer, similar **8** adequate, balanced, parallel, unbiased **9** identical **10** equivalent, tantamount **11** coextensive, comparative, counterpart, symmetrical **12** commensurate **13** corresponding

EQUALITY: **6** equity, parity **7** balance, isonomy **8** evenness, fairness **10** uniformity **11** egalitarian **12** impartiality

EQUALITY STATE: **7** Wyoming

EQUALIZE: **6** equate, square **7** balance **8** handicap **10** coordinate

EQUANIMITY: **4** cool **5** poise **6** aplomb **7** control **8** calmness, evenness, patience, serenity **9** composure, sang-froid **10** steadiness **11** tranquility

EQUATE: **5** liken, match **6** relate **7** balance, compare **8** equalize **9** associate **10** correspond

EQUATORIAL GUINEA:
capital: **5** Bioko **6** Malabo
cities: **4** Bata **5** Mbini **7** Rio Muni
continent: **6** Africa
ethnic groups: **4** Bubi, Fang
features: **5** Bioko **7** Annobon, Corisco, Rio Muni **11** Elobey Chico **12** Elobey Grande
languages: **4** Bubi, Fang **7** Spanish
monetary unit: **5** franc **6** ekuele
water: **8** Atlantic **12** Gulf of Guinea

EQUESTRIAN: **5** rider **8** horseman **9** horseback **10** horsewoman

EQUIDISTANT: **6** center, middle **7** central, halfway

EQUILIBRIUM: **5** poise **7** balance **8** symmetry **9** composure, stability **10** steadiness

EQUIP: **3** arm, rig **4** deck, gear **5** array, dress, endow, ready, stock **6** attire, outfit, supply **7** appoint, furnish, prepare, provide, qualify **8** accouter

EQUIPMENT: **4** gear **5** goods, tools **6** tackle **8** armament, fixtures, material, supplies **9** apparatus, machinery **10** provisions **11** accessories, instruments **12** contraptions **13** paraphernalia

EQUITABLE: **4** even, fair, just **5** equal, moral **6** honest **7** ethical **8** unbiased **9** impartial, righteous **10** reasonable

EQUITY: **3** law **5** funds, stock, value **6** assets **7** honesty, justice **8** fairness **9** integrity **10** investment

EQUIVALENT: **4** peer, same **5** alike, match **7** similar **8** parallel **9** identical **10** comparable, reciprocal, substitute, synonymous, tantamount **11** counterpart **13** proportionate

EQUIVOCAL: **4** hazy **5** vague **7** clouded, dubious, evasive, muddled, obscure, unclear **8** doubtful **9** ambiguous, uncertain **10** ambivalent, indecisive **12** inconclusive, questionable, undetermined

EQUIVOCATE: **3** con, fib, lie **5** avoid, dodge, elude, evade, hedge, parry **6** escape, palter, weasel **7** deceive, quibble **8** sidestep **9** pussyfoot **11** prevaricate

ERA: **3** age **4** date, term, time **5** cycle, epoch, stage **6** period **10** generation

ERADICATE: **4** raze **5** erase, trash **6** delete, remove, uproot **7** abolish, destroy, expunge **8** demolish **9** eliminate, extirpate **10** annihilate, obliterate **11** exterminate

ERASE: **4** blot **5** annul, blank **6** cancel, delete, efface, negate, remove **7** abolish, destroy, expunge, scratch **9** eliminate, eradicate **10** neutralize, obliterate

ERE: **5** prior **6** before, rather

ERECT: **4** make **5** build, exalt, raise, rigid, stiff **6** create **7** elevate, upended, upright **8** assemble, standing, straight, vertical **9** construct, establish, fabricate **13** perpendicular

ERGO: **4** then **5** hence **9** therefore **12** consequently

ERODE: **4** rust, wear **5** decay **6** abrade **7** corrode, crumble, destroy **11** deteriorate **12** disintegrate

EROTIC: **3** hot **4** lewd, sexy **5** bawdy, kinky, spicy **6** ardent, carnal, fleshy **7** amatory, sensual **8** indecent, prurient, romantic **9** erogenous, salacious, seductive **10** passionate **11** stimulating

ERR: **3** sin **4** goof, muff, slip **5** lapse, stray, wrong **6** bungle, wander **7** blunder, deviate, mistake, stumble **8** misjudge **10** transgress **12** miscalculate

ERRAND: **4** task **5** chore **7** mission **10** assignment

ERRANT: **6** astray, roving **7** erratic, roaming **8** drifting, shifting, straying **9** deviating, wandering **10** meandering **11** misbehaving

ERRATIC: **4** wild **5** queer, wacky **6** errant **7** bizarre, strange, unusual, wayward **8** aberrant, peculiar, unstable, volatile **9** arbitrary, eccentric, fluctuant, irregular, uncertain, wandering **10** capricious **12** inconsistent **13** unpredictable

ERRONEOUS: **5** false, wrong **6** faulty, untrue **7** inexact **8** mistaken **9** incorrect, misguided **10** inaccurate

ERROR: **4** flub, muff, slip, typo **5** boner, fault, fluff, lapse, wrong **6** fumble, miscue, slipup **7** blooper, blunder, default, fallacy, falsity, misplay, mistake, offense **9** oversight, violation **10** inaccuracy **13** misconception transgression

ERSATZ: **4** fake, sham **5** bogus, phony **9** imitation, synthetic **10** artificial, substitute **11** counterfeit

ERSTWHILE: **6** bygone, former, whilom **7** earlier **8** formerly, previous **9** preceding

ERUDITE: **4** wise **7** learned **8** cultured, educated, studious **9** scholarly **11** intelligent

ERUDITION: **6** wisdom **8** learning, literacy **9** education, knowledge **10** refinement **11** scholarship **12** studiousness

ERUPT: **4** boil, emit, gush, spew, vent **5** burst, eject, expel, spout, spurt **7** explode, release **8** detonate **9** discharge

ERUPTION: **4** rush **5** blast, storm **8** ejection, outbreak, outburst **9** commotion, explosion **10** outpouring **12** inflammation

ESCALATE: **4** grow, rise **5** climb, mount **6** ascend, expand, extend **7** advance, amplify, broaden, enlarge **8** heighten, increase **9** intensify

ESCAPADE: **4** lark, romp **5** antic, caper, fling, folly, prank, stunt **6** vagary **9** adventure

ESCAPE: **3** lam **4** bolt, duck, flee, leak, shun, skip, slip **5** avoid, dodge, elope, elude, evade, shake, spill **6** decamp, emerge, eschew, outlet, rescue **7** evasion, getaway, outflow, vamoose **8** breakout **9** desertion, disappear, diversion **10** liberation **12** sidestepping

ESCARGOT: **5** snail

ESCHEW: **4** shun **5** avoid **6** escape **7** abandon, abstain, refrain **8** renounce

ESCORT: **4** beau, date, lead, show **5** guard, guide, steer, usher **6** attend, convoy, gigolo, squire **7** conduct **8** cavalier, chaperon, outrider **9** accompany, attendant, bodyguard, companion, entourage, safeguard

ESCRITOIRE: **4** desk **9** davenport, secretary **12** writing table

ESCUTCHEON: **4** arms **5** crest **6** shield

ESKIMO: **5** Aleut, Inuit **7** Amerind *items:* **3** ulu **5** husky, igloo, kamik, kayak, parka, tupek, tupik, umiak **6** kashim, mukluk **8** malamute

ESOTERIC: **6** arcane, mystic, occult, secret **7** obscure, private **8** abstruse **9** recondite **10** mysterious **12** confidential

ESP: **7** insight **9** intuition, telepathy **10** perception, sixth sense **11** second sight **12** clairvoyance, precognition **22** extrasensory perception

ESPECIAL: **5** chief **6** unique **7** notable **8** intimate, peculiar, uncommon **9** important **10** particular **11** exceptional, outstanding, significant **13** distinguished, extraordinary **14** characteristic

ESPECIALLY: **6** mainly **9** eminently, expressly, primarily **10** remarkably, singularly **11** exclusively, principally **12** specifically

ESPIONAGE: **6** spying **12** surveillance **14** reconnaissance

ESPOUSE: **3** wed **4** back, mate **5** adopt, boost, marry, unite **6** defend, pledge, uphold **7** betroth, embrace, further, promote, support **8** advocate, champion

ESPRIT: **4** elan, zest **5** vigor **6** morale, spirit **10** cleverness **12** intelligence **13** sprightliness

ESPRIT DE CORPS: **6** morale **10** fellowship, solidarity **11** camaraderie

ESPY: **3** see **4** find, spot, view **5** sight, watch **6** detect, notice **7** discern, glimpse, observe **8** discover

ESSAY: **3** try **4** seek, test, work **5** paper, piece, story, theme, trail **6** effort, thesis **7** article, attempt, venture, writing **8** critique, endeavor, exertion, treatise **9** editorial, narrative, undertake **10** experiment, exposition **11** composition **12** dissertation

ESSENCE: **4** core, crux, gist, life, odor, root, soul **5** being, fiber, heart, point **6** nature, spirit **7** cologne, element, extract, meaning, nucleus, perfume, quality **9** attribute, character, existence, fragrance, principle, substance **10** distillate, extraction **12** constitution, significance

ESSENTIAL: **4** main, must **5** basic, chief, vital **7** crucial **8** cardinal, inherent **9** important, necessary, principal, requisite **10** elementary, imperative, sine qua non **11** fundamental, requirement **12** prerequisite **13** indispensable

ESTABLISH: **4** base, show **5** build, erect, found, plant, prove, start **6** create, decree, ground, ratify, secure, settle, verify **7** appoint, approve, clarify, confirm, install, instate, provide, situate **8** colonize, discover, document, generate, identify, initiate, organize, validate **9** ascertain, determine, institute, originate, predicate **10** accomplish, constitute **11** corroborate **12** substantiate

ESTABLISHED: **4** firm **6** stable **7** certain, fixture **8** accepted **10** entrenched **13** authenticated

ESTABLISHMENT: **5** elite, house, plant **7** company, concern, factory **8** business, Old Guard **9** authority, the system **10** enterprise, government **11** bureaucracy, corporation, institution, ruling class **12** organization

ESTATE: **4** home, rank, will **5** acres, class, manor, money, order, villa **6** assets, domain, ground, legacy, status **7** bequest, bracket, demesne, echelon, effects, fortune, grounds **8** hacienda, holdings, position, property, standing **9** endowment, situation **10** belongings, plantation **11** inheritance, latifundium

ESTEEM: **4** deem **5** count, favor, honor, judge, pride, prize, value, worth **6** admire, credit, regard **7** account, believe, cherish, respect **8** approval, consider, venerate **9** reckoning, reverence **10** admiration, appreciate, estimation

ESTIMABLE: **4** good **5** solid **6** worthy **8** laudable **9** admirable, deserving, honorable, respected, venerable **11** commendable, meritorious **12** praiseworthy

ESTIMATE: **4** rank, rate **5** assay, gauge, guess, judge, prize, value **6** figure, reckon, survey **7** average, believe, compute, opinion, surmise **8** consider, evaluate, forecast **9** appraisal, calculate, quotation **10** assessment, projection **11** approximate, computation

ESTIMATION: **4** view **5** honor **6** belief, esteem, regard **8** judgment **9** valuation **10** arithmetic, impression

ESTONIA:
capital: **7** Tallinn
cities: **5** Narva, Tartu

ESTOP: **3** bar **6** impede **7** prevent **8** obstruct, prohibit

ESTRANGE: **4** part **5** sever, split **6** divert **7** divorce **8** alienate, disunite, separate **9** disaffect **10** antagonize

ET CETERA: **3** and, etc **4** et al **7** and so on, what not

ETCH: **4** draw **5** carve, stamp **7** engrave, impress, imprint, portray **8** inscribe

ETERNAL: **6** always **7** ageless, endless, forever, lasting, undying **8** constant, enduring, immortal, infinite, timeless **9** boundless, continual, deathless, perpetual, unceasing **10** changeless, perdurable **11** everlasting, neverending **12** interminable **13** uninterrupted

ETERNAL CITY: **4** Rome

ETERNITY: **3** age **4** aeon **7** forever **8** blue moon **9** afterlife **10** perpetuity **11** immortality **12** timelessness

ETHER: **3** air, gas, sky **7** element, heavens, solvent **8** compound **10** anesthetic, atmosphere

ETHEREAL: **4** airy **5** filmy, light **6** aerial, divine **7** fragile, refined **8** delicate, heavenly, vaporous **9** celestial, spiritual, unearthly **10** intangible

ETHICAL: **4** just **5** moral **8** virtuous **9** equitable, honorable, righteous **10** aboveboard **13** conscientious

ETHICS: **5** ideal, mores **6** belief, morals, values **7** conduct, customs **9** integrity, standards **10** deontology, principles

ETHIOPIA:
capital: **10** Addis Ababa
cities: **5** Assab **6** Asmara **7** Eritrea, Massawa **8** Dire Dawa
continent: **6** Africa
ethnic groups: **5** Oromo, Tigre **6** Amhara, Sidama
features: **4** Haud **5** Aksum **6** Gondar, Ogaden **7** Danakil **8** Lalibela **10** Rift Valley
languages: **5** Galla, Tigre **7** Amharic
monetary unit: **4** birr
water: **3** Omo **8** Blue Nile

ETHNIC: **5** pagan **6** racial **7** heathen **8** cultural **10** background

ETIQUETTE: **4** form **5** usage **7** conduct, decorum, manners **8** behavior, courtesy, protocol **9** amenities, propriety, punctilio **10** politeness **11** formalities

ETYMOLOGY: **6** origin **7** history **10** derivation, word origin

EUCHARIST: **8** oblation **9** communion, sacrament
container: **3** pyx **5** cruet **7** ampulla, chalice **8** ciborium **9** ostensory **10** monstrance

EULOGIZE: **4** laud **5** bless, exalt **6** praise **7** glorify **9** celebrate

EULOGY: **5** paean **6** homage, praise **7** acclaim, address, oration, tribute **8** encomium **9** panegyric **10** salutation **12** commendation

EUPHONY: **5** sound **6** melody, rhythm **7** harmony

EUPHORIA: **5** bliss **7** ecstasy, elation **9** happiness, well-being **10** jubilation **12** exhilaration

EUROPE:
cities: **4** Kiev, Rome **5** Milan, Paris **6** Athens, Berlin, London, Madrid, Moscow, Vienna, Warsaw **7** Hamburg **8** Budapest, Istanbul **9** Barcelona, Leningrad **10** Birmingham, Manchester
countries: **5** Italy, Malta, Spain **6** Cyprus, France, Greece, Monaco, Norway, Poland, Sweden **7** Albania, Andorra, Austria, Belgium, Denmark, Finland, Germany, Hungary, Iceland, Ireland, Romania **8** Bulgaria, Portugal **9** San Marino **10** Luxembourg, Yugoslavia **11** Netherlands, Switzerland, Vatican City **12** Great Britain **13** Liechtenstein **14** Czechoslovakia
countries, partial: **6** Russia, Turkey
features: **4** Alps **5** Urals **6** Forest **7** Balkans **8** Bohemian, Caucasus, Pyrenees **9** Apennines **11** Carpathians, Mount Elbruz **12** Sierra Nevada
water: **3** Don **5** Onega, Volga **6** Danube, Ladoga, Vanern **7** Dnieper **13** Mediterranean

EVACUATE: **4** flee **5** clear, empty, expel, leave **6** decamp, desert, remove, vacate **7** abandon **8** hightail

EVADE: **4** duck, hide, shun **5** avert, avoid, ditch, dodge, elude, hedge, parry, shirk **6** escape, eschew **8** maneuver, sidestep **9** pussyfoot **10** equivocate

EVALUATE: **4** rank, rate, test **5** check, grade, judge, weigh **6** assess, survey **8** appraise, consider, estimate **9** ascertain, criticize

EVALUATION: **5** assay **7** opinion **8** analysis, critique, judgment **9** appraisal **10** estimation **14** interpretation

EVANESCE: **4** fade **6** vanish **8** dissolve **9** disappear, dissipate, evaporate

EVANESCENT: **7** evasive, melting **8** fleeting, fugitive **9** ephemeral, temporary, transient, vanishing **10** transitory

EVANGELIST: **4** John, Luke, Mark **6** Graham **7** apostle, Matthew, Roberts **8** disciple, preacher **10** missionary, revivalist

EVAPORATE: **4** melt **5** dry up, steam **8** dissolve, evanesce, vaporize **9** dehydrate, disappear

EVASIVE: **3** sly **5** cagey, vague **6** shifty, tricky **7** devious, elusive, elusory, unclear **8** slippery **9** ambiguous, deceitful **12** noncommittal **13** prevarication

EVE: **4** dusk **6** female, sunset **7** evening, sundown **9** preceding
husband: **4** Adam
inhabited: **12** Garden of Eden
sons: **4** Abel, Cain, Seth

EVEN: **4** fair, flat, just, tied **5** aline, equal, exact, flush, grade, level, match, still **6** direct, indeed, placid, smooth, square, stable, steady **7** abreast, flatten, regular, uniform **8** balanced, moderate, parallel **9** equitable, impartial **10** consistent, continuous **11** homogeneous **12** proportional

EVENING: **3** eve **4** dusk **6** soiree, sunset **7** bedtime, sundown **8** eventide, twilight **9** nightfall

EVENT: **4** case, fact, fate, feat, game **5** doing, match **6** affair, result **7** contest, miracle, outcome **8** disaster, incident, landmark, occasion, offshoot, scenario **9** adventure, happening, milestone **10** experience, occurrence, phenomenon, tournament **11** achievement, catastrophe, celebration, competition, consequence

EVENTFUL: **4** busy **7** crucial, fateful, notable **8** exciting **9** important, memorable, momentous **11** significant

EVENTUAL: **5** final, later **6** future **7** ensuing **8** possible, ultimate **9** resulting **10** concluding, inevitable

EVENTUALLY: **7** finally, someday **8** in the end, sometime **10** ultimately

EVER: **6** always **7** anytime, forever, usually **9** eternally **10** constantly, invariably **11** continually, perpetually **12** consistently

EVERGREEN: **4** tree **5** fresh, holly, plant, shrub **7** conifer **8** enduring **9** mistletoe
variety: **3** fir **4** pine **5** cedar, heath, savin **6** larche, laurel, spruce **7** hemlock, juniper **12** rhododendron

EVERGREEN STATE: **10** Washington

EVERLASTING: **7** durable, endless, eternal, forever, lasting, tedious, undying **8** constant, enduring, eternity, immortal, infinite, timeless **9** continual, incessant, perennial, perpetual, unceasing **12** imperishable **13** uninterrupted

EVERY: **3** all **4** each **5** whole **6** entire **7** equally

EVERYBODY: **3** all **6** people **8** everyone

EVERYDAY: **5** daily, plain, usual **6** common **7** mundane, routine **8** ordinary **9** customary **11** commonplace **13** unimaginative

EVERYTHING: **3** all **5** total **9** aggregate

EVERYWHERE: **9** prevalent, worldwide **10** throughout **11** extensively, omnipresent

EVICT: **4** oust **5** eject, expel **6** bounce, remove **7** dismiss **10** dispossess

EVIDENCE: **4** clue, show **5** goods, proof, token, trace **6** attest **7** display, exhibit, hearsay, witness **8** indicate, manifest **9** testimony **10** illustrate **13** documentation

EVIDENT: **5** clear, plain **6** patent **7** certain, glaring, obvious, visible **8** apparent, manifest **10** conclusive, noticeable **11** conspicuous, transparent **12** unmistakable

EVIL: **3** bad, sin **4** base, foul, mean, vice, vile **5** crime, curse, wrong **6** sinful **7** baleful, corrupt, hideous, hurtful, immoral, satanic, vicious **8** calamity, damnable, demoniac, depraved, devilish, disaster, iniquity, mischief, sinister **9** malicious, nefarious, offensive, worthless **10** affliction, flagitious, malevolent, misfortune, pernicious, wickedness **11** heinousness

EVILDOER: **5** crook, felon **6** sinner **7** villain **8** criminal **10** malefactor **12** transgressor

EVIL EYE: **3** hex **4** jinx **5** stare **6** whammy

EVIL SPIRIT: **5** demon, devil **7** incubus **8** succubus

EVINCE: **4** show **5** prove **6** reveal **7** display, exhibit, express **8** disclose, indicate, manifest **11** demonstrate

EVOKE: **4** call **5** educe **6** arouse, awaken, elicit, excite, induce, recall, summon **9** stimulate

EVOLUTION: **6** change, growth **8** ontogeny, progress **9** flowering, phylogeny **11** advancement, development **13** metamorphosis **14** transformation

EVOLVE: **4** emit, grow **5** ripen **6** derive, devise, emerge, expand, mature, unfold **7** develop **8** increase **9** germinate

EWE: **6** animal **11** female sheep

EWER: **3** jug **6** vessel **7** pitcher **8** decanter **9** container

EXACERBATE: **5** anger, annoy, tease **6** enrage, worsen **7** provoke **8** increase, irritate **9** aggravate, infuriate **10** exasperate

EXACT: **4** even, fine, levy, true **5** sharp, wreak, wrest **6** compel, demand, elicit, extort, formal, square **7** careful, certain, command, correct, enforce, extract, literal, precise, require **8** accurate, critical, distinct, explicit, specific, verbatim **9** identical **10** methodical, meticulous, scrupulous **11** painstaking, punctilious

EXACTING: **5** fussy, picky **6** direct, severe, strict, taxing, trying **7** arduous, finicky **8** pressing, rigorous **9** demanding, difficult **10** burdensome, particular

EXACTLY: **4** just **5** fully, quite, right, truly **8** entirely **9** assuredly, certainly, literally **10** absolutely, accurately, altogether, faithfully, positively **12** specifically

EXAGGERATE: **4** brag **5** boast, color **6** overdo **7** amplify, distort, enlarge, inflate, magnify **9** embellish, embroider, fabricate, overstate

EXAGGERATED: **6** padded **8** inflated **9** overblown **10** histrionic **12** melodramatic

EXALT: **4** laud **5** elate, extol, honor, raise **6** praise, uplift **7** acclaim, applaud, commend, dignify, glorify, inspire, magnify, promote, worship **8** heighten **9** intensify **10** aggrandize **11** distinguish

EXALTATION: **5** bliss **7** delight, ecstasy, rapture **8** euphoria **9** transport **10** jubilation, veneration

EXAMINATION: **4** exam, oral, quiz, test **5** assay, audit, final, probe **6** biopsy, review, survey **7** autopsy, checkup, inquiry, midterm **8** analysis, blue book, research, scrutiny **9** catechism **10** comparison, inspection **11** exploration **13** interrogation, introspection, investigation

EXAMINE: **3** ask **4** scan, sift, view **5** check, grill, study, weigh **6** ponder, screen **7** canvass, dissect, explore, inquire, inspect, observe, palpate **10** scrutinize

EXAMINER: **6** censor, critic, tester **7** analyst, auditor, coroner, teacher **8** inquirer, reviewer **9** appraiser, inspector **12** interrogator, investigator

EXAMPLE: **4** case, copy **5** ideal, model **6** lesson, sample **7** pattern **8** instance, paradigm, specimen, standard **9** epitomize, precedent, prototype **11** description **12** illustration

EXASPERATE: **4** gall, rile **5** annoy, upset **6** bother, enrage, excite, nettle, ruffle **7** agitate, disturb, incense, inflame, provoke **8** irritate **9** aggravate **10** exacerbate

EXCAVATE: **3** dig **4** mine **5** scoop **6** burrow, dredge, hollow, shovel, tunnel **7** unearth

EXCEED: **4** beat, best, pass **5** excel, outdo, outgo **6** better, outrun, overdo **7** surpass **8** outshine, overstep, overtake, surmount **9** overshoot, transcend **12** preponderate

EXCEEDINGLY: **4** very **7** greatly **9** extremely **10** enormously, remarkably, strikingly **11** excessively **13** exceptionally

EXCEL: **4** best **5** outdo, shine **6** better, exceed **7** surpass **8** outclass, outrival, outstrip, superior **9** transcend

EXCELLENCE: **5** merit, worth **6** virtue **7** quality **9** greatness, supremacy **10** perfection **11** distinction, superiority **12** marksmanship

EXCELLENT: **4** fine, good, tops **5** bravo, bully, great, nifty, prime, super **6** famous, select, spiffy, worthy **7** capital, classic **8** generous, peerless, sterling, superior, terrific, top-notch, valuable **9** admirable, firstrate, wonderful **10** stupendous **11** magnificent, outstanding, superlative **12** transcendent, unparalleled

EXCEPT: **3** ban, bar **4** omit, only, save **6** exempt, reject, unless **7** besides, exclude, however **9** eliminate

EXCEPTION: **5** demur, quirk **6** oddity **7** anomaly, offense **8** omission **9** allowance, complaint, exclusion

EXCEPTIONAL: **4** rare **6** unique **7** special, unusual **8** abnormal, superior **9** irregular, wonderful **10** noteworthy, phenomenal, prodigious, remarkable **11** outstanding **12** unparalleled **13** extraordinary, unprecedented

EXCERPT: **4** cite, part **5** quote **6** sample **7** extract, passage, portion, section **9** selection

EXCESS: **4** glut, over, plus **5** extra, flood, gravy **7** nimiety, residue, surfeit, surplus **8** overflow, overkill, plethora **9** overboard, profusion, remainder **10** lavishness **11** prodigality, superfluity, superfluous **12** intemperance **13** overabundance **14** overindulgence

EXCESSIVE: **5** undue **7** copious, extreme, fulsome **8** enormous, needless, overdone, overmuch **9** exuberant, indulgent **10** exorbitant, immoderate, inordinate **11** extravagant, intemperate **12** unreasonable **14** unconscionable

EXCHANGE: **4** deal, swap **5** bandy, store, trade, truck **6** barter, dicker, market, switch **7** commute, network, traffic **8** commerce **9** transpose **10** conversion, quid pro quo, substitute, Wall Street **11** reciprocate, replacement

EXCISE: **3** tax **4** duty, edit, levy, toll **5** erase **6** charge, delete, remove, tariff **7** exscind, extract **9** eradicate, extirpate, surcharge **10** assessment

EXCITABLE: **5** jumpy **8** skittish, volatile, volcanic **9** emotional **10** hysterical **12** enthusiastic

EXCITE: **4** fire, move, spur, stir **5** elate, prime, rouse, upset **6** arouse, awaken, elicit, foment, incite, kindle, thrill **7** agitate, animate, inflame, inspire, provoke **8** energize **9** electrify, galvanize, stimulate, titillate **10** invigorate

EXCITED: **3** hot **5** eager **6** elated, heated, piqued **7** charged, fevered, frantic **8** ecstatic, frenzied **9** delighted

EXCITEMENT: **3** ado **4** flap, stir **5** furor **6** action, flurry, hubbub **7** turmoil **8** hysteria **9** adventure, commotion, confusion **10** hullabaloo **11** disturbance

EXCITING: **5** spicy **8** dazzling **11** provocative **12** breathtaking, exhilarating

EXCLAIM: **4** roar **5** blurt, shout, utter **6** assert **7** declare **8** proclaim **9** ejaculate **10** vociferate

EXCLAMATION: **3** aha, bah, boo, fie, gee, ugh, wow **4** ahem, alas, drat, egad, phew, pish, rats **5** bravo, humph, pshaw **6** eureka, hurrah, indeed, outcry **7** hosanna **9** expletive **10** hallelujah **12** interjection

EXCLUDE: **3** ban, bar **5** debar, eject, expel **6** banish, except, reject **7** boycott **8** preclude, prohibit, relegate **9** blackball, blacklist, eliminate, ostracize

EXCLUSIVE: **4** chic, posh, rare, sole **5** alone, aloof, elite, swank, whole **6** single **7** private **8** cliquish, complete, monopoly, snobbish **9** expensive, selective, undivided **10** limitative, restricted **11** independent **14** discriminative

EXCOMMUNICATE: **3** ban **5** expel **6** banish **7** defrock **8** anathema, unchurch

EXCORIATE: **4** flay, gall **5** chafe, scold, strip **6** abrade **7** condemn **8** chastise, denounce, lambaste **9** criticize

EXCRESCENCE: **4** knob, lump, wart **6** pimple **9** accretion, outgrowth **11** enlargement

EXCRUCIATING: **5** acute **6** severe **7** extreme, intense, painful **8** grueling, shooting **9** agonizing, harrowing, torturous **10** tormenting, unbearable

EXCULPATE: **4** free **5** clear **6** acquit, excuse, pardon **7** absolve, amnesty, dismiss, forgive, release **9** exonerate, vindicate

EXCURSION: **4** hike, ride, sail, tour, trek, trip, walk **5** jaunt **6** cruise, junket, outing, safari, sortie, voyage **7** journey **9** diversion **10** digression, expedition

EXCUSABLE: **6** venial **9** allowable **10** forgivable, pardonable **11** justifiable, permissible, warrantable

EXCUSE: **4** plea **5** alibi, remit **6** acquit, defend, exempt, pardon **7** absolve, apology, condone explain, forgive, indulge, justify, release **9** discharge, exculpate, exonerate, vindicate

EXECRABLE: **3** bad **4** base, foul, vile **5** awful **7** hateful, heinous **9** abhorrent, atrocious, repulsive, revolting, sickening **10** abominable, deplorable, detestable, horrifying

EXECRATE: **4** damn, hate **5** abhor, curse **6** detest, loathe **7** despise **8** denounce **9** imprecate

EXECUTE: **3** act, gas **4** hang, kill, obey, slay **5** cause, enact, lynch **6** behead, direct, finish, manage, murder **7** conduct, enforce, perform **8** complete **9** implement **10** accomplish, administer, guillotine **11** assassinate, electrocute

EXECUTION: **7** garrote, killing **10** completion **11** fulfillment, realization, transaction **12** consummation **13** strangulation

EXECUTIVE: **3** CEO, VIP **4** dean, head **6** ruling **7** manager, officer **8** director, official **9** governing, president **10** supervisor **12** entrepreneur **13** administrator **14** businessperson

EXECUTOR: **4** doer **5** agent **8** enforcer **13** administrator

EXEGESIS: **8** analysis, critique **10** exposition **11** explanation **14** interpretation

EXEMPLARY: **5** ideal, model **7** typical **8** sterling **9** admirable, classical, honorable **10** admonitory **11** commendable **12** illustrative, praiseworthy

EXEMPLIFY: **6** depict, embody, typify **7** clarify **9** epitomize, personify, represent, symbolize **11** demonstrate

EXEMPT: **4** free **5** clear, spare **6** excuse, immune **7** exclude, release **8** absolved, excepted, pardoned, relieved **9** discharge, exonerate

EXERCISE: **4** task, yoga **5** drill, exert, sit-up, study, train **6** bestow, effort, employ, lesson, parade, praxis, push-up, school **7** display, prepare, problem, provoke, utilize, workout **8** activity, aerobics, ceremony, exertion, maneuver, practice **9** athletics, condition, operation **10** discipline, exhibition, gymnastics, isometrics **11** performance **12** calisthenics

EXERT: **5** apply, drive, force, wield **6** employ, expend, strain, strive, thrust **8** exercise

EXERTION: **4** pull, toil, work **5** labor, pains, power **6** action, effort, energy **7** attempt, trouble **8** endeavor, strength, struggle **11** elbow grease

EXHALE: **4** emit, puff **5** expel, steam **6** expire **7** breathe, respire **9** evaporate

EXHAUST: **4** tire **5** drain, empty, fumes, gases **6** expend, overdo, tucker, weaken **7** deplete, fatigue **8** bankrupt, squander **9** discharge **10** impoverish

EXHAUSTED: **4** beat, dead, done, worn **5** spent, tired, weary **6** bushed, effete, pooped **7** emptied **8** consumed, dog-tired, finished

EXHAUSTIVE: **8** complete, sweeping, thorough **9** extensive, intensive **13** comprehensive

EXHIBIT: **3** air **4** fair, show **6** expose, flaunt, ostend, parade, reveal **7** display, feature, perform, present, viewing **8** disclose, evidence, manifest, showcase **11** demonstrate, performance

EXHIBITION: **4** expo **5** drill, event, march, sight **7** contest, display, pageant **8** ceremony, offering, showcase **9** spectacle

EXHILARATE: **5** cheer, elate **6** excite, uplift **7** animate, delight, enliven, inspire **9** stimulate **10** invigorate

EXHILARATION: **6** gaiety **7** ecstasy, jollity **8** euphoria, gladness **10** joyousness, liveliness **11** refreshment

EXHORT: **4** goad, prod, spur, urge, warn **5** plead, press **6** advise, incite, preach **7** caution **8** admonish, persuade **9** encourage

EXHUME: **3** dig **6** unbury **7** uncover, unearth **8** disinter

EXIGENCY: **3** fix, jam **4** need **5** pinch **6** crisis, pickle, plight **7** dilemma **8** juncture, quandary **9** emergency, necessity **10** difficulty **11** requirement

EXIGENT: **4** dire **5** vital **6** taxing, urgent **7** crucial **8** critical, pressing, rigorous **9** demanding, necessary **10** imperative

EXIGUOUS: **4** tiny **5** petty, small, spare **6** little, meager, scanty, skimpy, sparse **7** slender **10** diminutive, inadequate

EXILE: **4** oust **5** eject, expel **6** banish, deport, outlaw **7** outcast, refugee **8** fugitive **9** expulsion, nonperson, ostracize **10** banishment, expatriate **15** displaced person

EXIST: **4** last, live **6** endure, remain **7** breathe, survive **8** continue, maintain

EXISTENCE: **4** esse, life **5** being **6** entity **7** essence, journey, reality **9** actuality, animation

EXIT: **4** door, gate, vent **5** going, leave, split **6** avenue, egress, exodus, outlet, retire **7** opening, passage, retreat **9** departure **10** evacuation, withdrawal

EXODUS: **4** exit **6** escape, flight **7** leaving **9** migration **10** emigration

EXONERATE: **4** free **5** clear **6** acquit, excuse, exempt, pardon **7** absolve, dismiss, forgive, release **9** disburden, exculpate, vindicate

EXORBITANT: **5** steep, undue **8** abnormal, enormous **9** excessive, expensive **10** outrageous, overpriced **11** extravagant **12** preposterous, unreasonable

EXOTIC: **5** alien, kinky **7** foreign, strange, unusual **8** alluring, enticing, romantic, striking **9** different, elaborate, fantastic **10** mysterious, outlandish

EXPAND: **4** grow, open **5** swell, widen **6** dilate, extend, fatten, spread, unfold **7** amplify, augment, balloon, broaden, develop, distend, enhance, enlarge, inflate, magnify, stretch **8** escalate, increase, lengthen, multiply, mushroom **9** diversify, elaborate, expatiate, explicate

EXPANSE: **4** area, span **5** plain, range, reach, scope, space, tract **6** domain, extent, region, spread **7** breadth, stretch **8** distance **9** territory

EXPANSION: **6** growth **8** increase, widening **9** extension **10** dilatation **11** development, enlargement **13** proliferation

EXPANSIVE: **4** free **5** ample, broad, grand, great, large **6** genial, lavish **7** elastic **8** effusive, generous, outgoing, spacious **9** extensive, talkative **10** gregarious, widespread **11** extroverted **13** communicative, comprehensive, demonstrative

EXPATIATE: **4** rant **6** ramble, wander **7** descant, enlarge, expound **9** elaborate, sermonize

EXPATRIATE: **4** oust **5** exile, expel **6** banish, deport **7** outcast, refugee **8** displace, emigrant, relegate

EXPECT: **4** deem, feel, hope, want **5** await, guess, sense, think **6** assume, demand, reckon **7** presume, suppose **8** envision, forecast **9** calculate **10** anticipate

EXPECTANT: **5** alert, eager **7** hopeful, waiting **8** pregnant, watchful

EXPECTATION: **4** hope **6** belief **8** prospect **10** likelihood **11** possibility **12** anticipation

EXPEDIENT: **4** wise **6** method, proper, scheme, useful **7** politic, stopgap **8** possible, resource **9** makeshift, opportune **10** beneficial, profitable, worthwhile **11** appropriate **12** advantageous

EXPEDITE: **4** rush **5** hurry, press, speed **6** hasten **7** advance, quicken **8** dispatch **9** efficient **10** accelerate, facilitate

EXPEDITION: **4** tour, trek, trip **5** haste, jaunt, quest **6** patrol, safari, voyage **7** crusade, journey, mission **9** excursion **10** promptness **11** exploration

EXPEL: **4** oust, pass, spew **5** drive, eject, evict, exile **6** banish, deport, remove **7** dismiss, exclude **8** dislodge **9** discharge, eliminate **10** expatriate

EXPEND: **5** drain, spend, waste **7** consume, exhaust, indulge **8** disburse, squander **9** dissipate **10** distribute

EXPENDABLE: **6** excess **9** forgoable **10** disposable **11** replaceable **12** nonessential

EXPENDITURE: **4** cost **5** outgo **6** outlay **7** expense, payment **12** disbursement

EXPENSE: **4** cost, debt, loss, risk **5** price **6** charge, outlay, upkeep **8** overhead **9** sacrifice **10** forfeiture **11** expenditure

EXPENSIVE: **4** posh **5** steep **6** costly, lavish **7** upscale **8** valuable **10** exorbitant, high-priced, overpriced **11** extravagant

EXPERIENCE: **4** feel, have, know, live, view **5** event, sense, skill, taste, trial **6** affair, behold, endure, ordeal, suffer, wisdom **7** feeling, know-how, sustain, undergo **8** exposure, maturity, training **9** adventure, encounter, knowledge, seasoning **10** background **11** involvement

EXPERIENCED: **4** able, wise **5** adept, tried **6** expert, tested **7** veteran **8** familiar, seasoned **9** competent, practiced, qualified **10** accustomed **12** professional

EXPERIMENT: **4** test **5** assay, check, probe, trial **6** search **7** analyze **8** exercise, research **11** investigate, observation

EXPERIMENTAL: **9** empirical, tentative **10** contingent **11** exploratory, preliminary **13** developmental

EXPERT: **3** ace, pro **4** deft **5** adept **6** adroit, artist, master, pundit **7** capable, gourmet, skilled **8** schooled, virtuoso **9** authority **10** consultant, proficient, specialist **11** connoisseur, experienced **12** professional

EXPIATE: **5** amend, atone **7** appease, forgive, rectify **9** reconcile

EXPIRATION: **5** death **6** finish **7** passing **8** elapsing **10** exhalation **11** termination

EXPIRE: **3** die, end **4** emit, quit, stop **5** cease, expel, lapse **6** perish

EXPLAIN: **6** define, expand, unfold **7** clarify, expound, justify, unravel **8** annotate, construe, decipher, describe, manifest, simplify **9** elaborate, elucidate, explicate, interpret, translate **10** illuminate **11** rationalize

EXPLANATION: **5** brief, cause **6** answer, motive, reason **7** account, apology, history, meaning **8** exegesis **9** statement **10** commentary, exposition

EXPLETIVE: **4** oath **5** curse, swear **11** exclamation

EXPLICATE: **6** expand, unfold **7** clarify, explain, expound **8** annotate, construe **9** interpret

EXPLICIT: **4** open **5** clear, exact, frank, plain **6** direct **7** express, obvious, pointed, precise **8** absolute, accurate, definite, positive, specific **9** categoric **11** categorical, unambiguous, unequivocal **12** unmistakable

EXPLODE: **5** blast, burst, erupt **6** refute, spring **7** deflate, shatter, thunder **8** detonate, disprove, dynamite, mushroom **9** discharge

EXPLOIT: **3** act **4** bilk, coup, deed, feat, milk **5** abuse, bleed, stunt **6** misuse **7** promote, utilize **9** advertise, adventure **10** manipulate **11** achievement

EXPLORE: **3** try **4** test **5** chart, probe, scout **6** search, survey **7** analyze, examine **8** prospect, question, research **11** investigate

EXPLOSION: **3** pop **4** bomb, clap **5** blast **8** eruption, ignition, outburst **9** discharge **10** detonation

EXPLOSIVE: **3** TNT **4** bomb, mine **5** tense **6** amatol, charge, powder, stormy **7** grenade, lyddite, missile, payload **8** critical, dynamite, eruptive, strained, unstable, volatile **9** dangerous, fireworks, fulminate, guncotton **10** ammunition, propellant **13** nitroglycerin

EXPONENT: **6** backer, symbol **7** booster, example **8** advocate **9** supporter **11** protagonist **12** illustration

EXPOSE: **4** bare, open, risk **5** strip **6** betray, flaunt, reveal, unfold, unmask **7** display, divulge, exhibit, feature, publish, uncover, unearth **8** disclose, discover, endanger, unclothe **9** broadcast **10** jeopardize

EXPOSED: **5** prone **6** liable **10** vulnerable **11** susceptible, unprotected

EXPOSITION: **4** fair, mart, show **5** essay, piece **6** bazaar, report **7** account, article **8** analysis, exegesis **9** editorial **10** commentary, exhibition **11** explanation

EXPOSTULATE: **5** argue **6** debate, demand, object, oppose **7** discuss, dispute, protest **8** dissuade **11** remonstrate

EXPOSURE: **6** danger, hazard **7** outlook **9** discovery, liability, publicity, unmasking **10** confession, divulgence, revelation **11** orientation **13** vulnerability

EXPOUND: **5** state **6** define **7** clarify, explain, express **8** construe, describe **9** elucidate, explicate, interpret **10** illustrate

EXPRESS: **4** fast, show, vent **5** couch, rapid, speak, state, swift, voice **6** convey, denote, depict, direct, phrase **7** certain, declare, dictate, exhibit, expound, nonstop, signify **8** definite, describe, explicit, manifest **9** expatiate, symbolize, ventilate **10** articulate

EXPRESSION: **4** form, grin, show, sign, term, word **5** frown, idiom, motto, smile, smirk, sneer, token, trope, voice, wince **6** cliche, phrase, remark, symbol **7** diction, emotion, gesture, grimace **8** atticism, laconism, language **9** assertion, euphemism, statement **10** intonation, modulation **11** delineation **13** communication, manifestation

EXPRESSIONLESS: **4** dull **5** blank, empty, stony **6** stolid, vacant **7** deadpan **9** impassive

EXPRESSIVE: **5** vivid **6** lively, poetic **7** graphic, telling **8** colorful, dramatic, eloquent **9** evocative, revealing **10** meaningful, passionate **11** significant

EXPRESSLY: **4** just **7** clearly, plainly **9** purposely, specially **10** definitely, explicitly **13** unequivocally

EXPRESSWAY: **4** road **7** freeway, highway, thruway **8** turnpike **10** interstate **12** superhighway

EXPROPRIATE: **4** take **5** seize **7** impound **10** commandeer, confiscate

EXPULSION: **5** exile **7** ousting, removal **8** ejection, eviction **9** debarment, dismissal **10** banishment, suspension

EXPUNGE: **5** erase **6** cancel, delete, efface, remove **7** destroy **9** eliminate, eradicate **10** annihilate, obliterate

EXPURGATE: **4** blip, edit **5** bleep, purge **6** censor, screen **10** blue-pencil, bowdlerize

EXQUISITE: **4** keen, nice **6** choice, dainty **7** careful, elegant, intense, refined **8** charming, delicate, flawless, precious, striking **9** beautiful, delicious, excellent, recherche **10** attractive, fastidious, impeccable **11** outstanding

EXTANT: **5** alive **7** present **8** existing **9** surviving

EXTEMPORANEOUS: **5** ad-lib **7** offhand **8** informal **9** impromptu **10** improvised **11** spontaneous **14** unpremeditated

EXTEND: **4** grow, rise, span **5** bulge, grant, offer, range, widen **6** accord, bestow, deepen, dilate, expand, spread, unbend **7** amplify, augment, broaden, display, enlarge, proffer, prolong, stretch **8** continue, elongate, increase, lengthen, protract, protrude **10** adulterate, outstretch, perpetuate, supplement

EXTENSION: **4** area, stay, wing **5** annex, delay, reach, scope **6** branch, spread **8** addition, duration, reprieve **9** outgrowth **11** enlargement **12** postponement

EXTENSIVE: **4** vast, wide **5** ample, broad, large, major **7** immense, sizable **8** spacious, sweeping, thorough **9** capacious, prevalent **10** widespread **13** comprehensive

EXTENT: **4** area, body, bulk, size, writ **5** limit, range, reach, scope, space, sweep, width **6** amount, degree, spread **7** breadth, expanse, measure **8** distance, duration, increase, latitude, quantity **9** dimension, encompass, intensity, magnitude, territory **10** assessment

EXTENUATING: **9** lessening **10** justifying, mitigating, palliating, qualifying **11** diminishing

EXTERIOR: **4** rind **5** outer, shell **6** facade **7** coating, outside, surface **8** external **9** outermost

EXTERMINATE: **4** kill **7** abolish, destroy **8** decimate, fumigate, massacre **9** eliminate, eradicate, extirpate **10** annihilate, extinguish

EXTERNAL: **3** out **5** outer **7** foreign, outside, visible **8** exterior **9** extrinsic **10** peripheral **11** superficial

EXTINCT: **4** dead, gone, lost **6** bygone **7** archaic, defunct **8** obsolete, vanished **10** antiquated **11** disappeared **12** extinguished

EXTINGUISH: **3** end **5** douse, quash, quell, snuff **6** cancel, quench, stifle **7** abolish, destroy, eclipse, expunge, nullify, smother, trample **8** suppress **9** eliminate, suffocate **10** annihilate

EXTIRPATE: **5** erase, expel **6** excise, remove, uproot **7** abolish, destroy, extract **8** demolish **9** eradicate **10** annihilate **11** exterminate

EXTOL: **4** laud **5** bless, exalt **6** praise **7** applaud, commend, glorify **8** eulogize **9** celebrate **10** compliment

EXTORT: **5** cheat, exact, force, wrest **6** coerce, elicit, wrench **7** extract, squeeze **10** intimidate

EXTORTION: **5** graft **6** payoff, racket, ransom **8** chantage, pressure **9** blackmail, shakedown

EXTRA: **3** odd **4** more, over, plus **5** added, spare **7** reserve, special, surplus **8** leftover, superior **9** accessory, ancillary, lagniappe, unusually **10** additional **11** superfluous **12** supplemental

EXTRACT: **4** cite, cull, draw **5** educe, evoke, exact, quote, wring **6** deduce, elicit, extort, gather, obtain, remove, select **7** essence, excerpt, exhaust, squeeze **8** separate, withdraw **9** decoction, quotation **11** concentrate

EXTRACTION: **4** race **5** stock **6** origin **7** descent, lineage **8** ancestry, breeding **9** parentage

EXTRANEOUS: **5** outer **6** exotic **7** foreign **8** needless **9** extrinsic, pointless **10** immaterial, irrelevant **11** impertinent **12** adventitious, inapplicable

EXTRAORDINARY: **4** rare **6** gnarly, signal, unique **7** amazing, bizarre, notable, special, strange, unusual **8** abnormal, terrific, uncommon **9** fantastic, monstrous, wonderful **10** incredible, phenomenal, remarkable, stupendous, superhuman, tremendous **11** exceptional, outstanding

EXTRAVAGANT: **4** wild **5** fancy **6** costly, lavish, ornate **7** bizarre, fanatic, profuse **8** prodigal, reckless, wasteful **9** excessive, expensive, fantastic, grandiose, luxurious **10** exorbitant, flamboyant, overpriced, ridiculous **12** preposterous, unreasonable, unrestrained

EXTREME: **4** last, peak **5** final, harsh, limit, ultra **6** severe, utmost, zenith **7** ceiling, drastic, faraway, highest, intense, maximum, outward, radical, violent **8** advanced, farthest, greatest, terrible, terrific, ultimate **9** desperate, excessive, nth degree, outermost **10** conclusive, immoderate **11** culmination

EXTREMIST: **6** zealot **7** fanatic, radical **8** nihilist **9** anarchist **10** maximalist **13** revolutionary

EXTREMITY: **3** arm, leg, toe **4** apex, foot, hand, limb, tail **5** brink, limit, verge **6** border, crisis, danger, finger **8** backside, boundary, disaster, distress **9** necessity, outermost

EXTRICATE: **4** free **5** clear, loose **6** remove, rescue **7** extract **8** liberate, untangle **9** disengage **11** disentangle

EXTRINSIC: **5** alien **7** foreign, outside **8** external **10** extraneous **11** unessential **12** adventitious

EXTROVERTED: **8** friendly, outgoing, sociable **10** gregarious

EXTRUDE: **4** spew **5** eject, evict, expel **7** project **8** protrude

EXUBERANCE: **4** elan, life, zest **5** vigor **6** energy, spirit **8** vitality, vivacity **9** eagerness, profusion **10** enthusiasm, liveliness **11** zestfulness **12** exhilaration, extravagance **13** effervescence

EXUBERANT: **5** happy **6** lavish, lively **7** excited, fertile **8** animated, cheerful, effusive, fruitful **9** abounding, excessive, plentiful, vivacious **10** flamboyant, passionate

EXUDE: **4** emit, ooze, seep **5** sweat **7** display, excrete, exhibit, secrete **8** perspire **9** discharge

EXULT: **4** brag, crow **5** boast, cheer, gloat, revel **7** rejoice **8** jubilate **9** celebrate

EXULTANT: **5** happy **6** elated, joyous **8** ecstatic **9** delighted, overjoyed **10** triumphant

EYE: **4** iris, lamp **5** orbit, pupil **6** areola, cornea, peeper, retina **7** blinker
black: **6** shiner
disease: **6** iritis, myopia **8** cataract, glaucoma **10** strabismus **11** astigmatism **14** conjunctivitis

EYE-CATCHING: **6** marked **10** attractive, noticeable **11** conspicuous

EYEFUL: **4** view **6** beauty, looker **8** knockout

EYEGLASSES: **5** specs **6** lenses **7** goggles **8** contacts, monocles **9** lorgnette **10** spectacles

EYE-POPPING: **7** amazing **8** exciting **9** thrilling, wonderful **11** astonishing

EYESIGHT: **4** view **6** vision

EYESORE: **4** dump, mess **6** blight **7** blemish

EYEWITNESS: **7** witness **8** observer, onlooker **9** bystander, spectator

F

FABLE: **3** lie **4** myth, tale **5** story **6** legend **7** fantasy, fiction, parable **8** allegory, apologue, exemplum **9** falsehood, narrative **10** concoction

FABRIC: **3** nap, rep, web **4** felt, repp, weft, woof **5** cloth, fiber, grain **6** lining **7** bunting, texture **8** material, shirting **9** construct, structure
coarse: **3** mat **5** crash, gunny **6** burlap **7** hopsack
corded: **3** rep **4** repp **5** pique **6** calico, poplin **7** pinwale **8** corduroy
cotton: **4** jean, susi **5** chino, drill, swiss **6** madras **7** galatea, gingham, percale **8** chambray, nainsook
dealer: **6** draper, mercer
flag: **7** bunting
linen: **4** ecru **5** carde, crash **6** barras **7** buckram, cambric, drabbet, lockram, sinelon
lustrous: **4** lame, silk **5** moire, satin, surah **6** poplin, sateen **7** taffeta
plaid: **6** madras, tartan
printed: **5** batik, toile **6** calico, chintz, damask **7** challis **8** jacquard
satin: **5** panne, pekin **6** etoile
sheer: **4** lawn **5** gauze, swiss, voile **6** dimity, tissue **7** batiste, chiffon, organdy, organza
silk: **5** carde, crepe, ninon, satin, surah **6** pongee, samite **7** alamode, chiffon, taffeta **8** sarsenet, shantung
striped: **3** aba **4** abba **5** pekin **7** galatea, ticking **8** algerine
synthetic: **5** nylon, orlon, rayon **6** dacron **7** acrilan, acrylic, plastic **9** polyester
waterproof: **7** oil skin
wool: **5** baize, beige, casha, loden, serge, tweed **6** burnet, caddis, camlet, duffel, frisca, melton, merino, moreen, witney, woolen **7** bolivia, debeige, delaine, droguet, frisado, frizado, hernani, woollen, worsted **8** cataloon, harateen, mackinaw, rattinet, zibeline **9** catalowne, gabardine, grenadine, harrateen, montagnac, zibelline
woven: **4** weft **5** tweed, twill **6** tricot **7** blanket, damasse, textile

FABRICATE: **4** coin, make **5** build, frame **6** create, devise, invent **7** concoct, falsify, fashion, produce **8** contrive **9** construct, formulate **11** manufacture

FABULOUS: **7** amazing, awesome **8** mythical, terrific **9** fantastic, legendary, marvelous, wonderful **10** astounding, incredible, outrageous, phenomenal, remarkable **11** astonishing

FACADE: **4** face, fake, mask **5** front **6** veneer **8** disguise, pretense

FACE: **3** mug, pan **4** bear, dare, defy, mask, meet, puss **5** brave, cover, front, frown, honor, paint, stand, stare **6** border, facade, kisser, oppose, visage **7** dignity, feature, grimace, profile, surface **8** confront, envisage, exterior, tolerate **9** encounter, semblance **10** expression, silhouette **11** countenance, physiognomy

FACET: **4** part, side **5** angle, phase **6** aspect **7** feature

FACETIOUS: **5** comic, funny, witty **6** clever **7** amusing, comical, jesting, jocular **8** humorous **9** laughable, sarcastic **12** wisecracking

FACE-TO-FACE: **6** direct **7** affront, vis-a-vis **8** confront

FACILE: **4** able, easy, glib **5** adept, quick, slick **6** adroit, expert, fluent, simple **8** skillful **10** effortless, proficient

FACILITATE: **3** aid **4** ease, help **6** assist, foster **7** further, promote **8** expedite

FACILITY: **4** east **5** knack, poise, skill **7** ability, address, amenity **8** aptitude **9** dexterity, readiness **10** adroitness, capability, expertness, pliability

FACSIMILE: **3** fax **4** copy **7** replica **9** duplicate, imitation **12** reproduction

FACT: **4** data, deed **5** basis, datum, event, point, proof, truth **7** reality **8** evidence, specific **9** actuality, certainty, ipso facto **10** statistics **12** circumstance

FACTION: **4** band, bloc, clan, ring, sect **5** cabal, group, junto, party **6** circle, clique, schism **7** coterie, dispute, quarrel **8** intrigue **9** coalition, rebellion **10** dissension **11** confederacy

FACTIOUS: **8** fighting **9** dissident, insurgent, seditious **11** conflicting, contentious

FACTITIOUS: **4** sham **5** bogus, phony **9** synthetic, unnatural **10** artificial

FACTOR: **4** doer, gene **5** agent, cause, point **6** aspect, author, detail, reason **7** element **9** component **10** antecedent, ingredient **11** constituent, determinant **12** circumstance

FACTORY: **4** mill, shop **5** plant **8** building, business, workshop **9** sweatshop **11** cooperative, manufactory **13** establishment

FACTUAL: **4** real, true **7** correct, genuine, literal **8** accurate **9** authentic, objective

FACULTY: **4** gift, wits **5** flair, knack, power, skill, staff **6** talent **7** ability **8** aptitude, capacity, instinct, teachers **10** capability, department, professors, propensity **11** instructors

FAD: **4** chic, rage, whim **5** craze, hobby, quirk, thing **7** fashion **9** amusement

FADE: **3** dim **4** dull, pale, wane, wilt **5** abate, decay, taper **6** recede, vanish, weaken, wither **7** evansce, lighten, shrivel, swindle **8** diminish, discolor, dissolve, languish **9** disappear

FAIL: **4** bomb, flop, fold, lose, sink, wane **5** flunk, welsh **6** bungle, desert, falter **7** abandon, default, exhaust, founder **8** bankrupt, languish, miscarry **10** disappoint **12** unsuccessful

FAILING: **4** flaw **5** fault **8** drawback, weakness **10** deficiency, inadequate **11** shortcoming **12** insufficient

FAILURE: **3** dud **4** bust, flop, loss **5** decay, fault, lapse, lemon, loser **6** fiasco, fizzle **7** debacle, decline, default, neglect, washout **8** abortion, collapse, downfall, omission **9** breakdown **10** bankruptcy, deficiency, insolvency **11** delinquency, frustration, miscarriage **14** disappointment

FAINT: **3** dim **4** dark, pale, soft, thin, weak **5** dizzy, faded, fuzzy, swoon, timid, vague, woozy **6** feeble, gentle, hushed, sickly, slight **7** distant, languid, muffled, obscure, syncope, unclear **8** blackout, collapse, delicate, languish, listless, sluggish **11** lightheaded

FAIR: **4** calm, even, gala, just, mild **5** bazar, blond, clear, equal, light, right **6** bazaar, blonde, decent, honest, square **7** average, exhibit, pageant **8** adequate, carnival, charming, distinct, festival, handsome, mediocre, middling, pleasant, unbiased **9** beautiful, equitable, impartial, judicious, objective **10** aboveboard, enchanting, exhibition, reasonable, sufficient **11** indifferent **12** unprejudiced

FAIRLY: **5** fully, quite **6** gently, rather **8** actually, properly, somewhat **9** favorably, tolerably **10** absolutely, distinctly **11** courteously **12** legitimately

FAIRNESS: **4** duty **6** equity **7** honesty **8** equality **10** legitimacy **11** objectivity **12** impartiality

FAIRY: **3** elf, fay **4** peri, puck **5** dwarf, genie, gnome, pixie **6** goblin, spirit, sprite **7** banshee, brownie, gremlin, sylphid **10** leprechaun **11** enchantress

FAITH: **4** cult, hope, sect **5** creed, dogma, trust **6** belief, church, pledge **7** loyalty, promise **8** reliance, religion **10** acceptance, confidence, conviction, persuasion **12** denomination

FAITHFUL: **4** fast, firm, true **5** loyal, pious, tried **6** honest, loving, steady, trusty **7** devoted, sincere, staunch, upright **8** constant, reliable **9** patriotic, steadfast, veracious **10** dependable, unwavering **11** trustworthy

FAITHLESS: **5** false **6** fickle, hollow, unjust, untrue **7** atheist **8** disloyal, recreant, shifting, unstable, wavering **9** deceptive, skeptical **10** inconstant, perfidious, traitorous **11** disaffected, treacherous, unbelieving

FAKE: **4** hoax, scam, sham **5** bogus, cheat, fudge, phony **7** falsify, pretend, swindle **8** imposter, invented, spurious **9** imitation **10** fictitious, fraudulent **11** counterfeit, fabrication, manufacture

FAKIR: **4** monk, yogi **5** Hindu **6** Moslem **7** ascetic **9** mendicant

FALCON: **4** bird, eyas, hawk **5** hobby, saker **6** cannon, lanner, merlin, musket **7** tiercel **9** peregrine

FALL: **3** die, sag **4** dive, drip, drop, fail, flop, plop, ruin, sink, slip, trip **5** abate, crash, lapse, occur, slump, spill **6** autumn, buckle, perish, plunge, recede, season, settle, submit, topple, tumble **7** cascade, decline, degrade, depress, descend, plummet, stumble, subside **8** cataract, collapse, decrease **9** backslide, overthrow, surrender **10** capitulate, depreciate, disappoint **11** destruction, precipitate

FALLACIOUS: **5** false, wrong **6** untrue **8** delusive, illusory, mistaken **9** beguiling, deceitful, deceptive, erroneous **10** fraudulent, misleading

FALLACY: **4** flaw **5** error **7** mistake **8** illusion **9** falsehood **11** false notion **13** misconception, preconception

FALL BACK: **6** recede, recoil **7** retract, retreat

FALLEN: **4** dead, lost **5** slain **6** ousted, shamed, sinful **7** deposed, immoral **9** disgraced

FALL FOR: **6** desire **7** believe

FALL GUY: **4** dupe, fool, pawn **5** chump, patsy **6** sucker **9** scapegoat

FALLIBLE: **5** human **6** faulty, mortal, unsure **7** erratic **9** erroneous, imperfect **10** unreliable **12** questionable

FALLING OUT: **4** spat **5** fight **7** dispute **8** argument **9** resultant **12** disagreement

FALLOUT: **4** dust **6** debris **9** byproduct **11** radioactive

FALLOW: **4** idle **6** barren, unused **8** inactive, unseeded **11** undeveloped **12** uncultivated

FALSE: **4** fake, sham **5** bogus, guise, phony, wrong **6** hollow, pseudo, unreal, untrue **7** crooked, devious, feigned, inexact **8** disloyal, illusive, mistaken, recreant, spurious **9** concocted, deceitful, deceptive, dishonest, erroneous, faithless, imaginary, incorrect, insincere, pretended **10** apocryphal, artificial, fictitious, groundless, inaccurate, misleading, perfidious, untruthful **11** counterfeit, disaffected, treacherous **12** hypocritical

FALSEHOOD: **3** fib, lie **4** tale **5** fable, fraud, story **6** canard **7** fallacy, fiction, perfidy, perjury, untruth **9** deception, mendacity, treachery **10** dishonesty, inaccuracy **11** fabrication **12** misstatement

FALSIFY: **3** lie **4** fake **5** alter, belie, forge, fudge, twist **6** betray, doctor **7** mislead **10** adulterate **11** counterfeit **12** misrepresent

FALTER: **4** fail, reel **5** waver **6** bobble, boggle, totter **7** shudder, stagger, stumble, stutter, tremble **8** flounder, hesitate **9** vacillate

FAME: **5** glory, honor, kudos, rumor **6** renown, report **7** acclaim, stardom **9** celebrity, greatness, notoriety **10** popularity, reputation **11** distinction, recognition

FAMILIAR: **4** bold, cozy, easy, free, snug **5** aware, buddy, close, usual **6** chummy, common, versed **7** affable, routine **8** frequent, friendly, habitual, intimate, ordinary, sociable **9** customary **10** accustomed, acquainted, conversant **12** acquaintance, confidential

FAMILY: **4** clan, line **5** brood, class, group, tribe **7** kindred, lineage, progeny **8** ancestry, category, children **9** genealogy, household, offspring, relatives **10** generation **11** descendants

FAMINE: **6** dearth, hunger **8** scarcity, shortage **10** starvation

FAMOUS: **5** grand, known, noted **7** eminent, notable, storied **8** renowned **9** excellent, legendary, notorious, prominent **10** celebrated, recognized, successful **11** illustrious **13** distinguished

FAN: **4** buff, cool, leaf **6** blower, punkah, rooter, spread, winnow **7** admirer, booster, devotee, groupie **8** follower, windmill **9** flabellum, propeller **10** enthusiast

FANATIC: **5** bigot, crazy, ultra **6** maniac, zealot **7** devotee, radical

8 activist **9** extremist **10** enthusiast **11** extravagant

FANCIFUL: **5** ideal **6** dreamy, quaint, unreal **7** bizarre, strange **8** illusory, mythical, romantic **9** fantastic, imaginary, visionary, whimsical **10** capricious, chimerical **11** imaginative

FANCY: **4** idea, love, whim **5** crave, dream, humor, taste **6** deluxe, desire, lavish, liking, notion, ornate, vagary, vision, whimsy **7** caprice, chimera, conceit, elegant, fantasy, picture, romance **8** illusion, pleasure **9** capriccio, elaborate, expensive **10** conjecture, decorative, impression, ornamental, preference **11** embellished, imagination, inclination

FANDANGO: **4** tune **5** dance **7** Spanish **8** nonsense **10** tomfoolery

FANFARE: **4** pomp, show **7** display, panoply, tantara **8** ceremony, cheering **9** fireworks

FANNY: **4** rump **5** hiney **6** behind, heinie **8** buttocks, derriere

FANTASIZE: **6** invent **7** imagine **8** daydream, envision

FANTASTIC: **4** huge **5** weird **6** absurd, exotic, unreal **7** amazing, bizarre, massive, strange **8** enormous, fabulous, fanciful, terrific **9** excellent, grotesque, imaginary, whimsical, wonderful **10** capricious, chimerical, incredible **11** extravagant, imaginative, sensational **12** unbelievable

FANTASY: **4** idea, whim **5** dream, fancy **6** desire, mirage, vision **7** chimera, reverie, romance **8** illusion **9** invention **10** apparition **11** imagination **13** hallucination

FAR: **4** deep, long, much, wide **5** miles **6** remote **7** distant, greatly **8** outlying **12** considerably, inaccessible

FAR AND WIDE: **10** everywhere, far and near

FARAWAY: **6** dreamy, remote **7** distant, removed **9** oblivious **10** abstracted **11** preoccupied

FARCE: **4** joke, mime **6** comedy, parody, satire **7** mockery **8** nonsense, stuffing **9** burlesque, slapstick

FARCICAL: **5** funny, silly **6** absurd **7** amusing, comical **8** humorous **9** ludicrous **10** outrageous, ridiculous **11** nonsensical

FARE: **3** eat, fee **4** diet, food, path, rate, toll **5** price, token, track **6** charge, happen, manage, ticket, travel **7** journey, passage, proceed, prosper **8** customer, progress **9** passenger, provision

FAREWELL: **3** bye **5** adieu, adios, aloha, conge **7** cheerio, goodbye, parting, sendoff **8** sayonara, swan song **9** bon voyage, departure **10** salutation **11** valedictory

FARFETCHED: **6** forced **7** bizarre, dubious **8** doubtful, strained, unlikely **10** cockamamie, improbable **11** unrealistic **12** unbelievable

FARINA: **4** meal, mush **5** flour **6** cereal, starch

FARM: **4** land, plow, till **5** croft, dairy, field, plant, ranch, range **6** garden, grange, oyster, rancho, spread **7** harvest, kibbutz, kolkhoz, orchard **8** hatchery, vineyard **9** cultivate, homestead **10** plantation **11** cooperative

FARMER: **6** grower, tiller, yeoman **7** breeder, granger, planter, plowman, rancher **8** producer **9** harvester, plowwoman **10** cultivator, husbandman **12** sharecropper **13** agriculturist

FARMING: **7** grazing **9** gardening, husbandry **11** agriculture

FAR-OFF: **6** remote **7** distant, strange

FAROUCHE: **4** wild **5** surly **6** fierce, savage, sullen

FAR-REACHING: **4** wide **5** broad **9** extensive, universal

FARSIGHTED: **4** wise **6** shrewd **9** hyperopic, provident, sagacious **10** perceptive **11** clairvoyant

FARTHER: **6** beyond, longer, yonder **7** further, remoter

FARTHEST: **4** last **6** utmost **7** endmost, extreme, longest, outmost **10** lattermost

FASCICLE: **5** bunch **6** bundle **7** cluster **10** collection

FASCINATE: **4** draw **5** charm, rivet **6** absorb, allure, compel, thrill **7** attract, enchant, engross **8** entrance, interest, intrigue **9** captivate, mesmerize, spellbind

FASCINATION: **6** wonder **9** magnetism, obsession **10** attraction **12** astonishment

FASCISM: **6** Nazism **9** autocracy **12** dictatorship **15** totalitarianism

FASCIST: **6** Hitler **8** dictator **9** Mussolini

FASHION: **3** air, fad **4** form, look, make, mold, rage **5** build, craze, frame, guise, model, shape, style, trend, vogue **6** create, custom, design, invent, manner, method, tailor **7** compose, pattern **8** attitude, contrive **9** construct, etiquette, fabricate **10** appearance

FASHIONABLE: **3** hip, hot **4** chic, posh **5** smart, swank **6** modern, modish, trendy **7** a la mode, dashing, popular, stylish **10** newfangled **12** contemporary

FAST: **4** diet, easy, firm, held, true **5** bawdy, brisk, fixed, fleet, hasty, loose, quick, rapid, stuck, swift **6** active, flying, pronto, secure, speedy, stable, starve **7** abstain, hurried, refrain **8** enduring, faithful, reckless **9** immovable, permanent, steadfast **10** stationary, unyielding **11** expeditious, promiscuous

FASTEN: **3** fix, pin, set, tie **4** bend, bind, bolt, bond, clip, glue, hook, join, lace, link, lock, moor, nail, rope, seal, weld, wire **5** affix, brace, chain, clamp, clasp, cling, focus, hitch, latch, paste, rivet, strap, truss **6** adhere, anchor, attach, batten, cement, clinch, couple, direct, secure, solder, staple, tether **7** connect, padlock, tighten

FASTENER: **3** nut, peg, pin **4** bolt, clip, hasp, lock, nail, snap, stud, tack **5** catch, clamp, clasp, latch, rivet, screw, strap **6** buckle, button, staple, Velcro, zipper **7** bracket, padlock

FASTIDIOUS: **4** fine, nice **5** fussy **6** choosy, dainty **7** elegant, finical, finicky, refined **8** critical, delicate, exacting **9** demanding, difficult, exquisite, sensitive, squeamish **10** meticulous, particular

FAT: **3** oil **4** flab, lard, rich, suet **5** broad, cushy, heavy, large, obese, plump, pudgy, stout, thick, tubby **6** chubby, fleshy, grease, portly, rotund, stocky **7** blubber, fertile, obesity, opulent, paunchy **8** fruitful **9** cellulite, corpulent **10** overweight, potbellied, profitable, prosperous **11** elephantine

FATAL: **5** final **6** deadly, doomed, lethal, mortal **7** crucial, fateful, ruinous **8** critical, destined, terminal **9** incurable **10** calamitous, disastrous, pernicious **11** destructive **12** catastrophic

FATALITY: **5** death **8** accident, casualty

FATE: **3** end, lot **4** doom **5** karma **6** chance, kismet, result **7** destiny, fortune, outcome, portion **11** consequence **14** predestination

FATEFUL: **6** deadly **7** crucial, ruinous **8** critical, decisive, eventful **9** important **10** disastrous, inevitable **11** destructive, predestined, significant

FATHER: **3** dad, pop **4** abba, papa, sire **5** adopt, beget, daddy, friar, padre **6** author, create, old man, parent, parson, pastor, priest **7** creator, founder **8** generate, inventor, minister, reverend **9** confessor, originate, paternity, patriarch, procreate

FATHERLAND: **8** homeland **10** birthplace, motherland

FATHERLY: **6** kindly **8** paternal **10** benevolent, protective, supportive **11** patriarchal

FATHOM: **5** delve, grasp, solve **7** discern, measure **9** penetrate **10** comprehend, understand

FATIGUED: **4** beat **5** jaded, spend, tired **6** bushed **7** drained, languid, wearied **8** weakened **9** exhausted

FATTEN: **4** feed, lard **5** plump, stuff, swell **6** batten, enrich, thrive

FATTY: **4** oily **5** lardy, suety **6** greasy **7** pinguid **8** blubbery **9** sebaceous

FATUOUS: **5** inane, silly **6** stupid, unreal **7** asinine, foolish, idiotic, moronic, witless **8** delusive, imbecile **9** brainless **10** ridiculous **13** unintelligent

FAUCET: **3** tap **5** valve **6** nozzle, spigot **7** hydrant

FAULT: **3** sin **4** flaw, flub, slip, vice **5** blame, error, wrong **6** defect, foible, glitch **7** blemish, blunder, default, failing, frailty, mistake, neglect, offense **8** drawback, weakness **9** liability **10** deficiency **11** culpability, dysfunction, shortcoming **12** imperfection **13** transgression

FAULTFINDER: **5** cynic, momus **6** carper, censor, critic **9** nitpicker

FAULTLESS: **4** pure **5** right, whole **7** correct, perfect, precise, sinless **8** spotless **9** blameless, exemplary, foolproof, stainless **10** immaculate, impeccable **14** irreproachable

FAULTY: **3** bad **5** wrong **6** broken, marred **7** damaged **8** impaired **9** defective, erroneous, imperfect, incorrect **10** inaccurate **14** malfunctioning

FAUX PAS: **4** bull, goof, slip **5** boner, error, gaffe **6** bungle **7** blooper, mistake **8** solecism **9** indecorum

FAVOR: **4** gift, help, like **5** bless, grace **6** esteem, letter, oblige, prefer, reward, uphold **7** advance, service, support **8** advocacy, approval, befriend, courtesy, goodwill, kindness **9** patronage, privilege, subscribe **10** assistance, concession, indulgence **11** accommodate, approbation

FAVORABLE: **4** good, kind **6** benign **7** benefic, hopeful **8** friendly, gracious, pleasant, pleasing, positive **9** approving, opportune, welcoming **10** auspicious, convenient, propitious, reassuring **11** encouraging **12** advantageous **13** complimentary

FAVORITE: **3** pet **6** adored, choice, minion **7** beloved, popular, special **9** treasured **10** preference

FAVORITISM: **4** bias **8** nepotism **9** prejudice **10** partiality **14** discrimination

FAWN: **4** buck, deer **5** cower, crawl, kotow, toady **6** cringe, grovel, kowtow **7** flatter, truckle, wheedle **8** yearling **9** sycophant **10** ingratiate

FAY: **3** elf **5** fairy, pixie **7** brownie

FAZE: **5** abash, daunt **6** bother, puzzle, rattle **7** confuse, perplex **8** irritate **9** embarrass **10** disconcert

FEALTY: **4** duty **7** loyalty **8** devotion, fidelity **9** constancy **10** allegiance, obligation **12** faithfulness

FEAR: **5** alarm, doubt, dread, panic **6** dismay, fright, horror, phobia, terror **7** anxiety, concern **8** affright, distrust, venerate **9** agitation, reverence, suspicion **10** uneasiness **11** trepidation **12** apprehension **13** consternation
of animals: **9** zoophobia
of bees: **10** apiophobia
of being buried alive: **11** taphephobia
of blood: **10** hemophobia
of cats: **12** ailurophobia
of childbirth: **10** tocophobia
of choking: **11** pnigophobia
of confined spaces: **14** claustrophobia
of crossing bridges: **13** gephyrophobia
of crowds: **11** ochlophobia
of darkness: **11** nyctophobia
of death: **11** necrophobia
of dirt: **10** mysophobia
of dogs: **10** cynophobia
of drafts: **10** aerophobia
of dust: **12** amathophobia
of fear: **11** phobophobia
of fire: **10** pyrophobia
of germs: **14** microbiophobia
of ghosts: **12** phasmophobia
of heights: **10** acrophobia
of illness: **10** nosophobia
of injury: **14** traumatophobia
of insects: **12** entomophobia
of lightning: **13** astrapophobia
of loneliness: **12** eremiophobia
of marriage: **12** gametophobia
of mice: **10** musophobia
of mirrors: **14** eisoptrophobia
of money: **14** chrometophobia
of night: **11** nyctophobia
of old age: **13** gerascophobia
of open spaces: **11** agoraphobia
of pain: **10** algophobia
of poisoning: **12** toxicophobia
of poverty: **11** peniaphobia
of pregnancy: **14** maieusiophobia
of public speaking: **10** lalophobia
of sharks: **11** galeophobia
of sleep: **11** hypnophobia
of snakes: **13** ophidiophobia
of spiders: **13** arachniphobia
of strangers: **10** xenophobia
of thirteen: **17** triskaidekaphobia
of thunder: **12** brontophobia **13** tonitrophobia
of travel: **10** hodophobia
of water: **11** hydrophobia
of work: **10** ergophobia
of worms: **15** helminthophobia

FEARFUL: **4** dire **5** awful **6** afraid, aghast, scared **7** alarmed, chicken, ghastly, jittery, nervous, panicky, worried **8** dreadful, horrible, shocking, terrible **9** appalling, concerned, frightful, terrified, trembling **10** frightened, horrendous **11** distressing **12** apprehensive

FEARLESS: **4** bold **5** brave **6** daring, heroic **7** gallant, valiant **8** intrepid, unafraid **9** audacious, undaunted **10** courageous **11** adventurous

FEASIBLE: **5** cinch **6** doable, likely, viable **8** possible, suitable, workable **10** achievable, attainable, reasonable **11** conceivable

FEAST: **3** eat **4** dine, fete, gala, luau, meal **5** stuff, treat **6** dinner, fiesta, regale, repast **7** banquet, delight, holiday, indulge **8** carnival, festival

FEAT: **3** act **4** deed, neat, trim **5** stunt, trick **6** action **7** exploit, miracle, triumph **8** conquest **9** adventure **10** attainment **11** achievement, tour de force **12** masterstroke **14** accomplishment

FEATHER: **4** down, vane, wing **5** adorn, fluff, penna, plume, quill **6** fledge, fletch, osprey, pinion **7** panache, plumage, species **9** character

FEATHERBRAINED: **5** giddy, silly **6** simple **7** flighty, foolish **9** brainless **11** empty-headed

FEATHERWEIGHT: **5** boxer **7** trivial **8** wrestler **11** unimportant

FEATURE: **4** mark **5** angle, story, trait **6** aspect, column, detail, factor **7** element, outline **8** hallmark, headline **9** attribute, character, component, highlight, lineament **11** countenance **12** idiosyncrasy **14** characteristic

FECKLESS: **4** weak **5** slack **6** feeble, remiss **7** aimless, useless **8** careless **9** worthless **10** unreliable **11** ineffective, meaningless, purposeless **13** irresponsible

FECUND: **7** fertile **8** fruitful, prolific **10** productive

FEDERATION: **5** union **6** league **8** alliance **9** coalition, syndicate **10** consortion **11** association, partnership

FED UP: **5** bored **7** annoyed **9** disgusted, surfeited **12** dissatisfied

FEE: **3** tab, tax **4** cost, dues, fare, rate, toll, wage **5** price **6** charge, reward, salary, tariff **7** expense, payment, stipend, tuition **8** gratuity, retainer **9** allowance, emolument **10** assessment, commission, honorarium, percentage, recompense **12** compensation

FEEBLE: **4** lame, poor, puny, weak **5** faint, frail **6** ailing, flimsy, infirm, senile, sickly **7** fragile, invalid, languid **8** decrepit, disabled, helpless, impotent, inferior **10** inadequate **11** debilitated, ineffective

FEEBLEMINDED: **5** dotty **6** senile **7** foolish, moronic **10** halfwitted, irresolute

FEED: **3** eat, hay **4** bran, dine, fuel, grub, meal, oats **5** feast, grass, nurse **6** fatten, fodder, foster, supply **7** furnish, indulge, nourish, nurture, provide, satiate, satisfy, sustain **8** dispense **9** aggravate, replenish **10** strengthen

FEEL: **3** air **4** aura, deem, know, mood **5** grope, sense, think, touch **6** fumble, gather, handle, stroke, tingle **7** believe, discern, explore, suppose, texture **8** ambience, conclude, perceive **10** atmosphere, experience, understand

FEELER: **4** hint, test **5** probe **6** barbel **7** antenna **8** proposal, question, tentacle **10** prospectus **12** trial balloon

FEELING: **4** pain, pity **5** humor, sense, touch **6** morale, notion, warmth **7** emotion, opinion, passion **8** attitude, pleasure, sympathy **9** awareness, intuition, sensation, sentiment, suspicion **10** atmosphere, enthusiasm, experience, perception **11** inclination, sensitivity

FEET: **4** dogs, paws **6** hooves **11** extremities

FEIGN: **3** act **4** fake, sham **5** avoid, bluff **6** affect, assume, devise, invent **7** conceal, concoct, imagine, pretend **8** disguise, simulate **9** dissemble, fabricate, personate **11** counterfeit

FEINT: **4** bait, hoax, mask, ploy, ruse, wile **5** bluff, dodge, stall, trick **6** deceit, gambit **8** artifice, pretense **9** expedient

FEISTY: **6** frisky, lively, spunky **8** spirited **9** energetic **10** aggressive

FELICITATE: **4** hail **5** greet **6** praise, salute **7** commend **12** congratulate

FELICITOUS: **3** apt **5** happy **6** joyous **7** fitting **8** inspired, pleasing, suitable **10** delightful

FELICITY: **3** joy **5** bliss **7** ecstasy **9** happiness

FELINE: **3** cat, tom **4** lion, lynx, puma **5** civet, tiger **6** jaguar **7** cheetah, leopard, wildcat

FELL: **3** cut **4** chop, dire, down, hack, hide, hill, kill, moor, pelt, ruin, skin, very **5** cruel, field, floor, great, level, sharp **6** cleave, deadly, fierce, fleece, lethal, savage, shrewd, tumble **7** brutish, crashed, hideous, inhuman, tumbled **8** sinister, spirited **9** barbarous, ferocious, marshland, prostrate, slaughter **11** destructive

FELLOW: **3** boy, guy, lad, man **4** beau, chap, mate, peer **5** bloke, cadet, match **6** friend, hombre, person **7** brother, comrade, partner **9** associate, colleague, companion, gentleman

FELLOWSHIP: **5** grant, guild, order, union **7** company, society **8** alliance **10** fraternity, friendship, membership, sisterhood **11** association, brotherhood, camaraderie, corporation, familiarity, freemasonry, partnership

FELON: **4** evil **5** crook, cruel **6** outlaw **7** convict, culprit, whitlow **8** criminal, gangster, jailbird, offender **10** lawbreaker, malefactor

FELONY: **4** rape **5** arson, crime **6** murder **7** offense, robbery **8** burglary **10** kidnapping

FEMALE: **3** mom, Mrs **4** girl, lady, Miss **5** woman **6** mother, sister **8** daughter, feminine, ladylike **11** grandmother

FEMININE: **4** soft **6** dainty, female, tender **7** girlish, womanly **8** ladylike, womanish **10** effeminate

FEMME FATALE: **5** siren **7** charmer **9** temptress **10** seductress

FEN: **3** bog **4** moor **5** marsh **7** wetland **8** quagmire

FENCE: **4** coop, duel, gird, post, rail, wall **5** dodge, guard, hedge **6** defend, picket **7** barrier, defense **8** backstop, encircle, palisade, stockade, surround **9** barricade, enclosure

FENCING:
terms: **3** cut **4** duel, epee, foil, volt **5** appel, feint, parry, piste, saber, sword **6** fleche, foible, remise, thrust, touche **7** barrage, en garde, reprise, riposte **8** balestra, coquille, plastron, swording

FEND: **5** avert, avoid, guard, parry, repel **6** defend, resist **7** protect, provide, support **9** safeguard

FENDER: **5** frame, guard **6** buffer, bumper, screen, shield **7** cushion **8** mudguard **11** splashboard

FERAL: **4** wild **6** brutal, fierce, savage **7** untamed **9** barbarous, ferocious

FERMENT: **4** barm, brew, heat, stew, turn **5** churn, fever, froth, yeast **6** enzyme, excite, seethe, simmer, tumult, uproar **7** agitate, provoke **8** catalyst, disorder **9** commotion **10** exacerbate, excitement, turbulence

FEROCIOUS: **4** fell, grim, wild **5** cruel, feral **6** brutal, fierce, savage **7** extreme, inhuman, untamed, vicious, violent **8** barbaric, ravenous, ruthless **9** merciless, murderous **10** malevolent, relentless, sanguinary **12** bloodthirsty

FERRET OUT: **4** hunt, seek **5** probe, trace, track, trail **6** elicit, follow **7** uncover **9** ascertain

FERRY: **5** barge, carry **7** shuttle

FERTILE: **4** lush, rich **6** fecund, hearty, virile **7** teeming **8** abundant, fruitful, generous, pregnant, prolific **9** bountiful, exuberant, feracious, flowering, luxuriant, plentiful **10** productive, profitable

FERTILIZE: **4** lime **6** enrich **8** fructify **9** fecundate, pollinate **10** impregnate, inseminate

FERTILIZER: **4** dung **5** guano, humus, mulch **6** manure, pollen **7** compost, nitrate **8** nitrogen

FERVENT: **3** hot **4** warm **5** eager, fiery **6** ardent, fierce, raging **7** blazing, burning, glowing, intense, zealous **8** animated, vehement **9** emotional, impetuous **10** passionate **12** enthusiastic

FERVOR: **4** fire, heat, love, zeal **5** ardor, gusto **7** ecstasy, passion **9** eagerness, intensity, vehemence **10** enthusiasm, excitement **11** earnestness

FESTER: **3** rot **4** fret, grow **5** decay **6** rankle **7** blister, inflame **8** ulcerate **9** suppurate

FESTIVAL: **4** fair, fete, gala **5** feast, festa **6** fiesta **7** banquet, holiday, jubilee **8** carnival, jamboree **11** celebration

FESTIVE: **3** gay **4** gala **5** happy, merry **6** joyous, upbeat **7** jocular, playful **8** mirthful, sportive **9** decorated **10** frolicsome **11** celebratory

FESTIVITY: **4** gala **5** mirth **6** gaiety, hoopla **7** fanfare, jollity, revelry, whoopee **10** joyfulness **11** celebration, merrymaking **12** conviviality **13** entertainment

FETCH: **3** get **5** bring, ghost, sweep, trick **6** elicit, inhale, obtain **7** achieve, attract, deliver, realize **8** retrieve **9** stratagem **10** apparition

FETCHING: **6** lovely **8** alluring, charming, pleasing **9** appealing, beautiful **10** attractive **11** captivating

FETE: **4** ball, fair, gala **5** bazar, feast, party **6** bazaar, fiesta **7** banquet, holiday **8** carnival, festival **9** celebrate, entertain

FETID: **4** foul, rank **5** fusty, moldy, musty **6** putrid, rancid, rotten **7** corrupt, noisome, noxious **8** mephitic, stinking **9** offensive, repulsive **10** malodorous

FETISH: **4** idol, juju **5** charm, image, mania, totem **6** amulet, desire, voodoo **7** passion, sorcery **8** fixation, talisman **9** obsession

FETTER: **4** bind, bond, hold **5** block, chain **6** hamper, hobble, impede **7** confine, manacle, shackle, trammel **8** handcuff **9** restraint

FEUD: **3** row, war **4** duel, fray, tiff **5** broil, fight **6** enmity, grudge, strife **7** contest, dispute, quarrel **8** argument, conflict, vendetta **9** hostility **12** disagreement

FEVER: **4** fire **5** craze **6** desire, frenzy **7** ferment, pyrexia **8** delirium **10** excitement **11** temperature

FEVERISH: **4** warm **5** fiery **6** ardent, hectic **7** burning, excited, febrile, flushed, frantic, intense, pyretic **8** restless **9** obsessive, overeager

FEW: **4** less, rare, some **5** scant **6** meager, scarce, seldom, skimpy **7**

handful, limited **10** infrequent, occasional

FEY: **4** dead **5** elfin **9** fairylike, visionary, whimsical **11** clairvoyant **12** otherworldly

FIANCE, FIANCEE: **6** steady **7** engaged **8** intended **9** betrothed

FIASCO: **4** bomb, flop **7** blunder, debacle, failure, screwup, washout **8** disaster **11** catastrophe

FIAT: **4** rule, writ **5** edict, order, ukase **6** decree, dictum **7** command, mandate **8** sanction **9** ordinance **12** announcement, proclamation

FIB: **3** lie **4** tale **5** hedge, story **6** canard **7** untruth **9** half-truth **10** equivocate **11** fabrication, prevaricate

FIBER: **4** coir, cord, flax, hair, hemp, jute, lint, root, rope, wool **5** floss, grain, nylon, rayon, sisal **6** cotton, dacron, fabric, nature, string, thread, tissue **7** acrylic, essence, quality, texture **8** filament, roughage **9** character, fortitude, polyester

FIBROUS: **4** ropy **5** pulpy, tough **6** sinewy **7** stringy

FIBULA: **5** clasp **6** brooch **7** leg bone **8** lower leg

FICKLE: **6** shifty **7** erratic, flighty **8** critical, shifting, unstable, unsteady, volatile, wavering **9** faithless, frivolous, mercurial, unsettled, whimsical **10** capricious, changeable, inconstant **11** fluctuating, vacillating **12** inconsistent

FICTION: **4** book, myth, tale, yarn **5** drama, fable, novel **6** legend **7** fantasy, figment, romance **8** pretense **9** falsehood, invention, narrative **10** concoction **11** contrivance, fabrication

FICTITIOUS: **4** fake, sham **5** bogus, false, phony **6** unreal, untrue **7** assumed, created, feigned **8** fanciful, invented, mythical, spurious **9** imaginary **10** apocryphal, artificial **11** counterfeit

FIDDLE: **3** bow **5** cheat, touch **6** dabble, doodle, fidget, putter, tamper, tinker, trifle, violin **7** swindle **9** guardrail

FIDELITY: **4** love, oath **5** honor, troth **6** fealty **7** honesty, loyalty **8** devotion **9** adherence, constancy, integrity **10** allegiance **11** reliability **12** faithfulness **13** dependability

FIDGETY: **5** antsy, fussy, hyper, jumpy, wired **6** uneasy **7** anxious, jittery, nervous, restive, squirmy **8** restless **9** impatient **12** apprehensive

FIDUCIARY: **7** curator, trustee **8** guardian **10** depositary

FIELD: **4** area, mead, plot **5** catch, orbit, patch, range, realm, rowen, scope, track, tract **6** course, domain, garden, handle, meadow, racket, sphere **7** compass, diamond, entries, grounds, pasture, runners, stadium, terrain **8** clearing, gridiron, vineyard **9** grassland, specialty **10** background, department, discipline, occupation, playground, profession **11** competitors, contestants **12** battleground

FIELD GOAL: **5** score **6** basket

FIEND: **5** beast, brute, demon, devil **6** addict, maniac, savage **7** fanatic, incubus, monster **8** obsessed, succubus **9** barbarian, scoundrel

FIENDISH: **4** evil **5** cruel **6** wicked **7** demonic, satanic, vicious **8** demoniac, devilish, sinister **9** atrocious, barbarous, difficult **10** diabolical

FIERCE: **4** bold, fell, wild **5** cruel, feral, fiery **6** ardent, brutal, raging, savage **7** fervent, furious, intense, untamed, violent **8** ruthless, terrible **9** cutthroat, ferocious, merciless, truculent **10** aggressive, passionate, relentless, unpleasant **12** overpowering, uncontrolled

FIERY: **3** hot **6** ablaze, ardent, fervid, fierce, heated, spunky, torrid **7** blazing, burning, fervent, flaming, glowing, intense, peppery, violent **8** choleric, feverish, inflamed, spirited **9** excitable, flammable, hotheaded, impetuous, impulsive, irascible, irritable **10** mettlesome, passionate **11** inflammable, tempestuous **12** enthusiastic

FIESTA: **4** fete, gala **5** feast, party **7** holiday **8** carnival, festival **11** celebration

FIFTY-FIFTY: **4** even **6** shared **7** divided, equally

FIG: **3** rig **4** fico **5** eleme, fruit, pipal **6** ginger, mammee **7** syconus **8** sinconus, syconium

FIGHT: **3** box, row, war **4** bout, duel, feud, fray, grit, spat, tiff **5** argue, brawl, brush, clash, joust, melee, scrap **6** affair, affray, attack, battle, bicker, combat, debate, fracas, hassle, mettle, oppose, resist, rumble, spirit **7** contend, contest, dispute, grapple, quarrel, rivalry, scuffle, wrangle **8** argument, conflict, exchange, skirmish, squabble, struggle **9** encounter, withstand **11** altercation, controversy **12** disagreement **13** confrontation

FIGHTER: **5** boxer **7** battler, bruiser, duelist, soldier, warrior **8** pugilist, scrapper **9** combatant, contender, gladiator **10** competitor

FIGMENT: **5** dream **7** fantasy, fiction, phantom **8** illusion **9** invention **11** fabrication

FIGURATION: **4** form **5** shape **7** contour, outline **9** symbolism

FIGURATIVE: **6** florid, ornate **7** flowery **8** symbolic **10** emblematic **11** allegorical, descriptive **12** metaphorical

FIGURE: **3** sum **4** cost, rate **5** digit, price, total, value **6** amount, emblem, number, symbol **7** numeral, topiary **8** gargoyle **9** character, quotation

geometric: **4** cone, cube, lune **5** prism, rhomb, solid **6** circle, gnomon, isagon, isogon, oblong, sector, square **7** diagram, ellipse, lozenge, pelcoid, rhombus **8** crescent, hexafoil, pentacle, spheroid, triangle **9** rectangle

of speech: **5** adage, color, image, irony, trope **6** aporia, cliche, simile, tmesis **7** analogy, conceit, echoism, imagery, litotes, meiosis, paradox, zeugmaa **8** allegory, aphorism, atticism, metaphor, metonymy, oxymoron, platitude, pleonasm **9** euphemism, hyperbole, syllepsis **10** allocution, brachylogy, synecdoche **11** antiphrasis, malapropism, periphrasis **12** alliteration, onomatopoeia **13** amplification **15** personification

FIGUREHEAD: **5** dummy, front **6** puppet, stooge **9** nonentity **10** mouthpiece

FIGURE OUT: **5** crack, solve **6** decide, decode **7** resolve, unravel **8** decipher, discover, untangle **9** calculate **10** unscramble

FIJI:

capital: **4** Suva
cities: **6** Levuka **7** Lautoka
continent: **7** Oceania
ethnic groups: **6** Fijian, Indian **10** Melanesian, Polynesian
features: **6** Nararu **8** Viti Levu **9** Vanua Levu
languages: **5** Hindi **6** Fijian **7** English
monetary unit: **6** dollar
water: **12** Pacific Ocean

FILAMENT: **4** hair, harl, wire **5** fiber, stalk **6** strand, thread **7** tendril

FILCH: **3** rob **4** lift **5** heist, pinch, steal, swipe **6** pilfer, snitch **8** embezzle

FILE: **3** row **4** case, line, list, rank, tool **5** grind, index, order, store **6** column, drawer, folder, record, smooth **7** arrange, cabinet, catalog, sharpen **8** archives, classify, register

FILIBUSTER: **5** delay **9** talkathon **10** adventurer, opposition **12** stonewalling

FILL: **4** cram, feed, load, pack, plug, sate **5** caulk, crowd, earth, gorge, stock **6** charge, occupy, supply **7** distend, enlarge, execute, inflate, padding, pervade, satiate, satisfy, suffuse **8** capacity, complete, permeate, stuffing **9** replenish **10** accomplish **11** sufficiency

FILLET: **4** band, fish, meat, tape **5** crown, ridge, slice, snood, strip **6** ribbon, wreath **7** bandeau, chaplet, garland, molding **8** boneless, headband

FILL IN: **5** brief **6** inform **8** complete **9** interject **10** substitute **11** replacement

FILLING: **4** weft **6** center **7** amalgam, content, custard, mixture, wadding

FILLIP: **3** tap **4** flip **5** boost **6** charge, excite **8** stimulus **9** incentive

FILM: **4** blur, haze, mist, scum, skin, veil, x-ray **5** flick, layer, movie **6** record **7** coating, deposit, footage **8** negative, pellicle **9** celluloid **10** photograph **12** transparency

FILMY: **4** hazy **5** gauzy, milky, misty, wispy **6** dainty **7** clouded, fragile **8** finespun, gossamer

FILTER: **4** seep, sift **5** clean, drain, sieve **6** purify, refine, screen, strain **8** strainer **9** percolate **10** infiltrate

FILTH: **4** dirt, dung, muck, silt, slop, smut **5** grime, slime, trash **6** refuse, sewage **7** garbage **9** obscenity, pollution **10** corruption **11** pornography

FILTHY: **4** foul, lewd, vile **5** dirty, grimy, gross, nasty **6** grubby, impure, rotten, scummy, sleazy, sordid, vulgar **7** obscene, raunchy, squalor, unclean **8** polluted, wretched **9** offensive, repulsive, revolting **10** disgusting **12** scatological

FIN: **3** arm **4** hand, vane **5** pinna **6** dorsal **7** airfoil, flipper **9** appendage **10** stabilizer

FINAGLE: **4** rook **5** cheat, trick **6** scheme **7** connive, deceive, swindle

FINAL: **4** last **6** latter **7** extreme, supreme **8** absolute, crowning, decisive, farewell, ultimate **10** concluding, conclusive, definitive **11** terminating, unalterable

FINALE: **4** coda **5** finis **6** climax, ending, windup **7** closing **8** epilogue **10** conclusion **11** culmination

FINALIZE: **5** agree **6** finish, settle **8** conclude **10** consummate

FINALLY: **6** lastly **9** certainly **10** decisively, eventually, ultimately **11** irrevocably

FINANCE: **4** back, fund **5** endow, float, money, stake **7** banking, sponsor **8** bankroll, business **9** economics, subsidize **10** underwrite

FINANCES: **4** cash **6** budget, wealth **7** affairs, revenue **9** resources

FINANCIAL: **6** fiscal **7** markets **8** economic, monetary **9** pecuniary

FINANCIER: 6 backer, staker 7 sponsor 10 capitalist 11 underwriter 12 entrepreneur

FIND: 4 spot 5 catch, judge, solve 6 locate 7 bonanza, recover, uncover 8 treasure 9 ascertain, discovery

FIND GUILTY: 6 indict 7 condemn, convict

FIND INNOCENT: 6 acquit 7 absolve 9 exonerate, vindicate

FIND OUT: 4 hear 5 learn 6 detect, fathom, reveal 7 realize, unearth 8 discover, identify 9 ascertain

FINE: 4 good, levy, nice, pure, thin 5 bonny, clear, dandy, frail, great, mulct, nifty, sharp, sheer, silky, swell 6 amerce, bright, choice, dainty, minute, slight, subtle, tender 7 capital, damages, elegant, forfeit, fragile, penalty, powdery, precise, tenuous 8 absolute, delicate, granular, handsome, penalize, pleasant, skillful, splendid, superior, top-grade 9 admirable, beautiful, excellent, expensive 10 assessment, consummate, pulverized, punishment, reparation 11 exceptional, magnificent, outstanding

FINERY: 6 frills 7 apparel, clothes, gaudery, gewgaws, regalia 8 elegance, frippery 9 adornment, trappings 10 Sunday best

FINESSE: 4 tact 5 guile, savvy, skill 7 cunning, operate 8 artifice, delicacy, maneuver, subtlety 9 adeptness, dexterity, stratagem 10 artfulness, craftiness, manipulate, refinement 11 sensitivity

FINGER: 3 paw 4 feel, make, poke 5 digit, index, pinky, strum, thumb, touch 6 choose, dactyl, handle 8 identify, indicate, pinpoint 9 appendage, designate

FINGERPRINT: 3 dab 4 mark 8 identify 11 dactylogram
pattern: 4 arch, loop 5 whorl
study: 13 dactylography

FINICKY: 5 fussy, picky 6 choosy 7 finical 9 difficult 10 fastidious, nitpicking, particular

FINISH: 3 die, end 4 kill, stop 5 cease, close, finis, glaze, limit, stain 6 defeat, devour, windup 7 achieve, coating, deplete, destroy, execute, fulfill, lacquer, perfect, surface 8 finalize 9 culminate, terminate 10 accomplish, completion, conclusion, perfection

FINISHED: 4 done, gone, over, ripe 5 ended, kaput 6 closed, ornate, ruined 7 refined, through 8 consumed, polished 9 completed, concluded, exhausted, perfected 10 terminated 11 consummated

FINITE: 5 exact, fixed 7 bounded, limited 9 definable 10 measurable, restricted 11 impermanent

FINLAND:
capital: 8 Helsinki
cities: 4 Oulu 5 Lahti, Turku 7 Tampere 9 Rovaniemi
continent: 6 Europe
ethnic groups: 4 Finn, Lapp 5 Swede
features: 12 Arctic Circle 13 Abland Islands, Haltiatunturi
languages: 7 Finnish, Swedish
monetary unit: 6 markka
water: 4 Kemi, Oulu 5 Enare 7 Karelia

FIORD, FJORD: 5 firth, inlet, reach

FIR: 4 pine, wood 5 cedar 6 alpine 7 conifer, douglas 9 evergreen

FIRE: 3 can 4 burn, glow, heat, sack, zeal 5 ardor, arson, blaze, drive, fling, light, shoot, torch, vigor 6 arouse, attack, excite, fervor, flames, ignite, incite, kindle, launch, spirit 7 animate, dismiss, element, explode, fervour, in-

ferno, inflame, inspire **8** detonate, vivacity **9** discharge, holocaust, intensity, terminate **10** combustion, enthusiasm, illuminate **13** conflagration
god of: **4** Agni

FIREARM: **3** gun **5** piece, rifle **6** musket, pistol, weapon **8** revolver

FIREBUG: **8** arsonist **10** incendiary, pyromaniac

FIREPLACE: **5** ingle **6** hearth **7** furnace

FIREPROOF: **12** nonflammable **14** noncombustible

FIREWORKS: **6** rocket **7** display, trouble **8** sparkler **9** girandole **11** Roman candle **12** pyrotechnics

FIRM: **4** hard, sure **5** dense, exact, fixed, house, loyal, rigid, solid, sound, stiff, stout, tight **6** hearty, intent, outfit, stable, steady, strict, strong, sturdy **7** adamant, certain, compact, company, confirm, decided, durable, secured, settled, staunch, unmoved **8** anchored, business, constant, definite, faithful, fastened, resolute, unshaken **9** backboned, immovable, inelastic, steadfast **10** consistent, determined, enterprise, inflexible, unwavering, unyielding **11** corporation, established, partnership, substantial **12** conglomerate **13** establishment

FIRMAMENT: **3** sky **5** ether, vault **7** heavens **8** empyrean

FIRMNESS: **4** iron **7** density, resolve **8** solidity, strength, tenacity **9** stability, toughness **10** immobility, steadiness **11** consistency **15** impenetrability

FIRST: **4** head, high, main **5** ahead, alpha, chief, debut, onset, prime **6** eldest, maiden, primal **7** highest, initial, leading, premier, primary **8** earliest, foremost, original **9** beginning, primitive, principal, unveiling **10** aboriginal, primordial **11** fundamental

FIRSTBORN: **4** heir **6** eldest, oldest **13** primogeniture

FIRST-CLASS: **4** best **5** prime **6** finest, tip-top **8** five-star, superior, top-notch **9** excellent, exclusive, first-rate, shipshape, top-drawer, topflight

FIRSTHAND: **6** direct **10** eyewitness

FIRST STATE: **8** Delaware

FISCAL: **8** economic, monetary **9** budgetary, financial

FISH: **3** net **4** cast, gill, quab **5** angle, drail, seine, troll **7** gudgeon, poisson
catfish: **6** hassar **8** bullhead, hornpout, stonecat **9** sheatfish
cod: **3** bib **4** cusk, hake, ling **5** torsk **6** burbot, gadoid, tomcod **7** bacalao, beardie, pollock
combining form: **6** ichthy
concerning: **7** piscine **8** ichthyic **9** piscatory
eellike: **4** link, opah **5** moray **6** conger, cuchia **7** eelpout, lamprey
eggs: **3** roe **5** spawn
electric: **4** raad **7** torpedo **9** stargazer
extinct: **10** coelacanth
female: **4** raun **7** henfish
fin types: **4** anal **6** caudal, dorsal, median, paired, pelvic **7** adipose, ventral **8** pectoral
flat: **3** dab, ray **4** butt, dace, sole **5** bream, brill, fluke, skate **6** plaice, turbot **7** halibut, sanddab, sunfish, torpedo **8** flounder
food: **3** cod, eel **4** bass, carp, hake, scup, shad, sole, tile, tuna **5** skate, smelt, trout **6** baleen, caviar, salmon, tautog, wrasse **7** alewife, catfish, grouper, haddock, halibut, herring, pompano, sardine, snapper **8** flounder, mackerel, sea trout **9** barracuda, swordfish

game: **4** bass, pike, tuna **5** perch, trout **6** grilse, marlin, salmon, tarpon **8** pickerel **9** swordfish
grunt: **5** ronco, sargo **7** pigfish **8** porkfish **10** bluestripe
herring: **4** shad **5** sprat **7** alewife, sardine **8** pilchard
kind: **3** cod, dab, eel, gar, ray **4** carp, gass, hake, hiku, jocu, lant, mado, masu, meat, opah, orfe, pega, peto, pike, pogy, pout, scup, shad, sole, tuna, ulua **5** bream, brill, lance, midge, otter, perch, scrod, seine, shark, skate, smelt, sword, trout, umbra, wahoo **6** barbel, blenny, caribe, marlin, porgie, salmon, tarpon, turbot, wrasse **7** alewife, anchovy, catfish, dogfish, dolphin, haddock, herring, lamprey, machete, piranha, sunfish **8** flounder, mackerel, sturgeon
raw: **5** sushi **7** sashimi
rock: **4** rena **5** reina **8** bocaccio, buccacio, lionfish, rosefish
scaleless: **9** alepidote
shellfish: **4** clam, crab **6** mussel, oyster, shrimp **7** lobster **9** langouste **11** langoustine
young: **3** fry **4** parr **5** larva, smolt **6** alevin, grilse **10** fingerling

FISHERMAN: **5** eeler **6** angler, seiner, whaler **7** trawler **8** piscator **9** harpooner

FISHERY: **4** weir **7** cannery, piscary **8** hatchery

FISHY: **4** cold, dull **5** shady **8** doubtful, unlikely **10** farfetched, improbable, suspicious **11** implausible

FISSION: **8** breaking, reaction, scission **9** splitting **12** reproduction

FISSURE: **3** gap **4** flaw, leak, rift, rima, rime, seam, slit, vein **5** break, chink, cleft, crack, split **6** cranny, furrow, groove, lesion, schism **7** blemish, crevice, opening **8** aperture, cleavage, crevasse, division

FIST: **4** grip, hand, hold **5** grasp **6** clench, clutch, strike

FIT: **3** apt **4** able, bout, meet, rage, ripe, suit, well, whim **5** adapt, adept, alter, equip, happy, match, ready, right, shape, spasm, toned **6** adjust, attack, become, belong, frenzy, proper, robust, seemly, stroke, strong, suited, timely **7** adapted, capable, conform, correct, furnish, healthy, prepare, qualify, seizure, tantrum **8** adequate, becoming, dovetail, eligible, outbreak, outburst, paroxysm, suitable **9** befitting, competent, deserving, opportune, pertinent, qualified **10** applicable, convenient, convulsion, correspond, felicitous **11** accommodate, appropriate

FITFUL: **6** random **7** erratic **8** periodic, restless, sporadic, variable **9** haphazard, impulsive, irregular, spasmodic **10** capricious, convulsive **12** intermittent

FITNESS: **5** shape **6** health **7** decency, decorum **8** aptitude, capacity **9** condition, readiness **10** competence **11** suitability

FITTING: **4** meet, part **5** happy **6** proper, seemly **8** becoming, suitable **9** accessory, warranted **10** adjustment, applicable, attachment, instrument **11** appropriate

FIVE NATIONS: **6** Cayuga, Mohawk, Oneida, Seneca **8** Onondaga

FIVE-SIDED FIGURE: **8** pentagon

FIVE-YEAR PERIOD: **7** lustrum **12** quinquennium

FIX: **3** set **4** bind, glue, hold, mend, mess, moor, nail, seal, spay, spot **5** bribe, focus, imbed, limit, patch **6** adjust, anchor, arrest, assign, attach, cement, corner, couple, direct, fasten, neuter, pickle, repair, revamp, scrape, secure, settle **7** appoint, arrange, confirm, correct, dilemma, prepare, restore, station **8** renovate **9** attribute, determine, establish, influence, stabilize **10** difficulty **11** concentrate, predicament, recondition, reconstruct

FIXATION: **5** craze, quirk **6** fetish **9** addiction, obsession **11** fascination, infatuation

FIXED: **4** fast, firm **5** rigid, staid, still **6** agreed, frozen, intent, stable, steady **7** capture, certain, sessile **8** arranged, attached, constant, definite, embedded, explicit, fastened, immobile, resolute, stubborn **9** ascertain, immovable, incessant, permanent, unbending **10** inflexible, stationary, unwavering **11** prearranged

FIXTURE: **7** regular, shelves **8** counters **9** apparatus, appliance, equipment **10** attachment, furnishing

FIX UP: **5** equip **6** repair **7** arrange, furnish **8** beautify, renovate **9** refurbish

FIZZ: **4** foam **6** bubble **7** sparkle **11** carbonation **13** effervescence

FIZZLE: **4** bomb, fail, flop, hiss **6** fiasco **7** failure, misfire **8** collapse

FLABBERGAST: **4** stun **5** amaze, shock **8** astonish, confound, overcome, surprise **9** overwhelm

FLABBY: **3** fat, lax **4** limp, soft, weak **5** loose, unfit **6** doughy, feeble, sloppy **7** flaccid, sagging **8** toneless

FLACCID: **4** limp **6** flabby **7** hanging **8** drooping, weakened, yielding

FLAG: **4** fade, fail, iris, jack, pine, tire, turf, waft, waif, warn, wilt **5** droop, slump **6** banner, burgee, colors, emblem, ensign, guidon, motion, pennon, signal, symbol **7** cattail, decline, gesture, pendant, pennant **8** languish, masthead, Old Glory, standard, streamer **9** banderole, Blue Peter, oriflamme **10** Jolly Roger, Yellow Jack **11** deteriorate **15** Stars and Stripes

FLAGELLATE: **4** beat, flog, lash, whip **5** impel **6** cudgel, punish, thrash **7** scourge

FLAGITIOUS: **6** rotten, wicked **7** corrupt, heinous, vicious **8** criminal, flagrant, infamous **9** atrocious **10** scandalous, villainous

FLAGON: **3** cup, mug **5** stein **6** bottle, vessel

FLAGRANT: **3** bad **4** rank **5** gross **6** brazen, odious, wicked **7** blatant, glaring, hateful, heinous, obvious, violent **8** dreadful, shameful, shocking **9** atrocious, egregious, nefarious, notorious, offensive **10** flagitious, noticeable, outrageous **11** conspicuous **13** reprehensible

FLAIL: **4** beat, flog, lash, whip **5** swing **6** strike, thrash

FLAIR: **4** bent, dash, feel, gift, nose **5** knack, style, taste **6** talent **7** ability, panache **8** aptitude, elegance, keenness

FLAK: **5** abuse **9** artillery, complaint, criticism **10** dissension

FLAKE: **3** bit, nut **4** chip, peel, snow **5** fleck, scale, shred, strip **6** lamina, sliver **7** crumble, oddball **9** screwball

FLAMBOYANT: **5** showy, swank **6** flashy, florid, ornate, rococo **7** flowery **8** dazzling **9** glamorous **10** theatrical **11** extravagant, resplendent **12** ostentatious

FLAME: **4** beau, fire, glow **5** ardor, blaze, flare, flash, glare, lover, spark **6** kindle **7** burning, passion **9** boyfriend **10** girlfriend, sweetheart

FLANK: **4** meat, side **5** thigh **6** border

FLAP: **3** bat, fly, tab **4** clap, fuss, slap, waff, wave, wing **5** alarm, apron, flack, lapel, skirt **6** bangle, strike, tongue **7** flounce, flutter, swindle **9** appendage, commotion, operculum **11** disturbance

FLARE: **4** pass **5** blaze, erupt, flame, flash, fleck, glare, light, splay, torch, widen **6** dilate, expand, signal, spread **7** balloon, broaden, flicker **8** outburst

FLASH: **4** beam, bolt, dart, sign **5** blaze, burst, flame, flare, gleam, glint, jiffy, shake, spark **6** glance, second, signal, streak, vision **7** flicker, glimmer, glimpse, glisten, glitter, instant, shimmer, sparkle, twinkle **11** coruscation, scintillate

FLASHY: **4** loud **5** cheap, fiery, gaudy, jazzy, showy **6** brazen, glitzy, ornate, snazzy, sporty **8** dazzling **9** flaunting **10** flamboyant

FLASK: **4** ewer, vial **5** crock, frame **6** bottle, carafe, fiasco, flacon **7** alembic, matrass **9** container

FLAT: **3** low, mat, pad **4** dead, dull, even, fade **5** banal, bland, blunt, fixed, flush, level, plane, prone, stale, vapid **6** boring, dreary, flashy, smooth **7** decided, insipid, uniform **8** absolute, deflated, dwelling, lifeless, sluggish **9** apartment, colorless, downright, prostrate, tasteless, unvarying **10** horizontal, lackluster, monotonous

FLATTEN: **4** deck, roll **5** floor **6** defeat, deject, oblate, squash **7** depress, trample **8** compress **9** prostrate

FLATTER: **4** coax **5** adorn, charm, court **6** become, cajole, grovel, hammer, praise, smooge, soothe **7** adulate, beguile, blarney, enhance, wheedle **8** blandish, bootlick **10** compliment

FLATTERER: **5** toady **8** eulogist **9** sycophant **10** panegyrist **11** lickspittle

FLATTERY: **4** bosh **5** gloze, salve, taffy **6** butter, praise **7** palaver, puffery **9** adulation **10** compliment

FLAUNT: **4** brag, show, wave **5** boast, flash, strut, vaunt **6** hotdog, parade, reveal **7** display, exhibit **8** brandish **9** advertise

FLAVOR: **4** aura, odor, salt, tang, zest **5** aroma, sapid, sapor, savor, scent, spice, style, taste, touch **6** relish, season **7** essence, extract, perfume, quality **8** piquancy **9** fragrance

FLAVORING: **4** herb, salt **5** sauce, spice **6** orgeat, pepper **7** vanilla **8** additive **9** condiment, grenadine, seasoning

FLAVORLESS: **4** dull, flat **5** bland, stale, vapid **7** insipid **9** tasteless

FLAW: **4** hole, mark, rift, spot, vice, wind **5** cleft, crack, error, fault, flake, stain **6** defect, glitch, squall **7** blemish, default, fissure, mistake, scratch **8** fracture, fragment, weakness **9** deformity **11** shortcoming **12** imperfection

FLAWLESS: **5** ideal, sound **6** intact **7** perfect **8** spotless, unmarred **9** exquisite, faultless, undamaged **10** immaculate, impeccable

FLAY: **4** lash, peel, skin, whip **5** chafe, flail, slash, strip **6** assail, attack, fleece **7** reprove **9** castigate, criticize, excoriate **11** decorticate

FLECK: **3** dot **4** mark, spot **5** flake, speck **6** dapple, streak **7** freckle, speckle **8** particle

FLEDGLING: **5** chick, squab **6** novice **7** untried **8** beginner **10** apprentice, tenderfoot **13** inexperienced

FLEE: **3** fly, lam, run **4** bolt, jump, skip **5** elude, evade, scoot, scram **6** decamp, escape, vanish **7** abscond, scamper, vamoose **8** liberate **9** disappear, skedaddle

FLEECE: **4** bilk, dupe, fell, flay, rook, wool **5** cheat, fleck, shear, steal **6** fabric **7** deceive, defraud, plunder, swindle

FLEECY: **4** soft **6** fluffy, lanose, woolly

FLEER: **4** grin, jeer, mock **5** laugh, scoff, smirk, sneer, taunt **7** grimace

FLEET: **4** fast, navy, sail, spry, unit **5** agile, brisk, drift, float, hasty, quick, rapid, swift **6** abound, argosy, armada, nimble, speedy, vanish **7** caravan **8** flotilla **9** formation **10** evanescent, occasional

FLEETING: **5** brief **6** fading, volage **7** elusive, passing **8** fugitive **9** ephemeral, fugacious, momentary, temporary, transient **10** short-lived, transitory **11** impermanent

FLESH: **3** kin, man **4** beef, body, meat, pulp, race, skin **5** stock **6** muscle, realty **7** mankind **8** humanity **9** plumpness, substance **10** sensuality

FLESH-EATING: **11** carnivorous, creophagous

FLESHY: **3** fat **5** beefy, gross, heavy, obese, plump, pulpy, stout **6** bodily, carnal, chubby, portly **9** corpulent **10** overweight

FLEX: **4** bend **5** curve, tense **7** stretch **8** contract

FLEXIBLE: **4** limp, lush, soft **5** lithe **6** limber, pliant, supple **7** ductile, elastic, pliable, springy, willowy **8** bendable, yielding **9** adaptable, resilient, tractable, versatile **10** adjustable, manageable, responsive

FLICK: **3** hit **4** blow, film, flip, snap, toss **5** movie **6** fillip, propel **7** picture

FLICKER: **4** fail, flit **5** blink, flash, waver **6** gutter **7** flutter, glimmer, sparkle, tremble, twinkle **9** fluctuate, oscillate, palpitate, vacillate

FLIER: **3** ace **5** pilot **6** airman **7** aviator, leaflet **8** airwoman, circular, pamphlet

FLIGHT: **3** lam **4** bolt, rout, trip **5** flock, floor, scrap, story **6** escape, exodus, flying, hegira, voyage **7** fleeing, getaway, migrate, mission, shuttle, soaring **8** stampede, swarming **9** agitation, migration **10** trajectory

FLIGHTY: **5** barmy, ditzy, dizzy, giddy, swift **6** fickle **7** foolish **8** fleeting, skittish, unstable **9** impulsive, transient **10** capricious **11** lightheaded **13** irresponsible

FLIM-FLAM: **4** dupe, fool **5** cheat, trick **6** humbug, trifle **7** chicane, defraud, swindle **8** nonsense **9** bamboozle, deception, deceptive

FLIMSY: **4** lame, limp, weak **5** frail, gaudy, shaky **6** feeble, shoddy, sleazy, slight, wobbly **7** fragile, rickety, tenuous **8** baseless, delicate, gossamer **10** groundless, inadequate **11** dilapidated, superficial, transparent **13** insubstantial

FLINCH: **5** avoid, blink, cower, feign, start, wince **6** blench, cringe, quaver, recoil, shrink **7** retreat, shudder **8** withdraw

FLING: **4** cast, dart, dash, emit, fire, flip, hurl, toss **5** binge, chuck, flirt, heave, pitch, sling, spree, throw, whirl **6** affair, hurtle, launch, plunge, spirit **7** discard, flounce, scatter, splurge **8** catapult **9** overthrow

FLINTY: **4** hard **5** stern **6** steely **7** callous **8** rigorous **10** unyielding

FLIP: **4** flap, glib, leaf, pert, snap, spin, toss, turn **5** flick, throw, thumb, twist **6** browse, fillip, propel **10** somersault

FLIPPANT: **4** airy, glib, pert, rude **5** fresh **6** brassy, chatty **9** talkative **10** irreverent **13** disrespectful

FLIRT: **3** toy **4** flip, gibe, jest, mock, ogle, play, toss, vamp **5** dally, flick, fling, tease, throw, vixen **6** spring, trifle **7** trifler **8** coquette **9** philander

FLIRTATIOUS: **3** coy **4** arch **7** amorous **10** coquettish **11** provocative

FLIT: **3** run **4** dart, flow, move, rush, whiz **5** fleck, fleet, hover, hurry, quick, scoot, swift **6** nimble, scurry **7** flicker, flutter

FLOAT: **3** bob, fly **4** buoy, cork, flow, raft, ride, sail, soar, swim, waft **5** drift, drink, fleet, flood, glide, hover **6** launch, natant **7** pontoon **8** levitate **9** negotiate

FLOCK: **3** mob **4** bevy, gang, herd, pack, rush **5** brood, bunch, crowd, drift, drove, group, swarm **6** church, flight, gaggle, gather, legion **7** company **8** assembly, converge **9** gathering, multitude **10** collection **11** aggregation **12** congregation

FLOG: **3** tan **4** beat, belt, cane, hide, lash, whip, wool **5** fight, flail **6** cotton, larrup, paddle, strike, switch, thrash **7** scourge, trounce **8** chastise **9** castigate **10** flagellate

FLOOD: **4** bore, flow, flux, glut, gush, rush **5** spate, swamp **6** deluge, engulf, excess **7** surplus, torrent **8** alluvion, downpour, inundate, overflow, saturate, submerge **9** abundance, cataclysm, overwhelm **10** outpouring

FLOOR: **4** deck, drop, fell **5** level, story, tiles **6** defeat, ground **7** flatten, parquet **8** linoleum

FLOP: **3** dud **4** bomb, bust, fall, plop, rest **5** lemon, loser **6** fizzle, lounge, tumble **7** failure, washout **8** collapse, disaster

FLORAL: **7** flowery **8** blooming **10** blossoming, decorative

FLORENCE:
citizens: **5** Dante **6** Giotto **7** da Vinci **9** Boccaccio **12** Michelangelo
place: **5** Italy
ruled by: **6** Medici
sites: **5** Duomo, Pitti **7** Vecchio **10** Santa Croce **12** Ponte Vecchio **17** Santa Maria Novella

FLORID: **5** ruddy, showy **6** ornate, rococo, rufous **7** flowery, healthy **8** blooming, vigorous **10** figurative, flamboyant, rhetorical **11** embellished

FLORIDA:
bird: **11** mockingbird
capital: **11** Tallahassee
cities: **5** Miami, Tampa **12** Jacksonville
explorer: **11** Ponce de Leon
features: **7** Daytona **9** Lake Worth, Palm Beach **11** Disney World, Florida Keys **13** Cape Canaveral
flower: **13** orange blossom
native: **9** Floridian
nickname: **8** Sunshine
tree: **8** palmetto
water: **8** Atlantic **12** Gulf of Mexico

FLOTILLA: **4** unit **5** fleet, group **6** armada

FLOUNCE: **4** flap, leap **5** fling, stomp **6** bounce, prance, ruffle, spring **8** flounder, struggle

FLOUNDER: **4** keel, roll, toss **5** fluke **6** bobble, falter, fumble, grovel, muddle, wallow **7** blunder, flounce, plounce, stumble **8** flatfish, struggle

FLOURISH: **4** boom, brag, grow, rise, show, wave **5** adorn, bloom, boast, quirk, shake, vaunt **6** arrive, expand, flaunt, parade, thrive **7** blossom, burgeon, develop, display, fanfare, garnish, prosper, succeed **8** brandish, curlicue, increase, multiply, ornament **9** embellish **10** decoration

FLOUT: **4** gibe, jeer, mock **5** fleer, scoff, scorn, sneer, taunt **6** deride, insult, scount **7** affront, outrage **8** ridicule **9** disregard

FLOW: **3** ebb, run **4** flux, gush, pour, roll, rush, tide, well, wind **5** drain, drift, float, flood, glide, issue, river, spill, spurt **6** course, deluge, influx, oozing, ripple, stream **7** cascade, current, debouch, emanate, flutter, torrent **8** alluvion, inundate, movement, progress, sequence **9** circulate, discharge, streaming **10** continuity, outpouring

FLOWER: **3** bud **4** iris, lily, pink, posy, rose **5** aster, bloom, bluet, lilac, pansy, peony, phlox, tulip **6** annual, azalea, crocus, dahlia, hybrid, orchid, violet **7** blossom, jonquil **8** bluebell, camellia, daffodil, gardenia, geranium, hepatica, hibiscus, hyacinth, marigold, primrose **9** buttercup, carnation, gladiolus, narcissus, perennial **11** honeysuckle **13** chrysanthemum
part: **5** calyx, ovary, petal, sepal, stalk, style **6** anther, carpel, nectar, pistil, stamen, stigma **7** nectary, petiole **8** filament, peduncle, perianth, pericarp

FLOWERY: **5** fancy, windy, wordy **6** florid, ornate, rococo **10** euphuistic, figurative **11** embellished **13** grandiloquent

FLOWING: **4** flux **5** fluid, tidal **6** afflux, fluent, smooth **7** copious, current, cursive, gushing, rolling, rushing **8** abundant, spouting **9** abounding, emanating **10** continuous, effortless **13** uninterrupted

FLUB: **3** fat **4** muff **5** boner, botch, error, fluff **6** bungle **7** blunder

FLUCTUATE: **4** sway, vary, veer **5** shift, waver **6** change, seesaw **7** flutter, vibrate **8** undulate, unsteady **9** alternate, oscillate, vacillate

FLUE: **3** net **4** barb, pipe, tube **5** organ, stack **6** funnel, tunnel **7** channel, chimney, fishnet, passage

FLUENT: **4** glib **5** fluid **6** facile, liquid, smooth **7** copious, flowing, natural, verbose, voluble **8** eloquent, graceful, polished **9** talkative **10** articulate, effortless **12** smooth-spoken

FLUFF: **4** down, flub, flue, fuzz, lint, puff, soft **5** botch, error, froth **6** miscue **7** blunder, mistake **13** entertainment

FLUFFY: **4** airy, soft **5** downy, furry, fuzzy, light **6** creamy **8** feathery **9** frivolous

FLUID: **3** ink **4** milk, rasa **5** juice, runny, water **6** fluent, liquid, watery **7** flowing, fluible, fluxile, gaseous, pliable **8** flexible, floating, fluxible, graceful, shifting, unstable, variable **9** adaptable **10** changeable

FLUKE: **4** fish **5** blade, quirk **8** accident, blessing, flounder **9** trematode

FLUKY: **6** chance **8** shifting, unsteady, variable **9** uncertain **10** capricious

FLUNKY: **5** toady **6** drudge, lackey **7** footman, servant, steward **9** attendant

FLURRY: **3** ado **4** gust, stir, wind **5** alarm, burst, haste, panic, spurt, whirl **6** bother, bustle, hubbub, scurry, shower, squall **7** confuse, fluster, flutter **8** snowfall **9** agitation, commotion, confusion **10** excitement

FLUSH: 4 even, flat, glow, rose, wash **5** blush, color, flood, level, rinse, rouge, vigor **6** excite, lavish, mantle, redden, smooth, square, thrill **7** cleanse, opulent, redness **8** abundant, affluent, frighten, rosiness **9** abounding **10** prosperous **11** overflowing

FLUSHED: 3 red **4** pink, rosy, ruby **5** aglow **7** crimson **8** animated, feverish **10** prosperous **11** embarrassed

FLUSTER: 5 shake, upset **6** bother, flurry, fuddle, muddle, puzzle, rattle, ruffle **7** agitate, confuse, disturb, perplex, unhinge **8** befuddle, bewilder **9** frustrate **10** discompose

FLUTE: 4 fife, pipe, tube **5** crimp **6** furrow, goffer, zufolo **7** chamfer, channel, ocarina, piccolo, zuffolo **8** flautino **9** wineglass **10** instrument

FLUTTER: 4 flap **5** hover, shake **6** flurry, quiver, thrill **7** flicker, flitter, pulsate, vibrate **8** tingling **9** fluctuate

FLUX: 4 flow, fuse, melt, rush **5** flood, resin **6** fusion, motion, stream, unrest **7** flowing **8** additive **9** discharge, substance **11** fluctuation

FLY:
insect: **3** bug **4** gnat **5** horse, house, midge, sedge **6** hackle, tsetse **8** dipteron
movement: **4** flee, scud, soar, solo **5** glide, hover, pilot **6** aviate, breeze, escape

FLY-BY-NIGHT: 5 brief, shady **6** unsure **10** unreliable **12** questionable, undependable, unscrupulous **13** untrustworthy

FLYER: 3 ace **5** flier, pilot **7** aviator

FLYING BOAT: 8 seaplane

FLYING HORSE: 7 Pegasus

FLYING SAUCER: 3 UFO **9** spaceship **10** spacecraft

FLY IN THE OINTMENT: 5 catch, hitch **8** drawback **9** hindrance

FLY THE COOP: 4 bolt, flee **6** escape **8** hightail **9** skedaddle

FOAL: 4 colt **5** filly **9** fledgling, offspring

FOAM: 4 fizz, fume, head, scud, scum, suds, whip **5** cream, frost, froth, spume, yeast **6** aerate, bubble, lather **10** effervesce

FOB: 5 chain, cheat, trick **6** pocket, ribbon **7** deceive **8** flimflam, ornament

FOCAL: 4 main **7** central, nucleus **9** important, principal

FOCUS: 4 core **5** point, train **6** adjust, center, direct, fixate, hearth **8** converge **9** fireplace, spotlight **11** concentrate

FODDER: 3 hay **4** corn, feed, food, oats **5** straw **6** barley, forage, silage **7** alfalfa **9** provender **10** provisions

FOE: 5 enemy, rival **8** opponent **9** adversary **10** antagonist, competitor

FOG: 4 daze, film, haze, mist, murk, smog **5** bedim, brume, gloom, grass, muddy, vapor **6** nebula, stream, stupor **7** obscure **8** moisture, whiteout **9** confusion **10** cloudiness **12** bewilderment

FOGGY: 4 dark, dull, gray, hazy **5** dense, misty, murky, soupy, vague **6** cloudy, groggy, marshy **7** blurred, brumous, muddled, obscure, shadowy, unclear **8** confused, nubilous, overcast

FOIBLE: **5** fault, quirk **6** defect **7** failing, frailty **8** weakness **9** infirmity **10** deficiency **11** shortcoming **12** imperfection

FOIL: **4** balk, curb **5** blade, blunt, elude, evade, metal, sword, track, trail **6** baffle, boggle, defeat, defile, outwit, stooge, thwart **7** beguile, counter, obscure, prevent, repulse, setback **8** disgrace **9** frustrate, overthrow

FOIST: **4** dupe, fool, gull, hoax **5** cheat, fudge, **6** impose, thrust **7** deceive, palm off, swindle **8** hoodwink

FOLD: **3** pen **4** bend, fail, flap, loop, tuck, turn **5** clasp, close, crimp, drape, flock, lapel, layer, plait, pleat, ridge, yield **6** buckle, crease, double, groove, pucker, rimple **7** crinkle, crumple, embrace, plicate **8** collapse, envelope, surround, withdraw **9** corrugate, enclosure **10** intertwine

FOLDER: **4** case **5** cover **6** binder **7** leaflet **8** brochure, pamphlet

FOLIAGE: **6** growth, leaves **7** leafage, verdure **10** vegetation

FOLK: **4** clan **6** family, people **7** friends, kindred **9** relatives

FOLKLORE: **4** myth **5** tales **6** belief, custom, legend **7** history **9** tradition **12** superstition

FOLKS: **6** family, people **7** parents **9** relatives

FOLLOW: **3** dog, spy, tag **4** copy, hunt, next, obey, tail **5** adopt, after, chase, ensue, hound, stalk, trace, track, trail **6** comply, fathom, pursue, result, sequel, shadow **7** conform, imitate, observe, replace, succeed, support **8** supplant **9** accompany, alternate, supervene **10** comprehend, understand

FOLLOWER: **3** fan **5** pupil, toady **6** claque, minion, votary **7** acolyte, apostle, copycat, devotee, groupie, pursuer, retinue **8** adherent, believer, disciple, henchman, parasite, partisan, retainer **9** attendant, entourage, satellite, successor, sycophant **10** aficionado, enthusiast

FOLLOWING: **4** next **5** after, below, group, later, train **6** serial **7** ensuing **8** audience, trailing **9** afterward, clientele, gathering, resulting **10** posthumous, sequential, subsequent, succeeding, successive **13** consequential

FOLLY: **4** whim **5** revue **6** levity, lunacy **7** daffery, foolery, madness, mistake **8** nonsense **9** absurdity, craziness, frivolity, silliness **10** imprudence, wantonness **11** foolishness

FOMENT: **4** abet, goad, spur **5** rouse, start, stupe **6** arouse, excite, foster, incite **7** agitate, provoke **9** encourage, instigate

FOND: **4** dear, kind, warm **5** silly **6** ardent, caress, doting, liking, loving, tender **7** amorous, beguile, devoted, foolish, insipid, partial **8** desirous, enamored, sanguine, trifling **9** affection, cherished, credulous, indulgent **10** infatuated, passionate **11** inclination **12** affectionate

FONDLE: **3** hug, pet **4** feel, love, neck **5** clasp, grope **6** caress, coddle, cosset, cuddle, nestle, pamper, stroke **7** embrace, snuggle

FONDNESS: **4** love **5** naive, taste **6** regard **8** dearness, devotion, kindness, weakness **9** affection **10** attachment, preference, tenderness **11** foolishness

FONT: **4** type **5** basin, stoup **6** source, spring **8** fountain **10** receptacle

FOOD: **4** bite, chow, diet, eats, fare, grub, meat, nosh **5** bread, cheer **6** fodder, morsel, viands **7** aliment, edibles, handout **8** victuals **9** nutriment **10** provisions, sustenance **11** comestibles, nourishment
animal: **4** feed **5** grain, grass **6** fodder, forage **9** provender
lover: **7** epicure, gourmet

FOOL: **3** ass, kid, oaf, sap, toy **4** boob, butt, dolt, dope, dupe, fake, hoax, jerk, jest, joke, scam, simp **5** bluff, cheat, chump, clown, dunce, goose, idiot, moron, ninny, silly, spoof, tease, trick **6** dimwit, nitwit, outwit, stooge, sucker, tamper, victim **7** buffoon, coxcomb, deceive, fathead, mislead, pretend **8** comedian, dumbbell, hoodwink, imbecile, meathead **9** bamboozle, blockhead, schlemiel, simpleton **10** dunderhead, nincompoop

FOOL AROUND: **4** lark, play **5** dally **6** dawdle, putter **8** lallygag

FOOLHARDY: **4** bold, rash **6** daring **8** reckless, temerity **9** daredevil, impetuous **11** venturesome

FOOLISH: **4** daft, dumb, rash, zany **5** anile, batty, crazy, dizzy, goofy, inane, inept, nutty, silly **6** absurd, simple, stupid, unwise **7** asinine, fatuous, idiotic, witless **8** cockeyed, heedless **9** brainless, doddering, imprudent, ludicrous, senseless **10** boneheaded, indiscreet, irrational, ridiculous **11** harebrained, nonsensical **12** preposterous

FOOLISHNESS: **4** bunk **6** lunacy **8** drollery, insanity, nonsense **9** absurdity, horseplay, stupidity **13** senselessness

FOOLPROOF: **4** sure **7** certain **9** effective **10** infallible

FOOL'S GOLD: **6** pyrite

FOOT: **3** dog, pad, paw, pay **4** base, hoof **5** dance, meter, nadir, speed, total **6** bottom, defray, tootsy **7** flipper **9** extremity **11** measurement
care: **8** pedicure
doctor: **10** podiatrist **11** chiropodist
parts of human: **3** toe **4** arch, ball, heel, sole **5** ankle, digit **6** hallux, instep **7** minimus, toenail **14** Achilles tendon

FOOTBALL:
also called: **5** rugby **6** rugger, soccer **7** pigskin
officials: **6** umpire **7** referee
positions: **3** end **5** guard **6** center, kicker, punter, tackle **8** fullback, halfback, split end, tailback, tight end **10** cornerback, linebacker **11** quarterback, running back
terms: **4** down, pass, punt, sack **5** block, drive, flare **6** fumble, huddle, safety, tackle **7** defense, end zone, holding, kickoff, lateral, offense, offside, rushing **8** clipping, gridiron, uprights **9** field goal, scrimmage, secondary, touchback, touchdown **10** conversion **12** interception, interference

FOOTING: **4** base, rank **5** basis, place **6** status **7** balance, support, surface **8** foothold, position, standing **9** condition **10** foundation, groundwork **12** relationship

FOOTLOOSE: **4** free **8** carefree **10** unattached

FOOTNOTE: **9** reference **11** explanation **12** afterthought

FOOTPRINT: **5** spoor, trace, track **7** moulage **8** bootmark, footstep

FOP: **4** buck, dude **5** dandy, swell **6** dasher **7** coxcomb **8** cavalier, popinjay **9** exquisite **11** Beau Brummel **12** man-about-town

FOR: **5** after, being, since **6** during **7** because **8** favoring **9** supposing **10** concerning **11** considering

FORAGE: **3** oat, rye **4** corn, hunt, raid **5** grass, raven, scour, wheat **6** barley, fodder, millet, ravage, search **7** alfalfa, plunder, rummage **10** provisions

FORAY: **4** raid **6** attack, inroad, ravage, sortie **7** attempt, pillage **8** invasion **9** incursion

FORBEAR: **4** help, shun **5** avoid, cease, forgo **6** desist, endure, forego, resist **7** abstain, decline, refrain **9** withstand

FORBEARANCE: **5** mercy **8** patience **9** fortitude, tolerance **10** abstinence, moderation

FORBEARING: **4** easy, mild **6** gentle **7** clement, lenient **8** tolerant **9** forgiving, restraint **11** sympathetic

FORBID: **3** ban **4** defy, deny, fend, halt, stop **5** block, debar, taboo **6** censor, defend, enjoin, impede, refuse **7** deprive, gainsay, inhibit, prevent **8** disallow, preclude, prohibit **9** interdict, proscribe

FORBIDDEN: **5** taboo **6** banned, denied, vetoed **8** verboten **10** prohibited

FORBIDDING: **4** grim **5** gaunt, harsh, stern **6** fierce, odious, strict **7** ominous **8** menacing, sinister **9** offensive **10** unpleasant **11** prohibiting, threatening **12** disagreeable

FORCE: **3** pry **4** army, bang, cram, make, push, unit **5** cause, clout, corps, drive, exert, impel, might, pound, power, press, repel, stuff, wrest **6** coerce, compel, demand, effort, energy, extort, hammer, impact, insist, muscle, oblige, ravish, stress **7** ability, command, impetus, impulse, require **8** coaction, compress, gumption, momentum, obligate, persuade, pressure, regiment, strength, validity, violence **9** constrain, influence, restraint **10** constraint, constringe, detachment **11** necessitate **13** determination

FORCED: **5** slave, stiff **7** labored, stilted **8** strained **9** mandatory, reluctant **10** artificial, begrudging, compulsory, farfetched **11** constrained, involuntary

FORCEFUL: **6** mighty, strong, virile **7** dynamic, violent **8** dominant, emphatic, forcible, powerful, vigorous **9** assertive, effective

FORCIBLE: **5** stout, valid **6** mighty, potent **7** intense, telling, weighty **8** emphatic, forceful, incisive, powerful, puissant **9** energetic **10** aggressive, compulsory, impressive, obligatory, persuasive

FORE: **4** near **5** ahead, front, prior **6** former **7** earlier, forward **8** advanced **10** antecedent, previously

FOREARM: **4** ulna **6** radius **7** prepare

FOREBODE: **4** omen, warn **5** augur **6** divine **7** foresee, portend, predict, presage **8** foretell, prophesy **13** prognosticate

FOREBODING: **4** fear, omen **6** augury, gloomy **7** anxiety, feeling **8** sinister **10** prediction **11** presagement **12** apprehension, presentiment

FORECAST: **4** bode **5** guess, infer **7** foresee, fortune, outlook, predict, surmise **8** conclude, estimate, foretell, prophesy **9** horoscope, prognosis **10** anticipate, conjecture, prediction, prognostic, projection **11** calculation, meteorology **12** predetermine **13** prognosticate

FORECASTER: **4** seer **7** prophet **10** astrologer, soothsayer **11** Nostradamus **13** meteorologist

FOREFATHER: **4** sire **5** elder **7** founder **8** ancestor, forebear **10** antecedent, originator, progenitor

FOREFRONT: **4** lead **5** front **8** vanguard **9** beginning **10** prominence

FOREGO: **7** precede

FOREHEAD: **4** brow **5** frons, front **7** metopic **8** sinciput

FOREIGN: **5** alien **6** exiled, exotic, remote **7** distant, faraway, strange, unknown **8** barbaric, overseas **9** different, extrinsic, peregrine **10** extraneous, irrelevant, outlandish, unexplored **11** impertinent **12** inapplicable, incompatible, inconsistent, unaccustomed

FOREIGNER: **5** alien **8** outsider, stranger **9** barbarian, greenhorn, immigrant, outlander

FOREKNOWLEDGE: **9** intuition **10** prescience **11** premonition

FOREMAN, FOREWOMAN: **4** boss **5** chief **6** gaffer, leader **7** captain, headman, manager, steward **8** overseer **10** supervisor, taskmaster **11** chairperson **12** spokesperson

FOREMOST: **4** head, high, main **5** chief, first, forme, front, prime **7** highest, leading, supreme **9** principal **10** preeminent

FORENSIC: **5** legal **8** judicial **9** debatable **10** rhetorical **11** disputation **13** argumentative

FORERUNNER: **4** omen, sign **6** augury, herald **7** portent, symptom, warning **8** ancestor, forebear, presager **9** harbinger, messenger, precursor **10** forefather, originator, progenitor, prognostic **11** predecessor, trailblazer

FORESEE: **6** divine **7** predict **8** envision, forecast, foretell, prophesy **10** anticipate **13** prognosticate

FORESHADOW: **4** hint **5** imply **7** presage, suggest **8** indicate **9** adumbrate, prefigure

FORESIGHT: **6** vision, wisdom **7** caution **8** prudence **10** discretion, prescience, providence **11** forethought **12** anticipation, clairvoyance

FOREST: **4** bush, park **5** cover, glade, sylva, taiga, woods **6** jungle, timber **7** boscage, shelter, thicket **8** woodland **9** backwoods **10** wilderness

FORESTALL: **5** avert, delay, deter **6** hinder, thwart **7** prevent **8** preclude **10** anticipate

FORETELL: **4** bode, read, warn **5** augur **6** divine, figure **7** bespeak, portend, predict, presage **8** forecast, forewarn, prophesy, soothsay **9** predicate, prefigure **10** anticipate, vaticinate **13** prognosticate

FORETHOUGHT: **4** heed **5** sense **7** caution **8** judgment, planning, prudence **9** canniness, foresight, provident **11** preparation **12** anticipation **13** consideration, premeditation

FOREVER: **4** ever **6** always **7** endless **8** eternity **9** endlessly, eternally, perpetual **10** constantly **11** ceaselessly, continually, everlasting, permanently, unceasingly **12** interminably

FOREWARN: **4** flag **5** alert, augur **6** notify, signal **7** caution, portend

FOREWORD: **5** proem **7** preface, prelude **8** overture, preamble, prologue **12** introduction

FORFEIT: **4** fine, lose, loss **5** forgo **7** abandon, default, penalty **9** sacrifice, surrender **10** relinquish

FORGE: **4** copy **5** drive, pound, shape **6** smithy **7** advance, falsify, fashion **8** bloomery **9** fabricate, reproduce **11** counterfeit, manufacture

FORGERY: **4** fake, sham **5** fraud, phony **7** fiction **8** feigning **9** deception, imposture **11** counterfeit, fabrication

FORGET: **4** omit, skip **5** fluff **6** ignore **7** neglect, unlearn **8** overlook **9** disregard, unmindful **11** disremember

FORGETFUL: **6** remiss, sloppy **7** amnesic **8** careless, heedless **9** negligent, oblivious **10** distracted **11** inattentive

FORGIVE: **5** clear, remit **6** acquit, cancel, excuse, pardon **7** absolve, amnesty, commute, condone, release **9** exculpate, exonerate

FORGIVING: **4** kind **7** clement **8** merciful, placable **10** charitable **13** compassionate

FORGO: **5** waive **7** forfeit, forsake, neglect, refrain **8** renounce **9** sacrifice **10** relinquish

FORK: **4** stab, tine **5** angle, prong, split **6** bisect, branch, crotch, divide, pierce **7** utensil **10** divaricate **11** bifurcation

FORLORN: **4** lost **5** alone **6** abject, tragic **8** deserted, desolate, forsaken, helpless, hopeless, lonesome, rejected, solitary, wretched **9** abandoned, cheerless, depressed, desperate, destitute, miserable **10** despondent, dispirited, friendless **12** disconsolate, inconsolable

FORM: **4** body, kind, make, mode, mold, plan, rite, type **5** being, build, carve, frame, guise, image, model, shape, style, teach, write **6** adjust, create, design, figure, health, invent, letter, manner, mature, method, ritual, system **7** arrange, compose, conduct, confect, contour, develop, fashion, fitness, outline, pattern, produce, profile **8** ceremony, conceive, likeness, organize, physique, protocol, skeleton **9** construct, etiquette, fabricate, framework, structure **10** appearance, constitute, discipline, expression, regulation, similitude **11** application, arrangement, crystallize **13** configuration, questionnaire

FORMAL: **4** prim **5** fancy, stiff **6** proper, solemn **7** correct, nominal, orderly, precise, regular, stately, stilted **8** academic, affected, official, reserved **10** ceremonial, methodical, systematic **11** ceremonious, established, punctilious **12** conventional

FORMALITY: **4** rite **6** custom **7** gesture **8** ceremony, protocol **9** procedure, tradition **15** conventionality

FORMAT: **4** plan, size **5** shape, style **6** scheme **7** pattern **11** arrangement

FORMATION: **4** form, rank **6** makeup, parade, spread **7** deposit **9** structure **10** procession **11** composition, development **12** construction, organization

FORMATIVE: **6** pliant **7** plastic **14** impressionable

FORMER: **4** late, once, past **5** maker, prior **6** whilom **7** ancient, creator, earlier, onetime, quondam **8** departed, previous, sometime **9** erstwhile, foregoing **10** antecedent

FORMIDABLE: **4** hard **5** awful, tough **6** fierce, mighty **7** fearful **8** alarming, horrible, imposing, menacing, powerful, terrible **9** dangerous, difficult **10** impressive **11** challenging, threatening

FORMLESS: **5** arupa, crude, vague **7** anidian, chaotic **8** nebulous **9**

amorphous, shapeless **10** indistinct **12** disorganized

FORMULA: **4** code, rule **5** maxim **6** method, recipe, theory **8** equation **9** blueprint, direction, procedure

FORMULATE: **4** coin, plan **5** draft, frame, state **6** define, devise, invent **7** concoct, develop, express **9** originate

FORSAKE: **4** deny, flee, quit, shun **5** avoid, forgo, leave, spurn, waive **6** desert, disown, forego, refuse, reject, resign **7** abandon, discard **8** abdicate, disclaim, renounce, withdraw **9** surrender **10** relinquish

FORSAKEN: **6** jilted **7** forlorn, ignored **8** deserted, desolate, rejected **9** abandoned, neglected

FORSWEAR: **4** deny **6** recant, reject **7** abandon, disavow, gainsay, perjure, retract **8** abnegate, renounce

FORT: **4** base, camp **6** castle **7** bastion, bulwark, citadel, fortify **8** bastille, fortress, garrison **10** blockhouse, protection, stronghold

FORTE: **3** bag **5** knack, skill, thing **6** metier, talent **7** ability **8** aptitude, strength **9** specialty

FORTH: **4** away, into **6** abroad, onward **7** forward, outward

FORTHCOMING: **7** pending **8** expected, imminent **9** impending **10** inevitable **11** anticipated, approaching

FORTHRIGHT: **4** open **5** plain **6** candid, direct, honest **7** frankly **10** aboveboard, truthfully **15** straightforward

FORTHWITH: **3** now **6** pronto **7** quickly **8** directly **9** instantly, presently, therewith **11** immediately **12** straightaway

FORTIFICATION: **4** moat, wall **5** tower **6** buffer, castle, shield **7** barrier, bastion, bulwark, citadel, defense, parapet, rampart **8** fortress, garrison **9** barricade **10** protection, stronghold

FORTIFY: **3** arm, man **5** boost, brace **6** enrich, secure **7** confirm, prepare, support, sustain **8** bastille, embattle, energize, entrench **9** barricade, reinforce **10** invigorate, strengthen, stronghold

FORTITUDE: **4** grit, guts **5** heart, spunk, valor **7** bravery, courage, stamina **8** backbone, strength **9** endurance **10** resolution **12** perseverance **13** determination

FORTRESS: **4** fort **6** castle **7** barrier, citadel, rampart, redoubt **8** bastille, garrison **10** stronghold **13** fortification

FORTUITOUS: **5** fluky, lucky **6** casual, chance, random **9** unplanned **10** accidental, contingent, incidental **13** serendipitous

FORTUNATE: **4** good, well **5** happy, lucky **6** dexter, golden, timely **7** blessed, favored **8** gracious, thriving **9** favorable, promising **10** auspicious, profitable, prosperous, successful **12** advantageous

FORTUNE: **3** lot, pot **4** doom, fate, luck **5** worth **6** bundle, chance, estate, riches, wealth **7** bonanza, destiny, success **8** accident, treasure, windfall **10** prosperity **11** inheritance, possessions

FORTUNETELLER: **4** seer **5** gypsy **6** medium **7** palmist, psychic **10** soothsayer **11** clairvoyant

FORTY WINKS: **3** nap **5** sleep **6** siesta, snooze

FORUM: **5** court **6** medium **8** tribunal **9** symposium **11** marketplace

FORWARD: **3** aid **4** bold, help, send, ship, step **5** ahead, along, brash, eager, forth, front, hasty, pushy, ready, relay, remit **6** ardent, before, brazen, coming, hasten, onward, player, prompt **7** advance, deliver, earnest, extreme, further, leading, promote, radical, support **8** advanced, arrogant, champion, impudent, perverse, position, transmit **9** audacious, encourage, obtrusive, presuming **10** accelerate, aggressive, precocious **11** progressive

FOSSIL: **4** fogy **5** relic **7** antique, ichnite **8** ammonite, conodont, skeleton **9** coprolite **10** antiquated, impression

FOSTER: **4** back, feed, food, help, rear **5** house, nurse **6** assist, harbor **7** advance, cherish, further, nourish, nurture, promote, shelter, support, sustain **8** advocate, befriend **9** cultivate, encourage

FOUL: **4** base, lewd, vile **5** bawdy, dirty, grimy, gross, muddy, nasty, sully **6** defame, filthy, horrid, impure, odious, putrid, rotten, smelly, soiled, unfair, vulgar, wicked **7** abusive, blocked, corrupt, defaced, illegal, obscene, profane, raunchy, smeared, unclean, vicious **8** indecent, polluted, stinking, wretched **9** entangled, loathsome, nastiness, obnoxious, offensive, repulsive, revolting **10** detestable, disgusting, nauseating **12** contaminated, dishonorable, scatalogical **15** unsportsmanlike

FOUL-MOUTHED: **4** lewd, rude **5** dirty **6** vulgar **7** obscene, profane **9** offensive **10** scurrilous

FOUL PLAY: **5** crime **6** murder **7** illegal, killing **8** violence

FOUL UP: **4** goof **5** botch **6** bungle **7** blunder **9** mismanage

FOUND: **4** base, cast, rest **5** begin, board, build, endow, erect, start **6** create, depart, gather, launch **7** isolate **8** equipped, initiate, organize, provided **9** establish, institute, originate, supported

FOUNDATION: **4** base, foot, fund, pile, raft, root **5** basis **6** bottom, cellar, piloti **7** bedding, bedrock, charity, roadbed, society, support **8** donation, pedestal **9** endowment, institute **10** groundwork, substratum **11** corporation **12** organization, substructure

FOUNDER: **4** fail, fall, sink **6** author **7** creator, stumble **8** collapse, inventor, miscarry, submerge **9** architect, organizer, patriarch, supporter **10** forefather, originator

FOUNTAIN: **3** jet **4** well **5** fount, spray **6** geyser, source, spring, stream **7** bubbler **9** beginning, reservoir **10** wellspring

FOUNTAINHEAD: **6** origin, source **10** originator

FOUR HORSEMEN:
Apocalypse: **3** War **5** Death **6** Famine **10** Pestilence
Notre Dame: **9** Don Miller **10** Jim Crowley **11** Elmer Layden **16** Harry Stuhldreher

FOURSCORE: **6** eighty

FOWL: **3** hen **4** bird, cock, duck, game **5** chick, goose **6** turkey **7** chicken, rooster **8** pheasant

FOX: **3** sly **4** fool **5** trick **6** baffle, clever, crafty, outwit **7** confuse, Reynard, vulpine **10** attractive, intoxicate
female: **5** vixen
genus: **6** vulpes
young: **3** cub, kit, pup

FOXY: **3** sly **4** sexy **5** slick **6** astute, crafty, shifty, shrewd, sneaky **7** cunning, vulpine

FOYER: **5** lobby **8** anteroom, entrance **9** vestibule

FRACAS: **5** brawl, fight, melee, scrap **6** rumpus, uproar **7** dispute, quarrel **8** brouhaha, squabble **9** commotion **10** donnybrook **11** altercation, disturbance

FRACTION: **3** bit **4** part **5** break, chunk, piece, ratio, slice **6** little **7** section **8** breaking, division, fragment **9** component **10** proportion

FRACTIONAL: **5** small **7** partial **13** insignificant

FRACTIOUS: **4** mean **5** cross, testy **6** cranky, ornery, unruly **7** fretful, grouchy, peevish **8** perverse, snappish **9** irritable **10** rebellious **11** quarrelsome

FRACTURE: **3** gap **4** flaw, rend, rift **5** break, crack, fault, split, wound **6** breach **7** rupture **10** separation

FRAGILE: **4** fine, weak **5** frail **6** dainty, feeble, flimsy, slight **7** brittle, friable, slender, unsound **8** delicate **9** breakable, frangible

FRAGMENT: **3** bit **4** atom, chip, part, snip **5** chunk, crumb, flake, grain, piece, scrap, shred, trace **6** morsel, parcel, sliver **7** flinder, portion, remnant, shatter **8** fraction, particle, shrapnel, splinter

FRAGMENTARY: **6** broken **7** partial **9** scattered **10** incomplete **12** unsystematic

FRAGRANCE: **4** odor **5** aroma, scent, smell, spice **6** flavor **7** bouquet, incense, perfume **9** redolence

FRAGRANT: **5** balmy, spicy, sweet **6** aromal **7** odorous, perfumy, scented **8** aromatic, redolent **9** ambrosial, nectarous **10** delectable **11** odoriferous

FRAIL: **4** fine, puny, weak **6** feeble, flimsy, infirm, sickly **7** brittle, fragile, slender **8** delicate **9** breakable **10** vulnerable

FRAILTY: **4** flaw, vice **5** fault **6** defect, foible **7** blemish **8** delicate, weakness **10** peccadillo **11** fallibility **12** imperfection

FRAME: **4** body, form, mold, plan **5** build, draft, panel, raise, serve, shape, shell, truss **6** adjust, binder, border, casing, devise, encase, fabric, invent, manage, tenter **7** arrange, attempt, chassis, enclose, fashion, furnish, outline, portray, prepare, proceed, support **8** casement, contrive, physique **9** calculate, construct, fabricate, formulate, structure **11** incriminate

FRAME OF MIND: **4** bent, mood **8** attitude **11** disposition

FRAMEWORK: **4** plan, rack, sill **5** cadre **6** fabric, stroma, system **7** lattice, trestle **8** skeleton, studwork **9** structure **10** foundation **11** constraints

FRANCE:
also called: **4** Gaul **6** Gallia
ancient divisions: **5** Arles **6** Arelas **7** Arelate **8** Aquitane
artists: **4** Dore **5** Degas, Manet, Monet **6** Renoir, Seurat **7** Poussin
authors: **4** Gide, Hugo, Sand, Zola **5** Benda, Camus, Dumas **6** Balzac, Proust, Racine, Sartre **8** Flaubert, Rousseau, Stendhal, Voltaire **9** Descartes
capital: **5** Paris
cardinal: **7** Mazarin **9** Richelieu
cathedrals: **5** Rouen **6** Nantes, Rheims **8** Chartres **9** Notre Dame
cities: **3** Aix **4** Nice, Vimy **5** Aries, Arles, Brest, Dijon, Havre, Lille, Lisle, Lyons, Nancy, Nimes, Paris, Rouen, Tours, Vichy **6** Amiens, Calais, Cannes, Lemans, Nantes, Rheims, Toulon **7** Antibes, Avignon, Bayonne, Dunkirk, Limoges, Orleans **8** Bor-

deaux, Clermont, Grenoble, Lettavre, Rochelle, Toulouse **9** Marseille
combining form: **5** Gallo
composers: **5** Bizet, Ravel **6** Franck, Gounod **7** Berlioz, Debussy
delicatessen: **11** charcuterie
divisions: **6** canton **7** commune **10** department **14** arrondissement
drink: **6** cognac **8** bordeaux, burgundy **9** champagne
dynasties: **5** Capet **6** Valois **7** Bourbon, Orleans
features: **8** Bastille, Left Bank **9** Cote d'Azur **11** Eiffel Tower **13** Arc de Triomphe, Champs-Elysees
food: **4** Brie, pate **5** boeuf, crepe **6** canape, mousse, quiche **7** souffle **8** escargot, Muenster, Napoleon **9** Camembert, croissant, Roquefort
islands: **3** Yeu **4** Cite, Elba **5** Groix, Hyere **6** Comoro, Oleron, Tahiti, Ushant **7** Corsica, Leeward, Reunion **8** Belle Ile, Windward **10** Guadeloupe, Martinique **12** New Caledonia
kings: **3** roi **5** Capet, Louis
lakes: **6** Annecy, Cazaux, Geneva **7** Bourget
measure: **3** pot **4** aune, mine, muid, pied, sack, velt **5** arpen, carat, ligne, minot, pinte, point, pouce, velte **6** arpent, hemine, league, quarte, setier
monetary unit: **5** franc **7** centime
months: **3** Mai **4** Aout, Juin, Mars, mois **5** Avril **7** Fevrier, Janvier, Juillet, Octobre **8** Decembre, Novembre **9** Septembre
mountains: **4** Alps, Jura **5** Pelat **6** Vosges **7** Cote d'Or **8** Ardennes, Auvergne, Pyrenees **9** Mont Blanc
palaces: **6** Elysee **10** Luxembourg, Versailles **13** Fontainebleau
people: **6** Franks
philosophers: **4** Caro **5** Camus **6** Pascal, Sartre **8** Rousseau **9** Descartes
queens: **7** Eugenie **15** Marie Antoinette
rivers: **3** Ain, Lot, Lys **4** Aire, Aude, Cher, Eure, Gard, Gers, Loir, Oise, Orne, Saar, Tarn, Yser **5** Aisne, Drome, Eiser, Isere, Loire, Maine, Marne, Meuse, Rhine, Rhone, Saone, Sarre, Seine, Yonne **6** Allier, Ariege, Loiret, Mosell, Vienne **7** Garonne, Gironde
weights: **3** sol **4** gros, kilo, once **5** carat, livre, pound, tonne **6** gramme **7** tonneau **8** esterlin **9** esterling

FRANCHISE: **4** team **5** grant, right **7** charter, license **8** suffrage **9** privilege, territory **10** permission **13** authorization

FRANK: **4** curt, free, open **5** bluff, blunt, plain **6** candid, direct, honest **7** brusque, natural, profuse, sincere **8** carefree, explicit, outright, straight, truthful **9** ingenuous, outspoken **10** aboveboard, unreserved

FRANTIC: **3** mad **4** wild **5** rabid **6** hectic, insane, raving **7** berserk, excited, violent **8** deranged, frenzied **9** delirious, desperate **10** distracted, distraught, distressed

FRATERNAL: **6** social **8** friendly **9** brotherly

FRATERNITY: **4** club, frat **5** order, union **6** circle **7** society **10** fellowship **11** association, brotherhood

FRATERNIZE: **6** mingle **7** consort **9** affiliate, associate, socialize

FRAUD: **4** fake, gaff, scam, sham, wile **5** cheat, crook, faker, guile, knave, phony, quack, rogue, trick **6** deceit, hustle **7** swindle **8** artifice, flimflam, impostor, trickery **9** charlatan, chicanery, deception, imposture, pretender **10** imposition

FRAUDULENT: **4** fake, wily **5** bogus, false, snide **7** crooked, cunning **8** cheating, criminal, spurious **9** deceitful, deceiving, deceptive, dishonest, underhand **10** misleading **11** clandestine, counterfeit, treacherous

FRAUGHT: **5** laden **6** filled, loaded **7** charged, stuffed **9** abounding, upsetting

FRAY: **4** feud, riot, spat **5** alarm, brawl, broil, chafe, clash, melee, panic, ravel, shred **6** assail, attack, battle, combat, fracas, rumpus, strain, tumult **7** contest, dispute, frazzle, scuffle, unravel **8** conflict, frighten, skirmish **9** commotion **10** donnybrook **11** altercation

FRAZZLE: **4** fray **5** shred, upset **9** prostrate **10** exhaustion

FREAK: **4** geek, rave, whim **5** fancy, fiend, fleck, humor, prank, sport **6** addict, frolic, mutant, oddity, rarity, vagary, whimsy **7** bizarre, caprice, chimera, crochet, fanatic, monster **8** flimflam **9** eccentric **10** aberration, enthusiast **11** monstrosity

FREAKISH: **3** odd **5** weird **6** screwy **7** strange, unusual **8** abnormal, peculiar **9** arbitrary, whimsical **10** capricious, outlandish

FREE: **4** able, bail, idle, open, void **5** clear, loose, ready, spare, untie **6** acquit, devoid, exempt, gratis, immune, loosen, pardon, parole, remove, rescue, spring, unbind, vacant **7** absolve, deliver, handout, leisure, liberal, manumit, release, relieve, unbound, willing **8** abundant, detached, expedite, generous, handsome, liberate, separate, unburden, unfasten, unleased **9** available, discharge, disengage, exculpate, exonerate, extricate, footloose, liberated, separated, sovereign, unbridled, unchecked, unimpeded, unshakled **10** autonomous, democratic, emancipate, gratuitous, self-ruling, unattached, unconfined, unimpaired, unoccupied, unreserved **11** disencumber, disentangle, enfranchise, independent, spontaneous, uncommitted, untrammeled **12** uncontrolled, unrestrained, unrestricted **13** communicative, complimentary

FREEDOM: **4** ease **5** right, sweep **6** leeway **7** abandon, leisure, liberty, license, release **8** autonomy, facility, immunity, latitude, openness **9** exemption, frankness, readiness, salvation **10** generosity, liberation **11** flexibility, sovereignty, willingness **12** carte blanche, emancipation, independence

FREE-FOR-ALL: **4** fray, riot **5** brawl, fight, melee, scrap **6** battle, ruckus **8** brouhaha **10** donnybrook

FREELOADER: **5** leech **6** sponge **7** moocher **8** barnacle, parasite

FREELY: **6** easily **7** cleanly **9** bountiful **10** generously, unhindered **11** voluntarily **12** unchallenged **13** intentionally

FREETHINKER: **7** atheist, infidel, radical, skeptic **8** agnostic **9** libertine

FREE WILL: **6** choice **7** consent, freedom **8** volition **9** voluntary

FREEZE: **3** ice **4** halt, numb, stop **5** chill, frost **6** harden **7** congeal **8** preserve **11** anesthetize, refrigerate

FREEZING: **3** icy, raw **4** cold **5** gelid, nippy **6** arctic, bitter, frigid

FREIGHT: **4** bulk, haul, load **5** cargo, goods **6** lading **7** payload **8** contents, shipment **9** transport **11** merchandise

FRENETIC: **3** mad **4** wild **5** crazy, rabid **6** insane **7** excited, fanatic, frantic, furious, violent, zealous **8** demented, frenzied **9** delirious, obsessive **10** distracted, distraught, passionate

FRENZIED: **5** amuck **6** hectic, raging **7** berserk, excited, frantic, furious, rampage **8** feverish, frenetic **9** delirious **10** hysterical **12** uncontrolled

FRENZY: **3** fit, mad **4** rage **5** craze, furor, mania **6** lunacy, ruckus **7** frantic, madness, turmoil **8** delirium, insanity, maniacal **9** rampaging **10** excitement **11** distraction

FREQUENCY: **6** number **10** recurrence, regularity, repetition **11** persistence

FREQUENT: **5** haunt, often, usual, visit **6** attend, common, hourly **7** current **8** familiar, habitual, numerous, repeated **9** assiduous, continual, habituate, patronize, prevalent, recurrent **10** persistent

FRESH: **3** hot, new **4** bold, cool, more, pure, racy, rude, wise **5** added, brisk, clean, crisp, green, naive, novel, sassy, sweet, vivid **6** brazen, breezy, bright, lively, modern, recent, rested, unused **7** chipper, current, untried, vibrant **8** impudent, straight **9** different, energetic, sparkling, unspoiled **10** additional **11** smart-alecky **12** invigorating, presumptuous **13** inexperienced

FRESHEN: **5** renew **6** purify **7** cleanse, sweeten **9** deoderize, ventilate

FRESHMAN: **4** tyro **5** frosh, plebe **6** novice, rookie **7** recruit, student **8** beginner, neophyte, newcomer **10** apprentice, tenderfoot

FRET: **3** rub, vex **4** fray, fume, fuss, gnaw, mope, pout, rile, stew, sulk, wear **5** brood, chafe, erode, grate, worry **6** abrade, harass, nettle, ripple, ruffle, strait **7** agitate, agonize, consume, corrode, disturb, trouble **8** irritate **9** headdress

FRETFUL: **5** angry, cross, huffy, testy **6** crabby, cranky, ornery, repine **7** gnawing, peevish, pettish **8** captious, contrary, restless **9** impatient, irascible, irritable, plaintive, querulous **11** troublesome

FRIABLE: **5** crimp, crisp, flaky, mealy **7** brittle, crumbly, fragile

FRIBBLE: **6** trifle **7** fritter **9** frivolity, frivolous

FRICTION: **5** clash **7** chafing, rubbing **8** conflict, grinding **9** hostility **10** antagonism, disharmony, dissension, resistance **12** disagreement

FRIEND: **3** ami, pal **4** ally, amie, chum **5** amiga, amigo, buddy, crony **6** bon ami, cohort **7** comrade, partner **8** compadre, playmate, relative, sidekick **9** associate, attendant, bonne amie, companion, confidant **10** confidante **12** acquaintance

FRIENDLY: **4** fond, kind, warm **5** civil **6** chummy, genial **7** affable, amiable, cordial **8** amicable, gracious, intimate, peaceful, sisterly, sociable **9** brotherly, congenial, favorable **10** benevolent, comforting, hospitable, neighborly **11** warmhearted **13** companionable

FRIENDSHIP: **4** love, pact **5** amity **6** accord **7** harmony **8** alliance, goodwill, platonic **9** coalition **10** attachment, federation **11** association

FRIGATE: **4** boat, ship **6** vessel **7** warship **8** sailboat

FRIGHT: **3** awe **4** fear, funk **5** alarm, dread, panic, scare, shock **6** dismay, horror, terror **7** anxiety, startle, strange **9** unsightly **11** trepidation **13** consternation

FRIGHTEN: **5** alarm, appal, hazen, panic, scare, spook, upset **6** appall, rattle **7** horrify, petrify, startle, terrify, unnerve **9** discomfit, terrorize **10** discourage, intimidate

FRIGHTENED: **5** timid **6** afraid, frozen **7** chicken, fearful **8** skittish

FRIGHTFUL: **4** dire, grim **5** awful, hairy, scary **6** grisly, horrid, morbid, wicked **7** extreme, fearful, gashful, ghastly, hideous **8** alarming, daunting, dreadful, fearsome, horrific, shocking, sinister, terrific **9** excessive **10** horrendous, horrifying, terrifying **11** distressing

FRIGID: **3** icy, raw **4** cold **5** stiff **6** arctic, chilly, frosty, frozen **8** freezing **11** passionless, straitlaced **12** unresponsive

FRILL: **3** air **6** luxury, ruffle **7** amenity, flounce, pleated **8** furbelow

FRINGE: **3** hem, rim **4** brim, edge **5** brink, limit, verge **6** border, edging **8** trimming **9** outskirts, perimeter, periphery

FRIPPERY: **5** waste **6** finery **7** regalia, trivial **8** nonsense **10** flashiness **11** ostentation, pretentious

FRISK: **4** lark, leap, skip **5** brisk, caper, dance **6** cavort, curvet, frolic, gambol, prance, search **7** examine **8** caracole **9** shake down

FRISKY: **4** pert, spry **5** peppy **6** active, lively **7** chipper, coltish, playful **8** spirited **9** kittenish **10** frolicsome

FRITTER: **4** cake, idle **5** dally, shred, spend, waste **6** bangle, dawdle, trifle **7** consume, deplete, pancake **8** squander

FRIVOLITY: **4** jest **5** folly **6** levity **7** fribble **8** flummery, nonsense **10** coquetting

FRIVOLOUS: **5** giddy, inane, petty, silly **6** futile **7** fribble, shallow, trivial **8** carefree, flippant **9** childlike, pointless, senseless, worthless **11** impractical **13** insignificant **14** featherbrained

FROCK: **4** gown, robe, wrap **5** apron, dress, habit, smock, tunic **6** mantle

FROG: **4** newt, toad **6** anuran, peeper, ranine **7** croaker **8** bullfrog **9** amphibian **10** batrachian, salientian

FROLIC: **3** fun **4** lark, play, ramp, romp **5** caper, frisk, prank, revel, sport, spree **6** cavort, curvet, gaiety, gambol, prance **7** carouse, disport, scamper, wassail **9** amusement, merriment **10** masquerade, tomfoolery

FROLICSOME: **6** frisky, jovial, lively **7** jocular, playful, waggish **8** gamesome, sportive **10** rollicking **11** mischievous

FROM: **3** fro **7** against **9** beginning **10** separating

FRONT: **3** bow, van **4** brow, face, fore, head, lead, show **5** cover **6** before, dickey, facade, facing, manner, oppose **7** display, forward, outlook **8** anterior, demeanor, disguise, exterior, forehead, foremost **9** beginning **10** appearance, effrontery

FRONTIER: **4** edge **5** bound, march **6** border **7** outpost **8** boundary **9** backlands, backwoods, outskirts, perimeter, unsettled **10** borderline

FROST: **3** ice, nip **4** hoar, rime **5** chill **6** blight, freeze

FROSTY: **3** icy **4** cold, cool, rimy **5** gelid **6** arctic, frigid, frozen **7** glacial **8** chilling, freezing

FROTH: **4** barm, fizz, foam, scum, suds, surf **5** spume **6** lather

FROWARD: **5** balky, cross **6** ornery **7** adverse, peevish **8** contrary, perverse, petulant, stubborn **9** obstinate **10** headstrong **11** disobedient, unfavorable

FROWN: **4** fret, pout, sulk **5** glare, gloom, lower, scowl **6** glower

7 grimace 8 disagree 10 disapprove

FROWSY, FROWZY: 5 musty, seedy, stale 6 smelly 7 unkempt 8 slovenly 10 disheveled, disordered

FROZEN: 4 cold, numb 5 fixed, gelid, stiff 6 arctic, frappe, frigid 7 chilled, frosted, stopped 8 hardened, immobile 9 congealed, suspended 11 coldhearted, frostbitten 12 refrigerated

FRUGAL: 5 canny, chary, tight 6 meager, saving, stingy 7 careful, prudent, sparing, thrifty 9 provident 10 economical, unwasteful 11 inexpensive 12 parsimonious 13 penny-pinching

FRUIT:
berry: 9 blueberry, cranberry 10 blackberry, loganberry, strawberry 11 boysenberry
citrus: 4 lime 5 lemon, mango 6 citron, orange, pomelo 7 kumquat, maartje, satsuma, tangelo 8 mandarin 9 ortanique 10 clementine
exotic: 4 kiwi 5 guava, melon, papaw 6 durian, litchi, longan, loquat 8 rambutan, tamarind 9 cherimoya, persimmon, sapodilla 10 breadfruit, cantaloupe, gooseberry, granadilla, mangosteen 11 pomegranate 12 passion fruit
hard: 4 sloe 6 quince 9 crab apple, nectarine
other: 3 fig 4 pear 5 grape, olive, peach 6 almond, banana, cherry, squash 7 apricot, avocado, currant 8 cucumber 9 pineapple

FRUITFUL: 5 ample 6 fecund 7 fertile 8 abundant, blooming, prolific 9 plenteous, plentiful, rewarding 10 productive, profitable, successful, worthwhile 11 flourishing

FRUITION: 7 delight 8 pleasure 10 attainment, maturation 11 achievement, fulfillment, realization 12 satisfaction 13 actualization 14 accomplishment

FRUITLESS: 4 geld, vain 6 barren, futile 7 sterile, useless 8 abortive 9 infertile, pointless 10 profitless 11 ineffective, ineffectual, unrewarding 12 unproductive, unprofitable, unsuccessful

FRUMP: 4 dull, prim, snub, sulk 5 dowdy, flout, plain 6 sedate 9 unstylish 13 unfashionable

FRUSTRATE: 4 balk, dash, foil, vain, void 5 block, check, cramp, crimp, cross, crush, elude 6 baffle, blight, defeat, hinder, impede, outwit, stymie, thwart 7 fluster, nullify, prevent, useless 8 confound, unsettle 9 checkmate, discomfit 10 circumvent, disappoint, disconcert, dishearten, exasperate, neutralize 11 countermand

FRUSTRATION: 7 letdown, setback 8 vexation 10 bottleneck, irritation 12 discomfiture 14 disappointment

FRY: 4 cook 5 brown, grill, saute 6 sizzle 7 destroy 11 electrocute

FRYING PAN: 6 spider 7 browner, griddle, skillet

FUDDLE: 5 drink 6 jumble, muddle, tipple 7 confuse, fluster 10 intoxicate

FUDGE: 4 fake 5 candy, cheat, dodge, evade, hunch 6 humbug 7 falsify 8 contrive, nonsense 10 exaggerate, substitute 12 misrepresent

FUEL: 3 gas, oil 4 coal, coke, feed, wood 5 juice, stoke 6 charge, ignite, incite, petrol 7 nourish, sustain 8 charcoal, energize, gasoline, kerosene 9 petroleum 10 ammunition, propellant 11 combustible, inspiration

FUGITIVE: 4 AWOL 5 brief, exile 6 dodger, outlaw, wanted 7 elusive, escapee, fleeing, refugee, roaming, runaway 8 criminal, deserter, fleeting, vagabond **9** ephemeral, fugacious, transient **10** evanescent, transitory

FUHRER: **6** leader, tyrant **8** dictator **11** Adolf Hitler

FULFILL: **4** full, meet, suit **5** reach **6** answer, effect, finish, redeem **7** achieve, execute, perform, realize, satisfy **8** complete **10** accomplish, effectuate

FULFILMENT, FULFILLMENT: **8** crowning, fruition **10** attainment **12** consummation **13** gratification

FULGENT: **6** bright **7** radiant, shining **8** dazzling, flashing, luminous **9** brilliant

FULL: **4** good, rich **5** ample, clear, laden, plump, round, sated, total, uncut **6** entire, filled, packed **7** copious, crammed, crowded, glutted, perform, plenary, replete, stocked, stuffed, teeming **8** adequate, brimming, bursting, complete, resonant, thorough **9** capacious, plentiful, satisfied, surfeited **10** exhaustive **11** overflowing

FULL-BLOODED: **5** ruddy **6** florid **7** genuine **8** purebred, rubicund **12** thoroughbred

FULL-BLOWN: **4** lush, ripe **5** adult **6** all-out, mature **9** blossomed, developed

FULL-BODIED: **4** rich **6** potent, robust **7** intense **9** flavorful

FULL-FLEDGED: **6** expert, mature **7** genuine, plumage **9** developed **10** proficient

FULL-GROWN: **4** ripe **5** ready **6** mature **9** developed

FULLNESS: **5** scope **6** plenty **7** breadth, satiety **8** entirety **9** abundance, aggregate, amplitude, plumpness **10** completion, perfection, plentitude **12** completeness

FULLY: **5** amply, quite **6** enough, wholly **7** clearly, totally, utterly **8** entirely, outright **9** perfectly **10** abundantly, completely, positively **11** plenteously, plentifully **12** sufficiently

FULMINATE: **4** fume, rant **6** berate **7** explode **8** detonate **9** castigate

FULSOME: **4** foul, glib **5** gross, plump, slick, suave **6** wanton **7** copious, overfed **8** abundant, unctuous **9** insincere, offensive, repulsive, satiating, sickening **10** disgusting, flattering, nauseating **12** ingratiating

FUMBLE: **4** boot, flub, goof, muff **5** botch, error, grope **6** bobble, bumble, bungle, mumble **7** stammer **8** flounder **9** mishandle, mismanage

FUME: **4** boil, emit, foam, odor, rage, rant, rave, stew **5** anger, smell, smoke, storm, vapor **6** exhale, seethe **8** fumigate **10** exhalation

FUN: **4** ball, game, glee, jest, joke, play **5** antic, blast, happy, mirth, sport **6** gaiety **8** clowning, hilarity, laughter, nonsense, pleasure **9** amusement, diversion, enjoyment, festivity, horseplay, merriment **10** recreation, tomfoolery **13** entertainment

FUNCTION: **3** job **4** duty, goal, role, task, work **5** feast, party **6** action, affair, object, office **7** benefit, mission, operate, purpose, service **8** activity, business, capacity, ceremony, occasion **9** festivity, gathering, operation, reception **10** occupation, profession, providence **11** celebration

FUNCTIONAL: **6** useful **7** working **9** operative, practical

FUND: **4** back, foot, pool **5** endow, stock, store, trust **6** source, supply **7** capital, deposit, finance, reserve, support **8** bankroll **9** subsidize **10** foundation **12** accumulation

FUNDAMENTAL: **4** rule **5** basic, chief, first, major, vital **7** central, crucial, element, organic, primary, radical, theorem **8** cardinal, integral, original **9** component, essential, important, necessary, paramount, principle **10** elementary, underlying

FUNDS: **4** cash **5** money **6** assets, wealth **7** capital, profits, savings **8** currency **9** resources

FUNERAL: **4** mass, wake **5** rites **6** burial **7** cortege **8** ceremony, exequies, services **9** cremation, obsequies, sepulture
oration: **6** eulogy **7** tribute **8** encomium **9** panegyric **10** salutation
song: **4** taps **5** dirge, elegy **6** lament **7** requiem **8** threnody

FUNEREAL: **4** grim **5** bleak, grave **6** dismal, dreary, gloomy, solemn **7** doleful **8** dirgeful, grieving, mournful **10** depressing

FUNGUS: **4** cepe, mold, rust, smut **5** ergot, morel, tinea, yeast **6** agaric, chitin, mildew, oidium, telium **7** amanita, truffle **8** mushroom, organism, puffball **9** stinkhorn, toadstool

FUNK: **4** odor, rage **5** gloom, music, panic, smell **6** coward, flinch, fright, misery, recoil, shrink **8** frighten **10** depression **11** despondency

FUNNEL: **4** cone, move, pipe **5** focus **6** convey, siphon **7** channel, conduct **8** transmit

FUNNY: **4** zany **5** droll, queer, silly, weird **6** clever **7** amusing, bizarre, comical, curious, jocular, offbeat, strange **8** humorous, puzzling **9** hilarious, laughable, slapstick **10** hysterical, mysterious, outlandish **12** entertaining

FUR: **4** coat, hair, hide, pell, pelt, pile, skin, wool **5** brush, stole **6** pelage
kind: **3** fox **4** lamb, mink, seal **5** otter, sable **6** beaver, rabbit **7** raccoon **8** squirrel

FURBELOW: **5** frill **6** ruffle **7** falbala, flounce **8** ornament, trimming

FURBISH: **5** clean, scour, shine **6** polish, revive **7** improve, restore **8** renovate **11** recondition

FURIOUS: **3** mad **5** angry, irate, livid, rabid, upset **6** crazed, fierce, fuming, raging, stormy **7** boiling, enraged, frantic, steamed, violent **8** blustery, frenzied, incensed, vehement **9** impetuous, turbulent **10** boisterous **11** tempestuous

FURL: **4** coil, curl, fold, roll, wrap **5** truss **6** bundle, enfold

FURLOUGH: **5** leave **6** layoff, permit **8** vacation

FURNACE: **4** kiln, oven **5** forge, stove **6** boiler, heater **11** incinerator **13** reverberatory

FURNISH: **3** arm **4** feed, give, lend **5** array, cater, endow, equip, stock **6** afford, bestow, clothe, insure, outfit, render, supply **7** apparel, appoint, garnish, prepare, provide **8** decorate, transfer **11** accommodate

FURNISHINGS: **8** fittings, fixtures **9** equipment, furniture, trappings **10** appliances **11** accessories

FURNITURE: **3** bed **4** desk, sofa **5** chair, couch, hutch, table **6** bureau **7** armoire, cabinet, dresser, ottoman, tallboy **8** bookcase, credenza **9** davenport, equipment **10** chiffonier, decoration **11** furnishings **12** chesterfield **13** embellishment
styles: **4** Adam **6** boulle **7** Regency

8 Colonial, Sheraton **9** Queen Anne **11** Biedermeier, Chippendale, Elizabethan **12** Second Empire

FUROR: **3** fad **4** fury, rage, stir **5** craze, mania **6** bustle, frenzy, uproar **7** fashion, madness **8** hysteria **9** commotion, whirlwind **10** enthusiasm, excitement

FURROW: **3** rut **4** fold, plow **5** ditch, drill **6** crease, groove, hollow, rimple, trench **7** channel, crumple, wrinkle

FURTHER: **3** aid, and, yet **4** also, help, more, push **5** again, serve **6** assist, beyond, foster **7** advance, another, besides, farther, forward, promote **8** moreover **9** advantage **10** accelerate, additional, contribute **12** supplemental

FURTHERANCE: **4** help **7** pursuit **8** advocacy, facility, progress **9** promotion **10** assistance **11** advancement

FURTHERMORE: **3** and, too, yet **4** also **7** besides **8** likewise, moreover **12** additionally

FURTIVE: **4** foxy, wily **6** covert, crafty, secret, shifty, sneaky **7** evasive **8** mystical, sneaking, stealthy **10** undercover **11** clandestine **13** surreptitious

FURY: **3** ire **4** rage **5** anger, force, furor, rigor, vixen, wrath **6** frenzy **7** bluster, madness, passion **8** outburst, violence **9** intensity, vehemence **10** fierceness **11** indignation

FUSE: **4** bind, flux, join, link, meld, melt, weld **5** blend, merge, smelt, unite **6** mingle, solder **7** combine **10** amalgamate **11** incorporate

FUSION: **4** flux **5** music **6** merger **7** melting, mixture **8** alliance, blending, reaction **9** coalition **10** liquefying

FUSS: **3** ado, nag, row **4** crab, flap, fret, spat, stew, stir **5** annoy, gripe, upset, whine, worry **6** bother, bustle, fidget, hassle, pother, squawk, tumult **7** dispute, nitpick, protest, quarrel, sputter, trouble **8** argument, complain **9** commotion, confusion **10** disconcert **11** disturbance

FUSSY: **5** picky **6** choosy **7** fidgety, finicky **9** demanding, difficult **10** fastidious, meticulous, particular **11** painstaking

FUSTIGATE: **4** beat, lash, whip **6** cudgel, strike **9** castigate, criticize

FUTILE: **4** idle, vain **7** forlorn, useless **8** hopeless, trifling **9** exhausted, frivolous, fruitless, pointless, worthless **11** ineffective, ineffectual **12** unsuccessful

FUTURE: **5** later **6** coming, latter **7** ensuing **8** eventual, prospect **9** hereafter, impending, projected **11** forthcoming

FUZZ: **4** down, hair, lint, pile **5** fiber, fluff **6** police

FUZZY: **4** hazy **5** faint, vague **6** bleary, woolly **7** blurred, unclear **9** unfocused

G

GAB: **3** yak, yap **4** chat, talk **5** prate **6** gabble, gossip, jabber **7** blabber, chatter, prattle **12** conversation

GABBLE: **3** gab, yak, yap **4** blab, talk **5** prate **6** babble, cackle, drivel, gossip, jabber **7** chatter, clatter, twaddle **8** chitchat

GABLE: **4** wall **6** dormer, pinion

GABON:
capital: **10** Libreville
cities: **6** Masuku, Owendo **10** Port-Gentil **11** Franceville
continent: **6** Africa
ethnic groups: **4** Fang **8** Bapounon
features: **8** Iboundji **9** Lambarene **13** Trans-Gabonais
languages: **5** Bantu **6** French
monetary unit: **5** franc
water: **6** Ogooue

GABRIEL: **9** archangel, messenger
instrument: **4** horn **7** trumpet

GAD: **4** roam, rove, tool **5** prowl, stray **6** ramble, wander **7** meander, traipse **9** gallivant

GADFLY: **4** goad, pest **6** bother, critic **8** busybody, nuisance

GADGET: **4** tool **5** gizmo **6** device, doodad **7** gimmick, novelty **9** appliance, doohickey, invention **11** contraption, contrivance, thingamajig

GAELIC: **4** Celt, Erse, Gael, Scot, Sept **5** Irish **6** Celtic, goidel, kelpie **10** Highlander

GAFFE: **4** goof **5** boner **7** blooper, blunder, faux pas, mistake **11** misjudgment

GAG: **4** hoax, hush, joke **5** choke, heave, quiet, trick, vomit **6** muffle, muzzle **7** silence **8** obstruct, restrain, suppress **9** constrain, wisecrack

GAIETY: **3** fun, joy **5** mirth **6** finery, frolic **7** elation, jollity **8** vivacity **9** animation, festivity, geniality, happiness, merriment **11** celebration

GAIN: **3** get, net, win **4** earn, good, land, plus, reap **5** clear, reach **6** attain, effect, growth, income, obtain, profit, return, secure **7** achieve, acquire, advance, benefit, prevail, procure, realize **8** addition, dividend, increase, progress **9** accretion, advantage, increment **11** acquisition, improvement **12** accumulation

GAINSAY: **4** deny **6** impugn, negate, oppose, refute, resist **7** dispute **8**

disagree, disclaim **10** contradict, controvert

GAIT: **4** lope, pace, rack, step, trot, walk **5** amble, march, strut, tread **6** canter, gallop, stride

GAITER: **4** boot, shoe **5** chaps **6** puttee **7** legging **8** overshoe

GALA: **4** bash **5** feast, merry, party **6** affair, festal, fiesta **8** carnival, colorful, festival, function **11** celebration

GALE: **4** gust, wind **5** blast, storm **6** flurry, squall **7** tempest, typhoon **8** outburst **9** hurricane, windstorm

GALILEO GALILEI:
birthplace: **4** Pisa **5** Italy
field: **7** physics **9** astronomy

GALL: **3** bug, irk, rub **4** burn, fret, rile **5** annoy, chafe, cheek, nerve, spite **6** abrade, harass, pester, rancor, ruffle **7** inflame **8** acerbity, boldness, irritate, temerity, vexation **9** brashness, excoriate, impudence **10** bitterness, effrontery, exasperate

GALLANT: **4** beau, bold, game **5** blade, brave, lover, noble, showy, suave, swain **6** daring, heroic, polite, suitor **7** conduct, courtly, dashing, stately, valiant **8** cavalier, fearless, handsome, intrepid, polished, splendid **9** attentive, courteous, dignified **10** chivalrous, courageous **11** gentlemanly

GALLANTRY: **4** grit **5** valor **6** spirit **7** bravery, courage, heroism **8** chivalry, courtesy **9** attention **11** courtliness

GALLERY: **5** porch, salon **6** arcade, loggia, museum, piazza **7** balcony, exhibit, portico, veranda **8** audience **9** mezzanine, promenade **10** assortment, collection, grandstand, passageway, spectators

GALLEY: **4** boat, ship, tray **5** cuddy, proof **6** bireme, vessel **7** kitchen, rowboat, trireme **8** cookroom, scullery

GALLIVANT: **4** roam **5** flirt **6** ramble, travel, wander **7** traipse

GALLOP: **3** fly, jog, run **4** bolt, dart, gait, race, trot **5** hurry, scoot, speed **6** hasten, sprint, stride **7** tantivy

GALLOWS: **4** rope **5** noose **6** gibbet **7** hanging, potence **8** scaffold

GALORE: **4** lots **7** aplenty, copious **8** abundant **9** plentiful

GALOSH: **4** boot, shoe **6** rubber **8** overshoe

GALVANIZE: **4** coat, jolt, spur, stir **5** prime, rally **6** arouse, excite **7** inspire, provoke, startle **8** energize, motivate **9** electrify, stimulate

GAMBIA:
capital: **6** Banjul
cities: **5** Bakau **9** Serekunda **10** Georgetown
continent: **6** Africa
ethnic groups: **4** Fula **5** Wolof **8** Mandinka
features: **9** Karantaba
languages: **5** Wolof **7** English **8** Mandinka
monetary unit: **6** dalasi
water: **5** Niger **6** Gambia

GAMBIT: **4** move, plan, plot, ploy, ruse **5** trick **6** design, remark **7** gimmick **8** maneuver **9** stratagem

GAMBLE: **3** bet **4** dice, game, play, risk **5** hedge, stake, wager **6** chance, hazard **7** venture **9** speculate **10** jeopardize **11** uncertainty

GAMBLER: **5** dicer, shark **6** bookie, player **7** hustler, sharper **8** gamester **10** speculator

GAMBOL: **4** jump, lark, leap, play, romp **5** caper, frisk **6** cavort, frolic, prance, tumble **7** rollick

GAME:
ball: **4** golf, polo **5** catch, rugby **6** hockey, soccer, squash, tennis **7** cricket, croquet **8** baseball, football, handball, pingpong, softball **9** billiards **10** basketball
board: **5** bingo, chess, lotto **8** checkers, cribbage, Monopoly, Parchesi, Scrabble **10** backgammon
card: **3** pan, pig, sam, war **4** faro, fish, frog, skat, trio, tunk **5** chile, cinch, ombre, pedro, pitch, poker, rummy, samba, stops, whist **6** boodle, bridge, clubby, eights, euchre, fan tan, hearts, hombre, kaluki, memory, piquet, pounce, red dog, sevens, shasta, slough, smudge, spider **7** auction, authors, belotte, bezique, bolivia, canasta, cassino, Chicago, garbage, kalougi, low ball, old maid, pool nap, seven-up, shotgun, Uruguay, wipe-off **8** all fours, baccarat, big forty, canfield, chouette, conquian, crapette, cribbage, gin rummy, kaloochi, Klondike, Michigan, Napoleon, Oklahoma, pinochle, Saratoga, sixty-six, slapjack **9** accordion, arlington, black jack, forty-five, kalabrias, monte bank, newmarket, old sledge, play or pay, sir garnet, solitaire, spoil five, stud poker, twenty-one, vingt-et-un **10** blind tiger, crazy jacks, deuces wild, five finger, five or nine, klaberjass, panguingue, parliament, put and take, schafskopf, sheepshead, tournament **11** calculation, crazy eights, five hundred, red and black, Russian bank **12** forty thieves **13** concentration, dealer's choice, Michigan rummy **14** earl of Coventry, spite and malice
court: **6** pelota, squash, tennis **7** jai alai **8** handball **9** badminton **10** basketball, volleyball
racket: **5** bandy **6** squash, tennis **8** lacrosse **9** badminton
word: **4** ludi **5** ghost **7** anagram **8** acrostic, scrabble **9** crossword

GAMETE: **3** egg **4** ovum **5** sperm **6** zygote **8** oosphere **12** spermatozoon

GAMMON: **3** ham **4** bosh, dupe, talk **5** bacon, cozen, feign **6** delude, humbug **7** beguile, deceive, mislead

GAMUT: **4** span **5** field, orbit, range, reach, scale **6** extent, series **7** compass **8** spectrum **9** continuum

GANG: **3** mob **4** band, clan, club, crew, pack, ring, team **5** crowd, group, horde, posse **6** circle, clique, outfit **7** company, friends **9** syndicate

GANGLING: **4** tall **5** lanky, rangy **6** skinny **7** awkward

GANGSTER: **4** goon, hood, moll, punk, thug **5** crook, thief **6** bandit, gunman **7** mobster, ruffian **8** criminal, hooligan **9** desperado, racketeer

GAP: **4** flaw, hole, lull, pass, rift, void **5** blank, break, chasm, cleft, clove, crack, gully, notch, pause, space **6** breach, defile, divide, hiatus, ravine, vacuum **7** crevice, fissure, opening **8** aperture **9** disparity **10** separation **12** interruption **13** inconsistency

GAPE: **3** eye **4** gasp, gawk, gaze, ogle, peer, yawn **5** stare **6** goggle **8** oscitate **10** rubberneck

GAPING: **4** open, vast **5** broad, great **9** cavernous

GARB: **4** gear **5** array, dress, getup, guise, style **6** attire, bundle, clothe, custom, outfit **7** apparel, costume, fashion, raiment, threads **8** clothing, vestment **10** appearance

GARBAGE: **4** junk **5** offal, trash, waste **6** debris, litter, refuse, sewage **7** rubbish **11** meaningless

GARBLE: **4** cull, sift **5** color, twist **6** jumble, mangle **7** distort **8** disguise, misstate, scramble **12** misrepresent

GARDEN: **3** bed **4** Eden, lawn, park, plot, yard **5** arbor, field, patch, tract **7** nursery, terrace **8** parterre **9** cultivate, enclosure **10** greenhouse **12** conservatory
variety: **4** herb, rock, rose **5** water **6** cactus, flower, formal **7** English, hanging, kitchen, victory **8** floating **9** vegetable

GARDENER: **9** caretaker **10** landscaper **14** horticulturist

GARDEN STATE: **9** New Jersey

GARGANTUAN: **4** huge, vast **5** giant **7** immense, mammoth, massive, titanic **8** colossal, enormous, gigantic

GARGLE: **5** swish **8** irrigate **9** mouthwash

GARISH: **4** loud **5** cheap, gaudy, showy **6** bright, flashy, tawdry **7** glaring **9** tasteless **12** ostentatious

GARLAND: **3** bay, lei **4** band **5** crown, glory **6** corona, laurel, rosary, wreath **7** chaplet, coronet, festoon **8** accolade, decorate, headband **9** anthology

GARMENT: **3** don, tog **4** coat, garb, gear, gown, robe **5** adorn, cloak, dress, frock, getup, habit, jeans, pants, preen, primp, shift, shirt, skirt, toile, train **6** attire, blouse, clothe, invest, jacket, jersey, jumper, khakis, outfit **7** apparel, clothes, garment, sweater, toggery **8** clothing, coverall, ornament, overalls, trousers, vestment **9** vestiture **10** habiliment **12** accouterment
ancient: **4** toga **5** palla, simar, stola **6** chiton, kirtle, rochet, tabard
law: **4** robe
religious: **4** robe **5** cloth, habit **8** vestment

GARNER: **4** reap **5** amass, hoard, store **6** gather **7** acquire, collect **9** stockpile **10** accumulate

GARNET: **5** jewel, stone **8** essonite

GARNISH: **4** deck, trim **5** adorn, equip **7** enhance, furbish, furnish, improve **8** beautify, decorate, ornament **9** embellish **10** jardiniere

GARRET: **4** loft **5** attic **6** turret **10** watchtower

GARRISON: **4** fort, post **6** secure, troops **7** station **8** regiment

GARRULOUS: **5** gabby, talky, wordy **7** gossipy, voluble **8** babbling, rambling **9** talkative **10** loquacious

GAS: **4** tear **5** ether, inert, marsh, noble, oxane, ozone, radon, xenon **6** butane, ethane, helium, ketene, oxygen **7** ammonia, krypton, methane, mustard, propane **8** cyanogen, ethylene, hydrogen, laughing **9** acetylene **12** nitrous oxide **13** carbon dioxide **14** carbon monoxide **15** hydrogen sulfide

GASCON: **7** boaster **8** blowhard, braggart

GASH: **3** cut **4** slit **5** carve, cleft, slash, split, wound **8** incision **10** laceration

GASP: **4** blow, gulp, huff, pant **5** heave **6** inhale, wheeze **7** breathe, exclaim

GASTRONOME: **7** epicure, gourmet **9** bon vivant **11** connoisseur

GASTROPOD: **4** slug **5** snail **6** cowrie, limpet, volute **7** mollusk **8** pteropod

GATE: **3** bar, dam, way **4** door, exit, hole, pass, take **5** hatch, valve **6** access **7** opening, passage, postern

8 barbican, entrance, receipts **9** threshold, turnstile **10** attendance

GATEKEEPER: **5** guard **6** porter, sentry, warden **8** sentinel, watchman

GATEWAY: **4** arch **5** entry, pylon, toran **6** portal **8** entrance

GATHER: **4** cull, draw, herd, mass, meet, pick, reap **5** amass, bunch, crowd, flock, glean, group, infer, shirr, stack, swarm, think **6** assume, bundle, deduce, derive, garner, huddle, muster, reckon, select **7** collect, compile, convene, convoke, harvest, imagine, marshal, recruit **8** assemble, compress, conclude **10** accumulate, congregate, understand **11** concentrate

GATHERING: **4** bevy, stag **5** crowd, flock, party, rally **6** affair **7** company, meeting, roundup, turnout **8** assembly, function **9** concourse, multitude **10** assemblage, collection, convention **11** convocation **12** accumulation, congregation

GAUCHE: **5** crude, inept **6** clumsy **7** awkward, uncouth **8** bumbling, bungling, tactless **9** maladroit, unrefined **10** blundering

GAUDY: **4** loud **5** cheap, crude, showy **6** brazen, bright, flashy, flimsy, garish, ornate, tawdry, vulgar **7** glaring, splashy **8** festival **9** flaunting, tasteless **11** pretentious **12** ostentatious

GAUGE: **4** norm, size, test **5** judge, meter, scale **7** measure **8** estimate, evaluate, standard **9** barometer, benchmark, criterion, guideline, yardstick **10** instrument

GAUL:
also called: **6** Gallia **7** Belgium
conquered by: **6** Caesar
gods/goddesses: **4** Esus **7** Taranis **8** Belisama
place: **6** France

GAUNT: **4** bony, grim, lean, slim, thin **5** bleak, lanky **6** barren, hollow, meager, skinny **7** angular, haggard, scraggy, scrawny, slender **8** anorexic, desolate, rawboned, skeletal **9** emaciated **10** cadaverous, forbidding

GAUNTLET: **4** test **5** armor, glove, trial **6** ordeal **9** challenge, onslaught

GAUZY: **5** filmy, lucid, sheer **6** flimsy **8** delicate, gossamer **11** transparent

GAVEL: **4** maul, rent **6** hammer, mallet **7** tribute

GAWK: **3** oaf **4** gape, gaze, lout, ogle **5** glare, klutz, stare **6** goggle **7** eyeball **9** simpleton **10** rubberneck

GAWKY: **6** clumsy **7** awkward **8** bumbling, bungling, ungainly **9** lumbering, maladroit

GAY: **4** airy, glad **5** brisk, happy, jolly, merry, showy, vivid **6** blithe, bright, flashy, frisky, jocund, jovial, joyful, lively **7** chipper, festive, gleeful, jocular, lesbian, playful **8** animated, carefree, cheerful, colorful, mirthful, sportive **9** brilliant, dissolute, sprightly, vivacious **10** flamboyant, frolicsome, homosexual, licentious **12** lighthearted

GAZE: **3** eye **4** gape, gawk, leer, look, ogle, peek, peer, scan, view **5** glare, sight, stare, study, watch **6** admire, behold, glance, survey **7** observe **10** scrutinize **11** contemplate

GAZETTE: **5** paper **7** journal **9** newspaper **11** publication

GAZETTEER: **5** atlas, guide, index **10** dictionary

GEAR: **3** cam, cog **4** duds, garb **5** dress, equip, goods, stuff, tools **6** outfit, pinion, tackle, things **7** apparel, baggage, luggage, prepare, rigging **8** clothing, cogwheel, garments, materiel, property, sprocket, supplies **9** accessory, apparatus, equipment, mechanism, trappings **10** appliances, belongings, derailleur, implements, instrument **11** possessions **13** paraphernalia

GELATIN: **4** agar **5** Jell-O, jelly **7** dessert, protein, sericin **8** membrane **9** isinglass

GELATINOUS: **5** gummy **7** viscous **9** jelly-like **10** coagulated

GELD: **3** fix, tax **4** spay **5** alter **6** neuter, weaken **8** castrate **10** emasculate

GELID: **3** icy **4** cold **6** chilly, frozen **8** freezing

GEM: **4** jade, onyx, opal, ruby **5** agate, amber, bijou, cameo, jewel, lapis, pearl, stone, topaz **6** amulet, garnet, jasper, lazuli, zircon **7** asteria, citrine, diamond, emerald, hyalite, peridot **8** amethyst, gemstone, intaglio, marquise, sapphire, sardonyx, tigereye **9** moonstone, morganite, turquoise **10** aquamarine **11** alexandrite

GEM STATE: **5** Idaho

GEMUTLICH: **4** cozy, warm **6** genial **8** cheerful, friendly, pleasant **9** agreeable, congenial **11** comfortable

GENDARME: **7** soldier **13** police officer

GENDER: **3** sex **4** male, sort **5** class **6** female, neuter **7** epicene **8** identity

GENEALOGY: **7** descent, lineage **8** ancestry, heredity, pedigree **10** family tree

GENERAL: **4** rank, true **5** basic, broad **6** common, leader, public **7** average, generic, inexact, officer, popular, routine, typical **8** everyday, ordinary **9** commander, customary, prevalent, universal **10** prevailing, unspecific, widespread **11** approximate, diversified

GENERALIZE: **5** infer **6** derive, extend, spread **8** theorize **11** hypothesive

GENERALLY: **5** about, often **6** mainly, mostly **7** broadly, largely, overall, roughly **8** commonly, normally **9** primarily, typically **11** customarily, principally

GENERATE: **4** form, make, sire **5** beget, breed, cause, spawn, yield **6** create, induce **7** develop, produce **8** engender, initiate **9** originate, procreate, propagate

GENERATION: **3** age, era **4** span, time **5** peers **6** family, period **7** progeny **8** creation, lifetime **9** offspring, posterity **11** descendants, procreation

GENERIC: **6** common **7** general **9** universal **11** unspecified **13** comprehensive

GENEROSITY: **5** heart **7** charity **8** kindness, largesse **11** benevolence, hospitality **13** unselfishness

GENEROUS: **4** good, kind **5** ample, noble **7** fertile, helpful, liberal **8** abundant, gracious, spirited **9** bountiful, excellent, plenteous, unselfish **10** altruistic, benevolent, bighearted, charitable, freehanded, munificent, openhanded, thoughtful **11** considerate, kindhearted, magnanimous, warmhearted **12** humanitarian **13** philanthropic

GENESIS: **5** alpha, birth **6** origin **7** dawning **8** creation **9** beginning, inception **11** origination

GENETIC: **9** ancestral **10** hereditary

GENIAL: **4** mild, nice, warm **5** happy, sunny **6** benign, jovial, kindly **7** amiable, cordial, festive **8** cheerful, friendly, gracious, pleasant, sociable **9** congenial, gemutlich

GENIE: **5** demon, jinni **8** creature

GENIUS: **4** gift, whiz **5** brain, flair, knack **6** talent **7** ability, insight **8** aptitude **9** ingenuity, intellect **10** brilliance, creativity, mastermind **11** imagination

GENRE: **4** kind, type **5** genus, group, order, style **6** gender **7** species, variety **8** category **11** description **14** classification

GENTEEL: **4** nice, prim **6** formal, polite, urbane **7** elegant, refined, stylish **8** cultured, graceful, mannerly, polished **9** courteous **10** cultivated

GENTLE: **4** calm, easy, fair, kind, meek, mild, soft, tame **5** bland, faint, quiet, sweet, tamed **6** benign, docile, feeble, mellow, placid, polite, serene, tender **7** amiable, clement, gradual, lenient **8** harmless, moderate, peaceful, pleasant, soothing, tranquil **9** courteous, honorable, sensitive **10** chivalrous **11** considerate **13** compassionate

GENTLEMAN: **3** sir **4** lord **5** senor **6** mister, squire **7** esquire, gallant **8** cavalier, nobleman **9** caballero **10** aristocrat

GENTLEWOMAN: **4** lady **6** polite **8** gracious **9** attendant **11** considerate

GENTRY: **5** elite **7** society **8** nobility **9** landowner **10** upper class **11** aristocracy

GENUINE: **4** open, pure, real, true **5** plain **6** actual, honest **7** earnest, natural, sincere **8** bona fide, original, sterling **9** authentic, certified, heartfelt, intrinsic, unfeigned **10** legitimate **11** trustworthy **13** unadulterated

GENUS: **4** kind, type **5** genre, group, order, style **6** gender **7** species, variety **8** category **11** description **14** classification

GEOLOGY: **12** earth science
age: **7** Permian **8** Cambrian, Cenezoic, Devonian, Jurassic, Mesozoic, Silurian, Triassic **9** Paleozoic **10** Cretaceous, Cryptozoic, Ordovician **13** Mississippian, Pennsylvanian
division: **3** age, era **4** aeon **5** epoch **6** period
period: **6** Eocene **7** Miocene **8** Pliocene, Tertiary **9** Oligocene **10** Quaternary **11** Pleistocene

GEOMETRY: **4** cone, kite, lune, oval **5** acute, angle, chord, curve, prism, rhomb, right, solid **6** circle, euclid, gnomon, oblong, obtuse, radius, secant, sector, sphere, spiral **7** ellipse, evolute, hexagon, pyramid, rhombus, scalene, tangent, theorem **8** cylinder, diameter, heptagon, parabola, pentagon, sinusoid, triangle **9** ellipsoid, incidence, inscribed, isosceles, rectangle, trapezium **10** concentric, hypotenuse, octahedron, semicircle **11** equilateral, icosahedron, tetrahedron **12** dodecahedron **13** circumference, quadrilateral **14** parallelepiped

GEORGIA (U.S):
bird: **13** brown thrasher
capital: **7** Atlanta
cities: **5** Macon **6** Athens **8** Columbus, Savannah
explorer: **6** de Soto
features: **9** Blue Ridge **10** Okefenokee, Sea Islands
flower: **12** cherokee rose
native: **8** Georgian
nickname: **5** Peach **6** Empire

tree: **7** live oak
water: **8** Atlantic, Savannah **13** Chattahoochee

GEORGIA:
capital: **7** Tbilisi
cities: **6** Batumi **7** Rustavi, Sukhumi

GERM: **3** bud, bug **4** seed **5** spore, virus **6** embryo, origin, sprout **7** disease, microbe, nucleus **8** organism, parasite, pathogen **9** bacterium, beginning

GERMANE: **4** true **7** fitting, related **8** material, relative, relevant **9** pertinent **10** applicable **11** appropriate

GERMANY:
authors: **4** Mann, Marx **6** Brecht, Goethe **7** Lessing
capital: **4** Bonn **6** Berlin
cities: **5** Essen **6** Munich **7** Cologne, Leipzig **8** Mannheim **9** Frankfurt, Nuremberg, Stuttgart, Wiesbaden **10** Dusseldorf
composers: **4** Bach **5** Weber **6** Brahms, Handel, Wagner **7** Strauss **8** Schumann **9** Beethoven **11** Mendelssohn
dynasty: **5** Saxon **8** Habsburg
food: **4** kase **5** torte, wurst **7** stollen **9** bratwurst, Limburger **10** knockwurst **11** sauerbraten **12** pumpernickel **15** wiener schnitzel
island: **7** Frisian
lakes: **6** Alster, Muritz **9** Constance
leaders: **6** Hitler **8** Bismarck
monetary unit: **4** mark **6** kronen, thaler **7** pfennig **8** groschen
mountains: **3** Ore **4** Alps, Harz **11** Black Forest
people: **3** Hun **4** Goth, Slav, Sorb, Wend **5** Boche, Saxon **6** Teuton
rivers: **3** Inn **4** Elbe, Main, Oder, Ruhr **5** Donau, Mosel, Rhine, Saale **6** Danube **7** Moselle
seas: **5** North **6** Baltic

GERMINATE: **3** bud **4** grow **6** evolve, sprout **7** develop **8** generate, vegetate

GESTATION: **7** bearing **9** evolution, pregnancy **10** conception, maturation **11** development

GESTURE: **3** nod **4** sign, wave, wink **5** shrug, snook, token **6** action, curtsy, motion, salute, signal **8** courtesy **9** formality **10** expression, intimation, salutation **11** gesticulate **12** genuflection

GET: **3** bag, win **4** draw, earn, find, gain, grab, land, nail, take **5** annoy, beget, bring, catch, fetch, learn, reach, seize, upset **6** appear, attain, baffle, bother, collar, derive, fathom, induce, master, obtain, prompt, puzzle, secure, suffer **7** achieve, acquire, capture, possess, prepare, procure, realize, receive **8** contract, irritate, overcome, persuade, retrieve **9** ascertain, determine, influence **10** accomplish, comprehend, understand

GET ACROSS: **6** convey **8** convince **10** understand **11** communicate

GET AHEAD: **5** climb, excel **7** advance, prosper, succeed **8** flourish

GET ALONG: **4** cope, fare **5** agree, leave **6** manage **7** advance, succeed **8** progress

GET AT: **4** mean **6** attain, intend **7** suggest **8** discover **9** ascertain

GETAWAY: **3** lam **4** flee **5** elude **6** escape **8** breakout

GET BACK: **6** recoup, regain, return **7** recover, salvage **9** repossess

GET BY: **4** pass **5** exist **6** manage **7** survive **8** outstrip

GET DOWN: **5** enjoy **7** depress, descend, exhaust **8** dismount **10** discourage

GET IN: **5** enter **6** arrive, insert **10** infiltrate

GET OFF: **4** exit **5** leave, start **6** depart, escape **8** pleasure **10** effrontery **13** gratification

GET ON: **5** board, mount **6** embark **7** advance **8** continue, progress **9** harmonize

GET OUT: **4** exit, flee **5** avoid, dodge, leave, scram **6** escape, vacate **7** publish **8** evacuate **9** skedaddle

GET RID OF: **4** drop, dump **5** ditch **6** remove, unload **7** discard **8** jettison **9** repudiate **11** exterminate

GET TOGETHER: **4** meet **5** party, rally **6** social **7** convene, meeting **8** assemble **10** accumulate

GET UP: **4** rise **5** adorn, awake, dress, scale, stand, style **6** ascend **7** costume **8** disguise, generate

GEWGAW: **3** toy **6** bauble, doodad, trifle **7** trinket **10** knickknack

GHANA:
capital: **5** Accra
cities: **4** Tema **6** Elmina, Kumasi, Tamale **10** Bolgatanga **15** Sekondi-Takoradi
continent: **6** Africa
ethnic groups: **2** Ga **3** Ewe **4** Akan **12** Moshi-Dagomba
features: **7** Ashanti **8** Afadjato
languages: **3** Ewe **4** Akan **5** Mossi **7** English **9** Ga-Adangme
monetary unit: **4** cedi
water: **9** Lake Volta

GHASTLY: **4** grim, pale **5** lurid **6** grisly, pallid **7** deathly, fearful, hideous, macabre **8** dreadful, gruesome, shocking, terrible **9** appalling, frightful, repulsive, revolting **10** horrifying, terrifying

GHOST: **4** soul **5** demon, image, shade, spook **6** shadow, spirit, vision, wraith **7** banshee, eidolon, phantom, specter, visitor **8** phantasm, presence, revenant **10** apparition **11** poltergeist

GHOSTLY: **5** eerie, scary, weird **6** spooky **7** uncanny **8** spectral **9** spiritual **12** supernatural

GHOUL: **5** demon, fiend **7** monster, vampire **11** grave robber

GIANT: **4** huge, ogre, rahu **5** jumbo, titan, troll **7** Cyclops, Goliath, immense, monster, titanic **8** behemoth, colossus, enormous, gigantic, mammouth, powerful **9** Herculean, monstrous **10** gargantuan, tremendous

GIBBERISH: **6** babble, drivel, jabber, jargon **7** chatter, twaddle **8** nonsense **10** double-talk, mumbo jumbo **11** jabberwocky

GIBBOUS: **6** convex **7** rounded **8** kyphosis **11** hunchbacked, protuberant

GIBE: **4** jeer, mock, quip **5** fling, flirt, flout, scoff, sneer, swipe, taunt **6** deride, harass, heckle **7** sarcasm **8** derision, ridicule **9** wisecrack

GIDDY: **5** dizzy, faint, silly **6** fickle, volage **7** erratic, flighty **8** heedless, skittish **9** befuddled, doddering, frivolous, impulsive, whimsical **10** capricious **11** harebrained, vertiginous

GIFT: **4** bent, boon, dole **5** bonus, bribe, dower, dowry, favor, forte, grant, knack, prize, token **6** bounty, genius, legacy, reward, talent **7** ability, aptness, benefit, faculty, handout, largess, memento, present, subsidy, tribute **8** aptitude, bestowal, blessing, donation, giveaway, gratuity, keepsake, offering, pittance, souvenir **9** endowment, gratitude, specialty **10** compliment **12** contribution

GIFTED: **4** deft **5** smart **6** adroit, bright, clever **9** brilliant, ingenious **10** proficient **11** intelligent

GIG: **3** job **4** boat, work **5** spear, stint **7** demerit, rowboat **8** carriage **10** engagement

GIGANTIC: **3** big **4** huge, vast **5** giant, large **6** mighty **7** immense, mammoth, massive, titanic **8** colossal, enormous, towering **9** monstrous **10** gargantuan, prodigious

GIGGLE: **5** laugh **6** cackle, teehee, titter **7** chuckle, snicker, snigger

GILD: **4** deck **5** adorn **6** enrich **7** overlay **8** brighten, decorate **9** embellish

GILL: **4** girl **5** brook **6** ravine, stream, wattle **10** sweetheart **11** measurement

GIMCRACK: **3** toy **5** cheap, gaudy **6** bauble, flimsy, gewgaw, trifle **7** trinket **8** ornament **9** frivolous, tasteless **10** knickknack

GIMMICK: **4** ploy, ruse **5** angle, catch, twist **6** device, gadget, scheme **8** maneuver **9** stratagem **11** contrivance

GIN: **4** game, pump, rack, trap **5** snare **6** device, liquor **7** alcohol, machine **8** beverage **10** intoxicant

GINGER: **3** pep, vim **5** brown, color, plant, spice, spunk, vigor **6** mettle, revive **7** rhizome **8** spirited **10** liveliness

GINGERBREAD: **4** cake **5** gawdy **6** cookie **8** trimming **9** elaborate **10** ornamented **11** superfluous **13** embellishment

GINGERLY: **6** warily **7** charily, timidly **8** daintily **9** carefully, guardedly **10** cautiously, delicately **11** reluctantly **12** fastidiously, suspiciously

GINGHAM: **5** cloth **6** fabric **8** chambray

GIRD: **4** belt, bind, hoop, jeer, loop, mock **5** brace, endow, equip, sneer **6** circle, clothe, fasten, remark, secure **7** enclose, prepare **8** encircle, ridicule, surround **9** encompass, reinforce **10** strengthen

GIRDER: **4** beam **5** brace, truss **6** binder **7** support

GIRDLE: **3** hem **4** band, bark, belt, bind, ring, sash **5** girth, strap **6** bodice, circle, corset **7** environ **8** cincture, encircle **9** waistband **12** undergarment

GIRL: **3** gal, sis **4** coed, dame, lass, maid, miss **5** chick, wench, woman **6** damsel, female, tomboy **7** colleen, servant **8** daughter, immature **9** debutante **10** sweetheart **13** inexperienced

GIRL FRIDAY: **4** aide **8** employee **9** assistant, secretary

GIRLFRIEND: **6** steady **7** fiancee **10** sweetheart

GIRLISH: **5** sissy **8** immature, juvenile, maidenly, youthful

GIRTH: **4** band, belt, bulk, size **5** cinch, strap, width **6** girdle **7** compass, measure **8** boundary, encircle **13** circumference

GIST: **4** core, crux, idea, pith **5** basis, drift, heart, point, theme, topic **7** essence, meaning **9** substance **12** significance

GIVE: **4** bear, bend, cede, dole, emit, fold, hand, pass, show **5** allow, apply, break, endow, grant, issue, serve, throw, yield **6** accord, afford, bestow, commit, confer, convey, devote, donate, extend, impart, notify, permit, render, supply, weaken **7** address, crumble, furnish, perform, present, proffer, propose, provide, stretch **8** bequeath, collapse, dispense, manifest, transfer **9** sacrifice, vouchsafe **10** administer, contribute, elasticity, resilience **11** communicate

GIVE AND TAKE: **8** exchange **10** compromise

GIVE AWAY: **4** leak **5** spill **6** betray, donate, reveal **7** divulge, present **8** disclose, telltale **9** sacrifice

GIVE BACK: **4** echo **6** rebate, recede, return **7** cutback, replace, restore **9** reinstate

GIVE FORTH: **4** emit **5** issue **6** exhale **9** discharge

GIVE IN: **5** yield **6** relent, resign, submit **7** abandon, concede, succumb **8** collapse **9** surrender

GIVEN: **5** fixed, prone **6** stated **7** assumed **8** inclined **10** accustomed

GIVE OFF: **4** emit, vent **5** exude **6** effuse **7** emanate, radiate, release **9** discharge

GIVE OUT: **4** deal, emit, fail, tire **5** issue **6** weaken **7** divulge, publish, release **8** collapse **10** distribute

GIVER: **5** donor **10** benefactor **11** contributor **14** philanthropist

GIVE UP: **4** cede, part, quit, stop **5** cease, forgo, spare, waive, yield **6** devote, resign, retire, reveal, vacate **7** abandon, despair, forsake, present, succumb **8** abdicate, renounce **9** sacrifice, surrender **10** relinquish

GIVE WAY: **5** yield **6** buckle **7** crumple, retreat **8** collapse, withdraw **10** relinquish

GIZMO: **5** thing **6** device, gadget **9** invention **10** instrument **11** contraption

GLACIAL: **3** icy **4** cold **5** gelid, polar **6** arctic, frigid, frozen **7** distant, hostile **8** freezing **10** unfriendly

GLACIER: **6** icecap **7** iceberg

GLAD: **5** eager, happy, merry **6** blithe, bright, elated, joyful, joyous **7** beaming, pleased, tickled, willing **8** cheerful **9** delighted, gratified, satisfied **11** exhilarated **12** lighthearted

GLADDEN: **5** cheer, elate **6** please **7** delight, gratify **10** exhilarate

GLADE: **4** dell, vale **5** marsh **6** hollow **7** opening **8** clearing

GLADIATOR: **5** boxer **7** athlete, fighter **9** combatant, disputant

GLADNESS: **3** joy **4** glee **5** bliss, mirth **6** gaiety **7** delight **8** pleasure **9** happiness **12** exhilaration

GLAMOROUS: **6** classy, exotic **7** elegant **8** alluring, charming **9** seductive **10** attractive, glamourous **11** captivating, charismatic, fascinating

GLAMOUR: **4** aura **5** charm, magic **6** appeal, beauty, glamor **7** glitter, mystery, romance **9** magnetism

GLANCE: **4** gaze, kiss, peek, peep, scan, skim, wink **5** brush, flash, glint, graze, shave **6** bounce, browse, careen, gander, squint **7** glimmer, glimpse, twinkle **8** ricochet

GLAND: **5** liver, lymph **6** pineal, thymus **7** adrenal, eccrine, mammary, parotid, thyroid **8** apocrine, ductless, exocrine, pancreas, prostate **9** endocrine, holocrine, lachrymal, merocrine, pituitary, sebaceous **10** suprarenal **11** parathyroid
enlarged: **4** bubo **7** adenoma
secretes: **5** sebum **6** smegma **7** hormone
study: **13** endocrinology

GLARE: **4** beam, gaze, glow **5** blaze, frown, scowl, shine, stare **6** dazzle, glower **7** glisten, glitter, radiate

GLARING: **4** loud, rank **5** clear, gaudy, gross, plain, vivid **6** brazen, bright **7** blatant, burning, evident, intense, obvious, visible **8** apparent, flagrant **10** noticeable **11** conspicuous

GLASS: **3** mug **4** lens, pane, pony **5** crown, Pyrex, stein **6** bumper, goblet, jigger, mirror, rummer **7** opaline, snifter, tankard, Tiffany, tumbler **8** schooner **9** Waterford
concerning: **6** vitric
gem-making: **5** paste **6** strass

GLASSES: **5** specs **6** shades **7** goggles, monocle **8** bifocals, pince nez **9** lorgnette **10** binoculars, spectacles

GLASSY: **4** hard **5** dazed, sharp, slick **6** smooth **8** lifeless, polished, vitreous **10** lackluster, unwavering, unyielding

GLAZE: **4** blur, coat **5** cover, glare, gloss **6** enamel, finish, glance, luster, polish **7** burnish, overlay, varnish, vitrify

GLEAM: **3** ray **4** beam, glow **5** flash, glint, gloss, sheen, shine **7** glimmer, glitter, shimmer, sparkle, twinkle **8** radiance **9** coruscate **10** brightness, brilliance **11** scintillate

GLEAN: **4** cull, reap **6** garner, gather **7** collect, harvest **10** accumulate

GLEE: **3** joy **5** mirth **6** gaiety **7** delight, ecstasy, elation **8** gladness, hilarity, pleasure **9** happiness, joviality, merriment **11** playfulness **12** cheerfulness

GLEN: **4** dale, dell, vale **5** glade **6** canyon, hollow, valley **10** depression

GLIB: **4** easy **5** quick, ready, slick, suave **6** facile, fluent, smooth **7** offhand, voluble **8** eloquent, flippant, slippery **9** impromptu, insincere **10** articulate, nonchalant, talktative **11** superficial

GLIDE: **4** flow, sail, scud, skim, slip, soar **5** coast, drift, slide **7** slither **8** glissade, volplane

GLIMMER: **4** beam, glow **5** blink, flash, gleam, trace, waver **6** glance **7** flicker, glimpse, glisten, glitter, sparkle, twinkle

GLIMPSE: **4** espy, look, peek **5** flash, trace **6** gander, glance **7** glimmer

GLINT: **5** flash, gleam, trace **6** glance, luster **7** glisten, glitter, sparkle **10** brightness **11** scintillate

GLISTEN: **4** glow **5** flash, gleam, glint **6** glance, luster **7** flicker, glimmer, glitter, shimmer, sparkle, twinkle **11** coruscation

GLITCH: **4** snag **5** error **7** problem **11** malfunction

GLITTER: **4** glow, pomp, show **5** flash, gleam, sheen, shine **6** luster, tinsel **7** glamour, glimmer, glisten, sparkle, twinkle **8** radiance, splendor **9** pageantry **10** brilliance **11** coruscation, scintillate

GLOAT: **4** bask, brag, crow **5** exult, strut, vaunt **7** rejoice **9** celebrate

GLOBAL: **6** all-out **7** general **8** sweeping **9** spherical, universal, worldwide **10** widespread **13** comprehensive, international

GLOBE: **3** map, orb **4** ball **5** earth, round, world **6** planet, sphere

GLOBULE: **4** ball, bead, drop, tear **6** bubble **7** droplet **8** particle, spherule

GLOOM: **4** dusk **5** blues, cloud, frown **6** misery, sorrow **7** despair, dimness, sadness **8** darkness, doldrums **9** dejection, murkiness, pessimism **10** cloudiness, depression, desolation, melancholy **11** unhappiness **12** hopelessness

GLOOMY: **3** dim, sad, wan **4** blue, dark, dour, down, drab, glum, grim **5** black, bleak, brown, dusky, moody, murky **6** broody, cloudy, dismal, dreary, morose, solemn, somber, sullen **7** forlorn, obscure, unhappy **8** dejected, desolate, downcast, overcast **9** cheerless, darkening, depressed, miserable **10** depressing, despondent, foreboding, melancholy, tenebrific **11** pessimistic **12** disconsolate, disheartened

GLORIFY: **4** laud **5** adore, bless, deify, exalt, extol, glory, honor, vaunt **6** praise, revere, uplift **7** acclaim, clarify, dignify, elevate, idolize, magnify, worship **8** eulogize, sanctify **9** celebrate **10** consecrate **11** apotheosize, immortalize

GLORIOUS: **5** grand, great, noble **6** bright, famous, superb **7** eminent, notable, radiant **8** ecstatic, esteemed, majestic, renowned, splendid, stunning **9** brilliant, wonderful **10** celebrated, delightful **11** illustrious, magnificent

GLORY: **4** fame, halo **5** boast, exult, honor, kudos, pride, revel **6** homage, praise, renown **7** dignity, triumph **8** grandeur, splendor **9** greatness, pageantry **10** admiration, brilliance, effulgence, reputation **11** distinction **12** magnificence, resplendence

GLOSS: **4** buff, glow, mask **5** glaze, gleam, sheen, shine **6** enamel, finish, luster, polish, remark, veneer **7** burnish, comment **8** annotate, disguise, footnote, palliate **9** sleekness **10** brightness, camouflage, commentary, definition **14** interpretation

GLOSSY: **5** shiny, showy, silky, sleek **6** bright, glazed, smooth **8** lustrous, polished **10** glistening

GLOVE: **4** mitt **5** cover **6** boxing, mitten **8** baseball, gauntlet

GLOW: **4** beam **5** ardor, blush, flame, flush, glare, gleam, gloss, shine **6** fervor **7** glimmer, glisten, passion, twinkle **8** radiance **9** intensity **10** brightness

GLOWER: **4** look, sulk **5** frown, glare, scowl, stare

GLOWING: **3** hot **5** alive, fiery, vivid **6** ardent, heated, raving **7** blazing, burning, fervent, lambent, radiant **8** luminous **10** candescent, passionate **12** enthusiastic **13** complimentary

GLUCOSE: **5** sugar **6** starch **7** dextrin, maltose, sucrose **8** dextrose **14** monosaccharide

GLUE: **3** fix, gum **4** join **5** epoxy, paste, stick **6** adhere, attach, cement, fasten **7** plaster **8** adhesive, mucilage

GLUM: **4** dour **5** moody **6** dismal, gloomy, morose, sullen **8** dejected **9** depressed, saturnine **10** melancholy

GLUT: **4** cloy, fill, jade, sate **5** feast, flood, gorge, stuff **6** deluge, excess **7** engorge, satiate, surfeit, surplus **8** overfeed, overload, saturate

GLUTINOUS: **4** ropy **5** gluey, gummy, slimy **6** sticky, viscid **7** viscous **8** adhesive

GLUTTON: **3** hog, pig **6** gorger **8** gourmand **9** chowhound, overeater

GLUTTONOUS: **6** greedy **7** bulimic, swinish **8** ravenous **9** excessive, voracious

GNARLED: **4** bent **6** knotty, rugged **7** crabbed, knotted, peevish, twisted **9** distorted, misshapen, roughened

GNASH: **4** bite, gnaw **5** chomp, grind

GNAT: **3** fly **4** pest **6** insect, punkie **7** no-see-um

GNAW: **3** eat **4** bite, chew **5** chomp, graze, munch, worry **6** bother, devour, harass **7** corrode, torment, trouble **8** irritate, ruminate **9** beleaguer

GNOME: **3** elf **4** pixy **5** adage, dwarf, fairy, maxim, motto, troll **6** goblin, kobold, sprite **7** gremlin **8** aphorism, creature

GNOSTIC: **4** sage, wise **6** clever, shrewd **7** knowing **10** insightful

GO ABOUT: **6** tackle **8** approach **9** undertake

GOAD: **3** egg **4** edge, move, prod, push, spur, urge **5** drive, impel, prick, sting, tease **6** arouse, coerce, incite, needle, prompt **7** inflame **8** catalyst, irritate, pressure, stimulus **9** instigate, stimulate

GO-AHEAD: **4** okay **7** consent **10** green light, permission **12** enterprising **13** assertiveness, authorization

GO AHEAD: **7** advance, proceed **8** continue

GOAL: **3** aim, end **4** mark **5** score, tally **6** basket, object, target **7** mission, purpose **8** ambition **9** intention, objective **10** aspiration **11** destination

GO ALONG: **5** agree **6** concur **9** accompany, cooperate

GO AROUND: **5** avoid **8** argument **10** circumvent

GO ASHORE: **4** land **6** debark **9** disembark

GO ASTRAY: **3** err **6** wander **8** miscarry

GOAT: **3** ram, tur **4** ibex **5** goral **6** alpaca, chamal **7** markhor **8** ruminant
concerning: **6** capric **7** caprine, hircine
constellation: **9** Capricorn
female: **5** nanny
hair: **6** angora, mohair
male: **4** buck **5** billy
young: **3** kid **8** yeanling

GO AWAY: **4** exit, scat, shoo, wane **5** leave, scram **6** begone **9** disappear

GOB: **3** wad **4** lump, mass **5** chunk, mouth **6** sailor **8** quantity

GO BACK: **6** betray, desert, recede, return **7** regress, retract, retreat

GOBBLE: **4** gulp, wolf **5** gorge, scarf, stuff **6** devour, guzzle, snatch

GO BEFORE: **4** lead **7** precede **8** antecede

GO-BETWEEN: **5** agent, envoy, fence, proxy **8** delegate, emissary, mediator **9** messenger, moderator **10** negotiator, translator **12** intermediary

GOBLET: **3** cup **5** glass **6** vessel **7** chalice **9** wineglass

GOBLIN: **3** elf, fay, hag **4** bogy **5** demon, dwarf, fairy, gnome, troll **6** hobbit, kobold, sprite **7** brownie, bugbear, gremlin **8** barghest **10** leprechaun

GO BY: **4** pass, snub **6** comply, elapse **7** proceed

GO-CART: **5** buggy, wagon **8** stroller

GOD:
Egyptian: **2** Ra **3** Geb, Set, Shu **4** Amon, Ptah **5** Horus, Thoth **6** Anubis, Osiris
Greek: **3** Pan **4** Ares, Eros, Zeus **5** Atlas, Hades, Hymen, Pluto **6** Apollo, Cronus, Hermes **7** Phoebus, Theseus **8** Dionysus, Halcyone, Heracles, Poseidon, Tantalus **9** Asclepius, Narcissus **10** Hephaestus
Roman: **3** Dis **4** Jove, Mars **5** Cupid, Hymen **6** Apollo, Faunus, Saturn, Vulcan **7** Bacchus, Jupiter, Mercury, Neptune, Phoebus **11** Aesculapius

GODDESS:
Egyptian: **3** Nut **4** Isis **6** Hathor, Tefnut **8** Nephthys
Greek: **4** Hera **5** Irene **6** Athena, Hestia, Pallas, Psyche **7** Artemis,

Demeter, Pandora **9** Aphrodite **10** Persephone
Roman: **3** Pax **4** Juno **5** Ceres, Diana, Venus, Vesta **7** Minerva **10** Proserpina

GODFATHER: **3** don **5** drink **7** sponsor

GODFORSAKEN: **6** dismal, remote **7** forlorn **8** desolate, wretched **9** miserable

GODLESS: **4** evil **6** unholy, wicked **7** immoral, impious, profane **8** agnostic, depraved, undevout **9** atheistic **11** irreligious, unspiritual

GODLY: **4** holy **5** moral, pious **6** devout, divine, sacred **9** celestial, religious, righteous

GO DOWN: **4** drop, fall, keel **6** plunge, topple **7** decline, descend **8** collapse, diminish, submerge

GODSEND: **4** boon, gift **7** benefit **8** blessing, windfall

GO-GETTER: **6** dynamo **7** hustler **8** achiever

GOGGLE: **3** eye **4** leer, peer, roll **5** glare, stare

GOING: **3** way **4** exit, fare, road **5** bound **6** access **7** current, headway, running, working **9** condition, departure **10** passageway, prevailing

GO INTO: **5** delve, enter **6** review **7** analyze, examine, explore **9** undertake **11** investigate, participate

GOLD: **3** bar, oro **4** gilt **5** aurum, color, ingot, metal, money **6** nugget, riches, wealth, yellow **7** bullion, element **8** standard, treasure
black: **3** oil
cloth: **4** lame
exploration: **8** prospect
fool's: **6** pyrite

GOLDEN: **4** gilt, good, rich **5** auric, blond, straw, tawny **6** blonde, bright, yellow **7** aureate, caramel, radiant, shining **8** lustrous, precious, splendid **9** excellent, favorable, promising **12** advantageous

GOLDEN AGE: **5** peace **6** period **9** happiness **10** prosperity

GOLDEN FLEECE:
assisted: **5** Jason, Medea
guarded by: **6** dragon
keeper: **6** Aeetes
kept at: **7** Colchis
ship: **4** Argo
stolen by: **5** Jason **9** Argonauts

GOLDEN STATE: **10** California

GOLD MINE: **7** bonanza **10** mother lode, profitable

GOLDSMITH: **7** artisan, jeweler **8** lapidary **9** artificer, craftsman

GOLF:
terms: **3** par, pin **4** fade, fore, hole, iron, putt, wood **5** apron, bogey, carry, divot, links, match, round, wedge **6** birdie, caddie, mashie, putter, stroke, stymie **7** brassie, niblick **8** handicap **11** double eagle

GOLIATH: **5** giant
killed by: **13** stone and sling
killer: **5** David
Philistine: **7** warrior
place of death: **4** Elah

GOMER:
father: **7** Diblaim
husband: **5** Hosea

GONDOLA: **3** car **4** boat **5** barge **6** basket

GONE: **4** away, dead, done, left, past **5** spent **6** absent **7** extinct, missing **8** consumed, deceased, departed, finished, vanished **9** exhausted

GONE BY: **3** ago, o'er **4** over, past

GONE WITH THE WIND:
author: **16** Margaret Mitchell
cast: **10** Clark Gable **11** Vivien Leigh **12** Leslie Howard **14** Hattie

McDaniel, Thomas Mitchell **16** Butterfly McQueen **17** Olivia de Havilland
characters: **5** Mammy **6** Big Sam, Prissy **11** Gerald O'Hara, Rhett Butler **12** Ashley Wilkes **13** Melanie Wilkes, Scarlett O'Hara

GOOD: **4** able, boon, braw, fine, full, gain, kind, nice, pure, real **5** ample, brave, bully, moral, nifty, pious, right, sound, valid **6** benign, devout, expert, giving, honest, intact, polite, profit, proper, useful, virtue **7** benefit, ethical, genuine, helpful, liberal, quality, trained, upright **8** becoming, blessing, decorous, friendly, gracious, handsome, interest, morality, pleasant, pleasing, reliable, skillful, splendid, suitable, virtuous **9** agreeable, bountiful, competent, enjoyable, excellent, favorable, fortunate, reputable, righteous, well-being, wonderful **10** acceptable, auspicious, beneficial, benevolent, charitable, excellence, gratifying, profitable, prosperity, sufficient **11** pleasurable, respectable, unblemished, well-behaved **12** considerable, satisfactory
French: **3** bon **4** bien
Spanish: **5** bueno

GOOD-BYE: **4** ta-ta **6** so-long **7** cheerio, parting **8** farewell, godspeed, swan song
French: **5** adieu
Hawaiian: **5** aloha
Italian: **11** arrivederci
Japanese: **8** sayonara
Spanish: **5** adios

GOOD-FOR-NOTHING: **3** bum **6** loafer **7** useless, wastrel **8** scalawag **9** worthless **11** rapscallion

GOOD-HUMORED: **4** warm **5** funny, happy, merry **7** affable, amiable **8** cheerful, pleasant **9** congenial

GOOD-LOOKING: **4** fair, sexy **5** bonny **6** comely, pretty **8** gorgeous, handsome **9** beautiful **10** attractive, impressive **11** captivating

GOOD-NATURED: **4** kind, mild **6** genial **7** amiable, helpful **8** cheerful, friendly, pleasant **9** agreeable, gemutlich **10** benevolent, charitable

GOODNESS: **3** gee, wow **5** grace **6** purity, virtue **7** decency, honesty **8** morality **9** integrity **10** excellence, generosity **11** benevolence **13** wholesomeness

GOODS: **4** gear **5** cargo, stock, stuff, wares **6** things **7** chattel, effects, freight **8** durables, evidence, property **9** inventory, trappings **10** belongings **11** commodities, information, merchandise, possessions **13** paraphernalia

GOOD TASTE: **11** discernment **14** discrimination

GOODWILL: **5** amity, favor **7** charity **8** altruism, kindness, sympathy **10** friendship, generosity **11** benevolence, helpfulness **12** friendliness, philanthropy

GOOF: **3** err **4** boob, fool, slip **5** botch, error, shirk, spoil **6** fumble **7** blunder

GO OFF: **4** exit **5** leave **7** explode **8** detonate **9** discharge

GOOFY: **5** crazy, silly **7** foolish **10** ridiculous

GO ON: **6** behave, endure, happen **7** persist, proceed **8** continue

GOON: **3** sap **4** boob, thug **6** oafish, stupid **7** hoodlum

GOOSE: **4** bird **5** ninny, solan **7** widgeon **9** screwball, simpleton
concerning: **8** anserine **9** grossular
group: **4** raft **5** flock **6** gaggle

male: **6** gander
young: **7** gosling

GOOSE EGG: **3** zip **4** zero **5** zilch **6** naught **7** nothing

GO OUT: **4** date, exit **5** cease, leave **6** darken, expire **10** extinguish

GO OVER: **5** study **6** review **7** analyze, examine, retrace **8** rehearse **11** investigate

GOPHER STATE: **9** Minnesota

GORE: **4** stab **5** blood, filth, slime **6** pierce **7** carnage **8** massacre **9** slaughter

GORGE: **4** fill, glen, pass, sate **5** chasm, gulch, gully, stuff **6** canyon, defile, devour, gobble, gullet, ravine, throat, valley **7** overeat, satiate **8** crevasse **10** gluttonize, gormandize **11** overindulge

GORGEOUS: **5** grand **7** elegant, opulent **8** dazzling, glorious, handsome, splendid, stunning **9** beautiful, exquisite, luxurious **10** attractive, delightful, impressive **11** magnificent, resplendent

GORGON: **6** Medusa, Stheno **7** Eurayle
father: **7** Phorcys
hair: **6** snakes
mother: **4** Ceto

GORILLA: **3** ape **4** thug **7** primate **10** anthropoid
group: **4** band
leader: **10** silverback

GORY: **6** bloody, creepy **8** horrible **9** murderous **10** sanguinary **12** bloodstained **13** bloodcurdling

GOSPEL: **5** Bible, creed, dogma, truth **6** belief **8** doctrine, teaching **9** scripture

GOSSAMER: **4** airy, thin **5** gauzy, sheer **6** flimsy **8** delicate **10** diaphanous

GOSSIP: **4** blab, chat, dirt, talk **5** imply, rumor, snoop **6** babble, gabble, magpie, tattle **7** hearsay, prattle, scandal, slander **8** busybody, informer, meddling **9** chatterer, grapevine **10** defamation, newsmonger, talebearer, tattletale **11** scuttlebutt

GOTHAM: **11** New York City

GOTHIC: **5** crude **6** fierce **8** barbaric, Germanic, medieval, Teutonic **12** architecture

GO THROUGH: **5** audit, brave **6** endure, search **7** consume, examine **8** squander, tolerate **9** penetrate, withstand **10** experience

GO TO: **3** see, use **4** rely **5** visit **8** frequent

GOUGE: **4** hole, tool **5** cheat, fraud **6** chisel, extort, groove, hollow **7** defraud **10** overcharge

GO UNDER: **4** fail, fold, sink **8** bankrupt, submerge

GOURD: **4** pepo **5** fruit, melon, plant **6** bottle, sponge, vessel **8** calabash, cucurbit **9** colocynth **10** gooseberry **11** chilacayote

GOURMAND: **7** glutton, gourmet **11** trencherman

GOURMET: **6** critic **7** epicure **8** gourmand **9** bon vivant **10** gastronome **11** connoisseur

GOUT: **4** blob, clot, drop **5** taste **6** blotch **7** podagra

GOVERN: **3** run **4** curb, head, lead, rule, sway **5** guide, order, reign, steer **6** bridle, direct, manage **7** command, conduct, control, dictate, oversee, preside **8** dominate, regulate, restrain **9** determine, influence, supervise **10** administer

GOVERNESS: **5** nanny, tutor **6** duenna **8** mistress

GOVERNMENT: **3** law **4** rule **5** power **6** regime **7** conduct **8** guidance, ministry, republic **9** authority, coalition, hierarchy **10** Big Brother, governance, hereditary, management, regulation **11** aristocracy, bureaucracy, ruling class **12** jurisdiction
by all members equally: **12** pantisocracy
by all-powerful dictator: **10** absolutism
by all-powerful monarch: **10** absolutism
by all-powerful ruler: **9** autocracy
by church: **10** hierocracy
by dictator: **15** totalitarianism
by elderly ruler: **12** gerontocracy
by few: **9** oligarchy
by five rulers: **9** pentarchy
by king, queen: **8** monarchy
by men: **10** patriarchy
by one ruler: **12** dictatorship
by the military: **11** stratocracy
by the people: **9** democracy
by the wealthy: **10** plutocracy
by three rulers: **11** triumvirate
by two rulers: **7** dyarchy **10** diumvirate
by women: **10** matriarchy **11** gynecocracy
without: **7** anarchy

GOVERNOR: **3** bey **4** lord **5** chief, pilot, ruler **6** regent **7** captain, manager, viceroy **8** director, official **9** executive, regulator **10** gubernator, magistrate

GO WITHOUT: **4** deny, lack **7** abstain

GOWN: **4** robe **5** dress, frock, habit **7** clothes, garment

GRAB: **4** grip, hold, snag, take **5** catch, clasp, grasp, pluck, seize **6** arrest, clutch, collar, corral, snatch, tackle **7** capture

GRACE: **4** ease, form, tact **5** adorn, charm, favor, mercy, poise, skill, style **6** allure, beauty, enrich, polish, prayer, thanks, virtue **7** agility, balance, dignify, dignity, finesse, manners **8** beautify, blessing, elegance, goodness, kindness **9** dexterity, embellish, privilege **10** benedicite, comeliness, compassion, loveliness, permission, refinement **11** forgiveness

GRACEFUL: **4** airy, easy, fine **5** agile **6** comely, fluent, gainly, limber, lovely, nimble, seemly, slinky, smooth, supple **7** elegant, flowing, lissome, willowy **8** charming, delicate, eloquent **9** beautiful **10** attractive

GRACELESS: **4** ugly **5** cruel, gawky, inept **6** clumsy, klutzy **7** awkward **9** inelegant **10** outlandish

GRACIOUS: **3** gee, wow **4** good, kind, mild **5** civil, happy, suave **6** benign, giving, kindly, polite, urbane **7** affable, cordial **8** debonair, generous, mannered, merciful, pleasing, sociable **9** benignant, congenial, courteous **10** benevolent, charitable, hospitable **11** considerate **13** compassionate

GRADATION: **4** rank, step **5** level, stage **6** ablaut, degree, nuance **8** grouping, position, sequence **9** variation **10** difference, succession **11** arrangement **14** classification

GRADE: **4** bank, mark, rank, size, sort, tilt **5** class, level, order, pitch, slant, slope, stage **6** ascent, degree, rating **7** flatten, incline, inspect **8** category, classify, division, evaluate, gradient, grouping, standard, standing

GRADE A: **4** tops **5** great, prime, super **8** superior, top-notch **9** excellent, first-rate **10** first-class

GRADIENT: **4** ramp **5** angle, pitch, slope **6** ascent, vector **7** descent, incline **9** steepness

GRADUAL: **4** slow **6** gentle, steady **7** regular **8** creeping **10** continuous **11** progressive

GRADUATE: **4** pass **6** alumna **7** advance, alumnus, measure, qualify **8** classify **9** calibrate

GRAEAE: **4** Enyo **5** Deino **6** Graiae **8** Pephredo
father: **7** Phorcys
goddess of: **3** sea
mother: **4** Ceto
sisters: **6** Gorgon, Medusa, Stheno **7** Euryale

GRAFT: **4** join **5** unite **6** fasten, payola, splice **7** implant **8** kickback **9** extortion **10** corruption, transplant

GRAIL: **3** cup **4** bowl, Holy **5** plate **6** vessel **7** chalice, platter

GRAIN: **3** rye **4** bran, corn, grit, malt, meal, oats, rice, seed, wale **5** chaff, fiber, flour, grist, maize, speck, straw, trace, wheat **6** barley, cereal, fodder, kernel, pellet **7** granule, modicum, texture **8** particle
comb. form: **5** grani-
container: **3** bin, pit **4** silo **6** hopper **7** granary **8** elevator
disease: **5** ergot
pile: **4** rick **5** shock, stook

GRAM: **6** metric, weight

GRAMMAR: **6** syntax **8** paradigm **11** linguistics
case: **6** dative **8** ablative, genitive, vocative **10** accusative, nominative, possessive
error: **8** solecism
explain: **5** parse

GRAND: **4** epic, main **5** chief, great, large, lofty, noble, regal, showy **6** august, famous, superb **7** elegant, exalted, immense, stately, sublime, supreme **8** fabulous, glorious, imposing, majestic, splendid, terrific **9** dignified, excellent, grandiose, sumptuous, venerable **10** impressive **11** illustrious, magnificent **13** comprehensive

GRAND CANYON STATE: **7** Arizona

GRANDE DAME: **14** respected woman

GRANDEUR: **4** pomp **5** glory, state **7** majesty **8** elegance, eminence, nobility, regality, splendor, vastness **9** greatness, immensity, loftiness, sublimity **10** augustness, importance **11** distinction **12** magnificence

GRANDFATHER: **4** male **5** elder **8** ancestor **9** patriarch

GRANDILOQUENT: **6** turgid **7** flowery, pompous **8** inflated **9** bombastic **10** histrionic **11** pretentious

GRANDIOSE: **4** epic **5** lofty **6** turgid **7** pompous, splashy, stately **8** imposing **9** ambitious, bombastic **10** impressive, monumental, theatrical **11** extravagant

GRANDMOTHER: **6** female, granny **8** ancestor **9** matriarch

GRANGE: **4** farm **5** lodge, ranch **7** granary, society

GRANITE: **4** rock **5** stone **6** aplite **7** haplite, igneous **8** enduring **9** steadfast

GRANITE STATE: **12** New Hampshire

GRANT: **4** boon, cede, gift, give **5** admit, allot, allow, award, bonus, yield **6** accede, accord, afford, bestow, confer, patent, permit, remise **7** concede, consent, present, promise, subsidy **8** donation, transfer **9** admission, authorize, endowment, franchise, privilege, undertake, vouchsafe **10** concession, permission **11** acknowledge, scholarship **13** appropriation

GRANULATE: **5** crush, grind, pound **9** pulverize

GRANULE: **4** spot **5** grain **6** pellet **7** crystal **8** fragment, particle

GRAPE:
cluster: **10** racemation
cultivation: **11** viniculture, viticulture
dried: **6** raisin
harvest: **5** yield **7** vintage
juice: **4** dibs, must, sapa, stum, wine

GRAPES OF WRATH:
author: **13** John Steinbeck
cast: **10** Henry Fonda **11** Jane Darwell **13** John Carradine
director: **8** John Ford

GRAPH: **3** map **4** plan, plot **5** chart **6** scheme, sketch **7** diagram **9** character

GRAPHIC: **5** clear, lucid, vivid **6** strong, visual **7** precise **8** detailed, explicit, incisive, lifelike, striking **9** realistic **10** compelling, expressive **11** picturesque

GRAPPLE: **4** grab, grip, hold, hook **5** clasp, grasp, seize, sport **6** clinch, combat, tussle **7** contend, grapnel, wrestle **8** struggle

GRASP: **4** grab, grip, hold, take **5** catch, clamp, clasp, seize, snare **6** clench, clinch, clutch, fathom, master, snatch **7** embrace, grapple, insight, realize **10** comprehend, understand

GRASPING: **4** avid **6** greedy **7** miserly, selfish **8** covetous **9** rapacious **10** avaricious, prehensive **12** apprehension

GRASS: **3** hay, pot **4** lawn, reed, turf **5** sedge, spike, sward **6** fescue, sorrel **7** esparto, hassock, herbage, pasture **9** marijuana, pasturage
concerning: **10** gramineous
clump: **5** divot **6** tuffet **7** hassock, tussock
land: **3** lea **4** veld **6** llanos, meadow, pampas, steppe **7** prairie, savanna

GRASSLAND: **3** lea **4** veld **5** field, range, veldt **6** llanos, meadow, pampas, plains, steppe **7** pasture, prairie, savanna

GRATE: **4** fray, fret, rasp **5** annoy, chafe, grill, grind, mince, pound, shred **6** abrade, nettle, offend, scrape **8** irritate **9** fireplace, framework, pulverize

GRATEFUL: **8** indebted, pleasing, thankful **9** agreeable, gratified **12** appreciative

GRATIFICATION: **6** reward **7** comfort, delight, elation **8** gratuity, pleasure **9** enjoyment **11** contentment, fulfillment **12** satisfaction

GRATIFY: **4** feed, sate **5** adorn, amuse, humor **6** coddle, pamper, please **7** appease, content, delight, flatter, gladden, indulge, satisfy

GRATING: **4** bars, grid **5** grill, harsh, raspy **6** grille, hoarse **7** jarring **8** gridiron, grinding, strident **9** dissonant, offensive

GRATIS: **4** free **10** gratuitous **13** complimentary

GRATITUDE: **6** praise, thanks **11** recognition, testimonial **12** appreciation, gratefulness, indebtedness, thankfulness

GRATUITOUS: **4** free **6** gratis, wanton **8** baseless, costless, needless, unearned **9** voluntary **10** groundless **11** unjustified, unnecessary, unwarranted **13** complementary

GRATUITY: **3** fee, tip **4** dole, gift **5** bonus, favor, token **6** bounty **7** cumshaw, present **8** courtesy, offering **10** compliment, recompense **11** benefaction **12** contribution

GRAVE: **4** dire, grim, plot, tomb **5** death, sober, staid, stamp, vault **6**

gloomy, sedate, severe, solemn, somber, urgent **7** crucial, earnest, serious **8** critical **9** important, mausoleum, momentous, sepulche

GRAVEL: **4** dirt, grit, sand **6** bother **7** confuse, pebbles, perplex **8** irritate

GRAVESTONE: **6** marker **8** monument **9** tombstone

GRAVEYARD: **7** ossuary **8** boneyard, catacomb, cemetery, hypogeum **10** churchyard, necropolis **12** potter's field

GRAVITATE: **4** drop, lean, move, tend **6** settle **7** attract, descend **8** approach, converge

GRAVITY: **4** pull **5** force **7** dignity, urgency **8** enormity, pressure **9** heaviness, influence, magnitude, solemnity **10** importance **11** consequence, seriousness, weightiness **12** significance **13** momentousness
formulated theory: **6** Newton

GRAVY: **5** juice, money, sauce **6** profit **8** windfall

GRAY: **3** dim, old **4** ashy, dark, drab, dull, grey **5** ashen, bleak, color, dingy, hoary, slate **6** dismal, leaden **7** clouded, elderly, neutral, silvery **8** grizzled, overcast **9** cheerless, venerable **10** achromatic, battleship

GRAY MATTER: **6** brains **9** intellect **11** nerve tissue

GRAZE: **4** feed, gnaw, skim **5** brush, shave, touch **6** abrade, browse, forage, glance, scrape **7** pasture **8** ricochet

GREASE: **3** fat, oil **4** lard, soil **5** money, smear, suint **7** lanolin **8** ointment **9** influence, lubricant, lubricate

GREASY: **4** oily, rich **5** dirty, fatty, slick **6** salved **7** pinguid, smeared **8** slippery, unctuous **10** oleaginous

GREAT: **3** big **4** huge, vast **5** ample, chief, grand, large, noble, super **6** famous, heroic **7** awesome, capital, eminent, exalted, extreme, immense, intense, mammoth, titanic **8** almighty, colossal, elevated, enormous, gigantic, powerful, renowned **9** elaborate, excellent, extensive, honorable, important, wonderful **10** celebrated, delightful, omnipotent, remarkable **11** magnificent, outstanding **12** aristocratic **13** distinguished

GREAT BEAR: **9** Big Dipper, Ursa Major **13** constellation

GREAT DIVIDE: **7** Rockies **14** Rocky Mountains **17** Continental Divide

GREATER: **4** more **6** better, beyond, bigger, larger **8** mightier, superior

GREATEST: **4** best, most **6** utmost **7** extreme, maximum, optimal, supreme **8** champion **9** paramount

GREAT LAKE: **4** Erie **5** Huron **7** Ontario **8** Michigan, Superior

GREBE: **4** bird, fowl **5** diver **8** dabchick
family: **13** Podicipedidae

GREECE:
alphabet: **3** chi, eta, phi, psi, rho, tau **4** beta, iota, zeta **5** alpha, delta, gamma, kappa, omega, sigma, theta **6** lambda **7** epsilon, omicron, upsilon
also called: **5** Ellas **16** Hellenic Republic
authors: **5** Homer **6** Pindar **8** Menander **9** Euripedes, Sophocles **12** Aristophanes
capital: **6** Athens
cities: **4** Elis **5** Corfu **6** Delphi, Sparta **7** Corinth, Olympia, Pira-

eus **8** Salonika, Thessaly **9** Gallipoli
dialects: **5** Doric, Elean, Eolic, Ionic **6** Aeolic
divisions: **6** Attica, Thrace **8** Thessaly **9** Macedonia
drinks: **4** ouzo **7** Metaxis, retsina
food: **8** moussaka **9** souvlakia **10** shish kabob
giant: **4** Otus
goddesses: **3** Ara, Ate, Eos **4** Alea, Enyo, Gaea, Gaia, Hebe, Hera, Nike **5** Horae, Irene, Metis, Niobe, Vesta **6** Athena, Eirene, Hecate, Hekate, Hestia, Selena **7** Artemis, Astarte, Demeter, Nemesis **9** Aphrodite **10** Persephone
gods: **3** Dis, Pan **4** Ares, Eros, Hera, Zeus **5** Cupid, Hades, Pluto **6** Apollo, Cronus, Hermes, Hestia, Kronos, Triton **7** Bacchus, Demeter **8** Dionysus, Poseidon
gulfs: **7** Argolis, Corinth, Laconia, Saronic **8** Messenia, Salonika, Taronaic **9** Strymonic
islands: **3** Ios **5** Chios, Corfu, Crete, Delos, Melos, Naxos, Paros, Samos, Syros, Zante **6** Andros, Ithaca, Lemnos, Lesbos, Rhodes, Skyros **7** Mykonos **10** Cephalonia, Samothrace
kings: **5** Minos **6** Nestor **9** Agamemnon **11** Constantine
leaders: **10** Papandreou **11** Constantine
mathematicians: **6** Euclid **10** Archimedes, Pythagoras
measure: **3** pik **4** bema, piki, pous **5** baril, chous, cubit, diote, doron, maris, pekhe, podos, pygon, xylon **6** acaena, bacile, barile, cotula, dichas, gramme, hemina, koilon, lichas, milion, orgyia, palame, pechys, schene, xestes **7** amphora, chenica, choemix, cyathos, diaulos, metreta, stadium, stremma **8** condylos, daktylos, dekapode, dolichos, palaiste, plethron, stathmos **9** hemiekton, oxybaphon
monetary unit: **6** lepton **7** drachma
mountains: **3** Ida **4** Idhi, Oeta, Ossa **5** Athos **6** Othrys, Pelion, Pindus **7** Helicon, Olympus **8** Taygetus **9** Parnassus **10** Erymanthus
people: **5** Greek **6** Cretan, Dorian, Ionian **7** Aeolian, Hellene, Spartan **8** Athenian
philosophers: **4** Zeno **5** Galen, Plato **6** Thales **8** Diogenes, Socrates **9** Aristotle **10** Pythagoras
regions: **5** Crete **6** Aegean, Athens, Epirus, Ionian, Thrace, Vardar **7** Central **8** Thessaly **9** Macedonia **11** Peloponnese
rivers: **4** Arta **6** Peneus, Struma **7** Alpheus **8** Achelous, Cephisus
seas: **5** Crete **6** Aegean, Ionian **13** Mediterranean
weight: **3** mna, oke **4** mina, obol **5** livre, pound **6** diobol, kantar, obolos, obolus, talent **7** chalcon, drachma **8** diobolon

GREED: **6** excess **7** avarice, craving **8** cupidity **10** indulgence **11** selfishness

GREEDY: **4** avid **5** eager **6** stingy **7** miserly, piggish, selfish **8** covetous, edacious, ravenous **9** voracious **10** avaricious, gluttonous, gormandize, insatiable **11** acquisitive

GREEN: **3** new, raw **4** lime, lush **5** color, crude, fresh, grass, naive, young **6** callow, common, tender, unripe **7** emerald, verdant **8** blooming, gullible, immature **9** unskilled, untrained **10** aquamarine, developing, unseasoned **11** flourishing **13** inexperienced

GREENBACK: **4** bill, cash **5** bread, dough, money **8** bank note, currency **10** paper money

GREEN-EYED: **7** envious, jealous

GREENHORN: **4** tyro **6** novice **7** amateur, recruit **8** beginner, neophyte, newcomer **10** apprentice, tenderfoot **13** inexperienced

GREENHOUSE: **7** nursery **8** hothouse, orangery **12** conservatory

GREENLAND:
capital: **4** Nuuk **8** Godthaab
ethnic groups: **3** Ita **6** Danish, Eskimo **10** Ammassalik
explorer: **10** Eric the Red
languages: **10** Ammassalik **11** Greenlandic

GREEN LIGHT: **8** approval **9** clearance **10** permission

GREEN MOUNTAIN STATE: **7** Vermont

GREET: **4** hail **7** address, receive, welcome **9** recognize **11** acknowledge

GREETING: **3** bow, nod **4** kiss **5** aloha, hello, toast **6** curtsy, salute **7** ovation, welcome **9** reception **10** salutation **11** compliments **12** introduction

GREGARIOUS: **6** social **8** friendly, outgoing, sociable **9** convivial **11** extroverted

GREMLIN: **3** elf, fay, imp **5** fairy, gnome, troll **6** goblin, kobold, sprite

GRENADA:
capital: **9** St. George's
cities: **9** Grenville **12** Hillsborough
ethnic groups: **5** Carib **7** African
features: **9** Grand-Anse, Great Pool **11** St. Catherine
islands: **9** Carriacon **15** Petit Martinique
languages: **6** French **7** English
monetary unit: **6** dollar
place: **9** Caribbean
water: **14** Annandale Falls

GRENADE: **4** bomb **5** shell **7** missile **8** fireball **9** explosive, pineapple

GRID: **4** bars, mesh **5** grate **7** network **8** gridiron **9** framework

GRIDDLE CAKE: **7** hotcake, pancake **8** flapjack **10** battercake **11** flannel cake

GRIDIRON: **4** grid **5** field **7** grating, network **8** football **9** framework, structure

GRIDLOCK: **3** jam **6** backup **10** stagnation

GRIEF: **3** woe **4** harm, hurt, pain **5** agony, dolor, tears, trial **6** regret, sorrow **7** anguish, chagrin, despair, emotion, sadness, trouble **8** distress, hardship **9** annoyance, grievance, heartache, suffering **10** affliction, depression, heartbreak **11** bereavement, frustration, lamentation

GRIEVANCE: **4** beef **5** grief, gripe, stink, wrong **6** injury **7** protest **8** hardship **9** complaint, injustice **10** affliction **11** indignation

GRIEVE: **3** rue **4** ache, harm, hurt, pain, pine, wail, weep **5** mourn **6** bemoan, lament, sadden, sorrow, suffer **7** afflict **8** distress

GRIEVOUS: **3** sad **4** dire, sore **5** grave, sorry **6** bitter, severe, tragic, woeful **7** heinous, hurtful, intense, painful, serious **8** shocking **9** atrocious **10** burdensome, calamitous, deplorable **11** distressing

GRIFTER: **5** fraud **6** con man **7** scammer **8** swindler **9** con artist **12** bunco-steerer

GRILL: **4** cook, pump, sear **5** broil, grate, probe **6** grille **7** griddle **8** barbecue, question **11** inquisition, interrogate, third-degree **12** cross-examine

GRIM: **4** dire, dour, glum **5** angry, bleak, cruel, fixed, harsh, rigid, stern **6** brutal, dismal, fierce, gloomy, grisly, horrid, savage, somber, sullen **7** adamant, furious, ghastly, hideous, ominous **8**

dreadful, hopeless, horrible, ruthless, sinister **9** ferocious, loathsome, merciless, repulsive **10** forbidding, inexorable, relentless, unyielding **11** unrelenting

GRIMACE: **3** mug **4** face, mock, moue **5** fleer, frown, scowl, smirk, sneer **6** rictus **10** expression

GRIME: **4** crud, dirt, gook, gunk, smut, soil, soot **5** filth

GRIN: **4** beam **5** fleer, smile, smirk **10** expression

GRIND: **3** rut **4** beat, chew, grit, mill, mull, plod, sand, whet **5** chore, crush, gnash, grate, labor, pound, shape **6** abrade, crunch, drudge, groove, polish, powder, smooth, weaken **7** oppress, routine, sharpen **9** pulverize, triturate **12** disintegrate

GRIP: **4** hold, vise **5** brace, clamp, clasp, cleat, grasp, rivet, seize **6** clench, clinch, clutch, handle **7** control, embrace, grapple, mastery **9** constrict, fascinate, handshake, mesmerize **10** perception **13** comprehension

GRIPE: **4** beef, fret, fuss **5** annoy, grasp, groan, whine **6** grouse, squawk **7** grumble, protest **8** complain, irritate **9** bellyache, complaint, grievance, objection

GRISLY: **4** gory, grim **5** awful **6** bloody **7** hideous, macabre **8** dreadful, gruesome, horrible **9** frightful **10** abominable, terrifying

GRIT: **4** dirt, guts, sand **5** moxie, nerve, pluck, spunk **6** gravel **7** bravery, courage, pebbles **8** backbone, tenacity **9** fortitude **10** resolution **12** perseverance **13** determination

GROAN: **4** moan, sigh **5** gripe, grunt, whine **6** bellow, lament **7** grumble **8** complain

GROG: **3** rum **5** drink **6** liquor **7** alcohol

GROGGY: **5** dazed, dizzy, drunk, shaky, tipsy, tired **6** sleepy, wobbly **8** confused, sluggish, unsteady

GROOM: **4** comb, tend, tidy **5** brush, clean, dress, preen, shave, train **6** spouse **7** educate, equerry, hostler, husband, marshal, nurture, prepare, servant **9** assistant **11** horsekeeper

GROOVE: **3** rut **4** slot **5** canal, chase, flute, grind, shaft **6** crease, furrow, gutter, hollow, rabbet, sulcus **7** chamfer, channel, routine **10** excavation **11** indentation

GROOVY: **4** cool, neat **6** modern **9** copacetic, excellent, wonderful

GROPE: **3** paw **4** feel, poke **5** probe **6** fondle, handle, search **7** examine, explore, grabble

GROSS: **3** all, big, fat, sum **4** bulk, foul, lewd, mass, rank, rude, ugly **5** burly, crass, crude, dense, great, heavy, large, obese, plain, rough, thick, total, whole **6** brutal, carnal, coarse, entire, filthy, greasy, impure, sleazy, vulgar **7** beastly, brutish, callous, glaring, massive, obscene, obvious, swinish, uncouth **8** apparent, cloddish, flagrant, indecent **9** egregious, offensive, repulsive, unrefined **10** indefinite, outrageous, scurrilous

GROTESQUE: **4** ugly **5** antic, eerie, weird **6** absurd **7** bizarre **8** abnormal, deformed, fanciful, freakish **9** fantastic **10** ridiculous **11** incongruous **12** preposterous

GROTTO: **3** den **4** cave, hole **5** vault **6** burrow, cavern, hollow, recess

GROUCH: **4** crab **5** crank, grump **6** grouse **7** grumble **8** sourpuss **10** bellyacher, complainer, crosspatch

GROUCHY: **5** surly, testy **6** crusty, touchy **9** irritable **12** cantankerous

GROUND: **4** base, dirt, down, land, root, soil, turf **5** beach, earth, field, train **6** bottom, estate, reason, strand **7** country, flatten, premise, terrain **8** initiate, restrict **9** landscape, territory **10** discipline, foundation

GROUNDHOG DAY:
location: **12** Pennsylvania, Punxsutawney

GROUNDLESS: **4** idle **5** false **6** flimsy, untrue **9** illogical, unfounded **10** unprovoked **11** unjustified, unwarranted

GROUNDS: **4** lees, park, zone **5** basis, dregs, proof **6** campus, domain, reason **7** premise, pretext **8** evidence, property **11** information

GROUNDWORK: **4** base, root **5** basis **6** source **7** support **8** planning, practice, training **10** foundation **11** cornerstone, preparation **12** fundamentals **13** preliminaries

GROUND ZERO: **4** site **6** target

GROUP: **3** lot, mob, set **4** band, bevy, club, crew, file, gang, herd, link, pool, ring, sect, size, sort, team **5** batch, bunch, cabal, class, clump, drove, flock, genus, party, squad, tribe **6** assort, bundle, circle, clique, family, galaxy, gather, huddle **7** arrange, cluster, collect, combine, company, consort, faction **8** assemble, assembly, category, classify, division, organize **10** assemblage, collection, congregate **11** aggregation **12** conglomerate, organization

GROUPIE: **3** fan **8** follower **9** supporter

GROUSE: **4** bird, fret **5** gripe, quail **6** grouch **7** grumble **8** complain, pheasant, squealer **9** bellyache, grievance, ptarmigan

GROVE: **4** bush, wood **5** brake, copse **6** pinery **7** boscage, coppice, orchard, thicket **8** woodland

GROVEL: **3** beg **4** fawn **5** abase, cower, crawl, toady **6** cringe, kowtow, wallow **7** wheedle **8** bootlick **9** brownnose **10** sycophancy

GROW: **3** age, bud, wax **4** rise **5** edify, raise, swell, widen **6** become, evolve, expand, extend, mature, sprout, thrive **7** advance, augment, blossom, develop, enlarge, nourish **8** flourish, increase, multiply, mushroom **9** cultivate, skyrocket

GROWL: **4** bark, gurr, howl **5** gnarl, grunt **6** mutter, rumble **7** grumble

GROWN-UP: **3** man **5** adult, elder, woman

GROWTH: **4** lump, rise **5** polyp, surge, swell, tumor **6** cancer **8** increase, parasite, progress, swelling **9** evolution, expansion **10** prosperity **11** advancement, development, enlargement **12** augmentation

GRUB: **3** bum, dig, eat **4** chow, comb, feed, food, plod, root, worm **5** larva, mooch, scour, stump **6** drudge, maggot, search, sponge **7** uncover **8** victuals **10** provisions

GRUBBY: **4** foul **5** dirty, grimy, seedy **6** filthy, grungy, shabby, soiled **7** scruffy, unkempt **8** slovenly **10** disheveled

GRUDGE: **4** envy **5** pique **6** hatred, malice, rancor **8** complain **9** animosity **10** resentment **12** spitefulness

GRUELING: **4** hard **6** brutal, fierce, taxing, tiring **7** arduous **9** demanding, difficult, punishing, strenuous

GRUESOME: **4** gory, ugly **5** awful, gross **6** grisly, horrid, morbid **7** ghastly, macabre **8** horrible **9** repugnant, repulsive, revolting

GRUFF: **4** curt, rude, sour **5** bluff, blunt, harsh, rough, short, surly **6** abrupt, crusty, hoarse, severe, snippy **7** brusque, throaty **8** impolite

GRUMBLE: **4** crab, fret, fuss **5** croak, gripe, groan, growl, snarl, whine **6** grouch, grouse, mumble, murmur, repine, rumble, squawk **7** protest **8** begrudge, complain **9** bellyache

GRUMPY: **5** cross, moody, surly, testy **6** crabby **9** crotchety, irritable **12** cantankerous

GRUNGY: **5** dirty, grimy **6** shabby **7** rundown

GRUNT: **4** fish **5** groan, snort, sound **7** dessert **11** infantryman

GUAM:
capital: **5** Agana
cities: **4** Apra
languages: **7** English **8** Chamorro
location: **7** Pacific

GUARANTEE: **4** bail, bond, seal, word **5** swear **6** assure, insure, pledge, surety **7** certify, endorse, promise, warrant **8** contract, covenant, guaranty, security, warranty **9** agreement, assurance, insurance, vouchsafe **11** certificate

GUARANTOR: **6** backer, patron **7** insurer, sponsor **8** bailsman **11** underwriter

GUARD: **4** care, fend, herd, keep, mind, tend, ward **5** watch **6** defend, escort, jailer, keeper, patrol, police, sentry, shield, warden **7** defense, lineman, lookout, protect **8** conserve, preserve, restrain, security, sentinel, watchdog, watchman **9** chaperone, custodian, protector

GUARDED: **4** safe, wary **5** leery **7** careful **8** cautious, discreet, reserved, shrouded **9** protected, tentative **10** supervised, suspicious

GUARDHOUSE: **4** brig, jail **5** clink **6** prison

GUARDIAN: **5** angel **6** escort, keeper, parent, warden **7** curator, trustee **8** defender, shepherd, watchdog **9** attendant, caretaker, chaperone, custodian, protector **11** conservator

GUARDIANSHIP: **4** care **5** trust **7** custody **8** tutelage **11** safekeeping

GUATEMALA:
capital: **13** Guatemala City
cities: **13** Puerto Barrios, Quezaltenango
continent: **14** Central America
ethnic groups: **4** Itza, Ixil, Maya **5** Xinca **7** Mestizo
features: **4** Agua **5** Fuego, Tikal **6** Tacana **7** Atitlan **9** Maya ruins, Tajumulco **10** Acatenango, Santa Maria **11** Sierra Madre
languages: **5** Mayan **7** Spanish
monetary unit: **7** quetzal
water: **6** Izabal **7** Atitlan **9** Peten Itza

GUERRILLA: **7** fighter, soldier **8** partisan, saboteur

GUESS: **4** shot, stab **5** fancy, hunch, infer, think **6** assert, assume, deduce **7** believe, imagine, presume, suppose, surmise, suspect **8** conclude, estimate **9** speculate **10** conjecture, prediction **11** hypothesize

GUEST: **6** caller, client, friend, lodger, patron **7** boarder, visitor **8** customer

GUFF: **3** lip **4** sass **5** mouth **6** humbug **7** baloney **8** malarkey, nonsense **10** balderdash

GUFFAW: **4** howl, roar **6** heehaw **8** laughter **10** horselaugh **12** cachination

GUIDANCE: **4** help, hint **6** advice **7** auspice, conduct, control, counsel **9** direction **10** leadership, management, suggestion **11** instruction, supervision

GUIDE: **4** buoy, clue, lead, mark, rein, rule, show **5** model, pilot, reign, scout, steer, teach, tutor, usher **6** bridle, convey, convoy, direct, escort, govern, leader, manage, master, rudder **7** adviser, captain, control, example, marshal, monitor, teacher **8** director, instruct, landmark, navigate, polestar, regulate, shepherd **9** chaperone, conductor, influence, itinerary, regulator **10** bellwether, instructor, manipulate, mastermind, pathfinder **11** inspiration, superintend

GUIDEBOOK: **4** text **6** manual **7** catalog **8** Baedeker, handbook **9** directory, itinerary **12** instructions

GUILD: **4** club **5** order, trade, union **6** league **7** society **8** alliance, sorority **10** federation, fellowship, fraternity, profession, sisterhood **11** association, brotherhood

GUILE: **4** wile **5** cheat, fraud **6** deceit **7** cunning, slyness **8** trickery **9** chicanery, duplicity, stratagem, treachery **10** cleverness, craftiness

GUILELESS: **5** naive **6** candid, honest **7** artless, genuine, natural **8** innocent, truthful **10** aboveboard

GUILLOTINE: **6** behead, maiden **9** execution **10** decapitate

GUILT: **3** sin **5** blame, fault, shame **6** regret **7** offense **9** liability **10** wickedness **11** criminality, culpability

GUILTLESS: **4** free, pure **5** clean, clear **7** sinless **8** innocent, spotless **9** blameless **10** immaculate

GUILTY: **6** liable, nocent **7** ashamed **8** blamable, culpable **9** condemned, convicted **11** responsible **12** incriminated

GUINEA:
capital: **7** Conakry
cities: **4** Labe **6** Kankan **9** N'Zerekore
continent: **6** Africa
ethnic groups: **6** Foulah **7** Malinke **8** Soussous
features: **5** Nimba **12** Fouta Djallon
island: **3** Los **5** Tombo
languages: **4** Peul **5** Mande **6** French
monetary unit: **5** franc
water: **4** Milo **5** Niger **6** Bafing, Gambia **7** Senegal **8** Konkoure

GUINEA-BISSAU:
capital: **6** Bissau
cities: **6** Mansoa **11** Sao Domingos
continent: **6** Africa
ethnic groups: **4** Fula **7** Balante, Manjaca **8** Mandinka
features: **7** Bijagos
languages: **7** Crioulo **10** Portuguese
monetary unit: **4** peso
water: **4** Geba

GUINEVERE:
husband: **10** King Arthur
lover: **11** Sir Lancelot
position: **5** Queen

GUISE: **3** air, hue **4** garb, mask, mien **5** cloak, color, cover, dress, habit, shape **6** aspect, attire, manner **7** costume, fashion **8** behavior, pretense **9** semblance **10** appearance, masquerade

GULCH: **4** rift **5** chasm, ditch, gorge, gully **6** arroyo, canyon, divide, hollow, ravine, valley

GULF: **3** bay, gap **4** cove **5** abyss, basin, bayou, chasm, inlet, sound **7** opening **9** whirlpool **10** separation

GULF STATES:
countries: **4** Iran, Iraq, Oman **5** Qatar **6** Kuwait **7** Bahrain **11** Saudi Arabia **18** United Arab Emirates

states: **5** Texas **7** Alabama, Florida **9** Louisiana **11** Mississippi

GULL: **3** gyp, mew **4** bird, dupe, fool **5** cheat, trick **6** sucker, teaser, victim **7** cheater, deceive, defraud, mislead **8** hoodwink **9** bamboozle

GULLET: **3** maw **4** neck **6** throat **9** esophagus

GULLIBLE: **5** green, naive **6** sucker **8** innocent, trusting **12** unsuspecting

GULLIVER'S TRAVELS:
author: **13** Jonathan Swift
character: **14** Lemuel Gulliver
inhabitants: **6** giants, Laputa, Yahoos **7** wise men **8** Lilliput **10** Houyhnhnms **11** Brobdingnag, small people **13** Houyhnhnmland
lands: **6** Laputa **8** Lilliput **11** Brobdingnag **13** Houyhnhnmland

GULLY: **5** chasm, ditch, gorge, gulch **6** hollow, ravine, valley **7** channel, couloir **11** watercourse

GULP: **4** swig **5** choke, quaff, scarf, swill **6** devour, gobble, guzzle **7** swallow

GUM: **4** glue, hive, kino **5** cheat, myrrh, resin, stick, trick **6** chicle, mastic, tissue **7** bilsted, chewing, gingiva **8** adhesive, mucilage **10** eucalyptus **11** masticatory **12** frankincense

GUMMY: **5** gooey **6** sticky, viscid **7** viscous **8** adhesive **9** glutinous

GUMPTION: **4** guts **5** nerve, sense, spunk **6** spirit **7** courage **10** enterprise, initiative

GUMSHOE: **3** cop **4** dick **6** sleuth **7** sneaker **8** flatfoot **9** detective **12** investigator **13** police officer

GUN: **3** rod, Uzi **4** Colt **5** piece, rifle, speed, tommy **6** cannon, heater, magnum, musket, pistol, weapon **7** firearm, Gatling, shotgun **8** howitzer, revolver **9** derringer, equalizer, forty-five, Remington **10** accelerate, Winchester **11** thirty-eight **14** Smith and Wesson

GUNMAN: **6** hit man, killer, sniper **7** torpedo **8** assassin, gunwoman, hit woman **10** gunslinger, triggerman **12** triggerwoman

GUNNER: **7** shooter, soldier **8** marksman, rifleman **12** artilleryman **14** warrant officer

GUNTHER:
killer: **9** Kriemhild
kingdom: **8** Burgundy
sister: **7** Gutrune **9** Kriemhild
uncle: **5** Hagen
wife: **8** Brunhild **10** Brunnhilde

GURGLE: **5** sound, swash **6** babble, bubble, burble, murmur **7** sputter

GURU: **5** guide, swami **6** master, mentor **7** mahatma, teacher **9** maharishi

GUSH: **4** flow, pour, rush **5** burst, flood, prate, spate, spout, spurt, surge **6** effuse, stream **7** blather, cascade, chatter **10** outpouring

GUSHY: **8** effusive **9** emotional **11** sentimental **12** enthusiastic **13** demonstrative

GUST: **4** blow, gale, puff, rush, waft, wind **5** blast, draft, surge, whiff **6** breeze, flurry, squall **8** outburst, paroxysm **9** explosion

GUSTO: **4** elan, zeal, zest **5** heart, taste **6** fervor, relish **7** delight, passion **8** appetite, pleasure **10** enthusiasm **12** appreciation, exhilaration

GUT: **5** belly, clean, level, strip, tummy **6** innate, paunch, ravage **7** abdomen, innards, plunder, stomach **9** intuitive **10** disembowel, eviscerate, midsection **11** instinctive

GUTLESS: **4** weak **5** timid, wimpy **7** chicken **8** cowardly **9** spineless

GUTS: **4** grit **5** moxie, nerve, spunk **6** spirit **7** courage **8** boldness **9** fortitude

GUTSY: **4** bold, game **5** brave **6** plucky, robust, spunky **7** gallant, valiant **8** fearless, intrepid **9** audacious, undaunted **10** courageous **11** uninhibited

GUTTER: **4** duct **5** ditch, drain, eaves, gully **6** cullis, groove, trench, trough **7** channel **9** rainspout

GUTTURAL: **4** deep **5** gruff, harsh, velar **6** hoarse **7** grating, rasping, throaty **8** gravelly

GUY: **3** kid, man **4** chap, cord, male, rope **5** bloke, buddy, cable, chain, guide **6** fellow, person

GUYANA:
capital: **10** Georgetown
cities: **7** Charity **8** Mabaruma **10** Enterprise **12** New Amsterdam
continent: **12** South America
ethnic groups: **7** African **10** East Indian
features: **6** Acarai **7** Kaietur **9** Pacaraima **12** Mount Roraima
languages: **7** English **10** Amerindian
monetary unit: **6** dollar
water: **6** Cuyuni, Potaro **7** Berbice **9** Essequibo **10** Courantyne **11** Kaietur Fall

GUZZLE: **4** bolt, gulp, slop, swig **5** drink, gorge, quaff, slosh, swill **6** devour, imbibe, tipple **11** gourmandize

GYMNAST: **6** jumper **7** acrobat, athlete, tumbler
famous: **10** Bart Connor, Cathy Rigby, Kim Zmeskal, Kurt Thomas, Olga Korbut **12** Mitch Gaylord **13** Mary Lou Retton, Nadia Comaneci

GYMNASTICS: **5** sport **8** exercise, tumbling **10** acrobatics **11** competition **12** calisthenics
equipment: **3** mat **5** horse, rings **10** trampoline, uneven bars **11** balance beam **12** parallel bars **14** horizontal bars
events: **5** vault **10** still rings, uneven bars **11** balance beam, Pommel horse **12** parallel bars **13** floor exercise **14** horizontal bars

GYP: **4** bilk, burn **5** cheat, steal **6** rip off **7** deceive, defraud, swindle **8** swindler **9** bamboozle **10** overcharge

GYPSY: **4** calo **5** nomad **6** Gitana, Gitano, roamer, Romany **7** czigany, Tzigane, vagrant, zingara, zingaro **8** Bohemian, wanderer

GYRATE: **4** spin, turn **5** twirl **6** rotate, spiral **7** revolve **9** circulate

H

HABEAS CORPUS: **4** deed, writ **5** order **7** mandate **8** mandamus **9** judgement

HABERDASHERY: **3** hat **4** shop **5** store

HABILIMENT: **4** garb, gown **5** dress **6** attire **7** apparel, clothes **8** clothing **9** trappings

HABIT: **3** rut, use, way **4** garb, gown, mode, suit, vice, wont **5** dress, guise, usage **6** attire, custom, groove, handup **7** apparel, bearing, clothes, costume, garment, pattern, routine **8** demeanor, practice, tendency **9** addiction, mannerism **10** propensity **11** disposition **12** idiosyncrasy

HABITANT: **7** denizen, dweller **8** resident

HABITAT: **3** den **4** cave, flat, home, nest **5** abode, haunt, house, place **8** locality **9** apartment, territory **11** condominium, environment

HABITUAL: **5** fixed, usual **6** common, inborn, wonted **7** chronic, natural, regular **8** familiar, ordinary **9** customary **10** accustomed, inveterate **11** established, traditional

HABITUATE: **3** use **5** inure, teach, train **6** addict, school, season **7** instill, prepare **8** accustom **9** acclimate **11** familiarize

HACIENDA: **4** farm **5** house, ranch **6** estate **10** plantation

HACK: **3** cab, cut **4** chop, jade **5** coach, cough, horse, slash **6** cabbie, drudge, haggle, lackey, manage, mangle, strike, writer **7** butcher, taxicab **8** carriage, hireling **9** mutiliate

HACKNEYED: **4** worn **5** banal, trite, vapid **6** common **7** cliched, routine **8** everyday, outdated, outmoded **10** threadbare **11** commonplace, stereotyped

HADES: **3** pit **4** hell **5** abyss, Sheol **6** Tophet **7** Avernus, Gehenna **8** Tartarus **10** underworld **11** netherworld
god: **3** Dis **4** Yama **5** Orcus, Pluto
goddess: **6** Hecate
river: **4** Styx

HAG: **3** bog, nag **5** biddy, crone, demon, marsh, shrew, swamp, witch **6** beldam **7** hellcat **8** quagmire **9** sorceress

HAGAR:
servant of: **5** Sarah
son: **7** Ishmael

HAGGARD: 4 bony, lank, lean, pale, thin, worn 5 drawn, gaunt, spent, tired 6 wasted 7 scraggy, scrawny 8 careworn, fatigued, harrowed 9 exhausted, suffering

HAGGLE: 4 deal, hack 5 cavil 6 badger, barter, bicker, chisel, dicker, higgle 7 bargain, chaffer, dispute, quarrel, stickle, wrangle 9 negotiate

HAIL: 4 ahoy 5 greet, honor, shout, sleet 6 accost, batter, praise, salute, signal, summon, volley 7 acclaim, applaud, barrage, torrent 9 originate 10 compliment, salutation 13 precipitation

HAIR: 3 fur, mop 4 barb, curl, mane, shag 5 tress 7 bristle, cowlick 8 filament
aid: 3 bow, gel 4 comb, ruff 5 brush, frill, spray 6 mousse, ribbon 8 barrette
concerning: 6 crinal 9 capillary
disease: 8 dandruff, psilosis
facial: 5 beard 6 goatee 8 whiskers 9 moustache, sideburns
fake: 3 rug, wig 6 switch, toupee
loss: 8 alopecia, baldness
style: 3 bob, bun 4 Afro, buzz, coif, perm, pouf 5 bangs, braid, butch, queue 6 hairdo, marcel, Mohawk, moptop 7 beehive, chignon, cornrow, crew cut, flattop, Mohican, page boy, pigtail, ringlet, shingle 8 bouffant, cornrows, ducktail, frizette, ponytail 9 pompadour 10 dreadlocks

HAIRDRESSER: 6 barber 7 friseur 8 coiffeur, colorist 10 beautician

HAIRLESS: 4 bald 6 smooth 7 tonsure 8 depilous, glabrous

HAIR-RAISING: 5 eerie 8 exciting 9 thrilling 10 terrifying 12 breathtaking

HAIRY: 5 bushy, furry, fuzzy, risky 6 chancy, fluffy, pilose, shaggy 7 bristly, hirsute 9 dangerous, difficult, harrowing, hazardous 11 treacherous

HAITI:
capital: 12 Port-au-Prince
cities: 8 Gonaives, Les Cayes 10 Cap-Haitien
ethnic groups: 7 African
explorer: 8 Columbus
features: 10 Hispaniola
island: 9 La Tortuga
languages: 6 Creole, French
location: 9 Caribbean
monetary unit: 6 gourde

HALCYON: 4 bird, calm 5 happy, quiet 6 golden, placid, serene 8 carefree, peaceful, tranquil 9 contented, unruffled 10 kingfisher, prosperous

HALE: 4 drag, pull 5 hardy, hoist, sound, stout 6 hearty, robust, strong 7 healthy 8 vigorous 9 energetic

HALF: 4 part 6 moiety 7 divided, partial 8 division, fraction 10 fifty-fifty, incomplete

HALFHEARTED: 5 blase, faint, tepid 7 neutral, passive 8 listless, lukewarm 10 uninspired 11 indifferent 14 unenthusiastic

HALF-MOON: 4 arch 5 curve 8 crescent 9 semilunar

HALFWAY: 6 almost, center, middle, midway, nearly 7 midmost 8 moderate 9 partially 10 incomplete 12 compromising

HALF-WIT: 4 dolt, fool 5 dummy, dunce, idiot, moron 6 nitwit 8 numskull 9 blockhead, simpleton

HALF-WITTED: 4 dull 6 stupid 7 asinine, foolish 9 senseless 12 feebleminded

HALITE: 4 NaCl, salt 7 mineral 8 rock salt

HALL: **4** room **5** arena, entry, foyer, lobby, manor, odeum **6** atrium, parlor **7** chamber, gallery, hallway, passage, theater **8** anteroom, corridor, entrance **9** dormitory, vestibule **10** auditorium, passageway

HALLMARK: **4** seal, sign **5** stamp **6** symbol **14** characteristic

HALLOWED: **4** holy **6** sacred **7** blessed, revered **8** anointed **9** venerated **10** sanctified **11** consecrated

HALLUCINATION: **5** dream **6** mirage, vision **7** fantasy **8** delusion, illusion **10** aberration

HALO: **4** aura, glow, ring **5** crown, glory, light **6** circle, corona, nimbus **7** aureole **8** cincture, radiance

HALOGEN: **6** iodine **7** bromine, element **8** astatine, chlorine, fluorine

HALT: **3** end **4** foil, limp, stay, stem, stop **5** block, cease, hitch, pause, stand, waver **6** arrest, desist, hamper, hobble **7** inhibit, suspend **8** hesitate **9** interrupt, terminate **11** discontinue

HALTER: **4** rope **5** leash, noose, strap **6** bodice, bridle, fetter **8** restrain

HAM:
brother: **4** Shem **7** Japheth
father: **4** Noah
son: **4** Cush **6** Canaan **7** Mizraim

HAMLET: **4** burg, dorp, town **5** hamel, moray **6** thorpe **7** village
characters: **7** Horatio, Laertes, Ophelia **8** Claudius, Gertrude, Polonius
home: **7** Denmark **8** Elsinore
killer: **7** Laertes
writer: **11** Shakespeare

HAMMER: **3** hit, ram **4** bang, beat, maul, nail, tack, tamp **5** drive, pound, punch, shape **6** batter, defeat, pummel, strike, wallop **7** clobber **9** reiterate
type: **3** air, rip **4** claw, jack, tilt **5** gavel **6** beetle, fuller, mallet, plexor, sledge **7** hatchet **8** ballpeen **9** pneumatic **10** Warrington

HAMPER: **3** bin **4** clog, curb, foil, load, slow **5** block, cramp, crate **6** basket, fetter, halter, hinder, hobble, impede, stymie **7** confine, inhibit, manacle, pannier, shackle, trammel **8** encumber, handcuff, handicap, obstruct, restrain, restrict **9** container, embarrass, frustrate

HAND: **3** fin, paw **4** clap, claw, fist, give, help, lift, mitt, pass **5** grasp, knack, power, reach, share **6** clunch, helper, player, pledge, worker **7** ability, flipper, laborer, ovation, workman **8** applause, employee, pointers, transmit **9** appendage, extremity, indicator, signature **10** assistance, penmanship **11** craftperson, handwriting, participant
lines: **4** Fate, Head, Life **5** Heart
part: **4** palm **5** thumb **7** fingers

HANDBAG: **4** tote **5** purse **6** clutch, valise **7** satchel **8** gripsack, pochette, reticule **10** pocketbook

HANDBILL: **5** flier **6** dodger **7** leaflet **8** bulletin, circular, pamphlet **13** advertisement

HANDBOOK: **4** text **6** manual **9** directory, guidebook **11** enchiridion

HANDCUFFS: **5** irons **6** chains **7** fetters **8** manacles, shackles

HANDFUL: **3** few **4** some **8** quantity **9** difficult **10** scattering, sprinkling

HANDICAP: **4** edge, odds **6** burden, defect, hinder, impede **7** barrier **8** drawback, encumber, obstacle **9** advantage, embarrass, head start, hindrance, liability **10** disability, impediment, limitation **12** disadvantage

HANDICRAFT: **5** skill, trade **6** metier **7** artwork **8** vocation **11** workmanship

HANDKERCHIEF: **5** scarf **6** hankie **7** bandana **11** neckerchief

HANDLE: **3** lug, nob, paw, ply, use **4** ansa, bail, cope, deal, feel, grip, haft, hold, knob, name, stem **5** crank, grasp, grope, guide, helve, lever, shaft, steer, swipe, touch, treat, wield **6** direct, finger, holder, manage **7** control, moniker, operate **8** doorknob, handgrip, maneuver, nickname **10** manipulate

HAND OUT: **4** alms, give **6** bestow **7** charity **8** dispense **10** distribute

HAND OVER: **5** waive **6** donate **7** present, release **9** surrender **10** relinquish

HANDSOME: **4** fair, fine **5** ample, bonny **6** comely, dapper, pretty **7** copious, elegant, fitting, gallant, liberal, sizable, stylish **8** abundant, becoming, generous, gracious, stunning, suitable **9** beautiful, bountiful, dexterous, exquisite, plentiful **10** attractive **11** appropriate, fashionable, good-looking

HANDWRITING: **6** script, uncial **7** cursive **8** longhand **9** autograph, majuscule, minuscule, shorthand **10** amanuensis, griffonage, manuscript, penmanship **11** calligraphy, chirography

HANDY: **4** deft **5** adept, close, ready **6** adroit, clever, nearby, useful **7** central, close-by, helpful, skilled **8** adjacent, dextrous, skillful **9** available, dexterous **10** accessible, convenient

HANG: **3** pin, sag **4** deck, nail, pend, rest, tack **5** await, drape, droop, hinge, hover, lynch, noose, slope, stick, swing **6** append, dangle, depend **7** execute, stretch, suspend **11** inclination

HANGAR: **4** shed **6** garage **7** shelter **8** barracks

HANGDOG: **5** cowed **6** guilty, shifty **7** ashamed **8** defeated, downcast, sneaking **9** groveling **10** shamefaced **11** intimidated

HANGER-ON: **5** leech, toady **6** flunky, lackey, minion, sponge **7** dangler, groupie **8** follower, parasite **9** dependent, scrounger, sycophant **10** free-loader

HANGMAN: **4** game **11** executioner

HANG ON: **5** cling **6** clutch, endure **8** continue **9** persevere

HANG OUT: **4** date **6** hobnob, loiter **10** fraternize

HANGOUT: **3** bar, den **4** dive **5** haunt, joint **10** rendezvous

HANGOVER: **7** letdown, vestige **8** headache, holdover **9** crapulous **11** aftereffect

HANG-UP: **6** phobia **7** dilemma, problem **8** fixation, obstacle **9** obsession **10** inhibition **13** preoccupation

HANG UP: **5** delay **6** halted, hinder, impede **7** snagged, suspend

HANKERING: **4** itch, urge, want **6** desire, hunger, thirst **7** craving, longing **8** yearning

HANKY-PANKY: **7** devious **8** trickery **9** chicanery **11** mischievous

HAPHAZARD: **6** casual, chance, random **7** aimless, chaotic **8** careless, reckless, shipshod **9** arbitrary **10** accidental, disorderly, undirected **11** unorganized **13** helter-skelter

HAPLESS: **6** cursed, jinxed **7** unlucky **8** luckless, wretched **11** star-crossed, unfortunate

HAPPEN: **4** come, fall **5** occur **6** arrive, befall, betide, chance, result **7** develop, perhaps, stumble **9** eventuate, transpire **11** materialize

HAPPENING: **5** event, thing **6** affair **7** episode **8** incident, occasion **9** milestone **10** experience, occurrence, phenomenon

HAPPINESS: **3** joy **4** glee, weal **5** bliss, mirth **6** gaiety **7** delight, ecstasy, elation, Elysium, rapture **8** euphoria, felicity, gladness, pleasure **9** beatitude, enjoyment, eudaemony, transport **10** exaltation, prosperity **11** contentment **12** satisfaction

HAPPY: **3** apt, gay **4** cosh, glad, nice **5** lucky, merry, sunny **6** elated **7** blessed, chipper, content, fitting, pleased, radiant, willing **8** carefree, euphoric, gracious, jubilant, mirthful **9** contented, exuberant, fortunate, overjoyed, satisfied **10** felicitous, gratifying, prosperous **12** enthusiastic, providential

HAPPY-GO-LUCKY: **6** casual **8** carefree **9** easygoing **10** nonchalant, untroubled **11** unconcerned **12** lighthearted

HARANGUE: **4** rant, rave **5** orate, spiel **6** accost, hassle, screed, sermon, speech, tirade **7** address, lecture, oration **8** jeremiad, perorate, scolding

HARASS: **3** nag, try, vex **4** bait, fret, haze, jade, raid, ride, tire **5** annoy, beset, bully, chafe, chase, harry, hound, tease, weary, worry **6** assail, attach, badger, bother, hassle, heckle, impede, molest, obsess, pester, plague, scrape **7** afflict, agitate, disturb, exhaust, fatigue, perplex, provoke, torment, trouble **8** distract, distress, irritate **9** persecute, tantalize **10** intimidate

HARBINGER: **4** omen, sign **5** usher **6** herald, signal, symbol **7** portent, presage, shelter **9** messenger, precursor **10** forerunner, indication

HARBOR: **3** bay **4** cove, dock, gulf, hide, hold, port **5** basin, haven, inlet, nurse **6** billet, foster, refuge **7** believe, imagine, landing, lodging, mooring, nurture, protect, quarter, retreat, seaport, shelter **8** withhold **9** sanctuary

HARD: **3** bad, fit **4** cold, dear, firm, iron, mean, real, sour, true **5** close, cruel, dense, harsh, rigid, rocky, rough, solid, stern, stiff, stony **6** bitter, coarse, frozen, marble, robust, rugged, severe, stable, steely, strict, strong, uphill **7** adamant, adverse, arduous, callous, compact, durable, earnest, intense, lasting, violent **8** definite, diligent, granitic, grasping, obdurate, rigorous, ruthless, stubborn **9** demanding, difficult, energetic, inclement, intricate, laborious, petrified, practical, repelling, resentful, resistant, strenuous, stringent, unfeeling, wearisome **10** inflexible, oppressive, perplexing, persistent, relentless, unyielding **11** complicated, comportment, distressing, impregnable, insensitive, penetrating, persevering, unremitting **12** backbreaking, impenetrable, indisputable, intoxicating, strong-minded, unassailable

HARD-CORE: **5** loyal **7** devoted, graphic, staunch **8** explicit **9** dedicated **12** intransigent **14** uncompromising

HARDEN: **3** set **4** bake, cake, firm **5** inure, steel **6** cement, endure, freeze, ossify, season, settle, temper **7** congeal, petrify, stiffen, thicken, toughen **8** accustom, concrete, condense, indurate, solidify **9** acclimate, climatize, coagulate, fossilize **10** strengthen

HARDHEADED: **4** keen **6** mulish, poised, shrewd **7** willful **8** stubborn **9** pragmatic, realistic, sagacious, unbending **10** inflexible

HARDHEARTED: **4** cold, mean **5** cruel **7** callous **8** pitiless, uncaring **9** unfeeling **11** indifferent, insensitive

HARDIHOOD: **4** grit, guts, will **5** pluck, vigor **6** daring **7** bravery, courage, potency **8** audacity, boldness, strength **9** fortitude, impudence, insolence, stoutness **10** confidence, effrontery **11** intrepidity

HARD LINE: **4** firm **10** inflexible **14** uncompromising

HARDLY: **4** just **6** barely, rarely **7** faintly, harshly **8** scarcely, severely, somewhat, unfairly **9** painfully **12** infrequently

HARDSHIP: **5** grief, peril, rigor, trial **6** injury **8** accident, asperity, calamity, disaster, handicap **9** adversity, endurance, injustice, privation, suffering **10** affliction, difficulty, misfortune **11** catastrophe, tribulation

HARD TIMES: **5** slump **9** recession **10** depression

HARD UP: **4** poor **5** needy **9** desperate

HARDWARE: **5** tools **7** weapons **8** computer, fittings, fixtures **10** appliances

HARDWOOD: **3** ash, oak **4** teak **5** birch, maple **6** cherry, walnut **7** hickory **8** mahogany, sycamore

HARDY: **4** bold, firm **5** brave, burly, solid, stout, tough **6** daring, mighty, robust, rugged, strong, sturdy **7** durable, healthy, spartan **8** intrepid, resolute, vigorous **9** audacious **10** courageous

HARE: **4** jack, pika **5** lepus **6** malkin, rabbit **7** leporid
concerning: **8** leporine
female: **3** doe
male: **4** buck
young: **7** leveret

HAREBRAINED: **5** crazy, wacky **6** absurd, insane, stupid **7** asinine, foolish **8** mindless **9** senseless

HAREM: **5** serai **6** purdah, serail, zenana **8** seraglio **10** concubines

HARK: **4** hear, heed, obey **6** attend, listen, notice **7** whisper

HARLEQUIN: **5** clown **6** jester **7** buffoon

HARLOT: **4** base, doxy, lewd, slut **5** rogue, whore **6** beggar, wanton **7** jezebel **8** vagabond **10** prostitute

HARM: **3** ill, mar **4** bane, evil, hurt, maim, pain **5** abuse, wound, wrong **6** damage, impair, injure, injury, punish **8** mistreat, sabotage **9** undermine **10** disservice, infliction, misfortune

HARMFUL: **3** bad **5** fatal, nasty, toxic **6** deadly, unsafe **7** adverse, baneful, hurtful, noxious, ruinous **8** damaging **9** hazardous, unhealthy **10** pernicious **11** deleterious, destructive, detrimental **12** catastrophic

HARMLESS: **4** pure, safe **5** naive **6** gentle **8** innocent, nontoxic **9** innocuous, peaceable **11** inoffensive

HARMONIA:
daughter: **3** Ino **6** Semele
father: **4** Ares, Mars
husband: **6** Cadmus
mother: **5** Venus **9** Aphrodite

HARMONIOUS: **6** dulcet **7** attuned, cordial, musical, spheral, tuneful, unified, uniform **8** amicable, balanced, friendly, peaceful, sonorous **9** agreeable, congruous, melodious **10** compatible, concordant, rhythmical **11** cooperative, coordinated, symmetrical **12** proportional

HARMONIZE: **4** jibe, mesh, sing **5** adopt, agree, amity, blend, chime, match, music, rhyme, unify **6** accord, adjust **7** concert, consist, consort **9** correlate, integrate, reconcile **10** correspond **11** orchestrate

HARMONY: **4** tune **5** amity, music, order, peace, unity **6** chorus, melody **7** balance, concord, rapport **8** symmetry **9** agreement **10** accordance, conformity, consonance, friendship **11** cooperation, tranquility **12** togetherness **13** compatibility

HARNESS: **4** belt, gear, rein, tame, yoke **5** hitch **6** bridle, collar, muzzle, saddle, tackle **7** channel, control, enclose, utilize **9** equipment, trappings
bit types: **6** pelham **10** kimblewick **12** double bridle **13** fulmer-snaffle **14** egg-butt snaffle **16** loose-ring snaffle **20** double-jointed snaffle
part: **3** bit **4** flap, hame **5** reins, skirt, swell, trace **6** billet, bridle, collar, saddle, terret **7** blinder, crupper **9** bellyband, ridgeband **10** breastband, crownpiece, martingale

HARP: **4** lyre **5** dwell **6** repeat, trigon **9** harmonica, reiterate **10** instrument

HARPY: **5** Aello **7** Celaneo, Ocypete, Podarge
father: **7** Thaumas
head and trunk: **5** woman
mother: **7** Electra
wings, tail, and talons: **4** bird

HARROWING: **8** chilling **9** dangerous, traumatic, upsetting **10** disturbing, terrifying **11** frightening

HARRY: **4** raid, sack **5** annoy, steal, worry **6** attack, badger, bother, harass, harrow, hector, pester, plague, ravage **7** agitate, assault, bedevil, disturb, pillage, plunder, torment **8** distress

HARSH: **4** curt, grim, hard, mean, sour **5** acrid, brute, crude, cruel, gruff, nasty, raspy, rough, sharp, stark, stern **6** bitter, brazen, coarse, hoarse, severe, strict, unkind **7** austere, drastic, glaring, grating, jarring, pungent, rasping, raucous **8** acerbate, clashing, district, guttural, rigorous, strident, ungentle **9** dissonant, inclement, repellent, truculent, unfeeling **10** astringent, discordant, relentless, unpleasant **11** acrimonious

HARUM-SCARUM: **4** rash, wild **7** flighty, foolish **8** careless, reckless **11** harebrained **13** irresponsible

HARVEST: **4** crop, fall, pick, reap **5** amass, cache, crops, hoard, yield **6** autumn, gather **7** collect, produce **10** accumulate

HASH: **4** chop, mess **5** mix-up, mince **6** jumble, mangle, review **7** mixture **8** consider **10** hodgepodge

HASP: **4** gird, lock **5** clasp, close, latch **8** fastener

HASSLE: **3** row, try **4** beef **5** fight, hound **6** bother, harass **7** dispute, problem, quarrel, trouble **8** argument, squabble, struggle **9** commotion **10** discussion **11** altercation

HASSOCK: **4** pess **5** grass **7** cricket, cushion, ottoman, tussock **8** footrest **9** footstool

HASTE: **4** dash, rush, tear **5** hurry, speed **6** bustle, flurry, scurry **7** beeline, scamper **8** celerity, dispatch, rapidity **9** quickness, swiftness **10** expedition, nimbleness **12** precipitance **13** impetuousness

HASTEN: **3** run **4** bolt, dart, push, race, rush, trot **5** drive, fleet, hurry, press, speed, whisk **6** barrel, gallop, scurry **7** advance, scamper **8** expedite **10** accelerate **11** precipitate

HASTY: **4** fast, rash **5** brash, brief, eager, fleet, quick, rapid, swift **6** abrupt, nimble, speedy, sudden, urgent **7** cursory, hurried **8** careless, fleeting **9** hurrisome, impatient, impetuous, impulsive, irritable **11** expeditious, precipitous, thoughtless

HAT: **3** cap, fez, top **4** kepi, pith **5** beany, beret, busby, derby, miter, shako, toque **6** boater, bonnet, bowler, cloche, cornet, fedora, forage, helmet, panama, shovel, turban **7** bicorne, biretta, chapeau, pillbox, Stetson **8** headgear, kaffiyeh, sombrero, trencher, tricorne, yarmulke **9** sou'wester, stovepipe **11** mortarboard, tam-o-shanter
concerning: **9** castorial
making: **9** millinery

HATCH: **4** door, gate, plan, sire **5** breed, brood, cover **6** create, invent, parent **7** concoct, opening, produce **8** contrive, generate, incubate **9** floodgate, originate **11** compartment

HATCHET: **3** axe **8** tomahawk

HATCHET MAN: **4** goon **6** critic, killer **8** assassin, henchman, murderer, myrmidon

HATE: **5** abhor, scorn **6** animus, detest, rancor, revile **7** condemn, despise, disdain, dislike **8** aversion, loathing **9** abominate, animosity, hostility, malignity **10** antagonism **11** detestation

HATEFUL: **4** evil, foul, mean, ugly **5** nasty **6** bitter, odious, ornery, rotten **7** heinous, vicious **9** abhorrent, loathsome, malignant, obnoxious, offensive, repellent, revolting **10** abominable, detestable, disgusting, flagitious **13** reprehensible

HATRED: **5** odium, spite **6** grudge, malice, rancor **7** vitriol **8** aversion, contempt **9** animosity, antipathy, hostility, prejudice **10** abhorrence, bitterness, repugnance **11** abomination, detestation

HAUGHTINESS: **4** airs **5** pride **7** conceit, disdain, hauteur **8** snobbery **9** arrogance, loftiness

HAUGHTY: **4** airy, bold **5** aloof, lofty, noble, proud **6** lordly, snooty, uppity **7** distant, stately **8** arrogant, cavalier, scornful **9** conceited, egotistic, imperious **10** disdainful, fastidious **11** highfalutin, magisterial, overbearing, patronizing **12** contemptuous, supercilious **13** condescending

HAUL: **3** lug, tow, tug **4** cart, drag, draw, load, move, pull, tote **5** bring, cargo, catch, heave, truck **6** spoils **7** freight, harvest, schlepp **9** transport

HAUNCH: **3** hip, leg **4** buns, loin, rump **5** thigh **8** buttocks **9** posterior **12** hindquarters

HAUNT: **3** den **4** dive, lair, nest **5** ghost, skill, spook, visit, worry **6** custom, infest, obsess, pester, resort, spirit, wraith **7** habitat, hang out, pervade, terrify, trouble **8** frequent, frighten, manifest **9** clubhouse **10** hang around

HAUTEUR: **5** pride **6** uppity **7** disdain **8** snobbery **9** arrogance, conceited **10** snootiness **11** haughtiness

HAVE: **3** get, own **4** bear, fool, gain, hold, need **5** allow, beget, enjoy **6** accept, become, endure, obtain, permit, retain **7** acquire, contain, deceive, include, possess, receive, swindle, undergo **8** comprise **10** experience, understand

HAVEN: **4** hope, port **5** cover, inlet, oasis **6** asylum, harbor, refuge, relief **7** hideout, retreat, shelter **9** anchorage, roadstead, sanctuary

HAVOC: **4** ruin **5** chaos, waste **6** mayhem, ravage **7** destroy, pillage **8** disorder, upheaval **9** confusion, devastate **10** disruption **11** destruction, devastation

HAWAII:
beach: **7** Waikiki
bird: **4** nene **5** goose
capital: **8** Honolulu
cities: **4** Aiea, Hilo, Paia **5** Lihue, Maili **6** Kailua **7** Kanache, Wailuku
drinks: **4** kava
flower: **5** lehua **8** hibiscus
food: **3** poi **4** kalo, taro
gods: **4** Kane, Lono **5** Wakea **7** Kanaloa
islands: **4** Maui, Oahu **5** Kauai, Lanai **6** Hawaii, Niihau **7** Molokai **9** Kahoolawe
mountains: **3** Kea, Loa **5** Kaala **8** Mauna Kea, Mauna Loa **9** Lanaihale
nickname: **10** Aloha State
people: **6** Kanaka **10** Polynesian
tree: **5** Kukui **9** candlenut
volcano: **7** Kilauea **8** Mauna Kea, Mauna Loa **9** Punchbowl

HAWK: **4** bird, bush, kite, sell, spit, vend **5** astur, buteo, jingo, noble, shark **6** falcon, osprey, peddle **7** buzzard, harrier, puttock, vulture **8** caracara, militant **9** accipiter, warmonger
adult: **7** haggard
female: **6** formel
group: **4** cast
male: **6** tercel
young: **4** eyas

HAWKEYE STATE: **4** Iowa

HAY: **4** feed **5** chaff, grass, money, swath **6** fodder, forage **7** herbage **9** provender
second crop: **5** rowen **9** aftermath

HAYSEED: **4** hick **5** yokel **6** rustic **7** bumpkin **9** greenhorn **10** countryman

HAZARD: **4** dare, luck, risk **5** guess, peril, stake **6** chance, danger, gamble, mishap, threat **7** imperil, venture **8** accident, endanger, jeopardy, obstacle **9** adventure **11** possibility

HAZARDOUS: **5** hairy, risky **6** chancy, unsafe **8** insecure, perilous **9** dangerous, uncertain, unhealthy **10** precarious

HAZE: **3** fog **4** beat, daze, film, mist, smog **5** brume, cloud, devil, dream, scold, vapor **6** harass, trance, vapour **7** drizzle, obscure, reverie **8** frighten, initiate **9** persecute

HAZEL: **3** nut **4** bush, tree **5** brown, color, shrub **6** cobnut **7** filbert **8** brownish

HAZY: **4** dull **5** filmy, foggy, fuzzy, misty, murky, smoky, vague **6** cloudy, groggy **7** blurred, obscure, unclear **8** nebulous **9** ambiguous, uncertain **10** indistinct

HEAD: **3** top **4** bean, mind, pate, poll **5** caput, crown, skull **6** noggin, noodle **7** coconut, cranium
concerning: **8** cephalic
part: **4** lore **5** lorum, scalp **6** temple, vertex **7** coxcomb, cranium, occiput **8** sinciput

HEADACHE: **4** pain **6** megrim **7** problem, trouble **8** migraine **9** annoyance **10** cephalagia, difficulty **11** cerebralgia **12** cephalodynia

HEADBAND: **4** agal **5** tiara **6** fillet **7** coronet **8** frontlet

HEADDRESS: **3** cap, hat **4** hood **5** busby, crown, miter, tiara, toque **6** bonnet, helmet, turban **7** bandore, biretta, coronet **8** coiffure

HEADING: **5** title, topic **6** course, rubric **8** headline, subtitle **9** direction

HEADLAND: **4** cape, ness, peak **5** bluff, cliff, ridge, strip **10** promontory

HEADLINE: **5** title **6** banner **7** caption, feature, heading **8** streamer

HEADLONG: **4** rash **5** hasty, sheer, steep **6** abrupt **8** heedless, reckless **9** breakneck, dangerous, foolhardy, impetuous, impulsive **11** precipitate, precipitous

HEADMAN: **4** boss **5** chief **6** leader **7** captain, foreman **9** commander **10** supervisor

HEADMASTER: **4** dean **9** principal **13** administrator

HEADQUARTERS: **4** base, post **5** depot **6** center **7** command **8** precinct **10** operations

HEADSTONE: **6** marker **8** keystone, monument **9** tombstone **10** gravestone

HEADSTRONG: **4** rash **6** mulish, unruly **7** froward, violent, willful **8** stubborn **9** obstinate **10** bullheaded, determined, persistent **12** ungovernable

HEADWAY: **6** ground **8** distance, progress **11** improvement

HEADY: **4** rash **5** cagey, smart, swift **6** clever **7** prudent, willful **8** stirring **9** impetuous, thrilling **10** stupefying **11** domineering, overbearing, precipitate, stimulating **12** exhilarating, intoxicating

HEAL: **4** cure, free, mend **5** treat **6** remedy, repair **7** recover, restore **9** alleviate **10** convalesce, recuperate, regenerate **12** rehabilitate

HEALTH: **5** shape, vigor **7** fitness, stamina **8** euphoria, strength, vitality **9** condition, hardiness, soundness, well-being **11** disposition **12** constitution

HEALTHY: **3** fit **4** firm, hale, spry, trim, well **5** hardy, sound **6** active, hearty, robust, strong, sturdy **8** athletic, salutary, vigorous **9** wholesome **10** nourishing, nutritious, prosperous, salubrious

HEAP: **4** bank, bulk, dump, gobs, hill, lots, lump, mass, much, pile, slew **5** amass, clump, crowd, mound, stack **6** bundle, burrow, gather, jalopy, jumble, plenty **7** clunker, cluster **9** abundance, multitude, stockpile **10** collection, congestion **11** overflowing **12** accumulation

HEAR: **4** feel, obey **5** catch, learn **6** attend, detect, harken, listen, permit **7** hearken, receive **8** consider, discover, perceive **9** eavesdrop **11** participate

HEARING: **3** ear **4** test **5** probe, sense, sound, trial **6** report **7** earshot, inquiry, meeting **8** audience, audition, auditory **9** interview, knowledge **10** conference, discussion **11** arraignment, examination

HEARKEN: **4** hark, hear, heed **6** attend, harken, listen, notice **7** observe

HEARSAY: **4** talk **5** rumor **6** gossip, report **9** grapevine **11** information, scuttlebutt

HEART:

concerning: **7** cardiac, cordate, cordial **8** coronary **9** cordiform, pulmonary

disease: **5** bruit **6** attack, murmur **10** infarction, thrombosis

expand: **8** diastole

part: **4** vein **5** aorta **6** artery, atrium **7** auricle, chamber **8** vena cava **9** ventricle **10** myocardium **11** pericardium

study: **10** cardiology

test: **3** ECG, EKG **17** electrocardiogram

HEARTACHE: **3** rue, woe **4** pain, pang **5** grief **6** misery, regret, sorrow **7** anguish, despair, sadness

HEARTBEAT: **4** tick, time **5** force, pulse, throb **7** impulse **9** pulsation

fast: **11** tachycardia
irregular: **10** arrhythmia **11** palpitation
slow: **11** bradycardia

HEARTBREAK: **5** agony, grief **6** misery, regret, sorrow **7** despair **9** suffering **14** disappointment

HEARTBURN: **7** pyrosis **10** cardialgia **11** indigestion

HEARTEN: **5** cheer, rally **6** arouse, solace, spirit, uplift **7** inspire **8** embolden, energize, reassure **9** encourage, stimulate

HEARTFELT: **4** deep, real, true **6** ardent, honest **7** earnest, genuine, sincere **8** profound

HEARTH: **4** home **5** grate, house **7** brazier **8** fireside **9** fireplace

HEARTLESS: **4** cold, hard, mean **5** cruel **7** callous **8** hopeless, ruthless, uncaring **9** merciless, unfeeling **11** insensitive **13** unsympathetic

HEARTTHROB: **5** flame, honey **6** beauty **10** sweetheart **11** infatuation

HEARTY: **4** firm, hale, rich **5** ample, eager, hardy, sound **6** active, cheery, devout, robust, sailor **7** comrade, cordial, earnest, healthy, sincere, staunch **8** abundant, cheerful, complete, thorough, vigorous **9** energetic, wholesome **10** nourishing **11** substantial, unequivocal **12** enthusiastic

HEAT: **3** gun **4** bake, cook, fire, rage, warm, zeal **5** ardor, chafe, fever, roast, steam, toast **6** degree, energy, excite, ignite, simmer, stress, warmth **7** caloric, firearm, hotness, inflame, passion **8** pressure, warmness **9** intensity **10** excitement **11** temperature

HEATED: **3** hot **5** angry **6** ardent, bitter, fierce, stormy **7** excited, furious, intense **8** sizzling, vehement **9** emotional **10** passionate

HEATER: **4** oven **5** stove **6** boiler, pistol **7** furnace **8** fastball, radiator **9** convector

HEATHEN: **5** pagan **6** ethnic, paynim **7** atheist, gentile, infidel, skeptic **8** agnostic **11** nonbeliever, unconverted

HEAVE: **3** gag **4** haul, heft, hurl, lift, pant, pull, push, send, toss **5** bulge, fling, groan, hoist, pitch, raise, retch, throw, utter, vomit **6** launch, propel **7** elevate **11** regurgitate

HEAVEN: **3** sky **4** Eden, Zion **5** ether, glory **6** Canaan, utopia **7** Elysium, kingdom, Nirvana, Olympus **8** empyrean, eternity, paradise, Valhalla **9** happiness, hereafter, Shangri-la **10** afterworld **12** promised land **13** Abraham's bosom

HEAVENLY: **4** holy, lush **5** sweet, yummy **6** divine, lovely, sacred **7** angelic **8** blissful, ethereal, pleasant, supernal **9** angelical, beautiful, celestial, delicious **10** enchanting

HEAVENLY BEING: **5** angel **6** cherub, seraph **9** archangel

HEAVENLY BODY: **3** sun **4** moon, star **5** comet **6** equant, galaxy, planet **9** satellite **13** celestial body

HEAVY: **4** deep, dull, hard, huge, loud, slow **5** beefy, broad, bulky, burly, dense, gross, hefty, large, obese, rough, thick **6** coarse, gloomy, hearty, stodgy, strong **7** arduous, complex, doleful, intense, massive, onerous, popular, serious, villain, weighty **8** burdened, grievous, inactive, lifeless, overcast, pregnant, profound, sluggish **9** difficult, excessive, important, indulgent, laborious, lethargic, ponderous **10** afflictive, burdensome, cumbersome, despondent, oppressive, overweight **11** complicated

HEAVY-HANDED: **5** harsh **6** clumsy **7** awkward **8** bumbling, bungling, tactless **10** indiscreet, oppressive

HEAVYHEARTED: **3** sad **7** doleful, unhappy **8** dejected **9** depressed **10** despondent, melancholy

HEBREW: **3** Jew **6** kosher, Semite **7** Semitic **8** Hebraean **9** Israelite
alphabet: **3** mem, nun, sin, tav, taw, vav, waw, yod **4** alef, ayin, beth, goph, heth, kaph, resh, sade, shin, teth, yodh **5** aleph, gimel, sadhe, zayin **6** daleth, samekh **7** lamedth
god: **5** Jahve, Yahwe **6** Adonai, Elohim, Yahweh **7** Jehovah
hello: **6** shalom
month: **4** Adar, Elul **5** Iyyar, Nisan, Tebet **6** Kislew, Shebat, Tammuz, Tishri, Veadar **7** Heshwan
scholar: **8** Hebraist
school: **5** heder, schul

HECKLE: **4** bait, gibe, jeer, mock, ride **5** hound, taunt, tease **6** badger, bother, harass, hector, needle, pester **7** disrupt, torment **9** embarrass

HECTIC: **4** wild **6** fervid **7** chaotic, flushed, frantic **8** confused, exciting, feverish, frenzied, restless **9** unsettled

HECTOR: **4** bait, ride **5** bully, tease, worry **6** badger, harass, heckle, plague **7** bluster, swagger, torment **8** browbeat, dominate, irritate **10** intimidate
brother: **5** Paris **9** Polydorus
father: **5** Priam
killer: **8** Achilles
mother: **6** Hecuba
sister: **8** Polyxena **9** Cassandra
title: **6** prince
wife: **10** Andromache

HECUBA:
daughter: **8** Polyxena **9** Cassandra
father: **5** Atlas
husband: **5** Priam
son: **5** Paris **6** Hector **9** Polydorus

HEDGE: **4** bush, cage, coop **5** avoid, block, bound, dodge, evade, fence, guard **6** hinder, hurdle, waffle **7** barrier, enclose, protect **8** boundary, obstacle, obstruct, separate, sidestep, straddle, surround **9** pussyfoot

HEDONIST: **4** rake **7** epicure **8** sybarite **9** bon vivant, libertine **14** pleasureseeker

HEED: **4** care, hear, mind, note, obey, reck **5** study, watch **6** beware, harken, listen, notice, regard, remark **7** caution, concern, observe, respect, thought **8** consider **9** attention, diligence **10** cognizance **11** observation

HEEDFUL: **4** wary **5** alert, aware **7** careful, mindful **8** cautious, diligent, watchful **9** advertent, attentive, observant **11** considerate

HEEDLESS: **4** rash **6** remiss, unwary **7** foolish **8** careless, mindless, reckless **9** impetuous, imprudent, negligent, oblivious, unmindful **10** incautious, indiscreet, regardless, unthinking **11** harebrained, inadvertent, inattentive, thoughtless, unobservant **12** disregardful

HEEL: **3** cad, end **4** cant, knob, lean, list, tilt **5** knave, rogue, slant, swine **6** careen, rascal **7** dastard, incline, tyranny **9** scoundrel **10** oppression
bone: **9** calcaneus
weakness: **12** Achilles heel

HEFTY: **3** big **5** ample, beefy, bulky, burly, heavy, husky **6** brawny **7** massive, weighty **8** powerful **9** extensive **10** cumbersome **11** substantial

HEGEMONY: **7** control **9** authority, dominance, influence

HEIGHT: **4** acme, apex, peak **5** crest **6** climax, summit, zenith **7** ceiling, maximum **8** altitude, eminence, pinnacle **9** dimension, elevation **11** culmination, magnanimity

HEIGHTEN: **4** lift **5** boost, raise **6** accent, enrich, expand **7** advance, amplify, augment, bolster, elevate, enhance, magnify **8** increase **9** aggravate, intensify

HEINOUS: **4** evil **5** awful **6** crying, grisly, odious, wicked **7** hateful, hideous **8** flagrant, shocking, terrible **9** atrocious, malicious, monstrous, nefarious, sickening **10** abominable, detestable, horrifying, outrageous **11** unspeakable

HEIR: **3** son **5** scion **7** heiress, heritor **8** daughter **9** firstborn, inheritor, offspring, successor **11** beneficiary
unchallengeable: **12** heir apparent

HEL:
father: **4** Loki
goddess of: **5** death **10** underworld
mother: **9** Angurboda

HELEN OF TROY:
abduction began: **9** Trojan War
abductor: **5** Paris
father: **4** Zeus
husband: **8** Menelaus
mother: **4** Leda

HELICOPTER: **4** gyro **7** chopper **8** aircraft **9** eggbeater **10** whirlybird
inventor: **12** Igor Sikorsky

HELIOS:
drove: **7** chariot
father: **8** Hyperion
god of: **3** Sun
mother: **5** Theia

HELL: **3** pit **5** abyss, agony, Hades, Sheol **6** misery, Tophet **7** anguish, Avernus, Gehenna **8** Tartarus **9** hereafter, suffering **10** underworld **11** netherworld
ruler: **5** devil, Satan

HELLEN:
father: **9** Deucalion
kingdom: **8** Thessaly
mother: **6** Pyrrha
wife: **6** Orseis

HELLISH: **4** vile **6** brutal, wicked **7** stygian **8** devilish, diabolic, dreadful **10** detestable, diabolical, unpleasant

HELLO: **8** greeting **10** salutation

HELM: **5** steer, wheel **6** direct, helmet, tiller **10** leadership

HELMET: **6** casque, heaume, morion, salade, sallet **7** basinet **8** burgonet **9** headpiece

HELP: **3** aid, S.O.S. **4** abet, back, cure, hand, lift, mend **5** avail, boost, favor, serve, stead, treat **6** advice, assist, relief, remedy, repair, rescue, succor, worker **7** advance, benefit, improve, laborer, promote, relieve, servant, support, sustain **8** befriend, champion, employee, guidance **9** alleviate **10** assistance, contribute, strengthen **11** accommodate, cooperation

HELPER: **4** aide, ally **6** deputy, server **7** abettor, servant, striker **8** adjutant, employee **9** assistant, associate, coadjutor, samaritan, volunteer **10** apprentice, benefactor **11** subordinate

HELPFUL: **4** good, kind **6** caring, useful **8** adjuvant, friendly, valuable **9** auxiliary, practical **10** beneficial, neighborly, supportive **11** considerate, cooperative **12** advantageous, constructive

HELPLESS: **4** numb, weak **6** feeble, futile, unable **7** forlorn **8** hopeless, impotent **9** destitute, incapable, powerless **10** vulnerable **11** defenseless, incompetent, involuntary, unprotected

HELTER-SKELTER: **6** random **7** flighty, hastily, turmoil **8** confused, pell-mell **9** haphazard **10** carelessly, disorderly

HEM: **4** brim, edge, seam **5** cough, hedge, skirt **6** border, circle, edging, fringe, margin **7** confine, enclose, environ **8** surround, trimming **9** encompass

HEMLOCK: **4** herb, tree **5** tsuga **6** conium, poison

HEMP: **3** kef, kif, pua, tow **4** bang, flax, jute, kaif, rine **5** abaca, fiber, plant, sizal **6** ambary, fennel, manila **7** hashish **8** cannabis **9** marijuana

HEN: **3** pea **4** fowl **6** gorhen, nester, pullet **7** chicken **8** poularde **9** free-range, gallinule
home: **4** coop **5** caire
young: **6** pullet

HENCE: **4** away, ergo, thus **5** since **6** onward **9** therefore **11** accordingly **12** consequently

HENCHMAN: **4** goon, page, thug **6** lackey, minion **8** adherent, criminal, follower, myrmidon **9** attendant, bodyguard, supporter

HENNA: **3** dye **4** tree **5** brown, color, shrub

HENPECK: **3** nag **4** carp **6** harass **8** dominate

HENRY: **6** Henry I, Henry V **7** Henry II, Henry IV, Henry VI **8** Henry III, Henry VII **9** Henry VIII
2nd's enemy: **6** Becket
8th's wives: **4** Anne, Jane **9** Catherine, Katharine
reign: **7** England
surnames: **5** Anjou, Tudor **11** Bolingbroke, Plantagenet

HEPHAESTUS:
father: **4** Zeus
god of: **4** fire **12** metalworking
mother: **4** Hera
wife: **6** Charis **9** Aphrodite

HERA:
brother: **4** Zeus
husband: **4** Zeus
mother: **4** Rhea
son: **4** Ares **10** Hephaestus

HERALD: **4** omen, sign **5** crier, greet, usher **6** runner, signal, symbol **7** courier, declare, trumpet **8** announce, foretell, outrider, proclaim **9** broadcast, harbinger, messenger **10** forerunner, foreshadow **12** spokesperson

HERB: **3** rue **4** aloe, balm, dill, leek, mace, mint, sage **5** anise, basil, cumin, thyme **6** borage, chives, cloves, endive, fennel, garlic, hyssop, nutmeg, sesame **7** aniseed, bay leaf, caraway, cayenne, chervil, chicory, mustard, oregano, paprika, parsley, saffron **8** allspice, cardamom, cinnamon, hepatica, marjoram, rosemary, tarragon, turmeric **9** asafetida, coriander **10** watercress **11** chili powder, horseradish **12** bouquet garni
dangerous: **4** hemp, loco **6** conium **7** hemlock, henbane

HERBAGE: **5** grass **6** greens **7** pasture **10** vegetation

HERCULEAN: **4** huge, vast **5** giant **6** mighty, strong **7** immense, mammoth, titanic **8** colossal, enormous, gigantic, muscular, powerful

HERCULES: **8** Heracles, Herakles
companion: **5** Hylas
father: **4** Zeus
friend: **6** Iolaus
lover: **4** Iole
mother: **7** Alcmene

victim: **5** Hydra
wife: **4** Hebe **8** Deianira

HERD: **3** mob **4** clan, crew, gang, lead, pack **5** brood, bunch, crown, drift, drive, drove, flock, group, guide, horde, swarm, tribe **6** gaggle, gather, rabble **8** guardian, shepherd **10** assemblage, congregate

HERE: **3** now **5** ready **6** hither **7** present **9** attending

HEREAFTER: **4** hell **5** hence **6** beyond, future, heaven **9** afterlife **10** eventually, underworld

HEREDITARY: **6** family, inborn, innate, lineal **7** genetic **9** ancestral, descended, inherited **10** congenital

HEREDITY: **8** ancestry **9** tradition **11** inheritance

HERESY: **6** schism **7** dissent, opinion **9** blasphemy, defection **10** iconoclasm, infidelity **11** unorthodoxy **13** nonconformity

HERETIC: **7** infidel, skeptic **8** apostate, renegade **9** dissenter, miscreant **10** iconoclast, schismatic, unbeliever **13** nonconformist

HERITAGE: **6** custom, legacy **8** ancestry **9** tradition **10** birthright **11** inheritance

HERMES:
father: **4** Zeus
god of: **5** theft **7** cunning **8** commerce **9** invention
mother: **4** Maia
served as: **6** herald, scribe **9** messenger
winged hat: **7** petasos, petasus
winged sandals: **7** talaria

HERMETIC: **4** shut **6** occult, sealed, secret **8** airtight, mystical **9** alchemist

HERMIT: **5** loner **6** cookie **7** ascetic, eremite, recluse, stylite **8** anchoret, solitary **9** anchorite

HERMITAGE: **5** abbey **7** retreat **8** cloister, hideaway **9** monastery

HERO: **3** ace **4** idol, male, star **5** actor **6** legend, martyr **7** demigod, heroine **8** champion, sandwich **9** celebrity, conqueror **10** leading man **11** protagonist

HEROIC: **4** bold, epic **5** brave, great, gutsy, noble **6** daring, mighty **7** extreme, gallant, valiant **8** colossal, enormous, fearless, intrepid, unafraid **10** courageous **11** illustrious, lionhearted, magnanimous, outstanding **12** mythological

HEROIN: **3** fix **4** drug, junk, scag **5** horse, smack **8** narcotic

HEROINE: **3** ace **4** idol, star **6** female, legend, martyr **7** actress **8** champion **9** celebrity, conqueror **11** demigoddess, leading lady, protagonist

HEROISM: **5** valor **7** bravery, courage **8** chivalry, nobility **9** gallantry **11** intrepidity

HESITANT: **3** shy **5** chary, loath **6** afraid, unsure **7** halting, waiting **9** reluctant, skeptical, tentative, uncertain **10** indecisive, irresolute

HESITATE: **4** balk, wait **5** avoid, dally, delay, doubt, hedge, pause, stall, waver **6** falter **7** stammer **8** flounder, sidestep, straddle **9** pussyfoot, vacillate **13** procrastinate

HETEROGENEOUS: **5** mixed **6** motley, varied **7** diverse **8** assorted **9** different **10** dissimilar **13** miscellaneous

HEW: **3** cut **4** chip, chop, fell, hack, hold **5** carve, prune, shape **6** cleave, strike, stroke **7** fashion

HEX: **4** jinx **5** curse, spell **6** voodoo, whammy **7** bewitch, evil eye

HEYDAY: **3** joy, top **4** acme **5** prime **6** height, spring, zenith

HIATUS: **3** gap **5** break, pause **6** lacuna **7** interim, opening **8** aperture, interval **12** interruption

HIBERNATE: **4** hide **5** sleep **6** torpid **7** dormant **8** inactive, vegetate

HIBERNIA: **7** Ireland

HICK: **4** jake **5** yokel **6** rustic **7** bumpkin **8** gullible **10** provincial **15** unsophisticated

HIDDEN: **6** buried, covert, latent, masked, secret, unseen, veiled **7** covered, cryptic, obscure, recluse **8** esoteric, secluded, shrouded **9** concealed, invisible **10** mysterious, undetected **11** clandestine, undisclosed

HIDE: **4** bury, coat, duck, fell, mask, pelt, skin, stow, veil **5** cache, cloak, cover, ditch, stash **6** harbor, screen, shroud **7** abscond, conceal, eclipse, leather, protect, secrete, smuggle **8** disguise, palliate, suppress, withhold **10** camouflage

HIDEAWAY: **6** escape, refuge **7** hideout **8** secluded **9** hermitage

HIDEOUS: **4** grim, sick, ugly **5** awful, nasty **6** grisly **7** ghastly, macabre **8** dreadful, gruesome, horrible, shocking, terrible **9** appalling, grotesque, loathsome, revolting **10** abominable, detestable, horrendous, terrifying

HIDEOUT: **4** cave, lair **5** haven **6** refuge **7** retreat, shelter **8** hideaway **9** sanctuary

HIE: **4** rush **5** haste, hurry **6** hasten, scurry **8** expedite

HIGH: **4** dear, main, tall **5** acute, chief, grand, lofty, noble, sharp, steep **6** alpine, costly, raised, remote, shrill, stoned **7** crucial, eminent, exalted, psyched, soaring, violent **8** advanced, cheerful, elevated, euphoric, foremost, piercing, towering **9** admirable, expensive, extending, favorable, important, luxurious, prominent **10** malodorous, tumultuous **11** intoxicated

HIGH AND DRY: **8** helpless, marooned, stranded

HIGH-AND-MIGHTY: **4** vain **6** lordly **7** pompous **8** arrogant, superior **9** conceited, imperious **11** overbearing

HIGHBROW: **7** Brahmin, egghead **8** cultured **9** scholarly **12** intellectual

HIGH-HANDED: **5** bossy **6** lordly **8** arrogant **9** arbitrary **10** oppressive **11** domineering, overbearing

HIGH-HAT: **6** la-di-da **7** haughty **8** snobbish **12** aristocratic, supercilious **13** condescending

HIGH JINKS: **6** antics, pranks **7** playful **9** rowdiness

HIGHLIGHT: **5** focus **6** climax, stress **7** feature **9** emphasize

HIGH-MINDED: **5** moral **6** honest **7** ethical **9** honorable, righteous **10** principled

HIGH-PITCHED: **5** acute **6** shrill **7** shrieky **8** piercing

HIGH-POINT: **4** acme, apex **6** climax, summit, zenith **8** meridian, pinnacle **11** culmination

HIGH-PRESSURE: **8** forceful **9** insistent **10** aggressive, compelling, persistent

HIGH-PRICED: **4** dear **6** costly **8** precious **9** expensive **10** exorbitant

HIGH-SOUNDING: **4** arty **7** pompous **8** imposing **9** overblown **11** pretentious **12** ostentatious

HIGH-SPIRITED: **5** fiery, jolly, merry **6** lively **7** gallant, peppery **9** exuberant, vivacious **12** effervescent

HIGH-STRUNG: **4** edgy **5** hyper, jumpy, tense, wired **6** uneasy **7** jittery, nervous, uptight **8** restless, stressed **9** excitable

HIGHWAY: **4** path, pike, road **6** artery, course, street **7** beltway, freeway, parkway, thruway **8** causeway, turnpike **9** boulevard **10** expressway, interstate **12** thoroughfare
British: **11** carriageway
German: **8** autobahn

HIGHWAYMAN: **5** crook, rider, thief **6** bandit, outlaw, robber **7** brigand **8** criminal

HIKE: **4** snap, tour, trek, trip, walk **5** boost, march, raise **6** ramble, travel **7** journey, traipse **8** backpack, increase

HILARIOUS: **5** funny, merry **6** jovial **7** amusing, comical, jocular **8** humorous **9** ludicrous **12** entertaining

HILARITY: **4** glee **5** cheer, mirth **6** comedy, gaiety **8** hysteria, laughter **9** happiness, joviality, merriment

HILL: **4** bank, dune, fell, heap, holt, kame, knob, mesa, pile **5** bluff, butte, cliff, cover, knoll, morro, mound, slope **6** ascent **7** hillock, hogback, incline **8** eminence, highland, mountain **9** acclivity, elevation

HILLOCK: **4** hill, knob **5** knoll, morro, mound **7** hummock

HIMALAYAS:
animals: **3** yak **4** bear, goat **5** bhalu, panda, sheep **6** nahoor **8** antelope
highest peaks: **3** Api **6** Makalu **7** Everest **9** Annapurna **11** Nanga Parbat **13** Kangchenjunga
where: **4** Asia **5** Assam, Nepal, Tibet **6** Bhutan, Sikkim **7** Kashmir

HIND: **3** doe **4** back, deer, fish, stag **6** rustic, worker **7** bumpkin, laborer, peasant, venison **9** posterior

HINDER: **3** bar, dam **4** clog, curb, slow, stop **5** block, check, choke, cramp, delay, deter, stall **6** arrest, burden, detain, hamper, harass, impede, stymie **7** deprive, inhibit, prevent **8** handcuff, handicap, obstruct, prohibit, restrain **9** embarrass, foreclose, frustrate, interfere

HINDMOST: **4** last, rear **5** final **10** concluding

HINDQUARTERS: **4** rear, rump **8** buttocks, haunches **9** posterior

HINDRANCE: **4** clog, curb, snag, stop **5** block, check, delay, hitch **7** barrier, trammel **8** drawback, handicap, obstacle **9** deterrent, liability, restraint **10** difficulty, impediment, limitation **11** obstruction **12** interference, interruption

HINDU:
books: **4** Veda **6** Sastra, Tantra **11** Yajna-valkya
castes: **3** Dom, Mal, Meo **4** Dasi, Gola, Koli, Kori, Mali, Pasi, Teli **5** Goala, Palli, Sudra, Varna **6** Babhan, Soodra, Vaisya **7** Brahman **9** Kshatriya
clothing: **4** jama, sari **5** jamah, saree
deities: **3** dev **4** deva, devi
demons: **4** Bali, Bhut, Ketu, Rahu **5** Asura **6** Daitya, Ravana
followers: **3** Jat **4** Jain, Seik, Sikh **5** Jaina, Seikh **6** Banyan, Rajput
goddesses: **3** Sri, Uma, Vac **4** Devi, Kali, Shri, Vach **5** Durga, Gauri, Sakti, Shree, Ushas **6** Chandi, Matris, Shakti **7** Lakshmi, Parvati **9** Haimavati
gods: **4** Agni, Deva, Kama, Siva, Vayu, Yama **5** Asura, Shiva, Simia **6** Brahma, Ganesa, Skanda, Varuna **7** Ganesha, Hanuman, Krishna **10** Karttikeya

heaven: **5** dyaus
hell: **6** naraka
holy people: **4** sadh, yogi **5** atman, sadhu **6** saddhu
kings: **4** Nala **5** Sesha **6** Shesha
languages: **4** Pali, Urdu **5** Hindi, Tamil **8** Sanskrit **10** Hindustani
leaders: **5** Nehru **6** Gandhi, Sirdar
nobleman: **4** raja **5** rajah **8** maharaja
priest: **5** hotar
prince: **4** raja **5** rajah **8** maharaja **9** maharajah
princess: **4** rani
queens: **4** rani **5** ranee **8** maharani **9** maharanee
races: **4** Swat **5** Aryan
scriptures: **4** Veda **5** Sruti **6** Purana, Sastra, Smriti, Tantra **7** Shastra **12** Bhagavad-Gita
sects: **4** Babu, Koli, Sikh, Siva **5** Tamil **6** Aghori, Gentoo, Hindoo
teacher: **3** pir

HINGE: **3** pin **4** axis, hang, link, rest, turn **5** elbow, joint, mount, pivot, stand **6** depend **10** contingent

HINT: **3** cue, tip **4** clue, help, warn **5** imply, infer, tinge, touch, trace, whiff **6** advice, allude, moment, notion **7** inkling, mention **8** forewarn, innuendo, reminder **9** catchword, insinuate **10** indication, intimation, suggestion **11** insinuation

HIP: **4** coxa, wise **5** aware, loins **6** groovy, haunch, huckle, modern, pelvis **7** stylish **9** cognizant **11** fashionable **13** knowledgeable

HIPPIE: **5** rebel **7** beatnik **8** bohemian, longhair

HIPPODROME: **5** arena **7** stadium **8** coliseum

HIRE: **3** fee, use **4** book, rent **5** draft, lease, price, wages **6** employ, engage, enlist, retain, salary, select **7** appoint, charter, conduce, recruit, stipend **12** compensation

HIRELING: **4** grub, hack, thug **5** slave **6** minion **7** gorilla **9** mercenary

HIRSUTE: **5** bushy, hairy **6** coarse, shaggy, woolly **7** bristly **9** whiskered

HISS: **3** boo **4** hoot, jeer, whiz **5** sound **6** heckle **7** catcall **8** ridicule, sibilant **9** raspberry **10** assibilate

HISTORIAN: **6** writer **7** teacher **8** annalist **9** professor **10** chronicler **15** historiographer

HISTORIC: **5** famed **6** famous **9** important, memorable, momentous **10** remarkable **11** significant

HISTORICAL: **4** past **6** actual **7** ancient **10** chronicled, documented

HISTORY: **4** epic, past, tale **5** story **6** annals, change, events, memoir, record **7** account **9** biography, chronicle, genealogy, narrative, yesterday **10** yesteryear **13** recollections

HISTRIONICS: **6** acting **8** affected **9** dramatics, emotional **11** performance, theatricals

HIT: **3** bat, jab, ram, rap, tap **4** bang, belt, bump, bunt, club, conk, shot, slog, slug, sock, swat, wham **5** clout, drive, homer, knock, liner, pound, punch, smack, smash, touch **6** attain, batted, double, impact, single, strike, triple, wallop, winner **7** clobber, collide, home run, popular, success **8** bludgeon, grounder **9** sensation

HITCH: **3** tie, tug **4** halt, haul, hook, join, pull, snag **5** agree, catch, marry, thumb, unite **6** attach, fasten, glitch, hobble **7** connect, problem **8** drawback, obstacle **9** hindrance **10** difficulty, impediment **12** complication

HITHER: **4** here **5** close **6** nearer, toward **11** to this place

HITLER, ADOLF:
author of: **9** Mein Kampf
chosen race: **5** Aryan
country: **7** Germany
known as: **9** Der Fuhrer
party: **4** Nazi
reich: **5** Third

HIT MAN: **3** gun **6** killer **8** assassin, murderer **10** gunslinger

HIT-OR-MISS: **6** chance, random **7** aimless **9** desultory, haphazard

HIVE: **5** store, swarm **6** apiary, colony **10** accumulate

HOAGIE: **4** hero **8** sandwich **9** submarine

HOAR: **3** dew **4** aged, gray, rime **5** frost, musty, stale **7** ancient **9** venerable

HOARD: **4** heap, save **5** amass, stash, stock, store **6** gather, supply **7** acquire, reserve **8** treasure **9** stockpile **10** accumulate, collection

HOARSE: **3** dry, raw **5** gruff, harsh, raspy, rough **7** grating, raucous **8** gravelly, scratchy

HOARY: **3** old **4** aged, gray **5** dated, white **7** ancient **8** timeworn **9** canescent, venerable

HOAX: **3** gyp, kid **4** bilk, dupe, fake, fool, joke, sham **5** bluff, cheat, fraud, prank, spoof, sting, trick **6** humbug, hustle **7** deceive, gimmick **9** bamboozle, victimize **11** hornswoggle

HOBBLE: **4** clog, clop, gimp, limp **5** cramp, leash **6** falter, fetter, hamper, hinder, hog-tie, impede **7** shackle, shuffle, stagger, stumble **8** scramble

HOBBY: **3** fad **5** craft **7** pastime **8** activity, interest **9** avocation, diversion, enjoyment, obsession

HOBGOBLIN: **3** elf, imp, pug **4** ogre, puck **5** bogey, demon, fairy, spook **6** goblin, sprite **7** bugaboo, bugbear **10** apparition

HOBNOB: **3** mix **6** mingle **9** associate **10** fraternize

HOBO: **3** bum **5** tramp **6** beggar **7** drifter, migrant, vagrant **8** vagabond, wanderer

HOCKEY:
officials: **7** referee **8** linesman
positions: **4** wing **6** center, goalie **7** forward **10** defenseman, goaltender
started: **5** bandy **6** Canada **11** field hockey
terms: **3** box, net **4** goal, puck, rink **5** check **6** boards, period **7** faceoff, penalty **8** blue line, empty net **9** power play **10** center line **11** shorthanded

HOCUS-POCUS: **5** cheat, magic, spell **7** juggler **8** delusion, flimflam, trickery, wizardry **9** chicanery, deception, trickster **11** abracadabra, foolishness

HODGEPODGE: **4** mess, olio, stew **6** jumble, medley **7** mixture **8** mishmash **9** potpourri **10** hotchpotch, miscellany **11** combination

HOE: **3** dig **4** till, tool, weed **5** clean **9** cultivate

HOG: **3** pig, sow **4** arch, boar **5** sheep, swine **6** barrow, vulgar **7** glutton **9** boschvark, razorback **10** motorcycle

HOGSHEAD: **3** keg, vat **4** cask, drum **6** barrel, vessel

HOGTIE: **4** curb **6** fetter, hamper, impede **7** disrupt, shackle

HOGWASH: **4** bull, bunk **5** swill **7** baloney, rubbish **8** nonsense **9** poppycock

HOI POLLOI: **3** mob **5** dregs **6** rabble **8** populace, riffraff **9** the masses **12** the multitude **15** the common people

HOIST: **4** jack, lift **5** boost, crane, heave, raise, setup, winch **6** uplift **7** derrick, elevate **8** windlass

HOITY-TOITY: **5** dizzy, giddy **6** snooty **7** flighty, pompous **8** arrogant **9** frivolity, silliness **11** patronizing, pretentious, thoughtless

HOLD: **3** own **4** bear, bind, feel, fill, grip, have, hook, keep, pull, rely, stay **5** brace, carry, catch, clasp, cling, grasp, guard, pause, rivet **6** adhere, arrest, behold, clench, clinch, clutch, defend, detain, harbor, occupy, remain, retain, steady **7** contain, control, embrace, support, sustain **8** consider, continue, function, interest, leverage, maintain, postpone, preserve, suppress **9** entertain, influence, mesmerize, spellbind **10** possession

HOLD BACK: **3** dam **4** curb, stem, stop **5** check, deter, stall **7** abstain, contain, inhibit, refrain, repress **8** restrain

HOLD FAST: **5** cling, stick **6** clinch, secure

HOLD FORTH: **4** talk **7** exhibit, expound **8** continue, maintain

HOLDINGS: **4** land **6** assets, stocks **7** beliefs, capital **8** property

HOLD OFF: **4** stop **5** avert, defer, delay, repel **7** refrain **8** postpone, suppress

HOLD ON: **4** wait **5** cling **7** persist **8** continue

HOLD OUT: **4** last **6** endure, refuse **8** continue

HOLD UP: **3** rob **4** cope, halt, lift, prop **5** boost, check, delay, raise **6** detain, endure, impede, manage **7** robbery, support, sustain **8** obstruct, postpone **9** interrupt **10** burglarize

HOLE: **3** fix, gap, jam, pit **4** brig, cave, cove, deep, dump, flaw, jail, leak, mess, mine, nook, rent, slot, vent, void **5** abyss, chasm, fault, inlet, niche, shaft **6** burrow, cavern, cavity, cranny, crater, defect, grotto, hollow, pocket, prison, recess, tunnel, vacuum **7** chamber, dungeon, opening, orifice, passage **8** aperture **10** depression, difficulty, excavation **11** perforation, predicament

HOLIDAY: **4** fete, gala **5** feast, leave, merry **6** fiesta, outing **7** festive, holy day, liberty **8** festival, vacation **11** celebration

HOLINESS: **5** faith, piety **7** unction **8** devotion, divinity, sanctity **9** godliness, reverence, sanctuary **11** blessedness, saintliness **12** consecration **13** righteousness

HOLLAND: **11** Netherlands

HOLLER: **4** yell **5** gripe, shout **6** bellow **7** protest **8** complain

HOLLOW: **3** den, dip, pit **4** cave, cove, deep, dent, glen, hole, vain, void **5** basin, chase, empty, false, scoop, sinus **6** alcove, cavern, cavity, crater, cupped, curved, groove, pocket, socket, sunken, vacant, valley **7** chamber, concave, ghostly, muffled, unsound **8** alveolus, specious **9** cavernous, deceitful, depressed, faithless, pointless, worthless **10** depression, resounding, sepulchral, thunderous **11** meaningless

HOLLY: **4** holm, tree **5** shrub, swamp, yupon **6** desert, horned, hulver, summer **8** mountain **9** moonlight
genus: **4** ilex

HOLOCAUST: **4** fire **7** carnage, inferno **8** disaster, genocide, massacre **9** sacrifice, slaughter **11** destruction

HOLY: **5** moral, pious **6** devout, divine, sacred **7** angelic, blessed, devoted, perfect, revered, sainted, saintly **8** blissful, hallowed **9** religious, sanctuary, spiritual, venerated **10** immaculate, sacrosanct **11** consecrated **13** sanctimonious
oil: **6** chrism

HOLY COMMUNION: **8** viaticum **9** Eucharist, sacrament

HOLY ONE: **3** God **5** Allah, Jesus **6** Christ **7** Jehovah, Messiah **8** Mohammed

HOMAGE: **5** honor **6** esteem, praise, regard **7** loyalty, ovation, respect, tribute **8** devotion **9** adoration, obeisance, reverence **10** admiration, veneration

HOMBRE: **3** man **4** game **5** ombre **6** fellow

HOME: **4** farm, nest **5** abode, haunt, house **6** asylum, castle, estate, family **7** address, habitat, village **8** bungalow, domestic, domicile, dwelling **9** apartment, orphanage, residence **10** birthplace, habitation **11** condominium **12** neighborhood
sickness: **9** nostalgia

HOME BASE: **3** den **9** home plate **12** headquarters

HOMELY: **4** cozy, snug, ugly **5** homey, plain **6** kindly, simple **7** natural **8** domestic, familiar, friendly, intimate, ordinary **9** unsightly, welcoming **11** comfortable **12** unattractive **13** unpretentious

HOMER:
occupation: **4** poet
works: **5** Iliad **7** Odyssey

HOMESPUN: **5** plain **6** coarse, folksy, modest, simple **9** handwoven **13** unpretentious

HOMICIDE: **6** murder **7** killing **12** manslaughter **13** assassination

HOMILY: **4** talk **6** sermon **7** lecture, oration **8** assembly **9** discourse **11** exhortation

HOMO SAPIENS: **3** man **11** human beings

HOMOGENEOUS: **4** same **5** alike, equal **7** similar, uniform **10** comparable, compatible, consistent

HONCHO: **4** boss **6** leader **7** headman, manager

HONDURAS:
capital: **11** Tegucigalpa
cities: **7** Henecan, La Ceiba **12** Puerto Cortes, San Pedro Sula
continent: **14** Central America
ethnic groups: **6** Indian **7** Mestizo
features: **5** Copan **10** Bay Islands, Mayan ruins
languages: **7** Spanish
monetary unit: **7** lempira
water: **7** Pacific **8** Atlantic **13** Gulf of Fonseca

HONE: **4** moan, tool **5** whine, yearn **6** hanker, smooth **7** sharpen **9** whetstone

HONEST: **4** fair, just, open **5** frank, plain **6** candid, chaste, decent, proper, square **7** ethical, genuine, sincere, upright **8** bona fide, faithful, reliable, rightful, straight, truthful, virtuous **9** equitable, honorable, reputable, veracious **10** aboveboard, creditable, forthright, legitimate **11** respectable, trustworthy **13** conscientious **15** straightforward

HONESTY: **5** honor **6** equity, virtue **7** decency, justice, loyalty, probity **8** fairness, fidelity, goodness, veracity **9** integrity, rectitude, soundness **11** uprightness **12** truthfulness

HONEY: **3** mel **4** dear, fine, mead **5** sweet **6** nectar **7** darling **8** flattery, precious **9** sweetness **10** sweetheart *types:* **4** comb, sage, wild **8** mountain, sycamore **9** extracted, goldenrod **10** eucalyptus

HONEYED: **5** sweet **6** dulcet, sugary **8** charming, melleous **12** ingratiating

HONEYSUCKLE: **4** vine **5** plant, shrub **6** azalea **9** columbine
genus: **8** Lonicera

HONG KONG:
capital: **8** Victoria **12** Hong Kong City
cities: **7** Kowloon **8** Tsuen Wan
colony of: **7** Britain
continent: **4** Asia
features: **7** Kowloon **8** Victoria **14** New Territories **18** Stonecutters Island
languages: **7** Chinese, English
monetary unit: **6** dollar
water: **4** Mirs **5** Sheko **6** Canton **7** Repulse

HONKY-TONK: **3** bar **4** dive **5** music **6** tawdry **9** nightclub

HONOR: **4** fame, fete, laud **5** adore, award, exalt, glory, kudos, trust **6** credit, esteem, homage, praise, regard, revere **7** courage, dignify, dignity, ennoble, glorify, honesty, laurels, respect, tribute, worship **8** accolade **9** celebrate, character, integrity, obeisance, reverence **10** decoration, reputation **11** distinction, recognition **12** commendation

HONORABLE: **4** just **5** moral, noble, title **6** honest, worthy **7** ethical, upright **8** elevated, sterling **9** admirable, reputable **10** creditable **11** commendable, illustrious, respectable

HONORARIUM: **3** tip **6** reward **7** payment **8** gratuity **12** compensation

HOOD: **3** cap, hat, top **4** coif, cowl, goon, hide, mask, punk, thug **5** blind, bully, cloak, cover, scarf **6** almuce, bonnet, canopy, chapel, helmet, tippet **8** chaperon, covering, gangster, hooligan, liripipe

HOODLUM: **4** goon, punk, thug **5** crook, rowdy **7** gorilla, mobster **8** criminal, gangster, hooligan **10** delinquent

HOODWINK: **4** dupe, fool, rook **5** bluff, cheat, cozen, trick **6** delude **7** deceive, mislead, swindle **9** bamboozle, blindfold

HOOF: **3** paw **4** foot, walk **5** cleft, dance, tramp **6** cloven, unguis, ungula

HOOK: **3** arc, net **4** bend, gaff, hold, link, lock, trap **5** angle, catch, curve, hitch, motif, seize, snare, steal **6** anchor, fasten, pilfer, secure **7** capture **8** crotchet **9** captivate **10** enticement

HOOKED: **4** bent **6** hamate **7** devoted **8** addicted **9** compelled

HOOLIGAN: **4** hood, punk **5** bully **7** hoodlum, ruffian **10** delinquent

HOOP: **4** band, ring **5** clasp **6** basket, circle, wicket **7** circlet **8** encircle, surround **13** circumference

HOOPLA: **4** hype **6** jovial **9** publicity **10** boisterous, excitement

HOOSIER STATE: **7** Indiana

HOOT: **3** boo **4** hiss, howl, jeer, razz, yowl **5** shout, sound, taunt, utter, whoop **9** criticize, raspberry

HOP: **4** ball, jump, leap, limp, move, prom, skip, trip, vine **5** dance, hitch **6** bounce, flight, gambol, hobble, spring

HOPE: **4** want, wish **5** dream, faith, trust **6** aspire, belief, desire, expect **7** longing **8** ambition, optimism, prospect, reliance **10** aspiration **12** anticipation

HOPEFUL: **6** upbeat **7** budding **8** cheerful, sanguine **9** confident, expectant, promising **10** auspicious, optimistic **11** encouraging **12** enthusiastic

HOPELESS: **4** sunk, vain **6** futile, gloomy **7** crushed, forlorn, useless **8** downcast **9** depressed, desperate, incurable, pointless **10** despairing, despondent, impossible, remediless **11** ineffectual, pessimistic **12** disconsolate, incorrigible, irredeemable

HORDE: **4** clan, gang, pack **5** crowd, drove, group, swarm, tribe **6** throng **9** gathering, multitude

HORIZON: **4** edge **5** reach, realm **6** border, future, sphere **7** outlook, purview, skyline **8** prospect

HORIZONTAL: **4** flat **5** flush, level, plane, prone **8** parallel

HORMONE: **5** auxin **7** estrone, insulin, steroid **8** autacoid **9** cortisone, substance **10** adrenaline
female: **8** estrogen
male: **8** androgen **12** testosterone

HORN: **4** tuba, tusk **5** bugle, cornu, siren, spike **6** antler, cornet **7** antenna, trumpet **8** clarinet, trombone **9** saxophone **10** cornucopia, instrument **12** protuberance

HORNSWOGGLE: **4** dupe, fool **5** cheat, trick **7** deceive, swindle **9** bamboozle

HORNY: **4** hard **5** tough **8** ceratoid **9** calloused

HORRIBLE: **4** grim, mean, ugly, vile **5** awful, cruel, nasty **6** grisly, horrid **7** fearful, ghastly, heinous, hideous, ungodly **8** dreadful, gruesome, horrific, shocking, terrible **9** appalling, atrocious, frightful, harrowing, loathsome, obnoxious, repulsive, revolting **10** despicable, detestable, horrendous, unbearable, unpleasant **11** unspeakable

HORRIFY: **5** alarm, scare, shock **6** appall, dismay **7** terrify **8** frighten

HORROR: **4** fear **5** alarm, dread, panic **6** fright, hatred, terror **7** disgust, dislike **8** aversion **9** revulsion **10** abhorrence, repugnance, unpleasant **11** abomination, trepidation **12** disagreeable

HORS D'OEUVRE: **4** food **5** tapas **6** canape, caviar, relish **9** antipasto, appetizer

HORSE: **3** gee, nag **4** colt, foal, hack, jade, mare, plug, pony, prad, sire, stud **5** bronc, draft, filly, hobby, mount, pacer, pinto, steed **6** bronco, equine **7** caballo, cavallo, cavalry, charger, clipper, courser, gelding, hackney, mustang, saddler, sheltie, sleeper, stepper, trotter **8** palomino, stallion
Achilles: **7** Xanthus
breeds: **4** Arab, Barb **5** Shire **6** hunter, Morgan, Nubian, Tarpan **7** Arabian, Belgian, harness, Suffolk, trotter **8** Galloway, Normandy, Shetland **9** Percheron **10** Clydesdale **12** thoroughbred
castrated: **7** gelding
colors: **3** bay **4** pied, roan **5** morel, pinto **6** calico, dapple, sorrel **7** piebald **8** chestnut, palomino, schimmel
combining forms: **4** eque, equi **5** hippo
commands: **3** gee, haw, hup **4** whoa **6** giddap
concerning: **6** hippic
draft: **4** aver **5** aiver, hairy **10** Clydesdale
equipment: **3** bit **4** rein, tack **5** longe **6** saddle **7** blinder, harness
famous: **4** Mr. Ed **6** Silver, Trojan **7** Trigger **8** Comanche **11** Black Beauty
farm: **6** dobbin
gait: **3** run **4** lope, pace, rack, trot, vott, walk **5** amble **6** canter, gallop
genus: **5** equus
hair: **4** mane, tail

hide: **7** leather **8** cordovan
lover: **10** hippophile
male: **4** colt, stud **6** entire **7** gelding **8** stallion
measure: **4** hand
pair: **4** span, team **6** tandem
saddle: **3** cob **5** mount **7** palfrey **9** Appaloosa
shoer: **6** smithy **10** blacksmith
small: **3** cob, nag, tit **4** pony **5** bidet, genet **6** cayuse, garron **8** galloway, Shetland
war: **5** steed **7** charger, courser **8** destrier
wild: **6** bronco, brumby, tarpan **7** mustang
young: **4** colt, foal **5** filly **8** yearling

HORSEMAN: **5** rider **6** cowboy, gaucho, jockey, knight **8** buckaroo, cavalier **9** caballero **10** equestrian, roughrider **12** equestrienne

HORSEMANSHIP: **6** manege, riding **10** equitation
jump: **6** curvet **8** capriole
movements: **8** dressage
sidewalk: **4** volt
turn: **8** caracole **9** pirouette

HORSEPLAY: **8** clowning **10** buffoonery **12** roughhousing

HORSEPOWER: **4** pull **5** power **8** strength

HORTICULTURE: **7** farming **9** gardening **11** agriculture **12** floriculture

HOSE: **4** sock, tube, wash **5** water **6** drench, tights **7** hosiery **8** breeches **9** stockings

HOSPITABLE: **4** kind, warm **7** cordial **8** friendly, gracious, sociable **9** courteous, receptive **10** charitable, gregarious, neighborly **11** cooperative

HOSPITAL: **6** clinic **7** hospice, sickbay **9** infirmary, lazaretto **10** sanatorium **11** institution

HOSPITALITY: **6** warmth **7** welcome **10** cordiality **11** amicability **12** friendliness

HOST: **4** army **5** crowd, emcee, flock, guest, horde, owner, swarm **6** legion, myriad, throng **7** company, hostess, maitre d', manager **8** landlord **9** innkeeper, multitude **10** assemblage, proprietor **11** entertainer, interviewer

HOSTAGE: **4** pawn **7** captive **8** prisoner, security **9** guarantee

HOSTEL: **3** inn **5** hotel, lodge **7** shelter **11** caravansary

HOSTILE: **4** mean, sour **5** enemy **6** bitter **7** adverse, hateful, opposed, vicious, warlike **8** contrary, inimical, militant, venomous **10** malevolent, rebellious, unfriendly **11** belligerent, contentious **12** antagonistic

HOSTILITY: **3** war **4** feud **5** clash **6** animus, enmity, hatred, rancor **7** warfare **8** argument, fighting, friction **9** animosity, antipathy **10** aggression, antagonism, bitterness, opposition, resentment, resistance **14** unfriendliness

HOT: **4** warm **5** angry, eager, fiery, spicy **6** ardent, biting, erotic, fervid, heated, piping, raging, stolen, strong, sultry, torrid, trendy **7** aroused, blazing, boiling, burning, excited, fervent, glowing, intense, lustful, peppery, popular, pungent, violent **8** scalding, sizzling, tropical, vehement **9** excitable **10** attractive, blistering, passionate, sweltering **11** radioactive

HOT AIR: **4** talk **8** malarkey, nonsense **12** exaggeration

HOTEL: **3** inn, spa **5** fonda, lodge, motel **6** hostel, imaret, tavern **7** fleabag, hospice **9** flophouse, roadhouse **11** caravansary

HOTHEADED: **4** rash **5** fiery, hasty **6** touchy **9** impetuous **13** quick-tempered

HOT SPOT: **6** action, lively **7** popular **8** activity **9** nightclub

HOT-TEMPERED: **5** testy **6** cranky **7** peppery **9** excitable, hotheaded

HOT WATER: **3** fix, jam **6** pickle **7** trouble **10** difficulty **11** predicament

HOUND: **3** dog **4** bait, hunt, mutt, ride **5** annoy, chase, harry, stalk, track **6** addict, badger, bother, canine, harass, hassle, heckle **9** persecute
dog breed: **6** Afghan, basset, beagle **7** harrier, whippet **8** foxhound **9** dachshund, deerhound, greyhound, staghound, wolfhound **10** bloodhound, otterhound

HOUR: **4** time **6** period **8** distance, interval **11** measurement

HOUSE: **3** cot, hut **4** casa, dorm, dump, firm, flat, home, live, nest, roof, stow **5** abode, cabin, cover, hovel, igloo, lodge, manor, shack, shell, store, villa **6** burrow, casino, castle, church, duplex, family, grange, harbor, palace, reside, senate, shanty, temple **7** chateau, convent, cottage, council, mansion, quarter, rectory, shelter, theater **8** ancestry, audience, building, bungalow, congress, domicile, dwelling, tenement **9** apartment, dormitory, monastery, residence, structure, synagogue **10** habitation, parliament **11** accommodate, condominium, legislature

HOUSEBREAK: **3** rob **4** tame **5** steal, train **6** subdue **10** burglarize

HOUSEHOLD: **4** home **5** folks **6** common, family, menage **8** domestic, familiar, ordinary

HOUSEWIFE: **6** mother **9** container, homemaker, sewing kit

HOUSEWORK: **5** chore **7** cooking, dusting, ironing, washing **8** cleaning, drudgery, sweeping **10** laundering

HOUSING: **3** box, pad **5** frame, niche **6** casing **7** lodging, shelter **8** covering, dwelling **10** protection **14** accommodations

HOVEL: **3** hut, sty **4** dump, hole, shed **5** cabin, hutch, lodge, shack **6** burrow, pigpen, pigsty, shanty **8** dwelling

HOVER: **4** flit, hang **5** float, waver **6** linger **7** flutter **9** suspended

HOWEVER: **3** but, yet **5** still **6** except, though **7** despite **8** although **11** nonetheless **12** nevertheless **15** notwithstanding

HOWITZER: **6** cannon

HOWL: **3** bay, cry **4** bark, bawl, roar, yell, yowl **6** bellow, lament, scream, shriek, squeal **7** protest, ululate **9** complaint

HUB: **4** core, nave **5** focus, heart, pivot **6** center, middle **10** focal point

HUBBUB: **3** ado **4** flap, fuss, stir **5** noise **6** clamor, racket, rumpus, tumult, uproar **7** turmoil **8** brouhaha, disorder **9** commotion, confusion **11** disturbance, pandemonium

HUCKLEBERRY FINN:
author: **9** Mark Twain **13** Samuel Clemens
character: **3** Jim **8** Injun Joe **9** Aunt Sally, Tom Sawyer **12** Widow Douglas **13** Becky Thatcher, Judge Thatcher
river: **11** Mississippi

HUCKSTER: **4** sell **5** adman **6** dicker, hawker, vendor **7** haggler, hustler, peddler **11** salesperson

HUDDLE: **3** hug **5** crowd, group, hurry **6** confer, crouch, cuddle, gather, jumble, mingle **7** consult, embrace, meeting, scrunch, snuggle **8** assemble, converge **9** confusion **10** conference, discussion

HUE: **4** cast, form, tint, tone **5** color, shade, shout, tinge **6** aspect, depict, outcry **10** appearance, complexion

HUFF: **4** blow, brag, gasp, pant, puff, rage **5** anger, pique, storm **6** expire, temper **7** bluster, dudgeon, inflate **8** boasting

HUFFY: **5** cross, moody, windy **6** crabby, grumpy, snappy, touchy **7** annoyed, haughty, pettish **8** arrogant, offended, superior **9** conceited, indignant, irritated

HUG: **4** hold **5** clasp, cling, press **6** caress, clinch, cradle, cuddle, huddle, huggle **7** cherish, embrace, snuggle, squeeze, welcome **9** affection

HUGE: **3** big **4** epic, vast **5** giant, great, jumbo, large **6** heroic **7** immense, massive, monster, titanic **8** colossal, enormous, gigantic, imposing, oversize, towering **9** humongous, monstrous **10** gargantuan, monumental, tremendous **11** elephantine

HUGGER-MUGGER: **6** covert, muddle, secret **7** jumbled, secrecy **8** confused, hush-hush **9** confusion **10** disorderly **11** clandestine, concealment

HULK: **4** bulk, hull, loom, ship **6** clumsy **8** shambles, unwieldy

HULL: **3** pod **4** body, case, hulk, husk, mold, rind, shed **5** frame, shell **6** casing **8** covering, skeleton **9** structure

HULLABALOO: **3** ado, din **5** noise **6** hubbub, racket, tumult, uproar **10** excitement **11** pandemonium

HUM: **4** blur, buzz, purr, sing, whiz, zoom **5** croon, drone, sound, speed **6** murmur **7** vibrate

HUMAN: **3** man **5** being, child, woman **6** mortal, person **8** hominoid **9** earthling **10** homo sapien, individual

HUMANE: **4** kind **6** tender **8** merciful **9** forgiving **10** altruistic, benevolent, charitable **11** sympathetic **13** compassionate, philanthropic

HUMANITARIAN: **8** generous **10** benefactor, benevolent, charitable **14** philanthropist

HUMANITY: **3** man **4** life, race **5** mercy, woman **6** people **7** mankind, species **8** goodwill, kindness **9** mortality **10** compassion

HUMBLE: **3** low **4** mean, meek, mild, poor **5** abase, lower, lowly, quiet, shame **6** deject, demean, demure, little, modest, reduce, simple **7** bashful, ignoble, mortify **8** deferent, disgrace, reserved, sheepish **9** embarrass, humiliate **10** submissive, unassuming **13** unpretentious

HUMBUG: **3** gyp, kid **4** bosh, bull, bunk, flam, guff, hoax, sham **5** bluff, cheat, faker, fraud, fudge, phony, trick **6** bunkum, gammon, phooey **7** deceive, mislead, rubbish, swindle **8** flimflam, flummery, impostor, malarkey, nonsense, pretense **9** bamboozle, deception, imposture, stratagem **10** balderdash

HUMDINGER: **4** lulu **5** dandy, doozy, nifty **10** remarkable **12** lollapalooza **13** extraordinary

HUMDRUM: **4** blah, drab, dull **5** trite **6** boring, dreary **7** mundane, prosaic, routine **8** everyday **10** monotonous, uneventful, unexciting **11** commonplace, indifferent

HUMERUS: **4** bone **8** upper arm

HUMID: **3** wet **4** damp, dank **5** moist, muggy **6** clammy, sticky, sultry

HUMILIATE: **5** abash, shame **6** demean, humble, insult **7** degrade, mortify **8** belittle, disgrace **9** denigrate, embarrass

HUMILITY: **6** humble **7** modesty, reserve, shyness **8** meekness, mildness

HUMMING: **4** busy **5** brisk **6** lively **7** buzzing, hopping **8** bustling

HUMMOCK: **4** hill **5** knoll, mound, ridge

HUMOR: **3** wit **4** baby, joke, mood, whim **5** cater, fancy, fluid **6** banter, comedy, levity, makeup, pamper, temper **7** caprice, gratify, indulge, jesting, satisfy **8** clowning, drollery **9** amusement, funniness, lightness, merriment, wisecrack, wittiness **11** accommodate, disposition, inclination, personality, temperament

HUMORIST: **3** wag, wit **4** card **5** clown, comic, joker **6** jester **8** comedian

HUMOROUS: **3** wry **5** droll, funny, witty **6** ironic, jocose **7** amusing, comical, jocular **8** pleasant, sardonic **9** facetious, hilarious, laughable, satirical, whimsical **12** entertaining, protuberance **13** sidesplitting

HUMP: **4** bump, hill, lump **5** bulge, hunch, mound, ridge **7** hummock **8** swelling **10** projection **12** protuberance

HUMPBACK: **5** whale **7** gibbous **8** kyphosis **9** hunchback

HUNCH: **4** arch, bend, clue, hint, hump, idea, lump **5** chunk, shove, squat **6** crouch, huddle, notion, thrust **7** feeling, inkling **8** forecast **9** intuition, suspicion **11** premonition

HUNCHBACK OF NOTRE DAME:
author: **10** Victor Hugo
character: **9** Quasimodo

HUNDRED: **6** number **7** century, correct, precise **8** accurate, flawless **9** centenary **10** centennial **12** thoroughbred

HUNDRED PERCENT: **6** entire **7** genuine, perfect

HUNDRED YEARS: **7** century **9** centenary **10** centennial

HUNGARY:
capital: **8** Budapest
cities: **4** Pecs **6** Szeged **7** Miskolc **8** Debrecen
continent: **6** Europe
ethnic groups: **5** Gypsy **6** German, Magyar
features: **5** Tokay **9** Hortobagy **12** Bakony Forest **22** Transdanubian Highlands
languages: **6** Magyar **9** Hungarian
monetary unit: **6** forint
water: **4** Raba **5** Tisza **6** Danube, Theiss **9** Blaten See **11** Lake Balaton

HUNGER: **3** yen **4** ache, want **5** greed **6** desire, famine, thirst **7** craving, longing **8** appetite, yearning **9** hankering **10** starvation

HUNGRY: **4** avid **5** eager, empty **6** barren, greedy, hollow **7** craving **8** esurient, famished, starving **10** avaricious **11** unsatisfied

HUNK: **3** gob, wad **4** clod, glob, hump, lump, mass, slab **5** batch, block, built, chunk, clump, piece **6** nugget **7** portion **10** attractive

HUNT: **4** hawk, seek **5** chase, delve, drive, hound, probe, quest, shoot, stalk, track, trail **6** ferret, follow, forage, pursue, search **7** inquest, inquiry, rummage **9** persecute **11** inquisition **13** investigation

HURDLE: 4 jump, leap, snag, wall **5** bound, clear, hedge, throw **6** hazard, spring **7** barrier **8** handicap, obstacle, overcome, surmount **9** barricade, roadblock **10** impediment **11** obstruction **12** complication

HURL: 4 cast, fire, send, toss **5** chuck, fling, heave, pitch, sling, throw **6** hurtle, launch, propel **8** catapult

HURLY-BURLY: 6 action, bustle, hubbub, tumult, uproar **7** turmoil **8** activity **9** commotion, confusion

HURRAH: 3 joy **4** zeal **5** bravo, cheer, huzza, shout **7** applaud, approve, fanfare **9** commotion **10** enthusiasm, excitement **13** encouragement

HURRICANE: 4 gale, wind **5** storm **7** cyclone, monsoon, tempest, typhoon **9** windstorm **13** tropical storm

HURRY: 3 ado, fly, run, zip **4** bolt, dart, dash, pass, race, rush, trot, urge, whir **5** drive, haste, scoot, speed, whisk **6** barrel, hasten, hustle, motion, scurry, tumult **7** beeline, quicken, urgency **8** dispatch, expedite, highball **10** accelerate, make tracks

HURT: 4 ache, harm, maim, pain, sore **5** abuse, agony, grief, punch, smart, sting, upset, wound **6** bruise, damage, impair, injure, injury, offend, punish, scathe, strike, weaken **7** afflict, cripple, mangled, tarnish, torture **8** battered, bleeding, distress **9** detriment, suffering **11** heartbroken

HURTFUL: 4 evil, mean **5** cruel **6** deadly, unkind **7** baneful, harmful, noxious **8** damaging **9** injurious, malicious, poisonous **10** pernicious **11** deleterious, destructive, detrimental

HURTLE: 4 dash, hurl, race, rush **5** clash, fling, lunge, throw, whirl **6** charge, plunge **7** collide, scamper

HUSBAND: 3 man **4** keep, mate, save **5** groom, hoard, hubby, store **6** manage, spouse **7** partner, steward **8** conserve, helpmate **9** economize **10** bridegroom

HUSBANDRY: 6 thrift **7** economy, farming **9** frugality **10** management **11** agriculture, cultivation **12** conservation

HUSH: 4 calm, lull, mute **5** quiet, shush, still **6** muzzle, soothe **7** appease, silence **8** suppress **11** tranquility

HUSH UP: 5 cover **6** squash **7** conceal **8** suppress

HUSK: 3 pod **4** bark, bran, case, coat, hulk, hull, peel, rind, skin **5** scale, shell, shuck, strip **7** harvest **8** covering, envelope **9** framework

HUSKY: 3 big **4** deep, loud **5** beefy, burly, gruff, hefty, solid **6** brawny, stocky, strong **7** throaty **8** gigantic, growling **10** overweight

HUSSAR: 7 soldier **8** horseman **10** cavalryman

HUSSY: 4 jade, minx, slut **5** tramp, wench, woman **6** female, harlot **10** adulteress, prostitute

HUSTLE: 4 bolt, dash, move, push, race **5** drive, fraud, hurry, press, shove **6** bustle, deceit, hasten, jostle **7** solicit **8** scramble

HUSTLER: 6 dynamo, hooker, peeler, vendor **10** prostitute **12** streetwalker

HUT: 4 camp, crib, shed **5** cabin, house, hovel, hutch, lodge, shack **6** cabana, chalet, lean-to, shanty **7**

cottage, shelter, wickiup **8** building, bungalow

HUTCH: **3** bin, hut, pen **4** cage, coop **5** chest **6** coffer **8** cupboard

HYBRID: **5** blend, cross **7** mixture, mongrel **9** composite **10** crossbreed

HYDRANT: **6** faucet, spigot **8** fireplug

HYDROGEN: **3** gas **7** element

HYGIENIC: **4** good **5** clean **7** healthy, sterile **8** asceptic, sanitary **10** salubrious **11** disinfected

HYMN: **4** laud, sing, song **5** carol, chant, dirge, paean, psalm **6** anthem, prayer **7** chorale, glorify, introit, requiem **8** canticle **11** recessional **12** processional

HYPE: **5** boost **7** buildup, deceive, mislead, promote **9** advertise, publicity

HYPERBOLE: **10** distortion **12** exaggeration **13** embellishment, magnification, overstatement

HYPERCRITICAL: **5** fussy **7** carping **8** captious **10** scrupulous **12** faultfinding, overcritical

HYPNOTIC: **6** sleepy **8** comatose, enticing, soothing **9** soporific **12** somnifacient, spellbinding

HYPNOTIZE: **5** charm **6** allure, induce **8** entrance **9** captivate, mesmerize, spellbind

HYPOCRISY: **4** cant **6** deceit **7** bigotry **8** pretense **9** phoniness **11** insincerity

HYPOCRITE: **5** bigot, faker, phony, quack **6** humbug, poseur **7** two-face **9** charlatan, pretender **10** dissembler

HYPOCRITICAL: **5** false **7** bigoted, canting **8** captious, two-faced **9** deceitful, deceptive, dishonest, insincere **10** artificial, pretending **11** dissembling **13** sanctimonious

HYPOTHESIS: **5** guess **6** belief, system, theory, thesis **8** proposal **9** deduction **10** assumption **11** supposition

HYPOTHETICAL: **7** assumed **8** abstract, inferred **9** imaginary **10** contingent **11** presupposed, theoretical

HYSTERIA: **5** panic **6** frenzy **7** madness **8** delirium **10** excitement

HYSTERICAL: **4** wild **5** funny **6** crazed, raving **7** berserk, comical, excited, frantic **8** unnerved **9** emotional, hilarious **10** distraught, uproarious **11** overwrought

I

IBSEN, HENRIK:
country: **6** Norway
play: **6** Ghosts **8** Peer Gynt **11** Rosmersholm **10** Doll's House **11** Hedda Gabler, Love's Comedy, The Wild Duck **13** The Pretenders **16** The League of Youth, The Master Builder, When We Dead Awaken **18** Emperor and Galilean, John Gabriel Borkman

ICBM: **6** rocket, weapon **7** missile

ICE: **4** cool, floe, flow, geal, rime, rink **5** chill, frost, gorge, sleet **6** freeze, icicle, jewels **7** congeal, crystal, glacier **8** diamonds **10** permafrost **11** refrigerate

ICE CREAM: **4** soda **6** sorbet, sundae **7** cassata, dessert, parfait, sherbet, tofutti

ICELAND:
capital: **9** Reykjavik
cities: **7** Akranes **8** Akureyri
continent: **6** Europe
ethnic groups: **4** Celt **5** Norse **9** Icelandic, Norwegian
features: **5** Hekla **7** Althing, Surtsey **10** Thingvelir
languages: **8** Islenska **9** Icelandic
monetary unit: **5** krona
water: **5** Hvita **7** geysers, Jokulsa **10** Gulf Stream, hot springs

ICE SPORT: **6** hockey **7** curling, skating **12** speed skating

ICHNOGRAPHY: **3** map **9** floor plan **10** ground plan

ICING: **5** fudge, glace **7** coating, topping **8** frosting, marzipan **12** butterscotch

ICKY: **4** vile **5** gooey, gross **6** sticky **9** offensive, revolting **10** disgusting **11** distasteful

I, CLAUDIUS:
author: **12** Robert Graves

ICON: **4** idol **5** image **6** symbol **7** command, picture **8** portrait **12** illustration **14** representation

ICONOCLAST: **5** rebel **7** radical **9** dissenter **13** individualist, nonconformist, revolutionary

ICU: **17** intensive care unit

ICY: **4** cold **5** aloof, gelid, polar **6** arctic, frigid, frosty, frozen **7** distant **8** chilling, freezing **11** unemotional

IDAHO:
bird: **16** mountain bluebird
capital: **5** Boise
cities: **7** Ketchum **9** Pocatello **10** Idaho Falls **11** Coeur d'Alene

explorer: **5** Clark, Lewis
features: **8** Nez Perce **9** Sun Valley **11** Hell's Canyon **14** Rocky Mountains
flower: **7** syringa
native: **7** Idahoan
nickname: **8** Gem State
tree: **9** white pine
water: **10** Snake River **13** Shoshone Falls **14** Lava Hot Springs

IDEA: **4** hint, plan, view **5** fancy, ideal, image, point **6** belief, design, figure, notion, object, scheme, theory **7** concept, essence, fantasy, feeling, inkling, insight, opinion, thought **8** reaction **9** principle, suspicion **10** appearance, brainstorm, cogitation, conception, impression, perception, philosophy, reflection

IDEAL: **4** goal, norm **5** dream, model **7** classic, example, optimal, paragon, pattern, perfect **8** absolute, abstract, exemplar, flawless, standard **9** exemplary, imaginary, prototype, visionary **10** aspiration, conceptual, embodiment, perfection **11** theoretical **12** satisfactory

IDEALISM: **9** meliorism, principle **10** philosophy

IDEALIST: **7** dreamer, utopian **8** optimist, romantic **9** visionary

IDENTICAL: **4** same, self, twin **5** alike, equal **6** double **7** uniform **8** matching, selfsame **9** duplicate **10** equivalent, tantamount **13** corresponding

IDENTIFICATION: **5** badge **8** passport **9** labelling **11** classifying, description, fingerprint, recognition **12** verification

IDENTIFY: **3** tag **4** find, mark, name **5** brand, label **6** finger, verify **8** describe, diagnose, discover, pinpoint **9** associate, designate, establish, recognize

IDENTITY: **4** name, self **7** oneness **11** homogeneity, personality **13** individuality **15** characteristics

IDEOLOGY: **5** creed, dogma **6** ideals **7** beliefs, culture, outlook **8** doctrine **10** philosophy, principles

IDIOGRAPH: **6** symbol **8** logogram **9** trademark

IDIOM: **5** style **6** jargon, speech **7** dialect **10** expression, vernacular **12** idiosyncrasy

IDIOSYNCRASY: **5** habit, idiom, quirk **6** oddity **9** mannerism **11** peculiarity **12** eccentricity **14** characteristic

IDIOT: **4** dolt, dork, fool, jerk **5** ament, booby, dunce, moron **6** cretin, dimwit, nitwit, stupid **7** dullard, fathead **8** bonehead, imbecile **9** blockhead, simpleton

IDIOTIC: **4** daft **5** crazy, daffy, inane, silly **6** stupid **7** asinine, foolish **9** foolhardy, senseless **10** ridiculous

IDLE: **4** lazy, loaf, vain **5** dally, empty, relax, still, waste **6** barren, dawdle, futile, loiter, otiose, unused, vacant **7** aimless, trivial, useless **8** baseless, deserted, inactive, slothful, trifling **9** unfounded, worthless **10** motionless, stationary, unoccupied **11** ineffectual

IDLER: **3** bum **5** drone **6** loafer **7** flaneur, slacker, trifler **8** faineant, loiterer, sluggard **9** lazybones

IDOL: **3** god **4** hero, icon, star **5** image **6** symbol **7** goddess

IDOLIZE: **5** adore, honor **6** admire, revere **7** cherish, glorify, worship **8** canonize, venerate **12** spiritualize

IDYLLIC: **6** rustic, simple **7** bucolic **8** carefree, pastoral, peaceful, pleasing **9** unspoiled

IFFY: **5** dicey, risky **6** chancy **8** doubtful **9** uncertain, undecided, unsettled **10** capricious

IGNITE: **4** burn, fire, glow **5** blaze, light **6** excite, kindle **7** inflame **8** detonate

IGNOBLE: **3** low **4** base, lewd, mean, vile **5** plain **6** common **8** cowardly, infamous, shameful, unworthy, wretched **10** degenerate, despicable **11** disgraceful **12** dishonorable

IGNORAMUS: **4** dolt, fool **5** dunce, idiot, moron **6** nitwit **9** numbskull, simpleton

IGNORANT: **5** dense, green, naive, young **6** callow, stupid **7** shallow, unaware **8** nescient, untaught **9** unknowing, unlearned, unskilled, untutored **10** illiterate, uncultured, uneducated, uninformed **11** misinformed

IGNORE: **4** omit, snub **5** avoid, elide **6** forget, slight **7** neglect **8** discount, overlook **9** disregard **10** circumvent

ILIAD, THE: **4** epic, poem
author: **5** Homer
characters: **4** Ajax, Zeus **5** Dolon, Helen, Paris, Priam **6** Aeneas, Hector, Nestor, Thetis **8** Achilles, Diomedes, Odysseus, Poseidon **9** Agamemnon, Patroclus, Thersites
theme: **9** Trojan War

ILK: **4** kind, same, sort, type **5** breed, class, genus **6** family, nature

ILL: **3** bad **4** evil, harm, poor, sick **5** amiss, cruel, wrong **6** ailing, malady, plague, poorly, queasy, sickly, wicked **7** adverse, ailment, baneful, harmful, hostile, noxious, trouble, unlucky **8** diseased, disorder **9** adversity, condition, defective, unhealthy **10** affliction, indisposed, misfortune, unfriendly

ILL-ADVISED: **4** dumb, rash **5** brash, hasty **6** unwise **7** foolish **8** reckless **9** foolhardy, imprudent, misguided **11** thoughtless **12** shortsighted

ILL-AT-EASE: **6** uneasy, unsure **7** awkward, fidgety, nervous **8** restless **11** discomfited **13** uncomfortable

ILL-BODING: **4** dire, evil **7** unlucky **11** apocalyptic, unfavorable **12** inauspicious

ILL-BRED: **4** rude **5** crude **6** vulgar **7** boorish, uncivil **8** churlish, impolite **10** uncultured **12** discourteous

ILL-DEFINED: **3** dim **5** fuzzy, murky, vague **7** clouded, unclear **8** obscured **10** indistinct

ILLEGAL: **5** shady **6** banned **7** crooked, illicit, lawless **8** criminal, outlawed, smuggled, unlawful **9** felonious **10** bootlegged, contraband, prohibited **12** illegitimate

ILLEGIBLE: **5** faint **7** unclear **9** scribbled **10** unreadable **12** hieroglyphic **14** undecipherable

ILLEGITIMATE: **7** bastard, illegal, invalid **8** improper, spurious **9** illogical

ILL-FATED: **6** doomed, jinxed **7** unlucky **10** disastrous **11** unfortunate **12** misfortunate

ILL-FAVORED: **4** ugly **9** offensive, unsightly **12** unattractive **13** objectionable

ILL HEALTH: **6** malady **7** ailment **8** sickness

ILL-HUMORED: **5** cross, surly, testy **6** cranky, grumpy **7** grouchy **9** irritable

ILLIBERAL: **4** mean **6** biased, greedy, myopic, stingy, vulgar **7** bigoted, partial **9** hidebound **10** prejudiced **12** narrow-minded

ILLICIT: **7** crooked, illegal **8** criminal, improper, unlawful **9** forbidden **10** contraband, prohibited **11** clandestine

ILLINOIS:
bird: **8** cardinal
capital: **11** Springfield
cities: **6** Aurora, Peoria **7** Chicago, Decatur **8** Rockford **9** Champaign
explorer: **7** Jolliet, La Salle **9** Marquette
features: **6** Nauvoo **13** Cahokia Mounds, Dickson Mounds
flower: **6** violet
native: **6** Illini **11** Illinoisian
nickname: **12** Prairie State **13** Land of Lincoln
tree: **8** white oak
water: **4** Ohio, Rock **6** Wabash **8** Illinois, Kankakee **10** Des Plaines **11** Mississippi **12** Lake Michigan

ILLITERATE: **6** unread **8** ignorant **9** unlearned, untutored **10** uneducated, unlettered, unschooled

ILL-MANNERED: **4** rude **7** uncouth **8** impolite **10** ungracious **12** discourteous **13** disrespectful

ILL-NATURED: **5** cross, nasty, surly **6** crabby, cranky, ornery, touchy **8** spiteful **9** irritable, malicious **12** disagreeable

ILLNESS: **5** colic **6** malady **7** ailment, disease **8** disorder, sickness, syndrome **9** breakdown, complaint, infirmity **10** affliction, disability

ILLOGICAL: **5** crazy, nutty **6** absurd **7** invalid, unsound **9** senseless **10** groundless, irrational, unreasoned **12** inconsistent, preposterous, unreasonable **13** contradicting, unsubstantial

ILL-OMENED: **7** ominous **12** inauspicious

ILL-STARRED: **4** dire **7** fateful, ominous, unlucky **10** disastrous **11** unfortunate

ILL-SUITED: **5** unfit **10** mismatched, unbecoming **12** incompatible **13** inappropriate

ILL-TEMPERED: **4** mean, sour **5** angry, cross, curly **6** crabby, cranky **9** crotchety, irritable

ILL-TIMED: **7** awkward **10** malapropos **11** inopportune **13** inappropriate

ILL-TREATMENT: **4** harm **5** abuse **11** molestation **12** maltreatment

ILLUMINATE: **4** fire, glow **5** adorn, light **6** ignite, kindle, uplift **7** clarify, emblaze, enhance, explain, expound **8** brighten **9** celebrate, enlighten, highlight, irradiate, spotlight

ILLUMINATION: **5** gleam, light **7** insight **9** awareness, knowledge **10** brightness, brilliance **11** information **13** enlightenment

ILLUSION: **4** myth **5** dream, fancy **6** deja vu, mirage, vision **7** chimera, fallacy, fantasy, phantom **8** delusion **9** invention **10** apparition **13** hallucination, misconception

ILLUSIVE: **4** fake, sham **5** false **6** unread **7** seeming **8** apparent, illusory **9** deceitful, deceptive, imaginary **10** misleading

ILLUSTRATE: **4** draw, show **6** sketch **7** clarify, explain, picture, portray **8** decorate **9** elucidate, emphasize, exemplify, highlight, represent **11** demonstrate

ILLUSTRATION: **5** image, model **6** figure **7** analogy, cartoon, drawing, example, picture **8** instance, painting, vignette **13** demonstration

ILLUSTRIOUS: **5** famed, great, noble, noted **6** famous **7** eminent, exalted **8** glorious, renowned, splendid, striking **9** brilliant, exemplary, honorable, prominent **10** celebrated **11** magnificent, outstanding **13** distinguished

ILL-WILL: **5** spite, venom **6** animus, grudge, hatred, malice, spleen **7** dislike **9** animosity, hostility **10** resentment **11** malevolence

IMAGE: **4** copy, form, icon, idol **6** double, effigy, emblem, figure, memory, mirror, statue, symbol, vision **7** concept, picture, replica **8** likeness, portrait **9** facsimile, photocopy, semblance **10** appearance, impression, photograph, reflection **12** illustration **14** representation

IMAGINARY: **5** ideal **6** unreal **7** fancied **8** illusive, illusory, invented, mythical **9** dreamlike, fantastic, visionary **10** chimerical, fictitious **12** mythological

IMAGINATION: **5** fancy **6** vision **7** fantasy, figment, insight, thought **9** ingenuity **10** creativity **11** originality

IMAGINATIVE: **6** clever, dreamy **8** creative, fanciful, original **9** ingenious, inventive, visionary **10** innovative

IMAGINE: **5** dream, fancy, think **6** create, devise **7** believe, picture, presume, realize, suppose, surmise, suspect **8** conceive, envision **9** fantasize, visualize **10** comprehend, conjecture, understand **13** conceptualize

IMBECILE: **4** dolt, fool, jerk **5** dummy, dunce, idiot, moron, ninny, silly **6** dimwit, nitwit, stupid **7** fatuous **8** dumbbell **9** simpleton

IMBIBE: **4** down, soak, swig **5** drink, quaff **6** absorb, guzzle, tipple **7** consume, partake, swallow **10** assimilate

IMBROGLIO: **3** row **4** spat **5** brawl, fight **6** ruckus **7** dispute, quarrel **8** argument, squabble **11** altercation, embroilment **12** disagreement

IMBUE: **3** dye **4** soak **5** color, stain, steep, tinge **6** charge, infuse, invade **7** animate, inspire, instill **8** permeate, saturate **9** inoculate

IMITATE: **3** ape **4** copy, echo, mime, mock **5** bogus, clone, mimic **6** assume, mirror, parody **7** emulate, lampoon, pretend **8** resemble, simulate **9** duplicate **11** counterfeit, impersonate

IMITATION: **4** copy, fake, sham **5** bogus, phony **6** ersatz, parody **7** lampoon, replica **8** travesty **9** burlesque, emulation, synthetic **10** impression **11** resemblance **12** reproduction, substitution

IMMACULATE: **4** pure **5** clean **6** chaste **7** perfect, sinless **8** flawless, innocent, spotless, unsoiled **9** faultless, undefiled, unspoiled, unstained, unsullied **11** unblemished, uncorrupted, untarnished

IMMANENT: **6** innate **8** inherent, internal **9** intrinsic **10** subjective **11** instinctive

IMMATERIAL: **7** shadowy, trivial **8** bodiless, trifling **9** celestial, spiritual, unearthly **10** intangible, irrelevant **11** impertinent, incorporeal, inessential, meaningless, unimportant **12** metaphysical **13** inappropriate, insignificant, insubstantial, unsubstantial

IMMATURE: **5** green, young **6** callow, unripe **7** puerile **8** childish, juvenile, youthful **9** infantile **11** undeveloped **13** inexperienced

IMMEASURABLE: **4** vast **7** endless, immense **9** boundless, countless, unlimited **10** indefinite **11** inestimable **12** incalculable, unfathomable

IMMEDIATE: **4** near, next **5** close **6** abrupt, direct, sudden, urgent **8** adjacent, critical **9** proximate **10** succeeding **12** straightaway **13** instantaneous

IMMEDIATELY: **3** now **4** anon **6** presto **7** rapidly, shortly **8** directly, promptly **9** instantly

IMMEMORIAL: **3** old **7** ancient, archaic **8** dateless **11** prehistoric

IMMENSE: **4** good, huge, vast **5** grand, great, large **6** mighty **7** mammoth, massive, titanic **8** colossal, enormous, gigantic **9** excellent, extensive, monstrous **10** prodigious, tremendous **12** immeasurable

IMMERSE: **3** dip **4** bury, dunk, soak **5** bathe, douse **6** absorb, drench, occupy, plunge **7** baptize, engross **8** christen, saturate, submerge

IMMIGRANT: **5** alien **8** newcomer **9** foreigner

IMMIGRATE: **6** settle **7** migrate **8** colonize

IMMINENT: **5** close **7** brewing, looming, ominous **9** expecting, immediate, impending **10** inevitable **11** approaching, inescapable, threatening, unavoidable

IMMOBILE: **4** firm **5** fixed, inert, still **6** frozen, stable **8** anchored **9** immovable, steadfast **10** motionless, stationary

IMMODERATE: **7** extreme **9** boundless, excessive **10** exorbitant, inordinate **11** extravagant **12** unreasonable, unrestrained **14** unconscionable

IMMODEST: **4** bold, vain **6** brazen, coarse **8** arrogant, boastful, indecent, unchaste **9** conceited, shameless, unabashed

IMMORAL: **3** bad **4** evil **5** dirty, loose, wrong **6** impure, sinful **7** corrupt, vicious **8** depraved, indecent **9** dishonest, nefarious, unethical **10** degenerate, licentious **12** unscrupulous

IMMORTAL: **6** divine, famous **7** endless, eternal, forever, undying **8** enduring **9** ceaseless, deathless **11** everlasting, neverending **12** imperishable **14** indestructible

IMMOVABLE: **4** fast, firm **5** fixed, rigid, stuck **6** rooted **7** adamant **8** immobile, obdurate, stubborn **9** heartless, implanted, permanent, steadfast **10** inflexible, stationary, unshakable, unyielding

IMMUNE: **4** free, safe **6** exempt **7** guarded **9** protected, resistant **12** invulnerable, unresponsive

IMMUNITY: **7** amnesty, freedom, release **9** exemption, privilege **11** exoneration

IMMUNIZE: **7** protect **9** inoculate, vaccinate

IMMURE: **4** coop, jail, wall **6** entomb **7** confine, seclude **8** cloister, imprison **11** incarcerate

IMMUTABLE: **4** firm **5** fixed, solid **7** eternal **8** constant, enduring **9** permanent, unaltered **10** invariable, unchanging **12** unchangeable

IMP: **3** elf, fay **4** brat, puck **5** demon, devil, fiend, gnome, pixie, scamp, troll **6** goblin, sprite, urchin **7** gremlin **9** hobgoblin

IMPACT: **4** bang, blow, jolt, rock **5** brunt, crash, crush, force, pound, shock, smash **6** effect **7** contact **9** collision **10** concussion, impression **11** implication **12** consequences, significance

IMPAIR: **3** mar **4** harm, hurt **5** spoil **6** damage, hinder, impede, injure, lessen, reduce, weaken **7** afflict, blemish, cripple, devalue, vitiate **8** decrease, diminish, undercut **9** undermine

IMPAIRED: **6** broken, faulty, flawed **7** unsound **9** afflicted, imperfect

IMPALE: **4** gore, spit, stab **5** lance, spear, spike **6** pierce, skewer **8** puncture, transfix

IMPART: **4** give, lend, tell **5** admit, offer, share, yield **6** bestow, confer, convey, direct, expose, inform, render, reveal **7** divulge, inspire **8** announce, disclose, discover **11** communicate

IMPARTIAL: **4** fair, just **7** neutral **8** detached, unbiased **9** equitable, objective, unslanted **10** evenhanded **11** indifferent **12** unprejudiced

IMPASSE: **3** box, jam **6** pickle **7** dead end, dilemma **8** cul-de-sac, deadlock, gridlock, standoff **9** stalemate **10** blind alley, standstill

IMPASSIONED: **5** fiery **6** ardent, fervid **7** excited, fervent, intense, rousing, zealous **8** feverish, romantic, stirring **10** passionate

IMPASSIVE: **4** calm, cool **5** still, stoic **6** stolid **7** callous **9** apathetic, collected **10** impassible, insensible, motionless **11** emotionless, insensitive, unemotional, unflappable **14** expressionless

IMPATIENT: **3** hot **4** edgy **5** antsy, eager, hasty, itchy, testy **7** anxious, fidgety, fretful, hurried, nervous, peevish **8** restless **9** irascible, irritable **10** intolerant

IMPEACH: **5** blame **6** accuse, charge, indict **7** censure, dismiss **8** denounce **9** challenge, discredit **11** incriminate

IMPECCABLE: **5** exact, right **7** perfect, precise **8** flawless **9** exquisite, faultless **10** immaculate, infallible **11** unblemished

IMPECUNIOUS: **4** poor **5** broke, needy **8** indigent **9** destitute, penniless **12** impoverished

IMPEDE: **4** clog, curb **5** block, check, delay, deter **6** hamper, harass, hinder, stymie, thwart **7** disrupt **8** obstruct **9** interfere

IMPEDIMENT: **4** flaw, snag **5** hitch **6** defect, hurdle, malady **7** barrier **8** drawback, handicap, obstacle **9** detriment, hindrance **10** difficulty **11** obstruction

IMPEDIMENTA: **4** gear **7** baggage, luggage **8** supplies

IMPEL: **4** goad, move, push, send, urge **5** drive, force, press **6** compel, excite, incite, induce, prompt, propel **7** inspire **8** motivate **9** constrain, encourage, influence, instigate, stimulate

IMPENDING: **5** close **6** coming **7** looming, nearing **8** imminent, menacing **10** inevitable **11** approaching, forthcoming, threatening

IMPENETRABLE: **4** hard **5** dense, thick **6** sealed **8** airtight **10** impassable, impervious, mysterious **11** bulletproof, impermeable **12** unfathomable

IMPERATIVE: **4** duty, rule **5** order, stern, vital **6** urgent **7** command, crucial **8** absolute, critical, pressing, required **9** essential, mandatory, necessary **10** commanding, compulsory, peremptory **13** indispensable

IMPERCEPTIBLE: **5** faint, scant, small **6** slight, subtle **9** invisible **10** insensible, intangible, unapparent **12** undetectable, unnoticeable **13** inappreciable, indiscernible, insignificant

IMPERFECT: **6** faulty, flawed **7** damaged **8** impaired **9** blemished, defective **10** disfigured, incomplete, unfinished

IMPERFECTION: **4** flaw, kink **5** fault **6** defect **7** blemish, failing **8** weakness **10** deficiency, inadequacy **11** shortcoming

IMPERIAL: **5** regal, royal **6** kingly, lordly **7** stately **8** majestic **9** sovereign **11** domineering, magisterial

IMPERIL: **4** risk **6** expose, hazard **8** endanger **10** compromise, jeopardize

IMPERIOUS: **5** bossy **6** lordly, urgent **7** haughty **8** arrogant, despotic, pressing **10** commanding, oppressive, tyrannical **11** dictatorial, domineering, magisterial, overbearing **13** authoritative

IMPERMANENT: **7** passing **8** fleeting **9** ephemeral, temporary, transient **10** evanescent, perishable

IMPERSONAL: **4** cold **7** general, neutral **8** detached **9** impartial, objective **10** unfriendly

IMPERSONATE: **3** ape **4** copy, pose **5** mimic **6** mirror **7** imitate, portray

IMPERTINENCE: **4** sass **8** audacity, boldness, rudeness **9** insolence **10** brazenness, incivility **11** forwardness, irrelevance

IMPERTINENT: **4** rude **5** fresh, sassy, saucy **8** arrogant, impolite, impudent, meddling **9** audacious **11** illmannered **12** discourteous **13** disrespectful

IMPERTURBABLE: **4** calm, cool **6** placid, serene, stable **8** composed, tranquil **9** collected, unruffled **11** levelheaded, unexcitable, unflappable

IMPERVIOUS: **8** hermetic **10** impassable, watertight **11** impermeable **12** impenetrable, inaccessible

IMPETUOUS: **4** rash **5** eager, fiery, hasty, heady **6** abrupt, ardent, fervid, fierce, flashy, sudden **7** furious, hurried, rushing **8** forcible, headlong, heedless, vehement **9** impulsive, unplanned **11** precipitate, spontaneous

IMPETUS: **4** push, spur **5** drive, force **7** impulse **8** ambition, catalyst, momentum, stimulus **9** incentive

IMPIETY: **6** heresy **9** blasphemy, sacrilege **10** disrespect **11** reprobation, ungodliness **13** undutifulness

IMPINGE: **6** strike **7** collide, disturb, intrude **8** encroach, infringe, trespass

IMPIOUS: **6** sinful, unholy **7** godless, profane, ungodly **8** undevout **10** iniquitous, irreverent, unfaithful **11** blasphemous, irreligious

IMPISH: **5** fresh **6** elfish, elvish **7** naughty, playful, puckish **8** devilish **11** mischievous

IMPLACABLE: **5** cruel **8** ruthless **9** merciless **10** inexorable, ironfisted, relentless **11** immitigable, unrelenting **12** unappeasable

IMPLANT: **4** root **5** embed, graft, inset **6** enroot, infuse, insert **7** impress, ingrain, instill **9** establish, inculcate, inoculate, introduce **10** impregnate

IMPLAUSIBLE: **4** weak **5** fishy **6** flimsy **7** dubious, suspect **8** doubtful, unlikely **10** farfetched, improbable, ridiculous **13** unbelieveable

IMPLEMENT: **4** tool **5** agent, begin, start **6** device, gadget **7** enforce, execute, fulfill, machine, realize, utensil **8** complete **9** apparatus, appliance **10** accomplish, instrument **11** contraption

IMPLICATE: **4** link **5** frame, imply **6** accuse, charge **7** connect, embroil, involve, suggest **11** incriminate

IMPLICATION: **8** overtone **9** inference **10** assumption, suggestion **11** association, presumption **12** ramification

IMPLICIT: **4** real **5** fixed **7** implied **8** absolute, complete, inherent **9** suggested **10** understood **13** unquestioning

IMPLIED: **5** tacit **6** hinted **7** assumed **8** implicit, inferred, intended **9** indicated, intimated, suggested **10** insinuated, understood

IMPLORE: **3** ask, beg **4** pray, urge **5** plead **6** adjure, appeal **7** beseech, entreat, solicit **8** petition **10** supplicate

IMPLY: **4** hint, mean **5** infer **7** connote, presume, signify, suggest **8** comprise, indicate, intimate **9** insinuate **10** presuppose

IMPOLITE: **4** rude **5** blunt, crude, rough **7** ill-bred, uncivil **9** inelegant, unrefined **10** indecorous, unmannerly, unpolished **12** discourteous **13** disrespectful

IMPORT: **4** mean **5** drift, sense, value, worth **6** convey, denote, intent, thrust **7** purpose, signify **8** indicate **9** introduce, substance **12** significance

IMPORTANCE: **4** rank **5** worth **6** moment, weight **7** gravity, stature, urgency **8** emphasis, position, prestige, priority, standing **9** attention, dimension, influence, magnitude, relevance **10** prominence **11** consequence **12** significance

IMPORTANT: **5** grave, great, noted **6** urgent **7** eminent, epochal, pompous, serious **8** critical, decisive, powerful, valuable **9** essential, momentous, necessary, prominent, strategic **10** meaningful, noteworthy, preeminent **11** influential, significant **12** considerable, earthshaking

IMPORTUNE: **3** beg, vex **4** urge **5** annoy, plead, press **6** appeal, demand, insist **7** beseech, entreat, implore, solicit **8** petition **10** supplicate

IMPOSE: **4** levy, wish **5** apply, force, order **6** burden, charge, create, demand **7** command, dictate, intrude, obtrude **8** generate, infringe

IMPOSING: **5** burly, grand, royal **7** massive, stately **8** majestic, striking **9** grandiose **10** commanding, impressive **11** magnificent, outstanding

IMPOSITION: **3** tax **4** duty, fine, levy **5** fraud **6** burden, demand **9** deception, intrusion

IMPOSSIBLE: **6** absurd **8** hopeless **9** insoluble **10** unbearable, unfeasible **11** unthinkable **12** unacceptable, unattainable, unimaginable

IMPOST: **3** fee, tax **4** duty, levy, toll **6** charge, custom, surtax, tariff, weight **7** tribute **10** assessment

IMPOSTOR: **4** sham **5** cheat, faker, phony, quack **6** humbug **8** imitator **9** charlatan, pretender **10** mountebank **11** pettifogger **12** impersonator

IMPOSTURE: **4** copy, fake, ruse, sham **5** cheat, fraud, trick **6** deceit

7 swindle **8** artifice, quackery **9** deception, falsehood, imitation **10** imposition, masquerade, pretension **11** counterfeit

IMPOTENT: **4** weak **5** inept **6** barren, feeble **7** sterile **8** helpless **9** incapable, powerless **10** inadequate

IMPOUND: **5** seize, store **6** retain **7** collect, confine **10** accumulate

IMPOVERISH: **4** ruin **5** drain **6** beggar, reduce, weaken **7** deplete, exhaust **8** bankrupt

IMPOVERISHED: **4** poor **5** broke, empty, needy **6** barren, bereft **8** indigent **9** destitute, penurious **10** pauperized

IMPRACTICAL: **6** unwise **8** quixotic, romantic, unusable **9** illogical, visionary **10** idealistic, unfeasible **11** unrealistic **12** unattainable

IMPREGNABLE: **4** firm, hard **6** secure, strong, sturdy **8** shielded **10** invincible, unshakable **12** invulnerable

IMPREGNATE: **4** soak **5** imbue **6** charge, drench, infuse, leaven **8** permeate, saturate **9** fertilize, penetrate **10** inseminate

IMPRESARIO: **7** manager **8** director, producer

IMPRESS: **4** etch, move, sway **5** affix, brand, drive, pound, print, reach, stamp, touch **6** effect, hammer, indent, stress, thrill **7** engrave, imprint, inspire, opinion **8** reaction **9** electrify, emphasize, influence

IMPRESSION: **4** dent, idea, mark, view **5** image, print, sense, stamp, trace **6** belief, effect, impact **7** feeling, opinion, takeoff, thought **8** reaction **9** influence **13** impersonation

IMPRESSIONABLE: **7** plastic **8** gullible **9** teachable **10** responsive, vulnerable **11** susceptible

IMPRESSIVE: **5** grand **6** august, lavish, moving, solemn **7** telling **8** imposing, majestic, powerful, stirring, striking **9** luxurious, memorable **11** magnificent

IMPRINT: **4** etch, mark **5** press, stamp **6** effect, symbol **7** engrave **8** inscribe **9** signature **10** impression

IMPRISON: **4** cage, hold, jail **5** limit **6** arrest, detain, entomb, immure **7** confine, enclose, shackle **8** restrain **11** incarcerate

IMPROBABLE: **4** slim **8** doubtful, unlikely **12** questionable, unbelievable, unconvincing **13** inconceivable

IMPROMPTU: **6** sudden **7** offhand **9** impulsive **10** improvised, unexpected, unprepared **11** extemporary, spontaneous, unrehearsed

IMPROPER: **5** crude, unfit, wrong **6** unjust, vulgar **7** illegal, illicit **8** impolite, indecent **9** erroneous, ill-suited, incorrect, irregular, unethical **10** ill-advised, indecorous, indelicate, unbecoming, unsuitable **11** unbefitting **12** illegitimate **13** inappropriate

IMPROPRIETY: **5** error, gaffe **7** blunder, faux pas **8** solecism **9** barbarism **10** corruption **12** indiscretion

IMPROVE: **4** gain, grow, help, lift **5** edify **6** better, enrich, reform, uplift **7** advance, augment, benefit, correct, develop, elevate, enhance, recover, upgrade **9** cultivate **10** ameliorate, recuperate, strengthen

IMPROVIDENT: **4** rash **8** careless, prodigal, reckless, wasteful **9** imprudent, negligent **10** incautious, thriftless **11** extravagant, spendthrift **12** shortsighted

IMPROVISE: **3** jam **4** wing **5** ad-lib **6** devise, invent **8** contrive **11** extemporize

IMPROVISED: **7** offhand **9** impromptu, makeshift **11** extemporary, spontaneous, unrehearsed

IMPRUDENT: **4** rash **5** crazy **6** unwise **7** foolish **8** heedless, reckless **9** negligent **10** ill-advised, incautious **11** improvident, inadvisable

IMPUDENT: **4** bold, rude, wise **5** brash, fresh, sassy, saucy **6** brazen **7** forward **8** flippant, impolite, insolent **9** offensive, shameless **11** impertinent **13** disrespectful

IMPUGN: **4** deny **5** doubt, fight, knock **6** assail, attach, resist **7** gainsay **8** denounce, question **9** challenge **10** contradict

IMPULSE: **4** push, urge **5** drive, force, throb **6** motion, motive, thrust **7** impetus, resolve **8** catalyst, instinct, stimulus, tendency **10** propulsion

IMPULSIVE: **5** quick **6** sudden **7** offhand **8** forceful, headlong **9** impellent, impetuous, impromptu **11** involuntary, spontaneous **13** unpredictable

IMPUNITY: **7** freedom **8** immunity **9** clearance, exception, privilege

IMPURE: **4** foul, lewd, vile **5** dirty, gross **6** carnal, coarse, filthy, smutty, unholy **7** corrupt, defiled, diluted, obscene, tainted, unclean **8** indecent, inferior, polluted, unchaste **9** unrefined **10** desecrated, unhallowed **11** adulterated, unwholesome **12** contaminated

IMPUTE: **5** blame, count, refer **6** accuse, charge, credit, impart **7** ascribe **8** consider, intimate **9** attribute, implicate

INABILITY: **7** failure **8** weakness **9** impotence **10** inaptitude, incapacity, ineptitude **12** helplessness, incompetence

INACCESSIBLE: **5** aloof **6** closed, remote **7** distant, elusive **11** unavailable, unreachable **12** unattainable

INACCURACY: **4** goof **5** error **7** blunder, fallacy, mistake **11** imprecision

INACCURATE: **5** false, wrong **6** faulty, untrue **7** inexact **9** defective, erroneous, incorrect **10** discrepant, misleading, unreliable

INACTION: **8** deferral, idleness **9** indolence **10** inactivity, suspension

INACTIVE: **4** dull, idle, slow **5** inert, slack, still **6** latent, otiose, static, supine **7** dormant, languid, passive **8** indolent, sleeping, slothful, sluggish **9** lethargic, quiescent, sedentary **10** motionless, unemployed, unoccupied

IN ADDITION: **3** and, too **4** also, more, plus **7** besides, further **12** supplemental

INADEQUACY: **4** flaw, lack **8** shortage **9** inability **10** deficiency **11** shortcoming **12** inefficiency **13** insufficiency

INADEQUATE: **4** weak **5** short, small, unfit **6** little, meager, scanty, skimpy, sparse **7** wanting **9** deficient, imperfect **10** incomplete **11** ineffective, unqualified

INADMISSIBLE: **9** unwelcome **10** disallowed, immaterial, irrelevant **11** unallowable, unqualified **12** unacceptable

IN ADVANCE: **5** ahead **6** before, sooner **7** earlier

INADVERTENT: **8** careless, heedless **9** unwitting **10** accidental, unintended

INADVISABLE: **4** rash **5** risky **6** unwise **7** foolish **9** impolitic, imprudent **10** unsensible

INALIENABLE: **5** basic **6** inbred, sacred **7** natural **8** absolute, defended, inherent **10** inviolable

INAMORATA: **5** lover, woman **8** ladylove, mistress, paramour **10** sweetheart

INANE: **4** daft, dumb **5** empty, silly, vapid **6** jejune, stupid, vacant **7** asinine, fatuous, foolish, idiotic, vacuous **9** frivolous, illogical, pointless, senseless, worthless **10** ridiculous **11** nonsensical

INANIMATE: **4** dead, dull, flat **5** inert **6** stolid **8** lifeless **9** exanimate, inorganic, unfeeling **10** insensible

INANITY: **7** vacuity **8** nonsense, vapidity **9** absurdity, emptiness, frivolity **10** hollowness, triviality **11** foolishness **13** senselessness

IN ANY CASE: **6** anyway **10** regardless **11** nonetheless

INAPPLICABLE: **5** unfit **10** immaterial, inapposite, irrelevant **11** impertinent

INAPPROPRIATE: **5** inapt **8** ill-timed, improper, unsuited **9** unfitting **10** malapropos, unbecoming, unsuitable

INAPT: **4** flat **5** inept, undue **6** clumsy, gauche **7** awkward **8** ill-timed, improper **10** amateurish, inadequate, unsuitable **13** inappropriate

IN ARREARS: **3** due **5** owing **6** behind **7** overdue **10** delinquent

INARTICULATE: **4** dumb, mute **7** blurred, garbled, muffled, unvocal **10** hesitating, incoherent, speechless, stammering, tongue-tied **12** inexpressive

INARTISTIC: **9** graceless, inelegant, tasteless

INASMUCH AS: **3** for **5** since, while **7** because **11** considering

INATTENTION: **9** disregard **10** dreaminess, negligence **12** carelessness

INATTENTIVE: **3** lax **5** bored **6** absent, remiss **7** unaware **8** careless, heedless **9** forgetful, negligent, unheeding, unmindful **10** abstracted, distracted, unnoticing **11** preoccupied, unobserving

INAUGURATE: **4** open **5** begin, start **6** induct, launch **7** install, usher in **8** commence, initiate **9** auspicate, institute, introduce, undertake

INAUGURATION: **7** opening **9** inception, induction **10** coronation **12** commencement

INAUSPICIOUS: **4** dire, foul **7** adverse, ominous, unlucky **8** sinister **10** disastrous, foreboding **11** threatening, unfortunate, unpromising **12** unpropitious

INBORN: **5** basic **6** inbred, innate **7** natural **9** ingrained, inherited, intuitive **10** hereditary **11** instinctive

INBRED: **6** inborn, innate, native, primal **7** natural **9** intrinsic **10** congenital, deep-seated

INCA:
also: **9** Atahualpa
capital: **5** Cuzco
cities: **11** Machu Picchu
features: **5** Andes
gods/goddesses: **3** Sun **4** Inti **5** Choun, Iraya **6** Chasca **9** Uiracocha, Viracocha **10** Pachacamac
kingdoms: **4** Peru **5** Chile **7** Bolivia, Ecuador
language: **7** Quechua

INCALCULABLE: **7** immense **8** infinite **9** countless, limitless, uncertain **11** inestimable, innumerable, measureless, uncountable **12** immeasurable, incomputable **13** unpredictable

INCANDESCENT: **5** lucid **6** bright **7** glowing, intense, radiant, shining **8** electric, luminous **9** brilliant

INCANTATION: **4** jinx, rite **5** chant, charm, magic, spell **6** voodoo **7** sorcery **8** witchery **9** utterance **11** abracadabra, conjuration

INCAPABLE: **5** inept, unfit **6** unable **8** helpless **9** powerless, untrained **10** inadequate, unequipped **11** incompetent, unqualified

INCAPACITATE: **4** lame, maim **6** damage, disarm, hinder **7** cripple, disable **8** handicap, sideline **10** disqualify

INCAPACITY: **7** illness **9** inability **10** deficiency, ineligible

INCARCERATE: **4** jail **6** commit, detain, immure **7** confine **8** imprison **9** constrain

INCARNATE: **6** embody **8** manifest, tangible **9** actualize **11** materialize, personified **12** exteriorized

INCAUTIOUS: **4** bold, rash **5** hasty **8** careless, reckless **9** impetuous, imprudent, negligent **10** indiscreet **11** thoughtless

INCENDIARY: **5** rebel **7** firebug **8** agitator, arsonist **9** insurgent **10** pyromaniac, subversive **12** inflammatory

INCENSE: **4** balm, rile **5** anger, aroma, myrrh, scent, smell, spice **6** enrage, homage, incite **7** essence, perfume, provoke **8** irritate **9** fragrance, infuriate **12** frankincense
container: **6** censer **8** thurible

INCENTIVE: **4** goad, lure, spur, urge **5** spark **6** motive **7** impetus, impulse **8** catalyst, stimulus **10** allurement, enticement, incitement, inducement, motivation **11** inspiration **13** encouragement

INCEPTION: **4** dawn **5** onset, start **6** origin, source **7** arrival, kickoff **9** beginning **12** commencement

INCERTITUDE: **5** doubt **10** insecurity, skepticism **11** instability, uncertainty

INCESSANT: **6** steady **7** endless, eternal, nonstop **8** constant, unending **9** ceaseless, perpetual **10** continuous, persistent, relentless **11** unremitting

INCH: **4** move, unit **5** creep **6** length **11** measurement

INCHOATE: **5** vague **8** unformed, unshaped **9** amorphous, incipient, shapeless **10** incohesive, incomplete **11** rudimentary, unorganized

INCIDENT: **5** event, prone, scene **7** episode **8** accident, occasion **9** happening **10** contingent, occurrence

INCIDENTAL: **5** minor **6** casual, chance **7** related **9** accessory, ancillary, secondary **10** contingent, fortuitous, occasional **12** contributing, nonessential

INCIDENTALLY: **7** apropos **8** by the way **15** parenthetically

INCINERATE: **4** burn **5** parch **7** consume, cremate

INCIPIENT: **7** budding, initial, nascent **8** inchoate **9** beginning, inceptive **10** commencing, developing

INCISE: **3** cut **4** etch, mold **5** carve **6** chisel **7** engrave

INCISION: **3** cut **4** gash, scar, slit **5** notch, slash, wound

INCISIVE: **4** keen **5** acute, clear, crisp, sharp **6** biting **7** concise, cutting, mordant, precise **9** sarcastic, trenchant **11** intelligent, penetrating

INCITE: **4** abet, coax, goad, move, prod, spur, stir, urge **5** drive, impel **6** arouse, compel, entice, excite, foment, induce, prompt **7** agitate, animate, inflame, provoke, trigger **8** motivate **9** encourage, influence, instigate, stimulate

INCIVILITY: **7** uncivil **8** rudeness **10** disrespect **11** discourtesy, misbehavior **12** churlishness, impertinence

INCLEMENT: **3** raw **4** foul, hard **5** harsh, rough **6** brutal, severe, stormy **8** ruthless **10** unmerciful

INCLINATION: **4** bent, bias, hill, mind, rise, urge, will, wish **5** angle, fancy, grade, pitch, slant, slope **6** ascent, desire, liking **7** descent, leaning **8** affinity, appetite, druthers, fondness, gradient, tendency **9** acclivity, affection, proneness **10** attachment, partiality, preference, proclivity, propensity **11** disposition

INCLINE: **3** bow, dip **4** bend, bias, cant, hill, ramp, tend, tilt **5** grade, pitch, slant, slope, trend **6** prefer **7** dispose, leaning, upgrade **9** influence **10** predispose

INCLINED: **3** apt **4** wont **5** given, prone **6** biased, liable, likely, minded **7** leaning, tilting **11** predisposed

INCLUDE: **5** cover **6** enfold, insert **7** contain, embrace, involve **8** comprise **9** encompass **10** comprehend **11** incorporate

INCLUSIVE: **5** broad **6** global **7** general **8** umbrella **9** embracing, universal **11** surrounding **13** comprehensive

INCOGNITO: **7** unknown **8** nameless **9** anonymous, concealed, disguised **10** undercover **12** unidentified

INCOGNIZANT: **7** unaware **8** ignorant **9** oblivious, unknowing **10** uninformed

INCOHERENT: **7** muddled, unclear **8** muttered, rambling **9** illogical **10** disjointed, indistinct **11** incongruous, unconnected **12** disconnected, inarticulate, inconsistent **14** unintelligible

INCOME: **4** cash, gain **5** means, wages **6** profit, return, salary **7** revenue, royalty **8** earnings, interest, proceeds, receipts **9** emolument **10** commission **12** compensation

INCOMPARABLE: **7** supreme **8** peerless, superior **9** excellent, matchless, unrivaled **10** surpassing, unequalled **11** superlative, unsurpassed **12** unparalleled **15** incommeasurable

INCOMPATIBLE: **7** adverse, warring **8** clashing, contrary, opposite **10** discordant, mismatched **11** conflicting, disagreeing, incongruous **12** antagonistic, inharmonious **13** contradictory

INCOMPETENT: **5** inept, unfit **6** unable **7** lacking, useless **8** bungling, helpless **9** incapable, unskilled **10** unequipped **11** inefficient, unqualified

INCOMPLETE: **5** rough **6** broken, undone **7** divided, lacking, partial, wanting **9** defective, deficient, imperfect **10** inadequate, unfinished **11** fragmentary, undeveloped **12** insufficient

INCOMPREHENSIBLE: **7** unclear **8** abstruse, baffling **9** confusing **10** mysterious, perplexing, unreadable **11** unthinkable **12** impenetrable, unfathomable, unimaginable **13** inconceivable

INCONCEIVABLE: **7** strange **8** unlikely **10** improbable, incredible **11** unthinkable **12** unbelievable

INCONCLUSIVE: **4** open **5** vague **9** uncertain, undecided, unsettled **10** indefinite, unfinished, unresolved **12** undetermined

INCONGRUOUS: **5** alien **6** absurd **8** contrary **10** discordant, mismatched, unsuitable **11** conflicting **12** disagreeable, incompatible, inconsistent, inharmonious **13** inappropriate

INCONSEQUENTIAL: **5** minor, petty **6** measly, paltry, slight **7** trivial **8** picayune, trifling **10** irrelevant, negligible **11** meaningless, unimportant **13** insignificant

INCONSIDERABLE: **5** minor, petty, small **6** little, scanty, slight **7** trivial **10** negligible

INCONSIDERATE: **4** rash, rude **6** unkind **7** selfish, uncivil **8** careless, impolite **10** incautious, indiscreet, neglectful, ungracious **11** improvident, insensitive, thoughtless

INCONSISTENT: **6** fickle **7** erratic **8** unstable **9** dissonant, irregular, unsatable **10** capricious, discordant, discrepant **11** conflicting, incongruous, uncongenial **12** incompatible **13** contradictory, unpredictable

INCONSOLABLE: **7** crushed, forlorn **8** dejected **10** despondent **11** comfortless, heartbroken **12** disconsolate

INCONSTANT: **6** fickle, untrue **7** elusive, erratic, wayward **8** disloyal, variable **9** faithless, unsettled **10** capricious, changeable **11** fluctuating, uncommitted, vacillating

INCONTINENT: **7** lustful **8** unchaste **10** licentious **12** uncontrolled, unrestrained

INCONTROVERTIBLE: **7** certain **10** undeniable **11** irrefutable, unequivocal **12** indisputable **13** incontestable **14** unquestionable

INCONVENIENCE: **5** annoy **6** bother **7** trouble **8** nuisance **9** annoyance, disoblige, hindrance **10** discomfort, discommode, uneasiness **11** awkwardness, disturbance

INCONVENIENT: **7** awkward, unhandy **8** annoying **10** burdensome **11** inopportune, troublesome **12** embarrassing, inaccessible, unreasonable

INCORPORATE: **4** form, fuse, join, link **5** blend, merge, unite **6** embody **7** combine, include **9** associate, integrate **10** assimilate

INCORPOREAL: **4** airy **8** bodiless **9** spiritual, unearthly, unworldly **10** immaterial **11** disembodied **12** supernatural **13** unsubstantial

INCORRECT: **5** false, wrong **6** untrue **8** mistaken **9** erroneous **10** inaccurate

INCORRIGIBLE: **6** rooted **8** hardened, hopeless **10** unreformed **11** intractable, irreparable **12** ineradicable, unmanageable

INCORRUPTIBLE: **4** pure **5** loyal **6** honest **9** honorable, righteous **11** trustworthy, untouchable

INCREASE: **3** add, wax **4** gain, grow, hike, jump, rise, soar **5** boost, build, raise, surge, swell **6** accrue, dilate, double, enrich, expand, extend, gather, growth, irrupt, markup, triple **7** amplify, augment, broaden, enhance, enlarge, further, inflate, magnify, upgrade **8** addition, compound, flourish, heighten, multiply **9** advantage, aggravate, expansion, extension, increment, intensify, quadruple **10** accelerate, accumulate, aggrandize, appreciate, exaggerate, strengthen **11** development, enlargement, proliferate

INCREDIBLE: **6** absurd **7** amazing, awesome **8** fabulous, unlikely **9** wonderful **10** astounding, impossible, outlandish, remarkable **12** questionable, unbelievable **13** extraordinary

INCREDULOUS: **7** dubious **8** doubting **9** skeptical, uncertain **10** suspicious **11** mistrustful, unconvinced **12** disbelieving

INCREMENT: **4** gain **5** raise **6** growth **7** accrual **8** addition, increase **11** advancement **12** accumulation, augmentation

INCRIMINATE: **5** blame **6** accuse, charge **7** involve **9** implicate, inculpate

INCUBATE: **4** plan, plot **5** brood, cover, hatch **7** develop

INCUBUS: **5** demon **6** burden, spirit **9** nightmare

INCULCATE: **5** drill, teach **6** impart, infuse **7** implant, impress, instill, program **9** propagate **12** indoctrinate

INCULPABLE: **5** clean, clear **8** innocent **9** blameless, exemplary

INCULPATE: **5** blame **6** accuse, charge **7** involve **9** implicate **11** incriminate

INCUR: **4** gain **6** assume, obtain **7** acquire, sustain **9** encounter

INCURABLE: **6** deadly **7** chronic **8** hopeless, terminal **10** inoperable **11** irreparable **12** incorrigible, irremediable **13** uncorrectible

INCURSION: **4** raid **5** foray **6** attack **7** assault **8** invasion **11** penetration **12** infiltration

INDEBTED: **5** bound **6** liable **8** beholden, grateful **9** obligated **12** appreciative

INDECENT: **4** foul, lewd **5** dirty, gross, nasty **6** coarse, impure, smutty, vulgar **7** immoral, obscene, raunchy **8** improper, unseemly **9** offensive **10** indelicate, scurrilous, unbecoming

INDECIPHERABLE: **7** cryptic **8** scrawled **9** illegible **10** unreadable **12** hieroglyphic

INDECISION: **5** doubt **7** anxiety **8** wavering **10** hesitation **11** uncertainty, vacillation **12** irresolution

INDECISIVE: **5** shaky **7** dubious, unclear **8** hesitant, waffling **9** equivocal **10** indefinite, irresolute **12** inconclusive

INDECOROUS: **4** rude **5** gross **6** coarse **7** uncivil **8** impolite, improper **9** inelegant, offensive, unfitting **10** unbecoming **11** distasteful **13** inappropriate

INDEED: **5** truly **6** really, surely **8** actually, honestly **9** certainly, naturally **10** absolutely, admittedly, positively, undeniable **11** undoubtedly

INDEFATIGABLE: **6** dogged **8** diligent, tireless, untiring, vigorous **9** energetic, tenacious **10** persistent, relentless, unwearying **11** industrious, persevering **13** inexhaustible

INDEFENSIBLE: **7** invalid **9** pregnable, untenable **10** vulnerable **11** inexcusable, unprotected **12** unpardonable

INDEFINITE: **5** loose, vague **6** unsure **7** endless, inexact **8** doubtful, infinite **9** ambiguous, equivocal, tentative, uncertain, unlimited **10** indecisive, unspecific **12** inconclusive, undetermined

INDELIBLE: **4** fast **5** fixed **7** lasting **8** enduring **9** permanent **10** unerasable **11** unremovable **12** ineffaceable, inexpungible, uneradicable

INDELICATE: 3 raw 4 lewd 5 brash, gross 6 coarse, vulgar 7 uncouth 8 impolite, improper, indecent, tactless, unseemly 9 offensive, unrefined 10 unbecoming

INDEMNIFY: 3 pay 5 atone 6 insure 7 protect, satisfy 9 reimburse 10 compensate, recompense, remunerate

INDEMNITY: 9 exemption, insurance 10 protection, reparation 11 restitution 12 compensation

INDENT: 4 dint, mark, nick 5 inlay, notch, press, space, stamp 6 bruise, recess 7 depress, serrate

INDENTATION: 5 dinge, notch 6 cavity, dimple, groove, pocket, recess 9 indenture 10 impression

INDENTURE: 8 contract, document 9 agreement 11 indentation

INDEPENDENCE: 7 freedom, liberty 8 autonomy 11 sovereignty 12 emancipation 14 self-government

INDEPENDENT: 4 free 5 alone 8 separate 9 exclusive, liberated, sovereign 10 autonomous, nonaligned 11 self-reliant, unconnected 12 uncontrolled, unrestricted 13 self-governing 14 self-supporting

INDESCRIBABLE: 9 ineffable 11 indefinable, unspeakable 12 overwhelming 13 unexpressible

INDESTRUCTIBLE: 7 durable, lasting 8 enduring 9 immutable, permanent 11 unbreakable 12 unchangeable 13 nonperishable

INDETERMINATE: 5 vague 7 inexact, obscure, unclear 9 ambiguous, uncertain 10 indefinite, unresolved 12 inconclusive

INDEX: 4 file, list, mark 5 guide, table 6 symbol 7 catalog, measure, pointer 8 glossary, tabulate 9 indicator 11 alphabetize

INDIA:
capital: 8 New Delhi
cities: 4 Pune 6 Bombay, Kanpur, Madras, Nagpur 7 Lucknow 8 Calcutta 9 Ahmadabad, Bangalore, Hyderabad
continent: 4 Asia
ethnic groups: 6 Indian 9 Dravidian, Mongoloid
features: 4 Thar 5 Ghats 7 Andaman, Nicobar 8 Taj Mahal 9 Himalayas, Hindu Kush 11 Lakshadweep 12 Golden Temple
languages: 4 Urdu 5 Hindi, Oriya, Tamil 6 Sindhi, Telugu 7 English, Gengali, Kannada, Marathi, Punjabi 8 Assamese, Gujarati, Kashmiri, Sanskrit 9 Malayalam
monetary unit: 5 rupee
water: 5 Indus 6 Ganges 7 Marmada 11 Brahmaputra

INDIAN (AMERICAS): 6 red man 7 Amerind 14 Native American
Central/South American: 3 Ona, Uro 4 Ande, Cuna, Inca, Maya 5 Aztec, Bravo, Carib, Olmec 6 Arawak, Aymara, Kechua, Toltec 7 Guarani, Quechua, Zapotec
child: 7 papoose
housing: 5 hogan, lodge, tepee 6 teepee, wigwam 7 wickiup
leaders: 7 Cochise, Osceola, Pontiac, Sequoya 8 Geronimo, Hiawatha, Powhatan, Tecumseh 10 Crazy Horse 11 Sitting Bull
male: 4 buck 5 brave, chief 6 sannup
meeting: 6 powwow
money: 5 sewan 6 wampum
North American: 3 Kaw, Oto, Sac, Ute 4 Cree, Crow, Erie, Hopi, Ioni, Iowa, Otoe, Pima, Sauk, Tana, Taos, Yuma, Zuni 5 Aleut, Banak, Caddo, Creek, Huron, Kania, Kansa, Kiowa, Maidu, Miami, Omaha, Osage, Sioux 6 Apache, Cayuga, Dakota, Kansas, Lenape, Mohave, Mohawk, Mojave, Munsee, Navaho, Navajo, Nootka, Ojibwa, Oneida, Ottawa, Paiute, Pawnee, Pueblo,

Sambos, Seneca, Siwash **7** Abenaki, Arapaho, Arikara, Chilkat, Chinook, Choctaw, Dakotah, Keresan, Klamath, Mohegan, Mohican, Natchez, Pontiac, Shawnee, Tlingit **8** Apalachi, Cherokee, Cheyenne, Chippewa, Comanche, Delaware, Hitchiti, Illinois, Iroquois, Nez Perce, Onondaga, Sagamore, Seminole, Shoshoni **9** Algonquin, Apalachee, Blackfoot, Chickasaw, Menominee, Tuscarora, Winnebago **10** Muskhogean, Potawatomi **11** Massachuset **12** Narragansett

peace pipe: **7** calumet

INDIANA:
bird: **8** cardinal
capital: **12** Indianapolis
cities: **4** Gary **7** LaPorte **9** Fort Wayne, South Bend **10** Evansville, Terre Haute, Tippecanoe, Valparaiso
explorer: **7** LaSalle **9** Vincennes
features: **12** Indiana Dunes **15** Indianapolis 500, Wyandotte Cavern
flower: **5** peony
native: **7** Hoosier
nickname: **12** Hoosier State
tree: **11** tulip poplar
water: **11** Wabash River **12** Lake Michigan

INDICATE: **4** bode, mark, mean, read, show **5** augur, imply, infer, point, prove **6** attest, denote, evince, import, reveal **7** bespeak, betoken, display, gesture, signify, specify, suggest, testify **8** disclose, evidence, intimate, manifest, register **9** designate, symbolize **11** demonstrate

INDICATION: **4** clue, hint, note, omen, sign **5** proof, token, trace **6** notion, signal **7** auspice, inkling, symptom, warning **8** evidence **10** expression, intimation, suggestion **11** designation, forewarning

INDICATIVE: **8** symbolic **10** emblematic, expressive, suggestive **11** significant **14** representative

INDICT: **6** accuse, charge, summon **7** arraign, impeach **9** inculpate, prosecute **11** incriminate

INDIFFERENCE: **6** apathy **7** disdain, iciness **8** coldness, lethargy **9** aloofless, lassitude, unconcern **10** negligence **11** callousness, disinterest **12** carelessness **13** insensitivity

INDIFFERENT: **4** cold, cool, so-so **5** aloof, blase, stoic **6** casual, frigid **7** neutral, unmoved **8** careless, detached, heedless, listless, mediocre, uncaring **9** apathetic, incurious, unfeeling, unmindful **10** impervious, insensible, nonchalant, uninspired **11** unconcerned **12** uninterested

INDIGENOUS: **6** inborn, innate, native **7** endemic, natural **8** domestic, inherent, original **9** homegrown **10** aboriginal, congential **13** autochthonous

INDIGENT: **4** poor **5** needy **7** lacking, wanting **8** beggarly, homeless **9** destitute, penniless **11** impecunious **12** impoverished

INDIGESTION: **3** gas **9** dyspepsia, heartburn **10** flatulence

INDIGNANT: **4** sore **5** angry **6** miffed **7** annoyed, furious **8** incensed, steaming, wrathful **9** irritated **10** infuriated **11** disgruntled, exasperated

INDIGNATION: **3** ire **4** fury, rage **5** anger, pique **6** animus **7** disdain, umbrage **9** animosity **10** resentment **11** displeasure

INDIGNITY: **5** abuse, wrong **6** insult, slight **7** affront, offense, outrage **8** dishonor **9** injustice **11** discourtesy, humiliation **13** embarrassment

INDIGO: **3** dye **4** anil, blue, herb **5** color, shrub

INDIRECT: **5** vague **6** shifty, sneaky, zigzag **7** crooked, devious, erratic, oblique **8** circular, rambling, twisting **9** dishonest, secondary, underhand **10** circuitous, incidental, meandering, misleading, roundabout

INDISCERNIBLE: **5** faint **9** invisible **10** evanescent, impalpable, indistinct **12** unnoticeable **13** imperceptible, insignificant

INDISCREET: **4** rash **5** brash **6** unwise **7** foolish **8** careless, heedless, tactless **9** impolitic, imprudent **10** ill-advised, incautious **11** improvident, injudicious **13** inconsiderate

INDISCRETION: **4** slip **5** folly, lapse **7** mistake, stumble **10** unwariness **11** foolishness **12** carelessness

INDISCRIMINATE: **5** broad, mixed **6** motley, random, wanton **7** chaotic, jumbled, mingled **8** assorted, confused **9** haphazard, unplanned **11** unselective **12** disorganized, unrestrained

INDISPENSABLE: **5** basic, vital **6** needed **7** crucial, needful **8** cardinal **9** essential, necessary, requisite **10** imperative, obligatory **11** unavoidable

INDISPOSED: **3** ill **4** sick **6** ailing, averse, sickly, unwell **7** uneager **8** confined, hesitant **9** reluctant, unwilling **11** disinclined

INDISPOSITION: **6** malady **7** ailment, dislike, illness, malaise **8** disorder, sickness **9** infirmity **10** affliction, discomfort, reluctance, resentment

INDISPUTABLE: **4** sure **7** certain, obvious **8** apparent, definite, positive **10** conclusive, undeniable **11** indubitable **12** irrefragable, unmistakable **14** unquestionable

INDISSOLUBLE: **4** firm **7** binding, lasting **8** enduring **9** permanent **12** imperishable

INDISTINCT: **4** dark, hazy, weak **5** faint, misty, muddy, vague **6** cloudy **7** blurred, obscure, shadowy, unclear **8** confused **9** ambiguous, inaudible, undefined **10** indefinite

INDISTINGUISHABLE: **4** same **5** vague **7** unclear **9** identical **13** imperceptible

INDITE: **3** pen **5** write **7** compose, dictate

INDIVIDUAL: **3** one **4** self, sole, solo, unit **5** alone, being, thing **6** entity, mortal, person, single, unique **7** private, special **8** separate, solitary, somebody **9** exclusive **10** particular **11** distinctive

INDIVIDUALITY: **5** habit, seity **6** makeup, nature **7** feature **8** identity **9** character, mannerism **10** uniqueness **11** distinction, personality, singularity, temperament **14** indivisibility

INDIVIDUALLY: **5** alone, apart **10** personally, separately **13** independently

INDOCTRINATE: **5** imbue, teach, train **6** school **7** educate, instill, program **8** instruct **9** brainwash

INDOLENT: **4** idle, lazy **5** inert **6** torpid **8** inactive, listless, slothful, sluggish **9** lethargic **10** lackadaisy

INDOMITABLE: **6** dogged **7** staunch **8** intrepid, stalwart **9** steadfast, undaunted **10** courageous, invincible, unbeatable, unyielding **11** persevering **12** invulnerable, undefeatable

INDONESIA:
capital: 7 Jakarta
cities: 7 Bandung 8 Semarang, Surabaya 12 Tanjung Priok
continent: 4 Asia
ethnic groups: 5 Malay 7 Chinese 8 Irianese
features: 4 Bali, Java 5 Sumba, Timor 6 Lombok, Madura, Malaku 7 Sumatra 8 Belitung, Moluccas, Sulawesi 9 Irian Jaya, New Guinea 11 Lesser Sunda 12 Greater Sunda
languages: 5 Malay 8 Javanese 16 Bahasa Indonesian
monetary unit: 6 rupiah
water: 4 Bali, Java, Savu, Toba 5 Banda, Ceram, Timor 7 Celebes, Molucca 8 Kerintji 11 Indian Ocean

INDUBITABLE: 4 open, sure 7 assured, certain, evident 8 apparent, positive 10 conclusive, undeniable 11 unequivocal 12 indisputable, irrefragable 14 unquestionable

INDUCE: 3 get 4 coax, draw, lure, sway, urge 5 cause, impel, press, tempt 6 elicit, incite, prompt 7 actuate 8 convince, generate, motivate, persuade 9 encourage, influence

INDUCEMENT: 4 bait, hook, spur 6 carrot, motive, reason 8 stimulus 9 incentive 10 attraction, enticement 11 instigation 13 consideration

INDUCT: 5 admit, draft 6 enlist, enroll 7 install, instate, recruit 8 initiate, register 10 inaugurate

INDULGE: 4 baby 5 enjoy, favor, humor, spoil 6 coddle, cosset, oblige, pamper, please 7 cherish, delight, gratify, satisfy 11 accommodate, mollycoddle

INDULGENCE: 5 spree 6 excess, luxury 7 petting 8 clemency, fondness, hedonism, lenience 9 allowance, tolerance 10 compassion 11 forgiveness 13 gratification

INDULGENT: 4 easy, good, kind 6 benign,. gentle, tender 9 compliant, easygoing, pardoning 10 charitable, permissive

INDUSTRIOUS: 4 busy 5 eager 6 active 7 dynamic, zealous 8 diligent, sedulous 9 ambitious, assiduous, energetic, laborious 10 productive 11 hardworking 12 enterprising

INDUSTRY: 4 toil, work, zeal 5 field, labor 6 bustle, energy 7 pursuit 8 activity, business, commerce 9 ingenuity 10 occupation 13 determination, manufacturing

INEBRIATED: 5 drunk, tipsy 6 bombed, loaded, stoned, tanked, wasted 7 smashed 9 plastered 11 intoxicated

INEFFABLE: 5 taboo 6 divine, sacred 8 empyreal, ethereal 9 celestial 11 unspeakable, unutterable 12 transcendent 13 indescribable, inexpressible

IN EFFECT: 6 really 9 activated 10 absolutely

INEFFECTIVE: 4 vain, void, weak 5 inept 6 futile 7 useless 8 impotent 9 fruitless, worthless 10 inadequate 11 incompetent, ineffectual, inefficient, neutralized

INEFFECTUAL: 4 idle, vain, weak 6 futile, unable 7 useless 8 hopeless, impotent 10 inadequate, unavailing 11 ineffective, inefficient 12 insufficient, unproductive

INEFFICIENT: 5 inept 8 slipshod, unfitted, wasteful 9 unskilled 10 unprepared 11 incompetent, ineffective, ineffectual 12 disorganized, unproductive

INELASTIC: 5 rigid, stiff 6 stable 9 unbending 10 inflexible, unyielding 11 unadaptable

INELEGANT: **5** crass, crude **6** clumsy, coarse, common, gauche, vulgar **7** awkward **9** graceless, ungenteel, unrefined

INELIGIBLE: **5** unfit **8** unworthy **10** unsuitable **11** unqualified **12** disqualified, unacceptable

INELUCTABLE: **4** sure **6** doomed **7** certain **10** inevitable, unevadable **11** indubitable, inescapable, unavoidable

INEPT: **4** slow **5** inane, inapt, unfit **6** absurd, clumsy, gauche **7** awkward, foolish **8** bumbling, bungling, improper, unseemly, unsuited **9** pointless, unskilled **10** unbecoming **11** incompetent, ineffectual, inefficient **13** inappropriate

INEQUALITY: **4** bias **8** imparity **9** disparity, diversity, prejudice **10** difference, unevenness, unfairness **13** disproportion **14** discrimination

INEQUITY: **5** wrong **9** injustice **10** unfairness

INERT: **4** dead, idle, lazy, slow **5** quiet, slack, still **6** static, supine, torpid **7** languid, neutral, passive **8** immobile, inactive, indolent, lifeless, sluggish **9** apathetic, impassive, lethargic **10** motionless, phlegmatic, stationary

INERTIA: **8** idleness **9** indolence, lassitude, oscitancy, passivity, stillness **10** inactivity, quiescence

IN ESSENCE: **9** basically **10** ultimately **11** essentially, practically **13** fundamentally

INESTIMABLE: **8** precious, valuable **9** exquisite, priceless **10** invaluable **12** incalculable, unmeasurable

INEVITABLE: **4** sure **5** fated **6** doomed **7** assured, certain, decided, fateful **8** destined, imminent **9** impending, necessary **11** inescapable, unavoidable **13** unpreventable

INEXACT: **5** false, rough, vague **9** erroneous **10** inaccurate **12** undetermined

INEXCUSABLE: **5** wrong **9** untenable **11** blameworthy, intolerable, unallowable **12** indefensible, unforgivable **13** reprehensible

INEXHAUSTIBLE: **7** wearied **8** infinite, tireless **9** boundless, unlimited **10** unflagging

IN EXISTENCE: **5** alive **6** extant **9** surviving

INEXORABLE: **5** harsh, rigid, stiff, stony **6** dogged, strict **7** adamant **8** ironclad, resolute, rigorous **9** unbending **10** determined, inflexible, relentless, unyielding **11** intractable, unalterable, unrelenting **14** uncompromising

INEXPEDIENT: **6** futile, unwise **9** impolitic, imprudent **11** detrimental, inadvisable, injudicious, inopportune

INEXPENSIVE: **5** cheap **6** frugal **7** bargain, thrifty **9** low-priced **10** economical, reasonable

INEXPERIENCED: **5** green, naive, young **6** callow, rookie **7** untried **8** inexpert, unversed **9** unskilled, untrained, unworldly **10** sophomoric, unfamiliar **11** unpracticed **12** shortsighted, unaccustomed

INEXPERT: **5** crude, green **7** awkward **9** unskilled, untrained **11** unpracticed **13** inexperienced

INEXPLICABLE: **7** baffling, obscure, strange **8** abstruse, peculiar **9** ambiguous, enigmatic **10** mysterious **12** supernatural, unfathomable **13** inexplainable, unaccountable

INEXPRESSIVE: **4** dull, flat **5** blank, empty **6** devoid, vacant **9** impassive

INFALLIBLE: **4** sure **5** exact **6** divine **7** certain, perfect **8** flawless, reliable, unerring **9** faultless, foolproof, unfailing **10** dependable, impeccable

INFAMOUS: **4** base, evil **5** shady **6** odious **7** corrupt, hateful, heinous **8** shameful **9** atrocious, loathsome, miscreant, nefarious, notorious **10** degenerate, despicable, detestable, scandalous, villainous **12** contemptible, dishonorable

INFAMY: **5** odium **7** scandal **8** disgrace, dishonor, ignominy, reproach, shameful **9** discredit, disesteem **10** immorality

INFANCY: **5** start **6** outset **8** babyhood **9** beginning, childhood, inception **10** immaturity

INFANT: **3** kid **4** babe, baby **5** child, minor **7** bambino, neonate, newborn, toddler **8** bantling

INFANTILE: **7** babyish **8** childish, immature, juvenile, youthful **10** sophomoric

INFANTRYMAN: **7** dogface, soldier **8** doughboy

INFATUATED: **4** fond **7** charmed, foolish **8** enamored, inflamed, obsessed **9** enchanted **10** captivated, enraptured, enthralled

INFATUATION: **4** love **5** craze, crush, folly **7** madness, passion **9** obsession **10** attachment **11** fascination

INFECT: **5** spoil, taint **6** affect, damage, invade, poison **7** afflict, pollute **11** contaminate

INFECTION: **6** malady, plague **7** disease, illness **9** contagion **10** corruption, defilement

INFECTIOUS: **7** noxious **8** catching, epidemic **9** poisonous, spreading, vitiating **10** contagious **11** pestiferous, transmitted **12** communicable, pestilential, transferable

INFER: **4** hint **5** drive, glean, guess, imply, opine **6** assume, deduce, gather, reason **7** suppose, surmise **8** conclude, construe **9** ascertain, interpret, speculate

INFERENCE: **9** corollary, deduction, judgement **10** assumption, conclusion, conjecture, suggestion **13** understanding

INFERIOR: **4** base, cull, less, peon, poor **5** below, cheap, lower, minor, petty, worst **6** common, feeble, impure, lesser, minion, nether **7** unequal **8** mediocre, unworthy **9** auxiliary, secondary, underling **10** inadequate, second-rate, underneath **11** subordinate, substandard

INFERNAL: **4** evil **5** awful **6** cursed **7** demonic, hellish, satanic, stygian, vicious **8** damnable, devilish, fiendish, horrible **9** chthonian, tartarean **10** abominable, diabolical, underworld

INFERNO: **3** pit **4** fire, hell **5** abyss, Hades **9** holocaust **10** underworld **11** netherworld

INFERTILE: **6** barren **7** drained, sterile **8** depleted, impotent, infecund **9** fruitless, unbearing **12** unproductive

INFEST: **5** beset, flood, swarm **6** defile, invade, pester, plague, ravage **7** overrun

INFIDEL: **5** pagan **7** atheist, heathen, heretic, skeptic **8** agnostic **10** unbeliever

INFIDELITY: **6** breach **7** falsity, treason **8** adultery, betrayal **9** violation **10** disloyalty

INFILTRATE: **4** leak, seep **5** foist **8** permeate **9** penetrate **10** impregnate

INFINITE: **4** vast **7** endless, eternal, immense **9** boundless, countless, limitless, perpetual, unlimited **10** tremendous **11** illimitable **12** immeasurable, interminable

INFINITESIMAL: **4** tiny **5** small **6** little, minute **9** minuscule **11** microscopic **12** unnoticeable **13** insignificant

INFIRM: **4** lame, weak, worn **5** anile, frail **6** ailing, feeble, sickly **7** brittle, failing, fragile, unsound **8** decrepit, disabled **9** doddering **11** debilitated, vacillating

INFIRMARY: **6** clinic **8** hospital **10** dispensary

INFIRMITY: **4** flaw **5** decay **6** malady **7** ailment, disease, frailty, illness **8** sickness, weakness **9** condition **10** affliction, deficiency, feebleness **11** confinement **12** debilitation

INFLAME: **4** boil, burn, fire, heat, rile, stir **5** anger, annoy, chafe **6** arouse, enrage, excite, kindle **7** incense, provoke **8** irritate **9** aggravate, electrify, impassion, infuriate **10** exasperate

INFLAMMABLE: **5** fiery **6** ardent **8** burnable, volatile **9** excitable, hazardous, ignitable, irascible, irritable **10** incendiary **11** combustible

INFLAMMATION: **4** acne, boil, fire, gout **7** chafing **8** bursitis, swelling **9** arthritis, infection **10** irritation, phlegmasia **13** conflagration

INFLATE: **4** blow, pump **5** bloat, boost, elate, swell **6** dilate, expand **7** amplify, augment, balloon, distend, enlarge, magnify **8** increase **12** overestimate

INFLATED: **5** blown, tumid, wordy **6** turgid **7** flowery, pompous, swollen **9** bombastic, flatulent **10** rhetorical **11** exaggerated

INFLECTION: **4** bend, tone **5** curve, sound **6** accent, timbre **8** emphasis **9** variation **10** intonation **11** enunciation **12** articulation

INFLEXIBLE: **4** firm, hard **5** fixed, rigid, stiff **6** dogged, strict **7** adamant **8** obdurate, rigorous, stubborn **9** immovable, inelastic, steadfast, stringent, unbending **10** adamantine, headstrong, implacable, inexorable, relentless, unyielding **11** unadaptable **14** uncompromising

INFLICT: **4** dump **5** force, wreak **6** impose, strike, unload **7** deliver **8** dispense **10** administer, perpetrate

INFLUENCE: **4** fame, hold, lead, move, pull, rule, sway **5** alter, clout, force, impel, lobby, money, power **6** affect, aspect, compel, effect, govern, induce, motive, prompt, weight **7** attract, command, control, gravity, impress, inspire, mastery **8** dominion, leverage, persuade, pressure, prestige **9** authority, magnetism **10** ascendancy, inducement, prominence **11** connections

INFLUENTIAL: **6** potent, strong **7** leading **8** dominant, powerful **9** effective, important, momentous **11** significant **12** instrumental

INFLUX: **4** flow, tide **6** inflow, inrush **7** arrival **8** increase, invasion **9** incursion, inpouring **12** infiltration

INFORM: **4** blab, post, talk, tell **5** brief, train **6** advise, betray, notify, preach, snitch, squeal, tattle, update **7** apprise **8** acquaint, forewarn, instruct **9** advertise, enlighten **11** communicate, familiarize

INFORMAL: **5** frank, loose **6** casual, simple **7** natural, relaxed **9** easygoing **10** colloquial, unofficial **13** unceremonious

INFORMANT: **3** rat **4** fink, nark **5** sneak **6** canary, snitch, source **7** stoolie, tipster **8** informer **10** tattletale

INFORMATION: **4** clue, data, dope, news, word **5** facts, scoop **6** notice, report, wisdom **7** lowdown, tidings **8** feedback, material **9** direction, documents, knowledge **11** instruction

INFORMATIVE: **9** revealing **11** descriptive, educational, instructive **12** enlightening, illuminating

INFORMED: **3** hip **4** told, wise **5** aware **6** versed, warned **7** abreast, knowing **8** apprised, notified **10** conversant

INFORMER: **3** rat **4** fink, nark **5** sneak **6** canary, snitch, source **7** stoolie, tipster **9** informant **10** tattletale

INFRACTION: **5** crime, error **6** breach **9** violation **11** misdemeanor **12** encroachment, infringement **13** transgression

INFRASTRUCTURE: **4** base, root **6** ground **7** support **9** framework **10** foundation **12** substructure
systems: **5** power **7** schools **14** communications, transportation

INFREQUENT: **4** rare **5** scant **6** scarce, seldom, sparse **7** unusual **8** isolated, sporadic, uncommon **9** irregular **10** occasional **12** intermittent

INFRINGE: **5** break **6** breach, invade, meddle, offend **7** disobey, impinge, infract, intrude, violate **8** encroach, overstep, trespass **10** contravene

INFURIATE: **3** vex **4** rile **5** anger **6** enrage **7** incense, inflame, outrage, umbrage **8** irritate **9** aggravate

INFUSE: **4** fill, soak **5** imbue, plant, steep **6** impart, leaven **7** implant, inspire, instill, pervade **8** saturate **9** inculcate, introduce

INGE, WILLIAM: **6** author **10** playwright
wrote: **6** Picnic **7** Bus Stop

INGENIOUS: **5** acute, canny, sharp, smart, witty **6** adroit, bright, clever, crafty, gifted **7** cunning **8** creative, original, skillful, talented **9** brilliant, inventive **10** innovative **11** imaginative, intelligent, resourceful

INGENUOUS: **4** open **5** frank, naive **6** candid, honest, simple **7** artless, natural, sincere **8** innocent, trustful **9** childlike, guileless **10** unaffected **11** undisguised

INGEST: **3** eat **4** take **5** drink **6** absorb **7** consume, swallow

INGLORIOUS: **4** base **6** odious, shabby **7** corrupt, obscure **8** infamous, shameful **9** degrading **10** scandalous **11** disgraceful, ignominious **12** dishonorable

INGOT: **3** bar **4** mold **5** block

INGRAINED: **4** firm **6** inborn, inbred, innate, native, rooted **7** chronic **8** inherent **10** congenital, deepseated **11** established, fundamental

INGRATIATING: **4** oily, soft **5** sweet **6** smarmy **7** affable, fawning, gushing, servile, winsome **8** friendly, pleasing, unctuous **9** agreeable, appealing **10** flattering, obsequious **11** sycophantic

INGREDIENT: **4** item **5** piece **6** factor **7** element, essence **8** additive **9** component **11** constituent

INGRESS: **4** door **5** entry **6** access **7** opening **8** entrance **9** penetrate

INHABIT: **4** live **5** dwell, lodge **6** occupy, people, reside, settle, tenant **8** populate

INHABITANT: **6** inmate, native **7** boarder, citizen, denizen, dweller **8** colonist, occupant, resident

INHALE: **4** drag, puff **5** smell, sniff **6** devour **7** breathe, consume, inspire, respire

INHERENT: **5** basic **6** inborn, inbred, innate **7** genetic, natural **9** essential, ingrained **10** congenital, deeprooted, hereditary, indwelling **11** fundamental **14** characteristic

INHERIT: **3** get **6** obtain **7** acquire, receive

INHERITANCE: **4** gift **6** estate, legacy **7** bequest **8** heirloom, heritage **9** endowment, patrimony **10** birthright

INHIBIT: **3** bar **4** curb, stop **5** avert, check, cramp **6** forbid, hinder, impede **7** prevent, repress **8** prohibit, restrain, restrict, suppress **10** discourage

INHIBITED: **4** cold **6** frigid **7** guarded **8** reserved **10** controlled **12** unresponsive

INHIBITION: **6** hangup **7** barrier **8** obstacle **9** restraint **11** suppression

INHOSPITABLE: **4** rude **7** hostile **8** impolite **10** unfriendly, unsociable **11** unwelcoming

INHUMAN: **4** cold **5** cruel **6** brutal, savage **7** beastly, bestial, brutish, vicious **8** barbaric, ruthless **9** barbarous, ferocious, heartless, malicious, merciless, monstrous **10** diabolical **11** coldhearted

INIMICAL: **7** adverse, harmful, hostile, hurtful **8** contrary **9** injurious, repugnant **10** unfriendly **11** unfavorable **12** antagonistic

INIQUITOUS: **4** evil **6** sinful, unjust, wicked **7** corrupt, immoral **9** nefarious

INIQUITY: **3** sin **4** evil, vice **5** wrong **6** infamy **7** offense **9** depravity, injustice **10** immorality, miscreancy, wickedness

INITIAL: **5** basic, first **6** letter, maiden **7** leading, opening, primary **8** earliest, original **9** beginning, incipient **10** elementary **11** fundamental

INITIATE: **4** haze, open **5** admit, begin, found, start **6** induct, launch **7** install, trigger **8** commence **9** establish, introduce, originate **10** inaugurate **12** indoctrinate

INITIATION: **4** rite **5** onset **7** baptism **8** ceremony, entrance **9** beginning, induction **10** admittance, enrollment **11** investiture **12** commencement, introduction

INITIATIVE: **4** push **5** drive, moxie, spunk **6** action, energy **8** ambition, aptitude, gumption **9** eagerness **10** creativity, enterprise, enthusiasm, get-up-and-go

INJECT: **3** put **4** pump **5** force, imbue, shoot **6** insert **7** instill **8** mainline **9** inoculate, introduce, vaccinate

INJUDICIOUS: **4** dumb **6** unwise **7** foolish, unsound **9** imprudent **10** indiscreet **11** inadvisable

INJUNCTION: **4** writ **5** edict, order **6** behest, charge, decree, ruling **7** command, mandate, precept **9** directive

INJURE: **3** mar **4** harm, hurt, maim **5** abuse, spoil, wound, wrong **6** bruise, damage, impair, insult, offend **7** affront, assault **8** maltreat **9** disfigure

INJURIOUS: **7** abusive, harmful, hurtful **8** libelous **9** unhealthy **10** slanderous **11** detrimental

INJURY: **3** cut **4** blow, gash, harm, hurt, stab **5** break, wound, wrong **6** bruise, damage, insult, lesion, mayhem, sprain, trauma **8** fracture, hardship, swelling, whiplash **9** contusion, detriment, injustice **10** affliction, impairment, laceration, mutilation

INJUSTICE: **4** bias, harm, hurt **5** crime, wrong **6** breach, injury **8** iniquity **9** grievance, prejudice, violation **10** favoritism, inequality, unfairness, wickedness **11** miscarriage **14** discrimination

INKLING: **4** clue, hint, idea, lead **5** hunch, scent **6** notion **7** glimpse **9** suspicion **10** glimmering, indication, intimation

INKY: **4** dark **5** black, ebony, murky, raven **7** stained

INLET: **3** arm, bay **4** cove, gulf **5** basin, bayou, bight, creek, fiord, firth, fjord, inlay, sound **6** harbor, strait, stream **7** channel, estuary, narrows, opening, orifice, passage **8** entrance, waterway

IN LINE: **7** aligned **8** balanced, straight

INMATE: **3** con **5** felon, lifer **7** convict **8** occupant, prisoner **10** inhabitant

IN MEMORIAM: **8** honoring **10** in memory of **11** recognizing **13** commemorating

INMOST: **7** central, deepest **8** intimate **10** intestinal

IN MOTION: **6** active, moving **9** traveling

INN: **3** pub **4** khan **5** fonda, hotel, house, lodge, motel **6** hostel, resort, tavern **7** albergo, auberge, hospice **8** hostelry **9** roadhouse **11** caravansary

INNARDS: **4** guts **6** bowels **7** insides, viscera **8** stuffing

INNATE: **6** inborn, inbred, native **7** natural **8** inherent, internal **9** essential, ingrained, inherited, intrinsic **10** congenital, hereditary **11** instinctive

INNER: **4** deep **5** close **6** hidden, inside, inward, middle **7** central, private **8** esoteric, interior, internal, personal **9** concealed

INNKEEPER: **4** host **8** boniface, hosteler, landlord, publican **10** proprietor, victualler

INNOCENCE: **6** purity, virtue **7** naivete **8** chastity **9** freshness **11** sinlessness **12** spotlessness **13** blamelessness, guiltlessness

INNOCENT: **4** free **5** clean, naive **6** chaste, lawful, simple **7** artless, unaware, upright **8** harmless, ignorant, pristine **9** blameless, childlike, exemplary, greenhorn, guileless, guiltless, stainless, uncorrupt, unworldly **10** inculpable, unblamable, uninvolved

INNOCUOUS: **6** jejune, pallid **7** insipid **8** harmless **11** inoffensive, unoffending

INNOVATION: **6** change **7** novelty **9** departure, invention **11** vicissitude **12** introduction

INNOVATIVE: **8** creative, original **9** ingenious, inventive **12** contemporary

INNUENDO: **4** clue, hint **8** overtone **9** reference **10** intimation, suggestion **11** implication, insinuation

INNUMERABLE: **4** many **6** legion, myriad **8** infinite, numerous **9** countless **12** incalculable

INOCULATE: **5** imbue, steep **6** infuse, leaven **7** implant, protect **8** immunize **9** vaccinate

INOFFENSIVE: **4** safe **7** neutral **8** harmless **9** innocuous **11** unobtrusive

INOPERATIVE: **4** dead, idle **8** inactive **10** unworkable **13** countermanded

INOPPORTUNE: **8** contrary, ill-timed, untimely **11** impractical, unfortunate **12** inconvenient, unseasonable **13** inappropriate

INORDINATE: **5** undue **6** lavish, wanton **7** copious, extreme, surplus **8** overmuch **9** excessive **10** disorderly, exorbitant, immoderate, outrageous **11** extravagant, superfluous **12** unrestrained

INORGANIC: **5** azoic **7** mineral **8** lifeless **9** inanimate **10** artificial

IN PERPETUUM: **6** always **7** forever **9** eternally

IN PIECES: **6** broken, busted, ruined **7** damaged, smashed **9** destroyed, shattered

INQUEST: **5** probe **6** search **7** delving, finding, hearing, inquiry **11** examination **13** investigation

INQUIRE: **3** ask, pry **4** quiz, seek **5** grill, query, study **6** search **7** examine, explore **8** question **10** scrutinize **11** interrogate, investigate

INQUIRING: **7** curious **9** searching, wondering **13** investigative

INQUIRY: **5** audit, check, probe, query **7** hearing, inquest **8** analysis, question, research, scrutiny **9** interview **11** examination, inquisition **13** investigation

INQUISITION: **4** hunt **5** trial **6** search **7** inquest, inquiry **8** tribunal **11** prosecution **13** investigation

INQUISITIVE: **4** nosy **6** prying **7** curious **8** meddling, snooping **9** intrusive **10** interested, meddlesome **11** challenging

IN RE: **5** about **9** regarding **10** concerning **10** in regard to **11** in the case of **13** in the matter of

INROAD: **4** raid **5** foray **7** advance **8** invasion **9** incursion, intrusion **12** encroachment

INS AND OUTS: **5** ropes **6** quirks **7** details, winding **11** particulars

INSANE: **3** mad **4** daft, loco, nuts **5** batty, crazy, daffy, loony, manic, wacky **6** crazed, cuckoo, maniac, screwy **7** bizarre, lunatic, touched **8** demented, deranged, frenetic, paranoid **9** delirious, eccentric, psychotic **10** immoderate, irrational, unbalanced **14** psychopathetic

INSANITARY: **5** dirty **6** filthy **9** unhealthy **10** unhygienic **12** contaminated, unsterilized

INSANITY: **5** folly, mania **6** lunacy **7** madness **8** delirium, dementia, hysteria **9** psychosis **10** aberration **11** derangement, foolishness

INSATIABLE: **6** greedy **7** wanting **8** desiring **9** voracious **10** gluttonous **11** unsatisfied **12** unquenchable **13** unfulfillable

INSCRIBE: **4** etch, list, sign **5** brand, carve, print, stamp, write **6** chisel, enroll, indite, scroll **7** engrave, impress, imprint **8** dedicate

INSCRIPTION: **5** label, motto, title **6** legend **7** caption, epigram, epitaph, writing **9** autograph, signature **10** dedication

INSCRUTABLE: **5** blank **6** arcane, hidden, secret **8** abstruse, baffling **10** cabalistic, mysterious **12** impenetrable, inexplicable, unfathomable **13** inexplainable

INSECT: **3** ant, bee, bug, fly **4** flea, gnat, mite, moth, tick, wasp **5** aphid, louse, midge **6** beetle, cicada, earwig, hornet, mantis, spider, weevil **7** cricket, termite **8**

mosquito **9** arthropod, bumblebee, centipede **12** yellowjacket
larva: **5** naiad, nymph
part: **3** eye **6** cercus, chitin, feeler, tergum, thorax **7** abdomen, aculeus, antenna, ocellus **8** forewing, hindwing, mandible, spiracle **9** proboscis **10** ovipositor

INSECURE: **5** frail, loose, risky, shaky **6** afraid, flimsy, unsafe, unsure **7** rickety **8** perilous, unstable **9** dangerous, hazardous, uncertain **10** precarious, vulnerable **11** unconfident, unprotected **12** apprehensive

INSEMINATE: **3** sow **4** seed **7** implant **9** fertilize **10** impregnate, promulgate

INSENSATE: **4** dull **6** brutal **7** fatuous, foolish, witless **9** inanimate, senseless, unfeeling **10** insensible **11** unconscious

INSENSIBILITY: **4** coma **6** apathy, torpor, trance **8** dullness, lethargy **9** analgesia **10** inactivity **12** indifference

INSENSIBLE: **4** cold, numb **7** unaware **8** obdurate **9** inanimate, insensate, oblivious, unfeeling, unmindful **11** indifferent, unconscious **13** imperceptible, inappreciable **14** unintelligible

INSENSITIVE: **4** cold, numb **5** blase, crass **7** callous **8** deadened, hardened **10** impervious **11** indifferent, unconcerned **12** anesthetized, unresponsive

INSEPARABLE: **6** united **7** unified **8** attached, entwined **9** connected **11** indivisible

INSERT: **5** embed, enter, foist, imbed, inlay, inset **6** infuse **7** implant **9** introduce **11** intercalate, interpolate

INSIDE: **5** inner **6** lining, middle **7** indoors, innards, private **8** interior **9** intrinsic **10** intramural, surrounded **12** confidential

INSIDE OUT: **8** inverted, reversed **9** backwards

INSIDIOUS: **4** deep, foxy **5** snide **6** artful, sneaky, tricky **7** cunning, devious, harmful **8** alluring, guileful **9** concealed, deceitful **10** fraudulent **11** treacherous, underhanded

INSIGHT: **6** acumen, vision, wisdom **9** awareness, intuition **10** perception **11** discernment, observation, penetration **13** understanding

INSIGNIA: **4** mark **5** badge, crest, medal **6** emblem, stripe, symbol **10** decoration

INSIGNIFICANT: **4** puny **5** dinky, minor, petty, small **6** little, paltry **7** trivial **8** inferior, trifling **9** minuscule **10** immaterial, irrelevant **11** meaningless, unimportant **12** nonessential **13** unsubstantial

INSINCERE: **5** false, phony **6** hollow **7** feigned **8** guileful **9** deceitful, dishonest **10** backhanded, untruthful **12** hypocritical

INSINUATE: **4** hint **5** foist, imply **6** allude, infuse, insert **7** implant, suggest **8** indicate, intimate **9** introduce, penetrate

INSIPID: **3** dry **4** arid, blah, dead, dull, flat, tame **5** banal, bland, prosy, stale **6** boring, jejune **7** mundane, prosaic **8** lifeless, ordinary **9** pointless, tasteless **10** lackluster, monotonous, spiritless **11** commonplace **12** unappetizing **13** uninteresting

INSIST: **5** claim, press **6** assert, demand, expect **7** contend, require **8** maintain

INSISTENT: **4** firm **6** dogged **8** emphatic, forceful, resolute **9** assertive, incessant **10** unyielding

INSOLENCE: **4** gall **5** nerve **6** insult **7** hauteur **8** audacity, boldness, contempt **9** arrogance, impudence **10** brazenness, disrespect, effrontery, incivility **11** haughtiness, presumption

INSOLENT: **4** bold, rude **5** sassy, saucy **6** arrant, brazen **7** abusive, defiant **8** arrogant, impolite, impudent **9** audacious **10** ungracious, unmannerly **11** overbearing **12** contemptuous

INSOLUBLE: **8** baffling **10** mysterious, unresolved **12** inexplicable **13** unexplainable

INSOLVENT: **5** broke **6** busted, ruined **8** bankrupt **9** penniless **10** foreclosed **12** impoverished

INSOMNIA: **7** ahypnia **8** agrypnia **10** anhypnosis **11** wakefulness **12** restlessness **13** indisposition, sleeplessness

INSOUCIANT: **6** casual **8** carefree, heedless **9** easygoing **10** nonchalant, untroubled **11** indifferent, unconcerned **12** lighthearted

INSPECT: **4** scan, view **5** audit, check, probe, scout, study **6** survey **7** canvass, examine, observe **9** supervise **10** scrutinize **11** investigate

INSPECTION: **5** frisk **6** parade, review **7** checkup **9** appraisal **11** examination **12** surveillance **13** investigation

INSPIRATION: **4** idea, spur **5** flash, spark **6** animus, genius, vision **7** impulse, thought **8** afflatus, stimulus **9** incentive **10** brainstorm, creativity, motivation, revelation

INSPIRE: **4** fire, move, stir **5** cause, exalt, touch **6** affect, arouse, excite, prompt **7** animate, enliven, provoke **8** inspirit, motivate **9** encourage, galvanize, influence, stimulate **10** invigorate

INSTABILITY: **8** wavering **9** imbalance, shakiness **10** insecurity, volatility **11** fluctuation, inconstancy, uncertainty **12** unsteadiness **13** changeability **16** unpredictability

INSTALL: **3** lay **4** seat **5** place **6** induct, invest **7** furnish, instate **8** initiate, position **9** establish **10** inaugurate

INSTALLMENT: **4** part **7** chapter, episode, payment, section

INSTANCE: **4** case, show, suit, time **5** proof, refer **6** detail **7** example, request **8** occasion, specimen **9** exemplify, precedent **10** occurrence, suggestion **12** illustration

INSTANT: **4** fast, wink **5** flash, jiffy, quick, rapid, swift, trice **6** breath, direct, minute, moment, second, speedy, urgent **8** pressing **9** immediate, precooked

INSTANTANEOUS: **4** fast **5** quick, rapid, swift **6** direct, speedy **9** immediate

INSTANTLY: **3** now **6** pronto **8** directly, urgently **11** immediately

INSTEAD: **6** in lieu, rather **10** equivalent, preferably, substitute **13** alternatively

INSTIGATE: **4** abet, goad, move, plot, prod, push, spur, urge **6** excite, foment, incite, needle, prompt **7** provoke **8** initiate, motivate **9** encourage, influence, stimulate

INSTILL: **4** pour **5** imbue, infix **6** impart, infuse, insert **7** implant, impress **8** engender **9** inculcate, introduce

INSTINCT: **4** gift, idea, urge **5** hunch, knack, sense **7** feeling **8** aptitude, tendency **9** intuition

INSTINCTIVE: **6** inborn, inbred, innate **7** natural **8** inherent, visceral

9 automatic, ingrained 10 congenital, unacquired 11 involuntary, spontaneous

INSTITUTE: 4 rite, rule 5 begin, edict, enact, found 6 custom, launch, ordain 8 organize 9 establish, originate, tradition 10 inaugurate

INSTITUTION: 6 asylum, clinic, school, system 7 academy, college, fixture 8 business, hospital, seminary 10 foundation, university 12 conservatory

INSTRUCT: 4 lead, show, tell 5 brief, coach, drill, guide, teach, train, tutor 6 advise, direct, inform 7 apprise, command, counsel, educate 9 enlighten 10 discipline 12 indoctrinate

INSTRUCTION: 6 advice, lesson, method, recipe 7 formula 8 teaching, training, tutelage 9 education, schooling 10 directions 11 edification

INSTRUCTOR: 4 guru 5 coach, guide, tutor 6 mentor 7 teacher, trainer 8 lecturer 9 professor

INSTRUMENT: 6 abacus, octant, sector 7 sextant 8 calipers, computer, odometer 9 altimeter, atmometer, baroscope, cryometer, manometer, optometer, pedometer, pyrometer, salimeter, slide rule 10 almucantar, anemometer, bathometer, calculator, clinometer, cyclometer, densimeter, gravimeter, hydrometer, hygrometer, photometer, planimeter, protractor, tachometer, tachymeter, variometer, voltameter 11 actinometer, calorimeter, chronometer, pluviometer, polarimeter, seismograph, spherometer, tensiometer, velocimeter 12 electrometer, electroscope, magnetometer, spectrometer 13 Geiger counter, saccharometer

INSTRUMENTAL: 5 vital 6 useful 7 crucial, helpful 9 assisting, conducive, essential 11 influential 12 contributory

INSTRUMENTALITY: 5 agent, force, means 6 agency 7 channel, vehicle

INSUBORDINATE: 6 unruly 7 defiant, riotous 8 factious, mutinous 9 fractious, insurgent, seditious 10 rebellious, refractory, unyielding 11 disobedient, dissentious 12 recalcitrant, ungovernable

INSUBSTANTIAL: 4 airy, fine, weak 5 frail, small 6 flimsy 7 fragile 8 delicate 9 imaginary 10 immaterial, intangible

INSUFFERABLE: 7 hateful, painful 8 dreadful 9 agonizing 10 unbearable 11 intolerable, unendurable 12 excruciating

INSUFFICIENT: 5 short 6 meager, scanty, scarce, sparse 7 drained, lacking, wanting 9 deficient 10 inadequate, incomplete

INSULAR: 6 biased, narrow 7 bigoted 8 confined, isolated, secluded 10 prejudiced, provincial, restricted

INSULATE: 4 tape 5 cover 6 enisle, shield 7 isolate, protect 9 segregate, sequester

INSULT: 4 mock, slap, slur, snub 5 abuse, roast, scorn, shame, taunt, tease 6 deride, malign, offend, revile 7 affront, degrade, outrage, slander 8 belittle, disgrace, ridicule 9 humiliate 10 derogatory

INSURANCE: 8 coverage, security, warranty 9 assurance, indemnity, safeguard 10 protection

INSURE: 5 cover, guard 9 guarantee 10 underwrite

INSURGENT: 5 rebel 7 radical 8 mutineer, mutinous, resister, revolter **9** dissident, revolting **10** rebellious **13** insubordinate, revolutionary

INSURMOUNTABLE: **8** hopeless **10** impassable, impossible, invincible **11** insuperable **12** overwhelming

INSURRECTION: **4** coup, riot **6** mutiny, revolt **8** uprising **9** rebellion **10** revolution

INTACT: **5** sound, whole **8** complete, together, unbroken, unharmed, unmarred **9** undamaged, undefiled, uninjured, unscathed **10** unimpaired

INTANGIBLE: **5** vague **6** unreal **8** abstract, ethereal **10** immaterial, impalpable, indefinite, unapparent **13** unsubstantial

INTEGER: **5** digit **6** figure, number **11** whole number
types: **8** negative, positive

INTEGRAL: **4** full **5** basic, whole **6** entire **8** complete, finished **9** component, essential, necessary **11** constituent, fundamental **13** indispensable

INTEGRATE: **3** mix **4** join, link, mesh **5** blend, merge, unite **7** combine **8** organize **9** harmonize **10** coordinate **11** desegregate

INTEGRITY: **5** honor **6** candor, virtue **7** decency, honesty, probity **9** character, wholeness

INTEGUMENT: **4** aril, coat, hide, pelt, skin **8** covering, envelope

INTELLECT: **3** wit **4** mind **5** brain **6** acumen, genius, smarts **7** thinker **9** mentality **12** intelligence **13** understanding

INTELLECTUAL: **6** brainy, genius, mental **7** egghead, scholar **8** cerebral, highbrow, literati, studious

INTELLIGENCE: **4** news, word **6** acumen, ntoice, report, smarts, wisdom **8** aptitude, learning **10** brainpower, brilliance **11** information **13** understanding

INTELLIGENT: **4** wise **5** acute, alert, quick, smart **6** astute, bright **7** logical **8** sensible **9** brilliant, cognizant, ingenious **11** exceptional

INTELLIGIBLE: **5** clear, lucid, plain **8** apparent, definite, distinct **11** perspicuous **12** unmistakable

INTEMPERATE: **6** severe **7** violent **9** excessive, inclement **10** immoderate **11** drunkenness, extravagant **12** unrestrained

INTEND: **3** aim **4** mean, plan **6** design, expect, strive **7** attempt, propose, signify **8** dedicate **9** determine **11** contemplate

INTENDED: **5** meant **6** fiance **7** fiancee **8** proposed **10** calculated, deliberate

INTENSE: **4** deep, hard, keen **5** acute, vivid **6** ardent, fierce, severe, strong **7** burning, earnest, extreme, fervent, violent, zealous **8** powerful, profound, strained, vehement **9** consuming, excessive **10** blistering, passionate

INTENSIFY: **5** boost, exalt, mount **6** deepen **7** bolster, enhance, magnify, quicken, sharpen **8** escalate, heighten, increase **9** aggravate **10** accentuate, strengthen

INTENSITY: **4** fire, zeal **5** depth, force, power, vigor **6** energy, fervor **7** emotion, passion **8** strength **13** concentration

INTENT: **3** aim **4** bent, firm, rapt, will **5** eager, fixed, tense **6** design **7** decided, meaning, purpose, riveted **8** absorbed, diligent, resolute, watchful **9** engrossed, steadfast **10** determined **11** industrious, preoccupied

INTENTION: **3** aim, end **4** goal, hope, plan **5** drift, point **6** animus, motive, object **7** purpose **8** struggle **9** objective **11** designation

INTENTIONAL: **5** meant **7** planned, willing **9** voluntary **10** calculated, deliberate **12** premeditated

INTER: **4** bury **5** inurn, plant **6** entomb, inhume

INTERACT: **4** join, mesh **5** unite **9** cooperate, interface **10** coordinate **11** communicate

INTERBREED: **3** mix **5** cross **9** hybridize

INTERCEDE: **7** mediate **9** arbitrate, interpose, intervene, negotiate

INTERCEPT: **4** grab, stop, take **5** block, catch, seize **6** ambush, hijack **7** deflect **9** interrupt

INTERCHANGE: **4** swap **5** trade **6** barter, switch **7** commute, convert, network **8** exchange, junction **9** alternate **10** substitute, transposal **11** reciprocate

INTERCHANGEABLE: **10** compatible, equivalent, reversible, synonymous **11** convertible **12** transposable

INTERCOURSE: **6** coitus **7** contact **8** business, commerce, dealings **9** communion **10** connection, copulation, networking **12** conversation **13** communication

INTERDICT: **3** ban **4** halt, stop, veto **5** taboo **6** forbid, outlaw **7** inhibit, prevent **8** prohibit **9** proscribe

INTEREST: **4** good, grab, part **5** hobby, share, stake **6** appeal, behalf, credit, excite, points **7** benefit, concern, passion, pursuit, welfare **8** earnings, sympathy **9** advantage, curiosity, fascinate, influence **10** attraction, enthusiasm, investment, recreation

INTERESTED: **4** rapt **5** drawn, lured, taken **6** hooked **8** absorbed, involved **9** attentive, committed

INTERESTING: **10** compelling, enchanting, intriguing **11** captivating, stimulating **12** entertaining

INTERFERE: **4** foil **5** block, clash **6** hamper, hinder, impede, meddle, tamper **7** disturb, intrude **8** conflict, obstruct, sabotage **9** frustrate, intervene

INTERIM: **5** break, pause, spell **6** acting, hiatus **8** breather, interval, meantime **9** interlude, makeshift, temporary **10** pro tempore

INTERIOR: **4** core **5** inner, midst **6** center, inland, inside, within **8** domestic **9** heartland

INTERJECT: **6** insert **7** include **9** interpose, interrupt, introduce

INTERJECTION: **3** boo, hey, huh, rah, ugh, wow **4** ahem, alas, amen, egad, oops, ouch, phew, pooh, psst **5** golly, hello, yipes **6** cheers, hooray, hurrah, phooey, shucks **7** jeepers, whoopee **11** exclamation

INTERLACE: **3** mix **4** knit **5** braid, twine, weave **7** entwine **9** alternate **10** intertwine, interweave

INTERLOPER: **7** meddler **8** busybody, intruder **10** trespasser

INTERLUDE: **4** rest **5** break, farce, pause **6** hiatus, recess **7** episode, interim, respite **8** breather, interval **12** intermission

INTERMEDIARY: **5** agent **6** broker, medium, umpire **7** channel, referee **8** delegate, mediator **10** ambassador, arbitrator, negotiator

INTERMEDIATE: **4** fair, mean **6** common, median, middle **7** average, between, halfway **8** moderate **11** intervening

INTERMINABLE: **7** endless, eternal **8** constant, infinite, timeless **9** boundless, ceaseless, incessant, perpetual, unlimited **10** continuous **11** everlasting

INTERMINGLE: **5** blend **7** network **8** intermix **9** associate, socialize

INTERMISSION: **4** rest, stop, wait **5** break, pause **6** hiatus, recess **7** interim, respite **8** interval **9** cessation **10** suspension

INTERMITTENT: **6** broken, fitful **8** cyclical, episodic, hesitant, on and off, periodic, rhythmic, sporadic **9** irregular, recurrent **10** occasional **11** alternating

INTERN: **6** doctor, immure **7** student, trainee **8** resident **10** apprentice

INTERNAL: **4** home **5** inner **6** inward, within **8** domestic, enclosed, inherent **9** intrinsic **11** centralized

INTERNATIONAL: **6** global **7** worldly **9** universal, worldwide **12** cosmopolitan

INTERPOLATE: **3** add **5** alter, foist **6** change, inject, insert **8** estimate **9** introduce **11** intercalate

INTERPOSE: **6** insert **7** mediate **8** moderate **9** arbitrate, intercede, interfere, interject, intervene, introduce, negotiate

INTERPRET: **6** decode, define, render **7** clarify, explain, expound, unravel **8** construe, decipher, describe **9** explicate, translate **10** commentate, paraphrase, understand

INTERPRETATION: **6** intent **7** meaning, version **8** analysis, exegesis **11** explanation, translation **13** understanding

INTERROGATE: **3** ask **4** pump **5** grill, query **7** examine, inquire **8** question **11** investigate **16** cross-examination

INTERROGATION: **5** probe **7** inquest **9** catechism **11** inquisition

INTERRUPT: **4** halt, stop **5** break, cease, check, stall, upset **6** arrest, bother, hinder, inject, thwart **7** disturb, suspend **9** interfere **11** discontinue

INTERRUPTION: **3** gap **5** delay, pause **6** hiatus, lacuna **9** cessation, intrusion **11** disturbance **12** interference, intermission

INTERSECT: **3** cut **4** meet **5** cross **6** divide **8** converge, separate **10** crisscross

INTERSECTION: **6** corner **8** junction **10** crossroads **11** decussation

INTERSPERSE: **6** pepper **7** bestrew, scatter **10** distribute

INTERSTICE: **4** hole, slit **5** chink, crack, space **6** cranny **7** crevice, opening, orifice **8** aperture, interval

INTERTWINE: **4** lace, link **5** braid, twist **9** interlace **10** crisscross, interweave

INTERVAL: **3** gap **4** rest, span, term, time **5** break, delay, pause, phase, space **6** breach, hiatus, period, recess **7** interim, respite **9** interlude **12** intermission

INTERVENE: **6** settle **7** mediate **9** arbitrate, intercede, interpose, negotiate

INTERVIEW: **4** talk **7** consult, hearing, meeting **8** audience, audition, dialogue, question **10** conference **12** conversation **13** communication

INTERWEAVE: **3** mix **4** fuse, knit, link **5** blend, braid, plait, twist **6** mingle **9** interlace **10** intertwine

INTESTINAL FORTITUDE: **4** grit, guts **5** nerve, spunk **6** spirit **7** courage **8** backbone **9** endurance

INTESTINES: **4** guts **6** bowels **7** innards, insides, viscera **8** entrails

IN THE AIR: **5** above **7** skyward **8** overhead

IN THE BAG: **7** assured, certain **8** clinched, definite

IN THE BLACK: **8** thriving **10** profitable, prosperous, successful

IN THE DARK: **8** confused **9** uninformed

IN THE END: **7** finally **10** eventually **12** in conclusion **13** sooner or later

IN THE KNOW: **9** cognizant **13** knowledgeable

IN THE NEIGHBORHOOD: **5** close **6** almost, around **13** approximately

IN THE WAY: **7** nagging **10** bothersome, disturbing, meddlesome

INTIMACY: **6** warmth **8** fondness **9** affection, closeness **10** friendship, tenderness

INTIMATE: **4** cozy, dear, hint, snug **5** bosom, buddy, close, crony, imply **6** chummy, direct, inmost, loving, secret **7** devoted, private, signify, suggest, trusted **8** announce, familiar, friendly, informal, personal **9** associate, companion, confidant, insinuate **12** acquaintance, confidential

INTIMATION: **4** clue, hint **5** scent **6** notice **7** inkling, warning **8** innuendo, telltale **10** indication, suggestion **11** declaration **12** announcement

INTIMIDATE: **3** cow **4** ride **5** abash, bully, daunt, scare **6** badger, coerce, hector **7** overawe, swagger, terrify **8** bludgeon, browbeat, dominate, frighten, threaten **9** terrorize

INTO: **4** form **5** among, state, until **6** inside, toward **7** against, divisor **9** condition **10** interested

INTOLERABLE: **9** abhorrent, offensive **10** impossible, unbearable **12** excruciating, unacceptable

INTOLERANT: **6** biased, narrow **7** bigoted, hostile **8** dogmatic **9** fanatical, hidebound, impatient, outranged, sectarian **10** disdainful, prejudiced **12** contemptuous

INTONATION: **4** tone **5** chant, pitch, sound **6** accent, speech

INTONE: **4** cant, sing **5** croon, utter **6** recite **8** modulate **10** articulate

IN TOTO: **5** fully **7** totally **8** entirely **10** altogether, completely

INTOXICANT: **3** gin, rum **4** beer, dope, drug, wine **5** booze, vodka **6** liquor **7** alcohol, bourbon, whiskey **8** narcotic

INTOXICATED: **4** high **5** drunk, tipsy **6** bombed, buzzed, loaded, soused, stewed, stoned, tanked, wasted, zonked **7** excited, smashed **8** ecstatic, euphoric, polluted **9** plastered **10** inebriated

INTRACTABLE: **5** surly **6** mulish, ornery, unruly **7** willful **8** indocile, obdurate, perverse, stubborn **9** difficult, obstinate, pigheaded **10** headstrong, unyielding **11** disobedient, unteachable **12** cantankerous, intransigent, ungovernable, unmanageable

INTRANSIGENT: **7** willful **8** obdurate, stubborn **9** unmovable **10** inflexible, iron-willed, unyielding **12** pertinacious **14** uncompromising

INTREPID: **4** bold, game **5** brave, gutsy, nervy **6** daring, heroic **7** doughty, gallant **8** fearless, resolute, valorous, vigilant **9** bodacious, undaunted **10** courageous **11** adventurous

INTRICATE: **4** hard **6** daedal, knotty **7** arduous, complex, tangled **8** involved **9** difficult, elaborate, entangled **10** convoluted, perplexing **11** complicated **12** labyrinthine

INTRIGUE: **4** hook, plot **5** amour, angle, cabal, charm, rivet **6** absorb, affair, allure, appeal, brigue, design, excite, puzzle, scheme **7** liaison, romance **8** artifice, conspire, interest **9** fascinate, machinate **10** conspiracy **11** machination

INTRINSIC: **4** real, true **5** basic, inner **6** inborn, inbred, inmost, innate, native **7** genuine, natural **8** inherent **9** essential, ingrained, necessary **11** fundamental

INTRODUCE: **4** meet, show **5** begin, debut, enter, start, usher **6** broach, herald, induct, insert, launch, submit, unveil **7** pioneer, precede, preface, present, sponsor **8** announce, initiate, innovate **9** establish, insinuate, institute, originate, recommend **10** inaugurate **11** interpolate

INTRODUCTION: **4** lead **5** proem **6** primer **7** intrada, opening, preface, prelude **8** entrance, foreword, overture, preamble, prologue **9** beginning, inception, insertion **11** preparation **12** commencement

INTRODUCTORY: **5** first **7** initial **9** beginning, prefatory, preludial, prelusive **10** elementary **11** preliminary

INTROSPECTION: **10** meditation, reflection **12** self-analysis **13** contemplation

INTROVERT: **5** loner **6** inward **7** brooder **8** solitary

INTRUDE: **6** bother, impose, meddle **7** disturb, obtrude **8** encroach, infringe, overstep, trespass **9** interfere, interlope, interpose, interrupt

INTRUSIVE: **6** prying **7** curious **9** officious **10** aggressive, meddlesome **11** impertinent

INTUITION: **3** ESP **5** hunch, sense **7** feeling, insight **8** instinct **10** sixth sense **11** premonition, second sight

INTUITIVE: **6** innate **7** psychic **8** inherent **10** perceptive **11** clairvoyant, instinctive

INUNDATE: **5** drown, flood, swamp **6** deluge **7** overrun **8** overflow, submerge **9** overwhelm

INURE: **3** use **5** adapt, teach, train **6** harden, season **7** toughen **8** accustom **9** habituate **10** discipline **11** acclimatize, desensitize

IN USE: **11** functioning, operational

INVADE: **4** raid **5** seize, storm **6** assail, attack, infest **7** assault, intrude, overrun **8** encroach, infringe, trespass **9** interfere, penetrate

IN VAIN: **4** lost **8** futilely, hopeless **9** fruitless **13** purposelessly

INVALID: **4** null, void, weak **6** feeble, infirm, sickly **7** cripple, useless **9** unfounded, worthless **11** ineffective **12** unreasonable

INVALIDATE: **4** undo **5** annul, quash **6** cancel, negate, offset, revoke **7** abolish **9** undermine **10** neutralize

INVALUABLE: **4** rare **6** costly **8** precious **9** expensive, priceless **11** inestimable

INVARIABLE: **4** same **6** steady **7** uniform **8** constant **9** immutable, unfailing, unvarying **10** consistent, inflexible, unchanging, unwavering

INVARIABLY: **6** always **7** forever **9** regularly **11** continually, perpetually

INVASION: **5** foray **6** attach, influx, inroad **7** assault **9** incursion, intrusion, offensive, onslaught **12** encroachment

INVECTIVE: **5** venom **6** insult, tirade **7** abusive **8** berating, diatribe, reproach, scurrile **9** contumely **12** billingsgate, denunciatory, vituperation

INVEIGH: **4** rail **5** blame, scold **7** condemn, protest, upbraid **8** admonish, belittle, harangue, lambaste **9** castigate

INVEIGLE: **4** coax, lure **5** charm, decoy, tempt **6** allure, cajole, entice, entrap, seduce **7** wheedle **8** persuade **9** influence **10** manipulate

INVENT: **4** coin, form, vamp **5** frame **6** create, design, devise, evolve, patent **7** concoct, fashion, imagine, pioneer **8** conceive, contrive, discover, engineer, envision **9** fabricate, improvise, originate

INVENTION: **3** lie **6** gadget **7** fantasy, fiction **8** creation **9** discovery **10** brainchild, innovation **11** contraption

INVENTIVE: **5** adept **6** clever **7** fertile **8** creative, skillful **9** demiurgic, ingenious **10** innovative **11** resourceful

INVENTOR: **6** author, coiner **7** creator, pioneer **8** engineer **10** discoverer, originator

air conditioner: **7** Carrier
airplane: **6** Fokker, Wright
automobile: **6** Duryea
cosmetics: **16** Washington Carver
cotton gin: **7** Whitney
dynamite: **5** Nobel
electric motor: **9** Davenport
elevator: **4** Otis
film projector: **6** Edison
frozen food: **8** Birdseye
incandescent light: **6** Edison
internal combustion engine: **6** Lenoir **7** Daimler
microphone: **8** Berliner
motor: **5** Tesla
nylon: **6** DuPont
phonograph: **6** Edison
photo film: **7** Eastman
photocopying: **7** Carlson
polaroid: **4** Land
printing: **3** Hoe **9** Gutenberg
radio: **7** Marconi **8** de Forest **9** Armstrong
razor: **6** Schick
reactor: **5** Fermi
reaper: **9** McCormick
revolver: **4** Colt **9** Remington
rocket engine: **7** Goddard
rubber: **8** Goodyear
sewing machine: **4** Howe **6** Lester
steam engine: **4** Watt
steamboat: **5** Fitch **6** Fulton, Rumsey
telegraph signs: **5** Morse
telegraph: **7** Marconi
telephone: **4** Bell
television: **5** Baird **6** Nipkow **10** Farnsworth
typewriter: **7** Glidden
videotape: **5** Dolby **8** Ginsberg

INVENTORY: **4** list, roll **5** stock, store, tally **6** record, survey **7** backlog, itemize, reserve, summary **8** register **9** catalogue, checklist, stockpile **10** accounting, evaluation

INVERSE: **7** reverse **8** backward, contrary, inverted, opposite **10** reciprocal

INVERT: **4** flip, turn **5** alter **7** inverse, reverse **9** transpose **10** upside-down

INVEST: **4** gird, gown, lend, robe, wrap **5** adorn, cover, crown, dress, endow, endue, imbue **6** clothe, confer, ordain **7** besiege, envelop, install, instate **8** bankroll, surround

INVESTIGATE: **4** sift **5** audit, check, probe, study **6** search, survey **7** analyze, dissect, examine, explore, inquire, inspect **8** question, research **10** scrutinize

INVESTIGATION: **6** review **7** hearing, inquest, inquiry, legwork **8** analysis **10** inspection **11** inquisition

INVESTIGATOR: **5** agent **6** police, sleuth **7** auditor **8** examiner **9** detective, inspector **10** inquisitor, researcher

INVESTMENT: **4** loan **5** asset, money, share, stake, stock **7** backing, capital, venture **8** property **9** financing **11** speculation

INVETERATE: **5** fixed **6** innate, inured **7** chronic, settled **8** enduring, habitual, hardened **9** confirmed, ingrained **10** deep-rooted, deep-seated, entrenched **11** established

INVIDIOUS: **6** odious **7** envious, hateful, jealous, vicious **8** spiteful **9** repugnant **10** defamatory, detestable **14** discriminatory

INVIGORATE: **4** stir **5** pep up, renew **6** excite **7** animate, fortify, freshen, refresh **8** energize **9** stimulate **10** exhilarate, rejuvenate, revitalize, strengthen

INVIGORATING: **5** brisk **6** hearty, lively **7** bracing, charged, zestful **9** healthful, uplifting

INVINCIBLE: **8** powerful **10** unbeatable **12** invulnerable, undefeatable **14** indestructible

INVIOLABLE: **4** holy, pure **6** chaste, divine, sacred, stable **8** hallowed **11** consecrated, impregnable, unbreakable

INVISIBLE: **6** covert, hidden, unseen **9** disguised **10** indistinct, unapparent **12** unobservable **13** inconspicuous

INVITATION: **4** call, date, lure **5** offer **7** request **8** proposal **9** challenge **10** temptation **11** proposition

INVITE: **3** ask, bid **4** call, draw, urge **5** court **6** allure, entice, summon **7** attract, include, solicit, welcome

INVOCATION: **4** plea **6** litany, prayer, sermon **7** calling **9** conjuring **11** benediction, incantation

IN VOGUE: **7** a la mode, current, popular, stylish **11** fashionable

INVOICE: **4** bill, list **7** account, receipt **9** inventory, statement

INVOKE: **4** call, pray **6** appeal, muster **7** beseech, conjure, entreat, request, solicit **8** initiate, petition **10** supplicate

INVOLUNTARY: **6** forced, reflex **9** automatic, impulsive, reluctant, unwilling, unwitting **10** accidental, begrudging, compulsory, unintended **11** conditioned, instinctive, spontaneous, unconscious

INVOLVE: **4** hook, link, wrap **5** imply, snare, touch **6** commit, engage, entail, tangle **7** concern, embrace, embroil, include **8** comprise **9** associate, implicate **10** complicate, comprehend **11** incorporate

INVOLVED: **4** into **7** complex **8** absorbed, immersed **9** elaborate, entangled, intricate **10** interested **11** preoccupied **13** participating

INVULNERABLE: **6** immune **10** formidable, invincible, unbeatable **11** impregnable **14** indestructible

INWARD: **5** inner **6** inside **7** inbound, ingoing **8** familiar, interior, intimate **9** inflowing, intrinsic, spiritual **10** internally **11** penetrating

IN WHICH CASE: **4** then, when **9** whereupon

IODINE: **7** element **8** compound

ION: **4** atom
charge: **8** negative, positive
negative: **5** anion
positive: **6** cation, kation

IOTA: **3** bit **4** atom, whit **5** crumb, grain, shred, speck, trace **7** smidgen **8** particle

IOWA:
bird: **16** eastern goldfinch
capital: **9** Des Moines
cities: **8** Iowa City **9** Davenport, Sioux City **11** Cedar Rapids
explorer: **7** Jolliet **9** Marquette
features: **12** Effigy Mounds
flower: **8** wild rose
native: **5** Iowan
nickname: **12** Hawkeye State
tree: **3** oak
water: **11** Mississippi

IPSO FACTO: **11** by the fact of

IRAN:
capital: **6** Tehran
cities: **3** Qum **6** Abadan, Bandar, Kashan, Shiraz, Tabriz **7** Hamadan, Isfahan, Mashhad
deserts: **9** Dasht-e-lut **11** Dasht-e-Kavir
dynasty: **5** Qajar **6** Seljuk **7** Arsacid, Pahlavi, Safavid, Safawid **8** Parthian, Seleucid **9** Sassanian **10** Achaemenid
ethnic groups: **4** Arab, Kurd, Turk **5** Farsi
formerly: **6** Persia
gulfs: **4** Oman **7** Persian
islands: **5** Kharg, Qeshm **6** Abadan
lakes: **5** Niris, Tasht, Tuzlu, Urmia **6** Sistan **8** Nemekser
languages: **4** Luri, Zend **5** Farsi, Turki **6** Arabic **7** Baluchi, Kurdish, Persian **8** Armenian **11** Azerbaijani
monetary unit: **4** rial **5** dinar
mountains: **6** Alwand, Bazman, Elburz, Sahand, Taftan, Zagros **8** Damavand, Lalehzar, Poshtkuh **9** Hindu Kush
people: **3** Lur, Tat **4** Arab, Kurd, Turk **5** Kajar, Medes, Mukri, Tajik **6** Galchi, Gilani, Jewish, Shugni, Tadjik **7** Baluchi, Hadjemi, Persian **8** Armenian, Bactrian, Pasthian, Scythian **9** Bakhtiari
rivers: **4** Aras, Mand **5** Araks, Atrek, Karun, Safid **6** Gargan **7** Karkheh **9** Kizil Uzen
ruler titles: **3** mir **4** azam, khan, shah **5** mirza **6** atabeg, atabek, satrap, sultan
rulers: **5** Abbas, Cyrus **6** Darius, Xerxes **7** Jamshid, Jamshyd, Pahlavi **8** Khomeini **9** Giamschid **10** Artaxerxes
sea: **7** Arabian, Caspian

IRAQ:
capital: **7** Baghdad
cities: **5** Basra, Mosul
continent: **4** Asia
ethnic groups: **4** Arab, Kurd, Turk
features: **5** Eridu **7** Babylon, Nineveh **8** Poshtkuh **9** Al Hajaara, Ctesiphon **12** Syrian Desert
formerly: **9** Babylonia **11** Mesopotamia
languages: **6** Arabic **7** Kurdish **8** Armenian, Assyrian
monetary unit: **5** dinar
water: **6** Dalmaj, Tigris **7** Hindiya **8** Al Hammar **9** Euphrates **11** Persian Gulf, Shatt-al-Arab

IRASCIBLE: **5** angry, huffy, irate, surly, testy **6** crabby, cranky, ornery, snappy, touchy **7** fretful **8** choleric, snappish **9** impatient **10** passionate **11** belligerent, hot-tempered **12** cantankerous **13** quick-tempered

IRATE: **3** mad **5** angry, irked, livid, riled, wroth **6** fuming **7** annoyed, enraged, furious **8** incensed, provoked, wrathful **9** indignant, irascible

IRE: **4** fury, heat, rage **5** anger, annoy, wrath **8** vexation **9** infuriate, vehemence **10** conniption, exasperate, resentment

IRELAND:
accent: **6** brogue
also called: **4** Eire, Erin **5** Ierne **8** Hibernia **9** Innisfail **11** Emerald Isle
authors: **4** Shaw **5** Joyce, Swift, Wilde, Yeats **6** O'Casey **8** Sheridan
battle cry: **3** abu **4** aboo
bays: **4** Clew **5** Sligo **6** Bantry, Dingle, Galway, Mannin, Tralee **7** Donegal, Dundalk
capital: **6** Dublin
cities: **4** Cobh, Cork, Erne **5** Ennis, Sligo **6** Bangor, Galway, Tralee, Ulster **7** Belfast, Dundalk, Kildare **8** Kilkenny, Limerick **9** Killarney, Tipperary, Waterford **11** Londonderry **12** Dun Laoghaire
combining form: **7** hiberno
coronation stone: **7** Lia Fail
dance: **10** rinkafadda, rinncefada
fairy: **3** elf **4** shee **5** sidhe **7** banshee, banshie **10** leprechaun
features: **4** Tara **7** Blarney **9** Waterford
festival: **4** feis
flower: **8** shamrock
goddesses: **3** Lir **4** Badb, Bodb, Dana **6** Brigit **8** Morrigan
gods: **3** Ler **4** Ogma **5** Dagda **6** Aengus, Oengus **7** Angus Og
islands: **3** Man **4** Aran, Bear, Holy, Tory **5** Clare, Clear, Great, Magee **6** Achill, Dursey, Saltee, Whiddy **8** Inisheer **9** Inishmore
kings: **3** Rig **4** Bres, Finn **5** Ardri, Ronan **9** Brian Boru
lakes: **3** Doo, Key, Ree, Tay **4** Conn, Derg, Erne, Gara, Mask **5** ALlen, Barra, Capra, Leane, Lough, Neagh **6** Corrib **9** Killarney
language: **5** Irish **6** Gaelic **7** English
legislature: **4** Dail
militant group: **3** IRA
monetary unit: **5** penny, pound
nationalist group: **8** Sinn Fein
patron saint: **7** Patrick
people: **4** Erse, Gael, Pict **6** Celtic, Gaelic **9** Hibernian **11** Londonderry
rivers: **3** Lee, May **4** Bann, Deel, Erne, Nore, Suir **5** Avoca, Boyne, Clare, Feale, Foyle, Laune **6** Barrow, Liffey, Slaney **7** Shannon **10** Blackwater
seas: **5** Irish **8** Atlantic
terms of endearment: **5** aroon, aruin **7** acushla, asthore **9** avourneen, mavoureen
theatre: **5** Abbey
whiskey: **6** poteen **10** usquebaugh
writing system: **4** ogam **5** ogham

IRIDESCENT: **5** shiny **6** bright, pearly **8** colorful, lustrous, nacreous **9** prismatic **10** opalescent **13** kaleidoscopic **14** rainbow-colored

IRK: **3** bug, vex **4** rile **5** annoy, chafe, peeve, upset **6** abrade, bother, nettle, ruffle **7** disturb **8** irritate **9** aggravate

IRKSOME: **4** dull **6** boring **7** humdrum, painful, tedious **8** vexation **9** annoyance, weariness **10** unpleasant **11** troublesome

IRON: **4** hard **5** hardy, metal, press, steel, tough **6** ferric, fetter, robust, strong **7** element, harpoon **8** firmness, golf club, manacles, shackles, stubborn **9** appliance, handcuffs **10** inflexible, unyielding

IRON CITY: **10** Pittsburgh

IRONCLAD: **5** fixed, rigid **6** strict **7** warship **9** immutable, permanent **10** inflexible **11** irrefutable, unalterable

IRONHANDED: **4** firm **5** rigid **6** strict **8** despotic **10** controlled

IRONIC: **5** funny, witty **6** clever **7** cynical, mordant **8** contrary, sardonic **9** facetious, sarcastic, satirical **10** surprising

IRON OUT: **5** agree **6** settle **7** resolve **8** simplify **9** negotiate, reconcile **10** compromise, smooth over

IRONY: **5** humor, twist **6** satire **7** mockery, paradox, sarcasm

IROQUOIS:
formed: **10** Six Nations
tribe: **6** Cayuga, Mohawk, Oneida, Seneca **8** Onondaga **9** Tuscarora

IRRATIONAL: **5** crazy **6** absurd, insane, stupid, unwise **7** foolish **8** demented, mindless, unstable **9** fanatical, illogical, senseless, unfounded **10** ridiculous **12** preposterous, unreasonable

IRRECLAIMABLE: **4** lost **8** hopeless **9** abandoned **11** irreparable **12** incorrigible, irredeemable

IRRECONCILABLE: **7** opposed **10** discrepant **11** conflicting, incongruous **12** incompatible, inconsistent **14** uncompromising

IRREFUTABLE: **7** certain **8** ironclad, positive **10** conclusive, inarguable, undeniable **11** indubitable **13** unimpeachable

IRREGULAR: **3** odd **4** bent **6** broken, fitful, patchy, random, spotty, uneven, unlike **7** aimless, crooked, cursory, devious, erratic, unequal, wayward, weaving **8** aberrant, abnormal, atypical, lopsided, peculiar, sporadic, unstable, unsteady, variable **9** anomalous, desultory, eccentric, haphazard, imperfect, unsettled, zigzagged **10** changeable, elliptical, immoderate **12** asymmetrical, uncontrolled, unsystematic

IRREGULARITY: **4** flaw **7** anomaly **8** disorder **9** variation **10** arrhythmia, illegality, unevenness **12** imperfection, occasionally, periodically **13** helter-skelter **14** intermittently

IRRELEVANT: **7** foreign **9** pointless, unrelated **10** immaterial **11** impertinent, unconnected, unessential, unimportant **12** inapplicable, inconsequent **13** insignificant

IRREPARABLE: **6** broken, ruined **8** hopeless **9** destroyed, incurable **12** incorrigible, irredeemable, irreversible

IRREPRESSIBLE: **8** bubbling **9** ebullient, vivacious **12** effervescent, enthusiastic **13** uncontainable **14** uncontrollable

IRREPROACHABLE: **7** perfect **8** flawless, innocent, spotless **9** blameless, errorless, exemplary, faultless **10** immaculate, impeccable, inculpable **11** unblemished **13** unimpeachable

IRRESISTIBLE: **8** alluring, charming, powerful, stunning **9** seductive **10** compelling, enchanting **11** fascinating **12** spellbinding

IRRESOLUTE: **6** fickle, infirm, unsure **8** doubtful, hesitant, waffling, wavering **9** tentative, uncertain, undecided **10** indecisive, wishy-washy **11** fluctuating **12** undetermined

IRRESPONSIBLE: **7** foolish **8** carefree, careless, immature, reckless

10 unreliable 11 harum-scarum, thoughtless 12 undependable

IRREVERENT: **5** sassy **7** impious, ungodly **8** flippant, undevout **9** satirical **11** blasphemous **13** disrespectful

IRREVOCABLE: **4** firm **5** fated, final, fixed **8** constant **10** conclusive **11** intractable, unalterable **12** irreversible

IRRIGATE: **5** flood, water **7** moisten **8** inundate

IRRITABLE: **4** edgy **5** cross, fiery, moody, tense, testy **6** crabby, cranky, ornery, touchy **7** annoyed, fretful, grouchy, peevish **8** choleric **9** excitable, impatient **12** cantankerous, disagreeable

IRRITATE: **3** bug, irk, nag, rib **4** burn, fret, gall, goad, hurt, rile **5** anger, annoy, chafe, peeve, pique, sting, tease, upset **6** abrade, badger, bother, enrage, excite, harass, madden, needle, nettle, ruffle **7** disturb, incense, inflame, provoke **8** acerbate **9** aggravate, stimulate **10** exacerbate, exasperate

IRRITATION: **4** itch, rash, sore **7** chafing **8** vexation **9** annoyance **10** discomfort

ISAAC:
brother: **7** Ishmael
father: **7** Abraham
in: **12** Old Testament
mother: **5** Sarah
offered as: **9** sacrifice
son: **4** Esau **5** Jacob
wife: **7** Rebekah

ISHMAEL:
brother: **5** Isaac
father: **7** Abraham
mother: **5** Hagar
son: **5** Massa **8** Nebaioth

ISHTAR:
goddess of: **3** war **4** love **9** fertility
lover: **6** Tammuz

ISIS:
father: **3** Geb
goddess of: **9** fertility
husband: **6** Osiris
mother: **3** Nut
origin: **8** Egyptian

ISLAM:
believer: **6** Moslem, Muslim
church: **6** masjid, mosque
founder: **7** Mahomet **8** Mohammed, Muhammad
god: **5** Allah
holy sites: **5** Kaaba, Mecca **6** Medina
leaders: **4** Imam **5** Mahdi **6** mullah **9** ayatollah
people: **4** cadi, emir **5** begum, ghazi, hafiz, hajji, hakim, mufti, ulema **6** moolvi, sharif, sherif **7** dervish, muezzin **8** calendar, marabout
scriptures: **4** adat **5** Koran, Qur'an, sheri **6** sharia, sheria **7** Alcoran
sects: **4** Sufi **5** Shiah, Sunni **6** Shiite **7** Ismaili, Sunnite, Wahhabi

ISLAND: **3** cay, key **4** isle **5** atoll, haven **6** refuge, skerry **7** enclave, isolate, retreat **9** sanctuary **11** archipelago

ISLE OF MAN:
animal: **7** Manx cat
capital: **7** Douglas
cities: **4** Peel **6** Ramsey **10** Castletown
features: **8** Snaefell
government: **7** Tynwald
language: **4** Manx **7** English

ISOLATE: **6** detach, island, remove **7** confine, seclude **8** insulate **9** segregate, sequester **10** disconnect, quarantine

ISOLATED: **5** alone, apart **6** hidden, lonely, random, remote **7** insular, private **8** solitary, sporadic **9** scattered, unrelated

ISRAEL:
capital: **9** Jerusalem
cities: **4** Acre **5** Eliat, Haifa, Holon, Jaffa **6** Bat-Yam **7** Tel Aviv **8**

Ramat Gan **9** Beersheba **11** Petach Tikva
continent: **4** Asia
ethnic groups: **4** Arab **6** Jewish
features: **5** Judea **6** Masada **7** Galilee, Jericho, Megiddo, Samarig **8** Nazareth, West Bank **9** Bethlehem, Gaza Strip **11** Negev Desert **12** Golan Heights
languages: **6** Arabic, Hebrew **7** Yiddish
monetary unit: **6** shekel
water: **6** Jordan **7** Dead Sea **12** Lake Tiberias

ISSUE: **4** copy, emit, stem **5** arise, brood, focus, point, topic **6** emerge, matter, result, spread, supply **7** concern, declare, deliver, edition, outcome, release **8** argument, children, printing, question **9** broadcast, offspring **10** distribute **11** controversy, descendants, publication

ISTANBUL:
capital of: **13** Ottoman empire **15** Byzantine empire
features: **10** Blue Mosque, Golden Horn **11** Hagia Sophia
formerly: **14** Constantinople
place: **6** Turkey

ISTHMUS: **4** neck **5** strip **6** strait **7** passage, portage
important: **4** Suez **6** Panama **7** Corinth

ITALY:
artists: **4** Reni, Tisi **5** Colle, Lippi **6** Crespi, Giotto, Pisano, Titian **7** Bologna, da Vinci, di Paolo, Raphael, Tiepolo **8** Angelico, Cagliari, Ghiberti, Raimondi **9** Donatello **10** Botticelli **12** Michelangelo
authors: **4** Cato, Livy, Ovid **5** Pliny **6** Cicero, Horace, Seneca, Virgil **7** Terence **8** Petrarch, St. Jerome **11** Machiavelli, St. Augustine **14** Dante Alighieri
capital: **4** Rome
cheeses: **6** romano **7** fontina, riccota **8** Bel paese, parmesan **10** gorgonzola
cities: **4** Bari, Pisa **5** Genoa, Milan, Parma, Siena **6** Ancona, Foggia, Modena, Naples, Venice **7** Bologna, Catania, Ferrara, Leghorn, Messina, Palermo, Perugia, Ravenna, Trieste **8** Brindisi, Cagliari, Florence
composers: **5** Verdi **7** Bellini, Puccini, Rossini, Vivaldi **8** Mascagni **9** Donizetti, Scarlatti **10** Monteverdi
dialects: **6** Tuscan **8** Sicilian
enclaves: **9** San Marino **11** Vatican City
features: **4** Pisa **5** Sighs **7** Pompeii, Riviera, Vatican **8** Pantheon, St. Peters **9** Appian Way, Catacombs, Colosseum **13** Sistine Chapel
food: **5** pasta, pizza **6** gelato, salami, scampi **7** gnocchi, lasagna, ravioli, spumoni, tortoni **8** frittata, linguine **9** antipasto, manicotti **10** minestrone
gentleman: **3** ser **6** signor **7** signore
greeting: **4** ciao
gulfs: **5** Gaeta, Genoa **6** Venice **7** Salerno, Taranto
heel region: **6** Apulia
house: **4** casa **6** casino
islands: **4** Edie, Elba **5** Capri, Egadi, Ponza **6** Giglio, Ischia, Istria, Linosa, Lipari, Salina, Sicily, Ustica **7** Aeolian, Trieste **8** Lampione, Sardinia **9** Stromboli
lady: **5** donna **7** signora **9** signorina
lakes: **4** Como, Nemi **5** Garda **6** Albano, Lesina, Lugano, Varano **7** Bolsena **8** Maggiore **9** Bracciano, Trasimeno
leader: **4** duce
monetary unit: **4** lira **9** centesimo
months: **4** mese **5** Marzo **6** Agosto, Aprile, Giugno, Luglio, Maggio **7** Gennaio, Ottobre **8** Dicembre, Febbraio, Novembre **9** Settembre
mountains: **3** Bue **4** Alps, Etna, Rosa **5** Blanc, Corno **6** Cimone, Varano **7** Miletto, Pollino, Vet-

tore **9** Apennines, Dolomites, Maritimes
opera house: **7** La Scala
patron saint: **7** Francis
people: **5** Latin, Oscan, Roman **6** Sabine, Tuscan **7** Italian **8** Etruscan, Venetian
pre-Roman nation: **7** Etruria
regions: **6** Apulia, Latium, Marche, Molise, Sicily, Umbria, Veneto **7** Abruzzi, Liguria, Tuscany **8** Calabria, Campania, Lombardy, Piedmont, Sardinia **10** Basilicata
rivers: **4** Adda, Agri, Arno, Liri, Nera, Reno, Sele, Taro **5** Adige, Oglio, Parma, Piave, Tiber **6** Aterno, Belice, Isonzo, Mincio, Panaro, Sangro, Tanaro, Ticino **7** Pescara, Rubicon, Secchia **8** Volturno
Rome's hills: **7** Caelian, Viminal **8** Aventine, Palatine, Quirinal **9** Esquiline **10** Capitoline
rulers: **6** Brutus, Caesar, Pompey, Seneca **7** Crassus, fontina, Lepidus **9** Mussolini **10** Mark Antony
ruling families: **4** Este **5** Amati, Cenci, Savoy **6** Borgia, Medici, Orsini, Sforza **7** Spinola **8** Visconti
scientists: **5** Fermi, Volta **7** Galileo, Galvani, Marconi
seas: **6** Ionian **8** Adriatic, Ligurian **13** Mediterranean
secret society: **5** Mafia **7** Camorra **9** Carbonari
toe region: **8** Calabria
volcano: **4** Etna **7** Vulcano **8** Vesuvius **9** Stromboli

ITCH: **4** burn, urge **6** desire, hunger, thirst **7** craving, longing **8** appetite, tingling, yearning **9** hankering, sensation **10** irritation, scratching

ITEM: **4** part **5** entry, point, story, thing, topic **6** aspect, clause, detail, matter, object **7** account, article, feature, product **9** commodity, component, paragraph **10** particular **12** conversation

ITEMIZE: **4** list **5** count, tally **6** number, record **7** catalog **8** document **9** enumerate, inventory

ITINERANT: **6** roving **7** migrant, nomadic, roaming, vagrant **8** traveler, vagabond **9** transient, wandering, wayfaring **10** ambulatory **11** peripatetic

ITINERARY: **4** plan, tour **5** route **6** course **7** account, outline **8** schedule **9** guidebook

IVANHOE:
author: **14** Sir Walter Scott
characters: **4** Tuck **5** Isaac **6** Cedric **7** Rebecca, Wilfred **8** Guilbert **9** Robin Hood **10** Lady Rowena **11** King Richard

IVORY COAST:
also called: **11** Cote d'Ivoire
capital: **7** Abidjan **12** Yamoussoukro
cities: **3** Man **5** Daloa **6** Bouake **8** San Pedro
continent: **6** Africa
ethnic groups: **4** Bete **5** Baule **6** Senufo **7** Malinke
features: **5** Nimba **9** Kossou dam **13** Mounts du Toura
languages: **3** Kru **4** Akan **6** French **7** Malinke, Voltaic
monetary unit: **5** franc
water: **7** Bandama **9** Sassandra **10** Vridi canal

IVORY TOWER: **5** lofty **6** dreamy **7** retreat **9** visionary **11** impractical, unrealistic

IVY LEAGUE: **4** Yale **5** Brown **7** Cornell, Harvard **8** Columbia **9** Dartmouth, Princeton **12** Pennsylvania

J

JAB: **3** hit **4** blow, poke, prod **5** price, punch, swing **6** pierce, strike, thrust

JABAL:
brother: **5** Jubal
father: **6** Lamech
mother: **4** Adah

JABBER: **4** blab, chat **5** prate **6** babble, drivel, gossip **7** chatter, palaver **8** nonsense **9** gibberish

JACK: **3** man, tar **4** card, lift **5** boost, brace, knave, money, raise **6** fellow, sailor **7** laborer, support

JACKANAPES: **3** ape **6** monkey **7** coxcomb **8** impudent **9** conceited **11** mischievous

JACKASS: **4** dolt, fool, jerk, mule **5** burro, dunce, idiot **6** donkey **9** blockhead

JACKET: **3** ski **4** coat, Eton, hide, pelt, skin **5** denim, parka, shell **6** blazer, bolero, casing, combat, dinner, dolman, folder, reefer, safari, tuxedo, wammus, wampus, woolly **7** doublet, envelop, peacoat, spencer **8** cardigan, chaqueta, covering, guernsey, wrapping **9** habergeon **11** Windbreaker

JACK-OF-ALL-TRADES: **6** tinker **8** factotum, handyman **11** pantologist

JACKPOT: **4** pool **5** award, kitty, prize **6** reward **7** bonanza **8** windfall

JACOB:
brother: **4** Esau
daughter: **5** Dinah
father: **5** Isaac
grandfather: **7** Abraham
mother: **7** Rebekah
new name: **6** Israel
son: **3** Dan, Gad **4** Levi **5** Asher, Judah **6** Joseph, Reuben, Simeon **7** Zebulun **8** Benjamin, Issachar, Naphtali
wife: **4** Leah **6** Rachel

JADE: **3** gem, nag **4** plug, slut, tire **5** hussy, jewel, tramp, weary, wench **6** harass **7** fatigue, jadeite, jezebel, mineral **8** nephrite **10** spiritless

JADED: **4** worn **5** blase, spent, tired **6** dulled **7** wearied, worn-out **8** satiated **9** exhausted **11** indifferent

JAGGED: **5** harsh, rough, sharp, spiny **6** barbed, nicked, ragged, spiked, uneven **7** cutting, notched, pointed, toothed **8** bristled, indented, serrated, tattered **9** irregular

JAI ALAI: **4** game **5** sport
ball: **6** pelota
court: **6** cancha **7** fronton
racket: **5** cesta

JAIL: **3** can, jug, pen **4** book, brig, cell, keep **5** clink, joint, pokey **6** arrest, cooler, lockup, prison **7** dungeon, slammer **8** bastille, hoosegow, imprison, sentence, stockade **9** calaboose **11** incarcerate, reformatory **12** penitentiary

JAILBIRD: **7** convict **8** prisoner

JAILER: **5** guard **6** keeper, warden **7** turnkey

JAM: **4** bind, cram, hole, pack, push, stop **5** cease, crowd, crush, jelly, pinch, press, stuff **6** corner, pickle, scrape **7** dilemma, squeeze, trouble **8** compress, preserve, quandary **9** marmalade **10** congestion **11** predicament

JAMAICA:
capital: **8** Kingston
cities: **8** St. Andrew **10** Montego Bay **11** Spanish Town
ethnic groups: **7** African, Chinese **9** Caucasian **10** East Indian
explorer: **8** Columbus
features: **9** Port Royal **13** Blue Mountains
languages: **6** Creole **7** English **8** Jamaican
location: **9** Caribbean
monetary unit: **6** dollar
water: **8** Atlantic

JAMES: **7** apostle
brother: **4** John
disciple of: **5** Jesus
father: **7** Zebedee **8** Alphaeus
mother: **4** Mary **6** Salome

JANGLE: **4** ring **5** chime, clang, noise **6** bicker, hubbub, racket, rattle, uproar **7** clatter, discord, quarrel **8** irritate **11** altercation, reverberate

JANITOR: **5** super **6** porter **7** doorman **9** caretaker, custodian **10** doorkeeper **14** cleaningperson

JAPAN:
aborigine: **4** Ainu
also called: **5** Nihon **6** Nippon
baron: **6** daimio, daimyo
battle cry: **6** banzai
bays: **3** Ise **4** Miku, Tosa, Yedo **5** Amort, Mutzu, Osaka, Tokyo **6** Atsumi, Suruga, Toyama, Wasaka **7** Uchiura **8** Ishikari **9** Kagoshima, Shimabara
Buddha: **5** Amida, Amita
Buddhist festival: **3** Bon
Buddhist sects: **3** Zen **4** Jodo, Shin
capital: **5** Tokyo
cities: **3** Ome, Usa **4** Kobe, Naha **5** Kyoto, Osaka **6** Nagoya, Sendai **7** Okayama, Sapporo **8** Kawasaki, Nagasaki, Yokohama **9** Hiroshima
clothing: **4** geta, mino **5** haori **6** kimono, mompei
dancing girl: **6** geisha
drama: **3** noh **6** kabuki
drink: **4** mate, sake, saki
dynasty: **5** Meiji, Taira **6** Yamato **8** Fujiwara, Minamoto
food: **3** ayu, tai, ume **4** ansu, fugu, fuji **7** sashimi, tempura **8** chirimen, sukiyaki, teriyaki
goddesses: **6** Benten **9** Amaterasu
gods: **4** Kami **5** Ebisu, Hotei **6** Benten **7** Daikoku, Jurojin **8** Bishamon **10** Fukorokuju
governor: **6** shogun, taikun, tycoon
island groups: **3** Oki **4** Goto **5** Bonin **6** Marcus, Ryukyu **7** Okinawa, Volcano
islands: **3** Iki, Izu, Oki, Tsu **4** Yaku **5** Hondo **6** Honshu, Kyushu, Tanega **7** Iwo Jima, Okinawa, Shikoku **8** Hokkaido
Japanese-American: **5** Issei, Kibei, Nisei **6** Sansei
lakes: **4** Biwa, Suwa, Toya **6** Towada **8** Chuzenji, Kutchawa, Shikotsu **10** Inawashiro

leaders: **5** Jimmu, Jingo **6** Tanaka **7** Akihito, Izanagi **8** Hirohito
martial arts: **4** judo **6** karate **7** jujitsu, jujutsu
measure: **3** boo, cho **4** hiro, koku **5** shaku, tsubo
monetary unit: **3** sen, yen
mountains: **3** Uso, Zao **4** Kuju **5** Hondo, Iwaki, Nikko **6** Ontake **7** Shirane **8** Fujiyama, Sakhalin **9** Kirishima
musical instruments: **4** fuye, koto **5** tarko **7** samisen, truyume
plant: **3** udo **5** kudzu
poem: **5** haiku, hokku, tanka **6** haikai
porcelain: **5** Hizen, Imari
religion: **6** Shinto, Tendai **8** Buddhism **9** Shintoism **12** Confucianism
rivers: **4** Kiso, Tone, Yalu **5** Iwaki, Shira **6** Sumida, Tashio **7** Shinano **8** Ishikari, Tonegawa
seas: **3** Suo **5** Japan **6** Harima, Inland, Kumano, Sagami **7** Okhotsk, Pacific **8** Tsushima **9** East China
ship: **4** maro, maru
suicide: **7** seppuku **8** hara-kari, hara-kiri, hari-kari, kamikaze
sword: **5** catan **6** cattan, katana **8** wacadash
tea girl: **6** mousme
title: **4** kami **6** shogun
trees: **4** kiri, kozo, sugi **5** akeki, kiaki, yeddo **6** hinoki, keyaki, urushi **7** camphor **8** akamatsu **10** shirakashi
vehicles: **7** ricksha **8** rickshaw **10** jinricksha, jinrikisha
volcano: **3** Aso **4** Fuji **5** Asama, Iwate **6** Daisen, On-take
warrior: **7** samurai
writing: **4** kana **8** hiragana, katakana

JAPE: **4** fool, jeer, jest, joke, mock, quip **5** prank, trick

JAR: **3** jug, urn, vat **4** bump, jolt, olla, rock, stun, vase **5** clash, crash, cruet, grate, quake, shake, shock **6** bottle, impact, jangle, rattle, shiver, tremor, vessel **7** agitate, clatter, discord, startle **8** conflict, unsettle **9** collision, container

JARGON: **4** bull, bunk, cant **5** argot, idiom, lingo, slang **6** babble, drivel, pidgin **7** baloney, dialect, hogwash, palaver **8** malarkey, nonsense, shoptalk **9** gibberish, poppycock **10** balderdash, vocabulary **11** jabberwocky **12** gobbledygook

JARRING: **4** rude **5** harsh, rough **7** grating **9** dissonant **11** incongruous

JASMINE: **4** vine **5** plant, shrub **6** flower **7** perfume

JASON:
father: **5** Aeson
followers: **9** Argonauts
mother: **8** Alcimede, Polymede
quest: **12** Golden Fleece
ship: **4** Argo
teacher: **6** Chiron **7** Cheiron
wife: **5** Medea

JAUNDICED: **6** biased, yellow **7** bigoted, envious, hostile, jealous, tainted **9** skeptical **10** prejudiced

JAUNT: **4** hike, ride, spin, trip **6** cruise, junket, outing, picnic, ramble, stroll, voyage **7** journey **9** excursion **10** expedition

JAUNTY: **4** airy **5** perky, showy **6** dapper, frisky, lively, spruce **7** playful **8** animated, carefree, debonair **9** sprightly, vivacious

JAVANESE:
animals: **3** beo **5** adjag, rasse, ratel **6** teledu **7** bantens **8** jelerang
instruments: **5** saron **6** bonang, gender **7** gambang, gamelan **8** gamelang
plants: **4** upas **5** cubeb, duhal, kapok, sawah **6** antiar, fuyang, jambul, lomboy **7** gondang, jambool, talisay

JAVELIN: **4** dart **5** lance, spear, sport **6** weapon **7** harpoon

JAW: **4** bone, chat, chop, jowl, talk, vise **5** prate, scold **6** babble, berate, jabber **7** chatter, maxilla **8** converse, mandible **9** criticize, yakety-yak

JAYHAWK STATE: **6** Kansas

JAZZ: **4** cool, scat **5** bebop, music, swing **6** modern **7** ragtime **8** nonsense **9** animation, dixieland **10** enthusiasm **11** progressive **13** improvisation, miscellaneous

JAZZY: **4** sexy **5** fancy **6** flashy, lively, snazzy **8** exciting

JEALOUS: **4** wary **6** bitter **7** envious **8** covetous, watchful **9** greeneyed, resentful **10** possessive, protective, suspicious **12** apprehensive

JEER: **4** gibe, hiss, hoot, jabe, mock, razz **5** fleer, flout, scoff, sneer, taunt, tease **6** deride, heckle **7** catcall **8** ridicule

JEHOVAH: **3** God **4** JHWH, YHWH **6** Adonai, Jahveh, Yahweh

JEJUNE: **4** arid, dull, flat **5** banal, bland, empty, inane, trite, vapid **6** barren, meager **7** insipid, sterile **8** childish, immature, juvenile **9** innocuous **10** unexciting

JELL: **4** clot **5** shape **6** harden **7** congeal, thicken **8** solidify **9** coagulate **11** crystallize, materialize

JELLYFISH: **5** sissy **6** coward, medusa **7** milksop **8** man of war, weakling **10** pantywaist **12** coelenterate, invertebrate

JEOPARDIZE: **4** risk **6** expose **7** imperil, venture **8** endanger **10** compromise

JEOPARDY: **4** risk **5** peril **6** chance, danger, hazard **7** trouble **9** liability

JERICHO:
city of: **9** Palestine
destroyed by: **6** Joshua

JERK: **3** ass, oaf, tic **4** dope, fool, jolt, yank **5** dunce, idiot, lurch, spasm, twist **6** jiggle, quiver, reflex, snatch, twitch **7** wriggle

JERKY: **4** beef, meat **5** silly **6** bouncy **7** charqui, fidgety, foolish **9** twitching **12** intermittent

JERRY-BUILT: **5** cheap, shaky, tacky **6** flimsy, sleazy **7** unsound **10** inadequate

JERSEY: **3** cow **5** shirt **6** jacket, tricot **7** sweater **10** undershirt

JERUSALEM:
also called: **4** Sion, Zion **5** Salem
capital of: **6** Israel
conquerors: **4** Omar **5** Titus **6** Pompey **7** Saladin **9** Alexander **10** Chosroes II **14** Nebuchadnezzar
features: **4** Omar, Zion **7** Old City **8** Bethesda **10** Gethsemane **11** Wailing Wall **13** Dome of the Rock, Holy Sepulchre
holy city of: **6** Jewish, Muslim **9** Christian

JESSE:
father: **4** Obed
grandfather: **4** Boaz
son: **5** David, Eliab **7** Shammah

JEST: **3** fun, gag, kid **4** fool, hoax, jape, joke, josh, quip, razz **5** clown, laugh, prank, roast, sport, tease, trick **6** banter, japery, trifle **8** drollery **9** wisecrack

JESTER: **4** fool, zany **5** clown, comic **7** buffoon **8** comedian, humorist, jokester **9** harlequin, prankster, trickster **11** merry-andrew

JESUS: **4** Lamb **6** Christ, Savior **7** Holy One, Messiah, Teacher **8** Redeemer, Son of God
birthplace: **9** Bethlehem
death place: **9** Jerusalem

mother: **4** Mary
stepfather: **6** Joseph

JET: **4** dark, flow, gush, rush **5** black, ebony, raven, spout, spray, spurt **6** nozzle, stream **8** aircraft, airplane

JETTISON: **4** dump, hurl, shed **5** eject, scrap **6** unload **7** abandon, discard **9** eliminate

JETTY: **4** dock, pier, slip **5** berth, black, ebony, groin, wharf **10** breakwater

JEW: **6** Essene, Hebrew, Judaic, Semite **7** Judaist **9** Israelite

JEWEL: **3** gem **4** dear **5** adorn, charm, pearl, prize, stone **6** winner **7** darling **8** ornament, precious **9** brilliant **10** birthstone **11** masterpiece

JEWELRY: **4** band, gems, gold, ring **5** beads, chain, crown, tiara **6** amulet, anklet, brooch, locket **7** bangles, costume, pendant **8** bracelet, diamonds, earrings, lavalier, necklace **10** bijouterie

JEZEBEL: **4** jade, slut **5** hussy, tramp **7** trollop **8** slattern, strumpet **10** prostitute
father: **7** Ethbaal
husband: **4** Ahab
killed: **6** Naboth
killer: **4** Jehu

JIB: **3** arm **4** balk, boom, sail, stop

JIBE: **4** mesh, tack **5** agree, match, shift, tally **6** square **7** conform **8** dovetail **9** harmonize

JIFFY: **4** wink **5** flash, hurry, shake, trice **6** minute, moment, second **7** instant

JIGGER: **4** boat, mast, sail, shot **5** glass **6** device, gadget, tackle **9** doohickey

JIGGLE: **4** jerk, rock **5** shake **6** bounce, fidget, wiggle **7** agitate

JIHAD: **3** war **6** strife **7** crusade, holy war **8** campaign, struggle

JILT: **4** drop, dump **5** leave **6** betray, desert **7** abandon, deceive, discard, forsake

JIMMY: **3** pry **4** open **5** force, lever **7** crowbar

JINGLE: **4** ring, song **5** chime, clank, ditty, noise, rhyme, sound, verse **7** chinkle, clatter **8** limerick

JINX: **3** hex **4** damn **5** curse, spell **6** voodoo, whammy **7** bewitch, evil eye, nemesis

JITTERS: **6** dither, shakes **7** anxiety, fidgety, shivers, willies **10** uneasiness **11** butterflies, nervousness **13** heebie-jeebies

JITTERY: **4** edgy **5** jumpy, tense **6** goosey, uneasy **7** nervous **8** restless

JIVE: **3** kid **4** bunk, jazz, talk **5** dance, music, swing **6** jargon **9** deceitful **11** nonsensical

JOB: **4** duty, post, task **5** chore, craft, grind, stint, trade **6** career, racket **7** mission, pursuit **8** function, position, vocation **10** assignment, employment, livelihood, occupation, profession **11** performance **14** responsibility

JOB:
daughter: **5** Kezia **6** Jemima
father: **8** Issachar

JOBBER: **6** dealer **10** wholesaler **12** middleperson

JOCASTA:
daughter: **6** Ismene **8** Antigone
husband: **5** Laius **7** Oedipus
kingdom: **6** Thebes
married: **7** Oedipus
son: **7** Oedipus **8** Eteocles **9** Polynices

JOCKEY: **5** cheat, rider, trick **6** direct, driver, outwit **7** beguile **8** maneuver **10** manipulate

JOCOSE: **5** funny, merry, witty **6** joking **7** jocular, playful **8** cheerful, humorous **10** frolicsome

JOCULAR: **4** airy **5** funny, happy, jolly, merry, silly, witty **6** blithe, elated, jocose, jocund, joking, jovial, joyous, lively **7** amusing, comical, festive, gleeful, jesting, playful, waggish **8** animated, cheerful, humorous, mirthful, sportive **9** facetious, vivacious **10** frolicsome, rollicking **12** entertaining

JOCUND: **5** jolly **6** blithe, elated, jocose **7** jocular **8** cheerful **9** sprightly **12** lighthearted

JOG: **3** run **4** pace, poke, prod, push, trot **5** nudge **6** canter, jiggle, jostle, prompt, remind **7** refresh **8** activate, exercise **9** stimulate

JOHN THE BAPTIST:
baptized: **5** Jesus
father: **9** Zacharias
killer: **5** Herod
mother: **9** Elizabeth

JOIN: **3** mix, tie, wed **4** ally, bind, bond, fuse, glue, knit, knot, link, mate, pool, team, weld, yoke **5** annex, blend, enter, marry, merge, piece, touch, unite **6** attach, border, bridge, cantle, cement, couple, engage, enlist, enroll, fasten, mingle, relate, solder, splice, stitch, suture **7** combine, connect, consort **8** coalesce **9** accompany, affiliate, associate, interlock, volunteer **10** amalgamate **11** consolidate, participate

JOINT: **3** hip **4** bend, butt, crux, dive, knee, seam **5** ankle, elbow, hinge, point, wrist **6** mutual, prison, shared, united **7** hangout, knuckle **8** combined, communal, coupling, dwelling, junction, shoulder **10** connection **11** cooperative **12** articulation

JOIST: **4** beam, stud **5** brace **7** support

JOKE: **3** fun, gag, kid, rib **4** fool, goof, hoax, jape, jest, josh, quip **5** antic, crack, farce, prank, sally, stunt, tease **6** banter, parody, satire **7** buffoon, lampoon **8** clowning, escapade **9** wisecrack, witticism

JOKER: **3** wag, wit **4** card **5** clown, cutup **6** jester, stooge **8** comedian, humorist **9** prankster

JOLLITY: **3** fun **4** glee **5** cheer, mirth, revel **6** frolic, gaiety **7** revelry, whoopee **8** hilarity **9** amusement, festivity, jocundity, joviality, merriment **11** merrymaking

JOLLY: **5** merry **6** bouncy, jocose, jovial, joyful **7** chipper, jocular, playful **8** cheerful, jubilant, laughing, splendid, sportive **9** convivial **10** delightful

JOLT: **3** jar, jog **4** blow, bump, rock **5** floor, knock, shake, shock **6** impact, jostle **7** setback, startle **8** surprise **9** collision **10** concussion

JONAH: **7** prophet
father: **7** Amittai
swallowed by: **5** whale **9** large fish

JORDAN:
capital: **5** Amman
cities: **5** Aqaba, Irbid, Zarqa
continent: **4** Asia
ethnic groups: **4** Arab
features: **5** Petra **6** Jerash **10** Rift valley
languages: **6** Arabic
monetary unit: **5** dinar
water: **6** Jordan **7** Dead Sea

JOSEPH:
brother: **3** Dan, Gad **4** Levi **5** Asher, Judah **6** Reuben, Simeon **7** Zebulun **8** Benjamin, Issachar, Naphtali
father: **5** Asaph, Jacob **10** Mattathias

mother: **6** Rachel
stepson: **5** Jesus
wife: **4** Mary **7** Asenath

JOSH: **3** kid, rib **4** jape, jest, jive, joke, razz **5** spoof, tease **6** banter, needle

JOSHUA:
father: **3** Nun
succeeded: **5** Moses

JOSTLE: **3** jar, jog, vie **4** bump, jolt, push **5** crowd, elbow, nudge, shake, shove **7** collide **8** bulldoze

JOT: **3** bit **4** atom, iota, whit **5** grain, minim, speck, write **6** record, tittle **7** smidgen **8** scribble

JOUNCE: **4** bump, jolt **5** shake, shock **6** bounce, impact **9** collision

JOURNAL: **5** diary, paper **6** annals, ledger, memoir, record **7** account, almanac, blotter, gazette, logbook, tabloid **8** magazine, yearbook **9** chronicle, newspaper, scrapbook **10** periodical **11** observation, publication

JOURNALIST: **6** editor, writer **8** reporter **9** columnist **10** newsperson **11** broadcaster, commentator **13** correspondent

JOURNEY: **4** hike, ride, roam, tour, trek, trip, wend **5** drive, jaunt, route **6** course, junket, safari, travel, voyage **7** circuit, odyssey, passage, sojourn **9** adventure, excursion, migration **10** expedition, pilgrimage

JOUST: **4** bout, duel, tilt **6** combat **7** contest **10** tournament

JOVIAL: **5** happy, jolly, merry **6** cheery, elated, genial, jocose, jocund, joyous **7** chipper, festive, jocular **8** humorous, jubilant, mirthful, sociable **9** convivial **10** delightful

JOWL: **3** jaw **5** cheek **6** dewlap, wattle **8** mandible

JOY: **4** glee **5** bliss, mirth **6** gaiety, solace **7** delight, ecstasy, elation, rapture **8** felicity, gladness, pleasure **9** amusement, beatitude, enjoyment, festivity, happiness **10** excitement, jubilation **12** cheerfulness, exhilaration, satisfaction

JOYCE, JAMES: **6** author
wrote: **6** Exiles **7** Ulysses **9** Dubliners **12** Chamber Music **13** Finnegans Wake

JOYLESS: **4** blue, glum **6** dismal, gloomy **7** doleful, forlorn, unhappy **8** funereal **9** cheerless, depressed, miserable, woebegone **10** melancholy

JOYOUS: **4** glad **5** happy, jolly, merry **6** blithe, joyful, upbeat **7** blessed, festive, gleeful, jocular, pleased **8** cheerful, ecstatic, jubilant, mirthful **9** delighted, wonderful **12** heartwarming

JUBILANT: **4** glad **5** happy, jolly **6** elated, joyful, joyous **7** excited, pleased **8** exultant, thrilled **9** rejoicing **10** triumphant **11** celebrating

JUDAH:
brothers: **4** Levi **6** Joseph, Reuben, Simeon
children: **4** Onan
father: **5** Jacob
head of: **9** Sanhedrin
mother: **4** Leah
wrote: **6** Mishna

JUDAISM, JEWISH:
ascetic: **6** Essene
bread: **5** echem, matzo **6** hallah, matzoh **7** challah, matzoth **8** afikomen
candelabrum: **7** menorah
ceremony: **8** habdalah **10** bar mitzvah, bat mitzvah
clothing: **5** shawl, talis **7** tallith
community: **6** aljama **8** kehillah
confession: **5** Alhet **7** Ashamnu
Day of Atonement: **9** Yom Kippur

devil: **6** Belial
diet: **7** kashrut
doctrine: **6** Mishna **7** Mishnah **8** Kodashim
Feast of Lights: **7** Hanukah **8** Chanukah, Hanukkah
holidays: **5** Pesah, Purim **6** Pesach, Succos, Sukkos, Yom Tov **7** Sukkoth **8** Chanukah, Hanukkah, Lagbomer, Shabouth **9** Tishahbab, Yom Kippur **11** Rosh Hashana **12** Simhath Torah
land: **4** Zion
laws: **4** Chok, Tora **5** Torah **6** Chukah, Talmud **7** Halacha, Halakah **8** Kashruth
months: **4** Adar, Elul, Iyar **5** Nisan, Sivan, Tebet **6** Beadar, Kislev, Shebat, Tammuz, Tishri **7** Heshvan
New Year: **11** Rosh Hashana
Old Testament: **11** Hagiographa
patriarchs: **5** Isaac, Jacob **7** Abraham
prayer book: **6** mahzor, siddur **7** machzor
prayers: **5** Alenu, Shema **7** Geullah
prophets: **4** Amos, Ezra **5** Elias, Hosea, Jonah, Micah, Nahum **6** Daniel, Elisha, Haggai **8** Habakkuk, Jeremiah **9** Zechariah
sabbath: **8** Saturday
scarf: **5** abnet
scripture: **5** Torah
sects: **6** Essene, Hassid
skullcap: **6** kippah **7** yamilke **8** yarmulke
toast: **8** mazel tov
women's group: **8** Hadassah

JUDAS ISCARIOT: **7** traitor **8** betrayer
betrayed: **5** Jesus
disciple of: **5** Jesus
replacement: **8** Matthias

JUDGE: **3** ref, try, ump **4** deem, find, rank, rate, rule **5** bench, court, gauge, honor, weigh **6** assess, critic, decide, expert, gather, review, settle, umpire **7** condemn, justice, referee, suppose **8** assessor, conclude, consider, critique, estimate, mediator, sentence **9** appraiser, arbitrate, criticize, determine **10** adjudicate, arbitrator, chancellor, magistrate **11** connoisseur **12** intermediary

JUDGMENT: **4** fate, view **5** award, sense, taste **6** decree, reason, ruling, wisdom **7** insight, opinion, summary, verdict **8** analysis, decision, prudence, sentence **9** appraisal, criticism **10** assessment, astuteness, conclusion, discretion, evaluation, punishment, shrewdness **11** common sense, sensibility

JUDGMENT DAY: **8** doomsday **13** end of the world **14** day of reckoning

JUDICIAL: **5** legal **6** lawful **8** critical, official **9** impartial **13** distinguished **14** constitutional

JUDICIARY: **5** bench, court

JUDICIOUS: **4** fair, just, wise **5** sound **7** careful, knowing, prudent **8** cautious, rational, sensible **9** equitable, sagacious **10** diplomatic, discerning, reasonable, thoughtful **11** calculating

JUG: **3** can, jar **4** ewer, jail, toby **5** crock **6** bottle, carafe, cooler, flagon, lockup, prison, vessel **7** canteen, growler, pitcher **9** calaboose, container

JUGGLE: **5** alter **6** change, modify **7** falsify, mislead, shuffle **8** disguise **10** manipulate, reorganize

JUICE: **3** oil, sap **4** fuel **5** cider, fluid, funds, money **6** gossip, liquid, liquor, nectar **7** alcohol, essence **8** gasoline, vitality **10** succulence **11** electricity

JUICY: **4** oozy, racy **5** moist, runny, spicy **8** dripping, exciting, luscious

9 saturated, succulent **10** intriguing **11** provocative, tantalizing

JUMBLE: **4** heap, mess **5** chaos, shake **6** medley, muddle **7** clutter, confuse, mixture, shuffle **8** disarray, disorder, mishmash, scramble **9** potpourri **10** assortment, hodgepodge

JUMBO: **4** huge **5** large **7** mammoth, titanic **8** colossal, enormous, gigantic **9** monstrous **11** elephantine

JUMP: **3** hop **4** dive, leap, rise, skip **5** boost, bound, caper, clear, evade, lunge, lurch, vault **6** ambush, bounce, charge, flinch, hurdle, hustle, plunge, spring, upturn **7** startle **8** escalate, increase **9** parachute, skyrocket

JUMPER: **4** frog, shot, sled, toad **5** dress, smock **6** jacket **8** kangaroo

JUMPY: **5** antsy, tense **6** uneasy **7** anxious, jittery, nervous, spooked, uptight **8** restless **9** excitable **10** frightened **12** apprehensive

JUNCTION: **4** seam **5** joint, union **7** conflux, contact, meeting **8** crossing, juncture **9** gathering, interface **10** connection, crossroads, transition **12** intersection

JUNCTURE: **4** pass, time **5** hinge, joint, point, union **6** choice, crisis, linkup, moment **7** instant **8** junction, position **9** condition, emergency **10** crossroads

JUNGLE: **3** zoo **4** bush, maze **6** forest, jumble **9** labyrinth **10** wilderness

JUNIOR: **5** class, grade **6** lesser, second **7** student, younger **8** namesake **11** subordinate

JUNIPER: **4** cade, tree **5** retem, savin, shrub **6** sabine **9** evergreen
genus: **9** Juniperus

JUNK: **4** boat, dope, dump, ship **5** scrap, trash, waste **6** debris, heroin, litter, refuse **7** clutter, discard, garbage, rubbish, salvage **8** jettison

JUNKET: **4** tour, trip **5** feast, jaunt, party **6** outing, picnic **7** banquet **9** excursion

JUNO:
brother: **7** Jupiter
goddess of: **8** Pantheon
husband: **7** Jupiter
queen of: **6** heaven
son: **4** Mars

JUNTA: **5** cabal **7** coterie, council, faction **8** tribunal **9** committee **10** government

JUPITER:
discoverer: **7** Galileo
features: **12** Great Red Spot
moons: **3** Pan **4** Hera, Leda **5** Hades **6** Europa, Hestia **7** Demeter **8** Adrastea, Amalthea, Callisto, Ganymede, Poseidon
place: **5** fifth

JURISDICTION: **3** law **4** area, beat, zone **5** field, power, reach, scope, venue **6** bounds, county, domain, parish **7** command, control, diocese **8** district, dominion, precinct, province **9** authority, bailiwick, territory

JURY: **5** panel, peers **6** judges **8** tribunal **9** committee, makeshift

JUST: **3** due **4** even, fair, firm, meet, only, true **5** exact, legal, right, solid, valid **6** almost, barely, decent, hardly, honest, merely, normal, purely, simply **7** correct, ethical, fitting, upright **8** accurate, deserved, narrowly, recently, suitable, unbiased **9** befitting, equitable, impartial, objective **10** legitimate **11** trustworthy, undistorted

JUSTICE: **4** code **5** court, judge, truth **6** equity, virtue **7** hearing, honesty **8** fairness **9** atonement **10** litigation, magistrate, reparation **13** righteousness

JUSTIFICATION: **5** proof **6** excuse, reason **7** apology, defense, grounds **9** rationale **10** redemption **11** exoneration, explanation, vindication

JUSTIFY: **6** defend, excuse **7** account, approve, explain, support, warrant **8** sanction, validate **9** authorize, exculpate, vindicate **10** legitimize **12** substantiate

JUT: **4** butt **5** bulge, jetty **6** beetle, extend **8** elongate, lengthen, overhang, protrude **10** projection

JUVENILE: **5** green, minor, young **6** callow, infant, tender, unripe **7** growing **8** childish, immature, youthful **9** pubescent **10** adolescent **11** undeveloped

JUXTAPOSITION: **7** contact **8** abutment, nearness, touching **9** adjacency, proximity

K

KAFKA, FRANZ: **6** author
wrote: **7** Amerika **8** The Trial **9** The Castle **11** The Judgment: **16** In the Penal Colony, The Metamorphosis

KAISER: **5** ruler, title **7** emperor, monarch

KALE: **4** cole **5** money, plant **7** cabbage, collard **8** colewort

KALEIDOSCOPIC: **5** vivid **6** motley **7** diverse, protean **8** colorful, variable **10** changeable **11** fluctuating

KANGAROO: **3** roo **5** bilby **7** bettong, wallaby **8** bettonga, forester **9** marsupial
female: **3** doe, gin, roo
male: **4** buck
pouch: **9** marsupium
young: **4** joey

KANSAS:
bird: **17** Western meadowlark
capital: **6** Topeka
cities: **7** Wichita **10** Kansas City **12** Overland Park
explorer: **7** La Salle **8** Coronado
features: **9** Dodge City **11** Leavenworth, Pony Express
flower: **9** sunflower
native: **6** Kansan
nickname: **14** Sunflower State
tree: **10** cottonwood
water: **3** Kaw **5** Osage **6** Kansas, Saline **8** Arkansas, Cimarron

KAPUT: **6** broken, ruined **7** wrecked **9** destroyed **13** incapacitated

KARATE: **5** sport **10** martial art **11** self-defense
origin: **5** Japan

KARMA: **4** aura, fate **5** power **6** kismet **7** destiny, feeling **10** atmosphere, vibrations

KASHA: **4** mush **5** grain **6** groats **9** buckwheat

KAZAKHSTAN:
capital: **7** Alma-Ata
cities: **9** Karaganda **13** Petropavlovsk

KEATS, JOHN: **4** poet
wrote: **5** Lamia **8** Endymion, Isabella, To Autumn **15** The Eve of St. Agnes **16** Ode on a Grecian Urn

KEEL: **4** boat, fall, ship **5** barge, slump, upset **6** topple **7** capsize

KEEL OVER: **4** fall **5** faint, swoon **7** capsize **8** collapse, overturn

KEEN: **4** avid, fond **5** acute, alert, awake, boned, eager, sharp, vivid **6** ardent, astute, bewail, clever, fierce, severe, shrewd, strong **7** cunning, devoted, fervent, intense, pungent, zealous **9** sensitive, trenchant **10** interested, perceptive **11** intelligent, penetrating **12** enthusiastic

KEEP: **4** have, hold, tend **5** amass, block, board, delay, deter, guard, lodge, place, stock, store **6** arrest, detain, endure, manage **7** confine, contain, control, fulfill, observe, possess, prevent, reserve, shackle **8** maintain, obstruct, preserve, restrain, withhold **9** celebrate, safeguard

KEEP AT: **5** grind **6** endure, finish **7** persist **8** continue **9** persevere

KEEP BACK: **4** hold, save **5** check, delay **6** detain, forbid **7** reserve **8** postpone, withhold

KEEP COMPANY: **4** date **7** consort **9** associate **10** fraternize

KEEPER: **5** guard **6** escort, sentry, warden **7** curator, janitor, manager **8** guardian, sentinel **9** attendant, caretaker, chaperone, constable, custodian

KEEP OUT: **3** bar **5** evade **6** detain, reject **8** restrict **9** blacklist

KEEPSAKE: **5** relic, token **6** trophy **7** memento **8** reminder, souvenir **10** knickknack

KEG: **3** cag, vat **4** cade, cask, drum **6** barrel **8** hogshead **9** container

KELP: **5** algae, varec

KEMPT: **4** neat, tidy, trim

KEN: **4** lore, view **5** admit, grasp, scope, sight **6** vision, wisdom **7** insight **9** knowledge **10** cognizance, perception **11** recognition **13** understanding

KENNEL: **3** den **4** lair **5** sewer, drain, flock, pound **6** gutter **7** shelter **8** doghouse **9** enclosure

KENTUCKY:
bird: **8** cardinal
capital: **9** Frankfort
cities: **9** Covington, Lexington, Owensboro **10** Louisville **12** Bowling Green
explorer: **5** Boone **6** Harrod
features: **8** Fort Knox **11** Mammoth Cave **13** Cumberland Gap, Kentucky Derby
flower: **9** goldenrod
native: **10** Kentuckian
nickname: **14** Bluegrass State
tree: **6** coffee
water: **11** Lake Barkley **12** Kentucky Lake **14** Lake Cumberland

KENYA:
capital: **7** Nairobi
cities: **6** Kisumu, Nakuru **7** Mombasa **8** Kakemega
continent: **6** Africa
ethnic groups: **3** Luo **4** Arab **5** Asian, Kamba, Luhya **6** Kikuyu **8** Kelenjin
features: **10** Mount Kenya **11** Nyiri Desert **12** Olduvai Gorge **15** Great Rift Valley **16** Malindini Reserve
languages: **3** Luo **4** Meru **5** Luhya **6** Kikuyu **7** Swahili
monetary unit: **8** shilling
water: **6** Rudolf **8** Victoria **10** Lake Nakuru **11** Lake Turkana

KERCHIEF: **4** veil **5** scarf, shawl **6** hankie **8** babushka, bandanna, headrail **12** handkerchief

KERNEL: **3** nut, pit **4** core, germ, meat, pith, seed **5** grain, heart, issue, stone **6** center **7** essence, nucleus **9** substance

KEROUAC, JACK: **6** author
coined: **7** beatnik
wrote: **6** Big Sur **9** On the Road **10** Dharma Bums

KETCH: **4** boat **6** vessel **8** sailboat

KETTLE: **3** pan, pot, vat **6** hollow, teapot, vessel **7** stewpot **8** cauldron, flambeau **10** kettledrum

KETTLEDRUM: **5** naker, tabla, tabor **6** timbal **7** tambour, timpano

KEY: **3** cay **4** code, isle, main, quay, reef **5** guide, islet, pitch, scale, vital **6** answer, clavis, island, master, opener, ticket **7** address, central, digital, pivotal **8** critical, password, skeleton, solution, tonality **9** essential, important **11** explanation

KEYBOARD: **5** organ, piano **7** celesta, clavier **8** carillon, computer **9** accordion **10** clavichord, instrument, typewriter **11** harpsichord, synthesizer **13** word processor

KEYED UP: **5** eager, tense **7** excited, nervous **10** stimulated

KEYNOTE: **4** gist, idea, tone **5** basis, heart, theme, topic **7** essence, feature, measure **8** standard

KEYSTONE: **4** base, root **5** crown, wedge **7** support **8** mainstay **9** headstone, principle **10** foundation **11** cornerstone

KEYSTONE STATE: **12** Pennsylvania

KHAN: **3** inn **5** chief, ruler **7** emperor **8** hostelry, official **11** caravansary

KIBBUTZ: **4** farm **7** commune **10** collective, settlement
located: **6** Israel

KIBITZER: **5** snoop **7** meddler **8** busybody **9** buttinsky, spectator

KICK: **4** bang, blow, boot, fret, fuss, jolt, punt, snap, stop **5** boost, eject, gripe, growl, power, punch, whine **6** object, recoil, thrill **7** abandon, grumble, protest **8** complain, strength **9** enjoyment, sensation

KICKBACK: **4** gift **5** bribe, graft **6** payoff, payola **12** repercussion

KICKER: **5** twist **6** punter **7** pitfall **8** surprise

KICK IN: **3** add **4** give **6** donate **10** contribute

KICK OFF: **5** begin, start **6** launch **7** opening **8** commence **10** inaugurate

KICK OUT: **3** can **4** fire **5** eject, evict, expel **6** bounce, remove **7** dismiss **9** discharge

KICKSHAW: **5** treat **6** bauble, gadget, gewgaw, tidbit **7** trinket **8** delicacy

KID: **3** rag, rib **4** baby, dupe, fool, goat, hoax, joke, josh, razz, ride **5** bluff, child, spoof, tease, trick, youth **6** banter **7** deceive **8** juvenile **9** youngster

KIDNAP: **4** grab **6** abduct, hijack, nobble, snatch **7** capture **8** shanghai

KIDNEY: **4** kind, sort **5** organ
shaped: **8** reniform

KILL: **4** cull, halt, hang, numb, ruin, slay, veto **5** croak, lynch, shoot, waste **6** cancel, deaden, finish, murder, poison **7** crucify, destroy, execute, garrote, silence **8** dispatch, massacre, strangle, suppress **9** slaughter, suffocate **10** annihilate, asphyxiate **11** assassinate, electrocute, exterminate

KILLER: **5** tough **6** gunman, hit man, slayer, sniper **7** butcher, hangman **8** assassin, gangster, murderer **9** difficult **12** exterminator
whale: **4** orca **7** grampus

KILLING: **5** fatal **6** lethal, murder, profit **7** bonanza, carnage, cleanup, slaying, success **8** homicide **9** execution, martyrdom, slaughter **12** excruciating, manslaughter
of father: **9** patricide

of god: **7** deicide
of goddess: **7** deicide
of king: **8** regicide
of mercy: **10** euthanasia
of mother: **9** matricide
of parents: **9** parricide
of prophet: **8** vaticide
of race: **8** genocide
of self: **7** suicide
of sibling: **10** fratricide
of wife: **9** uxoricide

KILLJOY: **8** sourpuss **9** pessimist, worrywart **10** complainer, malcontent, spoilsport

KILL TIME: **4** idle **5** dally **6** dawdle **13** procrastinate

KILN: **4** bake, fire, oast, oven **5** glaze, stove **6** hearth **7** furnace

KIN: **4** clan, folk, race **5** blood, flesh, tribe **6** family **7** kindred, related, sibling **8** relative **9** relations **10** connection

KIND: **3** ilk **4** good, make, mild, soft, sort, type, warm **5** brand, breed, class, fiber, genre, genus, order **6** benign, blithe, gender, genial, gentle, goodly, humane, kidney, loving, nature, polite, tender **7** affable, amiable, clement, cordial, essence, lenient, species, variety **8** amicable, friendly, generous, gracious, merciful, obliging, sisterly, tendency **9** brotherly, favorable **10** benevolent, charitable, neighborly **11** considerate, description, sympathetic, warmhearted **12** affectionate, humanitarian **13** compassionate, philanthropic

KINDLE: **4** fire, glow, move, rise, stir **5** brood, flock, light, start **6** arouse, awaken, excite, ignite, incite, litter **7** animate, inflame, inspire, provoke **9** stimulate

KINDLING: **4** fuel **5** paper, twigs **6** sticks, tinder **8** firewood

KINDNESS: **4** help **5** mercy **6** bounty **7** charity **8** courtesy, goodwill, sympathy **10** assistance, compassion, generosity **11** beneficence, benevolence **12** philanthropy **13** understanding

KINDRED: **3** kin **4** folk, race **5** blood, flesh, tribe **6** allied, family **7** lineage, related, similar **8** affinity, ancestry **9** congenial **10** affiliated, connection **12** relationship

KING: **3** rex **4** czar, lion, tsar **5** ruler **6** leader, master **7** emperor, majesty, monarch **9** sovereign

KING ARTHUR:
father: **5** Uther
group: **10** Round Table
home: **6** Avalon, Camlan **7** Camelot, England **8** Caerleon, Cornwall, Tintagel **11** Glastonbury
knights: **3** Kay **6** Gareth, Gawain **7** Galahad, Mordred **8** Lancelot, Tristram **9** Percivale
lady: **4** Enid
mother: **7** Igraine
queen: **9** Guinevere
quest for: **9** Holy Grail
weapon: **9** Excalibur

KINGDOM: **5** realm **6** domain, empire, throne **7** country, dynasty, scepter **8** monarchy **9** territory **12** commonwealth

KINGLY: **5** noble, regal, royal **6** lordly, regnal **7** stately **8** imperial, majestic, splendid **9** imperious, sovereign

KINK: **3** odd **4** bend, curl, flaw, knot **5** cramp, crick, crimp, curve, hitch, quirk, snarl, spasm, twist **6** buckle, defect, far-out, twinge **7** bizarre, crinkle, strange, wrinkle **9** corkscrew **10** outlandish **11** peculiarity **12** complication, imperfection

KINKY: **3** odd **5** weird **6** curled, far-out, frizzy, warped **7** bizarre, deviant, strange, twisted **8** perverse

KIRIBATI:
capital: **6** Tarawa
cities: **7** Bairiki
ethnic groups: **10** Polynesian **11** Micronesian
features: **4** Line **6** Banaba, Rawaki **7** Gilbert, Phoenix **8** Kiribati **10** Kiritimati **11** Ocean Island, Tarawa Atoll **15** Christmas Island
languages: **7** English **10** Gilbertese
location: **7** Pacific
monetary unit: **6** dollar

KISMET: **4** doom, fate **7** destiny, fortune **12** circumstance

KISS: **4** buss, neck, peck **5** greet, smack **6** caress, French, salute, smooch **7** embrace **8** osculate

KIT: **3** bag, lot, rig, set **4** gear, pack **6** outfit, tackle, things **8** knapsack, supplies, utensils **9** container, equipment **10** collection **11** instruments

KITCHEN: **4** mess **6** galley **7** canteen, cuisine **8** scullery

KITE: **4** bird, hawk, sail, soar **5** check **10** hang glider
type: **3** box **6** conyne **7** Chinese, eddy bow **9** delta-wing, hexagonal

KITH AND KIN: **6** family **7** friends **8** siblings **9** relations, relatives **12** acquaintance

KITTENISH: **3** coy **6** frisky **7** playful **8** childish **10** coquettish **11** flirtatious, mischievous

KITTY: **3** cat **4** pool **6** kitten, stakes **7** jackpot

KLEPTOMANIAC: **5** thief **8** criminal, pilferer **10** shoplifter

KLUTZ: **3** oaf **6** clumsy, lummox, stupid **9** blockhead, schlemiel

KNACK: **4** feel, gift, head, nose **5** flair, forte, skill, trick **6** talent **7** ability **8** aptitude **9** dexterity, expertise **10** adroitness

KNAPSACK: **3** bag, kit **4** pack **8** backpack

KNAVE: **3** cad **4** jack **5** cheat, churl, fraud, rogue, scamp **6** rascal, varlet **7** lowlife, villain **9** miscreant, scoundrel, trickster **10** blackguard **11** rapscallion

KNEAD: **3** mix **4** fold, work **5** blend, press **6** aerate **7** massage, stretch **10** manipulate

KNEE: **5** joint **7** patella

KNEE-JERK: **6** reflex **8** expected **9** automatic **11** predictable, spontaneous

KNEEL: **3** bow **5** stoop **6** kowtow **7** curtsey **9** genuflect

KNELL: **4** bell, ring, toll **5** chime, sound **6** signal, summon **7** warning **8** proclaim

KNICKKNACK: **3** toy **5** curio **6** bauble, gadget, gewgaw, trifle **7** bibelot, novelty, trinket **8** gimcrack, ornament, souvenir **9** bric-a-brac, showpiece **10** decoration

KNIFE: **3** cut **4** stab, tool **5** blade, carve, lance, slash, slice, sword, wound **6** pierce, weapon **7** utensil **8** lacerate
types: **3** pen **4** bolo, dirk, shiv **5** bowie, bread, putty **6** butter, dagger, lancet, pocket, sickle **7** bayonet, cutlass, hunting, machete, scalpel **8** surgical **9** Swiss Army **11** switchblade

KNIGHT: **7** gallant, paladin **8** cavalier, champion, horseman **9** caballero, chevalier, companion, gentleman
attendant: **7** armiger, esquire

duel: **5** joust **10** tournament **12** tilting match
page: **6** varlet
title: **3** sir

KNIGHTHOOD: **4** rank **8** chivalry

KNIT: **4** bind, heal, join, mend, purl **5** plait, unite, weave **6** fasten, furrow, stitch **7** conjoin, connect, crochet, wrinkle **10** intertwine **11** consolidate, intermingle

KNOB: **4** bump, dial, heel, hill, knot, lump, node **5** bulge, knoll, lever **6** button, handle, pommel, switch **8** mountain **12** protuberance

KNOCK: **3** hit, rap **4** beat, blow, bump, jolt, lick, ping, push, slam **5** abuse, blame, clank, pound, smack, thump, whack **6** bounce, defeat, strike, topple **7** collide, setback **8** belittle, denounce **9** criticize, reprehend

KNOCK DOWN: **4** deck, drop, fell **5** floor, level **6** thrash **7** flatten, trample

KNOCK OFF: **4** copy, kill, stop **5** steal, waste **6** deduct, desist, finish, murder **7** achieve **8** complete, subtract **9** eliminate, imitation **11** assassinate, discontinue

KNOCKOUT: **4** kayo **6** beauty, eyeful, looker **7** stunner

KNOLL: **4** hill, knob, ring **5** knell, mound, sound **7** hillock

KNOT: **3** bow, tie **4** bond, burl, knob, knur, link, loop, lump, mesh, node, snag **5** braid, crowd, gnarl, group, hitch, knurl, snarl **6** nodule, puzzle, tangle **7** rosette **8** entangle **10** contortion **12** entanglement, protuberance
types: **4** flat **5** slide **6** granny, shroud, square **7** bowline, seizing **8** slipknot, surgeon's **9** half hitch **10** fisherman's, sheepshank, stevedore's **11** carrick bend, figure eight **12** rolling hitch **14** blackwall hitch

KNOTTY: **4** hard **5** bumpy **6** nodule, tricky **7** bunched, complex, gnarled **9** difficult, intricate **10** perplexing, puzzlingly **11** troublesome

KNOW: **3** ken, see **5** grasp **6** fathom **7** cognize, discern, profess, realize **8** identify **9** associate, recognize **10** comprehend, experience, understand **11** distinguish **12** discriminate

KNOW-HOW: **5** flair, knack, skill **6** talent **7** ability, mastery **8** aptitude **9** expertise, ingenuity, knowledge **10** capability, experience

KNOWING: **4** deep, wise **5** alive, aware, cagey, sharp, smart, witty **6** bright, clever, shrewd **7** gnostic, worldly **8** educated, informed, sensible **9** brilliant, cognitive, conscious, observant **10** deliberate, experience, perceptive, scholastic **11** intelligent, intentional **13** knowledgeable, sophisticated

KNOW-IT-ALL: **5** brash **6** smarty **8** wiseacre **11** wisenheimer

KNOWLEDGE: **4** data, lore **5** facts, grasp **6** wisdom **7** ability, inkling, know-how, science **8** learning **9** awareness, cognition, education, erudition **10** cognizance, experience, revelation **11** familiarity, information, instruction **12** intelligence **13** comprehension, enlightenment, understanding

KNOWLEDGEABLE: **4** wise **5** aware, smart **6** bright, clever, posted, versed **7** knowing **8** apprised, educated, familiar, informed **9** cognizant **10** acquainted **11** experienced

KNOWN: **6** famous **7** obvious, popular **8** familiar, renowned **9** notorious, prominent **10** recognized **12** acknowledged

KNUCKLE UNDER: **4** cave **5** yield **6** give in, submit **7** succumb **9** acquiesce, surrender **10** capitulate

KOOK: **3** nut **5** crazy, flake, wacko **7** lunatic **8** crackpot **9** eccentric, screwball

KOSHER: **4** pure **5** clean **6** proper **7** ethical, genuine **8** accepted **9** authentic **10** legitimate **11** permissible

KOWTOW: **4** fawn **5** cower, stoop, toady **6** grovel **8** bootlick **9** brownnose

KUDOS: **4** fame **5** award, glory, honor **6** credit, esteem, praise **7** acclaim, laurels **8** accolade, citation, prestige **10** admiration, decoration

KUNG FU: **10** martial art
origin: **5** China

KUWAIT:
capital: **6** Kuwait
cities: **5** Jahra **6** Ahmadi **7** Hawalli **8** Fahaheel **11** as-Salimiyah
continent: **4** Asia
ethnic groups: **4** Arab **6** Indian **7** Iranian, Kuwaiti **9** Pakistani
features: **5** Warba **7** Bubiyan, Failaka
language: **6** Arabic
monetary unit: **5** dinar

KYPHOSIS: **8** humpback **9** curvature, hunchback

KYRGYZSTAN:
capital: **7** Bishkek

L

LABAN:
daughter: 4 Leah 6 Rachel
father: 7 Bethuel

LABEL: 3 tab, tag **4** band, call, logo, mark, name **5** brand **6** define, design, ticket **7** sticker **8** classify, hallmark, insignia **9** designate **11** description **12** characterize **14** identification

LABOR: **4** task, toil, work **5** grind, slave, sweat **6** effort, stress, strive **7** agonize, travail, workers **8** drudgery, endeavor, exertion, industry, struggle **9** employees **10** childbirth **11** parturition, undertaking **12** contractions

LABORED: **5** heavy **6** forced **7** awkward, unclear **8** strained **9** difficult, strenuous, unnatural

LABORER: **4** hand, peon, serf **5** navvy, plebe **6** coolie, toiler, worker **7** workman **8** workhand **10** bluecollar

LABORIOUS: **4** hard **5** tough **6** uphill **7** arduous **8** diligent, rigorous **9** assiduous, difficult, effortful, strenuous **10** burdensome **11** hardworking, industrious, painstaking **12** backbreaking

LABYRINTH: **3** web **4** knot, maze, mesh **5** snarl **6** jungle, tangle **7** network **9** intricacy **10** complexity **12** entanglement
builder: **8** Daedalus
confined: **8** Minotaur

LACE: **3** net, tie **4** band, beat, bind, cord, lash **5** adorn, braid, plait, twine, unite **6** border, edging, fabric, fasten, punish, ribbon, string, thrash, thread **7** entwine, netting **8** decorate, trimming **10** embroidery, intertwine, shoestring

LACERATE: **3** cut **4** gash, slit, stab, tear **5** knife, lance, slice, wound **6** harrow, mangle, pierce **8** distress

LACHRYMOSE: **3** sad **5** teary, weepy **6** crying **7** tearful, weeping

LACK: **4** need, want **5** fault, minus **6** dearth **7** absence, deficit, failure, paucity, poverty **8** scarcity, shortage **9** emptiness, privation **10** deficiency, inadequacy **13** insufficiency

LACKADAISICAL: **4** blah, idle, lazy **7** languid **8** careless, listless **9** lethargic **10** spiritless, uninspired **11** halfhearted, unmotivated

LACKEY: **4** page, thug **5** toady **6** flunky **7** footman, gorilla, servant **9** attendant

LACKING: **5** short **6** absent **7** missing, wanting, without **8** deprived, impaired **9** deficient **10** inadequate **12** insufficient

LACKLUSTER: **4** drab, dull, flat **5** bland **6** boring **7** humdrum **8** lifeless **9** colorless **10** uninspired

LACONIC: **4** curt **5** blunt, brief, crisp, pithy, short, terse **7** compact, concise, pointed **8** succinct **9** condensed

LACQUER: **5** gloss **6** finish **7** coating, shellac, varnish

LACUNA: **3** gap **5** break, pause, space **6** cavity, hiatus **7** interim, opening **8** interval **10** depression

LACY: **5** fancy, sheer **6** frilly, ornate **7** elegant, netlike, weblike **8** delicate **11** transparent

LAD: **3** boy, kid, son **5** youth **6** shaver **8** juvenile **9** stripling, youngster **10** adolescent

LADEN: **5** taxed **7** saddled **8** burdened, hampered, weighted

LADLE: **3** dip **4** bail, pour **5** scoop, serve, spoon **6** dipper **7** cyathus **8** calabash

LADY: **4** dame, girl **5** madam, queen, woman **6** female, senora **7** duchess **8** baroness, countess, mistress, princess **10** noblewoman **11** gentlewoman

LADYLIKE: **6** polite, proper **7** elegant, genteel, refined **8** feminine, mannerly, matronly, polished **11** respectable

LAERTES:
father: **8** Polonius
sister: **7** Ophelia
son: **7** Ulysses **8** Odysseus
wife: **8** Anticlea

LAG: **4** drag, flag, tire **5** delay, stave, tarry, trail **6** dawdle, linger, loiter **7** slacken **8** slowdown, straggle **10** dillydally **13** procrastinate

LAGER: **3** ale **4** beer

LAGGARD: **4** mope, slow **5** idler **6** remiss **7** dawdler **8** dilatory, loiterer, slowpoke, sluggish **9** straggler

LAGNIAPPE: **3** tip **4** gift **5** bonus **7** benefit, largess, present **8** gratuity

LAIR: **3** den **4** nest **5** haunt **6** burrow, cavern, refuge **7** habitat, hideout, retreat, shelter **9** sanctuary

LAISSEZ-FAIRE: **6** policy **8** inactive, tolerant **9** economics, unconcern **10** philosophy **12** indifference, mercantilism

LAKE: **4** loch, mere, pond, pool, shat, tarn **5** bayou, lough, oxbow, shott **6** lagoon
concerning: **10** lacustrine
study: **9** limnology

LAM: **3** hit **4** bash, beat, flog **6** escape, flight, strike, thrash, wallop

LAMB: **3** ean **4** yean **5** agnus **7** fatling, hogling
concerning: **5** ovine
cuts: **3** leg, rib **4** chop, loin **6** breast **7** sirloin **8** shoulder **9** foreshank, hind shank, spareribs **10** rack of lamb
leg: **5** gigot
pet: **4** cade **6** cosset

LAMBASTE: **4** beat, drub, flay, whip **5** pound, scold **6** assail, berate, hammer, pummel, punish, thrash **7** clobber **9** castigate, criticize

LAMBENT: **6** bright **7** glowing, radiant, shining **8** luminous, lustrous **9** brilliant **10** flickering

LAME: **4** game, hurt, maim, weak **5** gimpy, stiff **6** feeble, flimsy **7** halting, limping **8** crippled, decrepit, deformed, disabled **9** defective **11** handicapped **12** incapacitate, unconvincing

LAMEBRAIN: **4** dope, fool **5** dunce, moron **6** nitwit, stupid **8** imbecile **9** blockhead

LAMECH:
daughter: **6** Naamah
father: **9** Methusael **10** Methuselah
son: **4** Noah **5** Jabal, Jubal **9** Tubalcain
wife: **4** Adah **6** Zillah

LAMENT: **3** cry, rue **4** howl, keen, moan, pine, sign, wail, weep **5** dirge, dolor, grief, mourn **6** bemoan, bewail, grieve, monody, outcry, plaint, regret, repent, repine, sorrow **7** condole, deplore, elegize, requiem **9** complaint

LAMENTABLE: **3** sad **4** dire **8** grievous **9** miserable, upsetting **11** distressing, unfortunate

LAMP: **3** arc, gas, oil **4** bulb, davy **5** floor, light, table, torch **7** lantern **8** electric **10** chandelier **12** incandescent

LAMPOON: **4** mock **5** farce, roast, squib **6** parody, satire **7** takeoff **8** satirize **9** burlesque **10** caricature, pasquinade

LANCE: **3** cut **4** dart, hurl **5** point, spear **6** launch, pierce, skewer, weapon **7** javelin

LANCELOT: **9** Launcelot
killed: **6** Gawain
legend: **9** Arthurian
lover: **6** Elaine **9** Guinevere
son: **7** Galahad

LAND: **3** lot **4** acre, soil **5** earth, grass, realm, shore, terra, tract **6** domain, estate, ground, meadow, parcel, realty **7** acreage, country, marches, pasture, terrene **8** alluvion **9** territory **10** real estate **11** reservation
concerning: **11** terrestrial
church: **5** glebe
elevated: **3** alp **4** hill, mesa **5** mound, ridge **7** plateau **8** mountain
features: **10** topography
inheritable: **4** alod, fief, odal **5** allod, ethel **8** allodium, appanage
measure: **3** are, rod **4** acre, mile, rood **5** meter, perch
perfect: **6** Goshen, Utopia **9** Cockaigne, Shangri-la
plowed: **4** farm **5** arada, arado, field, ranch **6** arable, fallow, furrow **7** orchard, thwaite, tillage
point: **4** cape, ness, spit
strip: **8** corridor **9** panhandle, peninsula
unused: **5** heath **6** desert, forest **9** wasteland

LANDLORD: **4** host **5** owner **6** lessor **9** innkeeper **10** proprietor

LANDMARK: **5** event **6** crisis **7** feature, remnant **8** monument, signpost **9** guidepost, milestone **11** achievement, cornerstone

LAND OF ENCHANTMENT: **9** New Mexico

LAND OF LINCOLN: **8** Illinois

LAND OF OPPORTUNITY: **8** Arkansas

LANDSCAPE: **4** view **5** mural, scene, vista **7** picture, scenery **8** painting, panorama **11** countryside

LANDSLIDE: **3** win **5** sweep **7** victory **8** lopsided **9** avalanche **10** eboulement

LANE: **3** way **4** path, race, road **5** aisle, alley, byway, strip, track **6** course, street **7** pathway **8** approach, footpath **10** passageway

LANGUAGE: **5** argot, idiom, lingo, slang **6** jargon, speech, tongue **7** dialect, diction, grammar **10** vernacular, vocabulary **11** linguistics
ancient: **4** Pali **5** Aryan, Latin **8** Sanskrit
classical: **5** Greek, Latin
concerning: **8** semantic
international: **2** od, ro **3** ido **5** koine **9** Esperanto **12** lingua franca
mixed: **6** creole, pidgin
Romance: **5** Latin **6** French **7** Catalan, Italian, Spanish **8** Rumanian **10** Portuguese

LANGUID: **4** dull, slow, weak **6** feeble, supine **8** drooping, inactive, indolent, listless, sluggish **9** apathetic, enervated, lethargic **10** spiritless **11** indifferent **13** lackadaisical

LANGUISH: **4** fade, fail, flag, pine, sink, wilt **5** droop, faint, waste **6** linger, repine, suffer, wallow, wither **7** decline **8** diminish **9** neglected **11** deteriorate

LANGUOR: **4** lazy **5** blues, ennui **6** apathy, dreamy, torpor **7** boredom **8** lethargy **9** lassitude **10** stagnation **12** listlessness

LANKY: **4** lean, slim, tall, thin **5** gaunt, gawky, rangy **6** gangly, meager, skinny **7** angular, scraggy, scrawny, slender **8** gangling

LANYARD: **4** cord, line, rope **6** gasket, string

LAOCOON:
killer: **7** serpent
vocation: **6** priest
warned of: **11** Trojan Horse

LAOMEDON:
father: **4** Ilus
killer: **8** Hercules
kingdom: **4** Troy
mother: **8** Eurydice
wife: **6** Strymo

LAOS:
capital: **9** Vientiane
cities: **5** Pakse **11** Savannakhet **12** Luang Prabang
continent: **4** Asia
ethnic groups: **3** Lao, Meo, Yao **4** Thai **8** Mon-Khmer
features: **11** Plain of Jars
languages: **3** Lao, Tai **9** Palaung-Wa
monetary unit: **6** new kip
water: **6** Mekong, Sabang

LAP: **4** lick, loop, wash, wrap **5** bathe, drink, orbit, round, slosh, slurp **6** circle, course, enfold, splash, swathe **7** circuit

LAPIDARY: **7** jeweler **8** engraver **10** delineated

LAPSE: **3** err, gap **4** fall, goof, lull, sink, slip **5** boner, break, error, fault, slide **6** expire, revert **7** blooper, blunder, failure, mistake **9** backslide, disregard, oversight **10** infraction, regression **11** deteriorate

LARCENY: **5** crime, theft **7** looting, robbery **8** burglary, stealing, thievery **9** pilfering **10** absconding, purloining **12** embezzlement
degree: **5** grand, petty

LARD: **3** fat, oil **4** coat, lace **5** cover, enarm **6** enrich, grease, tallow **7** garnish **9** embellish **10** shortening

LARDER: **6** cellar, pantry **7** buttery **8** cupboard **9** storeroom **10** provisions

LARGE: **3** big, fat **4** huge, vast **5** ample, broad, bulky, burly, giant, grand, great, heavy, hefty, hulky, jumbo, roomy **7** booming, copious, immense, liberal, mammoth, massive, pompous, sizable, titanic **8** colossal, enormous, generous, gigantic, sweeping, whopping **9** capacious, extensive, monstrous, plentiful **10** exorbitant, monumental **11** extravagant, far-reaching, substantial **12** considerable

LARGELY: **6** mainly, mostly **7** chiefly **9** generally, primarily **12** considerably **13** predominantly

LARGESS: **3** tip **4** gift, perk **7** charity, present **8** donation, gratuity **9** lagniappe **10** generosity **12** contribution

LARIAT: **4** rope **5** lasso, noose, reata **6** tether

LARK: **4** bird, dido, romp **5** antic, prank, spree **6** frolic **8** carousal, escapade **9** adventure

LARRUP: **4** beat, flog, whip **6** thrash **7** clobber **8** lambaste

LARVA: **3** bot, fly, loa **4** grub, spat, worm **5** naiad, nymph **6** botfly **7** atrocha, oestrid, tadpole **8** horsefly **11** caterpillar

LASCIVIOUS: **4** lewd **6** coarse, fleshy, steamy, wanton **7** lustful, obscene, sensual **8** indecent **9** lecherous, libertine, salacious, seductive **10** licentious, voluptuous

LASH: **4** beat, blow, flog, lace, whip **5** slash, smack, smite **6** assail, attack, berate, fasten, hammer, pummel, secure, strike, stroke, thrash **7** blister **8** chastise **9** castigate, criticize, horsewhip

LASS: **3** gal **4** girl, miss **5** woman **6** damsel, female, maiden **7** colleen **10** sweetheart

LASSITUDE: **5** blues, ennui **6** apathy **7** fatigue, languor **8** doldrums, lethargy **9** torpidity, weariness **10** drowsiness, enervation, exhaustion **12** listlessness, sluggishness

LAST: **3** end **4** tail **5** abide, final, omega, stand **6** endure, newest, remain, utmost **7** extreme, persist, survive **8** continue, eventual, farthest, furthest, hindmost, ultimate **9** climactic, persevere **10** concluding

LASTING: **6** stable, sturdy **7** chronic, durable, eternal, forever **8** constant, immortal, unending **9** classical, continual, incessant, perennial, permanent, unceasing **10** deeprooted **11** everlasting

LAST OF THE MOHICANS:
author: **19** James Fenimore Cooper
characters: **5** Magua, Uncas **7** Hawkeye **9** Cora Munro **10** Alice Munro **11** Natty Bumppo **12** Chingachgook
fort: **16** Fort William Henry

LATCH: **4** bolt, hook, lock **5** catch, clamp, close **6** button, fasten, secure **8** fastener

LATE: **3** new **4** dead, past **5** tardy **6** behind, former, recent **7** belated, delayed, lagging, overdue **8** deceased, departed **9** postponed **10** behindhand, unpunctual **12** contemporary

LATENT: **6** covert, hidden, secret **7** abeyant, dormant, passive **8** inactive, inferred **9** concealed, potential, quiescent **10** unrealized **11** undeveloped

LATER: **4** soon **5** after, newer **6** behind **7** ensuing **9** afterward, following, hereafter, posterior **10** succeeding **12** subsequently

LATERAL: **4** pass **7** oblique **8** flanking, sidelong, sideward, sideways

LATH: **4** slat **5** spale, stave, stick **8** forepole

LATHER: **4** foam, fuss, soap, suds, wash **5** cream, froth **6** bustle, hassle **7** bubbles **9** agitation, commotion

LATIN:
cases: **6** dative **8** ablative, genitive, vocative **10** accusative, nominative

literature: 7 classic
versions: 6 vulgar 7 vulgate

LATITUDE: 4 play, room 5 range, scope, width 6 degree, extent, leeway 7 breadth, freedom, liberty, measure 8 distance 9 elbowroom 12 independence

LATRINE: 5 privy 6 toilet 8 bathroom, lavatory, restroom

LATTER: 5 final 6 latest, modern, recent 10 concluding, subsequent, succeeding

LATTER-DAY SAINT: 6 Mormon

LATTICE: 4 door, gate, grid, mesh 5 frame 7 trellis 9 structure 13 configuration

LATVIA:
capital: 4 Riga
cities: 7 Jelgava, Jurmala, Liepaja 9 Liepaglja, Ventspils 10 Daugavpils
continent: 4 Asia
ethnic groups: 7 Latvian
languages: 7 Latvian
monetary unit: 12 Latvian ruble
water: 4 Ogre 5 Gauga 6 Salaca 12 Western Dvina

LAUD: 4 hymn, song 5 adore, extol, honor 6 admire, praise, revere 7 acclaim, applaud, commend, glorify 8 eulogize, venerate 10 compliment

LAUDABLE: 8 sterling 9 admirable, deserving, estimable, exemplary 11 commendable 12 praiseworthy

LAUGH: 4 crow, ha-ha, howl, mock, roar 5 snort 6 cackle, giggle, guffaw, hee-haw, nicker, scream, titter 7 chortle, chuckle, snicker 9 cachinate

LAUGHABLE: 5 comic, funny, merry, silly, witty 6 absurd 7 amusing, bizarre, comical, foolish, mocking, strange 8 farcical, humorous 9 facetious, hilarious, ludicrous 10 outrageous, ridiculous 12 entertaining

LAUGHINGSTOCK: 4 butt, dupe, fool 5 sport 7 mockery

LAUGHTER: 5 mirth 9 joviality, merriment 10 risibility

LAUNCH: 4 fire, hurl, open, toss 5 begin, eject, fling, heave, start, throw 6 propel 7 bombard 8 catapult, commence, premiere 9 discharge, introduce

LAUNDER: 4 wash 5 clean, scrub 8 disguise

LAURELS: 5 award, glory, honor, kudos 6 credit, praise 7 tribute 8 accolade 10 decoration 11 distinction, recognition 12 commendation

LAVA: 4 slag 5 ashes, magma 6 basalt, coulee, latite, scoria 7 cinders 8 obsidian

LAVATORY: 4 head, john 5 basin, privy 6 toilet 7 latrine 8 bathroom, washroom

LAVENDER: 5 color, lilac, plant 6 pastel, purple, violet

LAVISH: 4 free, lush, wild 5 grand, plush, spend, waste 6 bestow, shower 7 opulent, profuse 8 gorgeous, prodigal, reckless, splendid, squander 9 bountiful, excessive, expensive, exuberant, impetuous, luxurious 10 immoderate, unstinting 11 extravagant, magnificent, overindulge 12 unrestrained

LAW: 3 act, bar, lex, res 4 code, fiat, rule, suit 5 actus, canon, edict, mesne, sutra, ukase 6 custom, decree, dharma, suttah 7 justice, precept, statute 8 handicap, pandects, replevin, rescript 9 enactment, gravamina, ordinance, principle 10 litigation, regulation 11 commandment, legislation 12 consti-

tution, jurisdiction, proclamation **13** jurisprudence
concerning: **5** legal **7** canonic **8** judicial **9** canonical, judiciary **11** legislative
degree: **3** LLB, LLD
document: **4** deed, writ **6** capias, elegit
types: **4** case **5** civil **6** common, family **8** criminal **9** adjective **11** substantive **13** international
violation: **3** sin **4** tort **5** crime, malum **6** breach, delict, felony **7** offense **10** infraction
worker: **5** judge **6** jurist, lawyer **7** counsel, justice **8** advocate, attorney **9** barrister, solicitor **10** prosecutor

LAWBREAKER: **5** crook, felon **6** outlaw **8** criminal, offender, violator **10** delinquent

LAWFUL: **3** due **4** just **5** legal **6** kosher **8** official, rightful **10** authorized, legitimate **11** established, permissible **14** constitutional

LAWLESS: **4** lewd **6** unruly **7** chaotic, illegal, riotous **8** mutinous **9** barbarous, insurgent **10** anarchical, disorderly, ungoverned **12** illegitimate

LAWN: **4** park, plot, turf, yard **5** glade, grass **6** cotton, fabric **7** grounds

LAWSUIT: **4** case **5** claim **6** action **10** accusation, litigation

LAWYER: **7** counsel, shyster **8** advocate, attorney, commoner, defender **9** barrister, counselor, solicitor **10** mouthpiece, prosecutor **11** pettifogger

LAX: **4** easy, lazy, open **5** loose, slack, tardy, vague **6** casual, remiss, sloppy **7** lenient, relaxed **8** careless, inactive **9** negligent, oblivious, unmindful **10** delinquent, permissive, unconfined **12** disregardful, unrestrained, unstructured

LAY: **3** aim, bet, put, set **4** bury, cast, hymn, plot, poem, rest, song, tune **5** ditty, level, place, quiet, stake, still, wager **6** ballad, charge, devise, entomb, impose, melody, smooth **7** amateur, ascribe, contour, deposit, incline, produce, secular, subside **8** contrive, position, suppress **9** formulate

LAY ASIDE: **4** keep, save **5** scrap, table **6** shelve **7** abandon, neglect

LAY DOWN: **5** wager, yield **6** assert, define, give up **7** dictate, specify, succumb **9** surrender

LAYER: **3** bed, ply **4** film, fold, seam, skin, slab, tier **5** crust, depth, floor, level, scale, sheet, story **6** lamina, lining, veneer **7** bedding, blanket, coating, stratum **8** covering **10** substratum

LAY INTO: **5** scold **6** assail, attack **8** lambaste **9** criticize

LAY LOW: **4** duck, hide **5** cover, sneak **9** disappear **10** camouflage

LAYMAN: **4** laic **6** novice **7** amateur, secular **8** follower **11** parishioner **12** churchperson

LAYOFF: **4** fire, halt, stop **5** cease **7** cutback, release **8** furlough **9** discharge, dismissal, terminate

LAYOUT: **3** map **4** plan **5** draft, model, spend **6** design, invest **7** diagram, outline **8** disburse **9** blueprint **11** arrangement

LAY UP: **4** hide **5** amass, stock **6** injure **7** confine, disable **10** accumulate **11** hospitalize **12** incapacitate

LAY WASTE: **4** ruin **5** wreck **6** ravage **7** destroy **8** desolate **9** devastate **10** annihilate

LAZARUS:
resurrected by: **5** Jesus
sister: **4** Mary **6** Martha

LAZY: **3** lax **4** idle **6** torpid **7** loafing **8** faineant, inactive, indolent, slothful, sluggish **9** lethargic **13** lackadaisical, unindustrious

LEAD: **4** clue, head, lode, sign, star **5** ahead, carry, excel, first, guide, metal, pilot, steer, usher **6** bullet, convey, direct, escort, govern, manage **7** command, conduct, element, pioneer, precede, protect, surpass **8** evidence, graphite, instruct, persuade, shepherd **9** advantage, headliner, influence, principal, spearhead

LEAD ASTRAY: **4** lure **6** entice **7** beguile, corrupt, deceive

LEADEN: **4** dull, gray **5** heavy, inert **6** dreary, gloomy **7** languid **8** downcast, listless, sluggish **9** depressed

LEADER: **4** boss, duke, guru, head, line, lion, pope **5** chief, coach, elder, guide, pilot, rabbi, ruler **6** bishop, cantor, priest, shogun **7** captain, foreman, general, maestro, warlord **8** cardinal, champion **9** chieftain, commander, conductor, president, principal **10** bellwether **11** chairperson, trailblazer

LEADERSHIP: **4** helm **5** skill **7** command **8** guidance **9** authority, direction **10** initiative

LEADING: **4** arch, head, main **5** chief, first, prime **7** capital, central, guiding, initial, premier, stellar **8** dominant, foremost **9** paramount, principal **10** motivating **11** controlling **12** unparalleled

LEAD ON: **4** bait, goad, lure **5** flirt **6** entice, seduce **9** encourage

LEAF: **4** foil, page, scan, skim **5** blade, bract, folio, frond, petal, scale, stalk, thumb **6** browse, glance, insert, needle, spathe

LEAFLET: **5** flier, pinna, tract **7** booklet, handout **8** brochure, circular, handbill, pamphlet

LEAFY: **4** lush **5** green, shady **7** layered, verdant **8** abundant

LEAGUE: **5** class, guild, order, union **7** circuit, network 8 alliance, division **9** coalition **10** conference, federation, fellowship, sisterhood **11** association, brotherhood, confederacy

LEAH:
daughter: **5** Dinah
father: **5** Laban
husband: **5** Jacob
sister: **6** Rachel
son: **4** Levi **5** Judah **6** Simeon **8** Issachar

LEAK: **4** drip, flow, hole, ooze, seep, vent **5** crack, drain, spill **6** escape, reveal **7** channel, divulge, fissure, rupture, trickle **9** discharge

LEAN: **4** bare, bend, cant, lank, poor, rely, slim, tend, thin, tilt **5** curve, gaunt, lanky, scant, slope, spare **6** depend, meager, nonfat, prefer, scanty, skinny **7** incline, recline, scrawny, slender **8** pressure, rawboned **9** deficient, emaciated **10** inadequate **12** unproductive

LEANING: **4** bias **6** desire, liking **8** aptitude, tendency **9** prejudice **10** preference, propensity **11** inclination

LEAN-TO: **3** hut **5** shack **6** shanty **7** shelter

LEAP: **3** fly, hop **4** buck, jump, skip, soar **5** bound, caper, clear, frisk, lunge, surge, vault **6** ascend, bounce, cavort, gallop, gambol, hurdle, plunge, prance, spring **7** upswing **8** capriole, catapult, increase

LEARN: **4** find, hear **5** grasp, study **6** master **7** acquire, uncover **8** discover, memorize **9** ascertain **10** apprentice, understand

LEARNED: **4** read, wise **6** astute, versed **7** erudite **8** academic, educated, informed, lettered, literary **9** scholarly **10** cultivated **12** intellectual

LEARNER: **5** pupil **6** novice **7** scholar, student, trainee **8** beginner, disciple **10** apprentice

LEARNING: **4** lore **6** wisdom **7** culture, science **9** education, erudition, knowledge **10** discipline, experience, literature, philosophy **11** information, scholarship **13** comprehension

LEASE: **3** let **4** hire, rent **5** grant **7** charter **8** contract

LEASH: **4** bind, cord, curb, lead, rein, rope **5** chain, strap **6** bridle, choker, tether **7** control, harness **8** restrain

LEAST: **6** fewest, lowest **7** minimal, minimum, tiniest, trivial **8** shortest, smallest **9** slightest **11** unimportant

LEATHER: **3** tan **4** hide, skin, whip **5** strap **6** thrash
types: **3** kid **4** buff, napa **5** split, suede **6** skiver **7** chamois, cowhide, Morocco, rawhide **8** buckskin, cabretta, calfskin, cordovan, deerskin **9** chevrette, horsehide **11** pebble grain, Scotch grain

LEAVE: **4** cede, exit, flee, move, omit, quit, will **5** endow, forgo, scram, split **6** assign, decamp, depart, desert, embark, escape, permit, retire, vacate **7** abandon, exclude, forsake, getaway, holiday, liberty, license, vamoose **8** bequeath, emigrate, evacuate, furlough, vacation **9** allowance **10** permission, relinquish, sabbatical

LEAVEN: **5** imbue, raise, yeast **6** enzyme, infuse **7** ferment **8** catalyst **9** activator

LEBANON:
capital: **6** Beirut
cities: **4** Tyre **5** Sidon **7** Tripoli
continent: **4** Asia
ethnic groups: **4** Arab **8** Armenian **11** Palestinian
features: **4** Mzar **5** Aruba **6** Byblos **7** Sannine **8** Baalbeck **11** Bekka Valley, Mount Hermon **14** Chouf Mountains
languages: **6** Arabic, French
monetary unit: **5** pound
water: **5** Kebir **6** Litani **7** Orontes

LECHEROUS: **4** lewd **6** carnal **7** corrupt, goatish, lustful, raunchy **9** salacious

LECTERN: **4** desk **5** stand **6** podium **8** platform

LECTURE: **4** talk **5** class, scold, spiel **6** berate, lesson, preach, rebuke, sermon, speech **7** address, hearing, oration **8** admonish **9** discourse, reprimand, sermonize

LECTURER: **6** docent, reader **7** speaker, teacher **9** professor **10** instructor

LEDA:
daughter: **5** Helen **12** Clytemnestra
husband: **9** Tyndareus
lover: **4** swan, Zeus
son: **6** Castor, Pollux

LEDGE: **4** berm, edge, sill, vein **5** ridge, shelf **6** mantel **8** platform

LEDGER: **4** book **5** entry **6** record **9** headstone, tombstone

LEECH: **4** worm **6** sponge **8** barnacle, parasite **11** bloodsucker

LEER: **3** eye **4** look, lust, ogle **5** fleer, smirk, stare **6** goggle **7** grimace

LEERY: **4** wary **7** guarded **8** cautious **9** skeptical, uncertain **10** suspicious **11** distrustful

LEEWAY: **4** play, room **5** drift, space **6** margin **7** cushion **8** latitude **9** clearance, elbowroom, tolerance **11** flexibility

LEFT: **4** port, quit **7** liberal **8** departed, larboard **9** abandoned, remaining

LEFT-HANDED: **6** clumsy, gauche **7** awkward, dubious **8** southpaw **9** insincere, maladroit

LEFTIST: **7** liberal, radical **9** socialist **10** left-winger

LEFTOVER: **5** extra **6** excess, scraps **7** residue, surplus **8** leavings, remnants **9** remainder

LEFT-WINGER: **7** leftist, liberal, radical **9** socialist

LEG: **3** gam, run **4** limb, pole, prop, walk **5** brace, shank, stage, stake **6** bender, column, course **7** circuit, support **8** cabriole **9** appendage, drumstick
bone: **5** femur, tibia **6** fibula **7** patella, tarsals **11** metatarsals
muscle: **13** biceps femoris, gastrocnemius, rectus femoris **15** vastus lateralis **16** tibialis anterior

LEGACY: **4** gift **6** devise **7** bequest **8** heirloom, heritage **10** birthright, foundation **11** inheritance

LEGAL: **5** valid **6** lawful **8** juristic **9** allowable, juridical, statutory **10** authorized, legitimate **11** contractual, permissible **14** constitutional

LEGALIZE: **5** allow, enact **6** permit **7** license **8** sanction, validate **9** authorize

LEGAL TENDER: **4** cash **5** money **8** currency

LEGATE: **5** agent, envoy **6** consul, deputy, nuncio **8** delegate, emissary **10** ambassador **14** representative

LEGEND: **3** key **4** code, lore, myth, saga, tale **5** fable, story, table **7** fiction **8** folklore **9** tradition

LEGENDARY: **6** fabled, famous **7** storied **8** immortal, invented, mythical **10** celebrated, fictitious

LEGERDEMAIN: **5** magic **6** deceit **8** trickery **9** conjuring, deception **10** artfulness

LEGIBLE: **4** neat **5** clear **8** apparent, distinct, readable **11** discernible

LEGION: **4** army, many **5** flock **6** troops **7** various **8** numerous **9** countless, multitude

LEGISLATION: **3** act, law **4** bill **6** ruling **7** charter, statute **9** enactment, ordinance **10** regulation

LEGISLATOR: **7** senator **8** delegate, lawgiver, lawmaker **10** politician **14** assemblyperson, congressperson, representative

LEGISLATURE: **4** body, diet **5** house **6** senate **7** council **8** assembly, congress **10** parliament

LEGITIMATE: **4** fair, just, real, true **5** legal, sound, valid **6** cogent, lawful, proper, square **7** genuine **8** accepted, rightful **9** authentic, warranted **10** recognized

LEI: **6** wreath **7** flowers, garland
origin: **6** Hawaii

LEISURE: **4** ease, idle, rest, time **5** spare **6** chance **7** freedom, holiday **8** vacation **10** recreation, relaxation **11** convenience, opportunity

LEISURELY: **4** slow **6** calmly, casual **7** languid, relaxed **9** gradually, unhurried **10** deliberate

LEMON: **3** dud **5** fruit **6** citron **7** failure **9** defective

LEND: **4** give, loan **5** grant **6** afford, extend, impart, permit, supply **7** furnish, provide **11** accommodate

LENGTH: **4** span, term, time **5** range, reach **6** period, radius **7** compass **8** diameter, distance, duration, interval **9** dimension, longitude

LENGTHEN: **6** expand, extend **7** augment, produce, prolong, stretch **8** continue, elongate, increase, protract

LENGTHY: **4** long **5** wordy **6** padded **7** tedious **8** extended **10** protracted

LENIENT: **3** lax **4** easy, kind, mild **6** gentle **7** clement, sparing **8** merciful, relaxing, soothing, tolerant **9** assuasive, condoning, emollient, forgiving, pardoning **10** benevolent, charitable, permissive **11** sympathetic

LENS: **5** glass, optic **7** bifocal, contact, monocle **8** meniscus, trifocal **10** spectacles
curved inward: **7** concave
curved outward: **6** convex

LENTIGO: **4** spot **7** freckle

LEOPARD: **3** cat **7** cheetah, panther
located: **4** Asia **6** Africa

LEPRECHAUN: **3** elf **5** dwarf, fairy **6** sprite
origin: **13** Irish folklore

LESE MAJESTY: **5** crime **6** attack **7** offense

LESION: **3** cut **4** flaw, gash, sore **5** tumor, ulcer, wound **6** injury **7** abscess

LESOTHO:
capital: **6** Maseru
cities: **4** Hoek, Roma **7** Mohales, Quthing **8** Mafeteng **12** Teyateyaneng
continent: **6** Africa
formerly: **10** Basutoland
languages: **4** Zulu **5** Xhosa **7** English, Sesotho
monetary unit: **4** rand **6** maluti
native: **7** Basotho
water: **6** Orange **7** Caledon

LESS: **5** fewer, lower, minus **6** little **7** reduced, smaller **8** inferior **9** shortened **10** diminished

LESSEE: **6** renter, tenant

LESSEN: **4** ease, wane **5** abate, lower **6** dilute, impair, minify, narrow, reduce, shrink, soften, weaken **7** abridge, assuage, curtail, degrade, deplete, lighten, relieve, subside **8** belittle, condense, contract, decrease, diminish, downsize, minimize, mitigate, truncate **9** alleviate, attenuate, disparage **10** depreciate

LESSER: **5** lower, minor **7** reduced, smaller **8** inferior **9** secondary

LESSON: **4** task, text **5** class, model, moral, study **6** rebuke **7** example, lecture, message, reading, reproof, warning **8** exercise, practice **9** deterrent, education, reprimand **10** assignment, experience **11** instruction

LESSOR: **5** owner **7** grantor **8** landlord

LET: **4** hire, rent **5** allow, cause, grant, lease, leave **6** permit, suffer **7** approve, charter, license, release **8** tolerate **9** authorize

LETDOWN: **4** blow **5** slump **7** setback **8** drawback **10** anticlimax **11** frustration **14** disappointment

LET GO: **4** emit, fire, free, sack **7** dismiss

LETHAL: **5** fatal, toxic **6** deadly, mortal, poison **7** harmful **9** dangerous, poisonous

LETHARGIC: **4** dull, lazy, slow **5** heavy, inert **6** sleepy, torpid **7** languid **8** comatose, inactive, listless, slothful, sluggish **9** apathetic, enervated **10** lackluster

LETHARGY: **5** sleep **6** apathy, stupor, torpor **7** inertia, languor **8** laziness **9** lassitude **10** inactivity **11** impassivity **12** sluggishness

LET IN: **5** admit, enter **7** receive

LET OFF: **4** drop, free **5** spare **6** acquit, excuse, pardon **7** absolve, forgive **9** exonerate

LET ON: **4** hint **5** admit **7** confess, divulge, pretend, suggest **8** disclose, indicate **11** acknowledge

LETTER: **4** line, mail, note, sign **5** brief, chain, vowel **6** billet, screed, symbol **7** epistle, message, missive **8** dispatch, document, postcard **9** character, consonant **13** communication
large: **7** capital **9** majuscule, uppercase
small: **9** lowercase, minuscule

LETTUCE: **5** money **9** vegetable **10** greenbacks
types: **5** chalk, water **6** Boston, garden **7** iceberg, romaine

LETUP: **4** ease, lull, stop, wane **5** break, pause **7** slacken **8** diminish, slowdown **9** abatement, cessation, reduction

LEVEE: **4** bank, dike, dock, pier, quay **5** berth, jetty, ridge **6** durbar **7** landing **10** embankment

LEVEL: **3** aim **4** even, flat, rank, raze, same **5** equal, floor, flush, grade, layer, plane, point, stage, story **6** degree, direct, reduce, smooth, steady **7** aligned, destroy, flatten, matched, uniform **8** balanced, demolish, parallel, position **10** aboveboard, consistent, horizontal, straighten **13** proportionate

LEVELHEADED: **4** cool **5** sound **6** poised **8** composed, rational, sensible, together **9** collected, practical **10** reasonable

LEVER: **3** bar, lam, pry **4** jack, tool **5** jimmy, peavy **6** binder, peavey **7** crowbar, machine, treadle

LEVERAGE: **5** clout, power **6** credit, weight **9** advantage, influence

LEVI:
father: **5** Jacob
mother: **4** Leah
son: **6** Kohath, Merari **7** Gershom
tribe: **6** Levite

LEVIATHAN: **4** ship **5** giant, large **6** dragon **8** creature, enormous

LEVITATE: **4** lift, rise **5** float, hover **7** suspend

LEVITY: **3** fun **5** humor **6** humour, laughs **8** buoyancy, hilarity **9** amusement, frivolity, lightness, silliness **11** foolishness, inconstancy

LEVY: **3** fee, tax **4** duty, toll, wage **5** exact **6** assess, burden, charge, extent, impose, tariff **7** collect **10** assessment

LEWD: **4** base, racy, rude **5** bawdy **6** coarse, filthy, vulgar, wanton, wicked **7** lustful, obscene **8** indecent, unchaste **9** lecherous, salacious **10** lascivious, licentious, suggestive **12** pornographic

LEXICOGRAPHER: **6** author, editor **7** definer **8** compiler, linguist

LEXICON: **8** glossary, language, wordlist **9** morphemes, thesaurus **10** dictionary, vocabulary **11** onomasticon

LIABILITY: **4** debt, duty **5** blame, minus **6** burden **8** drawback, exposure **9** hindrance, proneness **10** obligation **11** shortcoming **14** accountability, responsibility

LIABLE: **3** apt **5** bound, incur, prone **6** likely **7** exposed, subject **8** inclined **10** answerable, penetrable **11** accountable, responsible, susceptible

LIAISON: **4** bond, link **5** amour, fling **6** affair **7** contact **8** intrigue, mediator **9** encounter **12** intermediary, relationship

LIAR: **5** cheat **6** fibber **8** deceiver, perjurer **10** fabricator **11** exaggerator, pseudologue **12** prevaricator

LIBEL: **5** smear **6** defame, malign, vilify **7** calumny, lampoon, scandal, slander **9** denigrate, discredit **10** calumniate, defamation

LIBERAL: **4** free, open **5** ample, broad **6** giving, lavish **7** lenient, profuse, radical **8** abundant, flexible, generous, handsome **9** bounteous, bountiful, plentiful **10** benevolent, charitable, freehanded, munificent, openhanded **11** broad-minded, progressive

LIBERATE: **4** free **5** clear **6** acquit, loosen, redeem, rescue, unbind **7** deliver, manumit, release, unchain **8** unfetter **9** discharge, unshackle **10** emancipate

LIBERIA:
capital: **8** Monrovia
cities: **8** Buchanan, Marshall **10** Greenville
continent: **6** Africa
ethnic groups: **3** Kru, Kwa, Vai, Vei **4** Kroo, Toma **5** Bassa, Gibbi, Greba **6** Krooby, Kruman **7** Krooboy, Krooman **15** Americo-Liberian
languages: **3** Kwa **7** English
monetary unit: **6** dollar
native: **8** Liberian
water: **5** Manna **8** Atlantic, San Pedro

LIBERTINE: **4** lewd, rake, roue **7** immoral, lustful **9** debauchee, dissolute **10** lascivious, libidinous, licentious, sensualist **11** freethinker

LIBERTY: **5** leave, right **6** choice **7** freedom, license **8** autonomy, furlough **9** privilege **10** permission **11** sovereignty **12** emancipation, independence

LIBIDINOUS: **4** lewd **6** carnal, wanton **7** lustful, satyric **9** libertine **10** lascivious

LIBRARY: **5** books **7** archive, gallery **10** anthenaeum **11** bibliotheca, institution, reading room

LIBYA:
capital: **7** Tripoli
cities: **6** Tobruk **8** Benghazi, Misurata
continent: **6** Africa
ethnic groups: **10** Arab-Berber
features: **5** Bette **6** Fezzan, Giofra **8** Al-Kufrah, Sabratha **9** Giararbub **11** Leptis Magna
language: **6** Arabic
monetary unit: **5** dinar
native: **6** Libyan
water: **5** Sidra, Sirte

LICENSE: **4** pass **5** allow, leave, proof **6** excise, laxity, patent, permit **7** charter, empower, freedom, liberty **8** passport, sanction, variance **9** authority, authorize, franchise, looseness **10** permission **11** certificate, entitlement, unrestraint

LICENTIOUS: **4** free, lewd **5** loose **6** amoral, carnal, unruly, wanton **7** immoral, lustful, obscene, satyric **8** depraved **9** dissolute, libertine **10** lascivious, libidinous, profligate **11** promiscuous **12** uncontrolled, unprincipled, unrestrained

LICIT: **5** legal **6** lawful **8** licensed **10** authorized, sanctioned **11** permissible

LICK: **3** hit, lap, win **4** beat, flog, whip **5** graze, punch, smack, speed, taste, trace **6** defeat, stroke, thrash, tongue **7** clobber, conquer, shellac, trounce **8** overcome, surmount

LICKETY-SPLIT: **4** fast **5** jiffy, speed **7** quickly, rapidly, swiftly

LID: **3** cap, top **4** curb, hood, plug, roof **5** cover, limit **7** maximum **9** restraint

LIE: **3** fib **4** bask, loll, rest, tale **5** exist, fudge, story **6** canard, deceit, invent, lounge, remain, repose, sprawl **7** beguile, deceive, distort, falsify, falsity, mislead, perjury, recline, untruth **8** languish, misstate, position, situated **9** deception, fabricate, falsehood, misinform, prostrate **10** dishonesty, equivocate, inveracity **11** fabrication, prevaricate

LIECHTENSTEIN:
capital: **5** Vaduz
cities: **6** Schaan **7** Balzers, Ruggell
continent: **6** Europe
ethnic groups: **7** Italian **9** Alemannic
features: **4** Alps **11** Rhine Valley
languages: **6** German **9** Alemannic
monetary unit: **5** franc

LIEN: **5** claim, right **6** charge **8** mortgage

LIEU: **5** place, stead **7** instead **10** substitute

LIFE: **4** path, soul, span, zest **5** being, cycle, human, moral, plant, vigor **6** animal, biosis, course, energy, entity, living, memoir, nature, period, spirit **7** essence, history, journey **8** vitality **9** animation, biography, existence **10** enthusiasm **11** development **13** autobiography

LIFELESS: **4** cold, dead, dull, flat **5** amort, empty, inert, spent, stiff, vapid **6** barren, static, torpid, wooden **7** defunct, extinct **8** deceased, inactive, listless **9** bloodless, inanimate, lethargic **10** lackluster, spiritless **11** uninhabited

LIFELIKE: **7** graphic **8** accurate **9** realistic, simulated **12** naturalistic

LIFETIME: **3** age, day **4** span **5** being **6** period **7** forever **8** duration **9** endurance, existence

LIFEWORK: **4** work **6** career **7** calling, purpose, pursuit **8** vocation **10** occupation, profession

LIFT: **3** aid, pry **4** hand, help, jack, rear, ride, rise, take **5** boost, crane, exalt, heave, hoist, mount, raise, steal, swipe, theft **6** ascend, aspire, pilfer, repeal, revoke **7** derrick, elevate, enhance, improve, purloin, rescind, support, upgrade **8** elevator, levitate, ligament **9** encourage, transport

LIGAMENT: **3** tie **4** band, bind, bond **6** tissue

LIGATURE: **3** tie **4** band, bond, cord, link, wire **7** bandage, binding **8** filament **10** connection

LIGHT: **4** airy, beam, bulb, dawn, deft, easy, fair, fire, glow, lamp, land, mild, moon, neon, soft **5** blond, faded, flame, flare, flash, happy, merry, perch, petty, shine, small, spark, sunny, torch **6** beacon, bright, candle, casual, dainty, gentle, ignite, kindle, lively, lucent, lumine, nimble, pastel, simple **7** animate, buoyant, fragile, glimmer, lantern, slender, sunrise, trivial **8** attitude, brighten, carefree, cheerful, daybreak, delicate, ethereal, graceful, illumine, luminary, luminous, portable, radiance, trifling, untaxing **9** frivolous **10** capricious, illuminate, weightless **11** fluorescent, undemanding
god: **3** Lug, Sol **4** Inti **5** Surya **6** Balder, Helios

measure: **3** lux **4** phot **5** lumen **7** candela
northern: **6** aurora
rainbow: **8** spectrum

LIGHTEN: **4** ease, fade **5** allay, gleam, shine **6** bleach, dilute, lessen, reduce, unload **7** gladden, relieve **8** brighten, decrease, jettison, unburden **9** alleviate **10** illuminate

LIGHT-HEADED: **5** dizzy, faint, giddy, silly, woozy **7** flighty **8** unsteady **9** delirious

LIGHTHEARTED: **4** glad **5** happy, merry **6** blithe, jovial, lively, upbeat **7** buoyant **8** carefree, cheerful, spirited, volatile **9** vivacious **10** untroubled

LIGHTLESS: **4** dark **5** black **6** gloomy

LIGHTLY: **6** easily, gently, mildly, softly, subtly **7** faintly **8** daintily, gingerly, tenderly **12** effortlessly

LIKABLE: **4** nice **6** genial **7** amiable **8** charming, friendly, pleasant **10** attractive, personable

LIKE: **4** love, same, wish **5** enjoy, equal, favor **6** admire, choose, prefer, relish **7** approve, cherish, endorse, related, similar, uniform **8** parallel **9** identical **10** compatible, equivalent, homogenous, preference, synonymous

LIKELIHOOD: **6** chance **8** prospect **10** appearance **11** possibility, probability

LIKELY: **3** apt **5** prone **6** liable **7** hopeful **8** destined, expected, feasible, inclined, possible, probable, suitable **9** promising **10** achievable, attainable, believable, presumably **11** conceivable

LIKENESS: **4** copy, twin **5** clone, guise, image **6** double, effigy, parity, statue **7** analogy, picture, replica **8** affinity, parallel, portrait **9** duplicate, facsimile, imitation, rendition, semblance **10** comparison, photograph, similarity, similitude **11** equivalence **12** reproduction

LIKEWISE: **3** and, too **4** also **5** ditto **7** besides **8** moreover **9** similarly **11** furthermore

LIKING: **4** lust **5** fancy, gusto, taste **7** delight **8** affinity, appetite, fondness, penchant, pleasure, tendency **9** affection **10** preference, propensity **11** inclination **12** appreciation

LILLIPUTIAN: **4** tiny **5** dwarf, petty, small **6** little, midget **7** trivial **10** diminutive, teeny-weeny

LILT: **3** air **4** move, sing, song, tune **10** intonation

LILY: **3** pad **4** aloe, ixia, pond, rain, sego, toad **5** calla, glory, magic, plant, tiger, water, yucca **6** flower, meadow, orange, spider **7** panther, western **8** climbing, flamingo, mariposa, mountain **9** butterfly, celestial
family: **9** liliaceae
genus: **6** Lilium

LILY-LIVERED: **5** timid **6** afraid, coward, yellow **7** chicken, gutless **12** fainthearted

LIMB: **3** arm, fin, leg **4** edge, twig, wing **5** bough **6** branch, member **7** flipper **8** offshoot **9** appendage, extension, extremity **10** projection, prosthesis

LIMBER: **4** spry **5** agile, lithe **6** loosen, pliant, supple **7** elastic, pliable **8** flexible, graceful **9** resilient

LIMBO: **5** dance **7** neglect, nowhere **8** oblivion

LIME: **4** tree **5** color, fruit, green, shrub **6** citrus **12** calcium oxide
in caves: **10** stalactite, stalagmite

LIMIT: **3** end, fix, set **4** curb, edge, goal, mete, term **5** bound, brink, check, fence, quota, verge **6** border, curfew, define, extent, finish, ration **7** barrier, ceiling, closure, confine, extreme, inhibit, maximum **8** absolute, boundary, conclude, contract, deadline, restrain, restrict, ultimate **9** constrain, extremity **12** circumscribe

LIMITED: **3** few, ltd **5** local, short **6** finite, narrow, scanty **8** confined, reserved **10** inadequate, restricted

LIMITLESS: **4** vast **7** endless, eternal **8** infinite, unending 9 boundless, countless **10** bottomless **12** immeasurable, unrestricted

LIMN: **4** draw **5** paint **6** depict **8** describe **9** delineate, represent

LIMP: **4** gimp, lame, soft, weak **5** hitch, loose **6** dodder, droopy, falter, feeble, flabby, flimsy, floppy, hobble, limber, wilted, wobble **7** flaccid, stagger **8** flexible **9** enervated

LIMPID: **4** pure **5** clear, lucid **6** bright, serene **8** distinct, pellucid **10** untroubled **11** crystalline, translucent, transparent **14** comprehensible

LINCOLN, ABRAHAM:
assassin: **15** John Wilkes Booth
children: **6** Thomas **10** Robert Todd **11** Edward Baker **14** William Wallace
debate: **14** Lincoln-Douglas
nickname: **9** Honest Abe **12** Railsplitter
presidential order: **9** sixteenth
speech: **17** Gettysburg Address
state represented: **8** Illinois
war: **8** Civil War
wife: **8** Mary Todd

LINE: **3** job, pad, row **4** axis, cord, dash, draw, file, mark, path, rank, rope, rule, seam, tier, wire **5** cable, goods, march, queue, route, stock, track, trade **6** border, column, course, family, groove, letter, method, policy, stitch, streak, string, stripe, stroke, suture, system **7** barrier, carrier, contour, descent, message, pattern, pursuit, scratch, wrinkle **8** ancestry, boundary, business, division, heredity, vocation **9** formation, principle, procedure **10** employment, occupation **13** configuration

LINEAGE: **4** clan, race **5** birth, blood, breed, stock, tribe **6** family, stirps **7** descent, kindred **8** ancestry, heredity, pedigree **9** forebears, genealogy **10** background

LINEMAN: **3** end **5** guard **6** center, tackle

LINEN: **4** brin, lawn **5** cloth, paper, toile **6** barras, damask, fabric, sheets, thread **7** bedding, brabant, cambric, dornick **8** articles, garments

LINER: **4** boat, ship **6** insert, vessel **8** airplane

LINE-UP: **4** list **5** slate **6** roster **8** schedule

LINGER: **3** lag **4** drag, idle, poke, stay, wait **5** cling, delay, dwell, mosey, tarry **6** dawdle, loiter, remain, trifle **7** fritter, survive **10** dillydally

LINGO: **4** cant **5** argot, idiom, slang **6** jargon, patter **7** dialect **8** language **10** vernacular, vocabulary

LINGUIST: **8** polyglot **9** pantoglot **10** grammarian **11** interpreter, philologist **13** lexicographer

LINIMENT: **3** oil **4** balm **6** arnica, lotion **8** ointment **11** embrocation

LINK: **3** tie **4** band, fuse, join **5** chain, group, hitch, nexus, unite **6** braced, couple, course, faster **7** combine, conjoin, connect, contact, involve, network **8** catenate **9** associate, component, implicate, interface **10** connection

LION: **3** cat **4** king, puma, star **5** simba **6** cougar, feline **7** notable **8** wildcats **9** celebrity
constellation: **3** Leo
group: **5** pride
young: **3** cub

LIONHEARTED: **4** bold **5** brave **7** valiant **8** fearless, intrepid **10** courageous

LIP: **3** rim, tip **4** brim, edge, kiss, wash **5** brink, mouth, spout, utter **6** border, labium, margin, nozzle **8** backtalk, labellum **9** insolence

LIQUEUR: **4** ouzo **5** creme **6** Kahlua **7** alcohol, cordial, ratafee, sambuca **8** amaretto, anisette, Drambuie **9** triple sec **11** benedictine **12** Grand Marnier

LIQUID: **5** fluid, juice **6** fluent, liquor, melted, nectar, watery **7** aqueous, extract, solvent **8** beverage, solution **9** available, dissolved **11** convertible

LIQUIDATE: **4** kill **5** clear, repay **6** murder, settle, square **7** abolish **8** amortize, dissolve **9** eliminate, terminate

LIQUOR: **3** ale, gin, rum, rye **4** beer, brew, grog, sake, wine **5** booze, drink, hooch, lager, stout, vodka **6** brandy, scotch **7** alcohol, bitters, bourbon, cordial, spirits, whiskey **8** beverage, cocktail **9** firewater, moonshine **10** intoxicant

LISSOME: **5** agile **6** limber, nimble, pliant **8** athletic, flexible, graceful

LIST: **3** tip **4** bill, cant, file, keel, lean, roll, tilt **5** brief, canon, chart, count, index, slate, slope, table **6** careen, census, docket, record, roster **7** arrange, catalog, incline, itemize, lexicon **8** glossary, manifest, register, schedule, tabulate **9** catalogue, directory, inventory **10** dictionary **11** enumeration

LISTEN: **4** hark, hear, heed, note, obey **5** audit **6** attend **7** monitor 8 overhear **9** eavesdrop **10** auscultate **11** concentrate

LISTLESS: **4** dull, lazy **5** bored, faint **6** drowsy, sleepy, supine **7** languid **8** heedless, careless, sluggish **9** apathetic, enervated, heartless, lethargic **10** spiritless **11** inattentive **12** uninterested

LITANY: **4** list **5** chant **6** prayer **7** recital, refrain **8** rogation **10** invocation **12** supplication

LITERAL: **4** real **5** exact **6** actual **7** factual, precise, prosaic **8** accurate, unerring, verbatim **9** authentic

LITERARY: **6** versed **7** bookish, erudite **8** educated, lettered, pedantic **9** scholarly **12** intellectual

LITERATURE: **5** books, essay, novel **6** poetry, thesis **7** article, fiction, letters **8** pamphlet, writings **9** biography **10** nonfiction

LITHE: **4** lean, slim **5** agile **6** clever, limber, nimble, pliant, supple, svelte **7** lissome, slender **8** flexible, graceful

LITHIUM: **7** element

LITHUANIA:
capital: **7** Vilnius
cities: **6** Kaunas **7** Siaulai **8** Klaipeda **9** Panevezys
continent: **6** Europe
ethnic groups: **4** Balt, Lett **5** Zhmud **6** Litvak, Polish **7** Russian, Yatvyag **10** Lithuanian
features: **5** Vilna **12** Kursiu Marios
languages: **5** Zmudz **10** Lithuanian
monetary unit: **3** lit **5** ruble
native: **10** Lithuanian
water: **5** Nemen

LITIGATION: **4** case, suit **5** trial **6** action **7** contest, dispute, lawsuit

LITTER: **3** bed **4** bier, junk, mess, pile **5** brood, couch, straw, trash, waste, young **6** debris, refuse **7** clutter, garbage, mullock, rubbish, rummage **8** disorder **9** offspring, stretcher

LITTLE: **3** wee **4** dash, mean, puny, tiny **5** crumb, dinky, minor, petty, pinch, small, speck, trace **6** petite, seldom, slight **7** stunted **9** miniature **10** diminutive **11** microscopic, unimportant **13** insignificant

LITTLE WOMEN:
author: **15** Louisa May Alcott
character: **6** Laurie **7** Jo March, Mr. Bhaer **8** Amy March, Meg March **9** Beth March **10** John Brooke

LITURGY: **6** ritual **7** service, worship **8** ceremony **9** sacrament

LIVABLE: **4** cozy, snug **8** bearable, suitable **9** endurable, habitable, tolerable **10** acceptable **11** comfortable

LIVE: **4** room **5** abide, board, dwell, exist, vivid **6** active, occupy, reside **7** animate, blazing, breathe, burning, dynamic, glowing, subsist, survive **8** continue, maintain, vigorous **9** energetic **10** experience, unexploded

LIVELIHOOD: **3** job **5** craft, trade **6** career, living **8** business, vocation **10** employment, occupation, profession, sustenance **11** subsistence

LIVELY: **4** airy, busy, spry **5** agile, alert, alive, brisk, eager, fresh, peppy **6** active, blithe, bright, cheery, chirpy, frisky, nimble, snappy **7** buoyant, buzzing, chipper, humming **8** animated, bustling, spirited, vigorous **9** energetic, sprightly, vivacious **11** industrious, stimulating **12** effervescent, enthusiastic

LIVER: **5** gland, hepar, organ **8** tomalley
disease: **9** cirrhosis, hepatitis **11** biliousness

LIVERY: **7** costume, uniform **8** clothing, insignia

LIVID: **4** pale **5** angry, ashen, bleak, irate **6** fuming, purple **7** bruised, enraged, furious **8** incensed **9** colorless **10** discolored

LIVING: **4** work **5** alive, being, bread, means, vital, vivid **6** income **8** animated **9** lifestyle, realistic **10** livelihood, sustenance **11** subsistence

LIZARD:
order: **8** Squamata
suborder: **10** Lacertilia
types: **3** dab, eft **4** adda, dabb, gila, newt **5** agama, anole, gecko, goana, skink **6** flying, iguana **7** monitor, saurian, tuatera, worrell **9** chameleon, galliwasp **10** horned toad **12** Komodo dragon

LOAD: **4** bear, clog, drag, haul, lade, pack, stow, tote **5** cargo, drain, flood, goods, stuff, weigh **6** bundle, burden, hamper, saddle, weight **7** freight, oppress **8** carriage, contents, encumber, pressure, shipment

LOAF: **4** idle, lazy **5** bread, slack **6** dawdle, loiter, lounge **10** dillydally

LOAFER: **3** bum **4** shoe **5** idler **6** slouch **7** lounger, vagrant **8** deadbeat, vagabond **9** lazybones

LOAN: **4** lend **6** borrow, credit **7** advance **8** mortgage **13** accommodation

LOATH: **6** averse, odious **7** against, counter **8** hesitant, inimical **9** reluctant, resisting, unwilling **11** disinclined

LOATHE: **4** hate **5** abhor, scorn, spurn **6** detest **7** deplore, despise, dislike **9** abominate

LOATHSOME: **4** foul, mean, ugly, vile **7** cloying, hateful, hideous **8** horrible **9** abhorrent, obnoxious, offensive, repugnant, revolting **10** abominable, deplorable, detestable, disgusting, nauseating **11** distasteful, undesirable

LOB: **3** hit **4** toss **5** heave, throw **6** launch, propel

LOBBY: **4** hall, room **5** foyer, pitch **7** advance, doorway, promote, solicit **8** anteroom, entrance, persuade **9** influence, vestibule

LOBSTER: **7** decapod **10** crustacean
liver: **8** tomalley
trap: **5** creel
types: **4** rock **5** black, Maine, spiny **6** Norway **8** American, European **11** grasshopper

LOCAL: **6** narrow, native **7** endemic, insular, limited, topical **8** confined, regional **9** homegrown **10** provincial, restricted **12** neighborhood

LOCALE: **4** area, site, zone **5** place, scene **6** domain, region, sector **8** district, locality, vicinity **12** neighborhood

LOCATE: **3** see **4** espy, find, seat, site, spot **5** dwell, stand, trace **6** detect, settle **7** situate, uncover **8** discover, pinpoint, position **9** establish

LOCATION: **4** area, site, spot **5** place, point, scene **7** habitat **8** bearings, position **9** situation **11** whereabouts

LOCH: **4** lake **5** lough

LOCK: **4** bolt, cage, curl, grip, hook, link, seal, tuft, wisp **5** clamp, latch, tress **6** fasten, secure **7** confine, ringlet **8** fastener

LOCKUP: **4** jail **5** clink, pokey **6** cooler, prison **7** slammer **8** hoosegow **9** calaboose **12** penitentiary

LOCUST: **6** cicada, insect **11** grasshopper
types: **4** bald **5** water **6** yellow **12** greenstriped **13** Rocky Mountain, seventeen-year

LODE: **4** lead, vein **6** strike **7** deposit, fissure

LODGE: **4** camp, club **5** board, cabin, couch, dwell, hotel, motel **6** bestow, encamp, harbor, hostel **7** chapter, cottage, shelter **8** domicile **11** accommodate, brotherhood

LODGING: **3** bed, hut, inn **4** camp, nest, room, tent **5** abode **6** tavern, teepee, wigwam **8** barracks, chambers, dwelling, hostelry, quarters **9** dormitory, longhouse, residence **10** habitation

LOFT: **5** attic, raise **6** dormer, garret, studio **7** balcony, gallery

LOFTY: **4** aery, epic, high, tall **5** grand, noble, proud, steep **6** aerial, mighty, raised **7** arduous, eminent, exalted, haughty, pompous, soaring, stately **8** arrogant, elevated, eloquent, generous, imposing, majestic **9** dignified **11** overbearing **13** condescending, distinguished

LOG: **4** wood **5** diary, stump **6** billet, record, timber **7** account, journal **8** register

LOGGER: **6** cutter **10** lumberjack **11** woodchopper

LOGIC: **5** sense **8** analysis **9** deduction, rationale, reasoning **10** connection, philosophy

LOGICAL: **4** wise **5** clear, sound, valid **8** coherent, rational, sensible **10** analytical, perceptive, reasonable **11** intelligent

LOITER: **4** idle, laze, loaf, loll **5** delay, tarry **6** dawdle, linger, lounge, slough, stroll **7** saunter **8** hesitate **10** dillydally

LOLL: **4** idle, loaf **5** droop, tarry **6** dangle, dawdle, loiter, lounge, slouch, sprawl **7** recline

LONDON:
features: **4** Soho **5** Acton **6** Big Ben **7** Adelphi, Alsatia, Mayfair, St. James **8** Hyde Park, Victoria **9** Battersea **12** Madam Tussaud **13** Tower of London **15** Trafalgar Square
native: **7** Cockney **8** Londoner
place: **7** England **12** Great Britain **13** United Kingdom
streets: **4** Bond **5** Fleet **7** Downing **9** Haymarket, Whitehall **10** Piccadilly
subway: **4** tube **11** underground
water: **6** Thames

LONDON, JACK: **6** author
wrote: **7** The Game **9** White Fang **10** Before Adam, Martin Eden, The Sea Wolf **12** The Star Rover **14** John Barleycorn **16** The Call of the Wild

LONE: **4** sole, solo **5** alone, apart **6** single, unique **8** isolated, secluded, solitary **10** individual

LONELY: **5** alone, apart **7** forlorn **8** deserted, desolate, forsaken, homesick, isolated, lonesome, secluded, solitary **9** abandoned, withdrawn **10** friendless

LONE RANGER, THE:
cast: **8** John Hart **12** Clayton Moore **14** Jay Silverheels
companion: **5** Tonto
creator: **13** George Trendle
horse: **6** Silver

LONE STAR STATE: **5** Texas

LONG: **4** ache, hope, lust, miss, pine, want **5** crave, yearn **6** desire, hunger, prolix, thirst **7** lengthy, tedious **8** eternity, extended, tiresome, unending **9** elongated, extensive **10** protracted **12** interminable

LONG-STANDING: **6** rooted **7** durable, lasting **8** enduring **9** continual, perpetual **10** persistent

LONG-SUFFERING: **7** lenient, patient **8** patience, tolerant **10** forbearing

LONG-WINDED: **5** spiel, wordy **6** prolix **7** diffuse, lengthy, verbose **8** rambling **9** garrulous, redundant **11** periphrasis

LOOK: **3** air, see **4** face, gape, gawk, gaze, leer, ogle, peek, peep, peer, scan, view **5** fleer, focus, glare, scout, sight, snoop, stare, watch **6** aspect, behold, expect, gander, glance, glower, goggle, notice, review, search, squint, visage **7** glimpse, inspect **8** demeanor **10** appearance, expression, scrutinize **11** observation **12** surveillance **14** characteristic, reconnaissance

LOOK AFTER: **4** tend **5** guard, watch **6** attend **7** protect, support

LOOK AT: **3** eye, see **4** gape, leer, view **6** behold, goggle **7** examine, inspect, observe

LOOK BACK: **6** recall, review **7** reflect **8** remember **9** hindsight, reminisce **10** retrospect

LOOK DOWN ON: **5** spurn **7** despise **8** dominate **9** patronize **10** condescend

LOOKER-ON: **7** witness **8** audience, observer **9** bystander, spectator

LOOK FOR: **4** hunt, seek **5** await **6** expect, pursue, search **8** research

LOOK INTO: **4** sift **5** check, probe, study **7** examine, explore, inspect **8** research **11** investigate

LOOK OUT: **4** mind **6** beware, notice **7** hearken

LOOKOUT: **4** post **5** guard, scout, vigil, watch **6** beacon, patrol, sentry **8** observer, sentinel **9** crow's nest **10** watchtower, widow's walk **11** perspective **12** surveillance

LOOK OVER: **4** scan, skim **6** browse, ignore, survey **9** disregard

LOOK UP: **4** seek **7** improve **8** discover, progress, research **10** recuperate

LOOM: **4** brew, dawn, hulk, near **5** tower, weave **6** appear, emerge, gather, impend **7** emanate, machine **8** threaten **9** implement **11** materialize

LOON: **3** nut, sap **4** bird, dolt

LOONY: **5** crazy, silly, wacky **6** insane **7** foolish, lunatic **8** demented, deranged

LOOP: **3** arc, bow, eye **4** bend, coil, curl, fold, kink, knot, ring, turn **5** curve, noose, picot, twirl **6** billet, circle, spiral **7** circuit **8** surround

LOOPHOLE: **3** out **4** slit **5** alibi **6** escape, excuse, outlet **7** opening **8** aperture

LOOSE: **3** lax **4** easy, fast, free, open, wild **5** apart, baggy, slack, vague **6** coarse, flabby, limber, random, undone, unlash, wobbly **7** immoral, movable, relaxed, unbound, uncaged, unchain, unhitch, unleash **8** careless, detached, insecure, separate, unstable **9** dissolute, liberated, unbridled, unchecked, untighten **10** indefinite, unattached, unconfined, unfastened **11** promiscuous **12** disconnected, unrestrained

LOOSE END: **6** detail **7** problem

LOOSEN: **4** ease, free, undo **5** relax, untie **6** unbind **7** relieve, slacken, unchain **8** liberate, unfasten **9** extricate **10** disconnect

LOOT: **3** rob **4** sack **5** booty, dough, money, prize, steal, strip, swipe **6** pilfer, ravage, snatch, spoils **7** pillage, plunder

LOOTER: **5** thief **6** robber **8** marauder, pillager **9** plunderer

LOP: **3** cut **4** clip, crop, flop, hang, snip, trim **5** droop, prune, slice **6** dangle **8** truncate **9** eliminate

LOPSIDED: **6** tipped, uneven, warped **7** crooked, leaning, unequal **8** cockeyed, unsteady **9** irregular **10** unbalanced

LOQUACIOUS: **5** gabby, noisy, wordy **8** babbling **9** garrulous, jabbering, talkative **10** chattering

LORD: **4** earl, king, peer **5** ruler **6** bishop, master, prince **7** marquis, royalty **8** governor, nobleman, seigneur **9** landowner **10** aristocrat

LORDLY: **5** bossy, grand, lofty, noble, proud, regal **6** august, uppity **7** haughty, stately **8** arrogant, cavalier, despotic, gracious, majestic, snobbish, superior **9** dignified, grandiose, honorable, masterful **11** dictatorial, domineering, magisterial, magnificent, overbearing **13** condescending, high-and-mighty

LORE: **4** myth, tale **5** fable **6** belief, custom, legend, wisdom **7** history **8** learning **9** erudition, knowledge, tradition **12** superstition

LORGNETTE: **8** eyeglass **10** opera glass

LOS ANGELES:
features: **9** Hollywood, Long Beach **12** Beverly Hills
nickname: **8** La-La Land **9** Hollywood
place: **10** California

LOSE: **4** fail, miss **5** elude, stray, waste **6** defeat, mislay, wander **7**

bereave, default, forfeit **8** displace, misplace **9** surrender

LOSER: **4** bomb, bust, flop **5** lemon **7** failure **8** deadbeat, underdog

LOSS: **4** cost, leak, ruin **5** death, price, waste **6** damage, defeat, injury **7** deficit, failure **8** accident, calamity, casualty, decrease, disaster **9** privation, sacrifice **10** affliction, misfortune **11** bereavement, deprivation, destruction

LOST: **4** dead, gone, rapt **6** absent, doomed, hidden, ruined, wasted **7** extinct, mislaid, missing, strayed **8** absorbed, confused, defeated, dreaming, obscured, perished **9** abandoned, destroyed, engrossed, forfeited, forgotten, perplexed **10** abstracted, squandered **11** disappeared, irrevocable, preoccupied

LOT: **4** doom, fate, heap, land, luck, plat, plot **5** batch, bunch, clump, field, group, share, tract **6** amount, bundle, chance, hazard, number, parcel, ration **7** destiny, fortune, portion **8** clearing, quantity **9** allotment, allowance **10** assortment, percentage

LOT:
father: **5** Haran
place of flight: **5** Sodom
sister: **6** Milcah
son: **4** Moab **5** Ammon
uncle: **7** Abraham

LOTION: **3** oil **4** balm **5** cream, salve **8** ablution, cleanser, liniment, ointment **11** moisturizer

LOTTERY: **5** lotto **6** chance, gamble, raffle **7** contest, drawing **10** sweepstake

LOUD: **5** gaudy, noisy, showy **6** brazen, flashy, vulgar **7** blaring, blatant, glaring, obvious, raucous, roaring, splashy **8** colorful, emphatic, piercing, strident, vehement **9** deafening, obnoxious, offensive, turbulent, unrefined **10** bigmouthed, blustering, boisterous, stentorian, thundering, tumultuous, vociferous **12** earsplitting, ostentatious

LOUISIANA:
bird: **7** pelican
capital: **10** Baton Rouge
cities: **7** Augusta **9** Lafayette **10** New Orleans, Shreveport **11** Lake Charles **12** Natchitoches
dialect: **6** creole
division: **6** parish
explorers: **6** de Soto, de Vaca, Pineda
features: **8** Driskill **9** Mardi Gras **11** plantations **13** French Quarter
flower: **8** magnolia
native: **5** Cajun **6** Creole **7** Acadian **11** Louisianian
nickname: **11** Creole State **12** Pelican State
tree: **7** cypress
water: **11** Mississippi

LOUNGE: **3** bar, pub **4** club, idle, loaf, loll, rest, sofa **5** couch, lobby, relax **6** loiter, parlor, saloon, slouch **7** recline

LOUSE: **3** cad, rat **5** knave **6** cootie, insect **9** scoundrel

LOUSY: **3** bad **4** poor **5** awful, dirty **6** rotten **8** horrible, terrible **10** pediculous

LOUT: **3** bow, oaf **4** bend, boor, clod, dolt, fool, twit **5** clown, klutz, stoop **6** curtsy, lummox **7** bumpkin **8** dumbbell **10** clodhopper

LOVABLE: **4** dear **5** sweet **6** cuddly, tender **7** winning **8** adorable, charming **9** endearing **11** captivating, enthralling

LOVE: **4** dear, like **5** adore, agape, fancy, flame **6** admire, caress, enamor **7** charity, cherish, embrace, feeling, idolize **8** devotion,

fondness, goodwill, precious **9** adoration, affection, valentine **10** enthusiasm, sweetheart **11** infatuation
god: **4** Amor, Eros **5** Cupid
goddess: **5** Venus **6** Hathor, Ishtar **7** Astarte **9** Aphrodite

LOVE AFFAIR: **5** amour **7** liaison, romance **10** enthusiasm **12** relationship

LOVELY: **4** cute, nice **5** sweet **6** pretty, tender **7** angelic **8** adorable, charming, graceful, pleasant **9** beautiful, delicious, exquisite **10** attractive, enchanting **11** captivating **12** irresistible

LOVER: **3** fan **4** beau, buff, wife **5** flame, Romeo **6** fiance, suitor **7** admirer, Don Juan, fiancee, husband **8** lothario, mistress, paramour **9** boyfriend, Cassanova **10** enthusiast, girlfriend, sweetheart

LOVESICK: **7** longing **8** yearning **10** moonstruck **11** languishing

LOVING: **4** fond, warm **6** caring, erotic, tender **7** amorous, devoted **8** faithful **10** benevolent, passionate **11** considerate **12** affectionate

LOW: **4** base, bass, blue, deep, down, glum, mean, rude, vile, weak **5** crude, cruel, dirty, faint, gross, nasty, quiet, short, small, under **6** coarse, common, filthy, humble, hushed, slight, sordid, vulgar **7** beneath, bestial, ignoble, muffled, nominal, reduced, shallow, unhappy **8** degraded, dejected, inferior, murmured, plebeian, unworthy **9** depressed, destitute, miserable, offensive, unethical, whispered, woebegone **10** economical, melancholy **11** undignified, unfavorable **12** contemptible

LOWBRED: **5** crude **6** coarse, common, vulgar **7** boorish **9** unrefined

LOW-DOWN: **4** base, mean, vile **9** depressed **10** despicable **12** contemptible

LOWER: **3** dip **4** drop, fall, mute, sink **5** abase, abate, below, demit, droop, glare, scowl, under **6** debase, demean, demote, glower, humble, lessen, nether, reduce **7** beneath, cheapen, degrade, depress, descend, devalue, immerse, subside **8** diminish, inferior, submerge **9** decreased, disparage, downgrade **10** depreciate

LOW-KEY: **6** subtle **7** relaxed, subdued **8** laid-back, softened **9** easygoing

LOWLAND: **4** flat, holm, vale **5** marsh, swamp **6** valley **7** bottoms

LOWLY: **4** base, mean, meek **5** plain **6** humble, modest, simple **7** ignoble, mundane, prosaic **8** ordinary **10** unassuming **11** commonplace

LOW-MINDED: **4** lewd **5** crude **6** coarse, vulgar **9** offensive

LOW POINT: **4** base, foot **5** worst **6** bottom

LOW-PRESSURE: **6** casual **7** relaxed **9** easygoing

LOW-PRICED: **5** cheap **7** bargain **10** discounted, economical **11** inexpensive

LOW-SPIRITED: **4** blue, down **6** gloomy **7** forlorn **8** dejected **9** depressed, woebegone **10** melancholy **11** crestfallen, discouraged

LOYAL: **4** firm, true **7** devoted, dutiful, staunch **8** faithful, reliable **9** patriotic, steadfast **10** dependable **11** trustworthy

LOYALTY: **4** bond **5** honor **8** devotion, fidelity **9** adherence **10** allegiance **12** faithfulness

LUBRICATE: **3** oil **6** anoint, grease, smooth **7** moisten

LUCID: **4** sane **5** clear **6** bright **7** beaming, crystal, evident, obvious, radiant, shining **8** luminous, pellucid, rational, sensible **9** brilliant **11** translucent, transparent **12** intelligible

LUCIFER: **5** devil, Satan **9** archfiend, Beelzebub

LUCK: **3** hit, lot, win **4** fate **5** break, fluke **6** chance, kismet **7** destiny, fortune, handsel, success **8** accident, blessing, fortuity **9** advantage **10** prosperity **11** opportunity

LUCKY: **5** canny, happy **6** golden, timely **7** charmed **9** fortunate, opportune **10** beneficial, propitious, prosperous, successful **12** providential

LUCRATIVE: **6** paying **7** gainful **8** fruitful **10** productive, profitable, worthwhile **11** moneymaking **12** remunerative

LUDICROUS: **4** zany **5** antic, awful, comic, crazy, funny, silly **6** absurd **7** bizarre, comical, foolish **8** farcical **9** laughable **10** ridiculous **11** nonsensical

LUG: **3** box, nut, tow, tug **4** buck, drag, draw, haul, pull, tote, worm **5** carry **6** schlep **9** transport

LUGGAGE: **4** bags, gear **5** truck **7** baggage **8** suitcase

LUGUBRIOUS: **4** dour **5** bleak **6** dismal, gloomy, morose **7** doleful **8** mournful **9** sorrowful, woebegone **10** depressing, melancholy

LUKEWARM: **4** cool **5** tepid **11** halfhearted, indifferent **12** unresponsive **14** unenthusiastic

LULL: **4** calm, ease, hush, stop, wane **5** allay, pause, quell, quiet, still **6** pacify, settle, soothe **7** compose, subside **8** breather, interval, serenity **11** tranquilize

LULLABY: **4** song **5** music **8** berceuse **9** sleepsong **10** cradlesong

LUMBER: **3** log **4** plod, wood **6** boards, burden, timber, trudge **7** blunder, shuffle, useless

LUMBERJACK: **6** cutter, logger **9** lumberman **11** woodchopper

LUMBER STATE: **5** Maine

LUMINARY: **3** sun, VIP **4** star **5** light **6** bigwig, planet **7** notable **8** eminence, somebody **9** celebrity, dignitary

LUMINESCENT: **6** bright **7** glowing, radiant, shining **8** gleaming, luminous **9** twinkling **10** glimmering, glistening **11** fluorescent

LUMINOUS: **5** clear, lucid, vivid **6** bright **7** beaming, evident, glowing, obvious, radiant, shining **9** brilliant, inspiring **11** illuminated, intelligent, luminescent, translucent, transparent

LUMMOX: **3** oaf **4** boor, lout **5** klutz **6** clumsy, stupid **7** bungler

LUMP: **3** gob, wad **4** bear, beat, blob, bulk, burl, cake, clot, heap, hunk, knob, knot, mass, welt **5** bulge, bunch, clump, tumor, wedge **6** endure, gobbet, growth, nodule, nugget **8** swelling **9** aggregate, withstand **12** protuberance

LUMPISH: **4** dull **5** bulky, heavy **6** clumsy, stupid **7** awkward **8** sluggish **10** cumbersome

LUMPY: **5** rough, thick **6** clumsy, uneven

LUNACY: **5** folly, mania **6** idiocy **7** madness **8** insanity **9** absurdity, craziness, silliness, stupidity **10** ineptitude **11** derangement, foolishness

LUNATIC: **3** mad **4** loco, zany **5** batty, crazy, kooky, loony, nutty, wacky **6** cuckoo, insane, madman, maniac, psycho **7** bananas, bonkers, unsound **8** crackpot, demoniac, deranged, maniacal, neurotic **9** psychotic, screwball **10** irrational, psychopath

LUNCHEONETTE: **4** cafe **5** diner **8** snack bar **9** cafeteria **10** restaurant **12** sandwich shop

LUNGE: **4** dive, jump, leap, rush, stab **5** barge, burst, lurch, surge **6** attack, charge, plunge, pounce, thrust

LUPINE: **5** plant **6** fierce **7** wolfish **8** ravenous **9** rapacious

LURCH: **4** jerk, jolt, reel, rock, roll, sway **5** lunge, pitch, weave **6** careen, plunge, swerve, teeter, totter **7** blunder, stagger, stumble **8** flounder

LURE: **4** bait, coax, draw, hook, trap **5** charm, decoy, tempt, trick **6** allure, appeal, cajole, entice, seduce **7** attract, beguile, capture **8** inveigle **9** captivate, fascinate **10** allurement, attraction, camouflage

LURID: **4** gory, grim, pale **5** ashen, fiery, gaudy, livid **6** gloomy, sallow, savage **7** ghastly, graphic, hideous, macabre **8** gruesome, horrible, shocking, terrible **9** appalling **11** sensational

LURK: **4** hide **5** creep, prowl, slink, sneak, snoop **6** ambush **11** unsuspected

LUSCIOUS: **4** rich, ripe **5** juicy, sweet, tasty, yummy **6** divine, ornate, savory **7** opulent, sensual **8** aromatic, delicate, heavenly, sensuous **9** delicious, exquisite, flavorful, succulent **10** appetizing, delightful, voluptuous **11** scrumptious

LUSH: **4** posh, rich, soft **5** drunk, fancy, grand, ritzy **6** deluxe, mellow **7** profuse, sensual **9** alcoholic, ambrosial, elaborate, epicurean, luxurious, succulent **10** delectable

LUST: **4** ache, long, urge, want **6** desire, hunger, thirst **7** craving, passion **8** appetite, cupidity, yearning **9** eroticism **10** aphrodisia

LUSTER: **5** glaze, glint, glory, gloss, sheen, shine **6** beauty, polish **7** sparkle **8** radiance, splendor **10** brightness, brilliance **11** distinction, iridescence

LUSTERLESS: **3** dim, wan **4** dead, drab, dull, flat **5** faded **6** gloomy **7** prosaic **8** lifeless **9** tarnished

LUSTFUL: **4** lewd **7** fulsome, itching **8** prurient **9** lecherous, salacious **10** passionate

LUSTROUS: **6** bright, glossy, sheeny **7** glowing, radiant, shining **8** dazzling, luminous, polished, splendid **9** brilliant, sparkling **10** glistening **11** illustrious

LUSTY: **5** hardy, merry, sound **6** hearty, joyous, mighty, potent, robust, rugged, strong, sturdy, virile **7** dynamic **8** powerful, vigorous **9** energetic

LUXEMBOURG:
capital: **10** Luxembourg
cities: **9** Dudelange **14** Esch-sur-Alzette
continent: **6** Europe
ethnic groups: **6** French, German
features: **7** Oesling **8** Ardennes
languages: **6** French, German **13** Letzeburgesch, Luxembourgish
monetary unit: **5** franc
water: **7** Moselle

LUXURIANT: **4** lush, posh, rank, rich **5** fancy, plush **6** deluxe, lavish, ornate **7** elegant, opulent, profuse **8** sensuous **9** exuberant, sumptuous **10** voluptuous **11** extravagant

LUXURIOUS: **4** lush, posh, rich **5** grand, plush **6** costly **7** elegant, opulent **8** affluent, sensuous, splendid **9** elaborate, expensive, indulgent, sumptuous **11** extravagant, magnificent

LUXURY: **5** bliss, frill **7** amenity, comfort **8** delicacy, hedonism, splendor **10** indulgence **12** extravagance

LUZON:
capital: **10** Quezon City
cities: **5** Gapan **6** Aparri, Manila **10** Cabanatuan
features: **3** Iba **5** Mayon
place: **11** Philippines

LYING: **4** flat **5** false, prone **6** supine **7** fibbing **9** deceitful, dishonest, reclining **10** fraudulent, mendacious, misleading, untruthful **11** treacherous

LYNCH: **4** hang, kill **6** murder **7** execute **8** string up

LYNX: **3** cat **6** bobcat **7** caracal, wildcat **9** catamount

LYRE: **4** harp **6** trigon **7** cithara **10** instrument

LYRIC: **3** ode **4** alba, odic, poem **5** melic, verse, words **6** poetic, rondel **7** musical, rondeau **8** madrigal, sonorous **9** dithyramb

M

MACABRE: **4** grim **5** eerie **6** grisly **7** ghastly **8** dreadful, gruesome, horrible **9** deathlike

MACBETH:
author: **18** William Shakespeare
character: **6** Banquo **7** Fleance, Macbeth, Macduff, Malcolm **10** King Duncan **11** Lady Macbeth **12** three witches
overthrown by: **7** Malcolm
victims: **6** Banquo **10** King Duncan **11** Lady Macduff

MACE: **3** rod **4** club **5** baton, spice, staff **6** mallet, weapon

MACEDONIA:
capital: **12** Thessalonica
cities: **6** Beroea **8** Philippi **9** Chaeronea
features: **5** Athos **7** Balkans, Dysorus **8** Olympiad, Pangaeus **12** Mount Olympus
gods/goddesses: **8** Dionysus
kings/queens: **6** Philip **7** Perseus **8** Galerius **9** Alexander, Antipater
place: **6** Greece **8** Bulgaria **10** Yugoslavia
water: **5** Axius **6** Lydias, Nestus **7** Strymon **9** Haliacmon

MACERATE: **4** mash, soak **6** soften **7** liquefy **8** emaciate, permeate, saturate

MACHETE: **5** blade, knife **6** sickle, weapon

MACHIAVELLI, NICCOLO: **6** author **9** statesman **11** philosopher
wrote: **9** The Prince **10** Discourses **11** The Mandrake

MACHIAVELLIAN: **4** foxy **6** crafty, tricky **7** cunning, devious **9** ambitious, deceitful **11** treacherous **12** unscrupulous

MACHINATION: **4** plan, plot, ruse **6** design, scheme **8** intrigue, maneuver **10** conspiracy **11** contrivance

MACHINE: **3** car **4** auto, tool **5** robot **6** device, engine, gadget **7** vehicle **8** computer, movement **9** apparatus, appliance, mechanism **10** automobile, instrument **11** contraption, contrivance **12** organization

MACHINE GUN: **5** Maxim **6** strafe, weapon **7** Garrand, Gatling **8** Browning, Thompson, Tommy gun **10** chatterbox

MACROCOSM: **5** world **6** cosmos, nature **8** totality, universe

MACULATE: **4** spot **6** impure **7** blemish, defiled, pollute, stained **8** blotched, speckled

MAD: **4** daft, loco, rage, wild **5** angry, crazy, irate, irked, livid, loony, rabid **6** frenzy, fuming, insane, ticked **7** bananas, enraged, foolish, frantic, furious **8** agitated, demented, deranged, frenetic, incensed, maniacal, outraged, unstable **9** desperate, fanatical, illogical, psychotic **10** distracted, distraught, infatuated, infuriated, irrational, unbalanced **12** unreasonable

MADAGASCAR:
animals: **5** indri, lemur **6** aye-aye, tanrec, tenrec
capital: **12** Antananarivo
cities: **7** Toliary **9** Toamasina **10** Tananarivo **11** Antseranana **12** Fianarantsoa
continent: **6** Africa
ethnic groups: **4** Arab **7** African **17** Malayan-Indonesian
island group: **7** Aldabra
languages: **6** French **8** Malagasy
monetary unit: **5** franc
native: **4** Bara, Hova **6** Merina **8** Betsileo, Malagasy, Sakalava **13** Betsimasaraka
water: **11** Indian Ocean

MADAM, MADAME: **3** Mdm, Mme., Mrs. **4** frau, lady **5** donna, title, woman **6** senora **8** mistress **10** chatelaine, salutation

MADCAP: **4** rash, wild **5** brash, crazy **6** stupid **7** flighty, foolish **8** reckless **9** impetuous, impulsive

MADDEN: **5** anger, upset **6** bother, enrage **7** incense, outrage, provoke, unhinge **9** infuriate

MADE: **5** built **7** created **8** compiled, invented, produced **9** contrived **10** artificial **11** constructed **12** manufactured

MADEIRA:
capital: **7** Funchal
features: **9** Pico Ruvio
islands: **7** Madeira **8** Desertas **9** Selvagens **10** Porto Santo
continent: **6** Africa
ruled by: **8** Portugal

MADEMOISELLE: **4** miss, Mlle **5** title, woman

MADE-TO-ORDER: **8** suitable **10** customized

MADE-UP: **6** unreal **7** created **8** invented **9** fictional, imaginary **10** fabricated

MADHOUSE: **5** chaos **6** asylum, bedlam, uproar **9** funny farm **10** sanitarium **11** pandemonium

MADMAN, MADWOMAN: **4** loon **6** maniac, psycho **7** lunatic **8** deranged **9** psychotic

MADNESS: **4** fury, rage **5** furor, mania **6** bedlam, frenzy, lunacy **7** ecstasy **8** delirium, delusion, dementia, insanity **9** amazement, furiosity **11** derangement

MAELSTROM: **4** eddy **5** storm, swirl **6** vortex **7** current, turmoil **8** upheaval **9** confusion, whirlpool

MAESTRO: **6** master **7** teacher **8** composer **9** conductor **10** bandleader

MAFIA: **4** gang **6** family **7** mafioso **10** underworld **10** Cosa Nostra

MAGAZINE: **5** cache, depot **6** digest, review, weekly **7** arsenal, chamber, gazette, journal, monthly **9** warehouse **10** depository, periodical, repository, storehouse **11** compartment, publication

MAGGOT: **3** bug **4** grub, whim, worm **5** larva **6** notion

MAGIC: **4** rune **5** charm, fairy, spell **6** mystic, voodoo **7** conjury, sorcery **8** illusion, witchery, wizardry **9** deception, sortilege **10** hocus-pocus, necromancy, witchcraft **11** enchantment, legerdemain

MAGICAL: **6** occult, spooky **8** charming **9** enchanted, marvelous **10** mysterious **11** fascinating **12** spellbinding

MAGICIAN: **5** brujo, genie, magus, witch **6** medium, Merlin, shaman, wizard **7** charmer, Houdini, juggler, warlock **8** conjurer, Mandrake, sorcerer **9** charlatan, enchanter **11** entertainer, necromancer, thaumaturge **13** fortuneteller

MAGISTERIAL: **5** bossy, lofty **6** august, lordly, stuffy **7** pompous, stately **8** arrogant, dogmatic, judicial **9** dignified, imperious **10** highhanded **11** dictatorial, domineering, overbearing **13** authoritative

MAGISTRATE: **5** chief, court, judge **6** archon, consul **7** alcalde, bailiff, justice **8** governor, official **13** administrator

MAGNANIMOUS: **3** big **4** free **5** lofty, noble **6** heroic **7** liberal **8** generous **9** eschewing, forgiving, honorable, unselfish, unstinted **10** altruistic, benevolent, chivalrous

MAGNATE: **4** lord **5** baron, mogul, nabob, noble, titan **6** bigwig, tycoon **13** industrialist

MAGNESIUM: **7** element

MAGNETIC: **5** polar **7** drawing, pulling **8** alluring, hypnotic **9** seductive **10** attractive **11** captivating, charismatic, mesmerizing

MAGNIFICENT: **5** grand, great, noble, regal **6** august, lavish, superb **7** elegant, exalted, opulent, stately, sublime **8** dazzling, glorious, gorgeous, imposing, majestic, splendid, striking **9** beautiful, brilliant, excellent, grandiose, wonderful **11** outstanding, resplendent

MAGNIFY: **4** laud **5** boost, swell **6** dilate, expand **7** amplify, augment, enhance, enlarge, inflate **8** eulogize, increase, multiply **9** aggravate, embellish, intensify, overstate **10** exaggerate **13** overemphasize

MAGNILOQUENT: **5** lofty **6** turgid **7** flowery, pompous **8** boastful **9** bombastic **13** grandiloquent

MAGNITUDE: **4** bulk, mass, size **5** range, space **6** extent, volume, weight **7** breadth, measure **8** eminence, quantity **9** dimension, greatness, intensity **10** importance, proportion **12** significance

MAGNOLIA STATE: **11** Mississippi

MAGNUM: **3** gun **6** bottle **7** firearm

MAGNUM OPUS: **7** classic **11** achievement, masterpiece **13** one's great work

MAGUS: **4** magi **6** wizard **8** magician, sorcerer

MAHOGANY: **4** tree, wood **12** reddish brown

MAIA:
father: **5** Atlas
mother: **7** Pleione
son: **6** Hermes **7** Mercury

MAID: **6** virgin **7** servant **8** domestic **9** attendant **11** housekeeper

MAIDEN: **3** new **4** girl, lass **5** first, missy **6** damsel, lassie, virgin **7** untried **8** earliest **9** inaugural, unmarried

MAIL: **4** post, send, ship **5** armor **6** letter, parcel **7** express, forward, package **8** dispatch, postcard **13** communication

MAIM: **4** lame, maul **6** batter, damage, injure, mangle **7** cripple, disable **8** massacre, mutilate **9** disfigure, dismember

MAIN: **4** duct, head, line, pipe **5** chief, first, grand, major, prime, vital **6** direct **7** capital, central, conduct, leading, purpose **8** absolute, critical, foremost **9** essential, important, paramount, principal **10** preeminent **11** predominant

MAINE:
bird: **9** chickadee
capital: **7** Augusta
cities: **4** York **6** Bangor **8** Lewiston, Ogunquit, Portland **9** Bar Harbor
explorer: **5** Cabot
features: **6** Acadia, Baxter **8** Cadillac **9** Katahadin, Sugarloaf **10** Campobello **11** Mount Desert
flower: **6** tassel **8** pine cone
nickname: **6** Lumber **8** Pine Tree
water: **4** Saco **6** Sebago **8** Allagush, Kennebec, Rangeley **9** Moosehead

MAINSTAY: **3** key **4** rope **5** brace **6** crutch, pillar **7** support **8** backbone **9** supporter

MAINTAIN: **4** avow, hold, keep **5** argue, claim, state **6** affirm, assert, avouch, defend, insist, manage, retain, supply, uphold **7** contend, control, declare, finance, justify, prolong, support, sustain, warrant **8** conserve, preserve **9** vindicate

MAINTENANCE: **4** care, keep **6** upkeep **7** alimony, repairs **10** livelihood, sustenance **12** conservation, preservation

MAIZE: **4** corn, milo **5** grain **6** yellow

MAJESTIC: **5** grand, lofty, noble, regal, royal **6** august, kingly **7** courtly, elegant, stately, sublime **8** imperial, princely, splendid, stunning **9** dignified, grandiose **10** impressive **11** ceremonious, magnificent

MAJOR: **3** big **4** main, rank **5** chief, great, vital **7** crucial, leading, officer, primary, serious, sizable **8** critical, foremost, superior **9** extensive, important, paramount, principal **11** predominant, significant **12** considerable

MAJORITY: **3** age **4** bulk, edge, mass, more, most **6** margin **7** greater **9** adulthood, seniority

MAKE: **4** bear, coin, earn, form, mark, mold **5** build, cause, erect, force, forge, frame, press, shape **6** attain, coerce, compel, create, effect, invent, render, secure **7** achieve, acquire, appoint, compose, fashion, prepare, produce, require, suppose **8** assemble, comprise, generate **9** construct, establish, fabricate, formulate, originate **10** accomplish, constitute, synthesize **11** manufacture

MAKE AMENDS: **5** atone **6** settle, square **9** reconcile **10** compensate

MAKE AWARE: **4** tell **6** inform, notify, reveal **8** disclose **9** enlighten

MAKE-BELIEVE: **4** fake, sham **5** dream, magic **6** unreal **7** charade, fantasy, fiction, pretend **8** imagined, simulate **9** imaginary, invention **10** playacting

MAKE CERTAIN: **5** check **6** assure **7** examine **9** guarantee **11** investigate

MAKE DEAL: **6** settle **10** compromise

MAKE DO: **6** accept, employ, endure **7** suffice, survive **9** improvise

MAKE EFFORT: **3** try **6** strive **7** attempt, venture **9** undertake

MAKE FUN OF: **3** rib **5** mimic, tease **6** parody **7** imitate **8** ridicule **9** embarrass

MAKE GETAWAY: **4** bolt, flee **6** escape

MAKE GOOD: **5** repay **6** arrive **7** achieve, fulfill, justify, succeed **9** reimburse **10** accomplish, compensate

MAKE HAPPY: **5** amuse **6** please **7** delight

MAKE HEADWAY: **7** achieve, advance, improve **8** progress

MAKE HOSTILE: **7** provoke **8** alienate **10** antagonize

MAKE ILL: **6** revolt, sicken **7** afflict, disgust, repulse **8** nauseate

MAKE INTO: **5** alter **6** change, reform **7** convert **9** transform

MAKE IT: **7** achieve, succeed, triumph **10** accomplish

MAKE KNOWN: **4** tell **6** advise, expose, notify, reveal, unveil **7** declare, divulge, publish, uncover **8** announce, disclose, proclaim **9** advertise, broadcast, publicize

MAKE LIGHT OF: **8** belittle **9** disparage **13** underestimate

MAKE MISTAKE: **3** err **4** goof **12** miscalculate

MAKE OF: **5** think **9** interpret, translate

MAKE OFF: **4** bolt, flee, skip **6** decamp, depart, escape **7** abscond, run away, scamper **9** skedaddle

MAKE OUT: **3** see **4** fare, kiss, neck **6** detect, gather, manage, notice **7** achieve, discern, observe, succeed **9** determine **10** accomplish, understand

MAKE OVER: **4** redo **5** amend **6** revamp **7** correct, remodel, restore **8** renovate

MAKE PUBLIC: **3** air **4** tell, vent **6** reveal **7** display, exhibit **8** announce, proclaim **9** broadcast, publicize

MAKER: **6** author **7** builder, creator **8** composer, inventor, producer **10** originator **12** manufacturer

MAKE SENSE: **5** clear, lucid **7** logical **12** intelligible **14** understandable

MAKESHIFT: **7** stopgap **8** slapdash **9** emergency, impromptu, temporary **10** improvised, substitute **11** alternative, provisional, replacement

MAKE STATEMENT: **6** remark **7** comment, explain, expound

MAKE SURE: **5** check **6** review, secure **9** ascertain, determine

MAKE TRACKS: **4** shoo **5** leave, scram **6** depart

MAKE UNEASY: **5** upset **7** disturb, trouble **10** discomfort

MAKE UP: **4** coin, mend **5** atone **6** create, devise, invent **7** arrange, compose, concoct, consist, pretend **8** assemble, complete **9** formulate, improvise, reconcile **10** conciliate

MAKEUP: **4** plan **5** blush, fiber, rouge, shape, style **6** format, powder **7** mascara **8** lipstick **9** character, cosmetics, structure **10** complexion **11** composition **12** constitution **13** configuration

MALADROIT: **5** inept **6** clumsy, gauche **7** awkward **8** bumbling, bungling, inexpert, tactless **9** impolitic **10** blundering, ungraceful **11** floundering

MALADY: **7** ailment, disease, illness **8** debility, disorder, sickness **9** complaint, distemper, infirmity **10** affliction

MALAISE: **7** anxiety, despair, disease, illness **8** sickness **9** lassitude **10** depression, melancholy

MALAPROPOS: **8** improper, untimely **10** irrelevant **11** inopportune **13** inappropriate

MALARIA: **4** ague **6** miasma **8** paludism, sickness **11** jungle fever
carrier: **8** mosquito **9** anopheles
treatment: **7** quinine **8** cinchona **10** cinchonine

MALARKEY: **6** drivel **7** hogwash **8** nonsense **10** balderdash **11** foolishness

MALAWI:
capital: **8** Lilongwe
cities: **5** Mzuzu, Zomba **8** Blantyre
continent: **6** Africa
ethnic groups: **5** Bantu, Chewa, Lomwe **6** Nyanja
features: **5** Nyika **7** Kasungu, Lengare **13** Mulanje Massif **15** Great Rift Valley
formerly: **9** Nyasaland
languages: **3** Yao **5** Chewa, Lomwe **7** English **8** Chichewa
monetary unit: **6** kwacha
water: **5** Shire **6** Malawi **7** Chilara, Malombe

MALAYSIA:
animals: **3** lar **4** lory **5** sarus, tapir, tsine **7** banteng, carabao **8** seladang **10** chevrotain
capital: **11** Kuala Lumpur
cities: **4** Ipoh **6** Penang **7** Kuching, Malacca **10** Georgetown **11** Johor Banaru **12** Kota Kinabalu
continent: **4** Asia
ethnic groups: **5** Malay **6** Indian **7** Chinese
features: **6** Gunong, Gunung **8** Kinabalu **9** Niah Caves
islands: **5** Sabah **7** Sarawak
languages: **5** Malay **6** Bahasa, Indian **7** Chinese, English, Tagalog **8** Malaysia
monetary unit: **7** ringgit
plants: **4** palm, siri, upas **5** sawah **6** kanari, nibong, sambal **7** talipot **8** rambutan
states: **5** Kedah, Negri, Perak, Sabah **6** Johore, Perlis **7** Malacca, Sarawak **8** Selangor, Sembilan
water: **3** Kra **7** Pacific **11** Indian Ocean

MALCONTENT: **5** rebel **6** grouch, uneasy **7** grouchy **8** agitator, grumbler, revolter **9** anarchist, insurgent **10** complainer, rebellious **11** disgruntled **12** discontented, dissatisfied, troublemaker

MALDIVES:
capital: **4** Male
language: **6** Divehi
place: **7** Pacific **11** Indian Ocean

MALE: **3** guy, man **5** manly **6** manful, virile **7** mankind, manlike, mannish **8** paternal **9** masculine

MALEDICTION: **4** cuss, jinx **5** curse **6** whammy **7** malison, slander **8** anathema **9** damnation **11** imprecation **12** denunciation

MALEFACTOR: **5** felon, knave **6** rascal **7** convict, culprit, villain **8** criminal, offender **9** scoundrel, wrongdoer **10** delinquent

MALEVOLENCE: **4** evil **5** spite **6** enmity, grudge, hatred, malice, malign, rancor, spleen, wicked **7** hateful, vicious **8** sinister **9** animosity, hostility, malicious **10** antagonism, bitterness, despiteful

MALFEASANCE: **5** crime **10** misconduct, wrongdoing **11** delinquency

MALFUNCTION: **4** flaw **6** glitch **7** failure, problem **9** breakdown

MALI:
capital: **6** Bamako
cities: **5** Dakar, Kayes, Mopti, Segou **8** Timbuktu
continent: **6** Africa
ethnic groups: **4** Moor, Peul **5** Mande **6** Tuareg **7** Bambara, Malinke, Songhai, Voltaic **8** Sarakole

features: **6** Sahara
languages: **6** French, Senufo **7** Bambara
monetary unit: **5** franc
water: **5** Niger **7** Senegal

MALICE: **4** bane, hate **5** spite **6** enmity, grudge, spleen **7** despite **8** meanness **9** animosity **10** bitterness, resentment **11** malevolence **12** spitefulness, vengefulness

MALICIOUS: **4** evil, mean **5** catty, nasty **6** bitter, wicked **7** harmful, hateful, vicious **8** sinister, spiteful, venomous **9** felonious, malignant, poisonous, rancorous, resentful **10** despiteful, malevolent, revengeful

MALIGN: **4** evil, foul, slur **5** libel, smear, stain **6** defame, revile, vilify **7** asperse, baleful, hateful, hurtful, slander, tarnish, traduce **8** backbite, belittle, derogate, mudsling, sinister, virulent **9** denigrate, injurious **10** calumniate, pernicious **11** detrimental, malevolence **12** antagonistic

MALIGNANT: **4** evil **5** fatal **6** wicked **7** hateful, noxious, vicious **8** diseased, fiendish, spiteful, venomous, virulent **9** cancerous, injurious, invidious, malicious, poisonous, rancorous **10** pernicious

MALINGER: **4** fake, loaf, sham **5** dodge, evade, shirk

MALL: **4** walk **5** alley, court, plaza **6** arcade, square **9** concourse, promenade

MALLEABLE: **6** pliant, supple **7** ductile, plastic, pliable **8** flexible **9** adaptable, complaint, tractable **14** impressionable

MALLET: **4** club, maul, tool **5** gavel **6** hammer
variety: **5** metal **6** rubber, wooden **7** croquet, plastic **10** carpenter's

MALNUTRITION: **6** scurvy **8** beriberi, cachexia **10** emaciation, starvation

MALODOROUS: **4** foul, rank, vile **5** fetid, funky **6** putrid, rotten, smelly **7** noisome, reeking, stenchy **8** stinking **9** offensive

MALPRACTICE: **10** misconduct, negligence **12** carelessness

MALTA:
capital: **8** Valletta
cities: **5** Qormi, Rabat **10** Birkirkara, Marsaxlokk
location: **13** Mediterranean
ethnic groups: **4** Arab **6** French **7** Italian
features: **4** Gozo **6** Comino
languages: **7** English, Maltese
monetary unit: **4** lira
native: **7** Maltese
ruled by: **4** Rome **6** Arabia, France **7** Britain, knights **8** Normandy **9** Phoenicia
water: **13** Mediterranean

MALTREAT: **4** harm **5** abuse **6** damage, injure, misuse **9** mishandle, victimize

MAMMAL: **3** cat **5** beast, ovine, swine **6** bovine, equine, feline, rodent **7** primate **8** edentate, ruminant, ungulant **9** carnivore, marsupial
aquatic: **4** seal **5** otter, whale **6** desman, dugong, manati, rytina, walrus **7** dolphin, manatee, narwhal, sea lion **8** cetacean, platypus, porpoise, sirenian **12** hippopotamus
arboreal: **5** lemur, sloth **6** cuscus, fisher, monkey **7** glutton, opossum, raccoon **8** banxring, kinkajou, lemuroid **9** orangutan
bovine: **3** bos, cow **4** bull, calf, zebu **5** bison, steer **7** taurine **8** longhorn
burrowing: **4** mole **6** badger, gopher, wombat **8** squirrel, suricate **9** armadillo

carnivorous: **3** cat, dog, fox **4** bear, lion, wolf **5** dingo, otter, panda, skunk, tiger **6** badger, coyote, weasel **7** raccoon **8** mongoose **9** carnivore
cud-chewing: **8** ruminant
domestic: **3** cat, dog **5** horse, sheep **6** cattle
edentate: **5** sloth **7** ant bear, tamadau **8** anteater, pangolin **9** armadillo
equine: **4** colt, foal, mare **5** filly, horse, zebra **8** stallion
extinct: **6** quagga, rytina **8** mastodon, stegodon
feline: **3** cat **4** lion, lynx, puma **5** ounce, tiger **6** bobcat, cougar, jaguar, ocelot, serval **7** leopard, panther
flying: **3** bat
gnawing: **3** rat **6** beaver, rodent **8** squirrel
herbivorous: **5** daman, tapir **6** bovine, dugong, equine **7** manatee **8** ruminant **9** orangutan **10** rhinoceros **12** hippopotamus
highest order: **7** primate
horned: **3** cow **4** gaur, goat, reem **5** bison **7** buffalo, unicorn **8** antelope, reindeer **10** rhinoceros
insectivorous: **3** bat **4** mole **5** shrew **6** tenrec **8** hedgehog
lagomorph: **4** hare **6** rabbit
lowest order: **9** marsupial **11** marsupialia
marsupial: **4** tait **5** koala **6** possum, wombat **7** opossum, wallaby **8** kangaroo **9** bandicoot
nocturnal: **3** bat **5** hyena, lemur, ratel, tapir **6** macaco, racoon, wombat **7** raccoon, tarsier **8** kinkajou, platypus
porcine: **3** hog, pig **4** boar **5** swine **7** peccary
primate: **5** lemur **6** baboon, gibbon, monkey **7** gorilla **8** marmoset **9** orangutan **10** chimpanzee
ruminant: **3** yak **4** deer, goat **5** bison, camel, llama, moose, okapi, sheep, steer **6** alpaca, cattle, chewer, vicuna **7** buffalo, giraffe, vicugna **8** antelope
toothless: **5** sloth **8** edentate, pangolin **9** armadillo
tropical: **5** coati, rhino **7** peccary **9** coatimodi **10** coati-mundi, rhinoceros
ursine: **4** bear **5** panda
vulpine: **3** fox **4** wolf

MAMMON: **4** gain **6** riches, wealth **7** avarice **11** possessions

MAMMOTH: **4** huge **5** giant, great, large **7** massive, titanic **8** colossal, enormous, gigantic **10** behemothic, gargantuan, monumental, stupendous

MAN: **3** guy **4** buck, chal, chap, gent, lord, male **5** bloke, chiel, guard, homme, human, valet **6** fellow, hombre, mensch, mister, mortal **7** husband **8** creature **9** anthropos, boyfriend **11** homo sapiens
castrated: **6** eunuch
combining forms: **4** andr, homo **5** andro, homin **6** homini
concerning: **5** human **6** humane, mortal
eccentric: **6** codger, geezer
mean: **4** ogre **5** knave **7** monster, ruffian, villain **10** curmudgeon
mechanical: **5** robot **9** automaton
poor: **6** pauper **7** peasant **8** beadsman, bedesman
primitive: **6** savage **8** urmensch
resembling: **7** android **10** anthropoid **15** anthropomorphic
rich: **5** Midas, nabob **6** tycoon **7** Croesus, magnate **9** plutocrat **10** capitalist **11** billionaire, millionaire
sciences: **9** ethnology **12** anthropology
short: **6** mankin, shrimp, squirt **8** homuncio **10** homunculus
young: **3** boy, lad **5** youth **6** varlet **8** springal **9** stripling

MANACLE: **4** band, bond, cuff **5** irons **6** chains **7** confine, control, fetters, shackle **8** handcuff **9** restraint

MANAGE: **3** run **4** boss, deal, fare, head, lead, rule **5** guide, order, steer **6** direct, govern, handle, muddle **7** conduct, control, execute, finagle, husband, operate, oversee, survive **8** contrive, dominate, engineer, maintain, maneuver, regulate **9** designate, supervise **10** accomplish, administer, manipulate

MANAGEMENT: **4** care **5** brass **6** agency, charge, policy **8** guidance, overseer **9** ordinance **10** conducting, executives, governance **11** generalship **14** administration

MANAGER: **4** boss, doer **6** gerent **7** curator, foreman, handler, steward **8** director, executor **9** executive, forewoman **10** supervisor

MANASSEH:
father: **6** Joseph
grandfather: **5** Jacob
mother: **7** Asenath
son: **4** Amon **6** Machir

MAN-AT-ARMS: **7** fighter, soldier, warrior

MANCHURIA:
cities: **5** Hulan, Kirin **6** Harbin, Mukden **8** Shenyang **9** Niuchwang
place: **5** China
provinces: **5** Jilin **9** Likaoning **12** Heilongjiang
water: **4** Amur, Liao, Yalu

MANDATE: **4** word, writ **5** brief, edict, order **6** behest, charge, decree **7** command, precept **8** sanction, warranty **9** directive **10** injunction, referendum **11** requisition

MANDATORY: **6** forced **8** required **9** essential, necessary **10** compulsory, imperative, obligatory

MANDIBLE: **3** jaw **4** beak **7** jawbone

MANEUVER: **4** move, plot, ploy **5** drill, pilot, steer, stunt, trick **6** deploy, jockey, scheme, tactic **7** exploit, finagle, finesse **8** contrive, engineer, exercise, navigate, outflank **9** stratagem **10** manipulate

MAN FRIDAY: **4** aide **8** employee **9** assistant

MANGER: **4** crib, rack **5** stall **6** cradle, stable, trough

MANGLE: **3** cut, mar **4** hack, maim, maul, ruin **5** spoil **6** batter, deform **7** butcher, cripple, presser **8** calender, lacerate, mutilate **9** disfigure, dismember

MANGY: **4** mean **5** dirty, seedy **6** filthy, scurvy, shabby **7** rundown, scruffy, squalid

MANHANDLE: **4** maul, push **5** abuse, bully **7** rough up **8** mistreat

MANIA: **4** fear, rage **5** craze **6** fetish, frenzy, hangup **7** madness, passion **8** delirium, disorder, fixation, insanity **9** addiction, obsession **10** compulsion **11** derangement, fascination, infatuation

MANIAC: **3** nut **6** crazed, insane, madman **7** fanatic, lunatic **8** crackpot, deranged, madwoman **9** psychotic **10** enthusiast, psychopath

MANIFEST: **4** bare, list, mark, open, show **5** clear, index, overt, plain, prove **6** embody, evince, expose, reveal **7** approve, declare, develop, display, evident, exhibit, express, glaring, obvious, signify, visible **8** apparent, discover, evidence, indicate, palpable **9** disclosed **10** noticeable **11** conspicuous, demonstrate, indubitable, materialize, undisguised **12** indisputable, unmistakable

MANIFESTATION: **4** sign **5** proof **7** display, example, meaning, symptom **8** epiphany **10** expression, revelation **12** presentation

MANIFESTO: **4** writ **5** edict, order **7** placard **8** policies **9** statement **10** intentions, principles **11** declaration **12** proclamation

MANIFOLD: **4** many **6** sundry **7** diverse, various **8** abundant, multiple, numerous **9** multifold, multiform

MANIPULATE: **3** rig, use **4** work **5** shape, swing, wield **6** handle, manage, scheme **7** control, exploit, finagle, operate **8** maneuver **9** influence

MANITOBA:
capital: **8** Winnipeg
cities: **7** Portage, St. James **10** St. Boniface
country: **6** Canada
flower: **6** crocus
water: **7** Dauphin **8** Manitoba, Winnipeg **9** Churchill **12** Saskatchewan, Winnipegosis

MANKIND: **4** male, race **5** flesh **6** female, humans, people **8** humanity **11** Homo sapiens

MANLY: **4** bold, male **5** brave **6** daring, manful, strong, virile **7** gallant, valiant **8** fearless, resolute **9** masculine, undaunted **10** courageous **11** lionhearted

MAN-MADE: **9** synthetic, unnatural **10** artificial

MANNA: **4** boon, gift **7** bonanza **8** delicacy, windfall

MANNEQUIN: **5** dummy, model **6** figure **7** manikin

MANNER: **3** air, way **4** form, kind, look, mien, mode, sort, tone **5** breed, habit, style **6** aspect, course, custom, method, system **7** bearing, conduct, fashion, species **8** attitude, behavior, category, demeanor, practice, protocol **9** character, etiquette, technique **10** appearance, deportment **11** formalities

MANNERED: **5** posed **6** formal **8** affected **10** artificial **13** self-conscious

MANNERISM: **5** habit, trait **7** bearing **11** affectation, peculiarity **12** eccentricity, idiosyncrasy **13** individuality

MANNERLY: **5** civil **6** polite **7** genteel **8** decorous, polished **9** courteous **10** respectful **11** well-behaved

MANNERS: **7** conduct, decorum **8** behavior, courtesy, protocol **9** amenities, etiquette **11** formalities

MANOR: **4** land **5** house, villa **6** castle, estate **7** chateau, mansion

MANSERVANT: **5** valet **6** butler, garcon **7** footman, steward **9** attendant

MANSION: **4** hall, home **5** abode, house, manor, villa **6** castle, estate, palace **7** chateau **8** dwelling **9** residence

MANSLAUGHTER: **5** crime **6** murder **7** killing **8** homicide

MANTA: **4** rays, wrap **5** cloak, cloth **6** fabric **7** blanket, shelter

MANTLE: **4** cape, coat, glow, hood, robe **5** brain, cloak, color, cover **6** capote, pinken, redden, screen **7** envelop **8** filament, mantilla

MANUAL: **4** book, text **5** guide **6** primer **8** handbook, keyboard, physical

MANUFACTURE: **4** fake, make, mold **5** build, forge **6** create, invent **7** concoct, prepare, produce **8** assembly **9** fabricate **10** synthesize

MANUMISSION: **6** rescue **7** freedom, release **10** liberation **12** emancipation

MANURE: **4** dung **7** compost **9** excrement **10** fertilizer

MANUSCRIPT: **4** copy **5** codex, draft **7** writing **8** document **11** composition, handwriting, typewritten

MANY: **4** gobs, much, tons **5** piles **6** legion, myriad, oodles, plenty, scores, sundry **7** diverse, several, various **8** abundant, manifold, multiple, numerous, populous **9** bountiful, countless, multitude **10** multiplied

MAORI:
animals: **3** poe, tui **4** weka
ethnic groups: **3** Ati **4** Hapu
home: **3** pah **5** whare **8** wharekai **12** wharewananga
place: **10** New Zealand
plants: **3** kai **5** mapau **6** manuka **9** tanehakas

MAP: **4** plan, plat, plot **5** atlas, chart, draft, globe, graph, image **6** design, sketch, survey **7** diagram, explore, outline, picture **9** blueprint, delineate **10** cartograph, projection

MAPLE: **4** tree, wood **5** shrub **6** flavor
genus: **4** Acer
kind: **5** sugar, swamp **6** sierra, silver **7** dogwood **8** Japanese, Sycamore

MAR: **4** blot, flaw, harm, hurt, mark, ruin, scar **5** botch, spoil **6** bruise, damage, deform, impair, injure, mangle **7** blemish, scratch, tarnish **9** disfigure

MARATHON: **4** race **5** event **7** contest **8** activity

MARAUD: **4** raid, rove **5** foray, steal **6** attack, ravage **7** pillage, plunder, ransack

MARAUDER: **6** bandit, looter, pirate, raider, robber **7** ravager **8** pillager **9** buccaneer, desperado, plunderer

MARBLE: **4** ball, cold, game, hard, rock **5** agate, stone **6** basalt, smooth **7** granite **8** dolomite **9** sculpture, unfeeling

MARCH: **4** file, hike, move, step, trek, walk **5** drill, strut **6** border, course, parade, stride, travel **7** advance, journey **8** boundary, frontier, progress, traverse **10** procession **11** advancement

MARCH SISTERS: **2** Jo **3** Amy, Meg **4** Beth
characters in: **11** Little Women

MARDI GRAS: **7** holiday **8** festival, occasion **10** fat Tuesday, New Orleans

MARE: **3** sea **6** equine **11** female horse

MARE'S NEST: **3** lie **4** hoax **5** fraud, trick **9** deception **11** complicated

MARGIN: **3** hem, lip, rim **4** brim, edge, room, side **5** brink, shore, verge **6** border, fringe, leeway **8** boundary, latitude **9** allowance, perimeter **11** indentation

MARGINAL: **5** small **7** minimal **10** borderline, negligible **11** unimportant **13** insignificant

MARIGOLD: **5** plant **6** flower
genus: **7** tagetes
kind: **4** wild **5** field, marsh, water **7** African

MARIJUANA: **3** pot, tea **4** dope, drug, hemp, herb, weed **5** ganja, grass, joint **6** reefer **8** cannabis, loco weed, mary jane **9** marihuana

MARINA: **4** dock **5** basin **8** boatyard

MARINE: **3** sea **5** naval, water **6** sailor **7** aquatic, marinal, mariner, oceanic, pelagic **8** maritime, nautical, seagoing **9** seafaring **11** leatherneck **13** oceanographic

MARINER: **3** gob, tar **6** sailor, seaman **7** swabbie **8** seafarer, seawoman, shipmate **9** navigator, yachtsman **11** yachtswoman

MARIONETTE: **3** toy **4** doll **6** puppet

MARITAL: **6** wedded **7** married, nuptial, spousal **9** connubial **11** matrimonial

MARK: **3** dot, tag **4** dent, dupe, fool, goal, heed, line, logo, nick, note, pock, scar, seal, sign, spot **5** badge, brand, chart, gauge, grade, image, label, point, score, spare, stamp, track, trait **6** denote, emblem, letter, notice, number, rating, strike, symbol, target, victim **7** betoken, blemish, feature, impress, imprint, measure, observe, symptom **8** ambition, identity, manifest, standard **9** attribute, character, criterion, designate, influence, objective, yardstick **10** importance, impression, indication **11** distinction, distinguish, inscription

MARK DOWN: **3** cut **5** lower, slash **6** reduce **9** devaluate

MARKED: **5** clear, fated, noted **6** tabbed, traced **7** evident, obvious **8** apparent, destined, distinct, striking **9** prominent **10** emphasized, identified, noticeable, pronounced **11** conspicuous

MARKER: **3** peg **4** flag, pole **5** arrow, guide, notch, stone **6** scorer, signal **7** counter, monitor **8** recorder **9** indicator, tombstone **10** gravestone

MARKET: **4** mall, mart, sale, sell, shop, vend **5** plaza, store **6** bazaar, outlet, peddle, square **8** boutique, emporium, exchange **9** wholesale **12** delicatessen

MARKETABLE: **6** wanted **7** salable **8** bankable, sellable, vendible **9** wholesome

MARKSMAN: **4** shot **6** sniper **7** deadeye **12** sharpshooter

MARMALADE: **3** jam **5** jelly **8** preserve

MAROON: **5** leave **6** desert, enisle, strand **7** abandon, forsake, isolate, reddish **8** purplish **9** shipwreck

MARQUEE: **4** tent **6** awning, canopy **9** signboard

MARRIAGE: **4** link **5** match, union **7** wedding, wedlock **8** alliance, espousal, nuptials **9** betrothed, connubial, matrimony **11** association
broker: **8** shadchan **9** schatchen **10** matchmaker

MARROW: **4** core, pith **6** inmost **7** essence, medulla **8** vitality **9** essential, substance

MARRY: **3** wed **4** join, link, yoke **5** hitch, unite **6** couple, pledge, splice **7** espouse **9** associate

MARS:
also called: **4** Area
concerning: **5** Arean **7** Martian
features: **3** red **4** Mare **5** Libya, Oasis **11** Olympus Mons
from sun: **6** fourth
god of: **3** war
probes: **6** Viking **7** Mariner
satellites: **6** Deimos, Phobos
sons: **5** Remus **7** Romulus

MARSH: **3** bog, fen **4** mire, moor **5** bayou, glade, swale, swamp **6** morass, palude, slough **7** slashes, wetland **8** quagmire **9** everglade

MARSHAL: **4** lead **5** align, array, guide, usher **6** deploy, direct, gather, muster **7** arrange, officer, sheriff **8** assemble, mobilize **9** constable

MARSUPIAL: **5** koala **6** possum, wombat **7** opossum, wallaby **8** kangaroo **9** bandicoot

MART: **4** fair, mall, shop **5** store **6** bazaar, market **8** emporium, exchange

MARTIAL: **7** hostile, warlike **8** militant, military **9** bellicose, combative **10** aggressive **11** belligerent

MARTIAL ART: **4** judo, sumo **5** kendo **6** aikido, karate, kung fu **7** jujitsu **9** tae kwon do
origin: **6** Orient

MARTINET: **6** tyrant **8** dictator **13** authoritarian **14** disciplinarian

MARTINIQUE:
capital: **12** Fort-de-France
features: **5** Pelee
place: **9** Caribbean **10** West Indies **14** Lesser Antilles

MARTYR: **5** saint **6** victim **7** torment **8** sufferer **9** persecute, sacrifice

MARTYRDOM: **7** anguish, torment, torture **9** suffering **10** affliction

MARVEL: **4** gape **6** admire, goggle, wonder **7** miracle, portent **8** astonish, surprise **9** curiosity, sensation **12** astonishment

MARVELOUS: **5** great, super **6** superb **7** amazing, awesome **8** fabulous, splendid, terrific, wondrous **9** excellent, fantastic, wonderful **10** incredible, stupendous **11** astonishing, magnificent, outstanding, sensational, spectacular **13** extraordinary

MARYLAND:
bird: **15** Baltimore oriole
capital: **9** Annapolis
cities: **7** Dundalk **8** Bethesda **9** Baltimore, Ocean City **10** Hagerstown **12** Silver Spring
explorer: **7** Calvert **9** John Smith
features: **5** Bowie **7** Pimlico **9** Preakness **11** Fort McHenry **12** Appalachians
flower: **14** black-eyed susan
native: **10** Marylander
nickname: **4** Free **7** Cockade, Old Line
tree: **8** white oak
water: **7** Potomac **8** Patuxent **13** Chesapeake Bay

MASCULINE: **4** male **5** brave, macho, manly **6** potent, robust, strong, virile **7** manlike **8** powerful, vigorous

MASH: **4** mess, mush, pulp **5** cream, crush, flirt, grind, smash **6** squash **7** mixture **8** scramble **9** pulverize

MASHER: **4** chap **5** flirt **9** womanizer

MASK: **4** face, hide, veil **5** cloak, cover, front, guise **6** facade, screen, shield **7** conceal, curtain **8** disguise **10** camouflage, masquerade

MASKED: **6** covert, latent **8** larvated **9** concealed, disguised, incognito

MASONRY: **5** trade **6** ashlar **9** brickwork, stonework

MASQUERADE: **4** mask **5** guise, party **6** masque **7** charade, pretend **8** disguise, pretense **10** camouflage **11** impersonate

MASS: **3** gob, jam, mob, sum **4** blob, body, bulk, clot, heap, knot, lump, pile, rite **5** batch, bunch, crowd, gross, group, mound, store, whole **6** bundle, gather, matter, prayer, volume **7** liturgy, service **8** assemble, majority, mountain **9** aggregate, magnitude, stockpile, substance **10** accumulate, assemblage, collection, congregate **11** agglomerate, composition, consolidate, measurement **12** congregation

MASSACHUSETTS:
bird: **9** chickadee
capital: **6** Boston
cities: **7** Concord **8** Brockton **9** Cambridge, Lexington, Worcester **10** New Bedford **11** Springfield
features: **3** MIT **7** Cape Ann, Cape Cod, Harvard **9** Nantucket **10** Berkshires, Tanglewood **12** Plymouth Rock **15** Martha's Vineyard
flower: **9** mayflower
nickname: **3** Bay **6** Old Bay **9** Old Colony
tree: **3** elm
water: **6** Nashua **7** Charles, Concord **9** Merrimack **10** Walden Pond **11** Connecticut

MASSACRE: **6** murder **7** carnage **8** butchery, genocide **9** bloodbath, slaughter **10** decimation **12** annihilation

MASSAGE: **5** knead, press **6** caress, stroke **7** rubbing **9** stimulate **12** manipulation

MASSIVE: **4** huge, vast **5** bulky, giant, gross, heavy, jumbo, large **7** immense, mammoth, titanic, weighty **8** colossal, enormous, gigantic, whopping **9** ponderous **10** boisterous, monumental **11** substantial

MAST: **3** cue **4** nuts, pole, spar **5** stick **6** forage **8** beechnut **9** flagstaff
lookout: **9** crow's nest
type: **3** top **4** fore, jury, main **5** lower **6** jigger, mizzen **10** topgallant

MASTER: **3** get **4** best, boss, down, guru, lick, lord, rule, sire, tame **5** chief, learn, ruler, swami, tutor **6** artist, defeat, doctor, expert, govern, subdue, wizard **7** acquire, captain, conquer, headman, maestro, prevail, skilled, teacher, triumph **8** champion, dominate, educator, overcome, overseer, regulate, surmount, vanquish **9** commander, craftsman, matriarch overpower, paramount, patriarch, subjugate **10** understand **11** connoisseur **12** professional

MASTERFUL: **4** able **5** adept **6** clever, expert **7** skilled **8** forceful, imperial **9** arbitrary, imperious **10** commanding, preeminent, proficient **11** crackerjack, dictatorial, domineering, overbearing **13** authoritative

MASTERMIND: **4** plan **6** artist, author, brains, expert, genius **7** planner **8** organize

MASTER OF CEREMONIES: **4** host **5** emcee **7** speaker **9** performer

MASTERPIECE: **5** jewel **7** classic **8** treasure **9** objet d'art **10** brainchild, magnum opus, masterwork, perfection **11** chef d'oeuvre

MASTERY: **4** rule **5** grasp, knack, skill **7** command, control, victory **8** conquest **9** expertise, influence, supremacy **10** domination **11** proficiency

MASTICATE: **4** chew **5** chomp, crush, gnash, grind, knead **6** crunch

MAT: **3** pad, rug **4** dull, felt, flat **5** doily, snarl **6** border, carpet, tangle, tatami **7** cushion **8** entangle **10** interweave, lackluster, lusterless

MATADOR: **6** torero **8** toreador **11** bullfighter

MATA HARI:
executed by: **6** French
guilty of: **9** espionage
occupation: **3** spy **6** dancer
spied for: **7** Germans
stage name: **21** Gertrude Margaret Zelle

MATCH: **3** fit, pit, tie **4** even, game, mate, meet, peer, pout, race, side, spar, team, twin, wick **5** equal, event, marry, rival, union **6** couple, oppose, spouse **7** compare, contest, counter **8** marriage, parallel **9** companion, correlate, duplicate, lookalike **10** coordinate, correspond, tournament **11** competition, counterpart, partnership

MATCHED: **4** even **5** equal **6** paired, teamed **11** coordinated

MATCHLESS: **5** alone **8** peerless, superior **9** exemplary, exquisite, unrivaled **10** unbeatable, unequalled **11** unsurpassed **12** incomparable. unparalleled

MATCHMAKER: **8** shadchan **9** schatchen **14** marriage broker

MATE: **3** pal, wed **4** chum, join, pair, peer, twin, wife **5** breed, buddy, equal, marry, match **6** cohort, couple, fellow, friend, spouse **7** comrade, consort, husband, partner **8** sidekick **9** associate, colleague, companion, confidant, procreate

MATERIAL: **4** data, gear, real, tool **5** cloth, facts, goods, stuff **6** bodily, fabric, matter, things **8** physical, relevant, tangible **9** apparatus, corporeal, equipment, essential, important, pertinent, substance **10** ingredient, meaningful **11** information, significant

MATERIALISM: **9** physicism **10** heterodoxy, pragmatism **14** utilitarianism

MATERIALISTIC: **6** greedy **7** worldly **8** banausic **10** possessive **11** acquisitive, unspiritual

MATERIALIZE: **4** loom, rise, show **5** shape **6** appear, emerge, evolve, happen **7** emanate **8** energize, manifest

MATERIEL: **4** gear **6** tackle **8** supplies **9** apparatus, equipment, machinery **10** provisions

MATERNAL: **4** kind **8** motherly **10** protective

MATERNITY: **9** gestation, pregnancy **10** motherhood **12** childbearing

MATHEMATICS:
branches: **7** algebra **8** analysis, calculus, geometry **9** computing, mechanics **10** arithmetic, statistics **12** trigonometry
mathematician: **6** Euclid, Thales **9** Khwarizmi **10** Archimedes, Pythagoras
symbols: **7** operand **12** multiplicand
terms: **4** root, sine, surd **5** digit, graph **6** cosine, scalar, sector, vector **7** decimal, problem, theorem **8** derivate, fraction **10** quaternion
types: **4** pure **7** applied

MATINEE: **4** play, show **5** movie **11** performance **13** entertainment

MATRIARCH: **5** queen, ruler **6** female, matron, mother **7** dowager

MATRICULATE: **4** join **5** admit, enter **6** enroll **8** register

MATRIMONIAL: **6** bridal **7** marital, married, nuptial **8** conjugal **9** betrothed, connubial

MATRIMONY: **5** union **7** wedlock **8** marriage, nuptials **12** connubiality

MATRIX: **3** die, mat **4** cast, form, mold, womb **5** model, shape **6** gangue **7** pattern **10** groundmass

MATRON: **4** dame **5** widow **6** female, mother **7** dowager **8** overseer **9** matriarch **11** housekeeper

MATTER: **4** body, gear, mail, mass, text **5** being, issue, sense, solid, stuff, thing, topic, waste, worry **6** affair, entity, object, source, thesis **7** concern, content, problem, signify, subject, trouble **8** business, elements, material, obstacle **9** discharge, substance **10** difficulty **11** constituent

MATTER-OF-FACT: **4** calm, cold, dull **5** frank **6** direct **7** literal, prosaic **9** objective, practical, pragmatic, realistic **10** impersonal, unaffected **11** unemotional

MATURE: **3** age **5** adult, grown, prime, ripen **6** evolve, mellow **7** blossom, settled **8** complete, seasoned **9** developed **10** considered

MATURITY: **7** manhood **9** adulthood, womanhood **10** experience, maturation **11** development

MAUDLIN: **5** corny, mushy, tipsy, weepy **7** mawkish, tearful **8** bathetic **9** emotional **10** lachrymose **11** sentimental

MAUL: **4** bash, beat, club, mace **5** abuse, gavel, pound, staff, stomp **6** batter, bruise, hammer, injure, mallet, mangle, pummel **9** manhandle

MAUNDER: **5** drift, stray **6** babble, drivel, mumble, mutter, ramble, wander **7** blather

MAURITANIA:
capital: **10** Nouakchott
cities: **4** Atar **5** Kaedi, Kaldi **8** Zouerate **10** Nouadhibou
continent: **6** Africa
ethnic groups: **4** Moor **5** Negro, Wolof **6** Poular **7** Sonunke **10** Arab-Berber
features: **6** Sahara
languages: **6** Arabic, French **14** Hassanya Arabic
monetary unit: **7** ouguiya
native: **11** Mauritanian
water: **7** Senegal

MAUSOLEUM: **4** tomb **8** catacomb, monument

MAUVE: **4** plum **5** lilac **6** purple, violet **8** lavender

MAVEN: **6** expert, master **11** connoisseur **12** professional

MAVERICK: **5** stray **8** bohemian **9** dissenter, unbranded **13** nonconformist

MAW: **4** craw, jaws **5** mouth **6** gullet **7** stomach

MAWKISH: **5** gushy, mushy, teary **7** insipid, maudlin **8** bathetic **9** emotional, nostalgic, sickening **11** sentimental

MAXIM: **4** rule, word **5** adage, axiom, gnome, moral, motto **6** saying, truism **7** precept, proverb **8** aphorism, doctrine **9** catchword

MAXIMUM: **4** apex, most, peak **5** limit **6** climax, utmost, zenith **7** ceiling, highest, optimum **8** greatest, ultimate **9** paramount **11** culmination

MAY: **3** can **4** must, wish **5** might, shrub **7** allowed **8** hawthorn, possible **9** permitted **10** likelihood

MAYBE: **7** perhaps **8** feasible, possibly **9** perchance **11** conceivable, possibility

MAYHEM: **4** maim **5** chaos **7** cripple **8** violence **9** commotion, confusion **11** pandemonium

MAZE: **3** web **4** mesh **6** jungle, puzzle, tangle **7** network, perplex, stupefy **8** bewilder, confound **9** confusion, labyrinth **10** hodgepodge

MEA CULPA: **7** my fault **10** I am to blame

MEADOW: **3** lea **4** mead, park, vega **5** field, heath, sward, veldt **7** pasture, prairie **9** grassland

MEAGER: **4** bare, lean, mere, poor, puny, slim, thin **5** gaunt, scant, small, spare **6** barren, feeble, little, measly, scanty, scarce, skimpy, sparse **7** lacking, starved **10** inadequate **12** insufficient

MEAL: **4** chow, feed, food, grub, menu **5** board, feast, flour, grain, lunch, snack **6** brunch, dinner, supper **7** banquet, cookout, potluck **8** victuals **9** breakfast

MEAN: 3 low, mid, par **4** base, evil, norm, poor, show, vile, want **5** argue, cruel, imply, nasty, petty, snide **6** abject, allude, coarse, common, convey, denote, design, humble, import, intend, median, medium, middle, narrow, ornery, paltry, sordid, stingy, unkind **7** average, express, hostile, ignoble, miserly, propose, purport, purpose, selfish, signify, suggest **8** beggarly, indicate, intimate, midpoint, spiteful **9** excellent, irascible, malicious, niggardly, penurious, symbolize, truculent **10** unpleasant **12** contemptible, intermediate

MEANDER: 4 roam, turn, wind **5** amble, curve, drift, snake, stray, twist **6** ramble, wander, zigzag

MEANING: 3 aim **4** gist, hint **5** drift, point, sense **6** import, intent, spirit **7** content, context, essence, message, purport, purpose **9** intention, knowledge, substance **10** definition, indication **11** acceptation, designation, translation **12** significance **13** signification, understanding

MEANINGFUL: 4 deep **5** heavy **6** useful **7** pointed **8** eloquent **9** important **10** expressive, worthwhile **11** significant **13** consequential

MEANINGLESS: 5 blank, empty **6** hollow **7** aimless, shallow, useless **9** senseless, worthless **11** unimportant **13** insignificant

MEANS: 3 way **4** mode, path, road **5** funds **6** assets, avenue, budget, income, manner, method, system, wealth **7** channel **9** resources **10** instrument **11** wherewithal

MEANTIME: 5 while **7** interim **8** interval **9** temporary

MEANWHILE: 10 concurrent **14** simultaneously

MEASLY: 4 puny **6** meager, paltry, skimpy **9** worthless **11** unimportant **12** contemptible **13** insignificant

MEASURE: 3 act, law **4** area, mete, rule, span, tape, time **5** clock, gauge, girth, meter, quota, rhyme, ruler, scale, share **6** amount, degree, length, ration **7** cadence, caliper, quantum **8** estimate, odometer, standard **9** benchmark, calculate, criterion, yardstick

area: **3** are **4** acre, foot, inch, mile, yard **5** meter **6** decare **7** hectare

capacity: **4** cask, gill, orna, peck, pint **5** liter, minim, quart **6** barrel, bushel, gallon **8** fluidram

cloth: **3** ell **4** yard

combining forms: **6** metric **8** metrical

electricity: **3** ohm **4** volt, watt **5** ergon, joule **6** ampere **10** horsepower

energy: **3** BTU, erg **5** joule **7** calorie **11** thermal unit

land: **3** are, rod **4** acre, area, mile, rood **6** decare **7** hectare, kiliare

length: **3** dra, ell, pik, rod **4** foot, inch, knot, mile, nail, yard **5** cubit, digit, meter **6** league, micron **9** decimeter, kilometer **10** centimeter, hectometer, millimeter

light: **7** candela **11** candlepower

liquid: **3** aam, keg **4** gill, pint **5** liter, pipet, quart **6** barrel, gallon, magnum, minims, runlet, tierce **7** pipette, rundlet **8** hogshead **9** kiloliter

loudness: **4** phon

medicinal: **4** dram **5** minim, ounce **7** scruple

metrics: **3** ton **4** gram **5** tonne **7** quintal **8** dekagram, kilogram **9** centigram, milligram

nautical: **4** knot **6** fathom

paper: **4** page, ream **5** quire, sheet

sound: **7** decibel

temperature: **4** term **6** calory, degree, Kelvin, therme **7** calorie, Celsius **10** centigrade, Fahrenheit
time: **3** day **4** hour, week, year **5** month, score **6** decade, minute, moment, second **7** century **10** millennium, nanosecond **11** microsecond, millisecond
water depth: **5** sound
weight: **3** ton **4** bale, dram, troy **5** carat, grain, liter, ounce, pound **7** scruple **9** kiloliter **10** hectoliter

MEASURED: **5** exact **6** gauged **7** careful, uniform, weighed **8** computed **10** calculated, deliberate, restrained **12** standardized

MEASUREMENT: **4** area, mass, size **6** amount, height, length, volume, weight **8** distance, quantity **9** dimension, frequency, magnitude **10** assessment **11** calculation, mensuration

MEASURING INSTRUMENT: **4** gage, tape **5** gauge, meter, ruler **7** caliper, sextant **9** baroscope, vinometer, yardstick **10** densimeter, gravimeter, protractor **11** actinometer, calorimeter, colorimeter, pluviometer, seismograph

MEAT: **4** beef, core, fare, food, gist, lamb, pork, veal **5** brawn, flesh, heart **6** marrow, muscle **7** essence, venison **8** victuals **9** nutriment **11** comestibles, nourishment
cut: **3** ham, leg, rib **4** chop, loin, rump **5** chuck, flank, liver, roast, round, steak **6** cutlet **7** sirloin **8** shoulder
grade: **3** top **5** first, prime **6** choice, grade A, second **10** commercial

MEATY: **4** rich **5** heavy, solid **11** interesting, significant, substantial

MECCA:
birthplace of: **8** Mohammed
features: **5** Kaaba **6** Zam-Zam **10** Black Stone **11** Great Mosque
holy city of: **5** Islam
place: **11** Saudi Arabia
port: **6** Jiddah

MECHANIC: **6** worker **7** artisan **8** operator **9** craftsman, machinist

MECHANICAL: **7** routine **9** automatic **10** uninspired **11** emotionless, instinctive, involuntary

MECHANISM: **4** gear, tool **5** catch, means, motor, slide **6** device, engine, gadget, method, system **7** process **9** apparatus, appliance, machinery, operation, technique **10** components, instrument

MEDAL: **5** award, badge **6** laurel, plaque, trophy, wreath **10** decoration
Olympic: **4** gold **6** bronze, silver

MEDDLE: **3** pry **5** snoop **6** butt in, dabble, impede, kibitz, tamper, tinker **7** intrude **9** interfere, intervene

MEDDLER: **5** snoop **8** busybody **9** buttinsky **10** tattletale

MEDDLESOME: **4** busy, nosy **6** prying **7** curious **8** snooping **9** intrusive, officious **10** impudicity **11** interfering

MEDEA:
father: **6** Aeetes
husband: **5** Jason
inhabited: **7** Colchis
known as: **8** princess **9** sorceress
mother: **5** Idyia
obtained: **12** Golden Fleece
son: **6** Medeus

MEDIA: **4** news **5** cable, press, radio **9** magazines, newspaper **10** publishing, television **14** communications

MEDIAL: **4** mean **6** center, median, middle **7** average, central **8** ordinary

MEDIAN: **4** mean, norm **6** center, medial, middle, midway **7** average **8** midpoint **12** intermediate

MEDIATE: **6** umpire **7** referee, resolve **8** moderate **9** arbitrate, intercede, interpose, intervene, negotiate **10** conciliate

MEDIATOR: **5** agent, judge **6** broker, umpire **7** referee **9** go-between, moderator **10** arbitrator, negotiator, peacemaker **11** intercessor **12** intermediary

MEDIC: **6** doctor, intern **7** surgeon **9** physician **12** practitioner

MEDICAL: **6** iatric **7** healing **8** curative **9** medicinal **10** corrective **11** Aesculapian, therapeutic
instruments: **6** lancet **7** cannula, forceps, scalpel **8** otoscope, speculum **9** aspirator, endoscope, iron lungs, kymograph, polygraph, retractor **10** audiometer, CAT scanner, osteoclast **11** stethoscope **13** defibrillator **18** electrocardiograph

MEDICINAL: **6** curing **7** healing, medical **8** salutary **10** medicative **11** Aesculapian, therapeutic **12** pharmaceutic

MEDICINE: **4** cure, drug, pill **5** serum, tonic **6** emetic, physic, potion, remedy, tablet **7** antacid, capsule, codeine, insulin, quinine, steroid, vaccine **8** antidote, diuretic, hypnotic, laxative, ointment, sedative, tincture **9** analgesic, cathartic, cortisone, injection, paregoric, soporific **10** antibiotic **11** alternative, amoxycillin, antitussive, expectorant **12** decongestant, prescription, tetracycline, tranquilizer **13** anti-coagulant, antihistamine
branches: **7** surgery, therapy, urology **8** internal **9** neurology, pathology **10** cardiology, geriatrics, gynecology, obstetrics, osteopathy, pediatrics, psychiatry, veterinary **11** dermatology, diagnostics, oral surgery, orthopedics **12** chiropractic, radiotherapy **13** endocrinology, ophthalmology, psychotherapy **15** general practice
cure-all: **7** panacea
fake: **7** placebo
untested: **7** nostrum

MEDICINE MAN: **6** doctor, healer, priest, shaman **8** sorcerer **9** physician **11** witch doctor

MEDIEVAL: **6** feudal, Gothic **8** Dark Ages **10** antiquated, Middle Ages
minstrel: **8** jongleur **10** troubadour
peasant: **4** serf
system: **9** feudalism
tax: **4** geld **5** tithe **6** murage **7** scutage
tournament: **5** joust **8** carousel
weapon: **5** lance, sword **8** crossbow

MEDIOCRE: **4** fair, mean, so-so **6** common, medium, normal **7** average **8** inferior, moderate, ordinary, passable **11** commonplace, indifferent

MEDITATE: **4** mull, muse, pore **5** dream, study, think, weigh **6** ponder **7** reflect, revolve **8** consider, ruminate **9** speculate **10** deliberate **11** contemplate

MEDITATION: **4** yoga **6** prayer **7** thought **9** mysticism **10** cogitation **11** examination **13** contemplation
chant: **6** mantra

MEDITERRANEAN SEA:
concerning: **9** Levantine
islands: **4** Elba **5** Capri, Crete, Ibiza, Iviza, Malta **6** Candia, Cyprus, Ebusus, Lesbos, Lipari, Rhodes, Sicily **7** Corsica, Majorca, Panaria **8** Balearic, Cyclades, Sardinia, Sporades **9** Stromboli **10** Dodecanese
linked to: **6** Red Sea **8** Atlantic **11** Indian Ocean
ports: **4** Nice, Oran **5** Genoa, Tunis **6** Beirut, Malaga, Naples, Sicily **7** Algiers, Tangier, Tel Aviv, Trip-

oli, Tunisia **8** Benghazi, Port Said, Valencia **9** Barcelona, Cartagena, Gibraltar, Marseille **10** Alexandria
subdivisions: **6** Aegean, Ionian **8** Adriatic **10** Tyrrhenian
weather: **7** gregale, mistral, sirocco **8** levanter

MEDIUM: **4** fair, mean, tool **5** agent, midst, music, organ, radio **6** medial, midway, normal **7** average, channel, climate, diviner, psychic, setting, vehicle, writing **8** magazine, mediator, moderate, ordinary, painting **9** newspaper, sculpture **10** atmosphere, instrument, television **11** clairvoyant, environment **12** intermediary **13** fortuneteller

MEDLEY: **4** olio **5** blend, combo **6** jumble **7** melange, mixture **9** patchwork, potpourri **10** assortment, collection, hodgepodge, miscellany **11** gallimaufry

MEDUSA:
father: **7** Phorcys
form: **6** Gorgon
killer: **7** Perseus
mother: **4** Ceto
offspring: **7** Pegasus **8** Chrysaor

MEEK: **4** mild, weak **5** lowly, timid **6** docile, gentle, humble, modest **7** patient, subdued **8** moderate, peaceful, reserved, resigned, sheepish, tolerant, yielding **9** spineless **10** submissive, unassuming **11** unassertive

MEET: **4** bump, duel, face, find, join **5** clash, cross, equal, event, greet, match, touch, tryst **6** battle, chance, comply, confer, gather, happen, proper **7** collide, connect, contact, contend, contest, convene, fitting, fulfill, satisfy **8** assemble, confront, converge, moderate, suitable **9** encounter, intersect **10** congregate, rendezvous, tournament **11** appropriate, competition

MEET HALFWAY: **4** deal **6** middle **7** bargain **10** compromise, settlement

MEETING: **4** date, moot **5** forum, rally, tryst, union **6** caucus, huddle, powwow, summit **7** harmony, session **8** adjacent, approval, assembly, conclave, congress, junction, showdown **9** agreement, encounter, gathering, symposium **10** conference, engagement, rendezvous **11** convocation **12** consultation **13** confrontation

MEGRIM: **4** whim **5** blues, fancy **7** caprice, vertigo **8** flounder, headache, migraine **9** dizziness **10** depression, melancholy **11** unhappiness

MELANCHOLY: **3** low, sad **4** blue, dull, glum **5** dumps, moody **6** dismal, dreary, gloomy, somber, woeful **7** despair, doleful, pensive, sadness, unhappy **8** downcast, funereal, tristful **9** cheerless, dejection, plaintive, sorrowful, woebegone **10** depressing, depression, desolation, despondent **11** downhearted **12** disconsolate

MELANGE: **5** combo **6** medley **7** mixture **8** mishmash **9** pasticcio **10** assortment, hodgepodge

MELD: **4** fuse, join **5** blend, merge, unite **7** combine **10** amalgamate **11** incorporate

MELEE: **3** row **4** fray, riot **5** brawl, clash, fight **6** affray, battle, fracas, ruckus **7** scuffle **8** dogfight, skirmish **9** commotion **10** donnybrook

MELIORATE: **6** better, soften **7** improve

MELLIFLUOUS: **5** sweet **6** golden, smooth, syrupy **7** honeyed, musical, sugared **8** pleasant

MELLOW: **4** aged, rich, ripe **5** juicy, ripen **6** mature, tender **7** matured, relaxed **8** softened, soothing **9** developed, unhurried

MELODIOUS: **6** dulcet **7** lyrical, melodic, musical, tuneful **8** canorous, pleasing **9** agreeable **10** harmonious

MELODRAMATIC: **5** corny, showy **9** emotional **10** theatrical **11** exaggerated, sensational

MELODY: **3** air, lay **4** aria, note, song, tune **5** ditty, lyric, music, theme **6** rhythm, strain **7** harmony, refrain **9** resonance

MELON: **4** musk, pepo **5** fruit, gourd, water **6** casaba, nutmeg, papaya, winter **8** honeydew, spanspek **10** cantaloupe

MELT: **4** bake, burn, cook, flow, flux, fuse, heat, thaw **5** blend, smelt, sweat, yield **6** render, scorch, soften **7** dwindle, liquefy **8** dissolve, perspire **9** dissipate **10** colliquate, deliquesce **12** disintegrate

MELVILLE, HERMAN: **4** poet **6** author **8** novelist
wrote: **4** Omoo **5** Typee **6** Pierre **7** Redburn **8** Moby Dick **9** Billy Budd **11** White Jacket **20** Bartleby the Scrivener

MEMBER: **3** arm, leg **4** limb, part **5** organ, piece **6** branch, fellow **7** chapter, element, portion, section, segment **8** division **9** affiliate, component, extremity **11** constituent

MEMBERSHIP: **4** club, seat **5** group **7** society **10** enrollment, fellowship, sisterhood **11** affiliation, association, brotherhood

MEMBRANE: **3** web **4** coat, film, leaf, skin **5** layer, sheet **6** lamina, sheath, tissue

MEMENTO: **5** relic, token **6** trophy **7** vestige **8** keepsake, reminder, souvenir **10** knickknack **11** remembrance

MEMOIR: **5** diary **6** record, report **7** account, journal **9** biography, narrative **10** commentary **11** confessions **12** recollection **13** autobiography

MEMORABLE: **7** lasting, notable, special **8** eventful, historic **9** important **10** celebrated, impressive, noteworthy, remarkable, remembered **11** illustrious, reminiscent **13** distinguished, extraordinary, unforgettable

MEMORANDUM: **4** note **5** brief, diary **6** agenda, letter, report **7** message, minutes **8** dispatch, notation, reminder **9** directive **12** announcement

MEMORIAL: **5** relic, token **6** memoir, plaque, record, shrine, statue, trophy **7** memento **8** ceremony, monument, souvenir **9** mausoleum **11** remembrance, testimonial **13** commemorative

MEMORY: **4** mind, rote **5** image **6** prompt, recall **9** recapture, retention **10** cognizance **11** remembrance **12** recollection, reminiscence **13** retrospection
book: **5** album, diary **7** journal **9** scrapbook
loss: **5** fugue, lethe **7** amnesia **8** oblivion

MENACE: **4** pest **5** peril **6** bother, danger, hazard, impend, threat **7** torment **8** jeopardy, threaten **12** troublemaker

MENACING: **7** looming **8** imminent **10** formidable **11** frightening **12** intimidating

MEND: **3** fix, sew **4** cure, darn, heal, help, knit **5** amend, patch **6** better, doctor, remedy, repair **7** correct, improve, rebuild, rectify, restore **8** renovate **9** refurbish **10** ameliorate, convalesce, recuperate

MENDACIOUS: **5** false, lying **6** untrue **7** fibbing **9** deceitful, dishonest **10** untruthful

MENDACITY: **3** lie **5** fraud **6** deceit **7** untruth **9** deception, falsehood **11** insincerity **13** falsification, prevarication

MENDELEVIUM: **7** element

MENDICANT: **4** monk **5** friar **6** beggar, pauper **8** vagabond **10** panhandler

MENIAL: **4** base, mean **5** lowly **6** humble, sordid **7** ignoble, servant, servile, slavish **9** degrading, demeaning **11** subservient, sycophantic

MENTAL: **4** mind **6** crazed, insane **8** deranged, unstable **9** cognitive, disturbed, psychotic **11** intelligent **12** intellectual

MENTAL DISORDER: **5** quirk **6** oddity **7** aphasia **8** delusion, insanity, neurosis, paranoia **9** psychosis **11** megalomania **12** hypochondria **13** schizophrenia

MENTAL INSTITUTION: **6** asylum **8** loony bin, madhouse **9** funny farm **10** sanatorium, sanitarium

MENTALITY: **4** mind **5** sense **6** acumen, makeup **8** attitude **9** reasoning **10** brainpower **11** discernment, rationality **12** intelligence

MENTION: **4** cite, hint, name **5** honor, imply, quote, refer, speak **6** allude, denote, inform, notice, record, remark **7** comment, specify, tribute **8** allusion, citation **9** reference, statement **10** indication **11** observation

MENTOR: **4** guru **5** coach, tutor **6** master **7** teacher, trainer **9** counselor **10** instructor

MENU: **4** card, list, meal **5** carte **6** dishes **7** cuisine, options, program

MEPHITIC: **4** foul **6** smelly **7** noxious **8** stinking **9** offensive, poisonous

MERCENARY: **4** hack **5** venal **6** greedy, sordid **7** soldier, warrior **8** covetous, hireling, vendible **11** legionnaire

MERCHANDISE: **4** line, sell, ware **5** goods, stock, wares **7** product, promote, staples **9** advertise, publicize **11** commodities

MERCHANT: **5** buyer **6** broker, dealer, jobber, seller, trader, vendor **7** peddler **8** exporter, purveyor, retailer, salesman **10** saleswoman, shopkeeper, wholesaler **11** businessman, storekeeper **13** businesswoman

MERCIFUL: **4** kind **6** benign, humane, tender **7** clement, lenient, sparing **9** forgiving, pardoning **10** charitable **11** sympathetic **13** compassionate

MERCILESS: **4** grim, mean **5** cruel, harsh **6** fierce, savage **8** inhumane, ruthless **9** ferocious, heartless **10** relentless, unyielding

MERCURIAL: **5** quick **6** adroit, clever, lively, shrewd **7** cunning, flighty **8** volatile **10** changeable, inconstant **11** fluctuating, quicksilver

MERCURY: **3** god **6** planet **7** element **9** messenger
god of: **6** travel **8** commerce, thievery

MERCY: **4** pity, ruth **5** grace **6** lenity **7** charity **8** blessing, clemency, goodwill, humanity, kindness, leniency, sympathy **9** tolerance **10**

compassion, generosity, tenderness **11** benevolence, forgiveness
killing: **10** euthanasia

MERE: **4** lake, only, pond, pool, pure, sole **5** limit, marsh, scant, sheer, small, stark, utter **6** entire, little, simple, slight **8** absolute, boundary **10** negligible **13** insignificant, unadulterated

MERELY: **4** just, only **5** quite **6** barely, simply, solely **7** utterly

MERETRICIOUS: **4** loud **5** cheap, gaudy, showy **6** flashy **7** blatant, glaring **9** deceptive **10** misleading

MERGE: **4** fuse, join, meld, pool **5** blend, unify, unite **6** absorb **7** combine **8** coalesce, converge **9** commingle, integrate **10** amalgamate, assimilate **11** consolidate, incorporate

MERGER: **5** union **8** alliance, takeover **9** coalition **11** combination, unification

MERIDIAN: **4** acme, apex, noon, peak **5** curve **6** apogee, circle, climax, summit, zenith **8** pinnacle **11** culmination

MERIT: **4** earn **5** award, worth **6** credit, desert, reward, virtue **7** deserts, deserve, dignity, stature, warrant **10** excellence

MERITORIOUS: **6** worthy **8** laudable **9** admirable, deserving, exemplary, honorable **11** commendable

MERRIMENT: **3** fun **4** glee **5** mirth **6** frolic, gaiety **7** jollity, revelry **8** laughter **9** amusement, enjoyment, festivity, joviality **10** jocularity **11** celebration, merrymaking **12** cheerfulness, conviviality

MERRY: **4** glad **5** happy, jolly, sunny **6** blithe, jocose, jocund, jovial, joyful, joyous, lively **7** festive, gleeful, jocular **8** cheerful, mirthful, pleasant **9** hilarious, sprightly, vivacious **10** frolicsome **12** lighthearted

MERRYMAKING: **5** jolly **6** frolic **7** festive, revelry **8** carousal, pleasure **9** amusement, enjoyment, festivity, merriment **11** celebration **12** conviviality

MESA: **4** peak **5** butte **7** plateau **8** mountain **9** tableland

MESH: **3** web **4** grid **5** agree, skein, snare **6** engage, screen, tangle **7** connect, ensnare, netting, network **8** entangle **9** harmonize, interlock **10** coordinate

MESMERIZE: **4** hold **5** charm **7** control **8** enthrall **9** captivate, fascinate, hypnotize, spellbind

MESOPOTAMIA:
also called: **10** Paddam Aram
capital: **7** Baghdad, Nineveh
cities: **5** Mosul **6** Nippur **7** Babylon, Edessan, Kerbela
features: **6** Jazira, Taurus, Zagros **9** Lesser Zab **10** Greater Zab
kingdoms: **5** Akkad, Sumer **7** Assyria, Babylon **9** Babylonia
kings/queens: **6** Darius **9** Alexander, Hammurabi
place: **4** Iraq
water: **6** Tigris **9** Euphrates **11** Persian Gulf

MESS: **4** food, hash, meal, mull, soil **5** botch, dirty, snafu **6** bungle, crisis, dabble, debris, fiddle, jumble, litter, muddle, pickle **7** clutter, crumple, dilemma, eyesore, rations, trouble, wrinkle **8** disarray, dishevel, disorder, scramble, shambles, wreckage **9** commotion, confusion **10** difficulty, hodgepodge **11** predicament

MESSAGE: **4** code, memo, news, note, wire, word **5** cable, moral, point **6** letter, report **7** epistle, meaning, mission, missive **8** bulletin, dispatch, telegram **10** communique, memorandum **11** information **13** communication

MESS AROUND: **4** fool, play **5** flirt **6** dabble, dawdle, fiddle, putter, tinker **10** experiment

MESSENGER: **4** page **5** angel, crier, envoy, gofer, miler **6** herald, legate, pigeon, runner **7** apostle, carrier, courier, mercury, prophet **8** delegate, emissary, minister **9** go-between, harbinger **10** ambassador, dispatcher, evangelist **12** intermediary

MESSIAH: **5** Jesus **6** Christ, leader, savior **11** anointed one

MESS UP: **3** err **4** goof, muff **5** botch, dirty **6** bungle **7** blunder, confuse **11** disorganize

MESSY: **5** dirty **6** sloppy, untidy **7** jumbled, unkempt **9** cluttered **10** disheveled, unpleasant

METAL:
ages: **4** iron **6** bronze, copper
alloys: **5** brass, steel
concerning: **3** ore **5** tinny **8** metallic **13** metalliferous
found in: **3** ore **7** mineral **8** compound
piece: **3** gad, pig **4** lode, seam, slag, slug, vein **5** dross, ingot, lemel, paten, stope **6** nugget, scoria, solder, spline **7** filings, scissel
protection: **4** mail **5** armor **9** chain mail
sheet: **4** leaf **5** lames, plate **6** lamina, tagger
types: **3** tin **4** gold, iron, lead, zinc **6** cerium, cobalt, copper, erbium, osmium, pewter, radium, silver, solium **7** cadmium, iridium, mercury, terbium, uranium, yttrium **8** lutecium, platinum **9** potassium
worker: **5** smith **7** riveter **8** tinsmith **9** goldsmith **11** coppersmith, silversmith

METAMORPHOSE: **5** alter **6** change, mutate **9** transform, transmute **11** transfigure

METAMORPHOSIS: **6** change **7** rebirth **8** mutation **9** evolution **10** alteration, conversion

METAPHOR: **5** image, trope **6** simile, symbol **7** analogy **8** allegory **10** comparison **14** figure of speech

METAPHYSICAL: **8** abstract, abstruse, esoteric **9** unearthly **10** immaterial, intangible **12** supernatural **13** philosophical **14** transcendental

METE: **4** dole, give **5** allot, bound, limit **7** measure **8** allocate, boundary, disburse, dispense **9** apportion **10** administer, distribute

METEORIC: **5** brief, rapid, swift **6** sudden **7** blazing **8** dazzling, flashing **9** celestial **11** spectacular

METEOROLOGIST: **10** forecaster, weatherman **12** weatherwoman

METER: **4** beat, time **5** music, swing, verse **6** rhythm **7** cadence, measure, pattern **11** arrangement, measurement
one-tenth: **9** decimeter
one-hundredth: **10** centimeter
one-thousandth: **10** millimeter
ten: **9** decameter
one hundred: **10** hectometer
one thousand: **9** kilometer

METHOD: **3** way **4** form, mode, plan, rule **5** means, order, style, usage **6** manner, system **7** fashion, formula, pattern, process, routine, science **8** approach, strategy **9** procedure, technique **13** modus operandi

METHODICAL: **5** exact **7** orderly, precise **9** organized **10** deliberate, meticulous, systematic

METICULOUS: **4** neat **5** exact, fussy **7** careful, finical, precise **8**

detailed, thorough **10** fastidious, methodical, scrupulous **11** painstaking, persnickety, punctilious

METIER: **4** line, work **5** craft, forte, trade **7** calling **8** business **9** specialty **10** occupation, profession

METRIC: **3** are, day, ton **4** gram, hour **5** carat, liter, meter, stere, tonne **6** ampere, kelvin, minute, radian, second **7** candela, hectare **8** decigram, dekagram, kilogram **9** centigram, deciliter, decimeter, dekaliter, dekameter, hectogram, kiloliter, kilometer, milligram, steradian **10** centiliter, centimeter, hectoliter, hectometer, milliliter, millimeter **15** micromillimeter
origin: **6** France
prefixes: **4** atto, deci, deka, giga, kilo, mega, nano, pico, tera **5** billi, centi, femto, hecto, micro, milli

METROPOLITAN: **4** city **5** urban **6** bishop **9** municipal **12** cosmopolitan

METTLE: **4** fire, guts **5** heart, nerve, spunk, vigor **6** makeup, spirit **7** bravery, courage, quality **9** character, fortitude **10** enthusiasm **11** temperament

METTLESOME: **5** brave, fiery **6** ardent, plucky, spunky **7** peppery, valiant **8** spirited

MEW: **4** cage, coop, meow **5** alley **6** street **7** conceal, confine, seagull **8** hideaway **9** courtyard, enclosure

MEXICO:
aborigine: **4** Maya **5** Aztec
also called: **8** New Spain
ancient cities: **4** Tula **10** Monte Alban **11** Teotihuacan **12** Tenochtitlan
capital: **10** Mexico City
cities: **4** Leon **5** La Paz, Tepic **6** Cancun, Juarez, Merida, Oaxaca, Puebla, Toluca **7** Durango, Orizaba, Tampico, Tijuana, Torreon **8** Acapulco, Culiacan, Ensenada, Mazatlan, Mexicali, Vera Cruz **9** Chihuahua, Monterrey **10** Hermosillo **11** Guadalajara **14** Puerto Vallarta
conqueror: **6** Cortes, Cortez
drinks: **4** chia **6** mescal, pulque **7** tequila
empires: **4** Maya **5** Aztec, Olmec **6** Mixtec, Toltec **7** Zapotec
estate: **8** hacienda
ethnic groups: **3** Mam **4** Cora, Maya, Seri, Xova **5** Aztec, Huave, Lipan, Nahau, Opata, Otomi, Yaqui, Zoque **6** Indian, Mixtec, Otonia, Toltec **7** Huastec, Mestizo, Mexican, Nahuatl, Spanish, Tepanec, Zacatec, Zapotec **8** Totonaco, Zaceteco **10** Cuitlateca, Cuitlateco
fiber: **4** pita **5** istle, sisal **6** catena
food: **4** taco **5** arepa, atole, chile, salsa **6** tamale **7** tostada **8** frijoles, tortilla **9** enchilada, guacamole **10** quesadilla
gods: **6** Tlaloc **12** Quetzalcoatl **14** Huitzilopochtl
heroes: **4** Diaz **6** Juarez
house: **5** jacal
islands: **6** Carmen, Cedros **7** San Jose, Tiburon
lakes: **7** Chapala, Texcoco **9** Patzcuaro
languages: **5** Mayan, Otomi **6** Mixtec **7** Mazahua, Mazatec, Nahuatl, Spanish, Totonac, Zapotec **8** Tarascan
leaders: **3** Gil **4** Diaz **5** Lopez, Villa **6** Juarez, Madero, Valdes, Zapata **8** Santa Ana **9** Montezuma, Rodriguez
monetary unit: **4** peso **6** dinero
mountains: **6** Colima, Toluca **7** Orizaba **11** Ixtacihuatl, Sierra Madre **12** Citlaltepetl, Popocatepetl
plants: **3** ule **4** chia **5** agave, amole, datil, jalap, otate, sotol **6** chaute, maguey, slavia **8** acapulco **9** sabadilla, sapodilla

revolutionaries: **6** Zapata **8** Carranza **11** Pancho Villa
rivers: **4** Mayo **5** Yaqui **6** Grande, Panuco, Penuco **7** Tabasco **8** Colorado
seas: **7** Pacific **8** Atlantic **9** Caribbean
volcano: **6** Colima **7** Jorullo **9** Paricutin **12** Popocatepetl

MEZZANINE: **5** floor, story **7** balcony

MICHELANGELO:
occupation: **4** poet **7** painter **8** sculptor **9** architect
painting: **6** Julius **10** Holy Family **13** Sistine Chapel
sculptor: **5** David, Moses, Pieta **7** Madonna, Victory

MICHENER, JAMES: **6** author
wrote: **6** Alaska, Hawaii, Mexico **8** Caravans, Sayonara **9** The Source **10** Centennial, Chesapeake **11** The Drifters

MICHIGAN:
bird: **5** robin
capital: **7** Lansing
cities: **5** Flint, Ionia **7** Detroit, Pontiac **8** Ann Arbor **9** Marquette **11** Grand Rapids **17** Saulte Sainte Marie
county: **3** Bay **4** Kent **6** Inghum **7** Berrien, Calhoun, Genesee **9** Kalamazoo
explorer: **5** Brule **6** Joliet **7** La Salle **9** Marquette
features: **7** Curwood, Holland **8** Dearborn, Mackinac, Mackinaw
fish: **10** brook trout
flower: **12** apple blossom
Indian: **6** Ottawa
island: **8** Mackinaw
lakes: **4** Burt, Erie **5** Huron, Torch **8** Houghton, Michigan, Muskegan **9** Menominee
mountain peak: **7** Curwood
nickname: **9** Wolverine **10** Great Lakes
rivers: **5** Huron **7** Au Sable **8** Manistee, Muskegan **9** Menominee
tree: **9** white pine
water: **13** Hiawatha Falls

MICROBE: **4** germ **8** bacillus, bacteria, organism, parasite **13** microorganism

MICROORGANISM: **4** germ **5** virus **6** aerobe **7** microbe **8** bacillus **9** bacterium, protozoan, spirillum

MICROSCOPIC: **4** tiny **5** small **6** little, minute **13** infinitesimal

MIDDAY: **4** noon **8** meridian, noontide

MIDDLE: **4** core, mean **5** belly, midst, waist **6** center, marrow, medial, median, mesial, midway **7** average, between, central, halfway **11** intervening **12** intermediate

MIDDLE-CLASS: **6** common **8** ordinary **9** bourgeois

MIDDLE EAST:
area: **4** Asia **5** Egypt **12** Balkan States
countries: **4** Iran, Iraq, Oman **5** Egypt, Qatar, Sudan, Syria, Yemen **6** Israel, Jordan, Kuwait **7** Bahrain, Lebanon **11** Saudi Arabia

MIDDLEMAN: **5** agent **6** broker, dealer, trader **7** liaison **8** huckster **9** go-between **11** distributor, middlewoman, salesperson **12** intermediary

MIDDLE-OF-THE-ROAD: **3** MOR **7** popular **8** moderate

MIDDLING: **4** fair, okay, so-so **6** common, medium **7** average **8** mediocre, moderate, ordinary **11** indifferent

MIDGET: **4** tiny **5** dwarf, pygmy, small **7** manikin **8** munchkin, Tom Thumb **9** miniature

MIDST: **4** core, mean **5** among, depth, heart, thick **6** center, medium, middle **7** between, halfway **8** midpoint

MIDWIFE: **9** assistant **11** accoucheuse **12** practitioner

MIEN: **3** air **4** aura, look **5** guise, style **6** aspect, ostent **7** bearing, conduct **8** attitude, behavior, carriage, demeanor, presence **9** mannerism, semblance **10** appearance, deportment **11** countenance

MIFF: **4** spat **5** anger, annoy, upset **6** bother, offend **8** irritate **9** displease

MIGHT: **5** clout, drawn, power **6** muscle **7** ability, control **8** strength **9** supremacy **10** capability, domination

MIGHTY: **4** able, huge, vast **5** great **6** heroic, potent, strong **7** massive, violent **8** enormous, forceful, imposing, powerful, stalwart, towering, vigorous **9** extensive **10** courageous, monumental, omnipotent, tremendous

MIGRAINE: **6** megrim **8** headache

MIGRANT: **5** mover, nomad **7** drifter **9** itinerant, transient

MIGRATE: **4** move, roam, rove, trek **5** drift **6** travel, wander **8** relocate

MIGRATION: **6** exodus, flight **7** journey, passage **8** diaspora, movement

MIGRATORY: **6** mobile, moving, roving **7** nomadic **8** seasonal **9** transient, wandering

MILADY: **4** chic **5** madam, title, woman **10** noblewoman **11** fashionable, gentlewoman

MILD: **4** clam, cool, easy, kind, meek, soft, tame, warm **5** balmy, bland **6** benign, docile, gentle, medium, smooth **7** clement, lenient **8** delicate, moderate, pleasant, soothing, tranquil **9** easygoing, forgiving, indulgent, temperate **10** forbearing, unassuming

MILDEW: **4** mold, must **6** blight, fungus

MILE: **3** air **4** land **6** square **7** statute **8** nautical **11** measurement

MILESTONE: **4** step **5** event **7** plateau **8** landmark, milepost **11** achievement, anniversary **12** breakthrough

MILIEU: **7** climate, setting **8** ambience **10** atmosphere **11** environment **12** surroundings

MILITANT: **7** defiant, fighter, martial, soldier, warlike, warring, warrior **9** bellicose, combative **10** aggressive

MILITARY:

area: **4** base, camp, fort **5** depot, field, front, lines **6** armory, sector **7** arsenal **8** barracks, quarters **9** beachhead **10** encampment

clothes: **4** kepi **5** sagum, shako **6** helmet **8** havelock

command: **4** halt **6** at ease, salute **9** attention

concerning: **7** martial, warlike

equipment: **4** jeep, tank **6** camion **7** caisson **8** catapult, materiel, ordnance

group: **4** army, file, line **5** cadre, corps, drill, force, guard, squad, troop **6** legion, parade, review **7** cavalry, company, echelon, platoon, reserve **8** division, regiment **9** battalion, formation

movement: **5** drive **6** tactic **7** advance **8** anabasis, campaign, maneuver, strategy **11** penetration

person: **4** aide **5** guard, major **6** patrol **7** captain, colonel, estafet, general, marshal **8** adjutant **9** brigadier, commander, gendarmes, subaltern **10** Green Beret, lieutenant **12** constabulary

prisoner: **3** POW
rank: **6** brevet **8** banneret

MILK: **4** draw **5** bleed, drain, empty, nurse **6** elicit, siphon, suckle **7** exhaust, exploit, squeeze
heat treatment: **14** pasteurization
sugar: **7** lactose
types: **4** skim **5** cream, dried, goat's, whole **6** butter, low fat **7** formula, mother's **8** powdered **9** condensed **10** evaporated, two-percent **11** homogenized, pasteurized
watery part: **4** whey **5** serum

MILKSOP: **4** wimp **5** pansy, sissy **6** coward **7** chicken **8** weakling **9** jellyfish **10** pantywaist **11** lightweight, milquetoast, mollycoddle, yellowbelly

MILKY: **4** meek, tame **5** timid, white **6** chalky, cloudy, gentle, pearly **7** lacteal, opaline **10** effeminate

MILL: **3** box **4** beat, roam **5** crush, dress, fight, grind, knurl, plant, shape **6** device, finish, polish, powder, thrash **7** factory, machine **8** building **9** granulate, pulverize, transform

MILLENNIUM: **6** utopia **8** paradise, serenity **9** golden age, happiness **10** prosperity **13** thousand years

MILLER, ARTHUR: **6** author **8** novelist **10** playwright
second wife: **13** Marilyn Monroe
wrote: **5** Focus **9** All My Sons **10** The Misfits **11** The Crucible **12** After the Fall **16** Death of a Salesman

MILLESIMAL: **10** thousandth

MILLET: **3** hay **5** grain, grass

MILLIGRAM: **11** measurement

MILLILITER: **11** measurement

MILLIMETER: **11** measurement

MILLISECOND: **4** msec, time

MILLSTONE: **4** load, tool **6** burden **7** chopper, grinder **10** affliction **14** responsibility

MIME: **4** copy **5** actor, clown, farce, mimic **6** jester, parody **7** actress, buffoon, imitate **9** pantomime, performer, represent **11** impersonate **13** entertainment

MIMEOGRAPH: **4** copy **10** duplicator

MIMIC: **3** ape **4** echo, mime, mock **5** actor **6** parrot **7** actress, copycat, copying, imitate, trouper **8** comedian, ridicule, simulate, thespian **9** burlesque **11** counterfeit **13** impressionist

MIMICRY: **4** echo **5** apism **6** parody **9** imitation, mimicking **10** camouflage **13** impersonation

MINCE: **3** cut **4** chop, dice, hash **5** grind, strut **6** refine **7** posture **8** minimize, moderate, restrain **9** euphemize, extenuate, subdivide

MINCING: **5** fussy **6** dainty, la-di-da **7** genteel **8** affected, delicate **11** persnickety, pretentious

MIND: **4** care, hate, heed, look, obey, tend, view, will **5** abhor, brain, guard, power, study, watch **6** behold, belief, beware, detest, memory, notice, object, psyche, reason, regard, sanity, senses, spirit **7** dislike, faculty, feeling, opinion, outlook **8** consider, instinct, remember, thoughts **9** intellect, mentality, sentiment **10** conviction **11** inclination **12** intelligence, recollection **13** concentration

MINDFUL: **5** alert, awake, aware **7** careful **8** cautious, sensible **9** attentive, cognizant, conscious, observant

MINDLESS: **5** silly **6** insane, stupid **7** asinine, foolish, idiotic **9** forgetful, negligent, oblivious, unattuned **10** regardless **11** inattentive, thoughtless **13** unintelligent

MINE: **3** dig, pit, sap **4** hole, lode, vein **5** cache, delve, drill, scoop, shaft **6** burrow, cavity, quarry, supply, tunnel **7** deposit, gallery, passage, unearth **8** colliery **9** explosive **10** excavation
types: **4** coal, gold, iron **5** strip **6** copper, quartz, silver **7** diamond, open pit, surface

MINER: **6** digger, sapper **7** collier, dredger **9** excavator **10** prospector

MINERAL: **3** ore, tin **4** coal, gold, iron, mica, opal, spar, talc **5** beryl, irite, topaz **6** barite, copper, garnet, iolite, silver, sulfur, zircon **7** alumite, apatite, ataxite, citrine, uralite **8** cinnabar, dolomite, feldspar **9** celestite, galactite, petroleum, turquoise **10** chalcedony, gadolinite, retinalite, tourmaline
combining forms: **3** ine, ite **4** lite, lith, lyte, xene **5** oryct **6** orycto
crystalline: **4** mica, spar **5** fluor **6** quartz, yenite **7** apatite, felsite, felspar, knopite **8** boracite, elaterin, felspath
deposit: **4** lode, nest, vein **6** placer
flaky: **4** mica
hard: **6** spinel **7** adamant, diamond **8** corundum
native: **3** ore
non-metallic: **4** spar **5** boron **6** gangue, gypsum, halite, iodine **8** asbestos, graphite
shiny: **4** gold **6** galena, pyrite, silver
soft: **4** talc **6** gypsum

MINGLE: **3** mix **4** fuse, join, meld **5** blend, merge, unite **7** combine, network **8** coalesce, compound, intermix **9** associate, circulate, commingle, socialize **10** amalgamate

MINIATURE: **4** mini, tiny **5** small, teeny **6** little, minute, petite, pocket **9** minuscule **10** diminutive **11** lilliputian, microscopic

MINIMAL: **4** bare **5** basic, least **7** minimum **8** littlest, smallest **9** slightest **13** insignificant

MINIMIZE: **6** lessen, reduce **8** belittle, decrease, diminish, downplay **9** disparage **10** depreciate

MINIMUM: **5** least, speck **6** lowest **7** minimal **8** littlest, smallest **9** slightest

MINION: **4** idol **6** dainty **7** darling **8** delicate, favorite, follower **9** dependent, sycophant **11** subordinate

MINISTER: **4** tend **5** agent, nurse, padre, rabbi, serve **6** afford, attend, clergy, cleric, curate, divine, father, parson, pastor, priest, supply **7** nurture, provide **8** chaplain, preacher, reverend **9** attendant, clergyman **10** administer, ambassador, evangelist **11** clergywoman **12** ecclesiastic

MINNESOTA:
bird: **4** loon
capital: **6** St. Paul
cities: **3** Ely **5** Edina **6** Duluth, Winona **7** St. Cloud **9** Rochester **11** Bloomington, Minneapolis
county: **4** Cass, Clay, Cook, Lake, Pine, Polk, Pope, Rice, Todd **5** Atkin, Dodge, Swift **6** Benton, Carver, Dakota, Ramsey, Roseau, Sibley, Wadena, Wilkin **7** Kanabee, Stearns **8** Hennepin
explorer: **4** Pike **6** Duluth **7** La Salle **8** Hennepin **9** Creysolon
features: **6** Mesabi **7** Misquah **10** Mayo Clinic, Vermillion **13** Eagle Mountain
flower: **11** lady slipper
Indian: **5** Sioux **6** Ojibwa **8** Chippewa
lakes: **3** Red **7** Bemidji **8** Superior
motto: **9** North Star

mountain peaks: **6** Cuyuna, Mesabi **10** Vermillion
nickname: **6** Gopher **9** North Star
rivers: **5** Rainy **7** St. Croix
tree: **7** red pine
water: **7** St. Croix **8** Red River **11** Mississippi **14** Minnehaha Falls

MINOR: **5** child, petty, small, youth **6** infant, little, slight **8** juvenile, teenager, underage **9** dependent, secondary **10** adolescent **11** subordinate, unimportant **13** insignificant

MINORITY: **5** group, youth **6** nonage **10** immaturity **11** adolescence

MINOS:
father: **4** Zeus
judge of: **10** underworld
kingdom: **5** Crete
mother: **6** Europa
wife: **8** Pasiphae

MINOTAUR:
father: **10** Cretan bull
form: **7** monster
home: **9** Labyrinth
killer: **7** Theseus
mother: **8** Pasiphae

MINSTREL: **4** bard, poet, show **6** harper, player, singer **7** gleeman **8** jongleur, musician **10** troubadour **11** entertainer, performance

MINT: **4** coin, heap, herb, mold, sage **5** basil, candy, fresh, money, stamp, thyme **6** bundle, hyssop, invent **7** fortune **8** brand-new, endeavor, lavender **9** excellent, fabricate, undamaged **11** manufacture

MINUS: **4** less **6** defect **7** lacking, without **8** negative, subtract **10** deficiency, diminished

MINUSCULE: **4** tiny **5** small **6** minute **10** diminutive **11** microscopic, unimportant **13** insignificant

MINUTE: **4** mite, time, tiny **5** exact, flash, jiffy, petty, shake, small, teeny **6** atomic, little, moment, record, second, slight **7** instant, precise **8** detailed, piddling, thorough, trifling **9** minuscule **10** blow-by-blow, immaterial, meticulous **11** lilliputian, microscopic, unimportant **13** insignificant

MINUTES: **5** notes **6** record **7** summary **11** proceedings

MINUTIAE: **5** items **6** trivia **7** details **10** ins and outs **11** odds and ends, particulars

MINX: **4** jade, slut **5** flirt, hussy, woman **8** coquette

MIRACLE: **4** feat, sign **6** marvel, wonder **7** mystery, portent **10** phenomenon

MIRACULOUS: **6** divine **7** amazing, magical **8** wondrous **9** marvelous, wonderful **10** mysterious **11** astonishing, spectacular **12** supernatural **13** extraordinary

MIRAGE: **5** dream **6** vision **8** delusion, illusion, phantasm **13** hallucination

MIRE: **3** bog, fen, mud **4** glar, muck, ooze, quag **5** delay, marsh, stall, swamp **6** define, slough, sludge, tangle **7** embroil **8** entangle **9** quicksand

MIRIAM:
brother: **5** Aaron, Moses
father: **5** Amram
mother: **8** Jochebed

MIRROR: **4** copy, echo **5** glass, image, mimic, model **7** emulate, imitate **8** exemplar, speculum **9** exemplify **10** reflection **12** looking glass

MIRTH: **3** fun, joy **4** glee **6** gaiety, levity, spleen **7** delight, jollity **8** gladness, hilarity, pleasure **9** amusement, festivity, frivolity, happiness, merriment **10** jocularity, joyousness **11** playfulness **12** cheerfulness

MISADVENTURE: **5** boner, error, lapse **6** mishap **7** blunder, debacle, faux pas **8** accident, disaster **9** adversity **11** catastrophe

MISANTHROPIC: **7** cynical **10** antisocial, unfriendly, unsociable **11** distrustful

MISAPPROPRIATE: **5** steal **6** misuse **7** swindle **8** embezzle

MISBEGOTTEN: **8** unlawful **10** fatherless **12** illegitimate

MISBEHAVE: **7** disobey **10** roughhouse, transgress

MISBEHAVIOR: **7** misdeed **10** disrespect, misconduct **11** impropriety, shenanigans

MISCALCULATE: **3** err **7** blunder **8** miscount, misjudge **9** overshoot **12** misinterpret, overestimate **13** underestimate

MISCARRIAGE: **5** botch **6** mishap **7** failure, misdeed, mistake **11** malfunction **13** mismanagement

MISCARRY: **3** err **4** fail, flop, lose **6** fizzle **8** backfire

MISCELLANEOUS: **5** mixed **6** motley, random, sundry, varied **7** diverse **8** assorted **9** scattered **13** heterogeneous

MISCELLANY: **5** blend, melee **6** medley **7** mixture, variety **9** anthology **10** assortment, collection, hodgepodge **11** combination, compilation

MISCHANCE: **6** mishap **8** accident **10** misfortune **11** catastrophe **12** misadventure

MISCHIEF: **4** evil, harm, hurt **5** prank **6** damage, injury **7** devilry, knavery, misdeed, roguery, trouble **8** deviltry **9** devilment, rascality **11** misbehavior, naughtiness, shenanigans

MISCHIEVOUS: **3** sly **4** evil **5** elfin **6** elfish, elvish, impish, tricky, vexing, wicked **7** harmful, knavish, naughty, playful, roguish, teasing, waggish **8** devilish, prankish, sportive, venomous **9** injurious

MISCONCEPTION: **5** error **7** fallacy, mistake **8** delusion **11** misjudgment

MISCONDUCT: **7** offense **8** disorder, misdoing **9** mismanage **10** wrongdoing **11** impropriety, malfeasance, misbehavior **13** transgression

MISCONSTRUE: **7** distort **8** misjudge **11** misconceive **12** miscalculate, misinterpret **13** misunderstand

MISCREANT: **5** knave, scamp **6** rascal, wretch **7** heretic, infidel, villain **8** evildoer, scalawag **9** scoundrel **10** blackguard, malefactor, unbeliever **11** rapscallion **12** transgressor

MISCUE: **4** slip **5** error, fluff **7** blooper, mistake

MISDEED: **3** sin **5** crime, fault **7** offense **8** mischief **9** violation **10** wrongdoing **11** delinquency, misdemeanor **12** indiscretion **13** transgression

MISDEMEANOR: **3** sin **5** crime, wrong **7** misdeed, offense **9** violation **11** criminality, delinquency **13** transgression

MISE-EN-SCENE: **4** site **6** locale **7** climate **8** ambience **10** atmosphere **11** environment **12** stage setting, surroundings

MISER: **5** churl **7** hoarder, niggard, scrooge **8** tightwad **9** skinflint **10** cheapskate, curmudgeon **12** pennypincher

MISERABLE: **5** sorry **6** abject, feeble, gloomy, shabby, woeful **7** doleful, forlorn, pitiful **8** hopeless, wretched **9** depressed, sorrowful, woebegone **10** despicable, discomfort, melancholy **12** disconsolate

MISERLY: **4** mean **5** cheap, close, tight **6** frugal, greedy, stingy **8** covetous **9** penurious, scrimping **10** avaricious, ironfisted **11** closefisted **12** parsimonious

MISERY: **3** woe **4** ache, pain **5** agony, gloom, grief **6** burden, sorrow **7** ailment, anguish, despair, sadness, torment, trouble **8** calamity, distress **9** adversity, suffering **10** affliction, depression, melancholy, misfortune **11** unhappiness

MISFORTUNE: **3** woe **4** dole, harm **5** curse **6** misery, mishap **7** tragedy, trouble **8** accident, casualty, calamity, disaster **9** adversity, mischance **10** affliction **11** catastrophe **12** misadventure

MISGIVING: **5** alarm, doubt, qualm **8** distrust **9** suspicion **11** uncertainty **12** apprehension

MISGUIDED: **5** wrong **6** misled **7** foolish **8** confused, mistaken **10** mismanaged **11** misdirected, misinformed

MISHANDLE: **4** muff **5** abuse, botch **6** bungle, fumble **8** maltreat **9** mismanage

MISHAP: **5** error **6** fiasco **7** blunder, tragedy **8** accident, casualty, disaster **10** misfortune **12** misadventure

MISHMASH: **6** jumble, medley **7** melange, mixture **8** pastiche **9** pasticcio **10** hodgepodge **13** heterogeneity

MISINFORM: **3** lie **7** deceive, mislead **8** misguide, misstate **9** misdirect

MISINTERPRET: **3** err **7** distort, misread **11** misconceive, misconstrue **12** miscalculate **13** misunderstand

MISJUDGE: **3** err **7** presume **8** misthink **11** misconceive, misconstrue **12** miscalculate, misinterpret, overestimate **13** underestimate

MISLAY: **4** lose **8** displace, misplace

MISLEAD: **4** bait, bilk, dupe, fool **5** bluff, cheat **6** betray, delude, seduce **7** beguile, deceive **8** hoodwink, inveigle, misguide **9** bamboozle, misdirect, misinform, mismanage

MISLEADING: **5** false **9** ambiguous, confusing, deceptive **10** fraudulent, inaccurate

MISMANAGE: **4** muff **5** botch **6** bungle **9** misgovern, mishandle **12** misinterpret

MISPLACE: **4** lose **6** mislay **8** displace, unsettle **10** disarrange

MISPLAY: **4** muff **5** error **6** bobble, fumble, miscue, renege

MISREPRESENT: **3** lie **5** feign, twist **6** wrench **7** deceive, distort, falsify, mislead **8** disguise, misstate

MISREPRESENTATION: **7** untruth **8** pretense **9** chicanery **12** exaggeration

MISS: **3** err **4** fail, flub, girl, lack, lady, lass, muff, omit, skip, want **5** avoid, fault, title, woman, yearn **6** desire, escape, female, forget, ignore, lassie, miscue **7** failure, misfire, mistake, neglect **8** omission, overlook **9** disregard **12** mademoiselle

MISSILE: **4** bomb, dart, I.C.B.M., Scud **5** arrow, spear **6** bullet, rocket, weapon **7** Patriot, torpedo **9** Minuteman **10** projectile, sidewinder, trajectile

MISSING: **4** AWOL, gone, lost **6** absent **7** lacking, omitted **9** misplaced

MISSION: **4** duty, goal, task **6** charge, errand **7** calling, embassy, purpose **8** ministry **9** objective **10** assignment, commission **11** undertaking

MISSIONARY: **7** apostle **8** promoter **9** converter **10** evangelist **12** propagandist

MISSISSIPPI:
bird: **11** mockingbird
capital: **7** Jackson
cities: **6** Biloxi **7** Natchez **8** Meridian **11** Hattiesburg
explorer: **6** de Soto
features: **9** Vicksburg **12** Indian mounds
flower: **8** magnolia
nickname: **5** Bayou **8** Magnolia
tree: **8** magnolia
water: **5** Pearl, Yazoo **6** Ozarks **8** Big Black **11** Mississippi

MISSIVE: **4** note **6** billet, letter, report **7** epistle, message **8** dispatch **10** memorandum

MISSOURI:
bird: **8** bluebird
capital: **13** Jefferson City
cities: **7** St. Louis **8** Hannibal **10** Kansas City **11** Springfield **12** Independence
explorer: **6** de Soto **7** La Salle
features: **11** Pony Express
flower: **8** hawthorn
native: **5** Piker **10** Missourian
nickname: **6** Show Me **7** Bullion
tree: **7** dogwood
water: **5** Osage **8** Missouri **9** Merrimack **11** Mississippi

MISSPENT: **6** wasted **9** frittered **10** misapplied, squandered

MISSTATE: **4** warp **5** color, twist **7** confuse, distort **12** misrepresent

MISSTATEMENT: **4** tale **7** falsity, untruth **9** falsehood **13** prevarication

MISSTEP: **4** trip **5** error **6** bungle, miscue, slipup **7** blooper, faux pas, mistake, stumble

MIST: **3** dew, fog **4** blur, damp, film, haze, murk, rain, smog **5** cloud **7** drizzle, obscure **8** moisture, sprinkle **12** condensation **13** precipitation

MISTAKE: **3** err **4** balk, slip **5** boner, error, folly **6** bungle, miscue, slipup **7** blooper, blunder, misstep **8** omission **9** oversight **11** misconceive **12** miscalculate, misinterpret

MISTAKEN: **5** false, wrong **8** confused **9** erroneous, incorrect, misguided **10** inaccurate **11** misinformed

MISTER: **3** man **5** senor, title **8** monsieur

MISTREAT: **4** harm **5** abuse **6** injure **7** outrage, violate **9** mishandle

MISTRESS: **4** dozy **5** lover **7** hostess **8** ladylove, paramour **9** concubine, courtesan, kept woman **10** chatelaine, sweetheart **11** housekeeper

MISTRUST: **5** doubt **6** wonder **7** concern, dubiety, suspect **8** question **10** skepticism **12** apprehension

MISTY: **4** hazy **5** filmy, foggy, musky, vague **6** bleary, vapory **7** blurred, clouded, obscure **10** indistinct **11** sentimental

MISUNDERSTANDING: **4** feud, spat **7** dispute, mistake, quarrel **8** argument, conflict, squabble **9** confusion **10** difference **12** disagreement **13** misconception

MISUSE: **5** abuse **7** exploit, outrage, pervert **8** maltreat, mistreat **10**

negligence **14** misapplication, misappropriate

MITE: **3** bit, bug **4** atom, iota, tick **5** minim, speck **6** acarid, insect, minute **7** smidgen **8** parasite, particle

MITIGATE: **4** calm, ease, tone **5** abate, quell, relax, slake **6** lessen, pacify, reduce, soften, soothe, temper **7** appease, assuage, cushion, lighten, placate, relieve, sweeten **8** diminish, moderate, palliate **9** alleviate

MIX: **4** fuse, join, link, stir, toss, whip **5** alloy, blend, cross, merge, unite **6** fusion, jumble, mingle **7** combine, concoct, confuse, consort, shuffle **8** coalesce, compound **9** associate, commingle, hybridize, socialize **10** amalgamate, crossbreed, interbreed **11** incorporate, intermingle

MIXED: **6** hybrid, impure, motley **7** blended, diverse, mongrel **8** assorted **12** inconclusive, intermingled **13** heterogeneous, miscellaneous

MIXTURE: **4** brew, hash, stew **5** batch, blend **6** fusion, medley **7** amalgam, melange **8** compound, mishmash **9** admixture, composite, potpourri **10** concoction, hodgepodge, miscellany **11** combination

MIX-UP: **4** mess **5** melee, snafu **6** tangle **7** mistake **8** disorder **9** confusion

MIX UP: **6** muddle **7** confuse, disrupt, disturb, fluster, perplex **8** confound, disorder

MIZZLE: **4** mist, rain **6** decamp, depart **7** drizzle **9** disappear

MNEMOSYNE:
daughters: **5** Muses
father: **6** Uranus
goddess of: **6** memory
mother: **4** Gaea

MOAB:
city: **3** Kir
god: **7** Chemosh
king: **5** Eglon, Mesha
native: **4** Emim **7** Moabite
place: **6** Jordan
water: **7** Dead Sea **11** River Jordan

MOAN: **3** cry, sob **4** wail, weep **5** groan, sough, whine **6** grieve, lament, simper **7** deplore, grumble **8** complain

MOAT: **5** ditch, fosse **6** trench **7** barrier, channel

MOB: **4** gang, herd, pack, ring **5** crowd, drove, flock, group, Mafia, swarm **6** clique, masses, rabble **8** populace, surround **9** gathering, multitude, syndicate

MOBILE: **5** fluid **7** movable **8** portable, unstable **9** migratory, sculpture **10** changeable, locomotive, travelling

MOBILIZE: **5** rally **6** gather, muster **7** marshal, prepare **8** activate, assemble

MOBSTER: **4** hood **7** hoodlum **8** criminal, gangster

MOBY DICK:
author: **14** Herman Melville
characters: **3** Pip **6** Daggoo, Parsee **7** Ishmael **8** Queequeg, Starbuck, Tashtego
form: **5** whale
pursuer: **11** Captain Ahab
ship: **6** Pequod

MOCK: **3** ape **4** copy, fake, jape, jeer, jibe, joke, sham **5** false, farce, fleer, mimic, scoff, scorn, sneer, taunt, tease **6** banter, deride, insult, parody **7** deceive, imitate, lampoon **8** ridicule **9** burlesque, imitation **10** artificial, caricature, disappoint, stimulated **11** counterfeit

MOCKERY: **4** joke, sham **5** farce, irony, spoof **6** parody, satire, trifle **7** sarcasm **8** derision, ridicule, travesty **9** burlesque, imitation **13** laughingstock

MOD: **4** chic **6** modern **7** offbeat, stylish **8** up-to-date **11** fashionable

MODE: **3** fad, way **4** chic, form, look, rage **5** flair, modus, order, state, style, trend, vogue **6** custom, manner, method, system **7** fashion, variety **8** approach, attitude **9** technique **10** appearance

MODEL: **4** copy, form, mold, plan, type, wear **5** build, gauge, ideal, shape **6** design, effigy, figure, mirror, parade, sitter, symbol **7** display, example, fashion, imitate, manikin, paragon, pattern, perfect, replica, typical, version **8** exemplar, paradigm, portrait, standard **9** archetype, blueprint, exemplary, facsimile, flugelman, mannequin, miniature, prototype **12** reproduction

MODERATE: **4** calm, ease, even, fair, mild, soft **5** abate, bland, lower, sober **6** gentle, lessen, medium, slight, soften, temper **7** average, control, mediate, prudent, qualify **8** balanced, decrease, diminish, mediocre, ordinary **9** alleviate, arbitrate, temperate **10** reasonable **12** conservative

MODERATION: **7** balance, control, measure **8** prudence **9** restraint **10** abstinence, diminution, limitation, steadiness, temperance **11** restriction

MODERATOR: **5** judge **6** umpire **8** chairman, mediator **10** arbitrator, chairwoman, peacemaker

MODERN: **3** new **5** novel **7** current **8** neoteric **10** avant-garde, prevailing **11** fashionable **12** contemporary

MODERNIZE: **6** update **7** improve, refresh **8** renovate **9** refurbish **10** rejuvenate, reorganize

MODEST: **3** coy, shy **4** meek, mild, prim **5** plain **6** chaste, decent, demure, humble, simple **7** average, bashful, unshowy **8** moderate, reserved, retiring, virtuous **9** diffident **10** reasonable, unassuming **11** unexcessive, unobtrusive **13** unpretentious

MODESTY: **6** virtue **7** coyness, reserve, shyness **8** humility **10** demureness **11** bashfulness

MODICUM: **3** bit **4** atom, iota **5** crumb, grain, minim, pinch **6** morsel, sliver **7** smidgen

MODIFY: **5** adapt, alter, limit **6** change, lessen, reduce, revise, rework, soften **8** mitigate, moderate **9** influence, transform **10** reorganize

MODISH: **4** chic **5** swank **6** snazzy, trendy **7** dashing, stylish, voguish **9** happening **11** fashionable **12** contemporary

MODULATE: **4** tone, tune **6** adjust, change, temper **8** regulate **9** harmonize

MODUS OPERANDI: **6** method, system **9** operation, procedure **12** organization

MOGUL: **4** bump, lord **5** baron, mound, ruler **6** Mongol, tycoon **7** magnate **8** autocrat **9** Mongolian, personage

MOHAMMED:
also called: **4** Imam **7** Mahomet, Mahound **8** Muhammed
book: **5** Koran
born: **5** Mecca
family: **3** Ali **5** Aisha, Hasan **6** Avesha, Ayesha, Fatima, Husain **7** Ibrahim, Khadija **8** Abdallah, Abu-Talib

flight: **6** Hegira, Hejira
followers: **6** Moslem, Muslim, Wahabi **8** Wahabite
founded: **5** Islam
lived in: **5** Mecca **6** Medina
successors: **5** Calif **6** Caliph **7** Abu Bakr

MOIETY: **4** half, part **5** piece, share **7** element, portion **8** fraction **9** component **11** affiliation

MOIL: **3** wet **4** mire, soil, spot, toil, work **6** churn, labor, moist, muggy, soggy, weary **6** meddle, sticky, watery **7** tearful, torment, trouble, turmoil **8** drudgery **9** agitation, commotion, confusion

MOIST: **3** wet **4** damp, dank **5** humid, muggy, rainy, soggy **6** clammy, sticky, watery **7** tearful

MOISTEN: **3** dip, wet **4** soak **5** water **6** anoint, dabble, dampen, sparge **8** humidify, irrigate, saturate, sprinkle

MOISTURE: **3** dew **4** mist, rain **5** vapor, water **6** liquid **7** drizzle, wetness **8** dampness, humidity **13** precipitation

MOKE: **4** dolt, dull **5** horse **6** boring, donkey

MOLD: **3** die **4** cast, form, make, must, plot, soil **5** adapt, humus, knead, model, shape, stamp **6** devise, fungus, mildew **7** fashion, moulage, pattern **9** character, sculpture, transform

MOLDOVA:
capital: **8** Kishinev
cities: **7** Beltsey **8** Tiraspol

MOLDY: **5** dated, fusty, hoary, musty, stale **6** rotten **8** decaying, mildewed

MOLE: **3** spy **4** mark, pier, wall **5** fault, jetty, sauce **6** burrow, growth, mammal, rodent, tunnel **8** excavate **9** birthmark **10** breakwater

MOLECULE: **3** bit, ion **4** atom, iota, part, unit **5** speck **8** fragment, particle

MOLEST: **3** vex **4** harm **5** abuse, annoy, tease **6** accost, assail, attack, bother, harass, misuse **7** disturb, torment, trouble **8** encroach **9** interfere

MOLLIFY: **4** calm, ease, lull **5** abate, quiet, relax **6** lessen, pacify, smooth, soften, soothe, temper **7** appease, cushion, placate, relieve, sweeten **8** mitigate, moderate **9** alleviate **10** conciliate **11** tranquilize

MOLLUSK:
classes: **8** Bivalvia **10** Amphineura, Gastropoda, Scaphopoda **11** Cephalopoda **14** Monoplacophora
eight-armed: **7** octopus
group: **8** pteropod
one shell: **8** univalve
parts: **4** foot **6** mantle, radula
shell: **4** test **5** cowry, testa **6** cockle, cowrie, testae **7** bivalve **8** univalve **9** chambered
shell-less: **4** slug
ten-armed: **5** squid
two shell: **7** bivalve
types: **4** clam, leda, slug, spat **5** chama, murex, snail, squid, whelk **6** chiton, cockle, limpet, mussel, oyster, tellin, winkle **7** abalone, etheria, octopus, scallop, seaslug **8** argonaut, shipworm **10** coat-of-mail, cuttlefish, razor shell **14** pearly nautilus

MOLLYCODDLE: **4** baby **5** spoil **6** pamper **7** indulge, milksop **8** recreant, weakling **13** overprotected

MOLT: **4** cast, shed **6** change **7** discard **8** exuviate

MOLTEN: **6** melted **7** glowing **8** seething **9** liquefied

MOMENT: **4** tick, time **5** flash, jiffy, point, stage, trice **6** import, minute, second, weight **7** element, instant **8** occasion **9** magnitude, twinkling **10** importance **11** consequence **12** significance

MOMENTARY: **5** brief, quick, short **7** passing **8** fleeting **9** ephemeral, immediate, transient **10** transitory

MOMENTOUS: **5** grave **7** crucial, epochal, fateful, pivotal, serious, weighty **8** decisive, eventful, historic **9** important, paramount **10** meaningful **11** significant **12** unparalleled

MOMENTUM: **5** drive, force **6** energy, motion, thrust **7** impetus **8** velocity

MOMMY: **3** mom **5** momma **6** mother, parent

MONACO:
capital: **11** Monaco-Ville
casino: **10** Monte Carlo
cities: **10** Monte Carlo **11** Fontvieille, La Condamine
continent: **6** Europe
dynasty: **8** Grimaldi
ethnic groups: **6** French **7** Italian **10** Monegasque
features: **7** casinos
languages: **6** French
monetary unit: **5** franc
people: **11** Monegasques
prince: **6** Albert **7** Rainier
princess: **5** Grace **8** Caroline **9** Stephanie
rulers: **5** Grace **6** Albert **7** Rainier **8** Caroline, Grimaldi
water: **13** Mediterranean

MONARCH: **4** czar, king **5** queen, ruler **6** despot, prince **7** emperor, empress, majesty **8** autocrat, princess **9** sovereign

MONASTERY: **5** abbey **6** friary, priory **7** convent, hospice, nunnery, retreat **8** cloister, lamasery, minister **9** sanctuary

MONASTIC: **6** oblate **7** ascetic, austere, monkish, recluse **8** celibate, secluded, solitary **13** contemplative

MONETARY: **6** fiscal **9** budgetary, financial, pecuniary **10** commercial

MONEY: **3** oof, tin, wad **4** bill, cash, coin, cush, dubs, dump, gelt, gilt, grig, jack, jake, kale, loot, lour, mina, moss, pelf, swag **5** blunt, brass, bread, chips, clink, dough, funds, livre, lucre, manna, moola, rhino, rocks **6** argent, boodle, change, dinero, flimsy, hansel, mammon, mazuma, moolah, riches, tender, wampum, wealth **7** capital, chattel, coinage, handsel, lettuce, ooftish, scratch, stipend **8** bankroll, currency, finances, hard cash **9** long green, resources **10** greenbacks **11** wherewithal
container: **4** arca, safe, till **5** chest **6** drawer **7** brazier **8** register
counterfeit: **5** bogus, queer **6** boodle
found: **5** trove **8** treasure
gift: **4** alms **7** bequest, charity **9** endowment
handler: **6** teller **7** cashier
lender: **6** banker, usurer **7** shylock **9** loanshark **10** pawnbroker

MONEYED: **4** rich **6** loaded **7** opulent, wealthy **8** affluent **10** prosperous

MONEYMAKING: **7** gainful **9** lucrative **10** profitable, successful, worthwhile

MONGER: **6** dealer, hawker, trader, vender, vendor **7** peddler **8** merchant **10** trafficker

MONGOLIA:
capital: **9** Ulan Bator **11** Ulaanbaatar
cities: **4** Urga **5** Kobdo **6** Darhan **7** Kirghiz **10** Choybalsan

continent: **4** Asia
features: **10** Gobi Desert **14** Altai Mountains
languages: **6** Turkic **7** Chinese, Russian **16** Khalkha Mongolian
monetary unit: **6** tugrik
native: **6** Mongol, Tartar **9** Mongoloid
rulers: **9** Tamerlane **10** Kublai Khan **11** Genghis Khan
water: **3** Pei **4** Onon **5** Peiho **7** Kerulen, Selenga **8** Hobdo Gol

MONGREL: **3** cur, dog **4** mutt **5** mixed **6** hybrid **9** crossbred, halfbreed

MONIKER: **4** name **5** label **6** handle **8** nickname

MONITION: **4** hint **5** order **6** caveat, notice **7** caution, summons, warning **8** citation **10** admonition, intimation **11** forewarning

MONITOR: **5** check, guard, track, watch **6** device, mentor, police, survey **7** adviser, control, observe, warship **8** reminder **9** counselor

MONK: **5** abbot, clerk, fakir, friar **6** votary **7** brother, eremite **8** anchoret, cenobite, monastic **9** anchorite
Buddhist: **4** lama **5** arhat, bonze **6** bhikhu **7** poongee **8** poonghee **11** bodhisattva
Eastern Orthodox: **7** caloyer, hegumen, starets
haircut: **7** tonsure
Hindu: **4** guru **9** sannyasin
Islamic: **4** Sufi **6** mystic
vow of silence: **8** Trappist

MONKEY:
genus: **5** cebus **8** alouatta
New World: **3** sai **4** saki **5** acari **6** ateles, coaita, couxia, grison, howler, miriki, samari, spider **7** ouakari, sapajou, tamarin **8** capuchin, marmoset, orabassu, squirrel **9** beelzebub
Old World: **4** douc **5** jocko, patas, potto, toque, waaag **6** baboon, bandar, grivet, guenon, langur, rhesus, vervet **7** macaque

MONKEYSHINE: **4** lark **5** antic, caper, prank, trick **9** highjinks, silliness **10** tomfoolery **11** foolishness, mischievous, shenanigans

MONKEY WRENCH: **4** tool **10** disruption

MONOCLE: **7** lorgnon **8** eyeglass, pince-nez

MONODY: **3** ode **4** poem, song **11** composition

MONOGRAM: **6** cipher, design, symbol **8** initials **9** character **14** identification

MONOGRAPH: **5** essay, tract **6** thesis **8** treatise **9** discourse **12** dissertation

MONOLITH: **5** block, stone **6** column, menhir, pillar, statue **8** monument

MONOLOGUE: **6** speech **7** address, lecture, oration **9** discourse, soliloquy

MONOPOLIZE: **6** absorb, corner, manage **7** consume, control, engross **8** dominate **9** preoccupy

MONOPOLY: **5** trust **6** cartel, corner **7** control **9** syndicate **10** consortium, domination **11** exclusivity

MONOTONOUS: **4** drab, dull, flat, same **6** boring **7** humdrum, mundane, routine, tedious, uniform **8** unvaried **9** wearisome **10** repetitive, unchanging **11** repetitious

MONOTONY: **6** tedium **7** boredom, humdrum **8** sameness **10** redundancy, uniformity

MONSTER: **3** roc **4** huge, ogre, yeti **5** beast, brute, demon, devil, fiend, freak, giant, harpy, hydra, lamia, naiad **6** afreet, dragon, Kraken, Medusa, nereid, savage, scylla, sphinx, zombie **7** centaur, chimera, Cyclops, Gorgons, vampire **8** behemoth, bogeyman, Cerberus, colossus, creature, gargoyle, Gigantes, werewolf **9** barbarian, scoundrel **11** hippocampus **12** Frankenstein

MONSTROSITY: **5** freak **8** abortion **11** miscreation **12** malformation

MONSTROUS: **4** huge, vast **5** awful, large **7** ghastly, heinous, hideous, immense, mammoth, massive, titanic **8** abnormal, colossal, deformed, enormous, gigantic, horrible, shocking **9** atrocious, fantastic, frightful, revolting, unnatural **10** diabolical, gargantuan, outrageous, stupendous, tremendous **12** overwhelming

MONTANA:
bird: **10** meadowlark
capital: **6** Helena
cities: **5** Butte **8** Billings, Missoula **10** Great Falls
explorer: **9** Verendrye
features: **11** Glacier Park **14** Rocky Mountains **15** Yellowstone Park **17** Custer Battlefield
flower: **10** bitterroot
nickname: **8** Treasure
tree: **13** ponderosa pine
water: **8** Flathead, Missouri **11** Yellowstone **13** Little Bighorn

MONTH: **5** lunar, solar **8** calendar, sidereal

MONUMENT: **4** tomb **5** cairn, token **6** marker, record, shrine, statue **7** memento, tribute **8** memorial, monolith, reminder **9** headstone, mausoleum, testament, tombstone **10** gravestone **11** remembrance

MONUMENTAL: **4** huge **5** great **7** awesome, epochal, immense, mammoth, massive **8** enduring, enormous, gigantic, historic **9** important, memorable **10** astounding, impressive, stupendous **11** significant

MOOCH: **3** beg, bum **5** cadge, drift, filch, skulk, sneak, steal **6** sponge, wander

MOOD: **4** aura, tone, vein, whim **5** humor **6** spirit, strain, temper **7** caprice, emotion, feeling **8** ambiance, attitude **10** atmosphere **11** disposition, inclination, temperament

MOODY: **5** angry, sulky, surly **6** crabby, fickle, gloomy, grumpy, moping, sullen, touchy **8** brooding **9** depressed **10** capricious, melancholy **13** temperamental

MOON: **3** orb **4** Luna
concerning: **5** lunar **6** lunate **7** selenic
gods/goddesses: **3** Sin **4** Luna **5** Diana, Tanit **6** Hecate, Hekate, Nannar, Salena, Selene, Tanith **7** Artemis, Astarte
month: **8** lunation
parts: **3** sea **4** mare, rill, scar **5** cleft, maria, rille **6** crater
phases: **3** new **4** cusp, dark, full, half **5** apsis **6** apogee, octant, phasis, waning, waxing **7** menisci, perigee **8** crescent, meniscus **11** last quarter **12** first quarter
satellite of: **5** Earth
spacecraft: **3** LEM **6** Apollo

MOONSHINE: **5** hokum, sauce **6** liquor **7** alcohol, bootleg, eyewash, whiskey **8** homebrew, nonsense **9** moonlight **10** bathtub gin **14** white lightning

MOONSTRUCK: **5** dazed **6** crazed, insane **12** sentimental

MOOR: **3** bog, fen, fix **4** dock **5** berth, heath, marsh, swamp **6** anchor, secure, tether **9** wasteland

MOORS:
center: **8** Alhambra
concerning: **7** Moorish **8** Moresque
ethnic groups: **5** Arabs **7** Berbers
from: **10** Mauritania
ruled: **5** Spain **11** North Africa

MOOT: **5** argue, plead, speak **6** broach, debate **7** discuss, dispute, meeting **8** argument **9** debatable, uncertain, undecided, unsettled **10** litigation, unresolved **11** contestable, problematic **12** questionable

MOP: **4** dust, hair, swab, wash, wipe **5** clean

MOPE: **4** fret, pout, stew, sulk **5** brood, droop, grump **6** dawdle, linger **7** despair

MOPPET: **3** kid **4** tyke **5** child **7** toddler **9** youngster

MORAL: **4** good, just, pure **5** axiom, maxim, motto, noble, point **6** chaste, decent, homily, honest, lesson, truism **7** ethical, message, proverb, upright **8** virtuous **9** honorable, righteous **10** aboveboard, principled, scrupulous

MORALE: **4** mood, zeal **5** state **6** spirit **7** outlook **8** attitude **10** confidence **11** disposition **13** esprit de corps

MORALITY: **5** honor, mores **6** ethics, virtue **8** goodness **9** integrity **10** principles **11** uprightness **13** righteousness

MORALS: **5** mores **6** habits **7** conduct **8** scruples **9** integrity, standards

MORASS: **3** bog, fen **4** mess **5** marsh, snarl, swamp **6** tangle **8** quagmire, wetlands **12** overwhelming

MORATORIUM: **3** ban **4** halt **5** delay **9** cessation **10** suspension

MORBID: **4** dark, grim, sick **6** gloomy, grisly, morose, sullen **7** painful **8** diseased, dreadful, gruesome, horrible **9** corrosive, malicious, saturnine, unhealthy **11** melancholic **12** pathological

MORDANT: **4** keen **5** sharp **6** biting **7** burning, painful, pungent **8** incisive **9** corrosive, malicious, sarcastic, trenchant

MORE: **4** also, plus **5** added, again, extra **6** better, larger, longer **7** another, farther, further, greater **8** expanded **9** increased **10** additional

MORE OR LESS: **5** about **6** around **9** generally **13** approximately

MOREOVER: **3** and, yet **4** also **7** besides, further **8** likewise **12** additionally

MORES: **4** code, ways **5** rules **6** ethics, usages **7** customs, manners **9** standards

MORIBUND: **5** death, dying **6** doomed, fading **8** decaying, obsolete **10** regressing, terminated

MORMON STATE: **4** Utah

MORNING: **4** dawn **5** sunup **6** aurora **7** sunrise **8** cockcrow, daybreak, forenoon

MOROCCO:
capital: **5** Rabat
cities: **3** Fez **5** Ceuta **6** Agadir, Meknes **7** Melilla, Tangier **9** Marrakesh **10** Casablanca
continent: **6** Africa
ethnic groups: **10** Arab-Berber
features: **14** Atlas Mountains
languages: **6** Arabic, Berber, French **7** Spanish
monetary unit: **6** dirham

native: **8** Moroccan
water: **17** Strait of Gibraltar

MORON: **4** boob, dolt, dull, fool **5** dunce, idiot **6** dimwit, stupid **8** imbecile, numskull **9** blockhead, ignoramus

MOROSE: **4** blue, dour, glum, sour **5** gruff, moody, sulky, surly **6** crusty, gloomy, moping, morbid, sullen **7** unhappy **8** choleric, churlish, dolorous **9** depressed, splenetic **10** melancholy

MORSE CODE:
inventor: **11** Samuel Morse
signal: **3** dot **4** dash

MORSEL: **3** bit **4** bite, crub, snap **5** piece, scrap, slice, snack, taste **6** fliver, nibble, tidbit **8** delicacy, fragment, mouthful

MORTAL: **3** man **4** deep, dire, grim **5** being, fatal, grave, human, woman **6** animal, deadly, finite, lethal **7** deathly, extreme **8** terminal, terrible **9** earthling **11** conceivable, destructive, unrelenting

MORTALITY: **5** death **7** carnage **8** fatality **9** bloodshed, humankind **12** ephemerality

MORTGAGE: **4** deed, hock, lien, loan, pawn **5** trust **6** pledge **8** contract **10** obligation

MORTIFY: **5** abase, abash, shame **6** appall, humble **7** chagrin, torment **8** disgrace **9** embarrass, humiliate **10** discipline

MORTUARY: **6** morgue **7** charnel **11** funeral home **13** funeral parlor

MOSAIC: **6** design **7** chimera, picture **8** diapered, intarsia **9** patchwork

MOSES:
brother: **5** Aaron
exodus from: **5** Egypt
father: **5** Amram
father-in-law: **6** Jethro
mother: **8** Jochebed
proclaimed: **15** Ten Commandments
sister: **6** Miriam
sons: **7** Eliezer, Gershom
successor: **6** Joshua
wife: **8** Zipporah
witnessed: **11** burning bush

MOSEY: **5** amble **6** linger, ramble, stroll **7** saunter, shuffle

MOSQUE: **6** church, masjid, shrine, temple **12** hall of prayer
balcony: **7** maqsura
lectern: **5** kursi
niche: **6** mihrab
platform: **5** dakka
pulpit: **6** minbar
south wall: **6** giblah
tower: **6** manara **7** minaret

MOSS: **3** bog **4** club, peat, rock **5** Irish, musci, plant, swamp **6** lichen, morass **7** Spanish **8** sphagnum **9** bryophyta, treebeard

MOSSBACK: **4** fogy **5** fogey, square **6** rustic **11** reactionary **12** conservative

MOST: **4** best, very **5** chief **6** nearly **7** biggest, highest, maximum **8** greatest, majority, ultimate **11** practically

MOSTLY: **5** often **6** mainly **7** chiefly, largely, overall **9** generally, primarily **11** essentially **13** predominantly

MOTE: **3** dot, may **4** atom, iota **5** crumb, might, scrap, speck **8** particle

MOTH:
hunter: **10** goatsucker
larva: **11** caterpillar
order: **11** Lepidoptera
relative: **9** butterfly
spot: **8** chloasma, fenestra
types: **4** hawk **5** tinea **6** mattet, miller, tineid **7** clothes **8** forester, silkworm **11** corn earworm

MOTH-EATEN: **4** worn **5** dated, faded, stale **6** shabby **7** archaic, decayed **8** decrepit **10** antiquated

MOTHER: **3** mom, mum **4** care, dame **5** mamma, mater, mommy, mummy, nurse **6** foster, matron, origin, pamper, parent, source **7** cherish, nurture, protect **9** matriarch **10** wellspring

MOTHER COUNTRY: **8** homeland **10** fatherland, motherland

MOTHERLY: **6** caring, gentle, tender **8** maternal **9** nurturing **10** comforting, protective

MOTIF: **4** idea **5** point, theme, topic **6** design, figure **7** pattern, subject **11** arrangement

MOTION: **4** flag, flow, flux, move, rate, stir, wave **5** speed, swing, tempo **6** action, beckon, signal **7** gesture, impulse, request, suggest **8** kinetics, movement, proposal, velocity **9** agitation, direction **10** suggestion **11** application, inclination, oscillation, proposition

MOTIONLESS: **4** calm, dead **5** inert, quiet, rigid, still **6** frozen, static **7** dormant **8** immobile, lifeless, stagnant, stagnate, tranquil **9** paralyzed, sedentary **10** breathless, stationary, transfixed

MOTION PICTURE: **4** film **5** flick, movie **6** cinema, screen

MOTIVATE: **4** fire, lead, move, stir **5** impel, spark **6** arouse, excite, induce **7** inspire, provoke **9** influence, stimulate

MOTIVATION: **5** drive **6** desire **7** impetus **8** ambition, catalyst, interest, stimulus **9** incentive

MOTIVE: **4** goal, spur **5** basis, cause, theme **6** desire, intent, object, reason **7** emotion, grounds, impulse, purpose **8** ambition, stimulus **9** incentive, intention, rationale

MOTLEY: **5** mixed **6** varied **7** dappled, diverse, mottled, piebald **8** assorted, pastiche **10** hodgepodge, variegated **11** diversified **12** multicolored **13** heterogeneous, miscellaneous

MOTOR: **3** car **4** auto, ride **5** buggy, drive **6** device, engine **7** machine **10** automobile, instrument

types: **5** steam **6** diesel, rotary, Wankel **7** turbine **8** compound, electric

MOTORMAN: **6** driver **8** engineer, operator **9** conductor

MOTTLED: **6** motley **7** dappled, diverse, piebald, spotted **8** blotched, speckled **9** checkered, splotched **10** variegated

MOTTO: **5** adage, axiom, maxim **6** byword, phrase, saying, slogan, truism **7** precept, proverb **8** aphorism **9** catchword, watchword **10** expression

MOUÉ: **3** mug **4** pout **7** grimace

MOUND: **4** bank, butt, dune, heap, hill, hump, mass, pile **5** cairn, knoll, mogul, stack **6** barrow, tuffet **7** bulwark, tumulus **9** elevation **10** embankment

MOUNT: **4** grow, hill, pony, rise, seat **5** climb, frame, horse, scale, stage **6** ascend, aspire **7** advance, augment, prepare **8** escalate, increase, mountain, position, straddle **9** intensify

MOUNTAIN: **3** alp, ben, kop **4** aret, berg, dagh, peak **5** butte, chain, crest, ridge **6** barrow, sierra, summit **7** volcano

animals: **3** kea **4** bear, dove, goat, ibex, lion, lynx, puma **5** eagle, finch, quail **6** bobcat, cougar, falcon, grouse, marmot **7** chamois, leopard **9** brambling, harlequin, peregrine **10** cacomistle, woodpecker

concerning: **5** alpen **6** alpine **7** etiolin **10** alpestrine, orological **11** mountainous
forests: **6** arctic, boreal, tundra **7** ice pack **8** snow line, tree line, tropical **9** deciduous, low alpine, temperate **10** coniferous
highest: **7** Everest
lake: **4** tarn
pass: **3** gap **4** cove, gate, ghat **5** gorge
plants: **3** ash, fei, fir **4** sorb **5** basil, rowan **6** laurel **8** centaury, chestnut, dogberry, wormwood **10** cloudberry
ranges: **4** Alps, Ghat, Ural **5** Andes, Coast, Rocky, Teton, White **6** Alatau **7** Rockies, Sierras **8** Cascades, Catskill, Pyrenees **9** Allegheny, Blue Ridge, Himalayas **10** San Jacinto **11** Appalachian, San Gorgonio
science: **7** orology **9** orography **10** orogenesis
snow: **4** neve **5** jokul
sport: **6** biking **8** alpinism **10** alpestrian **14** mountaineering

MOUNTAINOUS: **4** high, huge **5** hilly, rocky **6** alpine, rugged **8** gigantic

MOUNTAIN STATE: **7** Montana **12** West Virginia

MOUNTEBANK: **5** cheat, faker, fraud, phony, quack **6** hawker **7** hustler **8** impostor, swindler **9** charlatan, pretender

MOURN: **3** cry, rue **4** ache, keen, long, sigh, wail, weep **5** yearn **6** bemoan, grieve, lament, regret, sorrow **7** anguish, deplore

MOURNFUL: **5** black, sorry **6** rueful, somber, woeful **7** doleful, unhappy **8** dejected, funereal, grievous, saddened **9** plaintive, sorrowful **10** deplorable, depressing, lamentable, melancholy **11** distressing

MOURNING: **4** garb **5** dolor **7** anguish, despair, sadness **8** grieving **11** bereavement

MOUSE: **6** button, coward, murine, rodent, vermin **8** black eye

MOUSY: **3** shy **4** drab **5** quiet, timid **7** bashful

MOUTH: **3** gab, mug **4** beak, crow, sass, talk **5** boast, delta, speak, stoma, voice **6** cavity, funnel, kisser, mumble **7** crevice, estuary, orifice **8** aperture, back talk, bragging, entrance **9** spokesman **11** spokeswoman
part: **3** jaw **4** gums, lips, roof **5** floor, teeth, uvula **6** tongue **7** alveoli, pharynx

MOUTHFUL: **4** bite, gulp **5** piece, taste **6** morsel **7** portion

MOUTHPIECE: **6** lawyer **7** adviser **8** attorney **9** counselor, spokesman **11** spokeswoman **12** spokesperson

MOUTH-WATERING: **5** tasty **8** inviting **9** appealing, delicious, palatable **10** appetizing

MOVABLE: **5** loose **6** mobile, motile **8** portable, unstable, unsteady **10** ambulatory, changeable, detachable **13** transportable

MOVE: **3** act, run **4** deed, flow, goad, huge, lead, spur, stir, sway, turn, walk **5** budge, cause, crawl, drift, drive, glide, impel, leave, rouse, shift, start, touch **6** action, affect, alpine, arouse, change, excite, incite, induce, kindle, motion, prompt, propel, rugged **7** advance, animate, inspire, migrate, proceed, propose, suggest **8** evacuate, motivate, persuade, relocate, transfer **9** influence, instigate, stimulate, stratagem **10** alpestrine **11** mountainous

MOVEMENT: **5** drive, steps, trend **6** action, motion, rhythm, unrest

7 crusade, gesture **8** activity, campaign, mobility, stirring **10** locomotion

MOVE OUT: **5** leave **6** vacate **8** evacuate, withdraw

MOVE UP: **5** boost, climb, hoist, raise **6** ascend **7** advance, promote

MOVIE: **4** film **5** flick **6** cinema, screen **7** picture

MOVING: **8** arousing, exciting, gripping, pathetic, poignant, stirring, touching **9** affecting, emotional, provoking **11** stimulating **13** inspirational

MOW: **3** cut, lay **4** clip, crop, heap, mass, pile **5** level, stack

MOXIE: **4** grit, guts **5** heart, nerve, skill, spunk **6** energy, spirit **7** courage **8** backbone **10** initiative

MOZAMBIQUE:
capital: **6** Maputo
cities: **5** Beira **7** Nampula
continent: **6** Africa
ethnic groups: **5** Bantu
features: **13** Beira Corridor
languages: **5** Makua, Shona **6** malawi, Tsonga **7** African **10** Portuguese
monetary unit: **7** metical
water: **7** Limpopo, Zambezi

MOZART, WOLFGANG:
birthplace: **7** Austria **8** Salzburg
composition: **8** Idomeneo **9** Mitridate **11** Don Giovanni, Sparrow Mass **13** The Magic Flute, Trumpet Sonata
death place: **6** Vienna
occupation: **8** composer

MUCH: **4** lots, many, most, very **5** about, ample, great, heaps, loads **6** plenty, scores **7** greatly, sizable **8** quantity, uncommon **9** abundance, multitude **10** remarkable, sufficient **11** exceedingly **12** considerable

MUCILAGE: **3** gum **4** glue **5** paste **8** adhesive **9** substance

MUCK: **3** goo, mud **4** dirt, dung, gook, gunk, ooze **5** filth, slime, trash, waste **6** drudge, manure, refuse, sewage, sludge **7** garbage **10** complicate

MUD: **4** dirt, mire, mush, ooze, roil, silt, soil **5** slime **6** sludge

MUDDLE: **3** mix **4** daze, mess, muff, roil **5** addle, botch, chaos, muddy, snafu, snarl **6** boggle, bungle, fuddle, fumble, humble, pother, tangle **7** blunder, confuse, fluster, perplex, stumble, stupefy **8** befuddle, bewilder, confound, disorder, flounder, mishmash **9** mismanage **10** complicate

MUDDLED: **5** foggy, fuzzy, tipsy **6** cloudy **10** bewildered, incoherent **11** unorganized

MUDDY: **4** drab, hazy, miry **5** dirty, grimy, murky, soily, vague **6** cloudy, filthy, slushy, turbid **7** blurred, clouded, obscure, squalid, unclear **8** confused **9** besmeared, spattered

MUFF: **3** fur **4** blow, flub **5** botch, error **6** bungle, fumble, warmer

MUFFLE: **4** dull, hush, mute, wrap **5** shush **6** dampen, deaden, lessen, muzzle, shroud, soften, stifle **7** cushion, envelop, silence, smother **8** suppress

MUFFLER: **4** mask, muff **5** cover, scarf **8** silencer

MUG: **3** cup, tug **4** dope, dupe, face, fool, punk, puss **5** mouth, stein **6** flagon, kisser **7** assault, grimace, hoodlum, picture **10** photograph

MUGGER: **4** thug **5** thief **8** attacker **9** assailant, crocodile

MUGGY: **4** damp, dank **5** humid, moist **6** clammy, sticky **10**, sweltering

MULCH: **5** straw **6** litter, manure **7** compost

MULCT: **4** balk, fine, rook **5** cheat, steal **6** fleece, punish **7** deceive, defraud, forfeit, penalty, swindle **8** penalize

MULE: **4** jack **5** burro, hinny **6** donkey, hybrid **7** jackass, slipper, spinner, tractor **10** crossbreed

MULISH: **5** balky **6** ornery **8** stubborn **9** obstinate, pigheaded **10** determined, headstrong **11** intractable **12** recalcitrant

MULL: **4** heat, muse, stew **5** cloth, spice, think, weigh **6** dawdle, loiter, muslin, ponder, powder **7** reflect, sweeten **8** consider, ruminate **10** deliberate **11** contemplate

MULTICOLORED: **4** pied **6** motley **7** dappled, mottled **9** checkered **10** variegated

MULTIFARIOUS: **5** mixed **6** motley **7** diverse **8** assorted, multiple **9** versatile **13** heterogeneous, miscellaneous

MULTIPLE: **4** many **6** varied **7** several **8** assorted, manifold, numerous **12** multifarious

MULTIPLY: **4** grow **5** breed **6** spread **7** augment, burgeon, enlarge, magnify **8** compound, increase **9** procreate, reproduce

MULTITUDE: **3** mob **4** pack, army, heap, host, many, mass **5** array, crowd, drove, flock, horde, swarm **6** legion, myriad, public, scores, throng **8** populace **10** collection

MULTITUDINOUS: **4** many **7** crowded **8** abundant, numerous, populous **9** countless **10** voluminous **12** considerable

MUM: **4** mute **5** still **6** mother, silent **10** speechless **13** chrysanthemum

MUMBLE: **4** chew **5** mouth **6** murmur, mutter, patter, rumble **7** grumble, whisper

MUMBO JUMBO: **6** jargon **7** baloney, bugaboo **9** confusion, gibberish **10** hocus pocus

MUNCH: **3** eat **4** bite, chew **5** champ, chomp, grind **6** crunch **9** masticate

MUNDANE: **6** cosmic **7** humdrum, prosaic, routine, secular, worldly **8** everyday, ordinary **9** unearthly **11** commonplace, terrestrial

MUNICIPAL: **4** city, town **5** civic **7** borough **9** community

MUNIFICENT: **4** free **6** kindly, lavish **7** liberal **8** generous **9** bountiful **10** altruistic, benevolent, charitable, openhanded **12** humanitarian **13** philanthropic

MUNITIONS: **7** weapons **8** armament **9** equipment **10** ammunition

MURDER: **4** hang, kill, slay **5** lynch, waste **7** butcher, destroy, execute, killing **8** homicide, massacre, strangle **9** eliminate, slaughter **10** asphyxiate, guillotine **11** assassinate, electrocute, exterminate **12** manslaughter
baby: **11** infanticide
brother: **10** fratricide
father: **9** patricide
genocide: **9** holocaust
god: **7** deicide
king/queen: **8** regicide
mercy: **10** euthanasia
mother: **9** matricide
parent: **9** parricide
planned: **12** premeditated
ritual: **7** seppuku **8** hara-kiri
self: **7** suicide
sister: **10** sororicide
wife: **9** uxoricide

MURDERER: **6** killer, slayer **8** assassin, criminal **11** executioner, slaughterer

MURDEROUS: **5** cruel **6** bloody, brutal, deadly, lethal, savage **7** arduous, ruinous **9** difficult, ferocious, homicidal **11** destructive **12** bloodthirsty

MURKY: **3** dim **4** dark, gray **5** black, dense, foggy, fuzzy, mirky, misty, muddy **6** cloudy, dismal, dreary, gloomy **7** obscure **9** ambiguous, cheerless

MURMUR: **3** coo, hum **4** buzz, fret, moan, purr **5** brool, drone, groan, sound, utter **6** babble, mumble, mutter, repine, report **7** grumble, whisper **8** complain **9** undertone

MUSCLE: **4** beef, meat, thew **5** brawn, clout, flesh, force, might, power, sinew **6** tendon **8** strength **9** influence
arm: **5** bicep **6** flexor, tricep **8** extensor
back: **7** erector **15** latissimus dorsi
buttocks: **7** gluteus
calf: **13** gastrocnemius
chest: **8** pectoral
contraction: **10** convulsion
hip: **10** fascia lata
lack of: **6** ataxia
shoulder: **7** deltoid **9** trapezius **11** rotator cuff
stomach: **9** abdominal **15** rectus abdominis
thigh: **9** hamstring, quadricep, sartorius
twitching: **12** fibrillation

MUSCULAR: **5** burly, hardy, husky, thewy **6** brawny, mighty, robust, sinewy, strong **7** fibrous **8** athletic, powerful, stalwart, vigorous

MUSE: **4** dump, mull **5** brood, dream, think, weigh **6** ponder **7** reflect, reverie **8** absorbed, cogitate, consider, meditate, ruminate **10** deliberate **11** contemplate

MUSE:
father: **4** Zeus
form: **7** goddess
mother: **9** Mnemosyne
of astronomy: **6** Urania
of comedy: **6** Thalia
of dancing: **11** Terpsichore
of epic poetry: **8** Calliope
of history: **4** Clio
of love/lyric poetry: **5** Erato
of music: **7** Euterpe
of sacred poetry: **8** Polymnia
of tragedy: **9** Melpomene
relationship: **7** sisters
tamed by: **6** Apollo

MUSEUM: **7** archive, gallery, library **8** atheneum **10** collection, foundation, repository **11** institution
director: **7** curator

MUSH: **4** trek **5** crush, march, slush **6** drivel, travel **7** journey, pudding **8** cornmeal, flattery, porridge **11** amorousness **14** sentimentality

MUSHROOM: **5** fungi, morel, spore **6** fungus **9** toadstool **10** champignon **11** chanterelle
parts: **3** cap **4** gill, stem **5** stipe **6** pileus **7** annulus **8** basidium, hymenium, sterigma **12** basidiospore
poison: **7** amanita **8** mycetism **9** toadstool

MUSHY: **4** soft **5** corny, gooey, gushy, pulpy **6** slushy, spongy **7** mawkish **8** romantic **11** sentimental

MUSIC: **3** air, art **4** tune **7** harmony
abbreviations: **3** dim, sfz **4** espr, pizz, rall **5** cresc
animated: **4** vivo **6** vivace **7** allegro **9** spiritoso
arrangement: **7** ridotto
as written: **3** sta
bass lines: **5** GBDFA
bass spaces: **4** ACEG
beat: **4** time **5** ictus, meter, pulse, tempo **6** rhythm
bold: **6** audace
cadence: **4** half **6** plagal **7** perfect **9** deceptive, imperfect

change key: **10** modulation **13** transposition
chord: **5** tonic, triad **8** dominant **9** augmented **10** diminished
composition: **4** aria, hymn, solo **5** etude, psalm, suite **6** anthem **7** chorale, requiem **8** madrigal, postlude
dignified: **8** maestoso
disconnected: **8** staccato
dying away: **7** calando
embellished: **3** run **4** turn **5** trill **7** cadenza, mordent, roulade **8** arpeggio, flourish **9** grace note
emotional: **12** appassionato
ending: **4** coda
evenly: **10** equalmente
excited: **7** agitato **9** spiritoso
fast: **4** vite, vivo **5** tosto **6** presto, veloce, vivace **7** allegro **10** tostamente
faster: **7** stretto **11** accelerando
fastest: **11** prestissimo
flourish: **7** roulade
for eight: **5** octet
for five: **7** quintet
for four: **7** quartet
for nine: **5** nonet
for one: **4** soli, solo
for seven: **6** septet
for six: **6** sextet **7** sestole **8** sestolet
for three: **4** trio
for two: **3** duo **4** duet
forcefully: **7** furioso
freely: **9** ad libitum
gayly: **7** giocoso
gently: **5** dolce **7** amabile, amoroso **10** affettuoso
gods: **5** Brage **6** Apollo **7** Phoebus, Pythius **9** Musagetes
group: **4** band, trio **5** choir, combo **6** chorus **7** quartet **8** ensemble, symphony **9** orchestra
half: **5** mezzo
heavy: **7** pesante
held: **6** tenuto
hurried: **7** agitato
instrumental: **4** jazz **5** etude, fugue, march, polka, suite, swing, waltz **6** minuet, sonata **7** ragtime **8** concerto, fantasia, overture, rhapsody, serenade, symphony
joyous: **7** giocoso
leap: **5** salto
less: **4** meno
little: **4** poco
lively: **4** vite **6** vivace **7** allegro, animato, giocoso **9** capriccio
loud: **5** forte **10** fortissimo
louder: **9** crescendo
loudest: **10** fortissimo
lovingly: **7** amabile, amoroso
majestic: **8** maestoso
major key: **3** dur
mania: **9** melomania
melodic phrase: **9** leitmotif, leitmotiv
minor key: **4** moll
moderate: **7** andante **8** moderato
moderately loud: **10** mezzo forte
moderately soft: **10** mezzo piano
morning song: **6** aubade
movement: **4** moto
muse: **7** Euterpe
muted: **5** sorda, sordo
outdoor: **6** aubade
passionless: **6** freddo
patron saint: **7** Cecilia
plaintive: **7** dolente **8** doloroso
playful: **7** giocoso **10** scherzando
plucked: **9** pizzicato
quick: **4** vite, viva **5** tosto **6** presto, veloce, vivace **7** allegro, schnell **10** tostamente
quickening: **11** affrettando
refrain: **5** epode **8** repetend
repeat: **3** bis **6** ancoro
repeated: **3** bis **6** da capo **7** represa
sad: **7** dolente
sadly: **8** doloroso
sharp: **8** staccato **9** sforzando
silent: **5** tacet
sliding: **9** glissando
slow: **5** grave, largo, lento, tardo **6** adagio **7** andante **9** larghetto
slowing: **3** rit **6** ritard **10** ritardando **11** rallentando
smooth: **5** dolce **6** legato **8** grazioso

soft: **5** dolce, piano **10** pianissimo
softening: **10** diminuendo
softer: **11** decrescendo
softest: **10** pianissimo
solemn: **5** grave
spirited: **4** vivo **6** audace, vivace **7** animato **9** spiritoso
stately: **7** pomposo **8** maestoso
strong: **5** forte **10** fortissimo
sustained: **6** tenuto **9** sostenuto, sustenuto
sweet: **5** dolce
syllables: **3** Ela, sol **7** alamire
symbols: **3** bar, key, tie **4** clef, flat, note, rest, slur, turn **5** brace, cleft, presa, segno, sharp, staff **7** fermata, natural **8** ligature **9** alla breve **10** accidental
tender: **7** amabile, amoroso **10** affettuoso
throughout: **6** sempre
treble lines: **5** EGBDF
treble spaces: **4** FACE
unaccompanied: **9** a cappella
vocal: **4** aria, hymn **5** canon, chant, opera, round **6** anthem, ballad **7** cantata, chanson, chorale **8** madrigal, serenade
vocal part: **5** canto

MUSICAL: **4** show **5** revue **6** choral **7** lyrical, songful **8** operatic, rhythmic **9** melodious **10** harmonious **11** symphonious

MUSICAL INSTRUMENT: **4** drum, fife, gong, harp, horn, lute, lyre, oboe, reed, tuba **5** banjo, flute, organ, piano, viola **6** cornet, guitar, spinet, violin **7** bassoon, ocarina, piccolo, saxhorn, trumpet, ukelele, ukulele **8** castanet, clarinet, dulcimer, mandolin, trombone **9** euphonium, flageolet, saxophone **11** violoncello
ancient: **4** asor, lyre, rote **5** rotte **6** cither, rappel, sebaca **7** mandola, serpent, sistrum **9** pantaleon
brass: **4** horn, tuba **5** bugle **6** cornet, tromba **7** althorn, clarion, helicon, saxhorn, trumpet **8** altohorn, trombone **10** French horn
keyboard: **5** organ, piano **6** spinet **7** celesta, cembalo, clavier **8** calliope, melodeon **9** accordion **10** clavichord, concertina, pianoforte **11** harpsichord
medieval: **4** lute **5** naker, rebab, rebec, rocta, tabor **6** citale **7** chrotta, gittern, mandola **8** dulcimer, oliphant, recorder **10** clavichord, hurdy-gurdy
non-electric: **8** acoustic
percussion: **4** drum, gong **5** bells **6** maraca **7** cymbals, marimba, tympani **8** bass drum, castanet, triangle **9** snare drum, xylophone **10** kettledrum, tambourine, vibraphone **12** glockenspiel
reed: **4** oboe **7** bassoon **8** clarinet **9** harmonica, saxophone **11** English horn
Renaissance instruments: **4** viol **6** spinet **7** bagpipe, bandora, cittern, serpent **8** recorder **11** harpsichord
string: **3** oud, uke **4** asor, bass, harp, lute, lyre, vina, viol **5** banjo, cello, rebec, sitar, viola **6** fiddle, guitar, violin, zither **7** cittern, gittern, pandura, samisen, theorbo, ukelele, ukulele **8** autoharp, dulcimer, mandolin **11** harpsichord, violoncello
wind: **5** organ **6** cornet **7** althorn, bagpipe, bassoon, clarion, panpipe, piccolo, saxhorn, serpent, trumpet **8** altohorn, clarinet, recorder, trombone, zampogna **9** flageolet, harmonica, saxophone **10** French horn **11** sarrusphone
woodwind: **3** sax **4** fife, horn, oboe, reed, tuba **5** brass, bugle **11** English horn

MUSICIAN: **4** bard **5** piper, tenor **6** artist, player, singer **7** cellist, drummer, flutist, maestro, pianist, soprano **8** baritone, composer, minstrel, organist, virtuoso, vocalist **9** conductor, guitarist, performer, serenader, violinist **10** troubadour **11** entertainer, saxophonist

MUSING: **7** pensive **8** absorbed **9** pondering **10** meditative, reflective **13** introspective

MUSKET: **3** gun **5** fusil, rifle **6** weapon **7** carbine, firearm **9** matchlock

MUSKETEER: **7** soldier **9** bodyguard
famous: **15** Three Musketeers

MUSLIM/MOSLEM: **4** Moor, Moro **5** Islam **6** Muslim, Paynim, Shiite **7** Abadite, Islamic, Saracen **9** Mahometan, Mussulman **10** Mohammadan
ascetic: **4** sufi **5** fakir **6** fakeer **7** dervish
bible: **5** Coran, Koran **7** Alcoran
calendar: **5** Rabia, Rajab, Safar **6** Jumada, Shaban **7** Ramadan, Shawwal **8** Zu'lhijah, Zu'lkadah **9** Mulharram
call to prayer: **4** adan, azan
cap: **3** taj **5** kulah **6** kullah
caste: **5** mopla **6** moplah
convert: **5** ansar
council: **5** ulema
creed: **5** Sunna **6** Kelima **7** Kalimah
crusade: **5** jahad, jehad, jihad
demon: **5** afrit, Eblis, jinni **6** jinnee
fast: **7** Ramadan
festival: **3** Eed **6** Bairam
garment: **3** fez, taj **4** izar **5** ihram, kulah **6** chador, jubbah, turban
god: **5** Allah, Eblis
holy cities: **5** Mecca **6** Medina
judge: **4** cadi, cazi, imam, kazi **5** hakim, imaum
lawyer: **5** mufti
leader: **3** aga **4** amir, emir, said, seid, tola **5** ameer, begum, emeer, hakim, nawab, nawah, sayid **6** caliph, hakeem, sultan
monastery: **5** ribat, tekke **7** khankah
mosque: **6** masjid
mystic: **4** Sufi
non-believer: **5** Kafir **6** Kaffir
pilgrim: **4** haji **5** hadji, hajji
pilgrimage: **3** haj **4** hadj, hajj
priest: **4** imam **5** imaum **6** wahabi
religion: **5** Islam
saint: **3** Pir **5** Abdal **6** Santon **8** Marabout
salutation: **5** salam **6** salaam
sects: **5** Isawa **6** Senusi, Shiite, Wahabi **7** Abadite, dervish, Sunnite **8** Ahmadiya, Sifatite
shrine: **5** Caaba, Kaaba **6** Kaabeh
student: **5** softa
teacher: **3** pir **4** alim, imam **5** mulla **6** mullah **8** mujtahid

MUSS: **4** mess **5** chaos **6** jumble, ruffle, rumple **7** turmoil **8** dishevel, disorder, shambles **10** disarrange **11** disorganize

MUSSOLINI, BENITO: **6** Il Duce **7** Fascist **8** dictator **13** prime minister
allied with: **7** Germany
country: **5** Italy

MUST: **4** mold, need, stum, want **5** ought, shall **6** should **9** essential, necessity **10** obligation **11** requirement **12** prerequisite

MUSTER: **4** call **5** amass, crowd, rally **6** enlist, gather, invoke, roster, summon **7** collect, marshal, roundup **8** assemble, generate, mobilize, organize **10** accumulate, congregate

MUSTY: **4** aged, damp, dull, rank, sour **5** dirty, moldy, stale, tired, trite **6** filthy, rotten, smelly **7** spoiled, squalid **8** mildewed, timeworn **10** antiquated

MUTABLE: **6** fickle **7** erratic **8** variable, wavering **9** alterable, mercurial **10** changeable, inconstant, unreliable **11** fluctuating, vacillating

MUTATE: **4** vary **5** alter **6** change, modify **7** convert **9** transform

MUTATION: **6** change, mutant **7** anomaly **9** evolution, variation **11** vicissitude **13** metamorphosis

MUTE: **3** mum **4** dumb **5** quiet **6** deaden, muffle, muzzle, silent, soften **8** unspoken **9** voiceless **10** speechless

MUTILATE: **3** mar **4** hack, hurt, lame, maim **6** batter, damage, deface, injure, mangle **7** butcher, cripple, destroy **9** disfigure

MUTINEER: **5** rebel **7** radical **8** revolter **9** insurgent **10** malcontent, subversive

MUTINOUS: **6** unruly **7** lawless, riotous **9** seditious, turbulent **10** rebellious, tumultuous **11** disaffected, intractable **13** insubordinate **14** uncontrollable

MUTINY: **4** riot **6** revolt, strife **8** defiance, upheaval, uprising **9** rebellion **10** resistance **12** insurrection

MUTT: **3** dog **5** dunce, idiot **6** dimwit **7** mongrel **9** blockhead

MUTTER: **4** moan **5** growl **6** mumble, murmur, patter **7** grumble, whisper **8** complain

MUTTONCHOPS: **8** whiskers **9** burnsides, sideburns

MUTTONHEAD: **4** fool **5** dunce, idiot **6** stupid **9** blockhead

MUTUAL: **5** joint **6** common, shared **7** related **10** associated, collective, reciprocal **11** interactive

MUZZLE: **3** gag **4** cork, nose **5** cover, quiet, snout **7** censure, harness, repress, silence, squelch **8** restrain

MYANMAR:
capital: **6** Yangon **7** Rangoon
cities: **4** Pegu **5** Pagan **6** Mingun **8** Mandalay, Moulmein
continent: **4** Asia
ethnic groups: **4** Shan **5** Karen **6** Burman **7** Rakhine
features: **10** rain forest
formerly: **5** Burma
languages: **4** Shan **5** Karen **7** Burmese
monetary unit: **4** kyat
water: **8** Chindwin **9** Irrawaddy

MYOPIC: **5** blind **7** blurred **10** astigmatic, presbyopic **11** nearsighted **12** shortsighted

MYRIAD: **4** army, host, lots **5** flood **6** legion, scores **7** endless **9** countless **11** innumerable

MYRMIDON: **6** cohort, minion **7** servant **8** follower, henchman **9** attendant, sycophant **10** henchwoman

MYSTERIOUS: **4** dark **6** arcane, mystic, occult, secret **7** cryptic, curious, magical, strange, unknown **8** abstruse, esoteric, puzzling **9** concealed, enigmatic, recondite **11** inscrutable **12** inexplicable, supernatural, unfathomable

MYSTERY: **5** craft, novel, story, trade **6** enigma, puzzle, riddle, secret **7** arcanum, stumper **8** stickler, thriller, whodunit **9** conundrum **11** cliffhanger

MYSTIC: **4** seer **5** magic **6** occult, secret **7** cryptic, magical, obscure **8** esoteric, mystical, symbolic, wizardly **9** enigmatic, recondite, sorcerous, spiritual, visionary **10**

cabalistic, paranormal **12** supernatural

MYSTIFY: **5** stump **6** baffle, muddle, puzzle **7** confuse, perplex **8** befuddle, bewilder, confound **9** bamboozle

MYTH: **4** saga, tale **5** fable, story **6** legend **7** fantasy, parable **8** allegory, folklore **9** tradition

MYTHICAL: **6** fabled, unreal **8** invented **9** imaginary, legendary **10** fabricated, fictitious

N

NAB: **4** bust, grab, nail **5** catch, pinch, seize **6** arrest, collar, snatch **7** capture **9** apprehend

NABOB: **5** nawab **6** bigwig, deputy, tycoon **7** magnate, notable, viceroy **8** governor **9** dignitary

NAG: **4** fuss, goad, harp, jade, plug, prod, ride, urge **5** annoy, horse, hound, scold **6** badger, berate, bother, harass, heckle, hector, needle, pester **7** hackney, henpeck, torment **8** harangue, irritate **9** aggravate, racehorse

NAIAD: **5** nymph, plant

NAIL: **4** brad, claw, join, stud, tack, trap **5** affix, catch, pound, seize, spike, talon **6** arrest, clinch, collar, detect, expose, fasten, hammer, master, secure, strike **7** capture **8** fastener

NAIVE: **5** green **6** candid, simple **7** natural, artless **8** childish, gullible, innocent, trusting **9** guileless, ingenuous, unworldly **10** unaffected, unassuming, unschooled **13** inexperienced

NAKED: **4** bare, nude, pure **6** barren, unclad **7** exposed, obvious **8** disrobed, manifest, revealed, stripped **9** au naturel, disclosed, unclothed, uncovered, undressed **10** discovered, vulnerable **11** defenseless, unprotected

NAMBY-PAMBY: **4** weak **5** banal, inane **7** insipid, sapless **9** innocuous, spineless **10** wishy-washy **11** sentimental

NAME: **3** tab, tag **4** call, race, term **5** alias, brand, label, style, title **6** byline, choose, family, handle, select **7** agnomen, appoint, baptize, entitle, epithet, moniker **8** christen, classify, cognomen, delegate, deputize, identify, identity, nominate **9** celebrity, designate, headliner, personage, pseudonym, signature, sobriquet **10** reputation **11** appellation, designation, distinction **12** denomination, nomenclature

NAMELESS: **7** obscure, unknown **8** untitled **9** anonymous, incognito **13** indescribable, unmentionable

NAMELY: **3** viz **5** noted **8** scilicet **9** videlicet **10** especially **12** particularly, specifically

NAMIBIA:
capital: **8** Windhoek
cities: **5** Rundu **8** Rehoboth **9** Walvis Bay **10** Swakopmund

continent: **6** Africa
ethnic groups: **6** Damara, Herero, Ovambo **7** Kavango
features: **11** Namib desert **13** Caaprivi Strip **14** Kalahari desert
formerly: **15** South West Africa
languages: **7** English **9** Afrikaans
monetary unit: **4** rand
native: **8** Namibian
water: **11** Orange River

NANNY: **4** goat **5** nurse **11** maidservant

NAP: **3** nod **4** doze, fuzz, pour, rest, shag, wink **5** break, fluff, sleep **6** siesta, snooze **7** respite, shuteye, slumber **10** forty winks

NAPKIN: **5** cloth, doily, towel **6** diaper, linens **9** handcloth, serviette

NAPOLEON BONAPARTE:
birthplace: **7** Corsica
deathplace: **8** St. Helena
defeat: **4** Nile **7** Leipzig **8** Waterloo **9** Trafalgar
exiled to: **4** Elba **8** St. Helena
law: **14** Napoleonic Code
title: **6** consul **7** Emperor, general
victory: **3** Ulm **4** Jena **6** Wagram **7** Dresden, Marengo **8** Borodino **9** Friedland **10** Austerlitz
wife: **9** Josephine **11** Marie Louise

NARCISSISTIC: **4** vain **9** conceited **10** self-loving **11** egotistical **12** vainglorious

NARCOTIC: **3** LSD **4** dope, drug, junk **5** ether, opium **6** downer, heroin, opiate, valium **7** anodyne, cocaine, hashish **8** hypnotic, morphine, quaalude, sedative **9** marijuana, soporific **10** anesthetic, medication, painkiller **12** tranquilizer
law enforcer: **4** nark, narc
seller: **6** dealer, pusher, source **7** peddler **8** candy man

NARRATE: **4** tell **5** state **6** depict, detail, recite, relate, report **7** recount **8** describe **9** chronicle, discourse **12** characterize

NARRATIVE: **4** epic, myth, saga, tale **5** conte, story **6** legend **7** account, comment, episode, history **8** anecdote, dialogue **9** narration, statement

NARROW: **4** mean, slim **5** close, rigid, scant, small, sound, taper, tight **6** biased, lessen, little, meager, reduce, select, strait, strict **7** bigoted, cramped, limited, pinched **8** definite **9** confining, constrict, eliminate, hidebound, illiberal **10** inexorable, inflexible, prejudiced, restricted **11** reactionary

NARROWLY: **4** just **6** almost, barely, nearly

NARROW-MINDED: **5** petty **6** biased **7** bigoted, shallow **9** hidebound **10** intolerant, prejudiced

NASTY: **4** evil, foul, mean, ugly **5** awful, cruel, dirty, gross **6** filthy, vulgar, wicked **7** harmful, hateful, obscene, raunchy, squalid, vicious **8** horrible, indecent **9** loathsome, malicious, offensive, repugnant, repulsive, sickening **10** abominable, disgusting, nauseating, unpleasant

NATION: **4** race **5** state, tribe, union **6** people **7** country **8** republic **9** community, territory **11** sovereignty **12** commonwealth

NATIONAL: **6** ethnic, public **7** citizen, federal **8** domestic **9** political **10** nationwide **11** countrywide

NATIVE: **4** wild **5** local, natal **6** inborn, inbred, innate **7** citizen, endemic, natural **8** domestic, inherent, original, regional, resident **9** congenial, ingrained **10** aboriginal, congenital, inhabitant **13** autochthonous **14** constitutional

NATTY: **4** chic, neat, posh, tidy, trim **5** smart **6** dapper, spruce **11** fashionable

NATURAL: **4** easy, open, pure, wild **5** naive, plain, usual **6** candid, common, inborn, inbred, innate, native, normal, rustic **7** artless, general, genuine, organic, regular, sincere **8** accepted, expected, inherent **9** intuitive, primitive, unrefined **10** congenital, unaffected **11** anticipated, instinctive **12** illegitimate

NATURALIZE: **5** adapt, adopt **7** conform **8** accustom **11** acclimatize

NATURE: **4** kind, sort, type **5** earth, style **6** makeup **7** essence, quality **8** category, outdoors, property, universe **9** character **10** attributes **11** disposition, environment, temperament **12** constitution

NAUGHT: **4** zero **5** zilch **6** cipher **7** nothing, useless **9** worthless **12** nonexistence **13** insignificant

NAUGHTY: **3** bad **4** evil, lewd **6** unruly, vulgar, wicket **7** immoral, obscene, playful, wayward **8** fiendish, improper **10** disorderly **11** disobedient, mischievous

NAURU:
capital: **13** Yaren District
continent: **7** Oceania, Pacific
ethnic groups: **7** Chinese, Nauruan **15** Pacific Islander
features: **9** phosphate
formerly: **14** Pleasant Island
language: **7** Nauruan
monetary unit: **6** dollar
water: **7** Anibare, Pacific

NAUSEA: **6** hatred **7** disgust **8** loathing, sickness, vomiting **9** dizziness, revulsion **10** queasiness

NAUSEATE: **5** repel, upset **6** bother, loathe, revolt, sicken **7** disgust

NAUSEATING: **7** fulsome **8** qualmish **9** loathsome, offensive, repugnant, sickening **10** disgusting **11** distasteful

NAUTICAL: **5** naval **6** marine **7** aquatic, oceanic, pelagic **8** maritime **9** seafaring

NAVE: **3** hub **4** body, core **6** center, middle

NAVIGATE: **4** keel, sail **5** guide, pilot, steer **6** cruise, direct **7** journey, operate **8** maneuver

NAVIGATION: **7** nautics, sailing **8** piloting, shipping, voyaging, yachting **9** traveling **10** seamanship

NAVIGATOR: **5** pilot **6** airman, sailor, seaman **7** aviator, copilot, mariner **8** explorer

NAVY: **5** fleet **6** armada **8** flotilla

NAY: **3** not **4** deny **6** denial, refuse **7** against **8** moreover, negative

NEAR: **4** dear, nigh **5** about, close, handy, rival, touch **6** almost, around, beside **7** advance, looming, similar, vicinal **8** adjacent, approach, imminent, intimate **9** alongside, immediate **10** contiguous, convenient **11** approaching, neighboring **13** approximately

NEARBY: **5** close, handy **8** adjacent **10** accessible, convenient

NEARSIGHTED: **6** myopic **10** astigmatic **12** shortsighted

NEAT: **4** nice, prim, pure, tidy, tosh, trig, trim **5** clean, exact, great, kempt, natty **6** adroit, clever, dapper, spruce **7** concise, orderly, precise, refined **8** exciting, skillful, spotless **9** dexterous, organized, shipshape, undiluted **10** immaculate, meticulous **11** uncluttered **12** spick-and-span

NEB: **3** nib **4** beak, bill, nose **5** snout

NEBRASKA:
bird: **10** meadowlark
capital: **7** Lincoln
cities: **5** Omaha **11** Grand Island, North Platte
explorer: **5** Clark, Lewis
features: **14** Rocky Mountains
flower: **9** goldenrod
nickname: **4** Beef **10** Blackwater, Cornhusker **12** Tree Planters
tree: **10** cottonwood
water: **6** Platte **8** Missouri, Niobrara

NEBULA: **5** vapor **6** galaxy, nimbus

NEBULOUS: **4** hazy **5** foggy, misty, murky, vague **6** cloudy **7** obscure, unclear **9** ambiguous, uncertain **10** indefinite, indistinct

NECESSARILY: **8** perforce **9** certainly, naturally **10** inevitably **11** accordingly, indubitably, unavoidably, undoubtedly

NECESSARY: **5** vital **6** needed **7** crucial **8** integral, required **9** essential, important, mandatory, paramount, requisite **10** imperative, inevitable **11** fundamental, unavoidable **13** indispensable

NECESSITATE: **5** force, impel **6** oblige, compel, demand **7** command, require

NECESSITY: **4** food, must, need, want **5** water **7** shelter **8** clothing **9** essential **11** requirement **12** prerequisite

NECK: **3** pet **4** cape, kiss, nape **6** caress, cervix, collar, collum, fondle, scruff, strait **7** embrace, isthmus

NECK-AND-NECK: **3** tie **4** even **5** close **10** nip and tuck

NECKERCHIEF: **5** scarf **8** bandanna, kerchief **12** handkerchief

NECKLACE: **4** band, rope **5** beads, chain **6** choker, collar, locket, pearls, torque **7** jewelry, pendant, riviere **8** carcanet **9** lavaliere

NECKTIE: **4** band **5** ascot **6** bow tie, cravat **7** bolo tie, foulard **9** clip-on tie, string tie **10** four-in-hand

NECROLOGY: **8** obituary

NECROMANCY: **5** goety, magic **7** sorcery **8** wizardry **10** witchcraft **11** conjuration, enchantment, thaumaturgy

NECROPOLIS: **8** boneyard, cemetery **9** graveyard

NECTAR: **4** wine **5** drink, honey **6** amrita **8** ambrosia

NEED: **4** lack, must, want **5** crave, pinch, yearn **6** demand, desire, hanker, hunger, thirst **7** longing, poverty, require, urgency **8** distress, exigency, shortage, weakness **9** emergency, essential, extremity, necessity, requisite **10** compulsion, dependence, obligation **11** requirement

NEEDLE: **3** sew **4** darn, goad, prod, ride, shot **5** annoy, taunt, tease **6** badger, bother, harass **7** provoke, syringe **8** irritate
hole: **3** eye

NEEDLESS: **7** useless **9** excessive, pointless **10** gratuitous **11** inessential, superfluous, unnecessary

NEEDLEWORK: **6** sewing **7** crochet, sampler, tatting **8** applique, knitting, quilting **9** hardanger, stitching **10** embroidery

NEEDY: **4** poor **8** indigent **9** destitute, penniless **12** impoverished **13** disadvantaged

NE'ER-DO-WELL: **3** bum **5** idler, loser **6** loafer **7** wastrel **9** shiftless, worthless **11** incompetent

NEFARIOUS: **4** base, rank, vile **5** gross **6** rotten, sinful, wicked **7** corrupt, heinous, vicious **8** depraved, horrible, infamous **9** atrocious, miscreant **10** despicable, detestable, villainous **11** treacherous

NEGATE: **4** deny, undo, veto **5** annul, quash **6** impugn, revoke **7** abolish, gainsay, nullify, retract **9** repudiate **10** invalidate, neutralize

NEGATIVE: **3** nay, not **4** film, veto **5** blank, minus **7** adverse, neutral **9** resisting, skeptical **10** contradict **11** detrimental, pessimistic, unfavorable

NEGLECT: **4** fail, omit, slip **5** fault, shirk **6** bypass, forget, ignore, laxity, reject, slight **7** abandon, default, failure **8** discount, omission, overlook **9** disregard, oversight **11** inattention **12** carelessness

NEGLECTFUL: **5** slack **6** remiss **8** careless, heedless **9** unmindful **10** unwatchful **11** inattentive, thoughtless

NEGLIGEE: **4** robe **7** nightie **8** camisole, peignoir **9** nightgown

NEGLIGENT: **3** lax **5** slack **6** remiss **8** careless, derelict, heedless, slipshod **9** forgetful **10** delinquent **11** inattentive, indifferent, thoughtless **13** inconsiderate

NEGLIGIBLE: **4** slim **5** small **6** minute, remote **8** piddling, trifling **13** insignificant

NEGOTIATE: **4** deal **6** barter, debate, dicker, haggle, hurdle, manage, settle **7** arrange, bargain, discuss **8** contract, surmount, transact, traverse

NEGOTIATION: **4** deal **6** treaty **9** mediation **10** compromise

NEIGH: **5** sound **6** nicker, whinny

NEIGHBOR: **4** abut **5** touch, verge **6** adjoin, border, friend, nearby **7** address

NEIGHBORHOOD: **4** area, turf, zone **5** block **6** parish, region, street, suburb **7** section **8** district, locality, vicinity **9** community, territory

NEIGHBORLY: **4** kind **5** civil **6** polite **7** cordial, helpful **8** amicable, friendly, sociable **10** hospitable

NEMESIS: **5** rival **7** avenger **8** downfall, opponent **10** antagonist **11** destruction

NEOPHYTE: **4** tyro **6** novice, rookie **7** convert, learner, student, trainee **8** beginner, newcomer **9** greenhorn, proselyte **10** catechumen

NEPAL:
capital: **8** Katmandu **9** Kathmandu
cities: **5** Patan **6** Morang **7** Birganj, Pokhara **8** Bhadgaon **10** Biratnagar
continent: **4** Asia
ethnic groups: **6** Indian
features: **7** Lumbini **9** Himalayas **12** Mount Everest **18** Mount Kangchenjunga
language: **6** Nepali
monetary unit: **5** rupee
native: **6** Nepali **8** Napalese
water: **4** Kusi **5** Bheri, Tamur **6** Gandak **7** Karnali

NEPENTHE: **4** drug **6** opiate **8** narcotic

NEPTUNE: **3** sea **5** ocean **6** planet
god of: **3** sea
planet order: **6** eighth
spear: **7** trident

NERO:
burned: **4** Rome
death: **7** suicide
deserted by: **11** Praetorians
father: **8** Domitius
killed: **5** Lucan **6** Seneca **7** Octavia **9** Agrippina
kingdom: **4** Rome
mother: **9** Agrippina
successor: **5** Galba
title: **7** Emperor
wife: **7** Octavia, Poppaea

NERVE: **4** gall, grit, guts **5** brass, heart, moxie, pluck, spunk, vigor **6** daring, energy, spirit, tendon **7** bravery, courage, stamina **8** audacity, backbone, boldness, coolness, gameness, strength, temerity **9** encourage, fortitude, hardihood **10** brazenness, effrontery **11** presumption **12** fearlessness
cell: **6** neuron
cranial: **5** optic, vagus **6** facial **8** abducens **9** olfactory, trochlear **10** oculomotor, trigeminal **11** hypoglossal **13** statoacoustic **16** glossopharyngeal
ending: **8** effector, receptor
group: **8** ganglion

NERVELESS: **4** calm, cool, dead, weak **5** inert **7** fearful **8** cowardly **9** collected, powerless, spineless **10** controlled, spiritless

NERVOUS: **4** edgy **5** jumpy, nervy, shaky, tense, upset **6** touchy **7** anxious, fearful, fidgety, jittery, uptight **8** neurotic, skittish, unstrung **9** concerned, excitable, querulous, sensitive **12** apprehensive

NERVOUS SYSTEM: **5** ulnar **6** lumbar, median, radial, sacral, tibial **7** digital, femoral, sciatic **8** brachial, cervical, peroneal, thoracic **9** coccygeal, maxillary **10** mandibular, ophthalmic **11** intercostal

NERVY: **4** bold **5** brash, gutsy, jumpy, tense **6** brazen, cheeky, uneasy **7** fidgety, jittery, nervous, uptight **8** impudent **9** excitable

NEST: **3** den **4** cave, hive, home, lair **5** abode, aerie, brook, eyrie, group, haunt, nidus, swarm **6** colony, cuddle **7** lodging, retreat, shelter **9** residence

NESTLE: **5** embed, lodge **6** bundle, caress, cuddle, nuzzle **7** embrace, shelter, snuggle

NET: **3** bag, web **4** gain, hook, lace, make, mesh, take, trap, trim **5** catch, seize, snare, tulle, yield **6** entrap, profit **7** capture, ensnare, network, realize **8** entangle **9** reticulum
type: **4** drop, gill, keep **5** drift, seine, snood, trawl **7** landing, trammel

NETHER: **5** below, lower, under **7** beneath **8** inferior

NETHERLANDS:
also called: **7** Holland
artists: **3** Lis **4** Eyck, Hals **5** Appel, Bosch **7** van Gogh, Vermeer **8** Mondrian **9** Rembrandt
capital: **9** Amsterdam
cheese: **4** Edam **5** Gouda **6** Leyden **7** cottage
cities: **3** Ede, Urk **5** Breda, Delft, Hague, Lisse **6** Aalten, Arnhem, Leiden, Velsen **7** Haarlem, Limburg, Utrecht **8** Aalsmeer **9** Eindhoven, Groningen, Rotterdam
concerning: **5** Dutch
drink: **3** gin **8** anisette, schnapps
former colonies: **4** Java **6** Borneo **7** Celebes, Sumatra, Surinam **9** New Guinea **10** East Indies
islands: **5** Arroe, Arrou, Texel **7** Ameland, Frisian **8** Antilles, Vlieland **9** Schelling
lakes: **7** Haarlem **10** Ijsselmeer
leaders: **7** Beatrix, Juliana, William **10** Wilhelmina
legislature: **4** Raad
patron saint: **10** Willibrord
people: **5** Dutch **7** Flemish, Frisian **9** Hollander **12** Netherlander
rivers: **3** Eem, Lek **4** Leck, Maas, Rijn, Waal, Ysel **5** Donge, Meuse, Rhine, Schie, Yssel **6** Dommel, Ijssel, Kromme

NETTLE: **4** fret, rile **5** annoy, peeve, pique, upset **6** bother, ruffle, splice **7** agitate, provoke, trouble **8** irritate **10** exasperate

NETWORK: **4** grid, maze, mesh, rete **5** chain **6** matrix, system **9** circuitry, labyrinth, reticulum, structure **12** organization

NEUROTIC: **7** anxious, erratic, nervous, uptight **8** unstable **9** obsessive **10** compulsive

NEUTER: **3** fix **4** spay **5** alter **7** asexual, neutral **8** castrate **9** impartial, sterilize **12** intransitive

NEUTRAL: **4** flat, gray **6** neuter **8** balanced, detached, unallied, unbiased **9** colorless, impartial, undecided **10** achromatic **11** indifferent, nonpartisan **13** disinterested **14** expressionless

NEUTRALIZE: **4** stop **5** annul, block **6** cancel, negate, offset **7** balance, nullify **8** abrogate **9** frustrate **10** counteract

NEVADA:
bird: **16** mountain bluebird
capital: **10** Carson City
cities: **4** Reno **8** Las Vegas
explorer: **6** Carson **7** Fremont
features: **7** casinos, divorce **8** marriage **9** Hoover Dam **10** Great Basin **11** Lehman Caves **12** Mohave Desert
nicknames: **6** Silver **9** Sagebrush **10** Battle Born
trees: **5** pinon **15** bristlecone pine
water: **4** Mead **5** Tahoe **6** Carson **7** Pyramid **8** Colorado

NEVER-ENDING: **7** eternal, lasting **8** constant, immortal, infinite **9** continual, perpetual, unceasing **11** everlasting **13** uninterrupted

NEVERTHELESS: **3** but, yet **5** still **6** anyhow, withal **7** however **8** although **9** howsoever **10** regardless

NEW: **5** fresh, green, novel **6** latest, modern, recent, unused **7** current, rebuilt, revived, untried **8** improved, original, restored, untested **9** remodeled, renovated **10** additional, unexplored, unfamiliar **11** regenerated **12** contemporary, unaccustomed **13** inexperienced

NEW BRUNSWICK:
capital: **11** Fredericton
cities: **7** Moncton **9** Saint John
country: **6** Canada
explorer: **7** Cartier **9** Champlain
features: **5** Fundy **10** Campobello
flower: **6** violet
formerly: **6** Acadia
water: **7** St. Croix **9** Grand Lake **10** Bay of Fundy **11** St. John River

NEWCOMER: **4** tyro **6** novice, rookie **7** settler, upstart **8** beginner, neophyte **9** greenhorn, immigrant

NEW ENGLAND:
of West: **9** Minnesota
settler: **6** Yankee **7** Pilgrim, Puritan
states: **5** Maine **7** Vermont **11** Connecticut, Rhode Island **12** New Hampshire **13** Massachusetts

NEWFANGLED: **5** fresh, novel **6** latest, modern, unique **7** stylish **12** contemporary

NEWFOUNDLAND:
capital: **7** St John's
cities: **6** Gander **10** Mount Pearl **11** Corner Brook
country: **6** Canada
explorer: **5** Cabot
features: **8** Labrador **10** Bell Island, Fogo Island, Grand Banks
flower: **12** pitcher plant
water: **6** Gander **9** Belle Isle

NEW GUINEA:
cities: **3** Lae **4** Daru **5** Soron, Wewak **6** Madang, Rabaul **11** Port Moresby
countries: **14** Papua New Guinea
features: **6** Albert **8** Victoria **10** Wilhelmina
place: **7** Pacific **10** East Indies **14** Solomon Islands
province: **9** Irian Jaya, West Irian
water: **4** Huon **5** Papua

NEW HAMPSHIRE:
bird: **11** purple finch
capital: **7** Concord
cities: **6** Nashua **10** Manchester, Portsmouth
explorer: **5** Pring **9** Champlain
features: **9** Monadnock **14** White Mountains **15** Mount Washington
flower: **11** purple lilac
nickname: **7** Granite
tree: **10** white birch
water: **4** Saco **9** Merrimack **10** Piscataqua **11** Connecticut **17** Lake Winnipesaukee

NEW JERSEY:
bird: **16** eastern goldfinch
capital: **7** Trenton
cities: **6** Camden, Newark **8** Paterson **9** Elizabeth **10** Jersey City **12** Atlantic City
explorer: **6** Hudson **9** Verrazano
features: **7** Cape May, casinos **9** Palisades **11** Meadowlands
flower: **12** purple violet
nickname: **6** Garden
trees: **6** Ramapo, red oak **7** Raritan **8** Delaware, Tuckahoe
water: **6** Ramapo **7** Raritan **8** Delaware, Tuckahoe

NEWLY: **4** anew **6** lately **7** freshly **8** recently

NEW MEXICO:
bird: **10** roadrunner
capital: **7** Santa Fe
cities: **7** Roswell **9** Las Cruces **11** Albuquerque
explorer: **8** Coronado
features: **10** White Sands **11** Great Plains **14** Rocky Mountains **15** Carlsbad Caverns
flower: **5** yucca
nickname: **17** Land of Enchantment
tree: **5** pinon
water: **9** Rio Grande

NEWS: **4** dirt, poop, word **5** flash, scoop **6** canard, gossip, report **7** account, lowdown, release, tidings **8** bulletin, dispatch **10** communique, revelation **11** description, information **12** announcement, intelligence

NEWSMONGER: **6** gossip **7** tattler **8** busybody, reporter

NEWSPAPER: **5** daily, sheet **6** herald, weekly **7** gazette, journal, tabloid **8** biweekly **9** community **10** periodical **11** publication **12** metropolitan
edition: **4** home, mail **5** extra, final **6** Sunday **7** evening, morning **8** Saturday **9** afternoon

NEW TESTAMENT: **5** Bible
books: **4** Acts, John, Jude, Luke, Mark **5** James, Peter, Titus **6** Romans **7** Hebrews, Matthew, Timothy **8** Philemon **9** Ephesians, Galatians **10** Colossians, Revelation **11** Corinthians, Philippians **13** Thessalonians
Gospels: **4** John, Luke, Mark **7** Matthew

NEW YORK:
bird: **8** bluebird
capital: **6** Albany
cities: **7** Buffalo, New York **8** Syracuse **9** Rochester
explorer: **6** Hudson **9** Champlain **9** Verrazano
features: **9** Catskills **10** Fire Island, Long Island **11** Adirondacks
flower: **4** rose
native: **9** New Yorker
nickname: **6** Empire **9** Excelsior
tree: **10** sugar maple
water: **4** Erie **6** Geneva, Hudson, Mohawk, Placid **7** Ontario **8** Delaware **9** Champlain **10** St. Lawrence **12** Niagara Falls

NEW YORK CITY:
airports: **3** JFK **7** Kennedy **9** La Guardia
also called: **8** Big Apple
boroughs: **5** Bronx **6** Queens **8** Brooklyn **9** Manhattan **12** Staten Island

explorer: **6** Hudson **9** Verrazano
features: **8** Broadway **15** Statue of Liberty **16** World Trade Center **19** Empire State Building
native: **9** New Yorker
place: **7** New York
water: **9** East River **11** Hudson River

NEW ZEALAND:
animals: **4** mako **7** tuatara, tuatera
birds: **3** kea, moa, oii, poe, roa, tui **4** kaka, kiwi, koko, kulu, ruru, titi, weka **6** kakapo, takahe **7** apteryx, wrybill **8** bellbird
capital: **10** Wellington
cities: **5** Otaki, Taupo **6** Foxton, Oamaru, Picton, Timaru **7** Dunedin, Raetihi, Rotorua **8** Auckland, Hamilton **9** Ashburton, Greymouth, Masterton, Whangarei **10** Palmerston, Queenstown, Wellington **12** Christchurch
explorer: **4** Cook **6** Tasman
islands: **4** Cook, Niue, Otea **5** North, South **6** Bounty, Snares **7** Aukland, Chatham, Stewart, Tokelau **8** Auckland, Campbell, Kermadec **9** Antipodes **12** Great Barrier
lakes: **3** Ada **4** Gunn, Ohau **5** Hawea, Taupo **6** Pukaki, Sylvan, Tekapo, Wanaka **7** Brunner, Diamond, Kanieri, Okareka, Rotorua **8** Okataina, Paradise, Rotoaira, Wakatipu
languages: **5** Maori **7** English
monetary unit: **4** cent **6** dollar
mountains: **4** Alps, Cook, Eden, Flat, Owen **5** Allen, Chope, Lyall, Mitre, Ohope, Otari, Young **6** Egmont, Tasman **7** Pihanga, Ruapehu, Tauhera **8** Aspiring, Tauranga **9** Murchison **11** Remarkables
people: **5** Arawa, Dutch, Maori **7** British, Ringatu **10** Polynesian
rivers: **5** Leuin **6** Clutha **7** Manu Kau, Waikato **8** Kawakawa, Touranga, Wanganui
trees: **3** ake **4** hino, kopi, mako, miro, pelu, puka, rata, rimu, tawa, toro, toru **5** hinau, kauri, mahoe, maire, mapau, matai, ngaio **6** manuka, puriri, totara
volcanos: **6** Egmont **7** Ruapehu **9** Ngauruhoe

NEXT: **4** then **5** after **6** behind **7** closest, ensuing, nearest **9** adjoining, following, immediate **10** succeeding **12** subsequently

NEXT TO: **6** almost, beside **8** adjacent **9** adjoining, alongside, bordering **11** neighboring, practically

NEXUS: **3** tie **4** bond, core, link **5** union **6** center **7** network **10** connection

NIB: **3** pen, tip **4** beak, bill **5** point

NIBBLE: **3** eat **4** bite, chew, gnaw, peck, pick **5** crumb, snack, speck **6** morsel

NICARAGUA:
capital: **7** Managua
cities: **4** Leon **7** Corinto, El Bluff, Granada **9** Matagalpa **13** Puerto Cabezas
features: **6** Madera **9** Momotombo **11** Corn Islands **13** Mosquito Coast
language: **7** Spanish
monetary unit: **10** cordoba oro
native: **10** Nicaraguan
water: **4** Coco **7** Managua, San Juan **8** Tipitapa **9** Nicaragua **10** Fonseca Bay

NICE: **4** fine, good **5** exact, fussy, picky, swell **6** choosy, dainty, gentle, lovely, peachy, polite, proper, subtle, wanton **7** cordial, correct, elegant, finical, genteel, helpful, likable, precise, refined **8** accurate, charming, delicate, exacting, friendly, pleasant, pleasing, precious, skillful **9** agreeable, appealing, courteous, exquisite **10** delightful, discerning, fastidious, gratifying, particular, profligate **11** considerate, respectable, warmhearted

NICHE: **4** apse, nook **5** place, space **6** alcove, corner, cranny, hollow, recess **7** retreat **9** cubbyhole

NICK: **3** cut **4** chip, dent, dint, mark, slit **5** notch **7** scratch **11** indentation

NICKEL: **7** element

NICKNAME: **3** tag **5** label **6** agname, byword, handle **7** agnomen, moniker **8** cognomen **9** sobriquet
Abraham Lincoln: **9** Honest Abe
Al Capone: **8** Scarface
Andrew Jackson: **10** Old Hickory
Babe Ruth: **7** Bambino **12** Sultan of Swat
Charles Stratton: **8** Tom Thumb
Dwight Eisenhower: **3** Ike
Elizabeth I: **11** Virgin Queen
Elroy Hirsch: **9** Crazy Legs
Ernest Hemingway: **4** Papa
Erwin Rommel: **12** The Desert Fox
Frank Sinatra: **10** Ol' Blue Eyes
George Brummell: **4** Beau
Jimmy Durante: **7** Schnozz
Joe DiMaggio: **9** Joltin Joe
Joe Louis: **11** Brown Bomber
Martha Raye: **8** Big Mouth
Milton Berle: **11** Uncle Miltie
Napoleon Bonaparte: **5** Boney **14** Little Corporal
Oliver Cromwell: **8** Crum Hell
Queen Mary: **10** Bloody Mary
Richard I: **9** Lionheart
Richard Nixon: **10** Tricky Dick
Richard Starkey: **10** Ringo Starr
Robert Macgregor: **6** Rob Roy
Roy Bean: **12** Hanging Judge
Rudolph Valentino: **5** Sheik
Sydney Biddle Barrows: **14** Mayflower Madam
The Beatles: **7** Fab Four, Moptops
Thomas Jackson: **9** Stonewall
William Cody: **11** Buffalo Bill
Winston Churchill: **6** Winnie

NIFTY: **4** cool, neat **5** natty, sharp, smart, super, swell **6** peachy **7** stylish **8** terrific **9** excellent, marvelous **11** fashionable

NIGER:
capital: **6** Niamey
cities: **6** Maradi, Tahoua, Zinder
continent: **6** Africa
ethnic groups: **5** Hausa **6** Djerma, Fulani, Tuareg **7** Songhai
features: **5** Sahel **6** Sahara
languages: **5** Hausa **6** French, Fulani
monetary unit: **5** franc
water: **8** Lake Chad **10** River Niger

NIGERIA:
capital: **5** Lagos
cities: **4** Kano **5** Warri **6** Ibadan **7** Calabar **9** Ogbomosho **12** Port Harcourt
continent: **6** Africa
ethnic groups: **3** Ibo **5** Hausa **6** Fulani, Yoruba
features: **9** harmattan **10** rain forest
languages: **3** Ibo **5** Hausa **6** Yoruba **7** English
monetary unit: **5** naira
native: **8** Nigerian
water: **3** Oli **10** River Niger

NIGGARD: **5** cheap, miser, tight **6** stingy **8** scrimper **9** skinflint **10** avaricious **11** closefisted

NIGGARDLY: **4** mean **6** frugal, greedy, meager, scanty, stingy **7** miserly **8** grudging **10** avaricious **11** closefisted

NIGGLING: **5** fussy, petty **7** finicky **8** picayune, trifling

NIGH: **4** near **5** about, close **6** almost, beside, nearly **8** adjacent **11** neighboring, practically

NIGHT: **4** dusk **7** bedtime, evening, sundown **8** darkness, twilight

NIGHT BLINDNESS: **10** nyctalopia

NIGHTCLUB: **3** bar **4** spot **6** tavern **7** cabaret **9** honky-tonk **11** discotheque

NIGHTFALL: **3** eve **4** dusk **6** sunset **7** evening, sundown **8** gloaming, twilight

NIGHTINGALE: **6** thrush **7** warbler **8** philomel, songbird

NIGHTMARE: **5** demon, dream, fancy, fiend **6** horror, spirit, vision **7** incubus **8** succubus **12** apprehension

NIGHTSTICK: **4** club **5** baton, billy, staff **6** cudgel **8** bludgeon

NIHILISM: **5** chaos **7** anarchy **8** antheism, disorder **10** skepticism **11** lawlessness, repudiation **12** renunciation

NIL: **4** zero **5** nihil **6** naught **7** nothing **11** nonexistent

NILE:
also called: **6** Al-Bahr
dams: **5** Aulia, Gebel **6** Makwar **9** Aswan High
falls: **4** Owen **8** Victoria **9** Murchison
islands: **4** Roda
known as: **7** longest
lakes: **4** Tana **8** Victoria
parts: **4** Blue **5** White
ports: **4** Giza **5** Cairo, Luxor, Rejaf **6** Karnak **7** Memphis, Rosetta **8** Khartoum
tributaries: **6** Atbara, Kagera

NIMBLE: **4** deft, spry **5** agile, alert, brisk, fleet, quick, swift **6** active, adroit, clever, limber, lively **8** lissome, skillful **9** dexterous, sprightly

NIMBUS: **4** aura, halo **5** cloud, vapor **7** aureole **10** atmosphere

NIMROD: **6** hunter
father: **4** Cush
grandfather: **3** Ham
great grandfather: **4** Noah
kingdom: **6** Shinar

NINCOMPOOP: **4** boob, fool, jerk **5** idiot, moron, ninny **6** lummox, nitwit **8** imbecile **9** blockhead, simpleton

NIP: **3** cut, sip **4** bite, clip, dart, dash, dram, shot, snag, stop **5** blast, check, chill, clamp, drink, hurry, pinch, sever, snort, steal, sting **6** morsel, remove, snatch, thwart, twitch **7** curtail, squeeze **8** compress

NIPPER: **3** boy, lad **5** child **6** pliers **7** pincers **9** youngster

NIPPY: **4** cold **5** brisk, crisp, sharp **6** biting, chilly **7** cutting **8** freezing

NIRVANA: **3** joy **5** bliss **6** wisdom **7** harmony **8** paradise **9** condition, stability **10** compassion **12** emancipation

NITID: **6** bright, glossy, spruce **7** glowing, radiant **8** lustrous **11** resplendent

NITPICK: **4** carp **5** cavil **7** quibble **9** criticize

NITRATE: **4** salt **5** ester **6** sodium **8** compound **10** fertilizer

NITROGEN: **5** azote **7** element

NITTY-GRITTY: **4** crux, meat **5** heart **7** essence, lowdown **10** essentials

NITWIT: **4** dolt, dope, fool **5** dunce, idiot, ninny **7** pinhead **8** bonehead, imbecile **9** blockhead, simpleton **10** nincompoop

NIX: **4** veto **6** forbid, sprite **7** nothing, refusal

NOAH:
ark resting place: **6** Ararat
built: **3** ark
father: **6** Lamech
grandson: **4** Aram, Cush **6** Canaan
great grandson: **6** Nimrod
son: **3** Ham **4** Shem **7** Japheth
story of: **5** flood
symbol: **4** dove

NOBEL, ALFRED:
bequeathed: **10** Nobel Prize
invented: **8** dynamite
occupation: **7** chemist **8** engineer

NOBILITY: **7** dignity, peerage, royalty **8** eminence, prestige **9** integrity **11** aristocracy, exaltedness, magnanimity

NOBLE: **4** fine, free, good, just, pure **5** grand, ideal, lofty, moral, proud, regal **6** august, epical, heroic, kingly, lordly, worthy **7** eminent, ethical, exalted, gallant, queenly, stately, sublime **8** cavalier, elevated, generous, imperial, majestic, precious, princely, renowned, splendid, sterling **9** dignified, excellent, grandiose, honorable, righteous, venerated **10** idealistic, principled **11** illustrious, magnanimous, pureblooded **12** aristocratic **13** distinguished

NOBLEMAN: **4** duke, earl, lord **5** baron, count **6** knight, prince, varlet **7** baronet, emperor, grandee, marquis **8** archduke, viscount **9** gentleman, patrician **10** aristocrat

NOBLEWOMAN: **4** lady **5** queen **7** duchess, empress **8** baroness, contessa, countess, marquise, princess **9** marquises **11** archduchess, gentlewoman

NOBODY: **4** punk **5** scrub **6** cipher **7** upstart **9** jackstraw, nonentity

NOCTAMBULISM: **12** sleepwalking, somnambulism

NOCTURNAL: **5** night **7** nightly **9** nighttime

NOCUOUS: **6** deadly **7** harmful, noxious **8** damaging **9** dangerous, injurious

NOD: **3** bow, yes **4** bend, doze **5** agree, drift, sleep **6** beckon, drowse, motion, salute, signal **7** gesture, signify **8** approval, greeting **10** acceptance **11** acknowledge

NODE: **4** bump, knob, knot, lump **5** joint, point **6** growth, nodule **7** dilemma, granule **8** swelling **12** complication, protuberance

NOËL: **5** carol **8** yuletide **9** Christmas

NOGGIN: **3** cup, mug **4** head, pate **6** noddle

NOISE: **4** bang, boom, fuss, talk **5** blast, bruit, sound **6** babble, clamor, gossip, hubbub, racket, uproar **7** fanfare, thunder, yelling **8** shouting **9** commotion, explosion **11** pandemonium

NOISELESS: **4** mute **5** quiet, still **6** hushed, silent **8** deadened **9** inaudible

NOISEMAKER: **4** bell, horn **6** rattle **7** clapper, whistle

NOISOME: **4** foul, rank, vile **5** fetid, nasty **6** putrid, rancid **7** baneful, harmful, hurtful, noxious **8** stinking **9** dangerous, offensive, repulsive, revolting **10** disgusting, pernicious **11** destructive, distasteful, unwholesome

NOISY: **4** loud **6** lively **7** blatant, rackety, squeaky **8** clattery **9** clamorous, deafening, screaming, turbulent **10** boisterous, thunderous, tumultuous, vociferous **12** rambunctious

NOMAD: **6** roamer, roving **7** migrant **8** vagabond, wanderer **9** itinerant

NOMADIC: **8** drifting **9** itinerant, migratory, traveling, wandering **11** peripatetic

NOM DE PLUME: **5** alias **7** pen name **9** pseudonym

NOMENCLATURE: **4** list, name **8** glossary, language, taxonomy **9** catalogue, designate **10** vocabulary **11** appellation, designation, terminology **14** classification

NOMINAL: **4** mere **5** cheap, small **6** formal, slight **7** minimal, trivial **8** supposed **9** professed **10** ostensible **11** inexpensive, theoretical **13** insignificant

NOMINATE: **3** tap **4** call, name **5** elect, offer, slate **6** choose, select, submit **7** appoint, propose, specify **9** designate, recommend

NOMINEE: **7** hopeful **9** applicant, candidate

NONAGE: **5** youth **7** infancy **9** childhood **10** immaturity

NONBELIEVER: **5** pagan **7** atheist, doubter, heathen, infidel, skeptic **8** agnostic

NONCHALANT: **4** calm, cool, easy **5** blase **6** casual **7** offhand **8** careless **9** collected, easygoing, lethargic **11** indifferent, unemotional **13** imperturbable, lackadaisical

NONCOMBATANT: **8** chaplain, civilian

NONCOMMITTAL: **5** vague **7** evasive, neutral **8** reserved **9** ambiguous, tentative **10** indecisive, indefinite

NONCOMPLIANT: **6** unruly **8** stubborn **10** rebellious, unorthodox **11** belligerent, disobedient

NON COMPOS MENTIS: **6** insane **11** incompetent **14** not of sound mind

NONCONFORMIST: **5** rebel **6** hippie, weirdo **7** beatnik, dropout, oddball, radical **8** bohemian, maverick, renegade **9** dissenter, eccentric **10** unorthodox

NONCONFORMITY: **6** heresy **7** anomaly, dissent **9** disbelief, recusancy **10** dissidence **11** discordance, peculiarity

NONDESCRIPT: **4** dull **8** ordinary **11** commonplace, unmemorable **12** unimpressive **13** unexceptional

NONE: **3** nil **4** zero **5** zilch **7** nothing

NONENTITY: **4** zero **5** zilch **6** cipher, nobody **7** nothing **8** small fry **12** nonexistence

NONESSENTIAL: **7** trivial **8** deadwood **9** extrinsic **10** expendable, incidental **11** dispensable, unimportant, unnecessary **13** insignificant

NONESUCH: **7** paragon **8** paradigm **9** matchless, unequaled, unrivaled **12** unparalleled

NONETHELESS: **5** still **6** though **7** however **12** nevertheless

NONEXISTENT: **4** null **7** extinct, missing **8** baseless, imagined, mythical **9** fictional **10** groundless

NONOBSERVANCE: **6** laxity, slight **7** failure **9** disregard, violation **10** negligence

NO-NONSENSE: **4** hard **5** grave, rigid, stern **6** direct, strict **7** serious **9** demanding, efficient, practical **12** businesslike

NONPARTISAN: **4** fair, just **7** neutral **8** unbiased **9** equitable, impartial, objective **11** independent **12** unprejudiced

NONPLUS: **4** balk, faze **5** blank, stump **6** baffle, puzzle, rattle, stymie **7** confuse, fluster, perplex **8** bewilder, confound **9** dumbfound, embarrass, frustrate **10** disconcert

NONPROFESSIONAL: **4** laic, tyro **6** layman **7** amateur, dabbler **8** laywoman

NONRESISTANT: **4** meek **7** passive **8** tolerant, yielding **10** submissive

NONSENSE: **4** blah, bosh, bull, bunk, jive, junk, muck **5** folly, hooey, trash **6** antics, babble, bunkum, drivel, faddle, folder **7** baloney, blarney, blather, garbage, hogwash, inanity, rubbish, twaddle **8** flummery, malarkey, trumpery **9** absurdity, craziness, fandangle, frivolity, gibberish, poppycock, silliness **10** balderdash, flapdoodle, triviality **11** foolishness, jabberwocky, shenanigans

NONSENSICAL: **5** crazy, silly **6** absurd **7** asinine, foolish, idiotic **9** ludicrous **10** ridiculous **12** preposterous

NONSTOP: **6** direct **7** endless **8** constant **9** incessant **10** continuous **13** uninterrupted

NONVIOLENT: **6** irenic **7** passive **8** pacifist, peaceful

NOODLE: **4** bean, fool, head, pate **5** brain, dunce, gourd, ninny, pasta **6** noggin **9** blockhead, simpleton

NOOK: **4** cove, glen, hole **5** angle, niche **6** cavity, corner, cranny, recess **7** byplace, crevice, retreat **8** hideaway **9** cubbyhole

NOON: **4** apex **6** midday **8** meridian **12** twelve o'clock

NOOSE: **3** tie **4** bond, hang, loop, trap **5** hitch, lasso, snare **6** entrap, lariat **7** ensnare

NORM: **3** par **4** mean, rule **5** gauge, model, scale **6** median **7** average, pattern **8** standard **9** benchmark

NORMAL: **4** sane **5** sound, usual **6** common **7** average, natural, regular, routine, typical **8** expected, ordinary, standard, together **10** reasonable **11** traditional **12** compos mentis, conventional

NORMANDY:
capital: **5** Rollo
cities: **4** Caen **5** Rouen **6** Bayeux, Dieppe **7** Alencon, le Havre, Lixieux **9** Cherbourg, Deauville
features: **5** Omaha **6** Perche **9** Coteentin **10** Pays de Caux **12** Mont St Michel
kings/queens: **5** Rollo **7** Charles **14** Philip Augustus **19** William the Conqueror
place: **6** France
regions: **5** Basse, Haute
water: **14** English Channel

NORSE:
concerning: **6** Viking **8** Norseman, Teutonic **9** Icelandic, Norwegian **12** Scandinavian
explorer: **4** Eric
gods/goddesses: **3** Asa, Ase, Ran, Tiu, Tyr, Ull, Urd, Zio **4** Erda, Frey, Hler, Hoth, Loke, Loki, Odin, Surt, Thor, Vali **5** Aeger, Aegir, Baldr, Brage, Bragi, Donar, Freyr, Frigg, Gymir, Nanna, Othin, Vanir, Wodan, Woden, Wotan **6** Balder, Freyja, Frigga, Hoenir, Njorth, Surtur **7** Asynjur, Forsete, Forseti, Heimdal, Vitharr **9** Heimdallr, Hlorrithi
kings/queens: **4** Atli, Olaf

NORTH: **4** cold **5** polar **6** arctic

NORTH AMERICA:
cities: **7** Chicago, Detroit, Houston, New York, Toronto **8** Montreal **9** Monterrey, Vancouver **10** Los Angeles, Mexico City **11** Guadalajara **12** Philadelphia **13** Guatemala City
countries: **6** Canada, Mexico **9** Greenland **12** United States
explorers: **5** Cabot **8** Columbus

NORTH CAROLINA:
bird: **8** cardinal
capital: **7** Raleigh
cities: **9** Charlotte **10** Greensboro **12** Winston-Salem
features: **8** Cape Fear **9** Blue Ridge, Kitty Hawk **10** Great Smoky **11** Cape Lookout **12** Appalachians, Cape Hatteras **13** Roanoke Island
flower: **7** dogwood
nicknames: **7** Tar Heel **8** Old North **10** Turpentine
tree: **4** pine

water: **3** Haw, Tar **6** Phelps **7** Roanoke **8** Waccamaw

NORTH DAKOTA:
bird: **10** meadowlark
capital: **8** Bismarck
cities: **5** Fargo, Minot **10** Grand Forks
explorer: **9** Verendrye
features: **11** Garrison Dam, Peace Garden **14** Red River valley **15** Missouri Plateau
flower: **11** prairie rose
nicknames: **5** Sioux **11** Flickertail, Peace Garden
tree: **3** elm
water: **8** Missouri, Red River **9** Sakakawea

NORTHEASTER: **4** gale, wind **5** storm

NORTH KOREA:
capital: **9** Pyongyang
cities: **5** Nampo **6** Wonsan **8** Chongjin
continent: **4** Asia
ethnic groups: **6** Korean
language: **6** Korean
monetary unit: **3** won
water: **3** Nam **4** Yalu **7** Pacific

NORTH POLE:
concerning: **6** Arctic
explorer: **5** Peary

NORTH SEA:
arm: **9** Skagerrak
canal: **4** Kiel
joins: **12** Norwegian Sea **13** Strait of Dover
river: **5** Weser

NORTH STAR: **7** polaris **8** polestar

NORTH VIETNAM:
capital: **5** Hanoi

NORTHWEST TERRITORIES:
capital: **11** Yellowknife
country: **6** Canada
explorer: **7** Simpson **8** Franklin **9** Frobisher
features: **11** Miles Canyon
flower: **13** mountain avens
island: **6** Baffin
water: **5** James **6** Ungava **8** Amundsen **9** Baffin Bay, Hudson Bay, Mackenzie, Queen Maud **10** Coppermine, Coronation **13** Great Bear Lake **14** Great Slave Lake

NORWAY:
capital: **4** Oslo
cities: **6** Bergen **9** Stavanger, Trondheim
continent: **6** Europe
ethnic groups: **4** Lapp **6** Alpine, Baltic, Nordic **8** Germanic
features: **5** Sogne **6** fjords **8** Telemark **9** Hardanger **11** midnight sun **12** Arctic Circle **14** northern lights
languages: **4** Lapp **5** Norse **7** Finnish **9** Norwegian
monetary unit: **5** krone
native: **9** Norwegian
water: **3** Ena **4** Tana **6** Glomma **8** North Sea

NOSE: **3** pry, spy **4** beak, bill, conk, gift, poke **5** flair, knack, scent, smell, sniff, snoop, snoot, snout **6** detect, meddle, muffle, muzzle, nozzle **7** schnozz, smeller, sniffer **8** busybody **9** proboscis **11** investigate
variety: **3** pug **4** snub **5** Roman **7** Grecian **8** aquiline **9** retrousse

NOSE-DIVE: **3** dip **4** drop, skid **6** plunge **7** plummet

NOSEGAY: **4** posy **7** bouquet, flowers

NOSTALGIA: **7** longing **8** yearning **10** loneliness **12** homesickness, reminiscence **14** sentimentality

NOSTRADAMUS:
nationality: **6** French
occupation: **4** seer **6** author **7** prophet **9** physician **10** astrologer
wrote: **9** Centuries

NOSY: **6** prying **7** curious **8** snooping **9** intrusive **10** meddlesome **11** inquisitive

NOT: **3** nay **6** denial, hardly, nought **7** neither, refusal **8** negative **11** prohibition

NOTABLE: **3** VIP **5** baron, chief, mogul **6** bigwig, fabled, famous, leader **7** eminent, kingpin, magnate, storied **8** eventful, historic, luminary, somebody **9** celebrity, dignitary, memorable, superstar **10** noteworthy, remarkable **11** heavyweight, personality **13** distinguished

NOT ALIKE: **8** distinct **9** different **10** dissimilar **11** contrasting

NOTARIZE: **6** attest **7** certify **8** validate

NOTATION: **5** entry **6** record, system **7** marking **10** annotation, memorandum

NOT BRIGHT: **4** dark, dull **5** dense **6** cloudy **8** obscured

NOTCH: **3** cut, jab **4** dent, dint, gash, mark, nick, pass, step **5** level, score, tally **6** degree, groove, indent, record, scotch **7** serrate **8** incision, undercut **11** indentation

NOTE: **3** I.O.U., jot, key **4** bill, call, chit, heed, line, loan, mark, memo, name, song, tone, tune **5** draft, enter, money, pitch, scale, sound, token **6** billet, letter, minute, notice, record, remark, report, symbol **7** comment, epistle, message, missive, observe, voucher **8** annotate, currency, eminence, indicate, perceive, reminder, scribble, thank you **9** character, greenback **10** commentary, indication, memorandum, promissory, reputation **11** certificate, distinction, inscription, observation

NOTEBOOK: **3** log **5** diary **6** record **7** journal **8** register
types: **6** spiral **8** computer **9** looseleaf

NOTED: **6** famous **7** eminent **8** renowned **9** prominent **10** celebrated, recognized **11** illustrious **13** distinguished

NOTEWORTHY: **7** eminent, notable, special **9** important, memorable, prominent **10** meaningful, observable, remarkable **11** exceptional, outstanding, significant **12** considerable

NOTHING: **3** nil **4** free, null, zero **5** blank, nihil, zilch **6** cipher, naught, nought, trifle **7** useless **9** bagatelle, nonentity **12** unimportance

NOTHINGNESS: **4** void **5** death **6** vacuum **8** oblivion **9** emptiness

NOTICE: **3** ban, see **4** care, espy, heed, mark, mind, news, note, sign **5** greet, sense **6** advice, billet, caveat, poster, regard, remark **7** article, caution, comment, discern, leaflet, mention, observe, warning **8** apprisal, brochure, bulletin, citation, civility, obituary, pamphlet **9** attention, recognize **10** cognizance, disclosure, memorandum **11** acknowledge **12** announcement, proclamation **13** advertisement, consideration

NOTICEABLE: **5** clear **6** marked **7** evident, obvious, salient **8** distinct, striking **9** prominent **10** noteworthy, remarkable **11** conspicuous, outstanding, sensational **12** unmistakable

NOTIFY: **4** clue, post, tell, warn **5** brief **6** advise, inform, report, signal **7** apprise, declare, divulge, publish **8** acquaint, announce **9** broadcast, circulate **10** promulgate

NOTION: **4** clue, hint, idea, view, whim **5** fancy, image **6** belief, desire, theory, vagary **7** caprice, conceit, concept, inkling, insight, opinion, thought **9** intention **10** intimation **11** inclination **13** understanding

NOTORIETY: **4** fame **6** infamy, stigma **7** scandal **9** celebrity, publicity **10** reputation

NOTORIOUS: **3** bad **5** known **6** arrant, famous **7** blatant **8** apparent, flagrant, infamous **9** acclaimed **10** celebrated, scandalous, villainous **12** dishonorable, disreputable

NOT PARTICULARLY: **6** barely, hardly **8** scarcely

NOT QUITE: **6** almost, nearly

NOT REALLY: **8** doubtful **9** uncertain **12** questionable

NOTWITHSTANDING: **4** even **5** spite **7** against, howbeit, however **8** although **10** regardless **11** nonetheless **12** nevertheless

NOUN: **4** idea, name, word **5** place, thing **6** person
types: **6** common, proper **7** pronoun **8** personal

NOURISH: **4** feed, rear **5** nurse **6** foster, supply **7** cherish, develop, nurture, promote, support, sustain **8** maintain **9** cultivate, stimulate **10** administer, strengthen

NOURISHING: **6** hearty **9** healthful, wholesome **10** beneficial, nutritious

NOURISHMENT: **4** food, meat **7** ailment, support **8** nutrient **9** nutriment **10** provisions, sustenance

NOUVEAU RICHE: **7** parvenu, upstart **9** newly rich

NOVA SCOTIA:
capital: **7** Halifax
cities: **5** Truro **6** Sydney **9** Dartmouth
country: **6** Canada
explorer: **5** Cabot
features: **7** Fort Ann **10** Cabot Trail, Cape Breton
flower: **7** arbutus **9** mayflower
water: **5** Fundy

NOVEL: **3** new, odd **4** book **5** fresh, story **6** daring, modern, unique **7** fiction, romance, unusual **8** original, uncommon **9** different, paperback **10** avant-garde, innovative, newfangled **11** theoretical **12** contemporary

NOVELTY: **3** fad **6** bauble, change, gewgaw, oddity **7** trinket **10** innovation, knickknack **11** contraption

NOVICE: **4** punk, tyro **5** plebe, pupil **6** rookie **7** amateur, convert, learner, student, trainee **8** beginner, neophyte, newcomer **9** greenhorn **10** apprentice, tenderfoot

NOW: **4** soon **5** today **6** pronto **7** present **8** directly, promptly **9** forthwith, instantly **11** immediately **12** straightaway

NOW AND THEN: **6** seldom **9** sometimes **12** infrequently, occasionally, periodically

NOXIOUS: **5** fetid, toxic **6** deadly, lethal, nocent, putrid **7** baneful, harmful, hurtful, nocuous, noisome **8** stinking, virulent **9** dangerous, injurious, poisonous, revolting, unhealthy **10** pernicious **11** destructive, unwholesome

NUANCE: **5** shade, touch **6** degree, nicety **7** soupcon **8** subtlety **9** gradation, variation **10** refinement, suggestion

NUB: **4** bump, core, crux, gist, knob, knot, lump **5** bulge, point **6** kernel **7** essence, nucleus **9** substance **12** protuberance

NUCLEAR PARTICLE: **6** proton **7** neutron

NUCLEUS: **3** nub **4** core, crux, ring, seed **5** focus, spark **6** center, kernel

NUDE: **3** raw **4** bare **5** naked, stark **6** unclad **7** exposed **8** stripped **9** au naturel, unclothed, uncovered, undressed

NUDGE: **3** jab, jog **4** bump, poke, prod, push **5** elbow, shove, touch **6** jostle

NUGATORY: **4** idle, vain **6** futile, hollow **7** invalid, trivial, useless **8** trifling **9** worthless **11** ineffectual

NUGGET: **4** gold, hunk, lump, mass **5** chunk, clump

NUISANCE: **4** pest **5** thorn **6** bother, burden, plague **7** problem **8** headache **9** annoyance **10** irritation **12** exasperation **13** inconvenience

NULL: **4** void, zero **7** invalid, nothing, nullify, useless **9** worthless **11** ineffectual, nonexistent **13** insignificant

NULLIFY: **4** null, undo, veto, void **5** annul **6** cancel, negate, offset, renege, repeal, revoke, squash **7** abolish, rescind **8** abrogate **10** counteract, invalidate, neutralize

NULLITY: **4** zero **5** zilch **6** cipher, naught **7** nothing **9** nonentity

NUMB: **4** dead, dull, stun **5** blunt **6** deaden, freeze, stupid, torpid **8** paralyze **9** unfeeling **10** insensible **11** desensitize, indifferent, insensitive **12** anesthetized

NUMBER: **3** sum **4** herd, host, many, slew **5** array, bunch, count, crowd, digit, flock, group, horde, prime, quota, scads, score, swarm, tally, total **6** amount, bundle, cipher, factor, figure, myriad, symbol **7** compute, decimal, integer, numeral, several **8** cardinal, fraction, numerate, quantity **9** aggregate, calculate, character, multitude, numerator **10** percentage, proportion **11** denominator

NUMBERED: **5** fated **6** doomed, marked **7** limited **8** totalled **9** specified

NUMBERLESS: **6** myriad **7** endless **8** infinite, numerous **9** unlimited **12** immeasurable, incalculable

NUMBER ONE: **4** main **5** first **7** oneself **8** champion, dominant, foremost **9** important, numero uno

NUMERAL: **5** digit **6** cipher, figure, letter, number, symbol **7** integer

NUMERATE: **4** list **5** count, tally, total **6** number **9** calculate

NUMEROUS: **4** lots, many **5** large **6** untold **7** copious, diverse, several **8** abundant, infinite, multiple **9** extensive, plentiful **10** voluminous

NUMSKULL: **4** dolt, fool, jerk **5** dunce, idiot, ninny **6** nitwit **8** bonehead, imbecile **9** blockhead **10** nincompoop **11** knucklehead

NUN: **6** abbess, sister, vestal **7** devotee **8** prioress, votaress **9** anchorite, postulant

NUNCIO: **8** delegate, diplomat **9** messenger **10** ambassador **14** representative

NUNNERY: **5** abbey, order **7** convent **9** monastery **10** sisterhood

NUPTIAL: **6** bridal **7** marital, wedding **8** espousal, hymeneal **9** connubial **11** matrimonial

NURSE: **4** care, feed, rear, tend **5** nanny **6** attend, cradle, foster, harbor, suckle **7** cherish, nourish, nurture, promote **9** cultivate

NURSERY: **6** creche **8** playroom **9** preschool **10** greenhouse

NURTURE: **4** feed, rear, tend **5** nurse, raise, teach, train **6** foster, uphold **7** bolster, cherish, develop, educate, nourish, support **9** cultivate **10** strengthen

NUT: **3** bur, lug **4** core, head, kola, kook **5** acorn, betel, crank, hazel, loony, pecan **6** almond, cashew, cuckoo, maniac, peanut **7** fanatic, filbert, hickory, lunatic, oddball, utricle **8** crackpot **9** eccentric, pistachio, screwball **10** enthusiast, psychopath

NUTMEG STATE: **11** Connecticut

NUTRIMENT: **4** food **7** aliment, support **10** provisions, sustenance **11** nourishment

NUTRITION: **4** diet, food **10** provisions, sustenance **11** nourishment

NUTRITIOUS: **7** healthy **8** balanced **9** wholesome **10** nourishing, salubrious

NUTS: **3** mad **4** wild **5** batty, crazy, loony, nutty **6** insane **7** bananas, bonkers, touched **8** demented, deranged **9** eccentric **10** unbalanced

NUZZLE: **4** push **5** nudge **6** caress, cuddle, fondle, nestle **7** snuggle

NYMPH: **4** girl **5** deity, fairy, naiad, siren, sylph, woman **6** damsel, female, maiden, sprite **7** mermaid
lake: **5** naiad
mountain: **5** oread
sea: **6** nereid
tree: **5** dryad **9** hamadryad

O

OAF: **4** boob, boor, clod, dolt, fool, goof, goon, jerk, lout, lump **5** clown, dunce, idiot, moron **6** lummox, nitwit **8** bonehead, dumbbell **9** blockhead, foundling, simpleton **10** nincompoop

OAK: **4** tree, wood **5** shrub
color: **5** brown
fruit: **5** acorn
genus: **7** Quercus
variety: **3** bur, red **4** bear, live **5** black, holly, scrub, white **6** canyon, laurel, poison, willow **7** scarlet, western **8** bluejack, chestnut **9** blackjack **11** huckleberry

OAR: **3** row **4** pole **5** blade, rower, scull, sweep **6** paddle, propel
fulcrum: **7** oarlock
horizontal: **7** feather
oarsman: **5** rower **7** sculler **8** helmsman **9** gondolier
part: **4** grip, loom, stop **5** blade, shaft **6** sheath
types: **5** spade **6** needle

OASIS: **3** spa **4** wadi **5** haven **6** garden, refuge, relief **9** sanctuary

OAT: **5** grain, grass **6** cereal
genus: **5** avena

OATH: **3** vow **4** bond **5** curse, swear **6** appeal, pledge **7** promise **8** contract **9** affidavit, expletive, profanity, swearword, testimony **10** adjuration, obligation **11** affirmation

OATMEAL: **4** food **6** cereal, pablum **8** porridge

OBDURATE: **4** firm, hard **5** cruel, rigid, rough **6** rugged **7** adamant, callous **8** hardened, stubborn **9** immovable, obstinate, pigheaded, unbending, unfeeling **10** headstrong, impenitent, inflexible, insensible, persistent, unshakable, unyielding **11** hardhearted, intractable, unemotional

OBEDIENT: **4** tame **5** loyal **6** docile **7** abiding, duteous, dutiful, heedful, mindful, obeying **8** amenable, yielding **9** attentive, compliant, tractable **10** respectful, submissive **11** acquiescent

OBEISANCE: **3** bow **5** honor **6** curtsy, esteem, fealty, homage, kowtow, salaam **7** gesture, loyalty **9** deference, reverence **10** salutation, submission

OBELISK: **4** mark **5** pylon, shaft, tower **6** column, dagger, needle, pillar **8** monolith, monument

OBESE: **3** fat **5** heavy, plump, pudgy **6** chubby, fleshy, rotund **9** corpulent **10** overweight

OBEY: **4** mind **5** yield **6** accept, comply, follow, submit **7** conform, observe, respect **9** acquiesce

OBFUSCATE: **3** dim **4** blur **5** cloud **6** darken, garble, muddle, puzzle **7** confuse, obscure, perplex **8** bewilder

OBITER DICTUM: **6** remark **7** comment, opinion

OBITUARY: **6** eulogy **9** necrology **11** death notice **12** announcement

OBJECT: **3** aim, end **4** duty, goal, item, mark **5** argue, cavil, point, thing **6** design, doodad, gadget, intent, motive, oppose, reason, target, victim **7** dispute, essence, mission, protest, purpose **8** function **9** challenge, principle **10** disapprove **11** expostulate, thingamajig

OBJECTION: **5** cavil, demur, gripe **6** oppose **7** protest **8** argument, demurral **9** challenge, exception

OBJECTIONABLE: **4** vile **9** abhorrent, loathsome, offensive, repellent, revolting **10** deplorable, unpleasant **11** exceptional, undesirable **12** disagreeable, unacceptable **13** reprehensible

OBJECTIVE: **3** aim, end **4** duty, fair, goal, just **6** motive, target **7** mission, purpose **8** straight, unbiased **9** impartial, intention **12** unprejudiced

OBJET D'ART: **5** curio **6** bauble, gewgaw **7** bibelot, trinket

OBJURGATE: **5** abuse, chide, scold **6** berate, rebuke **7** reprove **8** execrate **9** castigate

OBLATION: **4** gift **8** offering **9** sacrifice **12** presentation

OBLIGATED: **5** bound **6** forced **8** indebted, required **9** committed

OBLIGATION: **3** vow **4** bond, debt, duty, loan, must, oath, onus **6** burden, pledge **7** promise **8** contract, mortgage, warranty **9** agreement, guarantee, liability **10** commitment, compulsion **11** requirement **12** indebtedness **14** responsibility

OBLIGATORY: **7** binding **8** enforced, required **9** essential, mandatory, necessary **10** compulsory **11** unavoidable

OBLIGE: **4** help **5** favor, force **6** assist, compel, please **7** gratify, require **8** obligate **9** constrain **10** contribute **11** accommodate, necessitate

OBLIQUE: **4** awry, bent **5** askew, cross, vague **6** angled, sloped, tilted **7** crooked, evasive, pitched **8** diagonal, inclined, indirect, sidelong, sideways, sidewise, slanting **9** underhand **10** backhanded, roundabout

OBLITERATE: **4** blot, raze **5** erase, waste **6** cancel, delete, efface **7** abolish, destroy, expunge **9** eliminate **10** annihilate, extinguish **11** exterminate

OBLIVION: **5** limbo **6** pardon **7** amnesty **9** emptiness, obscurity **11** nothingness **12** nonexistence **13** forgetfulness

OBLIVIOUS: **5** blind **7** unaware **9** unwitting **10** unnoticing **11** inattentive, preoccupied, unconscious **12** absentminded, disregardful

OBLONG: **4** oval **7** angular **9** elongated **10** elliptical **11** rectangular

OBLOQUY: **5** odium, shame **6** infamy **7** calumny, censure **8** contempt, disgrace, dishonor, ignominy **9** aspersion, invective **10** defamation **12** vilification

OBNOXIOUS: **4** foul, loud, vile **5** nasty **6** liable **7** hateful **8** annoying **9** abhorrent, offensive, repugnant, repulsive **10** detestable, unpleasant **13** reprehensible

OBSCENE: **4** foul, lewd, rank **5** bawdy, crude, dirty, gross, lurid, nasty **6** coarse, filthy, impure, smutty, vulgar **7** immoral, profane, raunchy **8** indecent **9** loathsome, offensive, repugnant, repulsive **10** disgusting, lascivious, licentious **11** foulmouthed **12** pornographic

OBSCURE: **4** blot, dark, hazy, hide, mask, veil **5** befog, blind, block, cloak, cloud, cover, foggy, murky, vague **6** cloudy, darken, gloomy, hidden, mystic, remote, screen, shield **7** becloud, blurred, conceal, confuse, cryptic, falsify, shadowy, unclear, unknown **8** disguise, mystical, puzzling, secluded **9** ambiguous, difficult, enigmatic, equivocal, forgotten, secretive, uncertain, undefined **10** caliginous, camouflage, indistinct, overshadow **11** complicated, unimportant **12** unnoticeable

OBSEQUIES: **5** rites **7** funeral, service **8** ceremony

OBSEQUIOUS: **5** slick **6** menial **7** fawning, servile, slavish **8** cowering, obedient, toadying **9** attentive, compliant, groveling, kowtowing **10** submissive **11** bootlicking, subservient, sycophantic

OBSERVANCE: **4** form, mark, rite **6** custom, regard, ritual **7** service **8** ceremony, practice **9** attention, formality, tradition **11** celebration, observation

OBSERVANT: **4** keen **5** alert, aware **7** mindful **8** vigilant, watchful **9** attentive **10** discerning, perceptive

OBSERVATION: **4** note, view **5** probe, study **6** notice, remark, survey **7** autopsy, comment, finding **8** scrutiny **9** attention, discovery **10** commentary, monitoring **11** examination **12** surveillance

OBSERVATORY: **5** tower **7** lookout **10** watchtower
famous: **4** Hale, Lick **6** Yerkes **7** Palomar, Whipple **11** Mount Wilson

OBSERVE: **3** eye, see **4** espy, heed, keep, look, mark, note, obey, spot, view **5** catch, honor, sight, study, watch **6** adhere, behold, comply, detect, follow, notice, regard, remark **7** comment, discern, monitor, respect, witness **8** perceive **9** celebrate, solemnize **11** commemorate

OBSESSED: **5** beset **6** dogged, hooked **7** fixated, haunted **8** consumed **9** dominated, engrossed **10** controlled, infatuated

OBSESSION: **5** craze, mania **6** fetish, phobia **7** craving, passion **8** fixation **10** attraction, compulsion **11** fascination, infatuation **13** preoccupation

OBSOLETE: **3** old, out **5** dated, passe **7** ancient, archaic, extinct, outworn **8** outmoded, timeworn **9** out-of-date **10** antiquated **12** old-fashioned

OBSTACLE: **3** bar **4** bump, snag **5** block, catch, hitch **6** hurdle **7** barrier **8** blockade, handicap **9** hindrance **10** difficulty, impediment **11** obstruction, vicissitude

OBSTINATE: **5** sulky, tough **6** dogged, mulish, sullen, unruly **7** staunch, willful **8** contrary, obdurate, perverse, stubborn **9** crotchety, pigheaded, steadfast, unbending **10** bullheaded, determined, headstrong, inflexible, muleheaded, persistent, refractory **11** intractable, opinionated **12** cantankerous, pertinacious, recalcitrant

OBSTREPEROUS: **4** loud **5** noisy **6** unruly **7** defiant, raucous **9** clamorous **10** boisterous, vociferous

OBSTRUCT: **3** bar, dam **4** clog, curb, plug, stop **5** beset, block, check, choke, close, delay **6** arrest, hamper, hinder, impede, oppose, retard, screen, shroud, thwart **7** barrier, congest, inhibit, prevent **8** blockade, encumber **9** barricade, interfere, interrupt **10** filibuster

OBSTRUCTION: **4** snag **5** delay, hitch **6** hurdle **7** barrier **8** gridlock, obstacle **9** hindrance, roadblock **10** difficulty, impediment **11** restriction

OBTAIN: **3** get, win **4** earn, gain, reap, take **5** reach **6** attain, gather, secure, sponge **7** achieve, acquire, capture, collect, procure, receive, succeed **8** purchase

OBTRUDE: **6** impose **7** intrude **8** infringe **9** interfere

OBTRUSIVE: **5** brash, pushy **7** forward, obvious, pushing **9** intrusive **10** aggressive, meddlesome, noticeable, protruding **11** impertinent **12** presumptuous

OBTUSE: **4** dull **5** blunt, crass, dense, round **6** opaque, stupid **8** ignorant **11** insensitive

OBVERSE: **4** face **5** front **8** opposite **10** complement **11** counterpart

OBVIATE: **4** ward **5** avert, avoid, dodge **7** prevent **8** preclude **9** forestall, interfere, intervene **10** circumvent

OBVIOUS: **5** clear, lucid, overt, plain **6** patent **7** blatant, evident, glaring, visible **8** apparent, distinct, manifest, palpable **11** conspicuous **12** unmistakable

OCCASION: **4** hint, time **5** event **6** chance, excuse, moment, reason **7** grounds, instant **8** ceremony, function, incident **9** condition, gathering, happening, milestone **11** celebration, opportunity

OCCASIONAL: **4** rare **5** stray **6** random, scarce **8** sporadic **9** scattered **10** infrequent

OCCASIONALLY: **6** hardly, rarely **9** sometimes **11** irregularly **12** periodically

OCCIDENTAL: **7** Western **9** Hesperian, Westerner

OCCLUDE: **4** clog, plug, seal **5** block, close **6** absorb, impede **7** prevent **8** obstruct

OCCULT: **5** eerie, magic, weird **6** arcane, hidden, secret, voodoo **7** cryptic, psychic **8** esoteric, mystical **9** concealed, recondite **10** mysterious **11** inscrutable, underground **12** supernatural

OCCUPANCY: **6** tenure **10** habitation, occupation

OCCUPANT: **6** inmate, lessee, renter, tenant **7** denizen, dweller **8** resident **10** inhabitant

OCCUPATION: **3** job **4** line, work **5** trade **6** career, metier, racket, tenure **7** calling, control, pursuit, seizure **8** business, industry, takeover, vocation **9** occupancy **10** employment, habitation, livelihood, profession

OCCUPIED: **4** busy **7** engaged, settled **8** absorbed **9** engrossed, inhabited, populated

OCCUPY: **4** busy, fill, take **5** dwell, seize **6** absorb, employ, engage, reside, tenant **7** fulfill, immerse, inhabit, involve, overrun, possess **8** populate **9** establish

OCCUR: **4** come, pass **5** exist **6** appear, arrive, befall, betide, chance, happen, result, strike **9** transpire **11** eventualize, materialize

OCCURRENCE: **4** case **5** event **6** affair **7** episode **8** accident, incident, occasion **9** condition, encounter, happening, situation **11** development **12** circumstance

OCEAN: **3** sea **4** brim, deep, main **5** brine, drink, water **6** Arctic, Indian **7** Pacific **8** Atlantic, vastness
biggest: **7** Pacific
movement: **4** tide
smallest: **6** Arctic

OCEANIA:
islands: **4** Fiji, Guam **5** Tonga **6** Hawaii, Malaya, Midway **7** Solomon, Western **8** Bora-Bora **9** Australia, Melanesia, New Guinea, Polynesia **10** Micronesia, New Zealand **12** New Caledonia, Western Samoa
located: **12** South Pacific

OCEANIC: **4** vast **6** marine **7** aquatic, pelagic **8** maritime, nautical **9** seafaring, thalassic

OCELOT: **3** cat **7** leopard, wildcat

OCTAVE: **4** cask, note, tone **5** eight, scale **8** interval

OCTAVIA:
brother: **8** Augustus
husband: **4** Nero **6** Antony

OCTOPUS: **7** mollusk **9** devilfish **10** cephalopod
genus: **7** octopus
tentacles: **5** eight

OCULAR: **3** eye **5** optic, sight **6** visual **7** visible **10** ophthalmic

ODD: **4** lone, rare **5** droll, funny, queer, weird **6** quaint, uneven, unique **7** bizarre, curious, offbeat, strange, unusual **8** abnormal, atypical, fanciful, freakish, peculiar, uncommon, unpaired **9** different, eccentric, irregular, unmatched **10** occasional

ODDBALL: **4** kook **6** misfit, oddity, weirdo **7** strange **8** crackpot, peculiar **9** eccentric

ODDITY: **5** quirk **7** anomaly **9** curiosity **10** phenomenon **11** abnormality **12** eccentricity, idiosyncrasy, irregularity **13** unnaturalness

ODDS: **4** edge **5** ratio **6** chance, degree **8** handicap, variance **9** advantage **10** likelihood, percentage **13** probabilities

ODDS AND ENDS: **4** bits, olio **6** jumble, motley, scraps **7** mixture **8** remnants, sundries **9** leftovers, potpourri **10** assortment, hodgepodge, miscellany

ODE: **4** epic, hymn, poem, song **5** lyric, psalm, verse **6** ballad, melody **8** canticle

ODIN: **5** Norse, Othin, Wodan, Woden
brother: **4** Vili
children: **3** Tyr **4** Hodr, Thor, Vali **5** Baldr **6** Balder, Baldur
father: **3** Bor
god of: **3** art, war **4** dead **6** wisdom **7** culture
home: **9** Gladsheim
horse: **8** Sleipner
magic ring: **8** Draupnir
maiden: **8** Valkyrie
mother: **6** Bestla
raven: **5** Hugin, Munin
spear: **7** Gungnir
throne: **10** Hlidskjalf
wife: **4** Fria, Rind **5** Frigg
wolf: **4** Geri **5** Freki

ODIOUS: **4** evil, foul, mean, vile **6** horrid, putrid, rotten **7** hateful, heinous, hideous **8** horrible, infamous, terrible **9** abhorrent, loathsome, obnoxious, offensive, repugnant, revolting, sickening **10** abominable, detestable, disgusting, forbidding

ODIUM: **4** blot, spot **5** shame, stain **6** hatred, malice, stigma **8** contempt, disgrace, dishonor **9** antipathy, disesteem **12** condemnation **14** disapprobation

ODOR: 4 fume, funk, tang **5** aroma, fumet, nidor, scent, smell, stink **6** esteem, flavor, repute, stench **7** bouquet, essence, perfume **8** effluvia **9** fragrance, redolence **10** reputation

ODOROUS: 4 dank, rank **5** balmy **6** smelly **7** pungent **8** aromatic, fragrant

ODYSSEUS: 7 Ulysses
dog: **5** Argus
father: **7** Laertes
herb: **4** moly
kingdom: **6** Ithaca
mother: **9** Anticleia
poem: **5** Iliad **7** Odyssey
son: **9** Telegonus **10** Telemachus **11** Polyporthis
war: **9** Trojan War
wife: **8** Penelope

ODYSSEY: 8 epic poem
author: **5** Homer
character: **4** Zeus **5** Arete, Argus, Circe **6** Athena, Helios, Hermes, Nestor **7** Calypso, Cyclops, Eumaeus, Ulysses **8** Alcinous, Menelaus, Nausicaa, Odysseus, Penelope, Poseidon, Tiresias **9** Anticleia **10** Polyphemus, Telemachus **11** Lotus-eaters **14** Laestrygonians

OEDIPUS:
daughter: **6** Ismene **8** Antigone
father: **5** Laius
foster father: **7** Polybus
foster mother: **8** Periboea
killed: **5** Laius **6** father
kingdom: **6** Thebes
married: **6** mother **7** Jocasta
mother: **7** Jocasta
son: **8** Eteocles **9** Polynices **10** Polyneices

OFF: 4 away, gone, slim **5** apart, aside, crazy, slack, wrong **6** abroad, absent, remote **7** distant, farther, removed **8** canceled, launched **9** eccentric, incorrect, postponed

OFFAL: 4 junk **5** trash, waste **6** debris, refuse **7** carrion, garbage, leaving, remains, rubbish

OFF-BALANCE: 5 topsy **6** uneven **8** lopsided, unsteady

OFF BASE: 5 wrong **8** mistaken **9** erroneous, incorrect

OFFBEAT: 3 odd **5** weird **6** unique **7** bizarre, strange, unusual **8** peculiar **9** different, eccentric

OFF-CENTER: 5 askew **7** strange **8** unsteady **9** eccentric, irregular **10** unbalanced

OFF-COLOR: 4 blue, lewd, racy **5** dirty, salty, spicy **6** purple, risque, vulgar **7** obscene **9** offensive **10** indelicate, suggestive

OFFEND: 3 sin, vex **4** harm, hurt, miff, zing **5** abuse, anger, annoy, pique, shock, upset **6** appall, attack, insult, nettle, revolt **7** disturb, mortify, outrage **8** dishonor, irritate, trespass **9** aggravate, displease **10** antagonize, transgress

OFFENDER: 5 crook **6** sinner **7** culprit **8** criminal

OFFENSE: 4 huff, tort **5** crime, fault, guilt **6** attack, breach, charge, felony **7** affront, assault, misdeed, umbrage **8** delictum, trespass **9** indignity, onslaught, violation **10** aggression, peccadillo, wrongdoing **11** delinquency, misdemeanor

OFFENSIVE: 4 foul, push, rank, rude, vile **5** fetid, gross, nasty **6** attack, coarse, horrid **7** assault, fulsome, hideous, noisome, obscene **8** gruesome, horrible, invading, invasion, off-color, storming **9** appalling, loathsome, obnoxious, repugnant, repulsive, revolting **10** aggressive, disgusting, nauseating, unpleasant **11** distasteful **12** disagreeable

OFFER: **3** bid **4** show **6** extend, feeler, pledge, reward, submit, tender **7** advance, attempt, commend, furnish, present, proffer, propine, propose, suggest **8** overture, proposal **9** ultimatum, volunteer **10** invitation

OFFERING: **4** alms, gift **7** charity, present, tribute **8** donation, oblation **9** sacrifice **12** contribution

OFFHAND: **4** curt **5** hasty **6** abrupt, casual, chance **8** careless, cavalier, informal **9** impromptu, unplanned **10** improvised **11** extemporary, spontaneous, unrehearsed

OFFICE: **3** job **4** duty, post, shop **5** berth, place **6** agency, bureau **7** service, station **8** building, business, capacity, function, position **9** bailiwick, situation **10** commission, department, occupation **11** appointment, workstation **14** responsibility

employee: **5** clerk **6** typist **9** secretary **10** bookkeeper, keypuncher **12** receptionist **13** data processor

equipment: **3** fax **4** desk **5** chair **6** copier **8** computer **9** telephone **10** calculator, typewriter **13** word processor

seeker: **7** hopeful, nominee **9** candidate

types: **3** box, law **4** bank **7** doctor's **8** business, dentist's **9** brokerage, insurance **10** accountant, real estate **12** governmental, journalistic **13** psychiatrist's

OFFICER: **4** aide **5** agent **7** captain, colonel, general, manager **8** director, official **9** executive, president, secretary, treasurer **10** lieutenant **13** administrator

army: **5** major **7** captain, colonel, general **8** adjutant, chaplain, sergeant **9** brigadier **10** lieutenant **13** quartermaster **14** surgeon general

law-enforcement: **3** cop **5** chief **7** bailiff, marshal, sheriff **9** constable, detective, patrolman, policeman **11** patrolwoman, policewoman

navy: **4** mate **6** ensign, mister **7** admiral, captain **9** commander, commodore **10** lieutenant

OFFICIAL: **4** aide, dean **5** agent, envoy, judge, mayor **6** formal, leader, umpire **7** genuine, manager, officer, referee **8** alderman, approved, bona fide, chairman, director, endorsed, minister **9** authentic, canonical, certified, constable, dignitary, executive, president, selectman **10** alderwoman, ambassador, authorized, bureaucrat, chancellor, councilman, legitimate, magistrate, sanctioned **11** comptroller, selectwoman **12** commissioner, councilwoman, notary public **13** administrator, authoritative **14** representative

OFFICIATE: **4** head **5** chair **6** direct, govern, umpire **7** command, oversee, preside, referee **8** moderate, regulate

OFFICIOUS: **4** busy **5** pushy **8** arrogant, impudent, informal, meddling, snooping **9** intrusive **10** impersonal, meddlesome, unofficial **11** efficacious, impertinent, interfering

OFFSET: **5** ledge **6** recess, redeem **7** account, balance **8** equalize **10** compensate, complement, counteract, neutralize

OFFSHOOT: **5** scion **6** branch, sprout **7** spin-off **9** by-product, outgrowth **10** derivative, descendant, subsidiary **11** consequence

OFFSPRING: **3** kid, son **4** heir, seed **5** brood, child, fruit, issue, scion, young **6** family, litter, result **7** outcome, produce, product, progeny

8 children, daughter **9** youngster **10** descendant, generation

OFF THE CUFF: **9** impromptu **11** spontaneous

OFF THE RECORD: **6** secret **7** private **10** restricted **11** undisclosed **12** confidential

OFTEN: **4** much **6** common **8** frequent **9** generally **10** constantly, frequently, repeatedly **11** continually

OGLE: **3** eye **4** gape, gaze, leer, look **5** stare **6** glance

OGRE: **5** beast, demon, fiend, giant, troll **6** tyrant **7** monster

OHIO:
bird: **8** cardinal
capital: **8** Columbus
cities: **5** Akron **6** Canton, Dayton, Toledo **9** Cleveland **10** Cincinnati, Youngstown
explorer: **7** La Salle
features: **12** Serpent Mound **18** Allegheny Mountains
flower: **9** carnation
nickname: **7** Buckeye
tree: **7** buckeye
water: **5** Miami **8** Lake Erie **9** Ohio River

OIL: **3** fat, gas **4** balm, coat, fuel, lube **5** cream, smear **6** anoint, chrism, grease **7** lanolin **9** lubricate, petroleum
products: **7** bitumen **8** gasoline, kerosene **9** chemicals **10** diesel fuel, lubricants, natural gas
types: **4** corn, palm **5** crude, fatty, motor, olive, whale **6** animal, butter, castor, sesame **7** cooking, linseed, machine, mineral, soybean **8** cod-liver **9** vegetable **10** cottonseed **11** lubricating

OILY: **4** glib, rich **5** bland, fatty, slick, suave **6** greasy, oleose, smooth **7** fulsome **8** slippery, unctuous **9** plausible **10** flattering, oleaginous

OINTMENT: **4** balm, nard **5** cream, salve **6** cerate, chrism, lotion, remedy **7** unguent **8** dressing, liniment, medicine **9** spikenard

OKAY: **3** yes **4** fine, pass **6** agreed, ratify **7** approve, consent **8** blessing **9** authorize **10** acceptable, permission

OKLAHOMA:
bird: **10** flycatcher
capital: **12** Oklahoma City
cities: **4** Enid **5** Tulsa **6** Lawton, Norman
explorer: **10** de Coronado
features: **6** Ozarks **17** Canadian mountains
flower: **9** mistletoe
Indians: **4** Otoe, Waco **5** Creek **7** Choctaw, Tawkoni, Wichita **8** Cherokee, Chicasaw, Seminole
native: **6** Sooner
nickname: **6** Sooner
tree: **6** redbud
water: **3** Red **8** Arkansas

OLD: **4** aged, past **5** dated, hoary, passe, stale **6** bygone, former, mature, senile, senior **7** ancient, antique, archaic, elderly, vintage, wornout **8** lifelong, medieval, obsolete, outdated, seasoned, timeworn **9** venerable **10** antiquated **11** experienced, traditional **12** antediluvian

OLD AGE: **6** dotage **8** caducity, maturity, senility **10** senescence **11** decrepitude, senectitude
medical branch: **10** geriatrics

OLD COLONY STATE: **13** Massachusetts

OLD FAITHFUL: **6** geyser

OLD-FASHIONED: **4** aged **5** corny, dated, drink, passe **6** bygone, quaint **7** ancient, antique, archaic, vintage **8** cocktail, obsolete, outdated **9** primitive **10** antiquated, fuddy-duddy **11** traditional

OLD HAND: **3** pro **6** expert, master **7** veteran

OLD HAT: **5** dated, passe, stale, trite **6** cliche **7** archaic, vintage **8** obsolete, outdated, shopworn, timeworn **10** antiquated

OLD LINE STATE: **8** Maryland

OLD MAID: **4** game **5** woman **8** spinster **10** fastidious

OLD TESTAMENT: **3** Job **4** Amos, Ezra, Joel, Ruth **5** Hosea, Jonah, Kings, Micah, Nahum, Songs, Tobit **6** Baruch, Daniel, Esther, Exodus, Haggai, Isaiah, Joshua, Judges, Judith, Psalms, Samuel, Sirach, Wisdom **7** Ezekiel, Genesis, Malachi, Numbers, Obadiah **8** Habakkuk, Jeremiah, Nehemiah, Proverbs **9** Leviticus, Maccabees, Zechariah, Zephaniah **10** Chronicles **11** Deuteronomy **12** Ecclesiastes **13** Song of Solomon **14** Ecclesiasticus

OLD WORLD: **6** Europe, formal **10** ceremonial **11** established, traditional **12** conventional

OLEORESIN: **3** oil **5** resin **7** copaiba **10** turpentine

OLIO: **4** hash, stew **6** jumble, medley **7** melange, mixture **8** mishmash **9** potpourri **10** collection, hodgepodge, miscellany

OLIVE: **3** oil **4** tree **5** color, fruit **11** yellow-green
genus: **12** Oleo europaea

OLLA: **3** jar, jug, pot **5** crock **9** container **11** earthenware

OLYMPICS: **5** games **6** sports **7** contest **8** festival **9** athletics
originated: **6** Greece

OMAN:
capital: **6** Muscat
cities: **7** Salalah
continent: **4** Asia
ethnic groups: **9** Omani Arab, Pakistani
features: **10** Kuria Muria **11** Jebel Akhdar **13** Masirah Island
language: **6** Arabic
monetary unit: **9** rial omani
native: **5** Omani
water: **11** Persian Gulf **14** Strait of Hormuz

OMEGA: **3** end **4** last **5** final **6** letter

OMEN: **4** bode, sign **5** token **6** augury **7** auspice, portent, presage, warning **8** bodement, forebode, prophecy **9** harbinger **10** foreshadow, indication, prediction **11** premonition

OMINOUS: **4** dark, dour, grim **6** dismal, doomed, gloomy **7** baneful, fateful, fearful, unlucky **8** menacing, sinister **9** dangerous **10** foreboding, portentous **11** apocalyptic, threatening

OMISSION: **4** skip **5** blank, chasm, error, lapse **7** elision, failure **8** ellipsis, overlook **9** exclusion, oversight **10** negligence

OMIT: **3** cut **4** drop, edit, miss, skip, slip **5** avoid, elide, spare **6** bypass, cancel, delete, except, forget, ignore **7** exclude, neglect **8** overlook **9** disregard, eliminate

OMNIBUS: **5** whole **7** vehicle **9** anthology, including **11** compilation

OMNIPOTENT: **5** deity, great **6** mighty **7** godlike, supreme **8** almighty, powerful **9** unequaled, unlimited **11** all-powerful

OMNIPRESENT: **7** allover **8** infinite **10** everywhere, ubiquitous **12** simultaneous

OMNISCIENT: **4** wise **7** learned **10** all-knowing **11** pansophical **13** knowledgeable

ON ACCOUNT: **5** since **6** credit **7** because, charged

ON AND OFF: **6** seldom **8** episodic **9** irregular, sometimes **12** infrequently

ON AND ON: **6** boring **7** endless, forever, tedious **10** repetitive **12** interminable

ON BOARD: **6** aboard, loaded **7** shipped

ON CALL: **5** alert, handy, ready **9** available

ONCE: **4** back, erst, past **6** before, former **7** already, earlier, quondam **10** previously

ONCE-IN-A-LIFETIME: **6** unique **7** special **12** unbelievable

ONCE IN A WHILE: **6** seldom **9** sometimes **12** occasionally

ONCE MORE: **4** over **5** again **6** repeat

ONCE-OVER: **4** look **6** survey **7** checkup **10** inspection **11** examination

ONCOMING: **7** looming **8** expected, imminent **9** impending **11** approaching

ONE: **3** uno **4** same, sole, unit **5** alone, digit, unite **6** number, person, single, unique, united **7** numeral **8** separate, solitary **9** different, undivided **10** individual

ONE BY ONE: **6** singly **10** separately **12** individually

O'NEILL, EUGENE: **6** author **9** dramatist **10** playwright
wrote: **3** Ile **4** Gold **11** The Hairy Ape **12** Ah, Wilderness, Anna Christie, Emperor Jones **13** Marco Millions **14** Days Without End **15** A Touch of the Poet, The Iceman Cometh **16** Beyond the Horizon, Strange Interlude, The Great God Brown **17** The Long Voyage Home **18** Desire Under the Elms **19** Bound East for Cardiff, Where the Cross Is Made **22** Mourning Becomes Electra

ONENESS: **5** union, unity **6** accord **7** concord, harmony **8** identity, sameness **9** integrity, wholeness **10** uniformity **11** singularity **14** indivisibility

ONE-OF-A-KIND: **4** rare **6** unique **8** original

ONEROUS: **4** hard **5** heavy **6** taxing **7** arduous **8** exacting, grueling, pressing, rigorous, toilsome **9** demanding, difficult, laborious, strenuous **10** burdensome, exhausting, oppressive **12** backbreaking

ONE-SIDED: **6** biased, uneven, unfair, unjust **7** partial **8** lopsided **10** prejudiced

ONE-TIME: **4** past **5** prior **6** former **7** quondam **8** previous

ONGOING: **7** current, endless **8** evolving **9** advancing, improving, operating, unfolding **10** continuous **13** uninterrupted

ON GUARD: **5** alert **7** careful **8** cautious, vigilant, watchful

ON HAND: **7** stocked **9** available **10** accessible, convenient

ONION: **5** plant
genus: **10** Allium cepa
types: **4** leek, wild **5** green, white **7** Bermuda, Danvers, shallot, Spanish, Vidalia **8** scallion

ONLOOKER: **5** gazer **6** viewer **7** witness **8** observer **9** bystander, sightseer, spectator **10** eyewitness, rubberneck

ONLY: **3** but, yet **4** just, lone, mere, sole **6** barely, except, merely, simply, single, singly, solely **7** however, totally **8** entirely, singular, solitary **9** unrivaled **10** individual **11** exclusively **12** nevertheless, unparalleled

ONRUSH: **4** flow, gush **5** flood, onset, surge **6** attack, deluge **7** assault **9** onslaught

ONSET: **4** dash, push **5** birth, start **6** attack, charge, onrush, origin **7** assault, attempt, dawning **8** outbreak **9** beginning, encounter, onslaught **12** commencement

ONSLAUGHT: **5** blitz, onset, storm **6** attack, onrush **7** assault **8** invasion **9** offensive

ONTARIO:
capital: **7** Toronto
cities: **6** London, Ottawa **7** Windsor **8** Hamilton **9** Kitchener
country: **6** Canada
features: **7** Ogidaki
water: **6** Thames **8** Lake Erie **9** Lake Huron **11** Lake Ontario **12** Lake Superior, Niagara Falls

ON THE BALL: **4** able **7** skilled **9** competent, qualified

ON THE BUTTON: **7** exactly **8** squarely **9** precisely **10** accurately

ON THE CONTRARY: **9** inversely **10** conversely, oppositely **11** contrasting

ON THE WHOLE: **9** generally **10** by and large

ONTO: **4** atop, over, upon **5** above, aware **6** toward **8** informed

ONUS: **4** duty, load, task **5** blame **6** burden, stigma, weight **9** liability **10** obligation **14** responsibility

ONWARD: **4** away **5** ahead, along **6** beyond **7** forward **9** advancing

OODLES: **4** gobs, heap, lots **5** loads, scads **9** abundance

OOMPH: **4** dash, elan **5** drive, vigor **6** energy, pizazz, spirit **7** stamina **8** strength, vitality **10** attraction

OOZE: **4** drip, emit, gook, leak, mire, muck, seep, slob, spew **5** exude, marsh, slime, weeze **6** escape, sludge **7** emanate, secrete **8** overflow, sediment **9** discharge

OPAL: **3** gem **5** jewel, stone **7** mineral
type: **4** fire **5** black, milky, noble, white **7** girasol, hyalite **8** menilite, precious **9** geyserite, harlequin **10** chalcedony

OPAQUE: **4** dark, dull **5** dense, muddy, vague **6** obtuse, stupid **7** blurred, clouded, obscure, unclear **8** nebulous **9** concealed **14** unintelligible

OPEN: **4** airy, ajar, free, hole, undo, wide **5** agape, begin, clear, crack, frank, naked, overt, plain, prone, start, untie **6** candid, direct, expand, expose, gaping, honest, patent, unbolt, unfold, unseal, unstop, unwrap, vacant **7** blatant, cleared, obvious, release, sincere, unclose, unlatch, vacated **8** apparent, commence, disclose, explicit, extended, flagrant, initiate, outdoors, revealed, unfasten, unlocked **9** available, objective, originate, uncovered, undecided **10** accessible, forthright, unreserved **11** extroverted, susceptible, unconcealed

OPEN-AIR: **7** outdoor, outside **8** alfresco, spacious

OPEN-AND-SHUT: **5** clear **7** evident, obvious **8** apparent

OPENHANDED: **4** free, kind **7** liberal **8** generous **9** bountiful, receptive **10** altruistic, benevolent, charitable

OPENHEARTED: **4** warm **5** frank **6** honest, kindly **7** sincere

OPENING: **3** gap **4** cave, door, gash, gate, hole, pass, rift, slit, slot, span, vent **5** break, cleft, crack, debut, mouth, space, start, width **6** breach, chance, cranny, hiatus, lacuna, launch, outlet, portal, window **7** crevice, fissure, orifice **8** aperture **9** beginning, threshold **11** opportunity, possibility **12** commencement

OPEN-MINDED: **4** fair, just **7** liberal **8** flexible, tolerant, unbiased **9** objective

OPENMOUTHED: **6** aghast, amazed, gaping **9** awestruck, insistent, surprised **10** astonished, confounded, vociferous

OPERA: **7** musical, theater **8** libretto
glasses: **7** lorgnon **9** lorgnette
singer: **4** diva **10** prima donna
types: **4** soap **5** comic, grand, light **7** chorale

OPERATE: **3** man, run **4** work **5** drive, pilot **6** manage **7** perform **8** function, maneuver **10** manipulate

OPERATION: **6** action, agency **7** process, surgery **8** business, exercise, function **9** influence, procedure **10** engagement, overseeing, production **11** transaction, undertaking

OPERATIVE: **4** hand, open **5** agent **6** active **8** workable **9** detective, effective, efficient **12** manipulative

OPERATOR: **5** agent **6** broker, dealer, driver **7** manager **8** computer, motorist **9** conductor, emergency, telephone **10** speculator **11** switchboard

OPEROSE: **4** hard **7** arduous **8** diligent **9** laborious **11** industrious

OPIATE: **4** dope, drug **5** opium **6** deaden, downer **8** hypnotic, narcotic, sedative **9** soporific **10** depressant **12** tranquilizer

OPINE: **4** deem, hold, view **5** judge, offer, state, think **6** regard **7** suppose, surmise **8** conclude

OPINION: **4** idea **5** guess, tenet, think **6** advice, belief, dictum, notion, theory **7** concept, feeling, thought **8** attitude, decision, doctrine, estimate, judgment **9** sentiment, viewpoint **10** conclusion, conjecture, conviction, evaluation, expression, hypothesis, impression, persuasion

OPINIONATED: **5** bossy **6** biased **7** adamant **8** dogmatic, stubborn **9** obstinate, pigheaded **10** bullheaded, inflexible **11** dictatorial, overbearing **14** uncompromising

OPIUM: **4** dope, drug, hops **5** poppy **6** heroin, opiate **7** codeine **8** laudanum **9** laudanine, soporific **10** cryptopine, intoxicant
produce: **8** morphine

OPOSSUM: **6** possum **9** marsupial
family: **11** Didelphidae **13** Phalangeridae

OPPONENT: **3** foe **5** enemy, rival **7** nemesis **9** adversary, assailant, combatant **10** antagonist, challenger, competitor, opposition

OPPORTUNE: **5** ready **6** timely **7** fitting **8** suitable **9** favorable, fortunate, well-timed **10** auspicious, convenient, seasonable **11** appropriate **12** advantageous

OPPORTUNITY: **4** hope, shot, stab, turn **5** break **6** chance **7** exploit, opening **8** fortuity, occasion **9** advantage

OPPOSE: **3** pit, vie **4** buck, defy, duel, face, meet **5** argue, block, cross, fight, front, match, rebel, repel **6** battle, combat, debate, differ, object, oppugn, resist **7** contest, counter, dispute, protest **8** conflict, confront, contrast, disagree, obstruct **9** encounter, withstand **10** contradict, controvert

OPPOSITE: **5** polar **6** across, contra, facing **7** adverse, antonym, counter, inverse, paradox, reverse **8** antipole, contrary, contrast, converse **9** antipodal, different **10** antipodean, antithesis **11** diametrical **12** antagonistic, antithetical, counterpoint **13** contradictory

OPPOSITION: 5 clash, enemy **6** strife **7** rivalry **8** defiance, struggle **9** animosity, encounter, hostility **10** antagonism, contention, resistance **11** competition, contrariety

OPPRESS: 5 abuse, crush, wrong **6** burden, harass, harrow, ravish, subdue, weight **7** afflict, depress, repress, smother, trample, trouble **8** distress, pressure, suppress **9** constrain, overpower, overthrow, overwhelm, persecute, subjugate **10** dishearten

OPPRESSION: 6 misery **7** tyranny **8** dullness **9** injustice, lassitude, suffering **10** affliction

OPPRESSIVE: 4 hard **5** bleak, cruel, harsh, heavy, muggy **6** dismal, gloomy, severe, taxing, vexing **7** onerous **8** stifling **10** burdensome, depressing, hardhanded **11** distressing, heavyhanded, overbearing, suffocating **12** overwhelming

OPPRESSOR: 4 czar **6** despot, tyrant **8** autocrat, dictator, martinet **13** authoritarian

OPPROBRIOUS: 7 abusive, hateful **8** infamous, scornful, shameful **9** invective, malicious, notorious **10** despicable, malevolent **11** disgraceful **12** contemptuous

OPPROBRIUM: 5 abuse, odium, scorn, shame **6** infamy **7** disdain, offense **8** contempt, disgrace, dishonor, ignominy, reproach **10** disrespect, scurrility

OPPUGN: 6 attack, oppose, resist **7** contend, dispute **8** question **10** contradict

OPT: 4 pick, take, vote **5** elect **6** choose, decide, prefer, select

OPTIMISTIC: 4 rosy **5** sunny **6** bright, upbeat **7** hopeful **8** cheerful, sanguine **9** confident, promising **10** idealistic **12** enthusiastic

OPTIMUM: 4 best, peak **5** ideal **6** height, zenith **7** maximum, supreme **8** greatest

OPTION: 4 item **5** right **6** choice **7** feature **8** decision, druthers **9** privilege, selection **11** alternative, prerogative

OPTIONAL: 8 elective, unforced **9** available, voluntary **11** alternative **13** discretionary, nonobligatory

OPULENT: 4 rich **5** gaudy, plush, showy, swank **6** lavish **7** elegant, profuse, wealthy **8** abundant, affluent, luscious **9** luxurious, plentiful **11** extravagant

OPUS: 4 book, work **5** study **8** creation **10** brainchild **11** composition, masterpiece

ORACLE: 4 sage, seer **5** maxim, sibyl **6** augury, medium **8** prophecy **10** prediction, revelation, soothsayer **11** clairvoyant

ORACULAR: 7 cryptic, obscure **8** divining, esoteric, mystical **9** enigmatic, prophetic **10** foreseeing, mysterious

ORAL: 4 vial **5** aloud **6** sonant, spoken, verbal, voiced **7** lingual, uttered **8** narrated, phonetic **9** unwritten **10** acroamatic, articulate

ORANGE: 4 tree **5** juice, plant
color: **5** coral, peach **6** salmon **7** apricot **9** red-yellow, tangerine **11** burnt orange
genus: **6** citrus
variety: **4** wild **5** blood, China, navel, sweet **6** Temple **7** Florida, Maltese, Seville **8** bergamot, mandarin **9** tangerine

ORANGUTAN: **3** ape **4** mias **5** satyr **7** primate **10** anthropoid
family: **8** Pongidae
species: **13** Pongo pygmaeus

ORATE: **5** speak, spiel, spout **6** recite **7** address, declaim, lecture **8** harangue **9** sermonize **10** filibuster

ORATION: **6** eulogy, lecture, sermon, speech **7** address, soapbox **9** discourse

ORATOR: **7** demagog, speaker **8** lecturer **9** demagogue **11** rhetorician, spellbinder **12** spokesperson

ORATORY: **6** chapel **8** rhetoric **9** elocution, eloquence, preaching **14** public speaking

ORB: **4** ball, ring **5** earth, globe **6** circle, ocular, planet, sphere **7** circuit, eyeball

ORBIT: **4** path **5** cycle, range, realm, scope, track **6** circle, course, radius **7** circuit, ellipse **8** dominion, rotation **9** influence **10** revolution

ORCHARD: **4** farm **5** arbor, grove, trees **6** garden **10** plantation

ORCHESTRA: **4** band **5** group **6** string **7** chamber, gamelan, maestro **8** ensemble, symphony **11** instruments **12** philharmonic
instrument: **4** bass, drum, gong, harp, tuba **5** bells, cello, flute, oboes, piano, viola **6** cornet, violin **7** piccolo, timpani **8** trombone, trumpets **9** clarinets, xylophone **10** French horn
leader: **9** conductor
section: **5** brass **6** string **8** woodwind **10** percussion

ORCHESTRATE: **5** score **7** arrange, compose **8** organize **9** harmonize **10** coordinate

ORCHID: **5** color, plant **6** flower, purple
variety: **4** baby, moth **5** cobra, snowy, vanda **6** cradle, Easter, spider **7** calypso, rainbow, scarlet **8** hyacinth **9** butterfly, Christmas, cymbidium **10** buttonhole

ORDAIN: **4** deem, name **5** allot, order **6** decree **7** appoint, arrange, command, conduct, destine, install, prepare **9** authorize, establish **10** commission, consecrate, constitute, predestine

ORDEAL: **4** test **5** grief, trial **7** tragedy, trouble **9** nightmare, suffering **10** experience **11** tribulation

ORDER: **4** club, fiat, form, kind, line, rank, rule, sect, sort, type **5** align, array, caste, chain, class, edict, genus, grade, group, guide, lodge, place, scale, shape **6** charge, decree, degree, demand, direct, enjoin, extent, graith, kilter, layout, line up, manage, method, ordain, sequel, series, system **7** arrange, bracket, command, control, dispose, mandate, process, request, routine, society **8** category, decision, neatness, organize, purchase, regulate, sequence, standing, tabulate **9** direction, directive, hierarchy, magnitude, ordinance, procedure **10** discipline, fellowship, injunction, procession, sisterhood, succession **11** alphabetize, arrangement, association, brotherhood, instruction, tranquility

ORDERLY: **4** aide, neat, snug, tidy, trim **5** exact, quiet **6** formal **7** precise, uniform **8** obedient, peaceful, tranquil **9** peaceable, regulated, shipshape **10** controlled, manageable, methodical, systematic **11** uncluttered, well-behaved **12** businesslike

ORDINANCE: **3** act, law **4** code, fiat, rite **5** canon, edict, order **6** decree, ruling **7** statute **9** enactment

ORDINARY: **4** so-so **5** usual **6** common, normal **7** average, mundane, natural, prosaic, regular, routine, trivial, typical **8** everyday, familiar, frequent, habitual, mediocre **9** customary **10** uneventful **11** commonplace, traditional **12** conventional **13** unexceptional

ORDNANCE: **4** guns **5** armor **6** cannon **7** weapons **8** firearms, supplies **9** armaments, artillery, equipment, torpedoes **10** ammunition

ORE: **3** tin **4** gold, iron, lead, rock, zinc **5** metal **6** bronze, copper, silver **7** mineral **8** platinum
deposit: **4** lode, mine, vein **7** bonanza

OREGON:
bird: **10** meadowlark
capital: **5** Salem
cities: **6** Eugene **8** Portland
explorer: **4** Gray **5** Clark, Lewis **9** James Cook
features: **5** coast **8** Cascades **11** Oregon Trail
flower: **5** grape
native: **6** Beaver
tree: **10** Douglas fir
water: **5** Snake **8** Columbia **10** Crater Lake **15** Willamette River

ORESTES:
father: **9** Agamemnon
killed: **9** Aegisthus **12** Clytemnestra
mother: **12** Clytemnestra
sister: **7** Electra **9** Iphigenia
wife: **8** Hermione

ORGAN: **4** tool **5** forum, means, voice **6** agency, medium **7** channel, journal, vehicle **8** magazine **9** newspaper **10** instrument, periodical **11** publication
human: **3** ear, eye **4** lung, nose **5** brain, heart, liver **6** kidney, tongue **7** stomach **8** pancreas **9** intestine
musical: **8** calliope, melodeon **9** accordion, harmonica, harmonium **10** hurdy-gurdy
pipe: **4** flue, reed

ORGANIC: **5** basic **6** inborn, living, simple **7** natural **8** inherent **9** healthful **11** fundamental **12** nonsynthetic **14** constitutional, interconnected

ORGANISM: **4** cell, germ, life **5** being, monad, plant, virus **6** amoeba, animal, entity, fungus, person **7** microbe, protist **9** bacterium, protozoan **10** individual

ORGANIZATION: **4** band, club, firm, team **5** group, guild, lodge, order, trade, union **6** agency, circle, format, league **7** company **8** alliance, business, planning **9** coalition, framework, institute **10** fellowship, profession, sisterhood **11** arrangement, association, brotherhood, cooperative, corporation, disposition, partnership **12** constitution, coordination **13** confederation, configuration, establishment
college: **4** frat **7** alumnus **8** sorority **10** fraternity
criminal: **4** gang **5** mafia **9** syndicate **10** Cosa Nostra
political: **4** bloc **5** party **7** machine
secret: **3** CIA, FBI, KGB **4** BPOE, Elks, frat **5** lodge, mafia, Moose **6** Masons **8** sorority **9** Maccabees **10** fraternity, Freemasons **11** underground
veterans: **3** AVC, DAV, GAR, SAR, VFW **6** AMVETS **14** American Legion

ORGANIZE: **4** plan **5** edify, found, index, set up, start **6** create, neaten **7** arrange, catalog, marshal **9** establish, formulate **10** coordinate, mastermind **11** systematize

ORGY: **4** bash, romp **5** binge, feast, fling, party, revel, spree **6** frolic **7** debauch, rampage **8** carousal **9** bacchanal **10** indulgence, saturnalia **11** merry-making

ORIENT: **4** Asia **5** adapt, align, Burma, China, India, Japan,

Korea **6** adjust, locate **7** conform, Far East, Vietnam **8** accustom, Hong Kong, Thailand **11** acclimatize, accommodate, familiarize

ORIENTAL: **4** Thai **5** Asian **6** Korean **7** Asiatic, Chinese, Eastern **8** Japanese **10** Vietnamese
animals: **4** zebu **5** rasse **6** tussah, tusseh, tusser **7** macaque, tussore
buildings: **3** dar **4** khan **5** serai, yamen **6** imaret, pagoda **11** caravansary
clothing: **3** aba **6** sarong
drink: **3** cha, tea **4** sake, saki, tuba **6** arrack
exercise: **4** judo, yoga **6** tai chi **8** jiujitsu
food: **3** ame, koi, soy, tai **4** para, rice **5** pilaf, pilau, salep **6** pilaff **8** beancurd
market: **3** sug, suk **4** souk **6** bazaar
plants: **3** tea **5** atlee, henna **7** cheenar **8** oleander
rulers: **3** aga **4** amir, baba, emir, khan, raja, shah **5** ameer, calif, emeer, nawab, pasha, rajah **6** caliph, huzoor, sultan
salutation: **5** saheb, salam **6** kowtow, salaam
storm: **7** monsoon
tale: **7** Ali Baba **13** Arabian Nights
vehicle: **4** sado **5** araba **7** ricksha **8** rickshaw **11** jinrickshaw
worker: **5** cooly, hamal **6** coolie

ORIFICE: **4** hole, slit, vent **5** crack, inlet, mouth **6** cavity, outlet **7** opening **8** aperture

ORIGIN: **4** root, seed **5** alpha, basis, birth, blood, cause, start **6** family, nature, parent, source, spring **7** genesis, lineage **8** ancestry, creation **9** beginning, evolution, inception, maternity, parentage, paternity **11** inspiration, provenience **12** commencement

ORIGINAL: **3** new **5** first, fresh, novel **6** native, oddity, primal, unique **7** genuine, initial, pioneer **8** creative, pristine **9** authentic, eccentric, inventive, primitive, prototype **10** aboriginal, forerunner, innovative **11** fundamental

ORIGINALITY: **9** freshness, ingenuity **10** cleverness, innovation **11** unorthodoxy **12** creativeness

ORIGINATE: **4** coin, make, rise, stem **5** arise, begin, birth, cause, found, start **6** create, devise, father, invent, launch, spring **7** develop, emanate, produce **8** commence, contrive, discover, generate, initiate **9** establish, formulate, institute, introduce **10** inaugurate

ORIGINATOR: **6** author, father, mother **7** creator, pioneer **8** inventor **9** initiator, innovator **11** trailblazer **12** fountainhead

ORION: **5** giant **6** hunter **13** constellation
killer: **7** Artemis
lover: **4** Eros
pursued: **8** Pleiades

ORKNEY ISLANDS:
capital: **8** Kirkwall
cities: **9** Skara Brae
islands: **3** Hoy **6** Pomona, Rousay, Sanday **8** Mainland, Stronsay
place: **8** Scotland
water: **9** Scapa Flow

ORMOLU: **3** tin **4** gilt, gold, zinc **5** alloy **6** copper **8** ornament

ORNAMENT: **4** deck, trim **5** adorn, jewel **6** amulet, attire, brooch, design, emboss, enrich, finery, flower, gewgaw **7** festoon, furbish, garnish, trinket **8** beautify, figurine **9** embellish, embroider **10** decoration, furnishing, knickknack

ORNAMENTAL: **5** fancy **6** chichi, dressy, florid, frilly, rococo **7** elegant **9** elaborate **10** decorative

ORNATE: **4** lush **5** fancy, showy **6** flashy, florid, glitzy, ornery, rococo **7** baroque, flowery, opulent **8** dazzling **9** elaborate, luxurious **10** flamboyant

ORNERY: 4 mean **5** nasty, surly **6** cranky **7** grouchy **8** contrary, stubborn **9** crotchety, irritable **12** cantankerous

OROTUND: 4 loud, rich **5** clear, showy **7** pompous **8** resonant, sonorous **9** bombastic **10** resounding, stentorian

ORPHAN: 4 waif **5** Annie **8** forsaken **9** abandoned, foundling

ORPHEUS:
buried at: **12** Mount Olympus
career: **8** musician
instrument: **4** lyre
killer: **7** Maenads
mother: **8** Calliope
traveled with: **5** Jason **9** Argonauts
wife: **8** Eurydice

ORT: 3 bit **5** crumb, scrap **6** morsel **7** remnant **8** fragment, leftover

ORTHODOX: 5 pious **6** devout, proper **7** correct **8** accepted, approved, standard **9** canonical, customary **11** traditional **12** conservative, conventional

ORYX: 6 pickax **7** gazelle, gemsbok **8** antelope
genus: **4** oryx
origin: **6** Africa

OSCILLATE: 4 rock, sway, vary **5** swing, waver **7** flicker, pulsate, vibrate **8** unsteady **9** fluctuate, palpitate, vacillate

OSCULATE: 4 buss, kiss, peck **5** touch **7** contact

OSIER: 3 rod **4** tree, twig, wand **6** willow **7** dogwood

OSIRIS:
brother: **3** Set **4** Seth
father: **3** Geb, Keb, Seb
killer: **3** Set **4** Seth **7** brother
mother: **3** Nut
sister: **4** Isis
sons: **5** Horus **6** Anubis
wife: **4** Isis

OSMOSIS: 7 passage **9** diffusion **10** absorption **12** assimilation

OSSIFY: 3 set **6** harden **7** petrify, stiffen, thicken **9** fossilize

OSSUARY: 3 urn **4** tomb **5** vault **10** receptacle

OSTENSIBLE: 5 clear **6** likely **7** alleged, implied, obvious, seeming **8** apparent, illusory, supposed **9** pretended, professed, purported

OSTENTATION: 4 show **5** eclat, flair **6** parade, splash **7** display **8** flourish, pretense **9** flaunting, pageantry, pomposity, spectacle **10** exhibition, flashiness **11** pretentious

OSTENTATIOUS: 4 loud **5** gaudy, showy **6** chichi, flashy, sporty, swanky **7** dashing, pompous, splashy **8** overdone **9** elaborate, flaunting, grandiose **10** flamboyant **11** extravagant, pretentious

OSTRACIZE: 4 oust, shun, snub **5** avoid, exile **6** banish, reject **7** exclude **9** blackball, blacklist, proscribe **10** expatriate

OSTRICH: 4 bird, rhea
family: **15** Struthio camelus
feather: **5** plume
feature: **10** flightless

OTHER: 4 else, more **5** added, spare **6** former **7** further **8** distinct, opposite **9** different **10** additional **11** alternative

OTHERS: 4 many, rest, some **9** everybody

OTHERWISE: 9 variously **10** contrarily, oppositely **11** differently **13** alternatively

OTIOSE: 4 idle, lazy, vain **5** empty **6** futile, hollow **7** laggard, sterile, surplus, useless **8** inactive, indolent, slothful **11** ineffective, superfluous

OTTER: **3** fur
genus: **5** lutra **7** enhydra

OTTOMAN: **4** seat, sofa **5** couch, divan **7** hassock **8** footrest **9** footstool

OTTOMAN EMPIRE:
capital: **8** Istanbul **14** Constantinople
concerning: **4** Turk **5** Osman **6** Othman
kings: **5** Osman **8** Mohammed, Suleiman
religion: **5** Islam
water: **8** Black Sea **13** Mediterranean

OUCH: **3** cry **4** darn, oops, pain **5** clasp, shoot **6** blazes, brooch **7** setting **11** displeasure

OUGHT: **4** duty, must, want **6** cipher, should **7** behoove **8** anything **10** likelihood, obligation **12** desirability

OUNCE: **5** uncia **6** weight **7** leopard, measure
kind: **4** troy **5** fluid **11** avoirdupois

OUST: **3** bar **4** fire **5** eject, evict, expel **6** banish, remove, topple, unseat **7** dismiss **8** dethrone **9** discharge, ostracize **10** dispossess

OUT: **4** away, gone **5** dated, forth, passe **6** absent, demode, public **8** exterior, external, revealed **9** published **10** antiquated **12** extinguished, unacceptable **13** unfashionable

OUTAGE: **7** failure **8** blackout, brownout **12** interruption

OUT-AND-OUT: **4** pure **5** sheer **6** arrant, entire **7** perfect **8** absolute, complete, outright **9** notorious **11** unequivocal **13** thoroughgoing

OUTBACK: **4** bush **5** rural **6** remote **7** country **10** wilderness

OUTBREAK: **4** fury, riot **5** burst, onset **6** mutiny, plague, revolt, ruckus **8** conflict, epidemic, eruption, uprising **9** beginning, commotion, explosion **12** insurrection

OUTBUILDING: **4** barn, shed **6** garage, stable **8** outhouse **10** storehouse

OUTBURST: **4** gale, gust, rage, tiff **5** scene **6** attack, blow-up, frenzy, tirade **7** tantrum, torrent **8** eruption, paroxysm **9** discharge, explosion **11** disturbance

OUTCAST: **3** bum **5** exile, leper **6** pariah **7** refugee, runaway, vagrant **8** banished, derelict, expelled, fugitive, rejected, vagabond **10** expatriate

OUTCLASS: **4** best **5** excel, outdo **6** exceed **7** surpass

OUTCOME: **4** fate **5** issue, score **6** effect, payoff, result, upshot **7** fallout **8** causatum, reaction **9** aftermath **10** conclusion **11** consequence

OUTCRY: **4** bawl, yell **5** alarm, noise, shout **6** clamor, hubbub, racket, scream, shriek, uproar **7** protest, screech **8** upheaval **9** complaint, objection

OUTDATED: **3** old **5** passe **6** demode, square **7** archaic **8** obsolete **10** antiquated **13** unfashionable

OUTDO: **3** top **4** beat, best **5** cream, excel, worst **6** better, defeat, exceed **7** surpass **8** outclass, outshine, overcome **9** transcend

OUTDOORS: **7** country, outside **8** alfresco, fresh air **9** in the open **12** surroundings

OUTER: **5** alien, ectal **6** beyond, remote **7** exposed, foreign **8** exterior, external **10** extraneous, peripheral

OUTERMOST: **4** last **5** final **6** utmost **7** extreme **8** farthest, remotest **9** periphery

OUTFIT: **3** kit, rig **4** gear, suit, team, unit **5** array, corps, dress, equip, getup, party, squad **6** attire, clothe, supply **7** company, furnish **8** business, clothing, ensemble **9** equipment, furniture, trappings **10** enterprise, provisions **12** organization

OUTGOING: **4** warm **6** former, genial **7** cordial, exiting, leaving **8** friendly, retiring, sociable **10** gregarious **11** extroverted **13** demonstrative

OUTGROWTH: **4** node **5** bulge, issue **6** branch, result, sequel, sprout **7** product **8** offshoot **9** offspring **10** derivative, projection **11** consequence, culmination

OUTHOUSE: **5** privy **6** toilet **7** latrine **11** outbuilding

OUTING: **4** hike, ride, trip **5** drive, jaunt **6** junket, picnic **8** vacation **9** excursion

OUTLANDISH: **3** odd **4** wild **5** alien, weird **6** exotic, remote **7** bizarre, foreign, strange, unusual **8** peculiar **9** barbarous, eccentric, fantastic **10** outrageous, unorthodox **11** extravagant

OUTLAST: **6** endure, remain **7** persist, prevail, survive

OUTLAW: **3** ban **4** stop **5** crook **6** bandit, banish, forbid **7** condemn, hoodlum **8** criminal, fugitive, gangster, prohibit **9** desperado, miscreant, proscribe

OUTLAY: **4** cost **6** charge **7** expense, payment **11** expenditure **12** disbursement

OUTLET: **4** door, exit, shop, vent **5** store **6** egress, escape, market **7** channel, opening, orifice, passage **8** aperture

OUTLINE: **3** map **4** form, plan **5** chart, draft, frame, shape, trace **6** border, figure, fringe, limits, sketch **7** contour, profile, rundown, summary **8** describe, skeleton, syllabus, synopsis **9** blueprint, delineate, perimeter **10** silhouette **13** configuration

OUTLOOK: **4** view **5** angle, slant, vista **6** aspect **8** attitude, forecast, prospect **9** direction, prognosis, viewpoint **10** perception **11** expectation, perspective, probability

OUTLYING: **4** afar **5** outer **6** remote **7** distant, faraway, removed **8** external

OUTMODED: **5** dated, passe **6** bygone, demode **7** archaic **8** obsolete, outdated **10** antiquated **12** old-fashioned

OUT OF CONTROL: **4** lost, wild **5** crazy **6** doomed, ruined

OUT-OF-DATE: **5** passe **7** archaic **8** obsolete, outmoded **10** antiquated **12** old-fashioned

OUT OF HAND: **4** wild **6** unruly **10** disorderly **12** uncontrolled, unmanageable

OUT OF LINE: **5** askew **6** uneven **7** crooked **10** exorbitant **12** unreasonable

OUT OF ORDER: **6** broken, faulty **9** defective **11** inoperative

OUT OF PLACE: **4** lost **7** mislaid **10** unsuitable **13** inappropriate

OUT OF THE BLUE: **6** sudden **10** unexpected, unforeseen **13** unanticipated

OUT OF THE ORDINARY: **4** rare **6** unique **7** unusual **10** phenomenal, remarkable **13** extraordinary

OUT-OF-THE-WAY: **6** far-off, remote **7** distant, obscure, removed **8** isolated, secluded

OUT OF TOUCH: **7** unaware **8** unstable **9** estranged **11** disoriented

OUTPOST: **7** station **8** boundary, frontier, position **10** settlement

OUTPOURING: **4** gush **5** flood **6** deluge, stream **8** outburst, overflow

OUTPUT: **4** gain, take **5** power, yield **6** energy, profit **7** harvest, turnout **10** production **11** achievement

OUTRAGE: **4** evil, harm, rile **5** abuse, anger, shock **6** insult, misuse, offend, ravish **7** affront, incense, offense **8** atrocity, illtreat, iniquity, mistreat **10** wrongdoing

OUTRAGEOUS: **4** base, vile **5** crazy, gross **6** brutal, horrid, wicked **7** extreme, heinous, obscene, ungodly **8** dreadful, flagrant, horrible, shocking **9** atrocious, excessive **10** abominable, debauching, despicable, exorbitant **11** unspeakable **12** unreasonable

OUTRÉ: **7** bizarre, strange **9** eccentric **11** extravagant **14** unconventional

OUTRIGHT: **4** flat **5** total, whole **6** direct, entire, openly **8** absolute, complete **9** forthwith, instantly **10** thoroughly, undeniable **11** unmitigated **13** unconditional

OUTRUN: **4** beat **6** defeat, exceed **7** surpass

OUTSET: **5** birth, start **6** origin **7** dawning **9** beginning **12** commencement

OUTSIDE: **4** slim **5** faint, small **6** facade, remove, slight **7** distant, slender **8** alfresco, covering, exterior, farthest, unlikely

OUTSIDER: **5** alien **7** outcast **8** stranger **9** foreigner, outlander

OUTSKIRTS: **4** edge **5** limit **6** sticks **7** fringes, outpost **8** boundary

OUTSPOKEN: **4** free, open **5** blunt, frank, vocal **6** candid, direct, honest **7** artless **8** explicit **10** unreserved **11** opinionated

OUTSPREAD: **4** free **5** broad **6** opened **8** expanded, unfolded **9** unlimited **10** widespread **12** unrestrained

OUTSTANDING: **5** famed, great, major, noted **6** famous, marked, superb, unpaid **7** eminent, notable, overdue **8** dominant, foremost, renowned, standout **9** prominent, unsettled **10** celebrated, impressive, noticeable, remarkable **11** exceptional, uncollected **13** distinguished

OUTSTRIP: **3** top, win **4** best, pass **5** excel, outdo **6** defeat, exceed **7** surpass **8** overtake **9** transcend

OUTWARD: **5** ectad, overt **6** formal **7** evident, obvious, visible **8** apparent, exterior, external **10** noticeable, ostensible **11** perceivable, superficial

OUTWEIGH: **6** exceed, offset **7** prevail, surpass **8** dominate, override **10** compensate, overshadow

OUTWIT: **3** fox **4** best, dupe, foil, fool **6** baffle, jockey, thwart **7** finagle **9** bamboozle, frustrate **10** circumvent **11** outmaneuver

OUZO: **7** cordial, liqueur
flavor: **5** anise
origin: **6** Greece

OVAL: **5** ovate, ovoid **6** oblong **7** ellipse **9** egg-shaped, spherical **10** elliptical

OVATION: **4** hand **6** homage, praise **7** acclaim, broiler **8** applause, cheering **9** laudation

OVEN: **4** kiln, oast **5** range, stove **6** calcar **7** broiler, furnace **9** microwave

OVER: **3** too **4** also, anew, atop, done, leap, past, upon **5** above, again, clear, ended, extra, midst, vault **6** across, beyond, excess, hurdle **7** elapsed, through **8** finished **9** completed, concluded, excessive **10** terminated, throughout **12** additionally

OVERABUNDANCE: **4** glut **6** excess **7** surfeit, surplus **8** plethora **9** profusion **11** superfluity

OVERALL: **5** total **6** mainly, mostly **7** largely **8** sweeping **9** extensive, generally, primarily **13** comprehensive

OVER AND ABOVE: **6** beyond **7** besides **10** additional

OVERBEARING: **5** bossy, cocky, proud **6** lordly **7** haughty, pompous **8** arrogant, bullying, dominant, insolent, superior **9** imperious **10** disdainful, high-handed **11** dictatorial, domineering, egotistical **12** overpowering

OVERBLOWN: **5** windy **7** flowery, profuse **8** inflated **9** bombastic, excessive **11** pretentious, superfluous

OVERBURDEN: **7** exhaust, oppress **8** encumber **9** overwhelm **10** overloaded

OVERCAST: **4** dark, dull, gray, hazy **5** foggy, heavy **6** cloudy, darken, gloomy, sullen **7** obscure **8** nebulous

OVERCHARGE: **3** gyp, pad **4** soak **5** cheat, stick **6** fleece **9** embellish, extortion

OVERCOAT: **5** benny, parka **6** capote, raglan, ulster **7** surtout, topcoat **8** raincoat **9** greatcoat, inverness **12** chesterfield

OVERCOME: **4** beat, best, lick **5** crush, daunt **6** appall, defeat, exceed, hurdle, master **7** conquer, prevail, triumph **8** suppress, surmount, vanquish **9** overpower, overwhelm, prostrate **10** speechless

OVERCONFIDENT: **5** brash, cocky **8** arrogant **12** presumptuous

OVERDO: **6** exceed **7** amplify, exhaust, fatigue, magnify **8** overwork **9** overstate **10** exaggerate

OVERDUE: **4** late **5** tardy **6** behind, unpaid **7** arrears, belated, delayed **10** delinquent **11** outstanding

OVEREAT: **5** gorge, stuff **7** indulge, satiate **10** gluttonize

OVERFLOW: **4** pour, slop, soak, swim **5** drain, flood, spate, spill **6** deluge, engulf, excess, outlet **7** cascade, overrun, surplus, torrent **8** alluvion, inundate, submerge **9** abundance, ebullient, exuberant

OVERGROWN: **4** huge, lush, rank, wild **5** dense **6** jungly **8** colossal **9** excessive

OVERHANG: **3** jut **5** bulge, drape, eaves, jetty **6** extend **7** overlap, project, suspend **8** protrude

OVERHAUL: **4** mend **6** doctor, repair, revamp **7** examine, rebuild, restore **8** renovate **11** recondition

OVERHEAD: **4** cost, rent, roof **5** above, aloft **6** aerial, outlay, upkeep **8** expenses **9** insurance

OVERINDULGENCE: **6** excess **8** gluttony **9** satiation **10** overeating **12** overdrinking

OVERJOYED: **5** happy **6** elated **7** charmed **8** ecstatic, euphoric, jubilant, thrilled **9** delighted

OVERKILL: **7** surplus **8** genocide **9** excessive, slaughter **11** destruction

OVERLAP: **4** flap **5** cover **8** overhang **9** imbricate

OVERLAY: **4** coat **5** cover, glaze, plate **6** spread, veneer **7** blanket **9** embellish **11** superimpose

OVERLOAD: **4** cram, glut **6** burden, excess **8** encumber, inundate

OVERLOOK: **4** miss, omit, skip **6** excuse, forget, ignore, manage, pardon, slight **7** absolve, forgive, inspect, neglect **8** chaperon **9** chaperone, disregard, supervise

OVERLORD: **4** czar **5** chief, ruler **6** despot, tyrant **7** emperor **8** suzerain

OVERPOWER: **4** beat, rout, stun **5** cream, crush **6** dazzle, defeat, deluge, master, subdue **7** clobber, conquer, trounce **8** bulldoze, overbear, overcome, vanquish **9** overthrow, overwhelm, subjugate

OVERRIDE: **4** veto **5** annul, quash **6** cancel, defeat, revoke **7** nullify, reverse

OVERRULE: **4** veto **8** abrogate, disallow, overturn **9** supersede **10** invalidate

OVERRUN: **4** raid **5** crush, swarm **6** defeat, exceed, infest, invade, ravage **8** inundate, massacre **9** devastate, overwhelm

OVERSEAS: **5** alien **6** abroad, exotic **7** foreign **11** ultramarine

OVERSEE: **3** run **4** rule **5** watch **6** direct, manage, survey **7** examine, inspect **8** shepherd **9** supervise

OVERSEER: **4** boss, head **5** chief **7** curator, foreman, manager **8** chaperon, director, guardian **9** chaperone, inspector **10** supervisor **13** administrator **14** superintendent

OVERSHADOW: **4** rule **5** cloud, cover, dwarf, shade **6** darken **7** obscure **8** dominate, outshine **9** obfuscate

OVERSIGHT: **4** care, skip **5** error, lapse, watch **6** charge, slipup **7** blunder, control, failure, mistake, neglect **8** omission **9** disregard **10** management, negligence **11** inattention, supervision **12** carelessness

OVERSTATE: **5** color **6** exceed, expand, overdo **7** amplify, inflate, magnify **9** embellish **10** exaggerate

OVERSTEP: **6** exceed **8** encroach, infringe, trespass, violate **10** transgress

OVERT: **4** open **5** clear **6** public **7** obvious, visible **8** apparent, manifest **11** unconcealed, undisguised

OVERTAKE: **4** pass **5** catch, reach **6** attain **8** approach, overhaul **9** apprehend

OVERTAX: **4** tire **6** burden, exceed, strain **7** exhaust **8** overload, overwork

OVERTHROW: **4** fell, foil, oust, raze, rout, ruin **5** upset **6** defeat, depose, remove, topple, tumble, unseat **7** conquer, destroy, dismiss **8** confound, demolish, dethrone, downfall, overcome, overturn, vanquish **9** discomfit, overpower, overwhelm, prostrate, rebellion **11** destruction

OVERTONE: **4** hint **7** meaning **8** innuendo **9** inference **10** intimation **11** association, implication, insinuation

OVERTURE: **5** proem **6** tender **7** opening, preface, prelude **8** approach, foreword, prologue, proposal **9** beginning **11** composition, proposition **12** introduction

OVERTURN: **3** tip **4** tilt, void **5** spill, upend, upset **6** topple **7** capsize, reverse, subvert **9** overthrow **10** invalidate **11** countermand

OVERWEENING: **4** vain **5** brash, pushy **7** haughty, pompous **8** arrogant, insolent **10** highhanded **11** egotistical **12** presumptuous

OVERWEIGHT: **3** fat **4** huge **5** ample, heavy, hefty, obese, plump, pudgy, tubby **6** chubby, portly **9** corpulent

OVERWHELM: **4** bury, sink, whip **5** amaze, crush, floor, swamp **6** defeat, deluge, engulf, puzzle **7** confuse, conquer, engross, oppress, overrun, smother **8** astonish, inundate, massacre, overcome, overturn, submerge **9** devastate, overpower, overthrow

OVERWORK: **3** tax **4** tire **5** labor **6** burden, strain **7** exhaust **12** exploitation

OVERWROUGHT: **5** weary **6** ornate, shaken **7** excited, nervous **8** agitated, frenzied, overdone **9** emotional, flustered **10** hysterical

OVERZEALOUS: **9** overeager **12** enthusiastic

OVID: **4** poet **6** writer
lived: **4** Rome
wrote: **6** Amores **8** Heroides **9** Art of Love **11** Ars Amatoria **13** Metamorphoses

OVULE: **3** egg **4** seed **6** embryo **7** seedlet **8** nucellus **11** integuments

OVUM: **3** egg **4** seed **5** spore **6** gamete **7** egg cell **8** oosphere

OWE: **3** due **5** incur **9** attribute

OWING: **6** mature, unpaid **7** payable **8** indebted **9** obligated **11** outstanding **12** attributable

OWL: **4** bird
family: **9** Strigidae, Tytonidae **12** Strigiformes
kind: **4** barn, hawk, hoot, snow **5** eagle, pigmy **6** horned **7** boobook, screech, spotted
species: **4** Bubo, Otus, Tyto **5** Strix **8** Phodilus **10** Glaucidium

OWN: **4** avow, have, hold **5** admit, allow **6** retain **7** confess, control, possess **8** maintain **9** recognize **10** individual **11** acknowledge

OWNER: **5** buyer **8** landlady, landlord **9** landowner **10** proprietor **11** titleholder

OWNERSHIP: **4** deed **5** claim, title **7** holding, tenancy **8** dominium **10** possession

OWN UP: **5** admit **6** accept **7** confess **11** acknowledge

OX: **3** cow, oaf, yak **4** aver, buff, bull, musk, zebu **5** beast, bison, steer **6** bovine **7** buffalo, bullock, taurine **8** seladang
extinct: **4** urus **7** aurochs
family: **7** Bovidae **14** Antilocapridae

OXIDE: **8** compound
aluminum: **4** ruby **7** alumina **8** sapphire
calcium: **4** calx, lime
element: **6** oxygen
iron: **4** rust **6** ferric **8** limonite **9** magnetite
sodium: **4** soda

OXIDIZE: **4** burn, heat, rust **7** corrode

OXYGEN: **3** air, gas **7** element

OYSTER: **7** bivalve, mollusk **9** shellfish
family: **9** Ostreidae
genus: **6** ostrea **11** crassostrea
product: **4** food **5** pearl, shell
type: **4** flat, rock, wild **6** native, tonged **9** bluepoint **10** saddlerock

OZARK STATE: **8** Missouri

P

PABULUM: **4** diet, food, fuel **7** support **8** nutrient **9** nutriment **10** sustenance **11** nourishment

PACE: **4** clip, gait, lick, move, rate, step, time, trot, walk **5** amble, count, march, speed, tempo, tread **6** canter, gallop, motion, strait **7** measure **8** getalong, progress

PACHYDERM: **7** mammoth **8** elephant, mastodon **10** rhinoceros **12** hippopotamus

PACIFIC: **4** calm, mild **5** quiet **6** gentle, irenic, placid, serene, smooth **8** peaceful, tranquil **9** appeasing, peaceable **10** harmonious

PACIFIC ISLANDS:
also called: **7** Oceania
groups: **8** Marianas, Marshall **9** Carolines
U.S. base: **4** Guam

PACIFIC NORTHWEST: **6** Oregon **10** Washington

PACIFIC OCEAN:
explorer: **6** Balboa
islands: **3** Aru, Lae, Yap **4** Guam, Sulu, Truk, Wake **5** Leyte, Malay, Samoa **6** Tahiti, Tulagi **8** Marianas, Marshall, Tasmania **9** Carolines, Marquesas

PACIFIST: **4** dove **8** appeaser **11** flower child, peacemonger **15** passive resister

PACIFY: **4** calm, lull, tame **5** abate, allay, quiet **6** serene, settle, soften, soothe, subdue **7** appease, assuage, mollify, placate **8** mitigate, moderate **9** reconcile **10** conciliate **11** tranquilize

PACK: **3** jam, mob **4** bale, band, cram, fill, gang, heap, load, pile, stow, tote **5** bunch, carry, crowd, flock, group, hoard, store, stuff, swarm, truss **6** bundle, parcel **7** baggage, compact, squeeze **8** knapsack **9** container

PACKAGE: **3** box **5** crate **6** bundle, packet, parcel **9** container

PACKED: **4** full **6** jammed, loaded **7** stuffed **9** congested **11** overcrowded, overflowing

PACKET: **4** boat **5** pouch **6** bundle, folder, parcel **7** package **8** envelope **9** container

PACT: **4** bond, deal **6** cartel, treaty **7** bargain **8** alliance, contract, covenant **9** agreement **11** arrangement **13** understanding

PAD: **3** mat, wad **4** plod, walk **5** fudge, quilt, stuff, tramp **6** buffer, fatten, muffle, pillow, tablet, trudge **7** amplify, bolster, cushion, inflate, protect **8** notebook **9** embellish, embroider, overstate **10** exaggerate, overcharge

PADDING: **6** filler, lining **7** packing, wadding **8** stuffing **10** protection

PADDLE: **3** oar, row **5** blade, scull, spank **6** dabble, racket, thrash

PADRE: **4** monk **6** father, pastor, priest **8** chaplain, minister

PADRONE: **4** boss **5** chief, owner **6** master **10** proprietor, supervisor

PAEAN: **4** hymn, pean, song **6** anthem, praise **9** laudation **11** acclamation

PAGAN: **7** gentile, heathen, heretic, infidel, skeptic **8** agnostic, hedonist, idolator **10** unbeliever **11** nonbeliever

PAGE: **4** beep, call, leaf **5** folio, sheet, valet **6** insert, squire, summon **7** bellboy, bellhop, footboy, servant **8** announce **9** attendant, messenger
left-hand: **5** verso
right-hand: **5** recto

PAGEANT: **4** pomp, show **6** parade **7** display, tableau **8** pretense **9** spectacle **10** exhibition, procession **11** celebration

PAGODA: **3** taa **5** tower **6** alcove, gazebo, shrine, temple **8** memorial, pavilion

PAID: **8** refunded, rewarded **10** reimbursed **11** compensated, indemnified

PAIL: **3** can **6** bucket, piggin, vessel **9** container **10** receptacle

PAIN: **4** ache, harm, hurt, pang, pest **5** agony, annoy, cramp, crick, grief, gripe, sting, upset, wound **6** bother, grieve, injury, strain, twinge **7** afflict, anguish, malaise, torment, torture, trouble **8** disquiet, distress, nuisance, soreness **9** heartache, suffering **10** affliction, discomfort, irritation, punishment **11** unhappiness

PAINFUL: **3** raw **4** sore **5** acute, angry, awful, sharp **7** hurting, irksome **8** annoying, grueling, piercing, stinging **9** agonizing, difficult, irritated, laborious, throbbing **11** troublesome **12** excruciating **13** uncomfortable

PAINSTAKING: **5** fussy **7** careful, precise **8** diligent, exacting, thorough **9** assiduous, laborious, strenuous **10** meticulous, scrupulous **11** punctilious **13** conscientious

PAINT: **4** coat, daub, gaud, limn, tint **5** brush, color, rouge, stain **6** depict, enamel, makeup **7** picture, pigment, portray, pretend, varnish **8** decorate **9** represent

PAINTER: **6** artist **7** artisan **9** decorator **11** illustrator

PAINTING: **3** art, oil **5** mural **6** canvas, design **7** drawing, picture **8** portrait **10** watercolor **11** composition
equipment: **5** brush, easel, knife, paint **6** canvas **7** palette
one-color: **8** monotint **10** monochrome
sacred: **4** icon **5** pieta, putto
schools: **3** pop **5** Dutch **6** French **7** Flemish, Spanish **8** abstract, Venetian **9** symbolism **10** Florentine, surrealism **13** expressionist, impressionist **17** postimpressionist
wall: **5** mural, putto **6** fresco, frieze

PAIR: **3** duo, two **4** dyad, mate, span, team **5** brace, deuce, match, twins, unite **6** couple **7** twosome

PAKISTAN:
capital: **9** Islamabad
cities: **6** Lahore **7** Karachi **8** Peshawar **9** Hyderabad **10** Faisalabad, Rawalpindi

continent: **4** Asia
ethnic groups: **4** Urdu **6** Pathan, Sindhi **7** Baluchi, Punjabi
features: **7** Tarbela **9** Himalayas, Hindu Kush **10** Khyber Pass, Thar Desert **11** Indus Valley **12** Godwin Austen
languages: **4** Urdu **6** Brahvi, Pushtu, Sindhi **7** Baluchi, Bengali, Punjabi
monetary unit: **5** rupee
native: **9** Pakistani
water: **4** Ravi **6** Chenab, Jhelum, Kundar, Sutlej **10** Arabian Sea, Indus River **11** Indian Ocean

PAL: **4** ally, chum, mate **5** amigo, buddy, crony **6** cohort, friend **7** comrade, partner **8** sidekick **9** associate, companion, confidant **10** accomplice

PALACE: **5** manor, villa **6** castle **7** alcazar, chateau, mansion **8** seraglio

PALADIN: **4** hero **6** knight **8** champion, douzeper **9** supporter

PALATABLE: **5** sapid, tasty **6** savory **8** heavenly, pleasing **9** agreeable, delicious, toothsome **10** acceptable, appetizing, delectable, delightful

PALATIAL: **4** lush, posh **5** plush, regal, ritzy **6** ornate **7** elegant, opulent, stately **8** imposing, majestic, splendid **9** grandiose, luxurious **11** magnificent

PALAVER: **3** gab **4** blab, talk **5** clack **6** babble, debate, jolery, parley **7** chatter, flatter, wheedle **8** chitchat, dialogue, flummery **10** conference, discussion **12** conversation

PALE: **4** ashy, dull, fade, lily, sick, weak **5** ashen, bleak, faint, fence, light, lurid, stake, white **6** anemic, blanch, chalky, feeble, pallid, pastel, picket, sickly, whiten **7** enclose, ghastly, haggard, insipid, whitish **8** diminish, encircle **9** bloodless, colorless, deathlike

PALESTINE:
also called: **8** Holy Land
concerning: **11** Palestinian
descendants of: **6** Canaan
holy site of: **5** Islam **7** Judaism **12** Christianity
place: **6** Israel
water: **11** Jordan River **13** Mediterranean

PALISADE: **5** bluff, cliff, fence, slope **7** barrier, defense, fortify, furnish **8** stockade, surround **9** enclosure

PALL: **4** bore, cloy, tire **5** cloak, cloud, gloom, weary **6** coffin, damper, shadow **7** disgust, insipid, satiate **8** covering

PALLET: **3** bed, cot **4** tool **7** blanket, palette **8** mattress, platform

PALLIATE: **4** calm, ease, hide, lull **5** cloak, cover, glaze, gloss **6** excuse, lessen, soften, soothe **7** conceal, mollify, relieve **8** diminish, disguise, mitigate **9** alleviate, extenuate, sugarcoat, whitewash **10** conciliate

PALLID: **3** wan **4** blah, dull, pale, thin **5** ashen, bleak, white **6** anemic, boring **8** lifeless **9** bloodless, colorless **10** monotonous

PALM: **4** hand, hide, leaf, tree **5** blade, shrub **6** thenar **7** conceal, triumph, victory **11** measurement
family: **6** Palmae **9** Arecaceae
reading: **9** palmistry **10** chiromancy **14** fortunetelling
variety: **3** fan, oil, wax **4** date, doom, hemp, rock, wine **5** ivory, royal, snake **6** bamboo, needle, pignut, silver, yellow **7** cabbage, coconut, feather, funeral, palmyra, weddell **8** mangrove, umbrella **9** butterfly, petticoat

PALMY: **4** rosy **5** sunny **6** serene **7** booming **8** glorious, pleasant **10** delightful, prosperous, successful **11** flourishing

PALOOKA: **3** lug **5** idiot **6** clumsy, lummox, stupid

PALPABLE: **4** real **5** clear, plain **6** patent **7** blatant, certain, evident, obvious, tactile **8** apparent, concrete, distinct, manifest, material, tangible **10** noticeable, ostensible **11** discernible, perceptible **12** recognizable

PALPITATE: **4** beat **5** pound, pulse, shake, throb **6** quiver **7** flutter, pulsate, tremble, vibrate

PALSIED: **6** atonic **7** crippled, shaking, spastic **8** disabled **9** paralyzed, trembling **11** debilitated

PALSY-WALSY: **6** chummy **8** friendly, intimate

PALTER: **3** fib, lie **6** babble, haggle, trifle **7** bargain, deceive, falsify, quibble **10** equivocate **11** prevaricate

PALTRY: **4** bare, base, poor, puny, vile **5** cheap, petty **6** flimsy, meager, shabby, trashy **7** pitiful, rubbish, trivial **8** picayune, piddling, trifling, wretched **9** worthless **11** unimportant **12** contemptible **13** insignificant

PAMPER: **3** pet **4** baby **5** humor, spoil **6** caress, coddle, cuddle, dandle, fondle **7** cherish, gratify, indulge, satiate **11** mollycoddle

PAMPHLET: **5** flyer, tract **6** folder, manual **7** booklet, handout, leaflet **8** brochure, bulletin, handbill

PAN: **4** face, move, scan, wash **5** basin **6** follow, kettle, review, vessel **7** skillet **8** denounce, ridicule **9** container, criticize
body: **3** man
father: **6** Hermes
god of: **5** herds, woods **6** flocks, nature **9** shepherds
instrument: **4** pipe, reed
legs: **4** goat
pursued: **6** Syrinx

PANACEA: **4** cure **6** elixir, remedy **7** cure-all, nostrum **8** nepenthe **10** catholicon

PANACHE: **4** dash **5** flair, plume, style **7** swagger **8** charisma

PANAMA:
canal builder: **9** de Lesseps
capital: **6** Panama
cities: **5** Colon, David **6** Balboa **8** Santiago **9** Cristobal **10** Portobello
continent: **13** Central America
ethnic groups: **6** Indian **7** Mestizo **9** Caucasian **10** West Indian
explorer: **6** Balboa
features: **3** Rey **8** Chiriqui **10** Miraflores **13** Barro Colorado
languages: **7** English, Spanish
monetary unit: **6** balboa
native: **10** Panamanian
water: **11** Panama Canal

PANCAKE: **5** blini, crepe **6** blintz **7** bannock, blintze, fritter, hotcake **8** flapjack, slapjack **9** jonnycake **11** griddlecake

PANDEMONIUM: **4** hell, riot **5** chaos, noise **6** bedlam, racket, tumult, uproar **7** clatter, turmoil **8** disorder **9** commotion, confusion, craziness **10** hullabaloo

PANDER: **4** bawd, pimp **5** cater **7** gratify **8** procurer

PANDORA:
created by: **4** Zeus **10** Hephaestus
husband: **10** Epimetheus
opened: **3** box, jar
released: **3** age, sin **5** death **8** sickness

PANEGYRIC: **6** eulogy, praise **7** tribute **8** citation, encomium **9**

laudation **11** acclamatory **13** complimentary

PANEL: **4** gore, jury **5** board, group **6** insert **7** section **9** committee, partition

PANG: **4** ache, pain, stab, tang **5** agony, cramp, smart, spasm, throb, throe **6** twinge, twitch **7** anguish, torment **8** distress **9** heartache **10** discomfort

PANHANDLE: **3** beg, bum **5** cadge **6** hustle **7** solicit

PANHANDLE STATE: **12** West Virginia

PANIC: **4** fear **5** alarm, chaos, crash, dread, scare, slump **6** dismay, frenzy, terror **7** anxiety, unnerve **8** hysteria, stampede **9** confusion, overreact **11** trepidation **13** consternation

PANORAMA: **4** view **5** range, scene, scope, sweep, vista **6** radius, survey **7** compass, horizon, picture, scenery **8** overview **11** perspective

PAN OUT: **4** work **5** click **6** happen **7** succeed

PANSY: **4** wimp **5** plant **6** flower, violet **7** chicken **10** heartsease

PANT: **4** ache, beat, blow, gasp, huff, puff, sigh, wish **5** heave, throb, yearn **6** desire, hunger, thirst, wheeze **7** breathe, pulsate **9** palpitate

PANTHER: **3** cat **4** puma **6** cougar, jaguar **7** leopard **12** mountain lion

PANTRY: **5** ambry **6** cellar, closet, galley, larder **7** butlery, buttery, kitchen, pannier **8** cupboard

PANTS: **5** chaps, jeans **6** chinos, denims, slacks **7** drawers **8** britches, knickers, trousers **9** bluejeans, corduroys **11** bell bottoms

PANTYWAIST: **4** wimp **5** sissy **7** milksop **8** weakling

PAPA: **3** dad, paw, pop **5** daddy, poppy **6** father

PAPAL: **8** papistic **9** apostolic **10** pontifical
ambassador: **6** nuncio
court: **5** Curia
vestments: **3** alb **4** sash **5** cross, miter, stole **7** cassock, crosier **8** chasuble, mozzetta, zuchetto

PAPER: **4** deed **5** essay, sheet, theme **6** report, thesis, tissue, vellum **7** article, diploma, writing **8** critique, document, treatise **9** monograph, wallpaper **10** assignment, exposition, stationery **11** composition, examination **12** dissertation
ancient: **7** papyrus
folding: **7** origami **8** kirigami
fragments: **8** confetti
money: **4** cash **5** bills, notes, scrip **10** greenbacks
newspaper: **5** daily **7** gazette, journal, tabloid **10** periodical **11** publication
reused: **8** recycled
size: **4** copy, demy **5** atlas, crown, folio, legal, royal **6** medium **7** emperor **8** elephant, foolscap, imperial

PAPOOSE: **4** baby **5** child **6** infant

PAPPY: **3** dad, paw, pop **4** soft **5** daddy, mushy, poppy **6** father, spongy **7** squishy

PAPUA NEW GUINEA:
capital: **11** Port Moresby
cities: **3** Lae **6** Madang, Rabaul
continent: **7** Oceania
ethnic groups: **6** Papuan, pygmie **7** Chinese **10** Australian, Melanesian, Polynesian
feature: **5** swamp
head of state: **7** monarch
islands: **7** Solomon **9** Admiralty, Louisiade, New Guinea **10** New Britain, New Ireland **11** Archipelago **12** Bougainville **14** D'Entrecasteaux

languages: **6** Papuan, pidgin **7** English **10** Melanesian
monetary unit: **4** kina
water: **10** Sepik River

PAR: **4** norm **5** equal **6** normal, parity **7** average, balance **8** equality, sameness, standard **11** equivalence

PARABLE: **4** myth, tale **5** fable, moral, story **6** legend **8** allegory, apologue

PARACLETE: **5** aider **8** advocate, consoler **9** comforter **10** Holy Spirit **11** intercessor

PARADE: **4** pomp, show **5** array, flash, march, strut **6** flaunt, review, stroll **7** caravan, display, exhibit, marshal **8** ceremony, flourish, grandeur **9** advertise, motorcade, pageantry, promenade, spectacle **10** exhibition, masquerade, procession, tickertape **13** demonstration

PARADIGM: **5** ideal, model **6** sample **7** example, pattern **9** prototype, yardstick

PARADISE: **4** Eden, Zion **5** bliss **6** Assama, Avalon, Canaan, heaven, reward, utopia **7** arcadia, delight, Elysium, nirvana **8** Valhalla **9** afterlife, Alfardaws, cloud nine, shangri-la **12** Promised Land

PARADOX: **6** enigma, puzzle **7** anomaly **9** absurdity **13** contradiction

PARAGON: **4** tops **5** cream, ideal, jewel, model **7** epitome, example, pattern **8** nonesuch, paradigm, ultimate **12** quintessence

PARAGUAY:
capital: **8** Asuncion
cities: **10** Concepcion **11** Encarnacion **18** Pedro Juan Caballero **20** Presidente Stroessner
ethnic groups: **6** Indian **7** mestizo **9** Caucasian
features: **5** swamp **9** Gran Chaco, Itaipu dam
languages: **7** Guarani, Spanish
monetary unit: **7** guarani
water: **3** Apa **4** Ypoa **11** Parana River **13** Paraguay River

PARALLEL: **4** even, like **5** agree, alike, equal, match **6** equate **7** abreast, compare, similar **8** analogue, relation **9** alongside **10** collateral, correspond, equivalent **11** correlation, counterpart

PARALLELOGRAM: **5** plane, rhomb **6** oblong, square **9** rectangle

PARALYZE: **4** halt, maim, numb, stun **6** deaden, freeze **7** cripple, destroy, disable, petrify **8** demolish **10** immobilize **12** incapacitate

PARAMOUNT: **5** chief, prime, ruler **6** master, utmost **7** highest, premier, supreme **8** cardinal, crowning, dominant, foremost, superior **9** principal **10** commanding, preeminent **11** predominant

PARAMOUR: **5** lover, Romeo **6** amoret, suitor **7** Don Juan, gallant **8** Casanova, mistress **9** concubine, courtesan

PARAPET: **4** wall **7** bulwark, railing, rampart **9** barricade **10** breastwork, embankment **12** embattlement

PARAPHERNALIA: **4** gear **6** tackle, things **8** supplies **9** apparatus, equipment, materials **10** belongings **11** accessories, furnishings **13** accoutrements, appurtenances

PARAPHRASE: **6** reword **8** rephrase, synopsis **9** interpret, summarize, translate **11** restatement **12** recapitulate

PARASITE: **3** bug **5** leech, toady, virus **6** sponge **7** moocher, sponger **8** bacteria, barnacle, deadbeat, hangeron, organism **9** dependent, sycophant **10** freeloader **11** bloodsucker

PARASOL: **6** canopy **8** sunshade, umbrella

PARCEL: **3** box, lot **4** crew, deal, dole, land, pack, part, plot, wrap **5** bunch, group, piece, tract **6** bundle, carton, divide, packet, ration **7** acreage, company, package, portion, section **8** fragment, property **9** apportion, container **10** distribute

PARCH: **3** dry **4** burn, char, sear **5** roast **6** scorch, wither **7** blister, shrivel **9** dehydrate, desiccate

PARCHMENT: **5** paper **6** scroll, vellum **7** diploma, papyrus **9** sheepskin

PARDON: **4** free **5** clear, grace, mercy, spare **6** excuse, exempt **7** absolve, amnesty, commute, condone, forgive, release **8** liberate, overlook, reprieve, tolerate **9** exculpate, remission, vindicate **10** absolution

PARE: **3** cut **4** clip, flay, peel, skin, trim **5** prune, shave, shear **6** reduce, remove **7** curtail **8** decrease, diminish **11** decorticate

PARENT: **3** dad, mom **4** mama, papa, sire **5** cause, daddy, spawn **6** author, father, mother, origin **7** forbear, produce **8** ancestor, begetter, forebear, generate, guardian **9** protector **10** forefather, progenitor

PARENTHETICAL: **9** bracketed **10** incidental, qualifying **11** explanatory

PAR EXCELLENCE: **7** supreme **8** superior **9** excellent **10** preeminent

PARIAH: **7** outcast **9** scapegoat **11** undesirable, untouchable

PARIS (CITY):
capital of: **6** France
features: **6** Louvre **8** Left Bank, Sorbonne **9** Notre Dame, Right Bank, Tuileries **10** Luxembourg, Montmartre **11** Eiffel Tower **12** Montparnasse **13** Champs Elysees
native: **8** Parisian
Roman name: **7** Lutetia
water: **10** River Seine

PARIS:
abducted: **5** Helen
caused: **9** Trojan War
family: **6** Hecuba, Oenone **7** Troilus **9** Cassandra
father: **5** Priam
judged: **4** Hera **6** Athena **9** Aphrodite
killer: **11** Philoctetes
prince of: **4** Troy

PARISH: **4** fold **5** flock **7** diocese **8** brethren **9** community **11** archdiocese, churchgoers **12** congregation, parishioners

PARITY: **6** equity **7** analogy, balance **8** equality, likeness **9** closeness **10** similarity **11** consistency, equivalence

PARK: **4** stop **6** forest, meadow, refuge **7** commons, grounds **8** preserve, woodland **9** sanctuary **10** playground

PARLANCE: **4** talk **5** idiom, lingo **6** speech, tongue **7** diction **8** language, phrasing, verbiage **12** conversation

PARLEY: **4** talk **5** speak, treat **6** confab, confer, debate, huddle **7** consult, discuss, palaver **10** conference, discussion **12** conversation

PARLIAMENT: **4** diet **5** court **6** senate **7** council **8** assembly, congress **9** gathering **10** assemblage **11** legislature

PARLOR: **4** room **5** salon **6** lounge **9** reception

PAROCHIAL: **5** petty **6** biased, narrow **7** bigoted, insular, limited **10** prejudiced, provincial, restricted

PARODY: **3** ape **4** copy, mock **5** farce, mimic, spoof **6** satire **7** imitate, lampoon, takeoff **8** travesty **9** burlesque **10** caricature, exaggerate

PAROXYSM: **4** fury, rage **5** spasm, throe **6** attack, frenzy **7** seizure, tantrum **8** eruption, outbreak, outburst **9** agitation **10** convulsion

PARROT: **3** ape **4** bird, copy, echo **5** mimic, polly **6** repeat **7** imitate
disease: **11** psittacosis
family: **7** Loridae **10** Cacatuidae **11** Psittacidae
variety: **4** lory **5** macaw **6** conure, kakapo, trogon **7** quetzal **8** cockatoo, lovebird, parakeet

PARRY: **4** fend, ward **5** avert, avoid, block, dodge, elude, evade, shirk **7** deflect **8** sidestep **10** circumvent

PARSIMONIOUS: **4** mean **5** cheap **6** frugal, meager, skimpy, stingy **7** chintzy, miserly, thrifty **9** illiberal, niggardly, penurious **10** avaricious, economical **11** tightfisted **13** penny-pinching

PARSON: **5** clerk **6** cleric, pastor, priest, rector **8** minister, preacher, reverend **9** clergyman

PART: **3** bit, cut **4** chip, half, item, role, side **5** allot, break, chunk, leave, piece, quota, sever, share, slice, split **6** behalf, cleave, detach, detail, divide, factor, member, parcel, ration, region, sector, sunder **7** disjoin, element, portion, section, segment **8** disperse, disunite, division, fraction, fragment, separate, withdraw **9** apportion, character, component **10** department, incomplete, ingredient **11** constituent, involvement, subdivision

PARTAKE: **3** eat **5** drink, share, taste **6** divide, engage, sample **7** consume **11** participate

PARTIAL: **6** biased, unfair **7** colored, favored, halfway, limited **8** inclined, one-sided, partisan **9** sectional **10** fractional, incomplete, prejudiced, unfinished **11** fragmentary, predisposed **12** inconclusive

PARTIALITY: **4** bias **5** fancy, slant, taste **7** leaning **8** affinity, fondness, interest, tendency **10** favoritism, preference **11** inclination

PARTICIPANT: **4** ally **6** cohort, fellow, helper, player **9** associate, colleague **10** accomplice **11** contributor **12** collaborator

PARTICIPATE: **4** join **5** enter, share **6** assist, concur, engage **7** partake, perform **8** complete **9** cooperate **10** contribute

PARTICLE: **3** ace, bit, dot, ray **4** atom, drop, iota, mite, mote **5** crumb, fleck, grain, piece, scrap, shred, speck, trace **6** morsel, tittle **7** element, granule, smidgen **8** fragment, molecule

PARTI-COLORED: **4** pied **6** motley **7** piebald **9** checkered **10** variegated

PARTICULAR: **4** fact, item, lone **5** fussy, picky, point, scoop **6** choosy, detail, minute, unique **7** careful, finicky, notable, precise, special, unusual **8** accurate, detailed, distinct, especial, exacting, itemized, peculiar, separate, specific, uncommon **9** selective **10** fastidious, individual, noteworthy **11** exceptional, persnickety **12** circumstance **13** extraordinary

PARTING: **5** adieu, split **7** breakup, goodbye **8** division, farewell, partisan **9** departure **10** factionary, separation

PARTISAN: **6** backer, biased, zealot **7** devotee, fanatic **8** adherent, advocate, champion, defender, disciple, follower, guerilla, stalwart **9** supporter **11** sympathizer

PARTITION: **4** wall **5** fence, panel **6** divide, screen, septum **7** barrier, portion, section **8** division, separate **9** allotment, severance **10** detachment, separation **11** compartment **12** distribution **13** apportionment

PARTLY: **7** halfway, notably **8** slightly, somewhat **9** partially **10** noticeably **12** incompletely **13** comparatively

PARTNER: **3** pal **4** ally, chum, mate, wife **5** buddy, crony **6** cohort, fellow, friend, helper, spouse **7** comrade, husband **8** sidekick, teammate **9** assistant, associate, colleague, companion **10** accomplice **11** confederate

PARTNERSHIP: **4** firm, gang, ring **5** union **6** cartel **7** cahoots, company **8** alliance, business, marriage **11** affiliation, association **12** conglomerate, organization

PARTS: **4** area, land **6** pieces, region, talent **9** territory

PARTURITION: **5** birth **8** delivery **10** childbirth

PARTY: **4** ball, bash, body, clan, crew, gala, orgy, ring, sect, side, stag **5** cabal, dance, force, group, squad, troop **6** affair, fiesta, outfit, person, picnic, shindy, shower, soiree, troupe **7** banquet, carouse, company, faction, shindig **8** alliance, occasion, wingding **9** bacchanal, coalition, defendant, festivity, gathering, plaintiff, reception **10** detachment, individual **11** association, celebration

PARVENU: **4** snob **7** upstart **8** arrogant, newcomer **12** nouveau riche

PASQUINADE: **5** farce **6** parody, satire **7** lampoon **9** burlesque

PASS: **3** die, end, gap, way **4** beat, flow, give, lane, omit, pace, skip, step, toss, wend **5** adopt, cease, enact, gorge, lapse, leave, occur, outdo, relay, throw, utter **6** canyon, convey, crisis, decree, elapse, exceed, expire, happen, ignore, perish, permit, ratify, ravine, ticket, travel **7** advance, approve, journey, passage, pathway, proceed, qualify, surpass **8** bequeath, exchange, furlough, juncture, outshine, overlook, progress, surmount **10** adjudicate, permission, suggestion **11** discontinue **13** authorization

PASSABLE: **4** fair, open **5** clear **8** adequate, mediocre **9** crossable, navigable, tolerable **10** acceptable, accessible, admissible, negotiable, travelable **12** satisfactory, unobstructed

PASSAGE: **4** belt, door, duct, exit, fare, gate, hall, lane, pass, path, road, text **5** aisle, alley, entry, gorge, piece, route, verse **6** access, atrium, avenue, burrow, course, egress, strait, travel, tunnel, voyage **7** channel, estuary, excerpt, gangway, journey, reading, transit **8** aqueduct, corridor, crossing **9** enactment, quotation, selection **10** permission, transition **11** legislation **12** ratification, transmission

PASS AWAY: **3** die **6** depart, expire, perish **7** decease, succumb

PASS BY: **4** omit, skip **6** ignore **7** abandon, neglect **8** overlook **9** disregard

PASSÉ: **4** aged, past **5** dated, faded **6** bygone, lapsed **7** ancient, archaic, demoded, extinct **8** obsolete, outdated, outmoded **10** antiquated **12** old-fashioned **13** superannuated

PASSENGER: **4** fare **5** rider **7** pilgrim **8** commuter, stowaway, traveler, wayfarer **10** hitchhiker

PASSING: **5** brief, death, quick **6** demise **7** cursory **8** adequate, elapsing, fleeting, illusive **9** ephemeral, exceeding, momentary, temporary **10** transitory

PASSION: **3** ire **4** fire, fury, heat, love, lust, rage, zeal **5** amour, anger, ardor, craze, gusto **6** desire, fervor, hunger, temper, thirst **7** craving, ecstasy, emotion, feeling **8** appetite, devotion, distress **9** adoration, eagerness, intensity, obsession **10** dedication, enthusiasm, sensuality **11** infatuation

PASSIONATE: **5** fiery **6** ardent, fervid, fierce, heated, steamy, sultry **7** amorous, fervent, flaming, intense, lustful, peppery, sensual **8** frenetic, romantic **9** hot-headed **10** hotblooded, stimulated **11** hot-tempered **12** affectionate, enthusiastic

PASSIVE: **5** inert, quiet, stoic **6** docile, stolid **7** dormant **8** inactive, lifeless, yielding **9** apathetic, compliant, lethargic, quiescent **10** phlegmatic, submissive **11** unassertive

PASS OFF: **4** palm **5** eject, foist **6** vanish **7** pretend

PASS ON: **3** die **6** convey, decide, depart **7** decease, succumb **8** transmit

PASS OUT: **5** faint, swoon **8** black out **9** circulate **10** distribute

PASS OVER: **4** omit, skip **6** forget, ignore **7** dismiss, neglect **8** overlook **9** disregard

PASSOVER: **5** Pasch **6** Pesach **7** Paschal
bread: **5** matzo **10** unleavened
feast: **5** Seder
length: **9** eight days

PASSPORT: **3** key **4** visa **5** conge **6** ticket **7** license, voucher **9** safeguard **11** credentials **14** identification

PASSWORD: **9** watchword **10** open sesame **11** countersign

PAST: **3** ago **4** gone, late, yore **5** after, ended, olden, prior **6** beyond, bygone, former, latter **7** expired, history **8** foregone, previous **9** antiquity, preceding, yesterday **11** antecedents

PASTA: **4** orzo, ziti **6** shells **7** gnocchi, lasagna, lasagne, ravioli **8** linguine, macaroni, rigatoni **9** manicotti, spaghetti **10** fettuccine, tortellini, vermicelli

PASTE: **4** beat, glue, pate, seal **5** affix, cream, patch, punch, stick **6** attach, batter, cement, fasten, strass, strike **8** adhesive, mucilage

PASTEL: **4** pale, soft **5** color, light **6** crayon **8** delicate, pastiche

PASTICHE: **4** olio **6** jumble, medley **8** mishmash **10** assortment, hodgepodge

PASTIME: **4** game **5** hobby, sport **7** leisure **8** activity **9** amusement, diversion **10** recreation, relaxation **13** entertainment

PASTOR: **5** padre, rabbi **6** parson, priest, rector **8** minister, preacher, reverend, shepherd **9** clergyman **11** clergywoman **12** ecclesiastic

PASTORAL: **4** poem **5** rural **6** rustic **7** bucolic, country, idyllic **8** agrarian **11** picturesque **14** ecclesiastical

PASTRY: **3** pie **4** baba, cake, flan, puff, tart **6** Danish, eclair, phyllo **7** baklava, fritter, goodies, strudel **8** delicacy, Napoleon, turnover **9** croissant

PASTURE: **5** agist, grass, range **6** meadow **7** feeding, grazing, herbage **10** retirement

PASTY: **4** dull, pale **5** ashen, gluey **6** chalky, pallid, sickly **8** adhesive **9** bloodless, unhealthy

PAT: **3** dab, tap **5** aptly, ideal, piece, touch **6** caress, soothe, strike, stroke, timely **7** apropos, exactly, fitting, readily **8** relevant, suitable **9** pertinent, rehearsed **11** opportunely

PATCH: **3** fix **4** darn, mend, plot, spot **5** chunk, clump, cover, piece, scrap **6** blotch, doctor, emblem, repair, revamp, settle **7** restore **8** insignia **13** reinforcement

PATCHWORK: **4** mess, olio **6** jumble, medley **7** melange, mixture **8** mishmash, pastiche **9** fragments **10** hodgepodge, miscellany

PATE: **3** pie **4** head, meat **5** brain, crown, paste **6** noggin, spread **9** intellect

PATELLA: **3** pan **4** bone, dish **7** kneecap

PATENT: **4** open, rank **5** clear, grant, gross, overt, plain **7** control, evident, license, obvious **8** apparent, distinct, flagrant, manifest **9** copyright, franchise, invention **10** protection **11** conspicuous **12** unobstructed

PATERNAL: **6** tender **8** fatherly **10** benevolent, protective

PATH: **3** way **4** fare, lane, line, road, walk **5** alley, byway, orbit, route, track, trail **6** artery, avenue, course, groove **7** passage **8** shortcut

PATHETIC: **3** sad **4** poor **5** sorry **6** moving, rueful **7** doleful, pitiful, useless **9** affecting, miserable **10** lamentable **13** heartbreaking

PATHOS: **4** pity **7** emotion, feeling **8** sympathy **9** poignancy, sentiment **10** tenderness

PATIENCE: **4** calm, cool **5** poise **8** stoicism, tenacity **9** composure, diligence, endurance, fortitude, tolerance **10** resolution, submission **11** resignation **12** perseverance

PATIENT: **4** case, meek, mild **7** subject **8** enduring, tireless **9** forgiving **10** persistent **13** long-suffering, understanding

PATIO: **4** deck **5** porch **6** piazza **7** terrace **9** courtyard

PATOIS: **4** cant **5** lingo **6** jargon **7** dialect **10** vernacular

PATRIARCH: **4** head, male, sire **5** chief, elder, ruler **6** father, leader **7** founder **8** ancestor **9** venerable
religious: **4** Adam, Noah **5** Isaac, Jacob **6** bishop **7** Abraham **9** dignitary

PATRICIAN: **5** noble **6** lordly **7** stately **8** highborn **9** blueblood **10** aristocrat, upper-class

PATRIMONY: **6** estate, legacy **8** ancestry, heritage **9** endowment **10** bequeathal **11** inheritance

PATRIOT: **8** jingoist, loyalist, partisan **9** flag-waver, volunteer **10** chauvinist **11** nationalist

PATROL: **5** guard, scout, watch **7** inspect, protect **8** garrison, sentinel **9** safeguard **10** detachment

PATRON: **4** host **5** angel, guest, owner **6** backer, client **7** manager, shopper, sponsor **8** advocate, champion, customer, guardian **9** protector, supporter **10** benefactor

PATRONAGE: **4** help **5** aegis, favor, trade **6** buying, custom **7** auspice, backing, subsidy **8** business **9** clientele, customers **10** assistance, protection **11** sponsorship **13** encouragement

PATRONIZE: **4** snub **5** deign, stoop **6** assist **7** promote, support **8** frequent **10** condescend

PATSY: **3** sap **4** dupe, pawn **5** chump **6** pigeon, sucker, victim **9** scapegoat

PATTER: **4** cant, drum, glib, move, talk **5** sound, speak, utter **6** babble, jabber, jargon, mumble, rattle **7** chatter, scuttle, tapping

PATTERN: **4** copy, form, mold, plan, trim **5** guide, ideal, model, motif, order, plaid **6** design, figure, format, method, sample, system **7** diagram, emulate, example, imitate, stencil **8** exemplar, markings, paradigm, sequence, specimen, template **9** archetype, prototype **11** arrangement

PAUCITY: **4** lack **6** dearth, guilty **7** poverty **8** scarcity, shortage, sparsity **10** scantiness **13** insufficiency

PAUL:
birthplace: **6** Tarsus
companion: **5** Silas, Titus **7** Artemas, Timothy **8** Barnabas **9** Trophimus
known as: **7** apostle
original name: **4** Saul
place of conversion: **8** Damascus
teacher: **8** Gamaliel
tribe: **8** Benjamin

PAUNCH: **3** gut **5** belly, bulge, tummy **7** abdomen, stomach **8** potbelly **11** breadbasket

PAUPER: **6** beggar **7** almsman **8** bankrupt, indigent **9** destitute, insolvent

PAUSE: **4** halt, lull, rust, stay, stop, wait **5** break, cease, comma, delay, hover, letup **6** breath, hiatus, layoff, recess **7** caesura, respite **8** breather, hesitate, interval **9** cessation **10** hesitation **12** intermission, interruption

PAVE: **4** tile **5** cover, floor **6** smooth **7** asphalt, overlie, prepare, surface **8** blacktop **10** macadamize

PAVILION: **4** dome, tent **5** kiosk **6** awning, canopy, gazebo, litter **8** covering **9** structure

PAW: **3** dad, pop, toe **4** feel, foot, grab, hand, maul **5** daddy, grope, touch **6** father, fumble, handle

PAWN: **4** dupe, fool, hock, tool **5** patsy **6** flunky, pledge, puppet, stooge, sucker **7** counter, hostage **8** guaranty **9** guarantee **10** chess piece

PAY: **3** fee, tip **4** ante, foot, hire, wage **5** atone, clear, grant, spend, yield **6** defray, income, outlay, profit, refund, return, reward, salary **7** satisfy, stipend, tribute **9** allowance, indemnify, liquidate, reimburse **10** commission, compensate, recompense, remunerate, settlement **11** reciprocate, retribution **12** compensation

PAYABLE: **3** due **5** owing **6** mature, unpaid **10** obligatory, receivable **11** outstanding

PAY BACK: **6** rebate, return **8** compound **9** reimburse, retaliate

PAY FOR: **3** buy **7** expiate **8** purchase

PAYLOAD: **4** haul **5** cargo **6** charge, weight

PAYMASTER: **6** bursar, purser **7** cashier **9** treasurer

PAYMENT: **3** fee, tax **4** cash, debt, dues, duty, fine, levy, toll **5** award, money, price **6** amends, rebate, return, reward, tariff **7** alimony, annuity, pension, premium, tuition **8** defrayal, requital **9** allowance, discharge **10** honorarium, recompense, remittance **11** expenditure **12** compensation

PAYOFF: **5** bribe, graft **6** climax, payola, profit, result, reward **7** outcome **10** conclusion, settlement **11** culmination, retribution

PAYOLA: **5** graft **6** payoff **7** bribery

PEACE: **4** calm, ease, pact, rest **5** amity, order, quiet, truce **6** repose, treaty **7** concord, harmony **8** ataraxia, serenity **9** agreement, armistice **10** equanimity, neutrality **11** contentment, tranquility **12** pacification

PEACEABLE: **6** gentle, irenic, placid **7** amiable, pacific **8** amicable, friendly, peaceful **10** nonviolent **11** undisturbed

PEACEFUL: **4** calm **5** quiet, still **6** irenic, placid, serene, silent, steady **7** halcyon, neutral **8** tranquil **9** peaceable **10** nonviolent **11** undisturbed

PEACEMAKER: **8** diplomat, mediator, pacifist, placater **10** ambassador, arbitrator, negotiator **11** conciliator

PEACH: **4** blab, tree **5** color, fruit **6** betray, snitch, squeal **8** informer, jimdandy **11** crackerjack
genus: **13** Prunus persica
variety: **4** Hale, Muir **6** Desert, Indian **7** Elberta, Persian **8** Champion **9** Alexander, freestone, Halehaven, nectarine **10** North China, South China

PEACH STATE: **7** Georgia

PEACHY: **4** fine, nice **5** dandy **6** divine **8** splendid **9** excellent, marvelous

PEAK: **3** alp, tip, top **4** acme, apex, cone, crag, roof **5** crest, crown, point, visor **6** apogee, climax, summit, zenith **7** maximum **8** aiguille, meridian, mountain, pinnacle, ultimate **10** perfection **11** culmination

PEAKED: **3** wan **4** pale, thin, weak **5** ashen, drawn, sharp **6** ailing, anemic, sickly, spiked **9** emaciated

PEAL: **4** bong, boom, clap, ring, toll **5** bells, blast, chime, noise **7** resound, thunder **11** reverberate

PEANUT: **4** mani, puny, seed **5** petty, pinda, plant, small **6** goober, pindal **8** earthnut **9** groundnut
genus: **15** arachis hypogaea

PEANUTS: **7** nothing **8** trifling **13** insignificant

PEAR: **4** tree **5** fruit
genus: **13** pyrus communis
shaped: **8** pyriform
variety: **4** Bosc **5** Melon **6** Garber, Gorham, Seckel **7** Kieffer **8** Bartlett **10** Chaumontel

PEARL: **3** gem **4** seed **5** color, jewel, nacre **6** orient **7** paragon **8** lustrous, margaric
found in: **6** oyster

PEARLY: **5** clear, ivory, milky **7** shining **8** nacreous **10** opalescent

PEASANT: **4** boor, esne, kern, peon, ryot, serf **5** churl, knave, kulak, swain **6** cotter, farmer, fellah, muzhik, rustic, toiler **7** bumpkin, laborer, lowlife, villein **10** countryman **12** sharecropper

PEBBLE: **4** rock **5** stone **6** gravel

PECCADILLO: **3** sin **5** error, fault **7** blunder, misdeed, mistake, offense **9** violation **10** wrongdoing **13** transgression

PECCANT: **6** erring, guilty, sinful **7** corrupt

PECK: **3** dot, jab, nag, tap **4** beak, bill, bite, buss, carp, hole, kiss, nose, pick **5** prick, smack **6** nibble, strike, stroke **7** measure **9** criticize

PECULATE: **5** steal **8** embezzle

PECULIAR: **3** odd **5** queer wacky, weird **6** unique **7** bizarre, curious, offbeat, strange, unusual **8** abnormal, singular **9** eccentric, exclusive **10** outlandish **11** distinctive **14** characteristic, distinguishing

PECULIARITY: **4** kink, mark **5** quirk, stamp, trait, twist **6** oddity **7** feature **9** attribute, character, mannerism **12** idiosyncrasy

PECUNIARY: **6** fiscal **8** economic, monetary **9** financial

PEDAGOGIC: **8** academic, tutorial **10** scholastic **11** educational, instructive **13** instructional

PEDAGOGUE: **5** tutor **6** pedant **7** teacher **8** educator **10** instructor **12** schoolmaster

PEDANTIC: **7** bookish, donnish, learned, precise **8** academic, didactic **9** schoolish **10** scholastic **13** hairsplitting

PEDDLE: **4** hawk, push, sell **5** pitch **6** canvas, piddle, retail **7** solicit **8** dispense, huckster

PEDESTAL: **3** leg **4** base, foot **5** stand **6** column, pillar, podium **7** support **10** foundation

PEDESTRIAN: **4** dull **5** banal, hiker **6** walker **7** humdrum, mundane, prosaic **8** everyday, ordinary, stroller **10** unexciting **11** commonplace **13** unimaginative, uninteresting

PEDIGREE: **4** line **5** breed, stock **7** descent, lineage **8** ancestry, heredity, heritage, purebred **9** bloodline, genealogy **12** thoroughbred

PEEK: **4** look, peep **5** snoop, watch **6** gander, glance **7** glimpse

PEEL: **4** bark, flay, hull, husk, rind, skin **5** cover, flake, scale, shuck, strip **6** remove, shovel **7** uncover **11** decorticate

PEEP: **3** spy **4** hoot, look, peek, peer **5** cheep, chirp, snoop, tweet, watch **6** glance, squeak **7** chatter, chirrup

PEEPHOLE: **4** slit, slot **5** judas **6** eyelet **7** crevice, eyehole, opening

PEEPING TOM: **6** voyeur

PEER: **3** pry **4** gape, gawk, gaze, look, mate, peep, show, view **5** equal, glare, juror, snoop, stare **6** emerge **7** comrade, inspect **8** nobleman **9** associate, companion **10** rubberneck **12** contemporary

PEERAGE: **4** rank **5** title **6** gentry **8** nobility **12** jurisdiction

PEERLESS: **7** supreme **9** excellent, matchless, unequaled, unrivaled **11** superlative **12** incomparable, unparalleled

PEEVE: **3** bug, irk, vex **4** rile **5** annoy **6** bother, nettle **7** disturb, provoke **8** irritate **9** aggravate **10** exasperate

PEEVISH: **4** mean **5** cross, huffy, surly, testy **6** cranky, crusty, ornery, sullen, touchy **7** carping, fretful, pettish, waspish **8** captious, contrary, critical, petulant, snappish **9** crotchety, fractious, irascible, irritable, obstinate, querulous **11** contentious, disgruntled **12** cantankerous, discontented

PEEWEE: **4** tiny **5** dwarf, small, teeny **6** little **9** miniature **10** diminutive **11** lilliputian

PEG: **3** fix, leg, nob, pin **4** join, plug **5** dowel, notch, prong, spike, stake, throw, tooth **6** attach, degree, secure **7** support **8** fastener, identify

PEGASUS:
carried: **12** thunderbolts
father: **8** Poseidon

form: **11** winged horse **13** constellation
mother: **6** Medusa
rider: **4** Zeus **11** Bellerophon

PEJORATIVE: **8** debasing, negative **9** demeaning, slighting **10** belittling, derogatory, irreverent **11** disparaging

PELAGIC: **6** marine **7** aquatic, oceanic **9** thalassic

PELEUS:
brother: **7** Telamon
father: **6** Aeacus
mother: **6** Endeis
seized: **6** Thetis
son: **8** Achilles
wife: **6** Thetis

PELICAN STATE: **9** Louisiana

PELLET: **3** wad **4** ball, mass, pill, rock, shot **5** bolus, stone **6** bullet, pebble

PELL-MELL: **5** chaos **7** turmoil **8** disarray, disorder, headlong **9** confusion, haphazard, hurriedly **10** heedlessly, recklessly **11** impetuously, pandemonium **13** helter-skelter

PELLUCID: **5** clear, plain **6** bright, limpid, simple **8** explicit, luminous **11** crystalline, translucent, transparent **14** comprehensible

PELOPS:
father: **8** Tantalus
feature: **13** ivory shoulder
killer: **8** Tantalus
son: **6** Atreus
wife: **10** Hippodamia

PELT: **3** fur **4** beat, belt, blow, cast, hair, hide, hurl, skin **5** hurry, pound, stone, whack **6** assail, batter, pummel, strike, thrash, thrust, wallop **7** clobber, rawhide

PELVIS:
part: **5** ilium, pubis **6** coccyx, sacrum **7** ischium **9** symphysis

PEN: **3** sty **4** cage, coop, crib, fold, jail, yard **5** fence, hutch, kraal, quill, write **6** author, corral, kennel, prison, stylus, writer **7** compose, confine, enclose **8** imprison, stockade **9** enclosure **12** penitentiary
types: **4** desk, reed **5** quill **6** marker **7** drawing, felt-tip **8** fountain **9** ball point **10** stylograph **11** highlighter

PENAL: **8** punitive, punitory **9** punishing **10** corrective **11** retributive **12** disciplinary

PENALIZE: **4** fine **6** amerce, punish **8** handicap **9** castigate **10** discipline

PENALTY: **4** fine, loss **5** mulct **7** damages, forfeit, penance **8** hardship **9** suffering **10** amercement, punishment **11** retribution **12** disadvantage

PENANCE: **7** penalty, remorse **9** atonement, expiation, suffering **10** absolution, contrition, repentance **11** compunction, forgiveness **13** mortification

PENCHANT: **4** bent, bias **5** fancy, knack, taste **6** liking **8** affinity, fondness, tendency **9** proneness **10** attraction, partiality, propensity **11** inclination **12** predilection

PENDING: **6** during **7** hanging **8** awaiting **9** dependent, undecided, unsettled **10** unresolved

PENDULOUS: **6** droopy **7** hanging, pendent **8** dangling **9** suspended, tentative

PENELOPE:
father: **7** Icarius
home: **6** Ithaca
husband: **7** Ulysses **8** Odysseus
mother: **8** Periboea
son: **10** Telemachus
suitor: **7** Agelaus
trick: **7** weaving

PENETRATE: **4** bore, stab **5** drill, drive, enter, imbue, prick, stick **6** absorb, fathom, insert, invade, pierce, thrust **7** discern, pervade **8** permeate, puncture **9** insinuate, perforate **10** comprehend, infiltrate, understand

PENETRATING: **4** deep, keen **5** acute, harsh, sharp **6** astute, shrewd **7** cutting, knowing **8** incisive, stinging **9** intrusive, pervasive, sagacious **10** insightful, perceptive **14** discriminating

PENGUIN: **3** auk **4** bird
family: **12** Spheniscidae
feature: **10** flightless

PENINSULA: **4** cape, neck **5** point **8** headland **10** chersonese

PENITENCE: **5** grief, qualm, shame **6** regret, sorrow **7** anguish, penance, remorse, scruple **8** distress **9** attrition, expiation **10** contrition, repentance **11** compunction

PENITENT: **5** sorry **6** shamed **8** contrite **9** regretful, repentant **10** remorseful **12** compunctious

PENITENTIARY: **3** can, jug, pen **4** brig, coop, jail, poky, stir **5** clink, joint **6** cooler, prison **7** slammer **8** stockade **9** calaboose **11** reformatory

PENMANSHIP: **6** script **7** writing **8** longhand **11** calligraphy, chirography, handwriting

PEN NAME: **5** alias **9** pseudonym **10** nom de plume

PENNANT: **4** flag, jack **5** color **6** banner, emblem, ensign, pennon, symbol **7** pendant **8** streamer **9** banderole

PENNILESS: **4** poor **5** broke, needy **6** busted **8** bankrupt **9** destitute, insolvent **11** impecunious **12** impoverished

PENNON: **4** flag, jack **5** color **6** banner, ensign, pinion, symbol **7** pennant **8** gonfalon, streamer

PENNSYLVANIA:
among: **16** Thirteen Colonies
bird: **12** ruffed grouse
capital: **10** Harrisburg
cities: **4** Erie **7** Reading **8** Scranton **9** Allentown **10** Pittsburgh **12** Philadelphia **16** Cumberland Valley
explorer: **11** William Penn
features: **7** Poconos **10** Gettysburg **11** Valley Forge **14** Mason-Dixon Line **18** Allegheny mountains
flower: **14** mountain laurel
native: **5** Amish **9** Mennonite **13** Pennsylvanian
nickname: **13** Keystone State
tree: **7** hemlock
water: **4** Ohio **8** Delaware **10** Schuylkill **11** Monongahela, Susquehanna

PENNY-PINCHING: **5** tight **6** stingy **7** miserly **9** niggardly, penurious **12** parsimonious

PENSION: **3** IRA **7** annuity, payment, subsidy, support **9** allowance **14** social security

PENSIVE: **4** blue **5** sober **6** dreamy, solemn **7** wistful **8** absorbed, thinking **9** pondering **10** meditative, melancholy, reflective, ruminating, thoughtful **11** preoccupied **13** contemplative, introspective

PENTHEUS:
father: **6** Echion
grandfather: **6** Cadmus
kingdom: **6** Thebes
mother: **5** Agave

PENT-UP: **6** stored **7** bridled, checked **9** inhibited, repressed **10** suppressed

PENURIOUS: **4** poor **5** tight **6** barren, frugal, stingy **7** miserly **8** indigent **9** destitute, niggardly **12** parsimonious **13** penny-pinching

PENURY: **4** need **6** dearth **7** poverty **9** indigence, privation **10** barrenness, scantiness **11** destitution **13** insufficiency

PEON: **4** hand, pawn, serf **5** slave **6** drudge **7** footman, laborer, peasant, servant **9** messenger

PEOPLE: **3** kin, men **4** clan, folk **5** laity, plebs, stock, tribe, women **6** family, humans, nation, public **7** inhabit, mankind, persons, society **8** citizens, humanity, populace, populate, subjects **9** commoners, community, multitude, plebeians **10** electorate **11** individuals, inhabitants, proletariat, rank and file

PEP: **3** vim **4** dash **5** getup, gusto, verve, vigor **6** energy, ginger, spirit **8** vitality **9** animation, briskness, hardihood **10** enthusiasm, invigorate, liveliness

PEPO: **5** fruit
variety: **5** gourd **6** squash **7** pumpkin **8** cucumber **10** cantaloupe, watermelon

PEPPER: **3** hot **5** fruit, plant, spice **8** exercise **9** condiment
genus: **5** piper
variety: **3** red **5** black, chili, green, sweet **6** cherry **7** cayenne, paprika **8** jalapeno, pimiento

PEPPERY: **3** hot **4** keen **5** fiery, sharp, spicy, vivid, zesty **6** biting, cranky, lively, snappy, spunky **7** pungent **8** choleric, poignant, spirited, stinging **9** irascible, sarcastic **10** passionate

PEPPY: **4** spry **5** alert, perky **6** active, lively **8** animated, spirited, vigorous **9** vivacious

PER: **3** for **4** each **6** apiece **7** through

PERAMBULATE: **4** roam, tour, walk **5** mosey **6** ramble, stroll **9** promenade

PERCEIVE: **3** see **4** feel, hear, know, mind, note, spot **5** grasp, sense, smell, taste, touch **6** behold, deduce, descry, detect, divine, notice **7** discern, observe, realize **8** discover, identify **9** apprehend, recognize **10** comprehend, understand **11** distinguish

PERCENTAGE: **3** cut **4** odds, part **5** piece, ratio, share, split **6** profit **7** portion **8** division, interest **9** allotment **10** proportion **11** probability

PERCEPTIBLE: **5** clear, lucid **7** obvious, visible **8** apparent, palpable, sensible, tangible **10** cognizable, detectable, noticeable **11** appreciable, discernible **12** recognizable

PERCEPTION: **4** idea **5** image **6** acumen **7** concept, insight, thought **8** judgment **9** awareness, intuition, sensation **13** understanding

PERCEPTIVE: **4** keen, wise **5** acute, alert, aware, sharp **6** astute **9** observant, sensitive **10** insightful

PERCH: **3** bar, peg, rod, sit **4** fish, land, pike, pole, seat **5** roost, squat, staff, stick **6** alight, branch, sauger, settle **7** balance

PERCOLATE: **4** brew, drip, ooze, seep, sift **5** leach **6** filter, strain **7** trickle **8** permeate **9** penetrate, transfuse

PERCUSSION: **4** blow, jolt **5** shock, sound **6** impact **9** collision

PERCUSSION INSTRUMENT: **4** drum, gong **5** bones, bongo, conga, tabor **6** chimes, claves, cymbal, maraca, timbal **7** marimba, timpani **8** triangle **9** castanets, xylophone **10** kettledrum, lithophone, tambourine, vibraphone **12** glockenspiel

PERDITION: **4** doom, Hell, ruin **5** hades **8** downfall **9** damnation **11** destruction **12** condemnation

PEREGRINATION: **4** trip **5** jaunt **6** hiking **7** journey, roaming, travels **10** expedition, traversing

PEREMPTORY: **5** bossy, final, harsh, rigid **6** urgent **7** decided **8** absolute, decisive, dogmatic, positive, rigorous **9** imperious, masterful **10** commanding, imperative **11** dictatorial, domineering, overbearing **13** authoritative **14** uncompromising

PERENNIAL: **5** fixed, plant **6** annual **7** durable **8** constant, enduring, geophyte, lifelong, timeless **9** continual, permanent, perpetual, recurrent, unceasing **10** changeless **12** neverfailing

PERFECT: **4** fine, holy, pure **5** exact, ideal, right, sound, whole **6** entire, expert, finish **7** correct, fulfill, improve, precise, realize, sinless, utopian **8** absolute, accurate, complete, finished, flawless, masterly, suitable, thorough, unerring, unmarred **9** blameless, excellent, exquisite, faultless, stainless **10** accomplish, consummate, immaculate, impeccable, unimpaired **11** culminating, unblemished, untarnished

PERFECTION: **4** acme, pink **5** ideal **7** fulness, paragon **8** fullness **10** excellence

PERFECTLY: **5** quite **7** totally **8** entirely, superbly **10** absolutely, altogether

PERFIDIOUS: **5** false, venal **6** shifty, untrue **8** disloyal **9** deceitful, dishonest, faithless **10** traitorous, unfaithful **11** disaffected, treacherous **13** untrustworthy

PERFORATE: **4** bore **5** drill, prick, punch, sieve, stamp **6** pierce, pounce **8** permeate, puncture **9** penetrate

PERFORM: **3** act **4** play, work **5** enact, exert **6** effect, render **7** achieve, execute, exhibit, fulfill, furnish, gesture, operate, present **8** complete, transact **9** dramatize **10** accomplish

PERFORMANCE: **3** act **4** deed, feat, play, show, test, work **5** stunt **6** acting, effect, review **7** benefit, concert, matinee, recital **8** ceremony, function **9** depiction, portrayal, rendition, spectacle **10** completion, efficiency, exhibition **11** fulfillment **12** consummation, presentation **14** accomplishment

PERFORMER: **4** doer, mime, star **5** actor **6** artist, player, worker **7** actress, artiste, trouper **8** musician, thespian **12** impersonator

PERFUME: **4** aura, balm, odor **5** aroma, myrrh, scent, smell, spice **6** flavor, sachet **7** bouquet, cologne, essence, incense, sweeten **9** fragrance, patchouli, potpourri, redolence

PERFUNCTORY: **7** cursory, routine **8** careless, listless, standard **9** automatic **10** mechanical, unthinking **11** indifferent, passionless, superficial **13** disinterested, lackadaisical

PERHAPS: **5** maybe **6** likely **7** suppose **8** feasibly, possibly, probably **9** perchance **10** imaginably **11** conceivably

PERIL: **4** risk, trap **6** crisis, danger, hazard, menace, threat **7** pitfall **8** endanger, exposure, jeopardy **9** adventure, liability **10** insecurity **11** uncertainty

PERILOUS: **5** dicey, hairy, risky **6** chancy, touchy, unsafe **8** unstable, unsteady **9** dangerous, hazardous **10** precarious **11** treacherous

PERIMETER: **4** brim, edge **6** border, fringe, margin **7** outline **8** boundary **9** periphery **13** circumference

PERIOD: **3** age, day, dot, era **4** date, hear, span, stop, term, time **5** close, cycle, epoch, point, spell, stage **6** decade, ending, season **7** century **8** duration, interval, semester **10** conclusion, generation **11** termination

PERIODICAL: **5** daily **6** annual, review **7** journal, tabloid **8** cyclical, magazine **9** newspaper, recurring, routinely **12** infrequently, intermittent, occasionally

PERIPATETIC: **6** mobile, roving **7** migrant, nomadic **8** rambling **9** itinerant, traveling, wandering **10** ambulatory

PERIPHERAL: **5** minor **7** distant **8** external **9** outermost, secondary **10** incidental

PERIPHERY: **4** brim, edge **5** ambit, limit **6** border, fringe **7** outside, surface **8** boundary, environs **9** outskirts, perimeter **13** circumference

PERISH: **3** die **4** fade, ruin **5** croak, decay **6** depart, expire, vanish **7** crumble, decease, succumb **8** pass away **9** disappear

PERIWINKLE: **4** herb **5** shrub, snail **6** mussel **9** evergreen
genus: **17** catharanthus vinca

PERJURE: **3** lie **7** deceive, falsify, mislead **10** equivocate **11** prevaricate

PERK: **4** gain **5** bonus, extra **7** benefit **8** gratuity **9** percolate **10** perquisite

PERK UP: **5** rally **6** revive **7** improve, refresh **8** brighten **10** convalesce, invigorate, recuperate

PERKY: **5** alert, brisk, happy **6** bouncy, bubbly, lively **8** animated, cheerful, spirited **9** vivacious

PERMANENT: **5** fixed **6** stable **7** diurnal, durable, endless, eternal, forever, lasting **8** constant, enduring, unending **9** perennial, perpetual **11** everlasting **12** imperishable **14** indestructible

PERMEABLE: **6** porous **8** passable **9** absorbent **10** penetrable, spongelike

PERMEATE: **4** fill, seep, soak **5** imbue **6** drench, filter **7** pervade **8** saturate **9** penetrate **10** infiltrate

PERMISSIBLE: **6** lawful **8** endorsed **9** allowable, permitted **10** acceptable, admissible, legitimate **12** unprohibited

PERMISSION: **5** grant, leave **6** permit **7** consent, liberty, license **8** approval **9** allowance **11** approbation, endorsement **13** authorization

PERMIT: **3** let **4** have, pass, visa **5** admit, allow, grant, leave **6** enable, suffer **7** condone, consent, license, warrant **8** furlough, legalize, passport, tolerate **9** authorize **10** permission

PERMUTATION: **5** shift **6** change **10** alteration **12** modification **14** transformation

PERNICIOUS: **4** evil **5** fatal, toxic **6** deadly, lethal, malign, mortal, wicked **7** baleful, baneful, harmful, hurtful, noxious, ruinous **8** damaging, venomous **9** injurious, pestilent, poisonous, unhealthy **11** deleterious, destructive, detrimental

PERORATE: **4** rant **5** orate, speak **7** address, declaim, lecture

PERPENDICULAR: **5** erect, plumb, sheer **7** upright **8** straight, vertical **10** horizontal

PERPETRATE: **4** pull **5** enact, wreak **6** commit **7** execute, perform

PERPETUAL: **7** endless, eternal **8** constant, enduring, unending **9** continual, incessant, perennial, permanent, unceasing **10** continuous **11** everlasting **13** uninterrupted

PERPETUATE: **4** keep **7** prolong, sustain **8** continue, maintain, preserve **10** eternalize **11** immortalize

PERPLEX: **5** amaze, beset, snarl, stump **6** baffle, boggle, cumber, muddle, puzzle, thwart **7** astound, bedevil, confuse, diffuse, embroil, mystify, nonplus **8** astonish, bewilder, confound, distract, entangle **9** bamboozle, dumbfound, obfuscate **10** complicate

PERQUISITE: **3** fee, tip **4** gain **5** right **6** income, profit **8** appanage, gratuity, proceeds **9** privilege **11** prerogative

PER SE: **5** alone **6** solely **11** essentially **13** fundamentally, intrinsically

PERSECUTE: **4** bait **5** abuse, annoy, harry, hound, wrong **6** badger, harass, heckle, pester **7** afflict, crucify, oppress, torment, torture **8** maltreat **9** victimize

PERSEPHONE:
abducted by: **5** Pluto
ate: **15** pomegranate seed
father: **4** Zeus
husband: **5** Hades, Pluto
lover: **6** Adonis
mother: **7** Demeter
queen of: **10** Underworld

PERSEUS:
borrowed: **6** helmet, shield, sickle, wallet **13** winged sandals
father: **4** Zeus
grandfather: **8** Acrisius
killed: **6** Medusa **8** Acrisius **11** grandfather
lived on: **8** Seriphos
mother: **5** Danae
saved: **9** Andromeda
wife: **9** Andromeda

PERSEVERANCE: **4** grit **5** drive, spunk **7** stamina **8** patience, tenacity **9** constancy, diligence, endurance **10** dedication, insistence, resolution **11** continuance, persistence **13** determination, steadfastness

PERSEVERE: **4** last **5** abide, stick **6** endure, pursue **7** persist, prevail **8** maintain

PERSIA:
animals: **4** cora **5** maral, miana **6** Bulbul, fallow **7** Karakul **9** Angora cat, astrakhan
capital: **9** Ctesiphon
captured: **4** Fars **5** India, Medes, Syria **8** Anatolia **9** Babylonia, Palestine **11** Afghanistan
cities: **6** Abadan **7** Bushire
gods/goddesses: **7** Anahita, Mithras
kings: **4** shah **7** Darius I **9** Darius III **13** Cyrus the Great
located: **4** Iran
people: **5** Aryan
religion: **5** Islam **14** Zoroastrianism
rugs: **4** Kali **5** Saruk, Senna **6** carpet, Sarouk **7** Isfahan, Ispahan, Teheran **8** Serabend

PERSIFLAGE: **6** banter **7** mockery **8** chaffing, flippery **9** frivolity

PERSIST: **4** last **5** abide **6** endure, insist, linger, remain **7** perdure, prevail, survive **8** continue **9** persevere

PERSISTENT: **5** fixed **6** dogged, gritty **7** durable **8** constant, diligent, enduring, obdurate, resolute, stubborn **9** assiduous, insistent, steadfast, sustained, tenacious **10** consistent, continuing, continuous, determined, relentless, unshakable **11** persevering

PERSNICKETY: **5** fussy **6** choosy **7** finicky **8** picayune **10** particular

PERSON: **3** guy, man, one **4** body, chap, life, self, soul **5** being, child, human, woman **6** entity, fellow, mortal **8** creature **9** earthling **10** individual
40-year-old: **14** quadragenarian
50-year old: **15** quinquagenarian
60-year-old: **12** sexagenarian
70-year-old: **14** septuagenarian
80-year-old: **12** octogenarian
90-year-old: **12** nonagenarian
100-year-old: **11** centenarian
admirable: **6** mensch
bad: **3** cad, yap **4** heel, toad **5** knave **6** varlet **7** bauchle, caitiff **8** anathema **10** blackguard
combining forms: **6** prosop **7** prosopo
crazy: **3** nut **7** lunatic **9** psychotic **10** monomaniac, psychopath
energetic: **10** ball of fire
engaged: **6** fiance **7** fiancee
enterprising: **8** go-getter
foolish: **3** sop **4** zany **5** clown **6** dotard **7** halfwit **9** simpleton
guilty: **7** culprit
important: **3** VIP **4** star **5** great **7** notable
learned: **6** pundit, savant
middle-class: **9** bourgeois **11** bourgeoisie
mixed blood: **5** metis **7** mestizo, mulatto **8** octoroon **9** half-breed
named after another: **8** namesake
non-Jewish: **7** gentile
skilled: **5** adept **6** artist, master, talent **7** artisan **8** mechanic
small: **4** runt **5** dwarf, sprat **6** midget, poppet
stupid: **3** ass **4** boob, clod, coot, dolt, fool, gump **5** dunce, moron **6** boodle, duffer, nitwit **7** dullard **8** bonehead, dumbbell, imbecile **9** blockhead, simpleton
stylish: **12** clotheshorse
wealthy: **3** nob **5** nabob **9** plutocrat **10** capitalist **11** millionaire
young: **8** chipling **9** stripling

PERSONABLE: **4** warm **7** affable, amiable, likable, shapely **8** charming, friendly, handsome, pleasant, sociable **9** easygoing **10** attractive

PERSONAGE: **3** VIP **5** being **6** bigwig, tycoon **7** magnate, notable **9** celebrity, dignitary **10** individual **11** heavyweight

PERSONAL: **5** privy **6** secret **7** private **8** intimate **10** individual, particular **12** confidential

PERSONALITY: **3** ego **4** star **5** trait **6** makeup, nature, psyche **8** behavior, charisma, emotions, identity **9** celebrity, character **11** disposition, temperament

PERSONIFY: **6** embody, typify **7** imitate **9** epitomize, exemplify, incarnate, represent, symbolize **11** externalize **12** characterize

PERSONNEL: **4** crew **5** staff **6** people, troops **7** workers **9** employees

PERSPECTIVE: **5** angle, vista **7** context, mindset, outlook **8** panorama **9** viewpoint **10** relativity **11** expectation

PERSPICACIOUS: **4** keen **5** acute, alert, savvy **6** astute, shrewd **9** observant **10** discerning, perceptive **11** clearheaded

PERSPICUOUS: **5** clear, lucid **7** crystal, obvious **8** apparent, distinct, luminous, manifest **11** conspicuous **12** intelligible

PERSPIRE: **5** exude, sweat **7** excrete, secrete

PERSUADABLE: **7** ductile **8** amenable, flexible **9** acceptive, malleable, tractable

PERSUADE: **4** coax, lead, lure, sway, urge **5** argue, tempt **6** allure, entice, induce, prompt, seduce **7** convert **8** convince, inveigle **9** brainwash, influence

PERSUASION: **4** cult, mind, pull, type, view **5** class, creed, faith **6** belief, church, school **7** faction **8** religion **9** character, sentiment **10** conviction, enticement **11** affiliation **12** denomination

PERSUASIVE: **5** slick **6** smooth **8** eloquent **9** effective, impelling, seductive **10** compelling, convincing **11** influential

PERT: **4** bold, spry **5** alert, alive, brisk, fresh, perky, sassy, saucy, smart **6** active, brazen, dapper, frisky, jaunty, lively **7** chipper, naughty **8** animated, insolent, spirited **9** audacious, energetic, sprightly, vivacious

PERTAIN: **5** apply, refer, touch **6** befall, belong, regard, relate **7** concern, connect **9** associate

PERTINACIOUS: **4** firm **6** dogged **8** stubborn **9** obstinate, tenacious **10** bullheaded, determined, headstrong, inflexible, persistent, unshakable

PERTINENT: **3** apt **6** proper, timely **7** apropos, fitting, germane, related **8** apposite, material, relative, relevant, suitable **9** connected **10** applicable **11** appropriate

PERTURB: **5** annoy, upset, worry **6** bother, pester **7** agitate, confuse, disturb, fluster, trouble **8** disorder, irritate, unsettle **10** disconcert

PERU:
animals: **4** paco, yutu **5** llama **6** alpaca **10** chinchilla
capital: **4** Lima
cities: **6** Callao **7** Iquitos **8** Arequipa, Chiclayo, Chimbate, Mollendo, Trujillo
conqueror: **7** Pizarro
continent: **12** South America
empire: **4** Inca
ethnic groups: **6** Indian **7** mestizo **9** Caucasian
features: **5** Andes, Nazca **8** Chanchan **11** Machu Picchu **13** Atacama Desert **15** Charin de Huantar
languages: **6** Aymara **7** Quechua, Spanish
liberators: **7** Bolivar, de Sucre
monetary unit: **6** new sol **8** nuevo sol
native: **8** Peruvian
water: **6** Amazon **12** Lake Titicaca

PERUSE: **4** read, scan **5** study **6** search, survey **7** analyze, examine, inspect **10** scrutinize

PERVADE: **4** fill **5** imbue **6** charge, spread **7** suffuse **8** permeate, saturate **9** penetrate

PERVASIVE: **6** common **7** general **8** dominant **9** extensive, prevalent, universal **10** widespread

PERVERSE: **5** balky **6** cranky, ornery, wicked **7** awkward, corrupt, deviant, diverse, forward, vicious, wayward **8** backward, contrary, crotched, depraved, petulant, stubborn **9** difficult, fractious, obstinate **10** degenerate, determined **11** contentious, wrongheaded

PERVERT: **4** ruin, warp **5** abuse, twist **6** debase, divert, garble, misuse, poison, weirdo **7** contort, corrupt, deprave, deviant, distort **8** misapply **9** desecrate, misdirect **10** adulterate, degenerate, demoralize **11** misconstrue **12** misinterpret, misrepresent

PERVERTED: **5** kinky **6** wicked **7** corrupt, immoral, twisted **8** abnormal **9** distorted, unnatural

PERVIOUS: **4** open **6** porous **9** permeable **10** accessible, penetrable **12** approachable

PESKY: **7** irksome **8** annoying **9** obnoxious, vexatious **10** bothersome, disturbing **11** troublesome **12** disagreeable

PESSIMISM: **5** gloom **7** despair **8** cynicism **10** melancholy **12** hopelessness

PESSIMIST: **5** cynic **7** killjoy, worrier **8** sourpuss **9** Cassandra **10** complainer **11** misanthrope

PESSIMISTIC: **5** bleak **6** gloomy **7** cynical **8** hopeless **10** despairing

PEST: **3** bug **4** bane **5** creep **6** bother, insect, plague, vermin **7** heckler, trouble **8** nuisance **9** annoyance **10** irritation, pestilence

PESTER: **3** bug, nag, rib **4** bait, ride **5** annoy, devil, harry, hound, tease **6** badger, bother, harass, plague **7** torment, trouble **8** irritate **9** aggravate, annoyance

PESTIFEROUS: **5** toxic **7** harmful **8** annoying, diseased, virulent **9** unhealthy **10** bothersome, pernicious

PESTILENCE: **4** evil, pest **6** blight, plague **7** disease, scourge **8** epidemic **11** destruction

PESTILENT: **6** deadly, lethal **7** harmful, noxious **9** dangerous **10** contagious, infectious, pernicious

PET: **3** cat, dog, hug **4** coax, dear, huff, kiss, neck, pony **5** horse, jewel, lover **6** animal, caress, coddle, cuddle, fondle, pamper, parrot, rabbit, stroke, turtle **7** beloved, cherish, darling, embrace, indulge, special **8** favorite, goldfish **9** cherished, favourite

PETER OUT: **4** fade, stop, wane **6** fizzle **7** dwindle **8** diminish

PETER PAN:
author: **11** James Barrie
character: **4** John, Nana **5** Wendy **7** Michael **9** Tiger Lily **10** Tinker Bell **11** Captain Hook
place: **14** Never-Never-Land

PETITE: **3** wee **4** tiny **5** small **6** dainty, demure, little **8** delicate **10** diminutive **11** lilliputian

PETITION: **3** ask, beg **4** call, plea, pray **5** apply, plead **6** appeal, invoke, prayer **7** address, beseech, entreat, implore, request, solicit **8** entreaty, proposal **10** supplicate **11** application

PETRIFY: **4** daze, numb, stun **6** appall, deaden **7** horrify, startle **8** frighten, paralyze **9** fossilize **10** immobilize

PETTICOAT: **4** kilt, slip **6** female **7** clothes **8** feminine **9** undercoat, underwear, waistcoat **10** underskirt

PETTIFOGGER: **6** lawyer **7** shyster **8** attorney

PETTY: **4** base, mean, puny **5** minor, small **6** little, measly, slight **7** shallow, trivial **8** childish, inferior, niggling, nugatory, picayune, piddling, trifling **9** frivolous **10** diminutive, irrelevant **11** inessential, unimportant **12** contemptible **13** insignificant **14** inconsiderable

PETULANT: **5** cross, gruff, huffy, moody, sulky, testy **6** crabby, cranky, sullen **7** fretful, grouchy, peevish, pettish **8** insolent, snappish **9** crotchety, impatient, irascible, irritable, querulous **10** displeased

PEW: **4** seat, slip **5** bench, stall

PHAEDRA:
died: **6** hanged **7** suicide
father: **5** Minos
husband: **7** Theseus
jealous of: **10** Hippolytus
mother: **8** Pasiphae
sister: **7** Ariadne
stepson: **10** Hippolytus

PHANTASM: **5** dream, ghost, shade **6** mirage, shadow, spirit, vision **7** eidolon, fantasy, specter **8** illusion **9** nightmare **10** apparition

PHANTOM: **5** ghost, image **6** spirit, vision, wraith **7** figment, specter **8** phantasm **13** hallucination

PHARMACIST: **7** chemist **8** druggist **10** apothecary

PHAROS: **6** beacon, signal **7** lantern **10** lighthouse

PHASE: **4** hand, look, part, side, time **5** angle, facet, stage **6** aspect, period **7** chapter, feature **8** position **9** condition **11** development

PHENOMENAL: **4** rare **5** super **6** unique **7** unusual **9** fantastic **10** incredible, remarkable **11** exceptional, outstanding, sensational **13** extraordinary, unprecedented

PHENOMENON: **4** fact **5** event **6** marvel, wonder **7** miracle, paradox **8** incident **9** actuality, happening, sensation **10** experience **11** abnormality

PHILANDERER: **4** wolf **5** flirt, lover **6** tomcat **7** swinger **9** adulterer, debaucher, womanizer

PHILANTHROPIC: **6** giving, humane **8** generous **10** altruistic, benevolent, charitable, openhanded **11** kindhearted, magnanimous **12** humanitarian

PHILANTHROPIST: **5** donor **6** patron **8** altruist **10** benefactor **11** contributor **12** humanitarian

PHILIPPIC: **6** screed, tirade **8** exchange, reproach

PHILIPPINES:
capital: **6** Manila
carriage: **9** carretola
chief: **4** dato **5** datto
cities: **3** Iba **4** Agoa, Bogo, Cebu, Debu, Naga, Palo **5** Albay, Davao, Pasay **6** Aparri, Baguio, Cavite, Ilagan, Tarlac **7** Dagupan **10** Quezon City
clothing: **4** baro, saya **6** camisa **8** padadion **10** balintawak
drink: **4** beno, vino **5** bubud **6** tampoy **7** pangasi
explorers: **7** Lagazpe **8** Magellan **10** Villalobos
food: **3** poi **4** baha, rima, sabu, taro **5** balut, copra **7** lacatan **9** pineapple
forts: **4** Cota, Gota, Kota **5** Lotta **10** Corregidor
islands: **4** Cebu, Cuyo, Jolo, Poro, Sulu **5** Batan, Bohol, Leyte, Luzon, Panay, Samar, Ticao **6** Culion, Lubang, Negros **7** Masbate, Mindoro, Palawan, Paragua **8** Mindanao **10** Corregidor
languages: **4** Moro **5** Bicol, Bikol, Tagal **6** Ibanag **7** Cebuano, English, Filipino, Ilocano, Spanish, Tagalog, Visayan **8** Filipino **9** Pampangan **10** Samar-Leyte **14** Panay-Hiligayon
liberator: **9** MacArthur
measure: **4** loan **5** braza, caban, catty, cavan, chupa, fardo, ganta, picul, punto **6** apatan, balita, lachsa, quinon
monetary unit: **4** peso
mountains: **3** Apo, Iba **4** Mayo, Taal **5** Albay, Askja, Hibok, Mayon, Pulog **7** Banahao
people: **3** Ata, Ati, Ita, Tao **4** Aeta, Atta, Etas, Moro, Sulu **5** Bicol, Bikol, Tagal, Vicol **6** Igorot, Timaua, Timawa **7** Bisayan, Tagalog, Visayan **8** Filipino, Igorrote **10** Philippino
presidents: **6** Aquino, Marcos
seas: **4** Sulu **5** Samar **7** Celebes, Pacific, Visayan **10** Philippine, South China
shrubs: **4** alem, nabo
volcanos: **3** Apo **4** Mayo **7** Canlaon
water: **4** Abra, Agno, Taal **5** Davao, Lanao, Magat, Pasig, Ragay **6** Agusan, Laoang **7** Cagayan **8** Mindanao, Pampanga

PHILOSOPHER: **4** sage **7** scholar, sophist, thinker **9** theorizer
American: **9** John Dewey **10** Felix Adler **11** Josiah Royce, Paul Til-

lich **12** William James **13** Charles Peirce, Rudolph Carnap
British: **10** Roger Bacon **12** Thomas Huxley **13** Jeremy Bentham **14** Herbert Spencer, John Stuart Mill, William of Occam **15** Alfred Whitehead
Chinese: **6** Lao-tzu **9** Confucius
French: **8** Voltaire **12** Auguste Comte, Denis Diderot, Henri Bergson **13** Pierre Abelard, Rene Descartes
German: **10** Georg Hegel **11** Karl Jaspers, Martin Buber **12** Immanuel Kant, Johann Fichte, Johann Herder **13** Edmund Husserl **15** Martin Heidegger **18** Arthur Schopenhauer, Friedrich Nietzsche **19** Gottfried von Leibniz **21** Friedrich von Schelling
Greek: **5** Plato **6** Thales **8** Socrates **9** Aristotle **10** Anaxagoras, Pythagoras
Indian: **6** Buddha **17** Siddhartha Gautama
Italian: **13** Giordano Bruno, Thomas Aquinas
Spanish: **8** Averroes, Ignatius **10** Maimonides
Swedish: **17** Emanuel Swedenborg
Swiss: **15** Huldrych Zwingli

PHILOSOPHICAL: **4** calm, deep, wise **5** stoic **6** serene **7** learned, logical **8** abstract, composed, profound, rational **9** temperate **10** reflective, thoughtful

PHILOSOPHY: **6** belief, school, theory, values, wisdom **7** outlook **8** attitude, doctrine, ideology **9** reasoning **10** conviction, principles
fields: **5** logic **6** ethics **8** axiology **10** aesthetics, psychology **11** metaphysics **12** epistemology
school: **4** yoga **5** Stoic **6** Modern **7** Eleatic, Gnostic, realism, Sophist **8** idealism, nihilism, Platonic **9** Epicurean **10** tabula rasa **11** materialism, Pythagorean, rationalism **12** Aristotelian **14** existentialism

PHLEGMATIC: **4** calm, cold, cool, dull, slow **5** aloof **8** composed, listless, sluggish **9** apathetic, impassive, lethargic **10** spiritless **11** indifferent, unemotional

PHOBIA: **4** fear **5** dread **7** anxiety **8** neurosis **9** obsession **12** apprehension

PHOEBE: **4** moon **5** Diana **7** Artemis **9** satellite

PHOEBUS: **3** Sol, sun **5** deity **6** Apollo

PHOENICIA:
capital: **9** Jerusalem
cities: **4** Tyre **5** Arvad, Sidon **6** Byblos, Ugarit **7** Berytus
colonies in: **5** Cadiz, Malta, Spain **6** Cyprus, Sicily **8** Carthage
conquered by: **4** Rome **9** Assyrians **17** Alexander the Great
gods/goddesses: **4** Baal **5** Tanit **6** Agenor, Baltis, Eshmun, Ishtar, Moloch, Tanith **7** Astarte
king: **7** Solomon
language: **5** Punic
located: **5** Syria **6** Canaan **7** Lebanon **9** Palestine **11** Mount Carmel
made: **5** cloth **7** jewelry **8** alphabet **9** furniture, purple dye
water: **13** Mediterranean **15** Eleutherus River

PHOENIX: **4** bird **6** statue, symbol **7** paragon

PHONETIC: **4** oral **5** vocal **6** spoken, voiced

PHONOGRAPH: **4** hi-fi **6** stereo **7** machine **8** victrola **9** turntable **10** gramophone
inventor: **12** Thomas Edison

PHONY: **4** fake, sham **5** bogus, false, fraud **6** unread **8** impostor, spurious **9** imitation **10** artificial, fictitious **11** counterfeit

PHOTOGRAPH: **3** mug **4** film, snap **5** image, pinup, slide **6** blowup, candid, record **7** picture, tintype **8** likeness, portrait, snapshot

PHOTOGRAPHER: **6** artist **9** cameraman **10** shutterbug

PHOTOGRAPHIC: **5** exact **7** precise **8** lifelike **9** cinematic **11** picturesque

PHRASE: **4** term, word **5** couch, idiom, motto, state, voice **6** cliche, saying, slogan **7** diction, present, proverb **8** verbiage **9** catchword **10** expression

PHRASEOLOGY: **5** style **6** manner, syntax **7** diction, wording **8** language, parlance

PHRIXUS:
father: **7** Athamus
mother: **7** Nephele
rode: **9** golden ram
sister: **5** Helle
stepmother: **3** Ino
wife: **9** Chalciope

PHYLACTERY: **5** charm **6** amulet **8** reminder, talisman

PHYSIC: **4** cure, drug, heal **5** treat **8** medicine **9** cathartic

PHYSICAL: **4** real **5** brute **6** bodily, carnal **7** natural, somatic, violent **8** concrete, material, tangible **9** corporeal **11** examination, substantial

PHYSICIAN: **3** doc **5** medic, quack **6** doctor, healer, intern, medico **7** surgeon **8** sawbones **10** consultant, specialist **12** practitioner

PHYSICIST: **9** hylozoist, scientist **10** naturalist **11** materialist

PHYSIOGNOMY: **4** face, look, mien **6** aspect, visage **7** feature **8** portrait **10** appearance, expression **11** countenance

PHYSIQUE: **4** body, form **5** build, frame, shape **6** figure, makeup **7** anatomy, muscles, stature **12** constitution

PIANO: **5** grand **6** player, softly, spinet, square **7** boudoir, clavier, pianola, quietly, upright **8** electric **10** clavichord, instrument, pianoforte
inventor: **10** Cristofori

PIAZZA: **5** patio, porch **6** square **7** balcony, portico, veranda **9** colonnade

PICAROON: **5** knave, rogue **6** pirate **9** buccaneer **10** adventurer, freebooter

PICAYUNE: **4** mean **5** petty, small **6** little, measly **7** trivial **8** piddling **11** unimportant

PICK: **4** best, cull, take, tool **5** cream, elect, elite, jimmy, pluck, prize **6** choice, choose, gather, prefer, select **7** bargain, harvest **8** druthers **10** preference

PICKET: **4** pale, post, rail **5** fence, guard, stake **6** patrol, strike, tether **7** boycott, lookout, striker **8** sentinel **9** protester **11** demonstrate

PICKLE: **3** fix, jam **4** bind, cure, dill, mess, peck **5** brine, sweet **6** capers, crisis, garlic, plight **7** chutney, dilemma, gherkin, trouble, vitriol **8** cucumber, marinate, quandary **11** predicament

PICKLED: **5** drunk **6** buzzed, juiced, soused, tanked, wasted **7** sloshed **10** inebriated **11** intoxicated

PICK ON: **4** bull, goad **5** tease **6** badger **7** torment **9** criticize

PICKPOCKET: **5** thief **6** cannon, digger, dipper, jostle, riffle, robber **8** cutpurse, friskers **11** fingersmith

PICK UP: **4** bust, gain, lift **5** hoist, learn, pinch, raise **6** arrest, garner, gather **7** acquire, collect, elevate, improve, procure, recover **8** increase **9** apprehend

PICKUP: **5** boost, truck **9** impromptu, stimulant **12** acceleration

PICKY: **5** fussy **6** choosy **7** finicky **10** meticulous, particular **11** persnickety

PICNIC: **4** snap **5** cinch **6** breeze, outing **7** cookout **8** barbecue, pushover

PICTURE: **4** copy, draw, film, icon, idea, show **5** flick, image, movie, photo, print, scene **6** canvas, depict, mosaic, pastel, sketch **7** cartoon, drawing, etching, explain, imagine, portray, tableau **8** conceive, describe, envision, likeness, painting, panorama, portrait, vignette **9** delineate, pictorial, portrayal, represent **10** illustrate, impression, photograph, watercolor **12** illustration

PICTURESQUE: **5** vivid **6** quaint, scenic **7** graphic **8** alluring, artistic, charming, striking **9** beautiful **12** photographic

PIDDLING: **5** petty, small **6** little, measly, paltry **7** trivial **8** picayune, trifling **13** insignificant

PIE: **4** tart **6** pastry **7** cobbler, dessert **8** crustade, turnover **9** blackbird

PIEBALD: **5** mixed **6** motley **7** dappled, mottled, spotted **10** variegated **11** varicolored **12** multicolored **13** heterogeneous

PIECE: **3** bit, cut, lot **4** hunk, join, mend, part, slab, unit **5** crumb, essay, flake, paper, patch, scrap, shred, slice, snack, story, strip **6** morsel, parcel, sample, sliver **7** article, portion, section, segment **8** assemble, creation, fraction, fragment, painting **9** component **10** exposition, percentage

PIECE DE RESISTANCE: **8** main dish **9** showpiece **11** centerpiece, masterpiece **14** accomplishment

PIECEMEAL: **6** patchy, spotty **7** gradual **11** fragmentary **12** intermittent

PIECE TOGETHER: **4** form, make **6** create **7** combine **8** assemble

PIER: **4** dock, pile, quay, slip **5** berth, jetty, wharf **6** column, pillar **7** landing, support **8** buttress, pilaster **10** breakwater

PIERCE: **3** cut **4** bore, gash, gore, hole, stab **5** break, drill, enter, lance, probe, slash, spear, spike, stick, sting, wound **6** broach, cleave, impale, tunnel **8** puncture **9** penetrate, perforate

PIERCING: **4** high, keen, loud **5** acute, clear, sharp **7** blaring, cutting, intense, painful, pungent, roaring **8** poignant **9** agonizing, deafening **10** screeching **12** earsplitting

PIETY: **5** ardor, faith **6** fealty, fervor **7** loyalty **8** devotion, fidelity, holiness, religion **9** godliness, reverence **10** devoutness

PIG: **3** hog **4** slob **5** swine **6** animal, mammal, porker **7** porcine
family: **6** Suidae
female: **3** sow
food: **3** ham **4** chap, pork **5** bacon **7** sausage **8** chitlins, trotters **9** pettitoes
litter: **6** farrow
male: **4** boar **6** barrow
young: **4** gilt, runt **5** shoat, shote **6** barrow, farrow, piglet

PIGEON: **4** bird, dove, dupe, fool, gull **5** chump, decoy pluck **8** squealer

clay: **4** bird, disk **5** skeet **6** target
family: **10** Columbidae
types: **5** fruit **6** homing, isabel, pouter **7** carrier, crowned, fantail **10** turtledove
young: **5** squab

PIGEONHOLE: **4** rank, slot **5** label, niche, shelf, store **6** assort, recess **7** arrange, catalog, cubicle **9** cubbyhole **11** compartment

PIGGISH: **5** dirty **6** filthy, greedy **7** selfish **8** stubborn **10** gluttonous

PIGHEADED: **5** dense **7** willful **8** perverse, stubborn **9** insistent, obstinate **10** headstrong, unyielding

PIGMENT: **3** dye **4** tint **5** color, paint, shade, stain **8** colorant

PIGPEN: **3** sty **4** dump, hole, mess

PIGSKIN: **7** leather **8** football

PIGTAIL: **5** braid, plait, queue **7** tobacco

PIKE: **4** fish, road **5** drive, point, spear, spike **6** summit **7** freeway, highway, parkway, thruway **8** tollgate **10** expressway

PIKER: **5** miser **7** gambler **8** tightwad **9** skinflint **10** cheapskate, speculator

PILASTER: **4** pier, post **6** column, pillar **7** support

PILE: **3** gob, jam, wad **4** cock, hair, heap, hill, load, mass, pyre, shag, wool, yarn **5** amass, crowd, flock, hoard, money, mound, stack **6** boodle, bundle, wealth **7** fortune **8** building **10** accumulate, collection

PILEUP: **5** crash, stack **8** accident **9** collision **12** accumulation

PILFER: **4** hook, lift, loot, take **5** filch, steal, swipe **6** finger, snitch **7** pillage, plunder, purloin **8** embezzle, shoplift **11** appropriate

PILGRIM: **5** hadji **6** palmer **7** pioneer, settler **8** crusader, traveler, wanderer, wayfarer **9** sojourner

PILGRIMAGE: **4** hadj, trip **6** voyage **7** crusade, journey, mission, sojourn **10** expedition

PILGRIM'S PROGRESS:
author: **10** John Bunyan
character: **4** Help **5** Piety, Sloth **6** Simple **7** Charity, Hopeful **8** Faithful, Mistrust, Prudence, Timorous **9** Christian **10** Discretion, Evangelist, Mr. Good-will, Mr. Legality **11** Presumption
location: **6** Vanity **8** Morality **10** Wicket-gate **13** Celestial City **14** House Beautiful

PILL: **4** ball, pest **5** bolus **6** pellet, pilule, tablet, troche **7** capsule, placebo **8** medicine, nuisance

PILLAGE: **4** lift, loot, raid **5** booty, pinch, rifle, steal, swipe **6** maraud, pilfer, ravage **7** despoil, plunder, ransack **8** trespass **9** depredate, desecrate, devastate **10** confiscate **11** appropriate

PILLAGER: **6** looter, vandal **8** marauder **9** plunderer **10** freebooter

PILLAR: **4** pier, pile, post, prop **5** shaft **6** leader **7** obelisk, support **8** mainstay, pedestal, pilaster **9** colonnade

PILLARS OF HERCULES: **9** Gibraltar, Jebel Musa

PILLOW: **7** bolster, cushion, padding, support **8** headrest

PILOT: **3** ace **5** flier, guide, scout, steer **6** airman, fly-boy, fly-gal, leader **7** aviator, operate **8** airwoman, coxswain, director, helmsman **9** conductor **10** helmswoman

PIMPLE: **3** zit **4** acne, boil **6** papule **7** abscess, blemish **9** blackhead, whitehead

PIN: **3** fix, peg **4** bind, bolt, clip, dart, join **5** affix, badge, clasp, dowel, rivet, stake **6** attach, brooch, cotter, fasten, secure **7** confine, jewelry **8** fastener, ornament

PINCE-NEZ: **7** lorgnon **9** lorgnette **10** eyeglasses, spectacles

PINCH: **4** bust, dash, drop, grab, lift, snip **5** cramp, filch, grasp, gripe, speck, steal, theft, tweak **6** arrest, collar, crisis, crunch, pickle, pilfer, snatch **7** squeeze **8** contract, juncture **9** apprehend, emergency **10** difficulty

PINCHBECK: **4** fake **8** spurious **9** imitation **11** counterfeit

PINE: **4** ache, flag, fret, mope, tree, want, wood **5** brood, crave, mourn, waste, yearn **6** desire, grieve, hunger, lament, repine, wither **7** agonize, dwindle **8** languish

feature: **4** cone **6** needle

genus: **5** pinus

variety: **3** fir, nut, red **4** blue, gray, jack, pond **5** cedar, giant, pinon, stone, sugar, white **6** Apache, Scotch, spruce **7** Cypress, foxtail, hickory **8** loblolly, mahogany, mountain, Weymouth **9** evergreen, Norwegian

PINE TREE STATE: **5** Maine

PING: **4** ting **5** clink, knock, noise, sound

PINHEAD: **4** fool, tiny **5** clown, dunce, small **6** stupid **13** insignificant

PINK: **3** cut **4** deck, rose, stab **5** blush, color, coral, plant, prick, prime **6** flower, pierce, salmon **7** blossom, flushed **8** decorate **9** carnation **10** perfection

PINNACLE: **3** top **4** acme, apex, peak **5** crest, crown, serac, spire **6** belfry, climax, height, summit, turret, zenith **11** culmination

PINPOINT: **3** aim, fix **4** spot **5** exact, point **6** finger, locate **7** precise **8** diagnose, identify **11** distinguish

PINTO: **3** car **4** pied **5** horse **7** mottled, piebald

PIONEER: **5** first **6** invent **7** initial, pilgrim, settler **8** colonist, discover, explorer, original **9** innovator **10** pathfinder **11** trailblazer **12** experimental

PIOUS: **4** holy **5** godly, loyal **6** divine, devout, worthy **7** saintly **8** faithful, priestly, reverent **9** dedicated, religious, spiritual **11** commendable **13** sanctimonious

PIPE: **4** cask, duct, flue, hose, main, peep, tube **5** briar, canal, drain, flute, sewer, spout, stack, tweet **6** leader, outlet, siphon, supply, trough **7** conduit, passage, whistle **8** aqueduct **9** conductor **10** instrument

PIPE DREAM: **4** hope, wish **7** fantasy **8** illusion

PIPSQUEAK: **4** runt **5** small, twerp **6** nobody

PIQUANT: **4** racy, tart **5** sharp, spicy, tangy, zesty **6** biting, bitter, snappy **7** peppery, pungent, zestful **8** poignant, stinging **9** flavorful, sparkling **11** provocative, stimulating

PIQUE: **4** fret, miff, rile **5** annoy, peeve, pride, sting **6** arouse, bother, excite, fabric, grudge, nettle, offend, strunt **7** incense, offense, provoke, umbrage **8** irritate, vexation **9** aggravate, annoyance, stimulate **10** exasperate, irritation, resentment **11** displeasure

PIRATE: **5** steal, thief **6** raider, robber, sea dog **7** corsair, sea wolf **8** marauder, picaroon **9** buccaneer, privateer **10** freebooter, plagiarize

famous: **4** Hook, Kidd **5** Flint **6** Bonney, Morgan **7** Hawkins **10** Blackbeard
flag: **10** Jolly Roger

PISTOL: **3** gun, rod **4** Colt **5** Luger **6** weapon, Webley **7** firearm, handgun **8** revolver **9** automatic, derringer **10** six-shooter

PIT: **4** hell, hole, mine, seed, sump, trap, well **5** abyss, chasm, grave, gully, shaft, stone **6** cavern, cavity, crater, hollow, oppose, trench **7** abaddon, counter, foxhole **8** contrast, downfall, pockmark **10** depression, underworld **11** indentation

PITCH: **4** cant, cast, hurl, line, rate, rock, roll, tilt, tone, toss **5** angle, curve, erect, fling, grade, heave, lunge, lurch, raise, slant, slope, sound, spiel, throw **6** accent, degree, plunge, seesaw, slider, totter **7** incline **8** changeup, fastball, forkball, knuckler, spitball **9** frequency

PITCHER: **3** jar, jug **4** ewer, olla, toby **6** carafe, hurler, tosser, vessel **7** creamer **8** decanter, southpaw **9** container **10** ballplayer

PITCH IN: **4** help, work **5** begin **9** cooperate, volunteer **10** contribute **11** participate

PITEOUS: **6** ruined, woeful **7** pitiful, pitying **8** merciful, pathetic **9** miserable

PITFALL: **4** risk, snag **5** peril, snare, traps **6** danger, hazard **7** springe **8** drawback

PITH: **4** core, crux, gist, meat, pulp, soul **5** fiber, force, heart, vigor **6** center, marrow **7** essence, nucleus **8** strength **9** substance **10** importance **12** significance

PITHY: **5** brief, crisp, meaty, short, terse **7** compact, concise, laconic, pointed **8** forceful, succinct **10** meaningful **11** significant

PITIFUL: **4** mean **5** sorry **6** dismal, moving, woeful **7** forlorn, piteous **8** pathetic, pitiable, wretched **9** miserable, sorrowful, suffering **10** despicable **12** commiserable, contemptible, heartrending

PITILESS: **5** cruel, stony **6** brutal, savage **7** callous, inhuman **8** ruthless **9** ferocious, heartless, merciless, unfeeling **10** relentless, unmerciful **11** hardhearted, insensitive **13** unsympathetic

PITTANCE: **3** bit **4** alms, dole, mite **5** scrap, trace **6** little, trifle **7** peanuts, smidgen

PITY: **5** crime, mercy, piety, shame **6** lament, pathos, solace **7** charity, comfort **8** clemency, sympathy **10** compassion, kindliness, tenderness **11** commiserate, forbearance **13** understanding

PIVOT: **4** axis, spin, turn **5** avert, focus, hinge, swing, swirl **6** center, rotate, swivel **7** fulcrum

PIVOTAL: **5** vital **7** central, crucial **8** critical, decisive **9** essential, important **11** determining

PIXIE: **3** elf, imp **5** fairy **6** goblin, rascal, sprite **7** brownie **10** leprechaun

PIZZAZZ: **5** flair **6** energy, spirit **8** dazzling **10** excitement **11** flamboyance

PLACARD: **4** bill, card, sign **6** notice, plaque, poster **7** affiche **8** announce, bulletin **13** advertisement

PLACATE: **4** calm **5** humor, quiet **6** pacify, soothe **7** appease, mollify **10** conciliate **11** tranquilize

PLACE: **3** lay, put, set **4** area, base, city, duty, home, post, rank, room, seat, site, spot, town, zone

5 house, locus, niche, plant, point, space, stick, store, tract **6** assign, bestow, invest, locale, locate, region, status **7** deposit, dispose, install, situate, station, village **8** allocate, dwelling, identify, locality, location, position, standing, vicinity **9** community, residence, situation **14** responsibility

PLACID: **4** calm, even, mild **5** quiet, still **6** gentle, irenic, serene **8** composed, peaceful, tranquil **9** collected, unruffled **11** undisturbed

PLAGIARIZE: **4** copy, lift **5** forge, steal **6** pirate, thieve **11** appropriate

PLAGUE: **4** bane, fret, gall, pest, rash **5** chafe, curse, harry, tease, worry **6** badger, bother, harass, hassle, pester **7** disease, scourge, torment, trouble **8** calamity, epidemic, irritate, nuisance, outbreak **9** annoyance, contagion, suffering **10** affliction, pestilence **11** infestation

PLAIN: **4** bald, bare, even, fair, moor, open, pure **5** basic, blunt, broad, clear, frank, gross, heath, homey, level **6** candid, coarse, direct, homely, honest, humble, meadow, modest, simple, steppe, tundra **7** austere, average, evident, genuine, glaring, legible, obvious, plateau, prairie, savanna **8** apparent, campaign, distinct, explicit, flatland, homespun, manifest, ordinary, straight **9** downright, outspoken, primitive, unadorned **10** unaffected, unassuming **11** nondescript, transparent, undisguised **12** unattractive, unmistakable **13** unembellished **15** straightforward

PLAINTIFF: **4** suer **7** accuser **8** litigant **10** prosecutor **11** complainant

PLAINTIVE: **3** sad **5** cross **6** rueful **7** doleful, elegiac, piteous, pitiful **8** dolorous, mournful **9** lamenting, sorrowful, woebegone **10** melancholy

PLAIT: **4** fold, knit, tuck **5** braid, pleat, weave **6** crease **7** pigtail **10** interweave

PLAN: **3** aim, map **4** form, game, idea, plot **5** chart, draft, frame, order, shape, think **6** agenda, budget, design, devise, intend, layout, method, policy, scheme, sketch, system **7** arrange, diagram, drawing, foresee, outline, program, project, purpose **8** conspire, contrive, engineer, organize, platform, schedule, strategy **9** blueprint, calculate, formulate, stratagem **10** brainstorm, conception **11** arrangement, contemplate, premeditate

PLANE: **3** jet **4** even, flat, tool **5** flush, grade, level **6** degree, smooth **7** stratum, surface **8** aircraft **10** horizontal

PLANET: **5** globe, world **12** heavenly body **13** celestial body
first: **7** Mercury
second: **5** Venus
third: **5** Earth
fourth: **4** Mars
fifth: **7** Jupiter
sixth: **6** Saturn
seventh: **6** Uranus
eighth: **7** Neptune
ninth: **5** Pluto
largest: **7** Jupiter
minor: **4** Hebe, Iris, Juno **5** Ceres, Flora, Vesta **6** Hygeia, Metios, Pallas **7** Astraea
ringed: **6** Saturn, Uranus **7** Jupiter, Neptune
smallest: **7** Mercury

PLANETARY: **6** global **7** earthly, erratic, nomadic, worldly **9** universal, wandering **11** terrestrial

PLANK: **4** deal, slab **5** board **6** lumber, timber **7** support **8** platform **9** duckboard

PLANNER: **7** creator **8** designer **9** architect, executive **13** administrator

PLANT: **4** arum, bush, fern, herb, root, seed, tree, vine, weed, wort **5** berry, flora, fruit, fungi, grain, grass, shoot, shrub, spice **6** annual, clover, flower, legume **7** herbage, sapling **9** perennial, vegetable **10** vegetation

angiosperm: **5** dicot **7** monocot

aquatic: **4** need **5** lotus, sedge **7** cattail, papyrus **9** water lily **10** watercress

body: **4** stem **6** cormus **7** thallus

bulbous: **4** lily **5** camas, onion, tulip **7** jonquil, quamash **8** hyacinth **9** narcissus

cactus: **5** dildo, nopal **6** cereus, mescal **7** opuntia, saguaro **11** prickly pear

carnivorous: **6** sundew **10** butterwort **12** pitcher plant, Venus Flytrap

climbing: **3** ivy **4** vine **5** betel, liana, vetch **6** byrony, derris, smilax **7** creeper, jasmine **8** bignonia, wisteria **12** morning glory, philodendron

coloring: **8** carotene **10** endochrome **11** chlorophyll, xanthophyll

combining forms: **4** phyt **5** chore, cocci, oecia, phyta, phyte, phyto

concerning: **6** agamic **7** botanic, vegetal **9** botanical **10** vegetative

cone-bearing: **3** fir, yew **4** pine **5** cedar **6** gingko, spruce **7** conifer, cypress, redwood

desert: **4** aloe **5** agave **6** alhagi, cactus, cholla **8** mesquite **9** paloverde **11** brittlebush

disease: **3** rot **4** gall, mold, rust, scab, smut **5** ergot **6** blight, mildew, mosaic **7** blister

evergreen: **3** fir **4** pine **6** spruce **8** boxberry, clubmoss **11** wintergreen

flowerless: **4** alga, fern, kelp, moss **6** fungus, lichen **7** seaweed **8** clubmoss **9** horsetail, liverwort

garden: **4** iris, lily, rose **5** aster, calla, canna, daisy, pansy, peony, phlox, poppy, stock, tulip, viola **6** bletia, celery, crocus, lupine, oxalis, zinnia **7** anemone, begonia, jonquil, lobelia, petunia, statice, verbena **8** bluebell, daffodil, dianthus, gardenia, geranium, hyacinth, larkspur, marigold, primrose, scabiosa, sweet pea **9** amaryllis, carnation, hollyhock **10** delphinium, gypsophila, snapdragon **11** forget-me-not **12** rhododendron **13** chrysanthemum

grain: **3** oat, rye **4** corn, rice, teff **5** maize, wheat **6** barley, millet **9** buckwheat

marsh: **4** reed **5** sedge **6** juncus **7** bulrush, cattail

medicinal: **4** aloe, sage **5** poppy, senna **6** fennel, garlic, ginger, ipecac, nettle **7** aconite, boneset, camphor, caraway, gentian, hemlock, henbane, juniper, lobelia, mullein, mustard, parsley, saffron **8** camomile, licorice, wormwood **9** chamomile, dandelion, monkshead **10** peppermint

microscopic: **4** mold **5** spore **6** diatom **9** bacterium **10** microphyte

native: **8** indigene

onionlike: **4** leek **5** chive **7** shallot **8** scallion

parts: **3** bud, bur, nut, pip, pod, rod **4** bine, boll, bulb, burr, node, pith, root, stem **5** cutin, fruit, grain, palet, radix, scion, shaft, sprig, stalk, stoma, trunk, xylem **6** button, caulis, cormus, flower, medula, phloem, stamen, stipel, stolon **7** cambium, rhizome, stomata, tendril **8** lenticel, meristem **9** cellulose **12** cholorophyll

poisonous: **4** atis, poke, upas **5** sumac **6** castor, datura **7** amanita, cowbane, tobacco **8** foxglove, larkspur, oleander **10** belladonna, nightshade

suffix: **4** ales **5** aceae, ineae

thorned: **4** rose **5** briar **6** cactus, nettle, teasel **7** thistle **9** cocklebur *young:* **4** cion **5** scion, shoot **6** sprout **7** cutting, vinelet **8** seedling

PLANTATION: **4** farm **5** ranch **6** colony, estate

PLAQUE: **4** disk, slab **5** badge, medal, patch, plate **6** brooch **8** memorial **9** nameplate **10** decoration

PLASTER: **4** coat, glue **5** cover, grout, paste, salve, smear **6** adhere, cement, gypsum, mortar, stucco **7** spackle **8** adhesive

PLASTIC: **4** soft **6** pliant **7** acrylic, ductile, elastic, pliable **8** flexible, moldable, yielding **9** adaptable, formative, malleable, synthetic

PLATE: **4** base, coat, disc, dish, pane **5** armor, cover, layer, panel, paten, scale **6** lamina, saucer **7** denture, lamella, serving **8** laminate, stratify

PLATEAU: **4** mesa **5** table **7** uplands **8** highland **9** elevation, milestone, tableland

PLATFORM: **4** base, dais, deck, plan, ramp, skid **5** chart, floor, forum, ledge, stage, stand **6** pallet, podium, policy, pulpit **7** estrade, program, rostrum, soapbox, terrace **8** position, scaffold **9** boardwalk, gangplank **10** objectives

PLATINUM: **4** gray **5** color **7** element

PLATITUDE: **6** truism **7** bromide, cliche **8** banality **9** triteness **10** shibboleth, triviality **11** commonplace

PLATO:
founded: **7** Academy
nationality: **5** Greek
occupation: **6** writer **7** teacher **11** philosopher
pupil: **9** Aristotle
teacher: **8** Socrates
work: **3** Ion **4** Laws, Meno **5** Crito **6** Phaedo, Sophist **7** Apology, Gorgias, Letters, Timaeus **8** Phaedrus, Republic **9** Politicus, Symposium

PLATONIC: **7** utopian **8** quixotic **9** spiritual, visionary **10** idealistic **11** theoretical **12** transcendent

PLATOON: **4** crew, team, unit **5** force, group, squad **6** outfit, patrol **7** battery, company **8** division **9** formation **10** detachment

PLATTER: **4** dish, tray **5** plate **6** record, salver **7** charger **8** trencher

PLAUDIT: **4** kudo **5** cheer **6** praise **7** acclaim **8** applause, approval **10** compliment **11** acclamation, approbation

PLAUSIBLE: **5** valid **7** logical **8** credible, specious **9** colorable **10** acceptable, believable, reasonable

PLAY: **3** act, fun, hit, toy **4** flop, game, give, jest, joke, romp, room, show **5** amuse, caper, dally, drama, enact, farce, flirt, opera, sport, stake, swing, wager **6** cavort, comedy, engage, fiddle, frolic, gamble, gambol, leeway, margin, oppose **7** carouse, contend, delight, disport, execute, musical, perform, portray, tragedy **8** pleasure **9** amusement, pantomime **10** manipulate, recreation, relaxation **11** impersonate, merrymaking, participate, performance **13** entertainment

PLAYBOY: **4** wolf **5** flirt, Romeo **7** swinger **8** Casanova **9** womanizer **11** philanderer

PLAY DOWN: **6** soften **8** belittle, minimize **9** underrate **11** deemphasize

PLAYED OUT: **4** beat **5** ended, spent, tired **6** bushed, pooped **7** drained **8** depleted, finished **9** exhausted

PLAYER: **4** jock, star **5** actor **7** actress, athlete, gambler **8** opponent, thespian **9** adversary, performer **10** competitor, contestant **11** entertainer, participant

PLAYFUL: **3** coy **5** funny, jolly, merry **6** blithe, frisky, lively **7** coltish, jocular, larkish **8** gamesome, humorous, spirited, sportive **9** kittenish, sprightly **10** frolicsome, rollicking **11** mischievous

PLAYMATE: **3** pal **4** chum **5** amigo, buddy **6** friend **7** comrade **9** companion

PLAYTHING: **3** toy **4** doll, game **6** gadget, trifle **7** trinket

PLAYWRIGHT: **6** author, writer **8** scripter **9** dramatist **10** dramaturge

PLAZA: **4** park **5** court, green **6** common, square **11** marketplace

PLEA: **4** suit **5** alibi **6** appeal, excuse, prayer **7** apology, pretext, request, solicit **8** argument, entreaty, overture, petition **11** explanation **12** supplication

PLEAD: **3** ask, beg **4** pray, urge **5** argue **6** appeal **7** beseech, entreat, implore, solicit **8** advocate, petition **9** importune **10** supplicate

PLEASANT: **4** fair, fine, good, mild, nice, warm **5** merry, sunny, sweet **6** genial, joyous, lovely **7** affable, amiable, amusing, cordial, jocular, likable, welcome, winsome **8** charming, engaging, friendly, gracious, grateful, humorous, pleasing **9** agreeable, appealing, congenial, enjoyable, favorable **10** delightful, gratifying, refreshing

PLEASANTRY: **3** fun **4** jest, joke, quip **6** banter, remark **7** gesture **8** greeting **9** witticism **10** jocularity, salutation

PLEASE: **4** grab, like, suit, will, wish **5** agree, amuse, elate, enjoy, humor **6** humour, thrill, tickle **7** content, delight, gladden, gratify, indulge, placate, satisfy **9** titillate

PLEASING: **4** glad, nice **6** liking **7** fawning **8** charming, inviting, pleasant **9** agreeable, desirable, enjoyable, favorable, palatable **10** attractive, delectable, delightful, enchanting **11** pleasurable

PLEASURABLE: **7** sensual **8** pleasing **9** enjoyable **10** delightful, gratifying, satisfying **12** entertaining

PLEASURE: **3** fun, joy **4** like, will **5** bliss, fancy, hobby, mirth, treat **6** choice, desire, gaiety, relish **7** comfort, delight, jollity **8** delicacy, felicity, fruition, gladness, hedonism **9** amusement, diversion, enjoyment, happiness, merriment, selection **10** preference **11** contentment, delectation **12** cheerfulness

PLEAT: **4** fold, kilt, shir, tuck **5** crimp **6** crease, gather, ruffle

PLEBEIAN: **4** base **5** lowly **6** coarse, common, homely, vulgar **7** ignoble, lowborn **8** commoner, everyday, ordinary **9** unrefined

PLEDGE: **3** IOU, vow **4** bind, gage, oath, pawn, seal, wage, word **5** swear, toast, troth, vouch **6** assure, commit, engage, surety **7** betroth, promise, warrant **8** contract, covenant, guaranty, mortgage, security **9** assurance, certainty, guarantee, insurance **10** collateral

PLEIADES:
constellation: **6** Taurus
daughters: **4** Maia **6** Merope **7** Alcyone, Calaeno, Electra, Sterope, Taygeta
father: **5** Atlas
mother: **7** Pleione

PLENARY: **4** full **5** whole **6** entire **8** absolute, complete **9** inclusive

PLENIPOTENTIARY: **5** agent **8** diplomat, emissary **10** ambassador **12** spokesperson

PLENTIFUL: **4** full, lush, rich **5** ample **6** galore, lavish, plenty **7** copious, fertile, liberal, opulent, profuse **8** abundant, affluent, fruitful, generous, swarming **9** abounding, bounteous, bountiful, exuberant, plenteous **11** extravagant, overflowing

PLENTY: **4** gobs, lots, much **5** ample, heaps, loads **6** enough, oodles, wealth **7** copious **8** fullness, generous, opulence **9** abundance, affluence, plentiful **10** exuberance, plentitude, prosperity **11** sufficiency

PLETHORA: **4** glut, many **5** flood **6** excess **7** surfeit, surplus **8** overflow **9** repletion **13** overabundance

PLEXUS: **3** web **4** mesh **6** system **7** network

PLIABLE: **4** easy, soft **5** lithe **6** docile, limber, pliant, supple **7** ductile, plastic, tactile **8** bendable, flexible, moldable, workable, yielding **9** adaptable, compliant, malleable, tractable **10** manageable, responsive

PLIANT: **4** soft **6** limber, supple **7** elastic, pliable **8** flexible, yielding

PLIGHT: **3** fix, jam **4** bind, word **5** pinch, state **6** crisis, pickle, pledge **7** betroth, dilemma, impasse, promise **8** quandary **9** condition, situation **10** difficulty **11** predicament

PLOD: **4** drag, grub, moil, plow, plug, slog, toil, work **5** grind, labor, stomp, tramp **6** drudge, trudge **7** schlepp **8** flounder, struggle

PLOT: **3** lot, map **4** land, mark, plan, plat **5** cabal, chart, grave, setup, story, theme, tract **6** design, devise, parcel, scheme **7** collude, connive, diagram, outline **8** conspire, contrive, engineer, intrigue, scenario **9** calculate **10** conspiracy **11** machination

PLOVER: **4** bird **5** wader **7** lapwing **8** killdeer **9** turnstone
family: **12** Charadriidae

PLOW: **3** dig **4** farm, mole, till **5** break, forge, press, smash **6** furrow, plough **8** bulldoze **9** cultivate

PLOY: **4** joke, move, ruse **5** trick **6** frolic, gambit, scheme, tactic **7** gimmick **8** maneuver, strategy

PLUCK: **3** tug **4** grit, guts, jerk, pick, pull, tear, yank **5** moxie, nerve, spunk, strip, strum **6** daring, finger, mettle, remove, snatch, spirit **7** bravery, courage, plunder **8** backbone, gameness **9** fortitude, hardihood **10** resolution

PLUCKY: **4** bold **5** brave **6** daring **7** valiant **8** fearless, unafraid **9** undaunted **10** courageous

PLUG: **3** dam, wad **4** bung, clog, cork, hack, push, seal **5** block, boost, close, stuff **7** fitting, mention, promote, stopper, stopple **9** advertise, persevere, plowhorse

PLUM: **4** find, tree **5** catch, color, fruit, prize, prune **6** carrot, purple, raisin, reward **8** dividend, windfall
genus: **6** prunus
variety: **3** hog **4** date, sloe, wild **5** black **6** cherry, Damson, ground, Indian **8** American, European, Oklahoma

PLUMB: **5** delve, probe, solve, sound **6** fathom, plunge, search, weight **7** explore, plummet, utterly **8** absolute, complete, directly, squarely, straight, vertical **13** perpendicular

PLUME: **5** crest, egret, preen, pride, prize, quill, token **7** feather, panache

PLUMMET: **3** dip **4** drop, fall, plop, sink **5** crash, plunk **6** plunge, tumble **7** decline, descend **8** downturn, nose-dive

PLUMP: **3** fat **4** back **5** ample, buxom, obese, round, stout, tubby **6** chubby, fleshy, portly, rotund **8** abundant

PLUNDER: **3** rob **4** loot, raid, sack **5** booty, goods, peach, pluck, raven, steal **6** fleece, forage, maraud, pilfer, pirate, rapine, ravage, ravish, spoils **7** pillage, ransack **9** devastate

PLUNDERER: **5** thief **6** bandit, looter, raider, vandal **7** ravager **8** marauder, pillager **10** freebooter

PLUNGE: **3** dig, dip **4** dive, duck, dump, fall, jump, rush, sink, swim **5** douse, drive, fling, lunge, souse **6** absorb, engulf, thrust, tumble **7** descend, immerse, plummet **8** submerge

PLUNK: **4** drop, sink, toss **5** place, pluck, sound, strum, throw **6** strike

PLURALITY: **4** bulk, most **7** variety **8** majority **9** advantage, multitude

PLUS: **4** more, perk **5** added, asset, bonus **6** expand **7** augment, helpful **8** addition, increase, positive **10** beneficial **12** advantageous

PLUSH: **4** lush, posh **5** fancy, ritzy, swank **6** deluxe, lavish **7** elegant, opulent **8** palatial **9** luxurious, sumptuous

PLUTO: **3** god **6** planet
brother: **4** Zeus
defeated: **6** Cronos
father: **6** Cronos
from sun: **5** ninth
kidnapped: **10** Persephone
kingdom: **5** Hades **10** underworld
mother: **4** Rhea
rescued by: **4** Ares, Zeus
satellite: **6** Charon
wife: **10** Persephone

PLUTOCRAT: **6** tycoon **7** magnate **9** moneybags **10** capitalist

PLUTONIC: **7** abyssal, igneous **8** infernal **9** cimmerian

PLY: **4** bend, fold, mold, urge, work **5** exert, layer, shape, steer, wield **6** comply, employ, handle, pursue **8** exercise, maneuver **9** importune, thickness **10** manipulate

POACH: **4** boil, cook **5** filch, steal **6** pilfer **7** plunder, trample **8** encroach, trespass

POCKET: **4** lift, lode, sack, tiny, vein, void **5** filch, pouch, sinus, small, steal **6** accept, cavity **7** compact, conceal, confine, enclose **8** portable **9** miniature **11** compartment

POCKETBOOK: **3** bag **4** poke **5** pouch, purse **6** wallet **7** handbag, satchel **8** billfold

POD: **3** bag, sac **4** case, hull, husk **5** flock, pouch, shell, shuck **6** cocoon, school, sheath **7** capsule, silicle **8** covering

PODIUM: **4** base, dais, wall **5** stage **6** pulpit **7** lectern **8** pedestal, platform

POE, EDGAR ALLAN: **4** poet **6** author, critic, editor, writer
wrote: **6** Eureka **7** Ulalume **8** Berenice, Politian, The Raven **9** Hans Pfaal **10** Annabel Lee

POEM: **3** ode **4** epic, rime, rune, song **5** ditty, elegy, idyll, ionic, lyric, rhyme, verse **6** ballad, eulogy, jingle, poetry, stanza, tercet **7** dimeter, rondeau **8** acrostic, doggerel, limerick, madrigal, threnody **11** composition **12** epithalamium

four-line: **8** quatrain
seven-line: **10** heptastich
eight-line: **7** triolet
fourteen-line: **6** sonnet

POET: **4** bard, muse, scop **5** odist, rimer **6** artist, author, lyrist, rhymer, writer **8** idyllist, lyricist, minstrel **9** balladist, rhymester, sonneteer, versifier

POETIC: **4** odic **6** dreamy, epical, epodic **7** idyllic, lyrical **8** dramatic, romantic, rhythmic **9** beautiful **11** imaginative

POIGNANT: **4** keen, sour **5** acute, sharp **6** astute, biting, bitter, moving, urgent **7** cutting, painful, piquant, pungent **8** incisive, piercing, stinging, touching **9** affecting **11** distressing

POINT: **3** aim, dot, nib, tip **4** apex, barb, beak, cape, crux, cusp, east, edge, gist, goal, horn, item, mark, noon, peak, pole, spot, time, west **5** angle, brink, drift, focus, imply, issue, level, locus, north, prove, refer, sense, south, speck, stage, tally, theme, topic **6** allude, degree, detail, direct, moment, motive, period, summit **7** article, element, feature, maximum, meaning, purpose, suggest **8** argument, emphasis, indicate, intimate, juncture, location, pinnacle, position, validity **9** objective **10** particular **12** significance

POINT-BLANK: **5** blunt, close, frank **6** direct **7** plainly **8** straight

POINTED: **4** fine, keen **5** acute, piked, sharp **6** biting, direct, marked, picked **7** actuate, concise, pronged **8** accurate, aculeate, piercing, poignant, stinging, striking **9** acuminate, sarcastic **11** conspicuous, penetrating

POINTER: **3** arm, dog, rod, tip **4** clue, dial, hand, hint **5** gauge, index, stick **9** indicator **10** suggestion

POINTLESS: **5** blunt, inane, silly **6** absurd, futile **7** useless **9** senseless **10** ridiculous **11** unnecessary **13** insignificant

POINT OF VIEW: **5** angle **7** opinion, outlook **8** attitude, position **11** perspective

POINT OUT: **4** show **5** refer **6** denote **8** identify, indicate

POISE: **4** calm, tact **5** grace **6** aplomb, steady **7** balance, bearing, dignity, support, suspend **8** calmness, elegance, maintain **9** assurance, composure, stability **10** confidence **11** equilibrium

POISON: **4** bane, evil, harm, kill **5** taint, toxin, venom, virus **6** cancer, debase, infect, murder, plague **7** arsenic, botulin, corrupt, cyanide, debauch, pervert, pollute, vitiate **8** bacteria, botulism **9** contagion **10** salmonella **11** contaminate

POISONOUS: **5** fatal, toxic **6** deadly, lethal **7** baneful, harmful, noxious **8** venomous, virulent

POKE: **3** dig, job, jog, lag, pry **4** blow, drag, prod, push, sack, stir **5** bulge, dally, delay, elbow, mosey, nudge, probe, punch, shove, snoop **6** awaken, bonnet, dawdle, loiter, meddle, putter, thrust **7** intrude **9** interfere **13** procrastinate

POKER: **3** bar, rod **4** game, iron **5** cards **6** gamble
hand: **4** pair **5** flush **8** straight **9** full house **10** royal flush **13** straight flush
term: **4** call, draw, fold **5** check, raise
variety: **4** draw, jack, stud **5** bluff, strip **8** baseball, straight

POKER-FACED: **5** sober **6** somber **7** neutral, serious

POKY: **4** dull, jail, slow **5** pokey, small **6** prison, shabby **7** cramped, slammer **8** confined, dawdling, frumpish

POLAND:
also called: **6** Polska **7** Polonia **8** Sarmatia
capital: **6** Warsaw
cities: **4** Lodz **6** Gdansk, Gdynia, Krakow, Lublin, Poznan **7** Wroclaw **8** Katowice, Szczecin **9** Bydgoszcz, Byelostok
continent: **6** Europe
dances: **5** polka **7** mazurka **9** polonaise
ethnic groups: **6** German, Polish **9** Ukrainian **11** Belorussian
features: **5** Tatra **8** Sudetens **11** Carpathians, Wolin Island
language: **6** Polish
monetary unit: **5** zloty
native: **4** Pole, Slav
water: **4** Oder **6** Neisse **7** Vistula **9** Baltic Sea

POLAR: **6** arctic **8** freezing, opposite **9** diametric **13** contradictory

POLE: **3** bar, rod **4** axis, beam, boom, mast, pike, post, spar, wand **5** caber, guide, nader, staff, stake, stick, totem **8** magnetic, position

POLESTAR: **5** guide **7** Polaris **9** north star

POLICE: **3** cop, law **4** fuzz, heat **5** bobby, guard, watch **6** govern, patrol **7** marshal, officer, protect, sheriff **8** flatfoot, gendarme **9** constable, detective, patrolman, policeman **11** patrolwoman, policewoman **12** constabulary

POLICY: **4** code, plan **6** action, course, custom, method, system, wisdom **7** program, tactics **8** contract, platform, sagacity, strategy **9** principle, procedure

POLISH: **3** rub, wax **4** buff **5** glaze, gloss, scrub, sheen, shine, slick **6** finish, glance, luster, refine, smooth **7** burnish, culture, furbish, perfect **8** brighten, elegance, simonize, urbanity **10** refinement **11** cultivation

POLISHED: **4** fine **5** civil, suave **6** polite **7** elegant, gallant **8** educated, gleaming **12** accomplished

POLITE: **4** bane **5** civil, suave **6** gentle, proper **7** correct, courtly, gallant, genteel, refined **8** cultured, mannerly, polished **9** attentive, courteous **10** cultivated, neighborly, respectful, thoughtful **11** complaisant, considerate

POLITIC: **4** wise **5** sharp, suave **6** adroit, artful, astute, crafty, shrewd **7** cunning, prudent, tactful **8** discreet, tactical **9** expedient, judicious **10** diplomatic **11** calculating

POLITICAL: **5** civic **11** legislative **12** governmental
activist: **4** hawk **7** radical **8** lobbyist, nihilist, peacenik **9** anarchist, demagogue, dissident, extremist, guerrilla
party: **3** GOP **4** Tory **5** Green, Labor **9** Communist, Socialist **10** Democratic, Republican
philosophy: **6** Maoism **7** Marxism **8** nihilism **9** anarchism, communism, democracy, extremism, socialism **10** capitalism, liberalism **12** collectivism, conservatism, laissez faire

POLITICIAN: **6** leader **7** senator **8** lawmaker **10** legislator **12** officeholder, statesperson **14** congressperson

POLL: **4** clip, head, list, trim **5** count, shear, tally **6** ballot, census, survey **7** canvass, listing, opinion **8** counting, register, sampling

POLLEN: **4** dust **6** powder **11** microspores

POLLINATE: **5** breed **9** fertilize

POLLUTE: **4** foul, soil **5** dirty, smear, stain, taint **6** defile, poison **7** corrupt, debauch, profane **9** desecrate **11** contaminate

POLLUTION: **4** smog **5** waste **8** impurity **11** desecration, uncleanness **13** contamination

POLLUX:
also known as: **10** Polydeuces
father: **4** Zeus
mother: **4** Leda
twin: **6** Castor

POLTERGEIST: **5** ghost **6** spirit **7** specter **8** phantasm **10** apparition

POLTROON: **6** coward, craven, wretch **7** chicken, dastard, milksop **8** weakling **11** yellowbelly

POLYGON:
three-sided: **8** triangle
four-sided: **8** tetragon
five-sided: **8** pentagon
six-sided: **7** hexagon
seven-sided: **8** heptagon
eight-sided: **7** octagon
nine-sided: **7** nonagon
ten-sided: **7** decagon
twelve-sided: **9** dodecagon

POLYNESIA:
bird: **4** lupe
food: **3** fei, ube **4** hevi, kava, rata
islands: **4** Cook, Fiji, Line **5** Samoa, Tonga **6** Easter, Ellice, Hawaii, Tahiti, Tuvalu **7** Phoenix, Tokelau **8** Kiribati **15** French Polynesia
language: **7** Tagalog
located: **7** Oceania
native: **10** Polynesian
plants: **3** ara, pia **4** ahia, avas, hala, tara, taro
water: **7** Pacific

POLYP: **5** coral, hydra, tumor **6** growth **7** anemone, hydroid **12** coelenterate

POMERANIA:
capital: **7** Stettin
cities: **5** Thorn, Torun **6** Anklam
islands: **5** Rugen **6** Usedom
part of: **6** Poland **7** Germany **11** East Germany
port: **6** Gdansk
water: **4** Oder **9** Baltic Sea

POMMEL: **4** beat, knob **5** pound **6** finial, handle, pummel, strike **9** saddlebow

POMP: **4** fare, form, show **5** pride, state, strut **6** parade, ritual **7** cortege, display, fanfare, glitter **8** ceremony, grandeur, splendor **9** pageantry, spectacle **10** ceremonial

POMPEII:
near: **6** Naples **8** Vesuvius
place: **5** Italy

POMPOUS: **4** vain **5** lofty, proud, puffy, pushy **6** la-di-da, uppish **7** bloated, haughty, orotund, stately, stilted **8** arrogant **9** bombastic, egotistic, flaunting, grandiose **10** pontifical **11** overbearing, pretentious **12** highfaluting, ostentatious **13** condescending, self-important

POND: **4** lake, mere, pool, tarn **5** basin **6** lagoon

PONDER: **4** mull, muse, pore **5** brood, dwell, study, think, weigh **6** reason, wonder **7** examine, mediate, reflect **8** appraise, consider, evaluate, meditate, ruminate **9** speculate **10** deliberate **11** contemplate

PONDEROUS: **4** dull **5** bulky, heavy, hefty, large **6** dreary **7** awkward, humdrum, labored, massive, tedious, weighty **10** cumbersome, monotonous

PONTIFF: **4** pope **6** bishop **8** pontifex

PONTIFICAL: **5** papal, puffy **7** pompous **8** arrogant, dogmatic **11** overbearing, pretentious

PONY: **3** nag **4** crib, trot **5** glass, horse, pinto **6** cayuse **7** mustang **9** racehorse
breed: **5** Welsh **6** Exmoor **8** Shetland

POOH-POOH: **3** boo **4** hiss, razz **5** knock, sneer **7** catcall, disdain, dismiss **9** raspberry

POOL: **3** car, pot **4** game, lake, mere, pond, tank, tarn **5** basin, funds, group, kitty, merge, share **6** cartel, lagoon, puddle, salina **7** combine, jackpot **9** billiards, reservoir, resources **10** natatorium **11** combination, cooperative

POOP: **4** deck, tire **5** scoop, stern **7** exhaust, fatigue **11** information

POOR: **4** bare, base, lean, mean **5** broke, cheap, empty, needy, seedy, sorry **6** abject, barren, cheesy, feeble, humble, hungry, meager, paltry, scanty, shabby, sparse, subpar **7** lacking, pitiful, squalid, unlucky **8** depleted, indigent, inferior, strapped **9** defective, destitute, emaciated, fruitless, infertile, insolvent, penniless, penurious **10** bankrupted, inadequate **11** impecunious, unfortunate **12** impoverished, insufficient **13** disadvantaged, insignificant **14** unsatisfactory **15** underprivileged

POORLY: **3** ill, low **4** mean **6** ailing, sickly, unwell

POP: **3** dad, hit **4** bang, shot, snap, sock, soda **5** burst, shoot **6** father, strike **8** beverage **9** explosion

POPE:
concerning: **5** papal
bishop of: **4** Rome
court: **5** Curia
crown: **5** mitre, tiara **11** triple crown
decree: **4** bull **8** rescript
descendant of: **7** St. Peter
elected by: **9** cardinals
envoy: **6** legate **7** nuntius **8** ablegate
first: **5** Linus, Peter
heads: **19** Roman Catholic Church
located: **7** Vatican **16** St. Peter's Basilica
pretender: **8** anti-pope
seal: **5** bulla
titles: **5** vicar **6** bishop, prince **7** primate **9** patriarch, sovereign, successor **10** archbishop, holy father **12** metropolitan **14** supreme pontiff

POPINJAY: **3** fop **5** dandy **6** parrot **7** coxcomb

POPLAR: **4** tree **5** abele, alamo, aspen, downy **6** balsam **9** tulip tree **10** cottonwood
genus: **7** populus

POPPY: **4** drug, herb **5** color, plant **6** flower
genus: **7** papaver
variety: **4** snow **5** black, opium **6** horned **7** Mexican **8** Oriental **10** California

POPPYCOCK: **3** rot **4** bosh, jive **5** trash **7** baloney, hogwash, rubbish **8** malarkey, nonsense **9** gibberish **10** balderdash

POPULACE: **3** mob **5** plebs **6** masses, people, public **7** society **9** multitude, plebeians **11** commonality

POPULAR: **5** cheap, noted **6** common, famous, sought, trendy **7** admired, current, favored **8** accepted, favorite **9** preferred, prevalent **10** celebrated, democratic, prevailing **11** fashionable

POPULARITY: **4** fame **5** favor, vogue **6** esteem **7** acclaim **9** celebrity, notoriety

POPULATE: **4** live **6** occupy, people, settle **7** inhabit **8** colonize

POPULATION: **6** people **7** society **8** citizens, denizens **9** residents **11** inhabitants

POPULOUS: **6** jammed **7** crowded **8** numerous, swarming **9** populated **12** multitudinal

PORCELAIN: **5** china **7** ceramic **11** crackleware, earthenware
famous: **5** Adams, Spode **7** Bristol, Chelsea, Limoges **8** Copeland **9** Davenport **10** Rockingham, Sunderland

PORCH: **4** stoa **5** lanai, plaza **7** balcony, gallery, portico, terrace, veranda **8** entrance, solarium, verandah **9** breezeway, colonnade

PORCINE: **7** hoggish, piggish **9** rapacious

PORE: **4** gaze **5** brood, stare, stoma, study **6** outlet, ponder, search **7** examine, foramen, opening, orifice, vesicle **8** meditate

PORK: **3** ham, pig **4** food, jowl, loin, meat **5** bacon, funds, swine **6** hamhog **8** shoulder, sowbelly

PORNOGRAPHIC: **4** lewd **5** dirty **6** smutty, steamy **7** obscene, raunchy **8** indecent **9** offensive

POROUS: **5** leaky **6** spongy **8** pervious **9** absorbent, permeable **10** penetrable

PORPOISE: **5** whale **6** mammal, seahog **7** dolphin **8** cetacean
genus: **8** phocaena

PORRIDGE: **4** mush, putu, samp **5** grits, grout, gruel **6** burgoo, skilly **7** crowdie, oatmeal, polenta, pottage **8** frumenty, loblolly

PORT: **4** city, dock, exit, gate, left, town, wine **5** haven **6** harbor, portal, refuge **7** landing, mooring, opening, shelter **8** boatyard, carriage, entrance, larboard, porthole **9** transport **10** deportment **11** destination

PORTABLE: **5** handy, light **6** mobile, pocket **7** movable **10** convenient, manageable

PORTAL: **4** arch, door, port **5** entry **7** doorway, gateway, opening, passage **8** entrance

PORTEND: **4** bode, omen **5** augur **6** herald **7** predict, presage **8** forecast, foretell, forewarn, indicate, prophesy **10** foreshadow

PORTENT: **4** clue, omen, sign **5** vibes **6** marvel, wonder **7** caution, miracle, prodigy, warning **9** foretoken **10** foreboding **11** premonition

PORTENTOUS: **7** looming, ominous, pompous, weighty **8** exciting **10** foreboding **11** pretentious, significant

PORTER: **3** ale **4** beer, brew **5** carry, hamal, stout **6** bearer, redcap, skycap **7** bellhop, carrier, gateman **9** transport **10** doorkeeper

PORTICO: **5** patio, porch **6** arcade, atrium, piazza **7** balcony, terrace, veranda, walkway **8** verandah **9** colonnade

PORTION: **3** bit, cut, lot **4** bite, deal, dole, fate, part **5** divvy, dowry, endow, piece, quota, ratio, share, slice **6** divide, kismet, moiety, parcel, ration **7** destiny, helping, measure, section, segment, serving **8** division, quantity **9** allotment, allowance, apportion **10** distribute, percentage

PORTLY: **4** fate **5** beefy, bulky, burly, grand, hefty, obese, plump, pudgy, stout **6** chubby, chunky, stocky **7** stately **8** majestic, striking **9** corpulent, dignified

PORTMANTEAU: **3** bag **6** valise **7** luggage **8** suitcase **9** gladstone

PORTRAIT: **5** image **6** sketch **7** account, drawing, picture **8** likeness, painting **10** photograph, similitude

PORTRAY: **3** act **4** copy, draw, limn, play, show **5** enact, frame, image, paint **6** depict **7** imitate, picture **8** describe **9** delineate, duplicate, represent, reproduce **11** impersonate

PORTUGAL:
capital: **6** Lisbon
cities: **4** Ovar **5** Braga, Porto **6** Guarda **7** Coimbra, Setubal
continent: **6** Europe
explorers: **3** Cao **4** Diaz
features: **5** Macau **6** Angola **7** Madeira **13** Azores Islands **15** Serra da Estrella
former colonies: **3** Diu, Goa **5** Damao, Timor **6** Angola, Guinea **7** Sao Tome **8** Principe **9** Cape Verde **10** Mozambique
language: **10** Portuguese
monetary unit: **6** escudo
native: **10** Portuguese
navigators: **6** da Gama **8** Magellan
water: **5** Douro, Minho, Tagus

POSE: **3** air, ask, sit **5** guise, model, offer, state, strut **6** baffle, puzzle, stance, submit **7** confuse, posture, present, propose **8** attitude, confound, position, question **9** mannerism **10** expression **11** affectation

POSEIDON:
also known as: **7** Neptune
brother: **4** Zeus **5** Hades, Pluto
causes: **11** earthquakes
controls: **5** waves, winds
father: **6** Cronus
fought: **6** Titans
god of: **3** sea **5** ocean **6** waters
mother: **4** Rhea
rescued by: **4** Zeus
symbol: **7** trident
wife: **10** Amphitrite

POSH: **4** chic **5** ritzy, smart **6** swanky **7** elegant, opulent **9** exclusive, luxurious

POSITION: **3** job, set **4** pose, post, rank, side, site, spot **5** angle, class, locus, niche, place, point **6** belief, locale, office, rating, stance, status **7** opinion, outlook, posture, stature **8** bearings, judgment, location, standing **9** condition, placement, situation, viewpoint **10** assignment, importance, standpoint **11** affirmation, disposition

POSITIVE: **4** firm, plus, real, sure **5** clear **6** actual, useful **7** assured, certain, decided, genuine, helpful **8** absolute, complete, decisive, definite, dogmatic, emphatic, explicit **9** assertive, confident, convinced, downright, empirical, practical **10** beneficial, conclusive, undisputed **11** affirmative, categorical, unequivocal, unqualified **12** unmistakable

POSSE: **4** band, gang **9** vigilante **11** search party

POSSESS: **3** own **4** bear, have, hold **6** occupy, retain **7** acquire, bewitch, control, inhabit **8** dominate, maintain

POSSESSED: **4** calm **6** cursed **7** haunted **8** consumed, demoniac, obsessed **9** collected

POSSESSION: **5** asset, goods, title **6** wealth **7** control, mastery **8** property **9** ownership, territory **10** belongings

POSSIBILITY: **4** odds **6** chance **8** prospect **9** potential **10** likelihood **11** contingency, eventuality, feasibility, probability

POSSIBLE: **6** likely, viable **8** feasible, probable, workable **9** potential **10** attainable, contingent, manageable **11** conceivable, practicable

POSSIBLY: **5** maybe **7** perhaps **8** probably **9** perchance

POST: **3** job, leg **4** base, beam, beat, fort, mail, mast, pole, send, stud **5** brief, place, stake, stilt **6** advise, assign, column, inform, notify, office, picket, pillar **7** courier, lookout, station, support **8** announce, dispatch, position **9** advertise, circulate, situation

POSTER: **4** bill, sign **6** banner, notice **7** affiche, placard, sticker **9** billboard, broadside **12** announcement **13** advertisement

POSTERIOR: **4** back, butt, hind, rear, seat, tush **5** after, fanny **6** behind, dorsal, hinder **8** backside, buttocks, derriere **9** following **10** subsequent, succeeding

POSTERITY: **5** heirs **6** family **8** children **9** offspring **11** descendants

POSTHASTE: **4** fast **6** pronto, speedy **7** quickly, rapidly, swiftly **11** expeditious

POSTPONE: **4** stay, wait **5** defer, delay, table **6** remand, shelve **7** adjourn, suspend **8** reprieve **13** procrastinate

POSTSCRIPT: **5** rider **6** sequel **8** appendix, footnote **9** appendage **10** attachment, supplement

POSTULATE: **5** axiom, claim **6** assert, assume, demand **7** element, premise, presume, require, suppose **9** principle **10** assumption, hypothesis, presuppose

POSTURE: **4** mien, pose **5** shape, state **6** manner, stance, status **7** bearing, display, feeling, outlook **8** attitude, carriage, demeanor, position, standing

POSY: **5** motto, verse **6** flower **7** blossom, bouquet, corsage, nosegay **9** sentiment

POT: **3** bet, cup, pan, urn **4** bowl, pool **5** basin, crock, decay, drink, kitty, shoot, wager **6** basket, kettle, toilet, vessel **7** caldron, fortune, tankard **8** cauldron **9** container, marijuana **11** deteriorate

POTABLE: **4** pure **5** clean, drink, fresh **6** liquor **8** beverage **10** unpolluted

POTASSIUM: **7** element **8** chemical, compound

POTATO: **3** yam **4** spud **5** plant, tater, tuber **6** murphy **9** vegetable
types: **4** chip **5** baked, Idaho, Maine, sweet, white **6** mashed, Russet **9** scalloped **11** french fries

POTBELLY: **5** stove **6** paunch **7** stomach **9** abdominal

POTENCY: **4** kick **5** force, might, power, vigor **6** energy, muscle **8** strength, vitality **9** authority, hardihood, influence

POTENT: **4** able **6** cogent, mighty, robust, strong, sturdy **7** control **8** forceful, powerful, vigorous, virulent **9** effective, efficient **11** influential

POTENTIAL: **6** latent **7** ability **8** aptitude, possible **9** concealed, promising **10** capability, unrealized **11** possibility, undeveloped

POTHER: **4** flap, fuss, stir **5** worry **6** bother, bustle, harass, hassle, uproar **7** turmoil **9** agitation, annoyance, commotion, confusion **11** controversy, disturbance

POTION: **4** brew, dose, dram, drug **5** draft, drink, tonic **6** remedy **7** mixture, philter **8** medicine

POTPOURRI: **4** olio, stew **5** blend **6** jumble, medley **7** melange, mixture **8** mishmash, pastiche **10** assortment, hodgepodge, miscellany, salmagundi

POTTER: **4** idle, mess, poke **6** cotter, dabble, dawdle, fiddle, loiter, putter, tinker, trifle **7** saunter **8** ceramist **10** ceramicist

POTTERY: **5** china, delft **8** ceramics, crockery **9** delftware, porcelain, stoneware **11** earthenware

POUCH: **3** bag, pod, sac **4** cyst, sack **5** purse **6** pocket **7** handbag, saccule, sporran **9** container, marsupium **10** pocketbook

POUF: **4** puff **7** ottoman **9** hairstyle

POULTICE: **7** plaster **8** compress, dressing **9** cataplasm **11** fomentation

POULTRY: **3** hen **4** duck, fowl **5** geese, goose, quail **6** grouse, pigeon, pullet, turkey **7** chicken, rooster **8** pheasant **9** partridge

POUNCE: **4** claw, dart, leap **5** pound, punch, stamp, surge, swoop, talon **6** attack, plunge, powder, spring, strike, thrust

POUND: **4** bang, bash, beat, blow, maul, sock, unit **5** clout, crush, grind, knock, smack, stomp, thump **6** batter, buffet, hammer, powder, pummel, strike, thrash, wallop, weight **7** clobber **8** malleate **9** pulverize

POUR: **4** emit, flow, gush, rain, spew, teem, vent **5** drain, empty, flood, spill, spout **6** decant, deluge, drench, effuse, stream **7** cascade **8** inundate **9** discharge

POURBOIRE: **3** tip **4** gift **8** gratuity **9** lagniappe

POUT: **4** fish, fret, mope, moue, sulk **5** brood, frown, grump, pique

POVERTY: **4** lack, need, want **6** dearth, penury **8** scarcity, shortage **9** pauperism, privation **10** inadequacy, scantiness **11** destitution **13** pennilessness **14** impoverishment

POVERTY-STRICKEN: **4** poor **5** broke **8** indigent **9** destitute, penniless, penurious **12** impoverished

POWDER: **4** bray, dust, film, snow, talc **5** crush, grind **6** crunch, pollen, pounce, talcum **8** cosmetic, medicine, sprinkle **9** explosive, granulate, pulverize

POWER: **3** arm, vis **4** guns, hand, rule, sway **5** brawn, clout, fight, force, might, money, right, steam, sword, vigor **6** agency, effort, empire, energy, muscle, status, throne, weight **7** ability, command, control, mastery, potency, stamina **8** capacity, dominion, prestige, strength, virility **9** authority, dominance, influence, intensity, supremacy **10** domination **11** sovereignty **12** jurisdiction

POWERFUL: **4** able, fast, **5** great, stout **6** brawny, mighty, strong **7** leonine **8** dominant **9** effective, herculean, important, versatile **10** convincing, dominating, invincible, omnipotent **11** efficacious, influential

POWERLESS: **4** weak **5** frail, unfit **6** feeble, supine **7** passive **8** crippled, helpless, impotent **9** powerless **10** vulnerable **11** defenseless

POWWOW: **4** talk **5** forum **6** confer, huddle **7** council, meeting **8** assembly, congress **10** conference, discussion

PRACTICABLE: **6** doable, usable **8** feasible, possible, workable **10** accessible, attainable

PRACTICAL: **5** handy, sound **6** usable, useful **7** skilled, veteran **8** feasible, possible, seasoned, sensible, workable **9** efficient, pragmatic, realistic **10** functional, proficient **11** pragmatical

PRACTICALLY: **4** most **6** almost, nearly **9** basically, virtually **11** essentially

PRACTICE: **4** play, plot, rote **5** drill, habit, trade, train, usage **6** custom, follow, manner, method, repeat, system **7** clients, perform, process, routine **8** business, exercise, rehearse **9** procedure **10** profession **11** preparation

PRACTITIONER: **5** agent **6** artist, doctor, healer, lawyer **12** professional

PRAGMATIC: **4** busy **6** active **7** logical, skilled **8** busybody, dogmatic, sensible **9** practical, realistic **10** meddlesome, systematic **11** utilitarian

PRAIRIE: **5** llano, plain **6** meadow, steppe **7** quamash, savanna **9** grassland

PRAIRIE STATE: **8** Illinois

PRAISE: **4** hail, laud, tout **5** adore, bless, exalt, extol, glory, honor, kudos **6** esteem, eulogy, extoll, homage, revere, salute **7** acclaim, adulate, applaud, commend, flatter, glorify, hosanna, magnify, plaudit, tribute, worship **8** accolade, appraise, blessing, eulogize, proclaim **9** adulation, celebrate **10** admiration, compliment, panegyrize **11** approbation **12** commendation, congratulate

PRAISEWORTHY: **7** stellar **8** laudable **9** admirable, deserving, exemplary **11** commendable, meritorious **13** complimentary

PRANCE: **4** romp **5** dance, strut **6** cavort, frolic, gambol, parade, sashay **7** flounce

PRANK: **4** joke, lark, whim **5** adorn, antic, caper, trick **6** curvet, frolic, gambol **7** caprice, hijinks **8** decorate, escapade, mischief **9** frivolity **11** monkeyshine, shenanigans

PRATE: **3** gab, yak **4** blab, chat, talk **5** boast, clash, utter **6** babble, drivel, jabber, tongue **7** chatter, prattle, twaddle

PRATTLE: **4** talk **5** prate **6** babble, cackle, jabber **7** blather, chatter, clatter **8** chitchat

PRAXIS: **5** habit **6** custom **8** exercise, practice **9** practical

PRAY: **3** ask, beg **5** plead **6** appeal, invoke **7** beseech, conjure, implore, request **8** petition **10** supplicate

PRAYER: **4** plea, suit **5** chant, grace, matin **6** appeal, litany, orison, vesper **7** request, worship **8** blessing, petition **9** epiclesis **10** confession, invocation **11** application, benediction, paternoster **12** supplication, thanksgiving

beads: **6** rosary

book: **5** bible **6** hymnal, missal **7** liturgy **8** breviary

PREACH: **5** teach **6** exhort **7** lecture, profess **8** advocate, humilize, moralize, proclaim **9** sermonize **10** evangelize

PREACHER: **6** parson, pastor **8** minister, reverend **9** pulpiteer **10** evangelist, missionary **12** ecclesiastic

PREAMBLE: **7** preface, prelude **8** foreword **12** introduction

PRECARIOUS: **5** risky, rocky **6** chancy, tricky **7** dubious **8** doubtful, insecure, perilous, unstable **9** dangerous, hazardous, uncertain **11** unwarranted

PRECAUTION: **4** care **8** prudence **9** foresight, safeguard **11** carefulness

PRECEDE: **4** lead, pace **6** forego **7** outrank, predate, preface, surpass **8** announce, antecede, antedate **9** introduce

PRECEDENCE: **4** rank **8** priority **10** importance, preference **11** superiority

PRECEDENT: **5** model **6** custom, ruling **7** example **8** decision, instance, standard **9** guideline, preceding

PRECEDING: **5** above, first, prior **6** before, former **7** earlier **8** anterior, previous **10** heretofore, precursory

PRECEPT: **3** law **4** code, rule, writ **5** axiom, brief, canon, dogma, edict, maxim, order **6** behest, decree **7** command, mandate, statute **8** doctrine, document **9** direction, ordinance, principle **10** injunction, regulation **11** commandment, fundamental

PRECEPTOR: **5** tutor **6** expert, mentor **7** teacher **10** instructor, specialist

PRECINCT: **4** beat **6** domain, sector **7** quarter **8** boundary, district, environs **9** territory **11** subdivision

PRECIOUS: **4** dear, rare **5** loved, picky **6** choice, costly, prized, valued **7** beloved, darling, fragile **8** adorable, delicate, favorite, valuable **9** cherished, expensive, exquisite, priceless, treasured **10** fastidious, particular **11** inestimable, overrefined

PRECIPICE: **4** crag, drop **5** bluff, cliff, ledge, steep **9** declivity

PRECIPITATE: **4** fall, hurl, rash **5** hasty, hurry, speed, throw **6** abrupt, hasten, madcap, sudden **7** hurried **8** expedite, headlong, reckless **9** impatient, impetuous, impulsive **10** accelerate, unexpected **11** precipitous

PRECIPITATION: **4** hail, mist, rain, snow **5** sleet **7** drizzle **8** downpour, moisture **9** hastening **11** impetuosity **12** condensation

PRECIPITOUS: **5** hasty, quick, rapid, sheer, steep **6** abrupt **11** precipitate

PRECIS: **6** digest **7** epitome, summary **8** abstract, synopsis **11** abridgement **12** condensation

PRECISE: **4** even, nice **5** exact, fixed, fussy, rigid, stiff **6** formal, proper, strict **7** careful, literal **8** accurate, definite, detailed, explicit, specific **9** faultless, stringent **10** fastidious, immaculate, meticulous, particular **11** painstaking, punctilious

PRECISION: **4** care **8** accuracy **9** attention, exactness **11** correctness

PRECLUDE: **3** bar **4** stop **5** avert, cease, close, debar **6** forbid, hinder, impede **7** exclude, inhibit, prevent **8** prohibit **11** discontinue

PRECOCIOUS: **5** fresh, sassy, smart **6** bright, gifted **8** advanced **9** premature **11** intelligent

PRECONCEPTION: **4** bias **6** nation **9** prejudice **10** assumption **11** presumption

PRECURSOR: **6** herald **8** ancestor, vanguard **9** harbinger, messenger **10** forerunner **11** predecessor, trailblazer

PREDATORY: **7** preying **8** ravenous **9** marauding, pillaging, rapacious, raptorial, vulturine **10** plundering, predacious **11** carnivorous

PREDECESSOR: **7** forbear **8** ancestor, forebear **9** precursor **10** forefather, foremother

PREDESTINATION: **4** doom, fate **7** destiny, fortune **13** preordination

PREDETERMINED: **5** fixed **6** agreed **7** decided, planned **10** deliberate **11** prearranged **12** premeditated

PREDICAMENT: **3** fix, jam **4** bind, hole, spot **5** pinch, state **6** corner, crisis, pickle, plight, scrape **7** dilemma **8** quandary **9** condition, emergency, situation **10** difficulty

PREDICATE: **4** aver, base, rest **5** imply **6** affirm, assert **7** declare, profess **8** proclaim **9** establish

PREDICT: **4** call, omen, read **5** augur, guess **6** divine **7** forbode, foresee, portend, suppose **8** envision, forebode, forecast, foretell, prophesy, soothsay **10** conjecture **13** prognosticate

PREDICTABLE: **4** sure **6** likely **7** certain **8** expected **11** anticipated

PREDICTION: **5** guess, hunch **7** insight **8** forecast, prophecy **9** foresight

PREDILECTION: **4** bent, bias **7** leaning, mindset **8** druthers, penchant, tendency **9** prejudice **10** partiality, preference, proclivity, propensity **14** predisposition

PREDISPOSED: **5** prone **6** biased **7** willing

PREDISPOSITION: **7** leaning **8** tendency **10** likelihood **11** inclination, willingness **12** predilection **14** susceptibility

PREDOMINANT: **4** main **5** chief **6** ruling **7** leading, primary **8** reigning, superior **9** important, paramount, prevalent, principal **10** dominating, prevailing **11** controlling, influential

PREDOMINATE: **4** lead, rule **6** govern, manage, master **7** command, prevail **8** domineer **9** sovereign

PREEMINENT: **4** best, main, star **5** chief, famed **7** capital, honored, stellar, supreme **8** dominant, renowned, superior, towering **9** prominent **10** unequalled, unrivalled **11** outstanding, unsurpassed **12** incomparable, unparalleled **13** distinguished

PREEMPT: **4** bump, take **5** seize, usurp **6** obtain **7** acquire **8** arrogate, displace **9** sequester **10** confiscate **11** appropriate

PREEN: **4** perk, trim **5** adorn, clean, dress, groom, plume, press, pride, primp, prune **6** neaten, smooth, spruce

PREFACE: **5** begin, front, proem **7** precede, prelude **8** commence, overture, preamble, prologue **9** introduce **11** explanation **12** introduction

PREFER: **3** opt **4** like, pick **5** elect, fancy, favor, raise **6** choose, desire, select **7** advance, promote

PREFERENCE: **4** bias **6** choice **8** druthers, priority **9** prejudice, selection, upgrading **10** favoritism, partiality, propensity **11** advancement **12** predilection

PREFIGURE: **4** hint **6** typify **7** imagine, presage, suggest **8** foretell, indicate **9** adumbrate, symbolize **10** foreshadow

PREGNANT: **4** rich **5** heavy **6** fecund **7** fertile, hopeful, replete, teeming, weighty **8** creative, fruitful, prolific **9** abounding, expecting, gestating, momentous, potential **10** meaningful **11** significant

PREHISTORIC: **7** ancient **10** immemorial

PREJUDICE: **4** bent, bias, harm, hurt **5** slant, taint **6** damage, hatred, hinder, impair, racism, sexism **7** bigotry, distort **9** influence **10** favoritism, partiality, prepossess **11** inclination, intolerance, prejudgment **12** predetermine, predilection **14** discrimination

PREJUDICIAL: **6** biased, unjust **7** harmful **8** contrary, damaging **9** injurious **11** detrimental, undermining **14** discriminatory

PRELATE: **5** abbot **6** abbess, bishop, priest **8** cardinal **9** dignitary **10** archbishop **12** ecclesiastic

PRELIMINARY: **5** basic, prior **7** initial, preface **8** previous **9** beginning, inductive, prefatory **10** antecedent, qualifying **11** exploratory, fundamental, preparatory **12** introductory

PRELUDE: **5** fugue, proem **7** opening, preface **8** foreword, overture **9** beginning **12** introduction

PREMATURE: **5** early **6** unripe **7** unready **8** immature **10** incomplete, precocious **11** undeveloped

PREMEDITATED: **7** planned, studied **8** intended **9** conscious, contrived **10** calculated, deliberate **11** intentional **13** predetermined

PREMIER: **5** chief, first **7** leading **8** earliest, foremost **9** beginning **13** prime minister

PREMIERE: **5** debut **7** opening **9** beginning, inaugural **11** performance

PREMISE: **6** thesis **7** presume **8** argument **9** postulate **10** assumption, hypothesis **11** proposition, supposition

PREMISES: **4** land, site **6** bounds, campus, layout **7** grounds **8** property

PREMIUM: **5** award, bonus, gravy, prime, prize **6** bounty, carrot, choice, reward **7** payment **8** superior **9** excellent **10** recompense **11** installment

PREMONITION: **4** omen, sign **5** hunch, vibes **7** feeling, warning **9** misgiving **10** foreboding, prediction **11** forewarning **12** apprehension

PREOCCUPIED: **4** lost **6** absent **7** engaged, wrapped **8** absorbed, immersed **9** engrossed, oblivious **10** distracted **12** absentminded

PREPARATION: **8** readying, training **9** alertness, foresight, readiness **10** concoction, foundation, groundwork **11** arrangement, composition

PREPARE: **3** arm, fit, fix **4** cook, edit, make, plan, suit **5** adapt, alert, coach, draft, equip, frame, groom, prime, ready, train **6** adjust, braced, devise, outfit, settle, supply **7** address, arrange, concoct, dispose, furnish, groomed, instant, prepped, provide, qualify, trained **8** compound, finished, instruct, rehearse **9** condition, construct, processed, rehearsed **10** strengthen **11** conditioned

PREPONDERANCE: **6** weight **7** command **9** dominance, supremacy **10** ascendancy, prevalence **11** superiority **12** predominance

PREPOSSESS: **4** bias **9** influence, prejudice, preoccupy **12** predetermine

PREPOSSESSING: **8** charming, handsome, pleasant **10** attractive, enchanting

PREPOSTEROUS: **5** crazy, silly **6** absurd, insane **7** bizarre, foolish **9** ludicrous, senseless **10** irrational, outrageous, ridiculous **11** nonsensical **12** unbelievable, unreasonable

PREREQUISITE: **4** must **9** condition, essential, mandatory, necessary, postulate **11** requirement

PREROGATIVE: **4** gift **5** grant, right **6** choice, option **8** immunity **9** advantage, exemption, privilege **10** birthright **11** preeminence

PRESAGE: **4** bode, omen, sign **5** augur, token **6** augury **7** betoken, feeling, portend, portent, predict, warning **8** forebode, forecast, foretell, forewarn, indicate, prophecy, prophesy, soothsay **9**

harbinger, intuition **10** indication, prediction, prescience, prognostic **11** premonition **12** apprehension, presentiment **13** prognosticate

PRESBYTER: **5** elder **6** pastor, priest **9** clergyman **11** clergywoman

PRESCIENCE: **7** presage **9** foresight **10** prediction **11** omniscience **13** foreknowledge

PRESCRIBE: **4** rule **5** allot, guide, limit, order **6** assign, define, direct, enjoin, ordain **7** appoint, command, control, dictate **9** authorize, designate, establish, recommend

PRESCRIPT: **3** law **4** rule **6** decree **7** command, statute **10** regulation

PRESCRIPTION: **4** drug **6** recipe, remedy **7** formula, mixture **8** medicine **9** direction

PRESENCE: **3** air **4** aura, cool, look, mien **5** being, poise **6** aspect, manner, spirit **7** bearing, company **8** calmness, demeanor **9** alertness, character, closeness, influence, occupancy, proximity, sangfroid **10** apparition, appearance, deportment

PRESENT: **3** now **4** gift, give, here, show **5** award, being, bonus, grant, offer, ready, today **6** allege, bestow, bounty, confer, donate, nearby, render, tender **7** address, current, display, exhibit, largess, perform **8** donation, existing, gratuity, manifest, nowadays **9** endowment, immediate, introduce, lagniappe **10** contribute, exhibition **11** demonstrate **12** contemporary

PRESENTABLE: **4** okay **6** decent, proper **7** stylish **8** suitable **10** acceptable **11** appropriate, respectable **12** satisfactory

PRESENTATION: **4** gift, show **5** award, debut, pitch **7** lecture **8** delivery **10** appearance, production **11** performance **13** demonstration

PRESENTIMENT: **5** vibes **7** feeling, presage **9** intuition **10** foreboding **11** expectation, premonition **12** apprehension

PRESENTLY: **3** now **4** anon **5** today **7** shortly **8** directly **9** currently **11** immediately

PRESERVATION: **4** care **6** saving **7** defense, storage **9** safeguard **10** protection **11** maintenance, safekeeping

PRESERVATIVE: **4** salt **7** alcohol, vinegar **8** chemical **9** saltpeter **12** formaldehyde

PRESERVE: **3** can, dry, jam **4** cure, keep, salt, save **5** guard, jelly, smoke, spare, store **6** defend, embalm, freeze, govern, pickle, retain, season, secure, shield, uphold **7** compote, mummify **8** maintain **9** dehydrate, safeguard **11** refrigerate

PRESIDE: **3** run **4** head **5** chair **6** direct, handle, manage **7** conduct, control, oversee **8** regulate **10** administer

PRESIDENT (U.S.):
first: **16** George Washington
second: **9** John Adams
third: **15** Thomas Jefferson
fourth: **5** Jemmy **12** James Madison
fifth: **11** James Monroe
sixth: **15** John Quincy Adams
seventh: **10** Old Hickory **13** Andrew Jackson
eighth: **14** Little Magician, Martin Van Buren
ninth: **20** William Henry Harrison
tenth: **9** John Tyler
eleventh: **13** James Knox Polk
twelfth: **13** Zachary Taylor
thirteenth: **15** Millard Fillmore

fourteenth: **14** Franklin Pierce
fifteenth: **13** James Buchanan
sixteenth: **9** Honest Abe **14** Abraham Lincoln
seventeenth: **13** Andrew Johnson
eighteenth: **19** Ulysses Simpson Grant
nineteenth: **15** Rutherford Hayes
twentieth: **13** James Garfield
twenty-first: **13** Chester Arthur
twenty-second: **10** Uncle Jumbo **15** Grover Cleveland
twenty-third: **16** Benjamin Harrison
twenty-fourth: **10** Uncle Jumbo **15** Grover Cleveland
twenty-fifth: **15** William McKinley
twenty-sixth: **5** Teddy **10** Rough Rider **17** Theodore Roosevelt
twenty-seventh: **11** William Taft
twenty-eighth: **9** Professor **13** Woodrow Wilson
twenty-ninth: **13** Warren Harding
thirtieth: **9** Silent Cal **14** Calvin Coolidge
thirty-first: **13** Herbert Hoover
thirty-second: **3** FDR **18** Franklin D. Roosevelt
thirty-third: **12** Harry S. Truman
thirty-fourth: **3** Ike **21** Dwight David Eisenhower
thirty-fifth: **3** JFK **21** John Fitzgerald Kennedy
thirty-sixth: **3** LBJ **19** Lyndon Baines Johnson
thirty-seventh: **19** Richard Milhous Nixon
thirty-eighth: **5** Jerry **10** Gerald Ford
thirty-ninth: **5** Jimmy **15** James Earl Carter
fortieth: **5** Dutch **12** Ronald Reagan
forty-first: **5** Poppy **10** George Bush
forty-second: **5** Bubba **14** William Clinton

PRESS: **3** hug, jam, mob, ram, tax **4** bear, bind, cram, iron, mash, pack, pile, push, rush, urge **5** bunch, crowd, crush, drive, force, horde, knead, media, steam, stuff, wring **6** bother, compel, crunch, gather, impact, roller, smooth, squash, throng, thrust **7** embrace, entreat, express, flatten, impress, imprint, squeeze **8** compress, pressure, reporter **9** constrain, emphasize, importune **10** journalist **13** correspondent

PRESS CONFERENCE: **7** hearing **8** briefing **9** interview **12** announcement

PRESSING: **5** acute **6** urgent **7** burning, crucial, serious **8** critical, exacting **9** immediate, important **10** imperative **11** importunate

PRESSURE: **4** heat, mass, pull, push **5** force, power **6** burden, duress, stress, weight **7** anxiety, squeeze, tension **10** constraint, difficulty, impression, oppression **11** compression

PRESTIGE: **4** fame, rank **5** honor, power **6** esteem, renown, status **7** dignity, respect, stature **8** eminence, position **9** influence **10** importance, prominence **11** distinction

PRESTIGIOUS: **5** famed **7** eminent, honored **8** renowned **9** prominent, respected **11** influential **13** distinguished

PRESTO: **4** fast **5** magic **7** quickly, rapidly **8** suddenly **13** instantaneous

PRESUMABLY: **6** likely **8** credible, probably **10** apparently, ostensibly, supposedly **11** doubtlessly, indubitably **14** unquestionably

PRESUME: **5** guess **6** deduce, gather, impose, reason **7** believe, suppose, surmise, venture **8** consider, infringe **9** postulate, speculate **10** conjecture

PRESUMPTION: **4** gall **5** brass, cheek, nerve **6** belief, daring **8** audacity, boldness, chutzpah **9** suspicion **10** effrontery **11** forwardness, speculation

PRESUMPTUOUS: **4** bold, rude, smug **5** brash, pushy **6** brazen, uppity **7** forward, haughty, pompous **8** arrogant, assuming, familiar, insolent **9** audacious, conceited, confident

PRESUPPOSE: **5** infer, posit **6** assume, reckon **7** believe, surmise **9** speculate

PRETEND: **3** act **4** fake, sham **5** bluff, claim, feign **6** affect, assume **7** deceive, imagine, imitate, profess **8** disguise, proclaim, simulate **11** acknowledge, counterfeit, impersonate

PRETENDER: **4** fake **5** faker, fraud, phony, quack **8** deceiver, imitator, impostor **9** charlatan, hypocrite **10** dissembler

PRETENSE: **4** fake, flam, mask, sham, show **5** claim, cloak, cover, feint, fraud, trick **6** excuse, facade **7** charade, fiction, pretext **8** disguise, imagined, occasion, smugness **9** deception, falsehood **10** appearance, assumption, brazenness **11** affectation, fabrication, insincerity, ostentation

PRETENSION: **4** airs **5** claim, title **7** charade, pretext **9** hypocrisy, showiness **12** ostentatious, snobbishness

PRETENTIOUS: **4** smug **5** gaudy, lofty, showy **6** flashy, ornate, turgid **7** flowery, pompous, splashy **9** conceited, grandiose, insincere, presuming **10** flamboyant **11** extravagant **12** highfaluting, ostentatious

PRETERNATURAL: **7** ghostly, unusual **8** abnormal, atypical, uncommon **9** unnatural **10** miraculous, mysterious **11** exceptional **12** supernatural **13** extraordinary

PRETEXT: **4** mask **5** cover, front **6** device, excuse **8** disguise, pretense **10** masquerade

PRETTY: **4** cute, fair **6** adroit, clever, comely, dainty, lovely **7** cunning, darling, dollish, elegant **8** alluring, graceful, handsome, skillful, terrible **9** appealing, beautiful, ingenious **10** attractive, moderately **11** captivating

PREVAIL: **3** win **4** beat, rule **5** reign **6** obtain **7** conquer, control, succeed, triumph **8** dominate, overcome, surmount

PREVALENT: **4** rife **6** common, ruling **7** current, general, popular, rampant **8** accepted, dominant, frequent, superior **9** pervasive **10** accustomed, prevailing, widespread **11** established, influential

PREVARICATE: **3** fib, lie **5** dodge, evade **6** palter **7** deceive, falsify, mislead **10** equivocate, exaggerate **12** misrepresent

PREVARICATION: **3** fib, lie **4** tale **7** untruth **9** deception, falsehood **10** dishonesty **11** fabrication

PREVENT: **3** bar, dam, gag **4** balk, bind, foil, stop, veto, ward, warn **5** avert, block, debar, deter, guard **6** arrest, defend, forbid, hamper, hinder, impede, resist, thwart **7** inhibit, repress **8** obstruct, preclude, prohibit, restrain **9** forestall, frustrate, intercept, interrupt **10** anticipate

PREVIEW: **4** show **6** sample **7** trailer **9** foretaste

PREVIOUS: **4** fore, past **5** early, prior **6** before, bygone, former **7** earlier, quondam **8** anterior, foregone **9** preceding, premature, unfounded **10** antecedent, beforehand, heretofore **11** precipitate

PREVIOUSLY: **4** back, once **6** before **7** already, earlier **10** heretofore

PREY: **4** food, game, hunt, kill **5** raven, seize **6** quarry, ravage, victim **7** capture, plunder **8** underdog

PRIAM:
daughter: **6** Creusa **8** Polyxena **9** Cassandra
killed in: **9** Trojan War
killer: **7** Pyrrhus **11** Neoptolemus
kingdom: **4** Troy
sons: **5** Paris **6** Hector **7** Helenus, Troilus **9** Polydorus
wife: **6** Hecuba

PRICE: **3** fee **4** cost, fare, rate **5** value, worth **6** amount, charge, damage **7** expense, penalty **8** evaluate **9** appraisal, sacrifice **10** assessment, estimation, punishment

PRICELESS: **4** rare **5** funny **6** costly, prized **7** amusing **8** precious, valuable **9** cherished, hilarious, treasured **10** invaluable **13** irreplaceable

PRICK: **3** cut, jag **4** bore, goad, ping, pink, prod, spur, stab, urge **5** point, smart, stick, sting, thorn **6** broach, cactus, nettle, pierce, prompt **7** pinhole **8** puncture **9** perforate, stimulate

PRICKLE: **4** barb **5** chill, point, spike **7** acantha, bristle **8** spiculum, tingling **9** sensation

PRICKLY: **5** burry, sharp, spiny **6** coarse, thorny, touchy **8** scratchy **9** irritable **11** complicated, troublesome

PRIDE: **4** best, crow, huff **5** boast, elite, glory, honor, jewel, plume, prime, valor **6** egoism, esteem, mettle, spirit, vanity **7** conceit, dignity, disdain, egotism, hauteur, respect **8** smugness, splendor **9** arrogance, cockiness, enjoyment, insolence, loftiness, vainglory **10** lordliness, self-esteem **11** amour propre, haughtiness **12** satisfaction **13** self-assurance

PRIDE AND PREJUDICE:
author: **10** Jane Austen
character: **5** Darcy **7** Bingley, Wickham **9** Mr. Collins **10** Jane Bennet, Mary Bennet **11** Kitty Bennet, Lydia Bennet **15** Elizabeth Bennet

PRIEST: **4** abbe, lama **5** friar, padre, rabbi, vicar **6** bishop, cleric, divine, father, flamen, pastor, rector, shaman **7** pontiff **8** minister, pontifex, preacher **9** churchman, clergyman, dignitary, presbyter **10** chancellor **11** churchwoman, clergywoman **12** ecclesiastic

PRIESTLY: **8** churchly, hieratic **10** sacerdotal **14** ecclesiastical

PRIG: **3** fop **4** prim **5** dandy, prude, thief **6** purist **7** filcher **8** pilferer **9** nitpicker **10** pickpocket

PRIGGISH: **4** prim, smug, vain **6** stuffy **7** pompous **10** complacent **11** straitlaced

PRIM: **4** neat, snug, tidy, trim **5** stiff **6** demure, formal, prissy, proper, stuffy, wooden **7** genteel, precise, prudish **8** decorous, straight **9** shipshape **10** ceremonial, particular **11** straitlaced

PRIMA DONNA: **4** diva, lead, star **7** actress **13** temperamental

PRIMARY: **4** main **5** basic, chief, first, prime, vital **6** direct, primal **7** central, initial, leading **8** dominant, earliest **9** essential, immediate, primitive, principal **10** elementary, underlying **11** fundamental

PRIMATE: **3** ape, man **5** human, lemur **6** baboon, bishop, mammal, monkey **7** gorilla **9** orangutan **10** anthropoid, chimpanzee, prosimians **11** Homo sapiens

PRIME: **4** best, dawn, main, pick, prep, size **5** bloom, chief, coach, cream, elite, ready, tutor **6** choice, heyday, school, spring **7** morning, prepare, primary, sunrise, supreme **8** daybreak, greatest, original, superior **9** essential, excellent, important, principal, undercoat

PRIMER: **4** book **5** basal **8** hornbook, textbook

PRIMEVAL: **5** early **6** primal **7** ancient **8** original **9** primitive **10** aboriginal, primordial **11** prehistoric

PRIMITIVE: **5** basic, crude, early, first **6** simple **7** ancient, archaic, primary **8** barbaric, original, pristine **9** elemental **10** aboriginal, antiquated, elementary, uncultured **11** fundamental, uncivilized, undeveloped

PRIMORDIAL: **5** early, first **6** primal **7** primary **8** original, primeval **10** elementary **11** fundamental

PRIMP: **5** adorn, groom, preen **7** dress up, gussy up **8** beautify, spruce up

PRINCE: **4** emir, raja **5** emeer, rajah, ruler **7** monarch, royalty **8** archduke, atheling, nobleman **9** potentate, sovereign

PRINCE EDWARD ISLAND:
capital: **13** Charlottetown
cities: **8** Sherwood **10** Summerside
country: **6** Canada
explorer: **7** Cartier
flower: **12** lady's slipper
formerly: **10** Isle St. John, Isle St.-Jean
water: **8** Atlantic

PRINCELY: **5** grand, noble, regal, royal **6** lavish, lordly **7** stately **9** sovereign **11** magnificent

PRINCE OF DARKNESS: **5** devil, Satan **7** Lucifer

PRINCESS: **5** queen **7** royalty **10** noblewoman

PRINCIPAL: **4** arch, dean, head, high, main, star **5** chief, first, money, prime **6** leader **7** capital, highest, primary, stellar **8** cardinal, champion, dominant, foremost **9** essential, important **10** headmaster, preeminent **11** outstanding **13** administrator

PRINCIPLE: **3** law **4** code, rule **5** axiom, canon, creed, honor, truth **6** belief, dictum, ethics, morals **7** element, essence, theorem **8** doctrine, teaching **9** integrity, standards **10** foundation **11** fundamental, uprightness

PRINT: **4** copy, film, font, text, type **5** stamp, write **6** fabric **7** edition, engrave, picture, publish **8** magazine **9** newspaper **10** impression, lithograph **11** publication

PRINTER: **7** machine **8** pressman **9** linotyper **10** compositor, presswoman, typesetter **11** typographer **12** lithographer

PRIOR: **4** past **6** before, former **7** earlier **8** anterior, previous **9** erstwhile, preceding **10** antecedent, precursory **11** preexisting, retroactive

PRIORITY: **4** rank **5** order **7** urgency **8** position **9** seniority **10** ascendancy, precedence, preference **11** superiority

PRISM: **3** gem **5** stone **6** figure **7** crystal **8** cylinder, spectrum

PRISON: **3** can, pen **4** brig, cell, hole, jail, keep, tank **5** clink, pokey **6** cooler, lockup **7** dungeon, slammer **8** bastille, hoosegow, stockade **9** calaboose **10** guardhouse **12** penitentiary
famous: **6** Attica **7** Spandau **8** Alcatraz, Sing Sing **10** San Quentin **11** Leavenworth

PRISONER: **3** con **5** lifer **6** trusty **7** captive, convict **8** detainee, jailbird
of war: **3** POW

PRISSY: **4** prim **5** fussy **6** stuffy **7** finicky, prudish **9** sissified, squeamish **10** effeminate **11** straitlaced

PRISTINE: **4** pure **5** clean, early, fresh **8** original **9** primitive, unspoiled, untouched **11** uncorrupted

PRIVACY: **7** privity, retreat, secrecy **8** solitude **9** isolation, seclusion

PRIVATE: **5** privy **6** closet, covert, hidden, hushed, inside, remote, secret **7** soldier **8** desolate, discreet, intimate, personal, secluded, solitary **9** concealed, nonpublic, reclusive **10** unofficial **11** clandestine, sequestered **12** confidential

PRIVATEER: **4** lack, ship **6** penury, pirate, vessel **7** corsair **8** distress **9** buccaneer, pauperism, privation **10** freebooter

PRIVATION: **4** loss, want **6** misery **7** absence, poverty **8** hardship **11** deprivation, destitution

PRIVILEGE: **4** boon **5** favor, grace, grant, honor, right **7** charter, freedom, liberty **8** immunity **9** advantage, allowance, exemption **10** birthright, concession, permission **11** entitlement, prerogative

PRIVILEGED: **5** elite, privy **6** immune, secret **7** allowed, special **8** eligible **10** authorized **12** confidential

PRIVY: **4** head **5** aware **6** covert, hidden, secret, toilet **7** latrine, private **8** informed, lavatory, outhouse **9** concealed, conscious **10** privileged **11** clandestine **12** confidential

PRIZE: **4** best, goal, pick **5** award, bonus, booty, catch, cream, crown, elite, jewel, medal, plate, prime, purse, spoil, stake, value **6** carrot, choice, esteem, payoff, reward, seized, trophy **7** jackpot, premium **8** leverage, treasure, winnings **10** appreciate

PRIZEFIGHT: **4** bout **5** match **7** contest **10** fisticuffs **11** boxing match

PRO: **3** for **4** whiz, with **6** expert, master **8** advocate, favoring **9** authority **10** supporting **12** professional

PROBABILITY: **4** odds, shot **7** chances **8** prospect **10** likelihood **11** credibility, possibility

PROBABLE: **7** logical, seeming **8** possible **10** believable, presumable, reasonable **11** conceivable

PROBABLY: **6** likely **8** apparent, feasible **10** imaginably, presumably, supposedly

PROBE: **4** poke, quiz, seek, sift, test **5** query, scout **6** search **7** examine, explore, inquiry **8** analysis, research **9** penetrate **10** instrument, scrutinize **11** exploration, investigate **13** investigation

PROBITY: **6** virtue **7** honesty **8** goodness, morality **9** integrity, sincerity **11** uprightness **13** righteousness

PROBLEM: **5** issue, poser **6** enigma, puzzle, riddle **7** dilemma, trouble **8** obstacle, quandary, question **9** situation **10** difficulty **12** complication, unmanageable

PROBLEMATIC: **4** moot **6** tricky **7** dubious **8** doubtful **9** ambiguous, debatable, uncertain, unsettled **10** disputable **12** questionable

PROBOSCIS: **4** beak, nose **5** organ, snoot, snout, trunk

PROCEDURE: **4** mode **6** course, custom, method, policy **7** formula, measure, process, program, routine **8** approach **9** technique

PROCEED: **4** flow, move, pass **5** arise, begin, march, start **6** derive, spring **7** advance, emanate **8** commence, continue, progress **9** originate

PROCEEDINGS: **6** doings **7** account, matters **8** activity, business, dealings **10** litigation

PROCEEDS: **4** gate, loot, take **5** split **6** income, profit, return **7** revenue **8** earnings, receipts, winnings

PROCESS: **4** cook, mode, step, writ **5** order, usage **6** course, manner, method, notice, policy, system **7** passage, prepare, routine, summons **8** function, practice, progress **9** evolution, operation, outgrowth, procedure, technique

PROCESSION: **4** file, line **5** march **6** column, course, litany, parade, series **7** caravan, cortege **9** cavalcade, formation

PROCLAIM: **4** call, mark, show, tell, toot **5** blare, sound, state, utter, voice **6** assert, blazon, herald, outcry, praise, preach **7** declare, divulge, exhibit, glorify, publish, trumpet **8** announce **9** advertise, broadcast, celebrate, ventilate **10** promulgate

PROCLAMATION: **3** ban **5** edict, ukase **6** decree, notice **7** mandate **9** manifesto, statement **11** declaration, publication **12** announcement, promulgation

PROCLIVITY: **6** talent **7** leaning **8** penchant, tendency **9** prejudice **10** partiality, propensity **11** disposition, inclination **12** predilection **14** predisposition

PROCNE:
changed into: **7** swallow
husband: **6** Tereus
sister: **9** Philomela
title: **8** princess

PROCRASTINATE: **4** wait **5** dally, defer, delay, stall **6** loiter **7** prolong **8** postpone

PROCREATE: **4** bear, sire **5** beget, spawn **6** father, mother, parent **7** produce **8** conceive, multiply **9** reproduce

PROCTOR: **5** agent **7** monitor **8** delegate **9** supervise **10** supervisor **14** representative

PROCURE: **3** get, win **4** find, gain, land **5** bring, score **6** attain, effect, induce, obtain, secure **7** acquire, promote, receive, solicit **8** purchase **10** accumulate

PROD: **4** goad, move, poke, push, spur, urge **5** elbow, nudge, shove **6** excite, incite, prompt **7** provoke **9** encourage, instigate, stimulate

PRODIGAL: **4** lush **6** lavish **7** opulent, profuse, spender, wastrel **8** abundant, wasteful **9** excessive, luxurious **10** gluttonous, profligate, squanderer **11** extravagant, spendthrift, squandering

PRODIGIOUS: **4** huge **5** giant, grand, large **6** mighty **7** immense, mammoth **8** colossal, enormous, fabulous, gigantic **9** fantastic, marvelous, wonderful **10** impressive, monumental, portentous, stupendous, tremendous **11** astonishing, spectacular **13** extraordinary

PRODIGY: **6** genius, marvel, wizard, wonder **7** miracle, natural, portent **10** phenomenon

PRODUCE: **4** bear, from, grow, make, show **5** beget, breed, build, cause, shape, stage, yield **6** create, effect, fruits, induce, parent, reveal **7** exhibit, harvest, present, staples **8** engender, generate, multiply **9** cultivate, fabricate, offspring, originate, procreate **10** vegetables **11** manufacture

PRODUCT: **4** item **5** goods, yield **6** device, effect, output, result **7** produce **8** offshoot **9** outgrowth **11** consequence, merchandise

PRODUCTION: **4** play, show **5** movie, yield **6** output **8** assembly **11** performance **13** manufacturing

PRODUCTIVE: **4** busy, rich **6** active, fecund, useful **7** fertile **8** creative, fruitful, prolific, valuable **9** energetic **10** worthwhile

PROEM: **7** opening, preface, prelude **8** foreword, prologue **12** introduction

PROFANE: **3** lay **4** foul, lewd **5** abuse, crude, dirty **6** coarse, debase, defile, filthy, smutty, unholy, vulgar, wicked **7** godless, impious, obscene, raunchy, secular, ungodly, worldly **8** temporal **9** desecrate **10** irreverent, unhallowed **11** blasphemous, uninitiated **12** sacrilegious, unsanctified

PROFANITY: **4** cuss, oath **5** curse, swear **9** expletive, obscenity

PROFESS: **4** avow **5** admit, claim, state, vouch **6** affect, affirm, assert **7** confess, declare, purport **8** announce

PROFESSION: **3** art, job **4** work **5** craft, faith, forte, skill, trade **6** career **7** calling **8** business, endeavor, vocation **10** employment, occupation **11** declaration

PROFESSIONAL: **3** ace, pro **4** paid **5** adept, hired, shark **6** expert, master **7** skilled, trained **10** proficient

PROFESSOR: **3** don **5** tutor **7** teacher **8** educator, emeritus, lecturer **10** instructor

PROFFER: **4** give **5** offer **6** extend, submit, tender **7** present, suggest **8** proposal

PROFICIENCY: **5** knack, skill **7** ability, advance, mastery **8** aptitude **9** adeptness, dexterity **10** capability, competence, efficiency, expertness

PROFICIENT: **4** able **5** adept **6** expert, master, versed **7** contour, outline, skilled **8** skillful **9** competent, efficient **10** silhouette **12** professional

PROFILE: **4** form, side **6** review, sketch **10** figuration **11** description **13** configuration

PROFIT: **3** net **4** gain, good, help, take **5** avail, lucre, money, yield **6** income, return **7** benefit, improve, killing, revenue, surplus **8** earnings, increase, interest, proceeds **9** advantage **12** remuneration

PROFITABLE: **6** useful **9** lucrative, rewarding **10** beneficial, productive, prosperous, worthwhile **12** advantageous

PROFLIGATE: **6** lavish, sinful **7** corrupt, immoral, spender, wastrel, **8** depraved, prodigal, wasteful **9** dissolute, libertine, reprobate **10** licentious **11** extravagant, spendthrift, squandering

PROFOUND: **4** deep, sage, wise **5** heavy **6** moving **7** abysmal, intense, serious **9** emotional, recondite, sagacious **10** bottomless, exhaustive, thoughtful **11** enlightened, farreaching, penetrating **12** intellectual, unfathomable **13** philosophical

PROFUSE: **4** lush **5** ample **6** galore, hearty, lavish **7** copious, opulent, replete, riotous **8** abundant, generous, prodigal **9** bountiful, excessive, exuberant, luxuriant, plentiful **10** munificent **11** extravagant

PROGENITOR: **6** parent **7** founder **8** ancestor **9** precursor **10** forefather, originator

PROGENY: **4** race, seed **5** blood, breed, brood, child, fruit **6** family, strain **7** lineage, product **8** children **9** offspring, posterity **10** generation **11** descendants

PROGNOSIS: **8** forecast, prophecy **9** diagnosis **10** prediction

PROGNOSTICATE: **5** augur **6** divine **7** portend, predict, presage **8** forebode, forecast, foretell, prophesy **10** foreshadow

PROGNOSTICATOR: **4** seer **5** augur **6** divine **7** diviner, prophet **10** soothsayer **13** fortuneteller

PROGRAM: **4** card, list, plan, show **5** slate **6** agenda, course, docket, notice, scheme **7** catalog, outline **8** bulletin, calendar, playbill, schedule, syllabus **9** broadcast, timetable **10** prospectus **12** presentation

PROGRESS: **4** fare, grow, move **5** march **6** course, growth **7** advance, circuit, develop, headway, improve, journey, passage, proceed **9** evolution, promotion **10** expedition **11** development, improvement **12** breakthrough

PROGRESSION: **5** chain, order, stage **6** course, growth, series, string **8** sequence **9** evolution **10** succession **11** development, improvement **12** continuation

PROGRESSIVE: **6** active, rising **7** forward, gradual, growing, liberal **9** advancing **10** continuing

PROHIBIT: **3** ban, bar **4** stop, veto **5** block **6** forbid, hinder, impede, outlaw **7** inhibit, prevent **8** disallow, restrict **9** interdict

PROHIBITED: **5** taboo **6** banned **7** illegal, illicit **8** unlawful, verboten **9** forbidden **10** restricted

PROHIBITIVE: **8** limiting **9** expensive **10** forbidding, oppressive **11** restrictive

PROJECT: **4** goal, hurl, idea, plan, send, task, work **5** bulge, fling, gauge, shoot, think, throw **6** beetle, design, device, devise, extend, launch, propel, scheme, vision **7** extrude, feature, imagine, pattern, prolong, venture **8** activity, contrive, forecast, lengthen, protrude **9** calculate, discharge, intention **10** assignment, enterprise **11** proposition, undertaking

PROJECTILE: **4** bomb, dart **5** arrow, shell, spear **6** bullet, rocket, weapon **7** missile, torpedo **9** impelling

PROJECTION: **3** arm **4** hook, tusk **5** bulge, guess, ledge, point, ridge **7** cornice, empathy **8** abutment, eminence, estimate, forecast, overhand **9** extension **10** prediction, protrusion **12** protuberance **13** approximation

PROLETARIAT: **5** plebs **6** masses, rabble **7** workers **8** laborers **9** commoners **10** commonalty **12** working class

PROLIFERATE: **4** grow **5** spawn **6** spread **8** escalate, increase, multiply, mushroom **9** procreate, propagate

PROLIFIC: **4** lush, rich **6** fecund **7** fertile **8** abundant, fruitful, spawning, swarming **9** abounding, plentiful, reductive **10** productive **11** proliferous

PROLIX: **5** wordy **7** diffuse, lengthy, tedious, verbose **8** tiresome **9** prolonged, redundant, wearisome **10** protracted

PROLOGUE: **5** proem **7** opening, preface, prelude **8** foreword, preamble **12** introduction

PROLONG: **4** last **5** stall **6** endure, extend **7** persist, stretch **8** increase, lengthen **10** perpetuate

PROLONGED: **6** prolix **7** delayed **8** drawn-out, extended **9** continued, sustained **10** lengthened, protracted

PROM: **4** ball **5** dance **9** promenade

PROMENADE: **4** ball, deck, walk **5** dance, party **6** marina, parade, stroll **7** gallery **9** boardwalk, reception

PROMETHEUS:
created: **10** Bronze Race
father: **7** Iapetus
mother: **7** Clymene
punished by: **4** Zeus
rescued by: **8** Heracles, Hercules
stole: **4** fire

PROMINENCE: **4** bump, fame, rank **5** crest **6** renown **8** eminence, nobility, pinnacle, prestige, salience, standing **9** celebrity, greatness, notoriety **10** importance, popularity, protrusion **11** distinction

PROMINENT: **5** famed, great **6** famous, marked **7** eminent, leading, notable, obvious, popular, salient **8** renowned, striking **9** important **10** celebrated, noticeable, projecting, protruding **11** conspicuous, illustrious, outstanding **12** unmistakable **13** distinguished

PROMISCUOUS: **4** fast **5** loose **6** casual, random, wanton **7** diverse, immoral **8** confused, unchaste **14** indiscriminate

PROMISE: **3** vow **4** band, oath, pawn, word **5** agree, grant, swear **6** assure, engage, ensure, pledge, plight **7** ability, betroth, outlook **8** contract, covenant, warranty **9** assurance, guarantee, potential **10** commitment, obligation **11** declaration

PROMISED LAND: **4** Zion **6** Canaan, heaven, utopia **8** paradise **10** California

PROMISING: **4** rosy **5** happy **6** bright, rising **7** hopeful **8** talented **11** encouraging

PROMISSORY NOTE: **3** IOU **4** bond **5** check **6** pledge

PROMONTORY: **4** bill, head, peak, scaw, spit **5** jutty, mount, point, ridge **8** headland **10** projection

PROMOTE: **3** aid **4** help, plug, push **5** boost, exalt **6** better, foster, prefer **7** advance, bolster, elevate, endorse, enhance, forward, further, sponsor **8** advocate, champion **9** encourage, patronize, publicize

PROMOTER: **5** agent **7** booster **8** advocate, lobbyist **9** organizer, proponent, supporter

PROMOTION: **4** hype **7** buildup, fanfare **9** elevation **11** advancement, advertising

PROMPT: **4** fast, goad, hint, move, prod, spur, urge **5** alert, nudge, quick, ready, swift **6** active, assist, excite, induce, needle, remind **7** forward, provoke **8** motivate, punctual **10** responsive **13** instantaneous

PROMULGATE: **5** sound **6** decree, notify **7** declare **8** announce, proclaim **9** advertise, broadcast **11** communicate

PRONE: **3** apt **4** flat, open **5** ready **6** liable, likely, supine **7** exposed, passive, willing **8** disposed, inclined, pronated **9** prostrate, reclining, recumbent **10** horizontal **11** susceptible

PRONG: **4** fork, hook, horn, spur **5** point, spike, spine

PRONOUN:
demonstrative: **3** any, its **4** that, this **5** these, those
interrogative: **3** who **4** whom **5** whose
personal: **3** her, him, our, she, thy, you **4** mine, ours, thee, them, they, your **5** their, thine
reflexive: **6** itself, myself **7** herself, himself, oneself, ourself **8** yourself **9** ourselves **10** themselves, yourselves
relative: **3** who **4** that
substantive: **3** who **7** whoever **9** whosoever
types: **8** personal, relative **9** reflexive **13** demonstrative

PRONOUNCE: **5** sound, speak, utter **6** affirm, decree **7** declare, deliver, phonate **8** announce, vocalize **9** enunciate, verbalize **10** articulate

PRONOUNCED: **5** clear **6** marked **7** evident **8** apparent, distinct **10** noticeable **11** conspicuous **12** unmistakable

PRONOUNCEMENT: **6** decree, dictum **8** judgment **9** broadcast, statement **11** declaration **12** announcement, proclamation, promulgation

PRONTO: **3** now **4** fast **7** quickly **8** promptly **11** immediately

PRONUNCIATION: **5** drawl, twang **6** accent, speech **9** elocution, phonology **12** articulation

PROOF: **4** test **5** trial **6** galley, reason **7** exhibit, probate **8** argument, evidence **9** testimony **10** indication, validation **11** credentials **12** confirmation, verification **13** certification **14** authentication

PROOFREADER MARK: **3** cap, rom **4** dele, ital, stet **5** caret, space

PROP: **3** leg **4** lean, stay **5** brace, shore, staff, stand, stilt, truss **7** bolster, support, sustain **8** buttress **10** strengthen

PROPAGANDA: **4** hype **6** hoopla **8** agitprop, doctrine **9** publicity **12** brainwashing, indoctrinate

PROPAGANDIST: **7** apostle **8** activist **9** advocator, proponent **10** missionary

PROPAGATE: **4** grow **5** breed, spawn **6** spread **7** develop, diffuse **8** generate, multiply, proclaim, transmit **9** broadcast, fecundate, procreate, publicize, reproduce **11** disseminate

PROPEL: **4** hurl, move, push, send, spur, urge **5** drive, force, shove, sling, throw **6** launch, prompt, thrust **7** project **8** catapult

PROPELLER: **3** fan, fin, oar **4** prop **5** blade, screw **6** driver, paddle

PROPENSITY: **4** bent, bias **5** fancy **6** liking **7** aptness, leaning **8** affinity, penchant, tendency **9** affection, prejudice, proneness **10** partiality, proclivity **11** disposition, inclination **12** predilection **14** susceptibility

PROPER: **4** able, fine, good, just, meet, prim, true **5** moral, right **6** chaste, decent, formal, honest, polite, strict, useful **7** correct, fitting, seeming **8** accurate, becoming, ladylike, suitable **9** advisable, allowable, befitting **10** acceptable, convenient **11** appropriate, respectable **12** conventional

PROPERTY: **3** lot **4** acre, land **5** goods, trait **6** assets, domain, estate, realty, riches, wealth **7** acreage, chattel, effects, feature, quality **8** dominion, holdings, premises **9** attribute, homestead, ownership **10** belongings, real estate **11** appropriate, possessions **14** characteristic

PROPHECY: **6** vision **7** portent **8** bodement, forecast **9** prognosis **10** divination, prediction, revelation **11** declaration, foretelling

PROPHESY: **4** warn **5** augur **6** divine **7** predict, presage **8** forebode, forecast, foreshow, foretell, soothsay **10** vaticinate **13** prognosticate

PROPHET: **4** seer **5** augur **6** medium, oracle **7** diviner **8** sorcerer **9** predictor **10** forecaster, soothsayer **11** clairvoyant, Nostradamus **13** fortuneteller
major: **6** Baruch, Daniel, Isaiah **7** Ezekiel **8** Jeremiah
minor: **3** Gad **4** Amos, Joel **5** Hosea, Jonah, Micah, Nahum **6** Haggai, Nathan **7** Malachi, Obadiah **8** Habakkuk **9** Zechariah, Zephaniah

PROPHETESS: **4** Anna **5** Sibyl **6** Huldah, Miriam, Pythia **7** Deborah, seeress **9** Cassandra, pythoness, sorceress

PROPHETIC: **5** vatic **6** mantic, mystic **7** fateful, fatidic, vatical **8** oracular **9** sibylline **10** divinatory, mysterious, predictive, prognostic, signifying **11** apocalyptic, foretelling **12** vaticinatory **13** foreshadowing

PROPINQUITY: **7** kinship **8** affinity, nearness, vicinity **9** closeness, proximity **10** connection, contiguity, solidarity **12** relationship, togetherness

PROPITIATE: **4** calm **5** adapt **6** pacify, soothe **7** appease, conform, mediate, placate **9** reconcile **10** conciliate

PROPITIOUS: **4** good, rosy **6** benign, kindly, timely **7** helpful **8** friendly, gracious **9** favorable, opportune, promising **10** auspicious, beneficial, prosperous **11** encouraging **12** advantageous

PROPONENT: **7** booster **8** champion, defender **9** protector

PROPORTION: **4** part, rate **5** ratio, share **6** degree **7** balance, harmony, measure, portion **8** relation, symmetry **9** dimension **10** percentage **11** correlation

PROPORTIONAL: **4** even **5** equal **8** relative **10** equivalent, reciprocal **11** comparative, correlative, symmetrical **12** commensurate **13** corresponding

PROPOSAL: **3** bid **4** idea, plan **5** draft, offer **6** design, motion, scheme **7** outline, project **8** overture, proposal, question **9** statement **10** prospectus **11** affirmation, undertaking **14** recommendation

PROPOSE: **4** hope, mean, move, plan, pose **5** offer, start, state **6** allege, design, intend, invite, submit, tender **7** purpose, suggest **8** nominate, propound **11** contemplate

PROPOSITION: **4** post, task **5** offer, point **7** premise, project, solicit **8** approach, overture, proposal, question **9** statement **10** suggestion **11** affirmation, undertaking

PROPRIETOR: **5** owner **6** master **8** landlord **11** titleholder

PROPRIETY: **4** code, rule **7** aptness, conduct, customs, decorum, manners **8** behavior, courtesy **9** attribute, etiquette **11** suitability

PROPULSION: **4** push **5** drive, force **6** thrust

PRORATE: **5** allot **6** assess, divide **7** portion **9** apportion **10** distribute

PROSAIC: **4** drab, dull, flat **5** trite **6** actual, common **7** factual, humdrum, insipid, literal, mundane, tedious **8** everyday, tiresome **9** colorless **10** lackluster, unexciting **11** commonplace, uninspiring **13** unimaginative, uninteresting **15** straightforward

PROSCRIBE: **3** ban **5** exile, taboo **6** banish, forbid, outlaw **7** condemn, exclude **8** denounce, prohibit, sentence **10** expatriate

PROSE: **5** essay, story **7** written **11** composition

PROSECUTE: **3** sue **4** wage **5** press **6** accuse, charge, indict, pursue **7** arraign **8** continue, litigate **9** persevere

PROSELYTE: **7** convert, recruit **8** neophyte **9** conscript

PROSIT: **5** drink, toast **6** salute **10** salutation

PROSPECT: **4** hope, mine, sift, view **5** buyer, delve, scene, vista **6** chance, vision **7** explore, outlook **8** customer, proposal **9** applicant, candidate **10** likelihood **11** possibility

PROSPECTIVE: **6** coming, future, likely **7** eminent **8** destined, expected, possible **9** potential **11** anticipated, forthcoming

PROSPER: **4** boom, gain **6** flower, thrive **7** augment, benefit, blossom, succeed **8** flourish, increase, progress

PROSPERITY: **4** boom **6** growth, riches, thrift, wealth **7** fortune, success, welfare **9** abundance, affluence

PROSPEROUS: **4** rich, rosy **5** happy, lucky, palmy **6** bright, timely **7** booming, halcyon, opulent, roaring, wealthy **8** affluent, blooming, thriving **9** favorable, fortunate, promising **10** propitious, successful **11** flourishing

PROSTITUTE: **4** bawd, moll, slut **5** abuse, bimbo, hussy, madam, tramp, wench, whore **6** chippy, debase, demean, floozy, gigolo, harlot, hooker **7** corrupt, hustler, trollop **8** call girl, catamite, strumpet **9** courtesan **10** licentious **12** street-walker

PROSTRATE: **3** bow **4** fell, weak **5** abase, floor, prone **6** beaten, fallen, supine **7** exhaust, flatten **8** helpless, overcome, paralyze **9** overthrow, overwhelm, powerless, reclining, recumbent **10** horizontal, submissive

PROSY: **4** dull **5** stale, trite **6** jejune **7** humdrum, prosaic, tedious **9** colorless **11** commonplace

PROTAGONIST: **4** hero, star **5** actor **6** leader **7** heroine, warrior **8** advocate, champion, defender **9** proponent, spokesman **11** spokeswoman

PROTECT: **4** fend, hide, save **5** guard, hedge, shade **6** backer, defend, harbor, insure, police, screen, shield **7** bulwark, cherish, cushion, shelter **8** advocate, champion, conserve, preserve **9** proponent, safeguard, supporter

PROTECTION: **4** care, fort, moat **5** aegis, armor, bribe, graft, guard, haven, smock **6** asylum, buffer, patent, safety, shield **7** auspice, barrier, defense, shelter **8** immunity, security **9** extortion, safeguard, sanctuary, shakedown **12** conservation, preservation

PROTECTOR: **5** armor, guard **6** patron, shield **7** paladin **8** advocate, champion, defender, guardian **10** benefactor

PROTEGE: **4** ward **5** pupil **7** student **10** apprentice

PROTEIN: **3** egg **4** meat, milk **5** beans **6** casein, cheese, enzyme, fibrin, histon **7** albumen, albumin **8** creatine, globulin, prolamin **14** macromolecules

PRO TEMPORE: **6** pro tem **7** interim **11** temporarily

PROTEST: **4** aver, avow, beef, deny, kick **5** demur, fight, gripe, rebel **6** affirm, assert, assure, combat, object, picket, revolt, strike **7** boycott, contest, declare, dispute, dissent, profess **8** complain, disagree **9** challenge, grievance, objection **11** remonstrate

PROTESTANT: **5** Amish **6** Mormon, Quaker **7** Baptist, Puritan **8** Anglican, Lutheran **9** Adventist, Calvinist, Mennonite, Methodist, Unitarian, Zwinglian **12** Episcopalian, Presbyterian **14** Congregational

PROTOCOL: **4** code **5** order, rules **6** custom **7** decorum, manners **8** behavior **9** etiquette

PROTOTYPE: **5** model **8** original **9** archetype **10** forerunner **11** predecessor

PROTOZOAN: **4** cell **5** ameba **6** amoeba **7** ciliate, euglena, stentor **8** organism **9** sporozoan **10** flagellate, plasmodium

PROTRACT: **5** defer, delay, stall **6** extend **7** detract, prolong, stretch **8** continue, elongate, lengthen **13** procrastinate

PROTRUDE: **3** jut **4** poke **5** bulge, swell **7** distend, extrude, project **9** interfere

PROTUBERANCE: **4** bump, hump, knob **5** bulge **8** swelling **9** outgrowth **10** projection, protrusion

PROUD: **4** smug **5** cocky, lofty, noble **6** lordly, snooty, stuffy, uppity **7** haughty, pompous, stately, valiant **8** arrogant, boastful, cavalier, imposing, pleasing, splendid **9** conceited, dignified, honorable **10** impressive, satisfying **11** overbearing **12** ostentatious, presumptuous, supercilious

PROVE: **4** test **5** argue **6** attest, verify **7** confirm, justify, sustain **8** convince, indicate manifest, validate **9** ascertain, establish **11** corroborate, demonstrate **12** substantiate

PROVENDER: **3** hay **4** chow, corn, feed, food, oats **5** grain, straw **6** fodder, forage, viands **10** provisions

PROVERB: **3** saw **4** word **5** adage, axiom, maxim, motto **6** byword, cliche, saying, truism **7** epigram, parable **8** allegory, aphorism

PROVERBIAL: **6** common, famous **9** customary, legendary **11** traditional **12** acknowledged, unquestioned

PROVIDE: **4** give **5** cater, equip, offer, stock, store, yield **6** afford, outfit, ration, render, supply **7** furnish, prepare, support **8** maintain **9** replenish, stipulate **10** contribute

PROVIDENCE: **6** thrift **7** economy **8** guidance, prudence **9** foresight, husbandry **10** precaution

PROVIDENT: **4** wise **5** canny **6** frugal, saving, shrewd **7** careful, prudent, sparing, thrifty **8** discreet, prepared **10** economical **11** foresighted

PROVINCE: **4** area, role, work, zone **5** arena, field, range, realm, scope, state, tract **6** colony, county, domain, region, sphere **7** country, pursuit **8** district

PROVINCIAL: **5** crude, local, rural **6** narrow, rustic **7** awkward, bigoted, bucolic, limited **8** homespun, regional **9** parochial **10** uncultured, unpolished **11** countrified

PROVISION: **4** term **5** catch, rider **6** clause **7** proviso **9** condition **11** stipulation **12** prerequisite

PROVISIONAL: **4** iffy **7** interim **9** dependent, makeshift, temporary, tentative **10** contingent **11** conditional

PROVISIONS: **4** chow, feed, food **5** board **6** fodder, forage, viands **7** rations **8** supplies, victuals **9** groceries, provender

PROVISO: **4** term **5** rider **6** clause **7** article **9** condition, provision **11** restriction, stipulation **12** prerequisite

PROVOCATION: **6** insult **7** offense **8** vexation **9** annoyance, grievance, incentive **10** incitement, irritation

PROVOCATIVE: **4** sexy **6** erotic **8** alluring, exciting **9** seductive **11** aggravating challenging, fascinating, tantalizing

PROVOKE: **3** bug, ire, vex **4** bait, move, rile, spur, stir **5** anger, annoy, cause, rouse, start, tease, upset **6** arouse, bother, excite, foment, harass, incite, insult, madden, prompt, ruffle **7** incense, inflame, inspire, outrage, perturb **8** generate, irritate **9** aggravate, challenge, galvanize, infuriate, instigate, stimulate

PROVOST: **4** head **5** chief **6** jailer, keeper **7** officer **8** director, official **9** executive **10** magistrate, supervisor **13** administrator

PROW: **3** bow **4** beak, fore, head **5** front

PROWESS: **4** grit **5** power, skill, valor **6** daring, talent **7** ability, address, bravery, courage, heroism **8** boldness, strength **9** dexterity

PROWL: **4** hunt, lurk, roam, rove **5** creep, sneak, stalk

PROXIMATE: **4** near, next **5** close **6** direct, nearby **8** imminent **11** forthcoming

PROXIMITY: **8** locality, nearness, vicinity **9** closeness, immediacy **10** contiguity **11** propinquity **12** togetherness **13** juxtaposition

PROXY: **4** vote **5** agent, vicar **6** deputy **7** proctor **8** assignee, delegate **9** alternate, authority **10** procurator, substitute **14** representative

PRUDE: **4** prig **5** priss **7** puritan **10** goody-goody

PRUDENCE: **6** thrift, wisdom **7** caution, economy **9** foresight, frugality **10** discretion **11** calculation, forethought

PRUDENT: **4** sage, wary, wise **5** canny **6** frugal, shrewd **7** careful, politic **8** cautious, discreet, rational, sensible **9** advisable, judicious, provident, sagacious **10** discerning, economical **11** circumspect, levelheaded

PRUDISH: **4** prim, smug **5** stern, timid **6** prissy, square, stuffy **8** priggish **9** Victorian **11** puritanical, straitlaced

PRUNE: **4** clip, crop, pare, plum, snip, thin, trim **5** dunce, fruit, idiot, plume, preen, shave, shear **6** reduce, remove, stupid **9** simpleton

PRURIENT: **4** foul, lewd **5** bawdy **6** carnal, coarse, erotic, impure **7** goatish, lustful, sensual **10** lascivious, passionate

PRUSSIA:
capital: **6** Berlin
cities: **4** Kiel **5** Emden, Essen, Halle **6** Aachen, Altena, Tilsit **7** Breslau, Munster **9** Frankfurt **10** Dusseldorf, Konigsberg
conquered by: **8** Bismarck
features: **7** Sudeten **11** Schneekoppe

islands: **5** Rugen **6** Usedom, Wollin
king: **8** Wilhelm I
part of: **6** Poland, Russia **7** Germany **10** Third Reich **14** Weimar Republic
was: **5** state **7** kingdom
water: **3** Ems **4** Kiel, Oder, Saar **6** Danzig **7** Vistula

PRY: **3** spy **4** lift, move, open, peek, peep, peer **5** force, jimmy, lever, prize, raise, snoop, twist **6** meddle **7** inquire, intrude **8** leverage, scrounge, separate **9** interfere

PSALM: **3** ode **4** hymn, poem, song **5** chant, verse **6** eulogy, praise **7** glorify **8** canticle

PSEUDO: **4** fake, mock, sham **5** bogus, false, phony **6** forged **8** spurious **9** imitation, pretended, simulated **10** artificial, fictitious **11** counterfeit

PSEUDONYM: **5** alias **6** ananym, anonym **7** pen name **8** nickname **10** nom de plume **11** nom de guerre

PSYCHE: **3** ego **4** mind, self, soul **6** spirit **8** superego **11** personality **12** subconscious

PSYCHE:
husband: **4** Eros
personifies: **4** soul
punished by: **9** Aphrodite

PSYCHIATRIST: **6** doctor, shrink **7** analyst **9** therapist **13** psychoanalyst
famous: **4** Jung **5** Adler, Binet, Freud **6** Piaget **7** Erikson, Johnson, Masters, Skinner

PSYCHIC: **6** medium, mental, mystic **7** sensile **8** cerebral **9** spiritual **10** telepathic **11** clairvoyant **12** supernatural

PSYCHOLOGICAL: **6** mental **8** cerebral **9** cognitive **10** subjective **12** experimental, subconscious **13** temperamental

PSYCHOTIC: **3** mad **4** nuts **5** crazy, loony **6** insane **7** lunatic **8** demented, schizoid, unhinged **10** disordered **12** psychopathic, unreasonable

PUB: **3** bar **6** saloon, tavern **7** gin-mill, rummery, taproom **8** grogshop

PUBERTY: **10** juvenility, pubescence **11** adolescence **12** youthfulness

PUBLIC: **4** open **5** civic, civil, known, overt, plain, state **6** common, masses, mutual, people, shared, voters **7** general, obvious, popular, society **8** citizens, communal, national **9** community, municipal **10** accessible, widespread

PUBLICATION: **4** book **5** paper **6** annals, digest **7** booklet, gazette, journal, tabloid **8** magazine, pamphlet **9** newspaper **10** periodical **11** declaration, information **12** announcement, notification, proclamation

PUBLICITY: **4** plug, type **5** press **6** hoopla **7** buildup, puffery, reclame, release, write-up **8** ballyhoo **9** attention, limelight, notoriety, promotion, spotlight **11** advertising

PUBLICIZE: **4** hype, plug, push, tout **5** pitch **6** spread **7** promote **9** advertise, broadcast **10** promulgate **12** propagandize

PUBLISH: **4** vent **5** issue, print **6** expose **7** declare, divulge, release **8** announce, proclaim **9** advertise, broadcast, propagate **10** promulgate

PUCK: **3** elf, fay, imp **4** disk **5** fairy **6** goblin, sprite **9** hobgoblin, prankster

PUCKER: **4** bind, fold, tuck **5** bulge, plait **6** cockle, crease, gather **7** crinkle, wrinkle **8** contract

PUCKISH: **6** impish, wicked **7** naughty, playful **10** mysterious **11** mischievous

PUDDING: **6** junket, mousse **7** custard, dessert, sausage, tapioca

PUDDLE: **4** pond, pool **5** plash **8** quagmire

PUDGY: **3** fat **5** dumpy, hefty, obese, plump, squat, tubby **6** chubby, chunky, rotund **8** roly-poly

PUERILE: **5** green, naive, young **6** callow, jejune **7** babyish, trivial **8** childish, immature, juvenile, youthful **9** infantile **10** sophomoric

PUERTO RICO:
belongs to: **12** United States
capital: **7** San Juan
cities: **5** Ponce **6** Dorado **7** Arecibo **8** Mayaguez **9** Aquadilla
explorer: **8** Columbus
features: **4** Mona **8** El Yunque **9** San German **10** Old San Juan **12** Cerro Puntita
languages: **7** English, Spanish
located: **10** West Indies
native: **8** Hispanic
water: **9** Caribbean

PUFF: **4** blow, brag, drag, draw, gust, pant, plug **5** bloat, boast, fluff, quilt, smoke, whiff **6** admire, breath, exhale, inhale, praise **9** publicize

PUFFED UP: **4** vain **5** proud **7** bloated, swollen **8** expanded, imposing, inflated **9** bombastic, conceited **11** pretentious

PUFFERY: **4** hype **6** praise **9** publicity

PUFFY: **4** soft **6** turgid **7** bloated, pompous, swollen **8** enlarged, expanded, inflamed

PUG: **3** dog **4** clay **5** boxer, knead, track **9** footprint

PUGILIST: **5** boxer **7** bruiser, fighter **12** prizefighter

PUGNACIOUS: **7** defiant, warlike **8** militant **9** bellicose, combative **10** aggressive, rebellious **11** belligerent, contentious, quarrelsome **12** antagonistic, cantankerous

PUISSANCE: **4** sway **5** clout, force, might, power, vigor **6** energy, muscle **7** potency **8** strength **9** influence

PULCHRITUDE: **5** grace **6** appeal, beauty **10** comeliness, loveliness **12** handsomeness

PULE: **3** cry **4** weep **5** whine **6** repine, snivel **7** whimper **8** complain

PULL: **3** lug, row, tow, tug **4** drag, draw, haul, jerk, rend, yank **5** clout, hitch, pluck, trawl, tweak **6** appeal, entice, propel, strain, uproot **7** attract, extract, gravity, schlepp, stretch **9** influence, magnetism **10** attraction, persuasion **11** fascination

PULL APART: **4** tear **5** split **6** detach, divide **8** separate **9** criticize

PULL DOWN: **4** raze **5** lower, wreck **7** destroy **8** demolish **9** dismantle **10** annihilate

PULLEY: **4** ring **5** block, wheel **6** sheave **7** machine

PULLMAN: **3** car **5** coach **7** luggage, sleeper **8** suitcase

PULL OFF: **4** yank **6** detach, manage **7** achieve, execute **10** accomplish

PULL OUT: **4** quit **5** leave **6** depart **7** retreat **8** evacuate, withdraw

PULL THROUGH: **5** rally **7** recover, survive, triumph

PULL UP: **4** halt, stop **5** pause **6** arrive, uplift

PULP: **4** curd, mash, mush, pith **5** crush, smash **6** pomace, squash, vulgar **9** pulverize

PULPIT: **4** dais, desk **5** chair, stage, stand **6** podium **7** lectern, rostrum **8** ministry, platform

PULSATE: **4** beat, pant **5** pound, pulse, throb, waver **6** quiver **7** flutter, vibrate **9** fluctuate, oscillate

PULSE: **4** beat **5** throb **6** rhythm **7** pulsate **9** vibration **11** oscillation, palpitation

PULVERIZE: **4** beat, mash, ruin **5** crush, flour, grind, mince, smash **6** crunch, powder **7** atomize, destroy, shatter **8** decimate, demolish **9** comminute, triturate **10** annihilate

PUMA: **6** cougar **7** panther **9** catamount **11** mountain cat **12** mountain lion

PUMMEL: **4** beat, maul, pelt **5** pound **6** batter, hammer, pommel, thrash, wallop

PUMP: **4** draw, jack, quiz **5** drain, grill **6** inject, siphon **7** stirrup, syringe **8** question **11** interrogate

PUMPKIN: **4** pepo, vine **5** fruit, gourd **6** squash **12** jack-o'-lantern
genus: **9** cucurbita

PUN: **4** joke, quip **5** knock **7** quibble **9** calembour, conundrum, equivoque, witticism **11** paronomasia, play on words

PUNCH: **3** box, hit, jab **4** bash, blow, cuff, hook, poke, prod, sock, swat, tool **5** drill, drink, paste, smack, vigor **6** energy, pierce, strike **7** clobber **8** beverage, puncture, uppercut **9** perforate **10** roundhouse

PUNCHY: **5** dazed, drunk **6** groggy **8** confused

PUNCTILIOUS: **5** exact, fussy **6** formal, proper **7** careful, correct, finicky, precise **8** punctual **10** ceremonial, meticulous, particular, scrupulous **11** painstaking **13** conscientious

PUNCTUAL: **5** exact **6** on time, prompt, timely **7** precise **8** reliable **11** punctilious

PUNCTUATE: **4** mark **5** break, point **6** accent, divide, stress **8** separate **9** emphasize interrupt

PUNCTUATION MARK: **3** dot **4** dash **5** brace, colon, comma, quote, slash **6** bullet, hyphen, period **7** bracket, obelisk **8** asterisk, ellipsis **9** semicolon **10** apostrophe **11** exclamation, parenthesis

PUNCTURE: **4** bore, gore, hole, slit, stab, vent **5** drill, prick, wound **6** pierce, riddle **7** deflate, rupture **10** depression **11** perforation

PUNDIT: **4** guru, sage **5** swami **6** critic, expert **7** scholar, teacher **12** intellectual

PUNGENT: **3** hot **4** keen, racy, rich, tart **5** acrid, acute, salty, sharp, smart, spicy, tangy, witty **6** biting, bitter, snappy, strong **7** caustic, cutting, peppery, piquant, pointed **8** aromatic, piercing, poignant, seasoned, stinging **9** flavorful **11** acrimonious, penetrating, provocative, stimulating

PUNISH: **4** cane, fine, flog, hurt, whip **5** abuse, scold, spank, strap **6** avenge, strike **7** chasten, consume, correct, dismiss, revenge, torture **8** admonish, chastise, penalize, sentence **9** castigate **10** discipline **11** incarcerate **13** excommunicate

PUNISHING: **4** hard **5** tough **6** brutal **8** grueling, punitive

PUNISHMENT: **4** loss **5** lumps **6** lesson **7** damages, penalty, penance, revenge **8** judgment **9** ostracism, suffering, vengeance **10** correction, discipline, forfeiture **11** castigation, retribution **12** chastisement

PUNITIVE: **5** penal **9** punishing **10** revengeful, vindictive **12** disciplinary

PUNK: **4** hood, thug **5** bully **6** novice, rookie, tinder **7** hoodlum, incense, ruffian **8** beginner, gangster, hooligan, inferior, kindling **9** worthless **10** delinquent, prostitute

PUNT: **4** boat, boot, kick **6** gamble, propel **11** indentation

PUNY: **4** tiny, weak **5** frail, minor, petty, small **6** feeble, little, measly, shrimp, sickly, slight **7** trivial **8** inferior, picayune **10** diminutive **13** insignificant

PUPA: **6** cocoon **9** chrysalis

PUPIL: **4** tyro **5** cadet **6** junior, novice, senior **7** learner, scholar, student, trainee **8** disciple, freshman, neophyte **9** sophomore **10** apprentice **13** undergraduate

PUPPET: **4** doll, dupe, pawn, tool **5** slave **6** flunky, stooge **7** manikin **10** figurehead, marionette

PUPPY: **3** dog **5** whelp **6** animal, canine

PURCHASE: **3** buy **4** earn **5** asset **6** obtain **7** acquire **8** property **10** investment **11** acquisition, procurement

PURCHASER: **4** pure, user **5** buyer, whole **6** patron **7** blessed, ethical, natural, shopper **8** consumer, customer, flawless, spotless **9** righteous **10** sterilized, unblamable, unpolluted **11** speculative, theoretical, unmitigated **14** uncontaminated

PURE: **4** fine, good, neat, nice, true **5** clean, clear, fresh, moral, utter **6** chaste, simple, virgin **7** genuine, perfect, refined, sincere, sinless, unmixed **8** absolute, complete, filtered, innocent, straight, virtuous **9** authentic, blameless, elemental, faultless, guiltless, stainless, unalloyed, undefiled, unsullied **10** immaculate **11** unblemished, uncorrupted **13** unadulterated

PUREE: **4** mush, soup **5** blend, paste

PURELY: **4** just **5** fully **6** simply, wholly **7** totally **10** absolutely, completely **11** essentially

PURGATORY: **4** hell **5** limbo **6** misery **9** expiation, suffering

PURGE: **3** rid **4** oust **5** clear, erase **6** purify, remove, unload **7** absolve, cleanse **9** eliminate, exculpate, exonerate, liquidate **11** exterminate, extirpation

PURIFICATION: **7** baptism, freeing, rebirth, washing **9** atonement, catharsis, cleansing, salvation **10** redemption **12** distillation

PURIFY: **4** wash **5** clean, clear, purge **6** filter, refine **7** absolve, baptize, cleanse, distill **8** fumigate **9** deodorize, disinfect, exonerate, sterilize

PURITAN: **5** prude **6** proper, strict

PURITANICAL: **4** prim **5** rigid, stern **6** strict, stuffy **7** austere, genteel, prudish **9** blue-nosed, Victorian **11** straitlaced

PURITY: **5** piety **8** chastity, holiness **9** innocence **10** continence, sanctitude **11** cleanliness

PURLIEU: **4** area **5** haunt **6** fringe **7** environ, hangout **9** outskirts, periphery **12** neighborhood

PURLOIN: **5** filch, pinch, steal, swipe **6** finger, pilfer, thieve **11** appropriate

PURPLE: **4** plum, racy, rank **5** color, grape, lilac, mauve, regal, royal **6** maroon, ornate, tryian, violet **7** cassius, magenta, reddish **8** imperial, lavender **9** elaborate

PURPLE HEART: **5** award, medal **10** decoration

PURPORT: **4** core, gist, mean **5** drift, point, sense **6** import, intent, object, thrust **7** meaning, profess, purpose **8** maintain **9** intention, rationale, substance **11** connotation, implication **12** significance

PURPOSE: **3** aim, use **4** duty, goal, mean, plan **5** point **6** aspire, design, intend, intent, motive, object, reason **7** mission, purport, resolve **8** ambition, function, proposal **9** intention, objective **10** aspiration, resolution **13** determination

PURPOSEFUL: **4** bent **5** fixed **6** intent **7** decided, staunch **8** resolute **9** conscious, determined, steadfast **10** calculated, persistent

PURPOSELESS: **6** random **7** aimless, useless **9** pointless, senseless, unplanned **11** floundering, meaningless, unnecessary **13** insignificant

PURPOSELY: **9** expressly, knowingly, willfully **11** consciously **12** deliberately **13** intentionally

PURR: **3** hum **4** sing **5** noise, sound **6** murmur

PURSE: **3** bag **4** knit, poke **5** money, pouch, prize, stake **6** pucker, wallet **7** handbag **8** winnings **10** pocketbook

PURSER: **6** bursar **7** cashier **9** treasurer **11** comptroller

PURSUE: **4** date, hunt, seek, tail **5** chase, court, ensue, hound, stalk, track, trail **6** badger, follow, harass **7** address, persist, proceed **8** continue **9** prosecute

PURSUIT: **4** work **5** chase, quest **6** career **7** calling **8** business, pleasure, vocation **9** following **10** occupation **11** undertaking

PURVEY: **5** cater, equip, serve **6** assist, supply **7** furnish, procure, provide **9** circulate

PUSH: **3** ram **4** bear, bunt, butt, cram, ding, goad, move, plug, prod, sell, urge **5** boost, crowd, crush, drive, elbow, force, forge, heave, hunch, impel, nudge, press, shove, vigor **6** coerce, effort, energy, expand, extend, hustle, jostle, launch, peddle, prompt, propel, thrust **7** advance, inspire, promote **8** bulldoze, gumption, increase, motivate, pressure, stimulus, vitality **9** advertise, incentive **10** initiative

PUSH AROUND: **5** bully **8** threaten **10** intimidate

PUSHCART: **5** wagon **7** trolley **8** handcart **11** wheelbarrow

PUSH OFF: **4** exit **5** leave, start **6** depart, launch **8** withdraw

PUSH ON: **7** journey, proceed **8** continue

PUSHOVER: **4** fool, snap **5** chump, cinch **6** breeze, sucker

PUSHY: **5** bossy, brash **9** ambitious, assertive, obnoxious **10** aggressive **12** presumptuous

PUSILLANIMOUS: **4** tame **5** timid **6** afraid **7** chicken, fearful, gutless **8** cowardly, timorous

PUSS: **3** cat, mug **4** face, girl **5** child, mouth, woman **6** kisser, kitten

PUSSYFOOT: **5** avoid, dodge, evade, hedge **6** tiptoe **8** sidestep

PUT: **3** fix, lay, set **4** call, cast, hurl, levy, rest, urge, word **5** bring, drive, force, impel, place, rivet, state, stick, throw, wager **6** assing, attach, bestow, fasten, impose, incite, induce, insert, invest, submit, thrust **7** deposit, express, propose, require, subject **8** estimate, position **9** attribute

PUT ASIDE: **5** store, table **6** forget **7** deposit **8** inferred

PUTATIVE: **7** alleged, assumed, reputed **8** accepted, believed, inferred, supposed

PUT AWAY: **4** bury, down, jail, kill **5** stash, store **6** commit, devour, finish **7** confine, consume, discard **11** incarcerate

PUT BACK: **6** demote, return **7** restore **9** reinstate

PUT DOWN: **3** log **5** enter, quash, quell **6** defeat, record, reject, subdue **7** condemn, consume, degrade, repress, silence **8** belittle, suppress **9** criticize, disparage, humiliate

PUT FORTH: **4** form, show **5** offer **7** produce, propose **10** constitute

PUT IN: **4** land **5** plant **6** insert **9** interpose

PUT OFF: **5** defer, delay, stall **6** linger, offend, shelve **7** discard, repulse **8** postpone

PUT ON: **3** act, add, don **4** fake, hoax, sham **5** apply, bluff, spoof, stage, tease, trick **6** attach, parody, satire **7** deceive, present, pretend **8** pretense **10** masquerade

PUT OUT: **4** rile **5** anger, annoy, douse, expel **6** bother, quench **7** discard, disturb, provoke, publish, smother, trouble **8** displace, irritate **9** discomfit **10** extinguish **13** inconvenience

PUTREFY: **3** rot **5** decay, spoil, taint **7** corrupt, crumble **9** decompose **11** deteriorate **12** disintegrate

PUTRID: **3** bad **4** foul, vile **6** rancid, rotten, smelly **7** noisome, spoiled **8** depraved, polluted, stinking **9** offensive **10** malodorous **12** contaminated, disagreeable

PUT THROUGH: **6** finish, manage **7** connect, undergo

PUT TOGETHER: **4** join **5** build, erect, unite **6** create **7** produce **8** assemble **9** construct

PUTTER: **4** loaf **6** dawdle, doodle, fiddle, loiter, tinker **7** fritter **8** golf club

PUT UP: **3** can **4** bunk, make **5** build, erect, house, lodge **6** harbor **9** construct **11** accommodate

PUZZLE: **4** code, maze, muse **5** addle, amaze, stump, upset **6** baffle, enigma, jigsaw, ponder, rattle, riddle **7** anagram, charade, confuse, disturb, mystery, mystify, nonplus, paradox, perplex **8** bewilder, confound, distract, entangle, intrigue **9** conundrum, crossword, difficult, dumbfound, frustrate, labyrinth **10** disconcert

PUZZLING: **6** knotty **7** unclear **8** involved **9** ambiguous, confusing, difficult **10** mysterious **11** bewildering

PYGMALION:
occupation: **8** sculptor
statue: **7** Galatea
wife: **7** Galatea
worshipped: **9** Aphrodite

PYGMY, PIGMY: **3** elf **4** pixy, runt, tiny **5** dwarf, gnome, pixie, short, small **6** midget, shrimp **7** trivial **10** chimpanzee **11** lilliputian, unimportant

PYLON: **4** arch, door, span **5** tower **6** column, marker **7** gateway **8** entrance, monument

PYRAMID: **4** heap, pile, tomb **5** stack **6** accrue, shrine **8** monument, ziggurat

PYRE: **4** fuel, heap **6** suttee **7** bonfire

PYROMANIAC: **7** firebug **8** arsonist **10** incendiary

PYROSIS: **9** heartburn **11** indigestion

PYROTECHNICS: **7** rockets **9** fireworks, sparklers **10** pyrotechny

PYTHON: **3** boa **5** snake
family: **10** Pythonidae

PYX: **3** box, pix **4** case **5** chest **6** casket, vessel **8** binnacle, ciborium **9** container **10** tabernacle

Q

QATAR:
capital: **4** Doha
cities: **6** Dukhan **7** Musayid
continent: **4** Asia
ethnic groups: **4** Arab **6** Indian **7** Iranian **9** Pakistani
languages: **6** Arabic **7** English
monetary unit: **5** riyal
water: **11** Persian Gulf

QUACK: **3** cry **4** duck, honk, sham **5** cheat, faker, fraud, phony, sound **8** impostor **9** charlatan, pretender **10** mountebank **13** counterfeiter

QUAD: **8** quadrant **10** quadrangle, quadruplet **12** quadraphonic

QUADRANGLE: **4** yard **5** court, forum **6** campus, square **9** enclosure

QUADRANT: **3** arc, bow **6** fourth **10** instrument

QUADRATE: **4** cube, suit **5** adapt, agree **6** adjust, square **7** conform **8** balanced **9** rectangle **10** correspond

QUAFF: **4** down, swig **5** drink **6** guzzle, imbibe, tipple **7** swallow

QUAGMIRE: **3** bog **4** trap **5** marsh, swamp **6** morass, pickle **7** dilemma, impasse, mudhole, problem **9** quicksand **11** predicament

QUAIL: **4** bird **5** colin, cower, quake, shake, wince **6** blench, cringe, flinch, recoil, shrink, tremor **7** shudder, tremble **8** bobwhite, gamebird, squealer **9** partridge
flock of: **4** bevy **5** covey

QUAINT: **3** odd **4** nice **5** weird **7** antique, archaic, bizarre, curious, offbeat, strange, unusual **8** charming, colonial, fanciful, peculiar **9** whimsical **10** unfamiliar **11** picturesque

QUAKE: **5** quail, shake, spasm, waver **6** jitter, quiver, shiver, tremor **7** shudder, tremble, vibrate **9** oscillate **10** aftershock, earthquake

QUAKER STATE: **12** Pennsylvania

QUALIFICATION: **5** skill **6** talent **7** ability, makings **8** aptitude, capacity **9** attribute, condition, endowment **10** capability, competence, credential, experience **11** requirement **12** prerequisite

QUALIFIED: **4** able **7** capable, limited, trained **8** eligible, equipped, licensed, skillful **9** certified **10** restricted

QUALIFY: **5** abate, adapt, alter, equip, limit, ready **6** change, enable, lessen, modify, permit, soften, temper **7** assuage, certify, empower, license **8** diminish, mitigate, restrain, restrict **9** authorize, condition **10** commission, habilitate

QUALITY: **4** rank, rate, sort **5** blood, class, grade, merit, power, taste, trait, value, worth **6** factor, nature, status, virtue **7** caliber, element, essence, feature, stature **8** capacity, nobility, position, property, superior **9** attribute, character, excellent **10** excellence

QUALM: **4** pall **5** doubt **6** nausea, regret, twinge, unease **7** anxiety, feeling, scruple **8** sickness **9** faintness, misgiving, suspicion **10** hesitation, indecision, insecurity, reluctance **11** reservation, uncertainty **12** apprehension

QUANDARY: **3** fix, jam **4** bind **6** crisis, pickle, plight, scrape **7** dilemma, impasse **8** quagmire **10** difficulty

QUANTITY: **3** bit, lot, sum, ton **4** atom, body, dose, dram, drop, iota, mass, size, slew, unit **5** batch, bunch, grain, shred, speck, total **6** amount, bushel, degree, dosage, extent, length, morsel, number, volume, weight **7** handful, portion, smidgen **9** allotment, allowance, magnitude, multitude

QUANTUM: **3** sum **4** unit **5** total **6** amount **7** measure, portion **8** quantity

QUARANTINE: **3** ban **7** confine, exclude, isolate **8** restrain, restrict **9** interdict

QUARREL: **3** row, war **4** beef, feud, fray, fuss, miff, spat, tiff **5** argue, brawl, clash, fight, scrap, words **6** bicker, fracas, hassle, ruckus, strife **7** discord, dispute, faction, rhubarb, wrangle **8** argument, conflict, disagree, squabble, vendetta **10** contention, difference, dissension **11** altercation, controversy **12** disagreement

QUARRELSOME: **5** fiery **6** ornery, unruly **7** hostile, scrappy **8** brawling, choleric, militant, petulant **9** bellicose, combative, irritable, litigious, rancorous **10** pugnacious **11** belligerent, contentious **12** antagonistic, cantankerous **13** argumentative

QUARRY: **3** dig, pit **4** game, mine, prey **5** chase, shape **6** source, square, victim

QUART: **4** unit **6** fourth, volume **7** measure
four: **6** gallon

QUARTER: **4** bunk, coin, quad, time, zone **5** house, lodge, mercy, phase, tract **6** billet, fourth, harbor, period, region, sector **7** barrack, housing, section, shelter **8** clemency, district, division, domicile, location, quadrant **9** direction **10** compassion

QUARTERS: **4** camp, digs, home, room **5** space **7** lodging, shelter, station **8** barracks, chambers **9** dormitory, residence

QUARTZ: **7** mineral
type: **4** onyx, opal, rose, sard **5** agate, chert, flint, smoky, topaz **6** jasper **7** crystal **8** amethyst, sardonyx **9** carnelian **10** bloodstone, chalcedony

QUASH: **4** beat, stop, undo, void **5** abate, annul, crush, quell **6** cancel, defeat, repeal, squash, subdue, vacate **7** abolish, destroy, nullify, retract, smother **8** abrogate, suppress **9** overthrow **10** extinguish, invalidate

QUASIMODO:
author: **4** Hugo
feature: **9** hunchback
occupation: **10** bell ringer
residence: **9** Notre Dame

QUAVER: **4** sway **5** quake, shake, waver **6** falter, quiver, shiver, wobble **7** shudder, tremble, vibrate **9** oscillate, vacillate

QUAY: **3** key **4** dock, slip **5** berth, jetty, levee, wharf **7** landing

QUEASY: **5** queer, timid, upset **6** groggy, uneasy **8** qualmish, troubled **9** nauseated, sickening, squeamish, uncertain, unsettled **13** uncomfortable

QUEBEC:
capital: **10** Quebec City
cities: **4** Hull **5** Laval **6** Verdun **8** Montreal **10** Sherbrooke **13** Trois-Rivieres
country: **6** Canada
explorer: **9** Champlain
flower: **4** lily
language: **6** French
originally: **9** New France
water: **9** Hudson Bay **10** St. Lawrence

QUEEN/EMPRESS: **3** ant, bee **4** card **5** ranee, ruler **6** regina **7** czarina, monarch **9** matriarch, sovereign **10** chess piece
of Egypt: **9** Cleopatra
of England: **4** Anne, Mary **6** Boleyn **8** Boadicea, Victoria **9** Elizabeth, Guinevere
of France: **7** Eugenie **9** Josephine **15** Marie Antoinette
of Greece: **11** Helen of Troy
of Hawaii: **10** Liliuokani
of Russia: **9** Catherine
of Scots: **4** Mary
of Spain: **8** Isabella
of the Netherlands: **7** Beatrix, Juliana **10** Wilhelmina

QUEER: **3** odd **5** eerie, faint, funny, giddy, weird **6** queasy **7** bizarre, curious, disrupt, erratic, strange, touched, unusual **8** abnormal, atypical, doubtful, fanciful, peculiar, puzzling, qualmish, singular, spurious **9** eccentric, fantastic, squeamish **10** suspicious, unorthodox **12** questionable **14** unconventional

QUELL: **4** calm, cool, curb, kill, stop **5** allay, check, crush, quash, quiet **6** defeat, obtund, pacify, quench, reduce, soothe, subdue **7** assuage, conquer, destroy, repress, silence **8** overcome, suppress **9** overpower, overwhelm **10** extinguish

QUENCH: **5** allay, douse, quell, slake **7** destroy, satisfy, smother, squelch **8** suppress **9** alleviate **10** extinguish

QUERULOUS: **5** cross, whiny **6** touchy **7** fretful, grouchy, peevish **8** petulant **9** grumbling, irritable **11** complaining **12** cantankerous, discontented

QUERY: **3** ask **4** quiz **5** doubt, probe **7** examine, inquiry **8** mistrust, question **9** catechize, challenge **11** inquisition, interrogate **13** investigation

QUEST: **4** goal, hunt, seek **5** probe **6** search, voyage **7** crusade, delving, examine, journey, mission, odyssey, pursuit, seeking **9** adventure **10** expedition **13** investigation

QUESTION: **3** ask **4** poll, pump, quiz **5** demur, doubt, drill, grill, probe, query **6** debate, demand **7** debrief, dispute, examine, inquire, inquiry, mystery, problem, scruple, suspect **9** catechize, challenge, interview, objection **11** examination, interrogate, proposition **13** interrogation, investigation

QUESTIONABLE: **4** moot **5** shady, shaky **6** unsure **7** dubious, suspect **8** arguable **9** ambiguous, equivocal, uncertain, undecided **10** disputable, improbable, unreliable **11** unconfirmed **13** controversial

QUEUE: **4** file, line **5** braid, chain, order, plait **6** column **7** pigtail **8** sequence **10** succession

QUIBBLE: **4** carp, spat **5** argue, cavil, dodge, evade **6** bicker, haggle, niggle **7** dispute, nitpick, wrangle **8** pettifog, squabble **9** complaint, criticism, objection **10** equivocate **12** equivocation

QUICK: **4** able, ASAP, deft, fast, keen, wise **5** acute, agile, alert, alive, brisk, eager, fiery, fleet, hasty, rapid, ready, sharp, swift **6** abrupt, active, clever, moving, nimble, prompt, snappy, speedy, sudden, volant **7** intense **8** animated, skillful, vigorous **9** dexterous, immediate, impatient, sensitive, sprightly **10** perceptive **11** expeditious **13** instantaneous

QUICKEN: **4** move, rush, stir **5** hurry, press, speed **6** arouse, excite, hasten, incite, revive, vivify **7** animate, enliven, provoke, refresh, sharpen **8** energize, expedite, motivate **9** stimulate **10** accelerate, invigorate

QUICKLY: **4** fast, soon **6** presto, pronto **7** briefly, rapidly **8** promptly, speedily **9** instantly

QUICKNESS: **4** pace **5** haste, speed **6** acumen **7** agility **8** velocity **9** dexterity

QUICKSAND: **4** trap **5** snare **8** quagmire **9** mercurial **11** quicksilver **13** unpredictable

QUICK-TEMPERED: **5** cross, fiery **6** touchy **7** angered **8** choleric, volatile **9** excitable, impatient **13** temperamental

QUICK-WITTED: **4** keen, wise **5** acute, alert, canny, savvy, sharp, slick, smart **6** astute, bright, clever **9** brilliant **10** perceptive **11** intelligent

QUIDNUNC: **6** gossip **8** busybody **11** rumormonger

QUID PRO QUO: **5** trade **8** exchange **9** tit-for-tat **10** equivalent **12** substitution

QUIESCENT: **4** calm **5** quiet, still **6** latent, placid, serene **7** dormant, passive **8** inactive, sleeping, tranquil **10** motionless **11** undisturbed

QUIET: **4** idle, mute, soft **5** quell, shush **6** docile, mellow, muffle, stable **7** passive **8** reserved **9** collected, inaudible, secretive **10** relaxation **11** sequestered

QUIETUS: **5** death **6** repose **7** decease, release **9** discharge **10** extinction **11** acquittance, dissolution

QUILL: **3** pen **5** spine **6** bobbin, pinion **7** calamus, feather **10** instrument

QUILT: **3** pad **5** cover **7** blanket **8** coverlet **9** bedspread, comforter, patchwork **11** counterpane

QUINTESSENCE: **4** core, gist, pith, soul **5** heart **6** spirit **7** epitome, essence **9** substance

QUINTESSENTIAL: **5** ideal, model **7** classic, typical **8** ultimate

QUIP: **3** gag, odd, pun **4** gibe, jest, joke **5** sally, spoof, taunt **6** banter, remark **7** curious, quibble **9** wisecrack

QUIRK: **4** band, kink, turn **5** crook, knack, trait, twist **6** groove, oddity, vagary **7** caprice, quibble **9** deviation, mannerism **10** aberration **11** peculiarity **12** eccentricity, equivocation

QUISLING: **6** puppet **7** traitor **8** turncoat

QUIT: **3** end, rid **4** calm, dead, drop, ease, free, hush, lull, mild, rest, stop, tame **5** allay, avoid, cease, clear, leave, peace, sober, still **6** acquit, depart, desert, desist, gentle, hushed, modest, placid, resign, retire, secret, sedate, serene, settle, silent, smooth, soothe **7** abandon, appease, compose, release, relieve, restful, retired, silence **8** abdicate, composed, inactive, peaceful, renounce, secluded, tasteful, tranquil, withdraw **9** alleviate, contented, noiseless, peaceable, quiescent, surrender, terminate, unruffled **10** motionless, relinquish **11** clandestine, discontinue, tranquilize, undisturbed

QUITE: **4** very, well **5** fully, truly **6** purely, really, wholly **7** exactly, totally **8** actually, entirely, somewhat **9** perfectly **10** absolutely, altogether, completely, positively, reasonably, thoroughly **12** considerably

QUITTER: **4** slag **6** coward **7** chicken, dropout, shirker, slacker **8** deserter

QUIVER: **4** beat, case, jerk **5** quake, quick, shake, spasm **7** flutter, shudder, twinkle **8** convulse **9** oscillate

QUIXOTIC: **6** dreamy, unread **7** utopian **8** fanciful, romantic **9** imaginary, impulsive, visionary, whimsical **10** capricious, idealistic **11** impractical

QUIZ: **3** ask **4** exam, jest, joke, mock, pump, test **5** probe **7** examine, inquire **8** question, ridicule **11** examination, interrogate

QUIZZICAL: **7** amusing, comical, curious, mocking, probing, teasing **9** bantering, eccentric, skeptical **11** inquisitive, questioning

QUOIN: **5** angle, wedge **8** keystone **11** cornerstone

QUONDAM: **4** once, past **6** bygone, former **7** onetime **8** sometime

QUOTA: **4** part **5** share, slice **6** divide, ration **7** portion **8** dividend, quantity **9** allowance **10** allocation, proportion

QUOTATION: **5** offer, price, quote **7** excerpt, passage **8** estimate **9** reference, selection

QUOTE: **4** cite, cost **5** refer **6** adduce, recite, repeat, retell, select **7** excerpt, extract, passage **9** quotation, reference, selection

QUOTIDIAN: **5** daily, usual **7** trivial **8** everyday, ordinary **11** commonplace

R

RABBI: **6** master, priest, rabbin **7** teacher **9** clergyman, Talmudist

RABBIT: **3** doe **4** buck, cony, hare **5** bunny, capon, coney **6** rodent **10** cottontail
family: **9** Leporidae

RABBLE: **3** mob **4** herd, scum **5** crowd, dregs, swarm, trash **6** coarse, ragtag **8** riffraff **11** commonality

RABBLE-ROUSER: **8** agitator **9** demagogue, firebrand **10** incendiary

RABID: **3** mad **4** wild **5** crazy **6** insane, raging **7** berserk, extreme, frantic, violent, zealous **8** demented, deranged, frenzied, maniacal **9** delirious, fanatical **10** irrational **12** enthusiastic **14** uncontrollable

RACE: **3** run **4** clan, dart, dash, drag, lane, line, meet, rush, type **5** blood, breed, brood, chase, class, creek, hurry, rally, relay, river, speed, stock, track, tribe **6** course, endure, family, hasten, hurdle, nation, people, slalom, sprint, strain, stream **7** channel, contest, culture, dynasty, kindred, lineage, pursuit, regatta, rivalry, running, scamper, species **8** marathon, pedigree **10** generation, passageway **11** competition, descendants, nationality, watercourse

RACECOURSE: **4** oval, path, ring, turf **5** track **6** course **7** paddock **10** hippodrome

RACHEL:
children: **6** Joseph **8** Benjamin
husband: **5** Jacob

RACISM: **4** bias **7** bigotry **9** apartheid, prejudice **11** segregation **14** discrimination

RACK: **3** bed, cut **4** bunk, gait, pace, pain, scud **5** score, shelf, sleep, stand, track **6** gantry, strain, wrench **7** afflict, agonize, antlers, bracket, oppress, stretch, torment, torture **9** framework, persecute, suffering **10** excruciate, receptacle

RACKET: **4** fuss, game, roar, work **5** babel, blare, noise, trick **6** bustle, clamor, hubbub, outcry, paddle, scheme, uproar **7** clatter **8** business, shouting **9** commotion **10** occupation, turbulence **11** disturbance

RACKETEER: **4** hood **5** crook **7** mobster **8** criminal, gangster

RACONTEUR: **8** narrator **10** anecdotist **11** storyteller

RACY: **4** lewd **5** brisk, crude, fiery, fresh, saucy, sharp, spicy, zesty **6** lively, ribald, risque, strong, vulgar **7** obscene, piquant, pungent **8** indecent, spirited, vigorous **10** suggestive

RADAR:
image: **4** blip
operates by: **10** radio waves

RADIANCE: **4** beam, glow **5** glare, gleam, glory, light, shine **6** luster, warmth **7** delight, glitter **8** splendor **9** happiness **10** brightness, brilliance, effulgence **12** luminescence

RADIANT: **5** happy **6** bright, lucent **7** beaming, glowing, lambent, shining **8** blissful, cheerful, luminous **9** brilliant **11** resplendent **12** incandescent

RADIATE: **4** beam, burn, emit, send **5** shine **6** extend, spread **7** diffuse, glisten, scatter, sparkle **8** manifest, transmit **9** circulate **10** illuminate

RADICAL: **4** root **5** basal, basic, rebel, ultra **6** primal **7** drastic, extreme, leftist, liberal, primary **8** agitator, cardinal, complete, nihilist, renegade **9** anarchist, essential, extremist, firebrand **10** iconoclast, subversive **11** fundamental **13** nonconformist, revolutionary

RADIO: **6** signal **7** boom box, walkman **8** portable, wireless **9** broadcast, shortwave **10** transistor
inventor: **5** Hertz **6** Branly **7** Fleming, Marconi

RADIUM: **7** element

RADIUS: **4** line, span **5** field, orbit, range, reach, spoke, sweep **6** extent **7** compass **8** boundary

RAFFISH: **4** wild **5** cheap, showy **6** flashy, rakish, tawdry, vulgar **7** uncouth, unkempt **8** carefree **9** worthless **14** unconventional

RAFFLE: **4** game **6** chance, debris, refuse **7** drawing, lottery, rubbish **8** gambling **10** sweepstake

RAFT: **3** lot, mat **4** heap, slew **5** barge, craft, float **7** pontoon **8** quantity **9** catamaran, transport **10** collection

RAFTER: **3** rib **4** beam **9** crossbeam

RAG: **3** kid, rib **4** jive, joke, josh, mock, razz, tune **5** annoy, cloth, scold, scrap, shred, tease **6** banter, harass, needle **7** remnant **9** newspaper **10** periodical

RAGAMUFFIN: **3** bum **4** hobo, waif **5** tramp **6** beggar, orphan **7** vagrant **8** vagabond **9** scarecrow **10** panhandler **14** tatterdemalion

RAGE: **3** fad, ire **4** boil, fume, funk, fury, rant, rave **5** anger, chafe, craze, furor, livid, mania, storm, style, wrath **6** choler, fervor, frenzy, latest, squall, temper **7** emotion, fashion, madness, passion, tantrum **8** acerbity, acrimony, hysteria, outburst, violence **9** animosity, vehemence **10** enthusiasm, irritation **11** indignation

RAGGED: **4** torn **5** dingy, seedy **6** frayed, shabby, shaggy, uneven **7** patched, unkempt **8** battered, frazzled, strident, tattered **9** defective, imperfect, irregular **10** threadbare **11** dilapidated

RAGING: **4** wild **5** angry, irate, rabid **6** fierce, stormy **7** fervent, furious, rampant, violent **8** incensed **9** ferocious **10** blustering **12** uncontrolled

RAGOUT: **4** hash, stew **7** goulash **8** pot-au-feu

RAGS: **4** duds **6** scraps, shreds **7** clothes, tatters

RAGTIME: **4** jazz **5** blues, music, swing

RAH: **5** cheer **6** hurrah **7** approve **13** encouragement

RAID: **4** bust, loot **5** foray, storm **6** attack, forage, harass, inroad, invade, maraud, pirate, ravage, sortie **7** assault, bombard, pillage, plunder, roundup, seizure **8** invasion **9** onslaught

RAIDER: **5** thief **6** bandit, looter, pirate **7** rustler **8** hijacker, marauder, pilferer, pillager **9** buccaneer, plunderer, privateer **10** freebooter, highwayman

RAIL: **3** bar **4** bird, post, rant, rate **5** abuse, chide, fence, plank, scold, track **6** attack, banter, berate **7** barrier **9** castigate, criticize

RAILING: **3** bar **5** fence, grate **6** paling, siding **7** barrier, support **8** banister

RAILLERY: **5** irony, sport **6** joking, parody, satire **7** kidding, razzing, teasing **8** badinage, chaffing, derision, ridicule, roasting **9** bantering **10** lampoonery, persiflage

RAILROAD: **4** line, push, rush **5** frame, metro, track, train **7** railway **9** transport
car: **5** coach, diner **6** engine, hopper, parlor, tender **7** caboose, gondola, Pullman, sleeper **10** locomotive
elevated: **8** monorail
station: **5** depot **8** terminal
underground: **6** subway

RAIMENT: **4** duds **5** dress **6** attire **7** apparel, threads **8** clothing, garments **11** habiliments

RAIN: **4** mist, pour **5** flood, storm **6** deluge, mizzle, shower **7** drizzle **8** downpour, sprinkle **10** cloudburst **12** thunderstorm **13** precipitation

RAINBOW: **3** arc, bow **4** band, iris **7** fantasy **8** illusion, spectrum **10** assortment
colors: **3** red **4** blue **5** green **6** indigo, orange, violet, yellow
goddess: **4** Iris

RAINCOAT: **3** mac **4** mack **6** poncho **7** slicker **8** overcoat **10** mackintosh, trenchcoat

RAINY: **3** wet **4** damp **5** moist **6** stormy
season: **7** monsoon

RAISE: **4** grow, hike, jump, levy, lift, pump, rear, rise, spur, stir **5** amass, boost, breed, build, crane, erect, evoke, hoist **6** arouse, ascend, awaken, create, excite, foster, gather, incite, leaven, muster, uplift **7** advance, augment, collect, elevate, enhance, inflate, nourish, nurture, procure, produce, promote, upheave **8** addition, heighten, increase **9** construct, cultivate, establish, intensify, introduce, promotion, propagate, resurrect, transcend **10** aggrandize

RAISIN: **6** muscat **7** sultana
dried: **5** grape

RAJA, RAJAH: **4** king **5** chief, ruler **6** prince **7** monarch **9** maharajah

RAKE: **4** comb, gain, tool **5** clear, grade, scour **6** forage, gather, rascal, scrape **7** examine, playboy, ransack, rummage, scratch, swinger **8** Casanova **9** debauchee, libertine, womanizer **11** inclination

RAKISH: **4** chic, lewd, wild **6** dapper, jaunty, sporty **7** dashing, immoral **8** debonair **9** dissolute **10** licentious **11** streamlined

RALLY: **4** drag, meet, mock, race, stir **5** rouse, unite **6** arouse, attack, awaken, charge, kindle, muster, revive **7** convene, refresh, restore, reunite, revival **8** assemble, comeback, mobilize, organize, recovery **9** challenge, encourage **10** convention, recuperate, rejuvenate, strengthen **11** improvement

RAM: **3** hit, tap **4** buck, bump, butt, cram **5** Aries, crash, drive, force, pound, sheep, stuff **6** animal, batter, hammer, strike, thrust **7** collide, plunger **8** bulldoze

RAMBLE: **3** gad **4** roam, rove, walk **5** drift, stray **6** babble, stroll, travel, wander **7** chatter, digress, meander, saunter **9** excursion, gallivant

RAMBLING: **6** wordy **7** cursory, lengthy, rolling **9** desultory, sprawling, wandering **10** digressive, discursive, incoherent **12** disconnected

RAMBUNCTIOUS: **4** loud, wild **5** rough, rowdy **6** active, unruly **7** raucous, untamed **10** boisterous, disorderly, tumultuous

RAMIFICATION: **3** arm **5** ramus **6** branch, result **8** division, offshoot **9** extension **10** divergence **11** consequence, development **12** complication

RAMP: **4** hill, rage, walk **5** apron, grade, slope **6** access, easing **7** incline **8** gradient, platform **9** gangplank

RAMPAGE: **5** binge, spree, storm **6** frenzy, uproar **8** violence

RAMPANT: **4** rife **6** fierce, raging **7** profuse, violent **8** dominant, epidemic **9** excessive, prevalent, unchecked **10** prevailing, widespread **11** extravagant, threatening **12** unrestrained **14** uncontrollable

RAMPART: **4** wall **5** agger **7** barrier, bastion, bulwark, defense, parapet **9** barricade **10** breastwork, embankment, protection **13** fortification

RAMSHACKLE: **5** shaky **6** flimsy, shabby **7** rickety **8** decrepit **9** crumbling **10** dissipated **11** dilapidated

RANCH: **4** farm **6** grange **8** estancia, hacienda **10** plantation

RANCHER: **4** hand **6** cowboy, farmer, gaucho **7** cowgirl, cowhand, cowpoke **8** shepherd **9** cattleman

RANCID: **4** rank **5** musty, nasty, stale **6** putrid, rotten, smelly **7** odorous, spoiled **8** stinking **9** offensive, repugnant, repulsive **10** malodorous, unpleasant

RANCOR: **5** spite **6** enmity, grudge, hatred, malice **9** animosity, hostility, vengeance **10** bitterness, resentment **11** hatefulness

RANDOM: **5** stray **6** chance **7** aimless **9** arbitrary, haphazard, hit-or-miss, unplanned **10** accidental, fortuitous, occasional **11** purposeless **14** indiscriminate

RANDY: **4** lewd **5** crude **6** coarse, vulgar **7** lustful **8** carousal **9** lecherous, libertine **10** disorderly, lascivious, licentious **11** uninhibited

RANGE: **4** ally, area, farm, line, rank, roam, rove, sort, span **5** align, ambit, field, gamut, orbit, order, plain, reach, realm, ridge, scope, space, stove, stray, sweep **6** bounds, domain, extent, length, limits, ramble, series, sphere, stroll, wander **7** arrange, compass, explore, horizon, pasture, purview, stretch, variety **8** classify, diapason, distance, latitude, province, spectrum **9** appliance, grassland, highlands **10** assortment, parameters

RANGER: **5** rover **6** warden **7** soldier, trooper **8** wanderer **9** policeman **11** policewoman

RANGY: **5** lanky, roomy **6** skinny **8** gangling, spacious **9** spindling

RANK: **3** row **4** foul, line, lush, rate, rile, sort, tier, type **5** array, caste, class, dirty, fetid, genus, grade, gross, order, place, range, score, space, utter, value **6** assort, coarse, column, degree, estate, filthy, gentry, rancid, rating, series, smelly, smutty, status, strong **7** arrange, caliber, dignity, echelon, extreme, fertile, obscene, precede, quality, rampant, raunchy, station, stature **8** absolute, abundant, ancestry, classify, division, evaluate, flagrant, position, prestige, standing **9** condition, downright, excessive, exuberant, formation, gradation, hierarchy, luxurious, offensive, overgrown, revolting, seniority **10** coordinate, malodorous, noticeable **11** arrangement, distinction **14** classification

RANK AND FILE: **6** masses, plebes, troops **7** militia **9** commoners **11** commonality, proletariat

RANKLE: **3** irk, vex **4** fret, gall, rile **5** annoy **6** fester, nettle, plague **7** inflame, torment **8** embitter, irritate **9** aggravate

RANSACK: **4** comb, loot, raid, rake **5** rifle **6** ravage, ravish, search **7** pillage, plunder, rummage **9** vandalize

RANSOM: **4** free, save **5** atone, price **6** redeem, rescue **7** deliver, expiate, release **8** liberate, retrieve **10** emancipate **12** compensation

RANT: **4** fume, huff, rave, yell **5** orate, range, storm **6** bellow, berate, tirade **8** harangue

RAP: **3** hit, tap **4** blow, chat, swat, talk **5** blame, knock, music, smite, speak, utter, whack **6** lyrics, rebuke, snatch, strike, thwack **8** sentence **9** criticism, criticize, reprehend, reprimand **10** discussion, punishment **11** communicate **12** conversation

RAPACIOUS: **6** fierce, greedy **7** wolfish **8** ravening, ravenous **9** ferocious, predatory, voracious, vulturous **10** avaricious, plundering

RAPACITY: **5** greed **7** avarice **8** cupidity, thievery **12** covetousness

RAPE: **4** file **5** abuse, spoil **6** attack, defile, ravage, ravish **7** assault, despoil, offense, pillage, plunder, violate **9** violation

RAPID: **4** fast **5** agile, brisk, fleet, hasty, quick, river, swift **6** abrupt, nimble, prompt, speedy, winged **7** hurried, instant **10** whitewater

RAPIDITY: **4** pace **5** speed **8** celerity, velocity **9** quickness, swiftness **10** promptness **12** acceleration

RAPINE: **5** seize **7** plunder

RAPPORT: **4** bond **5** unity **6** accord **7** harmony **8** affinity, scalawag **9** scoundrel **10** connection **11** rapscallion **12** relationship **13** compatibility

RAPSCALLION: **5** rouge, scamp **6** rascal **7** villain

RAPT: **4** deep **6** intent **7** charmed **8** absorbed, dreaming, ecstatic, immersed **9** delighted, enchanted, engrossed, entranced **10** captivated, enraptured, fascinated, spellbound **11** preoccupied, transported

RAPTURE: **5** bliss **7** delight, ecstasy, elation **8** euphoria, rhapsody **9** happiness **11** contentment, enchantment **12** exhilaration

RARE: **3** odd, raw **4** fine, thin **6** choice, exotic, scarce, seldom, select, unique **7** antique, limited, special, unusual **8** isolated, precious, uncommon, unlikely **9** beautiful, excellent, exquisite, priceless, underdone **10** infrequent, invaluable, occasional **11** distinctive, exceptional, uncustomary, undercooked **13** extraordinary

RAREFIED: **4** thin **5** lofty **7** diluted, reduced, refined, tenuous **8** diminish, esoteric **10** attenuated

RARELY: **5** extra **6** hardly, seldom **9** unusually **12** infrequently, occasionally **13** exceptionally

RARING: **4** keen **5** eager, ready **7** anxious **9** impatient

RARITY: **6** oddity, wonder **7** anomaly, antique **8** scarcity **9** curiosity

RASCAL: **3** cad **4** rake **5** devil, knave, rogue, scamp **7** villain **8** scalawag **9** miscreant, scoundrel, trickster **10** blackguard **11** rapscallion **12** troublemaker

RASH: **4** bold, wave **5** brash, flood, hasty, heady, hives **6** abrupt, daring, eczema, sudden, unwary, unwise **7** foolish **8** careless, epidemic, eruption, headlong, heedless, reckless **9** desperate, foolhardy, hotheaded, impetuous, imprudent, impulsive, unadvised, venturous **10** headstrong, incautious, irrational, unthinking **11** adventurous, precipitate, precipitous, temerarious, thoughtless, venturesome **13** adventuresome, irresponsible

RASP: **4** file **5** grate **6** abrade, scrape, wheeze **8** abrasive, irritate **10** hoarseness

RASPBERRY: **3** boo **4** hiss, razz **5** fruit, sound **7** catcall
genus: **5** rubus

RASPING: **5** harsh, raspy, rough **6** hoarse **7** grating, raucous

RAT: **4** fink, pest, scab, snot **6** defect, inform, rodent, snitch, vermin **7** stoolie, traitor **8** betrayer, deserter, informer, turncoat **11** stool pigeon

RATE: **3** fee, tax **4** clip, cost, earn, fare, pace, rank **5** class, grade, judge, merit, price, ratio, scale, scold, speed, tempo, value **6** amount, assess, charge, degree, tariff **7** account, expense, quality **8** appraise, classify, estimate, evaluate, standard, velocity **10** assessment, percentage, proportion

RATHER: **4** than **5** quite **6** choice, enough, sooner **7** exactly, instead **8** contrary, somewhat **10** accurately, moderately, preferably, preference, relatively **13** alternatively, significantly

RATIFY: **4** pass, seal **5** bless **6** affirm, uphold, verify **7** approve, confirm, consent, endorse **8** sanction, validate **9** authorize, establish

RATING: **4** mark, rank **5** class, grade, score **6** rebuke **8** scolding, standing **9** reprimand **10** evaluation **14** classification

RATIO: **4** rate **5** quota, share **6** degree **7** percent **8** fraction, relation **10** percentage, proportion **11** correlation **12** distribution

RATION: **4** dole, mete **5** allot, divvy, quota, share **6** divide **7** helping, measure, portion, serving **8** allocate **9** allotment, allowance **10** distribute

RATIONAL: **4** calm, cool, sane, wise **5** sound **6** stable **7** logical, prudent **8** balanced, sensible **9** collected, realistic **10** reasonable **11** intelligent, levelheaded

RATIONALE: **5** basis, logic **6** motive, reason **7** grounds **11** explanation

RATIONALIZE: **5** think **6** reason **7** explain, justify

RATTLE: **3** toy **4** chat, faze, stun **5** annoy, clack, noise, shake, sound, upset **6** babble, jabber, jangle, jiggle **7** chatter, clapper, clatter, confuse, fluster, perplex, unnerve **8** confound

RATTLEBRAINED: **5** dizzy, giddy, silly **6** stupid **7** flighty, foolish **9** frivolous, talkative **10** irrational

RATTY: **3** old **4** worn **6** shabby **7** decayed, unkempt **11** dilapidated

RAUCOUS: **4** loud **5** gruff, harsh, noisy, rough, rowdy **6** coarse, hoarse, unruly **7** blaring, braying, rasping **8** piercing, strident **10** boisterous, disorderly, tumultuous **11** cacophonous

RAUNCHY: **4** foul, lewd **5** dirty, grimy, gross **6** coarse, filthy, smutty, vulgar **7** obscene, unkempt **8** explicit

RAVAGE: **4** loot, raid, ruin, sack **5** crush, foray, havoc, spoil, waste, wreck **6** devour, forage **7** consume, despoil, destroy, overrun, pillage, plunder, ransack, scourge, trample **8** demolish, desolate **9** devastate **10** annihilate **11** devastation

RAVE: **4** rage, rant, roar, talk **5** blurb, storm **6** babble, jabber, ramble **7** bluster, declaim, enthuse

RAVEL: **4** fray, free **5** snarl **6** loosen, muddle, sleave, tangle, unwind **7** crumble, perplex, untwist **8** entangle, separate, untangle **10** complicate **11** disentangle

RAVEN: **3** jet **4** bird, crow **5** black, ebony **6** devour **7** consume **9** blackbird
genus: **6** corvus

RAVEN, THE: **4** poem
author: **13** Edgar Allan Poe
saying: **9** Nevermore

RAVENOUS: **6** greedy, hungry, lupine **7** starved **8** desirous, edacious, famished **9** predatory, rapacious, voracious **10** gluttonous, insatiable

RAVINE: **3** cut, gap **4** dell, glen, pass, rift, wadi, wady **5** abyss, canon, chasm, ditch, flume, gorge, gulch, gully, kloof, notch **6** arroyo, canyon, coulee, valley **7** crevice

RAVING: **3** mad **4** wild **6** fuming **7** berserk, ranting, violent **8** frenzied **9** delirious **10** irrational

RAVISH: **4** raid, rape **5** abuse, charm, force, seize **6** allure, defile **7** delight, despoil, enchant, pillage, plunder, violate **8** deflower, enthrall **9** captivate, enrapture, hypnotize, mesmerize, transport

RAW: **4** cold, damp, nude, rare, rude, sore **5** basic, bleak, crude, cruel, fresh, green, harsh, naked, stark **6** abrade, biting, chilly, coarse, unfair, unripe **7** cutting, natural, untried **8** immature, uncooked **9** unclothed, unexposed, unrefined, unskilled, untrained **10** unfinished, unprepared, unseasoned **11** uncivilized, unprocessed **12** uncultivated **13** inexperienced

RAWBONED: **4** lean **5** gaunt, lanky **7** angular, scrawny

RAY: **4** beam, beta, fish, line **5** alpha, flare, flash, gamma, gleam, light, shaft, shine, skate, trace **6** radial, streak, stripe, vision **7** radiate, sunbeam **8** moonbeam, particle **9** emanation, irradiate, radiation **10** indication

RAZE: **4** ruin **5** erase, level, shave, smash, wreck **6** efface, scrape **7** destroy, flatten, scratch, subvert **8** bulldoze, decimate, demolish **9** dismantle, overthrow **10** obliterate

RAZOR: **5** blade, knife **6** shaver **8** electric

RAZORBACK STATE: **8** Arkansas

RAZZ: **3** kid, rib **4** jest, joke **5** chaff, taunt, tease **6** banter, heckle, needle **8** ridicule **9** raspberry

REACH: **4** come, find, gain, move, span, sway **5** ambit, grasp, scope, touch **6** affect, amount, arrive, attain, extend, extent, strive **7** achieve, compass, contact, expanse, fulfill, purview, stretch **8** approach **9** influence, penetrate **10** accomplish

REACHABLE: **6** answer **8** possible, reaction, response **9** influence **10** accessible, impression, obtainable

REACT: **5** reply **6** answer, behave **7** counter, respond

REACTION: **5** reply **6** reflex **7** allergy, opinion **8** backlash, feedback **10** opposition

REACTIONARY: **7** diehard **8** orthodox **12** conservative **14** traditionalist

READ: **4** pore, scan, show, skim, tell **5** grasp, learn, proof, study **6** browse, descry, peruse, recite, relate **7** discern, express, foresee, predict **8** decipher, describe, foretell **9** interpret, translate **10** comprehend, understand

READABLE: **5** clear **7** legible **8** coherent, eloquent, engaging, pleasing **12** intelligible **14** comprehensible

READER: **6** editor, lector, primer **7** reciter, scholar **8** bookworm, lecturer **9** anthology **11** proofreader **12** elocutionist

READILY: **6** easily, freely **7** quickly **8** promptly, speedily **9** willingly **11** immediately

READINESS: **7** address, prowess **8** alacrity, facility **9** dexterity, eagerness, quickness **10** expedition, promptness, volubility **12** preparedness

READING: **6** lesson, review **7** lecture, perusal, recital, version **9** rendition **11** declamation

READY: **3** apt, fit, set **4** game, prep, ripe **5** adept, alert, eager, handy, prime **6** active, adroit, facile, fluent, likely, mature, prompt **7** fortify, prepare, willing **8** arranged, dextrous, equipped, organize, prepared, skillful **9** attentive, available, dexterous **10** convenient **11** expeditious

REAL: **4** pure, true **5** being, solid, valid **6** actual, honest **7** certain, factual, genuine, literal, serious, sincere **8** absolute, bona fide, concrete, existent, original, tangible **9** authentic, intrinsic, unfeigned **10** legitimate, unaffected

REALISTIC: **5** sound **7** genuine, graphic **8** lifelike, rational, sensible **9** practical **10** reasonable **11** down-to-earth **12** matter-of-fact **14** representative

REALITY: **4** fact **5** being, truth **9** existence, substance **11** tangibility **12** concreteness

REALIZATION: **9** awakening, awareness **11** achievement, culmination, fulfillment **13** understanding

REALIZE: **4** earn, gain **5** clear, reach, sense, think **6** attain, obtain, profit **7** achieve, acquire, fulfill, imagine **8** complete, conceive, envision **9** apprehend **10** accomplish, appreciate, understand

REALLY: **6** indeed **8** actually, honestly **9** assuredly, certainly, genuinely **10** absolutely, positively **11** indubitably **12** unmistakably **13** categorically

REALM: **4** area, land **5** field, range, world **6** circle, domain, empire, region, sphere **7** control, country, dynasty, kingdom **8** division, dominion, province **9** dimension, territory **10** department **12** jurisdiction

REANIMATE: **5** renew **6** revive **7** enliven, restore **10** revitalize **11** resuscitate **12** reinvigorate

REAP: **4** gain **5** glean **6** garner, gather, profit **7** acquire, collect, harvest **10** accumulate

REAR: **3** aft, end **4** back, butt, gain, last, lift, seat, tail, tend **5** after, breed, build, erect, fanny, nurse, raise, stern **6** astern, behind, bottom, foster, uphold **7** develop, educate, elevate, nurture **8** backside, buttocks, derriere **9** construct, cultivate

REASON: **3** why **4** goal, mind **5** argue, brain, cause, logic, sense, think **6** debate, figure, motive, ponder, sanity **7** account, discuss, grounds, meaning, purpose **8** argument, converse, judgment, occasion **9** deduction, discourse, incentive, intellect, intention, intuition, rational, speculate, wherefore **11** explanation, rationality, rationalize **13** justification, understanding

REASONABLE: **4** fair, just, wise **5** sound **6** modest **7** logical, prudent **8** feasible, moderate, rational, sensible **9** equitable, practical, tolerable **10** affordable **11** inexpensive, levelheaded

REASONING: **5** basis, logic **7** thought **8** analysis, argument, thinking **9** rationale

REASSURE: **5** cheer **6** uplift **7** comfort **8** convince **9** encourage, guarantee

REBATE: **6** lessen, reduce, refund **8** diminish, discount, kickback **9** abatement, deduction, reduction **13** reimbursement

REBEKAH:
father: **7** Bethuel
husband: **5** Isaac
mother: **6** Milcah
sons: **4** Esau **5** Jacob

REBEL: **4** riot, rise **6** mutiny, revolt, secede **7** radical **8** denounce, mutineer, renegade **9** adversary, anarchist, demagogue, insurgent **10** antagonist, iconoclast **13** insubordinate, revolutionary, revolutionist

REBELLION: **6** mutiny, revolt **8** defiance, outbreak, sedition, upheaval, uprising **10** revolution **11** disturbance **12** insurrection

REBELLIOUS: **6** unruly **7** defiant, rioting **9** alienated, seditious **11** disobedient **12** contumacious, incorrigible, recalcitrant **13** insubordinant

REBIRTH: **7** renewal, revival **11** renaissance **12** rejuvenation, resurrection **13** reincarnation

REBOUND: **4** echo, stot **5** carom **6** bounce, recoil, return, spring **7** reflect, resound **8** recovery, retrieve, ricochet **9** boomerang **10** resilience **11** reverberate

REBUFF: **4** snub **5** check, chide, rebut, repel, scold, spurn **6** ignore, rebuke, refuse, reject, slight **7** refusal, reprove, repulse **8** brushoff **9** disregard, reprimand

REBUKE: **4** beat, snub **5** check, chide, scold **6** berate, lesson **7** lecture, repress, reproof, reprove **8** admonish, chastise, reproach, restrain **9** castigate, criticize, reprehend, reprimand **10** admonition

REBUT: **5** repel, reply **6** rebuff, refute **7** confute, repulse **8** disprove **10** contradict, invalidate

RECALCITRANT: **4** wild **6** unruly **7** defiant, willful **8** stubborn **9** obstinate, resisting **10** headstrong, rebellious **11** disobedient **12** unmanageable **13** undisciplined

RECALL: **4** cite **5** annul, place **6** awaken, cancel, elicit, memory, remind, repeal, retain, revoke **7** extract, nullify, rescind, restore, retrace, retract **8** remember, withdraw **9** recognize, recollect, reconvene, reminisce **11** countermand

RECANT: **5** annul, unsay **6** abjure, cancel, renege, revoke **7** abandon, disavow, retract **8** abrogate, disclaim, renounce, withdraw **9** repudiate

RECAPITULATE: **5** recap **6** rehash, repeat, review **7** recount, restate **9** reiterate, summarize, synopsize **10** paraphrase

RECEDE: **3** ebb **4** fade **5** abate **6** depart **7** dwindle, regress, retract, retreat, subside **8** decrease, diminish, withdraw **10** retrograde

RECEIPT: **4** bill, slip, stub **6** notice **7** arrival, release, voucher **9** admission **10** acceptance

RECEIPTS: **4** cash, gate **5** money **6** income **7** profits, revenue **8** earnings, payments, proceeds

RECEIVE: **3** get **4** earn, take **5** admit, catch, greet **6** accept, derive, endure, obtain **7** acquire, collect, inherit, support, welcome **10** experience

RECEIVER: **4** heir **5** fence **9** collector, recipient, telephone **11** beneficiary

RECENT: **3** new **5** fresh **6** modern **7** current **8** neotenic **10** newfangled **12** contemporary

RECEPTACLE: **3** bin, box, can, cup, jar, tub, urn, vat **4** case, cell, tank, tray, vase **5** basin, chest, crate **6** basket, bottle, bucket, carton, holder, vessel **7** pitcher **8** canister **9** container **10** repository

RECEPTION: **3** tea **5** levee, party **6** affair, soiree **7** meeting, ovation, welcome **8** function, greeting **9** admission, gathering **10** acceptance, admittance **13** entertainment

RECEPTIVE: **4** open **8** amenable, friendly **9** sensitive **10** hospitable, interested, responsive **11** sympathetic

RECESS: **4** cave, cove, hole, nook, rest **5** break, cleft, crypt, niche, sinus **6** alcove, cavity, closet, cranny, hiatus **7** adjourn, respite, retreat **8** breather, interval, vacation **10** depression, suspension **12** intermission

RECESSION: **4** bust **7** decline **10** depression

RECHERCHE: **4** rare **5** fresh, novel **6** choice, exotic, forced **7** unusual **8** precious, superior, uncommon **9** exquisite, overblown **11** exceptional, pretentious

RECIPE: **7** formula, pattern, process **10** directions **12** instructions, prescription

RECIPIENT: **4** heir **5** donee **7** awardee, legatee **8** receiver **9** receptive **11** beneficiary

RECIPROCAL: **4** twin **6** mutual, shared **9** duplicate, exchanged **10** changeable, equivalent **11** correlative **13** complementary, corresponding **14** interdependent

RECIPROCATE: **4** swap **5** equal, match, repay, trade **6** return **7** requite **8** exchange **9** alternate, retaliate **10** correspond, recompense **11** interchange

RECITAL: **4** tale **5** story **6** report **7** account, concert, musical, program **9** narration, narrative, rehearsal **11** description, performance **12** presentation

RECITE: **4** list, read, tell **5** chant, quote, speak **6** relate **7** address, explain, narrate, recount **8** describe **9** enumerate **11** communicate **12** recapitulate

RECKLESS: **4** bold, rash, wild **6** daring, madcap **7** foolish **8** carefree, careless, headlong, heedless **9** dangerous, daredevil, impetuous, imprudent, negligent **10** neglectful, regardless **11** adventurous, indifferent, precipitate, temerarious, thoughtless **13** irresponsible

RECKLESSNESS: **7** abandon **9** disregard **11** desperation **13** foolhardiness

RECKON: **3** add, sum **4** deem, rate, rely, tell **5** count, guess, judge, tally, think, total **6** assume, cipher, figure, number, regard, repute **7** account, compute, suppose, surmise **8** consider, estimate, numerate **9** calculate, determine, enumerate **10** understand

RECKONING: **4** bill, cost, debt, rate **5** count, score, tally **6** charge **7** invoice **9** statement, summation **10** settlement **11** computation

RECLAIM: **4** save, tame **5** train **6** recall, reform, repair **7** recover, resolve, restore, salvage **9** refurbish, restitute **10** regenerate

RECLINE: **3** lay, lie **4** lean, loll, rest **5** relax, slope **6** lounge, sprawl **7** stretch **8** reposing **9** accumbent, recumbent

RECLINING: **4** flat **5** loner **7** recluse **10** troglodyte

RECLUSE: **3** nun **4** monk **6** hermit, hidden **7** eremite **8** secluded, solitary **9** anchoress, anchorite **10** cloistered **11** sequestered

RECOGNITION: **6** credit, notice **9** attention, awareness, gratitude **10** acceptance **11** remembering **14** identification

RECOGNIZE: **4** know, note, spot **5** admit, greet, honor **6** accept, notice, recall, remark, review, revise, salute **7** approve **8** identify, perceive, remember **9** apprehend **10** appreciate, understand **11** acknowledge, distinguish

RECOIL: **4** jerk, kick **5** blink, dodge, quail, wince **6** blench, flinch, shrink **7** retreat, reverse **8** withdraw

RECOLLECT: **4** cite **6** arouse, awaken, recall **7** bethink **8** remember **9** reminisce

RECOLLECTION: **6** memory, recall **9** anamnesis **11** remembrance **12** reminiscence **13** retrospection

RECOMMEND: **4** tout, urge **5** refer **6** advise, praise, second **7** counsel, endorse, entrust, propose **8** advocate **9** encourage, prescribe

RECOMMENDATION: **6** advice, urging **9** direction, reference **10** suggestion **11** instruction

RECOMPENSE: **3** pay **5** award, repay **6** amends, bounty, reward, salary **7** premium, recover **9** atonement, indemnify, reimburse, repayment **10** compensate, remunerate, reparation **11** reciprocate, restitution, retribution **12** compensation

RECONCILE: **5** adapt, atone **6** accord, adjust, pacify, settle, square **7** absolve, conform, expiate, mediate, placate, rectify, resolve, restore, reunite, satisfy **9** arbitrate, harmonize **10** conciliate, propitiate

RECONDITE: **4** dark, deep **6** arcane, hidden, mystic, occult **7** cryptic, obscure **8** abstruse, esoteric, profound **9** ambiguous, concealed, difficult **10** mysterious

RECONNAISSANCE: **6** survey **8** scouting **10** inspection **11** exploration, observation

RECONNOITER: **4** look **5** probe, scout **6** survey **7** examine, explore, inquire, inspect

RECONSIDER: **5** amend **6** modify, replan, revise **7** reflect, rethink **9** reexamine **10** reevaluate

RECONSTRUCT: **4** copy, mend **5** patch **6** repair **7** rebuild, restore **8** overhaul, renovate **10** reassemble, reorganize **11** recondition

RECORD: **3** log, tab **4** date, file, list, mark, memo, note, show, tape **5** album, annal, chart, diary, enter, entry, score **6** legend, memoir, report **7** account, catalog, history, journal, minutes **8** calendar, document, preserve, register **9** catalogue, chronicle, directory, videotape **10** background, experience, transcribe, transcript **11** achievement

RECORDER: **5** flute, judge **10** dictaphone

RECOUNT: **4** tell **5** state **6** convey, recite, rehash, relate, repeat **7** explain, narrate, portray **8** describe, rehearse **9** enumerate

RECOUP: **6** regain **8** retrieve

RECOVER: **5** amend, rally **6** recoup, reform, regain, rescue, retake **7** balance, reclaim, recruit, restore, salvage **8** retrieve **9** reimburse, repossess **10** compensate, convalesce, recuperate

RECOVERY: **4** cure, gain, heal, mend **6** redeem, revive, upturn **7** improve, procure, rebound **8** comeback **11** improvement **12** recuperation, rehabilitate **13** convalescence

RECREANT: **6** coward, craven, untrue, yellow **7** traitor **8** apostate, betrayer, cowardly, deserter, disloyal **9** faithless **10** spiritless, unfaithful

RECREATION: **4** game, play **5** hobby, sport **6** frolic, picnic **7** leisure, pastime **8** exercise, pleasure **9** amusement, diversion **10** relaxation **13** entertainment

RECRUIT: **4** tyro **5** draft, renew **6** enlist, enroll, gather, muster, novice, revive, rookie, supply **7** draftee, recover, restore, soldier **8** assemble, beginner, inductee, neophyte, newcomer **9** reinforce, replenish, volunteer **10** recuperate, strengthen

RECTANGLE: **5** plane **6** figure, oblong, square **13** parallelogram

RECTIFY: **3** fix **4** cure **5** amend, emend, right **6** adjust, purify, refine, reform, remedy, repair **7** correct, improve, rebuild, redress **10** straighten

RECTITUDE: **6** virtue **7** decency, honesty **8** goodness, morality **9** integrity **11** uprightness **13** righteousness

RECTOR: **6** cleric, pastor, priest **7** proctor **8** minister **9** clergyman, principal **10** headmaster **11** clergywoman

RECTORY: **5** manse **8** benefice, vicarage **9** parsonage **10** presbytery

RECUMBENT: **4** flat, idle **5** lying, prone **6** supine **7** resting **8** inactive **9** prostrate, reclining

RECUPERATE: **4** heal, mend **6** regain **7** improve, recover **10** convalesce

RECUR: **6** repeat, return **7** iterate, persist **8** reappear **9** reiterate

RECURRENT: **7** chronic, regular **8** cyclical, habitual **9** recurring, repeating, returning **10** repetitive **11** reappearing

RED: **4** pink, rosy, ruby, rust **5** blush, brick, color, coral, fiery, rouge, ruddy **6** bloody, cherry, claret, commie, maroon, titian **7** carmine, crimson, florida, glowing, leftist, magenta, radical, roseate, rubious, scarlet **8** blushing, burgundy, cardinal, cinnabar, inflamed **9** bloodshot, communist, vermilion

RED-BLOODED: **6** robust, strong **7** healthy **8** spirited **9** energetic

REDDEN: **4** glow **5** blush, color, flush, rouge, ruddy **7** crimson

REDEEM: **4** cash, free, save **5** atone, repay **6** defray, ransom, regain, rescue **7** balance, convert, fulfill, reclaim, recover, release, restore **8** exchange **10** compensate

REDEYE: **4** fish **6** flight, signal **7** whiskey

RED-FACED: **7** flushed **11** embarrassed

RED-HANDED: **6** caught, openly **9** blatantly

RED-HOT: **3** new **6** heated **7** burning, glowing, hippest, popular **8** sizzling **9** scorching **10** sweltering

RED-LETTER: **5** happy **6** banner **7** notable **9** memorable **10** noteworthy

REDOLENCE: **4** balm, odor **5** aroma, scent **7** bouquet, perfume **9** fragrance

REDOLENT: **5** balmy, spicy **6** savory **7** scented **8** aromatic, fragrant, perfumed **10** suggestive **11** reminiscent

REDOUBLE: **6** repeat **7** augment, enhance, magnify, retrace **8** heighten **9** intensify, reinforce

REDOUBT: **4** fort **7** bulwark **8** fortress **9** earthwork **10** breastwork, stronghold **13** fortification

REDOUBTABLE: **7** awesome, fearful **8** dreadful, fearsome, imminent **10** formidable **11** frightening, illustrious

REDOUND: **5** cause **6** accrue, recoil, return **7** resound **10** contribute **11** reverberate

RED PLANET: **4** Mars

REDRESS: **4** help **5** amend **6** adjust, change, negate, offset, reform, relief, remedy **7** correct, payment, rectify, relieve **9** indemnity, vindicate **10** counteract, recompense, reparation **12** compensation

REDUCE: **3** cut **4** bate, curb, diet, slow, thin, trim **5** abase, abate, level, lower, scale, slash **6** change, debase, defeat, demote, dilute, humble, impair, lessen, rebate, recede, subdue, weaken **7** abridge, conquer, curtail, degrade, deplete, dwindle, shorten **8** condense, contract, decrease, diminish, discount, emaciate, minimize, overcome **9** downgrade, humiliate, subjugate **10** annihilate, depreciate

REDUCTION: **6** rebate **7** cutback, decline **8** discount, markdown **9** abatement, attrition, shrinkage **11** contraction, curtailment, degradation, devaluation, downgrading, subtraction

REDUNDANCY: **7** surplus **8** pleonasm, verbiage **9** verbosity **10** flatulence, repetition **11** duplication, superfluity

REDUNDANT: **5** extra, wordy **6** prolix **7** copious, surplus, verbose **9** excessive, exuberant **10** irrelevant, loquacious **11** overflowing, reiterating, repetitious, superfluous **12** overabundant, tautological

REDWOOD: **4** tree **7** Sequoia **9** evergreen **10** coniferous

REED: **4** cane, dart, pipe, stem, tule **5** arrow, grass, plant, spear, stalk **10** instrument

REEF: **3** bar, key **4** bank, lode, vein **5** atoll, ledge, ridge, shoal **7** bioherm, sandbar

REEK: **4** emit, fume, funk, vent **5** exude, smell, smoke, steam, stink, vapor **6** stench **7** emanate

REEL: **4** drum, rock, roll, spin, sway, swim, turn **5** dance, lurch, shirl, spool, swing, waver **6** bobbin, careen, rotate, teeter, totter, wobble **7** spindle, stagger, stumble **8** windlass

REFER: **4** cite, name, send **5** guide, quote **6** advert, allude, appeal, assign, commit, confer, direct, impute, relate, submit **7** ascribe, consult, mention, specify **8** identify, transfer **9** attribute, recommend

REFEREE: **5** judge **6** umpire **7** adjudge, arbiter, mediate **8** mediator, official **9** determine, moderator **10** arbitrator **11** conciliator **12** intermediary

REFERENCE: **5** quote **6** aspect, remark, source **7** meaning, mention, respect **8** footnote, innuendo **10** connection **11** associating, credentials, implication, testimonial **14** recommendation
book: **5** atlas **6** manual **7** almanac **9** thesaurus **10** dictionary **12** encyclopedia

REFERENDUM: **4** poll, vote **7** mandate **8** election

REFINE: **4** edit **5** groom **6** better, filter, finish, polish, purify, smooth, strain **7** clarify, cleanse, distill, elevate, improve, perfect **9** cultivate

REFINED: **5** suave **6** polite, urbane **7** elegant, genteel **8** cultured, delicate, graceful, highbred, ladylike, polished **9** civilized, courteous, processed **10** fastidious **11** gentlemanly

REFINEMENT: **5** grace **6** finish, polish **7** culture, finesse **8** civility, elegance **9** filtering **12** purification **13** clarification

REFLECT: **4** cast, echo, muse **5** image, shine, study, think **6** divert, mirror, ponder, reason **7** deflect, express, imitate **8** cogitate, consider, meditate, ruminate **10** deliberate **11** contemplate

REFLECTION: **4** idea, view **5** image, light **7** opinion, thought **8** likeness, thinking **9** sentiment **10** absorption, appearance, cogitation, impression, meditation, rumination **12** deliberation **13** contemplation

REFLECTIVE: **7** pensive **9** pondering **10** meditative, ruminative, thoughtful

REFORM: **4** mend **5** amend, emend, renew **6** better, change, remedy, repair, revise **7** convert, correct, improve, rebuild, reclaim, rectify, redress, restore **10** reorganize **12** rehabilitate

REFRACTORY: **6** unruly **7** mullish, willful **8** contrary, perverse, stubborn **9** difficult, obstinate **10** bullheaded, headstrong, rebellious, unyielding **11** disobedient, intractable, opinionated **12** cantankerous, incorrigible, ungovernable, unmanageable, unresponsive

REFRAIN: **4** curb, halt, song, tune **5** avoid, cease, check, forgo, music **6** chorus, desist, forego **7** abstain, forbear, inhibit **8** restrain, withhold

REFRESH: **3** jog **4** cool, rest **5** cheer, renew **6** prompt, revise, revive, update **7** enliven, freshen, restore **8**

energize, recreate, renovate **9** modernize, reanimate, replenish, stimulate **10** invigorate, rejuvenate, strengthen

REFRESHING: **5** balmy, crisp, tonic **6** unique **7** bracing **9** different **10** enervating **12** exhilarating, invigorating

REFRESHMENT: **4** food **5** drink, snack, treat **6** regale **8** beverage, cocktail **9** collation

REFRIGERATE: **3** ice **4** cool **5** chill **6** freeze **12** air-condition

REFUGE: **4** home, port **5** cover, haven **6** asylum, covert, harbor, relief, resort, shield **7** hideout, retreat, shelter **8** hospital, immunity, resource **9** sanctuary **10** protection

REFUGEE: **5** exile **6** emigre **7** runaway **8** defector, fugitive **9** foreigner **10** expatriate

REFULGENT: **6** bright **7** glowing, radiant, shining **8** luminous **9** brilliant **11** resplendent

REFUND: **5** repay **6** rebate, return **8** kickback **9** indemnify, reimburse **10** remunerate **11** retribution

REFURBISH: **5** clean, renew **6** revamp, update **7** freshen, remodel, restore **8** brighten, renovate **11** recondition

REFUSAL: **6** denial, option **8** turndown **9** rejection **11** declination

REFUSE: **4** deny, junk, veto **5** dodge, evade, offal, repel, scrap, spurn, trash, waste, wrack **6** debris, forbid, litter, lumber, rebuff, reject **7** decline, disavow, garbage, rubbish **8** disallow, prohibit, withhold **9** excrement, repudiate

REFUTE: **4** deny **5** avoid, rebut **6** answer **7** confute, counter, silence **8** disclaim, disprove **9** discredit, overthrow **10** contradict, invalidate

REGAIN: **6** recoup, retake **7** recover **8** retrieve **9** recapture, repossess

REGAL: **5** grand, noble, royal **6** august, kingly, lordly **7** queenly, stately **8** imperial, imposing, majestic, princely, splendid **11** magnificent

REGALE: **5** amuse, feast, party **6** dinner, spread **7** banquet, delight **8** delicacy **9** entertain **11** refreshment

REGALIA: **4** love **5** crown, judge **6** accept, finery, regard **7** account, emblems, feature, opinion, scepter, symbols **8** insignia **10** particular, privileges, scrutinize **11** decorations, observation **12** appreciation, satisfaction

REGARD: **3** air, eye **4** care, deem, gaze, heed, hold, look, mind, note, view **5** assay, honor, think, treat, value, watch **6** admire, aspect, attend, behold, esteem, glance, homage, notice, remark, revere **7** adjudge, concern, observe, respect **8** consider, estimate, interest, relation **9** affection, attention, reference **10** admiration, appearance, estimation **11** contemplate **13** contemplation

REGARDFUL: **6** polite **7** careful, mindful **9** attentive, observant **10** thoughtful **11** considerate

REGARDING: **5** about, anent **7** apropos **10** concerning

REGARDLESS: **6** anyhow **7** despite **8** although, careless **9** negligent **10** neglectful **11** inattentive, indifferent, unconcerned **12** irrespective, nevertheless

REGATTA: **4** race **8** boat race **9** yacht race

REGENERATE: **5** renew **6** reborn, redeem, reform, revive **7** refresh, restore **8** recreate, renovate **9** reproduce **10** exhilarate, invigorate, revitalize

REGENT: **5** ruler **7** viceroy **8** director, governor, minister, official

REGIMEN: **4** diet, rule **6** system **7** control, process **9** procedure **10** government **14** administration

REGIMENT: **5** cadre, corps, order **6** troops **7** control **8** soldiers

REGION: **4** area, belt, part, zone **5** field, place, scope, tract **6** domain, sector, sphere **7** climate, country, kingdom, section, terrain **8** district, division, precinct, province, vicinity **9** territory **12** neighborhood

REGIONAL: **5** local **9** parochial, sectional **10** provincial **11** territorial

REGISTER: **4** book, file, join, list, roll, show **5** annal, diary, enter, entry, tally **6** agenda, docket, enlist, enroll, record, roster **7** blotter, catalog, certify **8** archives, calendar, indicate, schedule **9** chronical **10** membership

REGNANT: **6** ruling **8** reigning **9** prevalent, sovereign **10** widespread **11** predominant

REGRESS: **4** back **6** recede, return, revert **7** retreat, reverse **8** rollback, withdraw **10** retrograde **11** deteriorate

REGRET: **3** rue, woe **4** pang **5** demur, grief, mourn, qualm, sorry **6** grieve, lament, repent, repine, sorrow **7** anguish, deplore, remorse, scruple **8** distress **9** apologize, heartache **10** bitterness, heartbreak, repentance **11** compunction, lamentation **14** disappointment

REGRETFUL: **5** sorry **6** rueful, woeful **10** apologetic, deplorable, remorseful **12** disappointed

REGULAR: **4** even **5** daily, fixed, usual, utter **6** common, formal, normal, proper, serial, stated, steady **7** general, genuine, natural, orderly, routine, typical, uniform **8** complete, constant, everyday, faithful, habitual, ordinary, periodic, rhythmic, standard, thorough **9** automatic, continual, customary, recurrent **10** consistent, dependable, methodical, systematic **11** established

REGULATE: **4** pace, rule, time **5** clock, gauge, guide, order **6** adjust, direct, govern, manage, settle, temper **7** arrange, balance, conduct, control, correct, monitor, rectify **8** allocate, modulate, organize **9** establish **10** administer, discipline **11** standardize

REGULATION: **3** law **4** code, rule **5** canon, edict, order **6** decree **7** precept, statute **8** regiment **9** ordinance **11** requirement **12** codification

REGULATOR: **5** valve **6** switch **7** manager **8** director, governor **10** thermostat

REHABILITATE: **7** improve, recover, restore **8** renovate **9** reinstate **11** recondition

REHASH: **6** repeat **9** reiterate, summarize

REHEARSE: **4** test **5** drill, study, train **6** detail, recite, repeat, retell, review **7** narrate, prepare, recount, reenact **8** describe, exercise, instruct, practice **9** enumerate **12** recapitulate

REHOBOAM:
father: **7** Solomon
kingdom: **5** Judah **6** Israel
mother: **6** Naamah
son: **6** Abijah

REIGN: **4** rule **5** power **6** empire, govern, regime **7** command, control, kingdom, prevail **8** dominate, dominion, monarchy **9** authority, dominance, influence **11** predominate, sovereignty

REIMBURSE: **3** pay **5** repay **6** offset, recoup, refund, return **7** recover **9** indemnify **10** compensate, recompense, remunerate

REIN: **4** curb, slow, stop, turn **5** check, guide, leash, strap **6** bridle **7** compose, control, harness, repress **8** restrain, suppress **9** deterrent

REINDEER: **7** caribou
Santa's: **5** Comet, Cupid, Vixen **6** Dancer, Dasher, Donner **7** Blitzen, Prancer, Rudolph

REINFORCE: **4** back, prop **5** brace, shore **6** pillar **7** augment, bolster, fortify, support, toughen **8** buttress, energize **10** strengthen, supplement

REINSTATE: **6** recall, rehire, revive **7** restore **11** reestablish, reinstitute **12** rehabilitate

REINTRODUCE: **5** renew **6** revive **11** reestablish, reinstitute

REITERATE: **4** harp **6** rehash, repeat, resume, stress **12** recapitulate

REJECT: **4** deny, jilt, snub, veto **5** eject, repel, scorn, scrap, spurn **6** adjure, cancel, refuse **7** cashier, decline, discard, disdain, dismiss, forsake **8** castaway, disallow, jettison, renounce **9** blackball, eliminate, ostracize, reprobate, repudiate

REJECTION: **6** denial **7** refusal **8** turndown **9** exclusion, ostracism **12** disallowance

REJOICE: **5** elate, enjoy, exult, glory **6** please, relish **7** delight, gladden, triumph **8** jubilate **9** celebrate

REJOIN: **5** reply **6** answer, retort **7** respond, reunite **8** assemble

REJUVENATE: **5** renew **6** revive **7** refresh, restore **10** regenerate, revitalize **11** recondition **12** reinvigorate

REKINDLE: **5** renew **6** revive **7** relight **10** revitalize

RELAPSE: **4** sink, slip **6** revert, weaken **7** decline, regress, setback **9** backslide **10** degenerate, recurrence **11** deteriorate

RELATE: **4** link, tell **5** apply, refer, speak, state, touch **6** belong, convey, detail, recite, report, reveal **7** connect, express, narrate, pertain, recount **8** describe, disclose **9** associate, correlate

RELATED: **4** akin **5** joint **6** mutual **7** cognate, germane, kindred **8** parallel **9** connected, pertinent **10** affiliated, associated, synonymous **11** intertwined **13** correspondent **14** interconnected

RELATION: **3** kin **4** bond **5** ratio **6** family **7** account, kinship, kinsman, sibling **8** affinity, relative **9** kinswoman, reference **10** connection **11** affiliation, association, correlation

RELATIONSHIP: **4** bond, link **5** blood **7** kinship, rapport **8** alliance, marriage **10** connection, friendship **11** affiliation, association, correlation

RELATIVE: **3** dad, kin, mom, son **4** aunt **5** niece, tribe, uncle **6** cousin, family, father, mother, nephew, parent, sister **7** brother, kindred, kinsman, sibling **8** ancestor, daughter, grandson, relation, relevant **9** connected, dependent, kinswoman, pertinent **10** associated, comparable, contingent, grandchild **11** comparative, correlative, grandfather, grandmother, grandparent **13** corresponding, granddaughter, proportionate

RELAX: **4** calm, ease, idle, rest **5** abate, loose, slack **6** divert, lessen, loosen, lounge, mellow, reduce, simmer, soften, unbend, unwind **7** recline, relieve, slacken **8** meditate, mitigate, unclench

RELAXATION: **4** ease, rest **5** hobby **6** repose **7** leisure **8** calmness, pleasure **9** amusement, diversion **10** recreation **11** tranquility **13** entertainment

RELAXED: **4** calm, soft **5** loose **6** casual **7** lenient **8** carefree, informal **9** easygoing, leisurely **11** comfortable

RELAY: **4** post, race **5** carry, shift **7** deliver, forward, station **8** transfer, transmit **11** communicate

RELEASE: **4** bail, emit, free, news, trip, undo, vent **5** clear, remit, story, untie, yield **6** acquit, exempt, loosen, pardon, parole, ransom, rescue, spring, unbind, uncork **7** absolve, commute, deliver, disband, freedom, manumit, publish, relieve, unchain, unleash **8** liberate, mitigate, unfasten **9** discharge, disengage, eliminate, exonerate, extricate **10** emancipate, relinquish **11** publication

RELEGATE: **4** shun **5** exile, expel **6** assign, banish, charge, commit, deport, remove **7** dismiss, entrust **8** classify **9** downgrade, ostracize

RELENT: **4** bend, ease, melt, wane **5** abate, yield **6** comply, soften **7** slacken, subside **8** dissolve, moderate **9** acquiesce

RELENTLESS: **4** hard **5** harsh, rigid, stern **6** fierce, severe, strict **7** adamant **8** rigorous **9** ferocious, incessant, merciless, tenacious, unbending **10** continuous, determined, inexorable, inflexible, persistent, unyielding **11** unstoppable

RELEVANT: **3** apt **6** timely **7** apropos, fitting, germane, related **8** apposite, material **9** allowable, connected, pertinent **10** admissible, applicable, associated, correlated **11** appropriate, significant

RELIABLE: **5** loyal, solid, sound **6** proven, stable **7** devoted **8** constant, faithful, verified **11** responsible

RELIANCE: **7** loyalty **8** credence, mainstay

RELIC: **4** ruin **5** token **8** artifact, heirloom, keepsake

RELIEF: **3** aid **4** cure, food, lift **5** break **6** remedy, succor **7** respite, support **8** antidote, breather **9** diversion **10** assistance **11** alleviation

RELIEVE: **3** sub **5** relax **6** exempt, rescue, soothe **7** absolve, dismiss **8** palliate **10** substitute

RELIGION: **5** creed **6** church, belief **8** theology **9** orthodoxy **11** affiliation **12** denomination, spirituality
major: **3** Zen **5** Islam **6** Taoism **7** Jainism, Judaism **8** Buddhism, Hinduism **12** Christianity, Confucianism **13** Protestantism

RELIGIOUS: **3** nun **4** monk **5** moral **6** sacred **7** ethical, staunch **8** priestly, reverent **9** believing, righteous **10** pontifical **11** theological **13** sanctimonious **14** ecclesiastical

RELINQUISH: **6** vacate **7** release

RELISH: **4** love, wish **5** fancy, spice **6** desire **7** stomach **8** pleasure **9** condiment **10** appreciate

RELUCTANT: **4** wary **6** afraid **7** uneager **8** cautious

RELY: **4** bank, hope, lean, rest **5** count, trust **6** depend, expect, reckon **7** believe, confide, entrust

REMAIN: **4** bide, last, rest, stay, wait **5** abide, dwell, pause, stand, tarry **6** endure, linger, reside **7** outlast, persist, prevail, survive **8** continue

REMAINDER: **4** rest **5** scrap **6** excess **7** balance, remains, remnant, residue, surplus **8** leavings, leftover, residual, residuum, wreckage

REMAINS: **4** body, dust **5** ashes, ruins **6** corpse, debris, relics **7** cadaver, carcass, fossils, residue

REMARK: **3** say, see **4** barb, note, word **5** state **6** notice, regard, saying **7** comment, express, mention, observe, opinion **8** comeback, perceive **9** statement, wisecrack **10** animadvert, annotation, commentary, expression **11** observation

REMARKABLE: **6** signal, unique **7** notable, strange, unusual **8** smashing, striking, uncommon **9** momentous, wonderful **10** impressive, miraculous, noteworthy, noticeable, phenomenal **11** exceptional, outstanding **13** extraordinary

REMEDIAL: **7** healing **8** curative **9** antidotal, medicinal, remedying **10** corrective **11** reformative, restorative, therapeutic

REMEDY: **4** cure, drug, heal, help, herb, mend, pill **5** amend, right, salve **6** relief, repair **7** correct, cureall, nostrum, panacea, placebo, rectify, redress, relieve **8** antidote, curative, medicine, solution **9** alleviate, medicinal, treatment **10** assistance, corrective, medication

REMEMBER: **6** recall, record, remind, reward **7** bethink, mention **8** memorize, treasure **9** recognize, recollect, reminisce **11** commemorate

REMEMBRANCE: **4** gift **5** relic, token **6** memory, recall, trophy **7** memento, mention **8** keepsake, memorial, reminder, souvenir **11** testimonial **12** recollection, reminiscence

REMIND: **4** hint **5** alert, nudge **6** prompt, recall, stress **7** caution, suggest **9** emphasize

REMINDER: **4** hint, memo, note, prod, sign **5** relic, token **6** string **7** memento, warning **8** keepsake, souvenir

REMINISCE: **4** mull **6** recall, revive **7** reflect **8** remember **9** recollect

REMINISCENT: **9** nostalgic, remindful **12** recollective **13** retrospective

REMISS: **4** idle, lazy **5** slack, tardy **6** sloppy **7** laggard, languid, relaxed **8** careless, derelict, dilatory, heedless, inactive, indolent, slothful **9** forgetful, negligent, unmindful **10** delinquent, neglectful **11** inattentive, indifferent, thoughtless **13** irresponsible

REMISSION: **4** lull **5** break, pause **6** pardon, relief **7** release **9** abatement, cessation, lessening **10** absolution, diminution, subsidence **11** forgiveness

REMIT: **4** free, mail, send, ship, stop **5** abate, defer, relax, route, spend **6** cancel, desist, excuse, pardon, resign, return, shelve, submit **7** abandon, absolve, forgive, release, restore, slacken, suspend **8** abrogate, liberate, mitigate, moderate, postpone, transmit **9** surrender **10** compensate

REMNANT: **4** dreg, part, stub **5** crumb, piece, relic, scrap, shred, trace **7** balance, portion, remains, residue, vestige **8** fragment, leftover, residual **9** remainder

REMODEL: **6** change, revamp **7** rebuild **8** renovate **9** refurbish **11** recondition, reconstruct

REMONSTRANCE: **5** demur **6** rebuke **7** protest **8** reproach **9** challenge, complaint, objection

REMONSTRATE: **5** argue, fight **6** combat, object, oppose **7** dispute, profess, protest **8** complain, reproach **9** challenge, criticize **11** expostulate

REMORSE: **3** rue **5** grief, guilt, shame **6** regret, sorrow **7** anguish, penance **9** penitence **10** compassion, contrition **11** compunction

REMORSEFUL: **6** guilty **7** ashamed **8** contrite **9** regretful, repentant, sorrowful **10** apologetic

REMOTE: **3** far, off, old **4** afar, cold, cool, slim **5** alien, faint, small, vague **6** slight **7** distant, faraway, foreign, obscure, removed, slender **8** detached, isolated, secluded, separate, unlikely **9** unrelated, unsettled, withdrawn **10** improbable **12** inaccessible

REMOVE: **4** doff, fire, free, kill, move, oust, sack, void, weed **5** bench, erase, evict, expel, purge, strip **6** cancel, deduct, delete, depose, murder, retire, unseat, uproot **7** dismiss, extract, uncover **8** amputate, dislodge, displace, separate, transfer, withdraw **9** eliminate, eradicate **10** disconnect **11** assassinate, exterminate

REMOVED: **4** away **5** alone, aloof, apart **6** remote **7** distant, faraway, obscure **8** detached, isolated, separate **9** withdrawn

REMUNERATE: **3** pay **5** award **6** reward, settle **9** indemnify, reimburse, vouchsafe **10** compensate, recompense

REMUNERATION: **5** wages **6** bounty **7** payment, stipend **8** requital **9** emolument **10** commission, honorarium **12** compensation, satisfaction **13** gratification, reimbursement

REMUNERATIVE: **6** useful **7** gainful **9** lucrative **10** beneficial, profitable **12** advantageous

REMUS:
father: **4** Mars
killer: **7** Romulus
mother: **10** Rhea Silvia
twin brother: **7** Romulus

RENAISSANCE: **7** rebirth, revival **11** reawakening, reemergence **14** reconstruction

REND: **3** cut, rip **4** pull, rive, slit, tear **5** break, crack, sever, split, wrest **6** cleave, divide, mangle, pierce, sunder **7** disrupt, disturb, rupture, shatter **8** fracture, lacerate, separate **12** disintegrate

RENDER: **3** pay **4** give, make, show **5** grant, treat, yield **6** depict, return, submit **7** deliver, explain, furnish, inflict, payment, perform, portray, present, provide, restore **9** interpret, represent, translate **10** administer, contribute, relinquish

RENDEZVOUS: **4** date, meet **5** haunt, tryst **6** affair, gather, muster **7** hangout, retreat **8** assemble **9** gathering **10** engagement **11** appointment

RENDITION: **7** edition, version **8** delivery **9** depiction, portrayal **11** explanation, performance, translation **14** interpretation

RENEGADE: **5** rebel **6** outlaw **7** heretic, radical, traitor **8** apostate, deserter, fugitive, mutineer, recreant, turncoat **9** insurgent

RENEGE: **5** welsh **6** disown, revoke **7** decline **8** renounce, withdraw

RENEW: **6** extend, repair, repeat, resume, revamp, revive, update **7** freshen, rebuild, refresh, replace, restore **8** continue, maintain, renovate **9** modernize, replenish, stimulate **10** invigorate, regenerate, rejuvenate, revitalize **11** reestablish, resuscitate

RENOUNCE: **4** deny, quit **5** cease, forgo, waive **6** abjure, defect, desert, disown, forego, recant, reject, renege, repeal, resign **7** abandon, disavow, discard, forsake, retract **8** abdicate, abnegate, disclaim **9** repudiate, surrender **10** relinquish

RENOVATE: **4** redo **5** renew **6** repair, resume, revamp, revive, update **7** cleanse, furbish, refresh, restore **8** overhaul **9** modernize, refurbish **10** invigorate, redecorate **11** recondition

RENOWN: **4** fame, note **5** eclat, honor, kudos **6** status **7** acclaim **8** eminence, prestige **9** celebrity, notoriety **10** popularity, prominence, reputation **11** distinction

RENOWNED: **5** famed, great, known, noted **6** famous **7** notable **8** esteemed **9** prominent **10** celebrated **11** illustrious

RENT: **4** dues, gape, hire, hole, toll **5** cleft, crack, gorge, lease, share, split, yield **6** breach, income, profit, schism, sublet **7** fissure, opening, payment, revenue, rupture **8** division, fracture, sublease

RENUNCIATION: **6** denial **8** forgoing **9** eschewing, rejection **10** abjurement, disclaimer **11** abandonment, forswearing

REOPEN: **6** resume, revive **7** restart **9** reconvene **10** recommence **11** reinstitute

REORGANIZE: **7** rebuild **8** readjust **9** rearrange **10** regenerate **11** reconstruct

REPAIR: **3** fix **4** darn, heal, mend **5** patch, refit, renew **6** doctor, remedy, retire, revamp, revive, travel **7** correct, improve, journey, rebuild, restore, retread, service **8** overhaul, renovate

REPARATION: **6** amends, reward **7** damages, redress **8** requital **9** atonement, expiation, indemnity, repairing **10** recompense, settlement **11** restitution, retribution **12** compensation, remuneration, satisfaction

REPARTEE: **3** wit **5** humor, irony, reply **6** answer, banter, retort, satire **7** sarcasm **8** comeback

REPAST: **4** feed, food, meal **5** feast, snack, treat **6** dinner, eating, viands **7** banquet **8** victuals **11** refreshment

REPAY: **5** award **6** avenge, offset, refund, return, reward, square **7** balance, requite, restore **9** indemnify, reimburse, retaliate **10** compensate, recompense, remunerate **11** reciprocate

REPEAL: **4** lift, void **5** amend, annul, scrub **6** cancel, recall, revoke **7** abolish, nullify, rescind, retract, reverse **8** abrogate, renounce, withdraw **10** invalidate, revocation **11** countermand

REPEAT: **4** echo, harp **5** ditto, mimic, quote, recap, recur **6** parrot, recite, replay, resume, retell **7** iterate, recount, restate **9** duplicate, reiterate, reshowing **10** repetition **12** recapitulate

REPEATEDLY: **5** again, often **9** regularly **10** frequently **11** continually **12** continuously

REPEL: **4** beat, stop **5** check, spurn **6** combat, defend, offend, oppose, rebuff, refuse, reject, resist, sicken **7** decline, deflect, disgust, repulse, scatter **8** nauseate

REPELLENT: **4** foul **7** hateful, pugnant **9** loathsome, offensive, repulsive, revolting, sickening **10** nauseating

REPENT: **3** rue **5** atone **6** grieve, lament, reform, regret **7** deplore **8** penitent **9** apologize

REPENTANCE: **4** ruth **5** grief, guilt **6** sorrow **7** penance, remorse **9** atonement, attrition, penitence **10** contrition **11** compunction

REPENTANT: **5** sorry **6** rueful **8** contrite, penitent **9** regretful **10** remorseful

REPERCUSSION: **4** echo, flak **6** action, effect, impact, recoil, result **7** fallout, rebound **8** backlash **10** reflection **11** consequence **13** reverberation

REPETITION: **4** copy, echo, rote **6** repeat **7** recital **8** iterance, practice **9** iteration, rehearsal **10** recurrence, redundancy **11** duplication **12** reproduction

REPETITIOUS: **4** dull **5** wordy **6** boring **7** tedious **9** redundant

REPINE: **4** fret, moan, mope, wish **5** mourn, yearn **6** lament, regret **7** grumble, whimper **8** complain, languish

REPLACE: **4** oust **5** alter, renew, repay, reset **6** change, refund **7** relieve, restock, restore, succeed **8** supplant **9** reimburse, replenish, restitute, supersede **10** substitute

REPLENISH: **4** fill **5** renew, stock **6** refill, reload, supply **7** freshen, refresh, restock, restore

REPLETE: **4** full, rift **6** filled, gorged **7** bloated, glutted, stocked, stuffed **8** abundant, brimming, complete, satiated **9** abounding, surfeited

REPLICA: **4** copy **5** model **6** carbon **8** likeness **9** duplicate, facsimile **12** reproduction

REPLY: **5** rebut **6** answer, rejoin, repeat, retort, return **7** counter, respond **8** comeback, feedback, reaction, repartee, response, solution **9** rejoinder **10** correspond **11** replication

REPORT: **4** news, tell, word **5** brief, noise, rumor, state, story **6** advice, detail, digest, notice, recite, record, relate, tattle **7** account, article, comment, crackle, hearing, hearsay, message, narrate, recital, release, summary **8** announce, bulletin, describe, disclose, document **9** grapevine, narrative, statement **10** reputation **11** information

REPORTER: **8** stringer **9** newshound **10** newsperson **11** commentator **12** anchorperson

REPOSE: **3** ret **4** calm, ease, loaf **5** peace, quiet, sleep **6** lounge **7** comfort, compose, leisure, recline **8** calmness, serenity **9** quietness **10** inactivity, relaxation **12** requiescence, tranquillity

REPOSITORY: **4** file, safe, tomb **5** chest, depot, vault **6** closet, museum **7** capsule **8** magazine, treasury **9** warehouse **10** depository, storehouse

REPROACH: **4** blot, slur **5** abuse, blame, braid, chide, shame, taunt **6** rebuke, revile, vilify **7** censure, condemn, reprove, upbraid **8** admonish, besmirch, contempt, denounce, disgrace, dishonor **9** criticize, discredit, disrepute, reprimand **10** stigmatize **11** degradation

REPREHEND: **5** chide, scold **6** berate, rebuke **7** censure, reprove **8** admonish, denounce, disprove **9** criticize, reprimand

REPREHENSIBLE: **4** base, foul **6** sinful **7** heinous **8** blamable, criminal, culpable, shameful **11** condemnable, inexcusable

REPRESENT: **4** limn, mean, show **5** enact, image **6** denote, depict, embody, typify **7** exhibit, express, picture, portray, produce, signify **8** describe, simulate **9** delineate, epitomize, exemplify, interpret, personify, symbolize **10** illustrate **12** characterize

REPRESENTATION: **3** map **4** icon **5** chart, graph, image, model **6** effigy, sample, sketch, symbol **7** account, diagram, picture, protest **8** likeness **9** portrayal, statement **10** delegation, embodiment **12** illustration

REPRESENTATIVE: **5** agent, envoy, proxy **6** consul, deputy, legate, sample **7** attache, example, senator, typical **8** delegate, diplomat, emissary, executor, symbolic **9** messenger **10** ambassador, legislator, substitute **11** congressman **12** illustrative, spokesperson **13** congresswoman

REPRESS: **4** bury, curb, hush, mask, rein, stop **5** check, cover, crush, quell **6** bridle, muffle, squash, stifle, subdue **7** compose, conceal, control, inhibit, squelch **8** restrain, suppress, withhold **9** constrain, overpower

REPRESSION: **7** control **9** restraint **10** constraint, inhibition, smothering **11** suppression

REPRIEVE: **4** stay **5** defer, delay **6** pardon, relief **7** absolve, amnesty, respite, suspend **8** breather, clemency, postpone

REPRIMAND: **5** chide, scold **6** berate, punish, rebuff, rebuke **7** censure, chasten, lecture, reprove **8** admonish, chastise, reproach **9** castigate, criticize, reprehend **10** discipline

REPRISAL: **7** revenge **8** requital **11** counterblow, retaliation, retribution

REPROBATE: **4** evil **5** scamp, spurn **6** rascal, sinful, sinner **7** abandon, corrupt, immoral, vicious **8** blamable, castaway, denounce, depraved **9** blameable, condemned, criticize, miscreant, reprehend, scoundrel **11** disapproved **12** unprincipled **13** reprehensible

REPRODUCE: **4** copy **5** breed, clone, spawn **6** repeat **7** imitate **8** generate, multiply **9** duplicate, procreate, propagate, represent **11** proliferate

REPRODUCTION: **4** copy **7** replica **8** likeness **9** duplicate, facsimile, photostat **11** counterpart, procreation, propagation **13** proliferation

REPROOF: **5** blame **6** rebuke **8** reproach, scolding **9** reprimand **10** admonition **11** disapproval

REPROVE: **5** blame, chide, scold, shame **6** berate, rebuff, rebuke, refute **7** censure, condemn, upbraid **8** admonish, chastise, disprove, lambaste, reproach **9** castigate, criticize, reprehend, reprimand, reprobate

REPTILE: **4** frog, newt, toad, worm **5** knave, snake **6** iguana, lizard, turtle **7** creeper **8** dinosaur, tortoise **9** alligator, amphibian, crocodile **10** salamander

REPUBLIC: **5** state **6** nation **9** democracy **12** commonwealth

REPUBLIC, THE:
author: **5** Plato

REPUDIATE: **4** deny, void **5** annul, spurn **6** abjure, banish, cancel, disown, recant, refuse, reject, revoke **7** abandon, disavow, discard, forsake, retract **8** abrogate, disclaim, renounce **10** disinherit

REPUGNANCE: **5** odium **6** hatred **7** disgust, dislike **8** aversion, distaste, loathing **9** antipathy, hostility, repulsion, revulsion **10** abhorrence, antagonism, opposition **11** abomination, detestation **13** inconsistency

REPUGNANT: **4** foul, vile **5** nasty **6** horrid **9** obnoxious, offensive, repulsive, revolting, sickening **10** abominable, disgusting, unpleasant **12** disagreeable

REPULSE: **4** deny, snub **5** repel, spurn **6** defeat, rebuff, refuse, reject, revolt, sicken **7** disdain, disgust **8** nauseate **9** rejection

REPULSIVE: **4** foul, ugly, vile **5** nasty **6** odious **7** fulsome, hateful **9** abhorrent, offensive, repellent, repugnant, revolting, sickening **10** detestable, disgusting, nauseating, unpleasant **11** distasteful

REPUTABLE: **6** famous **7** notable **9** acclaimed, honorable **10** celebrated, creditable **11** respectable **13** distinguished

REPUTATION: **4** fame, name **5** eclat, glory, honor **6** credit, renown, repute **7** respect, stature **8** prestige, standing **9** character, notoriety **10** prominence **11** distinction **14** respectability

REPUTED: **7** assumed **8** believed, putative, regarded, supposed **10** considered **12** hypothetical

REQUEST: **3** ask, sue **4** pray, suit, wish **5** apply, offer, order **6** appeal, demand, invite **7** entreat, inquiry, solicit **8** petition **10** invitation, supplicate

REQUIEM: **4** hymn, mass, song **5** chant, dirge **7** service **8** threnody **11** composition

REQUIRE: **3** ask, bid **4** lack, need, want **5** claim, crave, exact, force, order **6** compel, demand, desire, expect, oblige **11** necessitate

REQUIRED: **6** forced, needed **9** essential, mandatory, necessary, requisite **10** compulsory, imperative

REQUIREMENT: **4** must **5** terms **9** condition, criterion, essential, formality, necessity **11** fulfillment **12** prerequisite

REQUISITE: **4** must, need **6** needed **8** required **9** condition, essential, necessity **12** precondition **13** indispensable

REQUISITION: **4** call, form **5** claim, order **6** demand **7** request **9** postulate **11** application

REQUITAL: **7** redress, revenge **8** reprisal **9** vengeance **11** retaliation, retribution

REQUITE: **5** atone, repay **6** avenge, return, reward **7** revenge, satisfy **9** indemnify, reimburse, retaliate **10** compensate, recompense **11** reciprocate

RESCIND: **4** lift, void **5** annul **6** cancel, renege, repeal, revoke **7** abolish, nullify, retract, reverse **10** invalidate **11** countermand

RESCUE: **4** free, help, save **6** ransom, redeem **7** deliver, release, salvage **8** liberate, recovery, retrieve **9** extricate **10** redemption **11** deliverance

RESEARCH: **5** probe, study **7** delving, inquiry **8** analysis **10** experiment **11** examination **13** investigation

RESEMBLANCE: **6** simile **7** analogy **8** affinity, likeness, parallel **9** closeness **10** comparison, similarity, similitude **11** counterpart **14** correspondence

RESEMBLE: **4** like **5** favor, match **6** mirror **7** similar **8** parallel, simulate

RESENT: **7** dislike **8** begrudge

RESENTFUL: **5** angry **6** bitter **7** envious, jealous

RESENTMENT: **4** hate **5** anger, pique, spite **6** animus, choler, grudge, hatred, malice, rancor **7** umbrage **8** acrimony **9** animosity, hostility, malignity **10** bitterness **11** displeasure, indignation

RESERVATION: **5** doubt, terms **7** booking, proviso **9** condition, provision, sanctuary, territory **11** stipulation

RESERVE: **4** book, hold, keep, save **5** spare, stock, store **6** assets, retain, supply **7** backlog, caution, modesty, savings, shyness, surplus **8** coldness, conserve, preserve, withhold **9** alternate, exception, reservoir, resources, reticence **10** discretion, substitute

RESERVED: **3** shy **4** cold **5** aloof **6** modest, sedate, silent **7** bashful, distant **8** backward, cautious, reticent **9** collected, inhibited, qualified, withdrawn **10** unsociable **11** constrained

RESERVOIR: **4** lake, pond, pool, tank **5** basin, store **6** source, supply **7** reserve **8** fountain **9** container, inventory, stockpile **10** repository

RESIDE: **4** live, room, stay **5** abide, dwell, exist, habit, lodge **6** endure, occupy, remain, settle **7** habitat, inhabit **8** domicile

RESIDENCE: **4** digs, home **5** abode, house, villa **6** castle, palace **7** habitat, lodging, mansion **8** domicile, dwelling **9** apartment, household, occupancy **10** habitation **11** condominium

RESIDENT: **6** lessee, native, tenant **7** citizen, denizen, dweller **8** habitant, occupant **10** inhabitant

RESIDUAL: **5** extra **7** surplus **8** leftover **9** remainder, remaining

RESIDUE: **4** silt, slag **5** ashes, waste **6** cinder, debris, excess, relics, scraps, sludge, sordes **7** balance, remains, remnant **8** leavings, residuum, sediment **9** remainder

RESIGN: **4** quit **5** demit, yield **6** submit, vacate **7** abandon, forsake **8** abdicate, renounce, withdraw **9** surrender **10** relinquish

RESIGNATION: **6** notice **7** modesty **8** patience **9** departure, endurance **10** submission, withdrawal

RESIGNED: **4** calm **6** gentle **7** passive, subdued **8** yielding **9** compliant **10** submissive

RESILIENT: **5** hardy, tough **6** strong **7** buoyant, elastic, springy **8** flexible, stretchy **9** adaptable, resistant **10** rebounding

RESIN: **3** gum, tar **4** aloe, balm, tolu **5** amber, copal, epoxy, myrrh, pitch, rosin, syrup **6** balsam **7** acrylic, ambrite **8** olibanum **9** colophony **12** frankincense

RESIST: **4** buck, defy, fend **5** rebel, repel **6** combat, defend, endure, impugn, oppose, refuse, thwart, wither **7** contest, dispute, prevent **8** obstruct, traverse **9** frustrate, withstand

RESISTANCE: **5** fight **6** rebuff **7** defense **8** defiance, movement, struggle **9** rebellion **10** opposition

RESOLUTE: **4** firm **5** fixed, loyal **6** ardent **7** adamant, staunch **8** faithful, resolved, stalwart, stubborn **9** obstinate, unbending, undaunted **10** determined, persistent, unflagging, unwavering

RESOLUTION: **4** goal, grit, will **5** heart, nerve, spunk **6** answer, intent, mettle, spirit **7** courage, purpose, resolve, verdict **8** backbone, decision, firmness, judgment, proposal, solution, strength, tenacity **9** fortitude, hardihood, objective, stoutness **10** conviction, resilience **11** decidedness **12** perseverance, resoluteness **13** determination, steadfastness

RESOLVE: **5** clear, solve **6** answer, change, decide, dispel, remove, settle, unfold **7** analyze, dispose, explain, unravel **8** conclude, decision, dissolve, separate **9** breakdown, determine, intention, willpower **10** conclusion, resolution

RESONANT: **4** deep, full, loud, rich **6** rotund **7** booming, echoing, ringing, vibrant **8** enhanced, powerful, profound, sonorous **9** bellowing **10** resounding, thunderous **11** intensified, reverberant

RESORT: **3** inn, spa **4** turn **5** apply, haunt, hotel, lodge, refer, visit **6** direct, refuge, repair **7** retreat, utilize **10** substitute **11** alternative

RESOUND: **4** echo, ring **5** clang, extol **6** praise **9** celebrate **11** reverberate

RESOUNDING: **7** vibrant **8** emphatic, forceful **10** thunderous

RESOURCE: **6** device, supply, wealth **7** ability, capital, reserve, stopgap **9** expedient

RESOURCEFUL: **3** apt **5** sharp **6** artful, clever **7** capable **8** creative, talented **9** ingenious **10** innovative **11** imaginative **12** enterprising

RESOURCES: **5** funds, means, money **6** assets, riches, wealth **7** capital, revenue, savings **8** property, reserves **11** possessions

RESPECT: **5** honor, value **6** admire, esteem, homage, regard, revere **7** concern, dignity, observe, tribute, worship **8** venerate **9** adoration, attention, reverence **10** admiration **11** recognition

RESPECTABLE: **4** good **6** decent, honest, proper, worthy **7** upright **8** adequate, becoming, decorous **9** admirable, honorable, reputable **10** aboveboard, sufficient **11** appropriate, presentable

RESPECTFUL: **5** civil **6** polite **7** dutiful **8** gracious, mannerly **9** courteous, upholding **11** considerate

RESPIRATION: **7** process **9** breathing **10** exhalation, inhalation

RESPIRE: **6** exhale, inhale **7** breathe, oxidate

RESPITE: **4** lull, rest, stay **5** break, delay, pause **6** recess **7** leisure **8** breather, reprieve **9** cessation, deferment **10** suspension **12** intermission

RESPLENDENT: **5** shiny **6** bright **7** blazing, glowing, radiant, shining **8** dazzling, glorious, lustrous, splendid **9** brilliant, refulgent **10** glittering **11** magnificent

RESPOND: **4** feel **5** react, reply, write **6** answer, behave, rejoin, retort, return **8** response **10** correspond **11** acknowledge

RESPONSE: **5** reply **6** answer, retort **7** respond **8** comeback, reaction

RESPONSIBILITY: **4** care, duty, onus **5** blame, fault **6** burden, charge, sphere **8** capacity, function **9** authority, liability **10** obligation **14** accountability

RESPONSIBLE: **6** liable, mature **8** amenable, reliable, sensible **9** reputable **10** answerable, dependable **11** accountable, levelheaded, trustworthy

RESPONSIVE: **4** warm **6** active **9** receptive, sensitive **11** kindhearted, sympathetic **13** compassionate

RES PUBLICA: **5** state **8** republic **12** commonwealth

REST: **3** lay, lie, nap, set, sit **4** base, calm, doze, ease, hang, lean, loll, lull, prop, rely, seat, stay, stop **5** hinge, pause, peace, quiet, relax, sleep, spell, stand **6** depend, desist, lounge, recess, retire, settle, siesta, unwind **7** balance, caesura, holiday, leisure, recline, refresh, remains, remnant, residue, respite, slumber, support, surplus **8** breather, interval, vacation **9** cessation, interlude, leftovers, remainder, stillness **10** foundation, inactivity, relaxation **11** hibernation, refreshment, tranquility **12** intermission

RESTAURANT: **3** inn **4** cafe **5** diner **6** bistro, eatery, tavern **7** automat, beanery, canteen, tearoom **8** barbecue, pizzeria **9** brasserie, cafeteria, chophouse, hashhouse **10** rotisserie, steakhouse **11** porterhouse, rathskeller **12** luncheonette

RESTFUL: **4** calm **5** quiet **6** serene **7** relaxed **8** peaceful, soothing, tranquil **9** reposeful **11** comfortable

RESTITUTION: **6** amends **7** redress **9** atonement, indemnity, repayment **10** recompense, reparation **11** restoration **12** compensation **13** reimbursement

RESTIVE: **4** edgy **5** balky, jumpy, tense **6** ornery, uneasy, unruly **7** fidgety, nervous, uptight **8** contrary, restless, stubborn **9** impatient **10** unyielding

RESTLESS: **7** anxious, worried

RESTORATION: **7** healing, revival **10** remodeling, renovation, reparation **11** restitution **14** rehabilitation

RESTORATIVE: **5** tonic **6** remedy **7** curable, healing **9** medicinal **10** corrective **11** therapeutic

RESTORE: **4** cure, heal, mend, save **5** renew, repay, right **6** redeem, remedy, repair, return, revive, update **7** rebuild, recover, rectify, refresh, replace **8** renovate **9** refurbish, reinstate **10** regenerate, revitalize **11** recondition, reconstruct, resuscitate **12** rehabilitate

RESTRAIN: **3** bar, dam, gag **4** bind, clog, cool, curb, hold, jail, rein, rule, stay, stem, stop **5** chain, check, cramp, deter, leash **6** arrest, bridle, detain, fetter, govern, halter, hamper, hinder, impede, muzzle, pinion, tether **7** abridge, abstain, command, confine, contain, control, curtail, harness, inhibit, prevent, repress, shackle, trammel **8** imprison, prohibit, regulate, restrict, suppress, withhold **9** constrain **12** circumscribe

RESTRAINED: **4** calm, tied **5** quiet **7** subdued **8** discreet, reserved **9** withdrawn **10** controlled

RESTRAINT: **7** control, embargo **10** abridgment, abstinence, constraint, limitation, moderation **11** confinement

RESTRICT: **3** bar, tie **4** bind, curb **5** bound, cramp, limit **6** hamper, impede, ration **7** confine, repress **8** contract, prohibit, restrain, straiten **9** construct **12** circumscribe

RESTRICTION: **4** rule **5** check, cramp, limit **9** condition, restraint **10** limitation, regulation **11** confinement, stipulation

RESULT: **3** end, sum **4** rise, stem **5** arise, ensue, score, total **6** answer, effect, finish, follow, happen, sequel **7** finding, opinion, outcome, proceed, product **8** conclude, decision, judgment **9** aftermath **10** conclusion, resolution **11** consequence

RESUME: **5** renew **6** regain, reopen, review **7** epitome, proceed, recover, restart, summary **8** continue, synopsis **9** biography, summarize **10** recommence **14** recapitulation

RESURGENCE: **7** rebirth, renewal, revival

RESURRECTION: **7** rebirth, revival **11** restoration **14** transformation

RESUSCITATE: **4** save **6** revive **7** restore **9** resurrect

RETAIL: **4** hawk, sell **5** trade **6** barter, market, peddle **8** dispense **10** distribute

RETAIN: **4** have, hire, hold, keep, save **5** grasp **6** absorb, employ **7** contain, possess, reserve **8** maintain, memorize, preserve, remember, restrain, withhold **9** recollect **10** commission

RETAINER: **3** fee **6** minion **7** servant **8** employee **9** appliance, attendant

RETALIATE: **5** repay **6** avenge, return, settle **7** counter, requite, revenge **11** reciprocate

RETALIATION: **8** reprisal, requital **9** vengeance **11** retribution

RETARD: **4** clog, slow **5** brake, delay, stunt **6** baffle, fetter, hamper, hinder, impede **7** inhibit, prevent **8** obstruct **10** decelerate

RETENTION: **6** memory, recall **7** holding, keeping **11** recognition, remembering **12** recollection

RETICENT: **5** quiet **6** silent **7** subdued **8** discreet, reserved, retiring **9** reluctant, secretive, unwilling, withdrawn **10** restrained

RETINUE: **4** band, crew **5** harem, staff, suite, train **6** escort **7** cortege, service **9** entourage, following, personnel, retainers **10** attendants, procession

RETIRE: **4** exit, quit, rest **5** leave, sleep **6** depart, recede, resign, vacate **7** pension, retreat **8** withdraw

RETIRING: **3** shy **4** meek **5** demur, quiet, timid **6** modest **7** bashful **8** reserved, reticent **9** diffident, withdrawn **10** unassuming **11** unassertive

RETORT: **4** quip **5** crack, rebut, repay, reply **6** answer, return **7** counter, respond **8** comeback, repartee, reprisal, response **9** retaliate

RETRACT: **4** back, deny **6** abjure, cancel, disown, recall, recant, remove, renege, repeal, revoke **7** disavow, rescind, retreat, reverse **8** renounce, withdraw **9** repudiate

RETREAT: **4** back, bolt, flee, lair, port **5** haven, leave **6** asylum, escape, harbor, recede, recess, refuge, resort, retire, shrink **7** abandon, getaway, privacy, shelter **8** hightail, solitude **9** departure, sanctuary, seclusion **10** evacuation, withdrawal

RETRENCH: **4** omit, save **5** slash **6** delete, lessen, reduce, remove **7** abridge, curtail, shorten **8** decrease, diminish **9** economize, eliminate

RETRIBUTION: **6** return, reward **7** justice, payback, revenge **8** reprisal, requital **9** vengeance **10** punishment, recompense **11** retaliation **12** compensation

RETRIEVE: **4** save **5** fetch **6** recall, recoup, regain, rescue, revive **7** reclaim, recover, restore, salvage **8** remember **10** recuperate

RETROGRADE: **4** sink, slip **5** lapse **6** recede, revert, worsen **7** decline, inverse, regress **8** backward, contrary, inverted, reversed **9** backslide, catabolic **10** degenerate, retrogress **11** deteriorate

RETROGRESS: **6** revert, worsen **9** backslide **10** degenerate, retrograde

RETROSPECT: **6** review **8** remember **9** flashback **11** contemplate **12** afterthought, recollection, reminiscence

RETROSPECTIVE: **6** review **8** backward **11** remembrance, retroactive

RETURN: **4** gain **5** gross, recur, repay, reply, yield **6** advert, answer, coming, income, profit, rejoin, render, report, retort, revert **7** recover, reprise, respond, restore, revenue, reverse, revisit, summary **8** comeback, earnings, reappear, requital, response **9** reinstate, repayment, retaliate, statement **10** recompense, recrudesce, recurrence **11** reciprocate, restoration **12** reappearance

REUBEN:
brothers: **4** Levi **5** Asher **6** Joseph **8** Benjamin
father: **5** Jacob
mother: **4** Leah

REUNITE: **6** rejoin **9** reconcile, reconvene

REVAMP: **5** renew **6** repair **8** renovate **9** replenish **10** rejuvenate **11** recondition, reconstruct

REVEAL: **4** bare, blab, leak, open, show, tell **5** admit, spill **6** betray, expose, impart, squeal, unmask, unveil **7** confess, confide, declare, develop, display, divulge, exhibit, publish, uncover, unearth **8** announce, decipher, disclose, discover, manifest, proclaim **11** communicate

REVEL: **4** bask, romp, sign **5** enjoy, feast, gloat, spree **6** frolic, relish **7** carouse, delight, indulge, rejoice, roister, rollick, shocker, telling, whoopee **8** carnival, carousal, festival **9** bacchanal, celebrate, eyeopener, festivity **10** revelation **11** inspiration, merrymaking

REVELATION: **6** vision **8** prophecy **9** discovery **10** apocalypse, disclosure **13** manifestation

REVELER: **6** ranter **8** bacchant, carouser **9** roisterer **10** merrymaker

REVELRY: **7** jollity, whoopla **8** carousal **9** festivity, high jinks, merriment **11** celebration, merrymaking

REVENANT: **5** ghost, repay **6** settle, spirit **7** phantom, revenge, specter **8** reprisal **9** vengeance, vindicate **10** apparition

REVENGE: **6** avenge **8** requital **9** retaliate **11** retaliation, retribution

REVENUE: **5** gains, wages, yield **6** assets, income, profit, return, salary **8** earnings, interest, proceeds, receipts, taxation **12** compensation

REVERBERATE: **4** echo, ring **5** repel **7** rebound, reflect, resound, thunder, vibrate

REVERE: **4** love **5** adore, exalt, honor, value **6** admire, esteem **7**

cherish, idolize, respect, worship **8** treasure, venerate

REVERENCE: **3** awe **4** fear **5** honor, piety **6** homage, praise, regard **7** worship **8** devotion **9** deference, obeisance **10** admiration

REVEREND: **4** holy **6** clergy, divine, parson, priest, sacred **8** clerical, minister **9** clergyman, monsignor, venerable

REVERENT: **5** pious **6** devout, humble, solemn **7** dutiful **9** religious

REVERIE: **5** dream **6** musing, trance **7** fantasy, thought **8** daydream **10** meditation **11** abstraction **13** contemplation

REVERSE: **4** turn, undo **5** annul, shift, upset **6** cancel, change, defeat, invert, renege, repeal, revoke **7** counter, nullify, rescind, retract **8** backward, contrary, converse, disaster, exchange, opposite, overturn **9** backtrack, transpose, turnabout **10** antithesis, misfortune **11** countermand

REVERT: **4** turn, undo **5** lapse, react **6** return **7** recover, regress, reverse **9** backslide **10** retrograde, retrogress

REVIEW: **4** edit **5** audit, recap, study **6** parade, survey **7** analyze, brushup, journal, rethink **8** analysis, critique, magazine, reassess, revision, synopsis **9** criticism, criticize, summarize **10** assessment, evaluation, inspection, periodical, reconsider, reevaluate, retrospect **11** examination **12** recapitulate

REVILE: **4** hate, slur **5** abuse, libel, scold **6** berate, debase, malign, vilify **7** slander, upbraid **8** belittle, reproach **9** blaspheme, castigate, criticize

REVISE: **4** edit, redo **5** alter, amend, emend **6** change, modify, reform, revamp, update **7** correct, improve, redraft, rewrite, upgrade

REVISION: **6** change **9** amendment, rewriting **10** alteration, correction

REVIVAL: **7** rebirth, renewal **10** resurgence **11** reawakening, renaissance **12** invigoration, rejuvenation, resurrection

REVIVE: **4** wake **5** rally, renew **6** arouse, return **7** enliven, freshen, recover, restore **8** energize, reawaken, rekindle, remember, revivify **9** galvanize, reanimate, refreshen, resurrect, stimulate **10** invigorate, recuperate, regenerate, rejuvenate **11** resuscitate **12** reinvigorate

REVOKE: **4** lift, void **5** annul, check, erase **6** abjure, cancel, recall, recant, renege, repeal **7** abolish, nullify, rescind, retract, reverse **8** abrogate, disclaim, renounce, restrain, withdraw **10** invalidate **11** countermand

REVOLT: **4** coup, riot **5** rebel, repel **6** mutiny, offend, resist **7** boycott, disgust, repulse **8** nauseate, renounce, sedition, uprising **9** rebellion **10** opposition, revolution **12** insurrection

REVOLTING: **4** ugly, vile **5** awful, gross, nasty **7** hideous **8** horrible, shocking **9** appalling, loathsome, offensive, repugnant, repulsive, sickening **10** disgusting, nauseating

REVOLUTION: **4** gyre, turn **5** cycle **6** revolt, unrest **7** circuit **8** gyration, outbreak, rotation, uprising **9** bloodshed, overthrow, rebellion **12** insurrection

REVOLUTIONARY: **7** fanatic, radical **9** extremist, insurgent **10** rebellious

REVOLVE: **4** roll, spin, turn **5** orbit, swing, twirl, wheel, whirl **6** circle, gyrate, ponder, rotate **7** reflect **8** consider, meditate, ruminate **10** deliberate

REVOLVER: **3** gun **4** Colt **5** Dewey **6** pistol, weapon **7** firearm, handgun

REVULSION: **4** hate **8** aversion, distaste, loathing **9** repulsion **10** abhorrence, repugnance, withdrawal **11** abomination, detestation

REWARD: **4** gift, meed, plum **5** award, bonus, crown, fruit, honor, medal, merit, perks, prize, repay, wages **6** bounty, carrot, profit, return, ribbon, salary, trophy **7** guerdon, premium, success **8** requital **9** indemnify **12** compensation, remuneration

REWARDING: **8** pleasing **10** beneficial, fulfilling, gratifying, profitable, satisfying, worthwhile

REWORK: **4** edit, redo **5** adapt, alter **6** modify, redraw, revamp, revise **7** redraft, reshape, rewrite

RHAPSODIC: **6** elated **7** excited **8** ecstatic **9** emotional, overjoyed **11** exhilarated **12** enthusiastic

RHEA:
brother: **6** Cronus
daughter: **4** Hera **6** Hestia **7** Demeter
father: **6** Uranus
husband: **6** Cronus
queen of: **6** Titans
saved: **4** Zeus

RHETORIC: **6** speech **7** bombast, oratory **9** discourse, elocution, eloquence, pomposity, verbosity, wordiness **11** flamboyance

RHETORICAL: **5** showy, wordy **6** florid, fluent, ornate **7** flowery **8** eloquent, sonorous **9** bombastic **10** articulate, figurative, flamboyant, oratorical **11** embellished

RHINE:
concerning: **7** Rhenish
linked to: **8** Black Sea **13** Mediterranean
located: **6** Europe **7** Germany **11** Netherlands, Switzerland
ports: **4** Bonn, Koln **5** Mainz **7** Cologne **8** Mannheim **9** Wiesbaden
rivers: **5** Rhone **6** Danube
rock: **7** Lorelei
tributaries: **3** Ill **4** Aare, Lahn, Main, Ruhr, Waal **7** Moselle

RHINOCEROS:
area of: **4** Asia **6** Africa
feature: **4** horn
herd: **5** crash

RHODE ISLAND:
among: **16** Thirteen Colonies
bird: **14** Rhode Island red
capital: **10** Providence
cities: **7** Newport **8** Cranston **9** Pawtucket **10** Woonsocket
explorer: **13** Roger Williams
features: **11** Block Island
flower: **6** violet
native: **13** Rhode Islander
nicknames: **10** Ocean State **11** Little Rhody
tree: **8** red maple
water: **8** Atlantic **16** Narrangansett Bay

RHODES:
capital: **6** Rhodes
features: **8** Colossus **10** Chelidonia
island group: **10** Dodecanese
island of: **6** Greece
water: **9** Aegean Sea

RHUBARB: **5** fight, plant **6** hassle **7** dispute, quarrel **8** argument, pie plant **10** discussion **11** controversy
genus: **5** rheum

RHYME: **4** poem, rune, song, tune **5** meter, verse **6** jingle, poetry **7** harmony, measure

RHYMER: **4** bard, poet **8** minstrel **9** poetaster, rhymester, versifier **10** troubadour

RHYTHM: **4** beat, flow, lilt, pace, time **5** meter, music, pulse, sound, swing, tempo **6** accent **7** cadence, measure **8** movement

RIALTO: **8** district **11** marketplace

RIB: **4** bone, jest, joke, purl, razz, stay, wale **5** costa, ridge, tease **6** banter

RIBALD: **4** lewd, rude **5** bawdy, crude, gross, rogue **6** coarse, filthy, risque, vulgar **7** obscene, raunchy, uncouth **9** offensive **10** irreverent

RIBBON: **3** bow **4** band, tape **5** award, braid, corse, prize, strip, taste **6** cordon, fillet, riband, stripe, trophy **7** bandeau, binding **8** streamer, trimming **9** banderole **10** decoration

RICE: **4** seed **5** grass, plant
dish: **5** pilaf, pilau **7** biryani, pudding, risotto **9** jambalaya
drink: **4** sake, saki
family: **11** Oryza sativa
field: **4** padi **5** paddy
variety: **4** wild **6** Indian **8** mountain

RICH: **4** dark, lush, posh **5** ample, flush, funny, heavy, sweet, vivid **6** absurd, costly, creamy, fecund, fruity, golden, hearty, lavish, loaded, mellow, ornate, potent **7** amusing, copious, fertile, filling, moneyed, opulent, orotund, upscale, wealthy **8** abundant, affluent, eloquent, humorous, luscious, powerful, valuable **9** abounding, bountiful, elaborate, expensive, flavorful, laughable, luxuriant, luxurious, plentiful, sumptuous **10** prosperous, ridiculous **11** comfortable

RICHES: **4** gold, pelf **5** booty, lucre, money, worth **6** assets, wealth **7** fortune **8** property, treasure **9** affluence, resources **11** possessions

RICKETY: **4** weak **5** shaky **6** feeble, flimsy, infirm, unsafe, wobbly **7** unsound **8** unstable, unsteady **9** tottering **10** ramshackle **11** dilapidated

RICOCHET: **5** carom **6** bounce, glance **7** rebound, reflect

RID: **4** free, shed **5** clear, empty, expel, shake **6** loosen, remove **7** abolish, cleanse, deliver, relieve **8** liberate, unburden **9** eliminate **11** disencumber

RIDDLE: **4** crux, maze, sift **5** rebus, sieve **6** enigma, pierce, teaser **7** charade, dilemma, mystery, perplex, problem **9** conundrum, perforate

RIDE: **4** spin, trip **5** drift, drive, float, hound, tease **6** badger, cruise, harass, heckle, needle, outing, travel **7** commute, journey, oppress, torment, torture **8** ridicule **9** excursion

RIDER: **6** clause, cowboy, driver, jockey **8** addendum, addition, appendix, horseman, motorist **9** amendment, passenger, performer **10** equestrian, horsewoman, supplement **11** endorsement

RIDGE: **3** rib **4** back, balk, bank, dune, hill, hump, reef, ruck, seam, spur, wale, wave, weal, welt **5** bluff, chine, costa, crest, esker, ledge, levee, range, spine, wedge **6** crease, summit **7** hogback, moraine, wrinkle **9** elevation **11** corrugation

RIDICULE: **3** guy, kid, rib **4** gibe, haze, jeer, mock, rage, razz, ride, twit **5** roast, sneer, taunt, tease **6** banter, parody, satire **7** lampoon, mockery, pillory, putdown, sarcasm **8** belittle, raillery, satirize **9** burlesque, humiliate **10** caricature

RIDICULOUS: **5** crazy, droll, funny, silly **6** absurd, stupid **7**

amusing, asinine, bizarre, comical, foolish, idiotic **8** nonsense **9** ludicrous **10** irrational, outrageous **12** preposterous, unbelievable

RIFE: **5** alive **6** active, common, raging **7** current, profuse, rampant, teeming **8** abundant, numerous, swarming **9** abounding, prevalent **10** prevailing, widespread **11** overflowing

RIFFRAFF: **3** mob **4** scum **5** dregs, trash **6** masses, rabble, refuse **7** garbage, rubbish

RIFLE: **3** arm, gun, rob **4** loot **5** steal **6** ravage, search, weapon **7** despoil, firearm, pillage, plunder, ransack, rummage
types: **5** Minie, Sober **6** Garand, Mauser, Sharps **7** carbine, Johnson **9** automatic, Remington, repeating **10** Winchester **11** Springfield

RIFT: **3** gap **4** flaw, rent **5** break, chasm, chink, cleft, crack, fault, split **6** breach, cleave, cranny, divide **7** blemish, fissure, opening, quarrel, rupture **8** crevasse, division, fracture **12** disagreement

RIG: **3** fix **4** gear, quip **5** cheat, dress, trick, truck **6** clothe, outfit, supply, tackle, tamper **7** arrange, costume, derrick, furnish, tractor **8** carriage, fittings **9** apparatus, equipment, machinery **10** manipulate **11** contraption

RIGHT: **3** due, fit **4** fair, good, just, real, sane, true, well **5** amend, clear, emend, legal, moral, sound, valid **6** common, equity, lawful, normal, patent, proper, square **7** correct, ethical, exactly, fitting, genuine, liberty, license, rectify, redress, restore **8** becoming, deserved, directly, easement, straight, suitable, virtuous **9** authentic, authority, faultless, favorably, franchise, precisely, privilege, vindicate **10** aboveboard, acceptable, accurately, obligation, perquisite, sufficient, thoroughly **11** appropriate, prerogative
right-handed: **7** dextral

RIGHT AWAY: **3** now **8** directly, urgently **9** instantly, presently **11** immediately

RIGHTEOUS: **4** good, holy, just, pure **5** godly, moral, pious **6** devout, honest, worthy **7** ethical, sinless, upright **8** faithful, reverent, virtuous **9** blameless, guiltless, religious **10** principled **13** conscientious

RIGHTFUL: **3** due **4** fair, just, true **5** legal **6** honest, lawful, proper **7** correct, fitting **8** deserved **10** legitimate **11** appropriate

RIGHT-WING: **11** reactionary **12** conservative

RIGID: **3** set **4** firm, hard, taut **5** fixed, sharp, solid, stern, stiff, tense **6** formal, severe, strait, strict **7** adamant, austere **8** exacting, rigorous, stubborn **9** immovable, stringent, unbending **10** inflexible, ironhanded, unyielding

RIGOR: **4** fury **5** trial **7** cruelty **8** hardship, severity **9** austerity, exactness, harshness, precision, sharpness, sternness, stiffness **10** difficulty, exactitude, strictness **13** inflexibility

RIGOROUS: **4** hard **5** exact, harsh, rigid, stern, stiff **6** brutal, rugged, severe, strict, trying **7** ascetic, correct, onerous, precise **8** accurate **9** inclement **10** burdensome, oppressive, relentless **11** challenging

RILE: **3** bug, vex **4** gall, roil **5** anger, annoy, peeve, upset **6** bother, needle, nettle **7** agitate, disturb, provoke **8** irritate **9** aggravate

RILL: **5** brook, creek, rille **6** stream, trench, valley **7** channel, rivulet

RIM: **3** lip **4** bank, brim, edge, ring, tire **5** brink, ledge, skirt, verge **6** border, flange, fringe, margin **7** horizon **8** boundary **9** perimeter **13** circumference

RIME: **3** ice **4** hoar, poem, rung **5** chink, cleft, crack, frost, rhyme, verse **6** freeze **7** crinkle, fissure

RIND: **4** bark, hull, husk, peel, skin **5** crust, shell **6** cortex **7** epicarp **8** covering **10** integument

RING: **3** eye, mob, rim **4** band, bell, belt, buzz, ding, dirl, echo, gang, halo, hoop, peal, toll, tore **5** anlet, arena, bezel, chime, clang, clank, clock, group, henge, knell, party, sound **6** border, boxing, cartel, circle, circus, clique, collar, collet, corona, gasket, girdle, jangle, jingle, summon, tingle, tinkle, washer **7** annulet, aureole, circlet, coterie, resound, ringlet, vibrate **8** bracelet, cincture, encircle, monopoly, surround **9** enclosure, syndicate, telephone **11** reverberate **12** organization

types: **3** key **4** band, nose **5** class **6** napkin **7** earring, wedding **10** engagement

RINGLEADER: **4** boss **10** instigator, mastermind

RING-SHAPED: **5** torus **6** toroid **7** annular, annulus **8** circular

RINSE: **4** lave, soak, wash **5** bathe, douse, flush, water **6** gargle, sluice **7** cleanse

RIOT: **4** howl, rage **5** brawl, fight, melee, revel **6** affray, bedlam, mutiny, revolt, rumble, scream, tumult, uproar **7** protest, quarrel, rampage, revelry, turmoil **8** carousal, disorder, outburst, uprising **9** commotion, confusion **10** donnybrook **11** disturbance, pandemonium

RIOTOUS: **4** loud, wild **5** noisy **6** stormy, unruly, wanton **7** profuse, rampant, violent **9** luxuriant, turbulent **10** boisterous, disorderly, rebellious **12** unrestrained

RIP: **3** cut **4** rend, rent, rive, slit, tear **5** shred, split **6** cleave, sunder **7** estuary **8** belittle, lacerate **9** criticize

RIPE: **3** fit **4** aged, wise **5** adult, grown, ideal, ready **6** mature, mellow, primed, timely **7** matured, skilled **8** complete, enriched, finished, seasoned, suitable **9** developed, favorable, opportune, perfected **10** consummate, seasonable **11** enlightened, experienced

RIPEN: **3** age **4** grow **5** bloom, fruit **6** evolve, flower, mature, mellow, season **7** develop, improve, perfect **8** heighten

RIPOSTE: **5** reply **6** retort, return, thrust **8** comeback, maneuver, repartee

RIPPLE: **4** comb, curl, fret, purl, riff, wave **6** dimple, motion, riffle, rimple, ruffle **7** crinkle, wrinkle **10** undulation

RISE: **4** flow, gain, grow, hike, lift, loom, soar, stem, well **5** arise, awake, begin, boost, climb, mount, raise, reach, rebel, stand, start, surge, swell, tower **6** amount, appear, ascend, ascent, aspire, attain, emerge, growth, revolt, thrive **7** advance, augment, elevate, emanate, prosper, succeed, surface **8** addition, flourish, increase, levitate, multiply **9** elevation, intensify, originate, promotion, skyrocket, transcend

RISIBLE: **5** droll, funny **7** amusing, comical **8** humorous **9** laughable, ludicrous **10** ridiculous

RISK: **4** dare, wage **5** brave, peril, stake **6** chance, danger, expose, gamble, hazard, plunge **7** imperil, venture **8** endanger, exposure, jeopardy **9** adventure, liability, speculate **10** jeopardize **11** possibility, uncertainty

RISKY: **4** bold **5** dicey, hairy **6** chancy, unsafe **8** perilous, ticklish **9** dangerous, hazardous, uncertain, unhealthy **10** precarious **11** speculative

RISQUÉ: **4** blue, lewd, racy, sexy **5** crude, dirty, lurid, salty, spicy **6** daring, vulgar **7** naughty, obscene **8** off-color **10** suggestive **11** provocative

RITE: **4** cult **6** ritual **7** liturgy, service **8** ceremony, occasion **9** formality, ordinance, procedure, sacrament, tradition **10** ceremonial, initiation, observance **11** celebration

RITUAL: **4** cult, rite **6** custom **7** liturgy, obsequy, routine **8** ceremony, practice **9** formality **10** observance

RITZY: **4** chic, posh **5** fancy **6** classy, spiffy **7** elegant **8** snobbish **9** expensive, luxurious **11** fashionable

RIVAL: **3** vie **4** peer **5** enemy, equal, match **6** oppose, strive **7** compete, contest, emulate, feuding **8** opponent, struggle **9** adversary, competing, contender **10** antagonist, challenger, competitor, contending, contestant

RIVALRY: **6** battle **7** contest **8** jealousy **10** opposition **11** competition

RIVE: **4** chop, plow, pull, rend, rift, tear **5** break, cleft, sever, split **6** cleave, divide, pierce, sunder, thrust **7** shatter **8** lacerate, splinter

RIVER: **3** ree, ria, rio, run **4** wady **5** bayou, brook, creek, waddy **6** slough, stream **7** channel, rivulet **8** effluent **9** sluiceway, streamlet **11** watercourse

arm: **4** fork **7** estuary **9** tributary
concerning: **5** amnic **7** fluvial, potamic **8** riverine **9** fluminous
dam: **4** weir
inhabitant: **9** amphibian, rheophile
island: **3** ait **4** holm
longest: **4** Nile **6** Amazon
mouth: **4** beal, lade **5** delta **7** estuary
part: **3** bed, ess **4** eddy, ford **5** mouth **6** alveus, rapids, source
sides: **4** bank, rand, ripa **5** levee

RIVET: **3** fix, pin **4** bolt **6** attach, fasten, secure **7** engross **8** fastener

RIVULET: **4** rill **5** brook, creek, river **6** runlet, stream **7** channel **9** streamlet

ROAD: **3** way **4** fare, lane, path, ride **5** agger, alley, drive, route, track, trail **6** artery, avenue, career, course, street **7** beltway, freeway, highway, journey, parkway, passage, railway, viaduct **8** causeway, pavement, railroad, speedway, turnpike **9** boulevard, concourse **10** expressway, interstate, throughway

ROADBLOCK: **7** barrier **8** blockade **9** barricade **11** obstruction

ROADHOUSE: **3** inn **5** hotel **6** hostel, tavern **9** nightclub **10** restaurant

ROAM: **4** rove **5** prowl, range, stray **6** ramble, stroll, travel, wander **7** meander **8** straggle **9** gallivant

ROAN: **5** color, horse **9** sheepskin

ROAR: **3** cry **4** bawl, bell, boom, hoot, howl, yell **5** growl, laugh, noise, shout, sound **6** bellow, clamor, holler, outcry, scream, shriek **7** thunder **8** shouting

ROAST: **3** fry **4** bake, burn, cook, razz **5** broil, grill, parch **6** banter **7** lampoon, swelter **8** lambaste, ridicule **9** criticize

ROB: **3** cop, mug **4** bilk, lift, loot, roll, take **5** bribe, filch, heist, pilch, pinch, pluck, reave, rifle, spoil, steal, strip, touch **6** hijack, hustle, pilfer, pirate, snatch, snitch, thieve **7** bereave, defraud, deprive, despoil, pillage, plunder, purloin, swindle **8** embezzle **10** burglarize

ROBBER: **4** yegg **5** crook, ghoul, thief **6** bandit, catman, mugger, outlaw **7** brigand, burglar, rustler **8** hijacker, marauder, swindler **9** bandolero, buccaneer, desperado, privateer **10** highwayman, pickpocket

ROBE: **4** cape, gown, toga, vest, wrap **5** array, cloak, cover, dress, habit, smock, tunic **6** clothe, invest, kimono, mantle, muumuu **7** chimere, costume, garment **8** clothing, negligee, vestment **9** housecoat

ROBIN HOOD:
companions: **9** Friar Tuck **10** Allan-a-Dale, Little John, Will Stutly **11** Will Scarlet
enemy: **19** Sheriff of Nottingham
known as: **4** hero **6** legend, outlaw
lived in: **14** Sherwood Forest
lover: **10** Maid Marian

ROBINSON CRUSOE:
author: **11** Daniel Defoe
companion: **9** Man Friday
inhabited: **6** island

ROBOT: **5** droid, golem **7** android, machine **8** humanoid

ROBUST: **4** firm, hale, hard **5** built, hardy, lusty, sound, stout **6** brawny, hearty, potent, rugged, sinewy, strong, sturdy **7** healthy, roaring **8** athletic, muscular, stalwart, thriving, vigorous **9** energetic, strapping **10** prosperous **11** flourishing

ROCK: **3** ore **5** agate, earth, flint, scree, shale, slate, stone **6** gravel, pebble, silica **7** diamond, granite **8** dolomite, obsidian
concerning: **6** petric **7** petrean
igneous: **4** boss, sial, sima, trap, tufa **5** trass **6** basalt, domite, latite **7** diabase, diorite, felsite, peridot
liquid: **4** lava, tufa, tuff
made of: **7** mineral **15** organic material
material: **4** sand **5** attle, talus **6** gossan **8** detritus, xenolith
part of: **5** crust
place: **4** crag, peak **5** cliff **7** moraine **10** promontory
science: **9** petrology
types: **7** igneous **11** metamorphic, sedimentary

ROCK BOTTOM: **4** poor **6** lowest **8** cheapest, inferior

ROCKER: **5** chair, skate **6** cradle, singer **8** musician

ROCKET: **4** soar, whiz, zoom **5** climb, tower **6** ascend **7** missile **8** starship **9** satellite **10** projectile, spacecraft **11** firecracker

ROCKY: **4** firm, hard, weak **5** dizzy, rough, shaky, solid, stony **6** craggy, rugged **8** doubtful, obdurate, stubborn, unstable, unsteady **9** uncertain **10** inflexible **12** discouraging

ROCKY MOUNTAINS:
also called: **7** Rockies
animals: **6** mazame **8** antelope **12** bighorn sheep
countries: **6** Canada, Mexico
peaks: **5** Logan, Pikes **6** Denali, Elbert **8** McKinley
ranges: **5** Teton, Yukon **6** Alaska **7** Wasatch
river: **8** Missouri
wind: **7** chinook

ROCOCO: **4** arty **5** gaudy **6** ornate **10** flamboyant **11** extravagant

ROD: **3** bar, gun, pin **4** axle, bolt, cane, pole, twig, wand, whip **5** baton, birch, perch, power, scion, shaft, spike, spoke, staff, stick, strip **6** bamboo, carbon, fasces, needle, pistol, poston, rattan, skewer, switch, toggle **7** crowbar, measure, scepter, spindle, support, tyranny **8** revolver **9** authority **10** correction, oppression, punishment

RODENT: **3** rat **4** cavy, cypu, hare, mole, vole **5** aguti, hutia, mouse, ratel, zokor **6** beaver, biting, gerbil, gopher, gundie, marmot, murine, rabbit, weasel **7** chincha, gnawing, hamster, leveret, muskrat **8** chipmunk, leporide, squirrel **9** guinea pig, porcupine, woodchuck **10** chinchilla, prairie dog **11** kangaroo rat
genus: **3** mus **5** lepus

RODEO: **7** roundup **8** festival **9** enclosure **10** exhibition **11** competition
events: **7** cutting **8** re-riding **10** bull-riding, calf-roping **11** bulldogging **13** broncobusting **14** steer-wrestling

RODOMONTADE: **4** brag, crow, rant **5** boast, pride **7** bluster, bombast **8** boastful, braggart **10** pretension **12** exaggeration **14** grandiloquence

ROE: **4** deer, eggs, hart, hind, milt **5** coral, spawn **6** caviar

ROENTGEN, WILHELM:
discovered: **4** X-ray
nationality: **6** German
occupation: **9** physicist

ROGATION: **3** law **4** rite **5** chant **6** decree, litany, prayer **7** worship **12** supplication

ROGUE: **5** cheat, devil, knave, scamp, shark, tramp **6** beggar, harlot, pirate, rascal, wander **7** cheater, culprit, lowlife, vagrant, villain **8** criminal, picaroon, scalawag, swindler, vagabond **9** miscreant, scoundrel, trickster **10** blackguard, delinquent **11** rapscallion

ROGUISH: **3** sly **5** pawky **6** bother, wanton **7** playful, provoke **8** devilish, prankish, sportive **9** aggravate, deceitful, dishonest **11** mischievous **12** unprincipled, unscrupulous

ROIL: **3** vex **4** foul, rile, stir **5** anger, annoy, muddy

ROLE: **3** bit, job **4** duty, lead, part, task **5** cameo, guise, title **6** aspect, office **8** business, capacity, function **9** character, portrayal **10** appearance **11** performance

ROLL: **3** bun **4** coil, file, flip, flow, gush, list, loop, roam, rock, spin, sway, toss, turn, wind, wrap **5** bread, coast, drift, glide, index, pitch, shift, surge, swing, swirl, table, wheel **6** bundle, danish, grovel, gyrate, roster, rotate, rumble, scroll, spiral, tumble, wallow, wander **7** flatten, proceed, revolve, swagger, trundle **8** cylinder, drumbeat, flounder, register, rotation, rumbling, undulate **9** croissant, directory, revolving **10** revolution **11** reverberate

ROLL BACK: **5** lower **6** reduce **7** retreat

ROLLICKING: **3** gay **4** wild **5** happy, merry **6** frisky, jovial, joyful, joyous, lively **7** jocular, playful, romping **8** cheerful **10** boisterous, frolicsome **12** lighthearted

ROLL IN: **4** land, mass **5** enter **6** arrive **10** accumulate

ROLL OUT: **5** begin, start **8** initiate

ROLL OVER: **5** defer **8** postpone, reinvest **11** renegotiate

ROLY-POLY: **3** fat **5** dumpy, obese, pudgy **6** chubby, portly, rotund

ROMAN, ROME:

1st triumvirate: **6** Caesar, Pompey **7** Crassus
2nd triumvirate: **6** Antony **7** Lepidus **8** Octavian
assembly: **5** forum **6** senate **7** comitia
chief god: **4** Jove **7** Jupiter
chief goddess: **4** Juno
clothing: **4** toga **5** palla, sagum, stola, stole, tunic
comedy writer: **6** Cicero **7** Plautus, Terence
concerning: **5** Latin **7** Italian **9** classical
conspirators: **6** Brutus **7** Cassius **8** Catiline
date: **4** Ides **5** Nones **7** calends, kalends
emperors: **4** Nero, Otho, Otto **5** Galba, Nerva, Titus, Venus **6** Caesar, Julian, Trajan **7** Hadrian, Maximus, Severus **8** Augustus, Caligula, Claudius, Domitian, Tiberius, Valerian **9** Caracalla, Vespasian **11** Constantine
empress: **7** Eudocia
epic: **6** Aeneid
fates: **4** Nona **5** Morta, Parca **6** Decuma
features: **5** Forum **6** Circus **7** Vatican **8** Pantheon **9** Catacombs, Colosseum **13** Sistine Chapel
founders: **5** Remus **6** Aeneas **7** Romulus
generals: **5** Sulla, Titus **6** Antony, Brutus, Marius, Pompey, Scipio **7** Crassus **8** Agricola, Octavian **10** Mark Antony **12** Julius Caesar
god of agriculture: **6** Saturn
god of dead: **4** Mors **5** Orcus
god of dreams: **8** Morpheus
god of fire: **6** Vulcan
god of heaven: **6** Uranus
god of love: **4** Amor, Cupid
god of mirth: **5** Comus
god of sea: **6** Pontus **7** Neptune, Proteus
god of sun: **3** Sol **6** Apollo
god of underworld: **3** Dis **5** Orcus, Pluto
god of war: **4** Mars **8** Quirinus
god of wealth: **6** Plutus
god of wind: **5** Eurus **6** Boreas
god of wine: **7** Bacchus
goddess of agriculture: **5** Ceres
goddess of beauty: **5** Venus
goddess of flowers: **5** Flora
goddess of hope: **4** Spes
goddess of hunting: **5** Diana
goddess of love: **5** Venus
goddess of marriage: **4** Juno
goddess of moon: **4** Luna
goddess of night: **3** Nox
goddess of peace: **3** Pax
goddess of underworld: **10** Proserpina
goddess of victory: **6** Vacuna
goddess of war: **7** Bellona
goddess of wisdom: **7** Minerva
greeting: **3** ave
hills: **7** Caelian, Viminal **8** Aventine, Palatine, Quirinal **9** Esquiline **10** Capitoline
historian: **4** Livy **5** Nepos
kings: **5** Ancus **7** Martius, Romulus, Servius, Tullius **13** Numa Pompilius **15** Tullus Hostilius **18** Tarquinius Superbus
military formation: **3** ala **6** alares, cohort, legion **7** maniple, phalanx
mountain: **8** Apennine
official: **5** augur, edile **6** aedile, censor, consul, lictor **7** praetor, prefect, tribune **8** irenarch, quaestor **9** nestorian
people: **5** Laeti **7** Sabines **8** plebians **10** patricians
philosophers: **4** Cato **6** Seneca
physicians: **9** archiater **11** Aesculapius
poets: **4** Ovid **5** Cinna, Lucan **6** Horace, Vergil, Virgil **7** Juvenal, Terence
port: **5** Ostia
river: **5** Tiber
slave: **9** Spartacus

statesmen: **4** Cato **5** Pliny **6** Caesar, Cicero, Seneca **7** Agrippa **8** Augustus, Maecenas

ROMAN CATHOLIC CHURCH:
center: **7** Vatican
church: **7** lateran
division of: **12** Christianity
group: **7** Jesuits
head: **4** pope
priest: **4** abbe **6** father **8** sacerdos **9** monsignor

ROMANCE: **4** gest, love, tale **5** amour, charm, court, fable, fancy, fling, geste, novel, story **6** affair **7** fantasy, fiction, liaison **9** adventure, courtship, sentiment **10** exaggerate

ROMANIA:
also called: **7** Rumania
capital: **9** Bucharest
cities: **4** Ciuj, Iasi **6** Braila, Brasov, Galati **9** Constanta, Timisoara
continent: **6** Europe
ethnic groups: **8** Romanian **9** Hungarian
features: **11** Carpathians **16** Transylvania Alps
languages: **6** German **8** Romanian **9** Hungarian
monetary unit: **3** lei, leu
native: **8** Romanian
water: **6** Danube **8** Black Sea

ROMANTIC: **5** mushy **6** ardent, dreamy, exotic, poetic, unreal **7** amorous **8** quixotic **9** imaginary, visionary **10** enchanting, fictitious, idealistic, passionate

ROMEO: **5** lover, wooer **7** Don Juan, gallant **9** Cassanova

ROMEO AND JULIET:
author: **18** William Shakespeare
characters: **5** Paris **6** Tybalt **8** Mercutio **13** Friar Laurence
families: **8** Capulets **9** Montagues
Juliet's death: **8** stabbing
Romeo's death: **6** poison

ROMP: **3** run, win **4** play, roil, skip **5** caper **6** cavort, frolic, gambol, prance **7** carouse, gammock, rollick **8** carousal **9** celebrate

ROMULUS:
father: **4** Mars
mother: **10** Rhea Silvia
reared by: **4** wolf
twin brother: **5** Remus

ROOF: **4** dome **5** crown, house, slate **6** canopy, palate, summit **7** ceiling, gambrel, shelter **8** covering

ROOK: **4** bilk, bird, crow **5** cheat, steal **6** castle, fleece **7** deceive, defraud, swindle **9** bamboozle

ROOKIE: **4** tyro **6** novice **7** trainee **8** beginner, newcomer **9** greenhorn **10** apprentice, tenderfoot

ROOM: **3** den **4** area, cell, digs, flat, hall, play **5** divan, foyer, lobby, lodge, place, range, salon, scope, space, study, suite **6** atrium, dining, leeway, living, margin, studio **7** boudoir, cabinet, chamber, cubicle, expanse, gallery, kitchen, library, lodging, nursery, opening, rotunda, theater **8** capacity, latitude, quarters **9** allowance, apartment, clearance, dormitory **10** auditorium **11** compartment, opportunity **13** accommodation

ROOMER: **5** guest **6** renter, tenant **7** boarder, dweller

ROOMY: **4** huge **5** ample, broad, large **7** sizable **8** generous, spacious **9** capacious, extensive **10** commodious

ROOST: **3** sit **4** land, nest **5** abode, perch, sleep **6** alight, settle **7** lodging

ROOSTER: **4** cock, male **7** chicken **11** chanticleer

ROOT: **3** dig **4** base, beet, bulb, clap, core, grub, rise, soul, stem **5** basis, cheer, grout, heart, plant, tuber **6** bottom, burrow, carrot, center, fasten, motive, origin, radish, reason, search, settle, source, turnip **7** applaud, essence, nucleus, radical, rummage, support **8** entrench **9** beginning, encourage, establish, sassafras **10** derivation, foundation, groundwork **11** fundamental

ROOT OUT: **4** stub **6** remove **7** abolish, destroy, extract, unearth **8** demolish **9** eradicate, extirpate **10** annihilate

ROPE: **3** guy, tie, tow **4** bind, cord, fast, hemp, line, stay, vang **5** bight, cable, lasso, leash, longe, noose, twine **6** binder, corral, fasten, halter, hawser, hobble, lariat, shroud, string, tether, thread **7** binding, bobstay, cordage, halyard, lanyard, marline, painter, towline **8** inveigle, lifeline

ROPES: **7** details **9** procedure **10** ins and outs

ROSARY: **5** beads **7** chaplet, prayers

ROSE: **3** gem, red **4** pink **5** blush, color, flush, rouge **6** flower, nozzle **7** rosette
class: **3** tea **4** wild **7** rambler **8** noisette **9** polyantha **10** floribunda
family: **8** Rosaceae
genus: **4** rosa
variety: **4** rock **5** Peace **6** Alpine, damask **7** Granada **8** Japanese, Talisman **9** Christmas **10** Rubrifolia, Santa Anita

ROSEATE: **3** red **4** pink, rosy **6** bright **7** hopeful **8** cheerful **9** promising **10** optimistic

ROSTER: **4** list, roll **5** index, slate **6** agenda, muster, record **7** catalog **8** register, schedule

ROSTRUM: **4** dais **5** snout, stage **6** podium, pulpit **7** lectern, tribune **8** platform

ROSY: **4** pink **5** fresh, ruddy, sunny **6** bright, florid **7** flushed, hopeful, reddish, roseate **8** blushing, cheerful, rubicund **9** favorable, promising **10** optimistic **11** encouraging

ROT: **4** bosh, bull, warp **5** chaff, decay, spoil, trash **6** perish **7** corrode, decline, putrefy, rubbish, twaddle **8** nonsense **9** breakdown, decompose, poppycock **10** degenerate **11** contaminate, deteriorate

ROTATE: **4** roll, spin, turn **5** orbit, pivot, twirl, wheel, whirl **6** circle, gyrate, swivel **7** revolve **9** alternate

ROTATION: **4** eddy, spin, turn **5** cycle **6** torque, vortex **10** revolution

ROTE: **4** list **5** learn, sound **6** memory, repeat, system **7** routine **9** automatic **10** instrument, memorizing, repetition

ROTTEN: **3** bad **4** evil, foul, rank, sour **5** fetid, lousy, nasty **6** putrid **7** corrupt, crooked, decayed, spoiled, tainted, unlucky, unsound, vicious **8** depraved, inferior, smelling **9** dishonest, offensive, putrefied **10** abominable, decomposed, unpleasant **13** disintegrated

ROTUND: **3** fat **5** beefy, obese, plump, pudgy, round, stout **6** chubby, chunky, portly, stocky **7** vibrant **8** roly-poly, sonorous **9** spherical **10** potbellied

ROUGE: **3** red **4** pink **5** blush, color, flush, paint **6** redden **8** cosmetic

ROUGH: **4** curt, hard, hazy, rude, wild **5** basic, blunt, bumpy, crude, gruff, hairy, harsh, lumpy, raspy, rocky, rowdy, stern, tough, uncut **6** abrupt, broken, choppy, coarse, craggy, hoarse, jagged, rugged, severe, stormy, uneven, vulgar **7** austere, boorish, bristly, inexact, outline, raucous, ruffled, sketchy, uncivil, uncouth, violent **8** churlish, scabrous **9** difficult, imperfect, inclement, manhandle, turbulent, unrefined **10** boisterous, incomplete, tumultuous, unpleasant, unpolished **11** approximate

ROUGHNECK: **4** hood, punk **5** bully, rowdy, tough **7** ruffian

ROUGHNESS: **7** crudity **8** acrimony **9** bumpiness, gruffness, wooliness **10** coarseness, unevenness **12** irregularity

ROUGH OUT: **4** plan **5** draft **6** sketch **7** outline **9** delineate

ROUGH UP: **4** bash **6** thrash **9** manhandle

ROUND: **4** ball, band, beat, bend, full, oval, ring, turn **5** ample, cycle, globe, orbed, orbit, plump, shape, wheel **6** arched, bullet, chubby, circle, curved, looped, nearly, rotund **7** circuit, perfect **8** circular, complete, globular, resonant, rotation, sonorous, unbroken **9** spherical **10** ammunition, revolution **11** approximate

ROUNDABOUT: **4** tour **5** wordy **6** detour, rotary, zigzag **7** curving, devious, evasive, winding **8** circular, indirect, verbiage **9** ambiguous, excursion, runaround **10** circuitous, meandering

ROUNDED: **5** bowed **6** convex, curved, rotund **8** balanced, circular, complete **9** estimated **10** labialized **12** approximated

ROUND OFF: **6** climax, finish **8** complete, conclude **9** culminate **11** approximate

ROUND ROBIN: **6** letter **8** petition **10** tournament **11** competition

ROUND UP: **4** herd **5** rally **6** gather **7** collect, marshal **8** assemble

ROUNDUP: **6** muster **7** herding, summary **8** assembly, branding **9** gathering **10** collection

ROUSE: **4** call, goad, move, stir, urge, wake **5** alarm, awake, raise, rally, roust, start, waken **6** arouse, awaken, bestir, excite, foment, kindle, revive **7** agitate, animate, disturb, enliven, provoke, startle, trigger **8** motivate **9** challenge, galvanize, intensify, stimulate **10** exhilarate

ROUST: **4** rout, stir **5** rouse **7** provoke **8** motivate **9** stimulate

ROUT: **3** mob **4** band, beat, lick, ream, riot, romp, root **5** cream, crowd, dregs, drive, eject, expel, gouge, knock, scoop **6** defeat, furrow, rabble, wallop **7** clobber, confuse, conquer, debacle, retreat, rummage, shellac, uncover **8** stampede, vanquish **9** confusion, discomfit, multitude, overpower, overthrow, overwhelm, thrashing **10** demoralize **11** disturbance, outmaneuver

ROUTE: **3** way **4** beat, lane, line, path, road, send, ship **5** guide, pilot, plans, track, trail **6** course, detour, rounds **7** beeline, channel, circuit, highway, parkway, passage **8** turnpike **9** direction, itinerary

ROUTINE: **3** rut **4** dull, rote **5** cycle, drill, grind, habit, usual **6** boring, course, groove, method, system **7** regular, typical **8** everyday, habitual, ordinary, practice, standard **9** customary, procedure, treadmill

ROVE: **3** gad **4** move, roam **5** drift, prowl, range, stray **6** ramble, stroll, wander **7** meander **8** straggle **9** gallivant

ROVER: **5** nomad **6** pirate **7** drifter, migrant, vagrant **8** maverick, traveler, wanderer **9** itinerant **10** freebooter

ROVING: **6** errant, mobile **7** aimless, cursory, nomadic **8** rambling **9** desultory, itinerant, wandering

ROW: **3** oar **4** beef, file, fray, fuss, line, list, pull, rank, sail, scud, spat, tier, tiff **5** align, brawl, fight, noise, order, scull **6** column, paddle, propel, ruckus, rumpus, series, uproar **7** dispute, quarrel, rhubarb **8** argument, sequence, squabble **9** commotion **11** altercation, disturbance

ROWBOAT: **4** dory **5** canoe, scull, skiff **6** dinghy, vessel, wherry

ROWDY: **4** punk, rude, wild **5** bully, noisy, rough, tough **6** unruly **7** hoodlum, ruffian **8** hooligan **9** roughneck **10** boisterous, disorderly, rebellious

ROYAL: **4** easy **5** elite, grand, noble, regal **6** august, kingly, lavish, superb **7** eminent, stately **8** imperial, majestic, princely, splendid **9** excellent, grandiose, monarchal, sovereign **11** magnificent

ROYALTY: **4** rank **5** power, share **7** kingdom **8** dividend, dominion, eminence, kingship, nobility, regality **9** queenship **10** percentage **11** sovereignty

RUB: **3** irk, vex **4** buff, fret, snag, swab, wear, wipe **5** annoy, chafe, glaze, gloss, grind, scour, scrub, shine, smear **6** abrade, anoint, caress, hurdle, nettle, polish, scrape, smooth, stroke **7** massage, problem **8** friction, irritate, obstacle **9** hindrance **10** difficulty, impediment

RUBBER: **4** band **7** elastic **8** flexible, galoshes, material, overshoe **9** resilient **10** stretching

RUBBERNECK: **4** gape, look **5** snoop, stare **6** survey

RUBBISH: **4** bosh, crap, junk, slop **5** bilge, offal, trash, waste **6** debris, drivel, garble, litter, refuse, rubble **7** garbage, hogwash, rummage **8** nonsense, riffraff **9** gibberish, poppycock, worthless **10** balderdash **11** foolishness

RUBE: **4** boor, dolt, hick, jake **7** bumpkin, hayseed, redneck **9** hillbilly **10** clodhopper

RUBICUND: **3** red **4** rosy **5** color, ruddy **6** florid **7** flushed, healthy, reddish

RUBIDIUM: **7** element

RUB OUT: **4** kill **5** erase **6** cancel, delete, murder **7** destroy **8** massacre **9** eliminate **10** annihilate, obliterate **11** assassinate

RUBY: **3** gem, red **5** color, jewel, stone **7** mineral

RUCKUS: **3** row **4** fray **5** brawl, fight, melee **6** fracas, ruffle, rumpus, uproar **7** dispute **9** commotion, confusion **10** donnybrook **11** altercation, disturbance

RUDDY: **3** red **4** rosy **6** florid **7** reddish **8** blushing

RUDE: **3** raw **4** curt, lewd **5** blunt, crass, crude, fresh, gross, harsh, rowdy, surly **6** abrupt, brutal, callow, clumsy, coarse, crusty, fierce, rugged, rustic, savage, vulgar **7** abusive, boorish, brutish, jarring, loutish, natural, obscene, uncivil, uncouth, violent **8** churlish, homespun, ignorant, impolite, impudent, untaught **9** barbarian, barbarous, inelegant, insulting, makeshift, primitive, unlearned, unrefined, unskilled, untrained **10** boisterous, discordant, unbecoming, uncultured, unfinished, ungracious, unladylike, unmannerly, unpolished **11** ill-mannered, uncivilized **12** discourteous **13** disrespectful, unceremonious

RUDIMENTARY: **5** basic **6** simple **7** initial, primary **9** beginning, elemental, vestigial **10** elementary **11** fundamental, undeveloped

RUBY: **7** crimson, flushed, pinkish, scarlet **8** rubicund, sanguine

RUE: **4** pity **5** dolor, grief, mourn **6** bewail, grieve, lament, regret, repent, sorrow, suffer **7** afflict, anguish, deplore, remorse **8** sympathy **10** compassion, repentance

RUEFUL: **3** sad **5** sorry **6** woeful **7** doleful, pitiful **8** contrite, mournful, penitent **9** depressed, plaintive, sorrowful **10** lamentable, melancholy

RUFFIAN: **4** hood, punk, thug **5** brute, bully, rowdy, tough **7** hoodlum **8** gangster, hooligan **9** cutthroat, roughneck, scoundrel

RUFFLE: **3** irk, vex **4** fray, fret, roil **5** annoy, crimp, plait, pleat, ruche, shake, upset **6** abrade, bother, nettle, riffle, ripple, ruckus **7** agitate, crinkle, derange, disturb, fluster, flutter, provoke, swagger, wrinkle **8** brandish, dishevel, disorder, drumbeat, irritate, unsettle **9** commotion, confusion **10** disarrange, discompose, intimidate

RUG: **3** mat **5** cover **6** carpet, toupee **7** drugget

RUGGED: **4** hard, rude, worn **5** bumpy, burly, hardy, harsh, rocky, rough, stern, surly, tough **6** brawny, brutal, craggy, fierce, jagged, robust, severe, stormy, strong, sturdy, trying, uneven **7** arduous, healthy, uncivil, uncouth, unkempt, violent **8** muscular, rigorous, vigorous, wrinkled **9** demanding, difficult, weathered **10** unpolished **11** mountainous

RUIN: **4** bane, bust, dash, doom, fall, harm, loss, maim, undo **5** botch, break, decay, havoc, level, skids, spoil **6** damage, deface, defeat, impair, injure, mangle, perish, ravage **7** deplete, despoil, destroy, shatter **8** bankrupt, calamity, collapse, decimate, demolish, disaster, downfall **9** confusion, crumbling, decadence, desecrate, disfigure **10** bankruptcy, desolation, impoverish, insolvency, subversion **11** destruction, devastation, dissolution

RUINOUS: **4** dire **5** fatal **7** adverse **8** damaging **10** calamitous, disastrous, pernicious, shattering **11** destructive, devastating **12** catastrophic

RULE: **3** law, way **4** head, lead, sway **5** axiom, canon, edict, guide, judge, maxim, order, reign **6** course, custom, decide, decree, direct, empire, govern, manage, method, policy, regime **7** command, conduct, control, dictate, formula, preside, prevail, regency, regimen, statute **8** decision, doctrine, dominate, domineer, dominion, practice, regulate, standard **9** authority, criterion, determine, direction, enactment, establish, influence, ordinance, principle, procedure **10** government, leadership, regulation **12** jurisdiction

RULE OUT: **3** bar **4** omit **6** except, forbid, refuse, reject **7** exclude, prevent **8** preclude **9** eliminate

RULER: **4** amir, boss, czar, emir, king, lord, shah, tsar **5** chief, queen, sheik **6** despot, dynast, ferule, leader, prince, regent, sultan, tyrant **7** emperor, empress, measure, monarch, pharaoh, viceroy **8** autocrat, dictator, governor, princess **9** commander, dominator, matriarch, president, sovereign, yardstick **12** straightedge

RULING: **5** edict, ukase **6** decree **7** central, finding, leading, popular, statute, verdict **8** decision, dominant, judgment **9** directive, enactment, prevalent **10** prevailing, resolution, widespread **11** controlling, predominant

RUM: **3** odd **4** grog **6** liquor **7** strange **8** beverage, peculiar
types: **4** dark **5** light **6** spiced **7** Bacardi, Jamaica **11** Puerto Rican

RUMBLE: **4** boom, clap, roar, roll, seat **5** crack, crash, fight, growl, noise, rumor **6** gossip, murmur, polish, uproar **7** grumble, resound, thunder **11** reverberate

RUMINANT: **3** cow, yak **4** deer, goat, oxen **5** bison, camel, llama, moose, sheep, steer, zebra **6** bovine, cattle **7** buffalo, chewing, giraffe **8** antelope **10** meditative **13** contemplative

RUMINATE: **4** chew, mull, muse, spew **5** brood, think **6** ponder **7** reflect **8** consider, meditate **9** masticate **10** brainstorm, deliberate **11** contemplate

RUMMAGE: **4** comb, hunt, junk, poke **5** trash **6** forage, gather, litter, muddle, search **7** clutter, collect, disturb, examine, explore, ransack, rubbish **8** disorder, upheaval **9** confusion, searching **10** disarrange

RUMMY: **4** game **5** drunk **6** barfly, boozer **8** drunkard **9** alcoholic

RUMOR: **4** buzz, news, talk, word **5** bruit, noise, story **6** canard, gossip, murmur, report, spread **7** hearsay, message, prattle, scandal, tidings, whisper **8** innuendo **9** grapevine **11** fabrication, scuttlebutt

RUMP: **4** butt, duff, rear, seat, tush **5** fanny **6** behind, bottom **7** keister **8** backside, buttocks, derriere, haunches

RUMPLE: **4** fold, muss **5** crimp, crush, plait **6** crease, ruffle, tousle **7** crinkle, crumple, scrunch, wrinkle **8** dishevel

RUMPUS: **3** row **4** fray, stir **5** brawl, melee **6** barney, clamor, fracas, hubbub, ruckus, uproar **7** rhubarb, scuffle **8** argument **9** commotion, confusion **11** disturbance

RUN: **3** fly, gad, jog, ply **4** bolt, dart, dash, emit, flee, flow, fuse, gait, hunt, move, norm, pace, pass, pour, race, roam, rove, rush, scud, spin, tear, tend, tour, trot **5** blend, brook, carry, chain, chase, cover, cycle, drive, evade, glide, going, haste, hurry, range, reach, river, route, scoot, score, speed, spurt, whisk **6** ascend, barrel, charge, course, escape, extend, gallop, govern, hasten, hustle, manage, pursue, scurry, spread, spring, sprint, stream, thrust **7** bootleg, cascade, command, compete, conduct, control, freedom, journey, liquefy, migrate, operate, proceed, publish, retreat, scamper, scutter, scuttle, smuggle, stretch, trickle, vamoose **8** continue, dissolve, duration, function, maneuver, scramble, sequence, stampede, traverse **9** challenge, skedaddle, territory, transport **10** accumulate, mastermind **13** configuration

RUN-AROUND: **6** detour **9** avoidance, diversion **10** roundabout **12** postponement

RUN AWAY: **4** bolt, flee, flow **5** elope, leave **6** decamp, desert, escape **8** stampede

RUNAWAY: **4** wild **6** truant **7** escaped, fleeing **8** fugitive **10** delinquent

RUN-DOWN: **5** seedy, tired, weary **6** shabby **7** squalid **8** deserted, fatigued, tattered **9** abandoned, exhausted, neglected **11** debilitated, dilapidated

RUN DOWN: **4** hunt, stop **5** chase, seize, trace **6** pursue, vilify **7** capture, collide, detract **8** belittle, ridicule **9** denigrate, disparage **10** depreciate

RUNDOWN: **5** recap **6** review **7** outline, summary **8** briefing, synopsis

RUNG: **3** bar, rod **4** step **5** round, spoke, tread **8** crossbar **10** crosspiece

RUN-IN: **4** tiff **5** brush, fight **6** battle **7** dispute **8** argument, skirmish **9** encounter **11** altercation **13** confrontation

RUN IN: **3** nab **4** bust **5** pinch **6** arrest, collar **9** apprehend

RUN INTO: **3** see **4** bump, meet **5** crash **7** collide **9** encounter

RUNNER: **4** vine **5** agent, blade, racer, scarf **6** carpet, jogger **7** courier, hurdler **8** fugitive, smuggler, sprinter **9** collector, messenger **10** marathoner

RUNNING: **5** going **7** flowing, working **9** operation **10** continuous **11** functioning **13** uninterrupted

RUN OFF: **4** flee, make **5** drain, elope, empty, print **6** escape

RUN-OF-THE-MILL: **5** usual **6** common **7** average, regular, typical **8** everyday, mediocre, ordinary

RUN OUT: **4** fail, flow, lose, stop, tire **5** empty, lapse, leave, peter, spill, waste **6** elapse, expire, finish, weaken **7** abandon, exhaust **9** terminate

RUNT: **5** dwarf, pygmy **6** midget, peewee, shrimp **10** homunculus **11** lilliputian

RUN THROUGH: **4** blow **5** check, waste **6** browse, pierce **7** consume, deplete, exhaust, inspect **8** rehearse, squander

RUNWAY: **4** path, ramp, road **5** strip, track **6** groove **7** channel **8** airstrip, platform **10** passageway

RUPTURE: **4** open, part, rent, tear **5** break, burst, split **6** breach, divide, hernia, sunder **7** disrupt, divorce, quarrel **8** division, fracture, puncture, separate **12** disagreement

RURAL: **6** rustic, simple **7** bucolic, country, idyllic, natural **8** Arcadian, geoponic, pastoral

RUSE: **4** hoax, ploy, wile **5** feint, fraud, trick, twist **6** deceit, scheme **7** gimmick **8** artifice, maneuver **9** deception, stratagem **10** subterfuge

RUSH: **4** bolt, dart, dash, flow, race, scud, tear, zoom **5** blitz, chase, flood, haste, hurry, press, scoot, speed, storm, surge **6** attack, bustle, charge, course, defeat, hasten, hurtle, hustle, plunge, streak, urgent **7** assault, rampage, scamper **8** pressure, scramble, stampede **9** onslaught, overpower

RUSSIA: **4** USSR **7** Muscovy
authors: **5** Gorki **7** Chekhov, Pushkin, Tolstoy **9** Pasternak **10** Dostoevsky
capital: **6** Moscow
cities: **4** Omsk, Orel, Perm **5** Kasan, Kazan, Pensa, Pskov **6** Moskva, Nizhni, Rostov, Sartov **7** Bataisk, Ivanovo, Kalinin, Rybinsk **8** Kostroma, Orenburg, Smolensk, Taganrog, Vladimir, Voronezh, Yaroslaf **14** Nizhny Novgorod
Communist groups: **9** Comintern, Politburo, Presidium **13** Supreme Soviet
composers: **9** Prokofiev **10** Stravinsky **12** Tschaikovsky **14** Rimsky-Korsakov
drink: **5** kvass, quass, vodka
family: **7** Romanov **9** Stroganov
food: **4** ikra **5** ikary **6** beluga, caviar **7** borscht

lakes: **4** Aral, Neva, Sego **5** Elton, Ilmen, Onega
languages: **5** Uzbek **7** Russian **8** Armenian, Georgian **9** Ukrainian **11** Azerbaijani, Belorussian
monetary unit: **5** ruble
mountains: **4** Ural **5** Altai **6** Pamirs **8** Caucasus
newspaper: **6** Pravda **8** Izvestia
peasant: **5** kulak, mujik **6** muzhik, muzjik
people: **3** Red **4** Russ, Slav **7** Cossack, Russine **9** Muscovite
republic: **5** Uzbek **6** Latvia **7** Armenia, Georgia, Kirghiz, Turkmen, Ukraine
revolutionist: **5** Lenin, Rykov **6** Stalin, Tomsky **7** Trotsky
rivers: **3** Don, Ili, Ner, Oka, Ros, Ufa **4** Amur, Duna, Kara, Lena, Neva, Orel, Sura, Svir, Ural **5** Dnepr, Dvina, Onega, Terek, Tobol, Volga **6** Donets, Irtish **7** Dnieper

RUST: **3** eat, rot **5** color, decay, erode **6** blight, canker **7** corrode, erosion, oxidize, tarnish **9** corrosion, oxidation **13** decomposition

RUSTIC: **4** boor, hick, jake, rube, rude **5** churl, crude, plain, rough, rural, yokel **6** coarse, farmer, simple, sturdy, sylvan **7** artless, bucolic, bumpkin, bushman, country, hayseed, natural, peasant, plowboy, plowman, redneck, uncouth **8** agrarian, agrestic, clownish, pastoral **9** agrestian, greenhorn, hillbilly, inelegant **10** clodhopper, countryman, unpolished **11** picturesque **12** backwoodsman

RUSTLE: **4** stir **5** haste, noise, sound, steal, swish **6** forage, swoosh **7** crackle, crinkle

RUSTLER: **5** thief **6** bandit, driver, robber **9** desperado

RUSTY: **5** rough **6** rugged, unused **7** decayed **8** corroded, sluggish **10** discolored **11** unpracticed

RUT: **5** ditch, grind, habit, track **6** furrow, groove, trench **7** channel, pattern, pothole, routine **11** indentation

RUTH: **4** pity **5** grief, mercy **6** regret, sorrow **7** remorse, sadness **8** sympathy **9** penitence **10** compassion, repentance
husband: **4** Boaz
lived: **4** Moab
mother-in-law: **5** Naomi
son: **4** Obed

RUTHLESS: **4** cold, mean **5** cruel **6** brutal, savage **7** vicious **8** pitiless **9** cutthroat, ferocious, heartless, merciless **10** relentless **13** unsympathetic

RWANDA:
capital: **6** Kigali
cities: **6** Butare **9** Ruhengeri
continent: **6** Africa
ethnic groups: **3** Twa **4** Hutu **5** pygmy, Tutsi
features: **7** Virunga **14** Mount Karisimbi
former name: **12** Ruanda-Urundi
languages: **6** French, Rwanda **7** Swahili **11** Kinyarwanda
monetary unit: **5** franc
native: **7** Rwandan
water: **4** Kivu **6** Kagera

RYE: **4** feed **5** grain, grass **6** cereal, whisky **7** whiskey

S

SABBATH: **6** Sunday **8** Saturday **10** seventh day

SABBATICAL: **5** leave **7** holiday **8** vacation

SABER: **4** kill **5** sword **6** injure **7** cutlass **8** scimitar

SABLE: **3** fur, jet **4** dark, pelt **5** black, ebony **6** dismal, gloomy, somber

SABOTAGE: **5** block, wreck **6** damage **7** destroy, disable, disrupt, subvert **9** undermine, vandalize **12** incapacitate

SAC: **3** bag **4** cyst, sack **5** pouch **6** cavity, pocket **7** vesicle

SACCHARINE: **5** sweet **6** sugary, syrupy **7** candied, cloying, honeyed **11** sentimental **12** ingratiating

SACERDOTAL: **6** sacred **8** clerical, priestly **9** apostolic, religious **11** ministerial

SACHET: **3** bag **5** pouch, scent **7** perfume **9** fragrance, potpourri

SACK: **3** bag, bed, rob, sac **4** base, fire, loot, poke, raid, wine **5** pouch, purse **6** burlap, pocket, ravage, tackle **7** dismiss, pillage, plunder, ransack **8** desolate **9** container, discharge, dismissal, terminate

SACRAMENT: **4** rite, sign **6** pledge, ritual, symbol **7** baptism, liturgy, penance **8** ceremony, covenant, marriage **9** communion, Eucharist, matrimony **12** confirmation

SACRED: **4** holy, pure **5** godly, pious **6** divine **7** blessed, guarded, saintly **8** hallowed, reverend **9** cherished, protected, religious, spiritual, undefiled, venerated **10** inviolable, sacrosanct, sanctified **11** consecrated

SACRIFICE: **4** bunt, deed, give, loss **5** forgo **6** devote, endure, homage, martyr, victim **7** forfeit **8** hecatomb, immolate, oblation, offering **9** surrender **10** concession

SACRILEGE: **3** sin **5** crime **7** impiety **8** iniquity **9** blasphemy, violation **11** desecration, irreverence, profanation

SACRILEGIOUS: **6** sinful **7** impious, profane **10** irreverent **11** blasphemous, irreligious

SACROSANCT: **6** divine, sacred **7** blessed **8** esteemed, hallowed, regarded, reverent **9** religious **10** inviolable

SAD: **3** bad, low **4** blue, dark, down, glum **5** grave, sober, sorry, trist **6** dismal, dreary, gloomy, solemn, somber, tragic, woeful **7** doleful, joyless, pitiful, unhappy **8** dejected, desolate, dolorous, downcast, grievous, mournful, pathetic, pitiable, wretched **9** cheerless, depressed, miserable, sorrowful, woebegone **10** calamitous, deplorable, despondent, dispirited, melancholy **11** heartbroken, unfortunate **12** disconsolate, heavy-hearted

SADDEN: **5** crush, upset **6** burden, deject **7** depress **8** dispirit **10** discourage, dishearten

SADDLE: **4** load, seat **5** mount **6** burden, howdah, impede **7** montura, pillion **8** encumber, restrict
parts: **3** eye **5** girth, skirt, tread **6** branch, cantle, pommel **7** stirrup
types: **6** cowboy **7** English, Western **10** sidesaddle

SADISTIC: **5** cruel **6** brutal **7** vicious **9** barbarous

SADNESS: **4** funk **5** blues, dumps, gloom **6** sorrow **7** anguish **9** dejection, heartache **10** depression, melancholy **11** unhappiness

SAFARI: **4** hunt, tour, trek, trip **7** journey **9** excursion **10** expedition **11** exploration

SAFE: **4** sure, wary **5** chest, clear, sound, vault **6** armory, secure, stable, unhurt **7** careful, guarded, prudent **8** cautious, discreet, harmless, nontoxic, shielded, unharmed **9** innocuous, preserved, protected, sheltered, strongbox, unscathed, untouched **10** dependable, depository **11** impregnable, trustworthy **12** conservative, invulnerable

SAFEGUARD: **6** convoy, defend, escort, harbor, secure, shield **7** bulwark, defense, protect **8** armament, preserve, security, umbrella **10** protection

SAFEKEEPING: **4** care **7** custody, storage **8** security **10** protection **12** conservation, preservation

SAFETY: **5** cover **6** asylum, refuge **7** freedom, shelter **8** security **9** assurance, sanctuary, touchback **10** protection

SAG: **4** bend, drop, flag, flop, lull, sink, wilt **5** droop, slide, slump **6** dangle, settle, slouch, weaken **7** decline, deflate **8** diminish, downturn, languish **9** downtrend

SAGA: **4** epic, myth, tale, yarn **5** story **6** legend **7** history **9** adventure, narrative

SAGACIOUS: **4** sage, wise **5** acute, cagey, quick, sharp, smart **6** astute, clever, shrewd **7** cunning, knowing, prudent, sapient **8** sensible **9** judicious **10** discerning, insightful, perceptive **11** intelligent, penetrating

SAGACITY: **6** acumen, wisdom **8** prudence, sapience **10** cleverness, perception, shrewdness **11** discernment **12** intelligence

SAGE: **4** guru, herb, mint, seer, wise **5** sound, spice **6** master, pundit, salvia, savant, shrewd, solemn **7** learned, prudent, sapient, scholar **8** profound, sensible **9** judicious, seasoning **10** discerning, perceptive **11** philosopher
of Chelsea: **7** Carlyle
of Concord: **7** Emerson
of Ferney: **8** Voltaire
of Monticello: **9** Jefferson

SAGITTARIUS: **4** sign **6** archer **13** constellation
born: **8** December, November

SAHARA DESERT:
countries: **4** Chad, Mali **5** Egypt, Libya, Niger, Sudan **7** Algeria, Morocco, Tunisia **10** Mauritania
features: **5** oases **6** hamada **9** Air Massif **13** Tibesti Massif **16** Ahaggar Mountains
inhabitant: **4** Arab **5** nomad **6** Berber, Tuareg
place: **11** North Africa
winds: **5** leste **6** gibleh

SAID: **3** say **4** such **5** quoth **6** quoted, spoken, stated **7** uttered **10** pronounced

SAIL: **3** fly **4** boat, dart, kaul, keel, move, scud, skim, soar, trip **5** drift, float, glide, sheet **6** canvas, cruise, voyage **7** journey **8** navigate **9** excursion
types: **3** jib **6** mizzen **7** balloon, spanker, topsail **8** foresail, mainsail, staysail **9** spinnaker

SAILBOAT: **4** yawl **5** craft, ketch, skiff, sloop, yacht **6** vessel **8** schooner **9** catamaran

SAILOR: **4** jack, salt, swab **5** middy **6** pirate, seaman **7** mariner **8** deckhand, seafarer, seawoman **9** yachtsman **10** bluejacket, midshipman **11** yachtswoman **12** midshipwoman

SAINT: **4** holy **6** martyr **7** paragon **8** altruist, canonize, enshrine
biography: **11** hagiography

SAINTLY: **4** good, holy **5** godly, pious **6** devout, divine **7** angelic, blessed, upright **8** heavenly, virtuous **9** religious, righteous, spiritual

SAKE: **3** end **4** gain, good, saki, wine **5** drink **6** behalf, motive, reason, regard **7** account, benefit, purpose, respect, welfare **8** beverage, interest **9** advantage, objective

SALAAM: **3** bow **4** bend **6** salute **8** greeting **9** genuflect, obeisance **10** salutation

SALACIOUS: **4** lewd **5** bawdy **6** wanton **7** lustful, obscene **9** lecherous **10** lascivious

SALAD: **6** greens
ingredients: **3** egg **5** fruit, olive, onion **6** carrot, celery, cheese, pepper, radish, tomato **7** cabbage, crouton, lettuce, parsley **8** cucumber, dressing, mushroom
types: **3** egg **4** tuna **5** chef's, fruit **6** Caesar, potato, tossed **7** chicken, seafood, Waldorf **8** macaroni **9** vegetable

SALAMANDER: **3** eft **4** newt **5** poker, stove **6** lizard, spirit, triton **7** axolotl, reptile, urodela **8** mudpuppy **9** amphibian **10** hellbender

SALARY: **3** fee, pay **4** hire **5** bacon, bread, wages **6** income **7** stipend **8** earnings **9** allowance, emolument **10** honorarium, recompense **12** compensation, remuneration

SALE: **4** deal **6** demand, market **7** bargain, rummage **8** discount, exchange, purchase, transfer **9** clearance, reduction **11** transaction

SALESPERSON: **5** agent, clerk **6** hawker, vendor **7** peddler **8** salesman **10** saleswoman

SALIENT: **6** marked, moving, signal **7** glaring, jumping, obvious **8** flagrant, striking **9** important, prominent, springing **10** noticeable, projecting, pronounced, protruding **11** conspicuous

SALINE: **5** briny, salty **8** brackish, solution

SALIVA: **4** spit **5** water **6** phlegm **7** spittle **10** salivation

SALLOW: **3** wan **4** pale **5** ashen **6** anemic, pallid, sickly **9** jaundiced, unhealthy, yellowish

SALLY: **4** dash, joke, leap, quip, trip **5** burst, erupt, jaunt, start **6** attack, charge, outing, retort, sortie, spring **7** journey, rushing **8** outburst **9** excursion, witticism

SALMAGUNDI: **4** hash **5** salad **6** jumble, medley **7** mixture **8** mishmash **9** potpourri **10** assortment, hodgepodge

SALMON: **4** fish, food, mort, pink **5** color, smolt
enclosure: **4** weir, yair
female: **4** raun **6** baggit **9** blackfish
genus: **5** salmo **12** oncorhynchus
male: **6** kipper **7** redfish
smoked: **3** lox
variety: **4** coho **7** chinook, Pacific, quinnat, redback **8** Atlantic, blueback, humpback
young: **4** parr **6** alevin, grilse

SALON: **4** hall, room, shop **5** group **6** parlor **7** gallery **8** showroom **9** gathering, reception **10** assemblage

SALOON: **3** bar, pub **4** hall **5** cabin **6** tavern **7** barroom, taproom **8** alehouse, groggery

SALT: **3** tar, wit **4** corn, cure **5** brine, humor, sharp, spice, witty **6** flavor, sailor, saline, seaman, season **7** element, piquant **8** compound **9** condiment, seasoning **12** preservative

SALTY: **4** racy **5** briny, spicy, witty **6** risque, saline **7** zestful **8** alkaline, brackish, colorful, flavored

SALUBRIOUS: **4** good **7** bracing, healthy, helpful **8** curative, salutary, sanitary **9** desirable, healthful, wholesome **10** beneficial **11** restorative **12** invigorating

SALUTARY: **6** useful **8** remedial **10** nutritious, salubrious **12** advantageous

SALUTATION: **3** ave, bow **4** hail, kiss **5** aloha, hello, howdy, toast **6** curtsy, salaam, salute **7** address, tribute, welcome **8** farewell, greeting

SALUTE: **4** hail, heil, wave **5** cheer, greet, honor **6** accost, praise, signal **7** address, applaud **9** recognize **10** compliment **12** congratulate

SALVAGE: **4** save **6** rescue **7** reclaim, recover, restore

SALVATION: **6** rescue **8** mainstay **10** liberation, redemption **11** deliverance **12** conservation, emancipation, preservation

SALVE: **4** balm, ease, heal **5** cream **6** anoint, cerate, lotion, remedy, soothe **7** assuage, relieve, unguent **8** flattery, medicine, ointment **9** alleviate

SALVO: **5** burst **6** volley **7** barrage, gunfire **8** outburst **9** cannonade **11** bombardment, reservation

SAME: **4** ibid, like, self, very **5** alike, ditto, equal, exact **7** similar **8** parallel **9** duplicate, identical **10** comparable, consistent, equivalent, invariable, synonymous, unchanging

SAMENESS: **5** unity **6** parity **7** oneness **8** likeness, monotony **10** similarity, uniformity **11** equivalence

SAMOA, WESTERN:
animals: **3** asi, ipo **4** lulu **6** ataata, sesele
capital: **4** Apia
cities: **8** Pago Pago
continent: **7** Oceania
ethnic groups: **6** Samoan **8** European **10** Euronesian, Polynesian
features: **4** lava
islands: **5** Upolu **6** Manono, Savaii **7** Apolima
languages: **6** Samoan **7** English
monetary unit: **4** tala
water: **7** Pacific

SAMPLE: **4** test **5** model, piece, taste **7** example, inspect, pattern, segment **8** instance, specimen **12** illustration

SAMSON:
betrayer: **7** Delilah
deathplace: **4** Gaza
title: **5** judge

SAMUEL:
anointed: **4** Saul
father: **7** Elkanah
mentor: **3** Eli
mother: **6** Hannah
title: **5** judge **7** prophet

SANCTIFY: **5** bless **6** anoint, purify **7** glorify **8** dedicate **10** consecrate

SANCTIMONIOUS: **4** holy, smug **5** pious **7** canting, preachy **9** insincere **11** pharisaical **12** hypocritical

SANCTION: **4** okay **5** allow **6** decree, permit, ratify **7** approve, boycott, confirm, consent, embargo, endorse, penalty, support **8** accredit, legalize **9** approbate, authorize, encourage **10** permission **11** endorsement **12** confirmation, ratification **13** authorization, encouragement

SANCTITY: **5** piety **6** purity, virtue **8** holiness **9** godliness, solemnity **10** sacredness **11** saintliness **13** inviolability, righteousness

SANCTUARY: **4** port **5** cover, haven, oasis **6** asylum, bemata, chapel, church, harbor, mosque, refuge, safety, shrine, temple **7** convent, retreat, sanctum, shelter **8** hideaway, preserve **9** monastery **10** protection, tabernacle

SAND: **4** grit, guts, silt **5** beach, nerve **6** gravel, smooth **7** courage, resolve, stamina **8** backbone **12** perseverance

SANDAL: **4** clog, shoe, zori **5** thong **7** slipper, talaria **8** flipflop, huarache, moccasin **10** espadrille

SANDBANK: **4** dune, reef, spit **5** mound, shoal **7** sandbar **8** hillside

SANDPIPER: **4** bird, knot, ruff **5** reeve, terek **6** dunlin, teeter **7** fiddler **8** triddler **10** beachrobin

SANDWICH: **3** BLT, sub **4** club, hero **5** lunch **6** canape, hoagie **7** grinder **9** hamburger, sloppy Joe, submarine **12** cheeseburger

SANDY: **5** blond **6** gritty, plucky, porous **7** powdery **8** brownish, granular, sabulous, shifting, unstable

SANE: **4** wise **5** lucid, sober, sound **7** healthy, logical **8** balanced, rational, sensible **9** sagacious **10** reasonable **11** levelheaded

SANGFROID: **5** poise **6** aplomb **8** calmness, coolness **9** composure **10** equanimity

SANGUINE: **3** red **4** fond, warm **5** happy, ruddy **6** lively, upbeat **7** buoyant, crimson, flushed, hopeful, scarlet **8** cheerful **9** confident, expectant **10** optimistic, passionate **12** enthusiastic

SANITARY: **5** clean **7** aseptic, sterile **8** hygienic, purified **9** healthful **11** disinfected

SANITY: **4** mind **5** sense **6** reason **7** balance **8** lucidity, saneness **9** soundness, stability **10** competency **11** rationality **12** intelligence

SAN MARINO:
capital: **9** San Marino
cities: **10** Serravalle
continent: **6** Europe
ethnic groups: **7** Italian **11** Sanmarinese
features: **11** Mount Titano
language: **7** Italian
monetary unit: **11** Italian lira
native: **11** Sanmarinese

SAO TOME AND PRINCIPE:
capital: **7** Sao Tome
cities: **9** Santa Cruz **12** Santo Antonio

continent: **6** Africa
ethnic groups: **6** Arican **10** Portuguese
language: **10** Portuguese
monetary unit: **5** dobra
water: **8** Atlantic **12** Gulf of Guinea

SAP: **4** dolt, dupe, fool, jerk, milk, ruin **5** chump, drain, fluid, idiot, juice, vigor **6** energy, health, impair, sucker, trench, tunnel, weaken **7** deplete, destroy, exhaust, subvert **8** enervate, vitality **9** blackjack, secretion, undermine **10** debilitate, devitalize

SAPID: **5** tasty **6** savory **7** zestful **8** engaging **9** palatable **10** flavorable

SAPIENT: **4** sage, wise **7** knowing, learned **9** sagacious **10** discerning **11** intelligent **13** knowledgeable

SAPLESS: **3** dry **4** lazy **8** withered **9** shriveled, spineless **11** devitalized

SAPLING: **4** tree **5** young, youth **8** seedling

SAPPHO: **4** poet
nationality: **5** Greek

SAPPY: **4** lush **5** juicy, moist, plump, silly **6** slushy, watery **7** foolish, mawkish **9** succulent **11** sentimental

SARAH:
husband: **7** Abraham
servant: **5** Hagar
son: **5** Isaac

SARCASM: **4** gibe, jeer **5** humor, irony, scorn, taunt **6** banter, satire **7** mockery **8** acerbity, acridity, needling, ridicule **9** criticism **10** lampooning

SARCASTIC: **5** sassy, sharp **6** biting **7** caustic, cutting, cynical, mocking **8** ironical, sardonic, scornful **9** corrosive, satirical **11** disparaging

SARDINIA:
capital: **8** Cagliari
continent: **6** Europe
features: **7** Nuraghi **13** Costa Smeralda
kingdom with: **8** Piedmont
language: **7** Catalan
region of: **5** Italy
water: **13** Mediterranean

SARDONIC: **7** caustic, cynical, jeering, mocking **8** scornful

SASH: **4** band, belt **5** frame, scarf **6** corset, girdle, ribbon **8** casement, cincture **9** waistband **10** cummerbund

SASHAY: **4** move, walk **5** glide, mince, strut **6** prance **7** flounce, swagger **9** excursion

SASKATCHEWAN:
bird: **6** grouse
capital: **6** Regina
cities: **8** Moose Jaw **9** Saskatoon **12** Prince Albert
country: **6** Canada
flower: **4** lily
water: **5** Rouge **7** Red Deer **8** Reindeer **9** Athabaska, Qu'Appelle, Wollaston **11** Assiniboine

SASSY: **4** bold, rude, wise **5** brash, fresh, saucy, smart **6** brazen, cheeky, jaunty, snippy **7** forward **8** impudent **9** sarcastic **12** discourteous **13** disrespectful

SATAN: **5** demon, devil, fiend **6** Belial **7** Lucifer, Old Nick, tempter **8** Apollyon **9** Beelzebub **11** fallen angel **14** Mephistopheles

SATANIC: **4** evil **5** cruel **6** wicked **7** demonic, heinous **8** devilish, fiendish, sadistic **9** malicious **10** diabolical

SATCHEL: **3** bag **4** case **5** pouch, purse **6** valise **7** handbag **8** reticule, suitcase

SATE: **4** cloy, glut **5** gorge, stuff **7** gratify, satiate, satisfy, surfeit **8** overfill

SATELLITE: **4** luna, moon **6** minion, rocket **7** sputnik **8** asteroid, follower, hanger-on, retainer **9** ancillary, attendant, dependent, sycophant **10** spacecraft, subsidiary

SATIATE: **4** cloy, glut, sate **5** gorge, stuff **6** quench **7** gratify, satisfy, surfeit **8** overfill

SATIRE: **5** irony, spoof **6** banter, parody **7** lampoon, mockery, sarcasm, takeoff **8** ridicule **9** burlesque **10** caricature

SATIRICAL: **5** witty **7** caustic, comical, cynical, mocking **8** farcical, ironical, sardonic **9** sarcastic **10** lampooning

SATIRIZE: **4** mock **5** mimic, spoof **6** deride, parody **7** lampoon **8** ridicule **9** criticize **10** caricature

SATISFACTION: **5** bliss **6** amends, relief **7** comfort, justice, payment **8** pleasure **9** atonement, enjoyment, happiness **10** recompense, reparation **11** contentment, fulfillment, restitution, vindication **12** compensation, remuneration **13** gratification

SATISFACTORY: **4** fair, good, okay **5** valid **6** decent, enough **7** average **8** adequate, passable **9** tolerable **10** acceptable, sufficient

SATISFY: **3** pay **4** fill, meet, sate, suit **5** clear, repay, serve **6** answer, defray, pacify, please, quench, settle, supply **7** appease, assuage, content, fulfill, gratify, indulge, satiate, suffice, surfeit **8** convince, persuade, reparate **9** discharge, indemnify **10** compensate, remunerate **11** accommodate

SATURATE: **3** sop, wet **4** fill, glut, soak **5** imbue, souse, steep **6** dampen, drench, imbrue **7** ingrain **8** permeate, submerge, waterlog **9** penetrate **10** impregnate

SATURN:
from sun: **5** sixth
rings: **4** ansa
satellites: **4** Rhea **5** Dione, Mimas, Titan **6** Phoebe, Tethys **7** Iapetus, Japetus **8** Hyperion **9** Enceladus

SATURNALIA: **4** orgy **5** feast, party, spree **7** revelry **8** festival **9** bacchanal

SATURNINE: **4** dour, dull, glum **5** grave, heavy **6** bitter, gloomy, morose, solemn, somber, sullen **7** passive **8** sardonic **10** melancholy

SAUCE: **4** sass **5** booze, gravy **6** flavor, liquor, relish **7** alcohol **8** dressing **9** condiment, seasoning
variety: **3** soy **5** apple, chili, curry, pesto **6** catsup, tartar, tomato **7** Colbert, ketchup, mustard, Newburg, Tabasco **8** barbecue, Bernaise, marinara, ravigote, remolade **9** blueberry, raspberry **10** Bordelaise, gooseberry, mayonnaise, strawberry **11** hollandaise, horseradish **14** Worcestershire

SAUCY: **4** bold, pert, rude, smug **5** brash, cocky, fresh, sassy **6** brazen, cheeky **7** defiant, forward **8** flippant, impudent, insolent **9** audacious **11** impertinent **13** disrespectful

SAUDI ARABIA:
capital: **6** Riyadh
cities: **4** Taif **5** Jidda, Mecca **6** Dammam, Jeddah, Medina
continent: **4** Asia
ethnic groups: **4** Arab
features: **10** Rubal Khali **11** Nafud desert
language: **6** Arabic
monetary unit: **5** riyal
water: **6** Red Sea **9** Aqaba Gulf **11** Persian Gulf

SAUL:
daughters: **5** Merab **6** Michal
enemy: **11** Philistines
father: **4** Kish

grandfather: **3** Ner
kingdom: **6** Israel
sons: **7** Abinoam **8** Jonathan
successor: **5** David
uncle: **3** Ner
wife: **7** Ahinoam

SAUNTER: **4** idle, roam, rove, walk **5** amble, dally, drift, mosey, stray **6** dawdle, loiter, lounge, ramble, sashay, stroll, wander **7** meander **8** ruminate, straggle **9** promenade

SAUSAGE: **5** frank, gigot, wurst **6** salami, wiener **7** baloney, bologna **8** drisheen, kielbasa, rolliche **9** bratwurst, pepperoni, rollichie **10** liverwurst **11** frankfurter, wienerwurst

SAVAGE: **4** grim, rude, wild **5** brute, crude, cruel, feral, harsh, rabid, rough **6** bloody, brutal, fierce, native **7** beastly, brutish, inhuman, untamed, vicious, violent **8** barbaric, demoniac, ruthless, sadistic **9** barbarian, ferocious, heartless, merciless, murderous, primitive, truculent **11** uncivilized **12** bloodthirsty, unrestrained

SAVANNA: **5** plain **8** savannah **9** grassland

SAVANT: **4** sage **6** expert, genius, master **7** scholar, wise man **12** intellectual

SAVE: **4** bank, free, keep, stow **5** amass, guard, hoard, skimp, spare, store **6** defend, except, redeem, rescue, retain, scrimp **7** deliver, deposit, husband, reclaim, reserve, salvage **8** conserve, maintain, preserve **9** economize, extricate, safeguard, stockpile **10** accumulate

SAVING: **6** frugal, rescue **7** barring, careful, prudent, thrifty **10** economical **12** conservation, preservation

SAVINGS: **5** funds, means **7** account **8** reserves **10** investment, provisions

SAVIOR: **4** hero **6** knight **7** messiah, rescuer **8** defender, guardian, redeemer **9** liberator, protector **11** emancipator

SAVOIR FAIRE: **4** tact **5** grace, poise **7** finesse, manners **8** elegance **9** composure, diplomacy **10** adroitness **11** worldliness

SAVOR: **4** odor, zest **5** aroma, scent, smack, smell, taste, tinge, trait **6** flavor, relish **7** essence, quality **8** piquancy **9** fragrance, sensation **10** experience

SAVORY: **5** salty, sapid, spicy, tasty **7** piquant, pungent **8** alluring, aromatic, flavored, pleasing **9** agreeable, palatable **10** appetizing, delectable **11** inoffensive, scrumptious

SAW: **3** cut, hew **4** tool, word **5** adage, axiom, maxim, motto **6** cliche, saying **7** epigram, proverb **8** aphorism, apothegm

SAY: **4** aver, call, show, talk, tell, vote **5** claim, imply, quote, speak, state, utter, voice **6** advise, affirm, answer, assert, convey, inform, recite, relate, remark, repeat, report **7** comment, declare, dictate, express, mention, respond, testify **8** announce, indicate, intimate **9** advertise, enunciate, insinuate, pronounce **10** articulate, asseverate **11** communicate

SAYING: **3** saw **5** adage, axiom, maxim, motto **6** byword, cliche, phrase, slogan, truism **7** epigram, proverb **8** aphorism, apothegm **10** expression

SCAB: **5** crust, mange **6** eschar **8** apostate, blackleg **9** scoundrel **13** strikebreaker

SCABBY: **4** base, mean, vile **5** mangy **6** crusty, scurvy, shabby **7** blotchy **10** despicable **12** contemptible

SCABROUS: **5** rough, scaly **6** coarse, knotty, rugged **9** difficult **11** treacherous

SCALAWAG: **5** rogue, scamp **6** rascal **9** miscreant, reprobate, scoundrel, trickster **11** rapscallion

SCALD: **4** burn, char, heat **6** blanch, scorch **7** parboil **9** criticize, excoriate

SCALE: **4** film, husk, peel, rate, rule, shed, size, skin **5** climb, crust, flake, gamut, mount, order, ratio **6** ascend, degree, lamina, spread, weight **7** balance, coating, measure, ranking **8** covering, escalate, regulate, spectrum **9** continuum, gradation, hierarchy **10** instrument, proportion **11** calibration

SCALE DOWN: **4** trim **5** limit **7** shorten **8** decrease, diminish, downsize, restrict

SCALE UP: **7** advance, augment **8** increase, lengthen

SCALLION: **4** leek **5** onion **7** shallot

SCAM: **4** dupe **5** cheat **7** defraud, swindle **9** victimize

SCAMP: **5** cheat, knave, rogue **6** rascal **7** villain **8** scalawag **9** prankster, reprobate, scoundrel **11** rapscallion

SCAMPER: **3** run **4** bolt, dart, dash, flee, race **5** hurry, scoot **6** frolic, hasten, scurry **9** skedaddle

SCAN: **4** skim, view **5** study **6** browse, glance, peruse, search, survey **7** examine, inspect, observe **10** scrutinize **11** contemplate, examination

SCANDAL: **5** odium, shame, stain **6** expose, gossip, infamy **7** calumny, outrage, slander **8** disgrace, ignominy, reproach **9** aspersion, discredit **10** defamation, detraction, opprobrium **13** embarrassment

SCANDALIZE: **5** shock, smear **6** appall, offend, revile, vilify **7** slander **8** disgrace, dishonor **9** embarrass **10** calumniate

SCANDALOUS: **7** heinous **8** libelous, shameful, shocking **9** offensive **10** defamatory, flagitious, outrageous, slanderous **11** disgraceful **12** disreputable

SCANDINAVIA:
explorer: **4** Eric
features: **3** amt **4** odal **5** fiord, fjeld, fjord
includes: **6** Norway, Sweden **7** Denmark, Finland, Iceland
languages: **6** Danish **7** Faroese, Finnish, Swedish **9** Icelandic, Norwegian
people: **4** Dane, Lapp **5** Norse, Swede **8** Norseman, Teutonic **9** Icelandic, Norwegian
rulers: **3** Ros **4** Atli **10** Varangians

SCANT: **4** lean **5** short, stint, tight **6** meager, scarce, scrimp, slight, sparse **7** limited, sparing, wanting **9** deficient **10** inadequate **12** insufficient

SCAPEGOAT: **4** dupe **5** patsy **6** victim **7** fall guy **9** sacrifice

SCAR: **3** cut **4** flaw, mark, scab **5** cliff, crack, wound **6** damage, deface, injury **7** blemish, scratch **8** cicatrix, pockmark **9** disfigure

SCARCE: **4** rare **5** scant, short **6** hardly, meager, seldom, sparse **7** unusual **8** uncommon **9** deficient **10** infrequent, occasional **12** insufficient

SCARCITY: **4** lack, want **6** dearth, famine **8** rareness, shortage, sparsity **10** deficiency, inadequacy, scantiness **11** infrequency **12** uncommonness **13** insufficiency

SCARE: **4** fear **5** alarm, dread, panic, shock, spook **6** fright **7** horrify, startle, terrify **8** affright, frighten, threaten **9** terrorize **10** intimidate

SCARED: **6** afraid **7** alarmed, fearful **8** startled **9** terrified **10** frightened

SCARF: **3** boa, cut, tie **4** sash, wrap **5** ascot, cover, gorge, shawl, stole **6** cravat, devour, groove, tippet **7** consume, muffler, necktie **8** babushka, bandanna **9** comforter **11** neckerchief

SCARLET: **3** red **4** lewd **5** bawdy, color **7** immoral, reddish **8** unchaste

SCARLET LETTER, THE:
author: **18** Nathaniel Hawthorne
characters: **5** Pearl **12** Hester Prynne **16** Arthur Dimmesdale **18** Roger Chillingworth
crime: **8** adultery

SCARLETT O'HARA:
book: **15** Gone with the Wind
home: **4** Tara
husband: **11** Rhett Butler

SCARY: **5** eerie, hairy **6** creepy, spooky **7** fearful, ghostly **8** alarming, chilling **10** horrifying, terrifying **11** frightening

SCAT: **4** beat, flee, shoo **5** scoot, scram **7** singing, vamoose

SCATHING: **5** harsh, sharp **6** biting, brutal, severe **7** burning, caustic, harmful, mordant, pointed **8** scalding, scornful, stinging **9** scorching

SCATTER: **3** sow **4** cast, rout **5** fling, spray, strew, waste **6** dispel, divide, shower, spread **7** bestrew, deflect, diffuse, disband, fritter **8** disperse, separate, splatter, sprinkle, squander **9** circulate, dissipate, diversity **10** distribute **11** disseminate **12** decentralize

SCATTERBRAINED: **4** zany **5** dizzy, giddy, silly **7** flighty **8** careless **9** forgetful, frivolous **12** absent-minded **13** irresponsible

SCATTERED: **6** sparse, spotty, strewn **7** erratic **8** isolated, sporadic **9** irregular **10** infrequent, widespread **12** interspersed

SCAVENGER: **3** rat **5** hyena **6** magpie **7** vulture **9** collector

SCENARIO: **4** plan, plot **6** script **7** outline, rundown, summary **8** synopsis **10** screenplay

SCENE: **4** site, spot, view **5** arena, place, scape, sight, venue, vista **6** locale **7** culture, display, episode, picture, quarrel, setting, tableau, tantrum **8** backdrop, incident, locality, location **9** commotion, landscape, spectacle **10** background

SCENERY: **4** view **5** decor, props **7** setting, terrain **8** backdrop **9** landscape **11** furnishings **12** surroundings

SCENIC: **8** dramatic **9** beautiful, panoramic **11** picturesque, spectacular **12** breathtaking

SCENT: **4** clue, nose, odor **5** aroma, smell, sniff, spoor, track, trail, whiff **6** detect, flavor **7** bouquet, essence, perfume **9** fragrance, redolence

SCEPTER: **3** rod **4** wand **5** baton, staff, stick **9** authority **11** sovereignty **12** jurisdiction

SCHEDULE: **4** card, list, plan, time **5** chart, slate, table **6** agenda, docket, roster **7** arrange, catalog, program, routine **8** calendar, organize, register **9** inventory, itinerary, timetable

SCHEME: **3** aim, web **4** list, plot **5** angle, cabal, order, plant, trick **6** design, device, devise, layout, system **7** collude, concoct, diagram, gimmick, outline, pattern, program, project, purpose, tactics **8** conspire, contrive, intrigue, maneuver, strategy **10** concoction, conspiracy **11** arrangement, contrivance, proposition

SCHEMING: **3** sly **4** foxy **6** artful, crafty **7** cunning **9** conniving, deceitful

SCHISM: **5** break, split **6** breach **7** discord, faction **8** disunion, division **10** disharmony, separation

SCHLEMIEL: **3** oaf **4** bozo, clod, dolt, fool, jerk **5** idiot **7** bungler **8** bonehead

SCHLEPP: **3** lug **4** drag, haul, jerk, pull **5** carry

SCHOLAR: **4** sage **5** brain, pupil **6** pedant, savant **7** bookman, egghead, learner, student **8** academic, bookworm **9** bookwoman, professor **12** intellectual

SCHOLARLY: **7** erudite, learned **8** educated, lettered, schooled, studious **12** intellectual

SCHOLARSHIP: **3** aid **5** grant **8** learning **9** education, erudition, knowledge

SCHOLASTIC: **6** versed **7** learned **8** academic, lettered **11** educational

SCHOOL: **3** law **4** high, lead, prep, view **5** coach, crowd, drill, faith, flock, group, guide, shoal, teach, train **6** belief, middle, public **7** academy, college, convent, educate, prepare, primary, private, seminar **8** doctrine, instruct, military, seminary **9** cultivate, institute, secondary **10** elementary, philosophy, university, vocational **11** institution **12** conservatory, kindergarten

SCHOOLBOOK: **4** text **5** atlas **6** primer **7** grammar **9** geography

SCHOONER: **4** boat, ship **5** glass, yacht **6** vessel **7** clipper

SCIENCE: **3** art **5** skill, study **9** education, erudition, knowledge, technique **10** discipline, technology

branches: **6** botany **7** biology, geology, physics, zoology **8** medicine **9** chemistry, geography, sociology **10** physiology, psychology **11** archaeology, cybernetics, mathematics **12** anthropology **13** social science

SCIENTIFIC: **5** exact **8** skillful **9** technical **10** methodical, systematic **12** experimental

SCINTILLA: **3** ray **4** atom, iota **5** flash, spark, speck, trace **7** glimmer **8** particle

SCINTILLATE: **5** charm, flash, gleam, shine **7** glimmer, glitter, sparkle, twinkle **9** coruscate

SCINTILLATING: **5** witty **6** bright, lively **8** animated, dazzling **9** brilliant **11** stimulating

SCION: **3** bud **4** heir, seed, twig **5** child **6** branch, sprout **7** progeny **8** offshoot **9** offspring, successor **10** descendant

SCISSORS: **6** shears **7** trimmer **8** clippers

SCOFF: **3** eat **4** jeer, jibe, mock, razz **5** chide, gorge, knock, steal, taunt, tease **6** deride, devour, gobble **7** despise **8** belittle, ridicule

SCOLD: **3** nag **4** haze, lash, rail, rant, rate **5** abuse, chide, shrew **6** berate, rebuke, revile, virago **7** reprove, upbraid **8** admonish, chastise, lambaste **9** castigate, criticize, reprehend, reprimand **10** vituperate

SCONCE: **4** fort, head **5** skull **6** noggin **7** bracket, shelter **9** earthwork **10** protection **11** candlestick

SCOOP: **3** dig **4** bail, beat, lade, lift, news **5** gouge, ladle, spoon, story **6** dipper, dredge, gather, hollow, shovel, vessel **8** excavate **9** exclusive

SCOOT: **3** run **4** bolt, dart, dash, flee, rush **5** hurry, scram **6** hustle, scurry **9** skedaddle

SCOPE: **4** area, goal, room, span **5** field, grasp, range, reach, sweep **6** domain, extent, intent, length, margin, sphere, vision **7** liberty, outlook **8** capacity, distance, latitude **9** dimension, extension, influence

SCORCH: **3** dry **4** burn, char, flay, sear **5** parch, scald, singe, toast **6** scathe, wither **7** blister, scourge, shrivel **8** lambaste **9** excoriate

SCORE: **3** add, cut, run, tab **4** debt, goal, line, mark, rate **5** count, grade, judge, notch, point, slash, tally, total **6** amount, attain, basket, grudge, number, reason, record, result, scotch, secure **7** account, arrange, average, outcome, scratch, succeed, summary **8** evaluate, incision **9** calculate, grievance, reckoning **10** accomplish, obligation **11** composition, orchestrate

SCORN: **4** jeer, mock, shun **5** flout, scoff, sneer, spurn **6** deride, reject **7** condemn, contemn, despise, disdain **8** contempt, derision, ridicule **9** ostracize

SCORNFUL: **7** abusive, haughty **8** arrogant, insolent **9** malicious, sarcastic **10** despicable, disdainful **11** disparaging **12** contemptuous

SCORPION: **6** onager **7** stinger **8** arachnid

SCOTCH: **3** cut, end **4** foil, stop **5** notch, score **6** hinder, injure, liquor, thwart, whisky **7** alcohol, scratch **8** obstruct

SCOTLAND:
authors: **4** Hogg, Moir **5** Burns, Scott **6** Barrie **9** Stevenson **10** Conan-Doyle
bay: **5** Scapa
capital: **9** Edinburgh
child: **4** dalt **6** scuddy **8** smatchet
cities: **3** Ayr **4** Duns, Oban **5** Alloa, Banff, Burgh, Leith, Perth, Troon **6** Dundee **7** Glasgow, Grunock, Paisley, Renfrew **8** Aberdeen, Dumfries, Stirling **9** Edinburgh, Inverness, St. Andrews **10** Kilmarnock
clothing: **3** tam **4** kilt, maud **5** toosh **6** fecket, tartan **7** arisard **8** Balmoral **11** Tam o'Shanter
drink: **5** scour **6** athole, whisky **8** whittier
explorer: **3** Rae
firth: **3** Tay **4** Kyle, Loch, Lorn **5** Clyde, Forth, Lorne, Moray **6** Linnhe, Solway **7** Dornoch **8** Cromarty, Pentland
food: **4** saps **5** briar, brose, scone **6** haggis, tammie **7** bannock
former name: **9** Caledonia
government: **13** United Kingdom
hill: **4** brae **6** strone
historian: **4** Hume **5** Skene
islands: **3** Rum **4** Aran, Bute, Eigg, Fair, Inch, Iona, Jura, Lona, Muck, Mull, Rhum, Skye, Uist **5** Arran **6** Harris, Orkney **8** Hebrides, Shetland
kings: **5** David, James **6** Duncan, Robert **7** Kenneth, Macbeth, Malcolm, Stuarts, William
lakes: **3** dee, Lin, Tay **4** Earn, Fyne, Gare, loch, Ness, Ryan **5** Leven, Lough, Nevis
languages: **4** Erse **6** Celtic, Gaelic, Keltic, Lallan **7** English, Lalland
mountains: **4** Hope **5** Nevis **7** Cheviot **8** Grampian **9** Highlands

patron saint: **6** Andrew
people: **4** Gael, Pict, Scot **5** Norse **8** Damnonii **9** Dammonian
plaid: **4** maud **6** tartan
queens: **4** Mary **8** Margaret
rivers: **3** Ayr, Dee, Don, Esk, Tay **4** Doon, Glen, Nith, Norn, Spey **5** Afton, Annan, Clyde, Garry, North, Tweed, Ythan **6** Teviot **7** Deveron
seas: **5** Irish, North **8** Atlantic, Hebrides
spirit: **5** kelpy **6** kelpie

SCOTT, SIR WALTER: **4** poet **6** author **8** novelist
nationality: **8** Scottish
wrote: **6** Rob Roy **7** Ivanhoe, Marmion **8** The Abbot, Waverley **9** The Pirate, Woodstock **10** Kenilworth **11** Redgauntlet, The Talisman **12** The Antiquary, Guy Mannering, The Monastery, Old Mortality **14** Quentin Durward

SCOUNDREL: **3** cad **5** cheat, crook, knave, rogue, scamp, thief **6** rascal, varlet, weasel **7** villain **8** scalawag **9** miscreant, reprobate **10** blackguard **11** rapscallion

SCOUR: **3** rub **4** buff, comb, rake, swab, wash **5** clean, hurry, scrub **6** forage, polish, scurry, search **7** cleanse, rummage **8** brighten, traverse

SCOURGE: **4** bane, beat, flay, flog, lash, whip **5** curse, slash **6** plague, punish, switch, thrash **7** afflict, torment **8** chastise, epidemic, lambaste **9** castigate, excoriate **10** affliction, infliction, punishment

SCOUT: **3** spy **5** guide, scoff, watch **6** patrol, search, survey **7** despise, explore, lookout, observe, pioneer **8** explorer, informer, vanguard **10** adventurer **11** investigate, reconnoiter

SCOWL: **5** frown, glare, lower **6** glower **7** grimace **10** disapprove, expression

SCRABBLE: **5** climb, grope, scape **7** clamber **8** scribble, struggle

SCRAGGLY: **6** coarse, ragged, shabby, shoddy, untidy **7** patched, unkempt **8** battered, tattered **9** irregular

SCRAM: **4** flee, scat, shoo **5** leave, scoot **6** decamp, depart **7** vamoose **9** skedaddle

SCRAMBLE: **3** mix **4** hike, move, push, race, rush **5** blend, climb, haste, upset **6** garble, hustle, jostle, jumble, muddle **7** clamber, confuse, contend, distort, scatter, shuffle **8** mishmash, struggle **10** disarrange

SCRAP: **3** bit, row **4** chip, drop, dump, junk, tiff **5** brawl, chuck, crumb, fight, grain, piece, shred, speck, waste **6** fracas, morsel, refuse, reject **7** abandon, discard, quarrel, remnant, scuffle **8** argument, fraction, fragment, jettison, leftover, squabble

SCRAPE: **3** row, rub **4** claw, hole, mess, rasp, spot **5** amass, erase, fight, grate, graze, shave **6** abrade, gather, pickle, remove, scrimp **7** corrode, dilemma, scratch, scuffle, trouble **10** difficulty **11** predicament

SCRATCH: **3** cut, dig, mar, rub **4** claw, feed, gash, line, mark, rasp **5** break, erase, money, write **6** injury, scotch, scrape, scrawl **7** exclude, expunge **8** abrasion, incision, scribble, withdraw **9** eliminate

SCRAWL: **5** write **6** doddle **7** scratch **8** scrabble, scribble, squiggle **11** handwriting

SCRAWNY: **4** bony, lean, thin **5** gaunt, lanky **6** meager, skinny **7** scraggy **8** rawboned

SCREAM: **3** cry **4** howl, roar, wail, yell, yowl **5** joker, shout **6** bellow, holler, shriek, shrill, squeal **7** screech **8** comedian

SCREECH: **4** yell **5** shout **6** outcry, scream, shriek, shrill, squeal

SCREEN: **4** cage, hide, mask, mesh, pass, pick, sift, veil, view **5** blind, cloak, cover, guard, shade, sieve **6** canopy, censor, defend, filter, shield, sifter **7** analyze, conceal, curtain, divider, examine, protect, shelter **8** evaluate, separate **9** partition **10** camouflage

SCREW: **4** bolt, turn **5** cheat, clamp, crimp, guard, horse, rivet, twist **6** attach, extort, fasten, salary, spiral, thread **7** contort, crumple, distort, squeeze, tighten, turnkey **8** pressure **9** bargainer, propeller

SCREWBALL: **4** bozo, goof, kook **7** dingbat, fanatic, saphead **8** bonehead, crackpot, dumbbell, lunkhead **9** blockhead, character, eccentric, numbskull

SCREW UP: **3** low **4** flub, muff **5** botch, spoil **6** bungle **9** mismanage

SCREWY: **4** nuts **5** batty, crazy, flaky, wacky **6** absurd, insane, whacky **7** cracked **8** peculiar **9** eccentric **10** unbalanced **11** impractical

SCRIBBLE: **4** draw, mark **5** write **6** doodle, scrawl **7** scratch **8** scrabble, squiggle

SCRIBE: **5** clerk **6** author, copier, editor, penman, writer **7** copyist **8** reporter **9** scrivener, secretary **10** amanuensis, journalist **11** transcriber

SCRIMMAGE: **4** game, play **5** fight **6** battle **7** contest **8** practice, skirmish

SCRIMP: **3** eke **4** save **5** skimp **6** scanty **9** economize

SCRIPT: **4** text **5** score **8** scenario **10** manuscript, penmanship **11** calligraphy, chirography, handwriting

SCROLL: **4** list, roll **6** scrawl, volute **7** papyrus, writing **8** document, schedule, streamer **9** parchment

SCROUNGE: **3** beg, bum **6** forage, search, sponge **8** freeload

SCRUB: **3** mop, rub **4** buff, drop, runt, stop, swab, wash **5** abort, clean, scour **6** cancel **7** abandon, cleanse **11** discontinue

SCRUFFY: **5** mangy, messy, rough, seedy **6** shabby, untidy **7** unkempt

SCRUMPTIOUS: **5** tasty, yummy **8** heavenly, luscious **9** delicious, exquisite, succulent **10** appetizing, delightful

SCRUPLE: **4** balk, iota, part **5** demur, doubt, pause, qualm, worry **6** weight **7** anxiety **8** question **9** misgiving **10** conscience, reluctance, uneasiness

SCRUPULOUS: **5** exact, fussy **6** honest, proper **7** careful, dutiful, precise, upright **8** cautious **9** honorable, reluctant **10** meticulous, particular, principled **11** painstaking, punctilious **13** conscientious

SCRUTINIZE: **3** eye **4** comb, scan, sift, view **5** audit, check, probe **6** survey **7** analyze, canvass, examine, inspect **11** investigate

SCRUTINY: **5** watch **7** observe **8** analysis **10** inspection **11** examination **12** surveillance **13** investigation

SCUD: **3** fly, run **4** dart, gust, skim, wind **5** cloud

SCUFFLE: **3** how, row **5** brawl, fight, melee, scrap **6** affray, fracas, strife, tussle **7** shuffle, wrestle **8** struggle **9** commotion

SCULPTOR: **6** artist, carver **8** chiseler
famous: **4** Gabo **5** Moore, Myron, Rodin, Smith **6** Pisano, Robbia, Zorach **7** Bernini, Cellini, da Vinci, Noguchi, Phidias, Picasso, Zadkine **8** Brancusi, Ghiberti, Hepworth **9** Donatello, Lipschitz, Remington, Roubillac **10** Giacometti, Praxiteles **11** Polycleitus **12** Michelangelo
tools: **4** file, peen, pick **5** gouge **6** banker, chisel, graver, hammer, mallet **7** gradine **9** boucharde

SCULPTURE: **3** art **4** bust, mold **5** carve, shape, totem **6** chisel, heroic, sculpt, statue

SCUM: **4** film, foam **5** algae, dregs, froth, slime, snake, trash, waste **6** rabble, refuse **7** residue **8** riffraff **10** impurities

SCURRILOUS: **4** foul, lewd, vile **5** dirty, gross **6** coarse, filthy, vulgar **7** abusive, obscene, raunchy **8** indecent **9** insulting, offensive **10** derogatory **11** disparaging

SCURRY: **3** run **4** dart, dash, race, rush **5** harry, hurry, scoot, speed, whisk **6** bustle, hasten, hustle, sprint **7** scuttle **9** skedaddle

SCURVY: **4** base, mean, vile **6** shabby **7** disease **9** scorbutic **12** contemptible

SCUTTLE: **4** dish, pail, ruin, sink **5** hatch, scrap **6** basket, bucket **7** abandon, destroy, discard, opening

SCUTTLEBUTT: **4** talk **5** rumor **6** gossip **7** hearsay **8** chitchat

SCYLLA:
antagonist: **10** Amphitrite
devoured: **7** sailors
father: **5** Nisus **7** Phorcys
form: **4** rock **7** monster
heads: **3** six
lover: **5** Minos **8** Poseidon
whirlpool: **9** Charybdis

SEA: **3** mer **4** blue, deep, meer **5** ocean
animals: **4** seal **5** polyp, whale **7** actinia
arm: **3** bay **4** gulf **5** bayou, firth, fjord, frith, inlet, lough **7** estuary
bottom: **3** bed
concerning: **5** naval **6** marine **7** oceanic, pelagic **8** maritime, nautical **9** aequoreal, thalassic
current: **4** surf, tide **8** undertow
dog: **6** fogbow, sailor **8** seafarer
goddesses: **3** Ran **4** Nina **8** Eurynome **9** Leucothea **10** Amphitrite
gods: **3** Ler **5** Aegir, Doris **6** Nereus, Triton **7** Neptune, Phorcus, Proteus **8** Palaemon, Poseidon
names: **3** Red **5** Black, Japan, North **6** Baltic, Bering, Yellow **7** Andaman, Okhotsk **9** Caribbean, East China **10** South China **13** Mediterranean
route: **4** lane
spray: **9** spindrift

SEAL: **3** cap **4** cork, plug, shut, sign **5** brand, close, sigil, stamp, token **6** animal, assure, attest, cachet, clinch, fasten, mammal, pledge, ratify, secure, signet, symbol **7** confine, sticker **8** finalize, hallmark, insignia, validate **9** assurance, carnivore, guarantee **10** consummate, waterproof **12** authenticate
coat: **3** fur **4** pelt
family: **8** Phocidae **9** Otariidae
male fur: **8** seecatch
school: **3** pod
young: **3** pup

SEAM: **3** hem, sew **4** bond, fold, join, line, mark, scar **5** cleft, crack, joint, layer, pleat, ridge **6** groove, suture **7** crevice, fissure, stratum, wrinkle **8** coupling **9** stitching **10** connection

SEAMAN: **4** sail, salt **6** sea dog **8** seafarer **10** midshipman

SEAMSTRESS: **5** sewer **6** tailor **10** dressmaker **12** needleworker

SEAMY: **4** base **5** rough, seedy **6** sordid **7** corrupt **10** unpleasant **11** unwholesome

SEANCE: **4** town **5** haven **6** ritual **7** meeting, seaport, session, sitting **9** gathering

SEAPORT: **4** port, town **5** haven **6** harbor

SEAR: **3** dry **4** burn, char, cook, mark, scar **5** brown, parch, singe **6** scorch, sizzle, wither **9** cauterize, dehydrate

SEARCH: **4** comb, drag, hunt, look, rake, seek, sift **5** check, delve, frisk, learn, probe, quest, rifle, scour, scout **6** ferret, forage, survey **7** canvass, dragnet, examine, explore, inquire, inspect, manhunt, ransack, rummage **8** research, scavenge, scrounge **10** scrutinize **11** exploration, investigate

SEA ROBBER: **6** pirate **7** corsair **9** buccaneer, privateer **10** freebooter

SEASHORE: **5** beach, coast **7** seaside **8** seaboard, seacoast

SEASICKNESS: **6** nausea **8** mal de mer **9** dizziness, wooziness **10** queasiness

SEASON: **3** add, age, dry **4** fall, salt **5** drill, inure, ripen, savor, spice, taste, train **6** accent, autumn, flavor, harden, mature, pepper, period, refine, school, soften, spring, summer, temper, winter **7** enliven, prepare **8** accustom, interval, marinate **9** embellish **11** acclimatize

SEASONABLE: **3** apt **4** ripe **5** sharp, spicy **6** mature, timely **7** apropos **8** relevant, suitable **9** favorable, opportune **11** appropriate

SEASONED: **5** tangy **7** veteran **8** flavored **11** experienced

SEASONING: **4** dill, herb, mace, sage, salt, zest **5** basil, gravy, onion, sauce, spice, thyme **6** celery, cloves, garlic, ginger, nutmeg, pepper, relish **7** mustard, oregano, paprika, parsley, vinegar **8** allspice, cardamom, dressing, marjoram, rosemary, seasoner **9** condiment

SEAT: **3** hub, pew, sit **4** base, home, rest, room, rump, site **5** bench, chair, floor, house, place, stool, usher **6** behind, bottom, center, lounge, settle, throne **7** capital, cushion, fulcrum, install, keister, ottoman, situate, station **8** backside, bleacher, buttocks, derriere, locality, location **9** banquette, posterior, residence **10** foundation, membership

SEAWEED: **4** agar, kelp, nori **5** dulse, plant, varec **6** delisk, desmid, talgae, tangle **8** agar-agar, gulfweed, rockweed, sargasso **9** carrageen, desmidian, Irish moss

SECEDE: **5** leave **6** desert **8** separate, withdraw **12** disaffiliate

SECLUDE: **4** hide **5** evict **6** remove, retire, screen **7** conceal, exclude, isolate, retreat **8** cloister, separate, withdraw **9** segregate, sequester **10** quarantine

SECLUDED: **5** alone, aloof **6** remote, secret **7** private **8** deserted, isolated, lonesome, solitary **9** reclusive, sheltered, withdrawn **11** sequestered

SECLUSION: **7** privacy, retreat **8** cloister, solitude **9** isolation, sanctuary **10** desolation, quarantine, withdrawal

SECOND: **3** aid **4** abet, back, help, next, time, wink **5** flash, jiffy, other **6** assist, deputy, double, moment, ratify, uphold **7** another, confirm, endorse, forward, instant, succeed, support **8** advocate, inferior **9** assistant, encourage, supporter **10** additional, substitute, understudy **11** subordinate

SECONDARY: **5** minor, small **6** backup, lesser **8** inferior **9** ancillary, auxiliary, dependent, satellite, tributary **10** derivative **11** subordinate, unessential

SECONDHAND: **4** used, worn **7** derived **8** borrowed **10** indirectly

SECOND-RATE: **5** cheap **6** common, shabby **8** inferior, mediocre **10** inadequate

SECRECY: **7** mystery, privacy, silence, stealth **9** closeness **10** covertness **11** concealment

SECRET: **4** dark, hide **5** privy **6** arcane, closet, covert, enigma, hidden, occult, remote, sneaky, veiled **7** clouded, cryptic, furtive, mystery, obscure, private, retired, unknown **8** discreet, esoteric, mystical, secluded, shrouded, stealthy **9** concealed, disguised, seclusion, underhand **10** classified, confidence, mysterious, undercover **11** camouflaged, clandestine, concealment **12** confidential **13** surreptitious

SECRET AGENT: **3** spy **4** mole **7** courier **8** emissary, saboteur **12** collaborator

SECRETARY: **4** aide, desk **5** clerk **6** typist **7** officer **8** official, recorder **9** assistant **10** amanuensis, chancellor

SECRETE: **4** bury, hide, ooze **5** cache, exude, filch, stash **6** screen **7** conceal **9** discharge

SECRETION: **3** gum, sap **4** bile, milk **5** juice, latex, mucus, sweat, tears **6** saliva **7** hormone

SECT: **4** clan, cult **5** faith, group, order, party **6** church, school **7** faction **8** religion **10** persuasion **12** denomination

SECTARIAN: **6** zealot **7** bigoted, heretic, limited **8** partisan **9** dissenter, factional, parochial **12** narrow-minded **13** non-conformist

SECTION: **4** area, part, zone **5** piece, slice, tract **6** branch, parcel, region, sector, sphere **7** portion, segment **8** category, division, locality, vicinity **9** territory

SECTOR: **4** area, zone **7** quarter, section **8** district, division

SECULAR: **3** lay **4** laic **7** earthly, profane, worldly **8** material, temporal **9** layperson **11** nonclerical **12** nonspiritual

SECURE: **3** get, tie **4** bind, bolt, easy, fast, firm, land, lock, moor, nail, safe, sure **5** chain, clamp, guard, solid, sound **6** anchor, assure, attach, cement, clinch, defend, fasten, insure, obtain, stable, strong **7** acquire, assured, certain, procure, protect, tighten **8** reliable, shielded, unharmed **9** confident, constrain, guarantee, safeguard **10** dependable

SECURITY: **4** bail **5** guard, trust **6** pledge, police, safety, shield, surety **7** defense, freedom, hostage, shelter **8** armament, warranty **9** assurance, guarantee, insurance, safeguard, sanctuary, stability **10** confidence, protection

SEDATE: **4** calm, cool, drug **5** grave, quiet, sober, staid, still **6** placid, proper, serene, solemn **7** earnest, serious, settled, subdued **8** composed, tranquil **9** collected, dignified, unruffled

SEDATIVE: **4** drug **6** downer, opiate **8** lenitive, narcotic, pacifier, relaxing, soothing **10** depressant, palliative **11** barbiturate **12** tranquilizer

SEDENTARY: **4** lazy **5** inert **6** seated **7** settled **8** inactive, sluggish **10** motionless, stationary

SEDIMENT: **4** crap, gunk, scum, silt, slag, soot **5** dregs, trash, waste **6** debris, refuse, sludge **7** deposit, grounds, residue **8** settling

SEDITION: **4** coup **6** mutiny, revolt, strife **7** protest, treason **8** uprising **9** rebellion **10** dissension, revolution, subversion **11** lawlessness **12** insurrection

SEDUCE: **4** coax, draw, lure **5** charm, tease, tempt **6** allure, entice **7** corrupt, debauch, mislead **8** deflower, inveigle **9** captivate

SEDUCER: **4** rake **5** Romeo **7** Don Juan, playboy **8** Casanova, lothario **9** womanizer **10** seductress **11** philanderer

SEDUCTIVE: **4** sexy **8** alluring, charming, enticing **9** desirable **10** attractive, enchanting, voluptuous **11** captivating, flirtatious, provocative

SEDUCTRESS: **4** vamp **5** siren **7** jezebel, Lorelei, seducer **9** temptress

SEDULOUS: **4** busy **6** active **8** diligent, untiring **9** assiduous, laborious, vivacious **10** persistent **11** industrious, painstaking, persevering

SEE: **3** eye, spy **4** date, espy, look, meet, peek, peer, seat, show, spot, view **5** catch, chair, guide, sight, stare, watch **6** attend, behold, descry, detect, escort, notice, vision **7** discern, examine, imagine, inspect, observe, undergo, witness **8** consider, discover, envision, identify, perceive **9** accompany, apprehend, ascertain, encounter, interview, visualize **10** anticipate, appreciate, comprehend, experience, scrutinize, understand

SEED: **3** bud, egg, pea, sow **4** core, germ **5** acorn, bulbs, grain, plant, spark, sperm, spore, voule **6** embryo, kernel, origin, source **7** progeny, scatter **8** ancestry, children **9** beginning, offspring, posterity **10** conception **11** descendants

SEEDY: **4** worn **5** mangy, messy, ratty, tacky **6** shabby, untidy **7** unkempt **8** decaying, decrepit, slovenly, tattered **9** neglected **10** bedraggled **11** debilitated

SEEK: **4** comb, hunt **5** court, delve, probe, quest, scout, sniff, trace **6** aspire, pursue, search **7** examine, explore, inquire, request, solicit **8** endeavor **9** undertake **11** investigate

SEEM: **4** look **5** imply, sound **6** appear **7** pretend **8** intimate **9** insinuate

SEEMING: **5** quasi **7** evident **8** apparent, illusory, presumed **10** ostensible

SEEMLY: **5** right **6** decent, proper, suited **7** correct, fitting **8** becoming, decorous, pleasing, suitable **9** befitting **10** acceptable, compatible **11** appropriate

SEEP: **4** drip, flow, leak, ooze **5** exude **6** spread **7** dribble, trickle **8** permeate **9** percolate **10** infiltrate

SEER: **5** augur, sybil **6** medium, mystic, oracle **7** diviner, prophet, psychic **8** sorcerer **9** predictor, sorceress **10** astrologer, forecaster, soothsayer **11** clairvoyant **14** prognosticator

SEESAW: **4** rock, sway **5** waver **6** teeter **9** alternate, fluctuate, vacillate **12** teeter-totter

SEETHE: **4** boil, foam, fret, fume, rage, stew, teem **5** churn, steam, steep **6** bubble, sizzle **7** bristle, smolder

SEGMENT: **4** part **5** piece, share, slice **6** divide, parcel **7** portion, section **8** division, fragment, separate

SEGREGATE: **4** part **6** detach, divide **7** isolate, seclude **8** insulate, separate **9** sequester **10** quarantine

SEISM: **5** quake **6** tremor **10** earthquake

SEIZE: **3** bag, grip, nab, net **4** bind, claw, grab, hook, take, trap **5** annex, catch **6** abduct, arrest, attack, clinch, collar, gather, hijack, kidnap, occupy, snatch, strike **7** afflict, capture, conquer, impound, possess, prehend **8** arrogate, overtake **9** apprehend **10** commandeer, comprehend, confiscate, understand **11** appropriate

SEIZURE: **3** fit **5** spasm, spell **6** attack, stroke **7** capture, episode **8** paroxysm **9** abduction **10** convulsion

SELDOM: **6** hardly, rarely **8** scarcely **10** uncommonly **12** infrequently, occasionally, sporadically

SELECT: **3** opt **4** best, cull, draw, name, pick, rare **5** elect, elite **6** choice, choose, chosen, decide, prefer **8** nominate, superior, topnotch **9** excellent, exclusive, preferred **10** handpicked

SELECTION: **4** pick, vote **5** draft **6** choice, option **7** excerpt, passage **10** collection, preference

SELECTIVE: **5** fussy, picky **6** choosy **7** careful, finicky **8** eclectic **10** particular **14** discriminating

SELF: **3** ego, own **5** being **6** myself, psyche **7** oneself **8** identity, personal **9** character, identical **11** personality **13** individuality

SELF-ABSORBED: **4** vain **11** egotistical **12** narcissistic

SELF-ASSERTIVE: **4** bold, sure **9** audacious, confident

SELF-ASSURED: **4** pose, smug **5** cocky **9** confident, unabashed

SELF-CENTERED: **7** selfish **10** egocentric **11** egotistical **12** narcissistic

SELF-COMPOSED: **4** calm **6** poised **9** collected

SELF-CONFIDENCE: **5** pluck, poise **6** aplomb **7** conceit **9** assurance, cockiness

SELF-CONSCIOUS: **6** uneasy, unsure **7** awkward, nervous **8** insecure **9** unnatural **13** uncomfortable

SELF-CONTROL: **4** will **5** poise **8** calmness, patience **9** composure, stability, willpower **10** constraint, discipline **12** forebearance

SELF-DEFENSE: **4** judo **6** karate, kung fu **8** fighting **10** protection

SELF-DENIAL: **7** ascetic **10** abstinence, asceticism **12** selflessness

SELF-ESTEEM: **5** pride **6** vanity **7** egotism **10** confidence **11** self-respect

SELF-EVIDENT: **5** clear, plain **7** glaring, obvious, visible **8** apparent **10** undeniable **11** unequivocal **12** unmistakable

SELF-EXPLANATORY: **5** clear, plain **7** evident, obvious **8** distinct, manifest **12** unmistakable

SELF-GOVERNING: **9** sovereign **10** autonomous **11** independent

SELF-IMPORTANCE: **6** egoism **7** conceit **9** pomposity, vainglory

SELF-IMPORTANT: **4** smug **6** stuffy **7** pompous **8** arrogant **9** conceited **11** egotistical

SELF-INDULGENT: **6** effete, greedy **7** miserly **9** sybaritic **10** hedonistic **12** parsimonious

SELFISH: **5** stingy **6** greedy **7** miserly **9** egotistic **10** egocentric **12** parsimonious

SELF-LOVE: **6** vanity **7** conceit **9** vainglory **10** narcissism

SELF-POSSESSED: **4** calm, cool, easy **6** poised **8** composed, reserved, tranquil **9** collected, confident

SELF-RELIANT: **5** hardy **8** resolute **11** independent

SELF-RESPECT: **5** pride, worth **6** vanity **7** dignity **10** confidence, self-esteem

SELF-RIGHTEOUS: **4** smug **7** canting, pompous, preachy **11** pharisaical **13** sanctimonious

SELF-SACRIFICING: **5** noble **6** heroic **7** gallant, helpful **8** generous **9** unselfish

SELF-SATISFACTION: **5** pride **8** smugness **11** contentment

SELF-SATISFIED: **4** smug, vain **5** proud **7** content **8** priggish **9** egotistic **10** complacent

SELF-SUFFICIENT: **4** smug **8** arrogant **9** competent, confident, efficient **11** independent

SELL: **4** deal, dump, hawk, push, vend **5** cheat, fetch, stock, trade **6** barter, betray, hustle, market, peddle, retail, supply, unload **7** auction, bargain, deliver, dispose **8** convince, persuade, transfer **9** negotiate, wholesale

SELLER: **5** agent **6** dealer, pusher, trader, vender, vendor **7** peddler **8** merchant, retailer, salesman **10** saleswoman, shopkeeper **11** salesperson, storekeeper **14** businessperson

SELL OUT: **5** cross, trick **6** betray **7** deceive, mislead

SEMBLANCE: **3** air **4** aura, copy, mask **5** image **6** aspect **7** analogy, bearing, feeling, modicum, pretext, showing **8** likeness, pretense **9** duplicate **10** apparition, appearance, similarity, similitude **11** resemblance **14** representation

SEMELE:
father: **6** Cadmus
lover: **4** Zeus
sisters: **3** Ino **5** Agave **7** Autonoe
son: **8** Dionysus
title: **8** princess

SEMESTER: **4** term **5** curse **6** period **7** session

SEMI: **4** half **7** partial

SEMIRAMIS:
husband: **5** Ninus
kingdom: **7** Babylon
title: **5** queen

SEMITE: **3** Jew **4** Arab **6** Hebrew **7** Moabite **8** Aramaean, Arameans, Assyrian **9** Canaanite, Ethiopian **10** Babylonian, Phoenician **12** Carthaginian

SENATE: **5** house **7** council **8** assembly **11** legislature

SENATOR: **8** lawmaker **9** statesman **10** legislator, politician

SEND: **4** emit, hurl, mail, ship **5** carry, drive, fling, issue, relay, route, throw **6** bestow, convey, launch, propel **7** address, consign, deliver, forward, inflict, project **8** delegate, dispatch, transmit **9** broadcast, discharge **10** commission

SEND FORTH: **4** emit **5** issue **8** dispatch

SENDOFF: **8** farewell **11** celebration

SENEGAL:
capital: **5** Dakar
cities: **5** Thies **7** Kaolack
continent: **6** Africa
ethnic groups: **5** Diola, Serer, Wolof **6** Fulani **8** Mandingo **10** Toucouleur
features: **6** Gounou
languages: **4** Peul **5** Serer, Wolof **6** French **7** Tukulor
monetary unit: **5** franc
native: **10** Senegalese
water: **6** Gambia **8** Atlantic **12** Senegal River

SENILE: **3** old **4** aged, weak **6** doting, feeble, infirm **7** ancient **8** decrepit **9** doddering **12** feebleminded

SENIOR: **4** head **5** doyen, elder, older **7** ancient, student **8** superior

SENIORITY: **4** rank **6** status, tenure **7** quality **8** priority, standing **10** precedence

SENSATION: **5** sense **6** marvel, thrill, tingle **7** emotion, feeling, scandal **9** bombshell **10** perception, phenomenon **11** sensibility

SENSATIONAL: **5** lurid, smash **6** superb **7** amazing **8** dramatic, exciting, glorious, shocking, stunning **9** emotional, marvelous, startling, thrilling **10** impressive, remarkable **11** outstanding, spectacular **12** breathtaking, electrifying

SENSE: **4** aura, feel, mind **5** grasp, point, sight, smell, taste, touch, worth **6** reason, wisdom **7** feeling, hearing, meaning, message, realize **8** judgment, perceive, prudence **9** apprehend, awareness, foresight, intuition, sensation, substance **10** anticipate, comprehend, definition, perception **11** sensibility **12** intelligence **13** consciousness, understanding

SENSE AND SENSIBILITY:
author: **10** Jane Austen
characters: **10** Lucy Steele **13** Edward Ferrars, Robert Ferrars **14** Colonel Brandon, John Willoughby
sisters: **14** Elinor Dashwood **16** Marianne Dashwood

SENSELESS: **4** dumb, numb **5** inane, nutty, silly **6** stupid **7** foolish, idiotic, moronic **8** comatose, deadened, mindless **9** illogical, oblivious, pointless, unfeeling **10** insensible, irrational, ridiculous **11** meaningless, nonsensical, purposeless, unconscious **12** unreasonable

SENSIBILITY: **7** feeling, insight **8** keenness **9** affection, awareness, rationale **10** perception

SENSIBLE: **4** keen, sane, wise **5** aware, smart, sound **6** tricky **7** knowing, logical, moronic, painful, prudent, psychic **8** rational, together **9** cognitive, cognizant, emotional, judicious, realistic, sensitive **10** discerning, perceptive, reasonable, responsive, ridiculous **11** intelligent

SENSITIVE: **4** keen, sore **5** acute, aware **6** tender, touchy, tricky **7** painful, psychic **8** delicate **9** emotional, receptive **10** perceptive, responsive **11** susceptible **14** impressionable

SENSUAL: **4** doom, lewd, sexy **6** carnal, coarse, erotic, fleshy, sexual, steamy **7** fleshly, lustful, worldly **8** physical, sensuous **9** seductive **10** licentious, voluptuous

SENSUOUS: **6** carnal **7** sensual **9** luxurious, sybaritic **10** hedonistic, passionate, voluptuous **11** pleasurable

SENTENCE: **4** term **5** edict **7** convict, penalty, stretch, verdict **8** penalize **10** punishment **12** condemnation

SENTENTIOUS: **5** brief, pithy, short, terse **7** concise, pompous **9** abounding **10** aphoristic, meaningful, moralistic **11** pretentious

SENTIMENT: **4** view **6** notion **7** emotion, feeling, leaning, meaning, opinion, thought **8** attitude, penchant, tendency **10** conviction, perception **11** disposition, inclination

SENTIMENTAL: **5** corny, gushy, mushy, sappy **6** loving, tender **7** maudlin, mawkish **8** romantic, touching **9** emotional, nostalgic **10** idealistic, lovey-dovey, moonstruck **12** affectionate

SENTINEL: **5** guard **6** keeper, patrol, sentry **7** lookout, soldier **8** watchman

SEPARATE: **4** cull, free, part, sift, sort, undo **5** alone, apart, break, halve, sever, space, split, strip **6** assort, cleave, detach, divide, remove, secede, single, sunder, unlink, winnow **7** disjoin, dissect, diverse, divorce, isolate, segment, unravel **8** abstract, alienate, detached, discrete, disperse, distinct, disunite, estrange, secluded, solitary, uncouple **9** dependent, different, discharge, disengage, dismember, disparate, eliminate, extricate, partition, segregate, sequester, subdivide **10** disconnect, distribute, quarantine, unattached **11** distinctive, distinguish, unconnected **12** disassociate, disconnected

SEPARATION: **4** gulf, wall **5** split **6** schism **7** breakup, divorce, parting **8** distance, division, fracture **9** apartheid, discharge, partition, severance **10** detachment **11** disjunction, segregation

SEPULCHER: **4** bury, tomb **5** crypt, grave, vault **6** entomb **10** necropolis, repository

SEQUEL: **5** chain, order **6** effect, result, series, upshot **7** outcome **8** offshoot, sequence **9** aftermath **10** conclusion, succession **11** consequence **12** continuation

SEQUENCE: **4** flow **5** chain, cycle, gamut, order **6** course, rhythm, sequel, series **7** episode, outcome **8** schedule **10** succession **11** progression

SEQUENTIAL: **4** next **6** serial **9** following **10** continuous, succeeding **11** consecutive **13** chronological

SEQUESTER: **5** seize **7** confine, isolate, seclude **8** insulate, separate **9** segregate **10** confiscate, quarantine

SERBIA:
capital: **8** Belgrade
cities: **7** Novi Sad **8** Pristina, Subotica
continent: **6** Europe
ethnic groups: **7** Serbian **8** Albanian
islands: **4** Mahe **7** La Digue, Praslin
languages: **7** Serbian **10** Serbo-Croat
provinces: **6** Kosovo **9** Vojvodina
was part of: **10** Yugoslavia
water: **6** Danube

SERE: **3** dry **4** arid **5** dried **6** burned **7** parched **8** droughty, scorched, withered **9** shriveled, waterless **10** desiccated

SERENE: **4** calm, cool, fair **5** clear, quiet, still **6** bright, placid, poised, sedate, smooth, steady **8** composed, peaceful, tranquil **9** collected, unclouded, unruffled **10** unobscured **11** undisturbed

SERENITY: 4 calm **7** balance **8** quietude **9** composure, stillness **11** tranquility **12** peacefulness

SERF: 4 peon **5** churl, slave **6** thrall, vassal **7** bondman, peasant, servant, villein **8** hireling

SERIAL: 9 continual, recurring **10** sequential, succeeding, successive **11** consecutive

SERIES: 4 list **5** chain, order, scale, train **6** column, course, sequel, string **8** category, sequence **10** continuity, succession **12** continuation

SERIOUS: 4 deep, grim, hard **5** grave, heavy, sober, staid **6** intent, sedate, severe, solemn **7** austere, crucial, earnest, intense, weighty **8** critical, pressing **9** difficult, humorless, important, momentous, unamusing **10** determined **12** businesslike

SERMON: 6 homily, lesson, speech **7** address, lecture **8** harangue **9** discourse, preaching **10** preachment

SERPENT: 5 devil, fiend, Satan, snake, viper **7** reptile **8** creature

SERPENTINE: 3 sly **4** wily **5** snaky **6** sneaky **7** crooked, devious, sinuous, winding **8** devilish, fiendish, tempting **10** convoluted, meandering

SERRATE: 6 jagged **7** notched, toothed **11** denticulate

SERVANT: 4 amah, cook, girl, help, maid, page **5** gofer, groom, nurse, slave, usher, valet **6** eunuch, flunky, garcon, helper, menial, squire, varlet, vassal **7** flunkey, footman **8** domestic, factotum, handmaid, retainer **9** attendant, chauffeur **11** chamberlain, chambermaid, housekeeper

SERVE: 3 aid **4** give, help, pass, suit, wait, work **5** avail, cater, ladle, offer, treat **6** answer, assist, attend, succor, supply **7** advance, benefit, deliver, further, requite, satisfy, suffice **8** function, minister **9** officiate **10** distribute

SERVICE: 4 duty, help, mass, rite **6** agency, bureau, employ, repair, sermon, supply **7** benefit, liturgy, setting, utility **8** ceremony, maintain **10** assistance, employment **11** maintenance

SERVICEABLE: 5 tough **6** useful **7** durable, helpful **8** valuable **9** effective, practical **10** beneficial, dependable, functional

SERVILE: 4 base, mean **6** abject, menial **7** fawning, ignoble, slavish **8** cringing, obedient, toadying **9** dependent, groveling **10** obsequious, submissive **11** bootlicking, subservient, sycophantic

SERVITUDE: 7 bondage, peonage, serfdom, slavery **9** captivity, vassalage **10** subjection **11** confinement, subjugation

SESAME: 3 til **4** seed **5** plant **8** password

SESSION: 4 term **5** round **7** meeting, sitting **8** semester **9** gathering **10** assemblage, conference, discussion

SET: 3 dry, fix, gel, lay, put, sit **4** band, bent, crew, firm, gang, jell, pose, prim, suit **5** adapt, align, brood, crowd, fixed, group, imbed, place, plant, range, ready, rigid, scene, solid, staid, start **6** adjust, anchor, assign, bundle, cement, harden, rooted, secure, series, settle, studio **7** appoint, arrange, bearing, confirm, coterie, decided, decline, deposit, dictate, limited, routine, scenery, settled, specify, station, stiffen **8** arranged, backdrop, fastened, location, position, prepared, regulate, resolved, solidify, stubborn **9** coagulate, designate, determine, establish, immovable, prescribe, stabilize **10** assortment, collection, determined, positioned, stationary **11** established, prearranged, unflappable

SET APART: **7** earmark, isolate, seclude **8** separate **9** segregate **11** distinguish

SET ASIDE: **4** void **5** annul, table **6** cancel, reject **7** discard, reserve **8** abrogate, overturn

SET BACK: **4** mire **5** delay **6** hinder **7** reverse

SETBACK: **4** loss **6** defeat, rebuff **8** obstacle, reversal **9** hindrance **10** impediment **14** disappointment

SET DOWN: **4** land **5** write **6** record **8** register **9** establish

SET FORTH: **5** begin, leave, start, state **7** explain, present

SET FREE: **6** loosen, pardon **7** release **8** liberate **9** extricate **10** emancipate

SETH:
brothers: **4** Abel, Cain
father: **4** Adam
mother: **3** Eve
son: **4** Enos

SET IN: **4** turn **5** begin **6** insert **8** commence

SET OFF: **5** start **7** explode **8** activate, detonate

SET OUT: **4** head **5** begin, start **6** embark, intend **8** commence, initiate **9** undertake

SET STRAIGHT: **6** revise **7** correct **9** enlighten

SETTING: **4** eggs **5** decor, scene **6** locale **7** scenery **8** ambiance, backdrop, location, mounting **9** framework, hardening **11** environment **12** surroundings

SETTLE: **3** pay, sag, set **4** calm, firm, land, live, nest, sink **5** clear, lodge, marry, perch, plant, quiet, solve **6** assign, decide, locate, pacify, reduce, render, secure, soothe **7** appoint, arrange, clarify, compose, confirm, deposit, dispose, provide, rectify, relieve, resolve, subside **8** colonize, conclude, populate, regulate **9** designate, determine, establish, habituate, reconcile, stabilize **10** adjudicate **11** accommodate, tranquilize

SETTLEMENT: **4** camp **6** colony, hamlet **7** outpost, payment, village **8** decision, sediment **9** agreement, community, residence **10** compromise, conclusion, habitation, regulation, resolution **11** arrangement **12** colonization, compensation **13** determination, establishment, reimbursement

SETTLER: **6** sooner **7** pilgrim, pioneer, planter **8** colonist **9** colonizer, immigrant **11** homesteader

SET-TO: **4** fray, spat **5** brawl, fight **6** fracas **7** dispute, quarrel, scuffle **8** argument, skirmish, squabble **11** altercation

SET UP: **4** open **5** begin, build, erect, found, start **6** create, launch **7** arrange **8** generate, organize **9** establish

SEVEN DWARFS: **3** Doc **5** Dopey, Happy **6** Grumpy, Sleepy, Sneezy **7** Bashful

SEVEN SEAS: **6** Arctic, Indian **9** Antarctic **12** North Pacific, South Pacific **13** North Atlantic, South Atlantic

SEVER: **3** cut **4** chop, hack, part, rend, slit **5** slice, split **6** cleave, depart, detach, divide, sunder **7** divorce **8** dissolve, disunite, separate **9** dismember **10** dissociate **12** disassociate

SEVERAL: 4 many, some **6** divers, sundry **7** diverse, handful, various **8** assorted, distinct, numerous **9** different **10** individual

SEVERE: 4 cold, dour, grim, hard **5** acute, bleak, cruel, grave, gruff, harsh, rigid, rough, sharp, sober, stern, stiff, tough **6** biting, bitter, brutal, coarse, deadly, fierce, sedate, simple, solemn, strict **7** austere, caustic, chronic, crucial, cutting, drastic, extreme, hostile, intense, painful, serious, violent **8** exacting, grueling, rigorous, scathing **9** dangerous, difficult, inclement, strenuous, stringent, unsparing **10** afflictive, astringent, blistering, inflexible, oppressive, relentless, unpleasant **12** excruciating

SEW: 4 bind, darn, join, mend, seam **5** baste, patch, unite **6** fasten, needle, stitch, suture, tailor **9** embroider

SEWAGE: 5 waste **6** sludge **9** excrement

SEX: 4 love, male **6** coitus, female, gender **8** affinity, intimacy **10** copulation, lovemaking **11** fornication, intercourse **12** reproduction

SEXLESS: 6 neuter, spayed **7** asexual **9** castrated

SEXUAL: 6 carnal, erotic, loving **7** amatory, sensual **8** intimate, venereal **10** passionate **12** reproductive

SEXY: 4 racy **5** spicy **6** erotic, risque, steamy **7** sensual **9** seductive **10** libidinous, suggestive **11** flirtatious

SEYCHELLES:
belongs to: **12** Commonwealth
capital: **8** Victoria
cities: **6** Misere **7** Cascade **9** Port Glaud
continent: **6** Africa
ethnic groups: **6** Creole
features: **12** Aldabra atoll **13** double coconut
languages: **6** French **7** English
monetary unit: **5** rupee
water: **11** Indian Ocean

SHABBY: 4 mean, poor, worn **5** cheap, dingy, faded, mangy, seedy, tacky **6** ragged, scummy, scurvy, sleazy **7** run-down, scrubby, unkempt, wrecked **8** beggarly, decrepit, tattered, unworthy **9** neglected **10** threadbare **11** dilapidated, disgraceful **12** contemptible, deteriorated

SHACK: 3 coe, hut **5** cabin, hovel **6** lean-to, shanty

SHACKLE: 3 tie **4** band, bind, curb, ring, rope **5** chain, cuffs, irons, leash **6** bridle, collar, fetter, hamper, hinder, hobble, hogtie, pinion, secure **7** confine, manacle **8** coupling, handcuff, restrain

SHADE: 3 dim, hue **4** cast, dark, hint, tint, tone, veil **5** color, cover, ghost, tinge, trace **6** awning, canopy, darken, degree, nuance, screen, shadow, shield, spirit, streak **7** curtain, eclipse, obscure, phantom, protect, shelter, specter, umbrage, vestige **8** coolness, darkness **9** gradation, variation **10** apparition, difference, overshadow, protection, suggestion

SHADOW: 3 dog **4** lurk, omen, tail **5** cloud, cover, ghost, gloom, image, shade, stalk, tinge, watch **6** darken, follow, pursue, shroud **7** obscure, phantom, remnant, shelter, suggest **8** forecast, penumbra **10** apparition, protection, reflection

SHADOWY: 3 dim **4** dark, hazy **5** faint, shady, vague **6** cloudy, dreamy, umbral **7** ghostly, obscure **8** adumbral **9** imaginary **10** indistinct **13** unsubstantial

SHADY: **5** fishy **6** hidden, risque **7** crooked, shadowy, suspect **8** doubtful **9** dishonest, unethical **10** suspicious **11** underhanded **12** questionable

SHAFT: **3** bar, ray, rod **4** axle, barb, beam, duct, flue, hole, vent **5** arrow, lance, spear **6** column, handle, pillar, tunnel **7** chimney, conduit, missile, obelisk, spindle **8** cylinder, monolith **9** diaphysis

SHAGGY: **5** bushy, furry, fuzzy, hairy, rough **6** woolly **7** ruffled, scrubby, unkempt **8** straggly, uncombed **9** whiskered

SHAKE: **3** jar, jog **4** free, jerk, jolt, move, rock, stir, sway, toss, wave **5** avoid, churn, drink, elude, quake, swing, upset, waver **6** dither, hustle, jiggle, joggle, jostle, quaver, quiver, rattle, remove, totter, tremor, waggle, weaken **7** agitate, chatter, disturb, fluster, shudder, startle, tremble, unnerve, vibrate **8** brandish, convulse, unsettle **9** fluctuate

SHAKE DOWN: **5** frisk **6** extort, search **7** squeeze **9** blackmail

SHAKESPEARE:

characters: **4** Bone, Iago, Iras, Lear, Puck, Snug **5** Biron, Cleon, Henry, Regan, Romeo, Speed, Timon **6** Banquo, Hamlet, Juliet, Oberon, Portia, Simple **7** Antonio, Cassius, Othello, Richard, Salerio, Shylock, Silence, Slender, Titania **8** Falstaff

children: **6** Hamnet, Judith **7** Susanna

home: **15** Stratford-on-Avon

plays: **6** Hamlet, Henry V **7** Henry IV, Henry VI, Macbeth, Othello, Tempest **8** King Lear **9** Henry VIII, Richard II **10** Richard III **12** Julius Caesar, Twelfth Night **14** Comedy of Errors, Romeo and Juliet **16** Merchant of Venice, Taming of the Shrew **18** Antony and Cleopatra

poetry: **13** Rape of Lucrece **14** Venus and Adonis

theatre: **5** Globe

wife: **4** Anne

SHAKE UP: **4** stir **5** shock, upset **6** remove **7** disturb **8** unsettle **10** reorganize

SHAKY: **4** weak **5** jumpy **6** infirm, unsafe, unsure, wobbly **7** fragile, nervous, rickety, suspect, unsound **8** doubtful, insecure, unstable, unsteady **9** tottering, trembling, uncertain, unsettled **10** precarious, unreliable **12** questionable

SHALE: **4** clay, rock **5** slate **8** sediment

SHALLOW: **4** weak **5** empty, shoal **6** flimsy, slight **7** cursory, surface, trivial **8** trifling **9** depthless, frivolous **11** superficial **13** unintelligent

SHALOM: **5** peace **8** farewell, greeting

SHAM: **4** copy, fake, hoax, mock **5** bluff, bogus, cheat, false, farce, feign, fraud, phony, trick **6** deceit, facade **7** deceive, feigned, forgery, mockery, pretend **8** flimflam, imposter, impostor, pretense, travesty, trickery **9** deception, hypocrisy, imitation, imposture, synthetic **10** artificial, fictitious, substitute **11** counterfeit

SHAMAN: **4** monk **6** healer, priest **7** angakok **9** mundunugu **11** medicine man, witch doctor

SHAMBLES: **4** mess **5** chaos, havoc **6** bedlam **8** disarray, disorder, wreckage **9** confusion

SHAME: **5** abash, guilt **6** stigma **7** chagrin, degrade, mortify **8** contempt, disgrace, dishonor, ignominy **9** embarrass, humiliate **12** unworthiness **13** embarrassment

SHAMEFUL: **4** base, mean **6** sinful **7** ignoble **8** indecent, shocking **9** atrocious, degrading, dishonest, offensive **10** deplorable, outrageous, scandalous **11** disgraceful, ignominious **12** contemptible, dishonorable, disreputable

SHAMELESS: **4** bold **5** brash **6** arrant, brazen **8** immodest, impudent **9** audacious, barefaced, unabashed **10** impervious, unblushing

SHANGHAI: **5** seize **6** abduct, coerce, compel, induce, kidnap

SHANGRI-LA: **6** heaven, utopia **8** paradise

SHANK: **3** leg **4** meat, shin, stem **5** shaft, stalk

SHANTY: **3** hut **5** cabin, hovel, lodge, shack **7** cottage

SHAPE: **4** bend, body, cast, form, look, make, mold, plan, tool, trim **5** adapt, build, carve, frame, image, model, order, state **6** aspect, chisel, create, design, devise, figure, format, health **7** arrange, conform, contour, develop, fashion, pattern, posture **8** contrive, physique **9** condition, determine, fabricate, structure **10** appearance **11** arrangement **13** configuration

SHAPELESS: **8** deformed, formless, nebulous, unformed, unshaped **9** amorphous, distorted, irregular, misshapen **10** indistinct

SHAPELY: **3** fit **4** neat, trim **5** built **6** comely **9** beautiful, distorted **10** curvaceous **11** symmetrical **12** proportioned

SHARE: **3** cut, lot **4** deal, dole, part **5** claim, divvy, piece, quota, ratio, split, stake **6** divide, ration **7** partake, portion **8** dividend, division, interest **9** allotment, allowance, apportion, plowshare **10** commission, distribute, percentage, proportion **11** participate

SHARED: **5** joint **6** common, mutual **8** communal

SHARK: **4** fish **5** cheat **6** expert, usurer **8** maneater, predator, swindler

kind: **4** blue, sand **5** tiger, whale, white **10** great white, hammerhead, shovelhead

SHARP: **3** sly **4** acid, cold, cute, fast, keen, sour, tart, wise **5** acrid, acute, adept, alert, brisk, canny, clear, crisp, edged, harsh, quick, salty, savvy, slick, smart, steep, swank, tangy, witty **6** abrupt, adroit, astute, barbed, biting, bitter, bright, classy, clever, crafty, expert, horned, jagged, peaked, severe, shrewd, shrill, strong, sudden **7** angular, austere, caustic, cunning, cutting, drastic, intense, painful, piquant, pointed, prickly, pungent, stylish, violent **8** distinct, handsome, incisive, piercing, poignant, promptly, stinging, vigilant **9** ingenious, precisely **10** attractive, discerning, perceptive, punctually **11** acrimonious, intelligent, penetrating, quick-witted **12** excruciating

SHARPEN: **4** edge, hone, whet **5** focus, grind, point, strop, taper **7** enhance **9** intensify, stimulate

SHARPSHOOTER: **6** sniper **8** marksman, rifleman

SHARP-SIGHTED: **4** keen **5** acute, alert, aware **9** attentive, observant **10** perceptive **11** penetrating

SHARP-WITTED: **4** keen, wise **5** smart, witty **6** bright, clever **10** discerning **11** intelligent

SHATTER: **4** dash, rend, ruin **5** blast, break, burst, crack, crash, quash, smash, split, wreck **6** damage **7** clatter, destroy, disable, scatter **8** demolish, fragment, splinter **9** dissipate, pulverize **10** annihilate

SHAVE: **3** cut, mow **4** crop, slip, trim **5** brush, cheat, graze, shear, slash **6** barber, divide, glance, reduce, scrape, sliver **7** portion, tonsure, whittle **8** separate, splinter

SHAWL: **4** cape, maud, wrap **5** cloak, cloth, fichu, manta, scarf, stole **6** mantle, serape **7** tallith

SHEAF: **5** bunch **6** bundle, quiver **7** cluster **10** collection

SHEAR: **3** cut **4** clip, crop, snip, trim **5** prune, sever, shave, strip **6** cleave, fleece, remove **7** scissor

SHEARS: **6** pruner **7** cutters **8** clippers, scissors, snippers, trimmers

SHEATH: **4** case, coat, skin **5** dress **7** capsule, wrapper **8** covering, envelope, scabbard

SHED: **3** cut, hut, rid **4** cast, cote, drop, emit, molt, part, peel, pour **5** cabin, hovel, repel, strew **6** divest, divide, reject, slough **7** cottage, diffuse, discard, emanate, radiate, scatter, shelter **8** disperse, exuviate, jettison, sprinkle

SHEEN: **5** glaze, gleam, gloss, shine **6** bright, finish, glossy, luster, polish **7** glisten, glitter, radiant, shimmer, shining **8** lustrous **9** shininess **10** brightness, glossiness **11** resplendent

SHEEP:
breed: **4** Horn **5** Welsh **6** Dorset, Galway, Merino, Oxford, Romney, Somali **7** Cheviot, Delaine, Iceland, Lincoln, Suffolk **8** Cotswold, mountain **9** Leicester **10** blackfaced, Shropshire
caretaker: **6** drover **8** shepherd
coat: **4** wool **6** fleece
family: **7** Bovidae
genus: **4** ovis
male: **3** ram **6** wether **10** bellwether
meat: **4** lamb **6** mutton
wild: **3** sha **4** arui **5** argal, urial **6** aoudad, argali **7** bighorn, mouflon
young: **3** hog, teg **4** lamb, tegg **8** yearling **9** shearling

SHEEPISH: **3** shy **4** meek, tame **5** timid **6** docile **7** abashed, bashful, passive **9** chagrined **11** embarrassed, unassertive

SHEEPSKIN: **4** bond **6** mouton **7** diploma, leather **9** parchment

SHEER: **4** fine, pure, thin, turn, veer **5** clear, steep, total, utter **6** abrupt, swerve **7** chiffon, deflect, deviate, unmixed, upright, utterly **8** absolute, gossamer, outright **9** downright, undiluted **10** altogether, completely, diaphanous **11** transparent, unqualified

SHEET: **3** pan, ply, tin **4** leaf, page, pane, rope **5** chain, layer, linen, paper, plate **6** shroud **7** coating, overlay, surface, tabloid **8** covering **9** newspaper

SHELF: **4** bank, rack, reef, sill, slab **5** layer, ledge, shoal **6** mantel **7** bedrock, bracket, counter, jutting, sandbar, stratum **8** sandbank

SHELL: **3** pod **4** boat, bomb, case, hull, skin **5** armor, crust, frame, scale, shard, shuck **6** bullet, defeat, rocket **7** bombard, capsule, grenade **8** covering, exterior **9** cartridge **10** ammunition, projectile

SHELLAC: **5** resin **6** batter, defeat, strike **7** trounce, varnish

SHELLEY, MARY WOLLSTONECRAFT: **8** novelist
father: **13** William Godwin
husband: **18** Percy Bysshe Shelley

mother: **18** Mary Wollstonecraft
nationality: **7** English
wrote: **12** Frankenstein

SHELLEY, PERCY BYSSHE: **4** poet
nationality: **7** English
wife: **25** Mary Wollstonecraft Shelley
wrote: **7** Adonais, Alastor **8** Queen Mab, The Cloud **10** Ozymandias, To a Skylark **13** Laon and Cythna, Mask of Anarchy **15** Defence of Poetry

SHELLFISH: **4** clam, crab **5** conch, prawn, snail, whelk **6** mussel, oyster, shrimp **7** lobster, mollusk, piddock, scallop **8** barnacle, crawfish, crayfish **10** crustacean

SHELL OUT: **3** pay **4** give **5** spend **6** expend **8** disburse **10** contribute

SHELTER: **3** den, hut, lee **4** barn, camp, cave, cote, fold, port, roof, shed, tent **5** cloak, cover, haven, house, hovel, shack, shade **6** asylum, burrow, covert, defend, garage, hangar, harbor, hostel, refuge, safety, screen, shield, trench **7** carport, cottage, defense, enclose, foxhole, hideout, hospice, lodging, protect, retreat, trailer **8** dwelling, hideaway, quarters, security, umbrella **9** harborage, safeguard, sanctuary **10** protection

SHELVE: **4** drop, hold **5** defer, delay, ledge, scrub, table **6** mantel, retire **7** arrange, dismiss, suspend **8** postpone **10** pigeonhole

SHEM:
brother: **3** Ham **7** Japheth
father: **4** Noah

SHENANIGANS: **4** game **5** antic, prank, stunt, trick **6** hijinx **8** mischief, nonsense **9** horseplay **10** tomfoolery **11** monkeyshine

SHEPHERD: **4** herd, lead, tend **5** drive, guard, guide, pilot, watch **6** attend, escort, herder, keeper, leader, pastor **7** teacher **8** herdsman, minister **9** caretaker, protector

SHERBERT: **3** ice **6** sorbet **7** dessert, sherbet

SHERIFF: **7** marshal, officer **9** constable
aide: **6** deputy **7** bailiff
group: **5** posse

SHERLOCK HOLMES: **6** sleuth **9** detective
companion: **8** Dr. Watson
creator: **19** Sir Arthur Conan Doyle
enemy: **8** Moriarty

SHERRY: **4** fino, port, wine **6** brandy **7** amoroso, oloroso

SHETLAND ISLANDS:
cities: **7** Lerwick **9** Sullom Voe
features: **4** pony **7** sweater
islands: **8** Mainland **12** Muckle Flugga
language: **5** Norse
place: **8** Scotland

SHIBBOLETH: **6** custom, phrase, saying, slogan, truism **8** password, practice **9** catchword, watchword

SHIELD: **4** fend, hide **5** aegis, armor, badge, cloak, cover, guard, house, pavis, shade, shell, targe **6** bumper, canopy, defend, harbor, screen, target **7** buckler, conceal, prevent, protect, shelter **8** armament **9** safeguard **10** escutcheon, protection

SHIFT: **4** jump, move, stir, swap, tack, tour, turn, vary, veer **5** alter, dodge, evade, fault, group, spell, stint, trick **6** change, divide, period, swerve, switch **7** arrange, convert, dispose, replace, shuffle **8** exchange, transfer **9** expedient, rearrange, stratagem, vacillate **10** conversion, substitute, subterfuge, transition **11** fluctuation

SHIFTLESS: **4** idle, lazy **8** inactive, indolent **11** incompetent, inefficient

SHIFTY: **5** cagey, shady, slick **6** crafty, sneaky, tricky **7** crooked, cunning, devious, evasive **8** scheming, slippery **9** conniving, deceitful, dishonest, underhand

SHILLY-SHALLY: **5** stall, waver **6** dawdle **7** halting **8** hesitate **9** fluctuate, vacillate **10** indecision **13** procrastinate

SHIMMER: **4** glow **5** blink, flash, gleam, shine **7** flicker, flutter, glimmer, glisten, sparkle, twinkle **9** coruscate **11** scintillate

SHIMMY: **5** dance, shake **6** wobble **7** chemise, vibrate

SHIN: **3** leg, run **4** move **5** climb, scale, shank, tibia **6** ascend, letter, scurry **7** scamper

SHINDIG: **4** ball, bash **5** dance, party **6** shindy **7** shebang

SHINDY: **4** ball, bash **5** dance, party, revel, spree **6** fracas, frolic, uproar **7** shindig **8** carousal **9** commotion **11** disturbance, merrymaking

SHINE: **3** ray, rub, wax **4** beam, buff, glow **5** blaze, excel, flash, glare, gleam, glint, glitz, gloss, light, sheen **6** dazzle, finish, luster, polish **7** glisten, glitter, radiate, reflect, shimmer, sparkle, twinkle **8** radiance, splendor **9** coruscate **10** illuminate

SHINER: **4** fish **6** bruise **8** blackeye

SHINY: **6** bright, glossy **7** beaming, glaring, radiant **8** gleaming, lustrous, polished **9** brilliant, sparkling **10** glistening

SHIP:
ancient: **5** knorr **6** galley **7** galleon, trireme
arctic: **6** sealer
armored: **7** carrack, cruiser **9** destroyer, ironsides, submarine
attendant: **7** steward
berth: **4** dock, slip
boat: **4** dory, life **5** barge, dingy **6** dingey, dinghy, tender **7** pinnace
capacity: **3** ton **7** tonnage
commercial: **5** liner, oiler **6** tanker, trader **9** freighter
crew: **4** hand, mate **5** bosun **6** purser, sailor **7** steward **8** engineer, helmsman **9** boatswain, navigator, steersman
fishing: **5** smack **6** hooker, lugger **7** trawler
fleet: **4** navy **6** armada **8** flotilla
floor: **4** deck
in repair: **7** drydock
left side: **4** port
oar: **6** bireme, galley, sampan **7** pinnace, rowboat, trireme
parts: **3** bow, ram **4** boom, brig, deck, helm, hold, hull, keel, mast, port, prow, sail **5** bilge, crane, davit, hoist, stern, waist, wheel **6** bridge, galley, rudder **7** bulwark, capstan, carling, keelson, scupper **8** bulkhead, porthole **9** gangplank, stateroom
pirate: **7** galivat
prison: **4** brig
rear: **3** aft **5** abaft, stern **6** astern
record: **3** log
right side: **9** starboard
room: **4** brig **5** cabin, salon **6** galley **7** caboose **10** forecastle
rope: **4** line **6** hawser **7** halyard, lanyard, painter, ratline
sailing: **4** brig, dhow, yawl **5** ketch, sloop, xebec **6** caique, chebec, lugger, saltie **7** caravel, galleon **8** schooner
submersible: **9** submarine **11** bathyscaphe
war: **3** sub **7** cruiser, flattop **9** destroyer, submarine **11** dreadnaught
window: **4** port **8** porthole

SHIPMENT: **4** load **5** cargo, goods **7** freight **8** delivery, purchase **11** consignment

SHIP OF FOOLS:
author: **19** Katherine Anne Porter
ship: **4** Vera

SHIPSHAPE: **4** neat, snug, tidy, trim **6** spruce **7** orderly

SLIPSHOD: **5** messy, seedy, tacky **6** shabby, shoddy, sloppy, untidy **8** careless, slovenly **9** neglected **10** disheveled

SHIRK: **4** duck **5** avoid, dodge, elude, evade, slack **7** neglect **8** sidestep

SHIRKER: **5** sneak **6** loafer **7** quitter, slacker **10** malingerer

SHIRT: **4** polo, sark, silk **5** dress, sport **6** blouse, jersey **8** pullover **10** turtleneck

SHIVER: **4** ague **5** break, chill, quake, shake **6** freeze, quiver, tremor **7** frisson, shatter, shudder, tremble, vibrate **8** fragment, splinter

SHOAL: **3** bar **4** bank, mass, reef **5** crowd, flock, group, horde **6** school **7** sandbar, shallow **8** sandbank

SHOCK: **3** jar **4** blow, bump, daze, jolt, stun **5** crash, fight, scare, shake, upset **6** appall, excite, impact, offend, trauma, tremor **7** astound, collect, disgust, disturb, horrify, outrage, ramrock, startle, terrify **8** astonish, paralyze, surprise **9** agitation, collision, electrify **10** concussion, earthquake

SHOCKING: **5** awful, lurid **6** grisly, horrid **7** ghastly, heinous, hideous **8** dreadful, horrible, stunning, terrible **9** appalling, atrocious, revolting **10** abominable, disgusting, outrageous, surprising **11** unspeakable

SHODDY: **4** base, poor **5** cheap, gaudy, seedy **6** cheesy, shabby, sleazy, sloppy **8** inferior **9** dishonest **11** dilapidated

SHOE: **4** boot, clog, flat, mule, pump **5** cleat, gilly, sabot, wader **6** brogan, brogue, galosh, loafer, oxford, patten, plight, sandal, status **7** blucher, chopine, slipper, sneaker **8** balmoral, buckskin, larrigan, moccasin, pantofle, platform, position **9** brodequin, pompootee **11** clodhoppers
maker: **4** snob **5** soler **7** cobbler, crispin

SHOO: **4** away, scat **5** leave, scram **6** begone

SHOOT: **3** bag, bud, fly, hit, pop, rus **4** bolt, cast, dart, dash, drop, emit, film, fire, grow, hunt, kill, move, plug, race **5** blast, bough, chute, drive, eject, hurry, scion, shell, snipe, spear, spray, sprig, spurt, throw, utter, wound **6** inject, launch, propel, riddle, strike, thrust **7** bombard, explode, project **9** discharge **10** photograph

SHOP: **3** buy **4** hunt **5** plant, store **6** browse, market, office, outlet, studio **7** factory **8** boutique, business, emporium, purchase **9** workplace

SHOPKEEPER: **6** vendor **8** merchant, retailer **11** businessman, storekeeper **13** businesswoman

SHOPLIFT: **4** palm **5** pinch, steal, swipe **6** pilfer

SHOPWORN: **5** faded, stale, trite **6** cliche, frayed **8** overused **9** tarnished

SHORE: **4** bank, land, prop **5** beach, brink, coast **6** strand **7** bolster, seaside, support **8** buttress, seaboard **9** coastline, reinforce, waterside **10** strengthen, waterfront

SHORT: **4** curt, rude **5** blunt, brief, crisp, hasty, scant, small, spare, squat, terse **6** abrupt, little, petite, scanty, scarce, skimpy, slight **7** briefly, compact, concise, curtail, stunted, summary **8** abridged, abruptly, succinct **9** condensed, crumbling, deficient, momentary **10** diminutive, inadequate, incomplete **11** abbreviated, compendious, lilliputian **12** insufficient

SHORTAGE: **4** lack, need **6** dearth **7** deficit **8** sparsity, underage **10** deficiency, inadequacy

SHORTCOMING: **4** flaw, vice **5** fault, lapse **6** defect **7** failure **8** drawback, weakness **10** deficiency, inadequacy **12** imperfection

SHORTEN: **3** bob, cut **4** chop, clip, trim **5** slash **6** lessen, reduce, shrink **7** abridge, curtail, deprive **8** condense, contract, decrease, diminish, truncate **10** abbreviate

SHORT-LIVED: **5** brief **7** passing **8** fleeting **9** momentary, temporary **10** unenduring

SHORTLY: **4** anon, soon **6** curtly, pronto **7** quickly **9** concisely, presently **11** immediately

SHORTSIGHTED: **4** rash **5** blind **6** myopic **7** foolish **8** careless, headlong **9** imprudent **11** nearsighted

SHORT-TEMPERED: **5** huffy, testy **6** cranky, grumpy, touchy **7** grouchy **8** snappish **9** irascible, irritable

SHOT: **3** pop, try **4** dose, jolt, slug, wear **5** blank, blast, drink, fling, guess, photo, shack, tired **6** bullet, chance, effort, pellet, ruined, stroke **7** attempt, gunfire, missile, opening **8** decrepit, marksman **9** exhausted, injection **10** ammunition, conjecture, projectile **11** intoxicated, opportunity

SHOULDER: **4** bank, edge, push, side **5** carry, elbow, joint, shove **6** accept, border, hustle, jostle **7** scapula, support
blade: **7** scapula

SHOUT: **3** cry **4** bark, bawl, call, crow, hoot, howl, roar, root, yell, yelp **5** blare, cheer, noise, whoop **6** bellow, clamor, hurrah, scream, shriek **7** acclaim, rejoice, screech **10** vociferate

SHOVE: **4** bump, cram, prod, push **5** drive, elbow, force, nudge, press, shunt **6** hustle, jostle, propel, thrust **8** shoulder

SHOVEL: **3** dig **4** tool **5** delve, scoop, spade, stage, train **6** assign, cinema **7** shuffle **8** excavate

SHOVE OFF: **5** leave **6** depart **7** vamoose

SHOW: **3** air, see **4** fair, film, lead, look, play, pomp, pose **5** coach, flash, flick, grant, guide, movie, prove, usher **6** allege, circus, confer, detect, direct, escort, evince, expose, flaunt, inform, locate, parade, reveal, submit, unveil **7** declare, display, divulge, exhibit, explain, perform, picture, present, produce, program, uncover **8** carnival, ceremony, disclose, evidence, flourish, indicate, instruct, manifest **9** accompany, burlesque, designate, establish, represent, semblance, symbolize **10** appearance, exhibition, exposition **11** demonstrate, materialize, opportunity, performance **13** demonstration, entertainment, motion picture

SHOWCASE: **7** cabinet, display, exhibit, vitrine

SHOWDOWN: **5** clash **6** climax, crisis **9** encounter **11** culmination **13** confrontation

SHOWER: **4** bath, pour, rain, wash **5** bathe, party, salvo, spray, storm, water **6** bestow, deluge, lavish, volley **7** barrage, bombard, drizzle, scatter **8** sprinkle **10** cloudburst

SHOW ME STATE: **8** Missouri

SHOW OFF: **4** brag **5** boast **6** flaunt, parade **7** display, exhibit

SHOWOFF: **6** hotdog **7** boaster **8** braggart

SHOWPIECE: **3** gem **5** jewel, pride, prize **8** treasure **11** masterpiece

SHOW UP: **4** come **5** shame **6** appear, arrive, defeat, expose **9** embarrass

SHOWY: **4** loud **5** gaudy, grand **6** flashy, garish, ornate, snazzy, swanky **7** dashing, glaring, opulent, pompous, splashy **8** gorgeous, overdone, splendid, striking **9** brilliant, flaunting **10** flamboyant **11** pretentious **12** ostentatious

SHRED: **3** bit, cut **4** iota, snip, tear **5** crumb, grain, ounce, piece, prune, scrap, speck, strip, trace **6** ribbon, sliver, tatter **7** smidgen **8** fragment, particle **9** pulverize

SHREW: **3** hag, nag **5** curse, harpy, scold, vixen **6** mammal, virago **8** spitfire **9** battleaxe, termagant, Xanthippe **11** vituperator

SHREWD: **3** sly **4** foxy, keen, wily, wise **5** acute, cagey, canny, harsh, sharp, slick, smart **6** artful, astute, biting, clever, crafty, subtle **7** careful, cunning, knowing, politic **8** piercing, sensible **9** ingenious, judicious, sagacious **10** contriving, discerning, farsighted, perceptive **11** calculating, intelligent, penetrating, sharpwitted **13** perspicacious

SHRIEK: **3** cry **4** howl, wail, yell **5** shout **6** holler, scream, shrill, squawk, squeal **7** screech

SHRILL: **4** high, keen, loud **5** acute, dwarf, noisy, sharp, sound, vivid **6** biting, piping, shriek **7** blaring, screech, seafood **8** piercing, strident **10** crustacean **11** high-pitched, penetrating

SHRIMP: **5** krill **6** peewee **9** shellfish

SHRINE: **3** box **4** case, naos, tomb **5** altar **6** chapel, chasse, church, hallow, temple **7** sanctum **8** memorial, monument **9** container, mausoleum, reliquary, sanctuary

SHRINK: **3** shy **4** wane **5** cling, cower, demur, quail **6** blench, cringe, flinch, huddle, lessen, recede, recoil, reduce, retire, weaken, wither **7** atrophy, curtail, retract, retreat, shorten, shrivel, swindle **8** condense, contract, decrease, hesitate, withdraw **9** construct **12** psychiatrist

SHRINKING: **3** coy, shy **5** timid **6** modest **7** bashful **8** retiring **9** declining

SHRIVE: **4** free **5** atone, purge **6** acquit, pardon, repent **7** absolve, confess, forgive

SHRIVEL: **3** age **4** wilt **5** parch, rivei, wizen **6** shrink, wither **7** wrinkle **9** dehydrate

SHROUD: **4** hide, pall, veil, wrap **5** cloak, cover, dress, shade, sheet, vault **6** clothe, enfold, screen, shadow **7** conceal, envelop, garment, shelter **8** cerement, clothing, covering, envelope, obstruct **9** cerecloth **12** graveclothes

SHRUB: **4** bush, tree **5** drink, hedge, plant **8** beverage
variety: **4** aloe, coca **5** cubed, holly, lilac **6** azalea, cassia, coffee, laurel **7** hemlock, jasmine **8** allspice, bar-

berry, buddleia, cinchona, euonymus, hibiscus, rosemary **9** blueberry, cranberry, forsythia, hydrangea, mistletoe, sagebrush **10** blackberry, elderberry **11** honeysuckle

SHUCK: **3** pod **4** husk, peel, shed **5** ditch, shell, strip **6** remove **7** discard **8** jettison **9** worthless

SHUDDER: **5** quake, shake **6** jitter, quiver, shimmy, shiver **7** flutter, frisson, tremble **8** convulse

SHUFFLE: **3** mix **4** gait, limp, move, walk **5** dance, evade, scuff, shift, shunt **6** change, jumble, muddle **7** shamble **8** scramble, sidestep **9** rearrange **11** disorganize **12** equivocation

SHUN: **4** balk, duck, snub **5** avoid, dodge, elude, evade **6** escape, eschew, ignore, reject **9** ostracize

SHUT: **3** bar **4** cage, lock, seal, snap **5** block, close **6** fasten, forbid, secure **7** confine, exclude **8** prohibit

SHUT DOWN: **4** stop **5** cease, close **7** abandon

SHUT IN: **3** pen **4** cage **5** fence **6** hemmed **7** confine **8** imprison **10** restrained, surrounded

SHUT OFF: **4** stop **6** refuse **7** isolate

SHUT OUT: **3** bar **5** evict **6** screen **7** exclude **8** blockade **9** ostracize

SHUTTER: **5** blind, cover, shade **6** screen

SHUTTLE: **4** loom **6** looper, travel **7** vehicle **9** transport, vacillate

SHUTTLECOCK: **4** bird **6** birdie
used in: **9** badminton

SHUT UP: **3** gag **4** hush **5** quiet, shush **7** silence

SHY: **3** coy **4** balk, meek, shun, wary **5** avoid, chary, cower, dodge, short, timid **6** demure, humble, modest, recoil, shrink **7** bashful, fearful, lacking, nervous **8** cautious, hesitant, reserved, retiring, secluded, sheepish **9** diffident, reluctant **10** inadequate, incomplete, shamefaced, unassuming **11** introverted, unassertive **12** insufficient

SHYLOCK: **9** loan shark **11** moneylender
author: **11** Shakespeare
hated: **7** Antonio
outwitted by: **6** Portia
story: **16** Merchant of Venice

SHYSTER: **6** lawyer **8** attorney **11** pettifogger

SIB: **3** kin **6** sister **7** brother, kindred, kinfolk, kinship, related, sibling **8** relative

SIBERIA:
animals: **5** manul, nelma, ounce, sable, saiga **6** argali **7** miniver, Samoyed
cities: **4** Enna, Omsk **5** Chita **7** Irkutsk **8** Baranaul **10** Khabarovsk **11** Krasnoyarsk, Novosibirsk
continent: **4** Asia
ethnic groups: **4** Yuit **5** Sagai, Tatar, Yakut **6** Tartar **7** Kirghiz **8** Yukaghir **9** Mongolian
features: **5** Altai, taiga, Urals **6** steppe, tundra **11** Urman Forest **20** Trans-Siberian Railway
place: **6** Russia
water: **3** Ili, Tom **4** Amur, Lena, Maya, Onon, Yana **5** Sobol, Tobol **6** Anadyr, Olensk **7** Yenisei

SIBLING: **3** kin, sib **6** sister **7** brother, kinfolk **8** relative

SIBYL: **4** seer **5** augur, witch **6** oracle **7** seeress **9** sorceress **10** prophetess **13** fortune-teller

SIC: **3** set **4** thus, urge **6** attack, incite

SICILY:
capital: **7** Palermo
cities: **3** Aci **7** Catania, Marsala, Messina **8** Syracuse

continent: **6** Europe
features: **4** Etna
islands: **5** Egadi **6** Lipari, Ustica **11** Pantelleria
native: **8** Sicilian
region of: **5** Italy
water: **5** Salso **6** Belice, Simeto **7** Platani **13** Mediterranean

SICK: **3** ill **4** down, pale, weak **5** frail, gross, lousy, unfit, upset, weary **6** ailing, infirm, insane, morbid, pining, unwell **7** longing, unsound **8** confined, diseased, feverish, impaired, infected, stricken **9** afflicted, bedridden, depressed, disgusted, nauseated, suffering, unhealthy **10** indisposed **11** debilitated

SICKEN: **5** shock, upset **6** affect, offend, revolt **7** disgust, repulse **8** nauseate

SICKLY: **3** ill **4** down, pale **5** faint, frail **6** ailing, feeble, infirm, poorly **7** invalid, languid **8** diseased **9** afflicted, unhealthy **10** lackluster **11** unwholesome

SICKNESS: **4** bout **6** malady **7** ailment, disease, illness **8** disorder, insanity, syndrome **9** condition, infirmity **10** affliction

SIDE: **3** top **4** area, back, edge, face, hand, join, left, line, part, team **5** agree, align, angle, facet, flank, front, minor, party, phase, right, slant, slope **6** aspect, behalf, border, bottom, margin, region, sector, stance **7** faction, lateral, opinion, posture, support, surface **8** alliance, district, position **9** coalition, direction, viewpoint **10** standpoint

SIDEBOARD: **5** table **6** buffet, closet **8** credenza, cupboard **9** furniture **10** cellarette

SIDE BY SIDE: **7** abreast **8** parallel, together **10** collateral, juxtaposed

SIDEKICK: **3** pal **4** chum **6** deputy, friend **7** comrade, partner **9** assistant, companion

SIDELINE: **5** bench, hobby **8** boundary, interest **9** avocation

SIDESLIP: **4** skid **5** slide **8** downward, sideways

SIDESTEP: **4** duck **5** avoid, dodge, evade, skirt **6** bypass, escape **10** circumvent

SIDETRACK: **5** delay, shunt, stall **6** divert, switch **7** deviate

SIDEWALK: **7** walkway **8** footpath **9** boardwalk

SIDEWAYS: **7** askance, lateral **8** crabwise, sidelong, slanting **9** alongside, broadside, laterally, obliquely **10** indirectly

SIDE WITH: **4** back, help, join **5** agree, favor **7** support **8** champion

SIDLE: **4** ease, edge, tilt, veer **7** saunter

SIEGE: **4** bout **5** beset, flock, spell **6** attack **7** assault, offense **8** blockade **9** onslaught

SIEGFRIED:
father: **8** Siegmund
killer: **5** Hagen
mother: **9** Sieglinde
sword: **7** Balmung
wife: **9** Kriemhild

SIEGMUND:
father: **7** Volsung
kingdom: **5** Signy
lover: **5** Signy
mother: **4** Liod **5** Hliod
son: **6** Sigurd **9** Siegfried

SIERRA LEONE:
capital: **8** Freetown
cities: **6** Kenema, Makeni
continent: **6** Africa
ethnic groups: **5** Mende, Temne **6** Creole
language: **7** English

monetary unit: **5** leone
water: **8** Adriatic

SIERRA NEVADA:
features: **7** Sequoia **8** Yosemite **11** King's Canyon
peaks: **4** Dana **7** Whitney
place: **10** California
site of: **8** gold rush

SIESTA: **3** nap **4** rest **5** sleep **6** snooze

SIEVE: **4** mesh, sift **6** basket, filter, riddle, screen, sifter, strain **8** colander, separate, strainer

SIFT: **4** bolt, comb, sort **5** probe, sieve **6** filter, refine, riddle, screen, search, strain, winnow **7** analyze, canvass, examine, inspect **8** separate **10** scrutinize **11** investigate

SIGH: **3** sob **4** ache, long, lust, moan, pant, wail **5** crave, groan, mourn, sough, yearn **6** exhale, grieve, lament **7** suspire **8** complain, languish

SIGHT: **3** aim, ken, see, spy **4** espy, look, mess, show, spot, view **5** scene **6** behold, glance, vision **7** display, eyesore, glimpse, observe, outlook, witness **9** spectacle **10** exhibition, perception, visibility **11** observation

SIGHTSEER: **7** tourist **8** observer **9** traveller

SIGN: **3** cue, nod **4** clue, hint, mark, note, omen **5** badge, brand, extol, image, index, proof, token, trace **6** banner, beckon, emblem, figure, motion, poster, signal, symbol, tattle **7** auspice, earmark, gesture, initial, lullaby, message, portent, presage, vestige, warning **8** evidence, inscribe, insignia, proclaim, serenade, standard, vocalize **9** authorize, autograph, billboard, guidepost, harmonize, indicator, signature, subscribe **10** expression, indication, prognostic, suggestion, underwrite **11** premonition **13** advertisement, constellation, demonstration

SIGNAL: **4** flag, horn, sign, toot, wave, wink **5** alarm, flare, image, siren, sound **6** buzzer, motion, notify **7** blinker, command, gesture, impulse, lantern, message, notable, presage, signify, warning, whistle **8** password **9** indicator, memorable, prominent **10** noticeable, remarkable **11** communicate, outstanding **13** extraordinary

SIGNATURE: **3** ink **4** hand, mark, name, seal, sign **5** stamp **9** autograph, trademark **11** John Hancock **14** identification

SIGNET: **4** mark, seal, sign **5** stamp **10** impression

SIGNIFICANCE: **5** merit, point, value **6** intent, weight **7** bearing, gravity, meaning, purport, purpose **9** influence, relevance **10** importance **11** consequence, seriousness

SIGNIFICANT: **4** main **5** great, large, valid **7** knowing, telling, weighty **8** critical, decisive, eloquent, powerful, symbolic **9** important, momentous, prominent **10** compelling, expressive, meaningful, noteworthy, suggestive **11** substantial **13** consequential

SIGNIFY: **3** nod **4** mean, sign, tell **5** imply, spell **6** convey, denote, import, intend, matter, reveal, signal **7** betoken, compare, connote, declare, express, suggest **8** announce, indicate, intimate, manifest, proclaim **9** insinuate, represent, symbolize **11** communicate

SIGN OFF: **3** end **4** stop **5** cease **7** approve **8** conclude

SIGN ON: **5** start **6** enlist **7** endorse

SIGN UP: **4** join, take **6** accept, enlist, enroll **8** register **9** subscribe, volunteer

SIGURD:
awakens: **8** Brynhild
father: **8** Siegmund
horse: **5** Grani
killed: **6** Fafnir
killer: **5** Hogni
mother: **7** Hiordis
wife: **6** Gudrun

SILAS MARNER:
author: **11** George Eliot
characters: **5** Eppie **10** Squire Cass **11** Dunstan Cass, Godfrey Cass **13** Nancy Lammeter
occupation: **14** hand-loom weaver
village: **7** Raveloe

SILENCE: **3** gag **4** calm, hush, kill, mute, stop **5** death, peace, quell, quiet, shush, still **6** deaden, defeat, muffle, muzzle, pacify, refute, squash **7** destroy, repress, secrecy, squelch **8** muteness, overcome, suppress **9** reticence, stillness **11** tranquility

SILENT: **3** mum **4** dumb, mute **5** quiet, still, tacit **6** hushed **8** discreet, inactive, reserved, reticent, taciturn, tranquil, unspoken **9** quiescent, secretive, unuttered, voiceless **10** speechless **11** tight-lipped, unexpressed **12** close-mouthed, unpronounced

SILHOUETTE: **5** shape **6** shadow **7** contour, outline, profile **8** portrait **10** figuration

SILICON: **7** element

SILK: **5** fiber, tulle **6** fabric, thread, mantua, pongee, samite, sendal, tussah **7** taffeta, tussore
fabric: **5** crepe, moire, ninon, pekin, satin, surah **6** velvet **7** chiffon, foulard **8** gossamer
produced by: **4** moth, worm **7** insects
raw: **5** grege **6** greige **7** marabou **8** marabout
sound: **8** froufrou
source: **6** cocoon
waste: **4** noil **5** floss
yarn: **4** tram

SILKY, SILKEN: **4** fine, soft **5** plush, silky, sleek, sweet **6** gentle, glossy, satiny, smooth **7** elegant **8** delicate **9** luxurious

SILL: **4** beam **5** bench, frame, ledge, shelf **9** threshold

SILLINESS: **5** folly **9** absurdity, craziness, goofiness **11** foolishness

SILLY: **4** daft, dumb **5** crazy, dazed, funny, giddy, goofy, inane, wacky **6** absurd, cuckoo, simple, stupid, unwise **7** asinine, fatuous, foolish, foppish, shallow, witless **8** childish, imbecile **9** brainless, childlike, frivolous, ludicrous, pointless, senseless, simpleton **10** irrational, ridiculous **11** harebrained **12** preposterous, simpleminded

SILVER: **4** coin, gray, pale **5** color, money, plate **6** argent **7** bullion, element, jewelry **8** argentum, lustrous, precious, sterling **9** argentine, tableware

SILVER-TONGUED: **4** glib **6** fluent **8** eloquent **10** oratorical

SILVERWARE: **7** cutlery, service **8** flatware
pieces: **4** fork **5** knife, spoon **8** teaspoon **10** tablespoon

SILVERY: **5** shiny **7** frosted **8** resonant **9** brilliant, melodious **10** argenteous, glittering, shimmering

SIMEON:
father: **5** Jacob
mother: **4** Leah
tribe: **10** Simeonites

SIMIAN: **3** ape **6** monkey **7** gorilla, primate **9** orangutan **10** anthropoid, chimpanzee

SIMILAR: **4** akin, like **5** alike **7** cognate, related, uniform **8** matching, parallel **9** semblance **10** comparable, resembling **11** homogeneous, resemblance **13** corresponding

SIMILARITY: **6** parity **7** analogy **8** affinity, likeness **9** closeness **10** comparison, similitude **11** correlation **12** relationship

SIMILARLY: **4** also, thus **7** equally **8** likewise

SIMILE: **7** analogy **8** metaphor **10** comparison, similitude

SIMILITUDE: **6** simile **7** analogy, parable, replica **8** allegory, likeness **9** semblance **10** comparison, similarity **11** counterpart, resemblance

SIMMER: **4** boil, cook, stew, warm **5** brood **6** bubble, seethe **7** ferment, smolder

SIMMER DOWN: **4** cool **7** collect, compose **8** suppress

SIMON: **5** Peter
disciple of: **5** Jesus
duty: **7** apostle
father: **5** Jonah
son: **5** Judas **8** Iscariot

SIMPER: **4** grin **5** smile, smirk, sneer **6** giggle **7** snicker

SIMPLE: **4** bare, dull, easy, mere, pure, real, slow **5** basic, cinch, dense, naive, naked, plain, stark **6** candid, common, homely, humble, modest, rustic, stupid **7** artless, austere, endless, foolish, genuine, idyllic, natural, sincere, unmixed **8** absolute, backward, childish, gullible, homemade, homespun, ignorant, innocent, ordinary, trifling **9** childlike, elemental, ingenuous, nitwitted, primitive, unadorned **10** effortless, elementary, manageable, unaffected, uneducated, uninvolved **11** uncluttered, unelaborate **12** uncompounded **13** inexperienced, uncomplicated, unembellished, unpretentious

SIMPLEMINDED: **4** dull, dumb, slow **5** naive, silly, thick **6** stupid **7** artless, idiotic, moronic **8** imbecile **13** unintelligent

SIMPLETON: **3** ass, daw, oaf **4** boob, clod, dolt, fool, loon, lout, simp **5** dunce, moron, ninny **7** dullard **8** dumbbell, imbecile, numskull **9** blockhead, ignoramus **10** nincompoop

SIMPLIFY: **6** reduce **7** clarify, explain, expound, shorten **9** interpret **10** generalize, streamline **11** disentangle

SIMPLY: **6** merely, openly **7** clearly, frankly, plainly **8** candidly, honestly **9** naturally **10** absolutely, completely

SIMULATE: **3** act, ape **4** copy **5** feign, mimic **6** affect **7** imitate, playact, pretend **8** resemble **9** dissemble, reproduce **11** counterfeit

SIMULATED: **4** fake **5** phony **7** manmade **9** imitation, synthetic **10** artificial, fictitious

SIMULTANEOUS: **8** together **10** coexisting, coinciding, concurrent, synchronal **11** synchronize **12** contemporary

SIN: **3** err **4** debt, envy, evil, lust, vice **5** anger, error, fault, guilt, pride, sloth, stray, wrong **6** felony, murder **7** misdeed, offense, violate **8** adultery, gluttony, iniquity, trespass **9** violation **10** immorality, peccadillo, transgress, wrongdoing **12** covetousness **13** transgression

SINCE: **3** ago, for, now **4** from, past **5** after, hence, later **7** already, because, whereas **8** inasmuch **9** afterward, therefore **11** considering **12** subsequently

SINCERE: **4** open, pure, real, true **5** frank **6** candid, devout, hearty, honest **7** artless, cordial, earnest, genuine, serious **8** faithful, truthful, virtuous **9** authentic, heartfelt, unfeigned **10** aboveboard, unaffected **12** wholehearted

SINCERITY: **6** candor **7** honesty **8** goodwill **11** earnestness, genuineness

SINE QUA NON: **7** element **9** condition, essential, necessity **13** indispensable

SINEW: **5** force, power, vigor **6** muscle, tendon **7** potency **8** strength, vitality

SINEWY: **4** firm, lean, wiry **5** tough **6** brawny, robust, strong **7** elastic, stringy **8** athletic, forceful, muscular, powerful, vigorous

SINFUL: **3** bad **4** evil, vile **5** wrong **6** erring, unholy, wicked **7** corrupt, immoral, ungodly **8** criminal, damnable, shameful **10** iniquitous **11** blameworthy **13** reprehensible

SING: **3** hum **4** cant, lilt, talk **5** carol, chant, chirl, croon, extol, yodel, yodle **6** betray, inform, intone, tattle, warble **7** confess, divulge, lullaby, rejoice, tweedle **8** proclaim, serenade, vocalize **9** harmonize

SINGE: **4** burn, char, sear **6** scorch

SINGER: **4** alto, bard, bass, diva, poet **5** basso, buffo, tenor **6** artist, cantor **7** artiste, chanter, crooner, soloist, soprano **8** baritone, minstrel, musician, songbird, vocalist **9** chanteuse, chorister, descanter **10** cantatrice, troubadour **11** entertainer

SINGING: **5** music **8** chanting, crooning
group: **4** band, duet, trio **5** choir, octet **6** chorus, sextet **7** octette, quartet **8** glee club

SINGLE: **3** hit, one **4** lone, part, sole, unit **5** alone, unwed **6** unique **7** uniform, unitary, unusual **8** bachelor, distinct, divorced, eligible, separate, singular, solitary **9** exclusive, unmarried **10** individual, unattached

SINGLE-HANDEDLY: **5** alone **10** unassisted **12** courageously

SINGLE-MINDED: **4** firm **5** rigid **7** staunch **8** resolute, stubborn **9** steadfast, unbending **10** determined, inflexible, persistent, relentless

SINGLE OUT: **4** pick **6** choose, prefer, select **11** distinguish

SINGULAR: **3** odd, one **4** lone, rare, sole, solo **5** alone, queer **6** single, unique **7** bizarre, curious, strange, unusual **8** isolated, peculiar, separate, solitary, uncommon **9** different, eccentric, fantastic, marvelous **10** individual, remarkable **11** exceptional **12** unparalleled **13** extraordinary, unprecedented

SINISTER: **4** dark, dire, evil, grim, left **6** malign, wicked **7** baleful, corrupt, ominous **8** devilish, menacing **9** dishonest, malicious, underhand **10** despicable, diabolical, disastrous, portentous **11** apocalyptic, frightening

SINK: **3** bog, dip, ebb, sag **4** dive, drop, fail, fall, ruin, wane **5** basin, drain, droop, lower, sewer, slope, slump, stoop **6** debase, drench, humble, plunge, thrust **7** capsize, decline, degrade, depress, descend, destroy, founder, immerse, plummet, subside, torpedo **8** cesspool, decrease, diminish, submerge, submerse, washbowl **11** deteriorate

SINKER: 3 bob **5** pitch **6** weight **8** doughnut

SINLESS: 4 good, holy, pure **6** chaste **7** perfect **8** innocent **10** immaculate

SINNER: 5 scamp, thief **8** evildoer, murderer **9** adulterer, miscreant, reprobate, wrongdoer **10** trespasser **12** transgressor

SINUOUS: 4 wavy **5** curvy, snaky **6** zigzag **7** bending, crooked, curving, devious, sinuate, winding **8** indirect, twisting **9** deviating **10** circuitous, convoluted, meandering

SINUS: 6 cavity, hollow, pocket, recess **7** channel, opening **10** depressing

SIP: 4 drop **5** drink, quaff, savor, taste **6** sample

SIPHON: 4 draw, pipe, pump, tube **5** drain **6** funnel

SIR: 4 king, lord **5** title **6** knight, master **7** address **8** monsieur

SIRE: 4 lord **5** breed, spawn, title **6** father, parent **7** creator **8** ancestor, begetter **10** forefather, procreator

SIREN: 4 bell, horn, vamp **5** alarm, lurer, nymph **6** signal **7** charmer, enticer, mermaid, whistle **9** temptress **10** seductress

SIROCCO: 4 wind
originates: **12** Sahara Desert

SISSY: 4 baby, wimp **6** coward **7** milksop **8** weakling **10** effeminate, pantywaist

SISTER: 3 nun **5** woman **6** female, friend **7** sibling **9** companion

SISTERHOOD: 4 bond **8** sisterly, sorority **10** friendship

SIT: 3 set **4** meet, pose, rest, stay **5** brood, perch, relax, roost, squat, weigh **6** endure, occupy, please, remain, repose, settle, unused **7** convene **8** assemble **10** deliberate

SITE: 4 area, ruin, spot **5** field, place, point, scene **6** locale, sector **7** setting **8** location, position **9** situation

SIT-IN: 5 march **6** strike **7** display, protest **13** demonstration

SIT ON: 6 confer **7** repress **8** postpone, suppress **9** reprimand

SIT OUT: 6 ignore **7** refrain

SITTING BULL:
battle: **13** Little Bighorn
fought: **13** General Custer
tribe: **5** Sioux

SITTING DUCK: 4 dupe **5** decoy **6** target, victim

SITUATE: 5 place **6** locate, settle **8** position **9** establish

SITUATION: 3 job **4** need, post, seat, site, spot **5** berth, place, point, state **6** locale, plight, status, strait **7** bargain, dilemma, posture, problem, station, vantage **8** locality, location, position, quandary **9** condition, direction, emergency **11** arrangement, predicament, whereabouts **12** circumstance

SIZABLE: 3 big **5** ample, hefty, large, roomy **8** spacious, whopping **9** extensive **11** substantial **12** considerable

SIZE: 4 area, mass **5** cover, grade, scope, total, width **6** amount, degree, extent, height, length, volume **7** breadth, caliber, expanse, measure **8** capacity, diameter **9** amplitude **10** dimensions **11** proportions

SIZZLE: **3** fry **4** burn, cook, hiss, sear **5** brown, grill **7** crackle, shrivel, sputter

SKATE: **3** nag, ray **4** fish **5** glide, horse, slide **6** fellow
type: **3** ice **6** figure, hockey, roller

SKEDADDLE: **4** bolt, flee **5** leave, scoot, scram, split **6** scurry **7** scamper, vamoose **8** hightail

SKELETON: **4** past **5** bones, coral, draft, frame, shell **6** sketch **7** outline, support **9** framework

SKEPTIC: **5** cynic **7** doubter, infidel, sceptic, scoffer **8** agnostic **10** questioner, unbeliever **11** disbeliever, freethinker

SKEPTICAL: **5** leery **7** cynical, dubious **8** doubtful, doubting **9** sceptical, uncertain **10** suspicious **11** questioning, unconvinced

SKEPTICISM: **5** doubt **7** concern, dubiety **9** disbelief, suspicion **11** uncertainty

SKETCH: **3** jot, map **4** draw, plan, play, skit **5** chart, draft, paint, scene, story, trace **6** apercu, design, doodle, layout **7** account, cartoon, diagram, drawing, outline, picture, summary **8** describe, skeleton **9** blueprint, delineate, depiction **11** description

SKETCHY: **4** hazy **5** crude, rough, vague **6** cloudy **7** shallow **10** incomplete, unfinished **11** preliminary, superficial

SKEW: **4** slip, turn, veer **5** angle, slant, twist **6** biased, glance, squint, swerve **7** blunder, distort, oblique **9** distorted **12** asymmetrical

SKEWER: **3** pin, rod **4** pick **5** lance, prick, truss **6** pierce, skiver **8** puncture **9** brochette

SKI: **5** glide, slide **6** runner, travel
lift: **4** j-bar, poma, t-bar **5** chair **7** gondola **10** helicopter

SKID: **3** log **4** drag, rail, shoe, skim, slip, veer **5** brake, coast, glide, plank, slide **6** pallet, runner, swerve, timber, tumble **7** plummet, spinout, support **8** platform, sideslip

SKIFF: **4** boat **6** dinghy **7** rowboat

SKIING: **5** sport
Alpine event: **6** slalom, Super G **8** combined, downhill **9** freestyle **11** giant slalom **16** super giant slalom
bump: **5** mogul
equipment: **4** skis **5** boots, poles **8** bindings, clothing
Nordic event: **8** combined **10** ski jumping **12** cross-country
skier: **9** Billy Kidd, Phil Mahre **10** Steve Mahre **11** Bill Johnson, Cindy Nelson **12** Alberto Tomba, Franz Klammer, Stein Eriksen **14** Marc Girardelli **15** Ingemar Stenmark, Jean Claude Killy, Rosi Mittermaier
technique: **7** skating **8** parallel, pedaling, snowplow, traverse **11** herringbone **12** sideslipping, sidestepping
turn: **4** stem, step **5** swing **6** wedeln **7** christy **8** parallel

SKILL: **3** art **4** gift **5** craft, knack, trade **6** method, talent **7** ability, address, cunning, finesse, knowhow, mastery, science **8** aptitude, artistry, capacity, deftness, facility, training **9** adeptness, dexterity, expertise, knowledge **10** adroitness, capability, competence, efficiency, experience, expertness, occupation, profession **11** proficiency

SKILLFUL: **3** apt **4** able, deft, good **5** adept, handy, sharp **6** adroit, artful, clever, crafty, expert, gifted **7** capable, cunning, learned, trained, veteran **8** tactical, talented **9** dexterous, ingenious, qualified **10** proficient **11** experienced **12** accomplished, professional

SKIM: **4** sail, scan, scud, skip **5** brush, carom, coast, float, glide, graze, ladle, scoop, shave, skate, study, throw **6** browse, glance **7** examine **8** ricochet

SKIMP: **4** save **5** pinch **6** scrape, scrimp **9** economize, sacrifice

SKIMPY: **4** lean, thin **5** scant, spare, tight **6** meager, scanty, sparse, stingy **7** scrimpy **10** inadequate **12** insufficient

SKIN: **3** fur **4** bark, case, coat, flay, hide, husk, peel, pell, pelt, rack, rind, scum, shed **5** cheat, crust, cutis, derma, layer, scale, scalp, shell, strip **6** callus, dermis, fleece, scrape, sheath, vellum **7** callous, coating, cuticle, defraud, sheathe, surface, swindle **8** covering, exterior, exuviate, membrane, pellicle, planking **9** epidermis **10** overcharge **11** decorticate
blemish: **4** mole, rash, wart **5** nevus **6** macula, stigma **7** freckle, lentigo **9** birthmark **10** strawberry
disease: **4** acne, rash **5** hives, mange **6** eczema **7** roseola **8** shingles **9** psoriasis, seborrhea **10** dermatitis
fold: **5** plica **6** frenum, wattle
layer: **3** fat **6** cirium, dermis **9** epidermis **18** subcutaneous tissue
parts: **4** pore, vein **5** nerve **6** artery, tissue **7** appilla **9** capillary, hair shaft **10** melanocyte, sweat gland **12** hair follicle

SKINFLINT: **5** miser **7** niggard **8** tightwad **10** cheapskate

SKINNY: **4** bony, lean, thin **5** lanky, scant, spare **7** scrawny, slender **8** skeletal **9** emaciated **11** underweight **12** malnourished

SKIP: **3** hip, hop **4** bolt, flee, gait, jump, leap, miss, omit, pass, skim, trip **5** avoid, bound, hooky, leave, vault **6** escape, glance, gambol, spring **7** abscond **8** overlook, ricochet **9** skedaddle

SKIPPER: **4** fish **5** coach **6** leader, master **7** captain, officer **9** butterfly, commander

SKIRMISH: **4** fray **5** brawl, brush, clash, fight, melee, scrap **6** action, battle, combat **7** contest, dispute, scuffle **8** conflict, struggle **9** encounter, scrimmage

SKIRT: **3** hem, rim **4** brim, duck, edge, jupe, kilt, maxi, mini, tutu **5** avoid, dodge, dress, evade, flank **6** border, bypass **7** fringer, garment **8** culottes, envelope, lavalava, sidestep **9** periphery, petticoat **10** fustanella, wraparound

SKIT: **3** act **4** joke, play **5** caper, revue, story **6** parody, sketch **9** burlesque

SKITTISH: **3** coy, shy **5** jumpy, timid **6** fickle, lively **7** bashful, fidgety, nervous, playful, restive **8** restless, unstable **9** excitable, frivolous, mercurial **11** lightheaded **13** irresponsible

SKULK: **4** hide, lurk **5** creep, evade, prowl, shirk, slink, sneak **8** malinger **9** pussyfoot

SKULL: **4** head, mind **5** brain, scalp

SKULLCAP: **4** kipa **6** beanie, kappel **7** calotte **8** yarmulke **9** zucchetto

SKULLDUGGERY: **6** crafty **8** trickery **9** chicanery

SKUNK: **5** cheat, knave **6** animal, defeat, mammal **7** polecat, shellac, stinker **9** scoundrel
genus: **8** mephitis

SKY: **3** air **4** jump **5** space, vault **6** welkin **7** heavens **8** empyrean **9** firmament

SKY-BLUE: **5** azure, color **7** celeste **8** cerulean

SKYLARKING: **6** antics **7** hijinks, playing, revelry **9** carousing, horseplay **10** frolicking **11** roughhousing

SKYLINE: **7** horizon, outline

SLAB: **4** hunk, lump, tile, wood **5** board, chunk, piece, slice **6** tablet **7** portion

SLACK: **3** lax **4** easy, idle, lazy, play, slow, soft **5** loose, relax, shirk, tardy **6** excess, leeway, loosen, remiss, sloppy **7** flaccid, relaxed **8** careless, dilatory, flexible, inactive, indolent, slothful, sluggish, unsteady **9** leisurely, lethargic, looseness, negligent **10** inadequate, neglectful **11** inattentive

SLACKEN: **4** ease, slow **5** abate, loose, relax **6** loosen, reduce, retard, temper, weaken **7** subside **8** decrease, diminish, moderate **9** untighten

SLACKER: **5** idler **6** loafer **7** dawdler, goof-off, laggard, shirker **8** sluggard **9** goldbrick

SLAG: **4** lava **5** ashes, dross **6** debris, embers, refuse, scoria **7** cinders, residue **9** recrement

SLAKE: **4** cool **5** abate, allay, loose, relax, slack **6** lessen, quench, reduce, subdue **7** appease, assuage, compose, crumble, gratify, refresh, relaxed, relieve, satisfy **8** decrease, mitigate, moderate **12** disintegrate

SLAM: **3** hit, rap **4** bang, beat, belt, blow, push, slug, swat **5** abuse, clash, crash, knock, pound, smack, smash, throw, thump **6** batter, impact, strike, wallop **7** clobber **9** criticize

SLAMMER: **3** can, jug, pen, pog **4** jail **5** clink, pokey **6** cooler, prison **8** hoosegow **9** calaboose **12** penitentiary

SLANDER: **4** slur **5** belie, libel, smear, sully **6** assail, defame, malign, vilify **7** asperse, calumny, distort, scandal, traduce **8** derogate, disgrace, dishonor, muckrake **10** defamation, scandalize **11** mudslinging **12** misrepresent

SLANG: **4** cant, jive **5** argot, lingo **6** jargon **7** dialect **8** language **9** vulgarity **10** vernacular, vituperate

SLANT: **3** tip **4** band, bank, bias, lean, skew, tilt, turn, veer, view **5** angle, aside, bevel, grade, pitch, point, slope **6** glance **7** decline, distort, incline, opinion **8** sideways **9** prejudice, viewpoint

SLAP: **3** hit, pat **4** blow, clap, cuff, swat, wham **5** crack, smack, spank **6** buffet, insult, strike, wallop **9** castigate, criticize

SLAPDASH: **5** hasty **6** sloppy **8** careless, reckless, slipshod **9** haphazard, impetuous

SLAPSTICK: **5** farce, funny **6** absurd, comedy, paddle **7** comical

SLASH: **3** cut **4** gash, hack, lash, slit **5** carve, knife, slice, wound **6** lessen, reduce, strike, stripe **7** butcher, curtail, shorten **8** decrease, diagonal **9** criticize **10** laceration

SLATE: **4** gray, list, rock, tile **5** board, color **6** ballot, record, roster, tablet, ticket **7** roofing **8** register, schedule **10** blackboard, chalkboard

SLATTERN: **3** hag **4** slob, slug **5** whore **7** trollop **10** prostitute

SLAUGHTER: **4** kill, maim, rout, slay **6** murder, pogrom **7** butcher, carnage, destroy, killing, trounce **8** butchery, decimate, massacre, mutilate **9** bloodbath, bloodshed, overwhelm **10** annihilate **11** destruction, liquidation

SLAUGHTERHOUSE: **8** abattoir, butchery, shambles **9** stockyard

SLAV: **4** Pole, Serb, Sorb, Wend **5** Croat, Czech **6** Bulgar, Slovak **7** Deniker, Russian, Serbian, Slovene **8** Bohemian, Croatian, Moravian **9** Bulgarian, Ruthenian, Ukrainian

SLAVE: **4** bond, serf, toil **5** grind, helot **6** drudge, thrall, toiler, vassal **7** bondman, captive, chattel, laborer, servant **8** bondsman **9** workhorse **10** bondswoman

SLAVER: **4** fawn **5** drool **6** drivel, saliva **7** dribble, slobber

SLAVERY: **4** work **5** grind, labor **7** bondage, helotry, serfdom **8** drudgery **9** captivity, servitude, thralldom, vassalage **12** enthrallment

SLAVISH: **4** bond, hard **6** abject, menial **7** servile **9** dependent, imitative **10** obsequious, oppressive, submissive, uninspired, unoriginal **11** subservient

SLAY: **4** do in, kill **5** snuff **6** murder, strike **7** butcher, destroy, execute **8** massacre **9** eliminate, overwhelm, slaughter **10** annihilate **11** assassinate

SLAYER: **6** killer **8** assassin, criminal, murderer **11** executioner

SLEAZY: **4** thin **5** cheap, seedy, tacky **6** flimsy, shabby, shoddy, tawdry, trashy **11** dilapidated **12** disreputable

SLED: **4** luge, pung **6** cutter, sledge, sleigh **7** bobsled, clipper, coaster **8** toboggan

SLEEK: **4** chic, oily **5** gloss, preen, shiny, silky, slick, slide, smart, suave **6** adroit, chisel, clever, crafty, glossy, polish, satiny, silken, smooth **7** cunning, stylish **8** slippery, unctuous **9** ingenious **10** attractive, glistening **11** fashionable

SLEEP: **3** nap **4** coma, doze, rest **5** crash, death, dream, sopor **6** catnap, drowse, repose, retire, siesta, snooze, stupor **7** slumber **8** estivate, lethargy **9** hibernate

SLEEPER: **3** spy **4** beam **5** horse **7** dormant, pajamas, Pullman, reposer **8** dormouse, long shot

SLEEPING: **6** asleep, latent **7** dormant **8** comatose, inactive **11** unconscious

SLEEPLESS: **5** alert **6** active **7** wakeful **8** restless, watchful **9** ceaseless **11** insomnolent

SLEEPLESSNESS: **8** insomnia **11** wakefulness **12** restlessness

SLEEPWALKER: **12** noctambulist, somnambulist

SLEEPWALKING: **12** noctambulism, somnambulism

SLEEPY: **4** dozy, dull **5** quiet, tired **6** drowsy **8** fatigued, hypnotic, inactive, listless, sluggish **9** exhausted, lethargic, somnolent **10** slumberous

SLEIGH: **4** luge, pung, sled **6** cutter, sledge **7** bobsled **8** toboggan

SLEIGHT: **3** sly **5** craft, skill, trick **7** agility, cunning, gimmick **8** artifice, deftness **9** deception, dexterity, quickness

SLENDER: **4** lean, slim, thin, trim, weak **5** faint, frail, lanky, lithe, scant, small, wispy **6** feeble, little, meager, minute, narrow, remote, skinny, slight, svelte **7** outside, tenuous, willowy **8** delicate

SLEUTH: **5** agent **7** gumshoe, tracker **9** detective **10** private eye **12** investigator

SLICE: **3** cut **4** gash, part, slit **5** carve, piece, quota, sever, share, wedge **6** course **7** segment **9** allotment

SLICK: **4** foxy, glib, neat, oily, tidy, wily, wise **5** cagey, sharp, slimy, smart **6** greasy, shrewd, tricky **8** magazine, unctuous

SLICKER: **4** dude **5** cheat **7** sharper **8** raincoat, swindler **9** trickster

SLIDE: **4** fall, flow, skid, skim, sled, slip **5** chute, coast, glide, hurry, scoot, skate, slope **6** sledge, stream **7** decline, incline, slither **8** downturn, glissade **9** downswing

SLIGHT: **3** cut **4** slim, snub, thin **5** frail, light, minor, scant, scorn, small **6** dainty, flimsy, ignore, little, meager, offend, rebuff, remote, scanty, skinny **7** disdain, fragile, neglect, nominal, slender, trivial **8** delicate, overlook, trifling **9** disparage, disregard **11** discourtesy, superficial, unimportant **12** contemptuous **13** insignificant

SLIGHTLY: **6** hardly **8** somewhat **9** slenderly **10** delicately, marginally

SLIM: **4** diet, lean, thin **5** gaunt, small, spare **6** meager, narrow, reduce, remote, scanty, skinny, slight, sparse, svelte **7** outside, slender, tenuous **10** negligible

SLIME: **3** mud **4** glop, gunk, mire, muck, ooze, scum, slop **5** filth **6** sludge

SLIMY: **4** foul, oozy, vile **5** gooey, mucky, muddy **6** clammy, filthy, scummy, vulgar **7** viscous **9** offensive, repulsive

SLING: **4** cast, hurl, send, toss **5** chuck, fling, heave, throw **6** launch, weapon **8** catapult **9** slingshot

SLINK: **4** lurk **5** creep, prowl, sneak, steal **6** weasel **7** slither

SLIP: **3** err, imp **4** dock, fall, flub, goof, muff, omit, pier, quay, skid, trip **5** berth, chute, elude, error, fault, glide, jetty, lapse, slide **6** bungle, elapse, harbor, miscue, mishap **7** blooper, blunder, faux pas, misstep, mistake, neglect, slither, stumble, voucher **8** lingerie, pinafore **9** oversight, petticoat, underwear **12** undergarment

SLIP AWAY: **4** pass **5** lapse **6** elapse, escape

SLIP BACK: **6** return, revert **7** regress, relapse

SLIPPER: **4** mule, pump, shoe **5** scuff **6** sandal

SLIPPERY: **3** icy **4** foxy, glib, oily **5** slick **6** crafty, greasy, shifty, smooth, sneaky, tricky **7** elusive, evasive **9** dishonest, uncertain **10** unreliable

SLIP-UP: **4** flub **5** error **6** bungle, miscue, mishap **7** blooper, blunder, mistake **8** omission **9** oversight

SLIT: **3** cut **4** gash, rent, tear **5** crack, sever, slash, slice, split **7** fissure, opening **8** aperture, incision

SLITHER: **4** lurk **5** crawl, creep, glide, prowl, slide, snake, sneak **6** grovel

SLIVER: **5** crumb, flake, shred, slice, thorn **8** fragment, splinter

SLOB: **3** hog, pig **6** sloven **8** slattern

SLOBBER: **4** gush, kiss **5** drool, froth **6** drivel, slaver **7** blubber, dribble, slabber **8** salivate

SLOGAN: **5** idiom, motto **6** jingle, phrase **9** catchword, watchword **10** expression

SLOOP: **4** boat, ship **5** smack **8** sailboat

SLOP: **3** mud **4** gulp, gush, mash, muck, ooze **5** slush, spill, swill, trash, waste **6** drivel, guzzle, refuse, sludge, splash **7** garbage, slobber

SLOPE: **4** bank, bend, cant, hill, lean, ramp, rise, tilt **5** angle, bevel, cliff, grade, pitch, slant **6** ascent **7** descent, incline **8** gradient **9** acclivity, declivity, obliquely **11** inclination

SLOPING: **5** askew **6** supine, tilted **7** leaning, oblique, pitched **8** downhill, inclined, slanting **9** declivous

SLOPPY: **5** dirty, messy, muddy **6** clumsy, slushy, untidy **7** unkempt **8** careless, slipshod, slovenly **10** disheveled

SLOSH: **3** mud **4** wade **5** slime, slush, spill **6** splash, wallow **8** flounder, splatter

SLOT: **3** gap **4** hole, slit **5** crack, niche, notch, space, track **6** groove, hollow **7** keyhole, opening **8** position

SLOTH: **4** lazy, pack **6** animal, apathy, torpor **7** languor **8** idleness, laziness, lethargy, slowness **9** indolence, lassitude, tardiness, torpidity **12** listlessness, sluggishness

SLOTHFUL: **4** idle, lazy **8** inactive, indolent, listless, sluggish **9** lethargic

SLOUCH: **4** bend, gait, idle, loaf, wilt **5** droop, hunch, stoop **6** lounge **7** laggard, posture, slacker

SLOVAKIA:
capital: **10** Bratislava
cities: **6** Kosice
continent: **6** Europe
ethnic groups: **6** Slovak **9** Hungarian
features: **11** Carpathians
languages: **6** Slovak **9** Hungarian
monetary unit: **6** koruna
was part of: **14** Czechoslovakia
water: **6** Danube

SLOVENIA:
capital: **9** Ljubljana
continent: **6** Europe
ethnic groups: **7** Slovene
languages: **9** Slovenian **13** Serbo-Croatian
monetary unit: **5** tolar
was part of: **10** Yugoslavia
water: **4** Sava **5** Drava

SLOVENLY: **4** lazy **5** dirty, dowdy, messy, seedy, tacky **6** grubby, grungy, ragged, sloppy, untidy **7** unkempt **8** careless, slipshod **10** disheveled, disorderly, slatternly

SLOW: **4** dull, late, lazy, poky **5** brake, delay, pokey, slack, tardy **6** behind, boring, hamper, hinder, impede, retard, simple, stupid **7** gradual, laggard, relaxed, slacken **8** backward, delaying, dilatory, dragging, inactive, plodding, sluggard, sluggish **9** leisurely, lingering, unhurried **10** decelerate, deliberate, phlegmatic **13** procrastinate, unintelligent

SLOWDOWN: **4** curb **5** brake, delay, slump **6** strike **7** falloff, setback **8** stoppage **10** inactivity **12** deceleration

SLOWPOKE: **4** slug **5** snail **7** dawdler, laggard **8** lingerer **9** straggler

SLOW-WITTED: **4** dull **5** dense **6** stupid **7** moronic

SLUDGE: **3** ice, mud **4** mire, muck, ooze, slop **5** filth, slime, slush, waste **7** residue **8** sediment

SLUG: **3** bat, hit **4** belt, disk, shot, slam, slow, sock, swat **5** drink, punch, smack, smash, snail **6** bullet, slouch, strike, wallop **7** clobber, mollusk **8** sluggard **9** gastropod

SLUGGARD: **4** lazy, slug **5** drone, idler **6** loafer, slouch **7** dawdler, laggard **8** faineant **9** lazybones

SLUGGISH: **4** dull, lazy, slow **5** heavy, inert, stiff **6** drowsy, leaden, supine, torpid **7** lumpish **8** dilatory, dragging, inactive, indolent, listless, slothful, sluggard, stagnant **9** apathetic, lethargic **12** unresponsive

SLUICE: **4** gate, gush, pour, soak, wash **5** douse, flume, flush, valve **6** stream, trough **7** channel, conduit, opening **8** irrigate **9** floodgate

SLUM: **4** dump **5** alley **6** barrio, ghetto **7** skid row **8** tenement

SLUMBER: **3** nap **4** coma, doze, rest **5** sleep **6** drowse, snooze **7** languor **8** dormancy, lethargy **9** hibernate

SLUMP: **3** dip, sag **4** drop, fall, sink, slip **5** droop, slide **6** plunge, slouch, topple **7** decline **8** collapse **9** downswing, downtrend, recession **10** depression

SLUR: **4** blur, soil, spot **5** slide, smear, stain, sully **6** defame, garble, insult, malign, mumble, slight, stigma **7** blacken, blemish, calumny, slander, traduce **8** disgrace, innuendo, reproach **9** aspersion, criticize, discredit, disparage **10** calumniate

SLUSH: **3** ice, mud **4** mire, pulp, slop, snow **6** drench, drivel, sluice

SLUT: **4** jade, minx **5** bimbo, hussy, tramp, wench, whore **6** floozy, harlot, hooker **7** jezebel **8** slattern **10** prostitute

SLY: **4** foxy, wily **5** cagey, sharp, slick **6** artful, clever, crafty, secret, shifty, shrewd, smooth, sneaky, subtle, tricky **7** cunning, devious, evasive, furtive, roguish **8** guileful, skillful, sneaking **9** deceitful, ingenious, secretive **11** mischievous, underhanded

SMACK: **3** hit, pat, rap **4** bash, belt, blow, boat, cuff, kiss, slap, sock **5** crack, noise, punch, sloop, smash, spank, taste, touch, trace, whack **6** flavor, heroin, strike **7** collide, exactly **8** directly, sailboat **9** precisely **10** suggestion

SMALL: **3** wee **4** mean, puny, slim, thin, tiny **5** dinky, faint, minor, petty, scant, short, teeny **6** humble, little, meager, mignon, minute, modest, narrow, petite, remote, slight **7** cramped, limited, minimal, selfish, slender, trivial **8** picayune, trifling **9** miniature, minuscule **10** diminutive, humiliated, negligible, undersized **11** microscopic, unimportant **13** insignificant

SMALL FRY: **4** fish, kids **8** children **11** unimportant

SMALL-MINDED: **4** mean **5** petty **6** narrow **7** bigoted, selfish **10** intolerant, prejudiced

SMALLER: **4** less **6** lesser **7** littler, shorter

SMALLEST: **5** least **6** lowest **7** tiniest **8** shortest

SMALL TALK: **6** babble, banter, gossip **7** prattle **8** chitchat **12** pleasantries

SMART: **4** ache, chic, hurt, neat, pain, posh, smug, wily, wise **5** acute, alert, brisk, canny, fresh, quick, sassy, sharp, slick, sting, throb, witty **6** active, astute, bright, clever, dapper, lively, shrewd, sporty, spruce, swanky, trendy **7** elegant, knowing, pungent, stylish **8** insolent, spirited, vigorous **9** brilliant, energetic **10** precocious **11** fashionable, impertinent, intelligent, resourceful

SMART ALECK: **5** clown **7** boaster, wise guy **8** braggart, wiseacre **11** wisenheimer

SMARTEN: **4** tidy **6** spruce **7** educate, improve **8** beautify, brighten

SMASH: **3** hit **4** bang, bash, belt, dash, jolt, slam, slug, sock **5** break, crack, crash, crush, press, whack, wreck **6** batter, defeat, impact, strike, wallop **7** clobber, destroy, shatter, success **8** accident, collapse, demolish **9** collision, pulverize, sensation **10** annihilate

SMASHED: **4** shot **5** drunk **6** broken, buzzed, soused, stewed, wasted, zonked **9** plastered **10** inebriated **11** intoxicated

SMASHUP: **5** crash, wreck **6** defeat, pileup **8** accident, collapse **9** collision

SMATTERING: **4** dash, drop **7** smidgen **10** sprinkling

SMEAR: **3** dab, mar, rub **4** blot, blur, coat, slur, soil, spot **5** cover, smash, stain, sully, taint **6** blotch, defame, defeat, defile, grease, malign, sample, smirch, smudge, spread, thrash, vilify **7** besmear, degrade, plaster, slander, spatter, splotch, trounce **8** besmirch, lambaste

SMELL: **4** aura, funk, fust, nose, odor, reek **5** aroma, flair, scent, sense, sniff, stink, trace, whiff **6** detect, stench **7** perfume **8** discover **9** fragrance

SMELLY: **4** foul, rank **5** fetid, funky **6** putrid, rotten **7** noisome **8** stinking

SMIDGEN: **3** bit **4** drop, mite **5** crumb, pinch, shred, speck, trace **8** particle

SMILE: **4** beam, grin **5** laugh, smirk, sneer **6** simper **10** expression

SMIRCH: **4** blot, soil **5** dirty, smear, stain, sully, taint **6** blotch, smudge **7** besmear, blacken, blemish, corrupt, country, degrade, pollute, tarnish **8** besmirch, disgrace, dishonor **9** bespatter, discredit **11** contaminate

SMIRK: **4** beam, grin, leer **5** smile, sneer **6** simper **7** grimace

SMITE: **3** hit **4** belt, dash, slap, sock, swat **5** knock, smack, whack **6** attack, buffet, defeat, strike, wallop **7** afflict, chasten, clobber, destroy **8** chastise

SMITHEREENS: **4** bits **5** atoms **6** crumbs, pieces **9** fragments, particles

SMITTEN: **8** affected, enamored, stricken **9** afflicted **10** infatuated

SMOKE: **4** fume, funk, haze, kill, loud, mist, pipe, puff, smog **5** cigar, steam, vapor **6** murder, smudge **7** perform **9** cigarette

SMOKY: **4** fumy, hazy **5** dingy, fumid, murky, sooty **6** cloudy **7** burning **9** blackened **10** smoldering

SMOLDER: **4** burn, fume **6** bubble, fester, seethe, simmer **7** smother **9** fulminate

SMOOTH: **4** calm, ease, easy, even, iron, flat, mild, pave, sand, soft **5** bland, level, plane, preen, press, silky, sleek, slick, suave **6** creamy, evenly, fluent, gentle, glossy, placid, polish, serene, sleeky, soothe **7** comfort, equable, flatten, flowing **8** civilize, hairless, palliate, pleasant, polished, soothing, tranquil **9** courteous, easygoing, unruffled **10** effortless, harmonious, methodical, persuasive, unwrinkled **11** undisturbed **13** uninterrupted

SMORGASBORD: **6** buffet **8** mishmash **10** hodgepodge

SMOTHER: **4** hide **5** choke, cover, quash **6** quench, shower, solder, stifle **7** conceal, repress **8** suppress

9 overwhelm, suffocate **10** asphyxiate, extinguish

SMUDGE: **4** blot, blur, smut, soil, soot **5** dirty, grime, smear, stain, sully **6** blotch, smutch **7** blemish, splotch

SMUG: **4** neat, tidy, trim **5** suave **6** spruce, stuffy **7** pompous **8** priggish **9** confident **10** complacent

SMUGGLE: **5** sneak **6** pirate **7** bootleg

SMUGGLER: **6** runner **8** criminal **10** bootlegger

SMUT: **4** dirt, muck, soil, spot **5** filth, grime, stain, sully, taint **6** smudge **9** obscenity **11** pornography

SMUTTY: **4** lewd **5** dirty, nasty, sooty **6** filthy, soiled, vulgar **7** obscene, raunchy **8** indecent **12** pornographic

SNACK: **3** bit, eat, tea **4** nosh **6** morsel, nibble **7** goodies **8** munchies **11** refreshment

SNAFU: **4** mess **5** chaos, snarl **6** muddle **8** entangle **9** confusion **11** predicament **12** complication

SNAG: **4** knot, nail, spot, tear, tree **5** catch, hitch, stump **6** branch, damage, glitch, hamper, hazard, hinder, hurdle, pickle, sawyer **7** barrier, problem **8** drawback, obstacle **9** hindrance **10** difficulty, impediment **11** obstruction

SNAIL: **4** slug **8** escargot, slowpoke **9** gastropod **10** periwinkle

SNAKE:
concerning: **8** viperine
killer: **8** mongoose
movement: **7** slither **8** creeping, undulant **10** concertina
order: **8** squamata
poison: **5** venom
related to: **6** lizard
study: **11** herpetology
suborder: **9** serpentes
types: **3** asp, nag, sea **5** adder, cobra, coral, grass, racer, viper **6** python, rattle, smooth, taipan **7** serpent **8** anaconda, moccasin **10** bushmaster, copperhead **11** constrictor, cottonmouth

SNAKY: **3** sly **4** evil **6** crafty, sneaky, zigzag **7** devious, sinuous, winding, wriggly **8** twisting, venomous **10** meandering, serpentine

SNAP: **3** ite, pop **4** bark, easy, hike, jerk, lock, take **5** break, catch, cinch, click, close, crack, latch, quick, seize, snarl **6** breeze, cookie, energy, fillip, snatch **7** crackle, sparkle **8** fastener, interval, pushover **9** crackling, crispness **10** elasticity, photograph

SNAP BACK: **6** revive **7** improve, rebound, recover

SNAPPISH: **4** curt, edgy **5** angry, cross, huffy, short, testy **6** crabby, cranky, touchy **7** grouchy, peevish **8** petulant **9** irascible, irritable **12** cantankerous

SNAPPY: **4** chic, fast **5** hasty, nasty, quick, rapid, smart, swank, swift **6** classy, dapper, lively, prompt, speedy, spiffy, sudden **7** stylish **9** energetic, irritable **11** fashionable

SNARE: **3** bag, net, web **4** bait, grin, land, lure, mesh, trap **5** catch, decoy, grasp, noose, seize **6** ambush, entoil, entrap, tangle **7** involve, pitfall **8** entangle, inveigle **9** deception **10** enticement **12** entanglement

SNARL: **3** arr, jam, web **4** bark, kink, knot, maze, mesh, mess, snap **5** chaos, gnarl, growl, scold, snare, twist **6** muddle, tangle **7** confuse, grumble, quarrel **8** entangle, infusion **10** complicate **11** predicament

SNATCH: **3** bit, nab **4** grab, nail, take, trap, yank **5** catch, grasp, piece, pluck, seize, snare, swipe, wrest **6** abduct, clutch, collar, kidnap, rescue **7** grabble **8** fragment

SNEAK: **4** lurk, worm **5** cower, crawl, creep, knave, prowl, skunk, slink, snake, snoop, steal **6** ambush, coward, rascal, secret, tiptoe **7** cheater, slither **9** scoundrel, underhand

SNEAKY: **3** sly **6** shifty **7** devious, furtive **8** sinister **9** dishonest **11** clandestine, underhanded **13** surreptitious

SNEER: **4** gibe, grin, jeer, leer, mock, snub **5** flout, scoff, scorn, smile, smirk, taunt **6** insult **7** condemn, disdain, grimace, lampoon, snicker **8** belittle, ridicule **10** expression

SNICKER: **5** laugh, sneer **6** giggle, hee-haw, teehee **7** chortle, chuckle, snigger, sniggle

SNIDE: **3** sly **4** base, mean **5** nasty **6** tricky **7** cynical, hateful **8** sinister, spiteful **9** insincere, malicious, sarcastic, underhand **12** contemptible

SNIFF: **4** nose **5** scent, smell, snoop, snuff, whiff **6** detect, inhale **7** sniffle, snuffle

SNIFTER: **4** dram, shot **5** drink, snort **6** goblet

SNIP: **3** bit, cut **4** clip, easy, trim **5** piece, scrap, shear, shred **7** shorten **8** fragment, incision, particle, separate

SNIPER: **6** gunman, killer **8** assassin, gunwoman, marksman **10** markswoman **12** sharpshooter

SNIPPY: **4** curt, mean, rude **5** bluff, blunt, brief, gruff, sharp, short **6** abrupt, snotty **8** snippety **11** fragmentary, impertinent

SNITCH: **4** tell **5** pinch, steal, swipe, thief **6** betray, inform, pilfer, tattle **7** tattler **8** informer, squealer

SNIVEL: **3** cry, sob **4** fret, weep **5** sniff, whine **7** blubber, sniffle, whimper **8** complain

SNOB: **5** toady **7** elitist, parvenu, upstart **9** pretender

SNOBBISH: **6** snooty, snotty, uppity **7** pompous **8** arrogant **11** overbearing, pretentious **12** ostentatious **13** condescending

SNOOP: **3** pry, spy **4** peek, peep, poke **5** prowl, sneak **6** meddle, search **7** meddler **8** busybody

SNOOTY: **6** snotty **7** haughty **8** snobbish **9** conceited, exclusive **11** egotistical, pretentious **12** supercilious

SNOOZE: **3** nap **4** doze **5** sleep **6** drowse, siesta **7** slumber **10** forty winks

SNORT: **4** blow, pant, puff **5** drink, grunt, laugh, snore, sound **7** breathe

SNOTTY: **4** rude **5** dirty, nasty **6** snooty **7** haughty **8** arrogant, impudent, snobbish **11** impertinent

SNOUT: **4** beak, nose **5** spout, trunk **6** nozzle **7** rostrum **9** proboscis

SNOW: **3** ice **4** firn, pelt **5** cover, opium, sleet, slush, storm **6** heroin, whiten **7** blanker, cocaine, deceive **8** blizzard **9** overwhelm

SNOW-BOUND: **7** trapped **8** isolated

SNOWY: **4** pure, soft **5** nival, white **6** fluffy, stormy, wintry **7** niveous **8** spotless

SNUB: **3** cut, nip **4** shun, slap, stop **5** quell **6** rebuff, rebuke, remark, slight **7** censure, neglect, repress **8** reproach, restrain **9** disregard, ostracize, reprimand

SNUFF: **4** odor **5** scent, smell, sniff, snort, whiff **6** detect, inhale **7** destroy, tobacco **8** adequate **10** extinguish

SNUG: **4** cozy, neat, safe, tidy, trim, warm **5** close, comfy, cushy, tight **6** cuddle, nestle, secure **7** compact, snuggle **8** intimate **9** seaworthy, sheltered **11** comfortable

SNUGGLE: **4** snug **6** bundle, cuddle, huddle, nestle, nuzzle

SOAK: **3** dip, sop, wet **4** dunk, ooze, seep **5** douse, drink, flood, imbue, souse, steep **6** absorb, drench, imbibe, imbrue, seethe **7** immerse, moisten **8** drunkard, marinate, permeate, saturate, submerge, waterlog **9** penetrate, percolate **10** impregnate, overcharge

SOAKED: **3** wet **5** soggy **6** sodden **8** drenched **9** saturated **11** waterlogged

SOAP: **4** suds, wash **5** bribe, money **6** lather **7** castile, solvent **8** cleanser, flattery **9** detergent

SOAR: **3** fly **4** lift, rise, sail **5** climb, float, glide, mount, tower **6** ascend, aspire **9** skyrocket, transcend

SOB: **3** cry **4** bawl, moan, wail, weep **6** boohoo, lament, snivel **7** blubber, whimper

SOBER: **4** calm, cool, dull, grim, sane **5** grave, quiet, sound, staid **6** ailing, gentle, humble, placid, sedate, solemn, somber, steady, subdue **7** earnest, regular, serious, subdued **8** composed, moderate, peaceful, rational, reserved **9** abstinent, collected, realistic, unruffled **10** abstemious, controlled, reasonable **11** disciplined **13** unimpassioned

SOBRIETY: **7** gravity **9** soberness, solemnity **10** abstinence, continence, moderation, temperance

SOBRIQUET: **5** alias **6** byname, handle **7** epithet **8** nickname **11** appellation

SO-CALLED: **7** alleged, nominal **8** supposed **9** pretended

SOCIABLE: **4** cozy **6** chummy, genial, social **7** affable, cordial **8** friendly, gracious, outgoing, pleasant **9** agreeable, congenial, talkative **10** gregarious, hospitable

SOCIAL: **5** party **6** genial, public **7** cordial **8** communal, friendly, pleasant, sociable **9** convivial, gathering **10** gregarious, hospitable, neighborly **12** entertaining **13** companionable

SOCIALIZE: **3** mix **5** party **6** hobnob, mingle **9** associate, entertain **10** fraternize

SOCIETY: **4** clan, club, gang **5** elite, guild, order, union **6** circle, gentry, league, people, public **8** alliance, sodality **9** community **10** fellowship, sisterhood **11** aristocracy, association, brotherhood, cooperation **12** civilization, organization **13** companionship

SOCIETY ISLANDS:
capital: **7** Papeete
cities: **6** Uturoa
explorer: **4** Cook
island groups: **7** Leeward **8** Windward
islands: **4** Maio **5** Tahaa **6** Moorea, Tahiti **7** Huahine, Maupiti, Mehetia, Raiatea **8** Bora-Bora, Tetiaroa **10** Tubuai Manu
place: **15** French Polynesia

SOCK: **3** bop, hit **4** beat, belt, blow, hose, shoe **5** punch, smack, smash, whack **6** comedy, sandal, strike, wallop **7** clobber, hosiery **8** stocking

SOCRATES:
birthplace: **6** Athens
method: **8** Socratic
nationality: **5** Greek
occupation: **7** teacher **11** philosopher
poison: **7** hemlock
pupil: **5** Pluto
wife: **8** Xantippe **9** Xanthippe

SOD: **3** guy **4** dirt, peat, soak, soil, turf **5** divot, earth, grass **6** fellow

SODA: **3** pop **5** drink, mixer, tonic **7** seltzer **8** beverage

SODALITY: **5** order, union, unity **6** league **7** society **10** fellowship, fraternity **11** association, brotherhood

SODDEN: **3** wet **5** drunk, heavy, moist, mushy, soggy **6** soaked, soused, stewed, stupid, torpid **7** bloated, doughty, steeped **8** drenched **9** saturated **11** intoxicated **13** unimaginative

SODIUM: **7** element

SODOM: **4** city
destroyed with: **8** Gomorrah
located: **9** Palestine

SOFA: **4** pouf **5** couch, divan, squab **6** chaise, lounge, settee **7** ottoman **8** sociable **9** banquette, davenport, sectional **10** confidante, meridienne **12** chesterfield

SOFT: **4** easy, limp, mild, snug, weak **5** balmy, bland, comfy, cushy, downy, faint, mushy, quiet **6** doughy, feeble, flabby, fluffy, gentle, gently, hushed, placid, pliant, silken, simple, smooth, spongy, supple, tender **7** cottony, lenient, lightly, squashy, squishy, subdued, velvety **8** cushiony, delicate, flexible, pampered, soothing, tranquil **9** temperate **10** peacefully **11** comfortable, sympathetic **12** affectionate **13** compassionate

SOFTEN: **4** bend, calm, ease, mash, melt **5** relax, yield **6** lessen, mellow, pacify, relent, soothe, subdue, temper, weaken **7** appease, assuage, cushion, mollify **8** attemper, diminish, macerate, mitigate **9** alleviate, tenderize

SOFTHEARTED: **4** kind, warm **6** humane, tender **8** merciful **9** forgiving **11** sympathetic **13** compassionate

SOGGY: **3** wet **4** damp, dull **5** heavy, humid, mushy **6** soaked, sodden **8** drenched **9** saturated **11** waterlogged

SOIGNE: **4** chic, neat **5** sleek **7** stylish **8** elegance, polished **11** fashionable, well-groomed

SOIL: **3** mud **4** blot, dirt, foil, land, loam, muck, ruin, soot **5** dirty, earth, grime, humus, shame, smear, stain, sully, taint **6** befile, defile, ground, spoilt **7** blacken, degrade **8** homeland

SOILED: **4** foul **5** dirty, faded, grimy **6** filthy **7** sullied **9** blemished

SOJOURN: **4** rest, stay, stop **5** abide, abode, delay, dwell, lodge, tarry, visit **6** travel **7** layover **8** stopover **9** residence, tarriance

SOLACE: **4** calm, **5** allay, cheer, peace **6** lessen, relief, soften, soothe **7** assuage, comfort, console **8** mitigate **9** alleviate, entertain **10** relaxation **11** consolation

SOLAR: **5** lunar **6** cosmic **7** stellar **8** empyreal **9** planetary **10** celestrial

SOLD: **4** gone **7** pleased **8** marketed **9** convinced, impressed

SOLDER: **4** fuse, join, mend, weld **5** braze, patch, unite **6** fasten

SOLDIER: **3** vet **4** swad **5** cadet, major, pilot, plebe, poilu **6** airman, gunner, marine **7** colonel, fighter, general, officer, private, recruit, trooper, veteran, warrior **8** airwoman, cavalier, commando, doughboy, sergeant **9** grenadier, guerrilla, mercenary, musketeer, warmonger **10** lieutenant, serviceman **11** infantryman, paratrooper **12** servicewoman **13** infantrywoman

SOLDIERLY: **4** bold **5** brave **6** heroic **7** martial, warlike **9** combative

SOLE: **3** one **4** fish, foot, lone, only **5** alone **6** lonely, single, unique **8** desolate, flatfish, isolated, solitary, unshared **9** exclusive, unmarried, unmatched

SOLECISM: **4** slip **5** error **7** blooper, mistake **11** impropriety, incongruity

SOLELY: **4** only **5** alone **6** barely, merely, purely, simply, singly, wholly **7** totally **8** entirely, uniquely **11** exclusively

SOLEMN: **4** holy **5** grave, quiet, sober, staid **6** august, devout, divine, formal, gloomy, ritual, sacred, somber **7** earnest, serious, stately, weighty **8** funereal, hallowed **9** dignified, religious **10** ceremonial, reflective, sanctified **11** ceremonious **13** distinguished

SOLEMNIZE: **4** mark **5** bless, exalt, honor **7** dignify, observe **8** sanctify, venerate **9** celebrate **11** commemorate

SOLICIT: **3** ask **4** call, plea, seek **5** crave **6** accost, demand, entice, hustle, peddle **7** beseech, canvass, implore, inquire, request **8** approach, petition **9** importune, panhandle **10** supplicate **11** proposition

SOLICITOUS: **4** keen **5** eager **6** ardent **7** anxious, careful, worried **8** desirous, troubled **9** concerned **10** meticulous, thoughtful **11** considerate

SOLICITUDE: **4** care, ease, heed **5** qualm, worry **7** anxiety, caution, concern **9** attention **10** uneasiness **11** carefulness **12** apprehension

SOLID: **4** firm, full, hard **5** dense, level, sound, stiff, thick, valid **6** rooted, rugged, secure, stable, strong, sturdy **7** compact, durable, lasting, weighty **8** constant, reliable, sterling, thorough, unbroken **9** unanimous **10** consistent, continuous, convincing, dependable **11** impermeable, trustworthy **13** uninterrupted

SOLIDARITY: **5** union, unity **7** harmony **8** cohesion **12** togetherness

SOLIDIFY: **3** dry, set **4** cake **5** unify **6** cement, harden **7** compact, stiffen, thicken **8** concrete, condense **9** coagulate **11** crystallize

SOLILOQUY: **6** speech **7** address **9** discourse, monologue

SOLITARY: **4** lone, only, sole **5** alone **6** lonely, remote, single **7** eremite, recluse **8** deserted, desolate, hermetic, isolated, lonesome, secluded, unsocial **9** abandoned, reclusive, withdrawn **10** antisocial, individual

SOLITUDE: **6** desert **7** privacy **9** aloneness, isolation, seclusion **10** desolation, loneliness, quarantine, remoteness, retirement, wilderness **13** reclusiveness

SOLO: **4** aria **5** alone **6** single **7** arietta **9** monologue **10** individual **12** singlehanded **13** unaccompanied

SOLOMON:
characteristic: **4** wise
father: **5** David
kingdom: **6** Israel
mother: **9** Bethsheba

son: **8** Rehoboam
temple: **6** Shamir
wife: **6** Naamah

SOLOMON ISLANDS:
capital: **7** Honiara
cities: **4** Gizo **7** Yandina
continent: **7** Oceania
ethnic groups: **10** Melanesian, Polynesian
explorer: **9** de Mendana
features: **5** Balbi
islands: **4** Buka, Gizo, Savo **7** Malaita **8** Choiseul **10** New Georgia **11** Guadalcanal, Santa Isabel **12** San Cristobal
languages: **6** Papuan **7** English **10** Melanesian, Polynesian
monetary unit: **6** dollar
water: **4** Huon, Kula **7** Pacific

SOLUTION: **3** key **6** answer, result **7** mixture, solvent **8** analysis, compound **9** discovery **10** resolution **11** explanation

SOLVE: **4** undo, work **6** decide, decode, fathom, settle, unfold, unlock **7** explain, resolve, unravel **8** decipher, dissolve, untangle **9** interpret **11** disentangle

SOLVENT: **7** diluent, soluble **11** dissolvable

SOMALIA:
capital: **9** Mogadishu
cities: **7** Berbera, Kismayu **8** Hargeisa
continent: **6** Africa
ethnic groups: **7** Hamitic
features: **12** Horn of Africa
languages: **6** Arabic, Somali **7** English, Italian
monetary unit: **8** shilling
native: **8** Somalian
water: **4** Juba **7** Shebeli **11** Indian Ocean

SOMBER: **4** dark, down, dull **5** bleak, dusky, gloom, grave, sober, staid **6** dismal, dreary, gloomy, solemn **7** earnest, serious **8** funereal **10** depression, melancholy

SOME: **3** any, few **4** bout, part **7** portion, several, unknown **8** quantity **10** remarkable **13** approximately, extraordinary

SOMEBODY: **3** VIP **7** someone **9** celebrity, dignitary, superstar

SOMEDAY: **7** anytime, finally **8** sometime **10** eventually **12** subsequently

SOMEHOW: **6** anyhow, anyway **11** unspecified

SOMETHING: **5** being, event **6** entity, object **7** whatnot **8** somewhat **10** remarkable

SOMETIME: **4** late, once **6** former **7** quondam, someday **8** formerly, previous

SOMETIMES: **10** frequently **12** occasionally, periodically **14** intermittently

SOMEWHAT: **6** partly, rather **8** bearably, slightly **9** partially **10** moderately **12** considerably **13** approximately

SOMNOLENT: **6** drowsy, sleepy **7** languid **8** fatigued, sluggish **9** lethargic

SON: **3** ben, boy, lad **4** fils, heir, male **5** child **6** native **8** disciple, relative **9** offspring **10** descendant

SONG: **4** aria, call, cant, glee, hymn, lied, noel, poem, rock, tune **5** blues, carol, chant, dirge, ditty, lyric, music, psalm, verse **6** anthem, ballad, chanty, chorus, melody, number, poetry, shanty, sonnet, strain **7** arietta, canzone, lullaby, shantey **8** canticle, pittance, serenade, threnody **9** cabaletta, roundelay **11** composition

SONGWRITER: **8** composer, lyricist, songster **9** songsmith

SONNET: **4** poem, song **5** verse

SONOROUS: **4** deep, full **5** noisy **7** orotund, ringing, vibrant **8** imposing, resonant **9** grandiose **10** impressive, resounding

SOON: **4** anon, fast **5** early, later, quick **6** speedy **7** hastily, quickly, readily, shortly **8** directly, promptly, speedily **9** forthwith, instantly, presently, willingly **11** immediately **13** expeditiously

SOONER STATE: **8** Oklahoma

SOOT: **4** coom, dirt, grit, smut **5** cabon, grime, smoke **6** smudge **7** blacken, residue **8** sediment

SOOTHE: **3** pat, pet **4** balm, calm, ease, hush, lull **5** allay, quiet, relax **6** pacify, settle, soften, solace, stroke **7** appease, assuage, comfort, compose, console, message, mollify, placate, relieve **8** mitigate **9** alleviate **11** tranquilize

SOOTHING: **4** mild **5** balmy, downy, sweet **6** gentle **7** anodyne, calming **8** lenitive, pleasant, sedative **9** appeasing **10** palliative **13** tranquilizing

SOOTHSAY: **7** portend, predict **8** forecast, foretell, prophesy

SOOTHSAYER: **4** seer **5** augur **6** oracle, wizard **7** diviner, prophet, seeress **10** forecaster **13** fortuneteller **14** prognosticator

SOOTY: **4** dark **5** black, dingy, dirty, grimy, murky **6** smutty **7** smeared **9** blackened

SOP: **3** dip, wet **4** dunk, soak **5** bribe, douse, steep **6** absorb, drench **7** milksop **8** saturate, weakling

SOPHISTICATE: **6** refine **8** civilize **10** adulterate **11** disillusion

SOPHISTICATED: **5** suave **6** mature, uptown **7** complex, refined, worldly **8** advanced, cultured, involved, seasoned **9** intricate **11** adulterated, experienced, worldly-wise **12** cosmopolitan

SOPHISTRY: **8** trickery **9** ambiguity, casuistry, deception **13** inconsistency

SOPHOCLES: **4** poet **6** author, writer **9** dramatist **10** playwright, politician
nationality: **5** Greek
wrote: **4** Ajax **7** Electra **8** Antigone **9** Ichneutai **11** Philoctetes **15** Oedipus Tyrannos **16** Oedipus at Colonus

SOPHOMORIC: **5** naive **7** foolish **8** immature, reckless **9** infantile **13** inexperienced

SOPORIFIC: **6** drowsy, sleepy **7** calming, nodding **8** hypnotic, narcotic, sedative **9** lethargic **10** slumberous **11** somniferous

SOPRANO: **6** singer, treble **8** falsetto **10** coloratura

SORCERER: **4** mage **5** witch **6** wizard **7** charmer, warlock **8** conjurer, magician **9** alchemist, occultist **11** necromancer

SORCERESS: **3** hag, hex **5** sibyl, siren, witch **9** pythoness **11** enchantress

SORCERY: **5** magic, spell **6** voodoo **8** witchery, wizardry **9** sortilege **10** divination, necromancy, witchcraft **11** enchantment, incantation, thaumaturgy

SORDID: **3** low **4** base, foul, mean, rank, vile **5** cheap, dirty, gross, nasty **6** abject, filthy, scurvy, wicked **7** corrupt, ignoble, selfish, servile **8** degraded, grasping, wretched **10** despicable **12** contemptible

SORE: **3** raw **4** pain **5** angry, ulcer, upset, vexed, wound **6** aching, bitter, bruise, lesion, severe, tender, touchy **7** abscess, angered, annoyed, hostile, hurting, painful **8** abrasion, annoying, grievous, infected, inflamed **9** irritated, sensitive, suffering, vexatious **10** affliction, discomfort, distressed, unpleasant **11** disgruntled, distressing **13** temperamental, uncomfortable

SORELY: **5** badly **7** greatly **8** woefully **9** extremely, painfully **10** grievously

SORORITY: **4** club **7** society **10** sisterhood **11** association **12** organization

SORREL: **4** dock, herb **5** color, plant **7** redwood, roselle **8** brownish

SORROW: **3** woe **4** bale, grieve, loss, moan, pity, weep **5** agony, dolor, grief, mourn **6** lament, misery, regret **7** anguish, despair, remorse, sadness, trouble **8** calamity, distress, hardship, mourning **9** heartache, suffering **10** affliction, discomfort, melancholy, misfortune **11** lamentation, tribulation, unhappiness

SORROWFUL: **3** sad **6** dismal, dolent, dreary, rueful, tragic **7** doleful, forlorn, grieved, painful, unhappy **8** dolorous, grievous, mournful **9** afflicted, depressed, lamenting, miserable, plaintive **10** lamentable, melancholy **11** distressing, heartbroken

SORRY: **3** bad, sad **4** mean, poor **5** cheap **6** cheesy, dismal, gloomy, paltry, regret, shabby, shoddy **7** pitiful, unhappy **8** contrite, grievous, mournful, pathetic, penitent, saddened, wretched **9** afflicted, miserable, regretful, repentant, worthless **10** apologetic, remorseful **11** disgraceful **12** contemptible, disappointed

SORT: **4** kind, part, race, rank, sift, suit, type **5** allot, batch, brand, breed, class, genus, grade, group, index, order **6** assign, choose, family, gender, manner, nature, screen, select **7** arrange, collate, conform, species, variety **8** classify, organize, separate, typecast **10** categorize, collection, distribute, pigeonhole **11** alphabetize, description, systematize

SORTIE: **4** raid **5** foray, sally **6** attack **7** assault, mission

SORTILEGE: **6** augury **7** sorcery **8** witchery **10** witchcraft **11** enchantment

SO-SO: **4** fair, okay **6** subpar **7** average **8** adequate, mediocre, middling, ordinary, passable **9** tolerable

SOT: **4** fool, lush **5** drunk, toper **6** boozer **7** tippler **8** drunkard **9** alcoholic, inebriate

SOUGHT: **6** hunted, needed, wanted **7** desired, pursued

SOUL: **4** body, life **5** atman, being, force, ghost, heart, human, saint **6** energy, marrow, person, pneuma, psyche, spirit **7** courage, essence **8** vitality **9** intellect, personage, substance **10** conscience, individual **11** inspiration

SOUND: **3** cry, fit **4** bang, bark, blow, boom, bray, buzz, clap, deep, echo, firm, good, meow, note, ping, purr, roar, safe, sane, test, thud, tone, toot, well, wise **5** alarm, audio, blare, chang, clang, clank, clonk, creak, hardy, inlet, legal, music, noise, pitch, plumb, probe, rhyme, snore, snort, sober, solid, utter, valid, voice, vowel, whole **6** accent, fathom, hearty, honest, intact, melody, patter, racket, robust, rustle, secure, signal, stable, strong, sturdy, timbre, tumult, uproar **7** clatter, clutter, crackle, declare, durable, earshot, euphony, examine, explore, harmony, healthy, hearing, logical, measure, perfect, ringing, sonance, trumpet, upright **8** accepted, announce, complete, flawless, orthodox, rational, reliable, sensible, shouting, thorough, unmarred **9** consonant, resonance, undamaged, vibration, wholesome **10** dependable, impression, unshakable **11** intelligent, investigate, levelheaded, trustworthy, undisturbed **13** reverberation

SOUNDNESS: **3** wit **5** truth **6** weight **8** solidity, strength **9** integrity, stability **10** durability, heartiness **11** correctness, healthiness

SOUND OFF: **4** brag, yell **5** boast, count, shout **7** speak up

SOUND OUT: **4** feel **5** probe, study **7** examine, explore **10** experiment **11** investigate

SOUP: **4** food **5** broth, puree **6** bisque, modify, potage **7** chowder **8** bouillon, consomme, gazpacho **11** predicament, vichyssoise **12** mulligatawny **13** bouillabaisse

SOUPCON: **4** dash, drop, hint **5** pinch, taste, tinge, trace **7** smidgen **8** particle, sprinkle

SOUR: **3** dry **4** dour, grim, keen, seed, tart **5** acerb, acide, acrid, sharp, tangy **6** acetic, bitter, crabby, cranky, rotten, turned **7** acetose, acetous, curdled, grouchy, spoiled, unhappy **8** vinegary **9** acidulate, acidulous, fermented, irritable **10** astringent, unpleasant **11** distasteful **12** disagreeable

SOURCE: **4** font, rise, root, well **5** basis, cause, fount, start **6** author, expert, origin, parent, spring **7** dawning **8** fountain **9** authority, beginning, inception, informant, wellspring **10** antecedent **12** fountainhead

SOURNESS: **7** acidity **8** acrimony, asperity, tartness **10** bitterness, discontent **12** irritability

SOURPUSS: **4** crab **5** crank, grump **6** grouch **7** killjoy **8** sorehead **10** complainer, spoilsport

SOUSE: **3** dip, sop, wet **4** duck, dunk, lush, soak **5** brine, douse, drink, drunk, steep, thump **6** attack, deluge, drench, pickle, plunge, pounce, strike **7** immerse, tippler **8** drunkard, preserve, saturate, submerge, waterlog **9** alcoholic

SOUTH: **5** Dixie **7** Sunbelt **11** Confederacy

SOUTH AFRICA:

bays: **5** Algoa, False, Table **6** Mossel **8** Saldanha

capital: **8** Cape Town, Pretoria **12** Bloemfontein

cities: **3** Aus **4** Mara, Stad **6** Durban, Soweto **8** Mafeking **9** Germiston **12** Bloemfontein, Johannesburg

colonist: **4** Boer

deserts: **5** Namib **8** Kalahari

enclave: **7** Lesotho

foreigner: **9** uitlander

languages: **4** Taal, Zulu **5** Bantu, Nguni, Sotho, Swazi, Tamil, Tonga, Venda, Xhosa **6** Telegu **7** Sesotho **9** Afrikaans

leaders: **4** Biko, Tutu **5** Botha, Malan, Smuts **6** Kruger, Rhodes **7** Mandela, Vorster **8** Verwoerd **9** Pretorius

legislative assembly: **4** raad

monetary unit: **4** rand **10** krugerrand

mountains: **3** Aux, Kop **5** Table **7** Kathkin **9** Stormberg

people: **3** San **4** Boer, Xosa, Yosa, Zulu **5** Bantu, Namas, Nguni, Pondo, Sotho, Swazi, Tembu, Venda, Xhosa **6** Damara, Kaffir **7** Bushmen, Swahili **9** Afrikaner,

Bechnuana, Hottentot **10** Afrikander
rivers: **3** Hex **4** Vaal **5** Nosob **6** Modder, Molopo, Orange **7** Caledon, Limpopo **8** Olifants
segregation: **9** apartheid
settler: **4** Boer

SOUTH AMERICA:
animals: **4** apar, paca **5** coati, coypu, llama, minah, sloth, tapir **6** alpaca, guanco, guemal, jaguar, vicuna **7** muscovy **8** anteater, puffbird **9** armadillo
countries: **4** Peru **5** Chile **6** Brazil, Guyana **7** Bolivia, Ecuador, Surinam, Uruguay **8** Colombia, Paraguay **9** Argentina, Patagonia, Venezuela
drink: **4** mate **6** chicha
dances: **5** mambo, samba **6** cha-cha
deer: **6** guemal, guemul
game: **6** pelota
garment: **6** serape
Indians: **3** Ges, Ona **4** Auca, Inca, Tama **5** Carib, Tapas **6** Arawak, Jivaro **7** Cayapos, Goyanas, Guatoan, Pampero, Tapuyan **8** Camacans, Coroados, Timbiras **9** Caingangs, Chaventes, Patagonia
island: **5** Aruba
languages: **3** Ona **7** Spanish **10** Portuguese
liberator: **7** Bolivar
measure: **4** vara **7** manzana
mountains: **5** Andes **6** Acarai, Parima
plain: **5** llano, pampa
plains dweller: **7** llanero
rain forest: **5** selva
rivers: **4** Para **5** Plata **6** Amazon **7** Orinoco
strait: **8** Magellan
weapon: **4** bola
wind: **7** pampero

SOUTH CAROLINA:
bird: **4** wren
capital: **8** Columbia
cities: **8** Rock Hill **10** Charleston, Greenville **11** Spartanburg
explorer: **10** de Gordillo
features: **9** Blue Ridge **10** Fort Sumter, Hilton Head **11** Myrtle Beach
flower: **15** yellow jessamine
nickname: **13** Palmetto State
tree: **8** palmetto
was: **6** colony
water: **6** Peedee, Saluda, Santee **8** Atlantic

SOUTH DAKOTA:
bird: **8** pheasant
capital: **6** Pierre
cities: **8** Aberdeen **9** Rapid City **10** Sioux Falls
explorer: **9** Verendrye
features: **8** Badlands **10** Black Hills, Crazy Horse **11** Great Plains **13** Mount Rushmore
flower: **12** pasqueflower
nickname: **6** Coyote **8** Sunshine **13** Mount Rushmore
tree: **6** spruce
water: **4** Oahe **5** James **7** Big Bend **8** Bigstone, Missouri, Traverse

SOUTH KOREA:
capital: **5** Seoul
cities: **5** Pusan, Taegu **6** Inchon, Taejon **7** Kwangju
continent: **4** Asia
ethnic groups: **6** Korean
features: **8** Soraksan **11** Chomsongdae **14** Popchusa Buddha
language: **6** Korean
monetary unit: **3** won
water: **9** Yellow Sea **10** Sea of Japan

SOUTH SEAS/PACIFIC:
ethnic groups: **5** Maori **6** Kanaka, Samoan **10** Melonesian, Polynesian **11** Micronesian
islands: **4** Bali, Fiji, Sulu **5** Samoa, Tonga **6** Tahiti **7** Society **8** Pitcairn **9** New Guinea
seas: **5** Coral **6** Tasman

SOUTH VIETNAM: **7** Vietnam
former capital: **6** Saigon
guerrillas: **8** Vietcong
holiday: **3** Tet

SOUTHEAST ASIA:
countries: **4** Laos, Siam **7** Myanmar, Vietnam **8** Cambodia, Malaysia, Pakistan, Sri Lanka, Thailand **9** Indonesia **10** Bangladesh **11** Philippines

SOUTH WIND: **5** notus **6** auster

SOUVENIR: **4** gift **5** relic, token **6** memory, trophy **7** memento **8** keepsake, reminder **11** remembrance

SOVEREIGN: **4** coin, free, king, lord **5** chief, queen, regal, royal, ruler **6** kingly, master, prince **7** emperor, empress, majesty, monarch, queenly, supreme **8** absolute, autocrat, dominant, imperial, princely, reigning, superior **9** governing, paramount, potentate **10** autonomous, omnipotent **11** controlling, independent, monarchical, unmitigated

SOVEREIGNTY: **4** rule, sway **5** power **7** control **8** autonomy, dominion **9** masterdom, supremacy **10** ascendancy, domination **12** independence, jurisdiction

SOVIET UNION: **6** Russia
former republics: **5** Uzbek **6** Latvia **7** Armenia, Georgia, Kirghiz, Turkmen, Ukraine
heroes: **5** Lenin **6** Stalin
news agencies: **4** Tass **6** Pravda **8** Izvestia
police: **3** KGB

SOW: **3** hog, pig **4** grow, seed, wine **5** drain, drill, plant, strew **6** sluice, spread **7** channel, implant, scatter **9** broadcast, germinate, propagate **11** disseminate

SPA: **5** baths, oasis **6** resort, spring

SPACE: **3** gap, sky **4** area, room, time, void **5** align, berth, blank, empty, ether, range, reach, scope, track, width **6** cavity, divide, extent, leeway, margin, period, region **7** arrange, breadth, expanse, freedom **8** capacity, distance, duration, headroom, interval, quantity, separate, universe **9** amplitude, apportion, clearance, elbowroom, territory **11** reservation

SPACECRAFT: **3** UFO **5** probe **6** module, rocket **7** capsule, shuttle **9** satellite

SPACIOUS: **4** huge, vast, wide **5** ample, broad, large, roomy **7** immense **8** enormous **9** capacious, expansive, extensive **10** commodious

SPADE: **3** dig **4** tool **6** shovel **11** playing card

SPAIN:
also called: **6** Espana, Iberia **8** Hispania
artists: **4** Dali, Goya, Miro **6** Ribera **7** El Greco, Murillo, Picasso **9** Velazquez
authors: **5** Cueva, Rojas **6** Encina, Ibanez **7** Alarcon **9** Cervantes
capital: **6** Madrid
cities: **5** Cadiz **6** Bilbao, Malaga **7** Granada, Seville **8** Valencia **9** Barcelona, Cartagena, Saragossa
conquerors: **3** Cid **7** Pizarro **12** conquistador
dances: **6** bolero **8** fandango, flamenco
dynasty: **7** Almohad, Umayyad **9** Almoravid
explorers for: **6** Balboa, Cortes **7** Mendoza, Pizarro **8** Columbus, Coronado
islands: **5** Ibiza **6** Canary **7** Majorca, Minorca **8** Balearic
kingdoms: **4** Leon **6** Aragon **7** Castile
kings: **6** Philip **7** Charles **9** Ferdinand **10** Juan Carlos
languages: **6** Basque **7** Catalan, Spanish **8** Balearic, Galician **9** Castilian, Valencian
leaders: **5** Godoy **6** Franco

monetary unit: **6** peseta
mountains: **4** Gata **5** Aneto, Rouch **6** Europa, Morena, Nevada, Toledo **7** Catalan, Iberian **8** Asturian, Pyrenees, Mulhacem **10** Cantabrian, La Maladeta, Pic de Netou **11** Guardarrama
natives: **5** Diego **6** Basque, Espana **7** Catalan, Espanol, Iberian
queens: **8** Isabella **9** Elizabeth
rivers: **3** ria, rio, Sil, Ter **4** Cega, Ebro, Esla, Lima, Mino, Muga, Tajo, Ulla **5** Douro, Tagus, Tinto **6** Aragon, Huerva **8** Guadiana **12** Guadalquivir

SPAN: **4** arch, link, rope, term, time **5** cover, cross, reach, scope **6** bridge, extent, fasten, fetter, length, period, spread **7** connect, measure, stretch, trestle **8** distance, duration, interval **9** extension

SPANGLE: **4** star, trim **5** adorn, flash, gleam **6** sequin **7** glimmer, glisten, glitter, shimmer, sparkle, twinkle **8** decorate, ornament, sprinkle **9** coruscate

SPANK: **4** belt, cane, flog, slap, sock, whip **5** smack **6** paddle, punish, strike, switch, thrash **8** chastise **10** discipline

SPANKING: **3** new **5** brisk, fresh, swift **7** dashing **8** vigorous **10** remarkable **11** exceptional

SPAR: **3** bar, box **4** beam, boom, gaff, mast, pole **5** argue, fight **6** bicker, rafter, strike, timber **7** contend, contest, dispute, quarrel, wrangle

SPARE: **4** bony, free, give, lean, part, save, slim, thin **5** avoid, extra, favor, gaunt, grant, lanky, skimp, stint **6** afford, excess, exempt, frugal, meager, scanty, scrape, scrimp, sparse **7** deprive, forbear, forgive, lenient, release, relieve, reserve, surplus **8** leftover, merciful, preserve, reprieve, withhold **9** duplicate, emergency **10** additional, substitute **11** accommodate, replacement

SPARING: **5** chary, scant **6** frugal, meager, saving, scanty, stingy **7** careful, lenient, prudent, thrifty **8** merciful **10** economical, forbearing **11** tightfisted **12** parsimonious

SPARK: **4** beau, fire, germ, glow, seed, stir **5** ember, flash, glint, grain, light, trace **6** excite, incite, kindle, suitor **7** flicker, gallant, glimmer, inspire, provoke, sparkle **8** motivate **9** instigate, scintilla, stimulate **11** scintillate

SPARKLE: **4** dash, glow **5** flash, gleam, glint, shine, spark **6** bubble, dazzle **7** flicker, glimmer, glisten, glitter, radiate, scatter, shimmer, spangle, twinkle **8** vivacity **9** coruscate **10** brilliance, effervesce, illuminate **11** scintillate **13** effervescence, scintillation

SPARKLING: **5** fizzy **6** bright, bubbly, lively **7** shining **8** animated, dazzling, flashing, gleaming **9** brilliant, twinkling **10** glistening, glittering, shimmering **12** effervescent **13** scintillating

SPARSE: **4** thin **5** scant, spare **6** meager, scanty, scarce, skimpy **8** sporadic **9** dispersed, scattered, uncrowded **10** inadequate, infrequent, occasional

SPARTA:
army: **4** mora
features: **11** Peloponnese
inhabitants: **5** serfs **6** helots **8** perioeci
kings/queens: **4** Leda **5** Helen **8** Leonidas, Menelaus **9** Tyndareus
people: **7** Dorians, Laconia
wars: **7** Persian **13** Peloponnesian
was: **9** city-state

SPARTAN: **5** brave, plain **6** frugal, simple **7** austere, laconic **8** rigorous **10** courageous **11** disciplined

SPASM: **3** fit, tic **4** pain, pang **5** cramp, crick, spell **6** attack, twitch **7** seizure **8** paroxysm **10** convulsion **11** contraction

SPASMODIC: **5** jerky **6** fitful, sudden **7** erratic **8** sporadic **9** excitable, irregular **10** convulsive **12** intermittent

SPAT: **3** row **4** beef, gush, rain, slap, tiff **5** fight, flood, scrap, smack, spate **6** bicker, gaiter, oyster, strike **7** dispute, mollusk, quarrel **8** squabble **11** altercation

SPATE: **4** flow, rush **7** torrent **10** outpouring

SPATTER: **4** slop, soil, spot **5** dirty, smear, spurt, sully **6** defame, shower, smudge, splash, spread **7** dribble, scatter, sputter **8** sprinkle

SPAWN: **4** eggs, germ, seed, sire **5** breed, fungi **6** create, father, parent, source **7** produce **8** engender, generate, multiply, mushroom **9** offspring, originate, procreate, reproduce **11** proliferate

SPEAK: **3** say **4** blab, chat, rant, talk, tell **5** blurt, drawl, drone, orate, shout, sound, utter, voice **6** convey, gabble, jabber, jibber, mumble, murmur, mutter, recite, remark, reveal, yammer **7** address, bespeak, bluster, comment, consult, declare, discuss, expound, express, lecture, stutter, testify, whisper **8** converse, harangue, intonate, proclaim, splutter, vocalize **9** discourse, enunciate, pronounce, ventilate, verbalize **10** articulate, equivocate **11** communicate, pontificate

SPEAKER: **6** orator, talker **8** lecturer, preacher **9** announcer, demagogue, spokesman **10** mouthpiece **11** rhetorician, speechmaker, spellbinder, spokeswoman **12** spokesperson

SPEAR: **4** bolt, bore, dart, stab **5** blade, gouge, lance, prick, shoot, spike **6** impale, pierce, skewer, strike, weapon **7** bayonet, harpoon, javelin, leister, trident **8** puncture **9** penetrate

SPEARHEAD: **4** lead **5** begin, start **6** create, direct, launch **7** advance, develop, pioneer **8** initiate **9** originate

SPECIAL: **4** dear, gala, rare **5** chief, extra **6** choice, select, unique **7** limited, notable, primary, unusual **8** distinct, favorite, peculiar, specific, uncommon **9** important, momentous **10** additional, designated, individual, noteworthy, particular, privileged, remarkable **11** distinctive, exceptional **12** extravaganza **13** distinguished, extraordinary

SPECIALIST: **3** ace **5** maven **6** doctor, expert, master **7** scholar **8** virtuoso **9** authority **10** consultant **11** connoisseur **12** professional

SPECIALIZE: **5** major, train **6** pursue **8** practice **11** concentrate

SPECIALTY: **4** game **5** focus, forte, skill **6** career, talent **7** earmark, feature, pursuit **8** aptitude **9** trademark **10** profession **11** masterpiece **13** concentration

SPECIES: **4** kind, race, sort, type **5** breed, brood, class, genre, genus, group, image, order **6** nature **7** variety **8** category, division **9** humankind

SPECIFIC: **5** exact **6** unique **7** limited, precise, special **8** clear-cut, concrete, definite, detailed, explicit **10** individual, particular **11** categorical, distinctive

SPECIFY: **4** list, name, tell **5** state **6** assign, define, detail **7** itemize, request **8** describe **9** designate, determine, enumerate, establish, stipulate **13** individualize

SPECIMEN: **4** case, mark, type **5** model **6** person, sample **7** exhibit **8** instance **9** prototype **10** individual **11** examination **12** illustration

SPECIOUS: **5** false, showy **6** glossy, hollow, untrue **7** colored, unsound **9** beguiling, deceptive, plausible **10** fallacious, misleading, ostensible **12** hypocritical, questionable

SPECK: **3** bit, dot **4** atom, blot, flaw, iota, mark, mite, spot, whit **5** crumb, fleck, grain, pinch, point, stain **6** defect **7** blemish, smidgen **8** molecule, particle

SPECTACLE: **4** show **5** event, scene, sight **6** marvel, parade, wonder **7** display, example, pageant **9** curiosity **10** exhibition, phenomenon **12** extravaganza

SPECTACLES: **6** lenses **7** glasses **10** eyeglasses

SPECTACULAR: **5** grand **7** amazing **8** dazzling, dramatic, fabulous, splendid, striking **9** elaborate, fantastic, marvelous, thrilling, wonderful **10** miraculous, stupendous, theatrical **11** astonishing, magnificent, sensational **12** breathtaking

SPECTATOR: **3** fan **6** viewer **7** witness **8** audience, beholder, kibitzer, observer, onlooker **9** bystander **10** eyewitness

SPECTER: **5** demon, ghost, image, shade, spook **6** spirit, vision, wraith **7** phantom **8** illusion, phantasm, prospect, revenant **10** apparition

SPECTRAL: **5** eerie, scary **6** creepy, spooky **7** ghostly, phantom, shadowy **9** unearthly **12** supernatural

SPECTRUM: **5** array, range **6** colors, series, sphere **8** sequence **9** continuum **12** distribution
colors: **3** red **4** blue **5** green **6** indigo, violet, yellow

SPECULATE: **4** risk **5** dream, guess, think **6** chance, gamble, ponder, reason, wonder **7** imagine, predict, reflect, surmise, venture **8** consider, ruminate, theorize **10** brainstorm, conjecture, deliberate **11** contemplate, hypothesize

SPECULATION: **4** risk **5** hunch **6** gamble, review, theory **7** surmise **9** guesswork, reasoning **10** conjecture, hypothesis, meditation **13** contemplation

SPECULATIVE: **4** iffy **5** risky **8** insecure **9** inquiring, uncertain **10** reflecting **11** conjectural, theoretical

SPECULATOR: **7** gambler **8** explorer, investor, theorist, venturer **11** philosopher

SPEECH: **4** talk **5** idiom, slang, spiel, voice **6** drivel, eulogy, homily, jargon, sermon, tirade, tongue **7** address, dialect, keynote, lecture, oration, oratory, prattle **8** colloquy, dialogue, harangue, jeremaid, language, rhetoric **9** monologue, narration, soliloquy, statement, utterance **10** allocution, expression, salutation, vernacular **11** valedictory **12** conversation, vocalization **13** verbalization

SPEECHLESS: **3** mum **4** dumb, mute **6** amazed, silent **7** shocked **9** astounded

SPEED: **3** rip, run, zip **4** clip, dash, fare, knot, pace, race, rate, rush, zoom **5** haste, hurry, tempo **6** barrel, gallop, hasten, hustle, propel **7** urgency **8** celerity, dispatch, expedite, hightail, informed, rapidity, velocity **9** briskness, quickness, swiftness **10** accelerate **11** precipitate

SPEEDY: 4 fast **5** brisk, fleet, hasty, quick, rapid, swift **6** nimble, prompt, snappy **7** express, hurried **10** supersonic **11** expeditious

SPELL: 3 hex **4** bout, free, jinx, mean, rest, tale, talk, tell, time, tour, trap, turn **5** charm, curse, hitch, magic, relay, shift, stint, trick, while **6** period, relate, relief, shammy, streak, trance, voodoo **7** bewitch, illness, relieve, seizure, signify, sorcery, stretch, suggest **8** duration, interval **9** interlude **10** constitute **11** abracadabra, conjuration, enchantment, fascination

SPELLBIND: 4 grip **5** charm **7** enchant, engross **8** enthrall, intrigue **9** fascinate, hypnotize, mesmerize

SPELLBOUND: 6 amazed, hooked **9** bewitched, enchanted, possessed **10** bewildered, captivated, enthralled, fascinated, transfixed

SPELL OUT: 6 define **7** clarify, explain, expound **8** describe **9** interpret

SPEND: 3 pay, use **4** blow, give, pass **5** drain, exert, waste **6** devote, elapse, expend, lavish, occupy, outlay, spread, spring **7** consume, deplete, exhaust, fatigue, splurge **8** allocate, disburse, squander **9** dissipate, sacrifice **10** distribute

SPENDTHRIFT 6 waster **7** spender, wastrel **8** prodigal **9** imprudent **10** profligate, squanderer

SPENT: 4 beat, used **5** tired, weary **6** effete, wasted **7** drained **8** consumed, depleted, fatigued, finished **9** enervated, exhausted

SPEW: 4 gush, ooze, spit **5** eject, exude, flood, heave, vomit **7** scatter **8** disgorge **11** regurgitate

SPHERE: 3 orb, sky **4** area, ball, rank, star **5** ambit, arena, class, field, globe, orbit, order, range, reach, realm, scope **6** circle, domain, planet **7** circuit, compass, stratum **8** business **9** bailiwick, influence, territory **12** jurisdiction

SPHERICAL: 5 orbic, round **6** global, rotund **7** globate, stellar **8** circular, globular, heavenly **9** celestial, orbicular

SPHINX:
asked: **7** riddles
body: **4** lion
father: **6** Typhon **7** Orthrus
head: **3** man, ram **4** hawk **5** woman
location: **4** Giza **6** Thebes
mother: **7** Echidna **8** Chimaera
mythology: **5** Greek **8** Egyptian

SPICE: 4 dash, herb, hint, kick, zest **5** aroma, scent, taste, tinge **6** accent, flavor, relish, season **7** perfume, pizzazz **9** condiment, fragrance, seasoning **10** excitement
variety: **4** mace, sage, salt **5** curry **6** cloves, ginger, nutmeg, pepper **7** mustard, oregano, paprika **8** allspice, cinnamon

SPICK-AND-SPAN: 3 new **4** neat **5** clean, fresh **7** orderly **8** spotless

SPICY: 3 hot **4** racy **5** balmy, fiery, juicy, salty, sharp, showy, tangy, zesty **6** erotic, risque, snappy **7** peppery, piquant, pungent, scented **8** aromatic, fragrant, seasoned, spirited **9** flavorful **10** scandalous, suggestive

SPIDER: 3 bug, pan **6** insect, trivet **8** arachnid **9** frying pan
common: **4** wolf **6** garden, hermit **7** jumping **9** tarantula **10** black widow
legs: **5** eight
nest: **5** nidus
order: **7** Araneae
trap: **3** web

SPIEL: **4** line **5** pitch **6** patter, speech **7** promote

SPIFFY: **4** chic, neat **5** sharp, slick, smart **6** classy, dapper, snappy, snazzy **7** stylish **11** fashionable

SPIGOT: **3** tap **4** plug, vent **5** spile, spout, valve **6** dossil, faucet, nozzle, outlet **7** stopper

SPIKE: **3** peg, pin, rod **4** horn, nail, peak, spit, stab, stud, tine **5** block, lance, point, prong, spear, spile, stake **6** antler, fasten, impale, injure, pierce, secure, skewer, thwart **7** bayonet, fortify **8** mackerel, puncture

SPILL: **4** blab, drip, drop, fall, flow, leak, roll, ruin, shed, slip, slop, tell **5** empty, spile, upset, waste **6** betray, reveal, splash, tumble **7** divulge, overrun, scatter **8** disclose, downpour, overflow

SPIN: **4** birl, gyre, reel, ride, roll, turn **5** drive, swirl, twirl, twist, whirl **6** extend, gyrate, rotate, spiral **7** narrate, prolong, revolve, trundle **8** protract **9** oscillate, pirouette **10** revolution

SPINAL COLUMN: **5** chine, spine **6** rachis **8** backbone **9** vertebrae
curvature: **8** kyphosis, lordosis, swayback **9** scoliosis **10** saddleback

SPINDLE: **3** pin, rod **4** axis, axle, stem **5** pivot, shaft, stalk **6** rachis **7** mandrel **8** baluster

SPINDLY: **4** weak **5** frail, lanky, rangy **6** skinny **7** slender **9** elongated

SPINE: **4** back **5** chine, crest, point, ridge, thorn **6** needle, rachis, spirit **7** courage, prickle, spicule **8** backbone **9** vertebrae, willpower **12** spinal column

SPINELESS: **4** soft, weak **5** timid **7** fearful **8** cowardly **10** indecisive **12** invertebrate

SPINE-TINGLING: **8** exciting **9** thrilling **11** suspenseful **12** electrifying

SPIN OFF: **7** outcome **8** offshoot **9** byproduct, outgrowth **11** divestiture

SPINSTER: **7** old maid **11** single woman

SPINY: **5** sharp **6** spiked, thorny **7** pointed, prickly **9** difficult

SPIRAL: **4** coil, curl **5** curve, whorl **6** gyrate **7** coiling, curving, helical, winding **8** circling, cochlear, twisting **9** corkscrew, spherical

SPIRE: **4** apex, cone, curl, peak **5** point, tower, twist, whorl **6** sprout, summit **7** steeple **8** pinnacle

SPIRIT: **3** elf, hag, imp **4** dash, elan, fire, guts, life, mood, puck, soul, will, wind, zeal **5** angel, atman, demon, drive, dryad, fairy, force, genie, ghost, ghoul, heart, moxie, oomph, oread, pluck, shade, spook, spunk, vigor **6** animus, breath, energy, esprit, goblin, intent, mettle, morale, psyche, sprite, temper, undine **7** banshee, bravery, courage, essence, gremlin, incubus, loyalty, meaning, passion, phantom, purport, specter **8** attitude, gumption, phantasm, strength, succubus, tenacity **9** animation, character, encourage, hobgoblin, substance, willpower **10** apparition, dedication, enterprise, enthusiasm, motivation, resolution **11** inspiration, poltergeist **12** cheerfulness **13** determination

SPIRITED: **4** bold, game **5** brave, brisk, eager, fiery, peppy **6** active, gritty, lively, spunky **7** chipper, dashing, valiant, zealous **8** animated, cheerful, fearless, intrepid, vigorous **9** audacious, dauntless, energetic, sprightly, vivacious **10** courageous, mettlesome **12** enthusiastic

SPIRITLESS: **4** cold, dull **5** vapid **6** broken **7** languid **8** dejected, downcast, lifeless, listless **9** apathetic, depressed, examinate, heartless **10** despondent, melancholy **13** lackadaisical

SPIRITS: **4** mood, tone **5** booze **6** liquor **7** alcohol, feeling **9** condition **11** disposition

SPIRITUAL: **4** holy, pure, song **5** godly **6** deific, devout, divine, sacred **7** angelic, psychic, saintly **8** cerebral, churchly, ethereal, material, platonic, spirited **9** religious, unworldly **10** sanctified **11** incorporeal **12** metaphysical, supernatural

SPIRITUOUS: **9** alcoholic, distilled

SPIT: **3** rod **4** emit, hawk, reef, spew **5** drool, eject, spear **6** broach, dagger, drivel, phlegm, saliva, skewer, sputum **7** dribble, slobber, spittle, sputter **8** splutter **9** brochette, discharge, peninsula, secretion **11** expectorate

SPITE: **4** envy, hurt **5** annoy, venom **6** enmity, grudge, hatred, malice, offend, rancor **7** dislike, ill-will, provoke, revenge **8** contempt **9** animosity, hostility, humiliate, malignity, vengeance **10** resentment **11** malevolence

SPITEFUL: **4** evil, mean **5** catty **6** bitter, ornery, wicked **7** envious, hostile, hurtful, vicious **8** annoying, venomous, virulent **9** malicious, malignant, rancorous, resentful **10** malevolent, vindictive **11** troublesome **12** antagonistic

SPITTING IMAGE: **4** twin **6** double, ringer **8** likeness **9** duplicate **11** counterpart

SPLASH: **4** dash, mark, plop, soak, spot, stir, wash **5** bathe, douse, spray **6** blotch, dabble, drench, impact, plunge, shower, squirt, strike, wallow **7** display, moisten, scatter, spatter **8** splatter, sprinkle **9** publicize

SPLASHY: **4** loud **5** gaudy, showy **6** flashy, ornate, snazzy **7** opulent **11** sensational, spectacular **12** ostentatious

SPLATTER: **4** dash, slop **5** douse **6** splash **7** spatter

SPLAY: **5** bevel, carve, slant, slope, widen **6** clumsy, expand, spread **7** awkward, display, fanlike, sloping **8** slanting **9** dislocate, obliquely

SPLEEN: **4** whim **5** anger, organ, spite, wrath **6** grudge, hatred, malice, rancor **7** caprice, dislike **9** hostility **10** melancholy, resentment

SPLENDID: **4** fine, good, rich **5** grand, lofty, regal, showy **6** bright, costly, lavish, superb **7** elegant **8** dazzling, glorious, gorgeous **9** admirable, beautiful, brilliant, excellent, exquisite, fantastic, grandiose, luxurious, marvelous, sumptuous **10** impressive, surpassing **11** illustrious, magnificent **12** praiseworthy

SPLENDOR: **4** pomp **5** eclat, gleam, glory, light, shine **6** beauty, bright, dazzle, luster, parade **7** display **8** elegance, grandeur, opulence, radiance **9** pageantry, showiness **10** brightness, brilliance, effulgence, excellence, luminosity **12** gorgeousness, magnificence, resplendence

SPLICE: **4** join, mesh **5** marry, merge, unite **6** attach, fasten, insert **7** connect, entwine **10** interweave

SPLINTER: **4** chip, rend **5** break, flake, slice, smash, split **6** shiver, sliver **7** shatter **8** fragment **12** disintegrate

SPLIT: **3** cut, rip **4** deal, fork, part, rend, rent, rive, tear **5** break, burst, cleft, crack, halve, leave, mixed, reave, slice **6** bisect, broken, cleave, divide, schism, sliver, sunder **7** destroy, divided, divorce, fissure, isolate, opening, portion, rupture, shatter **8** alienate, allocate, fragment, separate, splinter **9** fractured, segregate, separated, undecided **10** difference, distribute, separation

SPLOTCH: **4** blob, blot, dash, mark, spot **5** fleck, smear, stain **6** blotch, smudge **7** blemish

SPLURGE: **5** binge, fling, showy, spend, spree **6** bender, splash **7** display, rampage **10** indulgence

SPOIL: **3** mar, rot **4** baby, foul, harm, hurt, loot, ruin, sour **5** booty, decay, prize, taint, waste, wreck **6** coddle, cosset, damage, deface, defile, impair, injure, pamper, perish, ravage, squash, thwart **7** blemish, corrupt, crumble, destroy, indulge, pillage, plunder, pollute, violate, vitiate **8** pickings **9** decompose **10** adulterate **11** contaminate, mollycoddle, overindulge

SPOILS: **4** haul, loot, swag **5** booty, goods, prize **6** bounty **8** pickings **9** amenities

SPOKE: **3** bar, pin, rod **4** rung, talk **5** brace, stake **6** handle, radius, speech **7** uttered

SPOKEN: **4** oral, said, told **5** vocal **6** verbal **7** uttered **8** declared **9** announced, expressed, mentioned, unwritten **11** articulated **12** communicated

SPOKESPERSON: **5** agent **7** speaker, sponsor **8** advocate, champion, delegate, mediator **9** spokesman **10** mouthpiece **11** spokeswoman **14** representative

SPONGE: **3** bum, wet **4** swab, wash, wipe **5** bathe, dough, leech **6** animal, borrow **7** cleanse, drinker, moocher **8** drunkard, parasite, scrounge **10** freeloader

SPONGER: **7** moocher **8** chiseler, deadbeat, parasite **10** freeloader **11** bloodsucker

SPONGY: **4** soft **5** soggy **6** porous **7** springy **9** absorbent, cushioned

SPONSOR: **4** back **5** angel, stake **6** backer, patron, surety **7** finance **8** advocate, bankroll, champion, defender, guardian, promoter **9** godparent, proponent, supporter **10** advertiser

SPONSORSHIP: **3** aid **5** aegis **7** backing, support **8** advocacy, auspices **9** patronage

SPONTANEOUS: **4** free **6** native **7** natural, offhand **8** careless, unforced **9** automatic, impromptu, impulsive, unplanned **10** improvised **11** instinctive, involuntary, unrehearsed **14** unpremeditated

SPOOF: **4** fake, fool, hoax, joke, josh **5** bluff, cheat, prank, trick **6** parody, satire **7** deceive, lampoon, mockery, swindle **8** nonsense **9** wisecrack **10** tomfoolery

SPOOK: **3** spy **5** agent, ghost, haunt, scare **6** goblin, spirit **7** phantom, specter, startle **8** frighten **9** hobgoblin, terrorize **10** apparition

SPOOKY: **5** eerie, jumpy, scary, weird **6** creepy **7** ghostly, haunted, ominous, uncanny **8** chilling **10** mysterious **11** frightening

SPOOL: **4** reel **5** quill **6** bobbin **7** spindle **8** cylinder

SPOON: **3** oar, pet **4** kiss, lure, neck **5** ladle, scoop **6** fondle, paddle **7** utensil **10** silverware

SPOOR: **4** odor **5** scent, trace, track, trail **9** footprint

SPORADIC: **4** rare **6** random **8** isolated, periodic **9** desultory, irregular, scattered **10** infrequent, occasional **12** intermittent

SPORT: **3** don, fun, toy **4** butt, game, jest, joke, mock, play, romp, wear **5** dally, hobby, mirth **6** banter, frolic, gamble, racing **7** contest, display, exhibit, gambler, jesting, mockery, pastime **8** derision, exercise **9** amusement, athletics, diversion, plaything **10** pleasantry, recreation **11** competition **13** entertainment

types: **4** golf, pool **5** rugby **6** boccie, boxing, hiking, hockey, racing, rowing, skiing, soccer, squash, tennis **7** archery, bowling, cricket, croquet, cycling, fencing, fishing, hunting, jai alai, sailing, skating, surfing **8** baseball, football, handball, lacrosse, swimming, yachting **9** billiards, wrestling **10** basketball, gymnastics, horseshoes, volleyball **11** bobsledding, racquetball **13** weightlifting

SPORTIVE: **4** game **5** merry **6** frisky, lively, wanton **7** festive, jocular **8** frolicky **9** sprightly **10** frolicsome

SPORTY: **5** jazzy, showy, smart **6** casual, flashy

SPOT: **3** dot, fix, jam, job, see, spy **4** bind, blot, blur, find, flaw, mark, post, site, soil **5** fault, fleck, patch, place, point, smear, speck, stain, sully, taint **6** blotch, corner, defect, detect, locate, pickle, pimple, scrape, smudge, stigma **7** blemish, dilemma, freckle, smidgen, splotch **8** discolor, discover, handicap, identify, location, molecule, particle, pinpoint, position, quandary **9** recognize **10** difficulty **11** predicament

SPOTLESS: **4** holy, pure **5** clean **6** chaste **8** flawless, sanitary **9** blameless, stainless, undefiled, unsullied **10** immaculate, impeccable **11** unblemished, untarnished

SPOTLIGHT: **4** beam, fame **9** attention, highlight, limelight, publicity **10** floodlight

SPOTTED: **6** espied, marked, patchy **7** blotchy, dappled, noticed, smeared, smudged, stained, sullied **8** speckled **9** blemished, tarnished

SPOTTY: **5** dotty **6** patchy, uneven **7** blotchy, erratic **8** splotchy, sporadic **9** irregular **10** unreliable

SPOUSE: **4** mate, wife **5** bride, groom **7** consort, husband, partner **8** roommate **9** companion **10** bridegroom

SPOUT: **3** jet **4** brag, emit, flow, gush, nose, pipe, rant, spew **5** boast, chute, eject, expel, shoot, snout, spray, spurt **6** nozzle, outlet, spigot, squirt, stream, trough **7** conduit, declaim **8** fountain **9** discharge, waterfall

SPRAIN: **4** pull, tear, turn **5** twist **6** injury, strain, wrench

SPRAWL: **4** flop, loll **5** relax, slump **6** extend, lounge, slouch **7** recline, stretch **11** spread-eagle

SPRAY: **4** dust, hose, mist, spew, twig **5** shoot, sprig, strew, treat **6** branch, nozzle, shower, squirt, volley **7** bouquet, drizzle, scatter **8** fumigate, moisture, sprinkle **9** discharge, spindrift

SPREAD: **3** fan, jam **4** coat, farm, meal, open, seep, span **5** cover, feast, jelly, level, ranch, reach, rumor, smear, space, strew, table, widen **6** artile, branch, butter, dilate, dinner, expand, extend, extent, unfold, unfurl, unroll, unwind **7** banquet, broaden, compass, diffuse, divulge, enlarge, expanse, flatten, overlay, plaster, prolong, publish, radiate, scatter, stretch **8** disperse, escalate, expanded, extended, multiply, permeate, straddle **9** broadcast, circulate, dispersed, propagate **10** distribute **11** proliferate

SPREE: **4** bash, bout, lark, orgy, riot, romp, toot **5** binge, fling, revel **6** bender, frolic, shindy **7** debauch, rampage, shindig, splurge, wassail **8** carousal **10** indulgence

SPRIGHTLY: **3** fun, gay **4** airy, spry **5** agile, alert, alive, brisk, fresh, merry, peppy, perky, quick, sharp **6** active, clever, frisky, lively **7** buoyant, chipper, dynamic, playful, zestful **8** animated, spirited, sportive, vigorous **9** energetic, vivacious **10** frolicsome

SPRING: **3** hop, pop, spa **4** bolt, dart, font, head, jump, leap, rise, skip, stem, well **5** arise, begin, birth, bound, shoot, start, surge, vault, youth **6** appear, bounce, emerge, hurdle, motive, origin, recoil, season, source, uncoil **7** develop, estuary, release **8** fountain **10** elasticity, resilience **11** flexibility **12** fountainhead

SPRINGY: **6** bouncy, supple **7** elastic, pliable **8** flexible, stretchy **9** resilient **10** rebounding

SPRINKLE: **3** dot, wet **4** dust, rain, spot **5** shake, spray, strew, water **6** dabble, dredge, powder, shower, sparge, splash, squirt **7** drizzle, moisten, scatter, sparkle, spatter, speckle **11** intersperse

SPRINT: **3** run **4** dart, dash, race, rush **6** scurry **7** scamper

SPRITE: **3** elf, fay **5** demon, fairy, genie, ghost, gnome, pixie **6** goblin, spirit **7** brownie, essence, specter **9** hobgoblin **10** apparition, leprechaun

SPROUT: **3** bud **4** grow **5** bloom, shoot, spout, sprig **6** spring, thrive **7** burgeon, develop **8** offshoot, seedling **9** germinate

SPRUCE: **4** chic, neat, smug, tidy, tree, trim **5** natty, sharp, smart **6** dapper, spiffy **7** elegant, stylish **9** evergreen, shipshape **11** well-groomed

SPRY: **5** agile, brisk, perky, quick **6** active, frisky, lively, nimble, robust **7** chipper, healthy **8** spirited, vigorous **9** energetic, sprightly, vivacious

SPUD: **3** dig **4** tool **5** drill, spade **6** potato, shovel

SPUME: **4** foam, scum, suds **5** froth, spray

SPUNK: **4** grit, guts **5** flame, gleam, heart, moxie, nerve, pluck, spark **6** mettle, spirit **7** courage, passion **8** backbone, gumption **9** fortitude **10** doggedness, liveliness **13** determination

SPUNKY: **4** bold, game **5** brave, gutsy **6** plucky **8** spirited **10** courageous

SPUR: **4** goad, move, prod, push, stir, urge **5** cause, drive, impel, press, prick, ridge, spark, spike **6** arouse, excite, foment, incite, needle, prompt, propel **7** crampon, impetus, provoke, trigger **8** catalyst, motivate, stimulus **9** encourage, galvanize, incentive, instigate, stimulate

SPURIOUS: **4** fake **5** bogus, false, phony **6** forged, unreal **7** bastard, feigned **9** contrived, fictitious, imitation **10** apocryphal, artificial, fraudulent **11** counterfeit, unauthentic **12** illegitimate

SPURN: **4** kick, shun, snub **5** flout, scoff, tread **6** ignore, rebuff, refuse, reject, scrape, slight **7** contemn, decline, despise, disdain **9** disregard, repudiate

SPURT: **3** jet **4** dart, emit, flow, gush, rush **5** burst, erupt, expel, spout, spray, surge **6** sprout, squirt, stream **9** commotion, discharge

SPUTTER: **4** spit **6** falter **7** stammer, stumble

SPY: **3** pry, see **4** case, espy, mole, peep, view **5** agent, scout, sneak, snoop, watch **6** behold, descry, detect, meddle, notice, search **7** examine, inspect, observe, sleeper, snooper, stoolie **8** discover, informer, saboteur, stake out **10** scrutinize **11** secret agent

SPYING: **9** espionage, following, voyeurism **11** wiretapping **12** surveillance

SQUABBLE: **4** feud, spat, tiff **5** argue, brawl, fight, words **6** bicker **7** dispute, quarrel, wrangle **8** argument **11** altercation

SQUAD: **4** band, crew, team, unit **5** group **7** company **8** squadron

SQUADRON: **4** unit **5** fleet, squad **6** armada **9** battalion **10** escadrille

SQUALID: **4** base, foul, mean, ugly, vile **5** dingy, dirty, grimy, mangy, nasty, seedy **6** filthy, grubby, rotten, shabby, shoddy, sordid **7** unclean, unkempt **8** wretched **9** miserable, offensive, repulsive **10** disgusting, disheveled

SQUALL: **3** cry **4** bawl, gale, gush, gust, wind, yell **5** blast, shout, storm **6** flurry, scream, shower, shriek, squawk **7** bluster, trouble **9** commotion, windstorm **11** disturbance

SQUALOR: **4** dirt, mire **5** filth **7** neglect, poverty **9** seediness **11** squalidness **12** wretchedness

SQUANDER: **4** blow, burn **5** spend, waste **6** lavish, misuse **7** consume, fritter, scatter **8** disperse, misspend **9** dissipate **12** extravagance

SQUANDERER: **6** waster **7** spender, wastrel

SQUARE: **4** boxy, dull, even, fair, hick, jibe, just, park, tied, true **5** bribe, clear, court, dated, equal, exact, hunky, legal, match, plaza **6** adjust, common, direct, firmly, honest, settle **7** balance, ethical, genuine, resolve, satisfy, upright **8** cornball, straight **9** equitable, objective **10** clodhopper **11** marketplace, rectangular **12** conservative, conventional

SQUASH: **4** beat, cram, fall, game, mash, stop **5** crowd, crush, plant, pound, press, quash, quell **6** squish **7** flatten, squeeze, squelch **8** suppress **9** undermine, vegetable **10** annihilate, disconcert
variety: **5** acorn **6** banana, cushaw, summer, turban, winter **7** Hubbard **8** zucchini **9** crookneck

SQUAT: **5** broad, cower, dumpy, hunch, kneel, pudgy, stoop **6** chunky, crouch, settle, stocky, stubby **8** heavyset, thickset

SQUAWK: **3** cry **4** crow, fuss, hoot **5** blare, gripe **6** cackle, scream, yammer **7** grumble, protest, screech **8** complain **9** bellyache

SQUEAK: **3** cry **4** peep **5** cheep, chirp, creak, noise, sound **6** escape, inform, shriek, shrill, snitch, squeal

SQUEAL: **3** rat **4** blab, fink, howl, sing, yell **6** betray, inform, scream, shriek, shrill, snitch, squawk, squeak **7** protest, screech **8** complain

SQUEALER: **3** rat **4** fink **6** canary, pigeon, snitch **7** stoolie, traitor **8** informer

SQUEAMISH: **5** dizzy, fussy, shaky **6** afraid, dainty, modest, prissy, queasy **7** finical, finicky, prudish **8** nauseous, priggish, sickened **9** nauseated, sensitive **10** fastidious, scrupulous

SQUEEZE: **3** hug, jam **4** bear, cram, grip, pack **5** choke, clasp, crown, crush, force, juice, pinch, stuff, wring **6** clutch, cuddle, extort, squash **7** compact, embrace, extract, oppress, scrunch **8** compress, condense, pressure, strangle **9** constrict, influence **10** constraint **11** compression, predicament

SQUELCH: **5** crush, quash, quell, shush, stamp **6** muffle, squash **7** silence, smother **8** restrain, suppress

SQUIB: **4** skit **5** spoof **6** filler, parody, satire **7** lampoon **11** firecracker

SQUID: **7** mollusk, octopus **8** calamary **10** cephalopod, cuttlefish
genus: **6** loligo
secretes: **3** ink
tentacles: **3** ten

SQUIGGLE: **4** curl **5** twist **6** squirm, wiggle, writhe **7** wriggle

SQUINT: **4** bent, cast, look, peek, skew **5** trend **6** goggle **7** deviate, squinch **10** strabismus

SQUIRE: **5** guard, judge, lover, title **6** assist, escort, lawyer **7** gallant **8** chaperon **9** accompany, attendant, gentleman, landowner

SQUIRM: **4** toss, turn, worm **5** shift, twist **6** fidget, wiggle, writhe **7** contort, wriggle **8** squiggle

SQUIRREL: **4** hide **5** hoard, stash, store **6** rodent
family: **9** Sciuridae
genus: **7** sciurus

SQUIRT: **3** jet **4** emit, gush, runt **5** eject, spray, spurt, twerp **6** shower, splash, stream **7** spatter **9** pipsqueak

SRI LANKA:
capital: **7** Colombo
cities: **5** Galle, Kandy **6** Jaffna **7** Negombo **11** Trincomalee
continent: **4** Asia
ethnic groups: **4** Moor **5** Tamil **9** Sinhalese
features: **9** Adam's Peak **11** Polonnaruwa **12** Anuradhapura
former names: **6** Ceylon **8** Serendip **9** Taprobane
languages: **5** Tamil **9** Sinhalese
monetary unit: **5** rupee
water: **11** Indian Ocean

STAB: **3** cut, dab, try **4** dirk, gash, gore, pain, poke **5** fling, gouge, knife, lance, lunge, prick, spear, stick, whirl, wound **6** attack, dagger, pierce, plunge, strike, thrust **7** attempt, bayonet **8** incision, puncture **9** penetrate

STABILITY: **5** poise **7** balance **8** firmness, security, strength **9** constancy **10** permanence, stableness, steadiness **11** equilibrium, reliability **13** dependability, steadfastness

STABILIZE: **5** fixed, poise **6** secure, settle **7** balance **8** equalize, regulate

STABILIZER: **7** airfoil, balance, ballast

STABLE: **4** barn, fast, firm, mews, safe, sure **5** fixed, flock, solid, sound, stall **6** hangar, moored, poised, secure, steady, strong, sturdy **7** durable, lasting, staunch **8** anchored, balanced, constant, enduring, reliable, together **9** immutable permanent, resistant, steadfast, unvarying **10** dependable, stationary, unchanging, unwavering **11** established, trustworthy **12** unchangeable

STACK: **4** bank, flue, heap, load, lump, pile, rick, stow **5** bunch, group, mound **6** bundle, gather **7** arrange, chimney **10** accumulate

STADIUM: **4** bowl, ring **5** arena, field, stage **6** period **7** diamond **8** ballpark, coliseum, gridiron **9** gymnasium

STAFF: **3** rod **4** cane, club, crew, mace, pole, prod, rung, team, wand **5** aides, baton, force, group, stave, stick **6** cudgel **7** crosier, scepter, support, workers **8** caduceus, flagpole, servants **9** employees, entourage, personnel **10** assistants, associates

STAGE: **4** dais, play, show, step, tier **5** arena, enact, floor, grade, level, notch, phase, point, story **6** degree, period, pulpit **7** arrange, exhibit, perform, present, produce, rostrum, setting, theater **8** organize, platform **9** condition, dramatize, limelight, spotlight **11** orchestrate

STAGGER: **4** reel, rock, stun, sway **5** amaze, lurch, shake, shift, shock, stump, waver, weave **6** careen, hobble, totter **7** astound, startle, stumble **8** astonish, hesitate, surprise, unsettle **9** alternate, dumbfound, overpower **11** flabbergast

STAGNANT: **4** dull, foul, idle **5** inert, stale, still **6** static **7** dormant **8** inactive, sluggish, standing **9** lethargic **10** monotonous, motionless, stationary, unchanging

STAGNATE: **4** dull, rust **5** decay **6** fester, stifle **8** languish, vegetate **11** deteriorate

STAID: **4** cool **5** fixed, grave, sober **6** demure, sedate, solemn **7** earnest, serious, settled **8** composed, decorous **9** dignified, permanent **10** restrained

STAIN: **3** dye **4** blot, blur, flaw, mark, ruin, soil, spot, tint **5** brand, color, paint, smear, speck, sully, taint, tinge, trace **6** blotch, debase, defile, smudge, stigma **7** blemish, corrupt, pigment, tarnish **8** discolor, disgrace, dishonor, tincture **11** contaminate

STAINLESS: **4** pure **6** chaste **8** spotless, unsoiled **9** exemplary, unsullied, untainted **10** immaculate

STAKE: **3** bet, pot **4** ante, back, loot, pile, play, pole, pool, post, risk, take **5** claim, kitty, prize, purse, share, spike, stick, wager **6** chance, gamble, hazard, marker, picket, pledge, reward **7** finance, sponsor, venture **8** bankroll, interest, winnings **10** capitalize, investment

STALE: **4** flat, sour, worn **5** banal, corny, dusty, moldy, musty, passe, trite, vapid **6** cliche **7** decayed, humdrum, insipid, spoiled, wornout **8** shopworn, stagnant **9** hackneyed **10** monotonous, unoriginal **11** commonplace

STALEMATE: **3** tie **4** draw **5** check **7** impasse **8** deadlock, gridlock, standoff **10** standstill

STALK: **4** axis, hunt, prey, reed, stem **5** chase, shaft, track, trail **6** follow, menace, pursue, shadow **7** pedicle **8** peduncle

STALL: **3** bin, pew **4** halt, seat, stop **5** block, booth, brake, check, delay, stand **6** hamper, impede, manger, stable **7** cubicle, suspend **8** hesitate, obstruct, postpone **9** stonewall **10** dilly-dally, filibuster **11** compartment **13** procrastinate

STALWART: **4** bold, firm **5** brave, stout **6** brawny, mighty, robust, strong, sturdy **7** gallant, valiant **8** fearless, forceful, muscular, powerful, resolute **9** dauntless **10** courageous

STAMINA: **5** heart, vigor **6** energy **7** courage **8** backbone, strength, vitality **9** endurance, fortitude, tolerance **12** perseverance

STAMMER: **6** falter, fumble, jabber **7** sputter, stumble, stutter **8** hesitate

STAMP: **3** die **4** beat, cast, form, kind, mark, mint, mold, seal, type **5** brand, crush, drive, label, pound, press, print, stomp **6** hammer, signet, strike, symbol **7** earmark, impress, imprint, postage, sticker, trample **8** hallmark, identity, inscribe, postmark **9** character, signature **10** impression
collector: **11** philatelist

STAMPEDE: **4** bolt, riot, rout, rush **5** panic **6** charge, flight **7** overrun **8** inundate

STANCE: **5** stand **6** policy **7** posture, station **8** attitude, position **9** viewpoint

STANCHION: **4** beam, pole, post, prop, stay **5** brace **7** bolster, support, upright **9** framework

STAND: **4** base, bear, dais, face, halt, last, rack, rest, stop, wait **5** abide, arise, booth, easel, erect, frame, honor, kiosk, pause, poise, raise, slant, stain, table **6** belief, endure, podium, policy, remain, resist, stance, suffer, tripod, trivet **7** measure, opinion, prevail, station, stomach, support, undergo, weather **8** attitude, maintain, platform, position, tolerate **9** pavillion **10** resistance

STANDARD: **3** par **4** base, flag, mark, mean, norm, rule, unit **5** gauge, grade, ideal, level, model **6** banner, common, ensign, ethics, median, morals, normal, sample, signal **7** average, classic, example, measure, pattern, pennant, regular **8** accepted, gonfalon, ordinary **9** barometer, benchmark, criterion, customary, guideline, magnitude, principle, yardstick **10** touchstone **11** measurement, requirement

STAND FOR: **4** mean **5** allow, imply **6** endure, permit **7** signify **9** represent, symbolize

STAND-IN: **5** proxy **6** backup, double, second **9** alternate, surrogate **10** substitute, understudy

STANDING: **4** rank, term **5** erect, fixed, order **6** esteem, stance, static, status, tenure **7** dignity, dormant, footing, lasting, settled, station, upright **8** capacity, duration, eminence, inactive, location, position, prestige, stagnant, verticle **9** character, permanent **10** continuing, reputation, stationary

STANDOFF: **3** tie **4** draw **7** impasse **8** deadlock **9** stalemate

STANDOFFISH: **4** cold, cool **5** aloof **7** distant, haughty **8** reserved, solitary **9** reclusive, withdrawn **10** antisocial, unfriendly

STAND OUT: **4** loom **5** bulge **6** beetle, emerge **7** project **8** overhand, protrude **9** prominent **11** conspicuous

STANDPOINT: **4** side **5** angle, slant **6** aspect **7** opinion, outlook **8** attitude, position **9** direction, viewpoint

STANDSTILL: **4** halt, stop **5** delay, pause **7** impasse **8** deadlock, gridlock **9** cessation, stalemate

STANZA: **5** stave, verse **7** strophe **8** division

STAPLE: **4** core, item **5** basic, chief, fiber, goods **6** fasten **8** fastener, resource **9** commodity, necessary, principal **10** foundation **11** fundamental

STAR:
born from: **7** nebulae
cluster: **6** nebula
concerning: **6** astral **7** astrean, stellar **8** sidereal, stellate
exploding: **4** nova
gazer: **10** astrologer, astronomer, daydreamer
group: **6** galaxy, nebula **7** cluster **13** constellation
highest: **5** alpha
made of: **6** helium **8** hydrogen
north: **7** polaris **8** lodestar, polestar
shooting: **5** comet **6** meteor
types: **6** binary **8** red dwarf, red giant, variable **10** brown dwarf, supergiant, white dwarf **15** planetary nebula

STAR-CROSSED: **7** unlucky **11** unfortunate

STARCH: **4** push **5** drive, vigor **6** energy, mettle **7** stiffen **8** backbone, gumption, strength, vitality **9** formality, stiffness, substance

STARCHY: **4** prim **5** rigid, stiff **6** formal, proper

STARE: **3** eye **4** gape, gawk, gaze, leer, look, ogle, peer **5** focus, glare, glaze, watch **6** goggle **10** rubberneck

STARK: **4** bare, firm, grim, hard, nude, pure **5** bleak, blunt, crude, empty, harsh, naked, plain, rigid, stiff, tense, utter **6** barren, dreary, entire, robust, severe, strong, unclad, vacant, wholly **7** austere, extreme **8** absolute, complete, desolate, entirely, forsaken, stalwart, stripped, vigorous **9** downright, unadorned **10** unyielding

STARRY: **6** astral, bright **7** shining, stellar **8** luminous, lustrous, sidereal **9** celestial, sparkling **10** glittering, shimmering

STAR-SPANGLED BANNER: **4** flag, poem, song **6** anthem
author: **15** Francis Scott Key

START: **4** bolt, dart, dawn, form, head, jump, lead, leap, rush, turn **5** begin, birth, cause, enter, found, onset, pulse, rouse, wince **6** broach, create, embark, flinch, ignite, launch, recoil, source, spring, twitch **7** genesis, infancy, kickoff, opening, provoke, retreat, startle **8** activate, commence, generate, initiate **9** advantage, establish, instigate, introduce, originate, undertake **10** inaugurate **11** opportunity

STARTLE: **4** jump, stun **5** alarm, rouse, scare, shock, start, upset **6** excite **7** terrify **8** frighten, surprise

STARVED: **6** hungry **8** famished **9** emaciated **12** malnourished **14** undernourished

STASH: **4** bury, hide **5** hoard, store **7** conceal

STATE: **3** put, say **4** aver, body, mind, mode, mood, rank, tell, vent **5** phase, shape, style, utter **6** affirm, allege, assert, define, degree, empire, nation, nature, recite, relate, report, status, throne **7** account, country, declare, dignity, display, explain, expound, express, narrate, outlook, politic, posture, specify, spirits, stature, testify **8** attitude, capacity, ceremony, describe, eminence, grandeur, position, proclaim, property, propound, republic, standing **9** character, condition, enunciate, pronounce, situation, territory, verbalize **10** articulate, government **11** disposition **12** circumstance, commonwealth

STATE ABBREVIATIONS:
Alabama: **2** AL **3** Ala
Alaska: **2** AK **4** Alas
Arizona: **2** AZ **4** Ariz

Arkansas: **2** AR **3** Ark
California: **2** CA **3** Cal **5** Calif
Colorado: **2** CO **4** Colo
Connecticut: **2** CT **4** Conn
Delaware: **2** DE **3** Del
Florida: **2** FL **3** Fla
Georgia: **2** GA
Hawaii: **2** HI
Idaho: **2** ID **3** Ida
Illinois: **2** IL **3** Ill
Indiana: **2** IN **3** Ind
Iowa: **2** Ia
Kansas: **2** KS **4** Kans
Kentucky: **2** KY
Louisiana: **2** LA
Maine: **2** Me
Maryland: **2** MD
Massachusetts: **2** MA **4** Mass
Michigan: **2** MI **4** Mich
Minnesota: **2** MN **4** Minn
Mississippi: **2** MS **4** Miss
Missouri: **2** MO
Montana: **2** MT **4** Mont
Nebraska: **2** NE **4** Nebr
Nevada: **2** NV **3** Nev
New Hampshire: **2** NH
New Jersey: **2** NJ
New Mexico: **2** NM **4** N.Mex
New York: **2** NY
North Carolina: **2** NC **4** N.Car
North Dakota: **2** ND **4** N.Dak
Ohio: **2** OH
Oklahoma: **2** OK **4** Okla
Oregon: **2** OR **3** Ore **4** Oreg
Pennsylvania: **2** PA **4** Penn **5** Penna
Rhode Island: **2** RI
South Carolina: **2** SC **4** S.Car
South Dakota: **2** SD **4** S.Dak
Tennessee: **2** TN **4** Tenn
Texas: **2** TX **3** Tex
Utah: **2** UT
Vermont: **2** VT **3** Ver
Virginia: **2** VA **4** Virg
Washington: **2** WA **4** Wash
West Virginia: **2** WV **3** W.Va
Wisconsin: **2** WI **3** Wis
Wyoming: **2** WY **3** Wyo

STATE CAPITALS:
Alabama: **10** Montgomery
Alaska: **6** Juneau
Arizona: **7** Phoenix
Arkansas: **10** Little Rock
California: **10** Sacramento
Colorado: **6** Denver
Connecticut: **8** Hartford
Delaware: **5** Dover
Florida: **11** Tallahassee
Georgia: **7** Atlanta
Hawaii: **8** Honolulu
Idaho: **5** Boise
Illinois: **11** Springfield
Indiana: **12** Indianapolis
Iowa: **9** Des Moines
Kansas: **6** Topeka
Kentucky: **9** Frankfort
Louisiana: **10** Baton Rouge
Maine: **7** Augusta
Maryland: **9** Annapolis
Massachusetts: **6** Boston
Michigan: **7** Lansing
Minnesota: **6** St. Paul
Mississippi: **7** Jackson
Missouri: **13** Jefferson City
Montana: **6** Helena
Nebraska: **7** Lincoln
Nevada: **10** Carson City
New Hampshire: **7** Concord
New Jersey: **7** Trenton
New Mexico: **7** Santa Fe
New York: **6** Albany
North Carolina: **7** Raleigh
North Dakota: **8** Bismarck
Ohio: **8** Columbus
Oklahoma: **12** Oklahoma City
Oregon: **5** Salem
Pennsylvania: **10** Harrisburg
Rhode Island: **10** Providence
South Carolina: **9** Columbia
South Dakota: **6** Pierre
Tennessee: **9** Nashville
Texas: **6** Austin
Utah: **12** Salt Lake City
Vermont: **10** Montpelier
Virginia: **8** Richmond
Washington: **7** Olympia
West Virginia: **10** Charleston
Wisconsin: **7** Madison
Wyoming: **8** Cheyenne

STATELY: **5** grand, lofty, noble, regal, royal **6** august, formal, kingly, lordly **7** courtly, elegant, gallant **8** imperial, imposing, majestic **9** dignified, grandiose **10** impressive, statuesque **11** ceremonious, magnificent

STATEMENT: **4** bill, word **5** audit, claim, voice **6** dictum, record, remark, report, speech, truism **7** account, address, article, comment, epitome, invoice, paradox, preface, summary **8** sentence **9** affidavit, agreement, assertion, narrative, testimony **10** allegation, deposition, expression **11** certificate, declaration **12** presentation

STATEROOM: **5** cabin **11** compartment

STATESMAN, STATESWOMAN: **6** leader **8** diplomat, lawmaker, minister, official **10** legislator, politician

STATIC: **5** fixed, noise **8** immobile, inactive, stagnant **9** criticism, quiescent **10** motionless, stationary, unchanging **11** electricity **12** interference

STATION: **4** duty, post, rank, site, spot, stop **5** berth, depot, grade, place **6** degree **7** footing **8** location, position, standing, terminal **10** assignment, occupation, settlement **12** headquarters

STATIONARY: **5** fixed, stale, still **6** parked, static **7** riveted **8** anchored, immobile, stagnant **9** immovable, permanent, sedentary **10** motionless, unchanging

STATUE: **4** bust, icon **5** image **6** bronze, figure **8** colossus, figurine, likeness, memorial, monument **9** sculpture

STATUESQUE: **4** tall **5** regal **7** shapely, stately **8** majestic **9** beautiful, dignified

STATURE: **4** rank **5** place **6** height, status **7** ability, posture **8** eminence, position, prestige **10** importance, prominence, reputation

STATUS: **4** rank **5** class, merit, state **6** aspect, degree **7** dignity, posture, stature **8** position, prestige, standing **9** condition, situation **10** prominence

STATUTE: **3** act, law **4** bill, rule **5** edict, order **6** decree **7** measure, precept **9** enactment, ordinance **10** regulation

STAUNCH: **4** firm, true **5** loyal, sound **6** ardent, rugged, stanch, strong **8** faithful, reliable, resolute **9** steadfast **10** dependable **11** trustworthy

STAVE OFF: **4** ward **5** avert, block, repel

STAY: **4** bide, bunk, curb, halt, hold, live, prop, rest, rope, stem, stop, wait **5** abide, block, brace, cable, defer, delay, dwell, lodge, pause, stand, tarry, truss, visit **6** arrest, column, detain, endure, fasten, linger, remain, reside, secure, settle **7** appease, persist, satisfy, sojourn, support, suspend, sustain **8** continue, postpone, reprieve, restrain, stopover **9** deferment **10** permanence

STEADFAST: **4** firm, sure, true **5** fixed, loyal **6** ardent, intent, steady **7** adamant, staunch **8** constant, enduring, faithful, resolute, stubborn **9** tenacious **10** dependable, inflexible, relentless, unchanging, unflagging, unswerving, unyielding **12** wholehearted

STEADY: **4** beau, calm, even, firm, sure **5** fixed, flame, lover, sober **6** poised, stable, sturdy **7** careful, equable, nonstop, regular, staunch, uniform **8** balanced, constant, faithful, frequent, habitual, reliable, resolute, unshaken, untiring **9** boyfriend, incessant, stabilize, steadfast **10** continuous, cool-headed, deliberate, girlfriend, methodical, sweetheart, unswerving, unwavering **11** unfaltering **13** unfluctuating, uninterrupted

STEAK: **4** beef, meat
cuts: **3** rib **4** cube **5** chuck, strip, T-bone **6** minute **7** New York, sirloin **9** hamburger, Salisbury **10** tenderloin **11** filet mignon, porterhouse **13** chateaubriand

STEAL: **3** cop, gyp, rob **4** grab, hook, lift, loot, take **5** bribe, cheat, creep, filch, heist, pinch, poach, shaft, sneak, swipe, theft **6** abduct, divert, hijack, kidnap, pilfer, pirate, pocket, rustle, snatch, snitch, thieve **7** bargain, pillage, purloin, swindle **8** embezzle, peculate, shoplift **9** blackmail **10** burglarize, plagiarize **11** appropriate

STEALING: **5** crime, theft **6** piracy **7** forgery, larceny **10** plagiarism **11** shoplifting **12** embezzlement

STEALTHY: **3** sly **4** wily **5** quiet **6** covert, crafty, secret, sneaky **7** cunning, devious, furtive **8** slippery **9** secretive **10** undercover **11** clandestine **13** surreptitious

STEAM: **4** brew, cook, fume, heat, mist **5** force, might, power, smoke, vapor, vigor, water **6** energy, muscle **8** strength, vaporize

STEAMER: **4** boat, clam, ship **5** liner **9** steamboat, steamship **10** paddleboat

STEEL: **4** firm, gird, gray, rail **5** alloy, brace, color, nerve, sword **6** harden, smooth, strong **7** fortify **9** encourage, reinforce **10** strengthen

STEEP: **4** brew, high, soak, stew, tall **5** bathe, hilly, imbue, lofty, rapid, sharp, sheer, stiff **6** abrupt, drench, imbrue, raised **7** arduous, extract, extreme, immerse **8** elevated, headlong, saturate, waterlog **9** ambitious, difficult, excessive, expensive **10** exorbitant, impregnate **11** precipitous **13** perpendicular

STEEPLE: **5** spire, tower **6** belfry, cupola, fleche, turret **7** minaret **8** ziggurat **9** campanile

STEER: **4** bull, herd, lead, show **5** drive, guide, pilot **6** cattle, direct, govern, manage **7** captain, control **8** navigate, shepherd

STELLAR: **5** chief **6** astral, cosmic **7** leading, shining **8** heavenly **9** celestial, principal **11** outstanding

STEM: **3** dam, rod **4** axis, base, body, cane, curb, halt, reed, root, stop **5** arise, check, deter, shaft, stall, stock, trunk, tuber **6** branch, derive, hinder, impede, oppose, resist, spring, stanch, stolon **7** contain, control, counter, develop, emanate, pedicel, peduncle, petiole, prevent **8** restrain **9** originate, withstand

STENCH: **4** funk, odor, reek **5** fetor, smell, stink **7** malodor **9** redolence

STENOGRAPHY: **9** shorthand, stenotype **11** tachography **12** transcribing

STENTORIAN: **4** loud **7** blaring, orotund **8** sonorous **10** resounding

STEP: **4** gait, move, pace, rank, rung, walk **5** dance, grade, level, plane, round, stage, stair, strut, tread **6** action, course, degree, ladder, prance, stride **7** advance, measure, process **8** maneuver, movement **9** footprint, gradation, procedure, promotion **10** proceeding

STEP DOWN: **4** quit **5** leave **6** reduce, resign, retire

STEP IN: **5** enter **6** arrive **9** intercede, interfere, intervene

STEPPE: **5** plain **7** prairie, savanna **9** grassland

STEP UP: **5** boost, hurry **8** escalate, increase **9** intensify **10** accelerate

STEREOTYPE: **4** mold **7** pattern **8** standard, typecast **10** categorize, convention

STEREOTYPED: **5** trite **8** ordinary **9** hackneyed **12** conventional

STERILE: **4** arid, dead, geld **5** clean **6** barren **7** aseptic **8** hygienic, impotent, sanitary **9** fruitless, infertile **10** antiseptic, unfruitful **11** disinfected, ineffective **12** unproductive

STERILIZE: **3** fix **4** geld, spay **5** alter **6** change, neuter, purify **8** castrate, sanitize **9** disinfect **10** emasculate

STERLING: **4** pure, true **5** noble **7** genuine **8** flawless **9** admirable, authentic, excellent, honorable

STERN: **4** cold, dour, firm, grim, hard, rear **5** cruel, harsh, rigid, rough, stout, tough **6** fierce, gloomy, severe, strict, sturdy, unkind **7** austere, serious **8** resolute, rigorous **9** unbending, unfeeling **10** astringent, forbidding, inexorable, inflexible, relentless, tyrannical, unyielding **13** authoritarian, unsympathetic **14** uncompromising

STEW: **4** boil, brew, cook, fret, fume, fuss, hash, mess, olio, soup **5** anger, brood, sweat, tizzy, worry **6** dither, seethe, simmer **7** goulash, melange, swelter, turmoil **8** mishmash **9** commotion, confusion **10** excitement, hodgepodge, hotchpotch, miscellany

STEWARD: **5** agent, reeve **6** waiter **7** bailiff, curator, foreman, manager, officer, proctor **8** director, guardian **9** attendant, custodian, seneschal **10** magistrate **11** chamberlain **13** administrator

STICK: **3** bar, bat, bow, cue, fix, ram, rod **4** bind, cane, club, fuse, glue, goad, hold, mast, poke, pole, seal, stab, stem, stop, twig, wand **5** affix, baton, cling, mount, paste, place, prick, spear, staff, stalk, stall, stave, trunk **6** adhere, attach, branch, cement, cleave, cohere, cudgel, endure, fasten, ferule, fescue, impale, insert, pierce, strike, thrust, warder **7** buffalo, defraud, nonplus, penalty, persist, support **8** bludgeon, continue, puncture, tolerate **9** drumstick **10** overcharge

STICK-IN-THE-MUD: **6** square **8** mossback **12** conservative

STICKLER: **6** puzzle, riddle, zealot **7** fanatic, mystery, paradox

STICK OUT: **3** jut **4** poke **5** bulge **6** beetle, extend **7** extrude, project **8** protrude

STICKY: **4** damp, hard **5** gluey, gooey, hairy, humid, messy, muggy **6** clammy, sultry, syrupy, tricky, viscid **7** awkward, viscous **8** adhesive **9** difficult, glutinous **10** oppressive **12** embarrassing **13** uncomfortable

STIFF: **3** bum **4** body, dead, dull, firm, hard, sore, taut **5** drunk, fixed, grave, harsh, rigid, steep, stern, tense, thick, tough, tramp **6** bitter, clumsy, corpse, formal, frozen, loafer, severe, stanch, strong, sturdy, uneasy, wooden **7** arduous, awkward, cadaver, drastic, precise, stilted **8** drunkard, exacting, hardened, powerful, resolute, rigorous, starched, stubborn **9** difficult, excessive, inelastic, laborious, resistant, unbending, unnatural **10** cheapskate, inebriated, inflexible, unyielding **11** intoxicated **14** uncompromising

STIFFEN: **3** set **4** firm **5** brace, tense **6** benumb, harden, ossify **7** bolster, petrify, thicken **8** solidify **9** reinforce

STIFF-NECKED: **5** aloof **8** arrogant, stubborn **9** obstinate, pigheaded **10** bullheaded, unyielding

STIFLE: **3** gag **4** curb, stop **5** check, choke **6** muffle **7** inhibit, repress, silence, smother, trammel **8** restrain, strangle, stultify, suppress **9** interrupt, suffocate **10** asphyxiate

STIGMA: **4** blot, mark, scar, spot **5** brand, cloud, odium, shame, stain, taint **7** blemish **8** disgrace, dishonor, reproach

STIGMATIZE: **5** brand, smear **6** defame **7** censure, tarnish **9** denigrate, discredit

STILL: **3** but, mum **4** also, calm, even, hush, lull, stop **5** check, inert, quiet **6** gentle, hushed, pacify, placid, serene, settle, silent, soothe, though **7** appease, besides, however, silence, subdued **8** inactive, lifeless, likewise, moreover, peaceful, restrain, suppress, tranquil **9** noiseless, soundless **10** distillery, motionless, photograph, stationary, uneventful **11** nonetheless, undisturbed **12** nevertheless

STILT: **4** bird, pole, post **6** pillar **8** longlegs

STILTED: **4** prim **5** stiff **6** formal, stuffy, wooden **7** awkward, flowery, pompous **8** affected **9** unnatural **10** artificial

STIMULANT: **4** drug **5** tonic, upper **6** bracer **7** caffein **8** caffeine, catalyst **9** energizer, incentive **10** motivation

STIMULATE: **4** goad, move, spur, stir, urge **5** brace, elate, impel, rouse, spark, sting **6** arouse, excite, foster, incite, thrill **7** animate, enliven, inspire, provoke, quicken, trigger **8** activate, energize, motivate **9** encourage, galvanize, innervate, instigate **10** exhilarate, invigorate

STIMULATING: **5** brisk **8** exciting **10** intriguing, refreshing **11** interesting, provocative, titillating **12** electrifying, invigorating

STIMULUS: **4** goad, spur **5** boost, cause, sting **6** fillip, motive **7** impetus, impulse **8** catalyst **9** incentive **10** inducement, motivation, propellant **11** provocation

STING: **3** bit **4** burn, dupe, goad, hurt, itch, pain, poke, spur, tang, urge **5** anger, cheat, prick, smart, wince, wound **6** impale, incite, nettle, pierce, tingle **8** stimulus **9** stimulate

STINGING: **5** harsh, sharp **6** biting, bitter **7** burning, caustic, painful, piquant **8** aculeate, scathing **9** sarcastic **11** acrimonious

STINGY: **4** mean **5** cheap, tight **6** biting, frugal, greedy, meager, scanty, skimpy **7** chintzy, miserly, selfish, thrifty **9** illiberal, niggardly, penurious **10** avaricious, economical, ungenerous **11** closefisted, tightfisted **12** parsimonious

STINK: **4** funk, odor, reek **5** fetor, smell **6** stench **9** offensive

STINT: **3** job **4** duty, stop, task, term, tour **5** chore, quota, scant, serve, shift, skimp, spell, stunt **6** assign, scrimp **7** confine **8** restrain, restrict, withhold **9** economize, restraint **10** assignment, limitation **11** restriction

STIPEND: **3** fee, pay **4** wage **6** income, salary **7** payment, pension **9** allowance, emolument **10** recompense **12** compensation

STIPULATE: **5** agree, state **6** detail **7** arrange, bargain, promise, require, specify, warrant **8** contract, covenant, indicate **9** designate, guarantee

STIPULATION: **4** item **5** limit, terms **6** clause, demand, detail **7** article, proviso **9** agreement, condition, provision, situation **11** arrangement, requirement **12** precondition, prerequisite

STIR: **3** mix **4** fuss, goad, jail, move, poke, prod, spur, toss, wake, whip **5** awake, blend, budge, churn, furor, hurry, rally, rouse, shake, shift **6** arouse, awaken, bestir, bustle, excite, hubbub, incite, kindle, moment, motion, prison, racket, seethe, tumult, uproar **7** agitate, animate, disturb, flutter, inflame, inspire, provoke, quicken, trigger **8** activity, displace, energize, motivate, movement, scramble **9** challenge, commotion, electrify, galvanize, instigate, stimulate

STIRRING: **5** astir **6** active, lively, moving **7** rousing **8** exciting, movement **9** animating, inspiring, thrilling **11** interesting, stimulating **12** electrifying

STITCH: **3** bit, hem, sew **4** join, knit, mend, pain, pang, purl, seam **5** baste, crick, unite **6** fasten, suture **9** embroider

STOCK: **4** band, butt, folk, fund, have, herd, hope, line, post, race, stem **5** asses, banal, blood, breed, carry, equip, goods, hoard, house, store, tribe, trunk, trust **6** cattle, common, family, shares, staple, supply **7** animals, backlog, capital, descent, lineage, produce, provide, reserve **8** ancestry, ordinary, pedigree **9** customary, hackneyed, inventory, livestock, provision, replenish **10** assessment, assortment, confidence, estimation **11** certificate, commodities, commonplace, merchandise, traditional **12** accumulation

STOCKADE: **3** can, pen **4** jail **5** fence **6** cooler, corral, kennel, prison **7** barrier **9** enclosure **10** protection

STOCK EXCHANGE: **11** stock market

major: **5** Tokyo **6** London, NASDAQ **7** New York, Pacific **8** American **9** Frankfurt **12** Philadelphia

STOCKING: **4** hose, sock **6** nylons **7** hosiery

STOCKPILE: **4** heap **5** amass, hoard, store **7** backlog, reserve **9** inventory **10** accumulate

STOCKY: **3** fat **5** husky, obese, plump, solid, squat **6** chubby, chumpy, chunky, stocky, stubby, sturdy **7** compact **8** heavyset, thickset

STODGY: **4** blah, dull, flat, prim **5** heavy, tacky, thick **6** boring, dreary, sticky, stuffy **7** lumpish, pompous, starchy, tedious **8** thickset **10** monotonous, uninspired **12** indigestible **13** unimaginative, uninteresting

STOIC: **4** calm, cool **6** stolid **7** patient, unmoved **8** detached **9** impassive, unruffled **10** phlegmatic **11** indifferent, philosophic, unconcerned, unflappable

STOICISM: **8** patience **9** fortitude **11** impassivity **12** indifference **13** impassiveness

STOKE: **4** feed, fuel, poke, stir, tend

STOLE: **3** fur **4** cape, robe, took **5** scarf **6** swiped **8** vestment **9** embezzled

STOLEN: **5** taken **6** lifted, robbed, swiped **7** poached **8** pilfered **9** embezzled **10** shanghaied

STOLID: **4** dull, slow **5** blunt, dense, stoic **7** brutish, deadpan, passive **9** apathetic, impassive, unfeeling **10** impassable, phlegmatic **11** insensitive, unemotional, unexcitable

STOMACH: **3** gut **4** bear, craw, crop **5** belly, brook, pouch, stand, taste, tummy **6** desire, endure, omasum, paunch **7** abdomen, gizzard, midriff, mindlow **8** abomasum, appetite, potbelly, tolerate **9** manyplies, reticulum **10** midsection, psalterium **11** breadbasket, inclination

STOMP: **4** jazz **5** dance, music, stamp, tread **7** trample

STONE: **3** gem **4** crag, jade, onyx, opal, pelt, rock, ruby, sand, seed **5** block, brick, flint, jewel, slate **6** cobble, gravel, marble, market, pebble, quartz **7** boulder, crystal, diamond, granite, mineral **8** boundary, monolith, sapphire **9** petrified
cutter: **6** jadder

STONED: **4** high **5** drunk **6** zonked **7** drugged **9** plastered **10** inebriated **11** intoxicated

STONEWALL: **5** stall **6** rebuff, resist **8** stubborn **9** obstinate **10** filibuster

STONY: **4** cold, firm **5** blank, cruel, rigid, rocky, rough, stern **6** jagged **7** adamant **8** hardened, obdurate, pitiless **9** petrified, unfeeling **10** inexorable, inflexible, unyielding **14** expressionless

STOOL PIGEON: **3** rat **4** fink, nark **5** decoy **7** stoolie **8** informer **10** tattletale

STOOP: **3** bow, dip, sag **4** bend, duck, lean, sink, tilt **5** deign, hunch, kneel, lower, porch, slant, slump, squat, swoop, yield **6** crouch, debase, resort, slouch, submit **7** decline, degrade, descend, succumb **8** overcome, platform **9** staircase **10** condescend

STOP: **3** bar, dam, end **4** calk, call, clog, cork, curb, halt, lull, plug, quit, rest, seal, stay, stem **5** block, brake, break, catch, caulk, cease, check, choke, close, delay, pause, repel, stall, tarry **6** anchor, arrest, behold, cutoff, defeat, desist, detain, finish, hinder, period, stanch **7** adjourn, caesura, layover, prevent, sojourn, station, staunch, suspend **8** blockade, conclude, obdurate, obstacle, obstruct, postpone, prohibit, restrain, suppress, withhold **9** barricade, cessation, hindrance, roadblock, terminate **10** conclusion, standstill **11** discontinue, obstruction **12** intermission, interruption

STOPGAP: **6** resort **8** resource **9** expedient, impromptu, makeshift, temporary **10** substitute **1** provisional

STOPPAGE: **4** halt **6** strike **7** embargo, lockout, walkout **8** blockage, gridlock, shutdown **9** cessation **10** standstill **11** curtailment, obstruction **12** interruption

STOPPER: **3** lid, wad **4** cork, fill, plug

STORE: **3** can **4** bank, bind, deli, fund, hold, mart, pack, pile, save, shop, stow **5** amass, cache, hoard, house, stash, stock **6** bottle, freeze, garner, gather, market, outlet, secure, shoppe, supply **7** collect, deposit, provide, reserve **8** boutique, emporium, reserves, showroom, squirrel, supplies, treasure **9** abundance, replenish, reservoir, resources, stockpile, warehouse **10** accumulate, collection, commissary, provisions, repository **11** supermarket

STOREHOUSE: **4** barn, shed, silo **5** cache, depot, etape **6** armory **7** arsenal, granary **8** building, magazine **9** warehouse **10** commissary, depository, repository

STOREKEEPER: **6** grocer **8** merchant, purveyor **10** shopkeeper **14** businessperson

STORM: **4** blow, fume, gale, gust, hail, rage, raid, rain, rant, rave, roar, rush, wind **5** anger, burst **6** assail, attack, charge, hubbub, shower, squall, strike, tumult **7** assault, barrage, besiege, bluster, cyclone, monsoon, rampage, tempest, thunder, tornado, trouble, turmoil, twister, typhoon **8** blizzard, downpour, eruption, outburst, surprise, upheaval, violence **9** commotion, hurricane, lightning **10** cloudburst **11** bombardment, disturbance

STORMY: **4** dark, foul, wild **5** gusty, rainy, rough, snowy, windy **6** bitter, raging, torrid **7** furious, howling, violent **9** inclement, turbulent **10** blustering, passionate, tumultuous **11** tempestuous, troublesome

STORY: **3** fib, lie **4** epic, lore, myth, news, play, plot, saga, tale, yarn **5** alibi, conte, drama, fable, floor, novel, rumor **6** legend, record, report, sequel, serial **7** account, article, episode, history, narrate, parable, recital, version **8** allegory, anecdote, folktale, scenario **9** falsehood, narration, narrative, statement **11** description, fabrication

STORYTELLER: **4** bard, liar **6** author, fibber, writer **8** minstrel, narrator **9** raconteur

STOUT: **3** ale, fat **4** beer, bold, firm, hard **5** brave, bulky, burly, hardy, heavy, husky, obese, plump, proud, pudgy, solid, tough **6** brawny, fleshy, heroic, portly, robust, rotund, stable, stanch, steady, stocky, strong, sturdy **7** defiant, gallant, staunch, valiant, weighty **8** athletic, enduring, fearless, forceful, insolent, muscular, powerful, resolute, stalwart, thickset, vigorous **9** corpulent, steadfast, strapping **10** courageous, determined, overweight **11** lionhearted, substantial

STOUTHEARTED: **4** bold **5** brave **6** heroic **7** valiant **8** fearless, intrepid, unafraid **9** dauntless, undaunted **10** courageous **11** lionhearted

STOVE: **3** gas **4** coal, kiln, oven, wood **5** range, stave **6** heater **7** furnace **8** electric **9** microwave, potbelly

STOW: **4** cram, fill, hide, hold, load, pack, save, stop **5** cache, crowd, lodge, place, stack, stash, store **6** bundle **7** arrange, contain, quarter

STRADDLE: **5** hedge, mount **6** sprawl, stride **8** bestride **12** noncommittal

STRAGGLE: **4** roam, rove **5** drift, stray, trail **6** dawdle, ramble, wander **7** meander

STRAIGHT: **4** even, fair, neat, tidy **5** blunt, erect, frank, level, plain, rigid, sound **6** candid, direct, honest, square, unbent **7** aligned, beeline, correct, factual, nonstop, orderly, unmixed, upright **8** accurate, directly, honestly, reliable, sequence, truthful, unbroken **9** honorably, undiluted **10** aboveboard, continuous, methodical, successive **11** consecutive, immediately, traditional, undeviating, unqualified **12** continuously, conventional **13** uninterrupted

STRAIGHTEN: **5** align, level, order **6** unbend **7** arrange, compose, rectify, unravel, untwist

STRAIGHTFORWARD: **4** easy, even **5** blunt, frank, plain **6** candid, direct, honest, simple **7** genuine, sincere **8** clearcut, directly, outright **9** outspoken **10** aboveboard **11** trustworthy

STRAIN: **3** air, irk, try **4** ache, balk, hint, kind, line, ooze, pain, pull, push, race, sift, song, sort, tone, tune, turn, type, vein **5** blood, breed, class, drive, exert, force, grind, heave, labor, music, press, sieve, stock, sweat, trace, track, trail, trait, twist **6** burden, deform, effort, extend, family, filter, injure, injury, melody, purify, refine, screen, sprain, streak, stress, strive, weaken, wrench **7** anxiety, confine, distort, fatigue, lineage, squeeze, stretch, tension, trickle, variety **8** ancestry, exertion, pressure, separate, struggle, tendency **9** constrain, constrict **10** suggestion

STRAINED: **4** taut **5** tense, tight **6** forced, uneasy **7** intense, uptight **8** volatile, weakened, wrenched **9** explosive, pretended **10** farfetched **11** antagonized, overwrought

STRAIT: **4** bind, pass **5** inlet, pinch **6** crisis, plight **7** channel, dilemma, isthmus, narrows **8** juncture **9** crossroad, stressful **10** difficulty **11** predicament

STRAITLACED: **4** prim **5** rigid, stiff **6** formal, prissy, proper, strict **7** prudish **11** puritanical

STRAND: **4** bank **5** beach, coast, fiber, leave, shore, tress, wreck **6** desert, ground, maroon, string, thread **8** filament

STRANDED: **7** aground, beached **8** castaway, helpless, marooned **9** abandoned **11** shipwrecked

STRANGE: **3** new, odd **4** rare **5** alien, eerie, fishy, kooky, novel, queer, weird **6** exotic, freaky, quaint **7** bizarre, curious, erratic, foreign, oddball, offbeat, uncanny, unknown, unusual **8** abnormal, peculiar, puzzling, singular, uncommon **9** different, eccentric, fantastic, unnatural, wonderful **10** mysterious, outlandish, unexplored, unfamiliar **11** exceptional **12** unaccustomed **13** extraordinary

STRANGER: **5** alien, guest **6** novice **7** drifter, visitor **8** intruder, newcomer, outsider **9** foreigner, immigrant, outlander

STRANGLE: **4** kill **5** choke, quell **6** muffle, quelch, stifle **7** garrote, repress, smother, squelch **8** garrotte, restrict, suppress, throttle **9** suffocate **10** asphyxiate

STRANGLEHOLD: **4** grip **5** choke **8** monopoly, restrict, suppress

STRAP: **4** band, beat, belt, bind, cord, flog, lash, rein, whip **5** leash, strop, thong **6** punish, secure **7** harness

STRAPPING: **5** burly, hefty, husky, stout **6** brawny, robust, strong, sturdy **8** powerful

STRATAGEM: **4** plot, ploy, ruse, wile **5** angle, dodge, fraud, slant, trick **6** device, scheme **7** finesse, gimmick **8** artifice, intrigue, maneuver **9** chicanery, deception **10** artfulness **11** machination

STRATEGIC: **5** vital **6** clever **7** cunning, planned **8** critical, tactical **9** important, necessary **10** calculated

STRATEGY: **4** plan **6** course, design, method, policy, scheme, system **7** tactics **8** approach, artifice, intrigue **9** procedure **11** maneuvering

STRATUM: **3** bed **4** seam, tier **5** class, group, layer, level **8** division

STRAW: **3** hat, hay **4** pipe, tube **5** chaff, color, grain **6** trifle **9** worthless, yellowish **11** meaningless, unimportant

STRAWBERRY: **5** color, fruit, plant **7** carmine, reddish
genus: **8** fragaria

STRAY: **3** err **4** roam, rove, veer, waif **5** drift, range **6** errant, ramble, random, swerve, wander **7** deviate, digress, meander, runaway **8** aberrant, homeless, isolated, sporadic, straggle **9** abandoned, straggler **10** occasional

STREAK: **4** band, blot, dash, hint, line, mark, rush, vein, zoom **5** fleck, layer, shade, smear, speed, tinge, touch, trace, trait **6** series, smudge, strain, strake, stripe, stroke **10** suggestion

STREAM: **3** run **4** burn, flow, flux, gush, pour, race, roll, rush **5** bourn, brook, creek, drift, flood, flume, issue, river, speed, surge, water **6** bourne, course, runlet, runnel, sluice, spritz **7** channel, current, rivulet **8** continue, effluent **10** succession **11** watercourse

STREAMER: **3** jet **4** flag **6** banner, pennon **7** pendant, pennant **8** banderol, headline

STREAMLINED: **5** sleek **6** smooth **10** modernized, simplified **11** aerodynamic

STREET: **3** way **4** drag, lane, road **5** alley, court, drive **6** avenue **7** highway, parkway, roadway **8** turnpike **9** boulevard **12** thoroughfare

STREETCAR: **4** tram **7** trolley

STREETWALKER: **5** whore **6** hooker **7** hustler **8** strumpet **10** prostitute

STRENGTH: **4** beef, kick, thew, will **5** asset, brawn, clout, force, might, power, sinew, spunk, valor, vigor **6** energy, muscle, spirit **7** potency, stamina **8** backbone, capacity, firmness, vitality **9** advantage, endurance, fortitude, influence, intensity, stability, stoutness, substance, toughness, vehemence **10** durability, robustness, sturdiness

STRENGTHEN: **3** add **4** back, beef, bind, help, prop **5** brace, steel **6** endure **7** bolster, confirm, enhance, fortify, improve, nourish, support, sustain, toughen **8** energize, heighten **9** encourage, reinforce **10** invigorate

STRENUOUS: **4** hard **5** tough **6** ardent, taxing, uphill **7** arduous, zealous **8** vigorous **9** demanding, difficult, energetic, laborious **10** exhausting

STRESS: **4** pain **5** force, press, worry **6** accent, assert, burden, strain, trauma, weight **7** anxiety, tension, urgency **8** distress, emphasis, exertion, pressure **9** emphasize, intensity, underline **10** accentuate, importance, resistance **12** apprehension, significance

STRETCH: **3** run **4** span, time, walk **5** crane, range, reach, scope, spell, stint, tract, while **6** bridge, course, expand, extend, length, limber, period, sprawl, spread, strain **7** distend, expanse, prolong, tension, tighten **8** distance, elongate, flexible, interval, lengthen, sentence, tautness **9** extension **10** elasticity, exaggerate

STRETCHER: **3** bed, cot **5** dooly **6** gurney, litter

STREW: **3** sow **4** toss **6** litter, spread **7** diffuse, scatter **8** disperse, sprinkle **9** broadcast, circulate **11** disseminate

STRICKEN: **4** hurt, sick **6** harmed **7** injured, smitten, wounded **8** disabled **9** afflicted **13** incapacitated

STRICT: **4** hard, true **5** exact, harsh, rigid, stern, stiff, tense, tight, tough **6** narrow, severe **7** austere, perfect, precise, upright **8** absolute, accurate, complete, exacting, faithful, rigorous, straight **9** confining, stringent, unsparing **10** inexorable, inflexible, oppressive, scrupulous **11** punctilious, puritanical, restricting, strait-laced, undeviating **12** disciplinary **13** authoritarian

STRIDE: **4** gait, pace, step, walk **5** march, stalk **7** advance, headway **8** progress **11** improvement

STRIDENT: **4** loud **5** harsh, noisy **6** shrill **7** grating, jarring, raucous **8** piercing **10** boisterous, discordant, vociferous **11** cacophonous

STRIFE: **4** feud, fray, spat **5** brawl, fight **6** battle, combat, fracas, static, unrest **7** contest, discord, dispute, hurling, quarrel, turmoil **8** argument, conflict, friction, squabble, struggle, upheaval **10** dissension **11** altercation, competition, controversy

STRIKE: **3** bat, box, fan, hit, pop, rap **4** bang, bash, bean, beat, belt, bump, clap, conk, dint, find, flog, hurt, lash, pelt, poke, rout, ship, slam, slap, slug, sock, swat **5** clash, clout, crash, knock, pound, punch, slash, smack, smear, smite, spank, trend, whack **6** assail, attack, attain, batter, buffet, hammer, picket, pierce, punish, stroke, thrash, thrust, wallop **7** assault, boycott, collide, protest, uncover, walkout **8** discover, struggle **9** penetrate

STRIKE BACK: **7** counter **9** retaliate

STRIKE DOWN: **4** fell, kill **6** cancel **12** incapacitate

STRIKING: **5** showy **7** telling **8** dazzling, handsome, powerful, stunning **9** arresting, beautiful **10** attractive, compelling, noticeable, remarkable, surprising **11** conspicuous, outstanding

STRING: **3** row **4** band, cord, file, line, rope **5** chain, queue, train, twine **6** series, strand, thread **8** sequence **10** conditions, succession

STRING ALONG: **3** toy **4** dupe, fool, hoax **5** agree, bluff, cheat, dally, flirt **7** deceive

STRINGENT: **4** grim, hard **5** harsh, rigid, stern, tight **6** severe, strict **7** binding **8** exacting, forceful **9** demanding **10** inflexible **11** constricted, restrictive

STRINGY: **4** long, ropy, wiry **5** gluey, gummy, lanky, tough **6** sinewy **7** fibrous, slender, spindly **10** threadlike

STRIP: **3** bar, rob **4** band, bare, flay, husk, peel, shed, skin, tear **5** clear, pluck, scale, shred **6** denude, divest, expose, length, ravage, reduce, remove, reveal, runway, stripe **7** deprive, despoil, disrobe, pillage, plunder, segment, uncover, undress **8** unclothe **9** dismantle, excoriate

STRIPE: **4** band, blow, flog, kind, lash, line, mark, sort, type **5** breed, strip **6** border, design, ribbon, streak, strike, stroke **7** chevron, pattern **8** division **10** decoration

STRIPLING: **3** boy, lad **5** minor, youth **9** fledgling, youngster **10** adolescent

STRIPPED: **4** bare, nude **5** naked **6** unclad **7** exposed **8** deprived **9** undressed

STRIVE: **3** aim, try, vie **4** push, seek, toil, work **5** exert, fight, labor **6** battle, buffet, strain **7** attempt, compete, contend, emulate **8** endeavor, struggle **9** undertake

STROKE: **3** bat, fit, hit, pat, pet, rap, rub **4** beat, blow, chop, feat, lash, mark, shot, swat, walk **5** brush, fluke, knock, power, rower, throb, whack **6** caress, effort, fondle, impact, soothe, stride, wallop **7** massage **8** apoplexy, movement **11** achievement

STROLL: **4** gait, roam, rove, turn, walk **5** amble, mosey, stray, tramp **6** linger, ramble, wander **7** meander, saunter **9** promenade

STROLLER: **4** pram **5** actor, buggy, tramp **6** beggar **7** vagrant **8** carriage, vagabond, wanderer **9** performer **12** perambulator

STRONG: **3** fit, hot **4** able, bold, firm, hard, keen, tart **5** burly, clear, eager, great, hardy, sharp, solid, sound, spicy, stout, tough **6** active, ardent, biting, brawny, cogent, hearty, heroic, mighty, potent, robust, rugged, sinewy, stable, sturdy, virile **7** durable, fertile, intense, piquant, pungent, staunch, violent, zealous **8** athletic, distinct, emphatic, explicit, forceful, forcible, muscular, powerful, resolute, resonant, stalwart, vigorous **9** difficult, effective, energetic, important, strapping, tenacious, undiluted **10** convincing, courageous, determined, forthright, outrageous, persuasive, pronounced, remarkable **12** concentrated, overpowering, unmistakable

STRONG-ARM: **5** bully, force **6** coerce **7** assault **8** browbeat, violence **9** terrorize **10** intimidate

STRONGBOX: **4** safe **5** vault **6** coffer **10** depository

STRONGHOLD: **4** fort **6** bunker, castle **7** bastion, bulwark, citadel, fortify, redoubt **8** fortress, garrison

STRONG POINT: **5** forte **6** talent **8** strength

STRUCK: **3** hit **7** pounded, smacked **8** affected

STRUCTURE: **4** form **5** frame, house, tower **6** bridge, design, fabric, format, makeup, scheme, system **7** complex, edifice, network, pattern, pyramid, texture **8** building, skeleton **9** framework **10** components, hierarchy, morphology, skyscraper **11** arrangement, composition, fabricature **12** construction, organization

STRUGGLE: **3** try, tug, vie, war **4** cope, duel, feud **5** brawl, clash, fight, grind, labor **6** battle, combat, effort, hassle, resist, strife, strike, strive, tangle, tussle **7** agonize, attempt, contend, contest, flounce, grapple, scuffle, warfare, wrestle **8** conflict, endeavor, exertion, flounder, scramble, skirmish

STRUMPET: **4** slut **5** hussy, wench, whore **6** harlot **10** prostitute **12** streetwalker

STRUT: **4** brag, gait, walk **5** brace, swank **6** flaunt, parade, prance, sashay, stride **7** flounce, peacock, swagger **10** grandstand

STUB: **4** bump, butt, snag **5** crush, stump **7** receipt, remnant **9** remainder **10** extinguish **11** counterfoil

STUBBORN: **4** firm **5** fixed, rough, tough **6** dogged, mulish, ornery, sturdy **7** adamant, diehard, willful **8** obdurate, resolute **9** difficult, obstinate, pigheaded, unbending **10** bullheaded, determined, hardheaded, headstrong, inexorable, inflexible, persistent, refractory, relentless, unyielding **11** opinionated **12** unreasonable **14** uncompromising

STUBBY: **5** dumpy, puggy, short, squat, stout **6** chubby, stocky, stumpy **8** heavyset, thickset

STUCK: **5** fixed, glued **6** caught, frozen, joined **7** baffled, puzzled, saddled, stumped, stymied **8** fastened **9** perplexed

STUCK-UP: **4** vain **5** cocky **6** uppity **7** haughty **8** arrogant, snobbish **9** bigheaded, conceited **10** disdainful, egocentric

STUD: **3** dot, peg, pin **4** beam, boss, buck, dude, male, post **5** brace **6** button, pillar **7** support, upright

STUDENT: **5** eleve, pupil **6** junior, senior **7** educand, learner, scholar **8** disciple, freshman **9** classmate, sophomore **13** undergraduate
divinity: **10** theologian
law: **8** stagiary
medical: **6** intern
military: **5** cadet, plebe **10** midshipman
Oxford: **8** commoner
residence: **4** dorm **5** house **6** hostel **9** dormitory
Talmudic: **5** bahur

STUDIO: **4** shop **5** salon, study **6** office **7** atelier, bottega **8** workroom, workshop

STUDIOUS: **7** bookish, heedful, learned, studied **8** academic, diligent **9** assiduous, attentive, contrived, scholarly **10** deliberate **12** intellectual

STUDY: **4** cram, look, mind, pore, read **5** grind, learn, watch **6** lesson, office, peruse, ponder, review, studio, survey **7** analyze, canvass, dissect, examine, explore, inspect, library, reflect **8** analysis, consider, meditate, memorize, research **10** schoolwork, scrutinize **11** contemplate, lucubration **13** consideration

STUFF: **3** jam, pad, ram **4** cash, cram, fill, gear, junk, load, pack **5** crowd, force, money **6** fabric, matter, refuse, things **7** element, essence, objects, overeat, squeeze **8** material, nonsense, overfill, overload **9** principle, substance **11** overindulge, possessions

STUFFING: **6** filler **7** filling, innards, insides, padding **8** dressing, feathers **9** forcemeat

STUFFY: **4** dull, prim **5** close, fusty, humid, muggy, musty, stale, stout, sulky **6** proper, stodgy **7** airless, crammed, pompous **8** arrogant, resolute, stagnant, stifling **11** puritanical, straitlaced, suffocating **12** conservative **13** uninteresting

STULTIFY: **6** impair, impede, stifle **7** cripple, inhibit, nullify **10** ridiculous

STUMBLE: **3** err **4** fall, slip, trip **5** botch, error, lurch, spill **6** bumble, chance, falter, happen, topple, wallow **7** blunder, failure, stagger, stammer **8** discover, flounder, hesitate **9** encounter

STUMBLING BLOCK: **4** snag **5** catch, hitch **6** hurdle **7** barrier, problem **8** drawback, obstacle **9** hindrance **10** impediment **12** complication

STUMP: **3** end **4** butt, dare, foil, plod, snag, stab, stub **5** barge, block, clump **6** baffle, hobble, lumber, puzzle, stymie **7** confuse, mystify, nonplus, perplex, stumble **8** bewilder **9** challenge

STUN: **4** daze, numb **5** amaze, shock **6** dazzle, deaden **7** astound, stagger, startle, stupefy **8** astonish, bewilder, dumfound, paralyze, surprise **9** overpower, overwhelm **11** flabbergast

STUNNING: **6** lovely, pretty **7** stylish **8** dazzling, gorgeous, handsome, shocking, smashing, striking **9** beautiful, marvelous **10** attractive **11** spectacular

STUNT: **4** curb, deed, feat, skit **5** antic, blunt, check, dwarf, stamp, trick **6** hinder, impede, sketch **7** curtail, exploit, shorten **8** suppress **10** acrobatics, undersized **11** performance

STUPEFY: **4** dull, faze, numb, stun **5** amaze, daunt, shock **6** bemuse, benumb, dazzle, rattle **7** astound, confuse, nonplus, startle **8** astonish, bewilder, confound, surprise **9** overwhelm **11** flabbergast

STUPENDOUS: **4** huge **5** giant, great **6** superb **7** amazing, immense, massive **8** colossal, enormous, fabulous, gigantic, terrific, wondrous **9** fantastic, marvelous, monstrous, wonderful **10** astounding, incredible, miraculous, phenomenal, remarkable, tremendous **11** astonishing, spectacular **13** extraordinary

STUPID: **4** clod, dull, dumb, slow **5** dazed, dense, dizzy, dopey, dunce, idiot, inane, moron, silly **6** absurd, oafish, obtuse, simple, torpid, unwise **7** asinine, brutish, daffish, doltish, fatuous, foolish, foppish, idiotic, moronic, vacuous, witless **8** blockish, cloddish, dumbbell, footless, ignorant, imbecile, sluggish **9** brainless, dimwitted, insensate, lethargic, pointless, senseless, simpleton, stupefied, worthless **10** irrational **11** meaningless **13** irresponsible, unintelligent

STUPOR: **4** coma, daze **5** faint, sleep, sopor, swoon **6** apathy, torpor, trance **7** languor, slumber **8** hypnosis, lethargy, narcosis **10** anesthesia

STURDY: **4** firm **5** hardy, solid, sound, stiff, stout, tough **6** brawny, robust, rugged, stable, steady, strong **7** durable, healthy **8** athletic, muscular, obdurate, powerful, resolute, stalwart, stubborn, vigorous **9** strapping **10** courageous, determined, unyielding **11** substantial

STURM UND DRANG: **6** unrest **7** ferment, turmoil **12** restlessness
translation: **14** storm and stress

STUTTER: **7** sputter, stammer, stumble **8** hesitate

STY: **3** den, pen **4** boil, dump **5** hovel, shack **6** pigpen

STYGIAN: **4** dark **6** dreary, gloomy **7** hellish **8** funereal, infernal

STYLE: **3** air, fad, pen, way **4** chic, elan, garb, kind, mode, name, rage, sort, tone, type **5** class, craze, flair, genre, grace, title, vogue **6** design, format, gnomon, manner, method, needle, phrase **7** diction, fashion, panache, pattern, variety, wording **8** demeanor, elegance **9** technique **10** appearance

STYLISH: **3** hip **4** chic, posh **5** nifty, sharp, sleek, slick, smart **6** chichi, classy, dapper, dressy, latest, modern, modish, snazzy, spiffy, swanky, trendy **7** a la mode, dashing, swagger **11** fashionable

STYMIE: **4** stop **5** block, cramp, stump **6** hinder, impede, puzzle, thwart **7** prevent **8** obstruct **9** frustrate, stonewall

STYX:
boatman: **6** Charon
father: **7** Oceanus
form: **5** river
location: **5** Hades **10** Underworld
mother: **6** Tethys
price to cross: **4** obol

SUAVE: **5** bland, civil, slick **6** polite, smooth, urbane **7** cordial, fulsome, politic, refined, tactful, worldly **8** charming, cultured, gracious, mannered, polished, unctuous **9** agreeable, courteous **10** diplomatic, pleasant **13** sophisticated

SUB: **5** below, under **6** backup, second **7** standby **9** alternate, auxiliary, submarine **10** understudy **11** replacement

SUBALTERN: **7** servile **8** inferior **9** assistant, secondary **11** subordinate

SUBCONSCIOUS: **4** mind, self **6** psyche **9** intuitive **10** subliminal

SUBDIVIDE: **8** separate **9** partition

SUBDIVISION: **4** part **6** branch, sector **8** subclass **10** department, subsidiary **11** development

SUBDUE: **4** beat, calm, tame **5** allay, break, crush, floor, quash, quell, sober **6** defeat, disarm, dismay, master, mellow, quench, reduce, soften, soothe **7** conquer, control, repress, squelch **8** diminish, moderate, overcome, restrain, suppress, surmount, vanquish **9** captivate, overpower, subjugate

SUBDUED: **4** mild, soft, tame **5** quiet, sober **6** mellow, solemn **7** humbled **8** tempered **10** controlled, restrained

SUBJACENT: **5** lower **7** beneath **10** underlying

SUBJECT: **4** core, gist, serf, test **5** cause, field, issue, motif, point, prone, study, theme **6** expose, liable, matter, motive, submit, vassal **7** citizen, exposed **8** disposed, follower, governed, inferior, material, obedient, question **9** dependent **10** contingent, discipline, discussion, submissive **11** accountable, conditional, subordinate

SUBJECTIVE: **6** biased **8** abstract, illusory, personal **9** emotional **10** individual, prejudiced **13** introspective

SUBJUGATE: **4** tame **5** break, crush **6** compel, defeat, master, subdue **7** conquer, enslave, triumph **8** overcome, suppress, vanquish **9** overpower, overthrow

SUBLIME: **4** high, holy **5** exalt, grant, great, ideal, lofty, noble **6** divine **7** dignify, exalted, stately **8** elevated, glorious, heavenly, majestic, splendid **9** spiritual **10** impressive **11** magnificent

SUBMARINE: **4** boat, hero **5** diver **6** hoagie **7** grinder **8** sandwich **11** submersible

SUBMERGE: **3** dip **4** dive, dunk, sink **5** douse, drown, flood, souse, swamp **6** deluge, drench, engulf, plunge **7** immerse, obscure **8** inundate, submerse

SUBMISSION: **8** meekness, yielding **9** obedience, servility, surrender **10** compliance, humbleness **11** prostration, resignation **12** acquiescence

SUBMISSIVE: **4** meek, mild, tame **6** humble **7** dutiful, obeying, passive, servile, slavish, subdued **8** obedient, resigned, yielding **9** compliant, complying **11** acquiescent, subservient, unassertive **13** accommodating

SUBMIT: **3** bow **4** bend, cave, fall, give, obey, urge **5** abide, agree, claim, defer, offer, stoop, yield **6** comply, resign, tender **7** contend, deliver, knuckle, present, proffer, propose, succumb, suggest **9** acquiesce, surrender **10** capitulate

SUBORDINATE: **5** minor **6** junior, lesser, subdue, worker **7** control, servant, subject **8** inferior, servient **9** ancillary, assistant, auxiliary, dependent, secondary, subaltern **10** subsidiary **11** subservient **13** supplementary

SUBORN: **5** bribe **6** incite **7** procure **9** instigate

SUB ROSA: **8** covertly, secretly **9** obscurely, privately **14** confidentially

SUBSCRIBE: **4** give, sign **5** agree **6** accept, assent, attest, pledge **7** approve, consent, endorse, support **8** advocate, sanction **9** signature **10** contribute

SUBSEQUENT: **4** next **5** after, later **7** ensuing **9** following, resultant **10** succeeding, successive **11** consecutive

SUBSEQUENTLY: **5** after, later, since **9** following **10** afterwards **12** consequently

SUBSERVIENT: **6** menial **7** fawning, servile, slavish, subject **8** cringing, obeisant, resigned **9** accessory, ancillary, auxiliary, compliant, secondary, truckling **10** obsequious, submissive **11** acquiescent, subordinate

SUBSIDE: **3** ebb **4** calm, fall, lull, sink, wane **5** abate, lower, taper **6** lessen, settle, shrink **7** descend, dwindle, slacken **8** decrease, diminish, moderate, withdraw

SUBSIDIARY: **5** minor **6** back-up, branch **8** division **9** accessory, affiliate, ancillary, auxiliary, secondary, tributary **10** collateral, supplement **11** subordinate

SUBSIDY: **3** aid **4** gift, help **5** grant, money **7** backing, pension, support, tribute **9** allowance **10** assistance, honorarium, subvention **11** sponsorship **13** appropriation

SUBSIST: **4** live, stay **5** exist **6** endure, manage, remain **7** breathe, support, survive, sustain **8** continue, maintain

SUBSISTENCE: **4** keep **6** living **7** support **8** survival **9** allowance, existence, resources **10** hypostasis, livelihood, provisions, sustenance **11** maintenance

SUBSTANCE: **4** body, core, gist, mass, pith, soul **5** basis, being, focus, heart, means, stuff, thing, worth **6** burden, entity, estate, fabric, marrow, matter, object, riches, spirit, wealth **7** element, essence, meaning, purport, reality **8** backbone, material, property, solidity, strength **9** affluence, resources **10** ingredient **12** significance

SUBSTANTIAL: **3** big **4** firm, full **5** ample, large, solid, sound, stout **6** hearty, strong, sturdy **7** massive, sizable, weighty **8** abundant, affluent, generous, material, tangible, valuable **9** corporeal, important, momentous, plentiful **10** meaningful **11** significant **12** considerable

SUBSTANTIATE: **5** prove, vouch **6** assure, attest, verify **7** confirm, justify, support **8** validate **9** establish **11** corroborate, demonstrate, materialize **12** authenticate

SUBSTITUTE: **4** swap **5** extra, proxy **6** backup, deputy, double, ersatz, second, switch **7** replace, reserve, standby **8** exchange **9** alternate, imitation, makeshift, surrogate **10** artificial, understudy **11** alternative, replacement, succedaneum

SUBSTRUCTURE: **4** base **10** foundation, groundwork **14** infrastructure

SUBSUME: **7** contain, include, involve **8** classify **11** incorporate

SUBTERFUGE: **4** plan, ploy, ruse, sham **5** cheat, fraud, trick **6** device, refuge, scheme **7** evasion **8** artifice, pretense **9** chicanery, deception, stratagem **10** dishonesty

SUBTERRANEAN: **4** cave **6** cavern, hidden, secret **9** concealed **11** underground

SUBTLE: **3** sly **4** cagy, deft, foxy, keen, wily **5** acute, quiet, sharp, slick **6** artful, clever, crafty, expert, shrewd **7** cunning, devious, elusive, logical **8** abstruse, analytic, indirect, skillful **9** beguiling, deceptive, ingenious, insidious, intricate **10** perceptive

SUBTRACT: **4** town **5** minus, urban **6** deduct, remove **7** suburbs **8** diminish, discount, environs, withdraw **9** outskirts

SUBVERSION: **8** sabotage **9** overthrow **10** disruption **11** undermining

SUBVERSIVE: **9** insurgent **10** rebellious, treasonous

SUBVERT: **4** ruin **5** rebel, spoil, upset **6** debase, topple **7** corrupt, destroy **8** overturn, sabotage **9** overthrow, undermine **10** infiltrate

SUCCEED: **3** win **4** reap **5** click, score **6** attain, follow, master, thrive **7** achieve, fulfill, prevail, prosper, replace, triumph **8** flourish, overcome, surmount **10** accomplish

SUCCESS: **3** hit **4** fame **6** reward **7** arrival, fortune, triumph, victory **9** celebrity, happiness **10** attainment, prosperity **11** achievement **12** breakthrough

SUCCESSFUL: **6** proven **7** booming, wealthy **8** smashing, thriving **9** satisfied **10** prosperous, triumphant, victorious **11** flourishing **12** accomplished

SUCCESSION: **3** run **5** chain, cycle, order, train **6** course, series, string **8** sequence **12** continuation

SUCCINCT: **4** curt **5** blunt, brief, short, terse **6** direct **7** compact, concise, summary **9** condensed

SUCCOR: **3** aid **4** help **6** assist, refuge, relief, rescue **7** comfort, nurture, relieve, support **8** befriend, mitigate **9** alleviate **10** assistance

SUCCULENT: **4** lush **5** fresh, juicy, sappy, tasty **6** tender **8** luscious **9** delicious **10** appetizing **13** mouthwatering

SUCCUMB: **3** die **4** drop, fall, quit **5** yield **6** accede, expire, perish, submit **7** decease **8** collapse **9** surrender **10** capitulate

SUCH: **4** like, some, that **5** alike **7** similar **8** parallel, specific **10** comparable, equivalent

SUCK: **3** sip **4** draw **5** drink, nurse **6** absorb, engulf, imbibe, inhale **7** extract, suction

SUCKER: **3** sap **4** boob, dupe, fool **5** chump, leech, patsy **6** pigeon, victim **8** lollipop, pushover **9** schlemiel

SUCKLE: **4** feed, rear **5** nurse **6** foster **7** nourish, nurture

SUCKLING: **4** babe, baby **6** infant **8** unweaned

SUDAN:
capital: **8** Khartoum
cities: **4** Juba **5** Kosti **6** Atbara **7** al-Obeid, Kassala **8** Omdurman **9** al-Qadarif, Port Sudan **10** Wadi Medani
conqueror: **11** Mohammed Ali
continent: **6** Africa
ethnic groups: **4** Arab, Beja, Beri, Daza, Fula, Golo, Nuer, Sere **5** Fulah, Hausa, Mossi **7** Nubiyan

features: **9** Sudd swamp **11** Nubia Desert **12** Libyan Desert, Nuba Mountain
former name: **5** Nubia
languages: **3** Ewe, Ibo, Kru **4** Beja, Efik, Mole, Nuer, Tshi **5** Dinka **6** Arabic, Nubian, Yoruba **8** Mandingo **10** Kordofaman
monetary unit: **5** dinar, pound
native: **8** Sudanese
water: **4** Nile

SUDDEN: **4** fast, rash **5** hasty, quick, swift **6** abrupt, speedy **7** hurried, instant **9** immediate, impetuous, impromptu **10** surprising, unexpected, unforeseen **11** precipitate

SUDDENLY: **6** presto **7** quickly, swiftly **8** abruptly **12** unexpectedly

SUDS: **4** beer, foam, soap **5** froth **6** lather **7** bubbles

SUE: **3** beg, woo **4** seek **5** claim, court, plead **6** appeal, summon **7** beseech, contest, entreat, proceed, solicit **8** litigate, petition **9** prosecute **10** supplicate

SUEZ CANAL:
builder: **9** de Lesseps
connects: **6** Red Sea **13** Mediterranean
place: **5** Egypt
ports: **6** Tawfiq **8** Damietta, Ismailia, Port-Said

SUFFER: **4** ache, bear, hurt **5** allow **6** accept, endure, grieve, lament, permit, submit **7** agonize, anguish, undergo **8** languish, tolerate **10** experience

SUFFERING: **4** hurt, loss, pain **5** agony, dolor, grief **6** ailing, misery, sorrow **7** illness, passion, torture, travail **8** distress, sickness **9** adversity **10** affliction, discomfort

SUFFICE: **4** meet **5** serve **6** answer, enough **7** appease, fulfill, satisfy **10** sufficient

SUFFICIENT: **4** able, good **5** ample, valid **6** enough, plenty **7** suffice **8** abundant, adequate **9** competent, efficient, plenteous, plentiful, qualified **10** acceptable **11** substantial **12** commensurate, satisfactory

SUFFOCATE: **4** kill **5** burke, choke, drown **6** stifle **7** destroy, smother **8** strangle, suppress, throttle **10** asphyxiate

SUFFRAGE: **4** vote **5** right, voice **6** ballot, prayer **8** petition **9** consensus, franchise

SUFFUSE: **4** fill **5** color, cover, steep **6** charge, spread **8** saturate **9** interject, introduce **10** overspread

SUGAR: **4** cane **5** candy, maple, money **6** friose, fucose, gulose, xylose **7** caramel, glucose, lactose, maltose, sucrose, sweeten, tetrose **8** dextrose, fructose **9** muscovado, sweetener **10** sweetheart
artificial: **6** allose **7** glucose **9** cyclamate, saccharin

SUGARY: **5** sweet **6** sticky, syrupy **7** candied, honeyed **8** granular, pleasant **10** flattering

SUGGEST: **4** hint, move, urge **5** imply, infer **6** advise, allude, broach, submit **7** connote, propose **8** indicate, intimate, propound, theorize **9** insinuate, recommend

SUGGESTION: **4** hint, idea **5** shade, tinge, touch, trace **6** advice **7** opinion, pointer **8** approach, overtone, proposal **9** undertone **10** intimation **11** implication **14** recommendation

SUGGESTIVE: **4** racy, sexy **5** dirty **6** erotic, risque, vulgar **8** symbolic **9** evocative, seductive **10** expressive **11** provocative, titillating

SUICIDAL: **5** fatal **6** deadly, lethal **9** dangerous, depressed **11** destructive

SUIT: **4** garb, plea **5** adapt, agree, befit, cards, dress, group, habit, match, serve, trial **6** adjust, answer, appeal, attire, become, behove, follow, outfit, please, prayer, series, tailor **7** apparel, arrange, behoove, clothes, conform, costume, satisfy, suffice, uniform **8** courting, ensemble, entreaty, petition, wardrobe **9** harmonize **10** correspond, litigation, proceeding **11** accommodate

SUITABLE: **3** apt, due, fit **4** able, good, just **5** right **6** comely, proper, timely, useful, worthy **7** apropos, fitting, seeming **8** adequate, becoming, eligible, matching, relevant **9** befitting, competent, consonant, expedient **10** acceptable, compatible, consistent, convenient **11** appropriate

SUITCASE: **3** bag **4** grip **5** brief **6** valise **7** satchel **11** portmanteau

SUITE: **3** set **4** band, flat **5** chain, group, rooms, staff **6** series **7** retinue **8** chambers **9** apartment, entourage, followers, furniture **10** attendants

SUITOR: **4** beau **5** asker, lover, wooer **7** admirer, gallant **9** boyfriend

SULFUR: **7** element

SULK: **4** mope, pout **5** brood, frown, grump **6** glower **7** grumble

SULKY: **4** cart, glum **5** moody, surly **6** dismal, gloomy, grouty, sullen **7** grouchy, peevish **8** carriage **9** irritable, withdrawn

SULLEN: **4** dour, dull, glum, grim, slow, sour **5** black, cross, heavy, moody, pouty, sulky, surly **6** crabby, dismal, gloomy, morose, silent, somber **7** forlorn, fretful, grouchy, peevish, serious **8** brooding, churlish, petulant, sluggish **9** saturnine **10** depressing, melancholy, sourpussed

SULLY: **4** blot, soil **5** smear, stain, taint **6** debase, defile **7** corrupt, pollute, tarnish **8** disgrace

SULTRY: **3** hot **4** sexy **5** close, humid, lurid, muggy **6** torrid **7** burning, sensual **8** sizzling, stifling **9** scorching **10** oppressive, sweltering, voluptuous

SUM: **3** add **4** gist, mass **5** count, gross, tally, total, value, whole, worth **6** amount, extent, figure, height, number, result **7** integer, measure, numeral, summary **8** addition, entirety, quantity, totality **9** aggregate, calculate, epitomize, magnitude, summarize, summation

SUMATRA:
animals: **4** balu, napu, tanu **5** orang **9** orangutan
cities: **6** Padang **9** Benkuelen, Palembang
features: **7** Barisan **8** Kerintji
place: **5** Sunda **9** Indonesia
water: **4** Musi, Toba **5** Jambi, Rokan **6** Asakan **9** Indragiri

SUMMARIZE: **3** sum **5** recap **6** digest **7** abridge, shorten **8** abstract, condense, nutshell **9** capsulize, epitomize **12** recapitulate

SUMMARY: **3** sum **4** gist **5** brief, recap, terse **6** digest, precis, report, resume, review, survey **7** concise, epitome, outline, rundown **8** abstract, overview, scenario, succinct, syllabus, synopsis **9** breakdown, condensed, inventory, summation **10** abridgment, compendium **11** abridgement **12** abbreviation

SUMMATION: **3** sum **7** summary **8** addition **9** aggregate

SUMMER: **4** beam **6** lintel, season
house: **6** alcove, gazebo, pagoda **7** cottage, retreat **8** pavilion
time: **4** July, June **6** August **9** September

SUMMERY: **4** warm **5** sunny **7** estival **8** aestival

SUMMIT: **3** cap, tip, top **4** acme, apex, peak, roof **5** crest, crown **6** apogee, climax, height, vertex, zenith **8** meridian, mountain, pinnacle **11** culmination

SUMMON: **3** bid **4** beck, call, page **5** evoke, order, rally, rouse **6** beckon, gather, motion, muster, notice, signal **7** command, convene, warrant **8** assemble, mobilize, subpoena

SUMMONS: **4** call, writ **6** notice **7** warrant **8** citation, subpoena **12** notification

SUMPTUOUS: **4** lush, rich **5** grand, plush **6** costly, deluxe, lavish **7** elegant, opulent **8** splendid **9** beautiful, expensive, grandiose, luxurious **11** extravagant, magnificent

SUN: **3** Sol **4** bask, star **5** shine **8** daylight
god: **3** Lug, Sol, Utu **4** Inti **5** Horus, Surya **6** Apollo, Helios **7** Shamash **8** Hyperion

SUNDA ISLANDS: **4** Bali, Java **5** Sumba, Timor **6** Borneo, Flores, Lombok, Madura **7** Sumatra, Sumbawa **8** Belitung, Sulawesi

SUNDER: **3** cut **4** part, rend, rive **5** break, sever, slice, split **6** cleave, divide **8** disunite, separate

SUNDOWN: **4** dusk **6** sunset **7** evening **8** twilight

SUNDRY: **4** many **6** divers, myriad, varied **7** diverse, several, various **8** assorted, manifold, numerous, separate, sundered **9** different **12** multifarious **13** miscellaneous

SUNFLOWER STATE: **6** Kansas

SUNKEN: **5** below **6** hollow **7** lowered **9** depressed, submerged

SUNLESS: **4** dark **5** bleak, rainy **6** gloomy **8** overcast **9** cheerless

SUNLIGHT: **3** day **8** daylight, sunshine

SUNNY: **4** fair, warm **5** clear, happy, merry, shiny **6** bright, cheery, golden **7** beaming, shining, smiling **8** cheerful, pleasant **9** vivacious **10** optimistic

SUNRISE: **4** dawn **5** sunup **7** morning **8** daybreak, daylight

SUNSET: **3** eve **4** dusk **7** evening, sundown **8** twilight **9** nightfall

SUNSET STATE: **6** Oregon

SUNSHADE: **5** visor **6** awning, canopy **7** parasol **8** umbrella **9** sunscreen

SUNSHINE: **5** light **6** warmth **8** daylight, sunbeams **9** geniality, happiness **12** cheerfulness

SUNSHINE STATE: **7** Florida **9** New Mexico **11** South Dakota

SUP: **3** eat **4** dine **5** drink, feast, munch **6** supper **7** swallow **8** mouthful

SUPER: **4** cool, keen, neat **5** great **6** superb **8** terrific **9** excellent, fantastic, marvelous, wonderful **10** tremendous **11** outstanding, sensational **14** superintendent

SUPERABUNDANCE: **4** glut **5** flood **6** excess, plenty **7** surplus **8** overflow, plethora **11** superfluity

SUPERABUNDANT: **6** lavish **9** excessive, exuberant **11** overflowing

SUPERANNUATE: **5** passe **6** retire **8** obsolete, outdated **9** antiquate

SUPERB: **4** fine, rich **5** grand, noble, proud, regal **6** lordly **7** elegant, stately, supreme **8** glorious, imposing, majestic, splendid, standout **9** excellent, exquisite, grandiose, luxurious, marvelous, wonderful **11** magnificent, outstanding, sensational

SUPERCILIOUS: **5** lofty, proud **6** lordly, uppity **7** haughty **8** arrogant, cavalier, insolent, snobbish, superior **10** disdainful **11** overbearing **13** condescending

SUPERFICIAL: **5** hasty, trite **6** casual, flimsy, hollow, slight **7** cursory, shallow, surface, trivial **8** apparent **9** desultory **13** insignificant

SUPERFLUITY: **6** excess, luxury **7** surplus **8** plethora **9** abundance **11** overflowing, superfluous **12** extravagance **13** overabundance **14** superabundance

SUPERFLUOUS: **5** extra, spare **6** excess **7** surplus, useless **8** needless **9** excessive, redundant, worthless **10** gratuitous **11** extravagant, inessential, superfluity, unnecessary **12** nonessential **13** superabundant

SUPERHUMAN: **5** great **6** divine, heroic **7** godlike, uncanny **9** herculean **10** omnipotent **12** supernatural **13** extraordinary, preternatural

SUPERINTEND: **4** boss, lead **5** guide **6** direct, manage **7** control, oversee **8** regulate **9** supervise **10** administer

SUPERINTENDENT: **4** boss **5** chief, super **6** warden **7** foreman, manager **8** director, overseer **9** caretaker, custodian, forewoman, inspector **10** supervisor **13** administrator

SUPERIOR: **4** boss, fine, head **5** chief, elder, upper **6** better, choice, deluxe, higher, senior, uppity **7** exalted, greater, haughty, premium **8** arrogant, dominant, elevated, insolent, snobbish **9** exceeding, excellent, exquisite, marvelous **10** noteworthy, preeminent, surpassing **11** exceptional, predominant **12** supercilious **13** condescending

SUPERLATIVE: **4** best, peak **6** utmost **7** highest, optimum, supreme **8** greatest, peerless **9** excellent, excessive, unequaled, unmatched **11** exaggerated, outstanding, unsurpassed

SUPERMAN: **9** Clark Kent
characters: **8** Lois Lane **10** Jimmy Olsen, Perry White

SUPERNATURAL: **5** magic **6** divine, mystic, occult **7** psychic, uncanny **8** abnormal, mythical **9** celestial, spiritual **10** miraculous, paranormal, phenomenal, superhuman **13** extraordinary, preternatural

SUPERSEDE: **7** abandon, discard, replace, succeed **8** displace, override, supplant

SUPERSTITION: **4** fear **5** magic **6** notion, voodoo **8** idolatry **13** irrationality

SUPERVISE: **4** boss **5** check, guide **6** direct, govern, manage **7** conduct, inspect, monitor, oversee **8** regulate **10** administer **11** superintend

SUPERVISION: **4** care **7** control **8** guidance **9** oversight **10** management

SUPERVISOR: **4** boss **5** chief **7** foreman, manager **9** forewoman **13** administrator

SUPINE: **4** flat **5** inert, prone **6** abject **7** languid, passive, sloping **8** inactive, inclined, indolent, listless, sluggish **9** apathetic, lethargic, prostrate, reclining **10** horizontal **11** inattentive, indifferent

SUPPER: **3** tea **4** meal **6** dinner

SUPPLANT: **4** oust **5** eject, usurp **6** depose, remove **7** replace, succeed **8** displace **9** overthrow, supersede, undermine **10** substitute

SUPPLE: **5** agile, lithe **6** limber, nimble, pliant **7** elastic, lissome, plastic, pliable, springy **8** bendable, flexible, graceful, stretchy, yielding **9** adaptable, compliant, malleable, resilient, versatile

SUPPLEMENT: **3** add **5** annex, arider **6** extend **7** augment, enhance **8** addendum, addition, additive, appendix **9** accessory, reinforce, subsidize **10** attachment, complement, strengthen

SUPPLIANT: **5** asker **6** beggar, seeker, suitor **9** solicitor **10** beseeching, petitioner

SUPPLICATE: **3** beg **4** pray **5** crave, plead **6** adjure, appeal **7** beseech, entreat, implore, request, solicit **8** petition **9** importune

SUPPLICATION: **4** plea **6** appeal, prayer **7** request **8** entreaty, petition **12** solicitation

SUPPLY: **3** aid **4** feed, fund, give, help, load **5** cache, equip, hoard, stock, store, yield **6** afford, outfit, purvey, relief, source **7** fulfill, furnish, nourish, produce, provide, replace, reserve, satisfy **9** inventory, provision, reinforce, replenish, reservoir, stockpile **10** contribute

SUPPORT: **3** aid **4** back, base, beam, bear, help, keep, lift, post, prop, side, stay **5** boost, brace, carry, cheer, hinge, shore **6** anchor, assist, column, crutch, defend, endure, foster, living, pillar, relief, second, shield, splint, tripod, trivet, uphold, verify **7** alimony, backing, bolster, cherish, comfort, confirm, console, embrace, endorse, nourish, nurture, protect, provide, subsidy, sustain **8** abutment, advocate, buttress, champion, maintain, pedestal, sanction, tolerate **9** encourage, patronize, reinforce, subsidize, vindicate **10** assistance, foundation, friendship, protection, strengthen **11** corroborate, countenance **12** substantiate

SUPPORTER: **4** ally **5** brace **6** backer, bearer, patron **7** abettor, booster, sponsor **8** adherent, advocate, champion, defender, disciple, exponent, follower **9** proponent, suspender **10** benefactor

SUPPOSE: **4** deem **5** allow, guess, imply, infer, judge, think **6** assume, deduce, expect, gather, reckon **7** believe, imagine, perhaps, presume, surmise, suspect **8** conceive, conclude, consider, theorize **9** intention, speculate **10** conjecture, understand **11** expectation, hypothesize

SUPPOSED: **7** alleged, assumed, reputed **8** presumed, probable, putative **11** conjectural, speculative **12** hypothetical, suppositious

SUPPOSITION: **4** idea **5** guess **6** belief, notion, theory, thesis **7** opinion, surmise **9** postulate **10** assumption, conjecture, estimation, hypothesis, likelihood **11** implication, presumption, proposition, speculation

SUPPRESS: **4** curb, hide, keep, kill, snub, stop **5** check, choke, crush, quash, quell, shush, stunt **6** arrest, bottle, bridle, censor, harass, muffle, squash, stifle, subdue **7** abolish, compose, conceal, control, curtail, destroy, exclude, oppress, prevent, refrain, repress, silence, smother, squelch **8** prohibit, restrain, strangle, withhold **9**

overpower, overthrow **10** extinguish

SUPREMACY: **4** sway **5** power **7** command, control, mastery **8** dominion **9** authority, dominance, masterdom **10** ascendancy, domination **11** omnipotence, sovereignty, superiority **12** predominance

SUPREME: **4** best, last **5** chief, first, prime **6** mighty, superb, utmost **7** crucial, highest, leading, maximum **8** absolute, flawless, foremost, greatest, peerless, towering, ultimate **9** excellent, important, paramount, sovereign, unequaled, unrivaled **10** preeminent **12** unparalleled

SURCEASE: **4** quit, rest, stay, stop **5** defer, delay, pause **6** desist **7** refrain, respite **8** postpone **9** cessation **11** discontinue **12** interruption

SURCHARGE: **3** tax **4** levy **6** burden, excise, impost **8** overfill, overload **10** overcharge

SURE: **3** rue **4** fast, firm, safe **5** solid **6** really, secure, stable, steady, strong **7** assured, certain, decided, staunch **8** absolute, definite, enduring, positive, reliable, unerring **9** confident, convinced, steadfast, undoubted, unfailing **10** dependable, guaranteed, inevitable, infallible, unshakable **11** indubitable, trustworthy, unfaltering **12** indisputable

SURELY: **6** really **9** assuredly, certainly **10** absolutely, definitely, inevitably **11** indubitably **12** conclusively

SURE THING: **4** fact

SURETY: **4** bail, bond **6** pledge, surity **7** promise, sponsor **9** assurance, certainty, certitude, guarantee, guarantor **10** confidence

SURFACE: **3** top **4** area, face, pave, skin **5** cover, crust, facet **6** facade, finish, veneer **7** outside **8** boundary, exterior **9** periphery **10** appearance **11** superficial

SURFEIT: **4** cloy, cram, glut, sate **5** gorge, stuff **6** excess, supply **7** replete, satiate, satisfy, surplus **8** overfeed, overfill, overkill **9** satiation **11** overindulge, superfluity **13** overabundance **14** superabundance

SURGE: **4** gush, pour, rise, roll, rush, tide, wave **5** flood, heave, mount, swell **6** billow **8** increase

SURGEON: **6** doctor **8** sawbones **9** physician

SURINAME:
capital: **10** Paramaribo
cities: **10** Brokopondo **13** Nieuw Nickerie **14** Nieuw Amsterdam
continent: **12** South America
ethnic groups: **6** Creole **8** Javanese **11** Hindustanis
features: **10** Tumuc-Humac
formerly: **11** Dutch Guiana
languages: **5** Dutch **6** Sranan **7** English **11** Sranantonga
monetary unit: **7** guilder
water: **5** Itany **6** Maroni **8** Suriname **9** Corantijn

SURLY: **4** dour, glum, rude, sour **5** cross, gruff, sulky, testy **6** crabby, crusty, grumpy, morose, sullen **7** bearish, boorish, grouchy, haughty, uncivil **8** churlish **9** irritable **10** ill-humored **12** discourteous

SURMISE: **4** deem **5** guess, infer, judge **6** notion **7** attempt, believe, imagine, opinion, presume, suppose **8** conclude **9** deduction, inference **10** assumption, conclusion, conjecture **11** hypothesize, speculation

SURMOUNT: **3** top **4** best, leap, rise **5** clear, climb, excel, outdo, scale **6** ascend, defeat, exceed, hurdle, master, subdue **7** conquer, prevail, surpass, triumph **8** overcome, vanquish **9** transcend

SURPASS: **3** cap, top **4** beat, best **5** excel, outdo **6** better, exceed, outrun **7** eclipse, outlive, outpace, outrank **8** outclass, outreach, outshine, surmount **9** transcend **10** outperform, overshadow

SURPLUS: **5** extra, spare **6** excess **7** overage, reserve, surfeit **8** leftover, overflow, plethora **9** overstock, remainder **10** oversupply **11** superfluity

SURPRISE: **4** blow, stun **5** alarm, amaze, floor, seize, shock, storm **6** ambush, dazzle, rattle, wonder **7** astound, fluster, miracle, nonplus, perplex, startle **8** astonish, bewilder, confound, dumfound, overcome, unsettle **9** bombshell, curveball, overwhelm **10** unexpected **11** flabbergast

SURRENDER: **4** cede, fall **5** waive, yield **6** resign, submit, vacate **7** abandon, cession, concede, forsake, succumb **9** acquiesce **10** capitulate, relinquish, submission **12** capitulation

SURREPTITIOUS: **6** covert, hidden, secret, sneaky **8** stealthy **9** concealed **10** undercover **11** clandestine

SURROGATE: **5** proxy **6** backup, deputy **8** delegate **9** alternate, expedient **10** substitute **11** replacement

SURROUND: **4** belt, gird, loop, ring, wrap **5** beset, hedge, round **6** border, circle, corral, encase, engulf, invest **7** besiege, compass, embosom, enclose, envelop, environ **8** encircle, inundate **9** encompass **10** circumvent **12** circumscribe

SURROUNDINGS: **6** milieu **7** climate, setting **8** ambience, vicinity **10** atmosphere, conditions **11** environment **12** neighborhood

SURVEILLANCE: **5** track, vigil, watch **6** spying **7** lookout **8** stakeout **11** observation

SURVEY: **4** poll, scan, view **5** audit, gauge, study **6** assess, review, sample, search **7** canvass, examine, inspect, measure, oversee **8** analysis, consider, estimate, evaluate, prospect **9** summarize **10** compendium, exposition, inspection, scrutinize **11** description, examination **13** questionnaire

SURVIVAL: **5** relic **9** endurance **12** continuation

SURVIVE: **5** exist **6** endure, remain **7** outlast, outlive, persist, weather **8** continue **9** persevere

SUSCEPTIBLE: **4** open **5** naive, prone **6** liable **7** exposed, subject **8** affected, allergic, gullible, inclined, sensible **9** receptive, sensitive **10** influenced, responsive, vulnerable **14** impressionable

SUSPECT: **5** doubt, fishy, guess, shaky, think **6** wonder **7** accused, believe, dubious, imagine, presume, suppose, surmise **8** distrust, doubtful, mistrust, question, theorize **9** discredit, uncertain **10** disbelieve, suspicious, understand **12** questionable

SUSPEND: **3** bar **4** halt, hang, hold, stop **5** cease, debar, defer, delay, expel, hover, swing, table **6** dangle, shelve **7** adjourn **8** postpone, withhold **9** eliminate, interrupt **11** discontinue

SUSPENDERS: **6** braces, straps **7** garters **8** galluses **10** supporters

SUSPENSE: **5** worry **6** unease **7** anxiety, mystery, tension **8** doubtful **11** uncertainty **12** anticipation, apprehension

SUSPENSION: **4** halt, stay, stop **5** delay, pause **8** abeyance, stoppage **9** remission **10** moratorium **11** termination **12** intermission, interruption, postponement

SUSPICION: **4** hint **5** doubt, hunch, shade, tinge, touch, trace **6** notion **7** caution, concern, feeling, inkling, surmise **8** distrust, jealousy, mistrust **9** misgiving **10** intimation, skepticism, uneasiness **11** uncertainty **12** apprehension

SUSPICIOUS: **4** wary **5** fishy, leery, shady, shaky **7** suspect **8** doubtful **9** skeptical **10** farfetched **11** distrustful, mistrustful **12** questionable

SUSTAIN: **4** abet, back, bear, feed, help, prop **5** abide, brace **6** endure, foster, suffer, supply, uphold **7** bolster, comfort, confirm, console, contain, nourish, nurture, prolong, support, survive, undergo **8** continue, maintain, preserve, tolerate **9** encourage, withstand **10** experience, strengthen **11** corroborate

SUSTENANCE: **4** meat **5** bread, means **6** living, upkeep **7** aliment, support **9** nutrition **10** provisions **11** maintenance, nourishment, subsistence

SUTURE: **3** sew **4** line, seam **5** joint **6** stitch

SVELTE: **4** lean, slim, thin, trim **5** lithe **6** smooth **7** lissome, shapely, slender **8** graceful

SWAB: **3** mop **4** daub, wash, wipe **5** clean **6** cotton, sailor, scrupt, sponge **8** specimen

SWADDLE: **4** bind, warp, wrap **6** swathe **7** bandage **8** restrain, restrict

SWAG: **4** loot **5** booty, graft, money **6** bundle, spoils **7** curtain, festoon, plunder **10** decoration

SWAGGER: **4** brag **5** boast, bully, gloat, strut, swank, swell **6** hector, parade, prance, sashay **8** browbeat **9** gasconade **11** braggadocio, pontificate, swashbuckle

SWAIN: **3** boy **4** beau **5** lover, wooer **6** suitor **7** admirer, gallant **8** shepherd **9** boyfriend

SWALLOW: **3** eat, sip **4** bear, bird, down, gulp, swig, take **5** drink, quaff, swill **6** absorb, accept, devour, engulf, gobble, guzzle, imbibe, ingest, inhale **7** believe, consume, repress **8** chugalug, suppress, tolerate, withdraw

SWAMP: **3** bog, fen **4** mire, moor, moss, muck **5** bayou, flood, glade, marsh, swale **6** deluge, engulf, morass, muskeg, slough **8** inundate, overcome, quagmire, saturate, submerge **9** everglade, marshland, overwhelm

SWAN: **4** bird **7** whooper **9** trumpeter
family: **8** Anatidae
female: **3** pen
genus: **4** olor **6** cygnus
male: **3** cob
young: **6** cygnet

SWANK: **5** grand, ritzy, sharp, showy, strut **6** classy, snappy **7** elegant, stylish, swagger **11** fashionable, pretentious **12** ostentatious

SWANKY: **4** chic, posh **5** fancy, plush, smart **6** chichi, flashy, snappy, snazzy, spiffy **7** elegant **9** exclusive, glamorous, luxurious

SWAP: **5** trade **6** barter, switch **8** exchange **10** substitute

SWARM: **4** army, mass, move, pack, rush, shin, teem **5** crowd, drove, flock, group, horde **6** infest, myriad, throng **7** migrate, overrun, turnout **8** assemble **9** multitude **10** congregate

SWARTHY: **4** dark **5** dusky, swart **7** darkish **11** dark-skinned

SWASHBUCKLER: **6** pirate **7** ruffian, soldier **9** buccaneer, daredevil, swordsman **10** adventurer

SWAT: **3** bat, hit **4** bash, beat, belt, blow, slug **5** smack, smash, whack **6** strike, wallop **7** clobber

SWATHE: **4** bind, wrap **5** cover, drape **6** enfold **7** bandage, swaddle

SWAY: **4** bend, bias, lead, lean, move, reel, rock, rule, veer **5** clout, guide, power, reach, shake, swing, waver, weave **6** affect, direct, divert, govern, prompt, swerve, totter, waddle, wobble **7** command, control **8** dominion, motivate, persuade **9** authority, dominance, influence, oscillate, vacillate **11** fluctuation

SWAZILAND:
capital: **7** Mbabane
cities: **7** Big Bend, Manzini
continent: **6** Africa
ethnic groups: **4** Zulu **5** Bantu, Swazi
features: **7** Lowveld, Lubombo **8** Highveld
languages: **5** Swazi **7** English, Siswati
monetary unit: **9** lilangeni
water: **5** Usutu **6** Komati **8** Umbuluzl

SWEAR: **3** vow **4** bind, cuss, oath **5** curse, vouch **6** adjure, affirm, assert, attest, pledge, threat **7** declare, promise, testify **9** blaspheme, expletive

SWEAT: **4** emit, fume, ooze, seep, toil, work **5** exude, hoist, labor **6** drudge, endure, fleece, strain **7** agonize, excrete, extract, ferment, swelter **8** overwork, perspire, transude **11** diaphoresis **12** perspiration

SWEATY: **3** wet **6** clammy, soaked, sticky **8** dripping **10** perspiring

SWEDEN:
bread: **10** knackebrod
capital: **9** Stockholm
cities: **5** Malmo, Ystad **7** Uppsala **8** Goteborg, Nykoping, Vasteras **10** Norrkoping
continent: **6** Europe
ethnic groups: **4** Lapp **7** Finnish, Swedish
explorer: **5** Hedin
features: **7** Riksdag **10** Kebnekaise **12** Kjolen Sarjek
islands: **5** Oland **7** Gotland
language: **7** Swedish
monetary unit: **5** krona
song: **5** yodel
water: **3** Uri **5** Rhine **6** Geneva **7** Lucerne **8** Maggiore **9** Constance

SWEEP: **3** fly **4** bend, dart, span, zoom **5** broom, brush, clean, curve, glide, orbit, range, scope, scour, swoop, whisk **6** extend, extent, remove, search, vacuum **7** compass, stretch **8** traverse

SWEEPING: **3** all **4** vast **5** broad **7** general, radical **8** complete **9** embracing, extensive, inclusive **10** large-scale, widespread **13** comprehensive, thoroughgoing

SWEET: **4** dear, kind **5** candy, fresh **6** dulcet, gentle, lovely, pretty, sugary, syrupy **7** angelic, beloved, darling, dessert, honeyed, lovable, musical, scented, winsome **8** aromatic, charming, euphenic, fragrant, heavenly, luscious, pleasant, pleasing, soothing **9** agreeable, ambrosial, wholesome **10** attractive, confection, delectable, harmonious, thoughtful **11**

considerate, mellifluous **12** affectionate

SWEETEN: **4** mull **5** honey, renew, sugar **6** pacify, soften, soothe **7** appease, cleanse, enhance, freshen, perfume, relieve **8** increase **9** alleviate, disinfect, sugarcoat **10** conciliate

SWEETHEART: **4** beau, dear, doll, love **5** flame, honey, lover, swain **6** adorer, suitor **7** darling, fiancee **8** paramour, truelove **9** boyfriend, companion, dreamboat, inamorata, inamorato, valentine **10** girlfriend

SWEETS: **5** candy **7** goodies **8** desserts **9** preserves **10** sweetmeats **13** confectionery

SWEET TALK: **4** coax **7** blarney **8** cajolery, flattery **10** compliment

SWELL: **4** bulk, fine, good, grow, huff, keen, puff, rise, surf, wave **5** bloat, bulge, dandy, grand, nifty, super, surge **6** billow, dilate, expand, extend, groovy **7** amplify, augment, awesome, balloon, distend, enlarge, inflate, stylish **8** fabulous, increase, terrific **9** excellent, intensify, marvelous, wonderful **10** accumulate **11** fashionable **12** protuberance

SWELLING: **3** sty **4** boil, bubo, bump, corn, lump, node, wart **5** bulge, tumor **6** growth **7** abscess, gibbous **9** contusion, puffiness **12** inflammation

SWELTER: **4** boil, burn, fret, heat, stew **5** roast, sweat **6** wallow **8** languish, perspire **9** suffocate

SWELTERING: **3** hot **5** humid, muggy **6** sticky, sultry, torrid **7** airless, burning **8** sizzling, stifling **9** scorching **10** oppressive

SWERVE: **4** skew, turn, veer **5** avert, shift, stray **6** totter **7** deflect, deviate, digress, diverge **8** sidestep

SWIFT: **4** fast, reel **5** brisk, fleet, hasty, quick, rapid, ready **6** flying, prompt, pronto, snappy, speedy, sudden **8** headlong **10** barrelling **11** expeditious

SWIG: **4** gulp, sway **5** draft, drink, hoist, swash **6** guzzle

SWILL: **4** fill, mash, raft, slop, wash **5** drink, flood, rinse, swash **6** drench, guzzle **7** garbage, hogwash, rubbish **8** nonsense

SWIM: **3** dip **4** reel, spin, wade **5** float **6** abound, paddle

SWIMMING: **5** sport **6** natant **7** bathing **8** floating **9** dizziness
stroke: **4** back, side **5** crawl **6** breast **7** trudgen **9** butterfly, dogpaddle

SWINDLE: **3** con, gyp **4** bilk, dupe, fake, fool, rook, scam, sham **5** cheat, fraud, spoof, steal, trick **6** hustle **7** deceive, defraud **8** embezzle, flimflam **9** bamboozle, blackmail, shakedown, victimize

SWINDLER: **5** cheat, crook, knave, rogue, shark, thief **6** forger **7** grifter, scammer **8** chiseler, finagler, imposter, impostor **9** charlatan **10** mountebank

SWINE: **3** hog, pig, sow **4** boar **5** beast, brute

SWING: **4** beat, hang, move, rock, sway, turn, whip **5** knack, lurch, pivot, tempo, waver, whirl **6** dangle, handle, manage, rhythm, rotate, stroke, swivel, totter, wobble **7** flutter, suspend, trapeze, vibrate **8** maneuver, undulate **9** fluctuate, oscillate

SWIPE: **3** hit **4** bash, blow, lift, swat **5** filch, heist, lever, steal **6** pilfer, snatch, strike, stroke

SWIRL: **4** curl, eddy, roil, spin, turn **5** churn, curve, twirl, twist, whirl **6** rotate **9** whirlpool

SWISH: **4** cane, flog, hiss, posh, whip **5** smart, sound, swank **6** classy, rustle, strike, trendy **7** stylish **9** exclusive **11** fashionable

SWITCH: **3** rod **4** beat, flog, lash, swap, turn, twig, wand, whip **5** flail, shift, stick, trade **6** change, divert, strike **8** exchange, reversal, transfer **9** rearrange, sidetrack, turnabout **10** substitute

SWITZERLAND:
capital: **4** Bern
cheeses: **7** Gruyere **10** Emmentaler
cities: **5** Basel **6** Geneva, Zurich **8** Lausanne **9** Neuchatel
concerning: **5** Swiss **6** Suisse **7** Schweiz **8** Helvetia
continent: **6** Europe
features: **4** Alps, Jura **9** Apennines **10** Matterhorn **12** Dufourspitze
languages: **6** French, German **7** Italian
monetary unit: **5** franc
people: **4** Jung, Klee, Tell
song: **5** yodel
water: **3** Uri **5** Rhine **6** Geneva **7** Lucerne **8** Maggiore **9** Constance

SWIVEL: **4** spin, turn **5** pivot, swing, whirl **6** rotate

SWOLLEN: **5** blown, bulgy, puffy, tumid **6** paunch, turgid **7** bloated, bulging, pompous **8** enlarged, inflamed, inflated **9** bombastic, distended, increased, overblown, tumescent

SWOON: **4** coma, fade **5** faint, float, sleep **6** stupor **7** ecstasy, syncope **8** blackout, languish **11** overwhelmed

SWOOP: **4** dive, drop, grab **5** sweep **6** plunge, pounce **7** descend, plummet

SWORD: **4** dirk, epee, foil, kris **5** bilbo, blade, brand, saber **6** creese, cutlas, dagger, rapier, toledo, weapon **7** cutlass, hanbger **8** claymore, falchion, scimitar, yalaghan **10** broadsword

SWORDSMAN: **6** dueler, fencer **9** gladiator

SWORN: **5** bound **6** avowed **8** affirmed **9** confirmed

SYBARITE: **7** epicure **8** hedonist **10** sensualist, voluptuary

SYCOPHANT: **5** toady **6** fawner, flunky, lackey, stooge, yes-man **8** parasite **9** flatterer **10** bootlicker, brownnoser

SYLLABLE:
accented: **5** arsis
beginning: **6** prefix
deleted at end: **10** catalectic
deleted: **7** apocope
ending: **6** suffix, ultima
next to last: **6** penult
second to last: **10** antepenult
short: **4** mora **5** breve **7** apocope, elision, systole
unaccented: **6** atonic

SYLLABUS: **4** plan **6** digest, precis **7** outline, program, summary **8** abstract, synopsis **9** statement **10** compendium

SYLVAN: **5** shady, woody **6** rustic, wooded **10** forestlike

SYMBOL: **4** icon, logo, mark, sign, type **5** badge, creed, cross, image, motif, stamp, token, totem **6** emblem, figure, letter, mascot **7** diagram, gesture, numeral **9** attribute, character, trademark **10** hieroglyph, indication **14** representation

SYMBOLIZE: **4** mean **6** embody, mirror, typify **7** connote, express, signify, suggest **9** emblemize, epitomize, personify, represent **10** illustrate

SYMMETRICAL: **5** equal **7** regular **8** balanced **12** proportional **13** commensurable

SYMMETRY: **5** order **6** beauty, rhythm **7** balance, harmony **8** evenness **9** agreement, congruity **10** conformity, proportion **11** equilibrium

SYMPATHETIC: **4** kind, soft, warm **6** caring, humane, tender **7** pitying **8** amenable, friendly **9** benignant, condolent, congenial, consonant, sensitive **10** altruistic, comforting, responsive, thoughtful **12** affectionate **13** compassionate, understanding

SYMPATHIZE: **4** pity **7** condole, feel for, support **9** empathize **10** understand **11** commiserate

SYMPATHY: **4** pity **5** favor **6** accord, solace, sorrow, warmth **7** comfort, empathy, harmony, support **8** affinity, kindness **9** agreement **10** compassion, condolence, tenderness **11** sensitivity **13** commiseration, understanding

SYMPHONY: **4** band **5** music **7** concert, harmony **9** orchestra

SYMPOSIUM: **5** forum **6** debate, parley **7** banquet, meeting **10** conference, discussion

SYMPTOM: **4** ache, pain, mark, sign **5** fever, token **6** signal **7** warning **8** evidence, syndrome **10** indication

SYNAGOGUE: **4** shul **5** schul **6** church **8** assembly, building, religion **9** community **12** congregation

SYNCHRONIZE: **5** agree **6** concur **8** coincide **12** simultaneous

SYNCHRONOUS: **9** identical **10** coexistent, concurrent **11** concomitant **12** contemporary, simultaneous

SYNDICATE: **4** gang, pool, ring **5** chain, group, trust, union **6** cartel **7** company, council **8** alliance **9** coalition, committee **11** association, congomerate **12** organization

SYNDROME: **6** malady **7** ailment, disease, problem, symptom **8** disorder, sickness **9** condition

SYNOD: **4** body **7** council, meeting **8** assembly, conclave **9** committee **11** convocation

SYNONYMOUS: **4** like **5** alike **7** similar **9** identical **10** equivalent **13** correspondent **15** interchangeable

SYNOPSIS: **4** plan, view **5** brief **6** apercu, digest, precis, review **7** epitome, outline, rundown, summary **8** abstract, syllabus **10** compendium **11** abridgement

SYNTAX: **5** order, rules **6** system **7** pattern **9** structure **11** arrangement

SYNTHESIS: **5** blend, union, whole **7** forming **9** deduction, structure **11** combination, composition **12** organization

SYNTHESIZE: **4** fuse **5** blend **7** combine **9** integrate **10** amalgamate **11** incorporate, manufacture

SYNTHETIC: **7** man-made **8** prepared **9** contrived, unnatural **10** artificial, fabricated **11** constructed **12** manufactured

SYRIA:
ancient name: **4** Aram
capital: **8** Damascus
cities: **4** Hama **5** Horns **6** Aleppo **7** Antioch, Latakia
continent: **4** Asia
deity: **4** Baal **5** Allat **6** Mammon **7** Resheph
ethnic groups: **4** Arab, Kurd **5** Druse **7** Ansarie, Armeman, Saracen
features: **4** Dura **6** Ugarit **7** Palmyra **11** Mount Hermon **12** Golan Heights

languages: **6** Arabic **7** Kurdish **8** Armenian
monetary unit: **5** pound
native: **6** Syrian
water: **3** Asi **5** Merom **6** Barada, Jordan **7** Orontes **8** Tiberias **9** Euphrates

SYRUP: **7** glucose, sorghum, treacle **8** molasses **9** sweetness

SYSTEM: **4** code, plan, rule **5** order, setup, whole **6** manner, method, scheme, theory **7** network, pattern, process, regimen, routine **8** strategy **9** operation, procedure, technique **10** hypothesis, philosophy **11** aggregation, arrangement, orderliness **12** organization **14** classification

SYSTEMATIC: **4** neat **7** logical, ordered, orderly **8** designed **9** efficient, organized **10** analytical, methodical **12** businesslike, standardized

SYSTEMATIZE: **4** plan **5** order **6** design **7** arrange, catalog **8** classify, organize **9** methodize **11** alphabetize, rationalize

T

TAB: **3** tag **4** bill, clip, cost, flap, loop **5** check, label, price, score, strip, tally **6** market, record **7** account, invoice **8** bookmark **9** statement

TABBY: **3** cat **4** silk **5** kitty **6** fabric, gossip, kitten **8** spinster

TABERNACLE: **4** tent **5** niche **6** church, shrine, temple **7** shelter **9** reliquary, sanctuary **10** habitation **13** house of prayer

TABLE: **4** desk, fare, food, list, slab **5** bench, board, chart, defer, delay, graph, index, stand **6** buffet, record, shelve, spread **7** console, counter, lectern **8** appendix, schedule, synopsis, tabulate **9** furniture, secretary, sideboard **10** escritoire

TABLEAU: **4** view **5** image, scene **7** picture **11** description **12** illustration

TABLET: **3** pad **4** book, pill, slab **5** slate **6** pellet, plaque, troche **7** capsule, lozenge **8** medicine, notebook

TABLEWARE: **3** cup **4** bowl, disk, fork **5** china, glass, knife, plate, spoon **6** saucer **8** utensils **10** silverware

TABOO: **3** ban **4** tabu **6** outlaw **7** illegal **8** anathema **9** forbidden, restraint **10** prohibited, proscribed, regulation **11** prohibition, restriction **12** interdiction, unacceptable **13** unmentionable

TABULATE: **4** list, rank **5** chart, grade, index, order **6** figure **7** arrange **8** classify **10** categorize

TACIT: **6** silent **7** implied **8** allusive, implicit, inferred, unspoken **9** intimated, suggested **10** understood **11** unexpressed

TACITURN: **4** mute **5** aloof, quiet **6** silent **7** laconic, unvocal **8** reserved, reticent **9** withdrawn **10** speechless **12** closemouthed, unexpressive

TACK: **3** pin **4** brad, clap, link, nail, rope, slap, turn, veer **5** baste, shift, strip, unite **6** append, attach, course, fasten, method, secure, tackle, zigzag **7** bearing, connect **8** approach **9** thumbtack **10** deflection, digression, stickiness, supplement

TACKLE: **4** gear, sack, stop, tack **5** grasp, tools **6** attack, collar, launch, outfit, secure **7** attempt, derrick, grapple, harness, rigging

8 linesman, material 9 apparatus, encounter, equipment, undertake 13 accoutrements, paraphernalia

TACKY: 5 cheap, crude, dowdy, gaudy, messy, ratty 6 grubby, ragged, shabby, sticky, untidy, vulgar 7 unkempt 8 adhesive, slovenly 9 tasteless

TACT: 5 poise 6 acumen 7 finesse, suavity 8 delicacy, judgment 9 diplomacy 10 adroitness, discretion, perception, refinement, smoothness 11 discernment, savoir-faire, sensitivity 14 discrimination

TACTFUL: 5 suave 7 careful, politic 8 discreet, polished, skillful 9 sensitive 10 diplomatic, thoughtful 11 considerate

TACTICAL: 7 prudent, tactics 9 expedient 10 diplomatic

TACTICS: 4 plan 6 attack, method, policy, system 8 approach, maneuver, strategy 9 procedure, technique

TACTLESS: 4 rude 5 brash, crude, gruff 6 clumsy 8 careless, impolite 10 indiscreet 11 insensitive, thoughtless 12 discourteous, undiplomatic 13 inconsiderate

TAG: 3 add, dog, tab 4 flap, game, logo, mark, stub, tail 5 affix, badge, brand, label, motto, strip, title, touch 6 append, attach, fasten, follow, pursue, shadow, ticket 7 sticker, voucher 8 identify, identity, nickname 9 accompany, designate

TAHITI:
capital: 7 Papeete
ethnic groups: 10 Polynesian
explorers: 4 Cook 5 Bligh
features: 7 Orohena
place: 14 Society Islands 15 French Polynesia

TAIL: 3 end, tag 4 back, butt, last, rear, seat 5 cauda, stalk, trail 6 bottom, follow, pursue, rudder, shadow 7 retinue 8 backside, buttocks 9 appendage, extremity, posterior 10 conclusion

TAILOR: 3 sew 5 adapt, alter, shape, style 6 adjust, design, modify, sartor 7 conform, fashion 8 clothier 10 dressmaker, seamstress

TAINT: 4 blow, blur, harm, hurt, ruin, soil, spot, tint 5 cloud, color, dirty, imbue, prave, smear, spoil, stain, sully, tinge, touch, trace 6 damage, defile, infect, poison, smudge, stigma 7 blemish, corrupt, pollute, tarnish, vitiate 8 disgrace 9 discredit 11 contaminate

TAINTED: 6 impure, rotten, soiled 7 damaged, decayed, stained 8 diseased 12 contaminated

TAIWAN:
capital: 6 Taipei
cities: 6 Tainan, Taipei 7 Chilung, Keelung 8 Taichung 9 Kachsiung
continent: 4 Asia
ethnic groups: 7 Chinese 9 Taiwanese
formerly: 7 Formosa
island groups: 4 Mazu 5 Matsu 6 Jinman, Penghu, Quemoy 10 Pescadores
languages: 5 Hakka 6 Taiwan 15 Mandarin Chinese
monetary unit: 6 dollar
water: 5 Wuchi 6 Tachia 7 Pacific, Tanshui 12 East China Sea: 13 South China Sea

TAJIKISTAN:
capital: 8 Dushanbe
cities: 9 Khodzhent
continent: 4 Asia
ethnic groups: 5 Tajik, uzbek 7 Russian 9 Ukrainian
features: 13 Communism Peak
monetary unit: 5 ruble

TAKE: 3 buy, get, gyp, nab, net, try, win 4 bear, bilk, draw, gate, grab, grip, haul, have, rick, root, trap 5

adopt, avail, booty, carry, catch, charm, cheat, grasp, gross, infer, seize, share, snare, steal, swipe, touch, usurp **6** absorb, accept, affirm, attach, attack, attain, borrow, choose, convey, deduce, deduct, derive, endure, engage, income, kidnap, obtain, pilfer, pocket, prefer, profit, remove, secure, select, snatch, strike, submit **7** attempt, attract, capture, conduct, deceive, defraud, detract, enchant, extract, plunder, revenue, stomach, swallow, swindle, undergo **8** contract, proceeds, quantity, receipts, subtract, tolerate **9** accompany, apprehend, captivate, fascinate, transport, withstand **10** commandeer, confiscate, understand **11** appropriate

TAKE ABACK: **7** startle **8** astonish, surprise **9** overwhelm

TAKE ADVANTAGE: **4** dupe, fool **7** deceive, exploit

TAKE AFTER: **4** copy **6** follow **7** emulate, imitate **8** resemble, simulate

TAKE APART: **4** ruin **6** thrash **7** analyze, destroy, dissect **11** disassemble

TAKE AWAY: **5** minus, seize **6** deduct, lessen, reduce **7** detract **8** decrease, diminish, discount, subtract

TAKE BACK: **6** abjure, recant, renege, return **7** restore, retract, reverse **8** withdraw **9** repossess

TAKE CARE: **4** heed, mind **5** watch **6** beware

TAKE DOWN: **4** note **5** lower **6** humble, record, reduce **9** dismantle **10** transcribe **11** disassemble

TAKE EXCEPTION: **5** demur **6** object, oppose, resent **8** disfavor

TAKE FIVE: **4** rest **5** break, relax **6** unwind

TAKE FROM: **4** grab **5** seize **6** reduce **7** deprive **8** subtract

TAKE IN: **4** bilk, fool **5** grasp **6** absorb, accept, digest **7** deceive, defraud, embrace, include, shorten, swindle, welcome **8** hoodwink **10** comprehend, understand

TAKE IT: **6** endure **9** persevere

TAKE NOTICE: **4** heed, note **6** regard **7** observe **9** recognize

TAKE OFF: **4** doff **5** leave, strip **6** begone, decamp, depart, lessen, remove **7** vamoose **8** hightail

TAKEOFF: **5** climb, spoof **6** ascent, launch, parody, satire **7** lampoon, mockery **9** burlesque, departure, imitation **10** caricature

TAKE ON: **3** add **4** face, hire **5** adopt, fight **6** accept, assume, attack, battle, engage, oppose, tackle **7** acquire, embrace **8** shoulder **9** undertake

TAKE OUT: **4** date, kill, vent **6** escort, murder, remove **7** extract, unleash **8** withdraw **9** accompany, eliminate

TAKE OVER: **5** seize, usurp **9** overthrow **10** commandeer

TAKE PAINS: **6** strive **7** attempt **8** endeavor

TAKE STOCK: **5** audit, check, study **6** review, survey **7** examine **8** appraise **9** enumerate, inventory

TAKE TO: **4** like **5** enjoy, favor **6** admire

TAKE TURNS: **5** share **6** rotate **9** alternate

TAKE UP: **4** lift **5** adopt, hoist, raise, start **6** occupy, reduce, resume, tackle **7** elevate, embrace, shorten **8** commence, continue

TALE: **3** fib, lie **4** epic, gest, myth, saga, yarn **5** fable, geste, novel, rumor, story **6** canard, gossip, legend, report, speech **7** account, fiction, history, parable, romance, untruth **8** anecdote **9** falsehood, narration, narrative **11** fabrication **12** exaggeration

TALEBEARER: **4** fink **6** gossip, snitch **7** tattler **8** busybody, gossiper, informer, squealer **10** newsmonger, tattletale **11** rumormonger **13** scandalmonger

TALENT: **4** gift, nose **5** flair, forte, knack, power, skill **6** genius **7** ability, aptness, faculty, feature, passion **8** aptitude, capacity, charisma, strength **9** attribute, endowment, expertise, performer **11** proficiency **13** inventiveness

TALENTED: **4** able **5** adept, smart **6** clever, gifted **7** skilled **8** artistic **12** accomplished

TALE OF TWO CITIES:
author: **14** Charles Dickens
background: **16** French Revolution
characters: **7** Stryver **9** Dr. Manette **11** St. Evremonde **12** Lucie Manette, Sydney Carton **13** Charles Darnay, Madame Defarge
cities: **5** Paris **6** London

TALISMAN: **4** juju **5** charm, lucky, piece, token **6** amulet, fetish, grigri, mascot, scarab, symbol **11** rabbit's foot

TALK: **3** gab, yap **4** blab, bunk, chat, rant, rave **5** lingo, noise, prate, rumor, speak, utter, voice **6** babble, banter, confer, debate, gabble, gossip, huddle, inform, jargon, mumble, patter, powwow, reason, report, sermon, speech, tattle, tongue **7** address, chatter, confess, consult, council, dialect, discuss, express, hearsay, lecture, meeting, palaver **8** chitchat, colloquy, converse, dialogue, verbiage **9** discourse, interface, interview, monologue, negotiate, pronounce, symposium, verbalize **10** conference, discussion **11** communicate **12** conversation

TALKATIVE: **4** glib **5** gabby, vocal, wordy **6** chatty, mouthy **7** gossipy, verbose, voluble **8** flippant **10** loquacious

TALK BACK: **4** sass **5** reply **6** remark

TALK BIG: **4** brag, crow **5** boast, gloat

TALKER: **6** magpie, orator **7** babbler, debater, speaker **8** lecturer **9** chatterer **10** chatterbox

TALK OVER: **6** confer **7** consult, discuss **8** consider **10** deliberate

TALL: **4** fine, hard, high, long **5** giant, grand, great, lanky, large, lofty, rangy **7** skyhigh **8** boastful, elevated, gangling, towering **9** demanding, difficult, excellent **10** farfetched **11** exaggerated

TALLOW: **3** fat, wax **4** suet **5** smear

TALLY: **3** add, tab **4** jibe, list, mark, poll **5** agree, check, count, grade, label, match, notch, score, total **6** number, reckon, record **7** account, catalog, itemize **8** estimate, numerate, register, tabulate **9** reckoning **10** correspond **11** counterpart

TALON: **4** claw, hook, nail

TAMBOURINE: **4** drum **7** timbrel **10** instrument

TAME: **4** bust, curb, dull, meek, mild **5** bland, break, prune, timid, train **6** boring, docile, gentle, humble, manage, master, subdue **7** conquer, control, insipid, servile **8** amenable, domestic, dominate, harmless, obedient, suppress **9** civilized, compliant, tractable **10** cultivated, discipline, submissive, unexciting **11** domesticate, housebroken **12** domesticated **13** uninteresting

TAMPER: **3** fix, rig **5** alter, bribe **6** fiddle, meddle, tinker **7** corrupt **9** influence, interfere, intervene **10** manipulate

TAN: **3** sun **4** beat, flog, whip **5** beige, brown, color, cream, khaki, toast **6** bronze, switch, thrash **7** sunburn **10** discipline

TANG: **4** bite, hint, odor, pang, pike, ring, zest **5** aroma, prong, scent, shank, smack, sting, taste, tinge, trace, twang **6** flavor, relish, tongue **7** quality **8** piquancy **10** smattering **11** surgeonfish

TANGIBLE: **4** real **5** solid **6** actual **7** tactile, visible **8** concrete, material, palpable, physical **9** corporeal, touchable **11** perceptible, substantial

TANGLE: **3** jam, mat, web **4** coil, kink, knot, maze, mesh, trap **5** ravel, skein, snare, snarl, twist **6** entrap, jungle, muddle, sleave **7** embroil, ensnare, involve **8** argument **9** labyrinth **10** complicate, intertwine **11** altercation

TANK: **3** vat **4** jail, pond, pool **5** basin **6** weapon **7** cistern, vehicle **8** aquarium, cauldron **9** container, reservoir **10** receptacle

TANKARD: **3** cup, mug **5** flask, stein, stoup **6** flagon

TANKER: **4** boat, ship **5** oiler, truck

TANTALIZE: **4** bait **5** charm, taunt, tease, tempt **6** allure, entice, pester **7** provoke, torment **9** captivate, frustrate, titillate

TANTALUS:
children: **5** Niobe **6** Pelops
condemned to: **5** Hades
father: **4** Zeus
killed: **6** Pelops
stole: **6** nectar **8** ambrosia
title: **4** king

TANTAMOUNT: **4** same **5** alike, equal **8** parallel **9** identical **10** comparable, equivalent

TANTRUM: **3** fit **4** rage **5** anger, storm **7** rampage **8** outburst **10** conniption

TANZANIA:
capital: **11** Dar es Salaam
cities: **5** Moshi, Tanga **6** Dodoma, Mwanza **8** Zanzibar
continent: **6** Africa
ethnic groups: **7** African
features: **4** Meru **5** Gorge **7** Olduvai **9** Serengeti **10** Ngorongoro **16** Mount Kilimanjaro
islands: **5** Pemba **8** Zanzibar
languages: **7** English, Swahili
monetary unit: **8** shilling
water: **5** Nyasa **8** Victoria **10** Tanganyika

TAP: **3** bar, hit, rap **4** beat, draw, drum, open, pipe, plug **5** break, dance, draft, drain, empty, knock, spout, thump, touch, valve **6** broach, faucet, spigot, strike, uncork **7** barroom, connect **8** nominate, stopcock **8** penetrate **9** designate

TAPE: **4** band, bind, seal **5** video **6** fasten, record, ribbon, secure **7** bandage, binding

TAPER: **4** wick **5** abate, light **6** candle, lessen, narrow, reduce **7** dwindle **8** decrease, diminish **9** acuminate

TAPER OFF: **4** fade, wane **6** recede, weaken **7** subside **8** diminish

TAPESTRY: **5** arras **6** dosser **7** curtain, drapery, Gobelin, hanging

TAPROOM: **3** bar, pub **6** lounge, saloon, tavern **7** barroom

TAR: **5** pitch, taint **6** sailor, seaman **7** asphalt, mariner **8** seafarer **10** distillate

TARANTULA: **6** spider
family: **13** Theraphosidae

TARDY: **4** late, slow **5** slack **6** remiss **7** belated, delayed, lagging, overdue **8** dilatory, sluggish **10** behindhand, unpunctual

TARE: **4** weed **5** plant, vetch **6** weight

TARGET: **3** aim **4** butt, goal, mark **5** quota, sight **6** center, object, pigeon, victim **8** ambition, bull's-eye **9** intention, objective, scapegoat **11** destination

TARHEEL STATE: **13** North Carolina

TARIFF: **3** fee, tax **4** duty, levy, rate, toll **5** price **6** charge, system **7** expense **8** schedule **10** assessment, commission

TARNISH: **3** dim, mar **4** dull, fade, soil, spot **5** cloud, dirty, muddy, smear, spoil, stain, sully, taint **6** damage, darken, defile, injure, smirch, smudge **7** blemish, corrode, corrupt **8** besmirch, diminish, discolor **9** discredit **11** contaminate

TARPAULIN: **4** coat **5** cover **6** canvas **8** oilcloth **9** dropcloth, sailcloth

TARRY: **3** lag **4** bide, loll, rest, stay, wait **5** abide, dally, defer, delay, dwell, lodge, pause, visit **6** dawdle, linger, loiter, remain **7** sojourn **10** filibuster **13** procrastinate

TART: **3** pie **4** acid, girl, sour **5** acerb, sharp, tangy **6** bitter, pastry, severe, snappy **7** acerbic, cutting, piquant, pungent **8** poignant, turnover, vinegary **10** prostitute

TARTARUS: **4** hell **5** Hades **9** purgatory **10** underworld

TARZAN:
author: **18** Edgar Rice Burroughs
mate: **4** Jane
nurtured by: **4** apes
setting: **6** Africa

TASK: **3** job, tax **4** duty, load, test, toil, work **5** chore, labor, stint, study **6** burden, effort, errand **7** mission **8** function **9** objective **10** assignment, employment **11** undertaking

TASKMASTER: **4** boss **6** driver, master **7** foreman, monitor **8** martinet, overseer **9** forewoman **14** disciplinarian

TASTE: **3** bit, eat, sip, try, yen **4** bent, bite, dash, hint, tang, test, zest **5** flair, gusto, sapor, savor, scent, shade, smack, spice, style, tinge, touch, trace **6** desire, flavor, hunger, liking, nibble, palate, relish, sample, savour **7** partake, stomach **8** appetite, delicacy, elegance, fondness, mouthful, yearning **9** judgement **10** experience, partiality, preference, sprinkling, suggestion **11** discernment, inclination

TASTEFUL: **6** classy, savory **7** elegant, refined, stylish **8** pleasing **9** exquisite **10** attractive, delectable

TASTELESS: **4** dull, flat **5** bland, crude, gross, tacky, vapid **6** tawdry, vulgar **7** insipid, raunchy **9** inelegant, offensive, unrefined **10** disgusting, flavorless **11** unpalatable

TASTY: **5** sapid, yummy **6** savory **7** zestful **8** luscious **9** delicious, palatable, toothsome **10** appetizing, delectable, flavorsome **11** scrumptious

TATTERED: **4** torn **6** frayed, ragged, ripped, shabby, shaggy **7** squalid **8** frazzled **9** disrupted **10** disheveled, threadbare **11** dilapidated

TATTLE: **4** blab, chat, leak, talk, tell **5** prate **6** babble, report, snitch, squeal **7** chatter, hearsay, prattle

TATTLETALE: **7** stoolie **8** bigmouth, busybody, informer, squealer **10** talebearer **12** blabbermouth **13** whistleblower

TAUNT: **4** gibe, jeer, jibe, mock, razz **5** crack, reply, sneer, tease, tempt **6** banter, bother, deride, insult, offend **7** provoke, torment, upbraid **8** comeback, reproach, ridicule

TAURUS: **4** bull, sign **13** constellation
born: **3** May **5** April

TAUT: **4** firm, neat, snug, tidy **5** close, drawn, rigid, stiff, tense, tight **8** strained **9** stretched

TAVERN: **3** bar, inn, pub **6** bistro, lounge, saloon **7** barroom, cabaret, taproom **8** drinkery **9** roadhouse **10** restaurant **13** establishment

TAWDRY: **5** cheap, crass, gaudy, gross, showy, tacky **6** vulgar **7** chintzy **9** tasteless **11** pretentious

TAWNY: **3** tan **5** beige, brown, dusky, olive **6** bronze, tanned **7** swarthy **8** brownish

TAX: **3** fee **4** dues, duty, fine, levy, load, onus, toll **5** drain, tithe **6** accuse, assess, burden, charge, custom, demand, excise, impost, settle, strain, stress, tariff, weight **7** deplete, exhaust, expense **8** overload, reproach **10** assessment, difficulty, obligation **12** contribution
types: **3** gas, sin **4** city, geld, toll **5** sales, state **6** county, excise, income, luxury **7** federal, tallage **8** property **9** cigarette **11** corporation, inheritance **12** capital gains **14** Social Security

TAXICAB: **3** cab, car **4** hack, taxi **7** vehicle **10** automobile

TAXING: **5** tough **6** tiring, trying **7** onerous, wearing **9** demanding, difficult **10** burdensome **11** troublesome

TEA: **4** brew **5** drink, party **8** beverage, function **9** gathering, marijuana, reception **11** refreshment
time: **9** afternoon
variety: **4** herb, sage **5** Assam, green, Hyson, pekoe **6** Ceylon, ginger, Oolong, tisane **7** cambric, jasmine **8** Earl Grey, Paraguay, Souchong **9** sassafras **10** Darjeeling

TEACH: **4** show **5** coach, drill, edify, guide, train, tutor **6** direct, inform, preach, school **7** develop, educate, explain, instill, nurture, prepare **8** instruct **9** enlighten, inculcate **10** discipline **11** demonstrate **12** indoctrinate

TEACHER: **4** guru, prof **5** coach, guide, rabbi, swami, tutor **6** master, mentor, pundit **7** edifier, maestro, trainer **8** director, educator, lecturer, preacher **9** pedagogue, preceptor, professor **10** instructor **12** schoolmaster

TEACHING: **6** belief **7** precept **8** doctrine, pedagogy, training, tutelage **9** education, schooling **10** curriculum, discipline, philosophy **11** instruction

TEAM: **3** rig **4** club, crew, gang, join, pair, side, unit, yoke **5** brood, bunch, flock, group, merge, squad, staff, wagon **6** clique, couple, lineup, string **8** alliance, carriage, foursome, partners **9** associate, coalition **11** association, collaborate

TEAMMATE: **7** partner **9** associate, colleague **12** collaborator

TEAR: **3** cut, fly, rip, run **4** bolt, claw, dart, dash, gash, rage, rend, rent, rush, slit, weep **5** binge, break, crack, hurry, sever, shred, split, spree **6** bustle, cleave, damage, divide, injury, sprint, sunder, wrench **7** disrupt, droplet, eyewash, fissure, rupture **8** carousal, lacerate, separate **9** skedaddle

TEAR DOWN: **4** raze, ruin **5** level, smash, wreck **7** destroy, shatter **8** demolish **9** denigrate

TEARFUL: **3** sad **6** crying **7** maudlin, snively, sobbing, weeping **9** lamenting, sorrowful **10** blubbering, lachrymose, whimpering

TEASE: **3** irk, kid, nag, rag, vex **4** bait, card, coax, gibe, haze, josh, razz, twit **5** annoy, roast, taunt, worry **6** badger, bother, harass, heckle, needle, pester, plague, ruffle **7** bedevil, disturb, provoke, torment **8** irritate **9** aggravate, importune, tantalize **11** disentangle

TEASPOON: **3** tsp **7** stirrer, utensil

TECHNICAL: **10** industrial, mechanical, scientific **11** complicated, specialized **13** technological

TECHNIQUE: **3** way **4** mode **5** style **6** manner, method **7** fashion, formula, tactics **8** approach, delivery **9** execution, procedure

TEDIOUS: **3** dry **4** arid, dull, long, slow **5** bored **6** boring, dreary, prolix, tiring **7** boorish, humdrum, irksome, prosaic **8** tiresome **9** laborious, wearisome **10** exhausting, monotonous, unexciting **13** uninteresting

TEDIUM: **5** ennui **7** boredom, routine **8** dullness, monotony **10** dreariness **11** tediousness

TEEM: **4** fill, full, gush, lead, pack, pour **5** crawl, drain, empty, swarm **6** abound **7** bristle, produce, prosper **8** abundant, overflow

TEEMING: **4** full, rife **5** alive **7** bundant, crowded, replete **8** bursting, crawling, prolific, swarming **9** abounding, bristling, plentiful **11** overflowing

TEENY: **3** wee **4** tiny **5** small **6** minute **9** miniature **10** diminutive **11** microscopic

TEETER: **4** reel, rock, sway **5** lurch, waver **6** dangle, falter, quiver, seesaw, topple, totter, wobble **7** flutter, stagger, stammer, tremble **9** vacillate

TEETH: **5** fangs, tusks **6** molars **7** canines, ivories **8** dentures, grinders **12** pearly whites

TEETOTALER: **9** abstainer **14** prohibitionist

TEGMEN: **5** cover, plate **7** tympani **8** covering, forewing

TELAMON:
brother: **6** Peleus
father: **6** Aeacus
friend: **8** Hercules
member of: **9** Argonauts
mother: **6** Endeis
sons: **4** Ajax **6** Teucer

TELEGRAM: **4** wire **5** cable **6** letter **7** message

TELEGRAPH: **3** dot **4** dash **4** wire **5** cable, Morse **6** signal
inventor: **5** Morse

TELEMACHUS:
father: **8** Odysseus
helped: Odysseus
mother: **8** Penelope

TELEPATHY: **3** ESP **7** insight **10** sixth sense **11** premonition, second sight **12** clairvoyance

TELEPHONE: **4** buzz, call, dial, ring **5** glass **9** telescope **10** mouthpiece
inventor: **4** Bell

TELESCOPE: **6** finder **8** spyglass **10** instrument
inventor: **7** Galileo

TELEVISION: **3** box **4** tube **5** cable, telly **7** console **8** boob tube

award: **4** Emmy
frequency: **3** UHF, VHF
inventor: **5** Baird **8** Zworykin

TELL: **3** bid, say **4** blab, chat, deem, post, talk, warn **5** order, speak, state, utter **6** advise, assure, betray, decide, direct, inform, notify, number, recite, relate, repeat, report, reveal, tattle **7** command, confess, confide, dictate, discern, divulge, explain, express, mention, narrate, publish, recount, request **8** announce, describe, disclose, instruct **9** calculate, enumerate, recognize **10** articulate **11** communicate

TELLER: **3** ATM **5** clerk **7** cashier **8** informer, narrator **9** bank clerk

TELLING: **5** solid, sound, valid **6** cogent **7** crucial, decided **8** definite, forceful, powerful, striking **9** effective, important **10** conclusive, convincing **11** devastating, significant

TELL OFF: **5** chide, scold **6** rebuke **7** upbraid **9** criticize, reprimand

TELLTALE: **4** hint, sign **5** clock **6** gossip **7** tattler **8** busybody, informer, squealer **9** important, revealing **10** indication, suggestion, talebearer, tattletale

TEMERARIOUS: **4** bold, rash **5** brash **6** daring **8** heedless, reckless **9** foolhardy **11** adventurous, venturesome

TEMERITY: **4** gall **5** brass, cheek, nerve **8** audacity, boldness, rashness **10** effrontery **12** carelessness, heedlessness **13** foolhardiness **15** venturesomeness

TEMPER: **3** fit, ire **4** curb, ease, fury, heal, mind, rage, tone **5** adapt, anger, humor, wrath **6** adjust, attune, dander, dilute, harden, makeup, modify, season, soften, soothe, spirit **7** assuage, chasten, compose, control, emotion, moisten, passion, toughen **8** calmness, coolness, mitigate, moderate, outburst, regulate, restrain **9** composure **10** complexion, irritation, strengthen **11** disposition

TEMPERAMENT: **4** mood **5** humor, state **6** makeup, nature, spirit **7** emotion, outlook **8** attitude, tendency **9** character **10** complexion **11** disposition, personality, temperature **12** constitution

TEMPERAMENTAL: **5** moody **6** fickle, touchy **8** unstable, volatile **9** emotional, excitable, explosive, irritable, sensitive **12** undependable

TEMPERANCE: **7** control **8** sobriety **9** restraint **10** abnegation, abstinence, constraint, moderation **11** prohibition

TEMPERATE: **4** calm, cool, fair, mild, warm **5** fever, sober **6** gentle, medium, modest, steady, warmth **7** clement **8** moderate, pleasant **9** collected, continent, easygoing, unextreme **10** abstemious, reasonable, restrained **11** temperature, unexcessive

TEMPERATURE: **3** hot **4** cold **7** climate, degrees

TEMPEST: **4** gale, rage, wind **5** furor, storm **6** squall, tumult, uproar **7** turmoil **8** blizzard, upheaval **9** agitation, commotion, hurricane, windstorm **12** thunderstorm

TEMPEST, THE:
author: **11** Shakespeare
characters: **5** Ariel **6** Alonso **7** Antonio, Gonzalo, Miranda **8** Prospero **9** Ferdinand

TEMPESTUOUS: **4** wild **5** fiery, rough **6** heated, raging, stormy **7** furious, intense, violent **8** agitated

9 emotional, turbulent **10** blustering, tumultuous **12** uncontrolled

TEMPLE: **4** fane, naos **6** chapel, church, hieron, mosque, pagoda, shrine **8** forehead, pantheon, ziggurat **9** cathedral, sanctuary, synagogue **10** house of God, tabernacle

TEMPO: **4** beat, clip, pace, rate, time **5** meter, pulse, speed **6** timing **8** momentum

TEMPORAL: **3** lay **5** civil **7** earthly, mundane, passing, profane, secular, worldly **8** fleeting, material, physical **9** ephemeral, momentary, temporary **10** transitory

TEMPORARY: **5** brief, short **6** acting **7** interim, limited, stopgap **8** fleeting, temporal **9** ad interim, ephemeral, makeshift, tentative, transient **10** substitute, transitory **11** provisional

TEMPT: **3** try **4** bait, coax, dare, goad, lead, lure, risk **5** court, decoy **6** allure, entice, incite, induce, seduce **7** attract, provoke **8** intrigue, inveigle **9** tantalize

TEMPTATION: **4** bait, draw, lure **5** decoy **9** hankering, incentive, seduction **10** allurement, attraction, enticement, inducement **11** fascination

TEMPTRESS: **4** vamp **5** siren **7** Delilah, Jezebel, Lorelei, mermaid **9** sorceress **10** seductress **11** enchantress

TENACIOUS: **4** fast, firm **5** tough **6** dogged, spunky, strong, viscid **7** adamant, staunch **8** adhesive, cohesive, resolute, stalwart, sticking, stubborn **9** retentive, steadfast **10** determined, persistent, relentless, unshakable, unyielding **11** persevering

TENACITY: **4** guts **5** heart, nerve **7** courage **8** firmness, strength **9** diligence, toughness **10** resolution **11** persistence **12** cohesiveness, perseverance, stubbornness **13** determination

TENANT: **4** leud **6** holder, lessee, occupy, renter, vassal **7** boarder, dweller, inhabit **8** occupant **10** inhabitant **12** sharecropper

TEND: **4** care, lead, lean, mind, move, till, work **5** favor, guard, nurse, reach, serve, treat, watch **6** attend, direct, intend, likely, listen, manage, supply **7** incline, oversee, protect, provide **8** minister, shepherd, tendency **9** accompany, cultivate, gravitate, safeguard, supervise **10** administer, contribute

TENDENCY: **3** aim, set **4** bent, bias **5** drift, drive, habit, tenor, trend **6** course, custom, reflex, result **7** aptness **8** instinct, penchant, relation **9** direction, proneness **10** partiality, proclivity, propensity **11** disposition, inclination **12** idiosyncrasy

TENDER: **3** raw **4** fond, give, kind, mild, nice, soft, sore, warm, weak **5** frail, green, offer, young **6** aching, extend, feeble, gentle, humane, loving, submit, touchy **7** bruised, careful, fragile, painful, pitiful, present, proffer, propose, sparing, swollen **8** delicate, immature, inflamed, merciful, precious, proposal **9** sensitive, succulent **10** charitable **11** considerate, kindhearted, softhearted, sympathetic, warmhearted **12** affectionate **13** compassionate, inexperienced

TENDERFOOT: **4** tyro **6** novice, rookie **8** beginner, neophyte, newcomer **9** greenhorn **10** apprentice

TENDER IS THE NIGHT:
author: **16** F. Scott Fitzgerald
characters: **9** Dick Diver **11** Nicole Diver
setting: **6** Europe

TENDERNESS: **4** love **6** warmth **8** goodness, kindness, sympathy, weakness **9** affection **10** compassion, gentleness, lovingness **11** benevolence, sensitivity

TENDON: **4** band, cord **6** tissue **8** ligament **9** hamstring

TENDRIL: **4** coil, curl **5** clasp **6** cirrus **7** ringlet

TENEBROUS: **4** dark **5** dusky, murky **6** gloomy **7** obscure, ominous, shadowy

TENET: **4** rule, view **5** canon, creed, dogma, maxim **6** belief **7** opinion **8** doctrine, position, teaching **9** principle **10** conviction, philosophy

TENNESSEE:
bird: **11** mockingbird
capital: **9** Nashville
cities: **7** Memphis **9** Knoxville **11** Chattanooga, Clarksville
explorer: **6** de Soto, Joliet **7** La Salle **9** Marquette
features: **3** TVA **9** Graceland **12** Grand Old Opry **14** Smoky Mountains **15** Lookout Mountain
flower: **4** iris
nickname: **9** Volunteer
trees: **5** tulip **6** poplar
water: **12** Reelfoot Lake

TENNIS:
2-person: **7** singles
4-person: **7** doubles
also called: **10** lawn tennis
inventor: **7** British
officials: **7** referee
scoring: **4** love **5** deuce, forty **6** thirty **7** fifteen **8** set point **9** advantage **10** match point
terms: **3** ace, cut, let, lob, set **4** dink **5** fault, serve **6** racket, volley **7** service **8** backhand, forehand

TENNYSON, ALFRED LORD: **4** poet
nationality: **7** English
wrote: **4** Maud **6** Becket, Harold **7** Ulysses **10** Enoch Arden, In Memoriam **11** The Princess **12** Locksley Hall **15** Idylls of the King **16** The Death of Denone

TENOR: **4** copy, gist, tone **5** drift, sense, trend, voice **6** course, intent, nature, singer **7** essence, meaning, purport, purpose **8** tendency **9** direction, procedure, substance **10** transcript

TENSE: **4** edgy, firm, past, taut **5** jumpy, rigid, stiff, tight **6** aorist, future, queasy, uneasy **7** anxious, excited, intense, jittery, nervous, perfect, present, uptight **8** restless, strained, unnerved **9** preterite, stressful, stretched **10** pluperfect **11** conditional

TENSION: **5** force **6** spring, strain, stress **7** anxiety **8** exertion, pressure, tautness **9** hostility, tightness **10** uneasiness **12** apprehension

TENT: **3** pup **4** camp, plug **5** cover, lodge, tepee **6** bigtop, canopy, marque, teepee, wigwam **7** shelter **8** pavilion **9** tarpaulin **10** tabernacle

TENTACLE: **3** arm **4** limb **6** feeler **9** appendage

TENTATIVE: **4** iffy **5** trial **6** unsure **8** cautious, doubtful, hesitant, proposed **9** makeshift, temporary, uncertain, undecided **11** provisional, speculative, vacillating **12** experimental

TENUOUS: **4** slim, thin, weak **5** shaky **6** dilute, flimsy, narrow, slight, subtle **7** dubious, fragile **8** delicate, ethereal, gossamer **13** insignificant, insubstantial

TENURE: **4** grip, hold, term **5** grasp, reign **6** clutch **10** occupation, possession

TEPID: **4** cool, mild, warm **8** lukewarm, moderate **9** temperate **11** halfhearted, indifferent: **14** unenthusiastic

TEREBENE: **10** antiseptic **11** expectorant

TEREUS:
changed to: **4** bird **6** hoopoe
kingdom: **6** Thrace
raped: **9** Philomela
sister-in-law: **9** Philomela
son: **4** Itys
wife: **6** Procne

TERGIVERSATE: **5** hedge, shift **6** defect **7** shuffle **8** renounce **10** apostatize, equivocate

TERM: **3** dub, era **4** call, name, span, time, tour, word **5** bound, idiom, label, limit, spell, state **6** detail, jargon, period, phrase, tenure **7** entitle, session, stretch **8** boundary, duration, interval, semester **9** condition, designate, provision, trimester **10** definition, expression, limitation **11** stipulation

TERMAGANT: **5** shrew, vixen **6** virago **7** furious, hellcat, raucous **8** scolding **9** turbulent, Xanthippe **10** disorderly, tumultuous **11** quarrelsome

TERMINAL: **3** CRT, end **4** last **5** depot, fatal, final, limit **6** deadly, finish, lethal, screen **7** monitor, station **8** ultimate **9** extremity, incurable **10** concluding

TERMINATE: **3** end **4** call, drop, fire, halt, quit, sack, stop **5** cease, close **6** expire, finish, result **7** abolish, adjourn, confine, dismiss **8** complete, conclude, dissolve **9** discharge, eliminate **11** discontinue

TERMINATION: **3** end **5** close, finis, limit **6** finish, period, result, windup **7** outcome **8** boundary, finality, stoppage, terminus **9** cessation **10** completion, conclusion, expiration

TERMS: **5** price **7** details **9** agreement **10** conditions, provisions **11** limitations, particulars **12** relationship, stipulations **13** understanding

TERRACE: **4** bank, deck, roof **5** patio, porch **7** balcony, gallery, portico **8** platform **9** promenade

TERRA-COTTA: **4** clay **7** pottery **8** brownish

TERRA FIRMA: **4** land, soil **6** ground

TERRAIN: **4** turf **5** tract **6** domain, ground, region **7** contour **9** bailiwick, territory **10** topography **11** countryside, environment

TERRESTRIAL: **5** human **6** global **7** earthly, mundane, secular, terrene, worldly **9** planetary

TERRIBLE: **4** dire, grim **5** awful, tough **6** brutal, grisly, severe, tragic **7** fearful, ghastly, hideous, intense, painful, vicious **8** alarming, dreadful, gruesome, horrible, shocking, terrific **9** appalling, atrocious, harrowing, revolting, upsetting **10** disastrous, disturbing, horrifying, unpleasant **11** cataclysmal, frightening, unfortunate

TERRIER: **3** dog **10** hunting dog
breeds: **3** fox, toy **4** blue, Bull, Skye **5** Cairn, Irish, Welsh **6** Boston **7** English **8** Airedale, Scottish **9** Yorkshire **10** Australian, Bedlington, Manchester

TERRIFIC: **5** great, super **6** superb **7** amazing, fearful, immense, intense **8** alarming, dreadful, enormous, exciting, fabulous, glorious, smashing, terrible **9** appalling, fantastic, frightful, marvelous, upsetting, wonderful

10 disturbing, formidable, terrifying, tremendous **11** distressing, magnificent

TERRIFIED: **6** afraid, aghast, frozen, scared **7** alarmed **10** frightened

TERRIFY: **4** stun **5** alarm, haunt, scare, shock, upset **6** appall, menace **7** horrify, startle **8** frighten, threaten **9** terrorize **10** intimidate

TERRIFYING: **4** grim **5** awful, scary **6** horrid **7** ghastly, hideous **8** alarming, horrible **11** frightening

TERRITORY: **4** area, land, turf, zone **5** arena, field, tract **6** colony, domain, empire, extent, region, sector, sphere **7** terrain **8** district, environs, province **9** bailiwick **12** jurisdiction, neighborhood

TERROR: **3** awe **4** fear, pest **5** alarm, dread, panic **6** affray, fright, horror **7** anxiety **11** trepidation **13** consternation

TERRORIST: **4** goon, thug **5** rebel **6** bomber **8** alarmist **10** subversive **13** revolutionary

TERRORIZE: **5** abash, bully, scare **6** coerce, menace **7** oppress **8** browbeat, frighten, threaten **10** intimidate

TERSE: **4** curt, neat **5** brief, crisp, exact, pithy, short **6** abrupt **7** compact, concise, laconic, pointed **8** clearcut, incisive, succinct

TEST: **3** try **4** exam, quiz **5** assay, check, final, probe, prove, taste, trial **6** ordeal, refine, sample, verify **7** analyze, approve, examine, explore, midterm **8** appraise, audition, evaluate, rehearse, standard, validate **9** criterion, determine **10** experiment, touchstone **11** examination **12** authenticate, experimental

TESTAMENT: **4** will **5** credo, proof **6** belief, legacy **7** tribute **8** covenant, evidence **9** testimony

TESTER: **5** crown, frame **6** canopy, prover **7** assayer **8** examiner **9** inspector, validator **10** questioner

TESTIFY: **5** prove, swear **6** affirm, assert, attest, depone **7** certify, declare, express, profess, witness **8** indicate, proclaim

TESTIMONIAL: **5** honor, salvo **6** salute **7** plaudit, tribute **8** citation, evidence, memorial **9** testimony **10** credential **11** endorsement **12** commendation **14** recommendation

TESTIMONY: **5** facts, proof **6** attest, avowal **7** witness **8** evidence **9** affidavit **10** deposition **11** affirmation, declaration **12** confirmation

TESTY: **5** cross **6** cranky, crusty, grumpy, ornery, touchy **7** grouchy, peevish, uptight **8** choleric, snappish **9** irascible, irritable, obstinate **12** cantankerous

TETE-A-TETE: **4** chat, seat, sofa, talk **7** private **10** discussion **12** confidential, conversation

TETHER: **3** tie **4** band, rope **5** cable, chain, limit, scope **6** fasten, secure **7** manacle, shackle **8** restrain

TETHYS:
brother: **7** Oceanus
father: **6** Uranus
form: **8** Titaness **10** sea goddess
husband: **7** Oceanus
mother: **4** Gaea

TEUTONIC:
deities: **3** Eir, Hel, Tiu, Tyr, Ull **4** Erda, Frea, Frig, Norn, Odin, Thor **5** Aesir, Baldr, Brage, Donar, Othin, Tiwaz, Wodin, Wotan **6** Balder, Frigga, Saeter **7** Forseti **8** Heimdall

people: **4** Dane, Goth, Jute, Ubii **5** Angle, Dutch, Frank, Saxon **6** German, Gothic, Vandal **7** English, Lombard **9** Norwegian **10** Burgundian **12** Scandinavian
symbol: **4** rune

TEXAS:
bird: **11** mockingbird
capital: **6** Austin
cities: **6** Dallas, El Paso **7** Houston, Lubbock **9** Fort Worth, Galveston **10** San Antonio **13** Corpus Christi
explorer: **6** de Vaca **8** Coronado
features: **5** Alamo **7** Big Bend **11** Great Plains
flower: **10** bluebonnet
native: **5** Texan
nickname: **8** Lone Star
tree: **5** pecan
water: **3** Red **9** Rio Grande

TEXT: **5** motif, theme, topic **6** manual, motive **7** content, passage, subject **8** handbook, textbook, workbook **10** schoolbook

TEXTILE: **4** yarn **5** cloth, fiber, goods **6** fabric

TEXTURE: **4** feel, look, make **5** fiber, grain **6** fabric, nature **7** essence, quality, surface **9** character, structure **11** composition, consistency **12** constitution

THAILAND:
capital: **7** Bangkok
cities: **7** Ayuthia **9** Chiangmai, Sukkothai **11** Nakhon Sawan
continent: **4** Asia
ethnic groups: **4** Thai **7** Chinese, Siamese
features: **5** Khies **6** Phuket **8** Maelamun
languages: **3** Lao **4** Thai **5** Malay **7** Chinese
monetary unit: **4** baht
water: **6** Mekong **7** Salween **10** Chao Phraya

THALASSIC: **6** marine **7** aquatic, oceanic **8** maritime

THANK: **5** blame, bless **6** credit, praise **10** appreciate **11** acknowledge

THANKFUL: **7** obliged **8** grateful, indebted **9** contented **12** appreciative

THANKLESS: **8** heedless **9** miserable **10** ungrateful **11** unrewarding **12** unrecognized **13** unappreciated

THANKS: **5** grace **6** credit, praise **8** blessing **9** gratitude **11** recognition **12** appreciation, gratefulness

THANKSGIVING: **5** feast **7** holiday **11** celebration

THAT IS: **5** id est **9** videlicet

THAUMATURGY: **5** magic **7** alchemy, sorcery **10** witchcraft

THAW: **4** melt, warm **6** soften **7** defrost, liquefy **8** dissolve

THEATER: **4** hall **5** arena, drama, house, movie, odeum, stage **6** cinema **8** Broadway, coliseum **9** playhouse **10** auditorium, hippodrome **12** battleground
award: **4** Tony
group: **6** troupe **7** company
parts: **5** apron, wings **7** balcony, catwalk, gallery, upstage **9** backstage, green room **10** auditorium, footlights, proscenium **12** orchestra pit

THEATRICAL: **5** showy, stagy **6** flashy, staged **8** affected, dramatic, thespian **10** artificial, histrionic **11** ceremonious, exaggerated, extravagant, superficial **12** melodramatic

THEBES:
also called: **9** Niut-Ammon
features: **5** Luxor **6** Karnak **16** Valley of the Kings

founder: **6** Cadmus
kings/queens: **5** Aedon, Dirce, Laius, Niobe **7** Amphion, Jocasta, Oedipus **8** Eteocles, Pentheus **11** Tutankhamen **12** Amenhotep III
place: **5** Egypt
water: **4** Nile
worshipped: **4** Amen **5** Ammon

THEFT: **5** caper, crime, fraud, heist **6** piracy **7** larceny, mugging, robbery **8** burglary, filching, stealing, thievery **9** pilferage, pilfering **10** plagiarism, purloining **11** shoplifting **12** embezzlement

THEME: **4** idea, song, text, tune **5** essay, focus, paper, point **6** matter, melody, thesis **7** article, message, premise, subject **8** argument **9** discourse **11** composition **12** dissertation

THEMIS:
father: **6** Uranus
form: **8** Titaness
helped: **6** Pyrrha **9** Deucalion
mother: **4** Gaea
sent by: **4** Zeus

THEN: **4** next **5** again, hence, later **6** before **7** besides **8** formerly, suddenly **9** therefore, thereupon **11** accordingly **12** consequently

THENCE: **4** away **6** whence **9** therefrom **11** thenceforth

THEOLOGIAN: **6** clergy, cleric, curate, divine **7** scholar **11** philosopher **12** ecclesiastic

THEOLOGICAL: **4** holy **6** sacred **8** dogmatic **9** canonical, religious, spiritual **14** ecclesiastical

THEOREM: **3** law **5** axiom **6** belief, theory, thesis **8** doctrine **9** principle **10** hypothesis

THEORETICAL: **5** ideal **8** abstract, academic, unproved **10** analytical **11** speculative, unpractical **12** hypothetical **13** philosophical

THEORIZE: **5** think **7** suppose **9** formulate, postulate, speculate **10** conjecture **11** hypothesize

THEORY: **4** idea **5** guess, hunch **6** belief, nation, thesis **7** formula, surmise, theorem **8** analysis, doctrine, ideology **9** principle **10** assumption, conjecture, hypothesis, philosophy **11** explanation, speculation

THERAPEUTIC: **4** good **7** healing **8** remedial **10** beneficial

THERAPY: **6** remedy **7** healing **9** treatment

THEREAFTER: **9** following **10** afterwards **11** accordingly **12** consequently, subsequently

THEREFORE: **4** ergo, then, thus **5** hence, since **6** thence, whence **7** because **9** wherefore **11** accordingly **12** consequently

THEREUPON: **4** then **8** directly, suddenly **11** immediately

THERMAL: **3** hot **4** warm **5** tepid

THERMOMETER: **9** indicator, regulator **10** instrument, thermostat
types: **7** Celsius, mercury **9** cryometer, pyrometer **10** Fahrenheit **11** thermograph **14** thermoelectric

THESAURUS: **5** Roget **7** lexicon **10** dictionary, word finder
compiler: **5** Roget **6** Kipfer

THESEUS:
father: **6** Aegeus **8** Poseidon
killed: **8** Minotaur
kingdom: **6** Athens
lover: **7** Ariadne
mother: **6** Aethra
rescued by: **8** Hercules
son: **10** Hippolytus
united: **6** Attica
wives: **7** Phaedra **9** Hippolyte

THESIS: **5** essay, paper, point, theme **6** belief, theory **7** opinion, premise **8** argument **9** discourse, postulate **10** exposition, hypothesis **11** composition **12** dissertation

THESPIAN: **5** actor **6** player **7** actress, trouper **8** dramatic **9** performer **10** theatrical

THETIS:
ability: **13** shape-changing
form: **6** Nereid **10** sea goddess
husband: **6** Peleus
lover: **4** Zeus
son: **8** Achilles

THICK: **4** deep, dull, dumb, hazy, wide **5** broad, bulky, burly, dense, gross, heavy, husky, plump, solid, squat, tight **6** chummy, chunky, cloudy, coarse, filled, gloppy, obtuse, packed, stodgy, stupid **7** compact, crowded, intense, viscous **8** abundant, familiar, friendly, ignorant, intimate, swarming **9** brotherly, dimwitted, excessive, populated **10** indistinct, pronounced **11** substantial **12** concentrated, impenetrable

THICKEN: **3** gel, set **4** cake, clot, curd, jell **6** curdle, deepen, freeze, harden **7** congeal, stiffen **8** condense **9** coagulate, intensify

THICKET: **4** bosk, bush **5** brake, brush, clump, copse, grove, hedge, woods **6** growth, shrubs **7** boscage **9** brushwood, shrubbery **10** underbrush

THICKHEADED: **4** dull, dumb **5** dense **6** stupid **7** idiotic **8** ignorant **10** boneheaded **11** blockheaded

THICKNESS: **3** ply **5** girth, layer, sheet, width **7** density, stratum **8** diameter **9** dimension **11** consistency

THICKSET: **5** bulky, husky, squat, stout **6** chunky, stocky, stodgy, stubby, sturdy

THICK-SKINNED: **5** tough **7** callous **8** hardened **9** unfeeling

THIEF: **5** crook **6** bandit, looter, mugger, robber **7** burglar, filcher grifter, prowler, rustler, stealer **8** criminal, gangster, larcener **9** embezzler, larcenist, purloiner **10** highwayman, pickpocket, shoplifter **12** kleptomaniac

THIGH: **3** ham, leg **4** hock **5** femur, flank **6** gammon

THIN: **4** bony, fine, lank, lean, pale, poor, rare, slim, weak **5** acute, faint, gaunt, lanky, scant, sheer, spare **6** dilute, flimsy, gangly, hollow, meager, narrow, reduce, scanty, scarce, skimpy, skinny, slight, sparse, twiggy, watery, weaken **7** scrawny, slender, tenuous **8** anorexic, beanpole, gossamer, rarefied, skeletal **9** attenuate, emaciated, extenuate **10** inadequate **11** transparent **12** insufficient, unconvincing **13** unsubstantial

THIN MAN, THE:
author: **15** Dashiell Hammett
characters: **7** Morelli **11** Nora Charles **13** Arthur Nunheim **18** Christian Jorgensen
sleuth: **11** Nick Charles

THING: **3** act, fad **4** deed, feat, idea, item, junk, rage **5** craze, doing, event, forte, gizmo, point, shape, stunt, style, trait, vogue **6** action, affair, detail, device, entity, gadget, matter, notion, object, oddity, reason **7** article, concern, element, fashion, feature, quality **8** creature, incident, property, referent **9** apparatus, doohickey, happening **10** occurrence, phenomenon **11** contrivance **12** circumstance

THINGAMAJIG: **5** gizmo **6** device, doodad, gadget, widget **9** doohickey **11** contraption, thingamabob

THINGS: **4** duds, gear **5** goods, stuff **7** baggage, clothes, effects **8** chattels **10** belongings, conditions **11** possessions

THINK: **4** deem, feel, mull, muse **5** brood, guess, judge, sense, study, weigh **6** expect, intend, invent, ponder, reason, recall, reckon, regard, repute **7** believe, imagine, purpose, realize, reflect, resolve, ruminate, suppose, surmise, suspect **8** cogitate, conceive, conclude, consider, meditate, remember **9** cerebrate, entertain, formulate, speculate, visualize **10** anticipate, conjecture, deliberate, reconsider, understand **11** contemplate

THINKABLE: **6** likely **8** feasible, possible **10** believable, imaginable, reasonable **11** conceivable **14** comprehensible

THINKER: **4** mind, sage **5** brain **7** casuist, scholar, student **8** theorist **10** mastermind **11** philosopher **12** intellectual

THINKING: **6** bright **7** thought **8** judgment, rational, studious **9** engrossed **10** meditation, reasonable, reflective **12** deliberating **13** introspective, understanding

THINNESS: **6** rarity **7** tenuity **8** slimness **10** meagerness **11** shallowness

THIN-SKINNED: **5** sulky **6** touchy **9** sensitive **13** oversensitive

THIRD ESTATE: **8** populace **9** commoners **10** commonalty

THIRST: **3** yen **4** lust, wish **5** yearn **6** desire, hunger **7** aridity, craving, longing, passion **9** hankering

THIRSTY: **3** dry **4** arid, avid **5** eager **6** desire **7** anxious, craving, longing, parched **8** droughty **9** waterless **10** dehydrated

THISTLE: **4** weed **5** plant
genus: **7** carduus, cirsium **9** onopordum
variety: **3** bur **4** bull, star **6** Canada, cotton, Scotch, silver, teazel **7** Russian

THITHER: **5** there **6** beyond, toward, yonder

THONG: **4** band, lace, lash, rein, whip **5** leash, strap, strip **6** sandal, twitch

THOR:
father: **4** Odin
god of: **7** thunder
hammer: **8** Mjollnir
mother: **5** Jordh, Jorth
rode: **7** chariot
wife: **3** Sif

THORAX: **5** chest, trunk **6** breast **7** abdomen

THORIUM: **7** element

THORN: **4** pain, spur **5** point, spike, spine **6** splint **7** prickle, trouble **8** vexation **9** annoyance **10** discomfort, irritation

THORNY: **5** sharp, spiny, tough **6** barbed, sticky, tricky **7** bristly, pointed, prickly **9** difficult, vexatious **10** nettlesome, unpleasant **11** problematic, troublesome **13** controversial

THOROUGH: **4** full **5** exact, utter **7** careful **8** absolute, accurate, complete, detailed, finished **9** intensive **10** exhaustive, meticulous **11** painstaking **13** comprehensive

THOROUGHBRED: **5** horse **7** trained, unmixed **8** educated, purebred, well-bred **9** pedigreed **11** full-blooded

THOROUGHFARE: **4** path, road **6** artery, avenue, strait, street **7** channel, freeway, highway, parkway, passage, roadway **8** turnpike, waterway **9** boulevard **10** expressway

THOROUGHGOING: **6** arrant **8** absolute, complete **9** out-and-out **11** unqualified

THOROUGHLY: **5** fully **7** totally, utterly **9** carefully, downright **10** absolutely, completely, throughout **11** efficiently, intensively **12** exhaustively, meticulously

THOUGH: **5** still, while **6** albeit **7** despite, granted, however, whereas **11** nonetheless **12** nevertheless

THOUGHT: **4** care, idea, mind, plan, view **5** image **6** belief, deemed, musing, notion, theory, trifle **7** anxiety, concept, judging, opinion, outlook, purpose **9** attention, deduction, inference, intention, reasoning, sentiment **10** cogitation, conception, meditation, reflection **11** cerebration, expectation, imagination, speculation **12** deliberation **13** concentration, consideration

THOUGHTFUL: **4** kind **6** caring, polite **7** careful, heedful, helpful, logical, mindful, pensive, prudent, serious **8** absorbed, gracious, sensible **9** attentive, courteous, regardful, sensitive **10** charitable, discerning, meditative, reflective, ruminative, solicitous **11** considerate, philosophic **12** intellectual **13** contemplative, introspective

THOUGHTLESS: **4** dull, rash, rude **5** brash, hasty, silly **6** remiss, stupid **7** foolish, selfish **8** careless, heedless, impolite, reckless, uncaring **9** negligent **10** neglectful, unthinking **11** inadvertent, inattentive, insensitive **12** discourteous **13** inconsiderate

THRALL: **4** serf **5** slave **6** vassal **7** bondage, bondman, captive, slavery, subject **9** servitude

THRASH: **4** beat, belt, bray, cane, flog, lash, lick, maul, pelt, rout, whip **5** flail, pound, spank, swing **6** batter, defeat, pummel, punish, strike, wallop **7** belabor, shellac, trounce **8** lambaste **10** flagellate

THREAD: **4** cord, flax, join, purl, silk, wire, wool, yarn **5** braid, fiber, floss, lisle, reeve, twine **6** attach, cotton, strand, string **7** connect **8** filament

THREADBARE: **4** used, worn **5** banal, corny, faded, stale, trite **6** frayed, ragged, shabby **7** cliched **8** everyday, tattered **9** hackneyed

THREADS: **4** duds **6** attire **7** clothes **8** clothing

THREAT: **4** risk **5** peril **6** caveat, danger, hazard, menace **7** warning **8** jeopardy **11** commination **12** intimidation

THREATEN: **3** cow **4** warn **5** augur, bully, scare **6** expose, menace **7** portend **8** endanger, frighten, pressure **9** terrorize **10** intimidate, jeopardize

THREATENING: **7** looming, ominous **8** alarming, imminent, lowering, menacing **9** dangerous, impending

THREE MUSKETEERS, THE:
author: **14** Alexandre Dumas
characters: **5** Athos **6** Aramis **7** Porthos **9** D'Artagnan
setting: **6** France

THRENODY: **4** poem, song **5** dirge, elegy **7** requiem

THRESHOLD: **3** eve **4** dawn, door, edge **5** brink, verge **6** outset **7** doorway, horizon, opening **8** doorsill, entrance **9** beginning

THRICE: **4** very **6** highly, triple **7** greatly **9** extremely, threefold

THRIFT: **6** saving **7** economy **8** prudence **9** austerity, frugality, husbandry, parsimony **11** sparingness **12** conservation

THRIFTLESS: **6** lavish, wanton **8** careless, prodigal, wasteful **10** immoderate **11** extravagant

THRIFTY: **6** frugal, saving, useful **7** careful, prudent, sparing **8** thriving **9** provident, scrimping **10** conserving, economical, prosperous **11** flourishing, industrious **12** parsimonious

THRILL: **4** bang, glow, kick, stir **5** flush **6** arouse, charge, excite, please, quiver, tingle, tremor **7** delight, tremble, vibrate **9** electrify, galvanize, stimulate

THRILLING: **7** awesome, intense **8** exciting, gripping, riveting, stirring **11** sensational, stimulating, titillating **12** breathtaking, electrifying

THRIVE: **4** boom, grow **7** blossom, burgeon, develop, improve, prosper, succeed **8** flourish, progress

THRIVING: **6** robust **7** healthy **8** blooming, prolific **9** flowering **10** prosperous, succeeding, successful **11** flourishing

THROAT: **3** maw **4** neck **5** gorge **6** gullet, larynx **7** passage, pharynx, trachea **8** windpipe **9** esophagus
fold of skin: **6** dewlap, wattle

THROATY: **4** deep **5** gruff, husky **6** hoarse **8** guttural

THROB: **4** ache, beat, drum, pant **5** pound, pulse, thump **6** quiver **7** flutter, pulsate, vibrate

THROE: **4** ache, pain, pang **5** agony, spasm **7** anguish, turmoil **8** disorder, struggle

THROMBUS: **4** clot **11** coagulation

THRONE: **4** rank, seat **5** chair, power **6** toilet **7** dignity, royalty **8** cathedra **9** authority **11** sovereignty

THRONG: **3** gag, jam, mob **4** fill, herd, host, mass, pack, push **5** bunch, crown, drove, flock, group, horde, press, swarm **6** stifle **7** smother **8** converge **9** concourse, multitude **10** assemblage

THROTTLE: **3** gag, gun **5** choke, valve **6** stifle **7** garrote, smother **8** strangle, suppress **9** suffocate **11** accelerator

THROUGH: **3** per, via **4** done, over, past, thru **5** about, among, ended **6** across, around, direct **7** between **8** finished, straight, washed-up **9** completed, concluded **10** terminated

THROUGHOUT: **4** amid **5** about **6** around, during **10** completely, everyplace, everywhere

THROW: **3** lob, peg, put **4** buck, cast, fire, flip, hurl, lose, pelt, shed, shot **5** chuck, flick, fling, force, heave, scarf, shawl, sling, whirl **6** baffle, launch, propel, submit, thrust, unseat **7** confuse, discard, dispose, nonplus, project, unhorse **8** catapult, unsettle **10** disconcert

THROW AWAY: **4** cast, dump **5** ditch, eject, scrap, waste **6** reject **7** abandon, discard, fritter **8** jettison, squander

THROW BACK: **5** check **6** revert **7** regress

THROW DOWN: **4** cast, drop, toss **5** fling **9** overthrow

THROW OFF: **4** emit, lose, slip **5** elude, evade, expel, shake, trick **6** divert, escape **7** confuse, mislead **8** distract

THROW OUT: **4** cast, emit, junk **5** chuck, eject, evict, expel, scrap **6** banish, reject, remove **7** discard **8** jettison **9** disengage

THROW OVER: **5** leave **6** desert, reject **7** abandon, forsake

THROW UP: **4** barf, puke **5** heave, retch, vomit **7** abandon, upchuck **10** relinquish **11** regurgitate

THRUST: **3** jab, ram **4** butt, meat, poke, push, stab **5** barge, drive, impel, onset, point, press, sense, shove **6** attack, charge, pierce, plunge, stress **7** assault, impetus, intrude, meaning **8** pressure, protrude **9** interject, interpose, onslaught, penetrate

THUD: **4** bang, blow, fall **5** clonk, clump, clunk, smack, sound, thump **6** strike

THUG: **4** goon, hood, punk **5** bully **6** gunman **7** hoodlum, mobster, ruffian, torpedo **8** assassin, criminal, gangster, hooligan **9** cutthroat

THUMB: **4** scan **5** hitch **6** browse, finger, pollex **9** hitchhike

THUMP: **3** bop, hit **4** bang, beat, blow, ding, drub, thud **5** knock, pound, punch, smack, sound, stump, throb, whack **6** strike, thwack, wallop

THUNDER: **4** bang, boom, clap, peal, rage, roar **5** crash, noise **8** cracking, drumfire, rumbling **9** fulminate

THUNDERBOLT: **4** boom **5** crack, flash **9** lightning

THUNDERING: **4** loud **5** large **6** mighty **7** booming

THUNDERSTRUCK: **5** agape **6** aghast, amazed **7** shocked, stunned **9** astounded, surprised **10** astonished, confounded

THUS: **3** yet **4** ergo **5** hence **9** therefore **11** accordingly **12** consequently

THWACK: **3** bop, hit, rap **4** bang, blow, sock **5** drive, force, knock, pound, smack, thump, whack **6** paddle, strike, thrash, wallop

THWART: **4** balk, curb, foil, stop **5** block **6** baffle, defeat, hamper, hinder, impede, oppose, outwit, resist, stymie **7** counter, prevent **8** obstruct **9** frustrate

THYESTES:
brother: **6** Atreus
father: **6** Pelops
kingdom: **7** Mycenae
mother: **10** Hippodamia
seduced: **6** Aerope
son: **9** Aegisthus

TIARA: **5** crown, miter **6** diadem **7** circlet, coronet **9** headdress

TIBET:
animals: **3** goa, sha, sus, yak **4** shou, zebu **5** kiang, manul, ounce, panda, takin **6** nahoor, tangun
capital: **5** Lhasa
lama: **5** dalai
mountains: **6** Kunlun **9** Himalayas
ruled by: **5** China
water: **5** Indus **7** Salween

TIBIA: **4** bone **5** flute **8** shinbone

TIC: **4** jerk **5** spasm **6** twitch **11** contraction

TICK: **3** dot, tap **4** beat, case, mark, mite, note, pest **5** click, count, cover, louse, sound, speck **6** degree, insect, moment, record, second **7** instant **8** mattress, parasite **11** bloodsucker

TICKET: **3** tag **4** card, list, note, pass, slip, stub **5** check, label, means, price, slate, token **6** ballot, choice, docket, notice, permit, record **7** license, receipt, sticker, summons, voucher **8** document, passport **9** admission, raincheck **11** certificate

TICKLE: **4** beat, play, stir **5** amuse, annoy, tease, touch **6** arouse, caress, divert, excite, please, stroke, thrill, tingle **7** delight **9** stimulate, titillate

TICKLISH: **5** risky **6** chancy, touchy, tricky **8** delicate, unstable, unsteady, volatile **9** dangerous, difficult, sensitive, uncertain **10** changeable, precarious **11** complicated

TIDBIT: **4** bite, item **5** goody, treat **6** morsel **8** delicacy

TIDE: **3** ebb **4** flow, flux, time, wave **5** drift, flood, surge, trend **6** course, season, stream **7** current **8** movement, undertow **9** direction **11** opportunity

TIDINGS: **4** news, word **6** advice **7** message **9** greetings **11** information **12** intelligence

TIDY: **4** fair, good, neat, smug, trig, trim **5** ample, clean, groom, large **6** spruce **7** healthy, orderly **8** adequate, diligent, spotless **9** organized, shipshape **10** immaculate, methodical **11** substantial, uncluttered **12** considerable, satisfactory

TIE: **3** rod, wed **4** band, beat, bind, bond, cord, draw, duty, even, join, knot, lace, link, rope **5** ascot, brace, chain, equal, hitch, marry, nexus, union, unite **6** anchor, attach, couple, cravat, fasten, hamper, hookup, pledge, secure, strain, string, tether **7** confine, connect, support **8** deadlock, ligature, restrict, standoff **9** constrain, fastening, interlace, stalemate **10** allegiance, connection, obligation **11** affiliation, association **12** relationship

TIER: **4** line, rank **5** class, grade, layer, level, stack, story **7** echelon, stratum **8** category, grouping

TIE UP: **4** rope, wrap **5** delay, snarl **6** fasten, hinder, secure **7** package

TIFF: **3** fit, row **4** huff, snit, spat **5** fight, scrap, tizzy, words **7** dispute, quarrel **8** argument, outburst, squabble **11** altercation **12** disagreement

TIGER: **3** cat, cub **4** lynx **6** cougar, feline, jaguar **7** leopard **9** carnivore

TIGHT: **4** busy, fast, firm, full, hard, neat, snug, taut, tidy, trim **5** bound, cheap, close, dense, drawn, drunk, fixed, solid, tense, tipsy **6** locked, narrow, packed, sealed, severe, steady, stingy **7** compact, concise, crowded, shapely, soundly **8** faithful, intimate **9** competent, condensed, difficult, plastered, stretched **10** impervious, inebriated **11** intoxicated **12** parsimonious **13** uncomfortable

TIGHTEN: **4** bind **5** crush, tense **6** clench **7** squeeze, stiffen, stretch **8** condense, contract **9** constrict

TIGHTFISTED: **5** cheap **6** frugal, greedy, stingy **7** thrifty **9** penurious **12** parsimonious

TIGHT-LIPPED: **3** mum **5** quiet **6** silent **8** discreet, reticent, taciturn **9** secretive **12** closemouthed

TIGHTWAD: **5** miser **6** scrimp **7** niggard, scrooge **9** skinflint **10** cheapskate

TILE: **4** slab **5** block, brick, drain, plate, slate **7** pantile, shingle

TILL: **3** dig, hoe, sow **4** draw, farm, plow, seed, tend, tray, turn, work **5** labor, vault **6** before, drawer, plough **7** develop, prepare **9** cultivate **12** cash register

TILLABLE: **6** arable **7** fertile **8** plowable **10** productive **12** cultivatable

TILLAGE: **4** land **11** agriculture, cultivation

TILLER: **4** hoer **5** lever, shoot **6** farmer **10** cultivator, husbandman

TILT: **3** tip **4** bias, cant, cock, duel, lean, list, tent **5** argue, crawl, fight, joust, pitch, shift, slant, slope, upend, upset **6** attack, awning, battle, canopy, careen, charge, combat, hammer, seesaw, thrust **7** contest, dispute, incline, scuffle **8** conflict, covering, gradient, skirmish **10** tournament **11** altercation

TIMBER: **3** rib **4** balk, beam, gate, logs, wood **5** board, cover, frame, plank, trees, woods **6** forest, girder, lumber, rafter **8** woodland

TIMBRE: **4** mood, tone **5** miter, pitch, sound **7** quality **9** character **10** intonation

TIME: **3** age, day, era **4** beat, book, date, hour, pace, past, rate, shot, span, term, tour, week, year **5** break, clock, cycle, epoch, month, phase, shift, speed, spell, stint, tempo **6** chance, decade, during, future, minute, moment, period, rhythm, season, second **7** century, instant, interim, measure, present, stretch **8** eternity, interval, schedule **9** continuum **10** chronology, millennium **11** opportunity

TIME AND AGAIN: **5** often **10** frequently, repeatedly

TIME-HONORED: **5** noble **7** eminent **8** accepted, reverend **9** respected

TIMELESS: **7** ageless, endless, eternal, lasting, undated **8** dateless, immortal, unending, untimely **9** ceaseless, continual, permanent, perpetual **10** continuous, intemporal **11** everlasting

TIMELY: **5** early **6** prompt, proper **7** fitting **8** punctual, relevant, temporal **9** favorable, opportune, pertinent, promising **10** auspicious, convenient, seasonable **11** appropriate **12** contemporary

TIMEPIECE: **4** dial **5** clock, watch **7** sundial **8** calendar, horologe, pendulum **9** hourglass, stopwatch **11** chronometer, chronoscope

TIMEWORN: **3** old **4** aged **5** dated, hoary, trite **7** ancient **8** battered **9** weathered **10** antiquated

TIMID: **3** coy, shy **4** meek, mild **5** mousy **6** afraid, gentle, modest **7** bashful, fearful, nervous **8** cowardly, hesitant, sheepish, timorous **9** diffident, spineless, tentative, uncertain, withdrawn **10** indecisive, irresolute, spiritless, unassuming **11** unassertive, vacillating **12** apprehensive, fainthearted

TIMOROUS: **4** meek **5** faint, timid **6** afraid **7** fearful **8** hesitant **9** shrinking, tentative, tremulous **10** shuddering **11** unassertive **12** apprehensive, fainthearted

TIN: **3** box, can, pan **5** metal **7** element, stannic, stannum **9** container

TINCTURE: **3** dye **4** cast, tint **5** color, imbue, shade, stain, taint, tinge, trace **6** elixir, imbrue **7** extract, pigment, vestige

TINDER: **4** fuel, punk, wood **8** kindling

TINE: **4** fork **5** point, prong, spike **6** branch

TINGE: **3** dye, hue **4** cast, dash, drop, hint, tint, tone **5** color, imbue, shade, smack, stain, touch, trace **6** flavor **7** pigment **8** coloring, tincture **10** suggestion

TINGLE: **4** burn, itch **5** sting **6** jingle, shiver, thrill, tickle, tinkle **7** tremble **9** sensation, stimulate

TINKER: **4** fuss, mend, mess **5** patch **6** dabble, fiddle, mender, potter, putter, repair **7** meddler

TINKLE: **4** ring **5** chime, chink, clink, plink, sound **6** dingle, jingle, signal, tingle

TINSEL: **4** sham **5** gaudy, showy **6** flashy, glossy, tawdry **10** decoration **11** pretentious

TINT: **3** dye, hue **4** cast, dash, hint, tone **5** color, shade, stain, tinge, trace **6** nuance **7** pigment **8** tincture **10** complexion

TINTINNABULATION: **5** chime, noise, sound **6** jingle **7** clangor, ringing **8** clanging

TINY: **3** wee **5** small, teeny, weeny **6** little, minute, peewee, petite, teensy **9** itty-bitty, miniature, minuscule **10** diminutive, negligible, pocket-size, teeny-weeny **11** lilliputian, microscopic

TIP: **3** cap, cue, end, tap, top **4** apex, barb, cant, clue, dump, fall, gift, hint, keel, lean, list, peak, rest, tilt **5** crown, empty, point, slant, slope, steer, touch, upset **6** advice, careen, reward, summit, topple, zenith **7** capsize, caution, crampit, deflect, ferrule, incline, warning **8** gratuity, overturn, pinnacle **9** overthrow **10** suggestion **11** information

TIPPLE: **4** grog **5** booze, drink **6** imbibe, liquor

TIPPLER: **3** sot **4** lush, soak, wino **5** drunk, souse, toper **6** boozer **7** drinker **8** drunkard **9** alcoholic

TIPSTER: **4** nark **6** pigeon, snitch **8** informer, squealer

TIPSY: **5** drunk, shaky, tight **6** groggy, loaded, soused, wobbly **7** drunken, smashed **8** unsteady **9** plastered **10** inebriated **11** intoxicated

TIPTOE: **5** creep, sneak **6** warily **7** quietly **8** cautious, stealthy **10** cautiously

TIPTOP: **4** best **5** elite, prime **7** supreme **8** superior **9** excellent, first-rate, uppermost **11** exceptional **13** extraordinary

TIRADE: **6** screed **7** lecture, ranting **8** berating, diatribe, harangue, jeremiad, outburst **9** invective, philippic **11** castigation

TIRE: **3** lag, rim, tax **4** band, bore, hoop, jade **5** drain, spare, weary, wheel **6** tucker, weaken **7** exhaust, fatigue **8** enervate, overwork **10** exasperate

TIRED: **4** beat, dead **5** bored, jaded, spent, weary **6** bushed, pooped, sleepy **7** drained, wearied **8** fatigued, tuckered, unrested **9** exhausted, lethargic **11** exasperated

TIRELESS: **4** busy **7** staunch **8** untiring **9** energetic, steadfast, unwearied, weariless **10** determined, unflagging **12** enthusiastic **13** indefatigable

TIRESIAS:
acted as: **4** seer **7** prophet **10** soothsayer **11** clairvoyant
advised: **7** Oedipus **8** Odysseus
blinded by: **6** Athena

TIRESOME: **4** dull, hard **6** boring, dreary, tiring **7** irksome, tedious **8** annoying **9** demanding, difficult, wearisome **10** irritating, monotonous **12** exasperating: **13** uninteresting

TISSUE: **3** web **4** film, lace, mesh, silk **5** cloth, gauze, paper **6** fabric, fascia, muscle, tendon **7** chiffon, network **8** filigree, ligament, membrane

TITAN:
defeated by: **4** Zeus
father: **6** Uranus
form: **6** giants **9** satellite
imprisoned in: **8** Tartarus
king: **6** Cronus
member: **4** Rhea **5** Atlas **6** Cronus, Phoebe, Tethys, Themis **7** Iapetus, Oceanus **8** Hyperion
mother: **4** Gaea

TITANIC: **4** huge, vast **5** giant, great, large **7** immense, mammoth **8** colossal, enormous, gigantic **9** humongous, monstrous **10** gargantuan **12** earthshaking

TITANIUM: **7** element

TITHE: **3** tax **4** levy **5** tenth **10** assessment, obligation

TITILLATE: **5** tease **6** arouse, excite, thrill, tickle **9** captivate, stimulate, tantalize

TITLE: **3** don, dub, Mrs, sir, tag **4** duke, earl, king, lady, miss, raja, rank, term **5** baron, claim, crown, label, madam, major, mayor, power, right, style **6** doctor, knight, madame, milady, prince, status, sultan **7** admiral, baptize, captain, caption, epithet, general, heading, senator **8** christen, governor, headline, position, princess, reverend **9** commodore, designate, monsignor, ownership, president, secretary **10** lieutenant, possession **11** appellation **12** denomination **13** vice-president **14** representative

TITTER: **5** laugh **6** cackle, giggle, teehee **7** chuckle, snicker

TITTLE: **3** dot, jot **4** atom, iota, mark, mite **5** fleck, speck **6** accent **8** particle

TITULAR: **7** nominal **8** so-called **10** in name only

TIZZY: **4** snit **6** dither, swivet

TOAD: **4** bufo, frog **6** anuran, peeper **7** tadpole **8** polliwog **9** amphibian, sycophant **10** salientian
family: **9** Bufonidae

TOADY: **4** fawn **6** flunky, kowtow, lackey, stooge **8** parasite, truckler **9** brownnose, flatterer, repulsive, sycophant **10** bootlicker

TOAST: **3** dry, tan **4** cook, heat, warm **5** bread, brown, drink, honor, melba, parch, skoal **6** cheers, pledge, prosit, salute **7** propose **9** celebrate

TOASTMASTER: **5** emcee **10** officiator

TOBACCO: **4** crop, leaf, shag, weed **5** cigar, plant, snuff **7** smoking **9** cigarette

TOBACCO ROAD:
author: **8** Caldwell
characters: **5** Pearl **6** Jeeter **9** Ada Lester, Lov Bensey **10** Bessie Rice, Dude Lester **12** Jeeter Lester **14** Ellie May Lester
setting: **7** Georgia

TOBIAS:
father: **5** Tobit
son: **8** Hycranus

TOBOGGAN: **4** luge, sled **7** bobsled, decline

TOCSIN: **4** bell, horn, sign **5** alarm, alert, siren **6** signal **7** warning

TODAY: **3** now **7** present **8** nowadays **9** on this day

TODDLE: **4** walk **6** stroll, waddle

TODDLER: **3** tot **4** tyke **5** child **6** infant

TO-DO: **4** flap, fuss, stir **5** fight **6** hoopla, hubbub, racket, rumpus, uproar **7** turmoil **8** brouhaha **9** commotion **10** excitement

TOE: **5** digit **6** dactyl **7** phalanx **9** appendage
big: **6** hallux

TOGA: **4** calm, cool, gown, robe, wrap **5** tunic **6** united **7** garment **8** combined, mutually, together **10** harmonious, integrated **12** collectively

TOGETHER: **6** fasten, unison **13** consecutively **14** simultaneously

TOGO:
cities: **6** Sokode **7** Kpalime
continent: **6** Africa
ethnic groups: **3** Ewe **4** Mina **5** kabye **6** Cabrai
features: **13** savanna plains
languages: **3** Gur, Kwa **6** French
monetary unit: **5** franc
water: **8** Atlantic

TOGS: **4** duds **6** attire, outfit, thread **7** apparel, clothes **8** clothing

TOIL: **4** moil, plod, plug, work **5** grind, labor, pains, slave, snare, sweat **6** battle, drudge, effort, strain, strife **7** travail **8** drudgery, industry, overwork, struggle

TOILER: **4** peon, serf **5** slave **6** worker **7** laborer **9** workhorse

TOILET: **3** can **4** head, john **5** dress, privy **6** attire, throne **7** commode, costume, latrine **8** bathroom, lavatory, outhouse, washroom

TOILSOME: **4** hard **6** tiring, uphill **7** arduous **9** difficult, laborious, strenuous, wearisome

TOKEN: **4** gift, mark, omen, sign **5** badge, medal, proof, relic **6** emblem, pledge, signal, symbol, trophy **7** memento, feature, gesture, minimal, nominal, portent, signify **8** evidence, keepsake, reminder, souvenir **9** symbolize **10** expression, indication **11** perfunctory, remembrance

TOLERABLE: **4** fair, so-so **6** decent **7** average, livable **8** adequate, bearable, passable **9** allowable, endurable, permitted **10** acceptable, sufferable, sufficient **12** satisfactory

TOLERANCE: **4** grit **5** mercy **7** stamina **8** leniency, patience, sympathy **9** endurance, fortitude, hardiness, threshold **10** compassion, indulgence **13** steadfastness, understanding

TOLERANT: **4** easy, soft **7** lenient, liberal, patient **8** enduring **9** forgiving, indulgent **10** forbearing, permissive **11** sympathetic **13** compassionate

TOLERATE: **4** bear, take **5** abide, allow, stand **6** accept, endure, permit, suffer **7** condone, sustain, swallow, undergo

TOLL: **3** fee, tax **4** cost, duty, levy, loss, peal, ring **5** chime, knell, sound **6** charge, damage, deaths, strike, tariff **7** customs, expense **8** announce **9** sacrifice **10** assessment, casualties **11** destruction

TOMATO: **5** fruit, plant **9** love apple, vegetable

TOMB: **5** crypt, grave, vault **6** dolmen, shrine **7** chamber, mastaba, tumulus **8** catacomb, cenotaph, monument **9** mausoleum, sepulcher

TOMBOY: **3** meg **4** girl **6** gamine, hoyden **8** spitfire

TOMBSTONE: **6** marker **8** memorial, monument **10** gravestone

TOME: **4** book **6** volume **9** portfolio **12** encyclopedia

TOMFOOLERY: **5** caper, prank **6** antics, frolic **8** malarkey, nonsense, tommyrot **9** horseplay, poppycock, silliness **11** foolishness

TOMMYROT: **4** bull, bunk, crap **5** trash **7** baloney, hogwash, rubbish **8** malarkey, nonsense **10** tomfoolery **11** foolishness

TOMORROW: **6** manana **9** the future

TOM SAWYER:
author: **9** Mark Twain
characters: **8** Injun Joe **9** Aunt Polly **13** Becky Thatcher **15** Huckleberry Finn

TOM THUMB: **5** dwarf **6** midget **11** lilliputian
real name: **14** Charles Straton

TON: **4** lots **5** heaps **6** weight

TONE: **4** cast, mood, note, tint **5** color, drift, humor, pitch, shade, sound, style, trend **6** accent, effect, health, manner, nature, nuance, spirit, temper, timbre **7** balance, quality **8** approach, attitude, modulate, strength **9** character **10** atmosphere, elasticity, inflection, intonation

TONE DOWN: **6** soften, subdue **8** mitigate, moderate

TONGA:
also called: **15** Friendly Islands
capital: **9** Nukualofa
cities: **6** Neiafu, Pangai
continent: **7** Oceania
ethnic groups: **6** Tongan **10** Polynesian
island groups: **5** Vavau **6** Haajai **9** Tonga-Tapu
languages: **6** Tongan **7** English
monetary unit: **6** paanga
water: **7** Pacific

TONGUE: **4** flap, lick, talk **5** lingo, speak, utter **6** creole, lingua, muscle, speech **7** dialect, glossal, lingula **8** language **10** vernacular
parts: **3** tip **4** apex, back **5** front **6** center

TONGUE-LASH: **5** scold **6** berate, rebuke **7** upbraid **8** reproach **9** castigate, reprimand

TONGUE-TIED: **6** silent **7** nervous **10** astonished, speechless **11** embarrassed

TONIC: **4** soda **5** boost **6** bracer, remedy **7** bracing **8** catalyst, medicine, roborant **9** refresher, stimulant **10** astringent, refreshing **11** restorative, stimulating **12** exhilarating, invigorating

TOO: **4** also, ever, more, over, very **5** along **6** indeed, overly **7** besides **8** likewise, moreover **9** extremely, immensely **11** exceedingly, excessively, furthermore **12** additionally

TOO LITTLE: **6** scarce **7** lacking **8** shortage **9** deficient **10** inadequate **12** insufficient

TOO MUCH: **6** excess **7** surplus **8** overflow **10** overcharge **12** overabundant **13** excessiveness

TOOL: **3** adz, awl, axe, saw, **4** adze, file **5** plane **6** hammer **7** cat's-paw, hatchet, utensil **9** implement
boring: **3** awl, bit, zax **4** pick **5** auger, chuck, drill **6** gimlet, reamer **11** countersink
bricklaying: **4** hock **5** float, level **6** hammer, trowel
carpentry: **3** adz, awl, bit, saw **4** rasp, vise **5** auger, brace, edger, lathe, level, plane, punch **6** chisel, gimlet, hammer, pliers, router, sander, square **7** handsaw, hatchet
cutting: **3** adz, axe, bit, hob, saw **4** adze **5** bezel, gouge, knife, razor **6** chisel, graver, reamer, shears **8** billhook, scissors
engraving: **5** burin **7** scauper
garden: **3** hoe **4** rake **5** edger, mower, spade **6** sickle, trowel, weeder
gripping: **4** vise **5** clamp, tongs **6** pincer, pliers, wrench **7** tweezer **11** screwdriver
holding: **4** vise **5** clamp
prehistoric: **4** celt **5** burin, flint **6** eolith **9** paleolith **10** palaeolith
striking: **4** maul **5** punch, wedge **6** hammer, mallet, pestle

woodworking: **3** adz, saw **4** adze **5** bevel, plane **6** chisel, hammer **7** edgeman, grainer, scauper, scriber

TOOT: **4** blow, honk **5** binge, shout, sound, spree **6** bender **7** declare, trumpet, whistle **8** proclaim

TOOTH: **4** dent, fang, snag, tine, tusk **5** ivory, molar, point **6** canine, cuspid **7** grinder, incisor, laniary **8** bicuspid, premolar

TOOTH AND NAIL: **7** eagerly **8** fiercely **9** fervently **10** vigorously **12** unrelentless

TOOTHLESS: **4** weak **6** futile **8** edentate **11** ineffectual

TOOTHSOME: **5** sapid, tasty **6** savory **8** luscious, pleasant, pleasing **9** delicious, palatable **10** appetizing, attractive

TOP: **3** ace, cap, lid, tip, toy **4** acme, apex, best, cork, dome, head, lead, peak, roof **5** chief, cover, cream, crest, crown, elite, excel, outdo, prime, prune **6** apogee, better, choice, exceed, leader, summit, vertex, zenith **7** ceiling, highest, maximum, notable, surface, surpass **8** covering, dominate, foremost, meridian, pinnacle, renowned, superior, surmount **9** beginning, excellent, uppermost **10** preeminent

TOPCOAT: **8** overcoat, raincoat **12** chesterfield

TOPIC: **4** item, text **5** issue, point, theme **6** matter **7** subject **8** argument, material, question **11** proposition

TOPICAL: **5** local **6** timely **7** current, limited **8** confined **9** temporary **10** subjective **12** contemporary

TOPNOTCH: **4** best **5** prime **6** finest **8** superior **9** excellent, first-rate **11** outstanding

TOPPING: **5** icing, sauce **6** plunge **7** garnish **8** frosting

TOPPLE: **4** fall, tilt **5** upset **6** defeat, falter, teeter, totter, tumble **7** capsize, overset, stumble **8** overturn **9** overthrow

TOPS: **4** aces, best **5** great, super **7** supreme **8** terrific **9** excellent, first-rate

TOPSY-TURVY: **5** askew **7** chaotic, jumbled **8** cockeyed, confused, inverted, reversed, upturned **9** cluttered **10** disordered, upside-down **12** disorganized

TORCH: **4** lamp **5** blaze, brand, flare, light **6** beacon **7** firebug, lantern **8** arsonist, flambeau **9** firebrand **10** flashlight, incendiary

TORMENT: **3** nag, rib, vex **4** pain, rack **5** agony, annoy, grill, harry, smite, tease **6** badger, bother, harass, harrow, heckle, misery, molest, pester, plague, punish, strain **7** afflict, agitate, agonize, anguish, bedevil, crucify, despair, tempest, torture, travail, trouble **8** distress, irritate **9** persecute, suffering, tantalize

TORN: **4** rent, slit **5** split **6** ripped, sliced **7** damaged, divided, mangled **8** shredded, wavering **9** lacerated, undecided

TORNADO: **4** wind **5** storm **6** funnel, squall **7** cyclone, twister, typhoon **9** hurricane, whirlwind

TORPEDO: **4** ruin, sink, thug **5** wreck **6** attack, damage **7** destroy, explode, missile **8** assassin, firework **9** cutthroat, explosive **10** projectile

TORPID: **4** dull, idle, lazy, numb **6** drowsy, static **7** dormant **8** benumbed, inactive, sluggish **9** apathetic, lethargic **10** motionless, slumberous **11** hibernating

TORPOR: **4** coma **5** sleep **6** apathy **7** languor, slumber **8** dormancy, dullness, laziness, lethargy **9** lassitude **10** inactivity, stagnation **12** listlessness, sluggishness

TORQUE: **4** turn **5** force, twist **6** collar **7** armband **8** necklace **10** revolution

TORRENT: **4** flow, gush, rush, tide **5** burst, flood **6** deluge, stream **7** cascade, channel, current, Niagara **8** cataract, downpour **9** turbulent, waterfall **10** cloudburst, inundation, outpouring

TORRID: **3** hot **4** arid **5** crime, fiery, rapid **6** ardent, heated, sultry **7** blazing, burning, fervent, hurried, intense, zealous **8** parching, sizzling **9** scorching **10** oppressive, passionate, sweltering **11** impassioned

TORT: **5** crime, wrong **6** damage, injury **8** iniquity

TORTOISE: **4** emyd **6** turtle **7** laggard **8** terrapin **9** chelonian **10** testudinal
breastplate: **8** plastron
shell: **8** carapace

TORTUOUS: **4** bent **5** snaky **6** curved, spiral, zigzag **7** complex, crooked, devious, sinuate, sinuous, winding **8** involved, twisting **9** deceitful **10** circuitous, convoluted, meandering, roundabout **11** complicated **12** labyrinthine

TORTURE: **4** beat, hurt, maim, pain, rack **5** abuse, agony, annoy, smite, wring **6** deform, harrow, mangle, punish **7** afflict, agonize, anguish, crucify, distort, torment **8** irritate, mistreat, mutilate **9** persecute **10** affliction, distortion, punishment **11** tribulation

TORY: **8** loyalist, royalist **11** reactionary **12** conservative

TOSS: **3** lob, mix **4** cast, flip, hurl, roll, turn **5** bandy, chuck, flick, fling, heave, pitch, serve, sling, throw, twist, upset **6** launch, propel **7** agitate, agonize, disturb **8** flounder

TOTAL: **3** add, sum, tot **4** full **5** equal, gross, tally, utter, whole, wreck, yield **6** amount, entire, figure, number **7** compute, concise, destroy, overall, summary **8** absolute, complete, comprise, demolish, entirety, thorough **9** aggregate, calculate **10** accumulate **13** comprehensive, unconditional

TOTALITARIAN: **7** fascist **8** absolute, despotic **10** autocratic, tyrannical **11** dictatorial **13** authoritarian

TOTE: **3** bag, lug **4** bear, cart, drag, haul, load, pack **5** carry, count, total **6** burden **9** summarize, transport

TOTEM: **4** pole **5** token **6** emblem, figure, symbol **14** representation

TOTTER: **4** fall, reel, rock, sway, toss **5** lurch, shake, waver **6** falter, quiver, seesaw, teeter, topple, wobble **7** stagger, stammer, stumble **8** unstable, unsteady **9** vacillate

TOUCH: **3** dab, hit, pat, paw, pet, rub, tag, tap **4** abut, blow, dash, feel, hand, hint, meet, move **5** brush, flair, grope, knack, nudge, reach, skill, style, taste, trace, trait, whiff **6** affect, border, caress, finger, fondle, handle, method, strike, stroke, tickle **7** contact, discuss, feeling, impinge, inspire, palpate, scratch, texture **8** tangible, tincture **9** influence, stimulate, tactility **10** manipulate, suggestion

TOUCHED: **4** nuts **5** crazy, nutty **6** insane **7** bizarre, bonkers **8** deranged, neurotic **9** eccentric

TOUCHING: **6** moving, tender **7** against, apropos, contact, meeting, piteous, tangent **8** abutting, adjacent, dramatic, stirring **9** adjoining, affecting, bordering, emotional **10** contacting, responsive **11** overlapping, sentimental, sympathetic **13** compassionate, heartbreaking

TOUCH OFF: **5** cause, light, start **7** explode **8** activate, detonate, initiate **9** discharge

TOUCHSTONE: **4** test **5** check, gauge, guide **7** example, measure **8** standard **9** barometer, benchmark, criterion, precedent, yardstick

TOUCH UP: **6** modify, polish, repair **7** enhance, improve, remodel **8** renovate

TOUCHY: **4** sore **5** cross, huffy, testy **6** crabby, cranky, grumpy **7** fragile, grouchy, peevish, uptight **8** delicate, ticklish, volatile **9** irascible, irritable, sensitive **10** precarious **11** thin-skinned **12** cantankerous **13** oversensitive, temperamental

TOUGH: **4** goon, hard, punk, thug **5** bully, hardy, harsh, rigid, rough, rowdy, stern, stiff **6** brutal, flinty, mulish, robust, rugged, severe, strict, strong, sturdy, taxing, uphill **7** callous, durable, hoodlum, ruffian, violent, viscous **8** enduring, hardened, hooligan, leathery, resolute, ruthless, stubborn, vigorous **9** demanding, difficult, laborious, obstinate, pigheaded, resilient, resistant, strenuous **10** aggressive, bullheaded, hardheaded, pugnacious **11** unfortunate

TOUGHEN: **5** drill, inure **6** anneal, harden, season, temper **7** stiffen **9** acclimate **10** strengthen

TOUPEE: **3** rug, wig **6** carpet **7** periwig **9** hairpiece

TOUR: **4** time, trek, trip, turn **5** jaunt, shift, spell, stint, visit, watch **6** course, travel, voyage **7** circuit, journey **9** barnstorm, excursion **10** expedition

TOUR DE FORCE: **4** feat **7** exploit **11** achievement, masterpiece **14** accomplishment

TOURIST: **7** visitor **8** traveler **9** sightseer **10** rubberneck **11** vacationist **12** excursionist, globetrotter

TOURNAMENT: **5** event, joust, match, sport **7** contest, tourney **11** competition

TOUSLED: **5** messy **6** sloppy **7** ruffled, rumpled, unkempt **10** disarrayed, disheveled, disordered

TOUT: **4** laud, plug, toot **5** exalt **6** herald, praise **7** acclaim, promote, solicit, trumpet **8** ballyhoo, proclaim **9** advertise, importune, publicize, recommend

TOW: **3** lug, tug **4** drag, draw, haul, pull, rope **5** cable, ferry, trail

TOWARD: **4** near **5** anent **6** coming, facing **7** against, apropos, forward, willing **8** favoring, obliging **9** regarding **10** beneficial, concerning, propitious **11** approaching

TOWER: **4** loom, rise, silo, soar **5** exalt, mount, raise, spire **6** ascend, belfry, castle, pillar, turret **7** minaret, overtop, steeple, surpass **8** brattice, dominate, monolith, outshine, overlook, ziggurat **9** campanile, transcend **10** skyscraper

TOWERING: **4** high, huge, tall **5** great, lofty, steep **7** intense, soaring, supreme **8** dominant, gigantic, imposing **9** excessive, monstrous, unequaled **10** preeminent **11** outstanding **12** overpowering

TOWN: **4** burg, city **5** bourg **9** residents **10** metropolis, settlement **12** municipality

TOXIC: **5** fatal **6** deadly, lethal **7** harmful **8** venomous **9** poisonous

TOY: **3** pet, top **4** ball, cars, doll, fool, game, play, tiny, whim **5** dally, flirt, model, sport, tease **6** bauble, blocks, cosset, frolic, gadget, gewgaw, little, puzzle, rattle, trains, trifle **7** novelty, pastime, trinket **9** miniature, plaything, teddybear **10** knickknack

TRACE: **4** clue, copy, dash, draw, drop, hint, hunt, line, mark, path, seek, sign **5** shade, speck, spoor, tinge, token, touch, track, trail **6** amount, deduce, detect, flavor, follow, locate, shadow, sketch **7** outline, remains, remnant, smidgen, soupcon, uncover, vestige **8** discover, evidence, quantity, tincture, traverse **9** ascertain, delineate, establish, footprint, reproduce, scintilla, suspicion **10** indication, suggestion

TRACHEA: **4** tube **8** windpipe

TRACK: **4** draw, find, hunt, line, mark, oval, path, rail, road, slot, wake **5** chase, route, scent, sight, trace, trail, tread **6** artery, avenue, course, follow, groove, pursue, search, shadow **7** circuit, vestige **8** footstep, speedway, traverse **9** ascertain, footprint **10** trajectory

TRACT: **3** lot **4** area, path, plot, zone **5** essay, field, range **6** course, estate, extent, parcel, region **7** expanse, leaflet, portion, stretch, terrain **8** brochure, pamphlet **9** territory **11** subdivision

TRACTABLE: **4** tame **6** docile, gentle, pliant **7** pliable **8** amenable, flexible, obedient, workable **9** compliant, malleable **10** governable, manageable **11** complaisant **12** controllable

TRACTATE: **5** essay, tract **6** thesis **8** treatise **9** discourse, monograph **12** dissertation

TRACTION: **5** power **6** stress **8** adhesion, friction **10** resistance

TRADE: **4** deal, sell, swap, work **5** craft, skill, track, trail **6** action, barter, employ, metier, switch **7** bargain, calling, pursuit, traffic **8** business, commerce, exchange, industry, practice, vocation **9** clientele, customers, patronage, patronize **10** handicraft, occupation, profession, substitute **11** transaction

TRADEMARK: **4** logo **5** brand, label **6** emblem, symbol **7** feature **14** characteristic

TRADER: **4** ship **6** dealer, seller **8** barterer, merchant **10** shopkeeper **11** salesperson, stockbroker **12** tradesperson

TRADITION: **4** code, lore, myth **6** belief, custom, legacy, legend **7** culture **8** folklore, heritage, practice **10** convention **11** institution

TRADITIONAL: **3** old **5** fixed, usual **6** common, rooted **7** popular **9** ancestral, classical, customary, unwritten **11** established **12** acknowledged

TRADUCE: **4** slur **5** smear **6** defame, malign, vilify **7** slander, violate **8** disgrace **9** denigrate **10** calumniate

TRAFFIC: **3** buy **4** push, sell **5** trade, truck **6** barter, doings, market **7** bootleg, freight, smuggle **8** business, commerce, dealings, exchange, gridlock **9** patronage, transport **10** bottleneck, congestion, passengers **13** communication

TRAGEDY: **4** doom **6** mishap, sorrow **8** accident, calamity, disaster, hardship **9** adversity **10** misfortune **11** catastrophe

TRAGIC: **3** sad **4** dire **5** awful, fatal **8** dreadful, horrible, terrible **10** disastrous **11** unfortunate **12** catastrophic

TRAIL: **3** dog, tow **4** drag, draw, hunt, mark, path, plod, tail, wake **5** chase, delay, hound, route, scent, spoor, stalk, trace, track, train **6** course, dawdle, follow, linger, pursue, shadow, stream, trudge **7** dwindle, traipse **8** footpath, straggle **9** footsteps **10** footprints

TRAIN: **3** aim, row **4** form, lead, line, lure, mold, rear, tail **5** break, breed, chain, coach, level, point, suite, teach, trace, track, trail, tutor **6** allure, convoy, direct, entice, harden, school, season, series, shaped, string, subway **7** caravan, conduct, cortege, develop, educate, prepare, retinue, sharpen **8** accustom, elevated, exercise, instruct, monorail, practice, rehearse, sequence **9** aftermath, condition, cultivate, entourage, following **10** attendants, discipline, locomotive, procession, succession **11** streamliner

TRAINED: **4** bred **5** aimed **7** skilled **8** educated, equipped, prepared, schooled **9** qualified

TRAINEE: **5** cadet, pupil **6** novice **7** student **10** apprentice

TRAINER: **5** coach, tutor **6** mentor **7** teacher **10** instructor **11** drillmaster

TRAINING: **4** diet **5** drill **8** breeding, exercise, practice, teaching **9** education, schooling **10** background, discipline, upbringing **11** instruction, preparation, supervision

TRAIPSE: **3** gad **4** drag, roam, walk **5** drift, trail, tread **6** ramble, trudge, wander **7** meander

TRAIT: **4** mark **5** habit, quirk **6** custom **7** feature, quality **8** hallmark, property, tendency **9** attribute, lineament, mannerism **11** peculiarity **12** idiosyncrasy **14** characteristic

TRAITOR: **3** rat, spy **4** mole **8** apostate, betrayer, defector, deserter, informer, recreant, renegade, turncoat

famous: **5** Judas **8** Quisling **14** Benedict Arnold

TRAITOROUS: **5** false **8** disloyal, mutinous, renegade **9** faithless **10** perfidious **11** treacherous, treasonable, unpatriotic

TRAJECTORY: **4** path **5** curve **6** course **7** missile **10** projectile

TRAM: **3** car **6** thread **7** gondola, trolley **8** cable car **9** streetcar

TRAMMEL: **3** net **4** clog **5** check, gauge **6** bridle, fasten, fetter, hamper, hinder, impede **7** compass, confine, prevent, shackle **8** obstruct, restrain **10** instrument

TRAMP: **3** bum, vag **4** hike, hobo, plod, roam, slut, step, walk **5** crush, march, pound, stamp, stomp, tread **6** gallop, harlot, trudge, wander **7** drifter, traipse, vagrant **8** derelict, vagabond **10** panhandler, prostitute

TRAMPLE: **5** crush, pound, stamp, stomp, tread **6** bruise, defeat, injure, squash **7** destroy, flatten **8** infringe **9** overwhelm

TRANCE: **4** coma, daze, muse **5** spell, swoon **6** stupor **7** ecstasy, enchant, reverie **8** daydream, hypnosis **9** catalepsy, enrapture, transport

TRANQUIL: **4** calm, cool, even, mild **5** balmy, quiet, still **6** gentle, hushed, placid, sedate, serene, steady **7** pacific, restful **8** composed, pastoral, peaceful, soothing **9** easygoing **10** motionless **11** undisturbed

TRANQUILITY: **4** calm **5** order, peace, quiet **7** harmony **8** ataraxia, serenity **9** composure, placidity **11** restfulness **12** peacefulness

TRANQUILIZE: **4** calm, lull **5** quell, quiet, relax **6** pacify, sedate, soothe, subdue **7** assuage

TRANSACT: **6** finish, handle **7** conduct, perform **8** complete, conclude, transfer **9** negotiate **10** accomplish

TRANSACTION: **4** deal, pact, sale **5** doing, trade **6** affair **7** bargain, venture **8** business, contract, covenant, exchange, purchase **9** agreement **11** undertaking

TRANSCEND: **4** soar **5** climb, excel, outdo, raise **6** ascend, exceed **7** elevate, surpass **8** outshine, outstrip, surmount

TRANSCENDENT: **7** supreme **8** superior **9** exceeding **10** preeminent, surpassing

TRANSCENDENTAL: **8** mystical **9** boundless, spiritual **10** surpassing

TRANSCRIBE: **4** copy **6** record **7** reprint, rewrite **8** decipher **9** duplicate, reproduce, translate

TRANSFER: **4** deed, give, move, pass, sale, send **5** carry, shift, trade **6** assign, change, convey, demise, orders **7** convert, deliver, dispose **8** delegate, relocate, transmit **9** transform, transport **10** abalienate, assignment **12** substitution, transmission

TRANSFIX: **5** lance, rivet, spear, spike, stick **6** impale, pierce **7** astound **8** astonish **9** captivate, fascinate, hypnotize, mesmerize, penetrate, spellbind

TRANSFORM: **4** turn **5** alter **6** change, mutate, revamp, switch **7** convert, remodel **11** reconstruct, transfigure **12** metamorphose

TRANSGRESS: **3** err, sin **5** lapse **6** offend **7** disobey, violate **8** infringe, overstep, trespass

TRANSGRESSION: **3** sin **5** crime, error **6** breach **7** misdeed, offense **8** trespass **9** violation **10** infraction, wrongdoing **11** misbehavior **12** disobedience, infringement

TRANSIENT: **5** brief, guest **6** change **7** passage, passing **8** fleeting, fugitive, temporal, traveler **9** ephemeral, itinerant, migratory, momentary, temporary **10** conveyance, evanescent, transitory **11** impermanent

TRANSIT: **6** travel **7** journey **8** movement **14** transportation

TRANSITION: **4** jump **5** phase, shift **6** change **7** passage **9** evolution **10** alteration, changeover, conversion **11** development

TRANSITORY: **5** brief **7** passing **8** fleeting, temporal **9** ephemeral, temporary, transient **10** evanescent **11** impermanent

TRANSLATE: **5** alter **6** change, decode, render **7** convert, explain, restate **8** decipher, rephrase **9** interpret **10** paraphrase, transcribe

TRANSLATION: **7** version **9** rendition **10** adaptation, paraphrase **11** explanation **14** interpretation, simplification

TRANSLUCENT: **5** clear, lucid, sheer **6** limpid, opaque **7** obvious **8** pellucid **9** unblurred **11** transparent

TRANSMISSION: **7** gearbox, message, sending **8** delivery, dispatch **9** broadcast **10** conveyance **13** communication

TRANSMIT: **4** emit, send, wire **5** carry, relay **6** convey, funnel, render, spread **7** channel, conduct **8**

televise, transfer **9** broadcast **10** dispatch **11** communicate

TRANSPARENT: **4** airy, open **5** clear, filmy, gauzy, lucid, plain, sheer **6** candid, glassy, limpid, lucent **7** evident, obvious **8** gossamer, luminous, pellucid **11** crystalline, translucent

TRANSPIRE: **5** occur **6** befall, emerge, happen, result **7** develop

TRANSPLANT: **4** move **6** uproot **8** displace, relocate, resettle, transfer **9** transport

TRANSPORT: **4** bear, boat, cart, haul, move, oust, send, ship, tote **5** bring, carry, exile, expel, ferry, truck **6** banish, convey, deport, fervor, thrill **7** delight, ecstasy, freight, rapture, smuggle, transit, vehicle **8** transfer **9** captivate, enrapture, happiness, piggyback **10** transplant

TRANSPORTATION: **4** fare **6** moving **7** carting, hauling, passage, vehicle **8** movement, shipment, shipping, trucking **10** conveyance

TRANSPOSE: **5** alter, shift **6** change, remove, switch **7** convert, reverse **8** exchange, transfer **9** transform **10** substitute **11** interchange

TRANSVERSE: **5** cross, pivot, shift **6** across, thwart, travel **7** oblique **8** diagonal **9** alternate, crosswise **10** horizontal

TRAP: **3** bag, net, pit, web **4** bait, cage, fool, lure, nail, ploy, seal, snag **5** catch, decoy, snare, trick **6** ambush, corner, hazard, seduce **7** capture, dragnet, ensnare, pitfall **8** artifice, confound, deadfall, inveigle, maneuver **9** roadblock, stratagem **10** conspiracy, enticement, temptation

TRAPPINGS: **4** gear **6** finery, things **7** apparel **8** trimming **9** caparison, equipment **11** decorations **13** paraphernalia

TRAPPIST: **4** monk
vow of: **7** silence **9** austerity

TRASH: **4** crap, dirt, junk, muck, scum **5** bilge, dregs, filth, tramp, waste, wreck **6** debris, drivel, litter, rabble, refuse, rubble **7** destroy, discard, garbage, hogwash, rubbish **8** malarkey, nonsense, riffraff, trumpery **9** vandalize **10** balderdash

TRASHY: **5** cheap, junky **6** flimsy, paltry **7** useless **8** riffraff, trumpery **9** worthless

TRAUMA: **5** shock, wound **6** injury, ordeal, stress **7** anguish **9** suffering

TRAVAIL: **4** toil, work **5** agony, labor, pains, pangs **6** effort, stress **7** anguish **8** distress, drudgery, exertion, struggle **9** suffering **10** childbirth **11** parturition, tribulation

TRAVEL: **3** run **4** flay, move, mush, ride, roam, tour, trek, trip, walk **5** coast, drive, jaunt, visit **6** cruise, junket, ramble, voyage, wander **7** commute, explore, journey, migrate, passage, proceed, sojourn **8** sightsee, traverse **9** excursion **10** expedition **11** peregrinate

TRAVELER: **4** hobo **5** nomad, tramp **7** pilgrim, rambler, tourist, voyager **8** commuter, explorer, vagabond, wanderer, wayfarer **9** itinerant, sightseer **10** adventurer **11** salesperson **12** globetrotter

TRAVERSE: **4** deny, pass, span **5** cross, rebut **6** bridge, hinder, oppose, refute, resist, swivel, thwart, travel, zigzag **7** examine, transom **9** crosswise, negotiate **10** contradict, crisscross

TRAVESTY: **4** sham **5** mimic **6** parody, satire **7** lampoon, mockery **8**

ridicule **9** burlesque, imitation **10** caricature, distortion, perversion **12** exaggeration

TRAWL: 3 net **4** drag, fish, line **5** troll **7** dragnet

TRAY: 5 board, plate **6** salver, server **7** coaster, platter

TREACHEROUS: 5 dirty, false, hairy, risky, snaky **6** chancy, tricky, unsafe **8** disloyal **9** dangerous, deceptive, difficult, dishonest, faithless, hazardous, insidious **10** perfidious, precarious, traitorous, unreliable **12** undependable, unscrupulous **13** untrustworthy

TREACHERY: 5 guile **6** deceit **7** perfidy, treason **8** betrayal, trickery **10** dishonesty, disloyalty, infidelity

TREACLE: 5 syrup **6** remedy **8** antidote, compound, molasses

TREAD: 4 gait, mark, pace, rush, step, walk **5** dance, march, press, stamp, stomp, trace, trail, tramp **6** groove, prance, stride, subdue **7** repress, traipse, trample **8** copulate **9** footprint, footsteps

TREASON: 6 mutiny, revolt **7** perfidy **8** betrayal, sedition **9** treachery **10** dishonesty, disloyalty

TREASURE: 4 find **5** cache, guard, hoard, money, pearl, prize, store, value **6** jewels, riches, wealth **7** cherish, fortune, worship **8** preserve **10** accumulate, appreciate, collection

TREASURER: 6 bursar, purser **7** cashier, curator, officer **9** financier **11** chamberlain, comptroller

TREASURY: 4 bank **5** chest, funds, vault **6** coffer, museum **8** archives, security **9** exchequer, thesaurus **10** depository, repository, storehouse

TREAT: 4 cure, heal **5** goody, snack **6** manage, tackle **7** delight, relieve **8** medicate, surprise **9** prescribe **11** refreshment

TREATISE: 5 essay, paper, study, tract **6** memoir, thesis **7** writing **9** discourse, monograph, narration **10** commentary, discussion, exposition **11** composition **12** dissertation

TREATMENT: 4 care, cure **5** usage **6** action, method, remedy **7** surgery, therapy **8** antidote, handling, strategy **9** procedure **10** management, medication **11** application

TREATY: 4 deal, pact **6** accord **7** concord **8** contract **9** agreement **10** settlement **11** arrangement, negotiation **13** understanding

TREBLE: 4 high **5** acute **6** shrill, triple **9** threefold

TREE: 3 ash, elm, fir, oak **4** palm, pine **5** beech, birch, cacao, carob, maple **6** banyan, locust, timber **8** magnolia

bark: **4** ross, tapa

Buddha's: **5** bodhi **6** botree

citrus: **4** lime **5** lemon **6** orange **8** bergamot **10** calamondin

combining forms: **3** dry **5** dendr

concerning: **8** arboreal

dwarf: **5** scrub **6** bonsai **7** abuscle **10** chinquapin

evergreen: **3** fir, yew **4** pine, titi **5** carob, cedar, holly, olive **6** balsam, carobe, pinyon **7** juniper, madrona, redwood, sequoia **8** tamarisk

flowering: **5** elder, sumac **6** acacia, mimosa, redbud **7** dogwood **8** oleaster, sourwood

fruit: **3** fig **4** gaub, lime **5** anona, apple, araca, lemon, olive, papaw, topes **6** banana, biriba, litchi, medlar, pawpaw, sapota **7** avocado, capulin, genipap, tangelo **8** tamarind **9** tangerine

hardwood: **3** oak **5** beech, birch, ebony **6** cherry **8** chestnut
nut: **4** cola, kola **5** hazel, pecan, pinon **6** almond, cashew **7** buckeye, filbert, hickory **9** pistachio
oil-yielding: **3** bel, ben, ebo **4** eboe, shea, tung **7** cajeput
palm: **4** coco, nipa **5** ratan **6** arengs, grugru, pinang, raffia, rattan **8** carnauba
parts: **4** bark, bole, knot, leaf, root, twig **5** trunk **6** branch
plantain: **4** pala **6** banana
shade: **3** ash, elm, oak **5** maple **6** linden, poplar **8** sycamore
softwood: **3** fir, lin **4** pine **5** alamo, ambay, balsa, cedar, linde **6** spruce, tupelo **8** black gum, corkwood
tropical: **4** ohia, sago, teak **5** areca, balsa, cacao **6** acajou, baobab, citrus **7** palmyra **8** allspice, mangrove, sweetsop **9** cherimoya
willow: **5** osier, sauch, saugh **6** poplar
worship: **11** dendrolatry
young: **7** sapling

TREK: **4** hike, trip **5** jaunt, march **6** travel, voyage **7** journey, migrate, odyssey **9** excursion **10** expedition

TRELLIS: **5** arbor **6** grille, screen **7** lattice, pergola **9** framework **11** latticework

TREMBLE: **4** fear **5** quake, shake **6** dodder, quaver, quiver, shiver, totter, tremor, wobble **7** flutter, shudder, vibrate **9** palpitate

TREMENDOUS: **4** huge, vast **5** giant, great, large **6** mighty **7** amazing, immense, mammoth, titanic **8** colossal, enormous, fabulous, gigantic, powerful, terrific, whopping **9** deafening, fantastic, marvelous, momentous, monstrous, wonderful **10** astounding, stupendous **12** overwhelming **13** extraordinary

TREMOR: **5** quake, shock **6** quaver, quiver, shiver **7** flutter, shaking **8** trembler **9** trembling, vibrating **10** earthquake

TREMULOUS: **5** aspen, timid **7** aquiver, excited, fearful, jittery, nervous, shaking **8** cowardly, timorous, wavering **9** quavering, quivering, shivering, trembling **11** palpitating

TRENCH: **3** cut **4** gash, moat **5** carve, chase, ditch, drain, fosse, gully, slash, slice **6** canyon, furrow, groove, gutter, trough **7** channel, foxhole **8** encroach **9** earthwork **10** excavation

TRENCHANT: **4** keen **5** acrid, crisp, sharp **6** biting **7** caustic, cutting, intense, mordant, pointed, probing **8** clear-cut, distinct, explicit, forceful, incisive, scathing, vigorous **9** effective, energetic, sarcastic **11** penetrating

TREND: **3** fad **4** bent, flow, mode, rage **5** craze, drift, style, vogue **6** course **7** current **8** movement, tendency **9** direction **11** inclination

TRENDSETTER: **6** leader **9** initiator, innovator **10** pacesetter **11** trailblazer

TRENDY: **3** hip **4** chic **7** faddish, popular, stylish **11** fashionable **12** contemporary

TREPIDATION: **4** fear **5** alarm, dread, panic **6** fright, tremor **7** anxiety, quaking, shaking **9** agitation, quivering, trembling **10** uneasiness **11** butterflies, disturbance, nervousness **12** apprehension **13** consternation

TRESPASS: **3** sin **5** poach **6** breach, invade, offend **7** intrude, offense **8** encroach, entrench, infringe **9** interlope, intrusion, violation **10** infraction, wrongdoing **12** encroachment **13** transgression

TRESPASSER: **7** invader **8** intruder, offender **9** infringer **10** encroacher, interloper **12** transgressor

TRESS: **4** curl, hair, lock **5** braid, plait **7** ringlet

TRESTLE: **4** beam **5** brace, horse, stand **7** support **8** sawhorse **9** framework

TRIAL: **3** try **4** case, pain, test **5** agony, cross, essay, pilot **6** ordeal, sample, tryout **7** anguish, attempt, contest, hearing, inquiry, lawsuit, trouble **8** analysis, crucible, endeavor, evidence, hardship, struggle **9** adversity, suffering **10** affliction, experiment, misfortune, visitation **11** examination, proceedings **12** probationary

TRIAL AND ERROR: **6** method **9** heuristic **10** experiment

TRIANGLE:
side: **10** hypotenuse
theorem: **11** Pythagorean
types: **7** scalene **9** isosceles **11** equilateral, right-angled

TRIANGULAR: **7** cuneate, deltoid, hastate **8** trigonal **10** trilateral

TRIBE: **4** band, clan, folk, race **5** group **6** family, people **7** kindred, lineage, society, village **8** division **11** association

TRIBULATION: **4** pain **5** agony, grief, trial **6** burden, misery, ordeal, sorrow **7** anguish **8** distress, hardship **9** adversity, suffering **10** affliction **11** persecution, unhappiness

TRIBUNAL: **3** bar **4** seat **5** bench, board, court, forum **8** assembly **9** committee

TRIBUTARY: **6** feeder, stream **9** accessory, ancillary, auxiliary, dependent, secondary **10** subsidiary **11** subordinate **12** contributory

TRIBUTE: **3** tax **4** duty, gift, levy **5** grant, salvo **6** assign, eulogy, praise, tariff **7** ovation, payment, respect **8** applause, citation, memorial **9** gratitude, laudation, panegyric **10** compliment, honoration, obligation **11** declaration, testimonial **12** accoladation, commendation

TRICE: **4** wink **5** blink, hoist, jiffy **6** moment, second, secure **7** instant **9** twinkling

TRICK: **3** fox, gag **4** bait, bilk, dupe, feat, fool, gull, hoax, jest, joke, lark, ruse, trap, wile **5** antic, bluff, catch, cheat, decoy, dodge, feint, fraud, guile, knack, prank, shift, skill, spell, stunt **6** ambush, deceit, device, method, outwit, secret **7** beguile, deceive, defraud, finagle, gimmick, mislead, pretext, sleight, swindle **8** artifice, delusion, escapade, flimflam, hoodwink, illusion, maneuver **9** bamboozle, chicanery, imposture, stratagem, technique **10** subterfuge **11** hornswoggle, legerdemain

TRICKERY: **4** scam **5** fraud **6** deceit, dupery **7** cunning, knavery, slyness **8** artifice, cheating, flimflam, quackery, trumpery **9** chicanery, deception, stratagem **10** dishonesty, hanky-panky, tomfoolery **11** shenanigans

TRICKLE: **4** drip, flow, leak, ooze, seep **7** distill, dribble **9** percolate

TRICKSTER: **5** cheat, joker **6** rascal **7** cheater, grifter **8** swindler **9** prankster

TRICKY: **3** sly **4** foxy, wily **5** slick **6** artful, crafty, shifty, sneaky **7** cunning, devious **8** delicate, unstable **9** deceitful, intricate, sensitive **10** misleading, precarious

TRIDENT: **4** fork **5** spear **6** weapon **7** scepter
holder: **7** Neptune **8** Poseidon
prongs: **5** three

TRIED: **4** used **5** known **6** proved, tested **8** approved, faithful, reliable **10** dependable **11** trustworthy **12** demonstrated

TRIFLE: **3** bit, jot, toy **4** dash, drop, hint, jest, play **5** dally, flirt, pinch, speck, touch, trace, trick, waste **6** bauble, dabble, dawdle, dibble, doodle, fiddle, fidget, frivol, gewgaw, little, putter **7** deceive, dessert, fribble, nothing, novelty, trinket **8** gimcrack **9** bagatelle, plaything **10** knickknack, suggestion, triviality

TRIFLING: **4** idle, mere, puny **5** banal, inane, petty, small **6** little, slight **7** measley, shallow, trivial **8** piddling **9** frivolous, worthless **10** immaterial, negligible **11** unimportant **13** insignificant

TRIG: **4** chic, neat, prim, prop, stop, tidy, trim **5** dandy, sharp, smart, stiff **6** classy, formal, spruce **7** dashing, stylish, support

TRIGGER: **5** cause, lever, spark, start **6** prompt **7** provoke, release **8** activate, generate, initiate **9** stimulate

TRILL: **4** roll **5** shake, sound, twirl **6** quaver, warble **7** tremolo, vibrate, vibrato

TRIM: **3** cut, lop **4** beat, chic, crop, deck, edge, edit, neat, snip, snug, thin, tidy, trig, whip **5** adorn, braid, cheat, chide, clean, dress, order, preen, prune, shape, shave, shear, slick, smart, whack **6** adjust, border, dapper, defeat, edging, fringe, modify, petite, reduce, spruce, thrash **7** balance, compact, curtail, furnish, garnish, orderly, shapely, shorten, slender **8** beautify, chastise, decorate, manicure, ornament **9** condition, embellish, shipshape **10** decoration **11** streamlined

TRIMMING: **4** lace **5** frill **6** border, edging, extras, fringe **7** cutting, pruning **8** clipping, ornament, reducing, trapping **10** decoration, embroidery **13** embellishment

TRINIDAD AND TOBAGO:
capital: **11** Port-of-Spain
cities: **5** Arima **11** San Fernando, Scarborough
continent: **12** South America
ethnic groups: **7** African **10** East Indian
features: **6** Galera
language: **7** English
monetary unit: **6** dollar
water: **5** Pitch

TRINITY: **4** trio **5** three, triad, trine **6** triune **7** trilogy **9** threesome
religious: **3** Son **6** Father **9** Holy Ghost

TRINKET: **3** toy **5** jewel **6** bauble, doodad, gadget, gewgaw, trifle **7** bibelot, novelty **8** gimcrack, ornament **9** bagatelle, doohickey, plaything, showpiece **10** knickknack **11** thingamabob, thingamajig

TRIO: **4** band **5** triad **6** triune **7** trinity **9** threesome

TRIP: **4** fall, hike, muff, skip, slip, spin, tour, trek **5** caper, catch, drive, error, jaunt, lapse, tread **6** bungle, cruise, errand, junket, outing, safari, tumble, voyage **7** blunder, journey, misstep, mistake, stumble **9** excursion **10** expedition

TRITE: **4** dull, worn **5** banal, corny, passe, silly, stale, tired, vapid **6** common, jejune **7** cliched, prosaic, routine, trivial **8** everyday, ordinary, shopworn, timeworn **9** hackneyed **10** threadbare, uninspired, unoriginal **11** commonplace, stereotyped **12** conventional

TRITURATE: **3** rub **5** crush, grind, pound **6** thrash **9** pulverize

TRIUMPH: **3** win **4** beat **5** exult, glory **6** defeat **7** conquer, mastery, prevail, succeed, success, victory **8** conquest, flourish **10** exultation, jubilation **11** achievement, celebration

TRIUMPHANT: **6** elated, joyous **8** exultant, exulting, glorious, jubilant **10** successful, victorious **11** celebrating

TRIVIAL: **5** banal, minor, petty, small, trite **6** little, measly, paltry, slight **7** nominal **8** ordinary, picayune, trifling **9** frivolous **10** incidental, negligible **11** commonplace, meaningless, superficial, unimportant **13** insignificant

TROILUS:
father: **9** King Priam
killer: **8** Achilles
kingdom: **4** Troy
lover: **8** Cressida
mother: **6** Hecuba

TROJAN:
concerning: **9** Dardanian
epic: **5** Iliad
horse builder: **5** Epeus
horse goal: **4** Troy
king: **5** Priam
war cause: **5** Helen
war heroes: **4** Ajax **5** Paris **6** Aeneas, Agenor, Hector **9** Agamemnon, Palamedes

TROLL: **4** fish, ogre, reel, roll, sing, turn **5** catch, dwarf, fairy, giant, gnome **6** goblin, patrol, ramble, sprite **7** gremlin, revolve **9** hobgoblin

TROLLOP: **4** slut **5** hussy, whore **6** floozy, harlot **10** prostitute **12** streetwalker

TROOP: **4** army, band, crew, gang, pack, unit **5** corps, crowd, drove, flock, group, march, squad **6** legion, outfit, troupe **7** battery, cavalry, company **8** infantry, military, soldiers **9** gathering **10** combatants

TROPE: **5** irony **6** simile **7** analogy **8** metaphor **9** hyperbole **10** comparison

TROPHY: **3** cup **5** award, booty, crown, honor, medal, prize **6** laurel, reward, ribbon **7** memento **8** citation, keepsake, memorial, souvenir

TROPICAL: **3** hot **4** warm **6** steamy, sultry, torrid **10** sweltering

TROT: **3** jog, run, tot **4** gait, pace, pony **5** hurry **6** canter, hasten **7** toddler

TROTH: **6** pledge **7** promise **8** fidelity, marriage **9** betrothal **10** engagement **11** declaration

TROUBADOUR: **4** bard, poet **6** singer **8** minstrel, musician **9** balladeer

TROUBLE: **3** ail, irk, try, vex, woe **4** care, fret, fuss, harm, heed, mess, pain, snag, spot, stir **5** anger, annoy, grief, labor, pains, upset, worry **6** bother, burden, crisis, danger, dither, effort, harass, impair, malady, matter, ordeal, pester, pickle, plague, plight, pother, scrape, sorrow, strife, unrest **7** afflict, agitate, ailment, anxiety, concern, dilemma, disturb, illness, perturb, torment, travail **8** aggrieve, calamity, disorder, distress, exertion, hardship, mischief, unsettle **9** adversity, commotion, complaint, interfere **10** difficulty, disability, discomfort, discommode, dissension, misfortune, uneasiness **11** displeasure, disturbance, predicament **13** inconvenience

TROUBLED: **5** fazed, upset **6** pained, uneasy **7** alarmed, fearful, plagued, puzzled, worried **8** bothered, harassed **9** afflicted, concerned, irritated, tormented **10** distraught, distressed

TROUBLEMAKER: **4** punk **5** knave **6** rascal **7** gremlin **8** agitator, nuisance **9** miscreant **10** instigator

TROUBLESOME: **5** pesky **6** trying, unruly, vexing, wicked **7** arduous **8** annoying, tiresome **9** demanding, difficult, upsetting, worrisome **10** bothersome, burdensome, disturbing, oppressive **11** problematic **12** inconvenient

TROUGH: **4** duct, moat **5** basin, canal, chute, ditch, drain, flume, gully **6** gutter, sluice, trench **7** channel, conduit **9** container

TROUNCE: **4** beat, flog, lick, rush, ship **5** cream, scold **6** defeat, hammer, pommel, thrash **7** clobber, conquer **9** overwhelm

TROUPE: **4** band **5** group **6** actors, outfit **7** company **10** performers

TROUPER: **5** actor **7** actress **8** thespian **9** performer **11** entertainer

TROUSERS: **5** jeans, pants **6** slacks **8** breeches, britches, knickers **9** dungarees **10** pantaloons

TROY:
also called: **5** Iliac, Ilian, Ilium, Troad, Troas **8** Teucrian
archaeologist: **10** Schliemann
concerning: **5** Iliac **6** Trojan
defender: **6** Aeneas
epic: **5** Iliad
fell to: **6** Greeks
founder: **4** Ilus, Tros
king: **5** Priam
part of: **9** Trojan War

TRUANT: **4** idle, lazy **5** stray **6** absent, loafer **7** missing, shirker, slacker **8** straying **10** neglectful

TRUCE: **4** halt **5** break, letup, pause, peace **7** respite **8** breather **9** armistice, cease-fire, cessation

TRUCK: **3** rig, van **4** cart, move **5** dolly, lorry, trade, trash **6** barter, peddle **7** bargain, rubbish, traffic, vehicle **8** business, commerce, dealings, exchange, handcart **9** negotiate, transport

TRUCKLE: **4** fawn **5** toady, yield **6** caster, cringe, grovel, kowtow, submit **7** servile, succumb, trundle **8** bootlick **10** submissive **11** apple-polish

TRUCULENT: **4** rude **5** cruel, harsh, rough, surly **6** brutal, fierce, savage **7** abusive, hostile, scrappy **8** bullying, militant, scathing **9** barbarous, bellicose, combative, ferocious **10** aggressive, pugnacious **11** belligerent **12** antagonistic, intimidating, vituperative

TRUDGE: **4** drag, hike, plod, slog, toil, trek, walk **5** march, tramp **6** hobble, lumber **7** schlepp, traipse

TRUE: **4** just, pure, real **5** exact, level, loyal, right, valid **6** actual, honest, lawful, proper, steady **7** certain, correct, devoted, dutiful, exactly, factual, genuine, precise, sincere, staunch, upright **8** accurate, bona fide, constant, faithful, reliable, resolute, rightful, truthful **9** authentic, essential, honorable, steadfast, unfeigned, veracious, veritable **10** dependable, legitimate **11** fundamental, trustworthy

TRUE-BLUE: **5** loyal **7** staunch **8** faithful, reliable **10** dependable

TRUELOVE: **5** lover **7** beloved **10** sweetheart

TRUISM: **5** adage, axiom, maxim, motto **6** cliche, saying **7** proverb **8** aphorism **9** platitude

TRULY: **4** very, well **6** indeed, really, surely, verily **7** exactly, rightly **8** actually, honestly **9** certainly, genuinely, literally, sincerely **10** absolutely, accurately, definitely, positively **13** unequivocally

TRUMPERY: **4** bosh **5** cheap, gaudy, showy, trash **6** cheesy, paltry, shoddy, tawdry **7** malarky, rubbish, useless **8** nonsense, trickery **9** deception, worthless

TRUMPET: **4** horn, tout **5** blare, bugle **6** cornet, herald **7** clarion, publish **8** proclaim **9** advertise **10** instrument

TRUNCATE: **3** cut, lop **4** crop, trim **5** prune, shear **6** lessen **7** abridge, curtail, shorten **8** condense **10** abbreviate

TRUNCHEON: **4** club **5** staff, stick **6** cudgel, weapon **8** bludgeon **9** billy club **10** nightstick

TRUNDLE: **4** cart, roll, spin, turn **5** dolly, twirl, wheel, whirl **6** caster, roller, rotate **7** revolve

TRUNK: **3** box **4** body, case, stem, tank **5** chest, snoot, snout, stalk, torso **6** locker, thorax **7** baggage, luggage **8** suitcase **9** container, proboscis

TRUSS: **3** tie **4** beam, bind, hold, pack, prop **5** strap **6** bundle, fasten **7** bracket, support, tighten **9** framework **10** strengthen

TRUST: **4** care, duty, hope, rely **5** faith, stock **6** assign, assume, belief, cartel, credit **7** believe, confide, consign, custody, loyalty, presume **8** business, credence, reliance, security **9** assurance, coalition, syndicate **10** commission, confidence, dependence, protection **11** safekeeping **12** organization **14** responsibility

TRUSTEE: **6** bailee **8** director, guardian, overseer **9** custodian, fiduciary **10** depository **13** administrator

TRUSTWORTHY: **4** safe, true **5** loyal, solid, sound, tried **6** honest, trusty **7** ethical, upright **8** credible, faithful, reliable, straight **9** authentic **10** aboveboard, believable, dependable **11** responsible **12** confidential

TRUSTY: **8** credible, faithful, reliable **10** dependable **11** trustworthy

TRUTH: **4** fact **5** axiom, scoop, sooth, troth **6** candor, gospel, truism **7** honesty, lowdown, loyalty, realism, reality **8** accuracy, fidelity, validity, veracity **9** agreement, integrity, sincerity **11** correctness, genuineness, uprightness **12** authenticity

TRUTHFUL: **4** open **5** frank **6** candid, honest, square, trusty **7** factual, sincere **8** accurate **9** veracious, veridical **10** aboveboard **11** trustworthy

TRY: **3** aim, irk, vex **4** hear, seek, stab, test, turn **5** annoy, assay, crack, essay, fling, judge, prove, taste, trial, upset, whack, whirl **6** bother, effort, harass, render, sample, screen, strain, strive **7** adjudge, afflict, agonize, attempt, contest, examine, partake, subject, torment, torture, trouble, venture **8** audition, endeavor, irritate, struggle **9** undertake **10** experiment **11** opportunity

TRYING: **4** hard **5** rough, tight, tough **6** taxing **7** arduous, irksome, onerous **8** annoying **9** demanding, difficult, strenuous, stressful **10** bothersome, burdensome, exhausting **12** exasperating

TRYST: **4** date **5** union, visit **7** meeting **9** agreement **10** engagement, rendezvous **11** appointment, assignation

TUB: **3** keg, vat **4** bath, boat, cask, ship, tank **5** barge, bathe, keeve **6** barrel, bucket, vessel **7** cistern **8** cauldron **9** container

TUBBY: **3** fat **5** jumbo, large, plump, pudgy **6** chubby, portly, rotund

TUBE: **4** duct, hose, pipe **5** chute, straw **6** subway, tunnel **7** cannula, conduit, pipette **8** cylinder, pipeline **10** television

TUBER: **3** yam **4** beet, bulb, root, stem, taro **5** jalap **6** potato, turnip **8** swelling **9** tubercule **12** protuberance

TUCK: **3** tap **4** beat, fold, food, save **5** cramp, pinch, pleat, stick, stuff **6** enfold, insert **7** shorten, tighten **8** contract, position

TUCKER: **4** poop, tire, wary, wilt **7** exhaust, fatigue

TUFT: **4** wisp **5** batch, beard, bunch, clump, group, mound **6** bundle, goatee, tassel **7** cluster **8** feathers

TUG: **3** lug, tow **4** boat, drag, draw, haul, pull, rope, toil, yank **5** chain, heave, labor, strap **6** drudge, effort, strain, strive **7** contend, contest, wrestle **8** struggle

TUITION: **4** cost **6** charge **8** teaching, tutelage **9** education **11** expenditure, instruction

TUMBLE: **4** fall, flip, roll, toss, trip **5** level, pitch, spill, twist, upset, whirl **6** jumble, plunge, rumple, topple **7** flatten, plummet, stumble **8** collapse, disorder **9** confusion, overthrow **10** disarrange, somersault

TUMBLER: **5** glass **6** goblet, pigeon, vessel **7** acrobat, gymnast

TUMBREL: **4** cart **5** wagon

TUMID: **5** puffy **6** turgid **7** bloated, bulging, pompous, swollen **8** enlarged, inflated **9** bombastic, distended, overblown, tumescent **11** protuberant

TUMOR: **3** wen **4** cyst, wart **5** gumma, polyp **6** cancer, growth, lipoma **7** bombast, sarcoma **8** hepatoma, melanoma, neoplasm, scirrhus **9** carcinoma, papilloma, sarcocele

TUMULT: **4** fray, fuss, riot, stew **5** brawl, noise **6** bedlam, dither, hassle, hubbub, outcry, racket, revolt, uproar **7** bluster, turmoil **8** disorder, outbreak, outburst, paroxysm, upheaval, uprising **9** agitation, commotion, confusion **10** excitement, hullabaloo, turbulence **11** disturbance, pandemonium

TUMULTUOUS: **4** wild **5** noisy, rough, rowdy **6** hectic, stormy, unruly **7** chaotic, furious, raucous, violent **8** agitated, confused **9** turbulent **10** boisterous, disorderly

TUN: **3** keg, vat **4** cask, drum, tank **6** barrel **8** hogshead **9** container

TUNE: **3** air, key **5** carol, ditty, piece, pitch, sound **6** accord, jingle, melody, number, strain, string **7** concert, concord, harmony, sonance **9** agreement, harmonize **11** disposition

TUNEFUL: **6** catchy, dulcet **7** lyrical, musical **8** rhythmic **9** melodious **10** harmonious

TUNIC: **4** coat, robe, toga **6** blouse, chiton, jacket, kirtle **7** surcoat

TUNISIA:
capital: **5** Tunis
cities: **4** Sfax **6** Sousse **7** Bizerte **8** Kairouan
continent: **6** Africa
ethnic groups: **4** Arab
features: **6** Djerba **8** Carthage **14** Atlas Mountains
languages: **6** Arabic, French
monetary unit: **5** dinar
water: **5** Gabes, Tunis **7** Bizerte **8** Hammamet **12** Shott el Jerid

TUNNEL: **4** adit, bore, mine, tube **5** shaft **6** burrow, subway **7** conduit **8** crawlway, excavate **9** underpass **10** passageway

TURBAN: **3** cap, hat **5** lungi **7** bandana **9** headdress

TURBID: **4** dark **5** dense, heavy, muddy, murky, thick **6** cloudy, impure **7** muddled, obscure, unclear **8** confused, polluted **9** unsettled **11** sedimentary

TURBULENCE: **4** fury **5** fight, havoc **6** fracas, frenzy, tumult, uproar **7** bluster, turmoil **8** disorder **9** agitation, commotion **11** disturbance

TURBULENT: **4** wild **5** bumpy, rough, rowdy **6** choppy, fierce, raging, stormy, unruly **7** chaotic, furious, rampant, violent **8** agitated, restless, unstable **9** unsettled **10** blustering, boisterous, rebellious, tumultuous **11** tempestuous **12** uncontrolled

TURF: **3** sod **4** area, soil **5** divot, earth, grass, track **6** ground, region **7** terrain **9** bailiwick, racetrack, territory **12** neighborhood

TURGID: **5** puffy, tumid **6** ornate **7** bloated, pompous, swollen **8** enlarged, inflated **9** bombastic, distended, grandiose, tumescent **11** pretentious **13** grandiloquent

TURKEY: **3** hen, tom **4** bird, fowl **5** poult **7** failure, gobbler

TURKEY:
capital: **6** Ankara
cities: **4** Enos, Homa, Sert, Troy, Urfa **5** Adana, Bursa, Izmir, Konya, Maras, Siirt, Sivas **6** Aintab, Edessa, Edirne, Elaziz, Marash, Samsun, Smyrna **7** Antioch, Broussa, Erzurum, Kayseri, Scutari, Uskudar **8** Istanbul, Stamboul **9** Byzantium **10** Adrianople **14** Constantinople
commander: **4** amir, emir **5** ameer, emeer, pacha, pasha **6** sirdar **9** seraskier
districts: **4** Pera **6** Angora, Thrace **7** Beyoglu, Cilicia **8** Anatolia **9** Asia Minor
drink: **4** boza, raki **5** airan, pasha, rakee **6** mastic
empire: **7** Ottoman
food: **4** hind **5** halva, pilaw **7** baklava **10** shish kebab
gulf: **3** Cos **5** Izmir **7** Antalya
languages: **6** Arabic **7** Kurdish, Turkish
leaders: **5** Osman **8** Suleiman
measures: **3** dra, oka, pik **4** draa, khat, kile, zira **5** berri, kileh, zirai **6** arshin, chinik, halebi
monetary unit: **4** lira **5** pound
mosque: **4** jami
mountains: **3** Ala **4** Alai, Dagh, Kara **5** Murat **6** Ararat **7** Aladagh
official: **4** amir, baba, emir **5** ameer, basha, pasha **6** bashaw, vizier **7** effendi, osmanli, subashi **8** subbassa
rivers: **3** Gok **4** Aras, Kura **5** Araks, Dicle, Gediz, Halys, Mesta, Sarus **6** Araxes, Delice, Seihun, Seyhan, Tigris **8** Maeander **9** Euphrates
ruins: **4** Troy **7** Ephesus **8** Pergamum
rulers: **3** aga, bey, dey **4** agha, khan **5** mudir, pasha **6** kehaya, sultan, vizier **7** chambul **9** president
seas: **4** Aral **5** Black **6** Aegean **7** Marmasa **13** Mediterranean
soldier: **5** nizam **8** janizary **9** janissary **11** bashi-bazouk
sultan: **3** Ali **5** Ahmed, calif, Selim **6** caliph **7** Bajazet, Ilderim, Saladin
sword: **7** yatagan **8** yataghan
weight: **3** oka, oke **4** aqui, dram, rotl **5** artal, cheke, kerat, obulu, ratel **7** drachma, quintal

TURKMENISTAN:
also called: **9** Turkistan
capital: **9** Ashkhabad
cities: **8** Chardzou
continent: **4** Asia
ethnic groups: **5** Uzbek **6** Kazakh **7** Russian **10** Turkmenian

features: **7** Kara Kum **9** Altyn Depe **10** Black Sands
languages: **7** Russian, Turkmen
monetary unit: **5** ruble
water: **8** Amu Darya

TURMERIC: **4** herb **5** plant, spice **9** bloodroot, condiment

TURMOIL: **4** riot, toil **5** chaos, upset **6** bedlam, hubbub, strife, tumult, unrest, uproar **7** anxiety, ferment, trouble **8** disorder, disquiet, distress, upheaval **9** agitation, commotion, confusion **10** turbulence **11** disturbance, pandemonium

TURN: **3** aim, bow, try **4** bend, bent, coil, deed, eddy, loop, move, plow, reel, ride, roll, spin, veer, walk, wind **5** alter, angle, cramp, crank, curve, hinge, pivot, point, round, scare, screw, shift, shirl, shock, spell, swing, swirl, train, twirl, twist, upset, weave, whack, wheel **6** branch, chance, change, circle, curdle, detour, direct, divert, gyrate, ponder, resort, rotate, sprain, swerve, switch, swivel, zigzag **7** attempt, capsize, convert, deflect, deviate, disgust, ferment, meander, reverse, revolve **8** gyration, nauseate, rotation, unsettle **9** alternate, excursion, negotiate, transform, variation **10** revolution **11** opportunity **12** metamorphose

TURN AROUND: **4** spin, time **5** shift **6** change, gyrate, rotate **7** revolve **8** reversal **9** aboutface

TURN ASIDE: **4** veer **5** avert **6** detour, divert, swerve **7** deflect

TURN AWAY: **5** avert, deter, repel **6** desert, divert, swerve **7** deflect, deviate, dismiss **8** distract

TURN BACK: **4** fold, halt, stop **5** repel **6** return, revert **7** retrace, retreat, reverse **10** retrogress

TURNCOAT: **3** spy **7** traitor **8** apostate, betrayer, defector, deserter, renegade

TURN DOWN: **5** lower, scorn, spurn **6** rebuff, refuse, reject **7** decline **9** repudiate

TURN IN: **3** rat **4** rest **6** betray, retire **7** deliver, produce **8** transfer

TURNING POINT: **6** climax, crisis **8** juncture **9** emergency, watershed

TURNIP: **5** plant **8** rutabaga **9** vegetable

TURN OFF: **4** bore, halt, stop **5** repel **6** detour, divert, unplug **7** deflect, disgust, repulse **8** alienate, nauseate, withdraw **11** disinterest

TURN ON: **5** begin, start **6** arouse, excite **7** enchant **8** activate, energize, initiate **9** stimulate

TURN OUT: **4** oust, rise **5** dress, equip, evict, expel **6** appear, arrive, clothe, emerge, outfit, result **7** produce **9** discharge **11** manufacture

TURNOUT: **5** crowd, quota, yield **6** output, volume **8** audience **9** gathering **10** attendance **12** productivity

TURN OVER: **4** flip, give, keel, roll **5** spill, upset **6** assign, invert, ponder, rotate, topple **7** deliver, entrust, reflect **8** consider, delegate, transfer **9** surrender **10** relinquish **11** contemplate

TURNPIKE: **7** freeway, highway, parkway, thruway **8** tollgate

TURN UP: **4** find, show **6** appear, arrive, detect, emerge **7** surface, uncover, unearth **8** discover, increase **11** materialize

TURPITUDE: **4** evil **8** baseness, vileness **9** depravity **10** wickedness **11** immortality

TURQUOISE: **5** color, stone **7** mineral **8** gemstone, sea-green **9** blue-green **10** aqua-marine **12** greenish-blue

TURRET: **5** lathe, spire, tower **6** belfry **7** minaret, steeple **8** gunhouse, gunmount

TURTLE: **6** cooter **7** reptile, snapper **8** shagtail, slowpoke, terrapin, tortoise **9** chelonian **10** loggerhead, testudinal **11** leatherback
breastplate: **8** plastron
shell: **4** mail **8** carapace

TUSK: **4** fang, tush **5** ivory, tooth **6** canine **7** incisor

TUSSLE: **4** spar **5** brawl, fight, scrap **6** battle, hassle **7** contest, scuffle, wrestle **8** conflict, skirmish, struggle

TUTELAGE: **7** tuition **8** guidance, teaching **9** schooling **11** instruction **12** guardianship

TUTOR: **4** guru **5** coach, drill, guide, teach, train **6** direct, mentor, school **7** prepare, teacher **8** educator, instruct **9** pedagogue **10** instructor

TUVALU:
capital: **8** Funafuti
continent: **7** Oceania
ethnic groups: **10** Polynesian
languages: **7** English **8** Tuvaluan
monetary unit: **6** dollar
water: **7** Pacific

TWADDLE: **4** bosh, bunk, chat, talk **5** prate **6** babble, drivel, gabble, jabber **7** blabber, chatter **8** nonsense, tommyrot **9** poppycock **10** balderdash

TWANG: **5** sound **7** resound **8** nasality **9** resonance, vibration

TWEAK: **4** jerk, pull **5** pinch, pluck, twist **6** adjust

TWEET: **4** peep **5** chirp **7** chirrup, twitter

TWERP: **4** brat, jerk **5** crumb, grunt **6** squirt **8** half-pint **9** pipsqueak

TWIG: **4** limb **5** scion, shoot, sprig, style **6** branch, notice **7** fashion, observe **8** offshoot **10** comprehend, understand

TWILIGHT: **3** eve **4** dusk **5** gloam **6** sunset **7** decline, evening, sundown **8** eventide, gloaming **9** nightfall **10** crepuscule

TWIN: **3** two **4** dual, pair **5** clone **6** couple, double **8** didymous **9** duplicate, fraternal, identical, lookalike **11** counterpart

TWINE: **4** coil, cord, knot, rope, vine, wind, wrap **5** braid, snarl, twist, weave **6** encurl, spiral, string, tangle, thread **7** wreathe **8** encircle, entangle **9** interlace **10** interweave

TWINGE: **4** ache, pain, pang **5** cramp **6** misery, stitch, twitch

TWINKLE: **4** flit, glow, wink **5** blink, flash, gleam, glint, shine **7** flicker, flutter, glimmer, glisten, glitter, shimmer, sparkle **10** illuminate **11** scintillate

TWIRL: **4** coil, gyre, kink, knot, spin, turn, worm, wrap **5** alter, braid, pivot, ravel, slant, snake, twist, whirl **6** gyrate, oddity, swivel, tangle, zigzag **7** falsify, revolve, wriggle **8** rotation, surprise **9** convolute, pirouette

TWIST: **4** bend, spin, turn, wind **5** crink, curve, gnarl, quirk, screw, tweak, twine, wring **6** spiral, squirm, thread, wrench, writhe **7** contort, distort, entwine, meander, revolve, tendril, torsion **8** squiggle **9** corkscrew, deviation **10** intertwine, interweave **11** peculiarity **12** misrepresent

TWISTED: **3** wry **4** awry, bent **5** wound **6** curled, knurly, warped **7**

braided, crooked, gnarled, tangled **8** wrenched **9** contorted, perverted **10** convoluted

TWISTER: **7** cruller, cyclone, tornado, typhoon **8** doughnut **9** whirlwind

TWITCH: **3** tic, tug **4** draw, jerk, pick, pull, yank **5** grasp, lurch, pluck, shake, spasm **6** clutch, snatch, twinge **7** shudder, tremble **9** vellicate **11** contraction

TWITTER: **4** chat, peep, sing **5** cheep, chirp, sound, tweet **6** giggle, titter **7** chatter, chirrup, chitter, flutter, tremble

TWO: **3** dos **4** dual, duet, dyad, pair, twin **6** binary, couple, double, number

TWO-FACED: **5** false **7** devious **9** deceitful, dishonest **11** treacherous, underhanded **12** hypocritical

TWOFOLD: **4** dual **6** bifold, binary, double, duplex, paired **7** diploid

TWOSOME: **3** duo **4** duet, pair **6** couple

TWO-TIME: **5** cheat **6** betray **7** deceive, mislead **11** double-cross

TWO-WHEELER: **4** bike **5** cycle **7** bicycle

TYCOON: **5** baron, mogul, nabob **6** bigwig **7** magnate **9** financier **13** industrialist

TYKE: **3** boy, cur, dog **5** child **6** squirt **7** mongrel

TYNDAREUS:
daughter: **12** Clytemnestra
kingdom: **6** Sparta
son: **6** Castor
wife: **4** Leda

TYPE: **4** case, font, form, kind, mark, mold, race, sign, sort **5** breed, class, genre, group, model, order, print, stamp **6** emblem, family, nature, strain, stripe, symbol **7** example, pattern, species, variety **8** category, classify, specimen **9** character **10** persuasion
style: **5** Didot, roman, Times **6** Bodoni, Futura, italic, modern, script **7** Century, cursive, Electra **8** boldface, standard **9** condensed, lightface **10** schoolbook **11** Baskerville

TYPHOON: **5** storm **7** cyclone, tornado, twister **9** hurricane

TYPICAL: **5** ideal, model, usual **6** common, normal **7** average, classic, regular **8** everyday, ordinary, standard **9** exemplary **11** commonplace **12** conventional **14** characteristic, representative

TYPIFY: **6** embody **9** epitomize, personify, prefigure, represent, symbolize **10** illustrate **12** characterize

TYRANNICAL: **5** cruel, harsh **6** brutal **8** despotic **9** imperious **10** oppressive **11** dictatorial, domineering **12** totalitarian

TYRANNIZE: **7** dictate, oppress, trample **8** dominate

TYRANNOUS: **8** despotic **10** autocratic, oppressive, repressive

TYRANNY: **5** rigor **7** fascism **9** autocracy, despotism **10** absolutism, oppression, repression **12** dictatorship

TYRANT: **4** czar **5** bully **6** despot **8** autocrat, dictator, martinet, overlord **9** oppressor

TYRO: **6** novice, rookie **7** amateur, trainee **8** beginner, neophyte, newcomer **9** greenhorn **10** apprentice, tenderfoot

U

UBIQUITOUS: **9** pervasive, universal **10** everywhere, widespread **11** omnipresent

UGANDA:
capital: **7** Kampala
cities: **5** Jinja, M'Bale **6** Masaka **7** Entebbe
continent: **6** Africa
ethnic groups: **5** Bantu **7** Nilotic, Sudanic **11** Nilo-Hamitic
features: **5** Elgon **14** Ruwenzori Range **15** Mount Margherita
languages: **3** Luo **5** Atero **7** English, Luganda, Swahili
monetary unit: **8** shilling
water: **6** Edward, George **8** Victoria **9** Owen Falls **10** Lake Albert

UGLY: **3** bad **4** base, foul, vile **5** awful, grave, gross, nasty, toady **6** cranky, gloomy, grisly, homely **7** beastly, crabbed, hideous, ominous, servile **8** gruesome, horrible, shocking, terrible, wretched **9** appalling, dangerous, frightful, grotesque, loathsome, offensive, repellent, repugnant, repulsive, revolting, unsightly **10** despicable, disfigured, disgusting, ill-favored, unpleasant **11** threatening, troublesome **12** disagreeable, unattractive

UKASE: **5** edict, order **6** decree **7** command, mandate **9** directive, ordinance **12** proclamation

UKRAINE:
capital: **4** Kiev
cities: **4** Lvov **6** Odessa **7** Donetsk, Kharkov **9** Drivoi Rog, Zaporozhe **14** Dnepropetrovsk, Knipropetrovsk
continent: **4** Asia
ethnic groups: **7** Russian **9** Ukrainian
features: **8** Crimeans **11** Carpathians
language: **9** Ukrainian
monetary unit: **10** karbovanet
water: **3** Bug **6** Donetz **7** Dnieper

ULCER: **4** boil, sore **6** canker, lesion **7** abscess
types: **6** peptic **7** gastric **8** duodenal

ULTERIOR: **5** later, privy **6** covert, hidden, secret **7** guarded, obscure, selfish **8** shrouded **9** concealed, enigmatic **10** subsequent, undivulged **11** undisclosed

ULTIMATE: **3** end **4** best, last, peak **5** final, grand **6** remote, utmost **7** capping, extreme, maximum, primary, supreme **8** absolute, eventual, farthest, greatest **9** elemental, paramount **10** conclusive, preeminent **11** fundamental **12** transcendent

ULTIMATUM: **5** offer, order, terms **6** demand, threat **11** requirement

ULTRA: **6** beyond **7** extreme, forward, radical **8** ultimate **9** excessive, fanatical **10** outlandish **11** extravagant

ULULATE: **3** cry **4** hoot, howl, wail **6** bellow, lament

ULYSSES:
author: **10** James Joyce
characters: **10** Molly Bloom **12** Leopold Bloom **14** Stephen Dedalus
dog: **5** Argos
enchantress: **5** Circe
enemy: **8** Poseidon
father: **7** Laertes
Greek name: **8** Odysseus
kingdom: **6** Ithaca
mother: **8** Anticlea
setting: **6** Dublin **7** Ireland
sons: **9** Telegonus **10** Telemachus
wife: **8** Penelope

UMBER: **5** brown, color **6** darken **7** shadowy **8** brownish, chestnut

UMBRAGE: **4** fury, hint, rage **5** anger, pique, shade, trace, wrath **6** grudge, offend, shadow **7** chagrin, incense, offense, outrage, shelter **9** animosity, infuriate, suspicion **10** protection, resentment **11** displeasure

UMBRELLA: **5** guard, shade **6** brolly, screen **7** parasol, protect, shelter **8** sunshade

UMPIRE: **4** rule **5** judge **6** decide **7** arbiter, referee **8** mediator **9** moderator **10** arbitrator, negotiator, peacemaker **11** adjudicator

UNABBREVIATED: **5** uncut, whole **8** complete **10** unabridged

UNABLE: **4** weak **5** inept **6** cannot **8** helpless, impotent **9** incapable, powerless **10** inadequate **11** incompetent, unqualified

UNABRIDGED: **5** uncut, whole **6** entire, intact **8** complete **13** unabbreviated

UNACCEPTABLE: **4** poor **5** lousy **8** below par, unworthy **9** deficient, unwelcome **10** inadequate, unsuitable **11** intolerable

UNACCOMPANIED: **4** solo, stag **5** alone **6** single **8** deserted, detached, isolated, solitary **9** abandoned

UNACCOUNTABLE: **6** exempt, immune, mystic **7** curious, strange, unusual **8** baffling, peculiar, puzzling **10** mysterious **12** inexplicable **13** irresponsible, unexplainable

UNACCUSTOMED: **3** new **4** rare **5** alien **6** exotic, novice **7** curious, foreign, strange, unknown, unusual **8** uncommon **10** unfamiliar **11** unpracticed **12** uninstructed **13** inexperienced

UNACQUAINTED: **7** strange, unaware, unknown **8** ignorant **9** unadorned **10** unfamiliar **13** inexperienced

UNADORNED: **4** bald **5** naked, plain, stark **6** barren, rustic, simple **7** austere **11** undecorated, unelaborate

UNADULTERATED: **4** pure **5** clean, uncut, utter **6** honest **7** genuine, unmixed **8** straight **9** unalloyed, undiluted, untainted **11** uncorrupted

UNADVISABLE: **5** silly **6** stupid, unwise **8** ignorant **9** imprudent **11** inadvisable

UNAFFECTED: **4** calm, cool, easy, real **5** naive, plain **6** simple **7** callous, genuine, sincere, unmoved **9** ingenuous, unchanged, unexcited, unruffled, untouched **10** impervious **11** indifferent, insensitive **12** uninfluenced

UNAFRAID: **4** bold **5** brave **6** daring **7** valiant **8** fearless **9** confident **10** courageous

UNAGGRESSIVE: **3** shy **4** meek **5** timid **7** passive **8** peaceful **11** unambitious

UNALIKE: **7** diverse **9** different **10** dissimilar

UNALLOYED: **4** pure **7** genuine, unmixed **8** complete **9** undiluted **11** unqualified **13** unadulterated

UNALTERABLE: **4** firm **5** fixed, rigid **9** permanent **10** inflexible **11** inalterable

UNAMBIGUOUS: **5** clear, plain **7** obvious **8** apparent, distinct, explicit, univocal **9** unblurred

UNAMBITIOUS: **4** lazy **8** slothful **12** unaggressive

UNANIMOUS: **5** solid **6** united **7** unified **8** agreeing **9** consensus, undivided **10** collective, harmonious **11** consentient, uncontested

UNANNOUNCED: **8** surprise, withheld **10** unheralded **11** undisclosed, unpublished **13** unanticipated

UNAPPEALING: **4** dull **5** plain, trite **6** dreary **10** disgusting, uninviting, unpleasant **12** unappetizing, unattractive

UNAPPETIZING: **5** gross **7** insipid **8** unsavory **9** tasteless **10** disgusting, uninviting **11** distasteful, unappealing

UNAPPROACHABLE: **4** cold **5** aloof **7** distant **8** superior **9** unequaled, withdrawn **10** unfriendly **11** unreachable, unsurpassed **12** inaccessible, incomparable

UNARMED: **4** bare **8** disarmed **11** defenseless

UNASKED: **6** wanton **8** unsought, unwanted **9** uninvited, unwelcome **11** unrequested

UNASSERTIVE: **3** shy **4** meek **5** timid **7** bashful **9** diffident **10** unassuming

UNASSUMING: **3** shy **4** meek **6** humble, modest, simple **7** bashful **8** reserved **9** diffident **11** unassertive

UNATTACHED: **4** free **5** loose **6** single **8** separate **9** unmarried **11** independent, uncommitted, unconnected

UNATTRACTIVE: **4** rude, ugly **5** plain **6** homely **8** frumpish **10** uninviting **11** unappealing, undesirable **12** unappetizing

UNAUTHENTIC: **4** fake **5** bogus, false **9** imitation, ungenuine **11** counterfeit

UNAUTHORIZED: **6** banned **7** illegal **8** outlawed, unlawful **9** unallowed **10** prohibited, unapproved, unofficial **11** unpermitted **12** unsanctioned

UNAVAILABLE: **5** taken **7** married **11** nonexistent **12** inaccessible

UNAVAILING: **4** vain **6** futile **7** useless **8** gainless **9** fruitless, pointless **11** ineffective **12** unproductive

UNAVOIDABLE: **5** fated **9** necessary **10** inevitable, obligatory **11** inescapable **13** unpreventable

UNAWARE: **8** heedless, ignorant **9** oblivious, unknowing **10** unapprised, unfamiliar, uninformed **11** incognizant **12** unsuspecting

UNBALANCED: **4** daft **5** shaky, wacky **6** crazed, insane, uneven, warped **7** unequal, unglued, unsound **8** demented, deranged, lopsided, troubled, unstable **9** disturbed, unsettled **10** irrational **12** asymmetrical

UNBEARABLE: **10** oppressive **11** intolerable **12** inadmissible, insufferable, unacceptable

UNBECOMING: **4** lewd, rude, ugly **6** homely **8** improper, indecent, unseemly, unworthy **9** inelegant, offensive, tasteless **10** indecorous, malapropos, unsuitable **11** disgraceful, unbefitting **12** unattractive **13** inappropriate

UNBELIEVABLE: **6** absurd **7** amazing **8** cockeyed, fabulous **9** fantastic **10** astounding, farfetched, impossible, improbable, incredible, remarkable **11** astonishing, harebrained, implausible, unthinkable **12** unimaginable **13** inconceivable

UNBELIEVER: **5** cynic, pagan **7** atheist, doubter, heretic, infidel, skeptic **8** agnostic **9** miscreant **11** freethinker, nonbeliever

UNBENDING: **4** firm **5** rigid, stern, stiff **6** strict **8** resolute, stubborn **9** inelastic, obstinate **10** inexorable, inflexible, relentless, unyielding

UNBIASED: **4** fair, just **6** honest **9** equitable, impartial, objective, unbigoted **11** nonpartisan **12** unprejudiced

UNBIND: **4** free, undo **5** untie **6** detach, loosen **7** absolve, release, unchain **8** liberate, unfasten **9** disengage **10** emancipate

UNBLEMISHED: **5** clean, whole **6** chaste, intact **7** perfect, unmarred **8** flawless, spotless **9** stainless, undamaged, unsullied **10** immaculate **13** unadulterated

UNBLOCK: **4** free, open **6** unclog, unstop

UNBOUND, UNBOUNDED: **4** free, open **5** freed, loose **6** untied **7** endless **8** released **9** boundless, limitless, unlimited **10** indefinite, unconfined **12** immeasurable, unrestrained

UNBRIDLED: **5** loose **8** unleased **9** unchecked **10** ungoverned **12** uncontrolled, unrestrained

UNBROKEN: **5** sound, whole **6** entire, intact **7** endless, untamed **8** unmarred **9** continual, undivided **10** continuous, sequential, successive, unimpaired **11** consecutive, unshattered **13** uninterrupted

UNBURDEN: **3** rid **4** dump, free **5** admit, empty **6** unload **7** confess, relieve, unbosom **10** relinquish

UNCALLED-FOR: **4** rude **6** wanton **7** foolish **8** impolite, needless **10** groundless **11** unessential, unjustified, unnecessary, unwarranted **12** discourteous, nonessential **13** disrespectful

UNCANNY: **5** eerie, weird **6** creepy, spooky **7** strange, unusual **9** fantastic, unnatural **10** incredible, mysterious, remarkable **11** exceptional **12** supernatural, unbelievable

UNCEASING: **7** endless, eternal **8** constant, unending **9** continual, incessant **10** continuous, persistent **11** everlasting

UNCEREMONIOUS: **4** curt **5** blunt, brief, hasty, short **6** abrupt, casual **8** familiar, informal **9** inelegant **11** thoughtless **13** inconsiderate

UNCERTAIN: **4** hazy, iffy, moot **5** vague **6** chancy, fitful, unsure **7** dubious, erratic, unclear **8** doubtful, hesitant, unsteady, variable **9** ambiguous, equivocal, tentative, undecided, unsettled **10** changeable, indecisive, indefinite, precarious, unresolved **11** speculative, unconfirmed, vacillating **12** questionable, undetermined **13** unpredictable

UNCERTAINTY: **4** risk **5** doubt, query, worry **6** gamble, wonder **7** concern, dubiety **8** suspense **9** ambiguity, confusion **10** hesitation, indecision, skepticism **11** ambivalence

UNCHAIN: **4** free **6** unbind **7** release **8** liberate **9** unshackle **10** emancipate

UNCHANGEABLE: **5** fixed, rigid **8** constant **9** immutable, steadfast **10** inflexible, invariable **11** unalterable

UNCHANGING: **4** same **5** fixed **6** stable, static, steady **7** eternal, uniform **8** constant **9** permanent, steadfast, unvarying **10** consistent, invariable, stationary

UNCHASTE: **4** lewd **5** loose **6** impure, wanton **7** immoral, obscene **8** immodest **9** debauched

UNCHECKED: **4** free, wild **5** loose **7** rampant, untamed **9** unbounded **12** unrestrained

UNCIVILIZED: **4** rude, wild **5** crass, crude, rough **6** abrupt, brutal, savage, vulgar, wicked **7** boorish, uncivil, uncouth **8** barbaric, impolite **9** barbarous, primitive, unrefined **10** uncultured, ungracious, unmannerly, unpolished **11** ill-mannered **12** discourteous, uncultivated **13** disrespectful

UNCLAD: **4** bare, nude **5** naked **8** disrobed **9** unclothed, undressed

UNCLEAN: **4** foul, vile **5** dirty, grimy, messy, soily **6** filthy, grubby, impure, sloppy **7** defiled, obscene, sullied, tainted **8** polluted, profaned, unchaste **11** unwholesome **12** contaminated

UNCLEAR: **3** dim **4** hazy **5** fuzzy, vague **6** blurry, cloudy, unsure **7** obscure, shadowy **8** confused **9** ambiguous, uncertain, unsettled

UNCLE TOM'S CABIN:
author: **19** Harriet Beecher Stowe
characters: **5** Eliza, Marks, Topsy **6** George **8** Uncle Tom **9** Little Eva **11** Simon Legree **14** Ophelia St. Clare **16** Augustine St. Clare
dealt with: **7** slavery **9** abolition
setting: **8** Kentucky **9** Louisiana

UNCLOTHE: **5** strip **6** divest, expose, reveal **7** display, disrobe, uncover, undress

UNCLOTHED: **4** bare, nude **5** naked **6** unclad **8** stripped **9** undressed

UNCLOUDED: **4** fair **5** clear, sunny **6** bright

UNCOLORED: **4** fair, just **5** plain **6** simple **8** unbiased **9** impartial, objective **12** unprejudiced

UNCOMBED: **5** messy **6** matted, sloppy, untidy **7** ruffled, unkempt **10** disheveled

UNCOMFORTABLE: **5** stiff, upset **6** uneasy **7** awkward, painful, prickly **8** troubled **9** miserable, suffering **11** distressful **12** excruciating

UNCOMMON: **3** odd **4** rare **5** novel **6** exotic, scarce, unique **7** bizarre, special, strange, unusual **8** abnormal, peculiar, unwanted **9** wonderful **10** infrequent, occasional, remarkable **11** exceptional **12** unaccustomed **13** extraordinary

UNCOMMUNICATIVE: **4** dumb **5** quiet **6** silent **8** reserved, reticent, taciturn **9** secretive, withdrawn **10** speechless, unsociable **12** close-mouthed, unresponsive

UNCOMPLICATED: **4** easy **5** basic, clear, plain **6** simple

UNCOMPLIMENTARY: **8** critical, negative **9** insulting **10** derogatory **11** disparaging **12** unflattering

UNCOMPROMISING: **4** firm **5** rigid, stern **6** strict **8** obdurate, stubborn **9** unbending **10** determined, inflexible, unyielding

UNCONCEALED: **4** bare, open **5** overt, plain **7** exposed, obvious, visible **8** apparent, revealed

UNCONCERNED: **4** cold, cool **5** aloof **7** distant, unmoved **8** carefree, composed, detached, uncaring **9** apathetic **10** impervious, nonchalant **11** indifferent, insensitive **12** uninterested

UNCONDITIONAL: **4** free **5** total **8** absolute, complete, explicit **11** categorical **12** unmistakable **14** unquestionable

UNCONGENIAL: **7** uncivil **9** repugnant **10** unfriendly **11** displeasing **12** discourteous **13** unsympathetic

UNCONNECTED: **7** severed **8** detached, separate **9** uncoupled, unrelated **10** irrelevant **11** impertinent **12** disconnected

UNCONQUERABLE: **6** innate, secure **9** resistant **10** invincible, unbeatable **11** impregnable **12** invulnerable

UNCONSCIONABLE: **7** extreme, immoral **8** criminal **9** excessive, unethical **10** immoderate, inordinate, outrageous **11** inexcusable, unjustified, unwarranted **12** unreasonable, unscrupulous

UNCONSCIOUS: **6** asleep, torpid, zonked **7** stunned, unaware **8** comatose, ignorant **9** automatic, lethargic, repressed, stupefied **10** insensible **11** inadvertent, involuntary **13** unintentional

UNCONSTRAINED: **4** easy, free **6** casual **7** natural, relaxed **8** informal **9** easygoing **11** spontaneous **13** demonstrative

UNCONTROLLABLE: **4** free, wild **6** unruly **9** irregular, unmanaged **10** hysterical, ungoverned **11** unregulated **12** uncontrolled, ungovernable, unmanageable, unrestrained **13** undisciplined

UNCONTROLLED: **9** unchecked **11** independent

UNCONVENTIONAL: **3** odd **5** crazy, loose, nutty, weird **6** casual **7** bizarre, offbeat, strange, unusual **8** atypical, Bohemian, informal, peculiar, uncommon **9** eccentric

UNCONVINCING: **4** weak **6** flimsy **7** suspect **11** implausible **12** questionable, unbelievable

UNCOOKED: **3** raw **9** au naturel

UNCOUPLE: **4** undo **5** loose **6** detach, unhook **7** release, unhitch **8** unfasten **10** disconnect

UNCOUTH: **4** loud, rude **5** crass, crude, gross **6** callow, clumsy, coarse, vulgar **7** awkward, boorish, loutish, raunchy, strange, uncanny, uncivil **8** desolate, ignorant, impolite, ungainly **9** inelegant, unrefined **10** mysterious, outlandish, uncultured, unpolished **11** uncivilized **12** discourteous, uncultivated **13** disrespectful

UNCOVER: **4** bare, open **6** detect, divest, expose, remove, reveal, unmask, unveil **7** display, disrobe, divulge, unbosom, undress, unearth **8** disclose, discover, unclothe

UNCOVERED: **4** bald, nude, open **5** naked **7** exposed **8** detected, stripped **9** disclosed

UNCRITICAL: **6** casual **7** inexact, offhand, pleased, shallow **8** careless, slipshod **9** imprecise **10** inaccurate **11** perfunctory, superficial **12** undiscerning

UNCTUOUS: **4** oily, rich, soft **5** fatty, soapy, suave **6** greasy, smarmy **7** gulsome **8** slippery **10** oleaginous

UNCULTIVATED: **4** arid, rude, wild **5** crass, crude, rough **6** coarse, savage **7** uncivil, uncouth **8** barbaric, unfarmed, unplowed **9** barbarous **10** uncultured **11** uncivilized, undeveloped

UNCULTURED: **4** rude **5** crass, crude **6** coarse, vulgar **7** boorish, uncouth **9** unrefined **10** unpolished **11** uncivilized **12** uncultivated

UNCUSTOMARY: **4** rare **6** unique **7** unusual **8** singular, uncommon, unwonted **11** exceptional **13** extraordinary

UNDAUNTED: **4** bold **5** brave **6** heroic **7** gallant, unfazed, valiant **8** fearless, intrepid, resolute, stalwart, unafraid **9** audacious, confident **10** courageous **11** unflinching

UNDECIDED: **4** moot, open **6** unsure **7** dubious **8** doubtful, hesitant, wavering **9** tentative, uncertain, unsettled **10** ambivalent, indecisive, irresolute, unresolved **11** fluctuating **12** undetermined

UNDECORATED: **4** bare **5** plain **6** simple **7** austere **9** unadorned **13** unembellished

UNDEFILED: **4** pure **5** clean **6** chaste **8** innocent, spotless, virtuous **9** stainless, unspoiled, unsullied **10** immaculate, unpolluted **11** unblemished, uncorrupted

UNDEMONSTRATIVE: **4** cold, cool **5** aloof **7** distant, laconic **8** reserved **10** restrained **11** indifferent, unemotional **12** inexpressive

UNDENIABLE: **4** sure, true **6** actual, proven **7** certain **8** decisive, definite, positive **10** conclusive, inarguable **11** irrefutable, unequivocal **12** indisputable, unassailable **13** incontestable

UNDEPENDABLE: **5** lower **6** lesser, pinned, unsafe **7** erratic, flighty, unsound **8** unstable, untrusty **9** secondary **10** capricious, unreliable **12** inconsistent **13** irresponsible, untrustworthy **13** unpredictable

UNDER: **3** sub **5** below, neath **6** nether **7** beneath **8** inferior **11** subordinate

UNDERCOVER: **6** covert, hidden, secret **7** furtive **8** stealthy **9** concealed, disguised, incognito **11** clandestine **12** confidential **13** surreptitious

UNDERCURRENT: **4** aura, eddy, mood **5** drift, sense **6** flavor **7** riptide **8** overtone, undertow **10** atmosphere, vibrations

UNDERESTIMATE: **8** belittle, minimize **9** disparage, underrate **10** undervalue **12** miscalculate

UNDERGARMENT: **3** bra **4** slip **5** teddy **6** bodice, briefs, girdle, shorts, undies **7** chemise, drawers, panties **8** bloomers, lingerie, skivvies **9** brassiere, chemilonn, petticoat, underwear

UNDERGO: **4** bear, feel, pass, take **5** brave, serve, yield **6** endure, suffer **7** subject, sustain, weather **8** tolerate **9** encounter, withstand **10** experience

UNDERGRADUATE: **4** coed **5** plebe **6** junior, senior **7** student **8** freshman **9** sophomore **13** underclassman, upperclassman

UNDERGROUND: **6** buried, hidden, secret **7** beneath, illegal **10**

subversive, undercover **11** clandestine **12** subterranean **13** revolutionary, surreptitious

UNDERHANDED: **3** sly **4** wily **5** shady **6** secret, shifty, sneaky, unfair **7** crooked, cunning, devious **9** deceitful, dishonest, unethical **10** fraudulent **11** clandestine, shorthanded, undermanned **12** unscrupulous

UNDERLINE: **4** mark **6** ascent, stress **7** caption, feature **9** emphasize **10** accentuate, underscore

UNDERLING: **4** serf **5** scrub **6** menial, minion **7** servant **8** hireling, inferior **11** subordinate

UNDERLYING: **5** basic, vital **6** bottom, latent **7** beneath, crucial, primary **8** cardinal, implicit **9** elemental, essential **11** fundamental

UNDERMINE: **4** foil, ruin **5** drain, erode, wreck **6** impair, thwart, weaken **7** corrupt, cripple, destroy, disable, sandbag, subvert **8** excavate, sabotage, threaten **9** frustrate **10** debilitate, demoralize

UNDERNEATH: **5** below, under **6** bottom **7** beneath, covered **9** underside

UNDERPIN: **4** prop **5** brace **7** bolster, support **8** maintain **10** strengthen **12** substantiate

UNDERPINNING: **4** base **5** basis **6** ground **7** support **10** foundation, groundwork **12** substructure

UNDERPRIVILEGED: **4** poor **5** needy **8** deprived **9** destitute **11** unfortunate **12** impoverished **13** disadvantaged

UNDERRATE: **7** devalue **8** belittle, discount, minimize **10** depreciate, underprice, undervalue **13** underestimate

UNDERSCORE: **4** mark **6** accent, stress **8** heighten **9** emphasize, italicize, underline

UNDERSIDE: **4** root, sole **5** belly **6** bottom **10** underneath

UNDERSIZED: **4** puny, tiny **5** short, small **6** little, petite **7** stunted **9** miniature

UNDERSTAND: **3** dig, get, see **4** know **5** catch, grasp, infer, learn, sense, solve, think **6** absorb, accept, decode, deduce, fathom, follow, gather, reason **7** discern, realize, surmise **8** conceive, perceive **9** apprehend, interpret, penetrate, recognize **10** appreciate, comprehend, conjecture, sympathize

UNDERSTANDABLE: **5** clear, lucid, plain **6** simple **7** logical **8** coherent **10** acceptable, reasonable **11** justifiable **12** intelligible, recognizable

UNDERSTANDING: **4** deal, grip, idea, pact **5** amity, brain, grasp, sense **6** accord, belief, kindly, notion, reason, treaty **7** concept, empathy, insight, knowing, meaning **8** attitude, judgment, sympathy **9** accepting, agreement, awareness, diagnosis, forgiving, intellect, intuition, knowledge, tolerance **10** acceptance, compassion **11** realization, sensitivity, sympathetic **12** intelligence **13** comprehension

UNDERSTATEMENT: **7** litotes **9** restraint **10** distortion **13** underestimate

UNDERSTOOD: **5** clear, lucid **6** unsaid **7** assumed, implied **8** accepted, implicit, inferred, presumed

UNDERSTUDY: **6** backup, double **9** alternate **10** substitute **11** replacement

UNDERTAKE: **3** try **4** dare, seek **5** begin, grant, seize, start **6** accept, assume, commit, engage, launch, pledge, strive, tackle **7** attempt, execute, perform, promise **8** commence, contract, covenant, endeavor, initiate, overtake, shoulder **9** guarantee

UNDERTAKING: **4** task **6** charge, effort **7** attempt, calling, project, promise, pursuit, venture **8** covenant, endeavor, struggle **9** adventure **10** commitment, enterprise, experiment **11** proposition

UNDERTONE: **4** aura, buzz, hint, mood **5** sense **6** flavor, mumble, murmur **7** feeling, whisper **8** overtone **10** atmosphere, suggestion **11** association

UNDERTOW: **4** eddy **6** vortex **7** riptide **9** whirlpool **12** undercurrent

UNDERVALUE: **8** belittle, minimize **9** disparage, underrate **10** depreciate **13** underestimate

UNDERWEAR: **3** bra **4** BVDs, slip **5** teddy **6** boxers, briefs, corset, diaper, girdle, T-shirt, undies **7** drawers, jockeys, panties **8** bloomers, lingerie, skivvies **9** brassiere, petticoat, union suit **10** underpants, undershirt **12** underclothes, undergarment

UNDERWORLD: **4** hell **5** abyss, Hades, Mafia, Orcus, Sheol **6** Erebus, Tophet **7** Avernus, Gehenna **8** gangland **9** antipodes, perdition, purgatory, syndicate **10** Cosa Nostra **11** netherworld
river: **4** Styx

UNDERWRITE: **4** back, sign **6** insure **7** endorse, finance, sponsor, support **8** bankroll **9** guarantee, subscribe

UNDESIRABLE: **5** unfit **7** outcast **8** disliked, unsought, unwanted **9** loathsome, offensive **10** uninviting, unpleasant, unsuitable, unwelcomed **11** displeasing, objectional **12** unacceptable **13** inappropriate

UNDETERMINED: **5** faint, vague **7** obscure, pending, unclear, unknown **8** doubtful, unproven **9** equivocal, undecided, unsettled

UNDEVELOPED: **5** crude, green **6** latent, unripe **7** archaic **8** backward, immature, untaught **9** primitive, unevolved **10** primordial, uneducated **12** uncultivated

UNDILUTED: **4** neat, pure **7** unmixed **8** straight **9** unalloyed **13** unadulterated

UNDISCIPLINED: **4** amok, wild **6** unruly, wanton **7** wayward **9** untrained **12** uncontrolled, ungovernable, unmanageable

UNDISCLOSED: **6** hidden, sealed, secret **9** concealed **10** unrevealed **12** confidential

UNDISGUISED: **4** open **5** frank, overt, plain **7** genuine, obvious **10** pronounced **11** unconcealed

UNDISPUTED: **4** sure **7** granted **8** accepted **10** conclusive, recognized, undeniable **11** irrefutable, uncontested **12** acknowledged, unchallenged, unquestioned

UNDISTINGUISHED: **5** plain **6** common **8** everyday, mediocre, ordinary **9** unnotable **12** unnoteworthy **13** unexceptional

UNDISTURBED: **4** calm **5** quiet **6** placid, serene **7** unmoved **8** peaceful, tranquil **9** unruffled, untouched **12** undistracted **13** uninterrupted

UNDIVIDED: **3** one **5** solid, total, whole **6** entire, united **8** absorbed, complete, unbroken **9** exclusive, unanimous **12** undistracted, wholehearted

UNDO: **4** free, open, ruin, void **5** annul, erase, loose, quash, untie, upset, wreck **6** cancel, defeat, negate, offset, outwit, unwrap **7** abolish, destroy, disjoin, nullify, release, reverse, unblock, uncover, unravel **8** abrogate, overturn, unfasten **9** disengage, undermine **10** disconnect, invalidate, neutralize

UNDOING: **4** doom, ruin **5** error **7** blunder **8** collapse, downfall, weakness **9** overthrow **10** misfortune **11** catastrophe, destruction **12** cancellation

UNDOUBTEDLY: **5** truly **6** indeed, really, surely **9** assuredly, certainly **10** positively, undeniably **11** indubitably **12** unmistakable

UNDRESS: **4** peel, shed **5** strip **6** divest, expose **7** disrobe, uncover, undrape **8** unclothe

UNDUE: **7** extreme, illegal **8** improper, needless, uncoming, untimely, unworthy **9** excessive, unfitting **10** exorbitant, immoderate, undeserved, unsuitable **11** unnecessary, unwarranted **12** unreasonable **13** inappropriate, unjustifiable

UNDULATE: **4** roll, sway, wave **5** swing, weave **6** ripple **9** fluctuate

UNDULY: **6** overly **9** extremely **11** excessively **12** immoderately, inordinately **13** extravagantly, unjustifiably, unnecessarily

UNDYING: **7** ageless, agelong, endless, eternal **8** constant, enduring, immortal, unending, unfading **9** continual, permanent, perpetual, unceasing **10** continuing, persistent **11** everlasting **12** imperishable

UNEARTH: **3** dig **4** find, show **5** learn **6** exhume, expose, reveal, uproot **7** divulge, uncover **8** disclose, discover, disinter, excavate

UNEARTHLY: **5** eerie, weird **6** spooky **7** awesome, ghostly, strange, uncanny, ungodly **8** ethereal, heavenly, spectral **9** fantastic **10** miraculous, mysterious, superhuman **12** supernatural **13** preternatural

UNEASINESS: **4** fear **5** alarm, doubt, dread, worry **6** unrest **7** anxiety, trouble **9** disbelief, misgiving **10** discomfort, discontent **11** displeasure, instability, nervousness, uncertainty **12** apprehension, restlessness **13** embarrassment

UNEASY: **4** edgy **5** jumpy, nervy, tense **6** afraid, unsure **7** alarmed, anxious, awkward, fidgety, nervous, uptight, worried **8** restless, troubled **9** concerned, difficult, perturbed, uncertain, unsettled **12** apprehensive **13** uncomfortable

UNEDUCATED: **6** simple, unread **8** ignorant, untaught **9** unlearned, untutored **10** illiterate, unlettered, unschooled

UNEMBELLISHED: **4** bare **5** plain **6** modest, simple **7** austere **9** unadorned **11** undecorated, unelaborate

UNEMOTIONAL: **4** cold, cool **5** stoic **6** formal **7** deadpan **8** reserved **9** heartless, unfeeling **11** coldhearted, indifferent, insensitive, unconcerned, unexcitable **13** unsympathetic

UNEMPLOYED: **4** idle **5** fired **6** canned **7** jobless, laid off **8** inactive, leisured **10** unoccupied

UNENDING: **6** steady **7** endless, eternal, lasting, undying **8** constant, infinite, timeless **9** continual, perpetual, unceasing **10** continuous **11** everlasting **13** uninterrupted

UNENLIGHTENED: **8** ignorant **9** unlearned **10** uninformed

UNENTHUSIASTIC: **4** cool **8** lukewarm **9** apathetic, unexcited **10** spiritless **11** indifferent, perfunctory **12** uninterested

UNEQUAL: **6** uneven, unfair, unjust **7** unalike, varying **8** lopsided, variable **9** different, irregular **10** dissimilar, inadequate, mismatched, unbalanced **11** fluctuating, inequitable **12** asymmetrical

UNEQUALED: **7** supreme **8** peerless **9** matchless, unmatched, unrivaled **10** surpassing **11** unsurpassed **12** unparalleled **13** unprecedented

UNEQUIVOCAL: **5** clear, plain **7** certain **8** absolute, decisive, definite, emphatic, explicit, positive **9** certainly **10** resounding **11** categorical, unambiguous **12** indisputable, unmistakable

UNERRING: **4** sure, true **5** exact **7** certain, perfect, precise **8** accurate, reliable **9** unfailing **10** dependable, infallible

UNETHICAL: **5** shady, wrong **6** amoral, sneaky **7** corrupt, crooked, immoral **9** dishonest, underhand **12** disreputable, unprincipled, unscrupulous

UNEVEN: **3** odd **4** bent **5** bumpy, rough **6** angled, jagged, rugged, spotty, tilted, unfair, unjust **7** crooked, unequal, unlevel, varying **8** lopsided **9** disparate, irregular **10** discrepant, ill-matched, unbalanced **11** fluctuating

UNEVENTFUL: **4** dull **6** boring, common **7** prosaic, routine **8** ordinary **10** monotonous **11** commonplace, unmemorable **13** insignificant, unexceptional

UNEXCEPTIONAL: **5** usual **6** common **7** prosaic, regular, typical **8** ordinary **10** uneventful **11** commonplace **12** conventional, satisfactory

UNEXCITED: **4** calm **5** level **7** unmoved **8** composed, tranquil **9** collected **11** unemotional

UNEXCITING: **4** blah, dead, dull **5** bland **6** boring **7** prosaic **10** lackluster

UNEXPECTED: **6** abrupt, sudden **9** impulsive, startling, unforseen, unplanned **10** accidental, staggering, surprising **11** unannounced **13** unanticipated, unpredictable

UNFADED: **3** new **5** fresh, shiny, vivid **6** bright **7** blazing, shining **8** colorful, flashing, polished

UNFAILING: **4** sure, true **5** loyal **7** certain, staunch **8** faithful, reliable, surefire, unerring **10** consistent, continuous, dependable, infallible, unchanging, unflagging **11** trustworthy **13** inexhaustible

UNFAIR: **4** foul **5** wrong **6** biased, uneven, unjust **7** partial, unequal **8** cheating, wrongful **9** dishonest, unethical **10** prejudiced **11** inequitable, underhanded, unfavorable **12** dishonorable **14** discriminatory

UNFAITHFUL: **6** untrue **7** infidel, unloyal **8** disloyal **9** dishonest, faithless **10** adulterous, inaccurate, traitorous, unreliable **11** treasonable **13** untrustworthy

UNFALTERING: **4** firm, sure, true **6** steady **8** enduring **9** steadfast **10** dependable **11** persevering **12** wholehearted

UNFAMILIAR: **3** new **6** exotic **7** curious, foreign, strange, unknown **8** unversed **9** different **10** uninformed **12** unaccustomed, unacquainted **13** inexperienced

UNFASHIONABLE: **5** dated, passe **6** frumpy **9** unstylish **10** antiquated

UNFASTEN: **4** free, open, undo **5** unpin, untie **6** detach, loosen, unhook, unlace, unlock, unsnap **7** unhitch **8** unbuckle, unbutton, unloosen **9** disengage

UNFATHOMABLE: **4** deep, vast **7** abysmal, complex **8** abstruse, baffling, profound **10** bottomless, mysterious **11** ungraspable

UNFAVORABLE: **3** bad **4** foul **6** unkind **7** adverse, hostile, unlucky **8** contrary, damaging, negative, untimely **11** detrimental, inopportune, unfortunate

UNFEASIBLE: **10** impossible, unworkable **11** impractical **12** unachievable, unattainable

UNFEELING: **4** cold, dull, hard, numb **5** cruel, harsh, stern, stony **6** brutal **7** callous **8** deadened, hardened, numbness, obdurate, ruthless **9** apathetic, heartless, merciless, senseless **10** insensible **11** cold-blooded, hardhearted, insensitive, unemotional **12** anesthetized **13** unsympathetic

UNFEIGNED: **4** real, true **6** honest **7** genuine, natural, sincere **9** heartfelt

UNFINISHED: **4** rude **5** crude, rough **6** undone **7** sketchy **8** immature **9** imperfect, unpainted, unstained **10** incomplete, unpolished **11** unassembled, undeveloped, unfulfilled

UNFIT: **4** sick, weak **5** inept **6** faulty, feeble, sickly **8** disabled, improper, unsuited **9** ill-suited, unhealthy, unskilled, untrained **10** blundering, ineligible, unprepared **11** handicapped, incompetent, ineffective, unqualified **12** incompatible **13** incapacitated, inexperienced

UNFLAGGING: **4** firm **6** steady **7** staunch **8** constant, tireless **9** steadfast, weariless **10** determined

UNFLAPPABLE: **4** calm, cool **7** relaxed **8** composed **9** collected, unruffled **11** unexcitable

UNFLINCHING: **4** firm **6** gritty **7** staunch **8** fearless, resolute **9** steadfast, tenacious, undaunted **10** relentless, unwavering, unyielding

UNFOLD: **4** open, show **5** solve **6** evolve, expand, flower, mature, reveal, spread, uncurl, unfurl, unroll, untuck, unwind, unwrap **7** blossom, clarify, develop, display, divulge, expiate, explain, release, resolve, uncover, unravel **8** describe, disclose **9** elaborate, explicate

UNFORCED: **6** casual **7** natural, relaxed, willing **9** easygoing, voluntary

UNFORESEEN: **6** sudden **10** accidental, surprising, unexpected, unimagined **11** unpredicted **13** unanticipated

UNFORTUNATE: **3** bad, sad **4** poor **6** cursed, dismal, doomed, jinxed, wretch **7** hapless, unhappy, unlucky **8** luckless, wretched **9** afflicted, miserable **10** calamitous, deplorable **11** inopportune, regrettable **12** inauspicious, unsuccessful

UNFOUNDED: **4** idle, vain **5** false **6** untrue **8** baseless, unproven **10** groundless, misleading **15** unsubstantiated

UNFRIENDLY: **4** cold, cool **6** remote **7** distant, hateful, hostile **8** unsocial **9** combative, malicious **10** antisocial, ungracious **12** antagonistic, inhospitable, unneighborly

UNFRUITFUL: **6** barren, wasted **7** sterile, useless **8** impotent, infecund **9** fruitless, infertile **11** unrewarding **12** unproductive, unprofitable

UNFURL: **4** open **6** expand, spread, unfold, unroll, unwind **7** develop, display

UNGAINLY: **5** gawky, lanky, stiff **6** clumsy, klutzy **7** awkward, uncouth **8** unwieldy **9** lumbering, maladroit

UNGENEROUS: **4** mean **5** close, harsh, petty, small **6** shabby, stingy **7** miserly, selfish **8** grudging **9** illiberal, penurious **12** parsimonious

UNGODLY: **6** impure, rotten, sinful, unholy, wicked **7** corrupt, immoral, impious, profane **8** depraved, dreadful **9** atrocious **10** outrageous **11** blasphemous, unbelieving, uncivilized **12** hypocritical

UNGOVERNABLE: **4** wild **6** unruly **8** mutinous **9** fractious, unbridled **10** disorderly, rebellious **11** disobedient, intractable **12** unmanageable **13** undisciplined **14** uncontrollable

UNGRACEFUL: **5** gawky, rusty **6** clumsy, coarse, vulgar **7** awkward **9** inelegant

UNGRACIOUS: **4** rude **5** gruff, short **7** uncivil, uncouth **8** churlish, impolite **9** offensive **10** unmannerly, unpleasant **11** thoughtless, unfortunate **12** discourteous, inhospitable **13** disrespectful

UNGRATEFUL: **7** ingrate, selfish **9** grumbling, repellent, repugnant, thankless **12** dissatisfied **14** unappreciative

UNGUARDED: **6** unwary **7** unalert **8** careless **9** imprudent, unmindful **10** incautious, indiscreet, vulnerable **11** defenseless, thoughtless, unprotected

UNGUENT: **4** balm **5** cream, salve **6** cerate, lotion **8** ointment **9** emollient, lubricant

UNGULATE: **3** cow, hog, pig **4** deer **5** camel, horse, llama, swine **6** cattle, hoofed **7** buffalo, giraffe **8** elephant, hooflike **10** rhinoceros **12** hippopotamus

UNHAMPERED: **4** free **5** clear **6** direct **9** unimpeded **11** uninhibited **12** unrestrained, unrestricted

UNHANDY: **5** inept **6** clumsy, klutzy **7** awkward **8** bumbling, fumbling **9** maladroit **10** cumbersome, unskillful

UNHAPPINESS: **3** woe **5** dolor, grief, worry **6** misery, sorrow **7** sadness **9** heartache **10** melancholy

UNHAPPY: **3** sad **4** blue **5** sorry **6** bummed, dismal, gloomy **7** forlorn, hurting, joyless, unlucky **8** dejected, downcast, saddened, wretched **9** depressed, miserable, sorrowful, woebegone **10** melancholy **11** unfavorable, unfortunate **12** inauspicious **13** inappropriate

UNHARMED: **4** safe **5** whole **6** intact, unhurt **8** harmless, unmarred **9** undamaged, unscathed, untouched **11** unblemished

UNHEALTHY: **3** ill **4** sick **5** frail, risky **6** chancy, feeble, sickly, unwell **7** noxious, unsound **8** diseased **9** dangerous, hazardous **10** unsanitary **11** detrimental, unwholesome

UNHEARD-OF: **4** rare **5** novel **6** unique **7** obscure, strange, unknown, unusual **8** uncommon **10** outrageous **12** unbelievable, undiscovered **13** extraordinary, unprecedented

UNHEEDING: **4** deaf **7** ignored **8** careless, heedless **9** forgotten, unmindful, unnoticed **10** unwatchful **11** inattentive, inobservant **12** disregarding

UNHESITATING: **5** eager, ready **6** prompt **9** immediate **10** forthright

UNHINGE: **5** upset **6** detach **7** fluster, unhitch **8** distract, separate, uncouple, unfasten, unsettle **9** disengage, unbalance **10** disconnect

UNHOLY: **4** evil **5** amiss **6** impure, sinful, wicked **7** corrupt, immoral, ungodly **8** depraved, fiendish, indecent **9** atrocious, malicious **10** irreverent, unhallowed **11** unchristian **12** unsanctified

UNHURRIED: **4** easy, slow **9** leisurely **10** deliberate, nonchalant

UNIDENTIFIED: **6** secret **7** unknown, unnamed **8** unmarked **9** anonymous **10** mysterious

UNIFICATION: **5** union, unity **6** hookup, merger **7** joining, linkage **8** alliance **9** coalition **11** combination **12** amalgamation **13** consolidation

UNIFORM: **4** even, like, suit **5** alike, dress, equal, level **6** attire, outfit, stable, steady **7** costume, orderly, regular, similar, stripes **8** constant **9** continual, unvarying **10** comparable, compatible, consistent, homogenous, invariable, systematic, unchanging

UNIFORMITY: **5** unity **7** harmony, oneness **8** equality, monotony, sameness **11** consistency, homogeneity

UNIFY: **4** ally, bind **5** merge, unite **6** couple **7** combine **8** organize **9** harmonize, integrate **10** centralize **11** consolidate, orchestrate, systematize

UNILLUMINATED: **3** dim **4** dark **5** murky **6** gloomy **7** obscure **9** lightless

UNIMAGINABLE: **9** fantastic **10** improbable, incredible **11** unthinkable **12** unbelievable **13** extraordinary, inconceivable, indescribable

UNIMAGINATIVE: **4** dull **5** trite **6** dreary **7** humdrum, prosaic, routine **9** hackneyed **10** pedestrian, uncreative, unexciting, uninspired, unoriginal **11** predictable

UNIMPAIRED: **4** free **5** sound, whole **6** intact, unhurt **8** unbroken, unharmed **9** undamaged, uninjured, unscathed

UNIMPASSIONED: **4** calm **6** placid, serene, steady **8** tranquil **9** impassive, unexcited **10** impersonal, phlegmatic **11** unemotional

UNIMPEACHABLE: **4** pure **5** clean **8** spotless **9** blameless, faultless, stainless, untainted **10** immaculate, impeccable **11** unblemished **12** unassailable **14** irreproachable, unquestionable

UNIMPORTANT: **5** minor, petty, small **6** little **7** trivial, useless **8** piddling **9** frivolous, worthless **10** immaterial, negligible **11** meaningless **12** nonessential **13** insignificant

UNINFORMED: **7** unaware **8** ignorant **9** oblivious, unadvised **10** uneducated **12** uninstructed

UNINHABITED: **5** empty **6** vacant **8** deserted, desolate, forsaken **9** abandoned **10** unoccupied

UNINHIBITED: **4** free **5** loose **6** candid **8** heedless, uncurbed **9** audacious, impulsive, liberated, outspoken **10** flamboyant, unhampered, unreserved **11** spontaneous **12** unrestrained, unsuppressed

UNINJURED: **5** sound, whole **6** intact, unhurt **8** unbroken, unharmed **9** undamaged, unscathed

UNINSPIRED: **4** dull **5** bland **6** boring, stodgy **7** unmoved **10** lackluster, uncreative, unoriginal **11** unimpressed **13** uninteresting

UNINTELLIGENT: **4** dumb **5** dense **6** obtuse, simple, stupid, unwise **7** asinine, foolish, idiotic **8** ignorant, mindless **9** senseless **10** uneducated

UNINTELLIGIBLE: **7** jumbled, muddled **8** puzzling **9** ambiguous, illegible **10** incoherent **11** meaningless **12** inarticulate, unfathomable

UNINTENTIONAL: **6** random **9** haphazard, unplanned, unwitting **10** accidental, fortuitous, undesigned, unintended **11** inadvertent **13** unanticipated

UNINTERESTED: **5** aloof, bored **8** listless **9** apathetic, unmindful, withdrawn **10** uninvolved **11** indifferent, unconcerned

UNINTERESTING: **3** dry **4** drab, dull, flat **5** stale **6** boring, dreary **7** humdrum, insipid, prosaic, tedious **8** tiresome **9** colorless **10** monotonous, uneventful, unexciting **13** unstimulating

UNINTERRUPTED: **7** endless **8** unbroken, unending **9** ceaseless, continual, sustained **10** continuous **11** consecutive, undisturbed

UNINVITING: **10** unpleasant, untempting **11** distasteful, unappealing, unwelcoming **12** unappetizing

UNION: **4** bloc, club **5** group, guild, local, order, unity **6** league, merger **7** joining, wedding **8** alliance, marriage, together **9** coalition, syndicate **10** connection, federation, fellowship, fraternity **11** association, brotherhood, partnership, unification **12** organization **13** confederation

UNIQUE: **3** odd **4** lone, only, rare, sole **5** alone **6** single **7** notable, special, strange, unusual **8** peculiar, peerless, singular, solitary, uncommon **9** matchless, unequaled, unrivaled **10** individual **11** distinctive, exceptional **12** incomparable, unparalleled **13** extraordinary, unprecedented

UNISON: **5** union, unity **6** accord **7** concert concord, harmony **9** agreement, consonant **10** concordant, together

UNIT: **3** ace, amp, BTU, one, ton **4** atom, bite, clan, foot, gram, hour, inch, item, mile, part, pint, volt, watt, yard, year **5** carat, digit, group, hertz, liter, meter, monad, ounce, pound, quart, squad, tribe, troop, whole **6** bushel, degree, entity, family, gallon, length, minute, module, outfit, second, weight **7** brigade, company, decibel, measure, platoon, section, segment **8** molecule, quantity **9** battalion, component **10** detachment, individual **11** measurement **12** denomination

UNITE: **3** mix, tie, wed **4** ally, band, bind, bond, fuse, join, link, meld, pair, pool, weld **5** affix, annex, blend, hitch, marry, merge, rally, unify **6** adhere, adjoin, attach, cement, couple, gather, mingle, solder, splice **7** combine, connect, consort, convene **8** assemble, coalesce, compound, condense, conspire, federate, organize, regulate, solidify **9** affiliate, aggregate, associate, cooperate **10** amalgamate, strengthen **11** consolidate, incorporate

UNITED: **6** allied, merged **7** unified **9** unanimous, undivided **10** collective, integrated **11** cooperative

UNITED ARAB EMIRATES:
capital: **8** Abu Dhabi
cities: **5** Dubai **6** Dubavy
continent: **4** Asia
ethnic groups: **4** Arab **6** Indian **7** Iranian **9** Pakistani
language: **6** Arabic

monetary unit: **6** dirham
water: **11** Persian Gulf

UNITED KINGDOM:
capital: **6** London
cities: **5** Leeds **7** Bristol, Glasgow **8** Bradford **9** Edinburgh, Liverpool, Sheffield **10** Birmingham, Manchester
comprises: **5** Wales **7** England **8** Scotland **15** Northern Ireland
continent: **6** Europe
ethnic groups: **5** Irish, Welsh **6** Ulster **7** English **8** Scottish
islands: **6** Caicos, Cayman **7** Bermuda, Channel, Leeward **8** Falkland, Hong Kong, Pitcairn, St. Helena **9** Ascension, Gibraltar, Isle of Man
languages: **5** Welsh **7** English
monetary unit: **5** pound

UNITED STATES:
capital: **12** Washington, DC
cities: **6** Boston, Dallas **7** Chicago, Detroit, Houston, Memphis, New York, Phoenix, San Jose **8** Honolulu, San Diego **9** Baltimore **10** Los Angeles, San Antonio **12** Indianapolis, Philadelphia, San Francisco
continent: **12** North America
language: **7** English
monetary unit: **4** cent, dime **5** penny **6** dollar, nickel **7** quarter
native: **8** American

UNITY: **5** peace, union **6** accord, unison **7** concord, consent, harmony, oneness **8** alliance, sameness **9** agreement, communion, congruity, wholeness **10** continuity, singleness, solidarity, uniformity **11** association, unification

UNIVERSAL: **5** broad, total, whole **6** common, cosmic, entire, global **7** general **8** accepted, constant, sweeping **9** boundless, customary, unlimited, worldwide **10** undisputed, widespread **11** omnipresent, unexcluding **13** comprehensive

UNIVERSE: **5** earth, world **6** cosmos, nature **8** creation **9** macrocosm **10** everything

UNIVERSITY: **6** school **7** academy, college **8** academie **11** institution
noted: **3** MIT **4** Duke, Yale **6** Oxford, Vienna **7** Chicago, Harvard **8** Berkeley, Columbia, Sorbonne, Stanford **9** Cambridge, Dartmouth, Notre Dame, Princeton **10** California

UNJUST: **5** cruel **6** biased, unfair **7** partial **8** improper, wrongful **9** dishonest **10** oppressive, prejudiced, undeserved **11** inequitable

UNJUSTIFIABLE: **5** undue **11** inexcusable, unwarranted **12** unforgivable

UNKEMPT: **4** rude **5** messy **6** grubby, shabby, shaggy, sloppy, untidy **7** ruffled, tousled **8** slovenly, uncombed **9** neglected, ungroomed **10** disarrayed, disheveled, disorderly, unpolished

UNKIND: **3** bad **4** mean, vile **5** cruel, harsh, nasty, rough, stern **6** brutal, severe, wicked **8** inhumane, uncaring, ungenial **9** malicious **10** unfriendly, ungenerous, ungracious, ungrateful **11** insensitive, unfavorable **13** inconsiderate

UNKNOWABLE: **8** mystical **10** mysterious **11** ungraspable **12** unfathomable **13** inconceivable

UNKNOWN: **5** alien **6** nobody **7** foreign, obscure, strange **8** nameless **9** anonymous, concealed, incognito, uncharted, unheard-of **10** unexplored, unfamiliar **12** uncelebrated, undiscovered, unidentified

UNLAWFUL: **5** taboo **6** banned **7** illegal, illicit, lawless **8** criminal, outlawed **9** forbidden **10** contraband, prohibited **12** illegitimate, unauthorized

UNLEARNED: **7** natural **8** backward, ignorant, untaught, unversed **9** untutored **10** illiterate, uneducated, unschooled **11** instinctive, uncivilized, unscholarly

UNLEASH: **4** free, vent **7** release **9** discharge

UNLETTERED: **8** ignorant, untaught **10** illiterate, uneducated, unschooled

UNLIKE: **6** uneven **7** diverse **8** clashing, contrary, distinct, opposite **9** different, unrelated **10** dissimilar **12** incompatible **13** heterogeneous

UNLIKELY: **5** unfit **6** absurd, remote, slight **8** doubtful, hopeless **10** improbable, unsuitable **11** unpromising **12** questionable, unbelievable, unimaginable

UNLIMITED: **4** huge, vast, wide **5** great, total **6** untold **7** endless **8** complete, infinite **9** boundless, countless, limitless, unbounded, undefined, universal **10** indefinite, unmeasured **12** immeasurable, unrestricted **13** comprehensive, unconditional, undeterminate

UNLOAD: **4** dump **5** eject, empty, trash **6** remove, unpack **7** deplane, deplete, discard, lighten, relieve **8** jettison, unburden **9** disburden, discharge, liquidate

UNLUCKY: **6** cursed, doomed, jinxed **7** hapless, unhappy **8** ill-fated, untoward **9** ill-omened, miserable **10** ill-starred **11** star-crossed, unfortunate **12** misfortunate

UNMANAGEABLE: **4** wild **6** unruly **9** fractious **10** disorderly, rebellious **11** disobedient **12** incorrigible, ungovernable **14** uncontrollable

UNMANLY: **5** sissy **7** gutless **8** cowardly, womanish **9** degrading **10** effeminate **11** unmasculine **12** dishonorable

UNMANNERLY: **4** rude **5** crude **6** coarse **7** boorish, uncivil, uncouth **8** impolite **10** ungracious **12** discourteous

UNMARRIED: **6** chaste, single **7** widowed **8** bachelor, celibate, divorced, eligible, unwedded **9** available **10** spouseless, unattached

UNMASK: **4** show **6** expose, reveal, unveil **7** uncloak, uncover **8** disclose, unshroud

UNMATCHED: **3** odd **6** unique **7** supreme **8** peerless **9** matchless, unequaled, unrivaled **12** unparalleled

UNMERCIFUL: **4** evil **5** cruel, harsh **6** brutal, severe **8** inhumane, pitiless, ruthless, uncaring **9** heartless, merciless **10** relentless **12** bloodthirsty

UNMINDFUL: **6** remiss **7** unaware **8** careless, heedless **9** forgetful, negligent, oblivious **10** neglectful **11** inattentive, thoughtless, unobservant

UNMISTAKABLE: **5** clear, plain **7** certain, evident, obvious **8** apparent, definite, distinct, explicit, positive **10** undeniable **11** unequivocal **12** undisputable

UNMITIGATED: **4** pure **5** sheer **6** arrant **7** unmixed **8** absolute, clearcut, unbroken **9** downright, undiluted **10** consummate, persistent, unmodified, unrelieved **11** unqualified

UNMIXED: **4** pure **5** sheer **6** simple **7** sincere **8** purebred, straight **9** pureblood, unalloyed **11** unmitigated **13** unadulterated

UNMOVED: **4** calm, cool, firm **5** stony **7** adamant, staunch **8** stubborn, unshaken **9** steadfast, untouched **10** unaffected **11** indifferent, unemotional **13** dispassionate

UNMOVING: **5** inert, still **6** static **8** immobile **10** motionless, stationary **11** unemotional

UNNAMED: **7** unknown **8** nameless, unmarked, unsigned **9** anonymous, incognito **10** unrevealed **12** unidentified

UNNATURAL: **4** fake **5** phony **6** forced **7** strange, uncanny **8** aberrant, abnormal, affected, freakish **9** anomalous, insincere, irregular, synthetic **10** artificial, fabricated, factitious **12** supernatural

UNNECESSARY: **5** extra **6** excess, lavish **7** surplus, useless **8** needless, optional, unneeded **9** redundant **10** gratuitous, unrequired **11** dispensable, superfluous, uncalled-for, unessential **12** nonessential

UNNERVE: **5** shake, spook, unman, upset **6** rattle, weaken **7** agitate, fluster, unhinge **8** castrate, distract, enervate, unsettle **9** undermine **10** emasculate, intimidate

UNNOTICED: **6** hidden, unseen **7** ignored, unnoted **9** neglected **10** overlooked, unobserved **11** disregarded **12** undiscovered, unrecognized

UNOBSERVANT: **5** blind **8** heedless, unseeing **11** inattentive

UNOBSTRUCTED: **4** free, open **5** clear **9** unimpeded **10** unhampered

UNOBTRUSIVE: **4** meek **5** quiet **6** humble, modest **8** reserved **10** unassuming **13** inconspicuous

UNOCCUPIED: **4** free, idle **5** empty **6** vacant **8** deserted, inactive **9** abandoned **11** uninhabited

UNOFFICIAL: **6** casual **8** informal **12** unauthorized, unsanctioned

UNORGANIZED: **5** loose, messy **7** chaotic, muddled **8** confused **9** haphazard **10** misorderly **12** disorganized **13** helter-skelter

UNORTHODOX: **6** unholy **7** radical, unusual **8** abnormal **9** eccentric, heretical **10** schismatic **13** nonconformist **14** unconventional

UNPAID: **3** due **7** donated, overdue **8** honorary **9** unsettled, voluntary **10** delinquent, gratuitous **11** outstanding

UNPALATABLE: **4** flat, weak **6** bitter **8** unsavory **9** repulsive, tasteless, uneatable **10** unpleasant **11** distasteful **12** disagreeable, unappetizing

UNPARALLELED: **5** alone **6** unique **8** peerless **9** matchless, unequaled, unmatched, unrivaled **11** exceptional, superlative, unsurpassed **13** unprecedented

UNPLANNED: **6** random **9** haphazard, impromptu **10** accidental, undesigned, unexpected, unintended **11** spontaneous **13** unintentional

UNPLEASANT: **3** bad **5** lousy, nasty **7** irksome, unhappy **8** annoying **9** abhorrent, obnoxious, offensive, repulsive **11** displeasing, distasteful, unpalatable **12** disagreeable

UNPOLISHED: **4** rude **5** crude, rough **6** coarse, rugged **7** boorish, uncivil, uncouth **8** impolite, tattered **9** inelegant, unrefined **10** uncultured, unfinished **11** uncivilized **12** discourteous

UNPOPULAR: **7** avoided, loathed, shunned, snubbed **8** detested, disliked, rejected **10** unaccepted, undesirable

UNPRECEDENTED: **3** new **5** novel **6** unique **7** unusual **8** abnormal, original, uncommon **9** unheard-of **11** exceptional **12** unparalleled

UNPREDICTABLE: **4** iffy **6** random **7** erratic **8** variable **9** arbitrary, irregular, uncertain, whimsical **10** capricious

UNPREJUDICED: **4** fair, just **8** straight, unbiased **9** equitable, impartial, objective, unbigoted **11** nonpartisan

UNPREPARED: **3** raw **6** asleep **7** napping, unaware, unready **8** uncooked **9** impromptu, surprised, unguarded **10** improvised **11** spontaneous, unrehearsed

UNPRETENTIOUS: **5** plain **6** humble, modest, simple **8** discreet **10** unassuming **11** unelaborate, unobtrusive

UNPRINCIPLED: **5** shady **6** amoral **7** corrupt, crooked, immoral **9** deceitful, dishonest, unethical **12** unscrupulous **14** unprofessional

UNPRODUCTIVE: **4** idle **6** barren, futile **7** sterile, useless **8** impotent, infecund **9** infertile **10** unfruitful **11** ineffective, inefficient

UNPROFESSIONAL: **6** shoddy, sloppy **7** amateur **8** inexpert **9** unethical, unskilled **12** unprincipled **13** inexperienced

UNPROFITABLE: **4** vain **6** barren **7** useless **8** gainless, hopeless **9** fruitless, pointless **10** unfruitful **11** unlucrative

UNPROGRESSIVE: **5** bleak **7** adverse **8** backward, ignorant, unlikely **9** benighted **11** undeveloped, unfavorable, unpromising **12** conservative, discouraging

UNPROPITIOUS: **7** adverse, ominous **8** contrary **11** threatening **12** antagonistic, inauspicious

UNPROTECTED: **6** unsafe **7** exposed, unarmed **8** helpless **9** dangerous, unguarded **10** vulnerable **11** defenseless, unsheltered

UNQUALIFIED: **4** bare, firm, sure **5** sheer, unfit, utter **6** unable **8** absolute, complete, definite, outright, thorough, unsuited **9** downright, incapable, unskilled, untrained **10** inadequate, unprepared **11** categorical, incompetent, unmitigated **13** inexperienced

UNQUESTIONABLE: **4** real, sure, true **5** clear **7** certain, evident, obvious **8** definite, positive **9** authentic **10** conclusive, undeniable **11** established **12** indisputable, unmistakable

UNRAVEL: **4** faze, undo **5** solve **6** unfold, unlace, unwind **7** resolve **8** decipher, separate, untangle **9** disengage, extricate **11** disentangle

UNREAL: **5** ideal **6** aerial, dreamy, fabled **7** fancied, surreal **8** fanciful, illusive, illusory, invented, mythical **9** fantastic, imaginary, pretended, visionary **10** artificial, fictitious **11** counterfeit, imaginative, nonexistent **12** unbelievable **13** insubstantial

UNREALISTIC: **5** silly **6** absurd **7** foolish **10** improbable, unfeasible **11** impractical

UNREASONABLE: **5** silly, undue **6** absurd, biased, unfair **7** foolish **9** excessive, fanatical, illogical, obstinate, senseless **10** exorbitant, headstrong, inflexible, irrational **11** extravagant, impractical, unwarranted

UNREFINED: **3** raw **4** rude **5** crass, crude, gross, rough **6** coarse, vulgar **7** boorish, uncouth **9** inelegant **10** uncultured, unpolished **11** uncivilized **12** uncultivated

UNREHEARSED: **7** offhand **8** informal **9** impromptu **10** improvised **11** extemporary, spontaneous

UNRELATED: **8** separate **9** disjoined **10** accidental, dissimilar **11** independent, unconnected **12** unassociated

UNRELENTING: **5** cruel, rigid **6** severe, steady **8** constant, rigorous, unabated **9** merciless, tenacious **10** continuous, determined, inflexible, persistent, relentless

UNRELIABLE: **5** false **6** tricky, unsafe **8** shifting, unstable **10** capricious **12** disreputable, questionable, undependable **13** irresponsible, unpredictable, untrustworthy

UNREMARKABLE: **5** plain **6** common **7** average, routine **8** ordinary **12** unsurprising

UNREMITTING: **8** constant, tireless **9** ceaseless, continual, incessant, perpetual, unceasing **10** persistent **11** persevering

UNREPENTANT: **7** callous **8** unatoned **9** unashamed **10** impenitent **11** remorseless **12** incorrigible

UNRESERVED: **4** open **5** frank **6** candid **8** outgoing **9** outspoken **11** unqualified **13** demonstrative

UNRESOLVED: **7** pending **8** unsolved, wavering **9** tentative, uncertain, unsettled **10** incomplete, indecisive, unanswered, unfinished **11** speculative **12** questionable

UNRESPONSIVE: **4** cold, cool **6** frigid **7** passive **9** unfeeling **11** insensitive, unemotional

UNREST: **5** chaos, tizzy **7** anarchy, anxiety, ferment, protest, tension, trouble, turmoil **8** disorder, disquiet, upheaval **9** commotion, confusion, rebellion **10** discontent, turbulence, uneasiness

UNRESTRAINED: **4** free, wild **5** blunt, frank, loose **6** candid, wanton **7** rampant **8** uncurbed **9** abandoned, audacious, dissolute, excessive, unbounded, unbridled, unchecked, unlimited **10** ungoverned, unhampered **11** extravagant, uninhibited **12** uncontrolled, unrestricted

UNRESTRICTED: **4** free, open **9** allowable, unlimited **10** accessible **12** unrestrained

UNRIPE: **5** green, young **6** callow **7** unready, verdant **8** immature, youthful **9** developed, premature **10** unseasoned **12** unseasonable

UNRIVALED: **6** unique **8** peerless, superior **9** unequaled, unmatched **10** undisputed **12** unparalleled

UNRUFFLED: **4** calm, cool **5** quiet **6** placid, poised, serene, smooth **8** composed, unshaken **9** collected **10** nonchalant, untroubled **11** undisturbed

UNRULY: **4** wild **5** rowdy **6** ornery, stormy **7** forward, lawless, raucous, restive, violent, wayward **9** difficult, fractious, obstinate, turbulent **10** boisterous, disorderly, headstrong, rebellious, tumultuous **11** disobedient, intractable **12** rambunctious, ungovernable, unmanageable

UNSAFE: **5** risky, shaky **6** chancy **7** exposed, unsound **8** insecure, perilous **9** dangerous, hazardous **10** unreliable, vulnerable **11** unprotected **13** untrustworthy

UNSATISFACTORY: **3** bad **4** poor **5** unfit **8** inferior **10** inadequate **11** inefficient **12** insufficient, unacceptable **13** disappointing

UNSAVORY: **4** flat **5** nasty **7** insipid **9** repugnant, revolting, sickening, tasteless **10** unpleasant **11** distasteful, unpalatable **12** disagreeable, unappetizing

UNSCATHED: 4 safe **5** sound, whole **6** intact, unhurt **8** unharmed, unmarked **9** uninjured, unscarred, untouched

UNSCHOOLED: 5 green, naive **8** ignorant, untaught **9** unlearned, untrained, untutored **10** illiterate, uneducated, uninformed, unlettered

UNSCRUPULOUS: 5 shady, venal **6** crafty **7** corrupt, crooked, devious, immoral **8** ruthless, sinister **9** deceitful, dishonest, unethical **11** underhanded **12** dishonorable, unprincipled

UNSEASONABLE: 6 unripe **8** abnormal, ill-timed, untimely **9** premature **10** malapropos **11** inopportune **13** inappropriate

UNSEASONED: 3 raw **5** bland, green **6** callow **8** immature **9** untrained

UNSEAT: 5 upset **6** depose, remove **7** replace **8** dethrone

UNSEEMLY: 5 cheap, crude, inept, rough **6** coarse, vulgar **7** boorish **8** improper, indecent **9** inelegant, offensive **10** unbecoming, unsuitable **11** distasteful, unbefitting **13** inappropriate

UNSEEN: 6 hidden **7** obscure **9** concealed, invisible, unnoticed **10** undetected, unobserved **12** undiscovered

UNSELFISH: 4 kind **6** giving **8** generous **10** altruistic, benevolent, charitable **11** magnanimous **12** humanitarian

UNSERVICEABLE: 7 useless **8** unusable **11** impractical **12** unfunctional

UNSETTLE: 5 spook, upset **6** bother, ruffle **7** agitate, derange, disrupt, disturb, fluster, trouble, unhinge, unnerve **8** confound, disorder, displace, disquiet **9** unbalance **10** discompose **11** disorganize

UNSETTLED: 5 tense **6** mobile, remote, shaken, unpaid **7** anxious, dubious, nervous, pending, unclear **8** bothered, restless, unstable, variable **9** debatable, uncertain, undecided **10** distracted, indecisive, unresolved **11** outstanding, unpopulated **12** undetermined

UNSHACKLE: 4 free **6** loosen **7** release, unchain **8** liberate, unfetter **10** emancipate

UNSHAKABLE: 4 firm **5** fixed **6** steady **7** abiding, adamant **10** unsinkable, unwavering **11** unflappable

UNSHAKEN: 4 calm, cool, firm, sure **6** poised, steady **7** unmoved **9** steadfast, undaunted **10** unaffected **11** levelheaded, unflinching

UNSHAPELY: 5 baggy, slack **8** deformed, formless **9** amorphous, shapeless

UNSIGHTLY: 4 ugly **6** homely **7** hideous **8** deformed **9** repulsive, revolting, sickening **12** unattractive

UNSKILLED: 5 green, inept **8** inexpert **9** untrained **10** amateurish, uneducated **11** incompetent **13** inexperienced

UNSKILLFUL: 5 inept **6** clumsy **7** awkward, unhandy **8** bungling, inexpert **9** maladroit **11** incompetent, inefficient **13** inexperienced

UNSOCIABLE: 3 shy **4** cold, cool **7** hostile **8** reserved, solitary **9** withdrawn **10** antisocial, unfriendly **11** introverted, standoffish

UNSOLICITED: **4** free **8** unsought **9** undesired, uninvited, voluntary **11** unrequested, volunteered

UNSOPHISTICATED: **4** pure **5** corny, crude, green, naive **6** callow, simple **7** artless, genuine, natural **8** innocent **9** ingenious, untutored, unworldly **13** inexperienced, uncomplicated

UNSOUND: **4** sick, weak **5** crazy, frail, hairy, risky, shaky, unfit **6** chancy, feeble, flawed, flimsy, insane, unsafe, wobbly **7** decayed, foolish, fragile, rickety **8** decrepit, deranged, diseased, impaired, insecure, unstable, unsteady, weakened **9** dangerous, defective, hazardous, imperfect, senseless, tottering **10** unbalanced **11** treacherous

UNSPARING: **6** giving **7** liberal **8** abundant, generous **9** bountiful **10** munificent, openhanded **11** extravagant

UNSPEAKABLE: **5** awful **6** wicked **7** hateful, heinous **8** alarming, shocking **9** appalling, atrocious, ineffable, loathsome, repulsive, revolting, sickening **10** disgusting, outrageous **11** indefinable, unutterable **12** unbelievable, unimaginable **13** inconceivable, indescribable, inexpressible

UNSPECIFIED: **5** vague **7** general **9** undefined **11** unmentioned **12** undetermined

UNSPOILED: **5** fresh **6** virgin **7** natural **8** pristine, unmarred, untapped **9** unsullied, untouched **11** unblemished, uncorrupted

UNSPOKEN: **4** mute **5** tacit **6** silent, unsaid **7** implied **8** implicit, inferred, invoiced **9** intimated, unuttered **10** understood

UNSTABLE: **5** loose, rocky, shaky **6** fickle, flimsy, shifty, tricky, wobbly **7** erratic, flighty, fragile **8** insecure, shifting, unhinged, unsteady, variable, volatile, wavering **9** eccentric, emotional, unsettled **10** changeable, inconstant, precarious, unreliable **11** fluctuating, vacillating **12** inconsistent

UNSTEADY: **5** dizzy, rocky, shaky, tippy **6** fickle, groggy, wiggly, wobbly **7** erratic, quivery, rickety, unsound, wayward **8** shifting, unstable, variable, wavering **9** teetering, unsettled **10** capricious, changeable, inconstant, unreliable **11** fluctuating, vacillating

UNSTUDIED: **5** naive **7** artless, natural **8** unforced, untaught, unversed **9** unlearned, untutored **10** unaffected, unschooled **11** extemporary, instinctive, spontaneous, unrehearsed

UNSUBSTANTIAL: **4** airy, slim, thin, weak **5** light **6** flimsy, slight, unread **7** fragile, lacking, nominal, tenuous, unsound **9** frivolous, imaginary, visionary **10** immaterial **11** implausible

UNSUBSTANTIATED: **10** unattested, unverified **11** unconfirmed, unsupported

UNSUCCESSFUL: **4** vain **6** futile **7** failing, hapless, unlucky **8** abortive, hopeless **9** fruitless **11** ineffectual, unfortunate **12** unprofitable

UNSUITABLE: **5** inapt, inept, unfit **7** useless **8** improper, untimely **10** inadequate, unbecoming **11** conflicting, unbefitting **12** unacceptable **13** inappropriate

UNSUITED: **5** inapt **8** unseemly **9** unfitting **12** incompatible **13** inappropriate

UNSULLIED: **4** pure **5** clean **8** pristine, spotless, unsoiled **9** undefiled **10** immaculate, unpolluted **11** unblemished, untarnished

UNSURE: **4** weak **5** shaky, timid **6** wobbly **7** unclear **8** doubtful, hesitant, insecure, unstable, unsteady **9** dangerous, hazardous, uncertain, undecided **10** borderline, indecisive **11** mistrustful, unconvinced, vacillating **13** untrustworthy

UNSURPASSED: **8** peerless **9** matchless, unequaled, unrivaled **10** unexcelled **12** unparalleled **13** unprecedented

UNSUSPECTING: **5** naive **6** unwary **7** unaware **8** gullible, innocent **9** credulous

UNSWAYED: **3** far **4** firm **8** unbiased **9** impartial, unbigoted **12** unprejudiced

UNSWERVING: **4** firm, true **6** steady **7** devoted, staunch **8** straight **9** dedicated, steadfast, undaunted **10** determined **11** unfaltering

UNSYMMETRICAL: **5** askew **6** uneven **8** lopsided **9** irregular **10** unbalanced

UNSYMPATHETIC: **4** cold, cool, mean **5** cruel, harsh, stony **7** callous, hostile **8** uncaring **9** heartless, repellent, unfeeling, unlikable **10** unpleasant **11** coldhearted, hardhearted, insensitive, unemotional **15** uncompassionate

UNTAMED: **4** wild **5** feral **6** savage **8** barbaric **9** unsubdued **11** uncivilized **12** rambunctious **13** undisciplined

UNTANGLE: **4** free **5** solve, untie **7** unsnarl, untwist **9** extricate **10** unscramble **11** disentangle

UNTARNISHED: **4** pure **5** clean, shiny **8** polished, spotless **9** unstained, unsullied, untainted **10** immaculate **11** unblemished

UNTAUGHT: **7** natural **8** ignorant **9** unlearned, untrained, untutored **10** illiterate, uneducated, unschooled **11** instinctive, spontaneous **12** uninstructed

UNTHINKABLE: **6** absurd, unique **10** impossible, incredible, outlandish **12** unbelievable **13** extraordinary, inconceivable

UNTHINKING: **4** rash **6** stupid, unwise **7** foolish **8** careless, heedless **9** impetuous, senseless, unmindful **11** inadvertent, insensitive, thoughtless **13** inconsiderate

UNTIDY: **5** dirty, messy **6** sloppy **7** tousled, unkempt **8** careless, littered, slipshod, slovenly, uncombed **10** bedraggled, disheveled, disordered **11** disarranged, uncluttered

UNTIE: **4** free, undo **6** before, loosen, unbind, unknot, unlace **7** unhitch **8** unfasten, untangle **9** disengage, extricate **11** disentangle **12** continuously

UNTIMELY: **5** early, inapt **8** improper, mistimed, unseemly **9** premature **10** unexpected, unsuitable **11** inopportune, unfortunate **12** unseasonable **15** inappropriately

UNTIRING: **6** steady **7** staunch **8** constant, resolute, tireless **9** incessant, tenacious **10** persistent, relentless, undeterred **11** persevering **13** inexhaustible

UNTOLD: **4** huge, many, vast **7** endless **8** enormous, numerous **9** boundless, countless, unrelated **10** staggering, unrevealed **11** innumerable, undisclosed **12** immeasurable, unimaginable

UNTOUCHED: **4** pure **5** sound, whole **6** intact, virgin **7** perfect **8** flawless, pristine, unharmed **9** unspoiled **10** immaculate **11** unscratched

UNTOWARD: **4** wild **6** unruly **7** adverse, awkward, unlucky **8** improper, unseemly **9** difficult, vexatious **10** irritating, unbecoming **11** intractable, troublesome, unfortunate **12** inconvenient, ungovernable, unmanageable, unpropitious **13** undisciplined

UNTRAINED: **3** raw **4** wild **5** green **6** novice **7** untamed **8** ignorant, inexpert, untaught **9** unskilled **10** amateurish, unprepared **11** unqualified **13** inexperienced, undisciplined

UNTRIED: **3** new **5** fresh, green **6** callow **8** immature, unproved, untested **11** unattempted **13** inexperienced

UNTROUBLED: **4** calm **6** placid, serene **7** halcyon, relaxed **8** carefree, peaceful, tranquil **9** easygoing, unruffled, unworried **10** unbothered

UNTRUE: **5** false, wrong **7** unloyal **8** disloyal **9** deceptive, dishonest, erroneous, faithless, incorrect **10** fictitious, inaccurate, misleading, unfaithful, untruthful

UNTRUSTWORTHY: **5** shady **6** shifty, tricky, unsafe **7** corrupt, crooked, devious **8** disloyal, slippery **9** deceitful, dishonest, unassured, unethical **10** unreliable, untruthful **12** disreputable, questionable, undependable **13** irresponsible

UNTRUTH: **3** fib, lie **4** hoax, tale, yarn **5** fable, story **6** canard **7** fallacy, falsity **9** falsehood **11** fabrication **13** prevarication

UNTRUTHFUL: **5** false, lying **9** deceptive, dishonest, insincere **10** fraudulent, mendacious, misleading

UNTUTORED: **5** naive **6** unread **7** natural **8** ignorant, untaught **9** unlearned **10** illiterate, uneducated, unschooled **12** uninstructed

UNTYPICAL: **3** odd **7** bizarre, strange, unusual **8** abnormal, uncommon

UNUSED: **3** new **4** idle **5** fresh **6** vacant **7** untried **8** untapped **9** remaining

UNUSUAL: **3** odd **4** rare **5** funny, novel, weird **6** unique **7** bizarre, offbeat, strange, typical **8** abnormal, distinct, peculiar, uncommon **9** anomalous, different, eccentric, untypical **10** phenomenal, refreshing, remarkable, surprising **11** exceptional **13** extraordinary

UNVARIED: **5** alike, fixed **6** steady **7** uniform **9** identical **10** monotonous **11** homogeneous

UNVARNISHED: **4** bald, bare **5** frank, plain, stark **6** candid, simple **9** unadorned **10** unfinished **11** undisguised **13** unembellished

UNVARYING: **5** fixed, plain **6** steady **7** uniform **8** constant **10** monotonous, unchanging **13** unfluctuating, uninterrupted

UNVEIL: **6** expose, reveal, unmask **7** divulge, exhibit, uncloak, uncover **8** announce, disclose

UNWARRANTED: **5** undue, wrong **6** unfair **8** baseless **9** unfounded **10** groundless, unprovoked **11** uncalled-for, unjustified **12** unreasonable

UNWARY: **4** rash **5** brash **7** unalert, unaware **8** careless, heedless, reckless **9** credulous, imprudent, unguarded **10** incautious **11** thoughtless **12** unsuspecting

UNWASHED: **4** base **5** dirty, dregs **6** filthy, grubby, soiled **7** unclean **8** plebeian **10** unscrubbed

UNWASTEFUL: **6** frugal **7** thrifty **9** efficient **10** economical, productive

UNWAVERING: **4** firm **6** stable, steady **7** staunch **8** constant, unshaken **9** dedicated, steadfast **10** consistent, determined, persistent, unchanging, unshakable **11** unfaltering, unflappable

UNWELCOME: **7** unasked **8** excluded, unsought, unwanted **9** undesired, uninvited, unpopular **10** unpleasant **11** distasteful **12** unacceptable **13** objectionable

UNWELL: **3** ill **4** sick **5** badly, frail **6** ailing, feeble, infirm, poorly, sickly **9** squeamish

UNWHOLESOME: **4** evil, foul **5** toxic **6** impure **7** baneful, corrupt, harmful, noxious, unclean, unsound **9** offensive, poisonous, repulsive, unhealthy **10** pernicious **11** deleterious, detrimental, unhealthful **12** insalubrious

UNWIELDY: **5** bulky, heavy **6** clumsy **7** awkward, weighty **8** ungainly **10** burdensome, cumbersome **12** unmanageable

UNWILLING: **5** loath **6** averse, forced **7** against, opposed, uneager **8** backward, hesitant **9** reluctant **11** disinclined, involuntary **13** uncooperative

UNWIND: **4** rest, undo **5** relax **6** loosen, uncoil, unroll **7** recline, unravel **8** untangle

UNWISE: **4** dumb **5** inane, inept, naive **6** stupid **7** foolish, unsound, witless **9** impolitic, imprudent, misguided, senseless **10** indiscreet, irrational **11** impractical, inadvisable, injudicious, thoughtless **13** irresponsible, unintelligent

UNWITTING: **7** unaware **8** innocent **9** unknowing, unplanned **10** accidental, unexpected, uninformed, unintended **11** inadvertent, involuntary **12** unsuspecting

UNWONTED: **4** rare **7** unusual **8** atypical, uncommon **10** infrequent **11** exceptional **12** unaccustomed, unimaginable **13** extraordinary

UNWORLDLY: **5** green, naive **6** dreamy, sacred **7** natural **8** abstract, ethereal, heavenly **9** celestial, spiritual, unearthly, unstudied, visionary **10** immaterial, unschooled **13** inexperienced

UNWORTHY: **4** base **5** unfit **7** beneath **8** blamable, shameful, unseemly **9** valueless, worthless **10** unbecoming, unsuitable **11** undeserving **12** contemptible, dishonorable

UNWRINKLED: **6** ironed, smooth **10** unfurrowed

UNWRITTEN: **4** oral **5** vocal **6** unsaid, verbal **8** accepted, unstated **9** customary **10** understood **11** traditional

UNYIELDING: **4** fast, firm, grim, hard **5** fixed, rigid, stern, stiff, stony, tough **6** steely, wooden **7** adamant **8** ironclad, obdurate, ruthless, stubborn **9** inelastic, obstinate, pigheaded, steadfast, tenacious, unbending **10** determined, headstrong, inflexible, relentless, unwavering **11** intractable **12** unsubmissive **14** uncompromising

UP-AND-COMING: **5** alert, eager **6** active **11** industrious **12** enterprising

UP-AND-DOWN: **6** seesaw, uneven **7** bobbing **8** vertical **11** vacillating **13** perpendicular

UPBEAT: **5** happy **6** cheery **7** hopeful **8** cheerful, positive, sanguine **10** optimistic

UPBRAID: **5** abuse, chide, scold **6** berate **7** censure, lecture, reprove **8** admonish, chastise, denounce, reproach **9** castigate, criticize, reprimand

UPCOMING: **6** future **7** looming, nearing **8** imminent **9** impending **11** approaching, forthcoming

UPDATE: **5** amend, renew **6** revise **7** restore **8** renovate **9** modernize, refurbish **10** rejuvenate

UPGRADE: **5** boost, raise, slope **6** ascent, uplift **7** advance, elevate, improve, incline **8** increase

UPHEAVAL: **5** storm **6** clamor, revolt, tumult **7** turmoil **8** disaster, shakeout **9** cataclysm, commotion, overthrow **10** revolution **11** catastrophe, disturbance

UPHILL: **4** hard **5** tough **6** rising, rugged, tiring **7** arduous **8** grueling, toilsome **9** ascending, difficult, laborious, strenuous **10** exhausting

UPHOLD: **4** back, bear, lift **5** brace, carry, raise **6** assert, assist, defend **7** confirm, promote, protect, support, sustain **8** advocate, champion, maintain **9** encourage, vindicate

UPKEEP: **6** budget, repair **7** support **8** expenses, overhead **10** sustenance **11** maintenance **12** preservation

UPLIFT: **4** lift, rock **5** edify, exalt, hoist, raise **7** elevate, improve, inspire, upgrade **9** enlighten **10** enrichment, illuminate **14** rehabilitation

UPON: **4** atop, over **5** about, above **7** against, astride **10** concerning, thereafter

UPPER: **4** drug, over **5** above, elite **6** higher, senior **7** topmost **8** elevated, overhead, superior **9** important, stimulant **11** amphetamine

UPPER CLASS: **5** elite **7** society **8** highbred **10** upper crust **11** gentrycracy

UPPER HAND: **4** edge **6** better **7** command **9** advantage, supremacy **11** superiority

UPPERMOST: **3** top **4** main **5** chief **6** senior **7** highest, leading, primary, supreme, topmost **8** dominant, foremost, greatest, loftiest **11** predominant

UPRIGHT: **4** fair, good, just, prop, true **5** erect, moral, noble, steep **6** honest, square **7** ethical, sincere **8** elevated, straight, vertical, virtuous **9** equitable, exemplary, honorable, righteous **10** aboveboard, principled **11** trustworthy **13** perpendicular

UPRIGHTNESS: **5** honor **6** virtue **7** dignity, honesty **9** integrity

UPRISING: **4** riot **6** ascent, mutiny, revolt, tumult **7** incline **8** upheaval **9** ascending, commotion, rebellion **10** insurgence, revolution **11** disturbance **12** insurrection

UPROAR: **4** fuss, riot, stir **5** brawl, chaos **6** bedlam, bustle, clamor, fracas, hassle, hubbub, mayhem, racket, tumult **7** clamour, ferment, turmoil **8** brouhaha, disorder, violence **9** commotion, confusion **11** disturbance, pandemonium

UPROARIOUS: **4** loud, wild **5** noisy **8** confused **9** hilarious, turbulent **10** boisterous

UPROOT: **4** move **6** remove **7** destroy **8** displace **9** eradicate, extirpate **10** annihilate, deracinate, transplant **11** exterminate

UPSET: **4** beat, turn **5** anger, annoy, shock, worry **6** bother, defeat, enrage, rattle, ruffle, topple, tumble **7** agitate, capsize, confuse, derange, disturb, fluster, incense, jumbled, outcome, reverse, subvert, trouble, unhinge, unnerve **8** capsized, surprise, unsettle **9** discomfit, embarrass, infuriate, overthrow **10** discompose, disconcert, disordered, distressed, overturned **11** disorganize, overwrought

UPSHOT: **5** limit **6** climax, effect, ending, finale, finish, result, sequel **7** outcome **9** aftermath **10** conclusion **11** consequence, culmination, termination

UPSIDE-DOWN: **7** chaotic, haywire, jumbled **8** backward, confused, inverted, reversed **10** topsy-turvy

UPSTANDING: **5** moral **6** honest **7** ethical, upright **8** vertical **9** honorable **10** principled **11** trustworthy

UPSTART: **4** snob **5** comer **7** parvenu **11** nouveau rich **12** presumptuous

UPSURGE: **4** boom, rise **6** upturn **7** advance, upswing **8** increase, recovery **11** improvement

UPTIGHT: **4** edgy **5** tense **6** uneasy

UP-TO-DATE: **6** modern **7** abreast

UPTURN: **7** advance, upsurge, upswing **8** increase, recovery **11** improvement

UPWARD: **5** above, lofty **6** higher, uphill **7** greater, skyward **9** ascending

URANIUM: **7** element **8** chemical
hazard: **5** toxic **11** radioactive

URBAN: **4** city, town **5** civic **7** central, oppidan **9** municipal **12** cosmopolitan, metropolitan

URBANE: **5** civil, suave **6** polite, smooth **7** affable, cordial, elegant, genteel, refined **8** cultured, debonair, polished **9** civilized, courteous **10** cultivated **12** cosmopolitan **13** sophisticated

URCHIN: **3** boy, elf, imp **4** brat, waif **5** child, gamin, scamp **8** hedgehog **10** delinquent, ragamuffin **11** guttersnipe

URGE: **3** egg, yen **4** coax, goad, prod, push, spur, sway **5** drive, force, hurry, impel, plead, press, shove **6** appeal, cajole, demand, desire, excite, exhort, incite, induce, insist, motive, needle, prompt **7** impulse, passion, provoke, request, solicit, suggest **8** advocate, appetite, persuade, pressure, weakness, yearning **9** encourage, importune, incentive, influence, recommend, stimulate

URGENCY: **4** need **6** stress **8** exigency, pressure **9** necessity **10** importance, insistence **11** desperation, seriousness

URGENT: **5** grave **7** clamant, crucial, exigent, serious **8** critical, pressing, required **9** demanding, essential, immediate, impelling, important, insistent, necessary **10** imperative

URIS, LEON: **8** novelist **12** screenwriter
nationality: **8** American
wrote: **5** Topaz **6** Exodus **7** Trinity **9** Battle Cry **10** Armageddon **13** The Angry Hills

URN: **3** jar **4** ewer, vase **6** vessel **7** capsule, cistern, ossuary, pitcher, samovar **9** container **10** cinerarium

URUGUAY:
capital: **10** Montevideo
cities: **5** Salto **8** Paysandu
continent: **12** South America
ethnic groups: **7** mestizo, mulatto, Spanish **9** Caucasian
language: **7** Spanish
monetary unit: **4** peso
water: **5** Negro **7** Uruguay **12** Rio de la Plata

USABLE: **4** open **5** handy **6** useful **7** helpful, working **8** valuable **9** available, practical **10** accessible, applicable, beneficial, convenient, functional **11** serviceable

USAGE: **4** form, mode, rule, wont **5** habit **6** custom, manner, method, system **7** formula, grammar **8** habitude, interest, practice **9** procedure, tradition, treatment **10** convention

USE: **3** try **4** duty, gain, good, hire, need, wont, work **5** apply, avail, exert, guide, habit, spend, treat, value, wield, worth **6** custom, demand, devour, employ, expend, handle, manage, occupy **7** benefit, consume, control, deplete, exhaust, exploit, mileage, operate, utility, utilize **8** accustom, exercise, function, handling, practice, regulate **9** advantage, habituate, privilege, treatment **10** capitalize, employment, manipulate **11** application, consumption, familiarize

USED: **8** accepted, consumed, shopworn, utilized **10** secondhand

USEFUL: **4** good **5** handy **7** helpful **8** valuable **9** effective, practical, pragmatic **10** beneficial, convenient, functional, profitable, worthwhile **11** serviceable **12** advantageous, multipurpose

USEFULNESS: **5** value **7** benefit, utility **9** advantage **10** efficiency **11** suitability **12** practicality

USELESS: **4** idle, vain, void **6** futile **8** helpless, hopeless, obsolete, outmoded **9** fruitless, pointless, worthless **10** unavailing, unworkable **11** incompetent, ineffective, ineffectual, inefficient **12** unproductive, unprofitable **13** impracticable, unserviceable

USHER: **4** lead, page, seat **5** guide, steer **6** attend, direct, escort, herald, porter **7** conduct, officer, precede, receive, servant **9** attendant, introduce, precursor **10** doorkeeper, gatekeeper, inaugurate

USUAL: **4** rife **5** trite **6** common, normal, wonted **7** average, general, natural, regular, routine, typical **8** everyday, familiar, frequent, habitual, ordinary, standard **9** customary **10** accustomed, prevailing **11** predictable, traditional **12** conventional

USURP: **4** take **5** seize, steal **7** preempt **8** arrogate **10** commandeer **11** appropriate

UTAH:
bird: **7** seagull
capital: **12** Salt Lake City
cities: **5** Ogden, Provo
explorer: **16** Franciscan friars
features: **6** Arches **10** Great Basin **11** Bryce Canyon **12** Mormon church **15** Colorado Plateau
flower: **8** sego lily
nicknames: **6** Mormon **7** Beehive
tree: **10** blue spruce
water: **8** Colorado

UTENSIL: **3** pan, pot **4** fork, tool **5** knife, spoon **6** gadget, grater **7** spatula **9** apparatus, appliance, equipment, implement **10** instrument, silverware

UTILITARIAN: **6** usable, useful **8** sensible **9** effective, efficient, practical, pragmatic, realistic **10** economical, functional

UTILITY: **6** profit **7** benefit, service **9** advantage, auxiliary, secondary **10** substitute, usefulness **11** convenience

UTILIZE: **3** use **6** employ **7** consume, exploit, harness **8** exercise **10** capitalize

UTMOST: **4** best **5** final **7** extreme, highest, maximum **8** absolute, farthest, greatest, ultimate **9** paramount

UTOPIA: **4** Eden, Zion **6** heaven **8** paradise **9** Shangri-la

UTOPIAN: **5** ideal **7** perfect **8** arcadian **9** imaginary, visionary **10** idealistic, unfeasible **11** impractical

UTTAR PRADESH:
capital: **7** Lucknow
country: **5** India

UTTER: **3** say **4** blat, dang, darn, emit, gasp, roar, talk, tell, vent **5** blurt, clack, croak, issue, sheer, shout, speak, stark, state, total, voice **6** assert, direct, entire, mumble, mutter, reveal **7** declare, deliver, divulge, exclaim, express, extreme, perfect, publish, whisper **8** absolute, complete, disclose, outright, vocalize **9** downright, enunciate, pronounce, verbalize **10** articulate, peremptory **11** unmitigated, unqualified

UTTERANCE: **4** talk, word **6** dictum, murmur, remark, speech **7** opinion, whisper **9** discourse, statement **10** expression, revelation **12** announcement, articulation, vocalization **13** verbalization

UTTERLY: **3** all **4** full, just, well **6** merely, wholly **7** totally **8** entirely **9** assuredly, perfectly **10** absolutely, altogether, completely, positively, thoroughly **13** diametrically

UTTERMOST: **6** utmost **7** extreme, maximum **8** farthest, remotest **11** furthermost

UZBEKISTAN:
capital: **8** Tashkent
cities: **5** Nukus **7** Bukhara **9** Samarkand
continent: **4** Asia
ethnic groups: **5** Uzbek **7** Russian
features: **13** Fergana Valley
formerly: **9** Turkestan
language: **5** Uzbek
monetary unit: **5** ruble
water: **8** Amu Darya, Syr Darya

V

VACANCY: **4** room, void **5** break, chasm, space **6** cavity, vacuum **7** opening, vacuity **8** position **9** emptiness **11** uninhabited

VACANT: **4** free, idle, open, void **5** blank, empty, inane, silly **6** barren, devoid, unused **7** deadpan, foolish, leisure, vacuous **8** deserted, unfilled **9** abandoned **10** disengaged, unemployed, unoccupied, untenanted **11** uninhabited **12** inexpressive **14** expressionless

VACATE: **4** quit, void **5** annul, clear, empty, leave **6** depart, repeal, retire **7** abandon, rescind **8** abrogate, dissolve, evacuate **10** relinquish **11** countermand

VACATION: **4** rest, trip **5** leave, spite **6** recess **7** holiday, leisure, liberty **8** furlough **10** sabbatical **12** intermission

VACCINATE: **7** protect **8** immunize **9** inoculate

VACILLATE: **4** rock, sway **5** shift, waver **6** seesaw, teeter, totter, wobble **7** flutter, stagger **8** hesitate **9** alternate, fluctuate, hem and haw, oscillate

VACILLATING: **6** unsure **7** swaying **8** hesitant, shifting, volatile, wavering **9** tentative, uncertain, vibrating **10** changeable, hesitating **11** fluctuating, oscillating

VACILLATION: **5** doubt, swing **7** swaying **8** wavering **9** faltering, vibration **10** feebleness, fickleness, indecision **11** fluctuation, uncertainty **12** irresolution **13** dillydallying

VACUITY: **4** void **5** blank, empty **6** stupid, vacuum **7** vacancy, vacuous **8** idleness, unfilled **9** emptiness **11** nothingness **13** unintelligent

VACUOUS: **5** clear, inane, silly **6** devoid, vacant

VACUUM: **4** void **5** space **6** cavity **7** vacuity **9** emptiness **11** nothingness

VAGABOND: **3** bum **4** hobo **5** rogue, rover, scamp, stiff, stray, tramp **6** beggar, wander **7** aimless, drifter, nomadic, vagrant, wayward **8** bohemian, deadbeat, drifting, wanderer, wayfarer **9** itinerant, transient, wandering, worthless **13** unpredictable

VAGARY: **4** kink, roam, whim **5** caper, fancy, prank, quirk, trick, waver **6** breach, notion, whimsy **7** caprice, conceit, fantasy, impulse

8 daydream, rambling **10** digression, divergence

VAGRANT: **3** bum **4** hobo, waif **5** idler, rover, tramp **6** beggar, roamer **7** nomadic, wayward **8** homeless, vagabond, wanderer **9** itinerant **10** panhandler **11** undesirable **12** unrestrained

VAGUE: **3** dim **4** dark, hazy **5** faint, foggy, fuzzy, loose, misty, muddy **6** bleary, blurry, cloudy, dreamy, opaque, unsure **7** obscure, shadowy, sketchy, unclear, unfixed **8** confused, nebulous **9** ambiguous, uncertain, unsettled **10** illdefined, indefinite, indistinct, unexplicit **11** unspecified **12** undetermined

VAIN: **4** idle **5** cocky, empty, petty, proud **6** flimsy, futile, hollow, otiose, snooty **7** foolish, haughty, stuckup, trivial, useless **8** arrogant, boastful, hopeless, nugatory **9** conceited, egotistic, frivolous, fruitless, senseless, worthless **10** egocentric, unavailing, unrewarded **11** egotistical, ineffective, ineffectual, unimportant **12** narcissistic, ostentatious, unprofitable, vainglorious

VAINGLORIOUS: **4** vain **5** cocky, proud **7** pompous **8** boastful, bragging, insolent **9** conceited **11** egotistical **12** narcissistic

VALE: **4** dale, dell, glen **5** adieu **6** valley **8** farewell

VALEDICTION: **5** adieu **6** speech **7** address, good-bye **8** farewell

VALEDICTORY: **5** final **7** good-bye, parting **8** farewell, terminal **9** departing

VALENTINE: **4** card, gift **5** heart **6** letter **10** sweetheart

VALET: **6** squire **7** dresser, equerry, servant **9** attendant **10** manservant

VALIANT: **4** bold **5** brave, gutsy, noble, stout **6** daring, heroic, strong, worthy **7** gallant **8** fearless, intrepid, powerful, stalwart, unafraid, valorous, vigorous **9** excellent, steadfast, undaunted **10** chivalrous, courageous **11** adventurous **12** stouthearted

VALID: **4** good, just, true **5** legal, right, solid, sound **6** lawful, strong **7** binding, genuine, healthy, telling, weighty **8** credible, powerful, verified **9** authentic, certified, confirmed, effective, efficient, realistic **10** compelling, conclusive, convincing, satisfying, sufficient **12** satisfactory

VALIDATE: **5** prove **6** verify **7** certify, confirm, justify **8** legalize, sanction **9** establish **12** authenticate, substantiate

VALIDITY: **5** force **6** weight **7** cogency, potency **8** strength **9** soundness, substance **10** legitimacy **11** genuineness **13** effectiveness

VALISE: **3** bag **7** baggage, luggage, satchel **8** suitcase **9** briefcase, haversack

VALLEY: **4** cove, dale, dell, glen, rill, vale **5** basin, chasm, combe, gorge, goyle, gulch, gully, swale **6** canyon, cirque, coulee, dingle, divide, hollow, ravine, strath, trough **10** depression

VALOR: **4** guts **5** heart, merit, nerve, spunk **6** spirit, virtue **7** bravery, courage, heroism, prowess **8** backbone, boldness, chivalry, tenacity **9** fortitude, gallantry **10** resolution **12** fearlessness

VALOROUS: **4** bold **5** brave, noble, stout **6** heroic **7** gallant, valiant **8** fearless, intrepid **9** dauntless **10** courageous

VALUABLE: **4** dear, rare **5** asset **6** costly, prized, useful **7** antique **8** heirloom, precious **9** cherished, expensive, important, priceless, treasured **10** beneficial, worthwhile **11** collectible, serviceable

VALUE: **4** cost, rate **5** avail, price, prize, worth **6** admire, assess, esteem, weight **7** account, apprise, apprize, cherish, expense, opinion, quality, respect, utility **8** appraise, estimate, evaluate, treasure **9** advantage, valuation **10** appreciate, assessment, estimation, importance, usefulness **11** distinction **12** significance

VALVE: **4** cock, flap, gate **6** faucet, outlet, spigot **7** shutoff, stopper **9** regulator

VAMOOSE: **4** scat **5** leave, scram **6** begone, decamp, depart **7** skiddoo **8** hightail **9** skedaddle

VAMP: **4** mend **5** flirt, patch, siren, tramp **6** repair, seduce **8** contrive **9** fabricate, improvise, temptress **10** seductress **11** enchantress

VAMPIRE: **3** bat **7** Dracula, monster, seducer **11** blackmailer, bloodsucker **12** extortionist

VAN: **4** cart, lead, wing **5** truck, wagon **6** camper **7** vehicle **8** vanguard **9** forefront

VANDAL: **6** looter, raider **7** hoodlum, ravager, ruffian **8** marauder, pillager **9** plunderer

VANDALIZE: **3** mar **5** trash, wreck **6** deface **7** destroy

VANE: **3** arm, fan **5** blade **6** device **7** feather **11** weathercock

VANGUARD: **7** leaders, leading **9** forefront **10** innovators **12** trailblazers

VANILLA: **4** bean **5** bland **7** extract **8** ordinary **9** flavoring **10** unexciting, unoriginal

VANISH: **4** exit, fade, melt **8** dissolve, evanesce, vaporize **9** disappear, evaporate, terminate **13** dematerialize

VANITY: **5** pride **6** egoism **7** cabinet, compact, conceit, egotism, foppery **8** futility, idleness **9** emptiness, pomposity, vainglory **10** narcissism **11** uselessness **13** worthlessness

VANITY FAIR:
author: **16** William Thackeray
characters: **10** Becky Sharp, Lord Steyne **12** Amelia Sedley, Joseph Sedley **13** George Osborne, Rawdon Crawley, William Dobbin **14** Gregory Osborne, Sir Pitt Crawley

VANQUISH: **4** beat, best, rout **5** crush, expel, quell **6** defeat, humble, master, reduce, subdue **7** conquer, subvert, trample **8** overcome, suppress, surmount **9** overthrow, subjugate

VANQUISHER: **6** master, victor, winner **8** champion **9** conqueror **10** subjugator

VANTAGE: **4** edge **9** advantage **11** superiority

VANUATU:
capital: **4** Vila
cities: **10** Luganville
continent: **7** Oceania
ethnic groups: **10** Melanesian, Polynesian **11** Micronesian
features: **9** volcanoes
islands: **5** Efate **8** Malekala **13** Espiritu Santo
languages: **6** French **7** Bislama, English
monetary unit: **4** vatu
water: **7** Pacific

VAPID: **4** dull, flat, lame, weak **5** bland, inane, trite **6** boring **7** insipid **8** lifeless **9** colorless, pointless, tasteless **10** flavorless, spiritless, unanimated, unexciting **11**

meaningless, uninspiring **13** unimaginative, uninteresting

VAPOR: **3** dew, fog, gas **4** haze, mist, smog **5** cloud, fumes, smoke, steam **6** breath, nimbus **8** humidity, moisture

VAPORIZE: **4** boil **8** condense **9** dissipate, evaporate

VAPOROUS: **4** airy, hazy **5** misty, vague, wispy **6** aerial, smoggy **8** ethereal, fleeting, volatile **13** insubstantial

VARIABLE: **6** fickle, fitful, shifty, uneven **7** diverse, unequal, variant, varying **8** unstable, unsteady, volatile, wavering **9** irregular, spasmodic, uncertain **10** capricious, changeable, inconstant **11** fluctuating

VARIANCE: **6** change **7** discord, dispute, dissent, quarrel **8** argument, conflict, disunity, division **9** deviation, variation **10** difference, dissension **11** discrepancy, fluctuation **12** disagreement

VARIATION: **5** shade **6** change **7** variety **8** variance **9** departure, deviation, disparity **10** difference **11** alternative **12** modification

VARIED: **5** mixed **6** motley **7** diverse, various **8** assorted **9** different **11** diversified **13** miscellaneous

VARIEGATED: **4** pied **6** calico, motley, varied **7** dappled, flecked, mottled, piebald, spotted **8** speckled **9** checkered, different **11** diversified, varicolored **12** multicolored

VARIETY: **4** kind, sort, type **5** brand, breed, class, genus **6** family, medley, strain **7** species **8** category **9** diversity, variation **10** assortment, collection, hodgepodge **11** subdivision

VARIOUS: **4** many **6** sundry, varied **7** diverse, several, unalike, variant **8** assorted, distinct, manifold, numerous, variable **9** countless, different, differing **10** changeable, dissimilar **12** multitudinal **13** miscellaneous

VARLET: **4** page **5** knave **6** helper, rascal, vassal **7** footman, servant **9** attendant, scoundrel **10** blackguard

VARNISH: **4** coat **5** gloss, japan, stain **6** finish, veneer **7** lacquer, shellac **9** embellish

VARY: **5** alter, shift **6** change, depart, differ, divide, modify, swerve **7** deviate, digress, dissent, diverge, qualify, variate **8** contrast, disagree, modulate **9** alternate, diversify, fluctuate, oscillate

VASE: **3** jar, pot, urn **4** ewer **6** crater, krater, vessel **7** amphora **9** container **10** jardiniere

VASSAL: **4** serf **5** helot, liege, slave **6** tenant, thrall, varlet **7** bondman, peasant, servant, servile, subject **9** dependent **11** beneficiary, subordinate

VAST: **4** huge, wide **5** ample, broad, giant, great, large **6** untold **7** endless, immense, massive, titanic **8** colossal, enormous, gigantic, spacious, whopping **9** boundless, capacious, extensive, unlimited **10** tremendous **11** farreaching

VAT: **3** bac, pit, tub, tun **4** back, beck, cask **5** basin **9** container

VATICAN CITY:
continent: **6** Europe
ethnic groups: **5** Swiss **7** Italian
features: **8** St. Peters **13** Vatican Palace **14** Castel Gandolfo
inhabitant: **4** Pope
languages: **5** Latin **7** Italian
monetary unit: **4** lira
place: **4** Rome **5** Italy

VAUDEVILLE: **4** show, skit **5** revue **7** theater **9** burlesque **13** entertainment

VAUDEVILLIAN: **5** actor, comic **6** dancer, singer **7** acrobat, juggler **8** comedian **9** performer **11** entertainer

VAULT: **3** box **4** arch, bend, cave, dome, jump, leap, roof, room, safe, soar, span, tomb **5** bound, clear, crypt, mount **6** cavern, cellar, crater, hurdle, spring **7** ceiling, chamber, dungeon **8** catacomb **9** mausoleum, storeroom, strongbox, structure **10** repository, strongroom

VAUNT: **4** brag, crow **5** boast, prate, strut **6** flaunt **7** display, exhibit **9** gasconade

VEER: **3** dip, yaw **4** bend, skew, sway, tack, turn **5** alter, avert, dodge, shift, twist **6** careen, change, depart, divert, swerve **7** deflect, deviate, digress

VEGETABLE: **3** pea, yam **4** bean, beet, corn, leek, okra, soya **5** chard, onion, plant **6** carrot, celery, endive, pepper, radish, squash, turnip **7** cabbage, lettuce, parsnip, rhubarb, romaine, shallot, spinach **8** broccoli, cucumber, eggplant, rutabaga, scallion **9** artichoke **11** cauliflower **14** Brussels sprout

VEGETARIAN: **5** vegan **10** fruitarian **11** herbivorous

VEGETATE: **4** grow, idle, loaf **5** decay **6** sprout **7** blossom **8** languish, stagnate **9** hibernate **11** deteriorate

VEGETATION: **5** flora **6** growth, plants **7** herbage, verdure **8** greenery, lethargy **10** inactivity **11** hibernation **12** listlessness

VEHEMENT: **3** hot **4** wild **5** angry, eager, fiery, rabid **6** ardent, fervid, fierce, heated, lively, raging, stormy, strong, urgent **7** fervent, furious, intense, violent **8** emphatic, forceful, vigorous **9** emotional, energetic, impetuous **11** impassioned, opinionated

VEHICLE: **3** ark, bus, cab, car, van **4** auto, jeep, sled, tank, taxi, tool, tram **5** buggy, float, lorry, means, sedan, sulky, train, truck, wagon **6** barrow, device, hansom, landau, sleigh, troika **7** chariot, minibus, minivan, tractor, trailer, trolley **8** carriage, rickshaw **9** ambulance **10** automobile, conveyance
children's: **5** buggy **6** walker **7** scooter **8** carriage, stroller, tricycle
two-wheel: **4** cart **5** sulky **7** bicycle

VEIL: **3** dim **4** hide, mask **5** cloak, cloud, cover, drape, guise, velum **6** enfold, mantle, screen, shield, shroud **7** conceal, curtain, netting, yashmak **8** disguise **10** camouflage

VEIN: **3** web **4** dash, duct, hint, lode, mind, mood, seam, tone, tube, vena **5** cleft, costa, crack, humor, shade, smack, spice, style, tinge, touch, trend **6** furrow, manner, nature, spirit, strain, streak, thread, venule, vessel **7** bonanza, channel, crevice, fissure, nervure, stratum **8** attitude, tendency **9** capillary, character **11** inclination, temperament

VELOCITY: **4** pace, rate **5** haste, speed **6** motion **7** headway **8** celerity, momentum, rapidity **9** quickness, swiftness **10** expedition **12** acceleration

VELUM: **4** veil **6** palate **8** covering, membrane

VELVET: **4** gain, silk **5** cloth, nylon, rayon **6** fabric, plushy, profit, velour **8** softness, winnings

VENAL: **5** hired **6** greedy **7** buyable, corrupt, crooked, salable **8** bribable, infamous, vendible **9** mercenary **11** corruptible **12** dishonorable, unscrupulous

VEND: **4** hawk, sell **5** trade **6** barter, market, peddle **8** huckster

VENDETTA: **4** feud **5** fight, gripe **7** dispute, quarrel

VENDOR: **6** dealer, hawker, seller, trader **7** peddler **8** huckster, merchant, retailer **11** salesperson **14** businessperson

VENEER: **4** coat, fact, mask, show, veil, wise **5** cover, front, gloss, layer **6** august, enamel, facade, facing, finish **7** admired, coating, elderly, overlay, revered, stately, surface, varnish **8** disguise, esteemed **9** dignified, respected

VENERABLE: **3** old **4** aged **5** hoary **7** ancient, antique **9** honorable

VENERATE: **5** adore, honor, prize, value **6** admire, regard, revere **7** cherish, respect, worship **9** reverence

VENERATION: **3** awe **5** honor, wrath **6** esteem **7** respect, worship **8** devotion **9** adoration, repayment, reverence, vengeance **10** admiration

VENEZUELA:
capital: **7** Caracas
cities: **8** Valencia **9** Maracaibo **12** Barquisimeto
continent: **12** South America
ethnic groups: **5** Carib **6** Timote **7** Italian, mestizo, Spanish **8** Guarauno **10** Portuguese
features: **5** Andes **9** Margarita **15** Guiana Highlands
language: **7** Spanish
monetary unit: **7** bolivar
water: **5** Paria **7** Orinoco **8** Valencia **9** Maracaibo, Tacarigua **10** Angel Falls

VENGEANCE: **7** revenge **8** reprisal, requital **11** retaliation, retribution

VENIAL: **4** mild **5** minor **6** slight **7** trivial **9** allowable, excusable, tolerable **10** forgivable, pardonable **11** unimportant

VENICE:
bridge: **6** Rialto
islands: **6** Rialto **8** San Marco **10** San Giorgio
resort: **4** Lido
water: **6** Brenta

VENISON: **4** deer, food, meat

VENOM: **5** anger, spite, toxin **6** hating, hatred, malice, poison, rancor **9** animosity **10** resentment

VENOMOUS: **4** evil, mean **5** toxic **6** deadly, lethal **7** baleful, baneful, hateful, hostile, vicious **8** poisoned, spiteful, virulent **9** malicious, malignant, poisonous, rancorous **12** antagonistic

VENT: **3** air **4** draw, emit, gush, hole, pipe, slit **5** eject, spout, state, voice **6** assert, avenue, outlet **7** express, opening, orifice, release, unleash **8** aperture **9** discharge **10** expression **11** communicate

VENTILATE: **3** air, fan **5** state, voice **6** aerate, debate, expose **7** discuss, examine, freshen **9** broadcast, circulate, oxygenate, publicize

VENTURE: **3** bet, try **4** dare, feat, risk **5** brave, essay, stake, wager **6** chance, danger, gamble, hazard **7** attempt, fortune, project **8** endeavor **9** adventure, challenge, speculate **10** enterprise, experiment, investment **11** speculation, undertaking

VENTURESOME: **4** bold, rash **5** brave, risky **6** daring, heroic **8** fearless, perilous, reckless, spirited **9** audacious, dangerous, foolhardy, hazardous **10** courageous **11** adventurous, speculative **12** enterprising

VENUE: **4** site **5** place, scene **6** ground, locale, thrust **7** setting

VENUS:
Earth's: **6** sister
form: **6** planet **7** goddess
from sun: **6** second
goddess of: **4** love **6** beauty
identified with: **9** Aphrodite

VERACIOUS: **4** true **5** valid **6** direct, honest **7** precise, sincere **8** accurate, truthful

VERACITY: **4** fact **5** truth **6** candor **7** honesty **8** accuracy, trueness **9** exactness, integrity, precision, sincerity **11** correctness, credibility **12** faithfulness, truthfulness

VERANDA: **5** lanai, patio, porch, stoop **6** piazza **7** balcony, portico, terrace **8** platform

VERBAL: **4** oral **5** vocal **6** spoken, stated **8** verbatim **9** talkative, unwritten **10** articulate

VERBALIZE: **3** say **4** talk, vent **5** speak, state, utter, voice **7** express **8** vocalize **10** articulate

VERBATIM: **6** orally, verbal **7** exactly, literal **9** precisely **10** accurately

VERBIAGE: **4** talk **7** chatter, diction, wordage **8** parlance **9** floridity, logorrhea, verbosity, wordiness **10** redundancy, repetition

VERBOSE: **5** gabby, windy, wordy **6** prolix **7** flowery **9** redundant, talkative **10** loquacious, repetitive **11** tautologous **13** grandiloquent

VERBOSITY: **9** loquacity, prolixity, wordiness **10** redundancy

VERBOTEN: **5** taboo **6** banned **9** forbidden **10** disallowed, prohibited

VERDANT: **5** fresh, green, naive **6** grassy, vernal **8** blooming, innocent **13** inexperienced

VERDI, GIUSEPPE: **8** composer
nationality: **7** Italian
operas: **4** Aida **6** Otello **7** Macbeth **8** Don Carlo **9** Rigoletto **10** La Traviata

VERDICT: **6** decree, ruling **7** finding, opinion **8** decision, judgment, sentence **10** assessment **13** determination

VERDURE: **8** greenery **9** freshness, greenness

VERGE: **3** hem, lip, rim **4** brim, edge, line, tend, wand **5** bound, brink, limit, point, range, scope, slope, staff **6** border, fringe, margin **7** horizon, incline **8** approach, boundary **9** threshold

VERIFICATION: **5** proof **8** averment **10** validation **11** affirmation **12** confirmation **13** certification

VERIFY: **4** back, test **5** audit, check, prove **6** affirm, attest, settle **7** certify, confirm, support **8** document, maintain, validate **9** establish **11** corroborate **12** authenticate, substantiate

VERILY: **4** amen, even **5** truly **6** indeed, really **7** factual **9** assuredly, certainly **11** confidently

VERITABLE: **4** real, true **5** valid **6** actual, honest **7** factual, genuine **8** bona fide **9** authentic, undoubted, veracious **11** indubitable

VERMILION: **3** red **5** color **7** scarlet **8** antimony, cinnabar

VERMIN: **4** ants, lice, mice, rats **5** fleas, flies, foxes, pests **6** animal, insect, snakes **7** bedbugs, rodents, termite, weasels **8** mosquito **9** centipede **11** cockroaches

VERMINOUS: **5** dirty **6** filthy **9** offensive, repulsive

VERMONT:
bird: **12** hermit thrush
capital: **10** Montpelier
cities: **5** Barre **7** Rutland **10** Burlington

explorer: **9** Champlain
features: **14** Green Mountains
flower: **9** red clover
nickname: **13** Green Mountain
tree: **10** sugar maple
water: **13** Lake Champlain

VERNACULAR: **4** cant **5** idiom, lingo, slang **6** jargon, patois, speech, tongue **7** dialect, endemic **8** language, parlance **10** colloquial

VERNAL: **5** fresh, young **6** spring **7** verdant **8** youthful **10** springlike

VERSATILE: **4** able **5** handy **6** adroit, gifted, mobile **7** skilled **8** flexible, talented, variable **9** adaptable **10** adjustable, changeable, proficient **11** resourceful **12** multifaceted

VERSE: **3** ode **4** poem **5** meter, rhyme, stave, stich **6** ballad, jingle, poetry, stanza **8** accustom, acquaint, limerick **11** composition, familiarize

VERSED: **5** adept, aware **6** taught **7** abreast, learned, skilled, trained **8** familiar, informed, schooled **9** au courant, competent, practiced, qualified **10** acquainted, proficient **11** experienced **12** accomplished **13** knowledgeable

VERSIFIER: **4** bard, poet **6** rhymer **8** minstrel **9** poetaster

VERSION: **4** side **5** story **6** report **7** account, edition **9** depiction, rendition, statement **10** adaptation, paraphrase **11** description, translation **14** interpretation

VERSUS: **7** against **8** contrast **11** alternative

VERTEBRA, VERTEBRAE: **4** back **5** chine, spine **7** spondyl **8** backbone **12** spinal column
parts: **4** axis, disk **5** atlas **6** caudal, coccyx, lumbar **8** cervical, thoracic

VERTEX: **3** top **4** apex, peak **5** crown, point **6** apogee, summit, zenith **8** pinnacle **11** culmination

VERTICAL: **4** acme **5** erect, plumb, sheet, steep **6** summit, vertex **7** upright **8** standing **13** perpendicular

VERTIGINOUS: **5** dizzy, giddy **7** turning **8** rotating, spinning, unstable, whirling **9** revolving

VERTIGO: **7** reeling **9** confusion, dizziness, giddiness **12** unsteadiness

VERVE: **3** pep, zip **4** dash, elan, fire, life, zeal, zest, zing **5** ardor, gusto, oomph, punch, vigor **6** bounce, energy, spirit, spring **7** ability, passion **8** vitality, vivacity **9** animation **10** enthusiasm, liveliness

VERY: **3** too **4** bare, mere, most, much, real, same, true **5** exact, ideal, quite, truly, utter **6** actual, deeply, highly, hugely, mighty, really **7** awfully, exactly, genuine, greatly, notably, precise, special **8** absolute, actually, complete, terribly, truthful **9** authentic, eminently, extremely, identical, precisely, veracious, veritable **10** absolutely, remarkably, strikingly, thoroughly **11** exceedingly **12** emphatically, surpassingly

VESICLE: **3** sac **4** cell, cyst **6** cavity **7** bladder, blister, utricle

VESPERS: **6** orison, prayer **7** service **8** evensong

VESSEL: **3** can, cup, jar, mug, pan, pyx, tub, urn, vat **4** boat, bowl, cask, drum, duct, ewer, olla, tank, tube, vase, vein **5** barge, basin, canoe, cogue, craft, cruse, flask, glass, liner, stein, yacht **6** barrel, beaker, bottle, carafe, crater, cutter, flagon, funnel, goblet, kettle, krater **7** caldron, cresset, pitcher, situlae, steamer, utensil **8** crucible **9** container **10** receptacle

VEST: **4** coat, robe **5** drape, dress, endow **6** clothe, jacket, jerkin **7** garment **9** waistcoat

VESTA:
form: **7** goddess
goddess of: **6** hearth
identified with: **6** Hestia

VESTAL: **3** nun **4** pure **6** chaste, virgin **8** virginal, virtuous

VESTIBULE: **4** hall **5** entry, foyer, lobby **6** cavity **7** channel, doorway, hallway, narthex, passage **8** anteroom, corridor, entrance **11** antechamber

VESTIGE: **4** hint, mark, path, sign **5** relic, scrap, shred, trace, track **7** remnant **8** evidence, footstep, tincture **9** footprint **10** indication

VESTMENT: **4** garb, gear, gown, hood, robe **5** dress, frock, tunic **7** cassock, garment, uniform, vesture **8** cincture, clothing, covering **10** habiliment

VESTURE: **5** cover **6** clothe **7** apparel, envelop, garment **8** clothing, vestment

VETERAN: **4** wise **6** expert, master **7** skilled **8** old-timer, seasoned **9** longtimer, practiced, weathered **11** disciplined, experienced **12** professional

VETO: **3** nix **4** deny, kill **5** quash **6** defeat, forbid, refuse, reject **8** disallow, negative, override, overrule, prohibit **11** disapproval

VEX: **3** bug, ire, irk **4** fret, fuss, gall, miff, rile, toss **5** anger, annoy, chafe, harry, spite, tease, upset, worry **6** bother, harass, needle, nettle, offend, pester, plague, puzzle, ruffle **7** afflict, agitate, dispute, disturb, perplex, provoke, torment, trouble **8** distress, irritate **9** aggravate, infuriate **11** disturbance

VEXATION: **5** pique **6** hassle **9** agitation, annoyance, weariness **10** harassment, irritation **11** aggravation

VEXATIOUS: **5** pesky **7** nagging **8** annoying, harassed **9** badgering, disturbed, upsetting **10** afflictive, bothersome, irritating, tormenting **11** aggravating, distressing, troublesome

VIA: **3** per, way **4** over, road, with **5** along **7** passage, through

VIABLE: **6** doable, living **8** feasible, possible, workable **10** applicable, reasonable **11** practicable

VIADUCT: **4** ramp **6** bridge **8** overpass

VIAL: **5** ampul, flask, phial **6** bottle **7** ampoule **9** container

VIANDS: **4** chow, eats, fare, feed, food, grub **7** edibles, vittles **8** victuals **10** provisions

VIBRANT: **5** alive, eager, vivid **6** bright, florid **7** dynamic, glowing, radiant **8** animated, colorful, resonant, sonorous, vigorous **9** brilliant, energetic, pulsating, throbbing, vivacious **10** resounding **12** electrifying, enthusiastic

VIBRATE: **3** jar **4** beat, echo, rock **5** pulse, quake, shake, swing, throb, trill, waver **6** quaver, quiver, ripple, shiver, thrill, tremor **7** agitate, flutter, resound, tremble **8** resonate **9** fluctuate, oscillate, vacillate **11** reverberate

VIBRATION: **4** vibe **5** quake, shake **6** quaver, quiver, thrill, tremor **7** flutter **9** pulsation, trembling **11** fluctuation, oscillation, vacillation **13** reverberation

VICAR: **5** proxy **6** cleric, pastor, priest **8** minister **9** clergyman **10** substitute **12** ecclesiastic

VICARIOUS: **9** delegated, surrogate **10** empathetic **11** substituted, sympathetic

VICE: **3** sin **4** evil, flaw **5** crime, fault, wrong **6** defect, foible **7** blemish, failing **8** iniquity, weakness **9** carnality, depravity, replacing **10** corruption, immorality **11** shortcoming **12** imperfection

VICE PRESIDENT: **4** Burr, Bush, Ford, Gore, King **5** Adams, Agnew, Dawes, Gerry, Nixon, Tyler **6** Arthur, Colfax, Curtis, Dallas, Garner, Hamlin, Hobart, Morton, Quayle, Truman, Wilson **7** Barkley, Calhoun, Clinton, Johnson, Mondale, Sherman, Wallace, Wheeler **8** Coolidge, Fillmore, Humphrey, Marshall, Tompkins, Van Buren **9** Fairbanks, Hendricks, Jefferson, Roosevelt, Stevenson **11** Rockefeller **12** Breckinridge
Adams, J.: **9** Jefferson
Adams, J.Q.: **7** Calhoun
also called: **4** veep
Arthur: **4** none
Buchanan: **12** Breckinridge
Bush: **6** Quayle
Carter: **7** Mondale
Cleveland: **9** Hendricks, Stevenson
Clinton: **4** Gore
Coolidge: **5** Dawes
Eisenhower: **5** Nixon
Fillmore: **4** none
Ford: **11** Rockefeller
Garfield: **6** Arthur
Grant: **6** Colfax, Wilson
Harding: **8** Coolidge
Harrison, B.: **6** Morton
Harrison, W.H.: **5** Tyler
Hayes: **7** Wheeler
Hoover: **6** Curtis
Jackson: **7** Calhoun **8** Van Buren
Jefferson: **4** Burr **7** Clinton
Johnson, A.: **4** none
Johnson, L.B.: **8** Humphrey
Kennedy: **7** Johnson
Lincoln: **6** Hamlin **7** Johnson
Madison: **5** Gerry **7** Clinton
McKinley: **6** Hobart **9** Roosevelt
Monroe: **8** Tompkins
Nixon: **4** Ford **5** Agnew
Pierce: **4** King
Polk: **6** Dallas
Reagan: **4** Bush
resigned: **5** Agnew **7** Calhoun
Roosevelt, F.D.: **6** Garner, Truman **7** Wallace
Roosevelt, T.: **9** Fairbanks
succeeded to president: **4** Ford **5** Tyler **6** Arthur, Truman **7** Johnson **8** Coolidge, Fillmore **9** Roosevelt
Taft: **7** Sherman
Taylor: **8** Fillmore
Truman: **7** Barkley
Tyler: **4** none
Van Buren: **7** Johnson
Washington: **5** Adams
Wilson: **8** Marshall

VICEROY: **5** nabob, ruler **6** satrap **8** governor **9** butterfly **14** representative

VICE VERSA: **5** again **8** contrary **10** conversely, oppositely **12** contrariwise

VICINITY: **4** area **5** close **6** nearby, region **8** ballpark, district, environs, locality **9** proximity **12** neighborhood, surroundings

VICIOUS: **3** bad **4** evil, foul, mean, vile, wild **5** cruel, nasty, wrong **6** fierce, rotten, savage, severe, wicked **7** beastly, corrupt, hateful, heinous, immoral, noxious, violent **8** debasing, depraved, fiendish, spiteful, terrible, vehement **9** atrocious, dangerous, ferocious, malicious, nefarious **10** corrupting, diabolical, iniquitous, villainous, vindictive

VICISSITUDE: **5** shift **6** change, switch **7** variety **8** mutation, reversal **9** diversity, variation **10** alteration, difficulty, mutability

VICTIM: **4** dupe, fool, goat, gull, prey **5** chump, patsy **6** stooge, sucker **8** casualty, fatality, pushover, sufferer, underdog **9** sacrifice, scapegoat

VICTIMIZE: **3** use **4** burn, dupe, gull **5** cheat, stiff, trick **7** deceive, exploit **8** hoodwink **9** bamboozle, persecute

VICTOR: **5** champ **6** master, winner **7** conquer **8** champion **9** conqueror **10** subjugator, vanquisher

VICTORY: **3** win **7** mastery, success, triumph **8** conquest **9** supremacy **10** ascendancy **11** achievement, superiority

VICTUALS: **3** rub **4** chow, eats, feed, food **5** meals **6** viands **7** edibles, vittles **8** supplies **10** provisions **11** comestibles, nourishment

VIE: **3** bet **5** fight, match, rival, stake, wager **6** endure, jostle, oppose, strive **7** compete, content

VIETNAM:
capital: **5** Hanoi
cities: **6** Da Nang **8** Haiphong **13** Ho Chi Minh City
continent: **4** Asia
ethnic groups: **3** Man, Meo **4** Cham, Thai **5** Khmer, Muong **7** Chinese **10** Vietnamese
features: **10** Cham Towers, Karst Hills
languages: **7** Chinese **10** Vietnamese
monetary unit: **4** dong
water: **6** Mekong **8** Red River

VIEW: **3** aim, eye, ken, see, spy **4** gaze, goal, look, peek, plan, scan **5** judge, scape, scene, sight, stare, watch **6** admire, aspect, behold, belief, notion, object, regard, survey, theory, vision **7** believe, canvass, examine, feeling, glimpse, inspect, observe, opinion, outlook, picture, profile, scenery, summary, thought, witness **8** attitude, consider, panorama, scrutiny, seascape **9** apprehend, landscape, objective **10** appearance, inspection, perception, scrutinize, standpoint **11** contemplate, examination, expectation

VIEWPOINT: **5** angle, scope, slant **6** belief, stance **7** feeling, opinion, outlook, posture **8** attitude, position **9** sentiment **11** perspective

VIGIL: **5** guard, watch **7** lookout, prayers, service **12** surveillance

VIGILANT: **4** agog, keen, wary **5** alert, awake, aware, sharp **6** shrewd **7** careful, wakeful **8** cautious, watchful **9** attentive, observant, sleepless

VIGNETTE: **5** scene, story **6** sketch **7** picture **8** scenario

VIGOR: **3** pep, vim, zip **4** bang, dash, fire, zeal, zing **5** drive, force, getup, might, moxie, oomph, power, punch, steam, verve **6** bounce, energy, growth, health, muscle, spirit **7** passion, potency, stamina **8** activity, strength, virility, vitality **9** animation, endurance, intensity **10** enthusiasm, invigorate

VIGOROUS: **4** hale, spry **5** brisk, eager, hardy, lusty, tough **6** hearty, lively, potent, robust, rugged, strong, sturdy **7** dashing, healthy, intense, vibrant **8** athletic, bouncing, muscular, powerful, spirited **9** effective, energetic, strapping, strenuous **11** efficacious

VILE: **3** bad, low **4** base, evil, foul, mean, ugly **5** lowly, nasty **6** coarse, filthy, impure, odious, sinful, sleazy, sordid, vulgar, wicked **7** corrupt, debased, hateful, ignoble, servile, vicious **8** depraved, horrible, shocking, wretched **9** degrading, loathsome, nefarious, obnoxious, offensive, repulsive, revolting, sickening, worthless **10** abominable, despicable, disgusting, unpleasant **12** contemptible

VILIFY: **4** slur **5** abuse, libel, smear **6** assail, attack, berate, debase, defame, malign, revile, slight **7** asperse, blacken, debauch, degrade, slander, traduce **8** belittle, denounce, disgrace, dishonor, mistreat, repreach **9** blaspheme, criticize, disparage

VILLA: **4** home **5** house, manor **6** castle, estate **7** chateau, mansion **8** dwelling **9** residence

VILLAGE: **4** burg, home, town **5** aldea, bourg, thorp, tribe, villa **6** hamlet, pueblo, suburb **7** borough **9** community **10** settlement **12** municipality

VILLAIN: **4** boor, lout **5** creep, demon, devil, heavy, knave, rogue, scamp **6** rascal, varlet **7** caitiff, lowlife **8** offender, scalawag, scelerat **9** miscreant, scoundrel **10** blackguard, delinquent, mountebank **11** rapscallion

VILLAINOUS: **3** bad, low **4** base, evil, mean, vile **6** rotten, vulgar, wicked **7** boorish, caddish, corrupt, vicious **8** criminal, depraved, horrible, wretched **9** dastardly, felonious **10** abominable, despicable, detestable **12** disagreeable

VILLAINY: **7** knavery **8** vileness **9** depravity **10** wickedness **11** viciousness

VIM: **4** dash, elan, fire, kick, push, zeal, zing **5** drive, force, oomph, vigor **6** energy, pepper, spirit **7** passion **8** strength, vitality **10** enthusiasm

VINDICATE: **4** free **5** clear, prove **6** acquit, assert, avenge, defend, excuse, uphold **7** absolve, justify, protect, revenge, support, sustain **8** advocate, maintain **9** exculpate, exonerate **12** substantiate

VINDICTIVE: **5** cruel, nasty **6** bitter, malign **8** spiteful, vengeful **10** revengeful **11** retaliatory, unforgiving

VINE: **3** hop, ivy **4** bine, soma **5** betel, briar, liana, plant **6** maypop **7** creeper, cupseed, jasmine, rambler **8** cucumber **9** grapevine, raspberry **10** blackberry, watermelon **11** honeysuckle

VINEGARISH: **4** sour, tart **6** biting, bitter **7** acerbic, pungent

VINTAGE: **3** old **4** aged, crop, rare, wine **5** dated, prize **6** choice, grapes **7** ancient, antique, harvest **8** selected, superior **9** classical **10** antiquated

VIOLATE: **4** rape **5** abuse, break, force, spoil, wrong **6** betray, breach, broach, defile, defoul, injure, insult, invade, offend, ravage, ravish **7** corrupt, debauch, disobey, disturb, outrage, pollute, profane **8** deflower, dishonor, encroach, infringe, trespass **9** desecrate, disregard, interrupt **10** transgress

VIOLATION: **5** crime **6** breach **7** assault, offense **9** sacrilege **10** illegality, infraction **11** delinquency, desecration **12** encroachment **13** transgression

VIOLENCE: **4** fury, gore, rage **5** clash, force **6** fervor, frenzy, uproar **7** assault, outrage, rampage **8** ferocity, fighting, savagery **9** bloodshed, brutality, intensity, onslaught, terrorism

VIOLENT: **4** wild **5** acute, fiery, harsh, heavy, rabid, rough, sharp **6** fierce, mighty, raging, savage, severe, stormy, strong **7** berserk, enraged, extreme, furious, intense, vicious **8** forceful, forcible, frenetic, inflamed, powerful, vehement **9** explosive, hotheaded, impetuous, turbulent **10** passionate, tumultuous **11** destructive, tempestuous

VIOLET: **5** color, mauve **6** flower, purple **8** lavender
variety: **4** pine **5** Parma, sweet, water **6** Alaska, alpine, Canada, garden, horned **7** African, Russian **8** Missouri, mountain, trailing

VIOLIN: **6** fiddle **10** instrument
plucking: **9** pizzicato
types: **3** kit **5** Amati **8** pochette **10** Guarnerius **12** Stradivarius

V.I.P.: **4** lion **6** bigwig, leader **7** big shot, notable, someone **9** celebrity, dignitary, personage

VIPER: **5** adder, cobra, snake **10** copperhead **11** rattlesnake

VIRAGO: **5** harpy, scold, shrew, vixen, woman **6** amazon **7** beldame **8** fishwife **9** termagant

VIRGIN: **3** new **4** pure **5** first, fresh **6** chaste, intact, maiden, modest, unused, vestal **7** initial **8** celibate, maidenly, pristine **9** unalloyed, undefiled, unsullied, untouched **10** unexplored **11** undisturbed **12** uncultivated **13** unadulterated

VIRGINAL: **5** fresh, snowy **6** chaste **8** innocent, virtuous **9** unsullied, untouched **10** immaculate **11** harpsichord

VIRGINIA:
bird: **8** cardinal
capital: **8** Richmond
cities: **7** Hampton, Norfolk **10** Chesapeake, Portsmouth **11** Newport News **12** Williamsburg **13** Virginia Beach
features: **8** Yorktown **9** Blue Ridge, Jamestown **10** Monticello, Shenandoah **11** Mount Vernon
first founded: **9** Jamestown
flower: **7** dogwood
native: **9** Virginian
nickname: **11** Old Dominion
tree: **7** dogwood

VIRGIN ISLANDS:
cities: **8** Road Town **15** Charlotte Amalie
explorer: **8** Columbus
island group: **7** Leeward
islands: **6** St. John **7** Anegada, St. Croix, Tortola **8** St. Thomas **11** Virgin Gorda **12** Jost van Dykes

VIRILE: **4** male **5** brave, macho, manly **6** potent, robust, strong **8** forceful, powerful **9** masculine

VIRILITY: **5** youth **9** freshness, greenness, innocence **12** inexperience

VIRTUAL: **5** tacit **7** implied **9** essential **11** fundamental

VIRTUALLY: **6** almost, nearly **7** totally **9** basically **11** essentially, practically

VIRTUE: **5** grace, honor, piety, power, valor **6** purity **7** courage, decency, honesty, quality **8** chastity, fidelity, goodness, morality **9** advantage, integrity **10** excellence, generosity **13** righteousness

VIRTUOSO: **4** whiz **6** artist, expert, savant **7** artiste **8** musician **10** dilettante **11** connoisseur

VIRTUOUS: **4** good, just, pure **5** moral, noble **6** chaste, honest, worthy **7** ethical, upright, valiant **8** innocent, spotless, virginal **9** exemplary, honorable, righteous, unsullied **10** moralistic, principled

VIRULENT: **5** harsh, toxic **6** bitter, deadly, lethal **7** cutting, hateful, hostile, noxious **8** spiteful, venomous **9** malignant, obnoxious, poisonous, sarcastic, unhealthy **10** infectious, irritating, vindictive **12** antagonistic

VIRUS: **3** bug **4** germ **5** venom **6** poison **7** disease, illness **8** sickness **9** infection

VISAGE: **4** face, look **6** aspect **8** features **10** appearance, expression **11** countenance

VIS-A-VIS: **4** date **6** escort, facing, versus **8** opposite **9** tete-a-tete **11** counterpart

VISCERA: **4** guts **7** innards, insides **8** entrails **10** intestines

VISCERAL: **5** inner **8** interior, profound **9** intuitive **11** instinctive

VISCOUNT: **5** title **8** nobleman

VISCOUS: **5** gobby, gooey, gummy, stiff, thick, tough **6** sticky, syrupy, viscid **8** adhering, adhesive, sticking **9** glutinous, tenacious

VISE: **4** tool **5** chuck, clamp, winch

VISIBLE: **4** seen **5** clear **6** visual **7** blatant, evident, glaring, obvious, seeable **8** apparent, manifest, revealed **10** noticeable **11** conspicuous, discernible, macroscopic, perceivable, perceptible

VISION: **4** view **5** dream, fancy, ghost, image, sight **6** beauty, mirage, seeing, spirit **7** concept, fantasy, imagine, phantom **8** eyesight, illusion **9** intuition **10** apparition, perception, revelation **11** perspective

VISIONARY: **4** seer **5** ideal **6** dreamy, unreal **7** dreamer, prophet, radical, utopian **8** delusory, idealist, quixotic, romantic **9** ambitious, fantastic, imaginary, stargazer **10** chimerical, idealistic **11** imaginative, impractical, philosopher, speculative

VISIT: **3** see **4** call, chat, stay, talk **5** apply, haunt **6** assail, avenge, bother **7** afflict, inflict, sojourn, trouble **8** converse, frequent, stopover, vacation

VISITATION: **4** call **5** trial **8** calamity, disaster

VISITOR: **5** guest **6** caller **7** company, tourist **9** sightseer **10** vacationer

VISTA: **4** view **5** range, scene, scope **7** outlook **8** panorama, prospect **11** perspective

VISUAL: **4** seen **5** chart, optic **6** ocular **7** optical, picture, seeable, visible **8** viewable **10** observable **11** perceptible

VISUALIZE: **3** see **4** view **5** fancy, think **7** foresee, imagine, picture, reflect **8** conceive, envision

VITAL: **5** alive, basic **6** lively, living, needed, urgent, viable **7** animate, crucial, dynamic, pivotal **8** animated, cardinal, critical, integral, vigorous **9** breathing, energetic, essential, important, necessary, requisite **10** imperative **11** fundamental, significant **12** invigorating **13** indispensable

VITALITY: **3** pep, vim **4** zest **5** drive, spunk, verve, vigor **6** energy, spirit **7** pizzazz, stamina **8** strength **9** animation, endurance **10** enthusiasm, liveliness

VITALIZE: **5** liven **6** excite **7** animate **8** activate, energize **9** stimulate **10** invigorate

VITIATE: **4** hurt, soil, undo, void **5** annul, spoil, taint **6** cancel, damage, debase, impair, injure, poison, weaken **7** abolish, blemish, corrupt, deprave, nullify, pervert, pollute, tarnish **8** sabotage **9** undermine **10** adulterate, invalidate, neutralize **11** contaminate

VITRIOLIC: **5** sharp **6** bitter **7** acerbic, burning, caustic **8** sardonic, scathing **12** antagonistic

VITUPERATE: **4** rail **5** abuse, curse, scold **6** berate, ensure, insult, rebuke, vilify **7** upbraid **8** lambaste, reproach **9** castigate, criticize

VITUPERATION: **5** abuse, blame **6** rebuke **7** censure, obloquy, railing **8** scolding **9** invective **10** revilement **11** castigation **12** vilification

VITUPERATIVE: **5** harsh **6** severe **7** abusive **8** critical, scolding **9** insulting, truculent **10** scurrilous, slanderous

VIVACIOUS: **3** gay **5** happy, merry, sunny **6** active, breezy, bubbly, lively, upbeat **7** playful, vibrant, zestful **8** animated, cheerful, spirited, sportive **9** exuberant, sprightly **12** lighthearted

VIVACITY: **4** dash, elan, fire, life, zeal **5** gusto, verve, vigor **6** energy **7** sparkle **9** animation **10** brilliance, enthusiasm **13** sprightliness

VIVID: **4** live, real, rich **5** alive, clear, lucid, sharp **6** active, bright, florid, lively, living, strong **7** glaring, glowing, graphic, intense, radiant, shining **8** animated, colorful, dramatic, lifelike, powerful, spirited, striking **9** brilliant **10** expressive **11** picturesque

VIVIFY: **6** revive **7** animate, enliven, quicken, refresh **10** invigorate

VIXEN: **3** fox **5** scold, shrew **6** virago **7** hellion, screech **8** fishwife **9** termagant

VOCABULARY: **4** cant **5** lingo, slang, terms, words **6** jargon, speech **7** dialect, diction, lexicon **8** glossary, language **9** thesaurus **10** dictionary **11** phraseology, terminology **12** nomenclature

VOCAL: **4** oral **5** blunt **6** direct, fluent, spoken, verbal, voiced **7** uttered **9** outspoken **10** articulate, expressive, resounding

VOCALIST: **4** alto **5** tenor **6** singer **7** caroler, soprano **8** baritone, musician, songster **9** performer **11** entertainer

VOCALIZE: **4** sing, talk **5** shout, speak, voice **6** convey **7** express **9** pronounce, verbalize **10** articulate **11** communicate

VOCATION: **3** art, job **4** call, work **5** craft, field, trade **6** career, racket **7** calling, pursuit **8** business **10** employment, occupation, profession

VOCIFERATE: **3** cry **4** bawl, call, howl, yell **5** shout, utter **6** bellow, clamor, holler, shriek **7** protest, screech

VOCIFEROUS: **4** loud **5** noisy **7** blatant **8** strident **9** clamorous, insistent, talkative **10** boisterous **11** loudmouthed

VOGUE: **3** fad **4** chic, mode, rage **5** craze, style, trend **6** custom, modish **7** fashion, popular **10** popularity **11** fashionable

VOICE: **3** air, say **4** alto, bass, talk, tone, vote, wish **5** mouth, sound, speak, tenor, utter **6** assert, choice, phrase, speech, tongue **7** declare, divulge, express, opinion, soprano **8** announce, baritone, language, proclaim, vocalize **9** pronounce, utterance, verbalize **10** articulate, expression **11** communicate
box: **6** larynx

VOICELESS: **3** mum **4** dumb, mute, surd **6** silent **7** aphonic, spirate **9** inaudible **10** speechless **12** inarticulate

VOID: **3** gap **4** bare, free, hole, null, veto, want **5** abyss, annul, avion, blank, drain, empty, leave, space **6** cancel, cavity, hollow, remove, vacant, vacate, vacuum **7** deplete, invalid, lacking, negated, nullify, opening, rescind, useless, vacuity, wanting **8** dissolve, evacuate **9** discharge, emptiness **10** unoccupied **11** countermand, ineffective, ineffectual, meaningless

VOLATILE: **4** airy, rash **5** moody **6** fickle, flying, lively, volage, volant **7** buoyant, elastic, erratic, flighty, gaseous, volatic **8** eruptive, fleeting, flippant, unstable, vaporous, variable **9** ephemeral, excitable, explosive, fugacious, transient **10** capricious, changeable, inconstant, transitory **12** lighthearted **13** temperamental

VOLITION: **4** will, wish **6** choice, desire, option **8** choosing, election **10** discretion, preference

VOLLEY: **4** shot **5** burst, round, storm **6** shower **7** barrage **8** drumfire **9** discharge

VOLTAIRE: **4** poet **6** writer **8** satirist **9** dramatist, historian **11** philosopher

pen name: **19** Francois Marie Arouet

wrote: **5** Irene, Zadig, Zaire **6** Brutus, Oedipe **7** Candide **8** Tancrede **9** La Pucelle, Le Mondain **10** La Henriade, Micromegas **16** Lettres anglaises **21** Lettres Philosophiques

VOLUBLE: **4** glib **5** vocal, wordy **6** fluent **7** twining **8** rotating, twisting **9** revolving, talkative **10** loquacious

VOLUME: **4** body, book, bulk, heap, mass, size **5** sound **6** scroll **7** content, edition **8** capacity, document, loudness, quantity, strength **9** aggregate, magnitude **10** dimensions **11** publication **13** amplification

VOLUMINOUS: **4** full, vast **5** ample, bulky, large **7** massive, several **8** abundant, numerous, spacious, swelling **9** cavernous, extensive

VOLUNTARY: **4** free **6** chosen, freely, unpaid **7** elected, unasked, willful, willing **8** elective, optional, unforced **9** volunteer, willingly **10** deliberate **11** intentional, spontaneous

VOLUNTEER: **5** offer **6** enlist, tender, unpaid **7** proffer, suggest **9** voluntary

VOLUNTEER STATE: **9** Tennessee

VOLUPTUOUS: **4** lush **5** buxom, curvy **6** erotic, wanton **7** sensual, shapely **8** luscious, sensuous

VOMIT: **4** barf, puke, spew **5** expel, heave, retch **7** throw up, upchuck **8** disgorge **11** regurgitate

VORACIOUS: **6** greedy, hungry **7** gorging **8** edacious, esurient, ravening, ravenous **9** consuming, rapacious **10** gluttonous, insatiable **12** unquenchable

VORTEX: **4** eddy, gyre **5** whirl **6** spiral **7** cyclone, tornado, twister **9** whirlpool, whirlwind **10** waterspout

VOTARY: **4** buff **6** addict, zealot **7** admirer, amateur, devotee, fanatic, habitue **8** adherent, believer, disciple, follower **10** aficionado, enthusiast, worshipper

VOTE: **4** poll, wish **5** elect, voice **6** choice, choose, confer, decide, ticket **7** declare **8** election, majority, suffrage **9** determine, franchise **10** plebiscite, referendum

VOTER: **7** citizen, elector **8** balloter, resident, taxpayer

VOUCH: **4** aver, back, cite **5** prove **6** affirm, assert, assure, attest, verify **7** certify, confirm, declare, endorse, sponsor, support, warrant, witness **8** maintain **9** establish, guarantee **12** authenticate, substantiate

VOUCHER: **4** bill, chit, note **5** proof **6** docket, ticket **7** receipt **9** affidavit, statement **10** credential **11** certificate

VOUCHSAFE: **4** give **5** award, deign, favor, grant, yield **6** bestow, permit **7** concede **10** condescend

VOW: **4** oath, wish, word **5** swear **6** assure, pledge, plight, prayer **7** declare, promise **8** covenant, dedicate **9** assertion

VOWEL:
contraction: **6** crasis **9** diphthong
deleted: **7** aphesis
diacritics: **5** breve, tilde **6** umlaut **8** dieresis **10** circumflex
sounds: **4** lene **6** ablaut, dental, labial **7** palatal
two: **6** digram **7** digraph

VOYAGE: **4** tour, trek **5** jaunt **6** cruise, travel **7** journey, passage **8** crossing **9** excursion **10** expedition, pilgrimage **11** undertaking

VULGAR: **4** base, lewd, rude, vile **5** crass, crude, dirty, gross **6** coarse, common, filthy, smutty **7** boorish, general, obscene, popular, profane, uncouth **8** barbaric, everyday, indecent, ordinary, plebeian **9** inelegant, offensive, revolting, tasteless, unrefined **10** vernacular **12** ostentatious, pornographic

VULGARITY: **8** rudeness **9** crassness, crudeness, impudence, indecency, obscenity, profanity **10** coarseness, commonness **11** discourtesy

VULNERABLE: **4** open, weak **6** liable, unsafe **7** exposed **8** insecure **9** unguarded **10** accessible, assailable **11** defenseless, susceptible, unprotected

VULPINE: **3** sly **4** foxy, wily **6** clever, crafty, tricky **7** cunning **8** skillful **9** ingenious **10** shrewdness

W

WACKY: **4** nuts, zany **5** batty, crazy, loony, silly **6** insane, screwy **7** cracked, foolish **8** demented, deranged **9** eccentric **10** irrational

WAD: **3** bat, pad **4** cram, heap, lump, mass, mint, pile, plug, roll **5** clump, stuff **6** boodle, bundle, insert, wealth **7** fortune, stopper **8** bankroll, compress

WADDLE: **4** sway, walk **6** hobble, totter, wiggle, wobble **7** shuffle

WADE: **4** ford, plod, toil, walk **6** drudge, trudge **7** proceed **8** struggle

WAFER: **4** cake, disk **5** candy **6** cookie **7** biscuit, cracker

WAFT: **4** blow, flag, gust, odor, puff, skim, wave **5** carry, drift, float, smell, whiff **6** breeze, convey, signal **7** flutter

WAG: **3** wit **4** card, move, stir, sway, zany **5** clown, comic, joker, shake, swing **6** jester, waddle, wiggle, wigwag **8** comedian, humorist, jokester **9** oscillate, prankster **11** wisecracker

WAGE: **3** fee, pay **4** hire **5** fight **6** engage, income, pursue, reward, salary **7** attempt, conduct, payment, stipend **8** earnings **9** allowance, emolument, undertake **10** honorarium, recompense **12** compensation

earner: **6** worker **7** laborer **8** employee

WAGER: **3** pot **4** ante, play **5** hunch **6** chance **9** challenge, speculate

WAGGISH: **5** droll, funny, merry, witty **7** comical, jesting, jocular, playful, roguish **10** frolicsome **11** mischievous

WAGGLE: **4** sway, wave **6** waddle, wiggle, wobble **8** brandish

WAGON: **3** car, van **4** cart, dray, tram, wain **5** buggy, coach, gilly, lorry **6** camion **7** caisson, chariot, fourgon, tumbril, vehicle **8** barouche, carriage, schooner **9** buckboard, Conestoga **10** chuckwagon

WAIF: **4** flag **5** stray **6** orphan **7** pennant, vagrant **8** homeless, wanderer **9** foundling **10** ragamuffin

WAIL: **3** cry, sob **4** bawl, fuss, howl, moan, weep, yell **5** whine **6** bemoan, lament, plaint **7** blubber, whimper **8** complain, undulate

WAIST: **5** shirt **6** blouse, bodice, middle **7** abdomen, corsage, midriff **10** midsection, undershirt

WAISTBAND: **4** belt, sash **6** girdle **8** cincture **10** cummerbund

WAIT: **4** bide, halt, rest, stay, stop, tend **5** cater, court, dally, delay, pause, serve, tarry **6** ambush, attend, expect, linger, loiter, remain **7** interim **8** hesitate, postpone **10** anticipate

WAITER: **4** tray **6** garcon, salver, server **7** footman, servant, steward **8** waitress **9** attendant

WAIVE: **5** allow, cease, defer, forgo, grant, leave, yield **6** excuse, reject, shelve **7** abandon, concede, dismiss, forbear, forsake, neglect, reserve **8** disclaim, postpone **9** disregard, surrender **10** relinquish

WAKE: **4** path, prod, stir, wave **5** arise, rouse, shake, track, trail, vigil, watch **6** arouse, awaken, excite, revive **7** freshen, passage, service **9** aftermath, stimulate **10** understand

WAKEFUL: **5** alert **7** careful **8** restless, vigilant, watchful **9** attentive, observant, sleepless

WALDEN:
author: **17** Henry David Thoreau
location: **7** Concord **13** Massachusetts
place: **4** pond

WALE: **3** rib **4** mark, weal, welt **5** grain, ridge, strip, weave, wheat **6** streak **7** texture

WALES:
also called: **5** Cymru **7** Cambria
capital: **7** Cardiff
cities: **6** Bangor **7** Swansea **8** Hereford, Pembroke **9** Worcester
counties: **5** Clwyd, Dyfed, Gwent, Powys **7** Gwynedd **12** Mid Glamorgan **13** West Glamorgan **14** South Glamorgan
emblem: **4** leek
features: **6** Berwyn
island: **8** Angelsey
language: **6** Cymric, Kymric **7** Cymraeg
native: **5** Cymry, Kymry, Taffy **8** Welchman
part of: **7** Snowdon **8** Cambrian **13** United Kingdom
water: **3** Dee, Wye **4** Bala, Teme **5** Teifi **6** Conway, Severn **8** Irish Sea **14** Bristol Channel

WALK: **4** foot, gait, hike, limp, pace, path, plod, ramp, roam, step, turn, wade **5** amble, jaunt, march, mince, slink, strut, trade, trail, tramp, tread **6** bobble, career, lumber, parade, patrol, prance, ramble, stride, stroll, strump, toddle, totter, travel, trudge, wander **7** circuit, flounce, gangway, pathway, saunter, shuffle, stretch, swagger, traipse **8** ambulate, crossing, exercise, footpath, traverse, vocation **9** promenade **10** profession **11** perambulate

WALKER: **5** hiker **8** stroller, wayfarer **10** pedestrian

WALKING: **5** afoot **6** hiking **7** roaming **8** ambulate, marching **9** strolling, strutting, wandering **10** ambulatory **11** digitigrade, plantigrade, promenading

WALKING STICK: **4** cane **5** staff, stilt, waddy **6** crutch **9** pikestaff

WALK OUT: **4** quit **5** leave **6** strike **7** protest

WALK OVER: **7** triumph, victory **8** conquest

WALL: **3** dam **4** dike **5** anger, cliff, fence, levee **6** immure, paries **7** barrier, curtain, defense, divider, enclose, parapet, rampart **8** blockade, distress, enceinte **9** barricade, enclosure, encompass, hindrance, partition **10** difficulty, ridiculous **13** fortification **14** unconventional

WALLABY: **6** animal **8** kangaroo **9** marsupial
location: **9** Australia
related to: **8** kangaroo

WALLET: **5** purse **8** billfold **10** pocketbook

WALLOP: **3** hit **4** bash, beat, belt, blow, lick, slam, slug, whip, whop **5** crash, pound, smack, smash **6** defeat, pummel, strike, thrash **7** clobber, shellac, trounce **9** collision

WALLOW: **4** bask, loll, roll, toss **5** glory, revel **6** billow, grovel **7** delight, indulge, stumble **8** flounder **9** luxuriate

WALTZ: **3** zip **5** dance, march, music, whirl **6** breeze **10** hesitation

WAN: **3** dim, sad **4** fade, pale, weak, worn **5** ashen, faint **6** anemic, dismal, feeble, gloomy, pallid, sickly **7** haggard, languid **8** blanched, paleness **9** bloodless, colorless, sorrowful **10** melancholy

WAND: **3** rod **4** mace, pole, twig **5** baton, sprig, staff, stick **6** switch **7** scepter **8** caduceus

WANDER: **3** gad **4** roam, roil, rove **5** amble, drift, range, shift, stray **6** ramble, stroll **7** deviate, digress, meander, saunter, traipse **8** straggle, traverse

WANDERER: **3** bum **5** nomad, rover **6** roamer **7** drifter, pilgrim, rambler, vagrant **8** traveler, vagabond **9** itinerant **11** beachcomber

WANDERING: **6** errant, roving **7** journey, migrant, nomadic, odyssey, roaming **8** drifting, rambling, straying **9** deviation, planetary, traveling **10** digressive, meandering

WANE: **3** ebb **4** fade, fail, sink, wilt **5** abate, decay, peter **6** absent, lessen, shrink, weaken, wither **7** decline, dwindle, subside **8** decrease, diminish

WANGLE: **4** fake, worm **6** juggle, obtain, wiggle **7** falsify, finagle, wriggle **8** contrive, engineer, maneuver **9** extricate **10** manipulate

WANT: **4** lack, miss, must, need, seek, wish **5** covet, crave **6** aspire, choose, dearth, demand, desire, hunger, penury, prefer, thirst **7** absence, longing, poverty, require **8** scarcity, shortage, yearning **9** deficient, necessity, privation **10** deficiency, inadequacy **11** deprivation, destitution, requirement

WANTING: **4** less **5** minus, short **6** absent, scanty, scarce **7** lacking, without **9** deficient, destitute **10** inadequate **11** unfulfilled **12** insufficient

WANTON: **4** fast, jade, lewd, slut **5** cruel, hussy, loose, merry, revel **6** frisky, frolic, harlot, lavish, trifle, unjust, unruly **7** fulsome, immoral, lustful, playful, sensual, spoiled, wayward **8** arrogant, careless, prodigal, spiteful, sportive, strumpet, unchaste **9** concubine, lecherous, luxuriant, malicious, merciless **10** capricious, frolicsome, gratuitous, licentious, malevolent, prostitute, voluptuous **11** extravagant, promiscuous **12** disregardful, overabundant, unprincipled, unrestrained **13** undisciplined

WAR: **4** feud **5** clash, fight, jihad **6** battle, combat, strife **7** contend, crusade, martial **8** conflict, struggle **10** blitzkrieg
god: **4** Ares, Mars, Odin, Thor **5** Ashur **15** Huitzilopochtli
goddess: **4** Enyo **6** Inanna, Ishtar **7** Bellona

WAR AND PEACE:
author: **10** Leo Tolstoy
characters: **8** Napoleon **12** Prince Andrei **13** Anatol Kuragin **14**

Natasha Rostova, Pierre Bezukhov **15** Platon Karatayev
setting: **6** Russia

WARBLE: 4 sing **5** carol, chant, chirp, trill, yodel **6** melody, quaver

WAR CRY: 5 motto, rally **6** phrase, slogan **8** Geronimo **9** watchword

WARD: 4 area, care, fend, halt, jail, zone **5** block, deter, guard, minor, parry, repel, watch **6** charge, defend, divert, prison, shield, stymie **7** custody, defense, deflect, fortify, prevent **8** corridor, district, garrison, guardian, precinct, watchman **9** safeguard **10** department, protection **12** guardianship

WARDEN: 5 guard **6** jailer, jailor, keeper, ranger, sentry **8** guardian, official, overseer, watchdog, watchman **9** constable, custodian **10** supervisor

WARD OFF: 4 fend, hold **5** avert, block, parry, repel **6** rebuff **7** prevent

WARDROBE: 5 chest, trunk **6** bureau, closet **7** apparel, armoire, cabinet, clothes, dresser, threads **8** costumes **12** clothespress

WAREHOUSE: 5 depot, store **7** shelter, storage **9** stockpile, stockroom **10** depository, repository, storehouse **11** accommodate

WARES: 4 line **5** goods, stock **8** articles, supplies **11** commodities, merchandise

WARFARE: 5 clash **6** strife **8** conflict, fighting, struggle **11** hostilities

WARINESS: 7 caution **9** suspicion **12** watchfulness

WARLIKE: 7 hawkish, hostile, martial **8** fighting, militant, military **9** bellicose, combative, soldierly **10** aggressive, pugnacious **11** belligerent **12** antagonistic

WARLOCK: 5 witch **6** wizard **8** conjuror, magician, sorcerer **9** archimage

WARM: 3 hot **4** cook, heat, keen, kind, mild, smug **5** balmy, close, eager, fiery, fresh, humid, sunny, tepid **6** ardent, genial, hearty, heated, kindly, lively, loving, tender, toasty **7** affable, amorous, clement, cordial, earnest, enliven, fervent, flushed, glowing, sincere **8** animated, friendly, generous, gracious, pleasant **9** excitable, heartfelt **10** overheated, passionate **11** kindhearted, sympathetic **12** affectionate, enthusiastic **13** compassionate, uncomfortable

WARMHEARTED: 4 kind **6** loving, tender **11** sympathetic **13** compassionate

WARMTH: 4 glow, heat, zeal **6** spirit **7** passion **8** kindness **9** affection **10** compassion, enthusiasm **11** hospitality, temperature

WARN: 3 tip **4** clue, tell **5** alarm, alert **6** advise, inform, notify, signal **7** apprise, caution, counsel, predict **8** admonish, threaten

WARNING: 4 hint, omen, sign **5** alarm **6** beware, caveat, lesson, signal **7** caution, portent **10** admonition **11** premonition

WARP: 4 beat, bend, bias, kink, line, rope, sway, turn **5** quirk, twist **6** buckle, damage, debase, deform, fasten, wrench **7** contort, deflect, distort, wrinkle **10** intertwine **12** misinterpret, misrepresent

WARRANT: 4 writ **5** claim, guard, order, proof, right **6** assert, defend, ensure, permit, pledge, reason, secure, uphold **7** grounds, justify, promise, protect, voucher **8** document, guaranty, sanction, subpoena **9** assurance, authority, authorize, guarantee, safeguard

10 commission, foundation, obligation, permission, protection **11** certificate **13** authorization, justification

WARRANTY: **6** pledge **7** promise **8** contract, guaranty, sanction, security **9** assurance, guarantee

WARRIOR: **4** hero **6** knight **7** fighter, soldier, trooper, veteran **9** combatant **13** serviceperson

WARSHIP: **6** cutter **7** cruiser, frigate, gunboat **8** corvette **9** destroyer, submarine **10** battleship **11** dreadnought
fleet: **6** armada **8** flotilla, squadron

WARY: **5** alert, cagey, canny, chary, leery **7** careful, guarded, mindful, prudent **8** cautious, discreet, vigilant, watchful **9** provident **10** suspicious **11** circumspect, distrustful

WASH: **3** lap, wet **4** bath, coat, flow, lave, roll, soap **5** bathe, clean, cover, drift, erode, float, rinse, scour, scrub, slosh, swirl **6** drench, purify, shower, sponge **7** cleanse, launder, laundry, shampoo **8** ablution, lustrate

WASHED-OUT: **4** pale **5** faded, spent, tired **6** effete **7** drained **8** depleted **9** colorless, exhausted

WASHED-UP: **4** done, shot **6** ruined **7** through **8** finished

WASHING: **7** bathing, laundry, rinsing, soaking **8** ablution, cleaning **9** showering

WASHINGTON:
bird: **15** willow goldfinch
capital: **7** Olympia
cities: **6** Tacoma **7** Seattle, Spokane
features: **8** Cascades **12** Mount Rainier **16** Olympic Mountains
flower: **12** rhododendron
nickname: **7** Chinook **9** Evergreen
tree: **7** hemlock
water: **8** Columbia

WASHINGTON, D.C.:
designed by: **7** L'Enfant
features: **7** Capitol **8** Pentagon **10** White House
water: **7** Potomac

WASHINGTON, GEORGE:
home: **8** Virginia **11** Mount Vernon
profession: **7** planter, soldier
vice president: **9** John Adams
wife: **6** Martha

WASHOUT: **4** flop **5** gully **6** fiasco **7** erosion, failure **8** disaster, downpour

WASP: **3** bee **6** insect **7** vespine
colony: **8** vespiary
variety: **4** sand, wood **5** paper **6** common, cuckoo, digger, hornet, spider **7** hunting **8** solitary **12** yellow jacket

WASPISH: **5** huffy, testy **6** crabby, ornery **7** fretful, peevish **8** petulant, snappish, spiteful **9** crotchety, irascible, irritable **12** cantankerous

WASSAIL: **5** binge, drink, feast, punch, revel, toast **6** frolic **7** carouse, revelry **8** carousal, festival **9** festivity, merriment **10** salutation **11** celebration

WASTE: **4** blow, bush, fail, idle, junk, kill, ruin, sack, soot **5** decay, dregs, trash **6** barren, debris, desert, devour, litter, murder, ravage, refuse, sewage, sludge, tundra, weaken, wither **7** atrophy, badland, consume, destroy, dwindle, exhaust, fritter, garbage, rubbish **8** demolish, desolate, emaciate, enfeeble, misspend, needless, squander **9** devastate, dissipate, excrement **10** wilderness **11** consumption, destruction, devastation, prodigality **12** extravagance, uncultivated

WASTE AWAY: **4** fail, wilt **5** decay **7** atrophy, corrode, decline

WASTED: **5** drunk, spent **6** stoned **7** decayed, haggard **8** needless, withered **9** emaciated, exhausted, shriveled **10** squandered **11** superfluous

WASTEFUL: **6** costly, lavish **8** careless, prodigal **10** thriftless **11** extravagant, improvident, spendthrift

WASTELAND: **5** marsh, swamp, wilds **6** desert **8** badlands **10** wilderness

WASTREL: **4** rake **5** idler **6** loafer, waster **7** vagrant **8** vagabond **10** profligate, squanderer **11** spendthrift

WATCH: **3** eye, see, spy **4** duty, look, mark, mind, scan, view, wait **5** focus, guard, stare, timer, vigil **6** defend, follow, notice, patrol, police, sentry **7** lookout, monitor, observe, oversee, protect **8** sentinel **9** timepiece **10** scrutinize **11** chronometer, supervision, surveillance

WATCHFUL: **4** keen, wary **5** alert, aware, chary, ready **7** careful, guarded, heedful **8** cautious, open-eyed, vigilant **9** attentive, wide-awake **11** circumspect

WATCHMAN: **5** guard, scout **6** keeper, sentry **7** flagman, lookout, spotter **8** sentinel **9** flagwoman **10** watchwoman

WATCHTOWER: **6** beacon **7** lookout, mirador **8** barbican, landmark **10** lighthouse **11** observatory

WATCHWORD: **3** cry **4** sign **5** motto **6** signal, slogan **8** password **11** countersign

WATER: **3** sea, wet **4** aqua, hose, lake, pond, pool, rain, soak, thin, well **5** brook, douse, drink, flood, fluid, oasis, ocean, river, spray, tears **6** deluge, dilute, drench, lagoon, liquid, puddle, splash, spring, stream **7** moisten **8** beverage, irrigate, moisture, saturate, sprinkle **9** reservoir

WATERCOURSE: **4** wadi **5** brook, canal, chute, creek, drain, flume, gully, inlet, river, shoot **6** gulley, gutter, ravine, sluice, stream, trench **7** channel, conduit, culvert, estuary **8** aqueduct, spillway

WATERED-DOWN: **4** thin, weak **5** mixed **7** diluted **8** weakened **10** diminished **11** adulterated

WATERFALL: **5** chute, falls **6** rapids **7** cascade, Niagara **8** cataract

WATERING HOLE: **3** bar, pub **5** oasis **6** lounge, resort, saloon, tavern **7** barroom, hangout **9** nightclub

WATERLESS: **3** dry **4** arid **7** thirsty **9** anhydrous **10** dehydrated

WATERLOG: **4** soak **6** drench, sodden **8** saturate

WATERPROOF: **6** sealed **8** airtight **10** impervious **11** impermeable

WATERY: **3** wet **4** damp, pale, thin, weak **5** fluid, moist, runny, soggy, teary **6** liquid, soaked, sodden **7** aqueous, diluted, insipid **9** colorless **11** adulterated

WATTLE: **3** rod **4** roof, skin, swig, tree, wall **5** fence, shrub, stick, twist **9** framework **10** intertwine, interweave

WAVE: **3** sea, wag **4** bore, coil, curl, flap, gush, rash, roll, surf, sway, tide, tube **5** crest, curve, eager, flood, greet, ridge, shake, surge, swell, swing, water **6** beckon, billow, influx, motion, ripple, roller, signal **7** breaker, flutter, gesture, tsunami, vibrate, winding **8** brandish, flourish, movement, outbreak, undulate, uprising, whitecap **9** fluctuate, vibration

WAVER: **4** reel, sway, vary **5** hedge, pause, shift, swing **6** change, falter, quaver, seesaw, teeter, totter, unsure, wiggle **7** flicker, flutter, stagger, tremble, vibrate **8** hesitate, unsteady **9** fluctuate, oscillate, vacillate

WAVERING: **6** fickle, unsure **8** unsteady, variable, waffling **9** undecided **10** hesitating, irresolute **11** vacillating **12** irresolution

WAVY: **5** bumpy, curly, snaky **6** coiled, curved **7** rolling, sinuate, sinuous **8** squiggly, undulant, unstable **11** vermiculate

WAX: **3** gum, oil **4** grow, rise **5** build, mount, swell, widen **6** become, expand, grease, polish **7** augment, cerumen, coating, enlarge, magnify **8** heighten, increase, paraffin

WAXEN: **4** pale, weak **6** pallid, smooth

WAXY: **4** pale **5** slick **6** smooth **7** pliable **8** lustrous, slippery, yielding **14** impressionable

WAY: **3** via **4** door, lane, mode, pass, path, plan, road, room, wont **5** alley, going, habit, means, order, route, style, track, trail **6** access, artery, avenue, career, course, custom, detour, manner, method, nature, policy, scheme, street, system **7** advance, fashion, journey, opening, passage **8** approach, distance, practice, progress, tendency **9** boulevard, direction, procedure, technique **12** idiosyncrasy

WAYFARER: **5** nomad **7** pilgrim, voyager **8** traveler **9** sojourner

WAYLAY: **4** trap **5** beset, slink **6** ambush, assail, attack **8** surprise **9** ambuscade, bushwhack, intercept

WAYWARD: **5** balky **6** errant, fickle, ornery, unruly **7** erratic, willful **8** contrary, stubborn, unsteady **9** arbitrary, irregular **10** capricious, headstrong, inconstant, refractory **11** disobedient, fluctuating, intractable **12** undependable, unmanageable **13** unpredictable

WEAK: **4** lame, puny, soft, thin, worn **5** faint, frail, shaky, wimpy, young **6** anemic, feeble, flimsy, infirm, tender, unsafe, watery **7** brittle, diluted, distant, exposed, fragile, pliable, rickety, unsound **8** cowardly, decrepit, helpless, impotent **9** dissolute, enervated, enfeebled, powerless, spineless, whispered **10** effeminate, inadequate, unaccented, unstressed, vulnerable **11** debilitated, defenseless, ineffective, unprotected **12** unconvincing

WEAKEN: **3** sap **4** fade, flag, thin, tire **6** damage, defeat, dilute, impair, lessen, reduce, soften **7** cripple, crumble, decline, depress, disable, exhaust, unnerve **8** diminish, enervate, languish, paralyze **9** extenuate, undermine **10** debilitate, devitalize **11** deteriorate

WEAKLING: **4** baby, wimp **5** ninny, sissy **6** coward **7** crybaby, milksop **8** pushover **10** pantywaist **11** milquetoast, mollycoddle

WEAKNESS: **4** flaw **6** defect, foible **7** ailment, frailty **8** appetite, debility, desirous, fondness **9** proneness **10** deficiency **11** inclination, shortcoming **12** imperfection **13** vulnerability

WEALTH: **4** gold, pelf, weal **5** funds, goods, means, money, power, worth **6** assets, riches **7** capital, fortune **8** holdings, opulence, property, treasure **9** abundance, affluence, resources **10** prosperity **11** possessions **12** accumulation

WEALTHY: **4** rich **6** loaded **7** moneyed, upscale **8** affluent **10** prosperous

WEAPON: **3** gun **4** claw, club, dart, dirk, tank, whip **5** arrow, knife, lance, rifle, saber, sling, spear, sword, talon **6** bomber, dagger, mortar, musket, pistol **7** bayonet, bazooka, carbine, firearm, machete, missile, shotgun, trident **8** armament, catapult, crossbow, revolver, tomahawk **9** artillery, boomerang, derringer, munitions

WEAR: **3** don, rub **4** fray, tire **5** annoy, chafe, drain, erode, grind, sport **6** abrade, attire, bother, endure, impair, pester **7** apparel, clothes, consume, corrode, durable, erosion, exhaust, exhibit, fatigue, frazzle, mileage **8** diminish, friction **9** corrosion **11** deteriorate

WEAR AWAY: **3** eat **4** gnaw, rust **5** erode **6** abrade **7** corrode

WEAR DOWN: **4** tire **5** drain, waste **6** reduce, weaken **7** exhaust, fatigue **8** friction

WEARISOME: **4** dull **6** boring **7** tedious **8** tiresome, toilsome **9** laborious, strenuous **10** exhausting

WEAR OUT: **4** tire **5** decay, waste **6** tucker **7** exhaust, fatigue

WEARY: **4** beat, tire, worn **5** annoy, bored, jaded, spent, timid, tired **6** bushed, plague, pooped, sleepy, tucker, weaken **7** drained, fatigue, irksome, tedious **8** fatigued, grievous, overwork, tiresome **9** disgusted, exhausted, overtired

WEATHER: **4** rust **5** brave, clime, erode **6** endure **7** climate, survive **8** discolor, elements, overcome **9** withstand **11** temperature **12** disintegrate
person: **10** forecaster **13** climatologist, meteorologist

WEAVE: **4** darn, join, knit, lace, loom, spin, sway **5** blend, braid, plait, twill, unite **6** careen, devise, wattle, wobble, zigzag **7** entwine, fashion, meander, stagger **8** contrive **9** interlace **10** crisscross, intertwine

WEB: **3** net **4** maze, mesh, trap **5** fiber, snare **6** fabric, tangle, tissue **7** ensnare, network, texture **8** entangle, gossamer, membrane **9** labyrinth **10** complexity **11** involvement

WED: **3** tie **4** join, link **5** blend, elope, hitch, marry, merge, unite **7** connect, espouse, pledged, spliced

WEDDING: **8** ceremony, espousal, marriage, nuptials, shivaree **11** celebration
people: **5** bride, groom, usher **7** best man **10** bridesmaid **11** maid of honor **13** matron of honor

WEDDING ANNIVERSARY:
1st: **5** clock, paper
2nd: **5** china **6** cotton
3rd: **5** glass **7** crystal, leather
4th: **4** silk **5** linen **9** appliance
5th: **4** wood **10** silverware
6th: **4** iron, wood
7th: **4** wool **6** copper
8th: **4** lace **5** linen **6** bronze
9th: **5** china **7** leather, pottery
10th: **3** tin **7** diamond **8** aluminum
11th: **5** steel **7** jewelry
12th: **3** gem **4** silk **5** pearl
13th: **3** fur **4** lace **7** textile
14th: **4** gold **5** ivory
15th: **5** watch **7** crystal
20th: **5** china **8** platinum
25th: **6** silver
30th: **5** pearl **7** diamond
35th: **4** jade **5** coral
40th: **4** ruby
45th: **8** sapphire
50th: **4** gold
55th: **7** emerald
60th: **7** diamond

WEDGE: **3** jam, pie **4** club, cram, lump, pack **5** block, crowd, stuff **7** squeeze **8** sandwich

WEDLOCK: **8** marriage, nuptials **9** matrimony **11** conjugality

WEE: **4** tiny **5** early, small, teeny **6** little, minute, teensy **9** miniature **10** diminutive **11** lilliputian, microscopic **13** infinitesimal

WEED: **3** hoe, pot **4** burr, dock, hemp, tare **5** vetch **6** darnel, nettle **7** purloin, ragweed, thistle, tobacco **8** plantain, purslane **9** buckthorn, cigarette, dandelion, horsemint, marijuana **11** undergrowth

WEEP: **3** cry, sob **4** bawl, drip, leak, moan, ooze, tear, wail **5** exude, mourn **6** bewail, boohoo, grieve, lament, yammer **7** blubber

WEIGH: **3** tax **4** bear, lift, load **5** count, hoist, judge, study, think **6** burden, ponder **7** analyze, balance, compare, examine, measure, portion **8** consider, evaluate, meditate **9** influence **11** contemplate **14** counterbalance

WEIGH DOWN: **4** load **5** press, worry **6** burden **7** depress, oppress **8** encumber, overload

WEIGHT: **3** bob, lot, tax, ton **4** beef, dram, gram, lade, load, mass, pull **5** carat, clout, flask, force, grain, ounce, pound, power, scale, stone, value, worth **6** anchor, barrel, burden, charge, impact, import, moment, saddle, sinker, stress **7** ballast, concern, density, gravity, oppress, scruple, tonnage, urgency **8** dumbbell, emphasis, encumber, kilogram, poundage, pressure **9** authority, centigram, heaviness, influence, magnitude, milligram **10** importance **11** consequence **12** forcefulness, significance **14** responsibility

WEIGHTINESS: **7** dignity, gravity **9** authority, heaviness, magnitude, solemnity **10** importance **12** significance

WEIGHTY: **3** fat **5** bulky, grave, heavy, hefty, large, massy, obese, solid, stout **6** portly, severe, solemn, taxing **7** massive, onerous, serious, telling **8** critical, powerful **9** corpulent, difficult, important, ponderous **10** burdensome, cumbersome **11** significant, substantial **12** considerable

WEIRD: **3** odd **4** fate, unco, wild **5** crazy, eerie, nutty, queer, scary **6** creepy, spooky **7** awesome, bizarre, curious, destiny, fortune, ghostly, predict, strange, uncanny, unusual **8** haunting, peculiar **8** abnormal **9** eccentric, unearthly, unnatural **10** mysterious, outlandish **12** supernatural

WELCOME: **3** hug **5** greet, hello **6** salute **7** cordial, desired, embrace, ovation, receive **8** greeting, pleasant **9** agreeable, desirable, handshake, reception **10** acceptable, refreshing, salutation, satisfying **11** comfortable, hospitality, pleasurable

WELD: **4** bind, fuse, join, link **5** unite **6** solder **7** combine, connect

WELFARE: **4** good, weal **6** health **7** benefit, success **8** progress **9** happiness, well-being **10** prosperity

WELL: **3** fit, pit, spa **4** fair, fine, flow, good, gush, hole, pool, sump **5** amply, fount, fully, lucky, quite, shaft, sound **6** cavity, fairly, gusher, hearty, indeed, nicely, robust, source, spring **7** happily, healthy **8** entirely, expertly, fountain, thriving **9** carefully, correctly, favorably, fortunate, perfectly, reservoir, wholesome **10** gratifying, intimately, personally, prosperous, reasonably, skillfully, splendidly, thoroughly **11** comfortable **12** satisfactory, successfully, sufficiently

WELL-BEHAVED: **6** polite **8** mannerly **9** courteous

WELL-BEING: **4** ease, good, weal **6** health **7** benefit, comfort, welfare **9** advantage, happiness **10** prosperity

WELL-BRED: **5** civil **6** polite **7** genteel, refined **8** cultured, mannerly, polished **9** courteous **10** cultivated **11** considerate

WELL-DEFINED: **5** clear **8** definite, distinct, outlined

WELL-DISPOSED: **6** kindly **7** willing **8** friendly **11** sympathetic

WELL-FAVORED: **6** pretty **8** handsome **9** beautiful **10** attractive **11** good-looking

WELL-FOUNDED: **4** good, just **5** sound **6** likely **7** factual **8** probable, rational **13** substantiated

WELL-GROOMED: **4** neat, tidy, trim **5** clean **6** dapper, spruce **9** shipshape **10** impeccable

WELL-GROUNDED: **5** valid **6** versed **9** supported **12** corroborated **13** substantiated

WELL-HEELED: **4** rich **7** wealthy **8** affluent **10** prosperous

WELL-KNOWN: **5** noted **6** common, famous **7** eminent, notable, popular **8** familiar, renowned **9** notorious, prominent **11** established, illustrious

WELL-MADE: **5** solid **6** sturdy **7** durable **8** flawless, reliable **10** dependable

WELL-MANNERED: **6** polite **7** genteel, refined **8** cultured, polished **9** courteous **10** cultivated

WELL-OFF: **4** rich, snug **5** lucky **6** loaded **7** wealthy **8** affluent, well-to-do **9** fortunate **10** prosperous, successful

WELLSPRING: **4** root **6** origin, source **8** fountain **9** beginning **12** fountainhead

WELL-TIMED: **6** timely **9** favorable, opportune **11** appropriate

WELL-TO-DO: **4** rich **7** wealthy, well-off **8** affluent **10** prosperous

WELT: **4** blow, bump, lash, lump, mark, wale, weal **5** ridge, wheal, wound **6** bruise, stripe, thrash

WELTER: **4** roll, toss, wilt **6** grovel, jumble, tumble, uproar, wallow, wither **7** turmoil **8** overturn **9** commotion, confusion

WENCH: **4** doxy, girl, lass **5** bimbo, hussy, tramp, whore, woman **6** damsel, maiden, wanton **7** jezebel, servant **8** strumpet **10** prostitute

WEND: **4** pass **5** alter, shift **6** change, stroll, travel **7** journey, proceed, saunter

WEST INDIES:
animals: **4** arar, paru, tody **5** hutia, pelon **6** agouti, arbalo, chigoe, mucaro **7** hicatee, pegador **9** picudilla
discoverer: **8** Columbus
features: **5** Pelee **10** Pico Duarte
groups: **7** Bahamas **14** Lesser Antilles **15** Greater Antilles
includes: **4** Cuba, Saba **5** Aruba, Haiti, Nevis **6** Tobago **7** Grenada, Jamaica, Leeward **8** Barbados, Trinidad, Windward **10** Hispaniola, Martinique, Puerto Rico, Santa Lucia **13** Virgin Islands **17** Dominican Republic
inhabitants: **5** Carib, Dutch **6** Arawak, Danish, French **7** African, British, Spanish, Swedish **10** Portuguese **12** Asian Indians
languages: **6** Creole, French **7** English, Spanish
plants: **4** ocra **5** ebony, yagua, yaray **6** gomart, grigri, grugru, papaya, pawpaw, vanglo **7** gadbush **8** cockspur **9** sapodilla
water: **9** Caribbean

WEST POINT: **7** Academy
location: **7** New York

river: **6** Hudson
student: **5** cadet, plebe **8** yearling

WEST VIRGINIA:
bird: **8** cardinal
capital: **10** Charleston
cities: **8** Wheeling **10** Huntington
explorer: **5** Boone **10** Washington
features: **9** Allegheny **12** Harpers Ferry
flower: **12** rhododendron
nickname: **8** Mountain
tree: **10** sugar maple
water: **9** Ohio River

WET: **4** damp, dank, dewy, rain, soak, wash **5** douse, foggy, humid, misty, moist, muggy, rainy, snowy, soggy, soppy, sweat, water, wring **6** dampen, drench, shower, soaked, sodden, splash, watery **7** moisten **8** dampened, dampness, drenched, irrigate, moisture, saturate, slippery, sprinkle **9** drizzling **11** waterlogged

WET BLANKET: **4** drag, drip **6** damper **7** killjoy **8** sourpuss **10** fuddy-duddy, spoilsport

WHACK: **3** bat, hit, try **4** bang, bash, beat, belt, blow, shot, slam, stab, turn **5** crack, fling, knock, pound, smack, smash, thump, whale **6** thwack, wallop **7** attempt, clobber

WHALE: **3** hit **4** beat **5** large, whack **6** mammal, strike, thrash **7** whopper **8** cetacean **9** abundance
air hole: **8** blowhole, spiracle
bone: **6** baleen **9** scrimshaw
fat: **7** blubber
flap: **5** fluke
food: **5** krill
school: **3** gam, pod
types: **4** orca **5** sperm, white **6** baleen, beluga, killer **7** finback, grampus **8** cachalot, humpback **9** mysticeti

WHAM: **3** hit **4** bang, blow, slam **5** crash, knock, smash, whack **6** strike, whammy

WHAMMY: **4** jinx **5** curse, spell

WHARF: **4** dock, pier, quay, slip **5** jetty, levee **7** landing

WHEAT: **5** durum, grain, grass, spelt **6** cereal **8** semolina
genus: **8** triticum

WHEEDLE: **3** con **4** coax, lure **5** charm, tempt **6** butter, cajole, entice **7** blarney, flatter **8** inveigle, persuade **9** influence, sweet-talk

WHEEL: **3** cam, cog, rim **4** disk, gear, helm, loop, reel, roll, spin, tire, turn **5** lathe, pivot, pully, rotor, round, rowel, swirl, twirl, whirl **6** caster, circle, roller, rotate, sheave **7** revolve **8** gyration, rotation, sprocket **9** treadmill **10** revolution

WHEEZE: **3** gag **4** gasp, joke, pant, puff **5** antic, prank, trick

WHELP: **3** cub, dog, pup **4** wolf **5** child, puppy **9** youngster

WHEN: **5** until, while **6** during, though **7** whereas **8** although **9** meanwhile

WHERE: **4** site, spot **5** place **8** location

WHEREAS: **4** when **5** since, while **6** though **7** because **11** considering

WHEREFORE: **3** why **9** therefore, thereupon **11** accordingly

WHEREUPON: **7** whereon **9** thereupon **12** consequently

WHEREVER: **8** anywhere **10** regardless **11** wheresoever

WHEREWITHAL: **5** funds, means, money **6** wealth **7** ability **9** financing, resources

WHET: **4** edge, hone, keen, stir **5** rouse **6** arouse, awaken, excite, incite **7** animate, provoke, sharpen **9** appetizer, stimulate

WHICH: **3** one, who **4** that, what **8** whatever

WHIFF: **4** gust, hint, odor, puff, waft **5** aroma, expel, scent, smell, sniff, tinge, trace **6** breath, inhale, stench **9** strikeout **10** inhalation

WHILE: **3** bit, yet **4** time **5** spell, until **6** during, period, though **7** interim, stretch, whereas **8** although, occasion

WHIM: **4** idea, mood **5** fancy, humor **6** desire, notion, trifle, vagary, vision **7** caprice, fantasy, impulse, thought **11** inclination

WHIMPER: **3** cry, sob **4** fuss, moan, pule, weep **5** whine **6** object, snivel, yammer **7** sniffle **8** complain

WHIMSICAL: **5** droll, funny **7** amusing, bizarre, comical, erratic, playful **8** fanciful, freakish **9** arbitrary, eccentric, fantastic, uncertain **10** capricious **13** unpredictable

WHIMSY: **4** idea, whim **6** notion, vagary **7** caprice, quality, thought

WHINE: **4** fret, fuss, mewl, moan, pule, wail **5** gripe **6** snivel, yammer **7** grumble, whimper **8** complain

WHIP: **3** rod, tan **4** beat, belt, cane, dart, dash, flog, hide, lace, lash, lick, push, urge **5** birch, flash, flick, spank, strap, swish, whisk **6** defeat, punish, stitch, strike, switch, thrash, wallop **7** clobber, conquer, provoke, rawhide, shellac, trounce **8** bludgeon **9** castigate **10** discipline, flagellate **13** cat-o-nine-tails

WHIR: **3** fly, hum **4** move, whiz **5** sound, swirl, swish **6** bustle **7** revolve, vibrate **9** commotion

WHIRL: **4** daze, reel, rush, shot, spin, stab, stir, turn **5** crack, hurry, pivot, swirl, twirl, whack, wheel **6** bustle, circle, flurry, gyrate, rotate, swinge, uproar **7** attempt, flutter, revolve **9** commotion, pirouette **10** revolution

WHIRLPOOL: **4** eddy **5** force, swirl, whorl **6** vortex **7** turmoil **9** Charybdis, maelstrom

WHIRLWIND: **4** stir **5** quick, swift **6** bustle, speedy **7** cyclone, tornado, twister, typhoon **9** hurricane, maelstrom **10** waterspout

WHISK: **3** fly, zip **4** race, rush, whip **5** hurry, scoot, speed, sweep **6** barrel, hasten, motion

WHISKERS: **4** hair **5** beard **6** goatee **7** stubble **8** bristles, mustache **9** sideburns, vibrissae

WHISKEY: **3** rye **4** corn **5** booze, drink, hooch, Irish **6** liquor, rotgut, Scotch **7** alcohol, bourbon, spirits **8** Canadian **9** moonshine **10** usquebaugh **11** mountain dew **14** white lightning
with beer: **11** boilermaker
with vermouth: **9** Manhattan

WHISPER: **4** buzz, hint **5** rumor, trace **6** murmur, mutter, rustle **7** breathe, confide **8** intimate **9** undertone **10** suggestion

WHISTLE: **4** hiss, pipe, toot, warn **5** flute, siren, sound, trill **6** signal **10** instrument

WHIT: **3** bit, jot **4** atom, dash, iota **5** crumb, shred, speck, trace **7** modicum, smidgen **8** fragment, particle

WHITE: **4** ashy, pale, pure **5** ashen, blank, clean, color, hoary, ivory, milky, snowy **6** albino, chalky, grayed, pallid, pearly **7** albumen, neutral, silvery **8** blanched, bleached, innocent, palliate, spotless **9** bloodless, Caucasian, colorless, marmoreal **11** impassioned, transparent

WHITEN: **4** fade, pale **5** frost **6** blanch, bleach **7** decolor, lighten **8** palliate

WHITENESS: **8** paleness **9** hoariness, pallidity

WHITEWASH: **5** paint **6** defeat **7** conceal **8** minimize, palliate **9** sugarcoat **10** camouflage

WHITHER: **5** place, where **6** result **8** position **9** condition

WHITTLE: **3** cut **4** pare, trim **5** carve, shape, shave **6** reduce, sculpt **8** decrease, diminish

WHIZ: **3** fly, hum, zip **4** bolt, buzz, dart, hiss, race, zoom **5** adept, hurry, speed, whisk **6** expert, genius, marvel, master, sizzle, whoosh, wizard **12** professional

WHOLE: **3** all, fit, sum **4** full, hale **5** cured, fixed, gross, sound, total, uncut **6** entire, healed, intact, unhurt **7** healthy, perfect, totally **8** absolute, complete, entirely, entirety, thorough, unbroken **9** aggregate, recovered, undamaged, undivided, uninjured, unscathed **10** unimpaired

WHOLEHEARTED: **4** sure, true **6** ardent **7** devoted, earnest, genuine, serious, sincere **8** complete, emphatic **9** committed, dedicated, steadfast, unfeigned **10** passionate, unreserved **12** enthusiastic

WHOLESALE: **4** bulk **7** massive **8** abundant, complete, discount, sweeping **9** extensive **10** widespread **13** comprehensive

WHOLESOME: **4** good, hale, pure, safe **5** clean, moral, sound **6** decent, hearty, honest, robust **7** ethical, healthy **8** hygienic, innocent, salutary, vigorous **9** healthful, uplifting **10** nourishing, nutritious, salubrious

WHOLLY: **3** all **4** well **5** fully, quite **6** solely **7** totally **8** entirely **10** altogether, completely, thoroughly **11** exclusively

WHOOP: **3** cry **4** crow, hoot, howl, urge, yell **5** cheer, shout **6** holler, hurrah

WHOPPER: **3** big, lie **5** story **7** untruth **9** falsehood **10** remarkable **11** fabrication

WHOPPING: **3** big **4** huge, very **5** giant, great, large **7** immense, mammoth, massive **8** colossal, enormous, gigantic

WHORE: **3** pro **4** slut **5** hussy, tramp, wench **6** harlot, hooker **8** strumpet **10** prostitute **12** streetwalker

WHORL: **4** coil, turn **5** swirl, twirl, twist **6** spiral **9** whirlpool

WHY: **3** how **5** cause, proof **6** motive, reason **7** mystery

WICKED: **3** bad **4** dark, evil, mean, vile **5** adept, awful, cruel, shady **6** adroit, clever, cursed, horrid, risque, rotten, severe, sinful, unholy, unjust **7** beastly, corrupt, harmful, heinous, hellish, immoral, intense, naughty, playful, vicious **8** criminal, depraved, devilish, diabolic, fiendish, sinister, skillful, spiteful, terrible **9** atrocious, dangerous, difficult, effective, heartless, malicious, nefarious, obnoxious, unethical **10** diabolical, outrageous, scandalous, suggestive, unpleasant, villainous **11** destructive, mischievous, troublesome **13** reprehensible

WICKER: **4** rope, twig **5** straw, withe, woven **6** branch

WICKET: **4** arch, door, gate, hoop **6** window **7** opening **8** entrance

WIDE: **3** off **4** full, vast **5** ample, broad, large, loose, roomy **6** astray **7** dilated, general, immense, liberal **8** expanded, spacious, sweeping **9** capacious, distended, expansive, extensive **10** commodious, inaccurate

WIDE-AWAKE: **4** keen **5** alert, aware, quick, sharp **8** vigilant, watchful **9** attentive, observant

WIDELY: **3** far **6** abroad **7** broadly **9** generally **11** extensively, universally

WIDEN: **4** grow, open, ream **5** swell **6** dilate, expand, extend, spread **7** broaden, enlarge, stretch **8** increase, multiply

WIDE-OPEN: **4** ajar, vast **7** exposed, lawless **9** expansive **12** unrestricted

WIDESPREAD: **4** rife **5** broad **6** common **7** general, popular **8** epidemic, sweeping **9** boundless, extensive, pervasive, prevalent, universal **10** acceptable, prevailing **12** unrestricted

WIDTH: **4** span **5** girth, range, scope **6** across, length **7** breadth, compass, measure **8** diameter, wideness **9** amplitude, magnitude, thickness

WIELD: **3** ply, use **4** deal, rule **5** exert, swing **6** direct, employ, handle, manage **7** command, conduct, control, operate, utilize **8** brandish, exercise **10** manipulate

WIFE: **3** Mrs. **4** frau, mate **5** bride **6** missus, spouse **7** consort, partner, uxorial **8** helpmate, helpmeet **9** companion

WIG: **3** rug **4** hair **5** scold **6** berate, carpet, peruke, rebuke, toupee **7** censure, periwig **8** pastiche **9** dignitary, hairpiece, reprimand **12** admonishment

WIGGLE: **4** worm **5** shake, twist **6** shimmy, squirm **7** wriggle **8** squiggle

WIGWAM: **4** home, tent **5** lodge, tepee **7** shelter, wickiup **8** dwelling

WILD: **3** mad **4** daft **5** crazy, dense, feral, nutty, rabid, risky, rough, rowdy **6** crazed, ferine, fierce, insane, madcap, native, raging, raving, savage, stormy, unruly **7** berserk, bestial, bizarre, chaotic, erratic, frantic, furious, intense, lawless, natural, rampant, riotous, uncivil, untamed, vicious, violent **8** carefree, frenetic, frenzied, reckless **9** barbarian, barbarous, delirious, dissolute, disturbed, fanatical, fantastic, ferocious, imprudent, neglected, overgrown, primitive, turbulent, unfounded **10** disorderly, inaccurate, irrational, licentious, outlandish, tumultuous, wilderness **11** disarranged, extravagant, impractical, uncivilized, uninhabited **12** enthusiastic, uncontrolled, uncultivated, unmanageable, unrestrained **13** irresponsible, undisciplined

WILDCAT: **4** lynx, well **5** risky **6** bobcat, feline, strike **7** caracal, illegal, unsound **12** unauthorized

WILDERNESS: **4** bush **5** waste **6** barren, desert, forest, jungle **7** outback **8** badlands **9** boondocks **10** wastelands

WILE: **4** coax, lure, pass, ploy, ruse **5** charm, guile, trick **6** deceit, entice **7** attract, cunning **8** artifice, maneuver, scheming, trickery **9** chicanery, stratagem **10** craftiness **11** shenanigans

WILL: **4** guts, mind, want, wish **5** endow, fancy, leave, spunk **6** bestow, choice, choose, decree, demand, desire, prefer **7** command, courage, longing, resolve **8** bequeath, pleasure, volition **9** testament **10** discipline, preference **11** inclination, self-control **12** instructions **13** determination

WILLFUL: **6** mulish, unruly **7** adamant **8** intended, stubborn **9** obstinate, pigheaded, voluntary **10** bullheaded, deliberate, headstrong **11** intentional **12** premeditated

WILLIAMS, TENNESSEE: **6** author, writer **9** dramatist **10** playwright
nationality: **8** American
wrote: **10** Camino Real **13** The Rose Tattoo **14** Battle of Angels, Garden District, Summer and Smoke **16** Cat on a Hot Tin Roof **17** Orpheus Descending, The Glass Menagerie **18** Suddenly Last Summer

WILLIAM THE CONQUEROR: **16** William the Norman
battle: **8** Hastings
father: **14** Robert the Devil
kingdom: **7** England
title: **4** king

WILLING: **4** fair, game **5** eater, prone, ready **8** amenable, desirous, disposed, inclined, obedient, unforced **9** agreeable, compliant, voluntary **10** consenting, deliberate **11** intentional

WILLINGNESS: **4** zeal **7** consent **8** alacrity **9** eagerness, readiness **10** compliance, enthusiasm

WILLOW: **4** tree, wood **5** shrub
genus: **5** salix
variety: **4** gray **5** black, osier, pussy, white **6** arroyo, autumn, beaked, laurel **7** prairie, sandbar, weeping **8** drooping

WILLOWY: **4** tall **6** limber, pliant, supple **7** lissome, slender **8** flexible, graceful

WILLPOWER: **4** grit **5** drive **8** strength **10** discipline, resolution **11** self-control **13** determination

WILLY-NILLY: **8** perforce **10** ambivalent, disordered, inevitable **11** haphazardly, unavoidable

WILT: **3** sag **4** drop, fade, flag, wane **5** droop **6** weaken, wither **7** dwindle, shrivel **8** collapse

WILY: **3** sly **4** foxy **5** cagey, canny, sharp **6** artful, astute, crafty, shrewd, smooth, sneaky, subtle, tricky **7** cleaver, cunning **8** scheming **10** streetwise

WIN: **3** get, net **4** beat, earn, edge, gain, take **5** charm, score, sweep, upset **6** attain, defeat, obtain, secure **7** achieve, acquire, capture, conquer, prevail, realize, succeed, triumph, victory **8** conquest, overcome **9** influence **10** accomplish

WINCE: **4** reel **5** cower, quail **6** cringe, flinch, recoil, shrink **7** gesture, grimace **8** movement

WIND: **3** air **4** bend, bise, blow, bora, clue, coil, curl, gale, gust, hint, loop, news, puff, reel, talk, turn, wrap **5** blast, crank, curve, draft, scent, smell, snake, storm, trade, twine, twist, weave, whiff **6** breath, breeze, circle, spiral, squall, writhe, zephyr, zigzag **7** chinook, cyclone, entwine, meander, monsoon, revolve, sirocco, tempest, tornado, typhoon, warning, wreathe, wriggle **8** blizzard, entangle **9** harmattan, hurricane, noreaster **10** intimation, suggestion, tramontana **11** geostrophic

WINDFALL: **4** boon, gain, luck **5** bonus, gravy **7** bonanza, fortune, godsend

WINDING: **5** snaky **6** spiral, zigzag **7** bending, coiling, crooked, curving, devious, sinuous, turning **8** flexible, indirect, rambling, twisting **9** intricate **10** convoluted, meandering, roundabout, serpentine

WINDOW: **3** bay, bow **4** rose **5** oriel **6** dormer, lancet **7** lucarne, lunette, opening, picture **8** aperture, casement, fanlight, jalousie, porthole, skylight, vasistas **9** mullioned **10** fanestella

WINDPIPE: **6** gullet, throat **7** airpipe, bronchi, trachea **9** esophagus

WINDSTORM: **4** gale **6** squall **7** cyclone, tornado, twister, typhoon **9** hurricane

WIND UP: **3** end **5** close **6** finish, settle **8** complete, conclude, finalize

WINDY: **4** airy **5** blowy, empty, gusty **6** breezy, drafty, stormy, wordy **7** lengthy, pompous, verbose **8** blustery, boastful, inflated, rambling **9** bombastic, garrulous, talkative **10** boisterous **11** tempestuous, unsheltered

WINDY CITY: **7** Chicago

WINE:
cellar: **6** bodega
concerning: **3** oen **4** oeno **5** vinic **6** vinous
container: **3** tun, vat **4** olpe **5** amula **6** carafe, fiasco, goblet, magnum **7** burette, chalice **8** decanter, jeroboam, oenochoe, wineskin
maker: **6** abkari **7** vintner **8** gourmand
server: **7** steward **9** sommelier
types: **3** dry, red **4** brut, port, rose, sake **5** Rhine, sweet, table, white **6** medium, Muscat, sherry **7** Chablis, Chianti, Madeira, Moselle, natural **8** Bordeaux, Burgundy, muscatel, sauterne, vermouth **9** fortified, sparkling, zinfandel
year: **7** vintage

WING: **3** arm, fly **4** hall, limb, sail **5** annex, flank, wound **6** branch, injure, pennon, pinion **7** airfoil, faction **8** addition, position, squadron **9** appendage, backstage, extension **10** protrusion

WINGED: **4** fast **5** alate, fleet, lofty, rapid, swift **7** sublime, wounded **8** elevated **9** feathered
horse: **7** Pegasus

WINK: **3** bat **5** blink, flash, flirt, gleam, sleep **6** minute, second, signal, squint **7** flicker, instant, nictate, slimmer, sparkle, twinkle **9** nictitate, twinkling

WINNER: **5** champ, first **6** victor **8** champion, medalist **9** conqueror

WINNIE-THE-POOH:
author: **7** AA Milne
characters: **3** Roo **4** Pooh **5** Kanga **6** Eeyore, Piglet, Tigger **16** Christopher Robin
illustrator: **13** Ernest Shepard

WINNING: **5** sweet **7** victory, winsome **8** charming, engaging **9** appealing **10** attractive, successful, triumphant, victorious

WINNOW: **3** fan **4** sort **5** sieve **6** remove, select **7** analyze, examine, extract, scatter **8** disperse, separate **9** eliminate

WINSOME: **4** cute **5** sweet **7** likable, lovable, winning **8** adorable, charming, engaging, pleasant **9** agreeable, appealing **10** attractive, delightful **11** captivating

WINTER: **4** cold **6** season **9** Jack Frost

WINTER'S TALE, THE:
author: **11** Shakespeare
character: **7** Camillo, Perdita **8** Florizel **9** Polixenes **11** King Leontes **13** Queen Hermione

WINTRY: **3** icy **4** cold **5** harsh, snowy **6** arctic, brutal, chilly, frigid, hiemal, stormy **8** chilling, freezing, hibernal **9** cheerless

WIPE: **3** dry, mop, rub **4** blow, gibe, jeer, swab **5** clean, erase, swipe, towel **6** cancel, delete, remove, sponge, stroke **7** abolish **10** annihilate, obliterate **11** exterminate

WIPE OUT: **5** erase **6** cancel, delete **7** abolish, destroy, expunge **8** massacre **9** devastate, eliminate, eradicate, slaughter **10** annihilate, obliterate **11** exterminate

WIRE: **3** rod **4** coil, line **5** cable **6** strand, thread **7** message **8** telegram **9** telegraph

WIRED: **5** bound **7** excited **8** equipped **9** circuited, connected **10** stimulated

WIRY: **4** lean, ropy, thin **5** agile, tough **6** limber, sinewy, strong **7** fibrous, stringy **8** muscular

WISCONSIN:
bird: **5** robin
capital: **7** Madison
cities: **6** Racine **8** Green Bay **9** Milwaukee
explorer: **7** Nicolet
features: **4** Door **5** Dells
flower: **10** wood violet
nickname: **6** Badger
tree: **10** sugar maple
water: **8** Michigan, Superior **9** Winnebago **11** Mississippi

WISDOM: **5** depth, sense **7** insight **8** instinct, judgment, sagacity **9** foresight, knowledge **10** astuteness, experience **12** intelligence **13** enlightenment, understanding **14** discrimination

WISE: **4** keen, sage, wary **5** alert, aware, brash, cagey, canny, cocky, fresh, sassy, slick, smart, sound, witty **6** astute, bright, clever, crafty, manner, method, shrewd, subtle, versed **7** advised, cunning, erudite, explain, knowing, learned, politic, prudent, sapient, skilled, tactful **8** discreet, flippant, informed, profound, sensible, skillful, tactical **9** cognizant, judicious, provident, sagacious, scholarly **10** discerning, insightful, perceptive, reasonable **11** calculating, circumspect, enlightened, experienced, intelligent **13** knowledgeable, sophisticated

WISECRACK: **3** gag **4** jest, joke, quip **5** sally **8** wiseacre **9** witticism

WISE GUY: **8** wiseacre **10** smart aleck **11** smartypants, wisecracker, wisenheimer

WISH: **4** envy goal, hope, itch, want, whim **5** crave, dream, fancy, yearn **6** desire, expect, hanker, hunger, prefer, thirst **7** longing, request **8** yearning **10** aspiration, preference

WISHBONE: **8** clavicle, furculum **9** formation **10** breastbone

WISHFUL: **5** eager **7** anxious, longing, wanting **8** desirous, yearning **9** desirable **12** enthusiastic

WISHY-WASHY: **4** thin, weak **5** bland, wimpy **6** jejune, watery **7** diluted, insipid **8** cowardly, listless, wavering **10** indecisive, spiritless **12** noncommittal

WISP: **4** band, hint, lock, thin, tuft **5** broom, brush, bunch, clean, flock, frail, piece, shred, trace, whisk **6** bundle, rumple, slight, strand **8** fragment **10** indication

WISPY: **5** frail **6** slight **7** slender **8** nebulous

WISTFUL: **3** sad **6** dreamy **7** craving, longing, pensive **8** yearning **9** nostalgic, woebegone **10** melancholy, reflective **11** daydreaming

WIT: **4** card, mind **5** comic, humor, irony, joker **6** acumen, brains, sanity, satire, senses, wisdom **7** balance, cunning, insight, punster, sarcasm **8** comedian, drollery, humorist, keenness, repartee, sageness **9** ingenuity, intellect, quickness **10** cleverness, perception **12**

intelligence **13** comprehension, understanding

WITCH: **3** hag, hex **5** crone, lamia, shrew, sibyl **6** beldam, wizard **7** warlock **8** magician, sorcerer **9** sorceress **11** enchantress, necromancer

WITCHCRAFT: **4** jinx **5** charm, magic, spell **6** occult, voodoo **7** sorcery **8** witchery, wizardry **9** conjuring, sortilege **10** black magic, necromancy **11** enchantment, thaumaturgy

WITH: **3** for **4** near, plus, upon **5** along, among **6** amidst, beside **9** alongside, including **12** accompanying

WITHDRAW: **4** quit, void **5** annul, leave **6** abjure, depart, detach, recall, recant, recede, remove, renege, retire, revoke, shrink **7** nullify, refrain, rescind, retract, retreat, scratch **8** abstract, alienate, evacuate, restrain **9** disengage

WITHDRAWAL: **4** exit **6** exodus **7** retreat **9** departure **10** evacuation, retraction **11** abandonment **12** cancellation

WITHDRAWN: **3** shy **5** aloof, quiet **6** hidden, remote **8** detached, isolated, secluded, solitary **9** reclusive **10** unsociable **11** abandonment, introverted **12** unresponsive

WITHER: **3** age **4** fade, stun, wane, wilt **5** decay, droop, waste, wizen **6** blight, shrink, weaken **7** atrophy, decline, shrivel, wrinkle **8** languish **9** dehydrate **11** deteriorate

WITHERED: **3** dry **4** arid, sere **5** faded **6** shrunk, wilted **7** sapless, stunned, wizened **8** wrinkled **9** shriveled

WITHHOLD: **4** curb, hide, keep **5** check **6** deduct, refuse, retain **7** abstain, conceal, forbear, refrain, repress, reserve **8** disallow, restrain, suppress

WITHIN: **4** into **5** among **6** during, inside, inward **7** indoors **8** interior, internal **10** intramural

WITH-IT: **4** cool **6** modern, modish, trendy **7** current, stylish **12** contemporary

WITHOUT: **5** minus **6** absent, beyond, except, unless **7** lacking, outside **9** outwardly **10** externally

WITHSTAND: **4** bear, cope, defy **5** brace, brave, fight **6** combat, endure, oppose, resist, suffer **7** contest, weather **8** confront, tolerate

WITLESS: **3** mad **5** crazy, silly **6** insane, simple, stupid **7** asinine, foolish, unaware **8** mindless **9** senseless **13** unintelligent

WITNESS: **3** eye, see **4** look, sign, spot, view **5** proof, vouch, watch **6** attend, attest, behold, notice **7** certify, confirm, endorse, observe, sponsor, testify **8** beholder, evidence, observer, onlooker, validate **9** bystander, signatory, spectator, subscribe, testifier, testimony **12** authenticate, substantiate

WITTICISM: **3** gag, pun **4** gibe, jest, joke, quip **5** sally **6** bon mot, remark **9** wisecrack

WITTY: **4** wise **5** comic, funny, sharp **6** bright, clever, jocose, jocund **7** amusing, jocular **8** humorous **9** facetious, ingenious, whimsical **13** scintillating

WITTY SAYING: **4** quip **6** bon mot **7** epigram **8** repartee **9** witticism **12** clever remark

WIZARD: **4** sage, seer **5** shark, witch **6** expert, genius, master, medium **7** diviner, prodigy, warlock **8** conjurer, magician, sorcerer **9** authority **11** clairvoyant, necromancer, thaumaturge **12** professional

WIZARD OF OZ:
author: **9** Frank Baum
characters: **4** Toto **7** Dorothy **9** Munchkins, Scarecrow **11** Tin Woodsman **12** Cowardly Lion
Good Witch: **5** North
setting: **6** Kansas
Wicked Witch: **4** West

WIZENED: **4** aged, lean **5** dried **6** silted **8** shrunken, withered **9** shriveled

WOBBLE: **4** sway **5** lurch, shake, waver, weave **6** quaver, shimmy, teeter, topple, totter **7** stagger, tremble

WOBBLY: **5** rocky, shaky **7** rickety **8** insecure, unstable, unsteady, wavering **10** unbalanced **11** vacillating

WOE: **4** dole **5** gloom, grief **6** dismay, misery, regret, sorrow **7** anguish, despair, tragedy, trouble **8** calamity, disaster, distress **9** heartache, suffering **10** affliction, heartbreak, melancholy, misfortune **11** unhappiness **12** wretchedness

WOEBEGONE: **4** blue, down **5** bleak **6** gloomy, shabby, woeful **7** forlorn **8** dejected, downcast, funereal, troubled **9** depressed **10** dispirited, melancholy **11** dilapidated

WOEFUL: **3** sad **4** dire **5** grave, sorry **6** dismal, paltry **7** pitiful, unhappy **8** dejected, downcast, mournful, wretched **9** depressed, miserable, sorrowful, woebegone **10** dispirited, melancholy **11** distressing **12** disconsolate **13** heartbreaking

WOLF: **4** bolt, gulp, lobo **5** hyena, scarf **6** animal, canine, coyote, gobble, lecher, lupine **7** Don Juan **8** Casanova, lothario, predator **9** womanizer **11** philanderer
genus: **5** canis
pack: **4** rout

WOLVERINE STATE: **8** Michigan

WOMAN: **4** dame, dona, frau, lady, wife **5** donna, femme, lover, madam **6** female, matron, milady **7** beloved, darling, fiancee, signora **8** fraulein, mistress, paramour **9** inamorata **10** sweetheart **11** gentlewoman
attractive: **4** doll **5** belle, filly, pinup, siren, sylph, Venus **6** beauty, eyeful, looker **7** charmer, stunner
combining form: **3** gyn
concerning: **7** gynecic **8** cynaecic **9** muliebral
dignified: **4** lady **5** queen **6** beldam, matron **7** beldame, dowager, heroine **8** princess **9** matriarch **10** grande dame
famous: **3** Eve **4** Meir, Mott **5** Curie, Stowe **6** Austen, Keller, Medusa, Teresa, Tubman **7** Anthony, Earhart, Pandora, Stanton **8** Victoria **9** Catherine, Cleopatra, Joan of Arc, Roosevelt **11** Nightingale
immoral: **4** slut **5** hussy, queen **6** chippy, giglet, giglot, harlot, wanton **7** cocotte, Jezebel, trollop **9** courtesan
intellectual: **7** seeress **12** bluestocking
objectionable: **3** hag **5** shrew, witch **6** gorgon, virago **9** grimalkin, termagant
old: **3** hag **4** dame **5** crone, frump **6** carlin, granny **7** dowager **8** grandame, spinster **9** termagant
pregnant: **7** gravida
strong: **5** titan **6** amazon, virago
unattractive: **3** bag, dog **4** drab **5** crone, dowdy, frump, witch **8** slattern
young: **4** girl, lass, miss **5** filly, wench **6** lassie, maiden **10** demoiselle

WOMANISH: **6** female **8** feminine **10** effeminate **11** unmasculine

WOMANIZER: **4** rake, wolf **7** Don Juan, seducer **8** Casanova **10** ladykiller **11** philanderer

WONDER: **3** awe **5** doubt, think **6** marvel, ponder, puzzle **7** miracle, prodigy **8** question, surprise **9** amazement, curiosity, reverence, sensation, speculate, uncertain **10** admiration, phenomenon **11** uncertainty **12** astonishment

WONDERFUL: **4** fine, good **5** great, super **6** lovely, peachy, superb **7** amazing, strange **8** fabulous, terrific **9** admirable, enjoyable, excellent, fantastic, marvelous **10** incredible, stupendous, surprising **11** astonishing, magnificent, sensational **13** extraordinary

WONT: **3** use **5** habit, usage **6** custom, likely, manner **8** practice **9** tradition **10** accustomed

WONTED: **4** used **5** usual **8** familiar **9** customary **10** accustomed, habituated **12** conventional

WOO: **3** sue **4** coax, seek **5** charm, court, spark, tempt **6** invite **7** address, entreat, solicit **9** importune

WOOD: **3** log **4** fuel **5** grove, hurst, trees, weald, xylem **6** driver, forest, insane, lumber, timber **8** golf club **10** timberland, unbalanced
variety: **3** ash, elm, oak **4** pine, teak **5** aspen, balsa, beech, birch, cedar, maple **6** bamboo, cherry, spruce, tinder, willow **7** hemlock, hickory, redwood **8** chestnut, kindling, mahogany **10** Douglas fir

WOODED: **5** uncut **6** jungly, sylvan **9** arboreous, lumbering

WOODEN: **4** dull, wood **5** heavy, rigid, stiff **6** clumsy, stolid **7** awkward **8** bumbling, lifeless, ungainly **9** unbending, unnatural **10** inflexible, spiritless, ungraceful **11** insensitive, unemotional

WOODLAND: **5** copse, grove, weald **6** forest **10** timberland

WOODSMAN: **6** hunter, logger **7** trapper **8** forester **10** lumberjack

WOODWORK: **5** doors **7** molding **8** paneling **9** finishing, staircase **10** windowsill

WOODY: **6** sylvan, xyloid **8** ligneous

WOOER: **4** beau **5** flame, lover **6** suitor **8** paramour **10** sweetheart

WOOL: **3** fur **4** coat, hair, yarn **5** fiber, tweed **6** duffel, fabric, fleece, frieze, mohair **7** flannel **8** cashmere, covering, material

WOOLLY: **4** soft **5** downy, hairy **6** blurry, fleecy, fluffy, lanate, lanose **7** unclear **8** confused, peronate **12** disorganized

WOOZY: **4** weak **5** dazed, dizzy, drunk, shaky **6** queasy **7** muddled **8** confused, nauseous

WORD: **3** vow **4** chat, dirt, news, poop, talk, term **5** adage, couch, edict, honor, maxim, motto, order, rumor, state, voice **6** advice, assent, avowal, decree, gossip, letter, notice, parole, phrase, pledge, remark, report, repute, ruling, saying, signal, speech **7** account, adjunct, bidding, command, comment, dispute, explain, express, lowdown, mandate, message, promise, proverb, summons, tidings **8** argument, audience, colloquy, dialogue, dispatch, password **9** assertion, direction, discourse, sobriquet, statement, ultimatum, utterance **10** expression **11** affirmation, declaration, information **12** consultation, intelligence **13** communication
action: **4** verb
book: **7** lexicon **9** thesaurus **10** dictionary
combining forms: **3** log **4** logo, onym
connective: **11** conjunction

group: **6** clause, phrase **8** sentence
imitative: **12** onomatopoeia
inventor: **6** coiner **9** neologist
misused: **8** malaprop, solecism **10** spoonerism **11** catachresis, malapropism
naming: **4** noun
new: **7** coinage **9** neologism, neoterism
opposite meaning: **7** antonym
origin: **7** history **9** etymology
root: **6** etymon
same backward/forward: **10** palindrome
same pronunciation: **7** homonym **9** homophone
same spelling: **7** homonym **9** homograph
scrambled: **7** anagram
shortened: **11** contraction **12** abbreviation
square: **10** palindrome
unnecessary: **8** pleonasm

WORD-FOR-WORD: **7** exactly **8** verbatim **9** literally

WORDINESS: **8** verbiage **9** prolixity, verbosity **10** redundancy **11** diffuseness

WORDY: **5** windy **6** chatty, turgid, verbal **7** lengthy **8** babbling **9** bombastic, talkative **10** palaverous, rhetorical

WORK: **3** act, job, till **4** duty, feat, line, mill, move, opus, task, tend, toil **5** chore, craft, exert, forte, grind, labor, pains, piece, skill, slave, solve, stint, sweat, trade **6** drudge, effort, muscle, output, racket, strain, thrive **7** attempt, calling, mission, operate, pattern, perform, pursuit, travail, trouble **8** activity, business, drudgery, endeavor, function, industry, struggle, vocation **9** cultivate, freelance **10** accomplish, commitment, employment, livelihood, manipulate, occupation, production, profession **11** achievement, composition, manufacture, performance, undertaking

WORKABLE: **6** useful, viable **8** feasible, possible **9** practical **10** functional

WORKADAY: **5** plain **7** mundane, prosaic, routine **8** everyday, ordinary **11** commonplace

WORKER: **4** doer, hand, help, peon, scab, serf **5** slave **6** toiler **7** artisan, laborer **8** commuter, employee, hireling, operator **9** operative, performer **10** apprentice **11** breadwinner, craftperson, proletarian

WORKING: **4** busy **6** active **7** engaged **8** employed, laboring, occupied **9** effective, operating **11** functioning

WORKING CLASS: **7** laborer **10** blue-collar **11** proletariat

WORKMANSHIP: **5** skill **7** ability, quality **8** artistry **9** expertise **11** performance **13** craftsmanship

WORK OUT: **5** solve, train **6** handle **7** develop, resolve, satisfy **8** exercise **9** formulate **10** accomplish, compromise

WORK OVER: **3** fix **4** beat, redo **6** repair, revamp, thrash

WORK UP: **6** arouse, excite, incite, refine **7** agitate, develop, enhance, improve **9** stimulate

WORKSHOP: **4** mill **5** plant **6** studio **7** factory **10** laboratory **13** establishment

WORLD: **4** life, race **5** earth, globe, realm **6** cosmos, domain, nature, people, planet **7** kingdom, mankind, society **8** creation, humanity, universe **9** macrocosm, microcosm **10** experience **11** environment

WORLDLY: **5** blase **6** carnal, mortal **7** earthly, knowing, mundane, secular, terrene **8** temporal **9** sublunary **11** terrestrial **12** cosmopolitan **13** materialistic, sophisticated

WORLD WARS:
alliance of I: **6** Allies **13** Central Powers
alliance of II: **4** Axis **6** Allies
allies in I: **3** USA **5** Italy, Japan **6** France, Greece, Russia, Serbia **7** Belgium, Britain, Romania **8** Portugal **10** Montenegro
allies in II: **5** Italy, Japan **7** Germany
battles in I: **5** Marne, Somme, Ypres **6** Verdun **7** Jutland
battles in II: **4** Orel **5** Bulge **6** Sicily **7** Cassino, Iwo Jima, Okinawa **8** Atlantic, Normandy **9** El Alamein
central powers in I: **6** Turkey **7** Germany **8** Bulgaria **14** Austria-Hungary
generals in I: **4** Foch **8** Pershing
generals in II: **6** Patton, Rommel **7** Bradley **9** MacArthur **10** Eisenhower, Montgomery
heroes in I: **4** York **12** Rickenbacker
treaty of I: **10** Versailles

WORLDWIDE: **6** global **7** general **8** catholic, pandemic **9** extensive, planetary, universal **10** ecumenical **13** international

WORM: **3** eel, lug **4** grub, inch **5** crawl, fluke, larva, leech, snake, sneak **6** maggot, mucker, squirm, wiggle, wretch **7** annelid, serpent, wriggle **8** flatworm, helminth, nematode, silkworm, squiggle, tapeworm **9** angleworm, arrowworm, earthworm, penetrate, roundworm, scoundrel, trematode **10** infiltrate, threadworm **11** caterpillar

WORN: **4** beat, shot, weak **5** drawn, spent, tired, weary **6** eroded, wasted **7** damaged, drained, haggard **8** fatigued, impaired **9** exhausted **11** dilapidated

WORN-OUT: **4** sere, shot, used **5** passe, spent, stale, tired, trite **6** effete, frayed, shabby **7** cliched, drained, useless **8** decrepit, depleted, impaired, overused, tattered **9** destroyed, exhausted, hackneyed **10** threadbare **12** deteriorated

WORRIED: **5** tense, upset **6** afraid, uneasy **7** anxious, nervous **8** bothered, troubled, unnerved **9** concerned **10** distraught, distressed

WORRY: **3** woe **4** care, faze, fear, fret, fuss, gnaw, stew **5** annoy, brood, dread, harry, upset **6** badger, bother, fidget, harass, hector, needle, pester, plague, pother, suffer **7** agonize, anguish, anxiety, bedevil, concern, despair, disturb, perturb, torment, torture, trouble **8** distress, struggle, unsettle **10** disconcert, uneasiness **11** disturbance

WORSEN: **4** sink, slip **5** decay, slide **7** decline, regress **8** diminish **10** exacerbate, retrogress **11** deteriorate

WORSHIP: **4** love **5** adore, exalt, honor, worth **6** admire, homage, prayer, revere **7** dignity, glorify, idolize, liturgy, respect, vespers **8** blessing, devotion, idolatry, oblation, offering, sanctify, venerate **9** adoration, celebrate, reverence **10** invocation, reputation, veneration

WORSHIPER: **6** adorer, votary **7** devotee **8** disciple **10** churchgoer

WORST: **3** bad **4** beat, best **5** least, outdo **6** defeat, lowest **8** inferior **9** overthrow **11** unfavorable

WORT: **4** herb, root **5** plant

WORTH: **4** cost, note **5** merit, price, value **6** assets, bounty, esteem, riches, virtue, wealth, weight **7** fortune, quality, stature **8** holdings **9** deserving, desirable, substance **10** excellence, importance, usefulness **11** equivalence, possessions **12** appreciation, significance

WORTHLESS: **3** low **4** base, idle, lazy, vain **5** cheap, junky **6** barren, cheesy, futile, paltry, trashy **7** fustian, trivial, useless **8** wretched **9** frivolous, fruitless, pointless, valueless **10** despicable **11** incompetent, ineffective, meaningless, unimportant **12** unproductive **13** insignificant

WORTHWHILE: **6** useful **7** helpful **8** valuable **9** important, lucrative **10** beneficial, productive, profitable **11** justifiable **12** constructive

WORTHY: **4** good **5** noble **6** honest **7** ethical, fitting **8** deserved, laudable, reliable, sterling, valuable **9** admirable, befitting, competent, deserving, estimable, exemplary, honorable, qualified, reputable, venerable **10** dependable **11** commendable, meritorious, respectable

WOUND: **3** cut **4** gash, harm, hurt, pain, stab, wing **5** break, slash, sting **6** bruise, damage, injure, injury, trauma **7** anguish, scratch **8** distress, puncture **9** contusion **10** affliction, laceration

WOW: **4** howl, rave **5** smash **7** success, triumph **8** pleasure **9** amazement

WRACK: **4** kelp, ruin **5** trash, wreck **6** avenge, defeat **7** destroy, seaweed, torment **8** calamity, decimate, wreckage **9** shipwreck, vengeance **11** destruction

WRAITH: **5** ghost **6** spirit, vision **7** phantom, shadowy, specter **10** apparition **12** doppelganger

WRANGLE: **4** spat, tiff **5** argue, brawl, fight **6** bicker, haggle, hassle, ruckus **7** dispute, quarrel, quibble **8** argument, squabble **11** altercation, controversy **12** disagreement

WRAP: **4** cape, fold, furl, hide, mask, roll, veil, wind **5** cloak, cover, drape, scarf, shawl, stole **6** bundle, encase, enfold, shroud, swathe **7** bandage, blanket, conceal, enclose, envelop, muffler, package **8** surround **10** camouflage

WRAPPER: **4** gown **5** cover **6** casing, folder, jacket **8** envelope

WRAP UP: **3** end **5** close **6** finish **7** package **8** complete, conclude

WRATH: **3** ire **4** fury, hate, rage **5** anger **6** temper **7** offense **9** animosity, hostility **10** resentment **11** indignation

WRATHFUL: **3** mad **5** angry **6** raging **7** enraged, furious **8** incensed **10** displeased, infuriated, vindictive

WREAK: **4** vent **5** cause, exact, force **6** avenge, punish **7** execute, inflict, revenge, unleash **9** vengeance

WREATH: **4** band **5** crown **6** laurel **7** chaplet, circlet, coronet, festoon, flowers, garland

WREATHE: **4** coil, curl, wind **5** twist **6** spiral **7** entwine **8** encircle

WRECK: **4** bash, hulk, ruin, undo **5** break, crash, level, ruins, smash, spoil, total **6** damage, jalopy, junker, mangle, pileup, ravage **7** clunker, destroy, disable, shatter, smashup **8** collapse, demolish, sabotage **9** undermine, vandalize **11** destruction, devastation

WRECKAGE: **5** ruins **7** flotsam, remains **8** remnants, shambles

WRENCH: **4** bend, jerk, pain, pull, tear, tool, turn, yank **5** Allen, pinch, twist, wrest, wring **6** injury, monkey, sprain, strain, twinge **7**

distort, spanner, squeeze **8** distress **10** distortion

WREST: **4** rend, take **5** exact, force, seize, usurp, wring **6** extort, snatch, wrench **7** distort, extract, squeeze, wrestle **8** disapply

WRESTLE: **3** tug **4** toil **5** fight **6** battle, squirm, strive, tangle, tussle **7** grapple, wriggle **8** struggle, scuffle

WRESTLING:
arena: **4** ring **8** palestra
holds: **6** nelson **8** headlock, scissors **10** half nelson
terms: **3** mat, pin **4** fall, hipe **8** takedown
types: **4** sumo **5** glima, sambo, yagli **9** freestyle, schwingen **10** Greco-Roman
weight classes: **9** flyweight **11** heavyweight, lightweight **12** bantamweight, middleweight, welterweight **13** featherweight **16** light-heavyweight **17** middle-heavyweight

WRETCH: **3** bum, dog **4** liar, scum, worm **5** brute, knave, loser, rogue, scamp, snake **6** beggar, pauper, rascal **7** ingrate, lowlife, outcast, villain **8** derelict, scalawag **9** miscreant, scoundrel **10** blackguard **11** rapscallion

WRETCHED: **4** base, foul, mean, poor, vile **5** sorry **6** abject, dismal, gloomy, paltry, rotten, scurvy, woeful **7** caitiff, doleful, forlorn, pitiful, unhappy **8** dejected, dreadful, inferior, pitiable, terrible **9** afflicted, miserable, sorrowful, woebegone, worthless **10** calamitous, deplorable, depressing, despicable, distressed, melancholy **11** unfortunate **12** contemptible

WRIGGLE: **4** ooze, turn, wind, worm **5** crawl, dodge, evade, slink, snake, twist **6** squirm, twitch, wiggle, writhe, zigzag

WRING: **5** choke, pinch, press, screw, twist, wrest **6** wrench **7** contort, extract, squeeze **8** compress, strangle

WRINKLE: **4** fold, idea, line, seam **5** crimp, fancy, pleat, ridge, trick **6** crease, furrow, notion, pucker, rimple **7** crimple, crinkle, crumple, gimmick, scrunch, shrivel **10** innovation **11** corrugation

WRINKLED: **5** lined **6** folded, rugose, rugous **7** creased **8** furrowed, puckered, unironed, withered **10** corrugated

WRIT: **5** breve, brief, order **6** decree **7** command, mandate, process, summons, warrant, writing **8** document, replevin, subpoena **10** injunction **12** habeas corpus

WRITE: **3** pen **4** note, sign **5** draft **6** author, create, indite, pencil, record, scrawl, scribe **7** compose, scratch **8** inscribe, scribble **9** autograph **10** correspond **11** communicate

WRITE DOWN: **4** note **5** enter **6** record **10** depreciate

WRITE OFF: **4** drop **5** lower **6** cancel, deduct **7** devalue **8** amortize, discount **9** downgrade **10** depreciate

WRITER: **4** hack, poet **6** author, critic, editor, scribe **7** copyist **8** composer, essayist, fabulist, lyricist, novelist, reporter, reviewer **9** columnist, dramatist, scrivener, wordsmith **10** biographer, journalist, playwright **12** calligrapher **13** correspondent

WRITHE: **4** bend, curl, jerk, toss, turn, worm **5** twist, wrest, wring **6** squirm, suffer, wiggle **7** agonize, contort, shrivel, wriggle **8** squiggle

WRITING: **4** book, play, poem, saga, skit **5** diary, essay, novel, paper, print, prose, verse, words **6** column, letter, script, thesis **7** article, epistle, journal **8** contract, document, graffiti, longhand **9** discourse, editorial, shorthand, signature **10** literature, manuscript, penmanship **11** calligraphy, composition, handwriting, inscription, orthography, publication, stenography **12** dissertation, transcribing **13** autobiography, hieroglyphics

WRONG: **4** awry, evil, harm, hurt, tort, vice **5** abuse, amiss, crime, error, false, unfit **6** astray, erring, faulty, injure, injury, malign, offend, sinful, slight, unfair, unjust, untrue, wicked **7** blunder, corrupt, crooked, defraud, illegal, illicit, immoral, inexact, misdeed, reverse, slander, twisted, vicious **8** dishonor, improper, iniquity, mistaken, opposite, tortuous **9** dishonest, erroneous, incorrect, injurious, injustice, misguided, prejudice, unethical, violation **10** inaccurate, iniquitous, unsuitable **11** inexcusable **12** unacceptable **13** inappropriate, miscalculated

WRONGDOER: **5** crook, felon **6** sinner **7** culprit **8** criminal, offender, violator **9** miscreant **10** lawbreaker, malefactor, trespasser **11** perpetrator **12** transgressor

WRONGDOING: **3** sin **4** evil **5** crime **7** misdeed, offense **8** iniquity **9** violation **10** misconduct **11** malpractice, misbehavior

WRONGFUL: **6** wicked **7** illegal, illicit **8** criminal, improper **9** dishonest, unethical **12** illegitimate

WROUGHT: **4** made **6** formed, molded, shaped, worked **7** created **8** hammered **9** fashioned, processed **10** ornamented **11** constructed **12** manufactured

WRY: **4** awry, bent **5** askew, avert **6** ironic, warped **7** amusing, crooked, cynical, twisted **8** perverse, sardonic **9** contorted, distorted, sarcastic

WUTHERING HEIGHTS:
author: **9** Ellis Bell **11** Emily Bronte
characters: **7** Hareton **10** Heathcliff, Mr. Earnshaw **11** Edgar Linton **15** Hindley Earnshaw **17** Catherine Earnshaw
setting: **7** England **9** Liverpool

WYOMING:
bird: **10** meadowlark
capital: **8** Cheyenne
cities: **6** Casper **7** Laramie
explorer: **6** Colter
features: **7** Rockies **10** Grand Teton **11** Yellowstone
flower: **10** paintbrush
native: **10** Wyomingite
nickname: **8** Equality
part of: **17** Louisiana Purchase
tree: **10** cottonwood
water: **11** Old Faithful

X

XANTHIPPE: **3** hag **4** harpy, scold, shrew **6** nagger, virago **8** fishwife **9** termagant
husband: **8** Socrates

XENON: **7** element

XENOPHON: **6** writer **7** soldier
nationality: **5** Greek
teacher: **8** Socrates
wrote: **8** Anabasis

XEROX: **4** copy **5** ditto **6** copier **9** duplicate, reproduce, trademark

XERXES:
battles: **6** Platae **7** Salamis **11** Thermopylae
destroyed: **6** Athens
kingdom: **6** Persia
title: **4** king

XMAS: **4** Noel, Yule **7** holiday **9** Christmas

X-RAY: **3** MRI **7** CAT scan, picture **8** actinism **11** Roentgen ray **13** radioactivity
inventor: **8** Roentgen
treatment: **12** radiotherapy

XYLOPHONE: **7** gambang, marimba **8** carillon **10** instrument, vibraphone

Y

YACHT: **4** boat, race, sail, ship **5** craft, ketch, racer, sloop **7** cruiser **8** sailboat

YAHOO: **4** boor, lout **5** beast, brute **6** savage **9** barbarian, roughneck

YAHWEH: **3** God **7** Creator, Jehovah **8** Almighty

YAK: **3** yap **4** chat, talk **6** babble, jabber, yammer **7** chatter, prattle

YALE UNIVERSITY:
location: **8** New Haven **11** Connecticut
mascot: **7** bulldog
named after: **9** Elihu Yale

YALTA:
location: **7** Ukraine
participants: **6** Stalin **9** Churchill, Roosevelt
significance: **10** conference

YAMMER: **3** cry, yap **4** chat, fuss, talk, yell **5** gripe, shout, whine **6** babble, scream, squawk **7** chatter, grumble, whimper **8** complain **9** bellyache

YANK: **3** tug **4** jerk, pull **5** pluck, wrest **6** snatch, twitch **7** extract

YANKEE: **4** Yank **6** gringo **7** soldier **8** doughboy **9** Easterner **12** Americanized

YAP: **3** gab, yak **4** bark, chat, yelp **5** scold **6** babble, gossip, jabber, rustic, yammer **7** bumpkin, chatter, lecture, prattle **9** hillbilly **10** clodhopper

YARD: **4** lawn, quad **5** court, garth, grass **6** garden, length **7** confine, grounds **9** curtilage, enclosure **10** playground, quadrangle **11** measurement

YARDSTICK: **4** rule **5** gauge, model, ruler **7** measure **8** standard **9** benchmark, criterion **10** touchstone

YARN: **4** tale, wool **5** fable, fiber, story **6** fleece, thread **8** anecdote **9** adventure, narrative **11** fabrication

YAW: **4** turn, veer **5** curve, weave **6** swerve, zigzag **7** deviate **8** unsteady

YAWL: **4** boat **5** dandy **6** vessel **8** sailboat

YAWN: **4** bore, gape, open **5** chasm **6** cavity, divide, drowse, tedium **7** opening

YAWP: **3** cry, yap **4** bark, bawl, fuss, talk, yelp **5** gripe **6** bellow, scream, squawk, yammer **8** complain

YEA: **3** aye, yes **4** okay, vote, yeah **5** truly **6** indeed **11** affirmative

YEAR: **4** time **5** cycle **6** period **7** vintage
types: **4** leap **5** lunar, solar **6** fiscal, school **7** natural **8** calendar, sidereal, tropical **10** sabbatical **12** astronomical

YEARLING: **6** animal **8** suckling **9** racehorse
age: **3** one
author: **7** Rawlings
characters: **4** Fawn, Jody
setting: **4** farm **7** Florida

YEARLY: **6** annual **8** annually, per annum **9** perennial, regularly

YEARN: **3** yen **4** ache, itch, long, lust, pine, pity, want, wish **5** crave **6** desire, grieve, hanker, hunger, thirst

YEARS: **3** age, era **4** time **7** oldness **8** agedness, senility **10** senescence

YEAST: **4** barm, foam **5** agent, froth **6** fungus, leaven **7** ferment **8** catalyst

YEATS, WILLIAM BUTLER: **4** poet **9** dramatist **10** playwright
founded: **12** Abbey Theatre
nationality: **5** Irish
wrote: **7** Deirdre **9** Byzantium, Crazy Jane, Purgatory **11** Lapis Lazuli **12** The Herne's Egg **13** Long-Legged Fly, The Secret Rose **15** In the Seven Woods, The Winding Stair **16** Responsibilities

YELL: **3** cry **4** call, howl, roar, wail, yowl **5** cheer, shout, whoop **6** bellow, holler, scream, shriek, squawk, squeal **7** protest, screech

YELLOW: **4** mean, yolk **5** amber, color, lemon, ochre, tinge **6** afraid, butter, canary, coward, craven, flaxen, golden, sallow **7** chicken, gutless, mustard, saffron, unmanly **8** cowardly **9** jaundiced **10** frightened, melancholy **11** sensational, treacherous **12** contemptible, dishonorable

YELLOWBELLY: **6** coward **7** chicken, quitter **8** poltroon

YELLOWISH: **5** sandy **6** creamy, flaxen, golden, tinged

YELP: **3** cry, yak, yap, yip **4** bark, hoot, howl **5** cheep, shout, sound **6** outcry, shriek, squeal **7** screech **8** complain

YEMEN:
capital: **5** Sanaa
cities: **4** Aden, Ta'iz **7** Al-Mukha **10** Al-Hudaydah
continent: **4** Asia
ethnic groups: **4** Arab **6** Indian **7** Negroid
islands: **5** Perim **7** Kamaran, Socotra
languages: **6** Arabic
monetary unit: **4** rial
water: **11** Bab-el-Mandeb

YEN: **4** ache, lust, pine, want **5** crave, money, yearn **6** desire, hanker, hunger, thirst **7** longing, passion **8** currency, languish **10** aspiration **11** inclination

YEOMAN: **5** churl, clerk **6** farmer, worker **7** servant **8** commoner **9** assistant, attendant **10** freeholder **11** subordinate

YES: **3** aye, oui, yea, yep, yup **4** okay, true, yeah **5** agree, Roger **6** assent, gladly, indeed, really **7** exactly, granted **9** assuredly, certainly, naturally, precisely **10** definitely, positively **11** affirmative **12** emphatically
French: **3** oui
German: **2** ja
Russian: **2** da
Spanish: **2** si

YESTERDAY: **4** past **6** before, bygone **7** earlier **8** recently **10** previously

YET: **3** but **4** also **5** along, still, until **6** except, though, withal **7** besides, despite, finally, further, however, someday **8** although, hitherto, sometime **10** eventually **11** furthermore, nonetheless **12** nevertheless

YIELD: **3** bow, net, pay **4** bear, bend, cave, cede, crop, fold, give, obey, quit **5** admit, agree, allow, defer, grant, stoop, waive **6** accede, afford, buckle, comply, income, kowtow, output, permit, profit, render, resign, return, reward, soften, submit, supply **7** abandon, concede, consent, crumple, harvest, produce, revenue, succumb, truckle **8** collapse, earnings, generate **9** acquiesce, surrender **10** capitulate, recompense, relinquish **11** accommodate, acknowledge

YIELDING: **4** meek, soft **6** docile, pliant, spongy, supple **7** elastic, passive, pliable **8** cracking, flexible, obedient **9** compliant, tractable **10** submissive **12** nonresistant

YODEL: **4** sing **5** carol, shout, trill **6** warble

YOGI: **5** fakir **6** mystic **7** ascetic

YOKE: **3** tie **4** bail, bond, join, link, pair, span, team, vice **5** brace, clamp, frame, hitch, marry, strap **6** burden, collar, couple, fasten **7** bondage, combine, enslave, harness, oppress, serfdom, slavery **8** crossbar, restrain **9** associate, servitude, thralldom **10** oppression

YOKEL: **3** oaf **4** boor, clod, hick, lout, rube **6** rustic **7** bumpkin, hayseed **10** clodhopper

YOLK: **6** yellow **8** vitellus

YONDER: **5** there **6** remote **7** distant, faraway, farther, further, thither

YOUNG: **3** new, raw **4** baby, weak **5** brood, child, fresh, green, minor **6** active, callow, infant, junior, litter, tender **7** budding, newborn, puerile **8** childish, ignorant, immature, juvenile, youthful **9** fledgling, infantile, offspring, pubescent, stripling, succulent **10** adolescent, unseasoned **11** undeveloped **13** inexperienced

YOUNGSTER: **3** boy, cub, kid, lad, pup, tot **4** babe, baby, colt, girl, lass, tike **5** child, filly, pupil, youth **6** junior **8** teenager **9** fledgling, stripling **10** adolescent

YOUTH: **3** bud **5** bloom, minor, prime **7** gossoon, puberty **8** juvenile, teenager **9** childhood, fledgling, innocence, stripling, youngster **10** adolescent **11** adolescence

YOUTHFUL: **3** new **5** fresh, green, young **6** active, boyish, callow **7** budding, girlish, puerile **8** childish, immature, juvenile, vigorous **10** adolescent

YOWL: **3** cry **4** bawl, howl, roar, wail, yell, yelp **5** sound **6** bellow, holler, scream, squall

YUGOSLAVIA:
capital: **8** Belgrade
cities: **5** Split **6** Rijeka, Skopje, Zagreb **9** Ljubljana
continent: **6** Europe
ethnic groups: **4** Serb **8** Albanian
features: **7** Dinaric **9** Dalmatian
languages: **7** Serbian **8** Albanian **9** Hungarian **10** Macedonian
monetary unit: **5** dinar
republics: **6** Bosnia, Serbia **7** Croatia **8** Slovenia **9** Macedonia **11** Herzegovina
water: **6** Danube **7** Shkoder

YUKON TERRITORY:
capital: **10** Whitehorse
cities: **4** Mayo **6** Dawson
country: **6** Canada
features: **8** Klondike **10** Mount Logan
water: **5** Yukon **8** Klondike

YULE: **4** Noel, Xmas **9** Christmas

Z

ZACHARIAS:
also called: **9** Zachariah
son: **14** John the Baptist
wife: **9** Elizabeth

ZAIRE:
capital: **8** Kinshasa
cities: **4** Boma **6** Matadj **7** Kananga **9** Kisangani **10** Lubumbashi
continent: **6** Africa
ethnic groups: **5** Bantu
features: **9** Ruwenzori
languages: **4** Luba **5** Kongo, Mongo **6** French, Rwanda
monetary unit: **5** zaire
water: **5** Zaire **6** Edward **10** Tanganyika **14** Mobutu Sese Seko

ZAMBIA:
capital: **6** Lusaka
cities: **5** Kabwe, Kitwe, Ndola **7** Chipata **10** Livingston
continent: **6** Africa
ethnic groups: **5** Bantu
features: **6** Kariba
languages: **5** Bantu **7** English
monetary unit: **6** kwacha
water: **7** Zambezi **13** Victoria Falls

ZANY: **4** card, dolt, fool **5** batty, clown, comic, crazy, daffy, dotty, funny, goofy, joker, loony, moron, nutty, wacky **6** madcap, screwy **7** bizarre, buffoon, comical, idiotic **8** clownish, comedian, humorous **9** eccentric, harlequin, ludicrous, simpleton, slapstick **10** outlandish

ZAP: **3** hit **4** kill **6** defeat, strafe, strike **7** bombard, destroy **9** irradiate

ZEAL: **4** fire, zest **5** ardor, drive, gusto **6** desire, fervor, spirit **7** passion **8** devotion **9** diligence, eagerness, intensity **10** enthusiasm, initiative, intentness **11** inclination **13** determination

ZEALOT: **5** bigot, fiend **6** votary **7** devotee, fanatic **8** disciple, follower, votaress **9** extremist **10** enthusiast

ZEALOUS: **4** avid, warm **5** eager, rabid **6** ardent, fervid **7** burning, devoted, earnest, fervent **8** frenetic, obsessed, spirited **9** dedicated **10** passionate **12** enthusiastic

ZEBULUN:
father: **5** Jacob
mother: **4** Leah
tribe: **11** Zebulunites

ZENITH: **3** cap, top **4** acme, apex, peak **5** crest, crown **6** apogee, climax, height, summit, vertex **8** meridian, pinnacle **11** culmination

ZEPHYR: **4** airy, wind, yarn **6** breeze, fabric

ZEPPELIN: **5** blimp **7** airship **9** dirigible

ZERO: **3** nil, nul, zip **4** void **5** aught, blank, zilch **6** cipher, naught, nobody, number **7** nothing, shutout **8** goose egg **9** nonentity **10** irrelevant **11** temperature

ZEST: **4** bite, kick, snap, tang, zeal, zing **5** gusto, punch, savor, smack, spice, taste **6** bounce, energy, flavor, relish **7** delight, passion **8** piquancy, pleasure **10** enthusiasm, excitement

ZESTFUL: **4** racy **5** flair, spicy **7** dynamic, panache, pungent **8** spirited, vigorous

ZESTY: **5** spicy, tangy **6** snappy **7** pungent **8** poignant, vivacity

ZEUS:
also called: **7** Alastor, Jupiter
father: **11** Titan Cronus
form: **4** bull, swan
lived: **5** Crete **12** Mount Olympus
loved by: **6** Europa
mother: **4** Rhea
oracle: **6** Dodona
relatives: **3** Ate, Gad **4** Ares, Hebe, Hera, Juno, Rhea **5** Arcas, Argus, Danae, Hades, Irene, Kjore, Metis **6** Aeacus, Apollo, Athena, Cronus, Hermes, Kronos, Semele, Tityus **7** Artemis, Astraea, Perseus **8** Dardanus, Despoina, Dionysos, Dionysus, Heracles, Hercules, Poseidon, Tantalus **9** Aphrodite **10** Hephaestus, Persephone, Proserpina **11** Helen of Troy, Persephassa
ruled: **5** earth **6** heaven
weapon: **11** thunderbolt

ZIGZAG: **4** tack, turn, worm **5** weave **6** swerve, wiggle **7** chevron, erratic, snaking, stagger, winding, wriggle **8** traverse **10** meandering **11** fluctuating

ZILCH: **4** zero **5** aught **6** naught **7** nothing **8** goose egg **9** nonentity

ZIMBABWE:
capital: **6** Harare
cities: **5** Gweru **6** Hwange, Kwekwe, Mutare **8** Bulawayo
continent: **6** Africa
ethnic groups: **5** Shona **7** Ndebele
features: **6** Hwange **8** Kalahari **13** Great Zimbabwe
languages: **5** Shona **7** English **9** Sinde Bele
monetary unit: **6** dollar
water: **7** Limpopo, Zambezi

ZINC: **5** metal **7** element
coat: **9** galvanize

ZING: **3** pep, vim, zip **4** dash, elan, zest **5** gusto, oomph, sound, vigor **6** energy, lively, spirit **9** criticize, vivacious **10** enthusiasm

ZION: **6** heaven, Israel, utopia **7** nirvana **8** paradise

ZIP: **3** fly, vim **4** buzz, dash, rush, whiz, zero, zest, zing, zoom **5** aught, gusto, hurry, speed, vigor, whisk, zilch **6** breeze, bustle, energy, naught **7** pizzazz **8** goose egg, vitality **10** enthusiasm

ZIPPY: **4** spry **5** agile, brisk **6** lively, snappy **9** sprightly

ZODIAC:
Aquarius: **10** Jan 20-Feb 19 **14** the Water Bearer
Aries: **6** the Ram **10** Mar 22-Apr 20
Cancer: **7** the Crab **12** June 23-July 23
Capricorn: **7** the Goat **10** Dec 23-Jan 19
Gemini: **8** the Twins **11** May 22-June 22
Leo: **7** the Lion **11** July 24-Aug 23
Libra: **9** the Scales **10** the Balance **11** Sept 24-Oct 23

Pisces: **9** the Fishes **10** Feb 20-Mar 21
Sagittarius: **9** the Archer **10** Nov 23-Dec 22
Scorpio: **10** Oct 24-Nov 22 **11** the Scorpion
Taurus: **7** the Bull **10** Apr 21-May 21
Virgo: **9** the Virgin **11** Aug 24-Sept 23

ZONE: **4** area, band, belt, path **5** realm, tract **6** region, sector, sphere **7** circuit, section, segment **8** district **9** territory

ZONKED: **4** high, stun **5** drunk **6** stoned, wasted **7** drugged **9** plastered **10** inebriated **11** intoxicated

ZOO: **4** park **6** aviary **8** vivarium **9** menagerie

ZOOM: **3** fly, hum, zip **4** buzz, dart, dash, rush, soar, whiz **5** climb, speed, swoop **6** streak

Prefixes

ABNORMAL: dys

ABOUT: amhi

ABOVE: hyper, super, supra

ACCESSORY: par, para

ACROSS: di, dia, trans

ADDITIONAL: super

ADVOCATING: pro

AFTER: meta, post

AGAIN: an, ana

AGAINST: ant, anth, anti, cat, cata, cath, cato, contra, kat, kata, kath, kato

AHEAD: pre

ALMOST: pen, pene

ALONGSIDE: par, para

ALTERNATE: counter

AMONG: inter

ANEW: an, ana

APART: dis

AROUND: ambi, circum, peri

ASUNDER: dis

AT THE FRONT: pre

AWAY FROM: ap, aph, apo

BACK: an, ana, retro

BEFORE: ante, pre, pro

BEFOREHAND: pre

BESIDE: par, para

BETWEEN: inter, intra

BEYOND: extra, praeter, preter, sur, trans, ultra

BOTH: ambi

CHEMICAL: ox, oxa

CHIEF: arch, archi

COMBATING: ant, anth, anti

CORRESPONDING: counter

DEPRIVED OF: dis

DETACHED: ap, aph, apo

DIFFERENT: ap, aph, apo

DIFFICULT: dys

DISEASED: dys

DOWN: cat, cata, cath, cato, kat, kata, kath, kato, nan, nano

EARLIER: ante

EXCESS: hyper

EXCESSIVE: sur
EXTREME: arch, archi
FAULTY: par, para
FORWARD: ante
FRONT: pro
GREAT: arch, archi
HALF: hemi, semi
HIGHER: super, supra
IMPROPER: mis
IN ADVANCE: pre
INCORRECT: mis
LATER: meta
LESS THAN: hypo
LOW-PITCHED: contra
LOWER: hypo
MISTAKEN: mis
NEAR: pros
NEARER: cis
NEARER TO: eph, epi
NEGATIVE: dis
NOT: non
ONE: uni
OPPOSED: dis
OPPOSING: ant, anth, anti
OPPOSITE: counter
OUTER: eph, epi
OUTSIDE: extra
OVER: eph, epi, extra, hyper, super, supra, sur
PARTIAL: demi, semi
PRIME: arch, archi
PRINCIPAL: arch, archi
PRIOR: ante, pro
RESEMBLING: par, para
RETALIATORY: counter
REVERSE: dis, dys
RIVAL: anth, anti
ROUND: peri
RULER: arch
SECONDARY: sub
SINGLE: uni
SUBSEQUENT: post
SUBSTITUTING: pro
SUCCEEDING: meta
SURROUNDING: circum, peri
THROUGH: di, dis, per
THROUGHOUT: per
TOGETHER: co, col, com, con, cor, sy, sym, syn
TOWARD: pros
TRANSCENDING: meta, supra
TRANSFORMATION: meta
TWO: du, duo, twi
UNDER: hypo, sub, intra
UNDERNEATH: intra
UNFAVORABLE: dys
UP: an, ana, sur
UPON: eph, epi
UPWARD: ano
WITH: co, col, com, con, cor, sym, syn
WITHIN: intra
WRONG: mis

Suffixes

ABUNDANCE: ose

ACCOMPLISHING: ive

ACT: ade, ance, ion, ure

ACTION: age, ance, ence, ing, ization

ACT UPON: ate

ADHERENT: ist, ite

ADJECTIVE: ular

AGENCY: ator, eer

AGENT: ator, eer, facient, fic, ier

ALCOHOL: itol

APPROXIMATELY: ish

ART: ery

BECOMING: escence, escent

BEGINNING: escent

BEING: ant, ent, ical, ure

BELONGING TO: an, ean, ian, ish

CAPABLE: able, ible

CAPABLE OF: ile

CAUSED BY: ical

CAUSING: able, facient, fic, ible

CHARACTER: ery

CHARACTERISTIC: ism

CHARACTERISTIC OF: ical, ish, ist, istic, istical

CHEMICAL: ane, ein, eine, ene, idin, ile, ine, ite, ole, olic, ose, ylene

CITIZEN: ese, ian, ist, ite

CITY: polis

COLLECTION: ery

COLLECTION OF: age

COMPOUND: ate

CONDITION: ance, ate, ence, ency, hood, ile, ism, ment, osis

CULT: ism

DEGREE: ity

DESCENDANT: ite

DIMINUTIVE: cle, cular, ette, ole, ule

DIRECTION: ling

DISEASE: itis, oma

DOCTRINE: ism

DOER: ast, ator, eer, facient, ier, ist, ster

EXISTING: ent

EXPERT: ician, ist

FEMALE: ine

FEMININE: ette

FIT: able, ible

FORM: ify

FORMATION: osis

FULL OF: ous

FUNCTION: ate, ure

GROUP: ery, ome

GROUP OF: ette

IMITATION: ette

INFERIOR: ling

INFLAMMATION: itis

INHABITANT: ese, ite

INSTRUMENT: tron

LANGUAGE: ese

LIKE: ose

LITTLE: ette

LITTLE ONE: el, elle, ium, kin, kins, ock

MAKE: fly

MARKED BY: ling

MINERAL: ite

MUSICAL INSTRUMENT: ina, ine

NATIVE: ite

OBJECT: ment

OFFICE: ate, dom, ship, ure

OFFSPRING: ite

OLD: ster

ORDINAL: eth, th

PARTICIPANT: ster

PERTAINING TO: ese, ile

PLACE: arium, ary, ery, orium

[illegible]ACE FOR: ory

PLACE OF: age

PLACES: aria

PLANT: acea

PLANTS: aceae, ales

PRACTICE: ery, ics, ism

PRACTIONER: ician

PROCESS: age, ence, ing, ion, ization, ment, osis, ure

PRODUCE: ade

PROFESSION: ship

QUALITY: ance, ancy, ence, ency, good, ice, ity, ness, ship

RANK: ate

REALM: dom

REFLECTING: escent

RELATED TO: ina, ine

RELATING TO: ative, ean, ese, ial, ical, ile, ine, ist, istic, istical, itious, ory

RESEMBLING: ular

RESULT: ization, ment

SERVING FOR: ory

SKILL: ics, ship

SMALL: ling

SMALL ONE: ula, ule, ulum, ulus

SPECIALIST: ician

SPECIALIZED IN: an, ean, ian

STATE: age, ance, ancy, ate, ation, dom, ence, ency, ery, hood, ion, ism, ity, ization, ment, ness, osis, ship

STEM: ome

STUDY: ics

STYLE: esque

SUBSTITUTE: ette

SUGAR: ose, ulose

SUPERLATIVE: est
SUPPORTER: ite
SWEET DRINK: ade
SYSTEM: ism
TENDENCY: itis
TENDING TOWARD: ive
THEORY: ism
THING: ant, orium
THINGS: oria
TRACE OF: ish
TRADE: ery
TRAIT: ism
TUMOR: oma
USER: ster
VACUUM TUBE: tron
WORTHY: able, ible
YOUNG: ster
YOUNGSTER: ling

Combining Forms

ABDOMEN: ventr, ventri, ventro

ABOUNDING: poly

ABOVE: super, supero

ACCELERATING: auxo

ACID: acet, aceto, oxy

ACORN: balan, balano

ACTION: praxia

ADHESION: anchyl, anchylo, ancyl, ancylo, ankyl, ankylo

AFFINITY: phily

AGAIN: pali

AGAINST: cat, cath, cata, kat, kata

AGRICULTURAL: agro

AIR: atm, atmo, pneumo

ALDEHYDE: ald, aldo

ALIKE: hom, homo, is, iso

ALL: amn, amni, pan, pano

ALONG: mon, mono, soli

ALTERNATIVE: allelo

AMBER: succin, succino

ANCIENT: archae, archaeo, arche, archeo, pale, paleo

ANGLE: anguli, angulo, gon

ANIMAL: zoic

ANKLE: tars, tarso

ANT: myrmec, myrmeco

ANTIMONY: stib, stibi, stibo

APE: pithec, pitheco, pithecus

APEX: apic, apici, apico

APPEAR: phaner, phanero

APPEARANCE: phany

APPETITE: orexia

ARCHETYPAL: prot, proto

ARISING: genous

ARM: brachi, brachio

ARMED: hoplo

AROUND: amph, amphi

ARRANGEMENT: tax, taxi, taxo

ART: techn, techno

ASS: ono

ASUNDER: dich, dicho

ATLAS: atlant, atlanto, atlo

AVIATION: aer, aero

AVOIDANCE: phob, phobo

BACK: dor, dori, not, noto, notus, opisth, opistho

BAD: cac, caco, mal

BALANCE: stato

BEAUTIFUL: calli, callo

BED: clin, clino

BEGINNING: acr, acro, akr, akro

BERRY: bacci, cocc, cocci, cocco

BEST: aristo

BILLIONTH: nano

BITTER: picr, picro

BLACK: atro, mel, mela, melo, argill

BLIND: typhl, typhlo

BLOOD: haem, haemo, hem, hema, hemi, hemo

BLUE: cyan, cyano

BOAT: scaph, scapho

BODY: dema, soma, somat, somato

BONE: oste, osteo

BOOK: biblio

BOTH: amph, amphi, ampho, bis

BRAIN: cerebr, cerebri, cerebro

BRANCHED: cladous

BREAST: mast, masto

BRIEF: brevi

BRIGHT: lampro

BRISTLE: chaet, chaeto, seti

BROAD: lati

BROOM: scopi

BRUSH: scopi

BUD: blast, blasto

BULK: onc, onco, onch

BULKY: hadr, hadro

BULL: taur, tauri, tauro

BUTTER: buryr, buryro

CAT: ailur, ailuro, celur, celuro

CATTLE: bovi

CAUDAL: ur, uro

CAUSE: aetio, aitio, etio

CAVITY: antr, antro

CECUM: typhl, typhlo

CELL: blast, cyt, cyte, cyto, gamet, gameto, phag, phage

CEMENT: lith

CHAIN: strept, strepto

CHAMBER: thalam, thalamo

CHEEK: bucco, mel, melo

CHEESE: case, caseo, tyr, tyro

CHEMICAL: amid, amido, amin, amino

CHEST: stern, sterno, steth, stetho, thorac, thoraci, thoraco

CHIEF: prot, proto

CHILD: paed, paedo, ped, pedo

CHIN: genio, mento

CHINA: sino

CHINESE: sinic, sinico

CHURCH: ecclesi, ecclesio

CLEFT: fissi, schisto, schiz, schizo

CLIMATE: meteor, meteoro

CLOSE: sten, steno

CLOSED: cleist, cleisto, clist, clisto

CLOSURE: cleisis, clisis

CLOT: thromb, thrombo

CLOUD: cirr, cirrhi, cirrho, cirri, cirro, nephel, nephelo, nepho, nimbo

CLUSTER: cym, cymo, kym, kymo

COAL: anthrac, anthraco

COLOR: chrom, chromo

COLORLESS: leuc, leuco, leuk, leuko

COMBINATION: hapt, hapto

COMPACT: pycn, pycno

COMPLETE: hol, holo, tel, tele, teleo

CONCEALED: adel, adelo

CONDITION: ance, ancy, blasty

CONTACT: hapt, hapto

CONTEMPORARY: ne, neo

CONTEST: machy

COPPER: chalc, chalco, chalk, chalko, cupr, cupro

CORRECT: orth, ortho

COUNTERFEIT: pseud, pseudo

COUNTERPART: pseud, pseudo

COVERED: crypt, crypto, krypt, krypto

CRAFT: techn, techno

CREEPING: herpet, herpeto

CROOKED: anchyl, anchylo, ancyl, ancylo, ankyl, ankylo

CROWN: corono, stephan, stephano

CRYSTAL: hedron

CUP: cotyl, cotyli, cotylo, cyath, cyatho

CURRENT: rheo

DARK: melan, melano, nyct, nycti, nycto

DEAD: abio

DECOMPOSITION: lysis

DEEP: bathy

DEER: cervi

DEFECTIVE: atel, atelo

DEFICIENCY: penia

DEFICIENT: privic

DENSE: pycn, pycno

DEPTH: bath, batho

DESCENDANT: ite

DESIRE: orexia

DEVELOPMENT: plkasia

DEVOURING: vorous

DIAPHRAGM: phren, phreni, phreno

DIFFICULT: mogi

DISEASE: agra, pathia, pathic, pathy

DISEASED: cac, caco

DISINTEGRATION: lysis

DISLIKE: mis, miso

DISTANT: tel, tele, teleo

DISTINCT: idio

DIVER: dyt, dyta, dytes

DIVERSE: vari, vario

DIVIDED: fid, fissi, schisto

DOCTRINE: logy

DOER: ist

DOG: cyn, cyno

DONKEY: ono

DOUBLE: bis

DOWN: cat, cath, cata, kat, kata

DREAM: oneir, oneiro, onir, oniro

DRUG: pharmaco

DRY: xer, xero

DULL: ambly, amblyo, brady

DWARF: nano

EAGLE: aet, aeto

EAR: aur, auri, ot, oto

EARING: vore

EARNEST: serio

EARTH: geo

EARTHQUAKE: seismo

EAT: phag, phago

EGG: ov, ovi, ovo

EMPTY: ken, keno

END: acr, acro, akr, akro, tel, tele, teleo

ENTIRE: hol, holo, integri, toti

ENVIRONMENT: ec, eco, oeco, oiko

EQUAL: aequi, equi, is, iso, pari

ERA: zoic

ERUPTION: anthema

EVEN: homal, homalo

EVERYWHERE: omni

EVIL: mal

EXAMINATION: opsy

EXISTENCE: ont, onto

EXTERNAL: ect, ecto, exo

EXTREMITY: acr, acro, akr, akro

EYE: irid, irido, ocul, oculo, opto, opy

EYELID: blephar, blepharo

FALSE: pseud, pseudo

FAT: adip, adipo, lip, lipo, seb, sebi, sebo, steat, steato

FATTY: lipar, liparo

FEAR: phob, phobo

FEATHER: penn, penni, penno, pinn, pinni, pter, ptero

FEELING: pathia, pathy

FEIGNED: pseud, pseudo

FEMALE: gyn, gyne, gyno

FEW: olig, oligo, pauci

FEWER: meio, mi, mio

FICTITIOUS: pseud, pseudo

FIFTH: quint, quinti

FIGHT: machy

FIN: pinn, pinni

FINE: lept, lepto

FINGER: dactyl, dactylo, digit, digiti

FIRE: igni, pyr, pyro

FIRST: prot, proto

FISH: ichty, pisci

FIXED: aplano, stato

FLAGELLUM: mastig, mastigo

FLAT: homal, homalo, plan, plani

FLUTE: aul, aulo

FONDNESS: phily

FOOD: sito, troph, tropho

FOOT: ped, pedi, pedo, pod, pode, podo

FOOTPRINT: ichn, ichno

FOREST: hyl, hylo

FORM: morph, morpho

FOUR: tessar, tessaro, tesser, tessera, tetr, tetra

FREEZING: cry, cryo

FRONT: antero

FRUIT: carp, carpia, carpium, carpus, fructi

FUNGUS: myc, mycete, myceto, myco

GAS: aer, aero, pneumo

GATE: pyl, pyle, pylo

GHOST: sci, scia, scio, skia

GIANT: megal, megalo

GILL: branch

GILLED: branchia

GLAND: aden, adeno, adren, adreno

GLANDULAR: aden, adeno

GLASS: hyal, hyalo, vitr, vitro

GLUE: coll, collo

GNAT: culic, culici

GOAT: capri

GOLD: auro

GOOD: agath, agatho

GOOSE: chen, cheno

GOVERNMENT: archy, cracy

GRAIN: cocc, cocci, sito

GRAPE: botry, botryo

GRAVE: serio

GREASE: sib, sibi, sibo

GREAT: marc, marco, meg, mega, megal, megalo

GROWTH: auxo

GUEST: xen, xeno

GUILDING: agague

GUMS: ulo

HABITAT: ec, eco, oeco, oiko

HAND: cheir, cheiro, chir, chiro, man, mani, manu

HARD: scler, sclera, sclero, stere, stereo

HARDENING: scler, sclera, sclero

HARE: lag, lago

HATRED: mis, miso, phobia

HEAD: cephal, cephalo, cephalus, crani, cranio

HEALING: iatric, iatrics, iatro, iatroly

HEAP: cumul, cumuli, cumulo

HEARING: acou, acouo, acousia, audio, oto

HEART: cardi, cardia, cardio

HEAVENS: uran, urano

HEAVY: bary, gravi, hadr, hadro

HEEL: calcaneo

HEIGHT: acr, acro, akr, akro, alt, hyps, hypsi, hypso

HIDDEN: adel, adelo, crypt, crypto, krypt, krypto

HIDE: derm, derma, dermo

HIGH: alti

HOLLOW: cel, celo, coel, coelo

HOLY: hagi, hagio, hier, hiero, sacr, sacro

HOMOGENEOUS: is, iso

HONEY: meli, mell, melli

HORN: cerat, cerato, com, kerat, kerato

HORNED: cera

HORSE: equi, hipp, hippo

HUMAN: anthrop, anthropo

HUNDRED: centi, hect, hecto

HUNDREDTH: centi

IDEA: ideo

ILLNESS: agro

IMAGE: eidolo, idolo, typ, typo

IMPERFECT: atel, atelo

INCOMPLETE: atel, atelo

INCREASE: auxo

INDIVIDUAL: idio

INNER: ent, ento

INSECT: entom, entomo

INSTRUMENT: labe

INTERMEDIATE: mes, meso

INTESTINE: enter, entero

IRIS: irid, irido

IRON: rerr, rerri, sider, sidero

IRREGULAR: anom, anomal, anomali, anomalo, anomo

IRREGULARLY: mal

JACKASS: ono

JAW: gnath, gnatho

JOINT: arthr, arthro, condyl, condylo

JUICE: opo

KERNEL: cary, caryo, kary, karyo

KEY: cleid, cleido

KIDNEY: nephr, nephro, ren, reni, reno

KILLER: cide

KIND: gen, geno

KNEE: gon

KNOB: tyl, tylo

KNOWLEDGE: gnosia, gnosis, gnosy, ics

LIGAMENT: desm, desmo

LAKE: limn, limni, limno

LAND: chor, choro, gaea, geo

LANGUAGE: gloss, glosso, glott, glotto, lingu, lingua, lingui, linguo

LARGE: macr, macro, meg, mega, megal, megalo

LAW: nom, nomo

LAYER: cline

LEAD: molybd, molybdo, plumb, plumbo

LEAF: phyll, phyllo

LEVEL: plan, plani, plano

LIFELESS: abio

LIGHT: luci, lumin, lumini, lumino, phos, phot, photo

LIKE: home, homeo, homoe, homoi

LILY: crinus

LINE: lineo, stich

LIP: labio

LISTENING: acou, acouo

LIVING: ont, onto, vivi

LIZARD: saur, sauro

LOCAL: top, topo

LOVE: eroto

LOVING: phil, phile, philo

LUNG: pneum, pneumo, pulmo

MAIDEN: partheno

MALE: andr, andro

MAN: anthrop, anthropo

MANIFEST: phaner, phanero

MANY: mult, multi, pluri, poly

MARRIAGE: gamy

MARRYING: gamous

MASS: onc, onch, onco

MASTER: arch

MATTER: hyl, hylo

MEASURING: metry

MEDICAL TREATMENT: atric, atrics, iatro, iatroly

MEMORY: mnem, mnemo

MIDDLE: mes, meso

MILK: lact, lacti, lacto

MILLION: meg, mega

MILLIONTH: micr, micro

MIND: menti, noo, phren, phreni, phreno, psych, psycho

MINERAL: lite, lyte

MITE: acar, acari, acaro

MODERN: ne, neo

MOISTURE: hygr, hygro

MONSTER: terat, terato

MOON: selen, seleni, seleno

MOSQUITO: culic, culici

MOTHER: matr, matri, matro

MOTLEY: par, pari, pary

MOUSE: my, mys, myo

MOUTH: or, ori, oro, stom, stoma, stome, stomo

MOUTHS: stomat, stomata

MUCH: mult, multi, poly

MUD: pel, pelo

MUSCLE: my, myo

NAME: omato, onym

NARROW: sten, steno

NATIVE: ite

NAVEL: omphal, omphalo

NEAR: juxta

NECK: ceric, cerici, cerico

NERVE: neur, neuro

NERVE TISSUE: gangli, ganglio

NEW: ne, neo

NIGHT: nyct, nycti, nycto

NINE: ennea

NIPPLE: mast, masto, papilli, papillio

NITROGEN: za, zaa, zao

NOSE: nas, nasi, naso, rhin, rhino, rhinus

NOVEL: caen, caeno, cen, ceno

NUCLEUS: cary, caryo, kary, karyo

NUMBER: arithmo

NUT: cary, caryo, kary, karyo

NUTRITION: troph, tropho

OCCULT: crypt, crypto, krypt, krypto

ODD: azygo

OFFSPRING: gen, geno, ped, pedo

OIL: ole, olei, oleo

OILY: lipar, liparo

OLD AGE: geront, geronto

ONE: mon, mono

OPENING: pora, pore, pyle

ORGAN: viscer, visceri, viscero

ORGANISM: ont, onto

OTHER: all, allo, heter, hetero

OUT OF: ect, ecto

OUTSIDE: ect, ecto, exo

OX: bovi

OYSTER: ostre, ostri, ostro

PAIN: agra, alg, algo, algia

PARALYSIS: plegia, plegy

PART: mer, mero

PARTICLE: plast

PARTURITION: toky

PATH: ode

PEAK: acr, acro, akr, akro

PECULIAR: idio

PEOPLE: dem, demo, ethn, ethno

PERFECT: tel, tele, teleo

PERSON: idio

PHENOMENA: ics

PHYSICIAN: iatrist, iatro, iatry

PICTURE: picto, pinac, pinaco

PIG: choerus

PILLAR: styl, stylo

PIPE: aul, aulo, siphon, siphoni, siphono, solen, soleno

PIT: bothr, bothro

PLACE: chor, choro, gaea, gea, loco, top, topo

PLANT: chore, phyt, phyta

PLEASANT: hedy

POEM: stich

POISON: toxic, toxico

POND: limn, limni, limno

POUCH: cyst, cysti, cystis, cysto

POVERTY: penia

POWER: dynam, dynamo

PRACTICE: ics

PRACTITIONER: path

PRESSURE: baro, piezo, tono

PRICKLY: echin, echino

PRIMARY: prot, proto

PRODUCER: gen, gene

PRODUCING: genetic

QUALITIES: ics

QUININE: chin, chino

RACE: ethn, ethno, gen, geno, phyl, phylo

RADIATING: actin, actini, actino

RAIN: hyet, hyeto, ombro, pluvi, pluvia, pluvio

RAINBOW: irid, irido

RAVEN: corax

RAY: actin, actini, actino

RECENT: caen, caeno, cen, ceno, ne, neo

RECIPROCAL: allelo

RECITAL: logue

RECOGNITION: gnosia, gnosis, gnosy

RECORD: gram, graph

RECURRING: ennial

RED: erythr, erythro, pyrrh, pyrrho, rhod, rhodo

REDUCTION: lysis

REMOTE: dist, disti, disto, palae, paleo, pale, paleo, tele, teleo

REPETITION: pali

REPRESENTATION: graphy

REPTILE: herpet, herpeto

RESEMBLING: form

RESPIRATION: pneumo

RESTING: stato

RIB: cost, costi, costo, pleur, pleuri, pleuro

RIBBON: taen, taeni, taeno

RICE: oryz, oryzi, oryzo

RIGHT: dextr, dextro, orth, ortho, rect, recti

RIVER: potam, potamo

ROCK: clast, ite, lite, lith, lyte, petr, petri, petro, phyre

ROD: rhabd, rhabdo

ROOF: steg, stego

ROSE: rhod, rhodo

ROTTEN: sapr, sapro

ROUGH: trachy

ROUND: globo

RULE: archy

RULER: arch

RUNNING: drom, dromo, dromous

SAC: cyst, cysti, cysto

SACRED: hagi, hagio, is, iso

SAW: serri

SCIENCE: ics, logy, ology, onomy, sophy

SEA: mer, pelag, pelago

SECOND: deut, deuto, deuter, deutero

SEED: sperm, sperma, spermi, spermo, spermat, spermato

SEIZURE: agra

SELF: aut, auto

SEPARATE: idio

SERPENT: ophi, ophio

SEVEN: hept, hepta, sept, septa

SEX: gen, geno

SHADOW: sci, scia, scio, skia

SHAGGY: dasy

SHAPE: morph, morpho

SHARP: oxy

SHEET: pallio

SHELL: conch, concho, oeco, ostrac, ostraco

SHIELD: aspid, aspido, aspis, scut, scuti

SHOOT: blast, blasto, thall, thalli, thallio

SHORT: brachy, brevi

SHOULDER: om, omo

SHRUB: thamn, thamno

SIDE: ali, later, lateri, latero, pleur, pleuri, pleuro

SIDES: ali

SIGHT: opsia, opsy

SILVER: argent, argenti, argento, argyr, argyro

SIMILAR: hol, holo, hom, home, homeo, homo, homoe, homoi

SINGLE: apl, aplo, hapl, haplo, mon, mono

SIX: hex, hexa, sex, sexi, sexti

SKILL: ics, techn, techno

SKIN: derm, derma, dermo, dermis

SLANT: clin, clino

SLEEP: hypn, hypno

SLOPE: cline

SLOW: brady

SMALL: lept, lepto, micr, micro, olig, oligo, parv, parvi, parvo

SMALLER: meio, mi, mio

SMELL: brom, bromo

SMOOTH: leio, lio, liss, lisso

SNAKE: ophi, ophio

SNOW: chio, chion, chiono

SODIUM: natr, natro

SOIL: agro, geo

SOLID: stere, stereo

SOLITARY: erem, eremo

SONG: melo

SOUL: psych, psycho, thym, thymo

SOUND: audio, phon, phone, phono, phonia

SOUTH: austr, austro, not, noto

SPECIALIST: ician, ist, logue

SPEECH: lalo, log, logo, phon, phono

SPHERICAL: globo

SPIDER: arachn, arachno

SPIRAL: helic, helico

SPIRIT: psych, psycho, thym, thymo

SPOT: macul, maculi, maculo

SPRING: cren, creno

SPROUT: blast, blasto, clad, clado

SPROUTING: blastic

STAIN: macul, maculi, maculo

STAR: astr, astro

STARCH: amyl, amylo

STEAM: atmid, atmido

STEM: caul, cauli, caulo

STICK: rhabd, rhabdo, stom, stoma, stomo

STOMACH: gaster, gastero, gastr, gastri, gastro

STONE: lith, litho

STOPPAGE: stasis

STRAIGHT: lineo, orth, ortho, rect, recti

STRAIN: tono

STRANGE: xen, xeno

STREAM: fluvio

STROKE: plegia

STRUCTURE: morph, morpho

STUPOR: narc, narco

SUBSTANCE: hyl, hylo, phane, state

SUFFERING: path, patho, pathia, pathy

SUGAR: gluc, gluco, glyc, glyco, saccharine, sacchari, saccharo, sucr, sucro

SULFUR: thi, thio

SUMMIT: acr, acro, akr, akro, apic, apici, apico

SUN: heli, helio

SUPPORTER: crat, ist, ite

SURFACE: bedron

SURGICAL REMOVAL: ectomy

SWEAT: hidr, hidro

SWEET: glyc, glyco

SWINE: hyo

SWOLLEN: phys, physo

TABLET: pinac, pinaco, plac, placo

TALK: logue

TALLOW: seb, sebi, sebo, stear, stearo, steat, steato

TAPEWORM: taen, taeni, taeno

TASTE: geusia

TEETH: odontia

TEN: dec, deca, decem, dek, deka

TENDENCY: philia, phily

TENDON: teno

TENTH: deci

TERRIBLE: din, dino

THEFT: klept, klepto

THEORY: logy

THERAPY: pathia, pathic, pathy

THICK: dasy, hadr, hadro, pachy

THIGH: mer, mero, merus

THIN: lept, lepto

THIRD: tri, trit, trito

THORN: acanth, acantho, acanthus, spini, spinio

THOUGHT: ideo, log, logo

THOUSAND: kilo

THREAD: mnemat, mnemato, nem, nema, nemo

THREE: ter, tri

THROAT: bronch, broncho

THUNDER: bront, bronto, ceraun, cerauno, kerauno

TICK: acar, acari, acaro

TIME: chronous, shron, shrono

TIN: stann, stanni, stanno

TIP: acr, acro, akr, akro, apic, apici, apico

TISSUE: hist, histo, hypho

TOE: dactyl, dactylo

TONE: phon, phono

TONGUE: gloss, glosso, lingu, lingua, lingui, linguo

TOOTH: dent, denti, dento, odont, odonto

TOP: acr, acro, akr, akro, apic, apici, apico

TOTAL: hol, holo, toti

TOUCH: hapt, hapto

TRACK: ichn, ichno

TRANSLUCENT: lyal, lyalo

TRANSMISSION: phoresis

TRANSPARENT: hyal, hyalo

TREATISE: logy

TREE: dendr, dentro, dendron

TRENCH: bothr, bothro

TRIANGULAR: trigon, trigono

TRIBE: phyl, phylo

TRILLION: treg, trega

TRILLIONTH: pico, troch, trocho, ventr, ventri, ventro

TROUGH: bothr, bothro

TRUE: orth, ortho

TUBE: siphon, siphoni, siphono, solen, soleno, syring, syringo

TUMOR: cele, gangli, ganglio, myom, myomo, onc, onch, onco

TWICE: bis, didym, didymo

TWIST: spir, spiri, spiro

TWISTED: strept, strepto

TWO: bin, duo

TWOFOLD: diphy, diphyo, dipl, diplo

TYPE: morph, morpho

UMBILICUS: omphal, omphalo

UNARMED: anopl, anoplo

UNEQUAL: anis, aniso

UNIFORM: is, iso

UNION: gamous, gamy, zyg, zygo

UNITED: gam, gamo

UNIVERSAL: cosm, cosmo, omni

UNIVERSE: cosm, cosmo

UNREAL: pseud, pseudo

UNTRUE: pseud, pseudo

UNUSUAL: anom, anomo

UPRIGHT: orth, ortho

URCHIN: echin, echnino

VAPOR: atm, atmo

VARIATION: all, allo

VARIOUS: part, parti, party

VEHICLE: mobile

VEIN: phleb, phlebo, ven, veni, veno

VERTEBRA: spondyl, spondylo, spondylus

VESSEL: angi, angio, arteri, arterio, vas, vascul, vasculo, vasi

VIEWING INSTRUMENT: scope

VINE: ampel, ampelo, viti

VINEGAR: acet, aceto

VIRGIN: parthen, partheno

VISCERA: splanchn, splanchno

VISIBLE: phaner, phanero

VISION: opia, opsy, opto, opy

VOICE: phon, phone, phono, phony

WAR: machy

WATER: hydr, hydro

WAVE: cym, cymo, kym, kymo

WAX: cer, cero

WAY: ode

WEAK: asthen, astheno, lept, lepto

WEALTH: plut, pluto

WEATHER: meteor, meteoro

WEB: hypho

WEIGHT: bar, baro

WELL: agath, agatho

WET: hygr, hygro

WHALE: cet, ceto

WHEEL: troch, trocho

WHILE: calli, callio

WHIP: mastig, mastigo, mastix

WHITE: alb, albo, cali, calio, leuc, leuco, leuk, leuko

WHOLE: hol, holo, integri, pan, pano

WHOLLY: toti

WIDE: eury

WILD: agrio

WILD BEAST: ther, thero

WIND: anem, anemo, venti, vento

WINDPIPE: bronchi, bronchio, trache, tracheo

WING: ali, pter, ptero

WITHIN: end, endo, ent, ento, eso

WOLF: lyc, lyco

WOMAN: gyn, gynaec, gynaeco, gyne, gynec, gyneco, gyno

WOMB: hyster, hystero, metr, metra, metro, uter, utero

WOOD: hyl, hylo, lign, ligni, ligno, xyl, xylo

WOOL: erio, lan, lani, lano

WORD: log, logo

WORK: erg, ergo

WORKER: ergat, ergato

WORLD: cosm, cosmo

WORM: helminth, helmintho, vermi

WORSHIP: latry

WOUND: traumat, traumato

WRIST: carp, carpo

WRITER: grapher

WRITING: grapho

YEAR: ennial

YELLOW: chrys, chryso, flav, flavo, lute, luteo, xanth, xantho

YOKE: zyg, zygo

YOLK: vitell, vitello